W9-BAG-795

Collectors' Information Bureau's

COLLECTIBLES

PRICE GUIDE

1993

COMPREHENSIVE VALUE GUIDE

Limited Edition: Plates • Figurines • Bells • Graphics • Ornaments • Dolls • Steins

Edited by
Diane Carnevale Jones

Collectors' Information Bureau
2420 Burton S.E.
Grand Rapids, Michigan 49546
(616) 942-6898

Acknowledgments

The Collectors' Information Bureau would like to thank the following persons who have contributed to the creation of this book: Dave Goodwin, Wm. C. Brown & Co.; Linda L. Joswick, Laurie Schaut and Joy Versluys all with Trade Typographers, Inc.

In addition, the C.I.B. would like to thank its panel of limited edition dealers, whose dedication has helped make our ever-expanding, 166-page Price Index possible. We wish we could thank them by name, but they have agreed that to be singled out in this manner might hinder their continued ability to obtain an unbiased view of the marketplace.

The executive director also wishes to express heartfelt appreciation to the following persons whose dedication, hard work and encouragement have made this book possible: Emily Eldersveld, Karen Feil, Ron Jedlinski, Susan K. Jones, Susan Knappen, Bruce Kollath, Bethany Kuiper, Debi Ley, Heio W. Reich, J.P. Smith, Jr., Carol Van Elderen and Cindy Zagumny.

Copyright 1993 © by Collectors' Information Bureau
Library of Congress Catalog Number: 83-61660. All rights reserved. No part of this work may be reproduced or used in any forms or by any means — graphics, electronic or mechanical, including photocopying or information storage and retrieval systems — without written permission from the copyright holder.

Printed in the United States of America.

ISBN: 0-930785-13-4 Collectors' Information Bureau

ISBN: 0-87069-700-5 Wallace-Homestead Book Company

CREDITS

Book Design and Graphics: Trade Typographers, Inc., Grand Rapids, Michigan

Contents

A Warm Welcome from The Collectors' Information Bureau

by Diane Carnevale Jones
Executive Director

In 1982, 14 collectible manufacturers became charter members of the Collectors' Information Bureau (CIB), which was formed to increase the public's awareness of the collectibles industry, an industry which has experienced extraordinary growth and collector enthusiasm in recent years. Today, the Collectors' Information Bureau is recognized as an authoritative source within the industry, providing the most accurate and up-to-date information on limited edition plates, figurines, bells, graphics, ornaments, dolls and steins. Entering its eleventh year, this not-for-profit organization has 80 member companies and reaches out to thousands of collectors across the country and around the world!

Books! Books! Books!

Collectors who enjoy reading about their hobby will enjoy the variety of books published by the Collectors' Information Bureau.

The Collectibles Market Guide & Price Index offers collectors nearly 600 pages of comprehensive information about most every aspect of collecting. Illustrated feature articles, a secondary market Price Index, manufacturer profiles, artist biographies and a complete listing of collector clubs are among the many topics covered in this ever-expanding edition. Rich color abounds on the cover and within the book, making this annual guide a 'must' for every collector.

The *Collectibles Price Guide*, published mid-year, features a Price Index listing over 30,000 active market prices based upon constant communication with a panel of expert retailers throughout North America, who buy and sell retired collectibles. Collectors who insure their artwork against theft and breakage, find this price guide an invaluable document, as well as hobbyists who buy and sell retired collectibles on the secondary market.

The Collectors' Information Bureau headquarters receives hundreds of phone calls from collectors who are interested in participating in the secondary market, yet need more information about the mechanics behind this venture. In an effort to educate collectors about this area, the Bureau makes available the *Directory to Secondary Market Retailers: Buying and Selling Limited Edition Artwork*. This book features a comprehensive listing of today's most respected secondary market dealers and exchanges nationwide, in addition to a practical guide outlining the basics of secondary market trading.

An exciting companion book to the *Directory to Secondary Market Retailers* will be introduced in July 1993. Entitled *Directory to Collectibles Retailers: Where to Shop for Collectibles*, this national dealer directory will feature hundreds of collectible stores, making it easier for collectors to locate stores while vacationing. Collectors who live in small towns without collectible shops will now be able to locate

The Collectibles Market Guide & Price Index

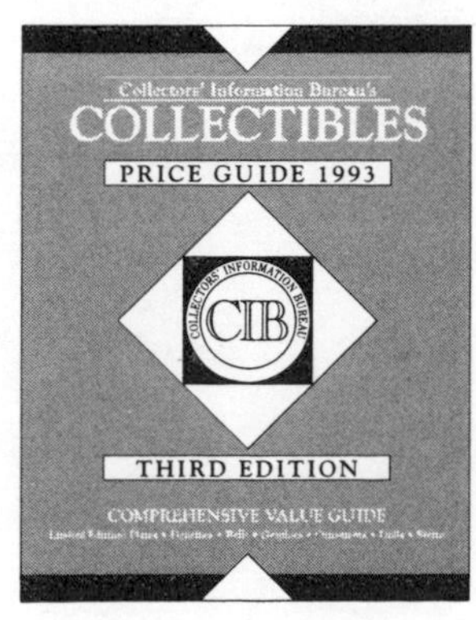

Collectibles Price Guide

Directory to Secondary Market Retailers

Directory to Collectibles Retailers

sources for their favorite collectibles. Each dealer listing will include complete information on location and lines carried by the stores.

Operation "Collector Hotline"

The Collectors' Information Bureau offers a hotline number to assist collectors with their difficult-to-answer questions. By calling (616) 942-9'CIB', collectors receive personal assistance in locating information on their favorite artists, phone numbers of manufacturers or perhaps values for their collectibles. Any questions that cannot be answered by phone are then directed to the research staff, who mail responses to collectors, once the information has been located.

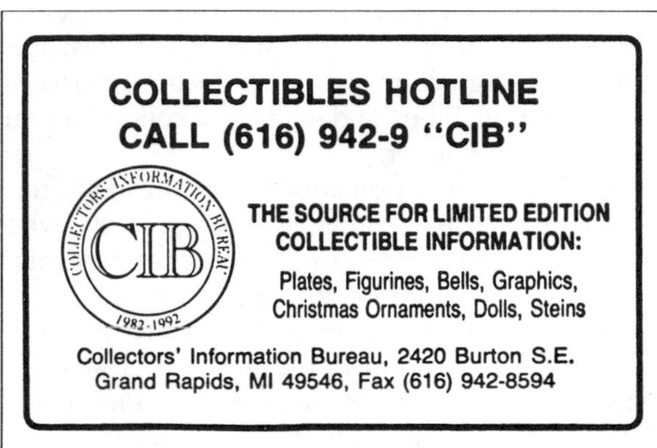

Media Blitz

The Collectors' Information Bureau is actively involved in the media, both in supplying collectibles information to the top 500 daily newspapers, in addition to writing several magazine columns for collectible publications. Executive Director Diane Carnevale Jones has also appeared on cable television and has participated in numerous radio talk shows on the subject of collecting.

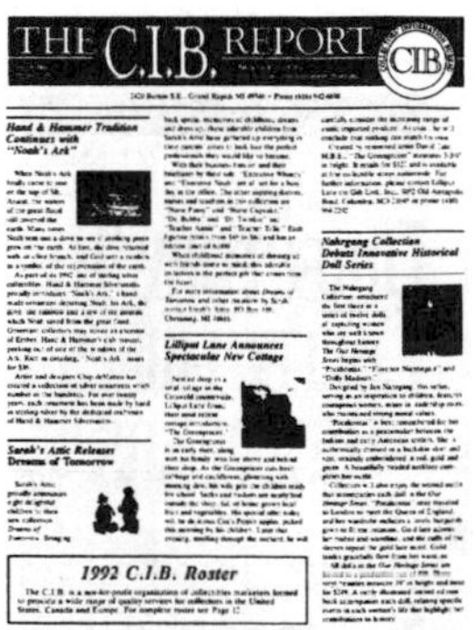

Newsletters, Collector Conventions and Seminars

The "C.I.B. Report" newsletter, published three times annually, contains the latest collectibles news, including recent product introductions, collector club activities, artist open houses, product retirement announcements and convention news. These 40-page color newsletters are distributed at national collector conventions, through retailers and directly to collectors who purchase CIB books.

The Collectors' Information Bureau's booth at the International Collectible Exposition was staffed by (L to R) Diane Carnevale Jones, Sue Knappen and Cindy Zagumny. This show, held each July in South Bend, Indiana and one other collector show held in the Spring on either the East or West Coast, is managed by McRand International, Ltd. of Lake Forest, Illinois.

The Collectors' Information Bureau, along with scores of manufacturers, exhibit at annual national collector conventions on the east and west coasts, as well as in South Bend, Indiana. Thousands of collectors attend these events, strolling through exhibition halls viewing recent product introductions, meeting the artists who create these products and attending seminars. The Collectors' Information Bureau is on hand to distribute newsletters, answer collectors' secondary market questions and to present seminars on this same topic.

The Collectors' Information Bureau looks to new opportunities and challenges as the organization continues to expand its services, offering accurate, up-to-date and educational information to collectors, retailers, manufacturers and the media. We remain "**the** source for limited edition collectibles information!"

1993 C.I.B. Members

Kurt S. Adler, Inc./ Santa's World
1107 Broadway
New York, NY 10010

Anheuser-Busch, Inc.
Retail Sales Department
2700 South Broadway
St. Louis, MO 63118

Annalee Mobilitee Dolls, Inc.
Box 708 Reservoir Road
Meredith, NH 03253

Armani
c/o Miller Import Corp.
300 Mac Lane
Keasbey, NJ 08832

Artaffects, Ltd.
P.O. Box 98
Staten Island, NY 10307

Artline
P.O. Box 811119
Boca Raton, FL 33481

The Ashton-Drake Galleries
9200 N. Maryland Avenue
Niles, IL 60714

Band Creations
28427 N. Ballard
Lake Forest, IL 60045

Marty Bell Fine Art, Inc.
9314 Eton Avenue
Chatsworth, CA 91311

The Bradford Exchange
9333 Milwaukee Avenue
Niles, IL 60714

Byers' Choice Ltd.
P.O. Box 158
Chalfont, PA 18914

Cast Art Industries, Inc.
1120 California Ave.
Corona, CA 91719

The Cat's Meow
2163 Great Trails Drive
Wooster, OH 44691

Christopher Radko
Planetarium Station
P.O. Box 770
New York, NY 10024-05393

Classic Carolina Collections/ C.U.I., Inc./DRAM TREE
1502 North 23rd Street
Wilmington, NC 28405

Creart
4517 Manzanillo Drive
Austin, TX 78749

The Crystal World
3 Caesar Place
Moonachie, NJ 07074

Department 56, Inc.
P.O. Box 44456
Eden Prairie, MN 55344-1456

The Walt Disney Company
500 South Buena Vista Street
Burbank, CA 91521-6876

Duncan Royale
1141 So. Acacia Avenue
Fullerton, CA 92631

Dynasty Doll
c/o Cardinal Inc.
P.O. Box 99
400 Markley Street
Port Reading, NJ 07064

Enesco Corporation
1 Enesco Plaza
Elk Grove Village, IL 60007

Fitz and Floyd Heirloom Collectibles Division
P.O. Box 815367
Dallas, TX 75381-5367

Flambro Imports
1260 Collier Road N.W.
Atlanta, GA 30318

Kevin Francis Inc.
P.O. Box 1267
Warren, MI 48090

The Franklin Mint
U.S. Route One
Franklin Center, PA 19091

Margaret Furlong Designs
210 State Street
Salem, OR 97301

GANZ
908 Niagara Falls Blvd.
North Tonawanda, NY 14120-2060

Gartlan USA, Inc.
15502 Graham Street
Huntington Beach, CA 92649

Georgetown Collection
866 Spring Street
Westbrook, ME 04092

Goebel United States
Goebel Plaza
P.O. Box 10, Rte. 31
Pennington, NJ 08534-0010

Goebel Miniatures
c/o Goebel United States
P.O. Box 10, Rt. 31
Pennington, NJ 08534-0010

Gorham Inc.*
P.O. Box 2010
Penndel, PA 19047-9010

The Hadley Companies
11001 Hampshire Avenue, S.
Bloomington, MN 55438

Hallmark Cards, Inc.
P.O. Box 412734
Kansas City, MO 64141-2734

The Hamilton Collection*
4810 Executive Park Court
Jacksonville, FL 32216-6069

Hand & Hammer Silversmiths
Hand & Hammer Collectors' Club
2610 Morse Lane
Woodbridge, VA 22192

Harbour Lights
8130 La Mesa Blvd.
La Mesa, CA 91941

Hawthorne Architectural Register
9210 N. Maryland Avenue
Niles, IL 60714

John Hine Studios, Inc.
4456 Campbell Road
P.O. Box 800667
Houston, TX 77280-0667

M.I. Hummel Club*
Division of Goebel Art GmbH
Goebel Plaza
P.O. Box 11
Pennington, NJ 08534-0011

Iris Arc Crystal
114 East Haley St.
Santa Barbara, CA 93101

Ladie & Friends, Inc.
220 North Main Street
Sellersville, PA 18960

The Lance Corporation
321 Central Street
Hudson, MA 01749

The Lawton Doll Company
548 North First
Turlock, CA 95380

Ron Lee's World of Clowns
2180 Agate Court
Simi Valley, CA 93065

Geo. Zoltan Lefton Company
3622 South Morgan St.
Chicago, IL 60609

LEGENDS
2665D Park Center Drive
Simi Valley, CA 93065

Lightpost Publishing
Ten Almaden Blvd., 9th Floor
San Jose, CA 95113

Lilliput Lane Limited
c/o Gift Link, Inc.
9052 Old Annapolis Road
Columbia, MD 21045

Lladro Collectors Society
43 W. 57th Street
New York, NY 10019

Seymour Mann, Inc.
225 Fifth Avenue,
Showroom #102
New York, NY 10010

Marina's Russian Collection, Inc.
507 N. Wolf Road
Wheeling, IL 60090

Maruri U.S.A.
7541 Woodman Place
Van Nuys, CA 91405

Mattel/Timeless Creations/ Annette Himstedt
333 Continental Blvd.
El Segundo, CA 90245-5012

June McKenna Collectibles Inc.
P.O. Box 846
Ashland, VA 23005

Michael's Limited
P.O. Box 217
Redmond, WA 98078-0217

Midwest Importers of Cannon Falls, Inc.
P.O. Box 20, Consumer Inquiries
Cannon Falls, MN 55009-0020

Miss Martha Originals Inc.
P.O. Box 5038
Glencoe, AL 35905

Nahrgang Collection
1005 First Avenue
Silvas, IL 61282

Napoleon USA, Inc.
P.O. Box 860
Oakes, PA 19456

Pemberton & Oakes
133 East Carrillo Street
Santa Barbara, CA 93101

PenDelfin Sales Inc.
750 Ensminger Road, #108
Box 884
Tonawanda, NY 14150

Polland Studios
P.O. Box 1146
Prescott, AZ 86302

Possible Dreams
6 Perry Dr.
Foxboro, MA 02035

Precious Art/Panton
110 E. Ellsworth Road
Ann Arbor, MI 48108

Reco International Corp.*
150 Haven Avenue
Port Washington, NY 11050

The Norman Rockwell Gallery
9200 Center for the Arts
Niles, IL 60714

Roman, Inc.*
555 Lawrence Avenue
Roselle, IL 60172-1599

Royal Copenhagen/ Bing & Grondahl
27 Holland Ave.
White Plains, NY 10603

Royal Doulton
700 Cottontail Lane
Somerset, NJ 08873

Sarah's Attic
126-1/2 West Broad
P.O. Box 448
Chesaning, MI 48616

Schmid
55 Pacella Park Drive
Randolph, MA 02368

Sheila's Inc.
P.O. Box 31028
Charleston, SC 29417

Silver Deer, Ltd.
4824 Sterling Drive
Boulder, CO 80301

Summerhill Crystal & Glass
P.O. Box 1479
Fairfield, IA 52556

Swarovski America Ltd.
2 Slater Road
Cranston, RI 02920

Terry Arts International, Inc.
109 Bushaway Road
Wayzata, MN 55391

United Design
P.O. Box 1200
Noble, OK 73068

VickiLane Design
3233 NE Cadet
Portland, OR 97220

*Charter Member

Questions—and Answers!
—*on Secondary Market Procedures*

by Diane Carnevale Jones

Q: How does the secondary market work?

A: 1. A collectible is introduced to the market and made available to collectors. Collectors may purchase the item through a retailer (in person or by mail or phone), or direct from the manufacturer/marketer (usually by mail or phone only). Items are sold at "original issue price," which is their retail price level. This method of selling is known as the "primary market."

2. After a period, which may vary from days to years, the collectible becomes "sold out." This means that neither the dealers nor the manufacturer/marketers have any additional pieces to sell to collectors on the primary market.

3. When a collector wishes to buy a piece which is "sold out," he or she must enter the "secondary market" to purchase it. Because the piece is no longer available at retail, the new buyer must locate someone who already owns it and pay whatever price the market will bear. Most buyers enlist the help of a dealer, exchange or matching service to help them in this process, while some place want ads in collectibles publications, or "network" with fellow collectors.

4. If new buyers continue to seek to acquire the piece long after its edition is sold out, the secondary market for that item may become stronger and stronger, and the price it can command may multiply over and over. Such market action is reported in price guides such as this one. Of course some collectibles never sell out completely, while others sell out but never attract sufficient demand to command a higher price than the issue-price level. Some collectibles peak soon after their editions close, while others remain dormant for years and then begin rising in value because of changing market dynamics.

Q: How do you determine when to sell collectibles on the secondary market?

A: I always tell collectors that if I knew the answer to this question, that I would be living in a luxurious condo in Florida soaking up the sun! You truly never know the *correct* time to buy or sell a collectible, once it has been retired. Once you've made up your mind, never look back and play the 'what if' game. For every time you make the right decision, there is probably another time that you may have guessed incorrectly.

Q: Once I decide to sell my collectibles, how shall I proceed?

A: If you own several collectibles, type an inventory of each item, including manufacturer, series, title, issue price, year of issue and artist. A secondary market value should be placed on each item, *before* you sell your collectibles. An informed collector, who knows the value of his/her collection, is a wise collector who won't be disappointed with the end result.

Q: How long will it take to buy or sell collectibles on the secondary market?

A: A lot longer that most people think! It is important to remember that for every seller, a buyer must be located. Timing is also important. A collectible that is in great demand, may not be readily available, or just the opposite: the one for sale is not in great demand! Some collectors can wait up to two years to locate a hard-to-find piece. There is a even waiting period for readily available items. Several weeks can elapse by the time buyers and sellers are contacted, collectibles are examined for authenticity and mint condition, checks are run through banks, and pieces are examined by potential buyers. Always check with the firm you are working with to get an idea of the procedure utilized to conduct buy-sell transactions.

Q: Should I buy duplicates of items I think may go up on the secondary market?

A: Experts suggest that first and foremost, collectors should buy what they like. If a collector follows this advice and a collectible does not rise in value, he owns a beautiful piece of artwork that he likes. Very few retailers will encourage collectors to buy duplicates for investment purposes. Collectors are likely to be disappointed if they have guessed incorrectly.

Q: Where do I locate secondary market values?

A: There are many excellent secondary market resources. *Make certain that your source keeps its pricing current.* There is nothing more disappointing than utilizing an old price guide to determine a value and selling price. The Collectors' Information Bureau publishes the most comprehensive and current price index for modern day limited edition plates, figurines (including cottages and crystal), bells, dolls, graphics, Christmas ornaments and steins. The index is published twice annually. Collectors are encouraged to contact the Collectors' Information Bureau when experiencing difficulty in locating values for rare pieces. The Bureau has an excellent research staff to assist in these cases.

Q: How shall I use price guides when buying and selling collectibles?

A: A price guide is only that—a guide to determine the approximate worth of an item. Some prices go up and down faster than a guide can be printed! Always use your good sense when reading a price guide. If you feel a price is outdated, check another guide or contact the Collectors' Information Bureau for other sources. Always remember that prices quoted in a price guide are for items in mint condition.

Q: What does the term 'mint condition' mean?

A: It can mean many things, depending upon the collectible. In all cases, the term, 'mint,' means not broken. For Christmas ornaments, the term means 'with the box.' The item cannot be chipped or faded by the sun. According to the glossary in the Collectors' Information Bureau's *Collectibles Market Guide & Price Index*, mint means 'a term originally related to the coin collecting hobby; this means that a limited edition item is still in its original, like-new condition, with all accompanying documents. The documents aforementioned include the Certificate of Authenticity and all other tags that originally accompanied the collectible.

Q: Does the original box make a difference in the secondary market sale of a collectible?

A: Read the following comments from retailers and exchanges across the country and be the judge of this very controversial 'box vs no box' theory:

Collectible Exchange, Inc. (New Middletown, OH): "Most collectors want the original box. Pieces without boxes normally sell at 10-20% less.

Dickens' Exchange (Metairie, LA): "Boxes are extremely valuable and their presence or absence does affect the value on the secondary market. One must remember that a piece will sell on the secondary market without a box, but always for approximately 10% less. The question is always asked: If I purchase this piece without a box, what will happen if I want to sell it later? Always remember that the same rule would apply. If you purchased it at a 10% discount, chances are you will sell it with a 10% discount at the time of sale."

Ellis in Wonderland (Sacramento, CA): "If you have two identical collectibles—one with the box and one without—the collector will always opt for the one with the box."

Collectibles etc., Inc. (Brown Deer, WI): "Except for some older items, most of our items are matched with the box. We have found that boxes do not matter to most people ... they just want the item and find storage a 'pain.' People who do save boxes have had to come up with 'creative' ways to store them. There are pros and cons for boxes. They are really handy when shipping to sell or when moving. Our Match Service finds it safer and convenient to have the boxes, but we do not insist. If the customer requires a box, we locate one. Satisfaction is guaranteed!"

The Kent Collection (Englewood, CO): "Boxes ARE important—for storage—for shipping—for giftwrapping—and one never knows which collector is going to insist upon original 'everything.' So we start with 'everthing.'"

Collector's Marketplace (Montrose, PA): "All original packaging is important. This includes tags, brochures, etc. The more complete the unit, the more the value."

Miller's Gift Gallery (Eaton, OH): "We do not feel that any packaging should come to play in the value of a collectible on the secondary market. The intrinsic value of a collectible item is in the figurine or material itself inclusive of its workmanship and artistry. The packaging is merely an effective means of transportation for the collectible."

Village Realty Miniature Properties (Fort Worth, TX): "Very important!! Not only do the pieces suffer a 15-20% devaluation ... they are very hard to sell without the original boxes to today's sophisticated collectors! Collectors are buying with an eye toward investment value. They not only look for boxes, but for excellent examples in the pieces themselves."

Q: Where should I look for help in buying or selling on the secondary market?

A: When collectors decide to buy or sell retired collectibles, they are often surprised to find they cannot return to the store from which they purchased their items. In fact, there are very few secondary market sources, in comparison to the tens of thousands of collectible gift stores located across the country. Collectors may also experience great difficulty in locating a source that specializes in a particular line of retired items. The Collectors' Information

Bureau decided to compile a comprehensive listing of secondary market sources to assist collectors in their quest for retired collectibles. These sources include retailers, exchanges, publications and show promoters. Located in the *Directory to Secondary Market Retailers: Where to Buy and Sell Limited Edition Artwork*, are unlimited contacts for plates, figurines, dolls, Christmas ornaments, bells, steins and graphics! Look up your favorite artist or company in the index and find one or more secondary market sources to contact for details. This secondary market directory is available in major bookstores and through the Bureau.

Q: Secondary market sources use different methods for transacting business. What do all of the terms mean?

A: The following are various terms used as descriptions by directory participants:

Buy outright: Firm will make a cash offer for the retired items. Typically, this offer is far less than the value in a price guide, because cash is offered up front, with no waiting on the collector's end. The business then accepts the merchandise as inventory and sells it as collectors contact them with their requests.

Buy/sell (exchange or brokerage): Buyers and sellers contact these businesses with their secondary market requests. The firm then matches buyers and sellers, usually, but not always, taking a commission from the seller. The firm takes on the liability during the entire exchange—making certain the piece in question is in mint condition—and making sure that the money is collected.

Consignment: A business accepts items from the collector and displays them or advertises them. The seller is then paid a commission, once the item is sold.

Locator service: This term usually refers to a business who specializes in doing research for a buyer looking for a retired collectible. This business normally does not do as much buying of collectibles, but only buys as needed.

Trade: Many collectors want to upgrade their collection by trading in the artwork they already own, for artwork they would prefer to own. Businesses may offer a combination of cash and merchandise for a retired item or offer a straight trade—merchandise, retired or primary, traded for the collector's pieces. Collectors should consider the trade carefully, making certain they are receiving an equitable trade. In many cases, collectors can quickly dispose of items they no longer want, for items (and cash) they prefer to own. Everyone can gain in this situation.

Q: How much should I expect to pay for selling my collectibles?

A: Commissions vary dramatically! In most cases, the seller ends up paying a commission on the item he sells. One of the only ways to avoid a 'third party' commission is to place an ad in a national collectibles publication. The cost of the ad is minimal and may bring successful results. Call the Collectors' Information Bureau for publications that accept secondary market advertisements. Many collectors question what they feel are exhorbitant commissions charged by 'third party' sources. However, if one takes into consideration the time, phone calls and research involved in a typical transaction, in addition to office space and other overhead, the commission does not appear as costly as initially indicated. Commissions vary from 5-50% for the most part. Collectors are encouraged to contact various sources until they have located a business with whom they feel comfortable working.

Q: How easy is it to sell large collections?

A: Selling large collections is very difficult! There are very few businesses who can afford to buy entire collections outright. Don't be surprised when a company offers you a fraction of their worth, when they are offering to buy outright for cash. There are some firms that will take collections on consignment (you give them the collection, and they pay you as the items are sold, minus a commission). Obviously, this method could take months to dispose of an entire collection.

Q: How do I know that I can trust these secondary market experts?

A: The Collectors' Information Bureau does not buy or sell collectibles on the secondary market. Therefore we have no way of guaranteeing a buy-sell transaction. Collectors must take full responsibility for researching their options, as they would in any business transaction. Be sure to ask for references!

Q: **More Questions?:** Contact the Collectors' Information Bureau at (616) 942-9242!

Collectors' Information Bureau's

PRICE INDEX•1993

Limited Edition: Plates • Figurines • Bells • Graphics • Christmas Ornaments • Dolls • Steins

This index includes several thousand of the most widely-traded limited editions in today's collectibles market. It is based upon interviews with more than a score of the most experienced and well-informed limited edition dealers in the United States, as well as several independent market advisors.

HOW TO USE THIS INDEX

Listings are set up using the following format:

Company		**Series**			
Number	**Name**	**Artist**	**Edition Limit**	**Issue Price**	**Quote**
❶		❷			
Enesco Corporation		**Retired Precious Moments Figurines**			
79-13-002	Praise the Lord Anyhow-E1374B	S. Butcher	Retrd.	8.00	75-125.00
❸❹❺	❻	❼	❽	❾	❿

❶ Company = Company Name

❷ Retired Precious Moments Figurines = Series Name

❸ 79 = 1979 (year of issue)

❹ 13 = Series number for Enesco Corporation. This number indicates that this series is the 13th listed for this particular company. Each series is assigned a series number.

❺ 002 = Item number within series. For example, this is the second listing within the series. Each item has a sequential number within its series.

❻ Praise the Lord Anyhow-E-1374B = Proper title of the collectible. Many titles also include the model number as well, for further identification purposes.

❼ S. Butcher = Artist's name. The first initial and last name is indicated most often, however a studio name may also be designated in this slot. (Example: Walt Disney).

❽ Retrd. = Retired. In this case, the collectible is no longer available. The edition limit category generally refers to the number of items created with the same name and decoration. Edition limits may indicate a specific number (i.e. 10,000) or the number of firing days for plates (i.e. 100-day, the capacity of the manufacturer to produce collectibles during a given firing period). Refer to "Open," "Suspd.," "Annual," and "Yr. Iss." under "Terms and Abbreviations" below.

❾ 8.00 = Issue Price in U.S. Dollars.

❿ 75-125.00 = Current Quote Price reflected may show a price or price range. Quotes are based on interviews with retailers across the country, who provide their actual sales transactions.

A Special Note to All Precious Moments Collectors: *Each ENESCO Precious Moments subject is engraved with a special annual mark. This emblem changes with each production year. The Collector value for each piece varies because of these distinctive yearly markings. Our pricing reflects an average for all years.*
A Special Note to All Hallmark Keepsake Ornament Collectors: *All quotes in this section are for ornaments in mint condition in their original box.*
A Special Note to All Department 56 Collectors: *Year of Introduction indicates the year in which the piece was designed, sculpted and copyrighted. It is possible these pieces may not be available to the collectors until the following calendar year.*

TERMS AND ABBREVIATIONS

Annual-Issued once a year

Closed-An item or series no longer in production

N/A -Not Available

Open-Not limited by number or time-available until manufacturer stops production, "retires" or "closes" the item or series

Retrd.-Retired

S/O-Sold Out

Set-Refers to two or more items issued together for a single price

Suspd.-Suspended (not currently being produced: may be produced in the future)

Undis.-Undisclosed

Unkn.-Unknown

Yr. Iss.-Year of issue (limited to a calendar year) 28-day, 10-day, etc.-limited to this number of production (or firing) days-usually not consecutive

Copyright 1993© by Collectors' Information Bureau. All rights reserved. No part of this work may be reproduced or used in any forms or by any means — graphics, electronic or mechanical, including photocopying or information storage and retrieval systems — without written permission from the copyright holder.

Company		Series			
Number	**Name**	**Artist**	**Edition Limit**	**Issue Price**	**Quote**
ANRI		**ANRI Wooden Christmas Bells**			
76-01-001	Christmas	J. Ferrandiz	Yr.Iss.	6.00	50.00
77-01-002	Christmas	J. Ferrandiz	Yr.Iss.	7.00	40-42.00
78-01-003	Christmas	J. Ferrandiz	Yr.Iss.	10.00	40.00
79-01-004	Christmas	J. Ferrandiz	Yr.Iss.	13.00	25-30.00
80-01-005	The Christmas King	J. Ferrandiz	Yr.Iss.	17.50	18.50
81-01-006	Lighting The Way	J. Ferrandiz	Yr.Iss.	18.50	18.50
82-01-007	Caring	J. Ferrandiz	Yr.Iss.	18.50	18.50
83-01-008	Behold	J. Ferrandiz	Yr.Iss.	18.50	18.50
85-01-009	Nature's Dream	J. Ferrandiz	Yr.Iss.	18.50	18.50
ANRI		**Juan Ferrandiz Musical Christmas Bells**			
76-02-001	Christmas	J. Ferrandiz	Yr.Iss.	25.00	80.00
77-02-002	Christmas	J. Ferrandiz	Yr.Iss.	25.00	80.00
78-02-003	Christmas	J. Ferrandiz	Yr.Iss.	35.00	75.00
79-02-004	Christmas	J. Ferrandiz	Yr.Iss.	47.50	60.00
80-02-005	Little Drummer Boy	J. Ferrandiz	Yr.Iss.	60.00	63.00
81-02-006	The Good Shepherd Boy	J. Ferrandiz	Yr.Iss.	63.00	63.00
82-02-007	Spreading the Word	J. Ferrandiz	Yr.Iss.	63.00	63.00
83-02-008	Companions	J. Ferrandiz	Yr.Iss.	63.00	63.00
84-02-009	With Love	J. Ferrandiz	Yr.Iss.	55.00	55.00
Artaffects		**Bells**			
87-01-001	Newborn Bell	R. Sauber	Unkn.	25.00	25.00
87-01-002	Motherhood Bell	R. Sauber	Unkn.	25.00	25.00
87-01-003	Sweet Sixteen Bell	R. Sauber	Unkn.	25.00	25.00
87-01-004	The Wedding Bell (White)	R. Sauber	Unkn.	25.00	25.00
87-01-005	The Wedding Bell (Silver)	R. Sauber	Unkn.	25.00	25.00
87-01-006	The Wedding Bell (Gold)	R. Sauber	Unkn.	25.00	25.00
Artaffects		**Bride Belles Figurine Bells**			
88-02-001	Caroline	R. Sauber	Unkn.	27.50	27.50
88-02-002	Jacqueline	R. Sauber	Unkn.	27.50	27.50
88-02-003	Elizabeth	R. Sauber	Unkn.	27.50	27.50
88-02-004	Emily	R. Sauber	Unkn.	27.50	27.50
88-02-005	Meredith	R. Sauber	Unkn.	27.50	27.50
88-02-006	Laura	R. Sauber	Unkn.	27.50	27.50
88-02-007	Sarah	R. Sauber	Unkn.	27.50	27.50
88-02-008	Rebecca	R. Sauber	Unkn.	27.50	27.50
88-02-009	Groom	R. Sauber	Unkn.	22.50	22.50
Artaffects		**Indian Brave Annual Bell**			
89-03-001	Christmas Pow-Pow	G. Perillo	Closed	24.50	30.00
90-03-002	Christmas Bells	G. Perillo	Closed	24.50	24.50
Artaffects		**Indian Princess Annual Bell**			
89-04-001	The Little Princess	G. Perillo	Closed	24.50	30.00
90-04-002	Little Madonna	G. Perillo	Closed	24.50	24.50
Artists of the World		**DeGrazia Bells**			
80-01-001	Los Ninos	T. DeGrazia	7,500	40.00	95.00
80-01-002	Festival of Lights	T. DeGrazia	5,000	40.00	85.00
Belleek		**Belleek Bells**			
88-01-001	Bell Ornament	Belleek	Open	38.00	38.00
89-01-002	Tower Ornament	Belleek	Open	35.00	35.00
90-01-003	Leprechaun Ornament	Belleek	Open	30.00	30.00
91-01-004	Church Ornament	Belleek	Open	32.00	32.00
92-01-005	Cottage Ornament	Belleek	Open	30.00	30.00
Belleek		**Twelve Days of Christmas**			
91-02-001	A Partridge in a Pear Tree	Belleek	Open	30.00	30.00
92-02-002	Two Turtle Doves	Belleek	Open	30.00	30.00
Bing & Grondahl		**Annual Christmas Bell**			
80-01-001	Christmas in the Woods	H. Thelander	Yr.Iss.	39.50	39.50
81-01-002	Christmas Peace	H. Thelander	Yr.Iss.	42.50	42.50
82-01-003	The Christmas Tree	H. Thelander	Yr.Iss.	45.00	45.00
83-01-004	Christmas in the Old Town	E. Jensen	Yr.Iss.	45.00	45.00
84-01-005	The Christmas Letter	E. Jensen	Yr.Iss.	45.00	45.00
85-01-006	Christmas Eve at the Farmhouse	E. Jensen	Yr.Iss.	45.00	45.00
86-01-007	Silent Night, Holy Night	E. Jensen	Yr.Iss.	45.00	45.00
87-01-008	The Snowman's Christmas Eve	E. Jensen	Yr.Iss.	47.50	47.50
88-01-009	The Old Poet's Christmas	E. Jensen	Yr.Iss.	49.50	49.50
89-01-010	Christmas Anchorage	E. Jensen	Yr.Iss.	52.00	52.00
90-01-011	Changing of the Guards	E. Jensen	Yr.Iss.	55.00	55.00
91-01-012	The Copenhagen Stock Exchange at Christmas	E. Jensen	Yr.Iss.	59.50	59.50
92-01-013	Christmas At the Rectory	J. Steensen	Yr.Iss.	62.50	62.50
93-01-014	Father Christmas in Copenhagen	J. Steensen	Yr.Iss.	62.50	62.50
Bing & Grondahl		**Christmas in America Bell**			
88-02-001	Christmas Eve in Williamsburg	J. Woodson	Yr.Iss.	27.50	100.00
89-02-002	Christmas Eve at the White House	J. Woodson	Yr.Iss.	29.00	75.00
90-02-003	Christmas Eve at the Capitol	J. Woodson	Yr.Iss.	30.00	30.00
91-02-004	Independence Hall	J. Woodson	Yr.Iss.	35.00	35.00
92-02-005	Christmas in San Francisco	J. Woodson	Yr.Iss.	37.50	37.50
93-02-006	Coming Home For Christmas	J. Woodson	Yr.Iss.	37.50	37.50
Brown & Bigelow Inc.		**A Boy and His Dog Silver Bells**			
80-02-001	Mysterious Malady	N. Rockwell	9,800	60.00	60.00
80-02-002	Pride of Parenthood	N. Rockwell	9,800	60.00	60.00
C.U.I./Carolina Collection/Dram Tree		**Sterling Classic**			
91-01-001	Small Tortoiseshell	J. Harris	10,000	100.00	100.00
91-01-002	Swallowtail	J. Harris	10,000	100.00	100.00
91-01-003	Camberwell Beauty	J. Harris	10,000	100.00	100.00
91-01-004	Large Blue	J. Harris	10,000	100.00	100.00
91-01-005	Peacock	J. Harris	10,000	100.00	100.00
91-01-006	Clouded Yellow	J. Harris	10,000	100.00	100.00
91-01-007	Mouse	J. Harris	10,000	100.00	100.00
91-01-008	Kingfisher	J. Harris	10,000	100.00	100.00
91-01-009	Barn Owl	J. Harris	10,000	100.00	100.00
Danbury Mint		**Various**			
75-01-001	Doctor and Doll	N. Rockwell	None	27.50	54.00
76-01-002	Grandpa Snowman	N. Rockwell	None	27.50	44.00
76-01-003	Freedom From Want	N. Rockwell	None	27.50	44.00
76-01-004	No Swimming	N. Rockwell	None	27.50	44.00
76-01-005	Saying Grace	N. Rockwell	None	27.50	44.00
76-01-006	The Discovery	N. Rockwell	None	27.50	44.00
77-01-007	The Runaway	N. Rockwell	None	27.50	40.00
77-01-008	Knuckles Down	N. Rockwell	None	27.50	40.00
77-01-009	Tom Sawyer	N. Rockwell	None	27.50	40.00
77-01-010	Puppy Love	N. Rockwell	None	27.50	40.00
77-01-011	Santa's Mail	N. Rockwell	None	27.50	40.00
77-01-012	The Remedy	N. Rockwell	None	27.50	40.00
Danbury Mint		**The Wonderful World of Norman Rockwell**			
79-02-001	Grandpa's Girl	N. Rockwell	None	27.50	29.50
79-02-002	Leapfrog	N. Rockwell	None	27.50	29.50
79-02-003	Baby-Sitter	N. Rockwell	None	27.50	29.50
79-02-004	Batter Up	N. Rockwell	None	27.50	29.50
79-02-005	Back to School	N. Rockwell	None	27.50	29.50
79-02-006	Gramps at the Reins	N. Rockwell	None	27.50	29.50
79-02-007	Friend in Need	N. Rockwell	None	27.50	29.50
79-02-008	Puppy in the Pocket	N. Rockwell	None	27.50	29.50
Danbury Mint		**The Norman Rockwell Commemorative Bell**			
79-03-001	Triple Self-Portrait	N. Rockwell	None	29.50	35.00
Enesco Corporation		**Precious Moments Annual Bells**			
83-01-001	Surrounded With Joy-E-0522	S. Butcher	Closed	18.00	60-75.00
82-01-002	I'll Play My Drum for Him-E-2358	S. Butcher	Closed	17.00	65-85.00
84-01-003	Wishing You a Merry Christmas-E-5393	S. Butcher	Closed	19.00	40-55.00
81-01-004	Let the Heavens Rejoice-E-5622	S. Butcher	Closed	15.00	165-180.
85-01-005	God Sent His Love-15873	S. Butcher	Closed	19.00	38-43.00
86-01-006	Wishing You a Cozy Christmas-102318	S. Butcher	Closed	20.00	38.00
87-01-007	Love is the Best Gift of All-109835	S. Butcher	Closed	22.50	30-44.00
88-01-008	Time To Wish You a Merry Christmas-115304	S. Butcher	Closed	25.00	40-45.00
89-01-009	Oh Holy Night-522821	S. Butcher	Closed	25.00	35-45.00
90-01-010	Once Upon A Holy Night-523828	S. Butcher	Closed	25.00	30-35.00
91-01-011	May Your Christmas Be Merry-524182	S. Butcher	Closed	25.00	32.00
92-01-012	But The Greatest Of These Is Love-527726	S. Butcher	Yr.Iss.	25.00	25-35.00
Enesco Corporation		**Precious Moments Various Bells**			
81-02-001	Jesus Loves Me-E-5208	S. Butcher	Suspd.	15.00	40-50.00
81-02-002	Jesus Loves Me-E-5209	S. Butcher	Suspd.	15.00	40-60.00
81-02-003	Prayer Changes Things-E-5210	S. Butcher	Suspd.	15.00	40-55.00
81-02-004	God Understands-E-5211	S. Butcher	Retrd.	15.00	40-75.00
81-02-005	We Have Seen His Star-E-5620	S. Butcher	Suspd.	15.00	40-50.00
81-02-006	Jesus Is Born-E-5623	S. Butcher	Suspd.	15.00	40-55.00
82-02-007	The Lord Bless You and Keep You-E-7175	S. Butcher	Suspd.	17.00	35-38.00
82-02-008	The Lord Bless You and Keep You-E-7176	S. Butcher	Suspd.	17.00	40-55.00
82-02-009	The Lord Bless You and Keep You- E-7179	S. Butcher	Open	22.50	35-55.00
82-02-010	Mother Sew Dear-E-7181	S. Butcher	Suspd.	17.00	35-50.00
82-02-011	The Purr-fect Grandma-E-7183	S. Butcher	Suspd.	17.00	35-50.00
Goebel/Schmid		**M. I. Hummel Collectibles Annual Bells**			
78-01-001	Let's Sing 700	M. I. Hummel	Closed	50.00	150-275.
79-01-002	Farewell 701	M. I. Hummel	Closed	70.00	75-165.00
80-01-003	Thoughtful 702	M. I. Hummel	Closed	85.00	85-160.00
81-01-004	In Tune 703	M. I. Hummel	Closed	85.00	100-155.
82-01-005	She Loves Me, She Loves Me Not 704	M. I. Hummel	Closed	90.00	120-150.
83-01-006	Knit One 705	M. I. Hummel	Closed	90.00	90-120.00
84-01-007	Mountaineer 706	M. I. Hummel	Closed	90.00	90-125.00
85-01-008	Sweet Song 707	M. I. Hummel	Closed	90.00	125.00
86-01-009	Sing Along 708	M. I. Hummel	Closed	100.00	125-200.
87-01-010	With Loving Greetings 709	M. I. Hummel	Closed	110.00	175-225.
88-01-011	Busy Student 710	M. I. Hummel	Closed	120.00	125.00
89-01-012	Latest News 711	M. I. Hummel	Closed	135.00	135.00
90-01-013	What's New? 712	M. I. Hummel	Closed	140.00	140-200.
91-01-014	Favorite Pet 713	M. I. Hummel	Closed	150.00	165-200.
92-01-015	Whistler's Duet 714	M. I. Hummel	Closed	160.00	160.00
93-01-016	Celestial Musician 779	M. I. Hummel	Yr.Iss.	50.00	50.00
Gorham		**Various**			
75-01-001	Sweet Song So Young	N. Rockwell	Annual	19.50	50.00
75-01-002	Santa's Helpers	N. Rockwell	Annual	19.50	30.00
75-01-003	Tavern Sign Painter	N. Rockwell	Annual	19.50	30.00
76-01-004	Flowers in Tender Bloom	N. Rockwell	Annual	19.50	40.00
76-01-005	Snow Sculpture	N. Rockwell	Annual	19.50	45.00
77-01-006	Fondly Do We Remember	N. Rockwell	Annual	19.50	55.00
77-01-007	Chilling Chore (Christmas)	N. Rockwell	Annual	19.50	35.00
78-01-008	Gaily Sharing Vintage Times	N. Rockwell	Annual	22.50	22.50
78-01-009	Gay Blades (Christmas)	N. Rockwell	Annual	22.50	22.50
79-01-010	Beguiling Buttercup	N. Rockwell	Annual	24.50	26.50
79-01-011	A Boy Meets His Dog (Christmas)	N. Rockwell	Annual	24.50	30.00
80-01-012	Flying High	N. Rockwell	Annual	27.50	27.50
80-01-013	Chilly Reception (Christmas)	N. Rockwell	Annual	27.50	27.50
81-01-014	Sweet Serenade	N. Rockwell	Annual	27.50	27.50
81-01-015	Ski Skills (Christmas)	N. Rockwell	Annual	27.50	27.50
82-01-016	Young Mans Fancy	N. Rockwell	Annual	29.50	29.50
82-01-017	Coal Season's Coming	N. Rockwell	Annual	29.50	29.50
83-01-018	Christmas Medley	N. Rockwell	Annual	29.50	29.50
83-01-019	The Milkmaid	N. Rockwell	Annual	29.50	29.50
84-01-020	Tiny Tim	N. Rockwell	Annual	29.50	29.50
84-01-021	Young Love	N. Rockwell	Annual	29.50	29.50
84-01-022	Marriage License	N. Rockwell	Annual	32.50	32.50
84-01-023	Yarn Spinner	N. Rockwell	5,000	32.50	32.50
85-01-024	Yuletide Reflections	N. Rockwell	5,000	32.50	32.50
86-01-025	Home For The Holidays	N. Rockwell	5,000	32.50	32.50
86-01-026	On Top of the World	N. Rockwell	5,000	32.50	32.50
87-01-027	Merry Christmas Grandma	N. Rockwell	5,000	32.50	32.50
87-01-028	The Artist	N. Rockwell	5,000	32.50	32.50
88-01-029	The Homecoming	N. Rockwell	15,000	37.50	37.50
Gorham		**Currier & Ives - Mini Bells**			
76-02-001	Christmas Sleigh Ride	Currier & Ives	Annual	9.95	35.00
77-02-002	American Homestead	Currier & Ives	Annual	9.95	25.00
78-02-003	Yule Logs	Currier & Ives	Annual	12.95	20.00
79-02-004	Sleigh Ride	Currier & Ives	Annual	14.95	20.00
80-02-005	Christmas in the Country	Currier & Ives	Annual	14.95	20.00
81-02-006	Christmas Tree	Currier & Ives	Annual	14.95	17.50
82-02-007	Christmas Visitation	Currier & Ives	Annual	16.50	17.50
83-02-008	Winter Wonderland	Currier & Ives	Annual	16.50	17.50
84-02-009	Hitching Up	Currier & Ives	Annual	16.50	17.50
85-02-010	Skaters Holiday	Currier & Ives	Annual	17.50	17.50
86-02-011	Central Park in Winter	Currier & Ives	Annual	17.50	17.50
87-02-012	Early Winter	Currier & Ives	Annual	19.00	19.00
Gorham		**Mini Bells**			
81-03-001	Tiny Tim	N. Rockwell	Annual	19.75	19.75
82-03-002	Planning Christmas Visit	N. Rockwell	Annual	20.00	20.00
Dave Grossman Designs		**Norman Rockwell Collection**			
75-01-001	Faces of Christmas NRB-75	Rockwell-Inspired	Retrd.	12.50	35.00
76-01-002	Drum for Tommy NRB-76	Rockwell-Inspired	Retrd.	12.00	30.00

Company		Series			
Number	**Name**	**Artist**	**Edition Limit**	**Issue Price**	**Quote**
76-01-003	Ben Franklin (Bicentennial)	Rockwell-Inspired	Retrd.	12.50	25.00
80-01-004	Leapfrog NRB-80	Rockwell-Inspired	Retrd.	50.00	60.00
Hallmark Galleries		**Enchanted Garden**			
92-01-001	Fairy Bunny (porcelain)	E. Richardson	9,500	35.00	35.00
Hamilton Gifts/Enesco		**Bells**			
92-01-001	Susanna 999377	M. Humphrey	Open	22.50	22.50
92-01-002	Sarah 999385	M. Humphrey	Open	22.50	22.50
92-01-003	Hollies For You 996095	M. Humphrey	Open	22.50	22.50
Kirk Stieff		**Musical Bells**			
77-01-001	Annual Bell 1977	Kirk Stieff	Closed	17.95	40-120.00
78-01-002	Annual Bell 1978	Kirk Stieff	Closed	17.95	70.00
79-01-003	Annual Bell 1979	Kirk Stieff	Closed	17.95	50.00
80-01-004	Annual Bell 1980	Kirk Stieff	Closed	19.95	50.00
81-01-005	Annual Bell 1981	Kirk Stieff	Closed	19.95	60.00
82-01-006	Annual Bell 1982	Kirk Stieff	Closed	19.95	60-120.00
83-01-007	Annual Bell 1983	Kirk Stieff	Closed	19.95	50.00
84-01-008	Annual Bell 1984	Kirk Stieff	Closed	19.95	35.00
85-01-009	Annual Bell 1985	Kirk Stieff	Closed	19.95	40.00
86-01-010	Annual Bell 1986	Kirk Stieff	Closed	19.95	40.00
87-01-011	Annual Bell 1987	Kirk Stieff	Closed	19.95	30.00
88-01-012	Annual Bell 1988	Kirk Stieff	Closed	22.50	35.00
89-01-013	Annual Bell 1989	Kirk Stieff	Closed	25.00	25.00
90-01-014	Annual Bell 1990	Kirk Stieff	Closed	27.00	27.00
91-01-015	Annual Bell 1991	Kirk Stieff	Closed	28.00	28.00
92-01-016	Annual Bell 1992	Kirk Stieff	Closed	30.00	30.00
Kirk Stieff		**Bell**			
92-02-001	Santa's Workshop Christmas Bell	Kirk Stieff	3,000	40.00	40.00
Lance Corporation		**Hudson Pewter Bicentennial Bells**			
74-01-001	Benjamin Franklin	P.W. Baston	Closed	Unkn.	75-100.00
74-01-002	Thomas Jefferson	P.W. Baston	Closed	Unkn.	75-100.00
74-01-003	George Washington	P.W. Baston	Closed	Unkn.	75-100.00
74-01-004	John Adams	P.W. Baston	Closed	Unkn.	75-100.00
74-01-005	James Madison	P.W. Baston	Closed	Unkn.	75-100.00
Lenox China		**Songs of Christmas**			
91-01-001	We Wish You a Merry Christmas	Unknown	Yr.Iss.	49.00	49.00
92-01-002	Deck the Halls	Unknown	Yr.Iss.	49.00	49.00
Lenox Collections		**Crystal Christmas Bell**			
81-01-001	Partridge in a Pear Tree	Lenox	15,000	55.00	55.00
82-01-002	Holy Family Bell	Lenox	15,000	55.00	55.00
83-01-003	Three Wise Men	Lenox	15,000	55.00	55.00
84-01-004	Dove Bell	Lenox	15,000	57.00	57.00
85-01-005	Santa Claus Bell	Lenox	15,000	57.00	57.00
86-01-006	Dashing Through the Snow Bell	Lenox	15,000	64.00	64.00
87-01-007	Heralding Angel Bell	Lenox	15,000	76.00	76.00
91-01-008	Celestial Harpist	Lenox	15,000	75.00	75.00
Lenox Collections		**Bird Bells**			
91-02-001	Bluebird	Unknown	Open	57.00	57.00
91-02-002	Hummingbird	Unknown	Open	57.00	57.00
91-02-003	Chickadee	Unknown	Open	57.00	57.00
92-02-004	Robin Bell	Unknown	Open	57.00	57.00
Lenox Collections		**Carousel Bell**			
92-03-001	Carousel Horse	Unknown	Open	45.00	45.00
Lladro		**Lladro Christmas Bell**			
87-01-001	Christmas Bell - L5458M	Lladro	Annual	29.50	125-200.
88-01-002	Christmas Bell - L5525M	Lladro	Annual	32.50	50-125.00
89-01-003	Christmas Bell - L5616M	Lladro	Annual	32.50	100-150.
90-01-004	Christmas Bell - L5641M	Lladro	Annual	35.00	40-100.00
91-01-005	Christmas Bell - L5803M	Lladro	Annual	37.50	37.50-56.00
92-01-006	Christmas Bell - L5913M	Lladro	Annual	37.50	37.50-75.00
Lincoln Mint		**Lincoln Bells**			
75-01-001	Downhill Daring	N. Rockwell	None	25.00	70.00
Museum Collections, Inc.		**Collectors Bells**			
82-01-001	Wedding/Anniversary	N. Rockwell	Open	45.00	45.00
82-01-002	25th Anniversary	N. Rockwell	Open	45.00	45.00
82-01-003	50th Anniversary	N. Rockwell	Open	45.00	45.00
82-01-004	For A Good Boy	N. Rockwell	Open	45.00	45.00
Reco International		**Special Occasions**			
89-01-001	The Wedding	S. Kuck	Open	15.00	15.00
Reco International		**Special Occasions-Wedding**			
91-02-001	From This Day Forward	C. Micarelli	Open	15.00	15.00
91-02-002	To Have And To Hold	C. Micarelli	Open	15.00	15.00
Reed & Barton		**Noel Musical Bells**			
80-01-001	1980 Bell	Reed & Barton	Closed	20.00	50.00
81-01-002	1981 Bell	Reed & Barton	Closed	22.50	45.00
82-01-003	1982 Bell	Reed & Barton	Closed	22.50	35.00
83-01-004	1983 Bell	Reed & Barton	Closed	22.50	45.00
84-01-005	1984 Bell	Reed & Barton	Closed	22.50	50.00
85-01-006	1985 Bell	Reed & Barton	Closed	25.00	40.00
86-01-007	1986 Bell	Reed & Barton	Closed	25.00	35.00
87-01-008	1987 Bell	Reed & Barton	Closed	25.00	30.00
88-01-009	1988 Bell	Reed & Barton	Closed	25.00	27.50
89-01-010	1989 Bell	Reed & Barton	Closed	25.00	27.50
90-01-011	1990 Bell	Reed & Barton	Closed	27.50	27.50
91-01-012	1991 Bell	Reed & Barton	Closed	30.00	30.00
92-01-013	1992 Bell	Reed & Barton	Closed	30.00	30.00
93-01-014	1993 Bell	Reed & Barton	Yr.Iss.	30.00	30.00
Reed & Barton		**Yuletide Bell**			
81-02-001	Yuletide Holiday	Reed & Barton	Closed	14.00	14.00
82-02-002	Little Shepherd	Reed & Barton	Closed	14.00	14.00
83-02-003	Perfect Angel	Reed & Barton	Closed	15.00	15.00
84-02-004	Drummer Boy	Reed & Barton	Closed	15.00	15.00
85-02-005	Caroler	Reed & Barton	Closed	16.50	16.50
86-02-006	Night Before Christmas	Reed & Barton	Closed	16.50	16.50
87-02-007	Jolly St. Nick	Reed & Barton	Closed	16.50	16.50
88-02-008	Christmas Morning	Reed & Barton	Closed	16.50	16.50
89-02-009	The Bell Ringer	Reed & Barton	Closed	16.50	16.50
90-02-010	The Wreath Bearer	Reed & Barton	Closed	18.50	18.50

Company		Series			
Number	**Name**	**Artist**	**Edition Limit**	**Issue Price**	**Quote**
91-02-011	A Special Gift	Reed & Barton	Closed	22.50	22.50
92-02-012	My Special Friend	Reed & Barton	Closed	22.50	22.50
93-02-013	Yuletide	Reed & Barton	Yr.Iss.	22.50	22.50
River Shore		**Rockwell Children Series I**			
77-01-001	School Play	N. Rockwell	7,500	30.00	75.00
77-01-002	First Day of School	N. Rockwell	7,500	30.00	75.00
77-01-003	Football Hero	N. Rockwell	7,500	30.00	75.00
77-01-004	Flowers for Mother	N. Rockwell	7,500	30.00	60.00
River Shore		**Rockwell Children Series II**			
78-02-001	Dressing Up	N. Rockwell	15,000	35.00	50.00
78-02-002	Future All American	N. Rockwell	15,000	35.00	52.00
78-02-003	Garden Girl	N. Rockwell	15,000	35.00	40.00
78-02-004	Five Cents A Glass	N. Rockwell	15,000	35.00	40.00
River Shore		**Norman Rockwell Single Issues**			
81-03-001	Looking Out to Sea	N. Rockwell	7,000	45.00	95.00
81-03-002	Spring Flowers	N. Rockwell	347	175.00	175.00
81-03-003	Grandpa's Guardian	N. Rockwell	7,000	45.00	45.00
Norman Rockwell Gallery		**Rockwell Christmas Bells**			
92-01-001	Good Girls & Boys	Rockwell-Inspired	N/A	24.95	24.95
Roman, Inc.		**The Masterpiece Collection**			
79-01-001	Adoration	F. Lippe	Open	20.00	20.00
80-01-002	Madonna with Grapes	P. Mignard	Open	25.00	25.00
81-01-003	The Holy Family	G. Notti	Open	25.00	25.00
82-01-004	Madonna of the Streets	R. Ferruzzi	Open	25.00	25.00
Roman, Inc.		**F. Hook Bells**			
85-02-001	Beach Buddies	F. Hook	15,000	25.00	27.50
86-02-002	Sounds of the Sea	F. Hook	15,000	25.00	27.50
87-02-003	Bear Hug	F. Hook	15,000	25.00	27.50
Roman, Inc.		**Annual Fontanini Christmas Crystal Bell**			
91-03-001	1991 Bell	E. Simonetti	Closed	30.00	30.00
92-03-002	1992 Bell	E. Simonetti	Closed	30.00	30.00
93-03-003	1993 Bell	E. Simonetti	Yr.Iss.	30.00	30.00
Roman, Inc.		**Annual Nativity Bell**			
90-04-001	Nativity	I. Spencer	Closed	15.00	15.00
91-04-002	Flight Into Egypt	I. Spencer	Closed	15.00	15.00
92-04-003	Gloria in Excelsis Deo	I. Spencer	Closed	15.00	15.00
93-04-004	Three Kings of Orient	I. Spencer	Yr.Iss.	15.00	15.00
Royal Copenhagen		**Christmas**			
92-01-001	The Queen's Carriage	S. Vestergaard	Closed	69.50	69.50
93-01-002	Christmas Guests	S. Vestergaard	Yr.Iss.	62.50	62.50
Sandstone Creations		**A Fantasy Edition**			
80-01-001	Little Prayer	T. DeGrazia	7,500	40.00	40.00
81-01-002	Flower Vendor	T. DeGrazia	7,500	40.00	40.00
XX-01-003	Wee Three	T. DeGrazia	7,500	40.00	40.00
XX-01-004	Party Time	T. DeGrazia	7,500	40.00	40.00
Schmid		**Berta Hummel Christmas Bells**			
72-01-001	Angel with Flute	B. Hummel	Yr.Iss.	20.00	75.00
73-01-002	Nativity	B. Hummel	Yr.Iss.	15.00	80.00
74-01-003	The Guardian Angel	B. Hummel	Yr.Iss.	17.50	45.00
75-01-004	The Christmas Child	B. Hummel	Yr.Iss.	22.50	45.00
76-01-005	Sacred Journey	B. Hummel	Yr.Iss.	22.50	25.00
77-01-006	Herald Angel	B. Hummel	Yr.Iss.	22.50	50.00
78-01-007	Heavenly Trio	B. Hummel	Yr.Iss.	27.50	40.00
79-01-008	Starlight Angel	B. Hummel	Yr.Iss.	38.00	45.00
80-01-009	Parade into Toyland	B. Hummel	Yr.Iss.	45.00	55.00
81-01-010	A Time to Remember	B. Hummel	Yr.Iss.	45.00	55.00
82-01-011	Angelic Procession	B. Hummel	Yr.Iss.	45.00	50.00
83-01-012	Angelic Messenger	B. Hummel	Yr.Iss.	45.00	55.00
84-01-013	A Gift from Heaven	B. Hummel	Yr.Iss.	45.00	75.00
85-01-014	Heavenly Light	B. Hummel	Yr.Iss.	45.00	75.00
86-01-015	Tell the Heavens	B. Hummel	Yr.Iss.	45.00	45.00
87-01-016	Angelic Gifts	B. Hummel	Yr.Iss.	47.50	47.50
88-01-017	Cheerful Cherubs	B. Hummel	Yr.Iss.	52.50	55.00
89-01-018	Angelic Musician	B. Hummel	Yr.Iss.	53.00	55.00
90-01-019	Angel's Light	B. Hummel	Yr.Iss.	53.00	53.00
91-01-020	Message From Above	B. Hummel	5,000	58.00	58.00
92-01-021	Sweet Blessings	B. Hummel	5,000	65.00	65.00
93-01-022	Silent Wonder	B. Hummel	5,000	58.00	58.00
Schmid		**Berta Hummel Mother's Day Bells**			
76-02-001	Devotion for Mothers	B. Hummel	Yr.Iss.	22.50	55.00
77-02-002	Moonlight Return	B. Hummel	Yr.Iss.	22.50	45.00
78-02-003	Afternoon Stroll	B. Hummel	Yr.Iss.	27.50	45.00
79-02-004	Cherub's Gift	B. Hummel	Yr.Iss.	38.00	45.00
80-02-005	Mother's Little Helper	B. Hummel	Yr.Iss.	45.00	45.00
81-02-006	Playtime	B. Hummel	Yr.Iss.	45.00	45.00
82-02-007	The Flower Basket	B. Hummel	Yr.Iss.	45.00	45.00
83-02-008	Spring Bouquet	B. Hummel	Yr.Iss.	45.00	45.00
84-02-009	A Joy to Share	B. Hummel	Yr.Iss.	45.00	45.00
Schmid		**The Littlest Light**			
93-03-001	The Littlest Light	B. Hummel	Open	15.00	15.00
Schmid		**Peanuts Annual Bells**			
79-04-001	A Special Letter	C. Schulz	10,000	15.00	25.00
80-04-002	Waiting For Santa	C. Schulz	10,000	15.00	25.00
81-04-003	Mission For Mom	C. Schulz	10,000	17.50	20.00
82-04-004	Perfect Performance	C. Schulz	10,000	18.50	18.50
83-04-005	Peanuts in Concert	C. Schulz	10,000	12.50	12.50
84-04-006	Snoopy and the Beagle Scouts	C. Schulz	10,000	12.50	12.50
Schmid		**Peanuts Christmas Bells**			
75-05-001	Woodstock, Santa Claus	C. Schulz	Yr.Iss.	10.00	25.00
76-05-002	Woodstock's Christmas	C. Schulz	Yr.Iss.	10.00	25.00
77-05-003	Deck the Doghouse	C. Schulz	Yr.Iss.	10.00	20.00
78-05-004	Filling the Stocking	C. Schulz	Yr.Iss.	13.00	15.00
Schmid		**Peanuts Mother's Day Bells**			
73-06-001	Mom?	C. Schulz	Yr.Iss.	5.00	15.00
74-06-002	Snoopy/Woodstock/Parade	C. Schulz	Yr.Iss.	5.00	15.00
76-06-003	Linus and Snoopy	C. Schulz	Yr.Iss.	10.00	15.00
77-06-004	Dear Mom	C. Schulz	Yr.Iss.	10.00	15.00

Company / Number	Series / Name	Artist	Edition Limit	Issue Price	Quote
78-06-005	Thoughts That Count	C. Schulz	Yr.Iss.	13.00	15.00
Schmid	**Peanuts Special Edition Bell**				
76-07-001	Bi-Centennial	C. Schulz	Yr.Iss.	10.00	20.00
Schmid	**Disney Annuals**				
85-08-001	Snow Biz	Disney Studios	10,000	16.50	16.50
86-08-002	Tree for Two	Disney Studios	10,000	16.50	16.50
87-08-003	Merry Mouse Medley	Disney Studios	10,000	17.50	17.50
88-08-004	Warm Winter Ride	Disney Studios	10,000	19.50	19.50
89-08-005	Merry Mickey Claus	Disney Studios	10,000	23.00	23.00
90-08-006	Holly Jolly Christmas	Disney Studios	10,000	26.50	26.50
91-08-007	Mickey & Minnie's Rockin' Christmas	Disney Studios	10,000	26.50	26.50
Schmid	**Lowell Davis Mini Bell**				
92-09-001	New Day	L. Davis	Yr.Iss.	10.00	10.00
Schmid/B.F.A.	**RFD Bell**				
79-01-001	Blossom	L. Davis	Closed	65.00	300-400.
79-01-002	Kate	L. Davis	Closed	65.00	300-400.
79-01-003	Willy	L. Davis	Closed	65.00	400.00
79-01-004	Caruso	L. Davis	Closed	65.00	300.00
79-01-005	Wilbur	L. Davis	Closed	65.00	300-350.
79-01-006	Old Blue Lead	L. Davis	Closed	65.00	275-300.
80-01-007	Cow Bell "Blossom"	L. Davis	Open	65.00	65.00
80-01-008	Mule Bell "Kate"	L. Davis	Open	65.00	65.00
80-01-009	Goat Bell "Willy"	L. Davis	Open	65.00	65.00
80-01-010	Rooster Bell "Caruso"	L. Davis	Open	65.00	65.00
80-01-011	Pig Bell "Wilbur"	L. Davis	Open	65.00	65.00
80-01-014	Dog Bell "Old Blue and Lead"	L. Davis	Open	65.00	65.00
Waterford Wedgwood USA	**New Year Bells**				
79-01-001	Penguins	Unknown	Annual	40.00	40.00
80-01-002	Polar Bears	Unknown	Annual	50.00	50.00
81-01-003	Moose	Unknown	Annual	55.00	55.00
82-01-004	Fur Seals	Unknown	Annual	60.00	60.00
83-01-005	Ibex	Unknown	Annual	64.00	64.00
84-01-006	Puffin	Unknown	Annual	64.00	64.00
85-01-007	Ermine	Unknown	Annual	64.00	64.00

CHRISTMAS ORNAMENTS

Company / Number	Series / Name	Artist	Edition Limit	Issue Price	Quote
Kurt S. Adler/Santa's World	**Fabriché™ Ornament Series**				
92-01-001	Hello Little One! W1561	KS. Adler	Open	22.00	22.00
92-01-002	Not a Creature Was Stirring W1563	KS. Adler	Open	22.00	22.00
92-01-003	Hugs And Kisses W1560	KS. Adler	Open	22.00	22.00
92-01-004	Merry Chrismouse W1565	KS. Adler	Open	10.00	10.00
Kurt S. Adler/Santa's World	**Smithsonian Institution Fabriché™ Ornament Series**				
92-02-001	Holiday Drive W1580	KS. Adler	Open	38.00	38.00
92-02-002	Santa On a Bicycle W1547	KS. Adler	Open	31.00	31.00
Kurt S. Adler/Santa's World	**Steinbach Ornament Series**				
92-03-001	The King's Guards ES300	KS. Adler	Retrd.	27.00	27.00
Kurt S. Adler/Santa's World	**Christmas in Chelsea Collection**				
92-04-001	Allison Sitting in Chair W2812	J. Mostrom	Open	25.50	25.50
92-04-002	Christina W2812	J. Mostrom	Open	25.50	25.50
92-04-003	Holly W2709	J. Mostrom	Open	21.00	21.00
92-04-004	Christopher W2709	J. Mostrom	Open	21.00	21.00
92-04-005	Amanda W2709	J. Mostrom	Open	21.00	21.00
92-04-006	Peony W2728	J. Mostrom	Open	20.00	20.00
92-04-007	Delphinium W2728	J. Mostrom	Open	20.00	20.00
92-04-008	Rose W2728	J. Mostrom	Open	20.00	20.00
92-04-009	Holly Hock W2728	J. Mostrom	Open	20.00	20.00
Kurt S. Adler/Santa's World	**Royal Heritage Collection**				
93-05-001	Nicholas W2923	J. Mostrom	Open	25.50	25.50
93-05-002	Patina W2923	J. Mostrom	Open	25.50	25.50
93-05-003	Sasha W2923	J. Mostrom	Open	25.50	25.50
93-05-004	Anastasia W2922	J. Mostrom	Open	28.00	28.00
93-05-005	Elizabeth W2924	J. Mostrom	Open	25.50	25.50
93-05-006	Charles W2924	J. Mostrom	Open	25.50	25.50
93-05-007	Caroline W2924	J. Mostrom	Open	25.50	25.50
93-05-008	Joella W2979	J. Mostrom	Open	27.00	27.00
93-05-009	Kelly W2979	J. Mostrom	Open	27.00	27.00
All God's Children	**Christmas Ornaments**				
87-01-001	Cameo Ornaments (set of 12)	M. Holcombe	Retrd.	12.00/ea	100.00/ea.
87-01-002	Doll Ornaments (set of 24)	M. Holcombe	Retrd.	14.00/ea	100.00/ea.
Anheuser-Busch, Inc.	**A & Eagle Collector Ornament Series**				
91-01-001	Budweiser Girl-Circa 1890's N3178	A.-Busch, Inc.	Open	15.00	15.00
92-01-002	1893 Columbian Exposition N3649	A.-Busch, Inc.	Open	15.00	15.00
93-01-003	Greatest Triumph N4089	A.-Busch, Inc.	Open	N/A	N/A
Anheuser-Busch, Inc.	**Christmas Ornaments**				
92-02-001	Clydesdales Mini Plate Ornaments N3650 (3 pc. set)	S. Sampson	Open	23.00	23.00
Annalee Mobilitee	**Christmas Ornaments**				
86-01-001	Clown Head	A. Thorndike	5,701	7.95	25.00
86-01-002	Angel Head	A. Thorndike	Unkn.	7.95	30.00
84-01-003	Snowman Head	A. Thorndike	13,677	7.95	25.00
82-01-004	Elf Head	A. Thorndike	1,908	2.95	25.00
85-01-005	Sun Ornament	A. Thorndike	1,692	6.50	25.00
84-01-006	Star Ornament	A. Thorndike	3,275	5.95	25.00
83-01-007	Gingerbread Boy	A. Thorndike	11,835	10.95	35.00
86-01-008	Baby Angel	A. Thorndike	N/A	11.95	35.00
85-01-009	3" Angel On Cloud	A. Thorndike	Unkn.	6.50	30.00
ANRI	**Ferandiz Message Collection**				
89-01-001	Let the Heavens Ring	J. Ferrandiz	1,000	215.00	215.00
90-01-002	Hear The Angels Sing	J. Ferrandiz	1,000	225.00	225.00
ANRI	**Ferrandiz Woodcarvings**				
88-02-001	Heavenly Drummer	J. Ferrandiz	1,000	175.00	225.00
89-02-002	Heavenly Strings	J. Ferrandiz	1,000	190.00	190.00
ANRI	**Disney Four Star Collection**				
89-03-001	Maestro Mickey	Disney Studios	Yr.Iss.	25.00	25.00
90-03-002	Minnie Mouse	Disney Studios	Yr.Iss.	25.00	25.00
Armani	**Christmas**				
91-01-001	1991 Christmas Ornament 799A	G. Armani	Retrd.	11.50	11.50
92-01-002	1992 Christmas Ornament 788F	G. Armani	Retrd.	23.50	23.50
93-01-003	1993 Christmas Ornament 829P	G. Armani	Yr.Iss.	25.00	25.00
Artaffects	**Annual Christmas Ornaments**				
85-01-001	Papoose Ornament	G. Perillo	Unkn.	14.00	65.00
86-01-002	Christmas Cactus	G. Perillo	Unkn.	15.00	50.00
87-01-003	Annual Ornament	G. Perillo	Unkn.	15.00	35.00
88-01-004	Annual Ornament	G. Perillo	Yr.Iss.	17.50	25.00
89-01-005	Annual Ornament	G. Perillo	Yr.Iss.	17.50	25.00
90-01-006	Annual Ornament	G. Perillo	Yr.Iss.	19.50	19.50
91-01-007	Annual Ornament	G. Perillo	Yr.Iss.	19.50	19.50
Artaffects	**Annual Bell Ornaments**				
85-02-001	Home Sweet Wigwam	G. Perillo	Yr.Iss.	14.00	14.00
86-02-002	Peek-A-Boo	G. Perillo	Yr.Iss.	15.00	15.00
87-02-003	Annual Bell Ornament	G. Perillo	Yr.Iss.	15.00	15.00
88-02-004	Annual Bell Ornament	G. Perillo	Yr.Iss.	17.50	17.50
89-02-005	Annual Bell Ornament	G. Perillo	Yr.Iss.	17.50	17.50
90-02-006	Annual Bell Ornament	G. Perillo	Yr.Iss.	17.50	17.50
91-02-007	Annual Bell Ornament	G. Perillo	Yr.Iss.	19.50	19.50
Artaffects	**Sagebrush Kids Bell Ornaments**				
87-03-001	The Fiddler	G. Perillo	Open	9.00	9.00
87-03-002	The Harpist	G. Perillo	Open	9.00	9.00
87-03-003	Christmas Horn	G. Perillo	Open	9.00	9.00
87-03-004	The Gift	G. Perillo	Open	9.00	9.00
87-03-005	Christmas Candle	G. Perillo	Open	9.00	9.00
87-03-006	The Carolers	G. Perillo	Open	9.00	9.00
Artaffects	**Kachina Ornaments**				
91-04-001	Sun Kachina	G. Perillo	Open	17.50	17.50
91-04-002	Old Kachina	G. Perillo	Open	17.50	17.50
91-04-003	Snow Kachina	G. Perillo	Open	17.50	17.50
91-04-004	Dawn Kachina	G. Perillo	Open	17.50	17.50
91-04-005	Kachina Mother	G. Perillo	Open	17.50	17.50
91-04-006	Totem Kachina	G. Perillo	Open	17.50	17.50
Artaffects	**Sagebrush Kids Collection**				
91-05-001	Tee-Pee Ornament	G. Perillo	Open	15.00	15.00
91-05-002	Tee-Pee Ornament	G. Perillo	Open	15.00	15.00
91-05-003	Shield Ornament	G. Perillo	Open	15.00	15.00
91-05-004	Moccasin Ornament	G. Perillo	Open	15.00	15.00
Artaffects	**Simple Wonders**				
91-06-001	Kim	C. Roeda	Open	22.50	22.50
91-06-002	Brittany	C. Roeda	Open	22.50	22.50
91-06-003	Nicole	C. Roeda	Open	22.50	22.50
91-06-004	Megan	C. Roeda	Open	22.50	22.50
91-06-005	Little Feather	C. Roeda	Open	22.50	22.50
91-06-006	Ashley	C. Roeda	Open	22.50	22.50
92-06-007	Sweet Surprise	C. Roeda	Yr.Iss.	15.00	15.00
Artists of the World	**De Grazia Annual Ornaments**				
86-01-001	Pima. Indian Drummer Boy	T. De Grazia	Yr.Iss.	27.50	350-450.
87-01-002	White Dove	T. De Grazia	Yr.Iss.	29.50	75-125.00
88-01-003	Flower Girl	T. De Grazia	Yr.Iss.	32.50	45-95.00
89-01-004	Flower Boy	T. De Grazia	Yr.Iss.	35.00	45-65.00
90-01-005	Pink Papoose	T. De Grazia	Yr.Iss.	35.00	45-95.00
90-01-006	Merry Little Indian	T. De Grazia	10,000	87.50	95-100.00
91-01-007	Christmas Prayer	T. De Grazia	Yr.Iss.	49.50	55.00
92-01-008	Bearing Gift	T. De Grazia	Yr.Iss.	55.00	55.00
93-01-009	Lighting the Way	T. De Grazia	Yr.Iss.	57.50	65.00
Bing & Grondahl	**Christmas In America**				
86-01-001	Christmas Eve in Williamsburg	J. Woodson	Closed	12.50	90-150.00
87-01-002	Christmas Eve at the White House	J. Woodson	Closed	15.00	15-60.00
88-01-003	Christmas Eve at Rockefeller Center	J. Woodson	Closed	18.50	18.50
89-01-004	Christmas in New England	J. Woodson	Closed	20.00	20-35.00
90-01-005	Christmas Eve at the Capitol	J. Woodson	Closed	20.00	25-45.00
91-01-006	Independence Hall	J. Woodson	Closed	23.50	23.50
92-01-007	Christmas in San Francisco	J. Woodson	Yr.Iss.	25.00	25.00
93-01-008	Coming Home For Christmas	J. Woodson	Yr.Iss.	25.00	25.00
Bing & Grondahl	**Santa Claus**				
89-02-001	Santa's Workshop	H. Hansen	Yr.Iss.	20.00	20.00
90-02-002	Santa's Sleigh	H. Hansen	Yr.Iss.	20.00	20.00
91-02-003	The Journey	H. Hansen	Yr.Iss.	23.50	23.50-45.
92-02-004	Santa's Arrival	H. Hansen	Yr.Iss.	25.00	25.00
93-02-005	Santa's Gifts	H. Hansen	Yr.Iss.	25.00	25.00
Buccellati	**Christmas Ornaments**				
86-01-001	Snowy Village Scene -2464	Buccellati	500	195.00	400.00
87-01-002	Shooting Star-2469	Buccellati	500	240.00	350.00
88-01-003	Santa Claus-2470	Buccellati	Closed	300.00	300.00
89-01-004	Christmas Tree-2471	Buccellati	750	230.00	230.00
90-01-005	Zenith-2472	Buccellati	750	250.00	250.00
91-01-006	Wreath-3561	Buccellati	750	300.00	300.00
92-01-007	Cherubs-3562	Buccellati	500	300.00	300.00

Carriage House: See Margaret Furlong Designs

Company / Number	Series / Name	Artist	Edition Limit	Issue Price	Quote
Cast Art Industries	**Dreamsicles Ornaments**				
92-01-001	Cherub With Moon-DX260	K. Haynes	Open	6.00	6.00
92-01-002	Praying Cherub-DX261	K. Haynes	Open	6.00	6.00
92-01-003	Cherub With Star-DX262	K. Haynes	Open	6.00	6.00
92-01-004	Cherub On Cloud-DX263	K. Haynes	Open	6.00	6.00
92-01-005	Bunny-DX270	K. Haynes	Open	6.00	6.00
92-01-006	Piggy-DX271	K. Haynes	Open	6.00	6.00
92-01-007	Raccoon-DX272	K. Haynes	Open	6.00	6.00
92-01-008	Squirrel-DX273	K. Haynes	Open	6.00	6.00
92-01-009	Bear-DX274	K. Haynes	Open	6.00	6.00
92-01-010	Lamb-DX275	K. Haynes	Open	6.00	6.00
Cazenovia Abroad	**Christmas Ornaments**				
68-01-001	Teddy Bear-P101TB	Unknown	Unkn.	9.00	34-45.00
68-01-002	Elephant-P102E	Unknown	Unkn.	9.00	34-45.00
68-01-003	Duck-P103D	Unknown	Unkn.	9.00	34-45.00
68-01-004	Bunny-P104B	Unknown	Unkn.	9.00	34-45.00
68-01-005	Cat-P105C	Unknown	Unkn.	9.00	34-45.00
68-01-006	Rooster-P106R	Unknown	Unkn.	10.00	34-45.00
68-01-007	Standing Angel-P107SA	Unknown	Unkn.	9.00	39-52.50
68-01-008	Tiptoe Angel-P108TTA	Unknown	Unkn.	10.00	34-45.00

Company Number	Series Name	Artist	Edition Limit	Issue Price	Quote
69-01-009	Fawn-P109F	Unknown	Unkn.	12.00	45.00
70-01-010	Snow Man-P110SM	Unknown	Unkn.	12.00	45.00
70-01-011	Peace-P111P	Unknown	Unkn.	12.00	45.00
70-01-012	Porky-P112PK	Unknown	Unkn.	15.00	45.00
71-01-013	Kneeling Angel-P113KA	Unknown	Unkn.	15.00	48-65.00
72-01-014	Rocking Horse-P114RH	Unknown	Unkn.	15.00	48-65.00
73-01-015	Treetop Angel-P115TOP	Unknown	Unkn.	10.00	37-50.00
74-01-016	Owl-P116O	Unknown	Unkn.	15.00	45.00
75-01-017	Star-P117ST	Unknown	Unkn.	15.00	45.00
76-01-018	Hatching Chick-P118CH	Unknown	Unkn.	15.00	45.00
77-01-019	Raggedy Ann-P119RA	Unknown	Unkn.	17.50	39-52.50
78-01-020	Shell-P120SH	Unknown	Unkn.	20.00	34-45.00
79-01-021	Toy Soldier-P121TS	Unknown	Unkn.	20.00	34-45.00
80-01-022	Burro-P122BU	Unknown	Unkn.	20.00	34-45.00
81-01-023	Clown-P123CL	Unknown	Unkn.	25.00	34-45.00
82-01-024	Rebecca-P124RE	Unknown	Unkn.	25.00	34-45.00
83-01-025	Raggedy Andy-P125AND	Unknown	Unkn.	27.50	39-52.50
83-01-026	Mouse-P126MO	Unknown	Unkn.	27.50	39-52.50
84-01-027	Cherub-P127CB	Unknown	Unkn.	30.00	39-52.50
85-01-028	Shaggy Dog-P132SD	Unknown	Unkn.	45.00	50.00
86-01-029	Peter Rabbit-P133PR	Unknown	Unkn.	50.00	50.00
86-01-030	Big Sister-P134BS	Unknown	Unkn.	60.00	60.00
86-01-031	Little Brother-P135LB	Unknown	Unkn.	55.00	55.00
87-01-032	Lamb-P136LA	Unknown	Unkn.	60.00	60.00
87-01-033	Sea Horse-P137SE	Unknown	Unkn.	35.00	26-35.00
88-01-034	Partridge-P138PA	Unknown	Unkn.	70.00	70.00
88-01-035	Squirrel-P139SQ	Unknown	Unkn.	70.00	70.00
84-01-036	Reindeer & Sleigh-H100	Unknown	Unkn.	1250.00	1500.00
89-01-037	Swan-P140SW	Unknown	Open	45.00	45.00
90-01-038	Moravian Star-P141PS	Unknown	Open	65.00	65.00
91-01-039	Hedgehog-P142HH	Unknown	Open	65.00	65.00
91-01-040	Bunny Rabbit-P143BR	Unknown	Open	65.00	65.00
91-01-041	Angel-P144A	Unknown	Open	63.00	63.00
91-01-042	Carousel Flag Horse-A301CFH	Herschell-Spillman	2,649	75.00	75.00
91-01-043	Dentzel Fishing Cat-A302CFC	Cernigliaro	2,649	75.00	75.00
91-01-044	Dentzel Flirting Rabbit-A303CFR	Cernigliaro	2,649	75.00	75.00
92-01-045	Humpty Dumpty-P145HD*	Unknown	Open	70.00	70.00
92-01-046	Looff Sneaky Tiger-A304LST	Looff	2,649	82.50	82.50
92-01-047	Herschell-Spillman Polar Bear-A305HPB	Herschell-Spillman	2,649	82.50	82.50
92-01-048	Parker Rose HorseA306PRH	C.W. Parker	2,649	82.50	82.50
Cybis	**Christmas Collection**				
83-01-001	1983 Holiday Bell	Cybis	Yr.Iss.	145.00	1000.00
84-01-002	1984 Holiday Ball	Cybis	Yr.Iss.	145.00	700.00
85-01-003	1985 Holiday Angel	Cybis	Yr.Iss.	75.00	500.00
86-01-004	1986 Holiday Cherub Ornament	Cybis	Yr.Iss.	75.00	500.00
87-01-005	1987 Heavenly Angels	Cybis	Yr.Iss.	95.00	400.00
88-01-006	1988 Holiday Ornament	Cybis	Yr.Iss.	95.00	375.00
Department 56	**Snowbabies Ornaments**				
86-01-001	Sitting, Lite-Up, Clip-On, 7952-9	Department 56	Closed	7.00	35-45.00
86-01-002	Crawling, Lite-Up, Clip-On, 7953-7	Department 56	Closed	7.00	12-35.00
86-01-003	Winged, Lite-Up, Clip-On, 7954-5	Department 56	Closed	7.00	35-45.00
86-01-004	Snowbaby on Brass Ribbon, 7961-8	Department 56	Closed	8.00	50-80.00
87-01-005	Moon Beams, 7951-0	Department 56	Open	7.50	7.50
87-01-006	Snowbaby Adrift Lite-Up, Clip-On, 7969-3	Department 56	Closed	8.50	30-55.00
87-01-007	Mini, Lite-Up, Clip-On, 7976-6	Department 56	Open	9.00	9.00
88-01-008	Twinkle Little Star, 7980-4	Department 56	Closed	7.00	30-45.00
89-01-009	Noel, 7988-0	Department 56	Open	7.50	7.50
89-01-010	Surprise, 7989-8	Department 56	Open	12.00	12.00
89-01-011	Star Bright, 7990-1	Department 56	Open	7.50	7.50
90-01-012	Rock-A-Bye Baby, 7939-1	Depatrment 56	Open	7.00	7.00
90-01-013	Penguin, Lite-Up, Clip-On, 7940-5	Department 56	Closed	5.00	10-30.00
90-01-014	Polar Bear, Lite-Up, Clip-On, 7941-3	Department 56	Closed	5.00	10-30.00
91-01-015	Swinging On a Star, 6810-1	Department 56	Open	9.50	9.50
91-01-016	My First Star, 6811-0	Department 56	Open	7.00	7.00
92-01-017	Snowbabies Icicle Star, 6825-0	Department 56	Open	16.00	16.00
92-01-018	Starry, Starry Night, 6830-6	Department 56	Open	12.50	12.50
Department 56	**CCP Ornaments-Flat**				
86-02-001	Christmas Carol Village, set of 3 (6504-8)	Department 56	Closed	13.00	33-45.00
86-02-002	Fezziwig's Warehouse	Department 56	Closed	4.35	N/A
86-02-003	Scrooge and Marley Countinghouse	Department 56	Closed	4.35	N/A
86-02-004	The Cottage of Bob Cratchit & Tiny Tim	Department 56	Closed	4.35	N/A
86-02-005	New England Village, set of 7 (6536-6)	Department 56	Closed	25.00	215.00
86-02-006	Apothecary Shop	Department 56	Closed	3.50	15-25.00
86-02-007	General Store	Department 56	Closed	3.50	15-45.00
86-02-008	Nathaniel Bingham Fabrics	Department 56	Closed	3.50	15-20.00
86-02-009	Livery Stable & Boot Shop	Department 56	Closed	3.50	15.00
86-02-010	Steeple Church	Department 56	Closed	3.50	15-115.00
86-02-011	Brick Town Hall	Department 56	Closed	3.50	15-50.00
86-02-012	Red Schoolhouse	Department 56	Closed	3.50	15-60.00
Department 56	**Christmas Carol Character Ornaments-Flat**				
86-03-001	Christmas Carol Characters, set of 3(6505-6)	Department 56	Closed	13.00	25-42.00
86-03-002	Bob Cratchit & Tiny Tim	Department 56	Closed	4.35	25-30.00
86-03-003	Scrooge	Department 56	Closed	4.35	25-30.00
86-03-004	Poulterer	Department 56	Closed	4.35	25-30.00
Department 56	**Village Light-Up Ornaments**				
85-04-001	Dickens' Village, set of 8 (6521-8)	Department 56	Closed	48.00	160-225.
85-04-002	Crowntree Inn	Department 56	Closed	6.00	20-35.00
85-04-003	Candle Shop	Department 56	Closed	6.00	20-35.00
85-04-004	Green Grocer	Department 56	Closed	6.00	20-35.00
85-04-005	Golden Swan Baker	Department 56	Closed	6.00	20-35.00
85-04-006	Bean and Son Smithy Shop	Department 56	Closed	6.00	15-35.00
85-04-007	Abel Beasley Butcher	Department 56	Closed	6.00	15-35.00
85-04-008	Jones & Co. Brush & Basket Shop	Department 56	Closed	6.00	35.00
85-04-009	Dickens' Village Church	Department 56	Closed	6.00	20-40.00
87-04-010	Dickens' Village, set of 6 (6520-0)	Department 56	Closed	36.00	155-165.
87-04-011	Blythe Pond Mill House	Department 56	Closed	6.00	20-40.00
87-04-012	Barley Bree Farmhouse	Department 56	Closed	6.00	15-25.00
87-04-013	The Old Curiosity Shop	Department 56	Closed	6.00	18-30.00
87-04-014	Kenilworth Castle	Department 56	Closed	6.00	18-28.00
87-04-015	Brick Abbey	Department 56	Closed	6.00	50-90.00
87-04-016	Chesterton Manor House	Department 56	Closed	6.00	25-57.00
87-04-017	Dickens' Village, set of 14 (6521-8, 6520-0)	Department 56	Closed	84.00	325-350.
87-04-018	Christmas Carol Cottages, set of 3 (6513-7)	Department 56	Closed	16.95	35-55.00
87-04-019	Fezziwig's Warehouse	Department 56	Closed	6.00	25-30.00
87-04-020	Scrooge & Marley Countinghouse	Department 56	Closed	6.00	15-25.00
87-04-021	The Cottage of Bob Cratchit & Tiny Tim	Department 56	Closed	6.00	15-25.00
86-04-022	New England Village, set of 7 (6533-1)	Department 56	Closed	42.00	325.00
86-04-023	Apothecary Shop	Department 56	Closed	6.00	15-30.00
86-04-024	General Store	Department 56	Closed	6.00	25-40.00
86-04-025	Nathaniel Bingham Fabrics	Department 56	Closed	6.00	30-35.00
86-04-026	Livery Stable & Boot Shop	Department 56	Closed	6.00	15-30.00
86-04-027	Steeple Church	Department 56	Closed	6.00	100-132.
86-04-028	Brick Town Hall	Department 56	Closed	6.00	30-47.00
86-04-029	Red Schoolhouse	Department 56	Closed	6.00	50-100.00
87-04-030	New England Village, set of 6 (6534-0)	Department 56	Closed	36.00	200-275.
87-04-031	Timber Knoll Log Cabin	Department 56	Closed	6.00	25-48.00
87-04-032	Smythe Woolen Mill	Department 56	Closed	6.00	45-60.00
87-04-033	Jacob Adams Farmhouse	Department 56	Closed	6.00	25-55.00
87-04-034	Jacob Adams Barn	Department 56	Closed	6.00	25-50.00
87-04-035	Craggy Cove Lighthouse	Department 56	Closed	6.00	100-140.
87-04-036	Weston Train Station	Department 56	Closed	6.00	25-48.00
87-04-037	New England Village, set of 13 (6533-1, 6534-0)	Department 56	Closed	78.00	495.00
Department 56	**Miscellaneous Ornaments**				
84-05-001	Dickens 2-sided Tin Ornaments, set of 6 (6522-6)	Department 56	Closed	12.00	165-260.
84-05-002	Crowntree Inn	Department 56	Closed	2.00	45.00
84-05-003	Green Grocer	Department 56	Closed	2.00	45.00
84-05-004	Golden Swan Baker	Department 56	Closed	2.00	45.00
84-05-005	Bean and Son Smithy Shop	Department 56	Closed	2.00	45.00
84-05-006	Abel Beasley Butcher	Department 56	Closed	2.00	45.00
84-05-007	Jones & Co. Brush & Basket Shop	Department 56	Closed	2.00	45.00
88-05-008	Christmas Carol- Scrooge's Head (5912-9)	Department 56	Closed	12.95	30-35.00
88-05-009	Christmas Carol- Tiny Tim's Head (5913-7)	Department 56	Closed	10.00	22-30.00
88-05-010	Christmas Carol- Bob & Mrs. Cratchit (5914-5)	Department 56	Closed	18.00	33-38.00
88-05-011	Balsam Bell Brass Dickens' Candlestick (6244-8)	Department 56	Closed	3.00	10.00
83-05-012	Snow Village Wood Ornaments, set of 6 (5099-7)	Department 56	Closed	30.00	N/A
83-05-013	Gabled House	Department 56	Closed	5.00	N/A
83-05-014	Swiss Chalet	Department 56	Closed	5.00	N/A
83-05-015	Countryside Church	Department 56	Closed	5.00	150.00
83-05-016	Carriage House	Department 56	Closed	5.00	N/A
83-05-017	Centennial House	Department 56	Closed	5.00	150.00
83-05-018	Pioneer Church	Department 56	Closed	5.00	N/A
Duncan Royale	**History Of Santa Claus**				
92-01-001	Santa I (set of 12)	Duncan Royale	Open	144.00	144.00
92-01-002	Santa II (set of 12)	Duncan Royale	Open	144.00	144.00
Enesco Corporation	**Precious Moments Ornaments**				
83-01-001	Surround Us With Joy-E-0513	S. Butcher	Yr.Iss.	9.00	60-65.00
83-01-002	Mother Sew Dear-E-0514	S. Butcher	Open	9.00	15-30.00
83-01-003	To A Special Dad-E-0515	S. Butcher	Suspd.	9.00	35-58.00
83-01-004	The Purr-fect Grandma-E-0516	S. Butcher	Open	9.00	15-30.00
83-01-005	The Perfect Grandpa-E-0517	S. Butcher	Suspd.	9.00	25-40.00
83-01-006	Blessed Are The Pure In Heart -E-0518	S. Butcher	Yr.Iss.	9.00	40-55.00
83-01-007	O Come All Ye Faithful-E-0531	S. Butcher	Suspd.	10.00	45-55.00
83-01-008	Let Heaven And Nature Sing-E-0532	S. Butcher	Retrd.	9.00	35-50.00
83-01-009	Tell Me The Story Of Jesus-E-0533	S. Butcher	Suspd.	9.00	35-55.00
83-01-010	To Thee With Love-E-0534	S. Butcher	Retrd.	9.00	30-60.00
83-01-011	Love Is Patient-E-0535	S. Butcher	Suspd.	9.00	40-55.00
83-01-012	Love Is Patient-E-0536	S. Butcher	Suspd.	9.00	35-70.00
83-01-013	Jesus Is The Light That Shines- E-0537	S. Butcher	Suspd.	9.00	45-60.00
82-01-014	Joy To The World-E-2343	S. Butcher	Suspd.	9.00	35-55.00
82-01-015	I'll Play My Drum For Him-E-2359	S. Butcher	Yr.Iss.	9.00	100-150.
82-01-016	Baby's First Christmas-E-2362	S. Butcher	Suspd.	9.00	25-70.00
82-01-017	The First Noel-E-2367	S. Butcher	Suspd.	9.00	40-65.00
82-01-018	The First Noel-E-2368	S. Butcher	Retrd.	9.00	40-65.00
82-01-019	Dropping In For Christmas-E-2369	S. Butcher	Retrd.	9.00	35-60.00
82-01-020	Unicorn-E-2371	S. Butcher	Retrd.	10.00	45-75.00
82-01-021	Baby's First Christmas-E-2372	S. Butcher	Suspd.	9.00	35-45.00
82-01-022	Dropping Over For Christmas-E-2376	S. Butcher	Retrd.	9.00	45-59.00
82-01-023	Mouse With Cheese-E-2381	S. Butcher	Suspd.	9.00	90-125.00
82-01-024	Our First Christmas Together-E-2385	S. Butcher	Suspd.	10.00	15-55.00
82-01-025	Camel, Donkey & Cow (3 pc. set)-E2386	S. Butcher	Suspd.	25.00	55-75.00
84-01-026	Wishing You A Merry Christmas-E-5387	S. Butcher	Yr.Iss.	10.00	35-45.00
84-01-027	Joy To The World-E-5388	S. Butcher	Retrd.	10.00	40-55.00
84-01-028	Peace On Earth-E-5389	S. Butcher	Suspd.	10.00	30-50.00
84-01-029	May God Bless You With A Perfect Holiday Season-E-5390	S. Butcher	Suspd.	10.00	25-50.00
84-01-030	Love Is Kind-E-5391	S. Butcher	Suspd.	10.00	30-50.00
84-01-031	Blessed Are The Pure In Heart-E-5392	S. Butcher	Yr.Iss.	10.00	40.00
81-01-032	But Love Goes On Forever-E-5627	S. Butcher	Suspd.	6.00	70-100.00
81-01-033	But Love Goes On Forever-E-5628	S. Butcher	Suspd.	6.00	60-110.00
81-01-034	Let The Heavens Rejoice-E-5629	S. Butcher	Yr.Iss.	6.00	200-250.
81-01-035	Unto Us A Child Is Born-E-5630	S. Butcher	Suspd.	6.00	40-65.00
81-01-036	Baby's First Christmas-E-5631	S. Butcher	Suspd.	6.00	45-60.00
81-01-037	Baby's First Christmas-E-5632	S. Butcher	Suspd.	6.00	45-70.00
81-01-038	Come Let Us Adore Him (4pc. set)-E-5633	S. Butcher	Suspd.	22.00	65-115.00
81-01-039	Wee Three Kings (3pc. set)-E-5634	S. Butcher	Suspd.	19.00	100-129.
81-01-040	We Have Seen His Star-E-6120	S. Butcher	Retrd.	6.00	55-80.00
85-01-041	Have A Heavenly Christmas-12416	S. Butcher	Open	12.00	20-30.00
85-01-042	God Sent His Love-15768	S. Butcher	Yr.Iss.	10.00	35-75.00
85-01-043	May Your Christmas Be Happy-15822	S. Butcher	Suspd.	10.00	22-45.00
85-01-044	Happiness Is The Lord-15830	S. Butcher	Suspd.	10.00	20-37.00
85-01-045	May Your Christmas Be Delightful-15849	S. Butcher	Open	10.00	15-35.00
85-01-046	Honk If You Love Jesus-15857	S. Butcher	Open	10.00	15-27.00
85-01-047	Baby's First Christmas-15903	S. Butcher	Yr.Iss.	10.00	38.00
85-01-048	Baby's First Christmas-15911	S. Butcher	Yr.Iss.	10.00	30-40.00
86-01-049	Shepherd of Love-102288	S. Butcher	Open	10.00	15-25.00
86-01-050	Wishing You A Cozy Christmas-102326	S. Butcher	Yr.Iss.	10.00	30-40.00
86-01-051	Our First Christmas Together-102350	S. Butcher	Yr.Iss.	10.00	15-39.00
86-01-052	Trust And Obey-102377	S. Butcher	Open	10.00	15-35.00
86-01-053	Love Rescued Me-102385	S. Butcher	Open	10.00	15-35.00
86-01-054	Angel Of Mercy-102407	S. Butcher	Open	10.00	15-35.00
86-01-055	It's A Perfect Boy-102415	S. Butcher	Suspd.	10.00	25-40.00
86-01-056	Lord Keep Me On My Toes-102423	S. Butcher	Retrd.	10.00	30-45.00
86-01-057	Serve With A Smile-102431	S. Butcher	Suspd.	10.00	20-35.00
86-01-058	Serve With A Smile-102458	S. Butcher	Suspd.	10.00	20-45.00
86-01-059	Reindeer-102466	S. Butcher	Yr.Iss.	11.00	150-250.
86-01-060	Rocking Horse-102474	S. Butcher	Suspd.	10.00	19-29.00
86-01-061	Baby's First Christmas-102504	S. Butcher	Yr.Iss.	10.00	22-40.00
86-01-062	Baby's First Christmas-102512	S. Butcher	Yr.Iss.	10.00	20-35.00
87-01-063	Bear The Good News Of Christmas-104515	S. Butcher	Yr.Iss.	12.50	25-35.00
87-01-064	Baby's First Christmas-109401	S. Butcher	Yr.Iss.	12.00	35-55.00
87-01-065	Baby's First Christmas-109428	S. Butcher	Yr.Iss.	12.00	35-45.00
87-01-066	Love Is The Best Gift Of All-109770	S. Butcher	Yr.Iss.	11.00	35-50.00
87-01-067	I'm A Possibility-111120	S. Butcher	Suspd.	11.00	29-49.00
87-01-068	You Have Touched So Many Hearts-112356	S. Butcher	Open	11.00	15-30.00
87-01-069	Waddle I Do Without You-112364	S. Butcher	Open	11.00	15-39.00

Company Number	 Name	Series Artist	 Edition Limit	 Issue Price	 Quote
87-01-070	I'm Sending You A White Christmas-112372	S. Butcher	Suspd.	11.00	20-25.00
87-01-071	He Cleansed My Soul-112380	S. Butcher	Open	12.00	19-25.00
87-01-072	Our First Christmas Together-112399	S. Butcher	Yr.Iss.	11.00	25-35.00
88-01-073	To My Forever Friend-113956	S. Butcher	Open	16.00	20-35.00
88-01-074	Smile Along The Way-113964	S. Butcher	Open	15.00	20.00
88-01-075	God Sent You Just In Time-113972	S. Butcher	Suspd.	13.50	25-35.00
88-01-076	Rejoice O Earth-113980	S. Butcher	Retrd.	13.50	35-45.00
88-01-077	Cheers To The Leader-113999	S. Butcher	Suspd.	13.50	20-35.00
88-01-078	My Love Will Never Let You Go-114006	S. Butcher	Suspd.	13.50	25-35.00
88-01-079	Baby's First Christmas-115282	S. Butcher	Yr.Iss.	15.00	25-35.00
88-01-080	Time To Wish You A Merry Christmas -115320	S. Butcher	Yr.Iss.	13.00	50-60.00
88-01-081	Our First Christmas Together-520233	S. Butcher	Yr.Iss.	13.00	20-28.00
88-01-082	Baby's First Christmas-520241	S. Butcher	Yr.Iss.	15.00	22-35.00
88-01-083	You Are My Gift Come True-520276	S. Butcher	Yr.Iss.	12.50	30-50.00
88-01-084	Hang On For The Holly Days-520292	S. Butcher	Yr.Iss.	13.00	30-45.00
89-01-085	Christmas is Ruff Without You-520462	S. Butcher	Yr.Iss.	13.00	25-45.00
89-01-086	May All Your Christmases Be White-521302 (dated)	S. Butcher	Yr.Iss.	17.50	25-35.00
89-01-087	Our First Christmas Together-521588	S. Butcher	Yr.Iss.	17.50	30.00
89-01-088	Oh Holy Night-522848	S. Butcher	Yr.Iss.	13.50	30-50.00
89-01-089	Make A Joyful Noise-522910	S. Butcher	Open	15.00	17.00
89-01-090	Love One Another-522929	S. Butcher	Open	17.50	20-25.00
89-01-091	I Believe In The Old Rugged Cross-522953	S. Butcher	Open	15.00	17.00
89-01-092	Peace On Earth-523062	S. Butcher	Yr.Iss.	25.00	75-105.00
89-01-093	Baby's First Christmas-523194	S. Butcher	Yr.Iss.	15.00	23.00
89-01-094	Baby's First Christmas-523208	S. Butcher	Yr.Iss.	15.00	25.00
90-01-095	Dashing Through The Snow-521574	S. Butcher	Open	15.00	15-18.00
90-01-096	Baby's First Christmas-523798	S. Butcher	Yr.Iss.	15.00	25.00
90-01-097	Baby's First Christmas-523771	S. Butcher	Yr.Iss.	15.00	25.00
90-01-098	Once Upon A Holy Night-523852	S. Butcher	Yr.Iss.	15.00	25-30.00
90-01-099	Don't Let the Holidays Get You Down-521590	S. Butcher	Open	15.00	15.00
90-01-100	Wishing You A Purr-fect Holiday-520497	S. Butcher	Yr.Iss.	15.00	20-35.00
90-01-101	Friends Never Drift Apart-522937	S. Butcher	Open	17.50	17.50
90-01-102	Our First Christmas Together-525324	S. Butcher	Yr.Iss.	17.50	20-28.00
90-01-103	Glide Through The Holidays-521566	S. Butcher	Retrd.	13.50	125-150.
90-01-104	May Your Christmas Be A Happy Home-523704	S. Butcher	Yr.Iss.	27.50	35-45.00
91-01-105	Our First Christmas Together-522945	S. Butcher	Yr.Iss.	17.50	25.00
91-01-106	Happy Trails Is Trusting Jesus-523224	S. Butcher	Open	15.00	15.00
91-01-107	The Good Lord Always Delivers-527165	S. Butcher	Open	15.00	15.00
91-01-108	Sno-Bunny Falls For You Like I Do-520438	S. Butcher	Yr.Iss.	15.00	30.00
91-01-109	Baby's First Christmas (Girl)-527092	S. Butcher	Yr.Iss.	15.00	15.00
91-01-110	Baby's First Christmas (Boy)-527084	S. Butcher	Yr.Iss.	15.00	15.00
91-01-111	May Your Christmas Be Merry (Ornament On Base)-526940	S. Butcher	Yr.Iss.	30.00	30.00
91-01-112	May Your Christmas Be Merry-524174	S. Butcher	Yr.Iss.	15.00	15.00
92-01-113	Baby's First Christmas-527475	S. Butcher	Yr.Iss.	15.00	15.00
92-01-114	Baby's First Christmas-527483	S. Butcher	Yr.Iss.	15.00	15.00
92-01-115	But The Greatest of These Is Love-527696	S. Butcher	Yr.Iss.	15.00	15.00
92-01-116	Our First Christmas-528870	S. Butcher	Yr.Iss.	17.50	17.50
92-01-117	But The Greatest of These Is Love-527734 (Ornament on Base)	S. Butcher	Yr.Iss.	30.00	30.00
92-01-118	Good Friends Are For Always-524131	S. Butcher	Open	15.00	15.00
92-01-119	Lord, Keep Me On My Toes-525332	S. Butcher	Open	15.00	15.00
92-01-120	I'm Nuts About You-520411	S. Butcher	Yr.Iss.	15.00	15.00

Enesco Corporation — Memories of Yesterday Ornaments

Number	Name	Artist	Edition Limit	Issue Price	Quote
88-02-001	Baby's First Christmas 1988-520373	M. Attwell	Yr.Iss.	13.50	25-30.00
88-02-002	Special Delivery! 1988-520381	M. Attwell	Yr.Iss.	13.50	25-45.00
89-02-003	Baby's First Christmas-522465	M. Attwell	Open	15.00	15-20.00
89-02-004	Christmas Together-522562	M. Attwell	Open	15.00	15-25.00
89-02-005	A Surprise for Santa-522473 (1989)	M. Attwell	Yr.Iss.	13.50	20-25.00
90-02-006	Time For Bed-524638	M. Attwell	Yr.Iss.	15.00	15-25.00
90-02-007	New Moon-524646	M. Attwell	Open	15.00	15-25.00
90-02-008	Moonstruck-524794	M. Attwell	Retrd.	15.00	15-20.00
91-02-009	Just Watchin' Over You-525421	M. Attwell	Open	17.50	17.50
91-02-010	Lucky Me-525448	M. Attwell	Open	16.00	16.00
91-02-011	Lucky You-525847	M. Attwell	Open	16.00	16.00
91-02-012	Star Fishin'-525820	M. Attwell	Open	16.00	16.00
91-02-013	S'no Use Lookin' Back Now!-527181(dated)	M. Attwell	Yr.Iss.	17.50	17.50
92-02-014	Merry Christmas, Little Boo-Boo-528803	M. Attwell	Open	37.50	37.50
92-02-015	I'll Fly Along To See You Soon-525804 (1992 Dated Bisque)	M. Attwell	Yr.Iss.	16.00	16.00
92-02-016	Mommy, I Teared It-527041 (Five Year Anniversary Limited Edition)	M. Attwell	Yr.Iss.	15.00	15.00
92-02-017	Star Light. Star Bright-528838	M. Attwell	Open	16.00	16.00
92-02-018	Swinging Together-580481 (1992 Dated Artplas)	M. Attwell	Yr.Iss.	17.50	17.50
92-02-019	Sailin' With My Friends-587575 (Artplas)	M. Attwell	Open	25.00	25.00

Enesco Corporation — Memories of Yesterday Society Member's Only Ornament

Number	Name	Artist	Edition Limit	Issue Price	Quote
92-03-001	With Luck And A Friend, I's In Heaven-MY922	M. Attwell	Yr.Iss.	16.00	16.00

Enesco Corporation — Enesco Treasury of Christmas Ornaments

Number	Name	Artist	Edition Limit	Issue Price	Quote
83-04-001	Wide Open Throttle-E-0242	Enesco	3-Yr.	12.00	35.00
83-04-002	Baby's First Christmas-E-0271	Enesco	Yr.Iss.	6.00	N/A
83-04-003	Grandchild's First Christmas-E-0272	Enesco	Yr.Iss.	5.00	N/A
83-04-004	Baby's First Christmas-E-0273	Enesco	3-Yr.	9.00	N/A
83-04-005	Toy Drum Teddy-E-0274	Enesco	4-Yr.	9.00	N/A
83-04-006	Watching At The Window-E-0275	Enesco	3-Yr.	13.00	N/A
83-04-007	To A Special Teacher-E-0276	Enesco	7-Yr.	5.00	15.00
83-04-008	Toy Shop-E-0277	Enesco	7-Yr.	8.00	50.00
83-04-009	Carousel Horse-E-0278	Enesco	7-Yr.	9.00	20.00
81-04-010	Look Out Below-E-6135	Enesco	2-Yr.	6.00	N/A
82-04-011	Flyin' Santa Christmas Special 1982-E-6136	Enesco	Yr.Iss.	9.00	75.00
81-04-012	Flyin' Santa Christmas Special 1981-E-6136	Enesco	Yr.Iss.	9.00	N/A
81-04-013	Sawin' Elf Helper-E-6138	Enesco	2-Yr.	6.00	N/A
81-04-014	Snow Shoe-In Santa-E-6139	Enesco	2-Yr.	6.00	N/A
81-04-015	Baby's First Christmas 1981-E-6145	Enesco	Yr.Iss.	6.00	N/A
81-04-016	Our Hero-E-6146	Enesco	2-Yr.	4.00	N/A
81-04-017	Whoops-E-6147	Enesco	2-Yr.	3.50	N/A
81-04-018	Whoops, It's 1981-E-6148	Enesco	Yr.Iss.	7.50	75.00
81-04-019	Not A Creature Was Stirring-E-6149	Enesco	2-Yr.	4.00	20.00
84-04-020	Joy To The World-E-6209	Enesco	2-Yr.	9.00	35.00
84-04-021	Letter To Santa-E-6210	Enesco	2-Yr.	5.00	30.00
84-04-022	Lucy & Me Photo Frames-E-6211	Enesco	3-Yr.	5.00	N/A
84-04-023	Lucy & Me Photo Frames-E-6211	Enesco	3-Yr.	5.00	N/A
84-04-024	Lucy & Me Photo Frames-E-6211	Enesco	3-Yr.	5.00	N/A
84-04-025	Lucy & Me Photo Frames-E-6211	Enesco	3-Yr.	5.00	N/A
84-04-026	Lucy & Me Photo Frames-E-6211	Enesco	3-Yr.	5.00	N/A
84-04-027	Lucy & Me Photo Frames-E-6211	Enesco	3-Yr.	5.00	N/A
84-04-028	Baby's First Christmas 1984-E-6212	Gilmore	Yr.Iss.	10.00	30.00
84-04-029	Merry Christmas Mother-E-6213	Enesco	3-Yr.	10.00	30.00
84-04-030	Baby's First Christmas 1984-E-6215	Enesco	Yr.Iss.	6.00	N/A
84-04-031	Ferris Wheel Mice-E-6216	Enesco	2-Yr.	9.00	N/A
84-04-032	Cuckoo Clock-E-6217	Enesco	2-Yr.	8.00	40.00
84-04-033	Muppet Babies Baby's First Christmas-E6222	J. Henson	Yr.Iss.	10.00	45.00
84-04-034	Muppet Babies Baby's First Christmas-E6223	J. Henson	Yr.Iss.	10.00	45.00
84-04-035	Garfield Hark! The Herald Angel-E-6224	J. Davis	2-Yr.	7.50	N/A
84-04-036	Fun in Santa's Sleigh-E-6225	J. Davis	2-Yr.	12.00	N/A
84-04-037	"Deer!" Odie-E-6226	J. Davis	2-Yr.	6.00	N/A
84-04-038	Garfield The Snow Cat-E-6227	J. Davis	2-Yr.	12.00	N/A
84-04-039	Peek-A-Bear Baby's First Christmas-E-6228	Enesco	3-Yr.	10.00	N/A
84-04-040	Peek-A-Bear Baby's First Christmas-E-6229	Enesco	3-Yr.	9.00	N/A
84-04-041	Owl Be Home For Christmas-E-6230	Enesco	2-Yr.	10.00	23.00
84-04-042	Santa's Trolley-E-6231	Enesco	3-Yr.	11.00	40.00
84-04-043	Holiday Penguin-E-6240	Enesco	3-Yr.	1.50	15-20.00
84-04-044	Little Drummer-E-6241	Enesco	5-Yr.	2.00	N/A
84-04-045	Happy Holidays-E-6248	Enesco	2-Yr.	2.00	N/A
84-04-046	Christmas Nest-E-6249	Enesco	2-Yr.	3.00	25.00
84-04-047	Bunny's Christmas Stocking-E-6251	Enesco	Yr.Iss.	2.00	N/A
84-04-048	Santa On Ice-E-6252	Enesco	3-Yr.	2.50	25.00
84-04-049	Treasured Memories The New Sled-E-6256	Enesco	2-Yr.	7.00	N/A
84-04-050	Up On The House Top-E-6280	Enesco	6-Yr.	9.00	N/A
84-04-051	Penguins On Ice-E-6280	Enesco	2-Yr.	7.50	N/A
84-04-052	Grandchild's First Christmas 1984-E-6286	Enesco	Yr.Iss.	5.00	N/A
84-04-053	Grandchild's First Christmas1984-E-6286	Enesco	Yr.Iss.	5.00	N/A
84-04-054	Godchild's First Christmas-E-6287	Enesco	3-Yr.	7.00	N/A
84-04-055	Santa In The Box-E-6292	Enesco	2-Yr.	6.00	N/A
84-04-056	Carousel Horse-E-6913	Enesco	2-Yr.	1.50	N/A
83-04-057	Arctic Charmer-E-6945	Enesco	2-Yr.	7.00	N/A
82-04-058	Victorian Sleigh-E-6946	Enesco	4-Yr.	9.00	N/A
83-04-059	Wing-A-Ding Angel-E-6948	Enesco	3-Yr.	7.00	50.00
82-04-060	A Saviour Is Born This Day-E-6949	Enesco	8-Yr.	4.00	12-20.00
82-04-061	Crescent Santa-E-6950	Gilmore	4-Yr.	10.00	50.00
82-04-062	Baby's First Christmas 1982-E-6952	Enesco	Yr.Iss.	10.00	N/A
82-04-063	Polar Bear Fun Whoops,It's 1982-E-6953	Enesco	Yr.Iss.	10.00	75.00
82-04-064	Holiday Skier-E-6954	J. Davis	5-Yr.	7.00	N/A
82-04-065	Toy Soldier 1982-E-6957	Enesco	Yr.Iss.	6.50	N/A
82-04-066	Merry Christmas Grandma-E-6975	Enesco	3-Yr.	5.00	N/A
82-04-067	Carousel Horses-E-6958	Enesco	3-Yr.	8.00	20-40.00
82-04-068	Dear Santa-E-6959	Gilmore	8-Yr.	10.00	17.00
82-04-069	Penguin Power-E-6977	Enesco	2-Yr.	6.00	15.00
82-04-070	Bunny Winter Playground 1982-E-6978	Enesco	Yr.Iss.	10.00	N/A
82-04-071	Baby's First Christmas 1982-E-6979	Enesco	Yr.Iss.	10.00	N/A
83-04-072	Carousel Horses-E-6980	Enesco	4-Yr.	8.00	N/A
82-04-073	Grandchild's First Christmas 1982-E-6983	Enesco	Yr.Iss.	5.00	73.00
82-04-074	Merry Christmas Teacher-E-6984	Enesco	4-Yr.	7.00	N/A
83-04-075	Garfield Cuts The Ice-E-8771	J. Davis	3-Yr.	6.00	N/A
84-04-076	A Stocking Full For 1984-E-8773	J. Davis	Yr.Iss.	6.00	N/A
83-04-077	Stocking Full For 1983-E-8773	J. Davis	Yr.Iss.	6.00	N/A
85-04-078	Santa Claus Balloon-55794	Enesco	Yr.Iss.	8.50	N/A
85-04-079	Carousel Reindeer-55808	Enesco	4-Yr.	12.00	35-40.00
85-04-080	Angel In Flight-55816	Enesco	4-Yr.	8.00	20.00
85-04-081	Christmas Penguin-55824	Enesco	4-Yr.	7.50	35.00
85-04-082	Merry Christmas Godchild-55832	Gilmore	5-Yr.	8.00	N/A
85-04-083	Baby's First Christmas-55840	Enesco	2-Yr.	15.00	N/A
85-04-084	Old Fashioned Rocking Horse-55859	Enesco	2-Yr.	10.00	N/A
85-04-085	Child's Second Christmas-55867	Enesco	5-Yr.	11.00	N/A
85-04-086	Fishing For Stars-55875	Enesco	5-Yr.	9.00	N/A
85-04-087	Baby Blocks-55883	Enesco	2-Yr.	12.00	N/A
85-04-088	Christmas Toy Chest-55891	Enesco	5-Yr.	10.00	N/A
85-04-089	Grandchild's First Ornament-55921	Enesco	5-Yr.	7.00	8.00
85-04-090	Joy Photo Frame-55956	Enesco	Yr.Iss.	6.00	N/A
85-04-091	We Three Kings-55964	Enesco	Yr.Iss.	4.50	N/A
85-04-092	The Night Before Christmas-55972	Enesco	2-Yr.	5.00	N/A
85-04-093	Baby's First Christmas 1985-55980	Enesco	Yr.Iss.	6.00	N/A
85-04-094	Baby Rattle Photo Frame-56006	Enesco	2-Yr.	5.00	N/A
85-04-095	Baby's First Christmas 1985-56014	Gilmore	Yr.Iss.	10.00	N/A
85-04-096	Christmas Plane Ride-56049	L. Rigg	6-Yr.	10.00	N/A
85-04-097	Scottie Celebrating Christmas-56065	Enesco	5-Yr.	7.50	25.00
85-04-098	North Pole Native-56073	Enesco	2-Yr.	9.00	N/A
85-04-099	Skating Walrus-56081	Enesco	2-Yr.	9.00	N/A
85-04-100	Ski Time-56111	J. Davis	Yr.Iss.	13.00	N/A
85-04-101	North Pole Express-56138	J. Davis	Yr.Iss.	12.00	N/A
85-04-102	Merry Christmas Mother-56146	J. Davis	Yr.Iss.	8.50	N/A
85-04-103	Hoppy Christmas-56154	J. Davis	Yr.Iss.	8.50	N/A
85-04-104	Merry Christmas Teacher-56170	J. Davis	Yr.Iss.	6.00	N/A
85-04-105	Garfield-In-The-Box-56189	J. Davis	Yr.Iss.	6.50	N/A
85-04-106	Merry Christmas Grandma-56197	Enesco	Yr.Iss.	7.00	N/A
85-04-107	Christmas Lights-56200	Enesco	2-Yr.	8.00	N/A
85-04-108	Victorian Doll House-56251	Enesco	Yr.Iss.	13.00	40.00
85-04-109	Tobaoggan Ride-56286	Enesco	4-Yr.	6.00	N/A
85-04-110	Look Out Below-56375	Enesco	Yr.Iss.	8.50	40.00
85-04-111	Flying Santa Christmas Special-56383	Enesco	2-Yr.	10.00	N/A
85-04-112	Sawin Elf Helper-56391	Enesco	Yr.Iss.	8.00	N/A
85-04-113	Snow Shoe-In Santa-56405	Enesco	Yr.Iss.	8.00	50.00
85-04-114	Our Hero-56413	Enesco	Yr.Iss.	5.50	N/A
85-04-115	Not A Creaturxe Was Stirring-56421	Enesco	2-Yr.	4.00	N/A
85-04-116	Merry Christmas Teacher-56448	Enesco	Yr.Iss.	9.00	N/A
85-04-117	A Stocking Full For 1985-56464	J. Davis	Yr.Iss.	6.00	N/A
85-04-118	St. Nicholas Circa 1910-56659	Enesco	5-Yr.	6.00	N/A
85-04-119	Christmas Tree Photo Frame-56871	Enesco	4-Yr.	10.00	N/A
90-04-120	Deck The Halls-566063	Enesco	3-Yr.	12.50	N/A
88-04-121	Making A Point-489212	G.G. Santiago	3-Yr.	10.00	N/A
88-04-122	Mouse Upon A Pipe-489220	G.G. Santiago	2-Yr.	10.00	12.00
88-04-123	North Pole Deadline-489387	Enesco	3-Yr.	13.50	N/A
88-04-124	Christmas Pin-Up-489409	Enesco	2-Yr.	11.00	N/A
88-04-125	Airmail For Teacher-489425	Gilmore	3-Yr.	13.50	N/A
86-04-126	1st Christmas Together 1986-551171	Enesco	Yr.Iss.	9.00	15-35.00
86-04-127	Elf Stringing Popcorn-551198	Enesco	4-Yr.	10.00	20-30.00
86-04-128	Christmas Scottie-551201	Enesco	4-Yr.	7.00	15-30.00
86-04-129	Santa and Child-551236	Enesco	4-Yr.	13.50	25-50.00
86-04-130	The Christmas Angel-551244	Enesco	4-Yr.	22.50	40-50.00
86-04-131	Carousel Unicorn-551252	Gilmore	4-Yr.	12.00	30-40.00
86-04-132	Have a Heavenly Holiday-551260	Enesco	4-Yr.	9.00	N/A
86-04-133	Siamese Kitten-551279	Enesco	4-Yr.	9.00	N/A
86-04-134	Old Fashioned Doll House-551287	Enesco	4-Yr.	15.00	N/A
86-04-135	Holiday Fisherman-551309	Enesco	3-Yr.	8.00	N/A
86-04-136	Antique Toy-551317	Enesco	3-Yr.	9.00	N/A
86-04-137	Time For Christmas-551325	Gilmore	4-Yr.	13.00	N/A
86-04-138	Christmas Calendar-551333	Enesco	2-Yr.	7.00	N/A
86-04-139	Merry Christmas-551341	Gilmore	3-Yr.	8.00	45.00
86-04-140	The Santa Claus Shoppe Circa1905-551562	J. Grossman	4-Yr.	8.00	15.00

CHRISTMAS ORNAMENTS

Company		Series			
Number	Name	Artist	Edition Limit	Issue Price	Quote
86-04-141	Baby Bear Sleigh-551651	Gilmore	3-Yr.	9.00	30.00
86-04-142	Baby's First Christmas 1986-551678	Gilmore	Yr.Iss.	10.00	20.00
86-04-143	First Christmas Together-551708	Enesco	3-Yr.	6.00	10.00
86-04-144	Baby's First Christmas-551716	Enesco	3-Yr.	5.50	10.00
86-04-145	Baby's First Christmas 1986-551724	Enesco	Yr.Iss.	6.50	30.00
86-04-146	Peek-A-Bear Grandchild's First Christmas-552004	Enesco	Yr.Iss.	6.00	23.00
86-04-147	Peek-A-Bear Present-552089	Enesco	4-Yr.	2.50	N/A
86-04-148	Peek-A-Bear Present-552089	Enesco	4-Yr.	2.50	N/A
86-04-149	Peek-A-Bear Present-552089	Enesco	4-Yr.	2.50	N/A
86-04-150	Peek-A-Bear Present-552089	Enesco	4-Yr.	2.50	N/A
86-04-151	Merry Christmas 1986-552186	L. Rigg	Yr.Iss.	8.00	N/A
86-04-152	Merry Christmas 1986-552534	L. Rigg	Yr.Iss.	8.00	N/A
86-04-153	Lucy & Me Christmas Tree-552542	L. Rigg	3-Yr.	7.00	25.00
86-04-154	Santa's Helpers-552607	Enesco	3-Yr.	2.50	N/A
86-04-155	My Special Friend-552615	Enesco	3-Yr.	6.00	N/A
86-04-156	Christmas Wishes From Panda-552623	Enesco	3-Yr.	6.00	N/A
86-04-157	Lucy & Me Ski Time-552658	L. Rigg	2-Yr.	6.50	30.00
86-04-158	Merry Christmas Teacher-552666	Enesco	3-Yr.	6.50	N/A
86-04-159	Country Cousins Merry Christmas, Mom-552704	Enesco	3-Yr.	7.00	23.00
86-04-160	Country Cousins Merry Christmas, Dad-552704	Enesco	3-Yr.	7.00	23.00
86-04-161	Country Cousins Merry Christmas, Mom-552712	Enesco	4-Yr.	7.00	23.00
86-04-162	Country Cousins Merry Christmas, Dad-552712	Enesco	4-Yr.	7.00	25.00
86-04-163	Grandmother's Little Angel-552747	Enesco	4-Yr.	8.00	N/A
87-04-164	Puppy's 1st Christmas-552909	Enesco	2-Yr.	4.00	N/A
87-04-165	Kitty's 1st Christmas-552917	Enesco	2-Yr.	4.00	25.00
87-04-166	Merry Christmas Puppy-552925	Enesco	2-Yr.	3.50	N/A
87-04-167	Merry Christmas Kitty-552933	Enesco	2-Yr.	3.50	N/A
86-04-168	I Love My Grandparents-553263	Enesco	Yr.Iss.	6.00	N/A
86-04-169	Merry Christmas Mom & Dad-553271	Enesco	Yr.Iss.	6.00	N/A
86-04-170	S. Claus Hollycopter-553344	Enesco	4-Yr.	13.50	50.00
86-04-171	From Our House To Your House-553360	Enesco	3-Yr.	15.00	40.00
86-04-172	Christmas Rattle-553379	Enesco	3-Yr.	8.00	50.00
86-04-173	Bah, Humbug!-553387	Enesco	4-Yr.	9.00	N/A
86-04-174	God Bless Us Everyone-553395	Enesco	4-Yr.	10.00	N/A
87-04-175	Carousel Mobile-553409	Enesco	3-Yr.	15.00	50.00
86-04-176	Holiday Train-553417	Enesco	4-Yr.	10.00	N/A
86-04-177	Lighten Up!-553603	J. Davis	5-Yr.	10.00	N/A
86-04-178	Gift Wrap Odie-553611	J. Davis	Yr.Iss.	7.00	15.00
86-04-179	Merry Christmas-553646	Enesco	4-Yr.	8.00	N/A
87-04-180	M.V.B. (Most Valuable Bear)-554219	Enesco	2-Yr.	3.00	N/A
87-04-181	M.V.B. (Most Valuable Bear)-554219	Enesco	2-Yr.	3.00	N/A
87-04-182	M.V.B. (Most Valuable Bear)-554219	Enesco	2-Yr.	3.00	N/A
87-04-183	M.V.B. (Most Valuable Bear)-554219	Enesco	2-Yr.	3.00	N/A
88-04-184	1st Christmas Together-554537	Gilmore	3-Yr.	15.00	N/A
88-04-185	An Eye On Christmas-554545	Gilmore	3-Yr.	22.50	30.00
88-04-186	A Mouse Check-554553	Gilmore	3-Yr.	13.50	40.00
88-04-187	Merry Christmas Engine-554561	Enesco	2-Yr.	22.50	25.00
89-04-188	Sardine Express-554588	Gilmore	2-Yr.	17.50	22.50
88-04-189	1st Christmas Together 1988-554596	Enesco	Yr.Iss.	10.00	N/A
88-04-190	Forever Friends-554626	Gilmore	2-Yr.	12.00	23.00
88-04-191	Santa's Survey-554642	Enesco	2-Yr.	35.00	45.00
89-04-192	Old Town's Church-554871	Gilmore	2-Yr.	17.50	20.00
88-04-193	A Chipmunk Holiday-554898	Gilmore	3-Yr.	11.00	N/A
88-04-194	Christmas Is Coming-554901	Enesco	3-Yr.	12.00	12.00
88-04-195	Baby's First Christmas 1988-554928	Enesco	Yr.Iss.	7.50	N/A
88-04-196	Baby's First Christmas 1988-554936	Gilmore	Yr.Iss.	10.00	N/A
88-04-197	The Christmas Train-554944	Enesco	3-Yr.	15.00	N/A
88-04-198	Li'l Drummer Bear-554952	Gilmore	3-Yr.	12.00	30.00
87-04-199	Baby's First Christmas-555061	Enesco	3-Yr.	12.00	N/A
87-04-200	Baby's First Christmas-555088	Enesco	3-Yr.	7.50	15.00
87-04-201	Baby's First Christmas-555118	Enesco	3-Yr.	6.00	N/A
87-04-202	Sugar Plum Bearies-555193	Enesco	2-Yr.	4.50	N/A
87-04-203	Garfield Merry Kissmas-555215	J. Davis	3-Yr.	8.50	30.00
87-04-204	Sleigh Away-555401	Enesco	3-Yr.	12.00	N/A
87-04-205	Merry Christmas 1987-555428	L. Rigg	Yr.Iss.	8.00	N/A
87-04-206	Merry Christmas 1987-555436	L. Rigg	Yr.Iss.	8.00	N/A
87-04-207	Lucy & Me Storybook Bear-555444	L. Rigg	3-Yr.	6.50	N/A
87-04-208	Time For Christmas-555452	L. Rigg	3-Yr.	12.00	N/A
87-04-209	Lucy & Me Angel On A Cloud-555487	L. Rigg	3-Yr.	8.00	35.00
87-04-210	Teddy's Stocking-555940	Gilmore	3-Yr.	10.00	N/A
87-04-211	Kitty's Jack-In-The-Box-555959	Enesco	3-Yr.	11.00	30.00
87-04-212	Merry Christmas Teacher-555967	Enesco	3-Yr.	7.50	N/A
87-04-213	Mouse In A Mitten-555975	Enesco	3-Yr.	7.50	N/A
87-04-214	Boy On A Rocking Horse-555983	Enesco	3-Yr.	12.00	18.00
87-04-215	Peek-A-Bear Letter To Santa-555991	Enesco	2-Yr.	8.00	30.00
87-04-216	Garfield Sugar Plum Fairy-556009	J. Davis	3-Yr.	8.50	12.50
87-04-217	Garfield The Nutcracker-556017	J. Davis	4-Yr.	8.50	30.00
87-04-218	Home Sweet Home-556033	M. Gilmore	3-Yr.	15.00	35-50.00
87-04-219	Baby's First Christmas-556041	Enesco	4-Yr.	10.00	20.00
87-04-220	Little Sailor Elf-556068	Enesco	3-Yr.	10.00	28.00
87-04-221	Carousel Goose-556076	Enesco	3-Yr.	17.00	40.00
87-04-222	Night Caps-556084	Enesco	2-Yr.	5.50	N/A
87-04-223	Night Caps-556084	Enesco	2-Yr.	5.50	N/A
87-04-224	Night Caps-556084	Enesco	2-Yr.	5.50	N/A
87-04-225	Night Caps-556084	Enesco	2-Yr.	5.50	N/A
87-04-226	Rocking Horse Past Joys-556157	Enesco	3-Yr.	10.00	20.00
87-04-227	Partridge In A Pear Tree-556173	Gilmore	3-Yr.	9.00	35.00
87-04-228	Carousel Lion-556025	M. Gilmore	3-Yr.	12.00	25.00
87-04-229	Skating Santa 1987-556211	Enesco	Yr.Iss.	13.50	N/A
87-04-230	Baby's First Christmas 1987-556238	Gilmore	Yr.Iss.	10.00	N/A
87-04-231	Baby's First Christmas 1987-556254	Enesco	Yr.Iss.	7.00	N/A
87-04-232	Teddy's Suspenders-556262	Enesco	4-Yr.	8.50	19.00
87-04-233	Baby's First Christmas 1987-556297	Enesco	Yr.Iss.	2.00	N/A
87-04-234	Baby's First Christmas 1987-556297	Enesco	Yr.Iss.	2.00	N/A
87-04-235	Beary Christmas Family-556300	Enesco	2-Yr.	2.00	N/A
87-04-236	Beary Christmas Family-556300	Enesco	2-Yr.	2.00	N/A
87-04-237	Beary Christmas Family-556300	Enesco	2-Yr.	2.00	N/A
87-04-238	Beary Christmas Family-556300	Enesco	2-Yr.	2.00	N/A
87-04-239	Beary Christmas Family-556300	Enesco	2-Yr.	2.00	N/A
87-04-240	Beary Christmas Family-556300	Enesco	2-Yr.	2.00	N/A
87-04-241	Merry ChristmasTeacher-556319	Enesco	2-Yr.	2.00	N/A
87-04-242	Merry ChristmasTeacher-556319	Enesco	2-Yr.	2.00	N/A
87-04-243	Merry ChristmasTeacher-556319	Enesco	2-Yr.	2.00	N/A
87-04-244	Merry ChristmasTeacher-556319	Enesco	2-Yr.	2.00	N/A
87-04-245	1st ChristmasTogether 1987-556335	Enesco	Yr.Iss.	9.00	18.00
87-04-246	Country Cousins Katie Goes Ice Skating-556304	Enesco	3-Yr.	8.00	30.00
87-04-247	Country Cousins Scooter Snowman-556386	Enesco	3-Yr.	8.00	30.00
87-04-248	Santa's List-556394	Enesco	3-Yr.	7.00	23.00
87-04-249	Kitty's Bed-556408	Enesco	3-Yr.	12.00	30.00
87-04-250	Grandchild's First Christmas-556416	Enesco	3-Yr.	10.00	N/A
87-04-251	Two Turtledoves-556432	Gilmore	3-Yr.	9.00	30.00
87-04-252	Three French Hens-556440	Gilmore	3-Yr.	9.00	30.00
88-04-253	Four Calling Birds-556459	Gilmore	3-Yr.	11.00	30.00
87-04-254	Teddy Takes A Spin-556467	Enesco	4-Yr.	13.00	35.00
87-04-255	Tiny Toy Thimble Mobile-556475	Enesco	2-Yr.	12.00	35.00
87-04-256	Bucket O'Love-556491	Enesco	2-Yr.	2.50	N/A
87-04-257	Bucket O'Love-556491	Enesco	2-Yr.	2.50	N/A
87-04-258	Puppy Love-556505	Enesco	3-Yr.	6.00	N/A
87-04-259	Peek-A-Bear My Special Friend-556513	Enesco	4-Yr.	6.00	30.00
87-04-260	Our First Christmas Together-556548	Enesco	3-Yr.	13.00	20.00
87-04-261	Three Little Bears-556556	Enesco	3-Yr.	7.50	15.00
87-04-262	Lucy & Me Mailbox Bear-556564	L. Rigg	4-Yr.	3.00	N/A
87-04-263	Twinkle Bear-556572	Gilmore	3-Yr.	8.00	N/A
87-04-264	I'm Dreaming Of A Bright Christmas-556602	Enesco	2-Yr.	2.50	N/A
87-04-265	I'm Dreaming Of A Bright Christmas-556602	Enesco	2-Yr.	2.50	N/A
87-04-266	Christmas Train-557196	Enesco	3-Yr.	10.00	N/A
88-04-267	Dairy Christmas-557501	M. Cook	2-Yr.	10.00	30.00
88-04-268	Merry Christmas 1988-557595	L. Rigg	Yr.Iss.	10.00	N/A
88-04-269	Merry Christmas 1988-557609	L. Rigg	Yr.Iss.	10.00	N/A
88-04-270	Toy Chest Keepsake-558206	L. Rigg	3-Yr.	12.50	30.00
88-04-271	Teddy Bear Greetings-558214	L. Rigg	3-Yr.	8.00	30.00
88-04-272	Jester Bear-558222	L. Rigg	2-Yr.	8.00	N/A
88-04-273	Night-Watch Cat-558362	J. Davis	3-Yr.	13.00	28.00
88-04-274	Christmas Thim-bell-558389	Enesco	Yr.Iss.	4.00	30.00
88-04-275	Christmas Thim-bell-558389	Enesco	Yr.Iss.	4.00	N/A
88-04-276	Christmas Thim-bell-558389	Enesco	Yr.Iss.	4.00	N/A
88-04-277	Christmas Thim-bell-558389	Enesco	Yr.Iss.	4.00	N/A
88-04-278	Baby's First Christmas-558397	D. Parker	3-Yr.	16.00	N/A
88-04-279	Christmas Tradition-558400	Gilmore	2-Yr.	10.00	25.00
88-04-280	Stocking Story-558419	G.G. Santiago	3-Yr.	10.00	23.00
88-04-281	Winter Tale-558427	G.G. Santiago	2-Yr.	6.00	N/A
88-04-282	Party Mouse-558435	G.G. Santiago	3-Yr.	12.00	30.00
88-04-283	Christmas Watch-558443	G.G. Santiago	2-Yr.	11.00	14.00
88-04-284	Christmas Vacation-558451	G.G. Santiago	3-Yr.	8.00	23.00
88-04-285	Sweet Cherub-558478	G.G. Santiago	3-Yr.	7.00	8.00
88-04-286	Time Out-558486	G.G. Santiago	2-Yr.	11.00	N/A
88-04-287	The Ice Fairy-558516	G.G. Santiago	3-Yr.	23.00	35.00
88-04-288	Santa Turtle-558559	Enesco	2-Yr.	10.00	35.00
88-04-289	The Teddy Bear Ball-558567	Enesco	3-Yr.	10.00	20.00
88-04-290	Turtle Greetings-558583	Enesco	2-Yr.	8.50	25.00
88-04-291	Happy Howladays-558605	Enesco	Yr.Iss.	7.00	15.00
88-04-292	Special Delivery-558699	J. Davis	3-Yr.	9.00	30.00
88-04-293	Deer Garfield-558702	J. Davis	3-Yr.	12.00	N/A
88-04-294	Garfield Bags O' Fun-558761	J. Davis	Yr.Iss.	3.30	N/A
88-04-295	Garfield Bags O' Fun-558761	J. Davis	Yr.Iss.	3.30	N/A
88-04-296	Garfield Bags O' Fun-558761	J. Davis	Yr.Iss.	3.30	N/A
88-04-297	Garfield Bags O' Fun-558761	J. Davis	Yr.Iss.	3.30	N/A
88-04-298	Gramophone Keepsake-558818	Enesco	2-Yr.	13.00	N/A
88-04-299	North Pole Lineman-558834	Gilmore	2-Yr.	10.00	N/A
88-04-300	Five Golden Rings-559121	Gilmore	3-Yr.	11.00	25.00
88-04-301	Six Geese A-Laying-559148	Gilmore	3-Yr.	11.00	25.00
88-04-302	Pretty Baby-559156	R. Morehead	3-Yr.	12.50	25.00
88-04-303	Old Fashioned Angel-559164	R. Morehead	3-Yr.	12.50	20.00
88-04-304	Two For Tea-559776	Gilmore	3-Yr.	20.00	28.00
88-04-305	Merry Christmas Grandpa-560065	Enesco	3-Yr.	8.00	N/A
90-04-306	Reeling In The Holidays-560405	M. Cook	2-Yr.	8.00	10.00
91-04-307	Walkin' With My Baby-561029	M. Cook	2-Yr.	10.00	N/A
89-04-308	Scrub-A-Dub Chipmunk-561037	M. Cook	2-Yr.	8.00	10.00
89-04-309	Christmas Cook-Out-561045	M. Cook	2-Yr.	9.00	10.00
89-04-310	Sparkles-561843	S. Zimnicki	3-Yr.	17.50	17.50
89-04-311	Bunkie-561835	S. Zimnicki	3-Yr.	22.50	22.50
89-04-312	Popper-561878	S. Zimnicki	3-Yr.	12.00	12.50
89-04-313	Seven Swans A-Swimming-562742	Gilmore	3-Yr.	12.00	23.00
89-04-314	Eight Maids A-Milking-562750	Gilmore	3-Yr.	12.00	23.00
89-04-315	Nine Dancers Dancing-562769	Gilmore	3-Yr.	15.00	23.00
89-04-316	Baby's First Christmas 1989-562807	Enesco	Yr.Iss.	8.00	20.00
89-04-317	Baby's First Christmas 1989-562815	Gilmore	Yr.Iss.	10.00	N/A
89-04-318	First Christmas Together 1989-562823	Enesco	Yr.Iss.	11.00	N/A
89-04-319	Travelin' Trike-562882	Gilmore	3-Yr.	15.00	15.00
89-04-320	Victorian Sleigh Ride-562890	Enesco	3-Yr.	22.50	22.50
91-04-321	Santa Delivers Love-562904	Gilmore	2-Yr.	17.50	17.50
89-04-322	Chestnut Roastin'-562912	Gilmore	2-Yr.	13.00	13.00
90-04-323	Th-Ink-In' Of You-562920	Gilmore	2-Yr.	20.00	20.00
89-04-324	Ye Olde Puppet Show-562939	Enesco	2-Yr.	17.50	17.50
89-04-325	Static In The Attic-562947	Enesco	2-Yr.	13.00	13.00
89-04-326	Mistle-Toast 1989-562963	Gilmore	Yr.Iss.	15.00	22.50
89-04-327	Merry Christmas Pops-562971	Gilmore	3-Yr.	12.00	12.00
90-04-328	North Pole Or Bust-562998	Gilmore	2-Yr.	25.00	25.00
89-04-329	By The Light Of The Moon-563005	Gilmore	3-Yr.	12.00	24.00
89-04-330	Stickin' To It-563013	Gilmore	2-Yr.	10.00	12.00
89-04-331	Christmas Cookin'-563048	Gilmore	3-Yr.	22.50	25.00
89-04-332	All Set For Santa-563080	Gilmore	3-Yr.	17.50	17.50
90-04-333	Santa's Sweets-563196	Gilmore	2-Yr.	20.00	20.00
90-04-334	Purr-Fect Pals-563218	Enesco	2-Yr.	8.00	8.00
89-04-335	The Pause That Refreshes-563226	Enesco	3-Yr.	15.00	18-35.00
89-04-336	Ho-Ho Holiday Scrooge-563234	J. Davis	3-Yr.	13.50	30.00
89-04-337	God Bless Us Everyone-563242	J. Davis	3-Yr.	13.50	30.00
89-04-338	Scrooge With The Spirit-563250	J. Davis	3-Yr.	13.50	30.00
89-04-339	A Chains Of Pace For Odie-563269	J. Davis	3-Yr.	12.00	20.00
90-04-340	Jingle Bell Rock 1990-563390	G. Armgardt	Yr.Iss.	13.50	30.00
89-04-341	Joy Ridin'-563463	J. Davis	2-Yr.	15.00	30.00
89-04-342	Just What I Wanted-563668	M. Peters	3-Yr.	13.50	13.50
89-04-343	Pucker Up!-563676	M. Peters	3-Yr.	11.00	11.00
89-04-344	What's The Bright Idea-563684	M. Peters	3-Yr.	13.50	13.50
90-04-345	Fleas Navidad-563978	M. Peters	3-Yr.	13.50	25.00
90-04-346	Tweet Greetings-564044	J. Davis	2-Yr.	15.00	15.00
90-04-347	Trouble On 3 Wheels-564052	J. Davis	3-Yr.	20.00	20.00
89-04-348	Mine, All Mine!-564079	J. Davis	Yr.Iss.	15.00	33.00
89-04-349	Star of Stars-564389	J. Jonik	3-Yr.	9.00	15.00
90-04-350	Hang Onto Your Hat-564397	J. Jonik	3-Yr.	8.00	15.00
90-04-351	Fireplace Frolic-564435	N. Teiber	2-Yr.	25.00	25.00
89-04-352	Hoe! Hoe! Hoe!-564761	Enesco	Yr.Iss.	20.00	40.00
91-04-353	Double Scoop Snowmouse-564796	M. Cook	3-Yr.	13.50	13.50
90-04-354	Christmas Is Magic-564826	M. Cook	2-Yr.	10.00	10.00
90-04-355	Lighting Up Christmas-564834	M. Cook	2-Yr.	10.00	10.00
89-04-356	Feliz Navidad! 1989-564842	M. Cook	Yr.Iss.	11.00	25.00
89-04-357	Spreading Christmas Joy-564850	M. Cook	3-Yr.	10.00	10.00
89-04-358	Yuletide Tree House-564915	J. Jonik	3-Yr.	20.00	20.00
90-04-359	Brewnig Warm Wishes-564974	Enesco	2-Yr.	10.00	10.00
90-04-360	Yippie-I-Yuletide-564982	K. Hahn	3-Yr.	15.00	15.00
90-04-361	Coffee Break-564990	K. Hahn	3-Yr.	15.00	15.00
90-04-362	You're Sew Special-565008	K. Hahn	Yr.Iss.	20.00	22.50

Company Number	Name	Series Artist	Edition Limit	Issue Price	Quote
89-04-363	Full House Mouse-565016	K. Hahn	2-Yr.	13.50	20.00
89-04-364	I Feel Pretty-565024	K. Hahn	3-Yr.	20.00	22.00
90-04-365	Warmest Wishes-565032	K. Hahn	3-Yr.	15.00	15.00
90-04-366	Baby's Christmas Feast-565040	K. Hahn	3-Yr.	13.50	13.50
90-04-367	Bumper Car Santa-565083	G.G. Santiago	Yr.Iss.	20.00	20.00
89-04-368	Special Delivery(Proof Ed.)-565091	G.G. Santiago	Yr.Iss.	12.00	12.00
90-04-369	Ho! Ho! Yo-Yo!(Proof Ed.)-565105	G.G. Santiago	Yr.Iss.	12.00	12.00
89-04-370	Weightin' For Santa-565148	G.G. Santiago	3-Yr.	7.50	7.50
89-04-371	Holly Fairy-565199	C.M. Baker	Yr.Iss.	15.00	40.00
90-04-372	The Christmas Tree Fairy-565202	C.M. Baker	Yr.Iss.	15.00	22.50
89-04-373	Christmas 1989-565210	L. Rigg	Yr.Iss.	12.00	38.00
89-04-374	Top Of The Class-565237	L. Rigg	3-Yr.	11.00	11.00
89-04-375	Deck The Hogs-565490	M. Cook	2-Yr.	12.00	14.00
89-04-376	Pinata Ridin'-565504	M. Cook	2-Yr.	11.00	N/A
89-04-377	Hangin' In There 1989-565598	K. Wise	Yr.Iss.	10.00	19.50
90-04-378	Meow-y Christmas 1990-565601	K. Wise	Yr.Iss.	10.00	15.00
90-04-379	Seaman's Greetings-566047	Enesco	2-Yr.	11.00	11.00
90-04-380	Hang In There-566055	Enesco	3-Yr.	13.50	13.50
91-04-381	Pedal Pushin' Santa-566071	Enesco	Yr.Iss.	20.00	N/A
90-04-382	Merry Christmas Teacher-566098	Enesco	2-Yr.	11.00	11.00
90-04-383	Festive Flight-566101	Enesco	2-Yr.	11.00	11.00
90-04-384	Santa's Suitcase-566160	Enesco	3-Yr.	25.00	25.00
89-04-385	The Purr-Fect Fit!-566462	Enesco	3-Yr.	15.00	35.00
90-04-386	Tumbles 1990-566519	S. Zimnicki	Yr.Iss.	16.00	40.00
90-04-387	Twiddles-566551	S. Zimnicki	3-Yr.	15.00	30.00
91-04-388	Snuffy-566578	S. Zimnicki	3-Yr.	17.50	17.50
90-04-389	All Aboard-567671	Gilmore	2-Yr.	17.50	17.50
89-04-390	Gone With The Wind-567698	Enesco	Yr.Iss.	13.50	30.00
89-04-391	Dorothy-567760	Enesco	Yr.Iss.	12.00	30.00
89-04-392	The Tin Man-567779	Enesco	Yr.Iss.	12.00	23.00
89-04-393	The Cowardly Lion-567787	Enesco	Yr.Iss.	12.00	23.00
89-04-394	The Scarecrow-567795	Enesco	Yr.Iss.	12.00	23.00
90-04-395	Happy Holiday Readings-568104	Enesco	2-Yr.	8.00	8.00
89-04-396	Christmas 1989-568325	L. Rigg	Yr.Iss.	12.00	N/A
91-04-397	Holiday Ahoy-568368	Enesco	2-Yr.	12.50	12.50
91-04-398	Christmas Countdown-568376	Enesco	3-Yr.	20.00	20.00
89-04-399	Clara-568406	Enesco	Yr.Iss.	12.50	15.00
90-04-400	The Nutcracker-568414	Enesco	Yr.Iss.	12.50	25.00
91-04-401	Clara's Prince-568422	Enesco	Yr.Iss.	12.50	12.50
89-04-402	Santa's Little Reindear-568430	Enesco	2-Yr.	15.00	25.00
91-04-403	Tuba Totin' Teddy-568449	Enesco	3-Yr.	15.00	15.00
90-04-404	A Calling Home At Christmas-568457	Enesco	2-Yr.	15.00	15.00
91-04-405	Love Is The Secret Ingredient-568562	L. Rigg	2-Yr.	15.00	15.00
90-04-406	A Spoonful of Love-568570	L. Rigg	2-Yr.	10.00	10.00
90-04-407	Christmas Swingtime 1990-568597	L. Rigg	Yr.Iss.	13.00	N/A
90-04-408	Christmas Swingtime 1990-568600	L. Rigg	Yr.Iss.	13.00	N/A
90-04-409	Bearing Holiday Wishes-568619	L. Rigg	3-Yr.	22.50	22.50
90-04-410	Smitch-570184	S. Zimnicki	3-Yr.	22.50	22.50
91-04-411	Twinkle & Sprinkle-570206	S. Zimnicki	3-Yr.	22.50	22.50
90-04-412	Blinkie-570214	S. Zimnicki	3-Yr.	15.00	15.00
90-04-413	Have A Coke And A Smile™-571512	Enesco	3-Yr.	15.00	30.00
90-04-414	Fleece Navidad-571903	M. Cook	2-Yr.	13.50	25.00
90-04-415	I Have a Navaho-Ho-Ho 1990-571970	M. Cook	Yr.Iss.	15.00	17.50
90-04-416	Cheers 1990-572411	T. Wilson	Yr.Iss.	13.50	N/A
90-04-417	A Night Before Christmas-572438	T. Wilson	2-Yr.	17.50	17.50
90-04-418	Merry Kissmas-572446	T. Wilson	2-Yr.	10.00	30.00
91-04-419	Here Comes Santa Paws-572535	J. Davis	3-Yr.	20.00	20.00
90-04-420	Frosty Garfield 1990-572551	J. Davis	Yr.Iss.	13.50	13.50
90-04-421	Pop Goes The Odie-572578	J. Davis	2-Yr.	15.00	30.00
91-04-422	Sweet Beams-572586	J. Davis	2-Yr.	13.50	13.50
90-04-423	An Apple A Day-572594	J. Davis	2-Yr.	12.00	12.00
90-04-424	Dear Santa-572608	J. Davis	3-Yr.	17.00	17.00
91-04-425	Have A Ball This Christmas-572616	J. Davis	Yr.Iss.	15.00	15.00
90-04-426	Oh Shoosh!-572624	J. Davis	3-Yr.	17.00	17.00
90-04-427	Little Red Riding Cat-572632	J. Davis	Yr.Iss.	13.50	33.00
91-04-428	All Decked Out-572659	J. Davis	3-Yr.	13.50	13.50
90-04-429	Over The Rooftops-572721	J. Davis	2-Yr.	17.50	28-35.00
90-04-430	Garfield NFL Los Angeles Rams-572764	J. Davis	2-Yr.	12.50	12.50
90-04-431	Garfield NFLCincinnati Bengals-573000	J. Davis	2-Yr.	12.50	12.50
90-04-432	Garfield NFLCleveland Browns-573019	J. Davis	2-Yr.	12.50	12.50
90-04-433	Garfield NFL Houston Oiliers-573027	J. Davis	2-Yr.	12.50	12.50
90-04-434	Garfield NFL Pittsburg Steelers-573035	J. Davis	2-Yr.	12.50	12.50
90-04-435	Garfield NFL Denver Broncos-573043	J. Davis	2-Yr.	12.50	12.50
90-04-436	Garfield NFLKansas City Chiefs-573051	J. Davis	2-Yr.	12.50	12.50
90-04-437	Garfield NFL Los Angeles Raiders-573078	J. Davis	2-Yr.	12.50	12.50
90-04-438	Garfield NFL San Diego Chargers-573086	J. Davis	2-Yr.	12.50	12.50
90-04-439	Garfield NFL Seattle Seahawks-573094	J. Davis	2-Yr.	12.50	12.50
90-04-440	Garfield NFL Buffalo Bills-573108	J. Davis	2-Yr.	12.50	12.50
90-04-441	Garfield NFL Indianapolis Colts-573116	J. Davis	2-Yr.	12.50	12.50
90-04-442	Garfield NFL Miami Dolphins-573124	J. Davis	2-Yr.	12.50	12.50
90-04-443	Garfield NFL New England Patriots-573132	J. Davis	2-Yr.	12.50	12.50
90-04-444	Garfield NFL New York Jets-573140	J. Davis	2-Yr.	12.50	12.50
90-04-445	Garfield NFL Atlanta Falcons-573159	J. Davis	2-Yr.	12.50	12.50
90-04-446	Garfield NFL New Orleans Saints-573167	J. Davis	2-Yr.	12.50	12.50
90-04-447	Garfield NFL San Francisco 49ers-573175	J. Davis	2-Yr.	12.50	12.50
90-04-448	Garfield NFL Dallas Cowboys-573183	J. Davis	2-Yr.	12.50	12.50
90-04-449	Garfield NFL New York Giants-573191	J. Davis	2-Yr.	12.50	12.50
90-04-450	Garfield NFL Philadelphia Eagles-573205	J. Davis	2-Yr.	12.50	12.50
90-04-451	Garfield NFL Phoenix Cardinals-573213	J. Davis	2-Yr.	12.50	12.50
90-04-452	Garfield NFL Washington Redskins-573221	J. Davis	2-Yr.	12.50	12.50
90-04-453	Garfield NFL Chicago Bears-573248	J. Davis	2-Yr.	12.50	12.50
90-04-454	Garfield NFL Detroit Lions-573256	J. Davis	2-Yr.	12.50	12.50
90-04-455	Garfield NFL Green Bay Packers-573264	J. Davis	2-Yr.	12.50	12.50
90-04-456	Garfield NFLMinnesota Vikings-573272	J. Davis	2-Yr.	12.50	12.50
90-04-457	Garfield NFL Tampa Bay Buccaneers-573280	J. Davis	2-Yr.	12.50	12.50
91-04-458	Tea For Two-573299	K. Hahn	3-Yr.	30.00	50.00
91-04-459	Hot Stuff Santa-573523	Enesco	Yr.Iss.	25.00	25.00
90-04-460	Merry Moustronauts-573558	M. Cook	3-Yr.	20.00	40.00
91-04-461	Santa Wings It-573612	J. Jonik	3-Yr.	13.00	13.00
90-04-462	All Eye Want For Christmas-573647	Gilmore	3-Yr.	27.50	40.00
90-04-463	Stuck On You-573655	Gilmore	2-Yr.	12.50	12.50
90-04-464	Professor Michael Bear, The One Bear Band-573663	Gilmore	3-Yr.	22.50	28.00
90-04-465	A Caroling Wee Go-573671	Gilmore	3-Yr.	12.00	12.00
90-04-466	Merry Mailman-573698	Gilmore	2-Yr.	15.00	30.00
90-04-467	Deck The Halls-573701	Gilmore	3-Yr.	22.50	25.00
90-04-468	You're Wheel Special-573728	Gilmore	3-Yr.	15.00	15.00
91-04-469	Come Let Us Adore Him-573736	Gilmore	2-Yr.	9.00	9.00
91-04-470	Moon Beam Dreams-573760	Gilmore	3-Yr.	12.00	12.00
91-04-471	A Song For Santa-573779	Gilmore	3-Yr.	25.00	25.00
90-04-472	Warmest Wishes-573825	Gilmore	Yr.Iss.	17.50	24.50
91-04-473	Kurious Kitty-573868	Gilmore	3-Yr.	17.50	17.50
90-04-474	Old Mother Mouse-573922	Gilmore	2-Yr.	17.50	20-32.00
90-04-475	Railroad Repairs-573930	Gilmore	2-Yr.	12.50	25.00
90-04-476	Ten Lords A-Leaping-573949	Gilmore	3-Yr.	15.00	23.00
90-04-477	Eleven Drummers Drumming-573957	Gilmore	3-Yr.	15.00	23.00
90-04-478	Twelve Pipers Piping-573965	Gilmore	3-Yr.	15.00	23.00
90-04-479	Baby's First Christmas 1990-573973	Gilmore	Yr.Iss.	10.00	N/A
90-04-480	Baby's First Christmas 1990-573981	Gilmore	Yr.Iss.	12.00	N/A
91-04-481	Peter, Peter Pumpkin Eater-574015	Gilmore	2-Yr.	20.00	20.00
90-04-482	Little Jack Horner-574058	Gilmore	2-Yr.	17.50	20.00
91-04-483	Mary, Mary Quite Contrary-574066	Gilmore	2-Yr.	22.50	32.50
91-04-484	Through The Years-574252	Gilmore	Yr.Iss.	17.50	17.50
91-04-485	Holiday Wing Ding-574333	Enesco	3-Yr.	22.50	22.50
91-04-486	North Pole Here I Come-574597	Enesco	3-Yr.	10.00	10.00
91-04-487	Christmas Caboose-574856	Gilmore	2-Yr.	25.00	25.00
90-04-488	Bubble Trouble-575038	K. Hahn	3-Yr.	20.00	20.00
91-04-489	Merry Mother-To-Be-575046	K. Hahn	3-Yr.	13.50	13.50
90-04-490	A Holiday 'Scent' Sation-575054	K. Hahn	3-Yr.	15.00	15.00
90-04-491	Catch Of The Day-575070	K. Hahn	3-Yr.	25.00	25.00
90-04-492	Don't Open 'Til Christmas-575089	K. Hahn	3-Yr.	17.50	17.50
90-04-493	I Can't Weight 'Til Christmas-575119	K. Hahn	3-Yr.	16.50	30.00
91-04-494	Deck The Halls-575127	K. Hahn	2-Yr.	15.00	15.00
90-04-495	Mouse House-575186	Enesco	3-Yr.	16.00	16.00
91-04-496	Dream A Little Dream-575593	Enesco	2-Yr.	17.50	17.50
91-04-497	Christmas Two-gether-575615	L. Rigg	3-Yr.	22.50	22.50
91-04-498	Christmas Trimmings-575631	Gilmore	2-Yr.	17.00	17.00
91-04-499	Gumball Wizard-575658	Gilmore	2-Yr.	13.00	13.00
91-04-500	Crystal Ball Christmas-575666	Gilmore	2-Yr.	22.50	22.50
90-04-501	Old King Cole-575682	Gilmore	2-Yr.	20.00	20.00
91-04-502	Tom, Tom The Piper's Son-575690	Gilmore	2-Yr.	15.00	33.00
91-04-503	Tire-d Little Bear-575852	L. Rigg	Yr.Iss.	12.50	12.50
90-04-504	Baby Bear Christmas 1990-575860	L. Rigg	Yr.Iss.	12.00	28.00
91-04-505	Crank Up The Carols-575887	L. Rigg	2-Yr.	17.50	17.50
90-04-506	Beary Christmas 1990-576158	L. Rigg	Yr.Iss.	12.00	12.00
91-04-507	Christmas Swingtime 1991-576166	L. Rigg	Yr.Iss.	13.00	13.00
91-04-508	Christmas Swingtime 1991-576174	L. Rigg	Yr.Iss.	13.00	13.00
91-04-509	Christmas Cutie-576182	Enesco	3-Yr.	13.50	13.50
91-04-510	Meow Mates-576220	Enesco	3-Yr.	12.00	12.00
91-04-511	Frosty The Snowman™-576425	Enesco	3-Yr.	15.00	15.00
91-04-512	Ris-ski Business-576719	T. Wilson	2-Yr.	10.00	10.00
91-04-513	Pinocchio-577391	J. Davis	3-Yr.	15.00	15.00
90-04-514	Yuletide Ride 1990-577502	Gilmore	Yr.Iss.	13.50	13.50
90-04-515	Tons of Toys-577510	Enesco	Yr.Iss.	13.00	13.00
90-04-516	McHappy Holidays-577529	Enesco	2-Yr.	17.50	17.50
90-04-517	Heading For Happy Holidays-577537	Enesco	3-Yr.	17.50	17.50
90-04-518	'Twas The Night Before Christmas-577545	Enesco	3-Yr.	17.50	17.50
90-04-519	Over One Million Holiday Wishes!-577553	Enesco	Yr.Iss.	17.50	23.00
90-04-520	You Malt My Heart-577596	Enesco	2-Yr.	25.00	25.00
91-04-521	All I Want For Christmas-577618	Enesco	2-Yr.	20.00	20.00
91-04-522	Things Go Better With Coke™-580597	Enesco	3-Yr.	17.00	17.00
91-04-523	Christmas To Go-580600	M. Cook	Yr.Iss.	22.50	22.50
91-04-524	Have A Mariachi Christmas-580619	M. Cook	2-Yr.	13.50	13.50
91-04-525	Christmas Is In The Air-581453	Enesco	Yr.Iss.	15.00	15.00
91-04-526	Holiday Treats-581542	Enesco	Yr.Iss.	17.50	17.50
91-04-527	Christmas Is My Goal-581550	Enesco	2-Yr.	17.50	17.50
91-04-528	A Quarter Pounder With Cheer®-581569	Enesco	3-Yr.	20.00	20.00
91-04-529	From The Same Mold-581798	Gilmore	3-Yr.	17.00	17.00
91-04-530	The Glow Of Christmas-581801	Enesco	2-Yr.	20.00	20.00
91-04-531	All Caught Up In Christmas-583537	Enesco	2-Yr.	10.00	10.00
91-04-532	Lights..Camera..Kissmas!-583626	Gilmore	Yr.Iss.	15.00	15.00
91-04-533	Sweet Steed-583634	Gilmore	3-Yr.	15.00	15.00
91-04-534	Dreamin' Of A White Christmas-583669	Gilmore	2-Yr.	15.00	15.00
91-04-535	Merry Millimeters-583677	Gilmore	3-Yr.	17.00	17.00
91-04-536	Here's The Scoop-583693	Enesco	2-Yr.	13.50	13.50
91-04-537	Happy Meal® On Wheels-583715	Enesco	3-Yr.	22.50	22.50
91-04-538	Christmas Kayak-583723	Enesco	2-Yr.	13.50	13.50
91-04-539	Marilyn Monroe-583774	Enesco	Yr.Iss.	20.00	20.00
91-04-540	A Christmas Carol-583928	Gilmore	3-Yr.	22.50	22.50
91-04-541	Checking It Twice-583936	Enesco	2-Yr.	25.00	25.00
91-04-542	Merry Christmas Go-Round-585203	J. Davis	3-Yr.	20.00	20.00
91-04-543	Holiday Hideout-585270	J. Davis	2-Yr.	15.00	15.00
91-04-544	Our Most Precious Gift-585726	Enesco	Yr.Iss.	17.50	17.50
91-04-545	Christmas Cheer-585769	Enesco	2-Yr.	13.50	13.50
91-04-546	Fired Up For Christmas-586587	Gilmore	2-Yr.	32.50	32.50
91-04-547	One Foggy Christmas Eve-586625	Gilmore	3-Yr.	30.00	30.00
91-04-548	For A Purr-fect Mom-586641	Gilmore	Yr.Iss.	12.00	12.00
91-04-549	For A Special Dad-586668	Gilmore	Yr.Iss.	17.50	17.50
91-04-550	With Love-586676	Gilmore	Yr.Iss.	13.00	13.00
91-04-551	For A Purr-fect Aunt-586692	Gilmore	Yr.Iss.	12.00	12.00
91-04-552	For A Dog-Gone Great Uncle-586706	Gilmore	Yr.Iss.	12.00	12.00
91-04-553	Peddling Fun-586714	Gilmore	Yr.Iss.	16.00	16.00
91-04-554	Special Keepsakes-586722	Gilmore	Yr.Iss.	13.50	13.50
91-04-555	Hats Off To Christmas-586757	K. Hahn	Yr.Iss.	22.50	22.50
91-04-556	Baby's First Christmas 1991-586935	Enesco	Yr.Iss.	12.50	12.50
91-04-557	Jugglin' The Holidays-587028	Enesco	2-Yr.	13.00	13.00
91-04-558	Santa's Steed-587044	Enesco	Yr.Iss.	15.00	15.00
91-04-559	A Decade of Treasures-587052	Gilmore	Yr.Iss.	37.50	37.50
91-04-560	Mr. Mailmouse-587109	Gilmore	2-Yr.	17.00	17.00
91-04-561	Starry Eyed Santa-587176	Enesco	2-Yr.	15.00	15.00
91-04-562	Lighting The Way-588776	Enesco	2-Yr.	20.00	20.00
91-04-563	Rudolph-588784	Enesco	2-Yr.	17.50	17.50
89-04-564	Tea For Two-693758	N. Teiber	2-Yr.	12.50	14.00
90-04-565	Holiday Tea Toast-694770	N. Teiber	2-Yr.	13.50	13.50
91-04-566	It's Tea-lightful-694789	Enesco	2-Yr.	13.50	13.50
89-04-567	Tea Time-694797	N. Teiber	2-Yr.	12.50	N/A
89-04-568	Bottom's Up 1989-830003	Enesco	Yr.Iss.	11.00	11.00
90-04-569	Sweetest Greetings 1990-830011	Gilmore	Yr.Iss.	10.00	10.00
90-04-570	First Class Christmas-830038	Gilmore	3-Yr.	10.00	10.00
89-04-571	Caught In The Act-830046	Gilmore	3-Yr.	12.50	12.50
89-04-572	Readin' & Ridin'-830054	Gilmore	3-Yr.	13.50	13.50
91-04-573	Beary Merry Mailman-830151	L. Rigg	3-Yr.	13.50	13.50
90-04-574	Here's Looking at You!-830259	Gilmore	2-Yr.	17.50	17.50
91-04-575	Stamper-830267	S. Zimnicki	Yr.Iss.	13.50	13.50
91-04-576	Santa's Key Man-830461	Gilmore	2-Yr.	11.00	11.00
91-04-577	Tie-dings Of Joy-830488	Gilmore	Yr.Iss.	12.00	12.00
90-04-578	Have a Cool Yule-830496	Gilmore	3-Yr.	12.00	12.00
90-04-579	Slots of Luck-830518	K. Hahn	2-Yr.	13.50	15.00
91-04-580	Straight To Santa-830534	J. Davis	2-Yr.	13.50	13.50
91-04-581	Letters To Santa-830925	Gilmore	2-Yr.	15.00	15.00
91-04-582	Sneaking Santa's Snack-830933	Gilmore	3-Yr.	13.00	13.00
91-04-583	Aiming For The Holidays-830941	Gilmore	2-Yr.	12.00	12.00
91-04-584	Ode To Joy-830968	Gilmore	3-Yr.	10.00	10.00
91-04-585	Fittin' Mittens-830976	Gilmore	3-Yr.	12.00	12.00
91-04-586	The Finishing Touch-831530	Gilmore	Yr.Iss.	10.00	10.00
91-04-587	A Real Classic-831603	Gilmore	Yr.Iss.	10.00	10.00

CHRISTMAS ORNAMENTS

Company Number	Name	Series Artist	Edition Limit	Issue Price	Quote
91-04-588	Christmas Fills The Air-831921	Gilmore	3-Yr.	12.00	12.00
91-04-589	Deck The Halls-860573	M. Peters	3-Yr.	12.00	12.00
91-04-590	Bathing Beauty-860581	K. Hahn	3-Yr.	13.50	13.50
92-04-591	Sparky & Buffer-561851	S. Zimnicki	3-Yr.	25.00	25.00
92-04-592	Moonlight Swing-568627	L. Rigg	3-Yr.	15.00	15.00
92-04-593	Carver-570192	S. Zimnicki	Yr.Iss.	17.50	17.50
92-04-594	A Rockin' GARFIELD Christmas-572527	J. Davis	2-Yr.	17.50	17.50
92-04-595	The Nutcracker-574023	Gilmore	3-Yr.	25.00	25.00
92-04-596	Humpty Dumpty-574244	Gilmore	2-Yr.	25.00	25.00
92-04-597	Music Mice-Tro!-575143	Enesco	2-Yr.	12.00	12.00
92-04-598	On Target Two-Gether-575623	Enesco	Yr.Iss.	17.00	17.00
92-04-599	Rock-A-Bye Baby-575704	Gilmore	2-Yr.	13.50	13.50
92-04-600	Queen of Hearts-575712	Gilmore	2-Yr.	17.50	17.50
92-04-601	Tasty Tidings-575836	L. Rigg	Yr.Iss.	13.50	13.50
92-04-602	Bearly Sleepy-578029	Gilmore	Yr.Iss.	17.50	17.50
92-04-603	Spreading Sweet Joy-580465	Enesco	Yr.Iss.	13.50	13.50
92-04-604	Ring My Bell-580740	J. Davis	Yr.Iss.	13.50	13.50
92-04-605	4 x 4 Holiday Fun-580783	J. Davis	2-Yr.	20.00	20.00
92-04-606	The Holidays Are A Hit-581577	Enesco	2-Yr.	17.50	17.50
92-04-607	Tip Top Tidings-581828	Enesco	2-Yr.	13.00	13.00
92-04-608	Christmas Lifts The Spirits-582018	Enesco	2-Yr.	25.00	25.00
92-04-609	A Pound Of Good Cheers-582034	Enesco	2-Yr.	17.50	17.50
92-04-610	Sweet as Cane Be-583642	Gilmore	3-Yr.	15.00	15.00
92-04-611	Sundae Ride-583707	Enesco	2-Yr.	20.00	20.00
92-04-612	The Cold, Crisp Taste Of Coke™-583766	Enesco	3-Yr.	17.00	17.00
92-04-613	Sew Christmasy-583820	Enesco	3-Yr.	25.00	25.00
92-04-614	Catch A Falling Star-583944	Gilmore	2-Yr.	15.00	15.00
92-04-615	Swingin' Christmas-584096	Enesco	2-Yr.	15.00	15.00
92-04-616	Mc Ho, Ho, Ho-585181	Enesco	3-Yr.	22.50	22.50
92-04-617	Holiday On Ice-585254	J. Davis	3-Yr.	17.50	17.50
92-04-618	Fast Track Cat-585289	J. Davis	3-Yr.	17.50	17.50
92-04-619	Holiday Cat Napping-585319	J. Davis	2-Yr.	20.00	20.00
92-04-620	The Finishing Touches-585610	T. Wilson	2-Yr.	17.50	17.50
92-04-621	Jolly Ol' Gent-585645	J. Jonik	3-Yr.	13.50	13.50
92-04-622	A Child's Christmas-586358	Enesco	3-Yr.	25.00	25.00
92-04-623	Festive Fiddlers-586501	Enesco	Yr.Iss.	20.00	20.00
92-04-624	La Luminaria-586579	M. Cook	2-Yr.	13.50	13.50
92-04-625	Cozy Chrismas Carriage-586730	Gilmore	2-Yr.	22.50	22.50
92-04-626	Small Fry's First Christmas-586749	Enesco	2-Yr.	17.00	17.00
92-04-627	Friendships Preserved-586765	K. Hahn	Yr.Iss.	22.50	22.50
92-04-628	Window Wish List-586854	Gilmore	2-Yr.	30.00	30.00
92-04-629	Through The Years-586862	Gilmore	Yr.Iss.	17.50	17.50
92-04-630	Baby's First Christmas 1992-586943	Enesco	Yr.Iss.	12.50	12.50
92-04-631	Firehouse Friends-586951	Gilmore	Yr.Iss.	22.50	22.50
92-04-632	Bubble Buddy-586978	Gilmore	2-Yr.	13.50	13.50
92-04-633	The Warmth Of The Season-586994	Enesco	2-Yr.	20.00	20.00
92-04-634	It's A Go For Christmas-587095	Gilmore	2-Yr.	15.00	15.00
92-04-635	Post-Mouster General-587117	Gilmore	2-Yr.	20.00	20.00
92-04-636	To A Deer Baby-587168	Enesco	Yr.Iss.	18.50	18.50
92-04-637	Moon Watch-587184	Enesco	2-Yr.	20.00	20.00
92-04-638	Guten Cheers-587192	Enesco	Yr.Iss.	22.50	22.50
92-04-639	Put On A Happy Face-588237	Enesco	2-Yr.	15.00	15.00
92-04-640	Beginning To Look A Lot Like Christmas-588253	Enesco	2-Yr.	15.00	15.00
92-04-641	A Christmas Toast-588261	Enesco	2-Yr.	20.00	20.00
92-04-642	Merry Mistle-Toad-588288	Enesco	2-Yr.	15.00	15.00
92-04-643	Tic-Tac-Mistle-Toe-588296	Enesco	3-Yr.	23.00	23.00
92-04-644	Heaven Sent-588423	J. Penchoff	2-Yr.	12.50	12.50
92-04-645	Holiday Happenings-588555	Gilmore	3-Yr.	30.00	30.00
92-04-646	Seed-son's Greetings-588571	Gilmore	3-Yr.	27.00	27.00
92-04-647	Santa's Midnight Snack-588598	Gilmore	2-Yr.	20.00	20.00
92-04-648	Trunk Of Treasures-588636	Enesco	Yr.Iss.	20.00	20.00
92-04-649	Festive Newsflash-588792	Enesco	2-Yr.	17.50	17.50
92-04-650	A-B-C-Son's Greetings-588806	Enesco	2-Yr.	16.50	16.50
92-04-651	Hoppy Holidays-588814	Enesco	Yr.Iss.	13.50	13.50
92-04-652	Fireside Friends-588830	Enesco	2-Yr.	20.00	20.00
92-04-653	Christmas Eve-mergency-588849	Enesco	2-Yr.	27.00	27.00
92-04-654	A Sure Sign Of Christmas-588857	Enesco	2-Yr.	22.50	22.50
92-04-655	Holidays Give Me A Lift-588865	Enesco	2-Yr.	30.00	30.00
92-04-656	Yule Tide Together-588903	Enesco	2-Yr.	20.00	20.00
92-04-657	Have A Soup-er Christmas-588911	Enesco	2-Yr.	17.50	17.50
92-04-658	Christmas Cure-Alls-588938	Enesco	2-Yr.	20.00	20.00
92-04-659	Dial 'S' For Santa-589373	Enesco	2-Yr.	25.00	25.00
92-04-660	Joy To The Whirled-589551	K. Hahn	2-Yr.	20.00	20.00
92-04-661	Merry Make-Over-589586	K. Hahn	3-Yr.	20.00	20.00
92-04-662	Campin' Companions-590282	K. Hahn	3-Yr.	20.00	20.00
92-04-663	Fur-Ever Friends-590797	Gilmore	2-Yr.	13.50	13.50
92-04-664	Tee-rific holidays-590827	Enesco	3-Yr.	25.00	25.00
92-04-665	Spinning Christmas Dreams-590908	K. Hahn	3-Yr.	22.50	22.50
92-04-666	Christmas Trimmin'-590932	Enesco	3-Yr.	17.00	17.00
92-04-667	Wrappin' Up Warm Wishes-593141	Enesco	Yr.Iss.	17.50	17.50
92-04-668	Christmas Biz-593168	Enesco	2-Yr.	22.50	22.50
92-04-669	Holiday Take-Out-593508	Enesco	Yr.Iss.	17.50	17.50
92-04-670	A Christmas Yarn-593516	Gilmore	Yr.Iss.	20.00	20.00
92-04-671	Treasure The Earth-593826	K. Hahn	2-Yr.	25.00	25.00
92-04-672	Toyful' Rudolph-593982	Enesco	2-Yr.	22.50	22.50
92-04-673	Take A Chance On The Holidays-594075	Enesco	3-Yr.	20.00	20.00
92-04-674	Lights..Camera..Christmas!-594369	Enesco	3-Yr.	20.00	20.00
92-04-675	Spirited Stallion-594407	Enesco	Yr.Iss.	15.00	15.00
92-04-676	A Watchful Eye-595713	Enesco	Yr.Iss.	15.00	15.00
92-04-677	Good Catch-595721	Enesco	Yr.Iss.	12.50	12.50
92-04-678	Squirrelin' It Away-595748	K. Hahn	Yr.Iss.	12.00	12.00
92-04-679	Checkin' His List-595756	Enesco	Yr.Iss.	12.50	12.50
92-04-680	Christmas Cat Nappin'	Enesco	Yr.Iss.	12.00	12.00
92-04-681	Bless Our Home-595772	Enesco	Yr.Iss.	12.00	12.00
92-04-682	Salute the Season-595780	K. Hahn	Yr.Iss.	12.00	12.00
92-04-683	Fired Up For Christmas-595799	Enesco	Yr.Iss.	12.00	12.00
92-04-684	Speedin' Mr. Snowman-595802	M. Rhyner	Yr.Iss.	12.00	12.00
92-04-685	Merry Christmas Mother Earth-595810	K. Hahn	Yr.Iss.	11.00	11.00
92-04-686	Wear The Season With A Smile-595829	Enesco	Yr.Iss.	10.00	10.00
92-04-687	Jesus Loves Me-595837	K. Hahn	Yr.Iss.	10.00	10.00
92-04-688	Merry Kisses-831166	Enesco	2-Yr.	17.50	17.50
92-04-689	Christmas Is In The Air-831174	Enesco	2-Yr.	25.00	25.00
92-04-690	To The Point-831182	Gilmore	2-Yr.	13.50	13.50
92-04-691	Poppin' Hoppin' Holidays-831263	Gilmore	Yr.Iss.	25.00	25.00
92-04-692	Tankful Tidings-831271	Gilmore	2-Yr.	30.00	30.00
92-04-693	Ginger-Bred Greetings-831581	Gilmore	Yr.Iss.	12.00	12.00
92-04-694	A Gold Star For Teacher-831948	Gilmore	3-Yr.	15.00	15.00
92-04-695	A Tall Order-832758	Gilmore	3-Yr.	12.00	12.00
92-04-696	Candlelight Serenade-832766	Gilmore	2-Yr.	12.00	12.00
92-04-697	Holiday Glow Puppet Show-832774	Gilmore	3-Yr.	15.00	15.00
92-04-698	Christopher Columouse-832782	Gilmore	Yr.Iss.	12.00	12.00
92-04-699	Cartin' Home Holiday Treats-832790	Enesco	2-Yr.	13.50	13.50
92-04-700	Making Tracks To Santa-832804	Gilmore	2-Yr.	15.00	15.00
92-04-701	Special Delivery-832812	Enesco	2-Yr.	12.00	12.00
92-04-702	A Mug Full Of Love-832928	Gilmore	Yr.Iss.	13.50	13.50
92-04-703	Have A Cool Christmas-832944	Gilmore	Yr.Iss.	13.50	13.50
92-04-704	Knitten' Kittens-832952	Gilmore	Yr.Iss.	17.50	17.50
92-04-705	Holiday Honors-833029	Gilmore	Yr.Iss.	15.00	15.00
92-04-706	Christmas Nite Cap-834424	Gilmore	3-Yr.	13.50	13.50
92-04-707	North Pole Peppermint Patrol-840157	Gilmore	2-Yr.	25.00	25.00
92-04-708	A Boot-iful Christmas-840165	Gilmore	Yr.Iss.	20.00	20.00
92-04-709	Watching For Santa-840432	Enesco	2-Yr.	25.00	25.00
92-04-710	Special Delivery-840440	Enesco	Yr.Iss.	22.50	22.50
93-04-711	I'm Dreaming of a White-Out Christmas -566144	Enesco	2-Yr.	22.50	22.50
93-04-712	Born To Shop-572942	Enesco	Yr.Iss.	26.50	26.50
93-04-713	Toy To The World-575763	Enesco	2-Yr.	25.00	25.00
93-04-714	Bearly Balanced-580724	Enesco	Yr.Iss.	15.00	15.00
93-04-715	Joyeux Noel-582026	Enesco	2-Yr.	24.50	24.50
93-04-716	Holiday Mew-Sic-582107	Enesco	2-Yr.	20.00	20.00
93-04-717	Santa's Magic Ride-582115	Enesco	2-Yr.	24.00	24.00
93-04-718	Warm And Hearty Wishes-582344	Enesco	Yr.Iss.	17.50	17.50
93-04-719	Cool Yule-582352	Enesco	Yr.Iss.	12.00	12.00
93-04-720	Have A Holly Jell-O Christmas-582387	Enesco	Yr.Iss.	19.50	19.50
93-04-721	Festive Firemen-582565	Gilmore	2-Yr.	17.00	17.00
93-04-722	Light Up Your Holidays With Coke-583758	Enesco	Yr.Iss.	27.50	27.50
93-04-723	Pool Hall-idays-584851	Enesco	2-Yr.	19.00	19.90
93-04-724	Bah Humbug-585394	Davis	Yr.Iss.	15.00	15.00
93-04-725	Chimer-585777	Zimnicki	Yr.Iss.	25.00	25.00
93-04-726	Sweet Whiskered Wishes-585807	Enesco	Yr.Iss.	17.00	17.00
93-04-727	Grade "A" Wishes From Garfield -585823	Davis	2-Yr.	20.00	20.00
93-04-728	Tree For Two-586781	Gilmore	2-Yr.	17.50	17.50
93-04-729	A Bright Idea-586803	Gilmore	2-Yr.	22.50	22.50
93-04-730	Baby's First Christmas 1993-585823	Gilmore	Yr.Iss.	17.50	17.50
93-04-731	My Special Christmas-586900	Gilmore	Yr.Iss.	17.50	17.50
93-04-732	Baby's First Christmas Dinner-587001	Enesco	Yr.Iss.	12.00	12.00
93-04-733	A Pause For Claus-588318	Enesco	2-Yr.	22.50	22.50
93-04-734	Not A Creature Was Stirring...-588663	Gilmore	2-Yr.	27.50	27.50
93-04-735	Terrific Toys-588644	Enesco	Yr.Iss.	20.00	20.00
93-04-736	Christmas Dancer-588652	Enesco	Yr.Iss.	15.00	15.00
93-04-737	Countin' On A Merry Christmas-588954	Enesco	2-Yr.	22.50	22.50
93-04-738	To My Gem-589004	Enesco	Yr.Iss.	27.50	27.50
93-04-739	Christmas Mall Call-589012	Enesco	2-Yr.	20.00	20.00
93-04-740	Spreading Joy-589047	Enesco	2-Yr.	27.50	27.50
93-04-741	Pitter-Patter Post Office-589055	Enesco	2-Yr.	20.00	20.00
93-04-742	Happy Haul-idays-589098	Enesco	2-Yr.	30.00	30.00
93-04-743	Hot Off ThePress-589292	Enesco	2-Yr.	27.50	27.50
93-04-744	Designed With You In Mind-589306	Enesco	2-Yr.	16.00	16.00
93-04-745	Seeing Is Believing-589381	Gilmore	2-Yr.	20.00	20.00
93-04-746	Roundin' Up Christmas Together-590800	Enesco	Yr.Iss.	25.00	25.00
93-04-747	Toasty Tidings-590940	Enesco	2-Yr.	20.00	20.00
93-04-748	Focusing On Christmas-590983	Gilmore	2-Yr.	27.50	27.50
93-04-749	Dunk The Halls-591009	Enesco	2-Yr.	18.50	18.50
93-04-750	Mice Capades-591386	Hahn	2-Yr.	26.50	26.50
93-04-751	25 Points For Christmas-591750	Enesco	Yr.Iss.	25.00	25.00
93-04-752	Carving Christmas Wishes-592625	Gilmore	2-Yr.	25.00	25.00
93-04-753	Celebrating With A Splash-592692	Enesco	Yr.Iss.	17.00	17.00
93-04-754	Slimmin' Santa-592722	Enesco	Yr.Iss.	18.50	18.50
93-04-755	Plane Ol' Holiday Fun-592773	Enesco	Yr.Iss.	27.50	27.50
93-04-756	Smooth Move, Mom-593176	Enesco	Yr.Iss.	20.00	20.00
93-04-757	Tool TIme, Yule TIme-593192	Enesco	Yr.Iss.	18.50	18.50
93-04-758	Speedy-593370	Zimnicki	2-Yr.	25.00	25.00
93-04-759	On Your Mark, Set, Is That To Go?-593524	Enesco	Yr.Iss.	13.50	13.50
93-04-760	Do Not Open 'Til Christmas-593737	Hahn	2-Yr.	15.00	15.00
93-04-761	Greetings In Stereo-593745	Hahn	Yr.Iss.	19.50	19.50
93-04-762	Tangled Up For Christmas-593974	Enesco	2-Yr.	14.50	14.50
93-04-763	Sweet Season's Eatings-594202	Enesco	Yr.Iss.	22.50	22.50
93-04-764	Have A Darn Good Christmas-594229	Gilmore	2-Yr.	21.00	21.00
93-04-765	The Sweetest Ride-594253	Gilmore	2-Yr.	18.50	18.50
93-04-766	Lights...Camera...Christmas-594369	Enesco	Yr.Iss.	20.00	20.00
93-04-767	Have A Cheery Christmas, Sister-594687	Enesco	Yr.Iss.	13.50	13.50
93-04-768	Say Cheese-594962	Gilmore	2-Yr.	13.50	13.50
93-04-769	Christmas Kicks-594989	Enesco	Yr.Iss.	17.50	17.50
93-04-770	Time For Santa-594997	Gilmore	2-Yr.	17.50	17.50
93-04-771	Holiday Orders-595004	Enesco	Yr.Iss.	20.00	20.00
93-04-772	T'Was The Night Before Christmas-595012	Enesco	Yr.Iss.	22.50	22.50
93-04-773	Sugar Chef Shoppe-595055	Gilmore	2-Yr.	23.50	23.50
93-04-774	Merry Mc-Choo-Choo-595063	Enesco	Yr.Iss.	30.00	30.00
93-04-775	Basketful Of Friendship-595098	Enesco	Yr.Iss.	20.00	20.00
93-04-776	Rockin' With Santa-595195	Enesco	2-Yr.	13.50	13.50
93-04-777	Christmas-To-Go-595217	Enesco	Yr.Iss.	25.50	25.50
93-04-778	Sleddin' Mr. Snowman-595275	Enesco	2-Yr.	13.00	13.00
93-04-779	A Kick Out Of Christmas-595373	Enesco	2-Yr.	10.00	10.00
93-04-780	Friends Through Thick And Thin-595381	Enesco	2-Yr.	10.00	10.00
93-04-781	See-Saw Sweethearts-595403	Enesco	2-Yr.	10.00	10.00
93-04-782	Special Delivery For Santa-595411	Enesco	2-Yr.	10.00	10.00
93-04-783	Top Marks For Teacher-595438	Enesco	2-Yr.	10.00	10.00
93-04-784	Home Tweet Home-595446	Enesco	2-Yr.	10.00	10.00
93-04-785	Clownin' Around-595454	Enesco	2-Yr.	10.00	10.00
93-04-786	Heart Filled Dreams-595462	Enesco	2-Yr.	10.00	10.00
93-04-787	Merry Christmas Baby-595470	Enesco	2-Yr.	10.00	10.00
93-04-788	Your A Hit With Me, Brother-595535	Hahn	Yr.Iss.	10.00	10.00
93-04-789	For A Sharp Uncle-595543	Enesco	Yr.Iss.	10.00	10.00
93-04-790	Paint Your Holidays Bright-595551	Hahn	2-Yr.	10.00	10.00
93-04-791	Goofy "Goals" For It-596019	Enesco	Yr.Iss.	15.00	15.00
93-04-792	Goofy Slam Dunk'-598027	Enesco	Yr.Iss.	15.00	15.00
93-04-793	Goofy Scores Again-598035	Enesco	Yr.Iss.	15.00	15.00
93-04-794	Goofy About Football'-596043	Enesco	Yr.Iss.	15.00	15.00
93-04-795	You Got To Treasure The Holidays, Man' -596051	Enesco	Yr.Iss.	25.00	25.00
93-04-796	Ariel's Under-The-Sea Tree-596078	Enesco	Yr.Iss.	22.50	22.50
93-04-797	Here Comes Santa Claws-596086	Enesco	Yr.Iss.	22.50	22.50
93-04-798	You're Tea-Lighting, Mom!-596094	Enesco	Yr.Iss.	20.00	20.00
93-04-799	Hearts A Glow-596108	Enesco	Yr.Iss.	18.50	18.50
93-04-800	Love's Sweet Dance-596116	Enesco	Yr.Iss.	29.50	29.50
93-04-801	Holiday Wishes-596124	Enesco	Yr.Iss.	17.50	17.50
93-04-802	Hangin Out For The Holidays-596132	Enesco	Yr.Iss.	15.00	15.00
93-04-803	Magic Carpet Ride-596140	Enesco	Yr.Iss.	25.00	25.00
93-04-804	Holiday Treasures-596159	Enesco	Yr.Iss.	18.50	18.50
93-04-805	Happily Ever After-596167	Enesco	Yr.Iss.	25.00	25.00
93-04-806	The Fairest Of Them All-596175	Enesco	Yr.Iss.	20.00	20.00
93-04-807	December 25...Dear Diary-596809	Hahn	2-Yr.	10.00	10.00
93-04-808	Wheel Merry Wishes-596930	Hahn	2-Yr.	15.00	15.00
93-04-809	Good Grounds For Christmas-596957	Hahn	Yr.Iss.	24.50	24.50
93-04-810	Ducking The Season's Rush-597597	Enesco	Yr.Iss.	17.50	17.50

Number	Name	Artist	Edition Limit	Issue Price	Quote
93-04-811	Here Comes Rudolph®-597686	Enesco	2-Yr.	17.50	17.50
93-04-812	It's Beginning To Look A Lot Like Christmas -597694	Enesco	Yr.Iss.	22.50	22.50
93-04-813	Christmas In The Making-597716	Enesco	Yr.Iss.	20.00	20.00
93-04-814	Mickey's Holiday Treasure-597759	Enesco	Yr.Iss.	12.00	12.00
93-04-815	Dream Wheels-597856	Enesco	Yr.Iss.	29.50	29.50
93-04-816	All You Add Is Love-598429	Enesco	Yr.Iss.	18.50	18.50
93-04-817	Goofy About Skiing-598631	Enesco	Yr.Iss.	22.50	22.50
93-04-818	A Toast Ladled With Love-830828	Hahn	2-Yr.	15.00	15.00
93-04-819	Christmas Is In The Air-831174	Enesco	2-Yr.	25.00	25.00
93-04-820	Delivered to The Nick In Time-831808	Gilmore	2-Yr.	13.50	13.50
93-04-821	Sneaking A Peek-831840	Gilmore	2-Yr.	10.00	10.00
93-04-822	Jewel Box Ballet-831859	Hahn	2-Yr.	20.00	20.00
93-04-823	A Mistle-Tow-831867	Gilmore	2-Yr.	15.00	15.00
93-04-824	Grandma's Liddle Griddle-832936	Gilmore	Yr.Iss.	10.00	10.00
93-04-825	To A Grade "A" Teacher-833037	Gilmore	2-Yr.	10.00	10.00
93-04-826	Have A Cool Christmas-834467	Gilmore	2-Yr.	10.00	10.00
93-04-827	For A Star Aunt-834556	Gilmore	Yr.Iss.	12.00	12.00
93-04-828	Watching For Santa-840432	Enesco	2-Yr.	25.00	25.00
Fitz and Floyd, Inc.	**Fitz and Floyd Annual Christmas Ornament**				
91-01-001	Plaid Teddy	M. Collins	Closed	15.00	15.00
92-01-002	Nutcracker Sweets	R. Havins	Closed	18.00	18.00
93-01-003	Charles Dickens' "A Christmas Carol"	T. Kerr	7,500	18.00	18.00
Fitz and Floyd, Inc.	**The Myth of Santa Claus**				
93-02-001	Russian Santa	R. Havins	7,500	18.00	18.00
Fitz and Floyd, Inc.	**The Twelve Days of Christmas**				
93-03-001	A Partridge in a Pear Tree	T. Kerr	7,500	18.00	18.00
Fitz and Floyd, Inc.	**Fitz and Floyd Baby's First Christmas**				
92-04-001	Rock-A-Bye Teddy	M. Collins	Closed	18.00	18.00
Flambro Imports	**Emmett Kelly Jr. Christmas Ornaments**				
89-01-001	65th Birthday	Undis.	Closed	24.00	40-100.00
90-01-002	30 Years Of Clowning	Undis.	Closed	30.00	125.00
91-01-003	EKJ With Stocking And Toys	Undis.	Closed	30.00	50.00
92-01-004	Home For Christmas	Undis.	Closed	24.00	30.00
Flambro Imports	**Raggedy Ann and Andy Ornaments**				
89-02-002	Raggedy Andy w/Gift Stocking	Undis.	Closed	13.50	18.00
89-02-002	Raggedy Andy w/Candy Cane	Undis.	Closed	13.50	18.00
Margaret Furlong Designs	**Musical Series**				
80-01-001	The Caroler	M. Furlong	3,000	50.00	100-125.
81-01-002	The Lyrist	M. Furlong	3,000	45.00	75-100.00
82-01-003	The Lutist	M. Furlong	3,000	45.00	75-100.00
83-01-004	The Concertinist	M. Furlong	3,000	45.00	75.00
84-01-005	The Herald Angel	M. Furlong	3,000	45.00	75-100.00
Margaret Furlong Designs	**Gifts from God**				
85-02-001	The Charis Angel	M. Furlong	3,000	45.00	100-200.
86-02-002	The Hallelujah Angel	M. Furlong	3,000	45.00	150-250.
87-02-003	The Angel of Light	M. Furlong	3,000	45.00	100.00
88-02-004	The Celestial Angel	M. Furlong	3,000	45.00	100-150.
89-02-005	Coronation Angel	M. Furlong	3,000	45.00	75-125.00
Margaret Furlong Designs	**Joyeux Noel**				
90-03-001	Celebration Angel	M. Furlong	10,000	45.00	45-55.00
91-03-002	Thanksgiving Angel	M. Furlong	10,000	45.00	45.00
92-03-003	Joyeux Noel Angel	M. Furlong	10,000	45.00	45.00
93-03-004	Star of Bethlehem Angel	M. Furlong	10,000	45.00	45.00
Ganz/Little Cheesers	**The Christmas Collection**				
92-01-001	Santa Cheeser Ornament	GDA/Thammavongsa	Open	14.00	14.00
92-01-002	Jenny Butterfield Ornament	GDA/Thammavongsa	Open	17.00	17.00
92-01-003	Myrtle Meadowmouse Ornament	GDA/Thammavongsa	Open	15.00	15.00
92-01-004	Little Truffle Ornament	GDA/Thammavongsa	Open	9.50	9.50
92-01-005	Jeremy With Teddy Ornament	GDA/Thammavongsa	Open	13.00	13.00
92-01-006	Abner Appleton Ornament	GDA/Thammavongsa	Open	15.00	15.00
Goebel United States	**Co-Boy Annual Ornaments**				
86-01-001	Coboy with Wreath	G. Skrobek	Closed	18.00	25.00
87-01-002	Coboy with Candy Cane	G. Skrobek	Closed	25.00	25.00
88-01-003	Coboy with Tree	G. Skrobek	Closed	30.00	30.00
Goebel United States	**Charlot Byj Annual Ornaments**				
86-02-001	Santa Lucia Angel	Charlot Byj	Closed	18.00	25.00
87-02-002	Christmas Pageant	Charlot Byj	Closed	20.00	20.00
88-02-003	Angel with Sheet Music	Charlot Byj	Closed	22.00	22.00
Goebel United States	**Charlot Byj Baby Ornaments**				
86-03-001	Baby Ornament	Charlot Byj	Closed	18.00	18.00
87-03-002	Baby Snow	Charlot Byj	Closed	20.00	20.00
88-03-003	Baby's 1st Stocking	Charlot Byj	Closed	27.50	27.50
Goebel United States	**Annual Ornaments**				
78-04-001	Santa (white)	Goebel	Closed	7.50	12.00
78-04-002	Santa (color)	Goebel	Closed	15.00	17-50.00
79-04-003	Angel/Tree (white)	Goebel	Closed	8.00	13.00
79-04-004	Angel/Tree (color)	Goebel	Closed	16.00	18-45.00
80-04-005	Mrs. Santa (white)	Goebel	Closed	9.00	14.00
80-04-006	Mrs. Santa (color)	Goebel	Closed	17.00	17-40.00
81-04-007	The Nutcracker (white)	Goebel	Closed	10.00	10.00
81-04-008	The Nutcracker (color)	Goebel	Closed	18.00	18-35.00
82-04-009	Santa in Chimney (white)	Goebel	Closed	10.00	10.00
82-04-010	Santa in Chimney (color)	Goebel	Closed	18.00	18.00
83-04-011	Clown (white)	Goebel	Closed	10.00	10.00
83-04-012	Clown (color)	Goebel	Closed	18.00	18-35.00
84-04-013	Snowman (white)	Goebel	Closed	10.00	10.00
84-04-014	Snowman (color)	Goebel	Closed	18.00	18-35.00
85-04-015	Angel (white)	Goebel	Closed	9.00	9.00
85-04-016	Angel (color)	Goebel	Closed	18.00	18-35.00
86-04-017	Drummer Boy (white)	Goebel	Closed	9.00	9.00
86-04-018	Drummer Boy (color)	Goebel	Closed	18.00	18.00
87-04-019	Rocking Horse (white)	Goebel	Closed	10.00	10.00
87-04-020	Rocking Horse (color)	Goebel	Closed	20.00	20.00
88-04-021	Doll (white)	Goebel	Closed	12.50	12.50
88-04-022	Doll (color)	Goebel	Closed	22.50	22.50
89-04-023	Dove (white)	Goebel	Closed	12.50	12.50
89-04-024	Dove (color)	Goebel	Closed	20.00	20.00
90-04-025	Girl In Sleigh	Goebel	Closed	30.00	30.00

Number	Name	Artist	Edition Limit	Issue Price	Quote
91-04-026	Baby On Moon	Goebel	Closed	35.00	35.00
Goebel United States	**Christmas Ornaments**				
87-05-001	Three Angels with Toys-(Set)	Goebel	Open	30.00	30.00
87-05-002	Three Angels with Instruments-(Set)	Goebel	Open	30.00	30.00
88-05-003	Snowman	Goebel	Open	10.00	10.00
88-05-004	Santa's Boot	Goebel	Open	7.50	7.50
88-05-005	Saint Nick	Goebel	Open	15.00	15.00
88-05-006	Nutcracker	Goebel	Open	15.00	15.00
86-05-007	Teddy Bear - Red Hat	Goebel	Open	5.00	5.00
86-05-008	Teddy Bear - Red Scarf	Goebel	Open	5.00	5.00
86-05-009	Teddy Bear - Red Boots	Goebel	Open	5.00	5.00
86-05-010	Angel - Red with Song	Goebel	Open	6.00	6.00
86-05-011	Angel - Red with Book	Goebel	Open	6.00	6.00
86-05-012	Angel - Red with Bell	Goebel	Open	6.00	6.00
86-05-013	Angel with Lantern (color)	Goebel	Open	8.00	8.00
86-05-014	Angel with Lantern (white)	Goebel	Open	6.00	6.00
86-05-015	Angel with Horn (color)	Goebel	Open	8.00	8.00
86-05-016	Angel with Horn (white)	Goebel	Open	6.00	6.00
86-05-017	Angel with Lute (color)	Goebel	Open	8.00	8.00
86-05-018	Angel with Lute (white)	Goebel	Open	6.00	6.00
88-05-019	Angel with Toy Teddy Bear	Goebel	Open	10.00	10.00
88-05-020	Angel with Toy Rocking Horse	Goebel	Open	10.00	10.00
88-05-021	Angel with Toy Train	Goebel	Open	10.00	10.00
88-05-022	Angel with Toys-(Set of three)	Goebel	Open	30.00	30.00
88-05-023	Angel with Banjo	Goebel	Open	10.00	10.00
88-05-024	Angel with Accordian	Goebel	Open	10.00	10.00
88-05-025	Angel with Violin	Goebel	Open	10.00	10.00
88-05-026	Angel with Music Set	Goebel	Open	30.00	30.00
Goebel/Schmid	**M.I. Hummel Annual Figurine Ornaments**				
88-01-001	Flying High 452	M.I. Hummel	Closed	75.00	125-135.
89-01-002	Love From Above 481	M.I. Hummel	Closed	75.00	80-135.00
90-01-003	Peace on Earth 484	M.I. Hummel	Closed	80.00	85-105.00
91-01-004	Angelic Guide 571	M.I. Hummel	Closed	95.00	95.00
92-01-005	Light Up The Night 622	M.I. Hummel	Closed	100.00	100.00
93-01-006	Herald on High 623	M.I. Hummel	Yr.Iss.	155.00	155.00
Goebel/Schmid	**M.I. Hummel Collectibles Annual Bell Ornaments**				
89-02-001	Ride Into Christmas 775	M.I. Hummel	Closed	35.00	35-85.00
90-02-002	Letter to Santa Claus 776	M.I. Hummel	Closed	37.50	37.50-50.00
91-02-003	Hear Ye, Hear Ye 777	M.I. Hummel	Closed	39.50	39.50
92-02-004	Harmony in Four Parts 778	M.I. Hummel	Closed	50.00	50.00
93-02-005	Celestial Musician 779	M.I. Hummel	Yr.Iss.	50.00	50.00
Goebel/Schmid	**M.I. Hummel Collectibles Miniature Ornaments**				
93-03-001	Celestial Musician 646	M.I. Hummel	Open	90.00	90.00
Gorham	**Archive Collectible**				
88-01-001	Victorian Heart	Gorham	Open	50.00	50.00
89-01-002	Victorian Wreath	Gorham	Open	50.00	50.00
90-01-003	Elizabethan Cupid	Gorham	Open	60.00	60.00
91-01-004	Baroque Angels	Gorham	Open	55.00	55.00
92-01-005	Madonna and Child	Gorham	Yr.Iss.	50.00	50.00
Gorham	**Annual Snowflake Ornaments**				
70-02-001	Sterling Snowflake	Gorham	Closed	10.00	250-325.
71-02-002	Sterling Snowflake	Gorham	Closed	10.00	90-125.00
72-02-003	Sterling Snowflake	Gorham	Closed	10.00	75-125.00
73-02-004	Sterling Snowflake	Gorham	Closed	10.95	65-110.00
74-02-005	Sterling Snowflake	Gorham	Closed	17.50	45-75.00
75-02-006	Sterling Snowflake	Gorham	Closed	17.50	30-75.00
76-02-007	Sterling Snowflake	Gorham	Closed	20.00	40-75.00
77-02-008	Sterling Snowflake	Gorham	Closed	22.50	30-70.00
78-02-009	Sterling Snowflake	Gorham	Closed	22.50	40-70.00
79-02-010	Sterling Snowflake	Gorham	Closed	32.80	40-70.00
80-02-011	Silverplated Snowflake	Gorham	Closed	15.00	75.00
81-02-012	Sterling Snowflake	Gorham	Closed	50.00	85.00
82-02-013	Sterling Snowflake	Gorham	Closed	37.50	45-75.00
83-02-014	Sterling Snowflake	Gorham	Closed	45.00	45-80.00
84-02-015	Sterling Snowflake	Gorham	Closed	45.00	45-75.00
85-02-016	Sterling Snowflake	Gorham	Closed	45.00	45-75.00
86-02-017	Sterling Snowflake	Gorham	Closed	45.00	45-60.00
87-02-018	Sterling Snowflake	Gorham	Closed	50.00	60.00
88-02-019	Sterling Snowflake	Gorham	Closed	50.00	50.00
89-02-020	Sterling Snowflake	Gorham	Closed	50.00	50.00
90-02-021	Sterling Snowflake	Gorham	Closed	50.00	50.00
91-02-022	Sterling Snowflake	Gorham	Closed	55.00	55.00
92-02-023	Sterling Snowflake	Gorham	Yr.Iss.	50.00	50.00
Gorham	**Annual Crystal Ornaments**				
85-03-001	Crystal Ornament	Gorham	Closed	22.00	22.00
86-03-002	Crystal Ornament	Gorham	Closed	25.00	25.00
87-03-003	Crystal Ornament	Gorham	Closed	25.00	25.00
88-03-004	Crystal Ornament	Gorham	Closed	28.00	28.00
89-03-005	Crystal Ornament	Gorham	Closed	28.00	28.00
90-03-006	Crystal Ornament	Gorham	Closed	30.00	30.00
91-03-007	Crystal Ornament	Gorham	Closed	35.00	35.00
92-03-008	Crystal Ornament	Gorham	Yr. Iss.	32.50	32.50
Gorham	**Baby's First Christmas Crystal**				
91-04-001	Baby's First Rocking Horse	Gorham	Open	35.00	35.00
Dave Grossman Creations	**Emmett Kelly Annual Figurine Ornaments**				
86-01-001	A Christmas Carol	B. Leighton Jones	Closed	12.00	12.00
87-01-002	Christmas Wreath	B. Leighton Jones	Closed	14.00	14.00
88-01-003	Christmas Dinner	B. Leighton Jones	Closed	15.00	15.00
89-01-004	Christmas Feast	B. Leighton Jones	Closed	15.00	15.00
90-01-005	Just What I Needed	B. Leighton Jones	Closed	15.00	15.00
91-01-006	Emmett the Snowman	B. Leighton Jones	Closed	15.00	25-30.00
92-01-007	Christmas Tunes	B. Leighton Jones	Closed	15.00	15.00
Dave Grossman Creations	**Gone With the Wind Ornaments**				
87-02-001	Tara	D. Geenty	Closed	15.00	45.00
87-02-002	Rhett	D. Geenty	Closed	15.00	45.00
87-02-003	Scarlett	D. Geenty	Closed	15.00	45.00
87-02-004	Ashley	D. Geenty	Closed	15.00	45.00
88-02-005	Rhett and Scarlett	D. Geenty	Closed	20.00	40.00
89-02-006	Mammy	D. Geenty	Closed	20.00	20.00
90-02-007	Scarlett (Red Dress)	D. Geenty	Closed	20.00	20.00
91-02-008	Prissy	R. Brown	Closed	20.00	20.00
92-02-009	Scarlett (Green Dress)	Rockwell-Inspired	Closed	20.00	20.00

CHRISTMAS ORNAMENTS

Company Number	Name	Series Artist	Edition Limit	Issue Price	Quote
Dave Grossman Designs		**Norman Rockwell Collection-Annual Rockwell Figurine Ornaments**			
78-01-001	Caroler NRX-03	Rockwell-Inspired	Retrd.	15.00	45.00
79-01-002	Drum for Tommy NRX-24	Rockwell-Inspired	Retrd.	20.00	30.00
80-01-003	Santa's Good Boys NRX-37	Rockwell-Inspired	Retrd.	20.00	30.00
81-01-004	Letters to Santa NRX-39	Rockwell-Inspired	Retrd.	20.00	30.00
82-01-005	Cornettist NRX-32	Rockwell-Inspired	Retrd.	20.00	30.00
83-01-006	Fiddler NRX-83	Rockwell-Inspired	Retrd.	20.00	30.00
84-01-007	Christmas Bounty NRX-84	Rockwell-Inspired	Retrd.	20.00	30.00
85-01-008	Jolly Coachman NRX-85	Rockwell-Inspired	Retrd.	20.00	30.00
86-01-009	Grandpa on Rocking Horse NRX-86	Rockwell-Inspired	Retrd.	20.00	30.00
87-01-010	Skating Lesson NRX-87	Rockwell-Inspired	Retrd.	20.00	30.00
88-01-011	Big Moment NRX-88	Rockwell-Inspired	Retrd.	20.00	25.00
89-01-012	Discovery NRX-89	Rockwell-Inspired	Retrd.	20.00	20.00
90-01-013	Bringing Home The Tree NRX-90	Rockwell-Inspired	Retrd.	20.00	20.00
91-01-014	Downhill Daring B NRX-91	Rockwell-Inspired	Retrd.	20.00	20.00
92-01-015	On The Ice	Rockwell-Inspired	Retrd.	20.00	20.00
Dave Grossman Designs		**Norman Rockwell Collection-Annual Rockwell Ball Ornaments**			
75-02-001	Santa with Feather Quill NRO-01	Rockwell-Inspired	Retrd.	3.50	25.00
76-02-002	Santa at Globe NRO-02	Rockwell-Inspired	Retrd.	4.00	25.00
77-02-003	Grandpa on Rocking Horse NRO-03	Rockwell-Inspired	Retrd.	4.00	12.00
78-02-004	Santa with Map NRO-04	Rockwell-Inspired	Retrd.	4.50	12.00
79-02-005	Santa at Desk with Mail Bag NRO-05	Rockwell-Inspired	Retrd.	5.00	12.00
80-02-006	Santa Asleep with Toys NRO-06	Rockwell-Inspired	Retrd.	5.00	10.00
81-02-007	Santa with Boy on Finger NRO-07	Rockwell-Inspired	Retrd.	5.00	10.00
82-02-008	Santa Face on Winter Scene NRO-08	Rockwell-Inspired	Retrd.	5.00	10.00
83-02-009	Coachman with Whip NRO-9	Rockwell-Inspired	Retrd.	5.00	10.00
84-02-010	Christmas Bounty Man NRO-10	Rockwell-Inspired	Retrd.	5.00	10.00
85-02-011	Old English Trio NRO-11	Rockwell-Inspired	Retrd.	5.00	10.00
86-02-012	Tiny Tim on Shoulder NRO-12	Rockwell-Inspired	Retrd.	5.00	10.00
87-02-013	Skating Lesson NRO-13	Rockwell-Inspired	Retrd.	5.00	10.00
88-02-014	Big Moment NRO-14	Rockwell-Inspired	Retrd.	5.50	6.00
89-02-015	Discovery NRO-15	Rockwell-Inspired	Retrd.	6.00	6.00
90-02-016	Bringing Home The Tree NRO-16	Rockwell-Inspired	Retrd.	6.00	6.00
91-02-017	Downhill Daring NRO-17	Rockwell-Inspired	Retrd.	6.00	6.00
92-02-018	On The Ice NRO-18	Rockwell-Inspired	Retrd.	6.00	6.00
Dave Grossman Designs		**Norman Rockwell Collection-Character Doll Ornaments**			
83-03-001	Doctor and Doll NRD-01	Rockwell-Inspired	Retrd.	20.00	30.00
83-03-002	Lovers NRD-02	Rockwell-Inspired	Retrd.	20.00	30.00
83-03-003	Samplers NRD-03	Rockwell-Inspired	Retrd.	20.00	30.00
Hallmark Galleries		**Enchanted Garden**			
92-01-001	Neighborhood Dreamer	E. Richardson	19,500	15.00	15.00
Hallmark Keepsake Ornaments		**1973 Hallmark Keepsake Collection**			
73-01-001	Betsey Clark 250XHD100-2	Keepsake	Yr.Iss.	2.50	85.00
73-01-002	Betsey Clark-First Edition 250XHD 110-2	Keepsake	Yr.Iss.	2.50	125.00
73-01-003	Manger Scene 250XHD102-2	Keepsake	Yr.Iss.	2.50	75.00
73-01-004	Christmas Is Love 250XHD106-2	Keepsake	Yr.Iss.	2.50	80.00
73-01-005	Santa with Elves 250XHD101-5	Keepsake	Yr.Iss.	2.50	75-85.00
73-01-006	Elves 250XHD103-5	Keepsake	Yr.Iss.	2.50	75.00
Hallmark Keepsake Ornaments		**1973 Keepsake Yarn Ornaments**			
73-02-001	Mr. Santa 125XHD74-5	Keepsake	Yr.Iss.	1.25	27.50
73-02-002	Mrs. Santa 125XHD75-2	Keepsake	Yr.Iss.	1.25	22.50
73-02-003	Mr. Snowman 125XHD76-5	Keepsake	Yr.Iss.	1.25	24.50
73-02-004	Mrs. Snowman 125XHD77-2	Keepsake	Yr.Iss.	1.25	22.50
73-02-005	Angel 125XHD78-5	Keepsake	Yr.Iss.	1.25	27.50
73-02-006	Elf 125XHD79-2	Keepsake	Yr.Iss.	1.25	24.50
73-02-007	Choir Boy 125XHD80-5	Keepsake	Yr.Iss.	1.25	27.50
73-02-008	Soldier 100XHD81-2	Keepsake	Yr.Iss.	1.00	22.00
73-02-009	Little Girl 125XHD82-5	Keepsake	Yr.Iss.	1.25	22.50
73-02-010	Boy Caroler 125XHD83-2	Keepsake	Yr.Iss.	1.25	29.50
73-02-011	Green Girl 125XHD84-5	Keepsake	Yr.Iss.	1.25	22.50
73-02-012	Blue Girl 125XHD85-2	Keepsake	Yr.Iss.	1.25	22.50
Hallmark Keepsake Ornaments		**1974 Hallmark Keepsake Collection**			
74-03-001	Norman Rockwell 250QX111-1	Keepsake	Yr.Iss.	2.50	80.00
74-03-002	Norman Rockwell 250QX106-1	Keepsake	Yr.Iss.	2.50	45-75.00
74-03-003	Betsey Clark-Second Edition 250QX 108-1	Keepsake	Yr.Iss.	2.50	45-78.00
74-03-004	Charmers 250QX109-1	Keepsake	Yr.Iss.	2.50	25-52.00
74-03-005	Snowgoose 250QX107-1	Keepsake	Yr.Iss.	2.50	75.00
74-03-006	Angel 250QX110-1	Keepsake	Yr.Iss.	2.50	65.00
74-03-007	Raggedy Ann and Andy(4/set) 450QX114-1	Keepsake	Yr.Iss.	4.50	75.00
74-03-008	Little Miracles (Set of 4) 450QX115-1	Keepsake	Yr.Iss.	4.50	55.00
74-03-009	Buttons & Bo (Set of 2) 350QX113-1	Keepsake	Yr.Iss.	3.50	50.00
74-03-010	Currier & Ives (Set of 2) 350QX112-1	Keepsake	Yr.Iss.	3.50	50.00
Hallmark Keepsake Ornaments		**1974 Keepsake Yarn Ornaments**			
74-04-001	Mrs. Santa 150QX100-1	Keepsake	Yr.Iss.	1.50	22.50
74-04-002	Elf 150QX101-1	Keepsake	Yr.Iss.	1.50	22.50
74-04-003	Soldier 150QX102-1	Keepsake	Yr.Iss.	1.50	21.50
74-04-004	Angel 150QX103-1	Keepsake	Yr.Iss.	1.50	27.50
74-04-005	Snowman 150QX104-1	Keepsake	Yr.Iss.	1.50	22.50
74-04-006	Santa 150QX105-1	Keepsake	Yr.Iss.	1.50	23.50
Hallmark Keepsake Ornaments		**1975 Keepsake Property Ornaments**			
75-05-001	Betsey Clark (Set of 4) 450QX168-1	Keepsake	Yr.Iss.	4.50	25-50.00
75-05-002	Betsey Clark (Set of 2) 350QX167-1	Keepsake	Yr.Iss.	3.50	40.00
75-05-003	Betsey Clark 250QX163-1	Keepsake	Yr.Iss.	2.50	40.00
75-05-004	Betsey Clark-Third Ed. 300QX133-1	Keepsake	Yr.Iss.	3.00	55-85.00
75-05-005	Currier & Ives (Set of 2) 250QX164-1	Keepsake	Yr.Iss.	2.50	16-40.00
75-05-006	Currier & Ives (Set of 2) 400QX137-1	Keepsake	Yr.Iss.	4.00	35-40.00
75-05-007	Raggedy Ann and Andy(2/set) 400QX 138-1	Keepsake	Yr.Iss.	4.00	65.00
75-05-008	Raggedy Ann 250QX165-1	Keepsake	Yr.Iss.	2.50	50.00
75-05-009	Norman Rockwell 250QX166-1	Keepsake	Yr.Iss.	2.50	75.00
75-05-010	Norman Rockwell 300QX134-1	Keepsake	Yr.Iss.	3.00	75.00
75-05-011	Charmers 300QX135-1	Keepsake	Yr.Iss.	3.00	20-40.00
75-05-012	Marty Links 300QX136-1	Keepsake	Yr.Iss.	3.00	35.00
75-05-013	Buttons & Bo (Set of 4) 500QX139-1	Keepsake	Yr.Iss.	5.00	30-47.50
75-05-014	Little Miracles (Set of 4) 500QX140-1	Keepsake	Yr.Iss.	5.00	30-50.00
Hallmark Keepsake Ornaments		**1975 Keepsake Yarn Ornaments**			
75-06-001	Raggedy Ann 175QX121-1	Keepsake	Yr.Iss.	1.75	35.00
75-06-002	Raggedy Andy 175QX122-1	Keepsake	Yr.Iss.	1.75	39.50
75-06-003	Drummer Boy 175QX123-1	Keepsake	Yr.Iss.	1.75	24.50
75-06-004	Santa 175QX124-1	Keepsake	Yr.Iss.	1.75	15-22.50
75-06-005	Mrs. Santa 175QX125-1	Keepsake	Yr.Iss.	1.75	21.50
75-06-006	Little Girl 175QX126-1	Keepsake	Yr.Iss.	1.75	19.50
Hallmark Keepsake Ornaments		**1975 Handcrafted Ornaments: Nostalgia**			
75-07-001	Locomotive (dated) 350QX127-1	Keepsake	Yr.Iss.	3.50	175.00
75-07-002	Rocking Horse 350QX128-1	Keepsake	Yr.Iss.	3.50	100-175.
75-07-003	Santa & Sleigh 350QX129-1	Keepsake	Yr.Iss.	3.50	200-275.
75-07-004	Drummer Boy 350QX130-1	Keepsake	Yr.Iss.	3.50	150.00
75-07-005	Peace on Earth (dated) 350QX131-1	Keepsake	Yr.Iss.	3.50	125-175.
75-07-006	Joy 350QX132-1	Keepsake	Yr.Iss.	3.50	175-275.
Hallmark Keepsake Ornaments		**1975 Handcrafted Ornaments: Adorable**			
75-08-001	Santa 250QX155-1	Keepsake	Yr.Iss.	2.50	55.00
75-08-002	Mrs. Santa 250QX156-1	Keepsake	Yr.Iss.	2.50	55.00
75-08-003	Betsey Clark 250QX157-1	Keepsake	Yr.Iss.	2.50	350.00
75-08-004	Raggedy Ann 250QX159-1	Keepsake	Yr.Iss.	2.50	300.00
75-08-005	Raggedy Andy 250QX160-1	Keepsake	Yr.Iss.	2.50	400.00
75-08-006	Drummer Boy 250QX161-1	Keepsake	Yr.Iss.	2.50	325.00
Hallmark Keepsake Ornaments		**1976 First Commemorative Ornament**			
76-09-001	Baby's First Christmas 250QX211-1	Keepsake	Yr.Iss.	2.50	30-95.00
Hallmark Keepsake Ornaments		**1976 Bicentennial Commemoratives**			
76-10-001	Bicentennial '76 Commemorative 250QX211-1	Keepsake	Yr.Iss.	2.50	75.00
76-10-002	Bicentennial Charmers 300QX198-1	Keepsake	Yr.Iss.	3.00	60.00
76-10-003	Colonial Children (Set of 2) 4 400QX 208-1	Keepsake	Yr.Iss.	4.00	40-65.00
Hallmark Keepsake Ornaments		**1976 Property Ornaments**			
76-11-001	Betsey Clark-Fourth Ed.300QX 195-1	Keepsake	Yr.Iss.	3.00	175.00
76-11-002	Betsey Clark 250QX210-1	Keepsake	Yr.Iss.	2.50	38-42.00
76-11-003	Betsey Clark (Set of 3) 450QX218-1	Keepsake	Yr.Iss.	4.50	50.00
76-11-004	Currier & Ives 250QX209-1	Keepsake	Yr.Iss.	2.50	40.00
76-11-005	Currier & Ives 300QX197-1	Keepsake	Yr.Iss.	3.00	42.00
76-11-006	Norman Rockwell 300QX196-1	Keepsake	Yr.Iss.	3.00	65.00
76-11-007	Rudolph and Santa 250QX213-1	Keepsake	Yr.Iss.	2.50	65-95.00
76-11-008	Raggedy Ann 250QX212-1	Keepsake	Yr.Iss.	2.50	65.00
76-11-009	Marty Links (Set of 2) 400QX207-1	Keepsake	Yr.Iss.	4.00	45.00
76-11-010	Happy the Snowman (Set of 2) 350QX216-1	Keepsake	Yr.Iss.	3.50	55.00
76-11-011	Charmers (Set of 2) 350QX215-1	Keepsake	Yr.Iss.	3.50	75.00
Hallmark Keepsake Ornaments		**1976 Decorative Ball Ornaments**			
76-12-001	Chickadees 225QX204-1	Keepsake	Yr.Iss.	2.25	50.00
76-12-002	Cardinals 225QX205-1	Keepsake	Yr.Iss.	2.25	55.00
Hallmark Keepsake Ornaments		**1976 Handcrafted Ornaments: Yesteryears**			
76-13-001	Train 500QX181-1	Keepsake	Yr.Iss.	5.00	155.00
76-13-002	Santa 500QX182-1	Keepsake	Yr.Iss.	5.00	175.00
76-13-003	Partridge 500QX183-1	Keepsake	Yr.Iss.	5.00	125.00
76-13-004	Drummer Boy 500QX184-1	Keepsake	Yr.Iss.	5.00	128-135.00
Hallmark Keepsake Ornaments		**1976 Handcrafted Ornaments: Twirl-Abouts**			
76-14-001	Angel 450QX171-1	Keepsake	Yr.Iss.	4.50	150-175.00
76-14-002	Santa 450QX172-1	Keepsake	Yr.Iss.	4.50	90-125.00
76-14-003	Soldier 450QX173-1	Keepsake	Yr.Iss.	4.50	80-120.00
76-14-004	Partridge 450QX174-1	Keepsake	Yr.Iss.	4.50	195.00
Hallmark Keepsake Ornaments		**1976 Handcrafted Ornaments: Tree Treats**			
76-15-001	Shepherd 300QX175-1	Keepsake	Yr.Iss.	3.00	90-150.00
76-15-002	Angel 300QX176-1	Keepsake	Yr.Iss.	3.00	125-195.
76-15-003	Santa 300QX177-1	Keepsake	Yr.Iss.	3.00	150-225.
76-15-004	Reindeer 300QX 178-1	Keepsake	Yr.Iss.	3.00	150.00
Hallmark Keepsake Ornaments		**1976 Handcrafted Ornaments: Nostalgia**			
76-16-001	Rocking Horse 400QX128-1	Keepsake	Yr.Iss.	3.50	160.00
76-16-002	Drummer Boy 400QX130-1	Keepsake	Yr.Iss.	3.50	155.00
76-16-003	Locomotive 400QX222-1	Keepsake	Yr.Iss.	3.50	185.00
76-16-004	Peace on Earth 400QX223-1	Keepsake	Yr.Iss.	3.50	195.00
Hallmark Keepsake Ornaments		**1976 Yarn Ornaments**			
76-17-001	Raggedy Ann 175QX121-1	Keepsake	Yr.Iss.	1.75	35.00
76-17-002	Raggedy Andy 175QX122-1	Keepsake	Yr.Iss.	1.75	39.50
76-17-003	Drummer Boy 175QX123-1	Keepsake	Yr.Iss.	1.75	22.50
76-17-004	Santa 175QX124-1	Keepsake	Yr.Iss.	1.75	23.50
76-17-005	Mrs. Santa 175QX125-1	Keepsake	Yr.Iss.	1.75	21.50
76-17-006	Caroler 175QX126-1	Keepsake	Yr.Iss.	1.75	27.50
Hallmark Keepsake Ornaments		**1977 Commemoratives**			
77-18-001	Baby's First Christmas 350QX131-5	Keepsake	Yr.Iss.	3.50	45-59.50
77-18-002	Granddaughter 350QX208-2	Keepsake	Yr.Iss.	3.50	150.00
77-18-003	Grandson 350QX209-5	Keepsake	Yr.Iss.	3.50	150.00
77-18-004	Mother 350QX261-5	Keepsake	Yr.Iss.	3.50	75.00
77-18-005	Grandmother 350QX260-2	Keepsake	Yr.Iss.	3.50	150.00
77-18-006	First Christmas Together 350QX132-2	Keepsake	Yr.Iss.	3.50	75.00
77-18-007	Love 350QX262-2	Keepsake	Yr.Iss.	3.50	95.00
77-18-008	For Your New Home 350QX263-5	Keepsake	Yr.Iss.	3.50	120.00
Hallmark Keepsake Ornaments		**1977 Property Ornaments**			
77-19-001	Charmers 350QX153-5	Keepsake	Yr.Iss.	3.50	50.00
77-19-002	Currier & Ives 350QX130-2	Keepsake	Yr.Iss.	3.50	55.00
77-19-003	Norman Rockwell 350QX151-5	Keepsake	Yr.Iss.	3.50	70.00
77-19-004	Disney 350QX133-5	Keepsake	Yr.Iss.	3.50	35-55.00
77-19-005	Disney (Set of 2) 400QX137-5	Keepsake	Yr.Iss.	4.00	75.00
77-19-006	Betsey Clark -Fifth Ed. 350QX264-2	Keepsake	Yr.Iss.	3.50	550.00
77-19-007	Grandma Moses 350QX150-2	Keepsake	Yr.Iss.	3.50	175.00
Hallmark Keepsake Ornaments		**1977 Peanuts Collection**			
77-20-001	Peanuts 250QX162-2	Keepsake	Yr.Iss.	2.50	65.00
77-20-002	Peanuts 350QX135-5	Keepsake	Yr.Iss.	3.50	35-50.00
77-20-003	Peanuts (Set of 2) 400QX163-5	Keepsake	Yr.Iss.	4.00	65.00
Hallmark Keepsake Ornaments		**1977 Christmas Expressions Collection**			
77-21-001	Bell 350QX154-2	Keepsake	Yr.Iss.	3.50	65.00
77-21-002	Ornaments 350QX155-5	Keepsake	Yr.Iss.	3.50	65.00
77-21-003	Mandolin 350QX157-5	Keepsake	Yr.Iss.	3.50	65.00
77-21-004	Wreath 350QX156-2	Keepsake	Yr.Iss.	3.50	65.00
Hallmark Keepsake Ornaments		**1977 The Beauty of America Collection**			
77-22-001	Mountains 250QX158-2	Keepsake	Yr.Iss.	2.50	30-55.00
77-22-002	Desert 250QX159-5	Keepsake	Yr.Iss.	2.50	30-55.00
77-22-003	Seashore 250QX160-2	Keepsake	Yr.Iss.	2.50	30-50.00
77-22-004	Wharf 250QX161-5	Keepsake	Yr.Iss.	2.50	30-50.00
Hallmark Keepsake Ornaments		**1977 Decorative Ball Ornaments**			
77-23-001	Rabbit 250QX139-5	Keepsake	Yr.Iss.	2.50	95.00
77-23-002	Squirrel 250QX138-2	Keepsake	Yr.Iss.	2.50	115.00
77-23-003	Christmas Mouse 250QX134-2	Keepsake	Yr.Iss.	3.50	85.00
77-23-004	Stained Glass 250QX152-2	Keepsake	Yr.Iss.	3.50	65.00

CHRISTMAS ORNAMENTS

Company / Number	Name	Series / Artist	Edition Limit	Issue Price	Quote
Hallmark Keepsake Ornaments		**1977 Colors of Christmas**			
77-24-001	Bell 350QX200-2	Keepsake	Yr.Iss.	3.50	35-55.00
77-24-002	Joy 350QX201-5	Keepsake	Yr.Iss.	3.50	35-60.00
77-24-003	Wreath 350QX202-2	Keepsake	Yr.Iss.	3.50	25-55.00
77-24-004	Candle 350QX203-5	Keepsake	Yr.Iss.	3.50	75.00
Hallmark Keepsake Ornaments		**1977 Holiday Highlights**			
77-25-001	Joy 350QX310-2	Keepsake	Yr.Iss.	3.50	25-55.00
77-25-002	Peace on Earth 350QX311-5	Keepsake	Yr.Iss.	3.50	45-75.00
77-25-003	Drummer Boy 350QX312-2	Keepsake	Yr.Iss.	3.50	70.00
77-25-004	Star 350QX313-5	Keepsake	Yr.Iss.	3.50	50.00
Hallmark Keepsake Ornaments		**1977 Twirl-About Collection**			
77-26-001	Snowman 450QX190-2	Keepsake	Yr.Iss.	4.50	55-65.00
77-26-002	Weather House 600QX191-5	Keepsake	Yr.Iss.	6.00	125.00
77-26-003	Bellringer 600QX192-2	Keepsake	Yr.Iss.	6.00	50-65.00
77-26-004	Della Robia Wreath 450QX193-5	Keepsake	Yr.Iss.	4.50	85-135.00
Hallmark Keepsake Ornaments		**1977 Metal Ornaments**			
77-27-001	Snowflake Collection (Set of 4)500QX 210-2	Keepsake	Yr.Iss.	5.00	95.00
Hallmark Keepsake Ornaments		**1977 Nostalgia Collection**			
77-28-001	Angel 500QX182-2	Keepsake	Yr.Iss.	5.00	125.00
77-28-002	Toys 500QX183-5	Keepsake	Yr.Iss.	5.00	110-145.
77-28-003	Antique Car 500QX180-2	Keepsake	Yr.Iss.	5.00	45-75.00
77-28-004	Nativity 500QX181-5	Keepsake	Yr.Iss.	5.00	130-175.
Hallmark Keepsake Ornaments		**1977 Yesteryears Collection**			
77-29-001	Angel 600QX172-2	Keepsake	Yr.Iss.	6.00	100-125.00
77-29-002	Reindeer 600QX173-5	Keepsake	Yr.Iss.	6.00	95-135.00
77-29-003	Jack-in-the-Box 600QX171-5	Keepsake	Yr.Iss.	6.00	100-125.00
77-29-004	House 600QX170-2	Keepsake	Yr.Iss.	6.00	85-115.00
Hallmark Keepsake Ornaments		**1977 Cloth Doll Ornaments**			
77-30-001	Angel 175QX220-2	Keepsake	Yr.Iss.	1.75	40-65.00
77-30-002	Santa 175QX221-5	Keepsake	Yr.Iss.	1.75	40-95.00
Hallmark Keepsake Ornaments		**1978 Commemoratives**			
78-31-001	Baby's First Christmas 350QX200-3	Keepsake	Yr.Iss.	3.50	50-75.00
78-31-002	Granddaughter 350QX216-3	Keepsake	Yr.Iss.	3.50	50.00
78-31-003	Grandson 350QX215-6	Keepsake	Yr.Iss.	3.50	50.00
78-31-004	First Christmas Together 350QX218-3	Keepsake	Yr.Iss.	3.50	45-55.00
78-31-005	25th Christmas Together 350QX269-3	Keepsake	Yr.Iss.	3.50	15-30.00
78-31-006	Love 350QX268-3	Keepsake	Yr.Iss.	3.50	50.00
78-31-007	Grandmother 350QX267-6	Keepsake	Yr.Iss.	3.50	50.00
78-31-008	Mother 350QX266-3	Keepsake	Yr.Iss.	3.50	27.00
78-31-009	For Your New Home 350QX217-6	Keepsake	Yr.Iss.	3.50	75.00
Hallmark Keepsake Ornaments		**1978 Peanuts Collection**			
78-32-001	Peanuts 250QX204-3	Keepsake	Yr.Iss.	2.50	50.00
78-32-002	Peanuts 350QX205-6	Keepsake	Yr.Iss.	3.50	75.00
78-32-003	Peanuts 350QX206-3	Keepsake	Yr.Iss.	3.50	50.00
78-32-004	Peanuts 250QX203-6	Keepsake	Yr.Iss.	2.50	50.00
Hallmark Keepsake Ornaments		**1978 Property Ornaments**			
78-33-001	Betsey Clark-Sixth Edition 350QX 201-6	Keepsake	Yr.Iss.	3.50	55.00
78-33-002	Joan Walsh Anglund 350QX221-6	Keepsake	Yr.Iss.	3.50	50-85.00
78-33-003	Spencer Sparrow 350QX219-6	Keepsake	Yr.Iss.	3.50	50.00
78-33-004	Disney 350QX207-6	Keepsake	Yr.Iss.	3.50	75.00
Hallmark Keepsake Ornaments		**1978 Decorative Ball Ornaments**			
78-34-001	Merry Christmas (Santa) 350QX202-3	Keepsake	Yr.Iss.	3.50	50.00
78-34-002	Hallmark's Antique Card Collection Design 350QX 220-3	Keepsake	Yr.Iss.	3.50	30-55.00
78-34-003	Yesterday's Toys 350QX250-3	Keepsake	Yr.Iss.	3.50	55.00
78-34-004	Nativity 350QX253-6	Keepsake	Yr.Iss.	3.50	150.00
78-34-005	The Quail 350QX251-6	Keepsake	Yr.Iss.	3.50	10-40.00
78-34-006	Drummer Boy 350QX252-3	Keepsake	Yr.Iss.	3.50	55.00
78-34-007	Joy 350QX254-3	Keepsake	Yr.Iss.	3.50	50.00
Hallmark Keepsake Ornaments		**1978 Holiday Highlights**			
78-35-001	Santa 350QX307-6	Keepsake	Yr.Iss.	3.50	95.00
78-35-002	Snowflake 350QX308-3	Keepsake	Yr.Iss.	3.50	50.00
78-35-003	Nativity 350QX309-6	Keepsake	Yr.Iss.	3.50	95.00
78-35-004	Dove 350QX310-3	Keepsake	Yr.Iss.	3.50	125.00
Hallmark Keepsake Ornaments		**1978 Holiday Chimes**			
78-36-001	Reindeer Chimes 450QX320-3	Keepsake	Yr.Iss.	4.50	60.00
Hallmark Keepsake Ornaments		**1978 Little Trimmers**			
78-37-001	Thimble Series (Mouse)-First Ed.250QX133-6	Keepsake	Yr.Iss.	2.50	250-300.00
78-37-002	Santa 250QX135-6	Keepsake	Yr.Iss.	2.50	55-75.00
78-37-003	Praying Angel 250QX134-3	Keepsake	Yr.Iss.	2.50	95.00
78-37-004	Drummer Boy 250QX136-3	Keepsake	Yr.Iss.	2.50	75-85.00
78-37-005	Set of 4 - 250QX355-6	Keepsake	Yr.Iss.	10.00	400.00
Hallmark Keepsake Ornaments		**1978 Colors of Christmas**			
78-38-001	Merry Christmas 350QX355-6	Keepsake	Yr.Iss.	3.50	80.00
78-38-002	Locomotive 350QX356-3	Keepsake	Yr.Iss.	3.50	75.00
78-38-003	Angel 350QX354-3	Keepsake	Yr.Iss.	3.50	35-55.00
78-38-004	Candle 350QX357-6	Keepsake	Yr.Iss.	3.50	125.00
Hallmark Keepsake Ornaments		**1978 Handcrafted Ornaments**			
78-39-001	Dove 450QX190-3	Keepsake	Yr.Iss.	4.50	85.00
78-39-002	Holly and Poinsettia Ball 600QX147-6	Keepsake	Yr.Iss.	6.00	85.00
78-39-003	Schneeberg Bell 800QX152-3	Keepsake	Yr.Iss.	8.00	199.00
78-39-004	Angels 800QX150-3	Keepsake	Yr.Iss.	8.00	325-400.
78-39-005	Carrousel Series-First Edition600QX 146-3	Keepsake	Yr.Iss.	6.00	350-400.
78-39-006	Joy 450QX138-3	Keepsake	Yr.Iss.	4.50	80.00
78-39-007	Angel 400QX139-6	Keepsake	Yr.Iss.	4.50	85.00
78-39-008	Calico Mouse 450QX137-6	Keepsake	Yr.Iss.	4.50	160-200.
78-39-009	Red Cardinal 450QX144-3	Keepsake	Yr.Iss.	4.50	150-175.
78-39-010	Panorama Ball 600QX145-6	Keepsake	Yr.Iss.	6.00	90-135.00
78-39-011	Skating Raccoon 600QX142-3	Keepsake	Yr.Iss.	6.00	75-95.00
78-39-012	Rocking Horse 600QX148-3	Keepsake	Yr.Iss.	6.00	65-95.00
78-39-013	Animal Home 600QX149-6	Keepsake	Yr.Iss.	6.00	150-175.
Hallmark Keepsake Ornaments		**1978 Yarn Collection**			
78-40-001	Green Boy 200QX123-1	Keepsake	Yr.Iss.	2.00	20.00
78-40-002	Mrs. Claus 200QX125-1	Keepsake	Yr.Iss.	2.00	19.50
78-40-003	Green Girl 200QX126-1	Keepsake	Yr.Iss.	2.00	17.50
78-40-004	Mr. Claus 200QX340-3	Keepsake	Yr.Iss.	2.00	20.00
Hallmark Keepsake Ornaments		**1979 Commemoratives**			
79-41-001	Baby's First Christmas 350QX208-7	Keepsake	Yr.Iss.	3.50	20-30.00
79-41-002	Baby's First Christmas 800QX154-7	Keepsake	Yr.Iss.	8.00	135-175.
79-41-003	Grandson 350QX210-7	Keepsake	Yr.Iss.	3.50	20-28.00
79-41-004	Granddaughter 350QX211-9	Keepsake	Yr.Iss.	3.50	28.00
79-41-005	Mother 350QX251-9	Keepsake	Yr.Iss.	3.50	15.00
79-41-006	Grandmother 350QX252-7	Keepsake	Yr.Iss.	3.50	14.50
79-41-007	Our First Christmas Together350-QX 209-9	Keepsake	Yr.Iss.	3.50	45.00
79-41-008	Our Twenty-Fifth Anniversary350QX 250-7	Keepsake	Yr.Iss.	3.50	15-19.00
79-41-009	Love 350QX258-7	Keepsake	Yr.Iss.	3.50	30.00
79-41-010	Friendship 350QX203-9	Keepsake	Yr.Iss.	3.50	17.50
79-41-011	Teacher 350QX213-9	Keepsake	Yr.Iss.	3.50	10-18.00
79-41-012	New Home 350QX212-7	Keepsake	Yr.Iss.	3.50	40.00
Hallmark Keepsake Ornaments		**1979 Property Ornaments**			
79-42-001	Betsey Clark-Seventh Edition350QX 201-9	Keepsake	Yr.Iss.	3.50	29.50
79-42-002	Peanuts (Time to Trim) 350QX202-7	Keepsake	Yr.Iss.	3.50	25.00
79-42-003	Spencer Sparrow 350QX200-7	Keepsake	Yr.Iss.	3.50	30.00
79-42-004	Joan Walsh Anglund 350QX205-9	Keepsake	Yr.Iss.	3.50	25-35.00
79-42-005	Winnie-the-Pooh 350QX206-7	Keepsake	Yr.Iss.	3.50	35.00
79-42-006	Mary Hamilton 350QX254-7	Keepsake	Yr.Iss.	3.50	15-30.00
Hallmark Keepsake Ornaments		**1979 Decorative Ball Ornaments**			
79-43-001	Night Before Christmas 350QX214-7	Keepsake	Yr.Iss.	3.50	29.50
79-43-002	Christmas Chickadees 350QX204-7	Keepsake	Yr.Iss.	3.50	29.00
79-43-003	Behold the Star 350QX255-9	Keepsake	Yr.Iss.	3.50	35-45.00
79-43-004	Christmas Traditions 350QX253-9	Keepsake	Yr.Iss.	3.50	32.50
79-43-005	Christmas Collage 350QX257-9	Keepsake	Yr.Iss.	3.50	30.00
79-43-006	Black Angel 350QX207-9	Keepsake	Yr.Iss.	3.50	10-20.00
79-43-007	The Light of Christmas 350QX256-7	Keepsake	Yr.Iss.	3.50	23.00
Hallmark Keepsake Ornaments		**1979 Holiday Highlights**			
79-44-001	Christmas Angel 350QX300-7	Keepsake	Yr.Iss.	3.50	85.00
79-44-002	Snowflake 350QX301-9	Keepsake	Yr.Iss.	3.50	40.00
79-44-003	Christmas Tree 350QX302-7	Keepsake	Yr.Iss.	3.50	75.00
79-44-004	Christmas Cheer 350QX303-9	Keepsake	Yr.Iss.	3.50	55.00
79-44-005	Love 350QX304-7	Keepsake	Yr.Iss.	3.50	87.50
Hallmark Keepsake Ornaments		**1979 Colors of Christmas**			
79-45-001	Words of Christmas 350QX350-7	Keepsake	Yr.Iss.	3.50	85.00
79-45-002	Holiday Wreath 350QX353-9	Keepsake	Yr.Iss.	3.50	39.50
79-45-003	Partridge in a Pear Tree 350QX351-9	Keepsake	Yr.Iss.	3.50	36-45.00
79-45-004	Star Over Bethlehem 350QX352-7	Keepsake	Yr.Iss.	3.50	65.00
Hallmark Keepsake Ornaments		**1979 Little Trimmer Collection**			
79-46-001	Thimble Series-Mouse 300QX133-6	Keepsake	Yr.Iss.	3.00	150-225.
79-46-002	Santa 300QX135-6	Keepsake	Yr.Iss.	3.00	55.00
79-46-003	A Matchless Christmas 400QX132-7	Keepsake	Yr.Iss.	4.00	75.00
79-46-004	Angel Delight 300QX130-7	Keepsake	Yr.Iss.	3.00	100.00
Hallmark Keepsake Ornaments		**1979 Handcrafted Ornaments**			
79-47-001	Holiday Scrimshaw 400QX152-7	Keepsake	Yr.Iss.	4.00	200-250.
79-47-002	Christmas Heart 650QX140-7	Keepsake	Yr.Iss.	6.50	95.00
79-47-003	Christmas Eve Surprise 650QX157-9	Keepsake	Yr.Iss.	6.50	55.00
79-47-004	Santa's Here 500QX138-7	Keepsake	Yr.Iss.	5.00	65.00
79-47-005	Raccoon 650QX142-3	Keepsake	Yr.Iss.	6.50	85.00
79-47-006	The Downhill Run 650QX145-9	Keepsake	Yr.Iss.	6.50	135-150.
79-47-007	The Drummer Boy 800QX143-9	Keepsake	Yr.Iss.	8.00	125.00
79-47-008	Outdoor Fun 800QX150-7	Keepsake	Yr.Iss.	8.00	100-150.
79-47-009	A Christmas Treat 500QX134-7	Keepsake	Yr.Iss.	5.00	85.00
79-47-010	The Skating Snowman 500QX139-9	Keepsake	Yr.Iss.	5.00	40-85.00
79-47-011	Christmas is for Children 500QX135-9	Keepsake	Yr.Iss.	5.00	83-95.00
79-47-012	Ready for Christmas 650QX133-9	Keepsake	Yr.Iss.	6.50	150.00
Hallmark Keepsake Ornaments		**1979 Collectible Series**			
79-48-001	Carrousel-Second Edition 650QX146-7	Keepsake	Yr.Iss.	6.50	150-200.
79-48-002	Thimble-Second Edition 300QX131-9	Keepsake	Yr.Iss.	3.00	150-195.
79-48-003	Snoopy and Friends 800QX141-9	Keepsake	Yr.Iss.	8.00	125.00
79-48-004	Here Comes Santa-First Edition 900QX 155-9	Keepsake	Yr.Iss.	9.00	400-550.
79-48-005	Bellringer-First Edition 10QX147-9	Keepsake	Yr.Iss.	10.00	325-400.
Hallmark Keepsake Ornaments		**1979 Holiday Chimes**			
79-49-001	Reindeer Chimes 450QX320-3	Keepsake	Yr.Iss.	4.50	75.00
79-49-002	Star Chimes 450QX137-9	Keepsake	Yr.Iss.	4.50	75.00
Hallmark Keepsake Ornaments		**1979 Sewn Trimmers**			
79-50-001	The Rocking Horse 200QX340-7	Keepsake	Yr.Iss.	2.00	15.00
79-50-002	Merry Santa 200QX342-7	Keepsake	Yr.Iss.	2.00	15.00
79-50-003	Stuffed Full Stocking 200QX341-9	Keepsake	Yr.Iss.	2.00	19.00
79-50-004	Angel Music 200QX343-9	Keepsake	Yr.Iss.	2.00	17.50
Hallmark Keepsake Ornaments		**1980 Commemoratives**			
80-51-001	Baby's First Christmas 400QX200-1	Keepsake	Yr.Iss.	4.00	20-40.00
80-51-002	Black Baby's First Christmas 400QX 229-4	Keepsake	Yr.Iss.	4.00	20-25.00
80-51-003	Baby's First Christmas 12QX156-1	Keepsake	Yr.Iss.	12.00	40-45.00
80-51-004	Grandson 400QX201-4	Keepsake	Yr.Iss.	4.00	25.00
80-51-005	Granddaughter 400QX202-1	Keepsake	Yr.Iss.	4.00	25.00
80-51-006	Son 400QX211-4	Keepsake	Yr.Iss.	4.00	17.00
80-51-007	Daughter 400QX212-1	Keepsake	Yr.Iss.	4.00	29.50
80-51-008	Dad 400QX214-1	Keepsake	Yr.Iss.	4.00	15.00
80-51-009	Mother 400QX203-4	Keepsake	Yr.Iss.	4.00	13.50
80-51-010	Mother and Dad 400QX230-1	Keepsake	Yr.Iss.	4.00	12.00
80-51-011	Grandmother 400QX204-1	Keepsake	Yr.Iss.	4.00	15.00
80-51-012	Grandfather 400QX231-4	Keepsake	Yr.Iss.	4.00	13.50
80-51-013	Grandparents 400QX213-4	Keepsake	Yr.Iss.	4.00	49.00
80-51-014	25th Christmas Together 400QX206-1	Keepsake	Yr.Iss.	4.00	12.50
80-51-015	First Christmas Together 400QX205-4	Keepsake	Yr.Iss.	4.00	15-25.00
80-51-016	Christmas Love 400QX207-4	Keepsake	Yr.Iss.	4.00	32.50
80-51-017	Friendship 400QX208-1	Keepsake	Yr.Iss.	4.00	16.00
80-51-018	Christmas at Home 400QX210-1	Keepsake	Yr.Iss.	4.00	29.00
80-51-019	Teacher 400QX209-4	Keepsake	Yr.Iss.	4.00	13.00
80-51-020	Love 400QX302-1	Keepsake	Yr.Iss.	4.00	50.00
80-51-021	Beauty of Friendship 400QX303-4	Keepsake	Yr.Iss.	4.00	55.00
80-51-022	First Christmas Together 400QX305-4	Keepsake	Yr.Iss.	4.00	25-55.00
80-51-023	Mother 400QX304-1	Keepsake	Yr.Iss.	4.00	35.00
Hallmark Keepsake Ornaments		**1980 Property Ornaments**			
80-52-001	Betsey Clark-Eighth Edition 400QX 215-4	Keepsake	Yr.Iss.	4.00	29.50
80-52-002	Betsey Clark 650QX307-4	Keepsake	Yr.Iss.	6.50	65.00
80-52-003	Betsey Clark's Christmas 750QX194-4	Keepsake	Yr.Iss.	7.50	25.00
80-52-004	Peanuts 400QX216-1	Keepsake	Yr.Iss.	4.00	20-25.00
80-52-005	Joan Walsh Anglund 400QX217-4	Keepsake	Yr.Iss.	4.00	21.00

Company		Series			
Number	**Name**	**Artist**	**Edition Limit**	**Issue Price**	**Quote**
80-52-006	Disney 400QX218-1	Keepsake	Yr.Iss.	4.00	25.00
80-52-007	Mary Hamilton 400QX219-4	Keepsake	Yr.Iss.	4.00	21-80.00
80-52-008	Muppets 400QX220-1	Keepsake	Yr.Iss.	4.00	25-37.50
80-52-009	Marty Links 400QX221-4	Keepsake	Yr.Iss.	4.00	15.00
Hallmark Keepsake Ornaments		**1980 Decorative Ball Ornaments**			
80-53-001	Christmas Choir 400QX228-1	Keepsake	Yr.Iss.	4.00	150.00
80-53-002	Nativity 400QX225-4	Keepsake	Yr.Iss.	4.00	125.00
80-53-003	Christmas Time 400QX226-1	Keepsake	Yr.Iss.	4.00	20.00
80-53-004	Santa's Workshop 400QX223-4	Keepsake	Yr.Iss.	4.00	15-30.00
80-53-005	Happy Christmas 400QX222-1	Keepsake	Yr.Iss.	4.00	28-40.00
80-53-006	Jolly Santa 400QX227-4	Keepsake	Yr.Iss.	4.00	30.00
80-53-007	Christmas Cardinals 400QX224-1	Keepsake	Yr.Iss.	4.00	35.00
Hallmark Keepsake Ornaments		**1980 Holiday Highlights**			
80-54-001	Three Wise Men 400QX300-1	Keepsake	Yr.Iss.	4.00	22.50
80-54-002	Wreath 400QX301-4	Keepsake	Yr.Iss.	4.00	85.00
Hallmark Keepsake Ornaments		**1980 Colors of Christmas**			
80-55-001	Joy 400QX350-1	Keepsake	Yr.Iss.	4.00	25.00
Hallmark Keepsake Ornaments		**1980 Frosted Images**			
80-56-001	Drummer Boy 400QX309-4	Keepsake	Yr.Iss.	4.00	10-20.00
80-56-002	Santa 400QX310-1	Keepsake	Yr.Iss.	4.00	20.00
80-56-003	Dove 400QX308-1	Keepsake	Yr.Iss.	4.00	25-35.00
Hallmark Keepsake Ornaments		**1980 Little Trimmers**			
80-57-001	Clothespin Soldier 350QX134-1	Keepsake	Yr.Iss.	3.50	45.00
80-57-002	Christmas Teddy 250QX135-4	Keepsake	Yr.Iss.	2.50	125.00
80-57-003	Merry Redbird 350QX160-1	Keepsake	Yr.Iss.	3.50	55.00
80-57-004	Swingin' on a Star 400QX130-1	Keepsake	Yr.Iss.	4.00	75.00
80-57-005	Christmas Owl 400QX131-4	Keepsake	Yr.Iss.	4.00	45.00
80-57-006	Thimble Series-A Christmas Salute 400QX 131-9	Keepsake	Yr.Iss.	4.00	150.00
Hallmark Keepsake Ornaments		**1980 Handcrafted Ornaments**			
80-58-001	The Snowflake Swing 400QX133-4	Keepsake	Yr.Iss.	4.00	45.00
80-58-002	Santa 1980 550QX146-1	Keepsake	Yr.Iss.	5.50	95.00
80-58-003	Drummer Boy 550QX147-4	Keepsake	Yr.Iss.	5.50	65-95.00
80-58-004	Christmas is for Children 550QX135-9	Keepsake	Yr.Iss.	5.50	95.00
80-58-005	A Christmas Treat 550QX134-7	Keepsake	Yr.Iss.	5.50	75.00
80-58-006	Skating Snowman 550QX139-9	Keepsake	Yr.Iss.	5.50	75.00
80-58-007	A Heavenly Nap 650QX139-4	Keepsake	Yr.Iss.	6.50	50.00
80-58-008	Heavenly Sounds 750QX152-1	Keepsake	Yr.Iss.	7.50	90.00
80-58-009	Caroling Bear 750QX140-1	Keepsake	Yr.Iss.	7.50	150.00
80-58-010	Santa's Flight 550QX138-1	Keepsake	Yr.Iss.	5.50	95.00
80-58-011	The Animals' Christmas 800QX150-1	Keepsake	Yr.Iss.	8.00	65.00
80-58-012	A Spot of Christmas Cheer 800QX 153-4	Keepsake	Yr.Iss.	8.00	160.00
80-58-013	Elfin Antics 900QX142-1	Keepsake	Yr.Iss.	9.00	225.00
80-58-014	A Christmas Vigil 900QX144-1	Keepsake	Yr.Iss.	9.00	110.00
Hallmark Keepsake Ornaments		**1980 Special Editions**			
80-59-001	Heavenly Minstrel 15QX156-7	Keepsake	Yr.Iss.	15.00	350-375.
80-59-002	Checking it Twice 20QX158-4	Keepsake	Yr.Iss.	20.00	175.00
Hallmark Keepsake Ornaments		**1980 Holiday Chimes**			
80-60-001	Snowflake Chimes 550QX165-4	Keepsake	Yr.Iss.	5.50	30.00
80-60-002	Reindeer Chimes 550QX320-3	Keepsake	Yr.Iss.	5.50	55.00
80-60-003	Santa Mobile 550QX136-1	Keepsake	Yr.Iss.	5.50	60.00
Hallmark Keepsake Ornaments		**1980 Collectible Series**			
80-61-001	Norman Rockwell-First Edition650QX 306-1	Keepsake	Yr.Iss.	6.50	225.00
80-61-002	Frosty Friends-First Edition650QX 137-4	Keepsake	Yr.Iss.	6.50	600-650.
80-61-003	Snoopy & Friends-Second Ed. 900QX 154-1	Keepsake	Yr.Iss.	9.00	95.00
80-61-004	Carrousel-Third Edition 750QX141-4	Keepsake	Yr.Iss.	7.50	155.00
80-61-005	Thimble-Third Edition 400QX132-1	Keepsake	Yr.Iss.	4.00	150-175.
80-61-006	Here Comes Santa-Second Ed.12QX 143-4	Keepsake	Yr.Iss.	12.00	115-175.00
80-61-007	The Bellringers-Second Edition15QX 157-4	Keepsake	Yr.Iss.	15.00	55-75.00
Hallmark Keepsake Ornaments		**1980 Yarn Ornaments**			
80-62-001	Santa 300QX161-4	Keepsake	Yr.Iss.	3.00	20.00
80-62-002	Angel 300QX162-1	Keepsake	Yr.Iss.	3.00	20.00
80-62-003	Snowman 300QX163-4	Keepsake	Yr.Iss.	3.00	20.00
80-62-004	Soldier 300QX164-1	Keepsake	Yr.Iss.	3.00	20.00
Hallmark Keepsake Ornaments		**1981 Commemoratives**			
81-63-001	Baby's First Christmas-Girl450QX 600-2	Keepsake	Yr.Iss.	4.50	20.00
81-63-002	Baby's First Christmas-Boy450QX 601-5	Keepsake	Yr.Iss.	4.50	20.00
81-63-003	Baby's First Christmas-Black450QX 602-2	Keepsake	Yr.Iss.	4.50	18-25.00
81-63-004	Baby's First Christmas 550QX516-2	Keepsake	Yr.Iss.	5.50	29.50
81-63-005	Baby's First Christmas 850QX513-5	Keepsake	Yr.Iss.	8.50	15.50
81-63-006	Baby's First Christmas 1300QX440-2	Keepsake	Yr.Iss.	13.00	30-49.00
81-63-007	Godchild 450QX603-5	Keepsake	Yr.Iss.	4.50	12.50
81-63-008	Grandson 450QX604-2	Keepsake	Yr.Iss.	4.50	23.00
81-63-009	Granddaughter 450QX605-5	Keepsake	Yr.Iss.	4.50	25.00
81-63-010	Daughter 450QX607-5	Keepsake	Yr.Iss.	4.50	15-25.00
81-63-011	Son 450QX606-2	Keepsake	Yr.Iss.	4.50	15-25.00
81-63-012	Mother 450QX608-2	Keepsake	Yr.Iss.	4.50	19.00
81-63-013	Father 450QX609-5	Keepsake	Yr.Iss.	4.50	12-15.00
81-63-014	Mother and Dad 450QX700-2	Keepsake	Yr.Iss.	4.50	12.50
81-63-015	Friendship 450QX704-2	Keepsake	Yr.Iss.	4.50	12.50-26.00
81-63-016	The Gift of Love 450QX705-5	Keepsake	Yr.Iss.	4.50	17.50
81-63-017	Home 450QX709-5	Keepsake	Yr.Iss.	4.50	14.50
81-63-018	Teacher 450QX800-2	Keepsake	Yr.Iss.	4.50	12.00
81-63-019	Grandfather 450QX701-5	Keepsake	Yr.Iss.	4.50	12.00
81-63-020	Grandmother 450QX702-2	Keepsake	Yr.Iss.	4.50	12.50
81-63-021	Grandparents 450QX703-5	Keepsake	Yr.Iss.	4.50	12.00
81-63-022	First Christmas Together 450QX706-2	Keepsake	Yr.Iss.	4.50	25.00
81-63-023	25th Christmas Together 450QX707-5	Keepsake	Yr.Iss.	4.50	15.00
81-63-024	50th Christmas 450QX708-2	Keepsake	Yr.Iss.	4.50	12.00
81-63-025	Love 550QX502-2	Keepsake	Yr.Iss.	5.50	19.50
81-63-026	Friendship 550QX503-5	Keepsake	Yr.Iss.	5.50	29.50
81-63-027	First Christmas Together 550QX505-5	Keepsake	Yr.Iss.	5.50	22.50
81-63-028	25th Christmas Together 550QX504-2	Keepsake	Yr.Iss.	5.50	19.50
Hallmark Keepsake Ornaments		**1981 Property Ornaments**			
81-65-001	Betsey Clark Cameo 850QX512-2	Keepsake	Yr.Iss.	8.50	30.00
81-65-002	Betsey Clark 900QX423-5	Keepsake	Yr.Iss.	9.00	30-65.00
81-65-003	Betsey Clark-Ninth Edition450QX 802-2	Keepsake	Yr.Iss.	4.50	25.00
81-65-004	Muppets 450QX807-5	Keepsake	Yr.Iss.	4.50	25-35.00
81-65-005	Kermit the Frog 900QX424-2	Keepsake	Yr.Iss.	9.00	80-95.00
81-65-006	The Divine Miss Piggy 1200QX425-5	Keepsake	Yr.Iss.	12.00	95.00
81-65-007	Mary Hamilton 450QX806-2	Keepsake	Yr.Iss.	4.50	19.50
81-65-008	Marty Links 450QX808-2	Keepsake	Yr.Iss.	4.50	15.00
81-65-009	Peanuts 450QX803-5	Keepsake	Yr.Iss.	4.50	25.00
81-65-010	Joan Walsh Anglund 450QX804-2	Keepsake	Yr.Iss.	4.50	15.00
81-65-011	Disney 450QX805-5	Keepsake	Yr.Iss.	4.50	22.00
Hallmark Keepsake Ornaments		**1981 Decorative Ball Ornaments**			
81-66-001	Christmas 1981 450QX809-5	Keepsake	Yr.Iss.	4.50	25.00
81-66-002	Christmas Magic 450QX810-2	Keepsake	Yr.Iss.	4.50	19.50
81-66-003	Traditional (Black Santa) 450QX801-5	Keepsake	Yr.Iss.	4.50	50-95.00
81-66-004	Let Us Adore Him 450QX811-5	Keepsake	Yr.Iss.	4.50	50.00
81-66-005	Santa's Coming 450QX812-2	Keepsake	Yr.Iss.	4.50	19.50
81-66-006	Christmas in the Forest 450QX813-5	Keepsake	Yr.Iss.	4.50	175.00
81-66-007	Merry Christmas 450QX814-2	Keepsake	Yr.Iss.	4.50	17.50
81-66-008	Santa's Surprise 450QX815-5	Keepsake	Yr.Iss.	4.50	19.50
Hallmark Keepsake Ornaments		**1981 Crown Classics**			
81-67-001	Angel 450QX507-5	Keepsake	Yr.Iss.	4.50	25.00
81-67-002	Tree Photoholder 550QX515-5	Keepsake	Yr.Iss.	5.50	25.00
81-67-003	Unicorn 850QX516-5	Keepsake	Yr.Iss.	8.50	23.00
Hallmark Keepsake Ornaments		**1981 Frosted Images**			
81-68-001	Mouse 400QX508-2	Keepsake	Yr.Iss.	4.00	20.00
81-68-002	Angel 400QX509-5	Keepsake	Yr.Iss.	4.00	45-65.00
81-68-003	Snowman 400QX510-2	Keepsake	Yr.Iss.	4.00	25.00
Hallmark Keepsake Ornaments		**1981 Holiday Highlights**			
81-69-001	Shepherd Scene 550QX500-2	Keepsake	Yr.Iss.	5.50	20-25.00
81-69-002	Christmas Star 550QX501-5	Keepsake	Yr.Iss.	5.50	10-24.50
Hallmark Keepsake Ornaments		**1981 Little Trimmers**			
81-70-001	Puppy Love 350QX406-2	Keepsake	Yr.Iss.	3.50	35-40.00
81-70-002	Jolly Snowman 350QX407-5	Keepsake	Yr.Iss.	3.50	50.00
81-70-003	Perky Penguin 350QX409-5	Keepsake	Yr.Iss.	3.50	60.00
81-70-004	Clothespin Drummer Boy 450QX408-2	Keepsake	Yr.Iss.	4.50	45.00
81-70-005	The Stocking Mouse 450QX412-2	Keepsake	Yr.Iss.	4.50	95.00
Hallmark Keepsake Ornaments		**1981 Hand Crafted Ornaments**			
81-71-001	Space Santa 650QX430-2	Keepsake	Yr.Iss.	6.50	80-125.00
81-71-002	Candyville Express 750QX418-2	Keepsake	Yr.Iss.	7.50	125.00
81-71-003	Ice Fairy 650QX431-5	Keepsake	Yr.Iss.	6.50	65-85.00
81-71-004	Star Swing 550QX421-5	Keepsake	Yr.Iss.	5.50	50.00
81-71-005	A Heavenly Nap 650QX139-4	Keepsake	Yr.Iss.	6.50	49.50
81-71-006	Dough Angel 550QX139-6	Keepsake	Yr.Iss.	5.50	80.00
81-71-007	Topsy-Turvy Tunes 750QX429-5	Keepsake	Yr.Iss.	7.50	75.00
81-71-008	A Well-Stocked Stocking 900QX154-7	Keepsake	Yr.Iss.	9.00	75.00
81-71-009	The Friendly Fiddler 800QX434-2	Keepsake	Yr.Iss.	8.00	45-75.00
81-71-010	The Ice Sculptor 800QX432-2	Keepsake	Yr.Iss.	8.00	95.00
81-71-011	Christmas Dreams 1200QX437-5	Keepsake	Yr.Iss.	12.00	225.00
81-71-012	Christmas Fantasy 1300QX155-4	Keepsake	Yr.Iss.	13.00	75.00
81-71-013	Sailing Santa 1300QX439-5	Keepsake	Yr.Iss.	13.00	250.00
81-71-014	Love and Joy 900QX425-2	Keepsake	Yr.Iss.	9.00	95.00
81-71-015	Drummer Boy 250QX148-1	Keepsake	Yr.Iss.	2.50	50.00
81-71-016	St. Nicholas 550QX446-2	Keepsake	Yr.Iss.	5.50	35-50.00
81-71-017	Mr. & Mrs. Claus 1200QX448-5	Keepsake	Yr.Iss.	12.00	125-150.
81-71-018	Checking It Twice 2250QX158-4	Keepsake	Yr.Iss.	22.50	195.00
Hallmark Keepsake Ornaments		**1981 Holiday Chimes**			
81-72-001	Snowman Chimes 550QX445-5	Keepsake	Yr.Iss.	5.50	25.00
81-72-002	Santa Mobile 550QX136-1	Keepsake	Yr.Iss.	5.50	40.00
81-72-003	Snowflake Chimes 550QX165-4	Keepsake	Yr.Iss.	5.50	25.00
Hallmark Keepsake Ornaments		**1981 Collectible Series**			
81-73-001	Rocking Horse - 1st Edition900QX 422-2	Keepsake	Yr.Iss.	9.00	500-595.
81-73-002	Bellringer - 3rd Edition 1500QX441-5	Keepsake	Yr.Iss.	15.00	85-95.00
81-73-003	Norman Rockwell - 2nd Edition850QX 511-5	Keepsake	Yr.Iss.	8.50	30-45.00
81-73-004	Here Comes Santa - 3rd Ed.1300QX 438-2	Keepsake	Yr.Iss.	13.00	225-245.
81-73-005	Carrousel - 4th Edition 900QX427-5	Keepsake	Yr.Iss.	9.00	75-95.00
81-73-006	Snoopy and Friends - 3rd Ed.1200QX 436-2	Keepsake	Yr.Iss.	12.00	75.00
81-73-007	Thimble - 4th Edition 450QX413-5	Keepsake	Yr.Iss.	4.50	125.00
81-73-008	Frosty Friends - 2nd Edition800QX433-5	Keepsake	Yr.Iss.	8.00	350-425.
Hallmark Keepsake Ornaments		**1981 Fabric Ornaments**			
81-74-001	Cardinal Cutie 300QX400-2	Keepsake	Yr.Iss.	3.00	19.00
81-74-002	Peppermint Mouse 300QX401-5	Keepsake	Yr.Iss.	3.00	32.50
81-74-003	Gingham Dog 300QX402-2	Keepsake	Yr.Iss.	3.00	15.00
81-74-004	Calico Kitty 300QX403-5	Keepsake	Yr.Iss.	3.00	5-15.00
Hallmark Keepsake Ornaments		**1981 Plush Animals**			
81-75-001	Christmas Teddy 500QX404-2	Keepsake	Yr.Iss.	5.50	22-25.00
81-75-002	Raccoon Tunes 550QX405-5	Keepsake	Yr.Iss.	5.50	22-25.00
Hallmark Keepsake Ornaments		**1982 Commemoratives**			
82-76-001	Baby's First Christmas-Photoholder 650QX 312-6	Keepsake	Yr.Iss.	6.50	24.50
82-76-002	Baby's First Christmas 1300QX455-3	Keepsake	Yr.Iss.	13.00	33-43.00
82-76-003	Baby's First Christmas (Boy)450QX 216-3	Keepsake	Yr.Iss.	4.50	20.00
82-76-004	Baby's First Christmas (Girl)450QX 207-3	Keepsake	Yr.Iss.	4.50	26.00
82-76-005	Godchild 450QX222-6	Keepsake	Yr.Iss.	4.50	17.50
82-76-006	Grandson 450QX224-6	Keepsake	Yr.Iss.	4.50	17.50
82-76-007	Granddaughter 450QX224-3	Keepsake	Yr.Iss.	4.50	20-30.00
82-76-008	Son 450QX204-3	Keepsake	Yr.Iss.	4.50	25.00
82-76-009	Daughter 450QX204-6	Keepsake	Yr.Iss.	4.50	25.50
82-76-010	Father 450QX205-6	Keepsake	Yr.Iss.	4.50	14-24.00
82-76-011	Mother 450QX205-3	Keepsake	Yr.Iss.	4.50	15.00
82-76-012	Mother and Dad 450QX222-3	Keepsake	Yr.Iss.	4.50	12.00
82-76-013	Sister 450QX208-3	Keepsake	Yr.Iss.	4.50	22.50
82-76-014	Grandmother 450QX200-3	Keepsake	Yr.Iss.	4.50	12.00
82-76-015	Grandfather 450QX207-6	Keepsake	Yr.Iss.	4.50	12-24.00
82-76-016	Grandparents 450QX214-6	Keepsake	Yr.Iss.	4.50	12.00
82-76-017	First Christmas Together 850QX306-6	Keepsake	Yr.Iss.	8.50	35.00
82-76-018	First Christmas Together 450QX211-3	Keepsake	Yr.Iss.	4.50	20.00
82-76-019	First Christmas Together-Locket 1500QX 456-3	Keepsake	Yr.Iss.	15.00	45.00
82-76-020	Christmas Memories 650QX311-6	Keepsake	Yr.Iss.	6.50	19.50
82-76-021	Teacher 450QX214-3	Keepsake	Yr.Iss.	4.50	10.00
82-76-022	New Home 450QX212-6	Keepsake	Yr.Iss.	4.50	19.00
82-76-023	Teacher 650QX312-3	Keepsake	Yr.Iss.	6.50	15.00
82-76-024	25th Christmas Together 450QX211-6	Keepsake	Yr.Iss.	4.50	14.00
82-76-025	50th Christmas Together 450QX212-3	Keepsake	Yr.Iss.	4.50	14-24.00
82-76-026	Moments of Love 450QX209-3	Keepsake	Yr.Iss.	4.50	14.00
82-76-027	Love 450QX209-6	Keepsake	Yr.Iss.	4.50	15.00
82-76-028	Friendship 450QX208-6	Keepsake	Yr.Iss.	4.50	15.00
82-76-029	Teacher-Apple 550QX301-6	Keepsake	Yr.Iss.	5.50	15.00

Company Number	 Name	Series Artist	 Edition Limit	 Issue Price	 Quote
82-76-030	Baby's First Christmas 550QX302-3	Keepsake	Yr.Iss.	5.50	19.50
82-76-031	First Christmas Together 550QX302-6	Keepsake	Yr.Iss.	5.50	27.50
82-76-032	Love 550QX304-3	Keepsake	Yr.Iss.	5.50	27.00
82-76-033	Friendship 550QX304-6	Keepsake	Yr.Iss.	5.50	24.50
Hallmark Keepsake Ornaments		**1982 Property Ornaments**			
82-77-001	Miss Piggy and Kermit 450QX218-3	Keepsake	Yr.Iss.	4.50	40.00
82-77-002	Muppets Party 450QX218-6	Keepsake	Yr.Iss.	4.50	40.00
82-77-003	Kermit the Frog 1100QX495-6	Keepsake	Yr.Iss.	11.00	75-95.00
82-77-004	The Divine Miss Piggy 1200QX425-5	Keepsake	Yr.Iss.	12.00	125.00
82-77-005	Betsey Clark 850QX305-6	Keepsake	Yr.Iss.	8.50	24.50
82-77-006	Norman Rockwell-3rd ed.850QX305-3	Keepsake	Yr.Iss.	8.50	18-36.00
82-77-007	Betsey Clark-10th edition450QX215-6	Keepsake	Yr.Iss.	4.50	29.50
82-77-008	Norman Rockwell 450QX202-3	Keepsake	Yr.Iss.	4.50	16-29.50
82-77-009	Peanuts 450QX200-6	Keepsake	Yr.Iss.	4.50	25.00
82-77-010	Disney 450QX217-3	Keepsake	Yr.Iss.	4.50	30-35.00
82-77-011	Mary Hamilton 450QX217-6	Keepsake	Yr.Iss.	4.50	17-21.00
82-77-012	Joan Walsh Anglund 450QX219-3	Keepsake	Yr.Iss.	4.50	18-27.00
Hallmark Keepsake Ornaments		**1982 Designer Keepsakes**			
82-78-001	Old World Angels 450QX226-3	Keepsake	Yr.Iss.	4.50	19.50
82-78-002	Patterns of Christmas 450QX226-6	Keepsake	Yr.Iss.	4.50	22.50
82-78-003	Old Fashioned Christmas 450QX227-6	Keepsake	Yr.Iss.	4.50	39.50
82-78-004	Stained Glass 450QX228-3	Keepsake	Yr.Iss.	4.50	19.50
82-78-005	Merry Christmas 450QX225-6	Keepsake	Yr.Iss.	4.50	15.00
82-78-006	Twelve Days of Christmas 450QX203-6	Keepsake	Yr.Iss.	4.50	39.50
Hallmark Keepsake Ornaments		**1982 Decorative Ball Ornaments**			
82-79-001	Christmas Angel 450QX220-6	Keepsake	Yr.Iss.	4.50	18.00
82-79-002	Santa 450QX221-6	Keepsake	Yr.Iss.	4.50	19.00
82-79-003	Currier & Ives 450QX201-3	Keepsake	Yr.Iss.	4.50	16.00
82-79-004	Season for Caring 450QX221-3	Keepsake	Yr.Iss.	4.50	20.00
Hallmark Keepsake Ornaments		**1982 Colors of Christmas**			
82-80-001	Nativity 450QX308-3	Keepsake	Yr.Iss.	4.50	40-46.00
82-80-002	Santa's Flight 450QX308-6	Keepsake	Yr.Iss.	4.50	30-39.50
Hallmark Keepsake Ornaments		**1982 Ice Sculptures**			
82-81-001	Snowy Seal 400QX300-6	Keepsake	Yr.Iss.	4.00	20-23.00
82-81-002	Arctic Penguin 400QX300-3	Keepsake	Yr.Iss.	4.00	12-19.50
Hallmark Keepsake Ornaments		**1982 Holiday Highlights**			
82-82-001	Christmas Sleigh 550QX309-3	Keepsake	Yr.Iss.	5.50	75.00
82-82-002	Angel 550QX309-6	Keepsake	Yr.Iss.	5.50	20-25.00
82-82-003	Christmas Magic 550QX311-3	Keepsake	Yr.Iss.	5.50	27.50
Hallmark Keepsake Ornaments		**1982 Handcrafted Ornaments**			
82-83-001	Three Kings 850QX307-3	Keepsake	Yr.Iss.	8.50	22.50
82-83-002	Baroque Angel 1500QX456-6	Keepsake	Yr.Iss.	15.00	150.00
82-83-003	Cloisonne Angel 1200QX145-4	Keepsake	Yr.Iss.	12.00	95.00
Hallmark Keepsake Ornaments		**1982 Brass Ornaments**			
82-84-001	Santa and Reindeer 900QX467-6	Keepsake	Yr.Iss.	9.00	45-50.00
82-84-002	Brass Bell 1200QX460-6	Keepsake	Yr.Iss.	12.00	15-22.50
82-84-003	Santa's Sleigh 900QX478-6	Keepsake	Yr.Iss.	9.00	24-30.00
Hallmark Keepsake Ornaments		**1982 Handcrafted Ornaments**			
82-85-001	The Spirit of Christmas 1000QX452-6	Keepsake	Yr.Iss.	10.00	125.00
82-85-002	Jogging Santa 800QX457-6	Keepsake	Yr.Iss.	8.00	35-45.00
82-85-003	Santa Bell 1500QX148-7	Keepsake	Yr.Iss.	15.00	60.00
82-85-004	Santa's Workshop 1000QX450-3	Keepsake	Yr.Iss.	10.00	85.00
82-85-005	Cycling Santa 2000QX435-5	Keepsake	Yr.Iss.	20.00	120-150.
82-85-006	Christmas Fantasy 1300QX155-4	Keepsake	Yr.Iss.	13.00	59.00
82-85-007	Cowboy Snowman 800QX480-6	Keepsake	Yr.Iss.	8.00	45-50.00
82-85-008	Pinecone Home 800QX461-3	Keepsake	Yr.Iss.	8.00	100-175.
82-85-009	Raccoon Surprises 900QX479-3	Keepsake	Yr.Iss.	9.00	150-175.
82-85-010	Elfin Artist 900QX457-3	Keepsake	Yr.Iss.	9.00	37.50-45.00
82-85-011	Ice Sculptor 800QX432-2	Keepsake	Yr.Iss.	8.00	75.00
82-85-012	Tin Soldier 650QX483-6	Keepsake	Yr.Iss.	6.50	39.50
82-85-013	Peeking Elf 650QX419-5	Keepsake	Yr.Iss.	6.50	32.50
82-85-014	Jolly Christmas Tree 650QX465-3	Keepsake	Yr.Iss.	6.50	75.00
82-85-015	Embroidered Tree - 650QX494-6	Keepsake	Yr.Iss.	6.50	25.00
Hallmark Keepsake Ornaments		**1982 Little Trimmers**			
82-86-001	Cookie Mouse 450QX454-6	Keepsake	Yr.Iss.	4.50	50-62.00
82-86-002	Musical Angel 550QX459-6	Keepsake	Yr.Iss.	5.50	100-125.
82-86-003	Merry Moose 550QX415-5	Keepsake	Yr.Iss.	5.50	49.50
82-86-004	Christmas Owl 450QX131-4	Keepsake	Yr.Iss.	4.50	35.00
82-86-005	Dove Love 450QX462-3	Keepsake	Yr.Iss.	4.50	55.00
82-86-006	Perky Penguin 400QX409-5	Keepsake	Yr.Iss.	4.00	35.00
82-86-007	Christmas Kitten 400QX454-3	Keepsake	Yr.Iss.	4.00	32.00
82-86-008	Jingling Teddy 400QX477-6	Keepsake	Yr.Iss.	4.00	40-48.00
Hallmark Keepsake Ornaments		**1982 Collectible Series**			
82-87-001	Holiday Wildlife-1st Ed. 700QX 313-3	Keepsake	Yr.Iss.	7.00	350-475.
82-87-002	Tin Locomotive-1st Ed. 1300QX 460-3	Keepsake	Yr.Iss.	13.00	525-650.
82-87-003	Clothespin Soldier-1st Ed. 500QX 458-3	Keepsake	Yr.Iss.	5.00	105-125.
82-87-004	The Bellringer-4th Ed. 1500QX 455-6	Keepsake	Yr.Iss.	15.00	75-100.00
82-87-005	Carrousel Series-5th Ed. 1000QX 478-3	Keepsake	Yr.Iss.	10.00	80-100.00
82-87-006	Snoopy and Friends-4th Ed.1000QX 478-3	Keepsake	Yr.Iss.	13.00	85.00
82-87-007	Here Comes Santa-4th Edition 1500QX 464-3	Keepsake	Yr.Iss.	15.00	95-125.00
82-87-008	Rocking Horse-2nd Ed. 1000QX 502-3	Keepsake	Yr.Iss.	10.00	300-375.
82-87-009	Thimble-5th Edition 500QX451-3	Keepsake	Yr.Iss.	5.00	75-80.00
82-87-010	Frosty Friends-3rd Ed. 500QX 451-3	Keepsake	Yr.Iss.	8.00	225.00
Hallmark Keepsake Ornaments		**1982 Holiday Chimes**			
82-88-001	Tree Chimes 550QX484-6	Keepsake	Yr.Iss.	5.50	49.00
82-88-002	Bell Chimes 550QX494-3	Keepsake	Yr.Iss.	5.50	30.00
Hallmark Keepsake Ornaments		**1983 Commemoratives**			
83-89-001	Baby's First Christmas 750QX301-9	Keepsake	Yr.Iss.	7.50	14.50
83-89-002	Baby's First Christmas 1400QX402-7	Keepsake	Yr.Iss.	14.00	34.50-37.50
83-89-003	Baby's First Christmas 450QX200-7	Keepsake	Yr.Iss.	4.50	20-25.00
83-89-004	Baby's First Christmas 450QX200-9	Keepsake	Yr.Iss.	4.50	20-25.00
83-89-005	Baby's First Christmas 700QX302-9	Keepsake	Yr.Iss.	7.00	25.00
83-89-006	Grandchild's First Christmas400Q 430-9	Keepsake	Yr.Iss.	14.00	34.50
83-89-007	Child's Third Christmas 450QX226-9	Keepsake	Yr.Iss.	4.50	19.00
83-89-008	Grandchild's First Christmas600QX 312-9	Keepsake	Yr.Iss.	6.00	20.00
83-89-009	Baby's Second Christmas 450QX226-7	Keepsake	Yr.Iss.	4.50	25.00
83-89-010	Granddaughter 450QX202-7	Keepsake	Yr.Iss.	4.50	22.50
83-89-011	Grandson 450QX201-9	Keepsake	Yr.Iss.	4.50	22.50
83-89-012	Son 450QX202-9	Keepsake	Yr.Iss.	4.50	24.50
83-89-013	Daughter 450QX203-7	Keepsake	Yr.Iss.	4.50	35-50.00

Company Number	 Name	Series Artist	 Edition Limit	 Issue Price	 Quote
83-89-014	Godchild 450QX201-7	Keepsake	Yr.Iss.	4.50	14.00
83-89-015	Grandmother 450QX205-7	Keepsake	Yr.Iss.	4.50	14.00
83-89-016	Mom and Dad 650QX429-7	Keepsake	Yr.Iss.	6.50	17.50
83-89-017	Sister 450QX206-9	Keepsake	Yr.Iss.	4.50	17.00
83-89-018	Grandparents 650QX429-9	Keepsake	Yr.Iss.	6.50	14.50
83-89-019	First Christmas Together 450QX208-9	Keepsake	Yr.Iss.	4.50	20.00
83-89-020	First Christmas Together 600QX310-7	Keepsake	Yr.Iss.	6.00	30-39.50
83-89-021	First Christmas Together 750QX301-7	Keepsake	Yr.Iss.	7.50	20.00
83-89-022	First Christmas Together- Brass Locket 1500QX 432-9	Keepsake	Yr.Iss.	15.00	40-45.00
83-89-023	Love Is a Song 450QX223-9	Keepsake	Yr.Iss.	4.50	20-25.00
83-89-024	Love 1300QX422-7	Keepsake	Yr.Iss.	13.00	29.50
83-89-025	Love 600QX310-9	Keepsake	Yr.Iss.	6.00	35.00
83-89-026	Love 450QX207-9	Keepsake	Yr.Iss.	4.50	25.00
83-89-027	Teacher 600QX304-9	Keepsake	Yr.Iss.	6.00	10.00
83-89-028	First Christmas Together 600QX306-9	Keepsake	Yr.Iss.	6.00	28.00
83-89-029	Friendship 600QX305-9	Keepsake	Yr.Iss.	6.00	14.50
83-89-030	Love 600QX305-7	Keepsake	Yr.Iss.	6.00	13.00
83-89-031	Mother 600Qx306-7	Keepsake	Yr.Iss.	6.00	14.50
83-89-032	25th Christmas Together 450QX224-7	Keepsake	Yr.Iss.	4.50	17.00
83-89-033	Teacher 450QX224-9	Keepsake	Yr.Iss.	4.50	14-20.00
83-89-034	Friendship 450QX207-7	Keepsake	Yr.Iss.	4.50	15.00
83-89-035	New Home 450QX210-7	Keepsake	Yr.Iss.	4.50	15.00
83-89-036	Tenth Christmas Together 650QX430-7	Keepsake	Yr.Iss.	6.50	20.00
Hallmark Keepsake Ornaments		**1983 Property Ornaments**			
83-90-001	Betsey Clark 650QX404-7	Keepsake	Yr.Iss.	6.50	29.50
83-90-002	Betsey Clark 900QX440-1	Keepsake	Yr.Iss.	9.00	27.50
83-90-003	Betsey Clark-11th Edition 450QX211-9	Keepsake	Yr.Iss.	4.50	30-50.00
83 90 004	Peanuts 450QX212-7	Keepsake	Yr.Iss.	4.50	22-24.00
83-90-005	Disney 450QX212-9	Keepsake	Yr.Iss.	4.50	30-50.00
83-90-006	Shirt Tales 450QX214-9	Keepsake	Yr.Iss.	4.50	22.50
83-90-007	Mary Hamilton 450QX213-7	Keepsake	Yr.Iss.	4.50	39.50
83-90-008	Miss Piggy 1300QX405-7	Keepsake	Yr.Iss.	13.00	195.00
83-90-009	The Muppets 450QX214-7	Keepsake	Yr.Iss.	4.50	50.00
83-90-010	Kermit the Frog 1100QX495-6	Keepsake	Yr.Iss.	11.00	35.00
83-90-011	Norman Rockwell-4th Edition750QX 300-7	Keepsake	Yr.Iss.	7.50	30-40.00
83-90-012	Norman Rockwell 450QX215-7	Keepsake	Yr.Iss.	4.50	42.50
Hallmark Keepsake Ornaments		**1983 Decorative Ball Ornaments**			
83-91-001	Currier & Ives 450QX215-9	Keepsake	Yr.Iss.	4.50	15-17.00
83-91-002	Christmas Joy 450QX216-9	Keepsake	Yr.Iss.	4.50	22.50
83-91-003	Here Comes Santa 450QX217-7	Keepsake	Yr.Iss.	4.50	40.00
83-91-004	Oriental Butterflies 450QX218-7	Keepsake	Yr.Iss.	4.50	15-20.00
83-91-005	Angels 500QX219-7	Keepsake	Yr.Iss.	5.00	22.00
83-91-006	Season's Greeting 450QX219-9	Keepsake	Yr.Iss.	4.50	20.00
83-91-007	1983 450QX220-9	Keepsake	Yr.Iss.	4.50	19.00
83-91-008	The Wise Men 450QX220-7	Keepsake	Yr.Iss.	4.50	30-39.50
83-91-009	Christmas Wonderland 450QX221-9	Keepsake	Yr.Iss.	4.50	95.00
83-91-010	An Old Fashioned Christmas450QX 2217-9	Keepsake	Yr.Iss.	4.50	15.00
83-91-011	The Annunciation 450QX216-7	Keepsake	Yr.Iss.	4.50	22.50
Hallmark Keepsake Ornaments		**1983 Holiday Highlights**			
83-92-001	Christmas Stocking 600Qx303-9	Keepsake	Yr.Iss.	6.00	39.50
83-92-002	Star of Peace 600QX304-7	Keepsake	Yr.Iss.	6.00	15.00
83-92-003	Time for Sharing 600QX307-7	Keepsake	Yr.Iss.	6.00	22-35.00
Hallmark Keepsake Ornaments		**1983 Crown Classics**			
83-93-001	Enameled Christmas Wreath 900QX 311-9	Keepsake	Yr.Iss.	9.00	12.50
83-93-002	Memories to Treasure 700QX303-7	Keepsake	Yr.Iss.	7.00	22.00
83-93-003	Mother and Child 750QX302-7	Keepsake	Yr.Iss.	7.50	34.50
Hallmark Keepsake Ornaments		**1983 Holiday Sculptures**			
83-94-001	Santa 400Qx308-7	Keepsake	Yr.Iss.	4.00	22-33.00
83-94-002	Heart 400QX307-9	Keepsake	Yr.Iss.	4.00	49.50
Hallmark Keepsake Ornaments		**1983 Handcrafted Ornaments**			
83-95-001	Embroidered Stocking 650QX479-6	Keepsake	Yr.Iss.	6.50	12-20.00
83-95-002	Embroidered Heart 650QX421-7	Keepsake	Yr.Iss.	6.50	19.50
83-95-003	Scrimshaw Reindeer 800QX424-9	Keepsake	Yr.Iss.	8.00	32.50
83-95-004	Jack Frost 900QX407-9	Keepsake	Yr.Iss.	9.00	54.50
83-95-005	Unicorn 1000QX426-7	Keepsake	Yr.Iss.	10.00	58-63.00
83-95-006	Porcelain Doll, Diana 900QX423-7	Keepsake	Yr.Iss.	9.00	20-30.00
83-95-007	Brass Santa 900QX423-9	Keepsake	Yr.Iss.	9.00	19.00
83-95-008	Santa's on His Way 1000QX426-9	Keepsake	Yr.Iss.	10.00	30-37.00
83-95-009	Old-Fashioned Santa 1100QX409-9	Keepsake	Yr.Iss.	11.00	50-65.00
83-95-010	Cycling Santa 2000QX435-5	Keepsake	Yr.Iss.	20.00	150.00
83-95-011	Santa's Workshop 1000QX450-3	Keepsake	Yr.Iss.	10.00	60.00
83-95-012	Ski Lift Santa 800QX418-7	Keepsake	Yr.Iss.	8.00	65.00
83-95-013	Hitchhiking Santa 800QX424-7	Keepsake	Yr.Iss.	8.00	39.50
83-95-014	Mountain Climbing Santa 650QX407-7	Keepsake	Yr.Iss.	6.50	34.50
83-95-015	Jolly Santa 350QX425-9	Keepsake	Yr.Iss.	3.50	35.00
83-95-016	Santa's Many Faces 600QX311-6	Keepsake	Yr.Iss.	6.00	30.00
83-95-017	Baroque Angels 1300QX422-9	Keepsake	Yr.Iss.	13.00	45-58.00
83-95-018	Madonna and Child 1200QX428-7	Keepsake	Yr.Iss.	12.00	18-39.50
83-95-019	Mouse on Cheese 650QX413-7	Keepsake	Yr.Iss.	6.50	45-48.00
83-95-020	Peppermint Penguin 650QX408-9	Keepsake	Yr.Iss.	6.50	35-48.00
83-95-021	Skating Rabbit 800QX409-7	Keepsake	Yr.Iss.	8.00	35-49.50
83-95-022	Skiing Fox 800QX420-7	Keepsake	Yr.Iss.	8.00	35-40.00
83-95-023	Mouse in Bell 1000QX419-7	Keepsake	Yr.Iss.	10.00	55-65.00
83-95-024	Mailbox Kitten 650QX415-7	Keepsake	Yr.Iss.	6.50	60.00
83-95-025	Tin Rocking Horse 650QX414-9	Keepsake	Yr.Iss.	6.50	40-43.00
83-95-026	Bell Wreath 650QX420-9	Keepsake	Yr.Iss.	6.50	27.50
83-95-027	Angel Messenger 650QX408-7	Keepsake	Yr.Iss.	6.50	95.00
83-95-028	Holiday Puppy 350QX412-7	Keepsake	Yr.Iss.	3.50	26-30.00
83-95-029	Rainbow Angel 550QX416-7	Keepsake	Yr.Iss.	5.50	125-135.
83-95-030	Sneaker Mouse 450QX400-9	Keepsake	Yr.Iss.	4.50	30-45.00
83-95-031	Christmas Koala 400QX419-9	Keepsake	Yr.Iss.	4.00	29.50
83-95-032	Caroling Owl 450QX411-7	Keepsake	Yr.Iss.	4.50	39.50
83-95-033	Christmas Kitten 400QX454-3	Keepsake	Yr.Iss.	4.00	35.00
Hallmark Keepsake Ornaments		**1983 Collectible Series**			
83-96-001	The Bellringer-5th Edition1500QX 403-9	Keepsake	Yr.Iss.	15.00	110-135.
83-96-002	Holiday Wildlife-2nd Edition 700QX 309-9	Keepsake	Yr.Iss.	7.00	40-75.00
83-96-003	Here Comes Santa-5th Edition1300QX 403-7	Keepsake	Yr.Iss.	13.00	200-225.
83-96-004	Snoopy and Friends-5th Ed.1300QX 416-9	Keepsake	Yr.Iss.	13.00	75.00
83-96-005	Carrousel-6th Edition 1100QX401-9	Keepsake	Yr.Iss.	11.00	47.50
83-96-006	Porcelain Bear-1st Edition700QX 428-9	Keepsake	Yr.Iss.	7.00	65-95.00
83-96-007	Clothespin Soldier-2nd Edition500QX 402-9	Keepsake	Yr.Iss.	5.00	40-45.00
83-96-008	Rocking Horse-3rd Edition1000QX 417-7	Keepsake	Yr.Iss.	10.00	175-250.
83-96-009	Frosty Friends-4th Edition800QX 400-7	Keepsake	Yr.Iss.	8.00	215-235.
83-96-010	Thimble - 6th Edition 500QX401-7	Keepsake	Yr.Iss.	5.00	35-45.00
83-96-011	Tin Locomotive - 2nd Edition1300QX 404-9	Keepsake	Yr.Iss.	13.00	225-270.

Company	Series				
Number Name		Artist	Edition Limit	Issue Price	Quote
Hallmark Keepsake Ornaments	**1984 Commemoratives**				
84-97-001	Baby's First Christmas 1600QX904-1	Keepsake	Yr.Iss.	16.00	40-55.00
84-97-002	Baby's First Christmas 1400QX438-1	Keepsake	Yr.Iss.	14.00	25-45.00
84-97-003	Baby's First Christmas 700QX300-1	Keepsake	Yr.Iss.	7.00	17.00
84-97-004	Baby's First Christmas 600QX340-1	Keepsake	Yr.Iss.	6.00	25-37.50
84-97-005	Baby's First Christmas-Boy450QX 240-4	Keepsake	Yr.Iss.	4.50	27.00
84-97-006	Baby's First Christmas-Girl450QX 340-1	Keepsake	Yr.Iss.	4.50	27.00
84-97-007	Baby's Second Christmas 450QX241-1	Keepsake	Yr.Iss.	4.50	27.50
84-97-008	Child's Third Christmas 450QX261-1	Keepsake	Yr.Iss.	4.50	20.00
84-97-009	Grandchild's First Christmas110QX 460-1	Keepsake	Yr.Iss.	11.00	15-33.00
84-97-010	Grandchild's First Christmas450QX 257-4	Keepsake	Yr.Iss.	4.50	14.00
84-97-011	Godchild 450QX242-1	Keepsake	Yr.Iss.	4.50	15.00
84-97-012	Grandson 450QX242-4	Keepsake	Yr.Iss.	4.50	20.00
84-97-013	Granddaughter 450QX243-1	Keepsake	Yr.Iss.	4.50	20.00
84-97-014	Grandparents 450QX256-1	Keepsake	Yr.Iss.	4.50	15.00
84-97-015	Grandmother 450QX244-1	Keepsake	Yr.Iss.	4.50	15.00
84-97-016	Father 600QX257-1	Keepsake	Yr.Iss.	6.00	12.00
84-97-017	Mother 600QX343-4	Keepsake	Yr.Iss.	6.00	12.50
84-97-018	Mother and Dad 650QX258-1	Keepsake	Yr.Iss.	6.50	17.00
84-97-019	Sister 650QX259-4	Keepsake	Yr.Iss.	6.50	10-15.00
84-97-020	Daughter 450QX244-4	Keepsake	Yr.Iss.	4.50	24.50
84-97-021	Son 450QX243-4	Keepsake	Yr.Iss.	4.50	20-25.00
84-97-022	The Miracle of Love 600QX342-4	Keepsake	Yr.Iss.	6.00	29.50
84-97-023	First Christmas Together 600QX342-1	Keepsake	Yr.Iss.	6.00	19.50
84-97-024	First Christmas Together 1600QX904-4	Keepsake	Yr.Iss.	16.00	65.00
84-97-025	First Christmas Together 1500QX436-4	Keepsake	Yr.Iss.	15.00	29.50
84-97-026	First Christmas Together 750QX340-4	Keepsake	Yr.Iss.	7.50	17.00
84-97-027	First Christmas Together 450QX245-1	Keepsake	Yr.Iss.	4.50	15-19.00
84-97-028	Heartful of Love 1000QX443-4	Keepsake	Yr.Iss.	10.00	45.00
84-97-029	Love...the Spirit of Christmas450QX 247-4	Keepsake	Yr.Iss.	4.50	24.50
84-97-030	Love 450QX255-4	Keepsake	Yr.Iss.	4.50	14.50
84-97-031	Ten Years Together 650QX258-4	Keepsake	Yr.Iss.	6.50	19.50
84-97-032	Twenty-Five Years Together650QX 259-1	Keepsake	Yr.Iss.	6.50	19.50
84-97-033	Gratitude 600QX344-4	Keepsake	Yr.Iss.	6.00	10.00
84-97-034	The Fun of Friendship 600QX343-1	Keepsake	Yr.Iss.	6.00	32.50
84-97-035	Friendship 450QX248-1	Keepsake	Yr.Iss.	4.50	15-24.00
84-97-036	A Gift of Friendship 450QX260-4	Keepsake	Yr.Iss.	4.50	15.00
84-97-037	New Home 450QX245-4	Keepsake	Yr.Iss.	4.50	60-107.50
84-97-038	From Our Home to Yours 450QX248-4	Keepsake	Yr.Iss.	4.50	12.00
84-97-039	Teacher 450QX249-1	Keepsake	Yr.Iss.	4.50	13-15.00
84-97-040	Baby-sitter 450QX253-1	Keepsake	Yr.Iss.	4.50	12.50
Hallmark Keepsake Ornaments	**1984 Property Ornaments**				
84-98-001	Betsey Clark Angel 900QX462-4	Keepsake	Yr.Iss.	9.00	29.50
84-98-002	Katybeth 900QX463-1	Keepsake	Yr.Iss.	9.00	18-25.00
84-98-003	Peanuts 450QX252-1	Keepsake	Yr.Iss.	4.50	20-25.00
84-98-004	Disney 450QX250-4	Keepsake	Yr.Iss.	4.50	25-33.00
84-98-005	The Muppets 450QX251-4	Keepsake	Yr.Iss.	4.50	29.50
84-98-006	Norman Rockwell 450QX251-4	Keepsake	Yr.Iss.	4.50	20.00
84-98-007	Currier & Ives 450QX250-1	Keepsake	Yr.Iss.	4.50	15-20.00
84-98-008	Shirt Tales 450QX252-4	Keepsake	Yr.Iss.	4.50	20-25.00
84-98-009	Snoopy and Woodstock 750QX439-1	Keepsake	Yr.Iss.	7.50	50-75.00
84-98-010	Muffin 550QX442-1	Keepsake	Yr.Iss.	5.50	20-30.00
84-98-011	Kit 550QX453-4	Keepsake	Yr.Iss.	5.50	20-30.00
Hallmark Keepsake Ornaments	**1984 Traditional Ornaments**				
84-99-001	White Christmas 1600QX905-1	Keepsake	Yr.Iss.	16.00	65-95.00
84-99-002	Twelve Days of Christmas1500QX 415-9	Keepsake	Yr.Iss.	15.00	95.00
84-99-003	Gift of Music 1500QX451-1	Keepsake	Yr.Iss.	15.00	75-95.00
84-99-004	Amanda 900QX432-1	Keepsake	Yr.Iss.	9.00	20-29.50
84-99-005	Holiday Jester 1100QX437-4	Keepsake	Yr.Iss.	11.00	25-33.00
84-99-006	Uncle Sam 600QX449-1	Keepsake	Yr.Iss.	6.00	35-43.00
84-99-007	Chickadee 600QX451-4	Keepsake	Yr.Iss.	6.00	37.50
84-99-008	Cuckoo Clock 1000QX455-1	Keepsake	Yr.Iss.	10.00	40-50.00
84-99-009	Alpine Elf 600QX452-1	Keepsake	Yr.Iss.	6.00	37.50
84-99-010	Nostalgic Sled 600QX442-4	Keepsake	Yr.Iss.	6.00	24.50
84-99-011	Santa Sulky Driver 900QX436-1	Keepsake	Yr.Iss.	9.00	32.50
84-99-012	Old Fashioned Rocking Horse750QX 346-4	Keepsake	Yr.Iss.	7.50	17.50
84-99-013	Madonna and Child 600QX344-1	Keepsake	Yr.Iss.	6.00	40.00
84-99-014	Holiday Friendship 1300QX445-1	Keepsake	Yr.Iss.	13.00	24.50
84-99-015	Peace on Earth 750QX341-4	Keepsake	Yr.Iss.	7.50	20-23.00
84-99-016	A Savior is Born 450X254-1	Keepsake	Yr.Iss.	4.50	19.50
84-99-017	Holiday Starburst 500QX253-4	Keepsake	Yr.Iss.	5.00	20.00
84-99-018	Santa 750QX458-4	Keepsake	Yr.Iss.	7.50	14.50
84-99-019	Needlepoint Wreath 650QX459-4	Keepsake	Yr.Iss.	6.50	15.00
84-99-020	Christmas Memories Photoholder 650QX 300-4	Keepsake	Yr.Iss.	6.50	24.50
Hallmark Keepsake Ornaments	**1984 Holiday Humor**				
84-100-001	Bell Ringer Squirrel 1000QX443-1	Keepsake	Yr.Iss.	10.00	25-35.00
84-100-002	Raccoon's Christmas 900QX447-7	Keepsake	Yr.Iss.	9.00	40-58.00
84-100-003	Three Kittens in a Mitten 800QX431-1	Keepsake	Yr.Iss.	8.00	44-50.00
84-100-004	Marathon Santa 800QX456-4	Keepsake	Yr.Iss.	8.00	40-50.00
84-100-005	Santa Star 550QX450-4	Keepsake	Yr.Iss.	5.50	40.00
84-100-006	Snowmobile Santa 650QX431-4	Keepsake	Yr.Iss.	6.50	30-35.00
84-100-007	Snowshoe Penguin 650QX453-1	Keepsake	Yr.Iss.	6.50	40-50.00
84-100-008	Christmas Owl 600QX444-1	Keepsake	Yr.Iss.	6.00	25-30.00
84-100-009	Musical Angel 550QX434-4	Keepsake	Yr.Iss.	5.50	43-60.00
84-100-010	Napping Mouse 550QX435-1	Keepsake	Yr.Iss.	5.50	45-50.00
84-100-011	Roller Skating Rabbit 500QX457-1	Keepsake	Yr.Iss.	5.00	29.00
84-100-012	Frisbee Puppy 500QX444-4	Keepsake	Yr.Iss.	5.00	44.50
84-100-013	Reindeer Racetrack 450QX254-4	Keepsake	Yr.Iss.	4.50	16.00
84-100-014	A Christmas Prayer 450QX246-1	Keepsake	Yr.Iss.	4.50	16.00
84-100-015	Flights of Fantasy 450QX256-4	Keepsake	Yr.Iss.	4.50	12-20.00
84-100-016	Polar Bear Drummer 450QX430-1	Keepsake	Yr.Iss.	4.50	20-35.00
84-100-017	Santa Mouse 450QX433-4	Keepsake	Yr.Iss.	4.50	39.50
84-100-018	Snowy Seal 400QX450-1	Keepsake	Yr.Iss.	4.00	14-19.00
84-100-019	Fortune Cookie Elf 450Q452-4	Keepsake	Yr.Iss.	4.50	39.50
84-100-020	Peppermint 1984 450Q452-1	Keepsake	Yr.Iss.	4.50	50.00
84-100-021	Mountain Climbing Santa 650QX407-7	Keepsake	Yr.Iss.	6.50	34.50
Hallmark Keepsake Ornaments	**1984 Limited Edition**				
84-101-001	Classical Angel 2750QX459-1	Keepsake	Yr.Iss.	27.50	110.00
Hallmark Keepsake Ornaments	**1984 Collectible Series**				
84-102-001	Nostalgic Houses and Shops-1st Edition 1300QX 448-1	Keepsake	Yr.Iss.	13.00	165-175.
84-102-002	Wood Childhood Ornaments- 1st Edition 650QX 439-4	Keepsake	Yr.Iss.	6.50	30-45.00
84-102-003	The Twelve Days of Christmas- 1st Edition 600QX 3484	Keepsake	Yr.Iss.	6.00	225-250.
84-102-004	Art Masterpiece - 1st Edition650QX 349-4	Keepsake	Yr.Iss.	6.50	13-25.00
84-102-005	Porcelain Bear - 2nd Edition700QX 454-1	Keepsake	Yr.Iss.	7.00	30-45.00
84-102-006	Tin Locomotive - 3rd Edition1400QX 440-4	Keepsake	Yr.Iss.	14.00	60-85.00
84-102-007	Clothespin Soldier -3rd Edition 500QX 447-1	Keepsake	Yr.Iss.	5.00	20-33.00
84-102-008	Holiday Wildlife - 3rd Edition 725QX 347-4	Keepsake	Yr.Iss.	7.25	20-34.00
84-102-009	Rocking Horse - 4th Edition 1000QX 435-4	Keepsake	Yr.Iss.	10.00	45-75.00
84-102-010	Frosty Friends -5th Edition 800QX 437-1	Keepsake	Yr.Iss.	8.00	45-60.00
84-102-011	Norman Rockwell - 5th Edition750QX 341-1	Keepsake	Yr.Iss.	7.50	20-35.00
84-102-012	Here Comes Santa -6th Edition1300QX 438-4	Keepsake	Yr.Iss.	13.00	72.50
84-102-013	The Bellringer - 6th & Final Ed.1500QX 438-4	Keepsake	Yr.Iss.	15.00	45.00
84-102-014	Thimble - 7th Edition 500QX430-4	Keepsake	Yr.Iss.	5.00	30-44.00
84-102-015	Betsey Clark - 12th Edition500QX 249-4	Keepsake	Yr.Iss.	5.00	35.00
Hallmark Keepsake Ornaments	**1984 Keepsake Magic Ornaments**				
84-103-001	Village Church 1500QLX702-1	Keepsake	Yr.Iss.	15.00	50.00
84-103-002	Sugarplum Cottage 1100QLX701-1	Keepsake	Yr.Iss.	11.00	45-52.00
84-103-003	City Lights 1000QLX701-4	Keepsake	Yr.Iss.	10.00	45-50.00
84-103-004	Santa's Workshop 1300QLX700-4	Keepsake	Yr.Iss.	13.00	62.50
84-103-005	Santa's Arrival 1300QLX702-4	Keepsake	Yr.Iss.	13.00	65.00
84-103-006	Nativity 1200 QLX700-1	Keepsake	Yr.Iss.	12.00	28.00
84-103-007	Stained Glass 800QLX703-1	Keepsake	Yr.Iss.	8.00	19.50
84-103-008	Christmas in the Forest 800QLX703-4	Keepsake	Yr.Iss.	8.00	15-19.50
84-103-009	Brass Carrousel 900QLX707-1	Keepsake	Yr.Iss.	9.00	55-85.00
84-103-010	All Are Precious 800QLX704-1	Keepsake	Yr.Iss.	8.00	25.00
Hallmark Keepsake Ornaments	**1985 Commemoratives**				
85-104-001	Baby's First Christmas 1600QX499-5	Keepsake	Yr.Iss.	16.00	35-45.00
85-104-002	Baby's First Christmas 1500QX499-2	Keepsake	Yr.Iss.	15.00	35-45.00
85-104-003	Baby Locket 1600QX401-2	Keepsake	Yr.Iss.	16.00	35-38.00
85-104-004	Baby's First Christmas 575QX370-2	Keepsake	Yr.Iss.	5.75	17.50
85-104-005	Baby's First Christmas 700QX478-2	Keepsake	Yr.Iss.	7.00	14.50
85-104-006	Baby's First Christmas 500QX260-2	Keepsake	Yr.Iss.	5.00	15-27.00
85-104-007	Baby's Second Christmas 600QX478-5	Keepsake	Yr.Iss.	6.00	29.50
85-104-008	Child's Third Christmas 600QX475-5	Keepsake	Yr.Iss.	6.00	28-31.00
85-104-009	Grandchild's First Christmas500QX 260-5	Keepsake	Yr.Iss.	5.00	12.00
85-104-010	Grandchild's First Christmas1100QX 495-5	Keepsake	Yr.Iss.	11.00	24.00
85-104-011	Grandparents 700QX380-5	Keepsake	Yr.Iss.	7.00	10.00
85-104-012	Niece 575QX520-5	Keepsake	Yr.Iss.	5.75	10.50
85-104-013	Mother 675QX372-2	Keepsake	Yr.Iss.	6.75	10.00
85-104-014	Mother and Dad 775QX509-2	Keepsake	Yr.Iss.	7.75	18.50
85-104-015	Father 650QX376-2	Keepsake	Yr.Iss.	6.50	11-13.00
85-104-016	Sister 725QX506-5	Keepsake	Yr.Iss.	7.25	14.50
85-104-017	Daughter 550QX503-2	Keepsake	Yr.Iss.	5.50	12-15.00
85-104-018	Godchild 675QX380-2	Keepsake	Yr.Iss.	6.75	8-10.00
85-104-019	Son 550QX502-5	Keepsake	Yr.Iss.	5.50	42.50
85-104-020	Grandmother 475QX262-5	Keepsake	Yr.Iss.	4.75	15-23.00
85-104-021	Grandson 475QX262-2	Keepsake	Yr.Iss.	4.75	24.50
85-104-022	Granddaughter 475QX263-5	Keepsake	Yr.Iss.	4.75	11-25.00
85-104-023	First Christmas Together 1675QX400-5	Keepsake	Yr.Iss.	16.75	20-25.00
85-104-024	Love at Christmas 575QX371-5	Keepsake	Yr.Iss.	5.75	37.50
85-104-025	First Christmas Together 675QX370-5	Keepsake	Yr.Iss.	6.75	20-24.00
85-104-026	First Christmas Together 1300QX493-5	Keepsake	Yr.Iss.	13.00	25.00
85-104-027	Holiday Heart 800QX498-2	Keepsake	Yr.Iss.	8.00	25.00
85-104-028	First Christmas Together 800QX507-2	Keepsake	Yr.Iss.	8.00	13.00
85-104-029	Heart Full of Love 675QX378-2	Keepsake	Yr.Iss.	6.75	8-10.00
85-104-030	First Christmas Together 475QX261-2	Keepsake	Yr.Iss.	4.75	17.50
85-104-031	Twenty-Five Years Together800QX 500-5	Keepsake	Yr.Iss.	8.00	10-20.00
85-104-032	Friendship 775QX506-2	Keepsake	Yr.Iss.	7.75	10.00
85-104-033	Friendship 675QX378-5	Keepsake	Yr.Iss.	6.75	9.50
85-104-034	From Our House to Yours 775QX520-2	Keepsake	Yr.Iss.	7.75	11.00
85-104-035	Teacher 600QX505-2	Keepsake	Yr.Iss.	6.00	19.50
85-104-036	With Appreciation 675QX375-2	Keepsake	Yr.Iss.	6.75	9.50
85-104-037	Special Friends 575QX372-5	Keepsake	Yr.Iss.	5.75	10.00
85-104-038	New Home 475QX269-5	Keepsake	Yr.Iss.	4.75	25.00
85-104-039	Baby-sitter 475QX264-2	Keepsake	Yr.Iss.	4.75	10.00
85-104-040	Good Friends 475QX265-2	Keepsake	Yr.Iss.	4.75	22.50
Hallmark Keepsake Ornaments	**1985 Property Ornaments**				
85-105-001	Snoopy and Woodstock 750QX491-5	Keepsake	Yr.Iss.	7.50	49.00
85-105-002	Muffin the Angel 575QX483-5	Keepsake	Yr.Iss.	5.75	24.00
85-105-003	Kit the Shepherd 575QX484-5	Keepsake	Yr.Iss.	5.75	24.00
85-105-004	Betsey Clark 850QX508-5	Keepsake	Yr.Iss.	8.50	22.50
85-105-005	Hugga Bunch 500QX271-5	Keepsake	Yr.Iss.	5.00	19.50
85-105-006	Fraggle Rock Holiday 475QX265-5	Keepsake	Yr.Iss.	4.75	20.00
85-105-007	Peanuts 475QX266-5	Keepsake	Yr.Iss.	4.75	25.00
85-105-008	Norman Rockwell 475QX266-2	Keepsake	Yr.Iss.	4.75	20-23.00
85-105-009	Rainbow Brite and Friends 475QX 268-2	Keepsake	Yr.Iss.	4.75	20.00
85-105-010	A Disney Christmas 475QX271-2	Keepsake	Yr.Iss.	4.75	22.50
85-105-011	Merry Shirt Tales 475QX267-2	Keepsake	Yr.Iss.	4.75	19.00
Hallmark Keepsake Ornaments	**1985 Traditional Ornaments**				
85-106-001	Porcelain Bird 650QX479-5	Keepsake	Yr.Iss.	6.50	30-40.00
85-106-002	Sewn Photoholder 700QX379-5	Keepsake	Yr.Iss.	7.00	22.50
85-106-003	Candle Cameo 675QX374-2	Keepsake	Yr.Iss.	6.75	10-15.00
85-106-004	Santa Pipe 950QX494-2	Keepsake	Yr.Iss.	9.50	22.50
85-106-005	Old-Fashioned Wreath 750QX373-5	Keepsake	Yr.Iss.	7.50	19.50
85-106-006	Peaceful Kingdom 575QX373-2	Keepsake	Yr.Iss.	5.75	15-18.00
85-106-007	Christmas Treats 550QX507-5	Keepsake	Yr.Iss.	5.50	15-24.00
85-106-008	The Spirit of Santa Claus -Special Ed. 2250QX 498-5	Keepsake	Yr.Iss.	22.50	70-95.00
85-106-009	Nostalgic Sled 600QX442-4	Keepsake	Yr.Iss.	6.00	19.50
Hallmark Keepsake Ornaments	**1985 Holiday Humor**				
85-107-001	Night Before Christmas 1300QX449-4	Keepsake	Yr.Iss.	13.00	32-45.00
85-107-002	Nativity Scene 475QX264-5	Keepsake	Yr.Iss.	4.75	25.00
85-107-003	Santa's Ski Trip 1200QX496-2	Keepsake	Yr.Iss.	12.00	60.00
85-107-004	Mouse Wagon 575QX476-2	Keepsake	Yr.Iss.	5.75	50-57.00
85-107-005	Children in the Shoe 950QX490-5	Keepsake	Yr.Iss.	9.50	35-50.00
85-107-006	Do Not Disturb Bear 775QX481-2	Keepsake	Yr.Iss.	7.75	20-25.00
85-107-007	Sun and Fun Santa 775QX492-2	Keepsake	Yr.Iss.	7.75	35.00
85-107-008	Bottlecap Fun Bunnies 775QX481-5	Keepsake	Yr.Iss.	7.75	33-45.00
85-107-009	Lamb in Legwarmers 700QX480-2	Keepsake	Yr.Iss.	7.00	18-20.00
85-107-010	Candy Apple Mouse 750QX470-5	Keepsake	Yr.Iss.	6.50	40-62.00
85-107-011	Skateboard Raccoon 650QX473-2	Keepsake	Yr.Iss.	6.50	36.50
85-107-012	Stardust Angel 575QX475-2	Keepsake	Yr.Iss.	5.75	35-38.00
85-107-013	Soccer Beaver 650QX477-5	Keepsake	Yr.Iss.	6.50	24.50
85-107-014	Beary Smooth Ride 650QX480-5	Keepsake	Yr.Iss.	6.50	15-23.00
85-107-015	Swinging Angel Bell 1100QX492-5	Keepsake	Yr.Iss.	11.00	25-37.00
85-107-016	Doggy in a Stocking 550QX474-2	Keepsake	Yr.Iss.	5.50	30-37.00
85-107-017	Engineering Mouse 550QX473-5	Keepsake	Yr.Iss.	5.50	20-25.00
85-107-018	Kitty Mischief 500QX474-5	Keepsake	Yr.Iss.	5.00	20-25.00
85-107-019	Baker Elf 575QX491-2	Keepsake	Yr.Iss.	5.75	27-30.00
85-107-020	Ice-Skating Owl 500QX476-5	Keepsake	Yr.Iss.	5.00	25.00
85-107-021	Dapper Penguin 500QX477-2	Keepsake	Yr.Iss.	5.00	20-28.00
85-107-022	Trumpet Panda 450QX471-2	Keepsake	Yr.Iss.	4.50	22-30.00

Company / Number	Name	Series / Artist	Edition Limit	Issue Price	Quote
85-107-023	Merry Mouse 450QX403-2	Keepsake	Yr.Iss.	4.50	18-22.00
85-107-024	Snow-Pitching Snowman 450QX470-2	Keepsake	Yr.Iss.	4.50	20-32.00
85-107-025	Three Kittens in a Mitten 800QX431-1	Keepsake	Yr.Iss.	8.00	34.50
85-107-026	Roller Skating Rabbit 500QX457-1	Keepsake	Yr.Iss.	5.00	19.00
85-107-027	Snowy Seal 400QX450-1	Keepsake	Yr.Iss.	4.00	16.00
Hallmark Keepsake Ornaments		**1985 Country Christmas Collection**			
85-108-001	Old-Fashioned Doll 1450QX519-5	Keepsake	Yr.Iss.	14.50	30-35.00
85-108-002	Country Goose 775QX518-5	Keepsake	Yr.Iss.	7.75	15-23.00
85-108-003	Rocking Horse Memories1000QX518-2	Keepsake	Yr.Iss.	10.00	12.00
85-108-004	Whirligig Santa 1250QX519-2	Keepsake	Yr.Iss.	12.50	20-25.00
85-108-005	Sheep at Christmas 825QX517-5	Keepsake	Yr.Iss.	8.25	24-30.00
Hallmark Keepsake Ornaments		**1985 Heirloom Christmas Collection**			
85-109-001	Keepsake Basket 1500QX514-5	Keepsake	Yr.Iss.	15.00	19-24.00
85-109-002	Victorian Lady 950QX513-2	Keepsake	Yr.Iss.	9.50	20-25.00
85-109-003	Charming Angel 975QX512-5	Keepsake	Yr.Iss.	9.75	24.50
85-109-004	Lacy Heart 875QX511-2	Keepsake	Yr.Iss.	8.75	28-30.00
85-109-005	Snowflake 650QX510-5	Keepsake	Yr.Iss.	6.50	20-25.00
Hallmark Keepsake Ornaments		**1985 Limited Edition**			
85-110-001	Heavenly Trumpeter 2750QX405-2	Keepsake	Yr.Iss.	27.50	95-100.00
Hallmark Keepsake Ornaments		**1985 Collectible Series**			
85-111-001	Windows of the World-1st Ed.975QX490-2	Keepsake	Yr.Iss.	9.75	85-95.00
85-111-002	Miniature Creche-1st Ed.875QX482-5	Keepsake	Yr.Iss.	8.75	30-60.00
85-111-003	Nostalgic Houses and Shops-Second Ed.-1375QX497-5	Keepsake	Yr.Iss.	13.75	55-71.00
85-111-004	Art Masterpiece-2nd Ed.675QX377-2	Keepsake	Yr.Iss.	6.75	15.00
85-111-005	Wood Childhood Ornaments-2nd Ed. 700QX472-2	Keepsake	Yr.Iss.	7.00	31-45.00
85-111-006	Twelve Days of Christmas-2nd Ed. 650QX371-2	Keepsake	Yr.Iss.	6.50	40-50.00
85-111-007	Porcelain Bear-3rd Ed.750QX479-2	Keepsake	Yr.Iss.	7.50	31-46.00
85-111-008	Tin Locomotive-4th Ed.1475QX497-2	Keepsake	Yr.Iss.	14.75	45-65.00
85-111-009	Holiday Wildlife-4th Ed.750QX376-5	Keepsake	Yr.Iss.	7.50	25-35.00
85-111-010	Clothespin Soldier-4th Ed.550QX471-5	Keepsake	Yr.Iss.	5.50	22-24.50
85-111-011	Rocking Horse-5th Ed.1075QX493-2	Keepsake	Yr.Iss.	10.75	40-60.00
85-111-012	Norman Rockwell-6th Ed.750QX374-5	Keepsake	Yr.Iss.	7.50	28-30.00
85-111-013	Here Comes Santa-6th Ed.1400QX496-5	Keepsake	Yr.Iss.	14.00	40-53.00
85-111-014	Frosty Friends-6th Ed.850QX482-2	Keepsake	Yr.Iss.	8.50	41-55.00
85-111-015	Betsey Clark-13th & final Ed.500QX263-2	Keepsake	Yr.Iss.	5.00	28-30.00
85-111-016	Thimble-8th Ed.550QX472-5	Keepsake	Yr.Iss.	5.50	30-37.00
Hallmark Keepsake Ornaments		**1985 Keepsake Magic Ornaments**			
85-112-001	Baby's First Christmas 1650QLX700-5	Keepsake	Yr.Iss.	16.50	40.00
85-112-002	Katybeth 1075QLX710-2	Keepsake	Yr.Iss.	10.75	42.50-47.50
85-112-003	Chris Mouse-1st edition1250QLX703-2	Keepsake	Yr.Iss.	12.50	55-85.00
85-112-004	Swiss Cheese Lane 1300QLX706-5	Keepsake	Yr.Iss.	13.00	45-78.00
85-112-005	Mr. and Mrs. Santa 1450QLX705-2	Keepsake	Yr.Iss.	14.50	85.00
85-112-006	Little Red Schoolhouse 1575QLX711-2	Keepsake	Yr.Iss.	15.75	85-95.00
85-112-007	Love Wreath 850QLX702-5	Keepsake	Yr.Iss.	8.50	30.00
85-112-008	Christmas Eve Visit 1200QLX710-5	Keepsake	Yr.Iss.	12.00	22-27.50
85-112-009	Season of Beauty 800QLX712-2	Keepsake	Yr.Iss.	8.00	20-30.00
Hallmark Keepsake Ornaments		**1986 Commemoratives**			
86-113-001	Baby's First Christmas 900QX412-6	Keepsake	Yr.Iss.	9.00	35-38.00
86-113-002	Baby's First Christmas Photoholder 800QX379-2	Keepsake	Yr.Iss.	8.00	22.50
86-113-003	Baby's First Christmas 600QX380-3	Keepsake	Yr.Iss.	6.00	20-25.00
86-113-004	Baby's First Christmas 550QX271-3	Keepsake	Yr.Iss.	5.50	27.00
86-113-005	Grandchild's First Christmas1000QX411-6	Keepsake	Yr.Iss.	10.00	16.00
86-113-006	Baby's Second Christmas 650QX413-3	Keepsake	Yr.Iss.	6.50	27.50
86-113-007	Child's Third Christmas 650QX413-6	Keepsake	Yr.Iss.	6.50	9-20.00
86-113-008	Baby Locket 1600QX412-3	Keepsake	Yr.Iss.	16.00	24.50
86-113-009	Husband 800QX383-6	Keepsake	Yr.Iss.	8.00	15.00
86-113-010	Sister 675QX380-6	Keepsake	Yr.Iss.	6.75	15.00
86-113-011	Mother and Dad 750QX431-6	Keepsake	Yr.Iss.	7.50	17.50
86-113-012	Mother 700QX382-6	Keepsake	Yr.Iss.	7.00	15.00
86-113-013	Father 650QX431-3	Keepsake	Yr.Iss.	6.50	13.00
86-113-014	Daughter 575QX430-6	Keepsake	Yr.Iss.	5.75	25-30.00
86-113-015	Son 575QX430-3	Keepsake	Yr.Iss.	5.75	20-28.00
86-113-016	Niece 600QX426-6	Keepsake	Yr.Iss.	6.00	10.00
86-113-017	Nephew 675QX381-3	Keepsake	Yr.Iss.	6.25	12.50
86-113-018	Grandmother 475QX274-3	Keepsake	Yr.Iss.	4.75	18.00
86-113-019	Grandparents 750QX432-3	Keepsake	Yr.Iss.	7.50	17.00
86-113-020	Granddaughter 475QX273-6	Keepsake	Yr.Iss.	4.75	22.50
86-113-021	Grandson 475QX273-3	Keepsake	Yr.Iss.	4.75	20.00
86-113-022	Godchild 475QX271-6	Keepsake	Yr.Iss.	4.75	10-14.50
86-113-023	First Christmas Together 1600QX400-3	Keepsake	Yr.Iss.	16.00	27.50
86-113-024	First Christmas Together 1200QX409-6	Keepsake	Yr.Iss.	12.00	20-24.00
86-113-025	First Christmas Together 7000QX379-3	Keepsake	Yr.Iss.	7.00	15-20.00
86-113-026	First Christmas Together 475QX270-3	Keepsake	Yr.Iss.	4.75	16-20.00
86-113-027	Ten Years Together 750QX401-3	Keepsake	Yr.Iss.	7.50	24.50
86-113-028	Twenty-Five Years Together800QX410-3	Keepsake	Yr.Iss.	8.00	24.50
86-113-029	Fifty Years Together 1000QX400-6	Keepsake	Yr.Iss.	10.00	18.00
86-113-030	Loving Memories 900QX409-3	Keepsake	Yr.Iss.	9.00	13-34.50
86-113-031	Timeless Love 600QX379-6	Keepsake	Yr.Iss.	6.00	24.50
86-113-032	Sweetheart 1100QX408-6	Keepsake	Yr.Iss.	11.00	39.50
86-113-033	Season of the Heart 4750QX270-6	Keepsake	Yr.Iss.	4.75	12.50
86-113-034	Friendship Greeting 800QX427-3	Keepsake	Yr.Iss.	8.00	15.00
86-113-035	Joy of Friends 675QX382-3	Keepsake	Yr.Iss.	6.75	12.50
86-113-036	Friendship's Gift 600QX381-6	Keepsake	Yr.Iss.	6.00	12.00
86-113-037	From Our Home to Yours 600QX383-3	Keepsake	Yr.Iss.	6.00	12.00
86-113-038	Gratitude 600QX432-6	Keepsake	Yr.Iss.	6.00	9.50
86-113-039	Friends Are Fun 475QX272-3	Keepsake	Yr.Iss.	4.75	30.00
86-113-040	New Home 475QX274-6	Keepsake	Yr.Iss.	4.75	22.50
86-113-041	Teacher 475QX275-3	Keepsake	Yr.Iss.	4.75	12.00
86-113-042	Baby-Sitter 475QX275-6	Keepsake	Yr.Iss.	4.75	10.00
Hallmark Keepsake Ornaments		**1986 Property Ornaments**			
86-114-001	The Statue of Liberty 600QX384-3	Keepsake	Yr.Iss.	6.00	15-33.00
86-114-002	Snoopy and Woodstock 800QX434-6	Keepsake	Yr.Iss.	8.00	30-38.00
86-114-003	Heathcliff 750QX436-3	Keepsake	Yr.Iss.	7.50	28-31.00
86-114-004	Katybeth 700QX435-3	Keepsake	Yr.Iss.	7.00	22.50
86-114-005	Paddington Bear 600QX435-6	Keepsake	Yr.Iss.	6.00	35-40.00
86-114-006	Norman Rockwell 475QX276-3	Keepsake	Yr.Iss.	4.75	24.50
86-114-007	Peanuts 475QX276-6	Keepsake	Yr.Iss.	4.75	24.50
86-114-008	Shirt Tales Parade 475QX277-3	Keepsake	Yr.Iss.	4.75	14.50
Hallmark Keepsake Ornaments		**1986 Holiday Humor**			
86-115-001	Santa's Hot Tub 1200QX426-3	Keepsake	Yr.Iss.	12.00	39.75
86-115-002	Playful Possum 1100QX425-3	Keepsake	Yr.Iss.	11.00	35.00
86-115-003	Treetop Trio 975QX424-6	Keepsake	Yr.Iss.	11.00	29.50
86-115-004	Wynken, Blynken and Nod 975QX424-6	Keepsake	Yr.Iss.	9.75	30-43.00
86-115-005	Acorn Inn 850QX424-3	Keepsake	Yr.Iss.	8.50	23-30.00
86-115-006	Touchdown Santa 800QX423-3	Keepsake	Yr.Iss.	8.00	40-43.00
86-115-007	Snow Buddies 800QX423-6	Keepsake	Yr.Iss.	8.00	32.50
86-115-008	Open Me First 725QX422-6	Keepsake	Yr.Iss.	7.25	25-30.00
86-115-009	Rah Rah Rabbit 700QX421-6	Keepsake	Yr.Iss.	7.00	39.50
86-115-010	Tipping the Scales 675QX418-6	Keepsake	Yr.Iss.	6.75	20-27.50
86-115-011	Li'l Jingler 675QX419-3	Keepsake	Yr.Iss.	6.75	26-35.50
86-115-012	Ski Tripper 675QX420-6	Keepsake	Yr.Iss.	6.75	23-27.00
86-115-013	Popcorn Mouse 675QX421-3	Keepsake	Yr.Iss.	6.75	28-47.00
86-115-014	Puppy's Best Friend 650QX420-3	Keepsake	Yr.Iss.	6.50	27.50
86-115-015	Happy Christmas to Owl 600QX418-3	Keepsake	Yr.Iss.	6.00	18-25.00
86-115-016	Walnut Shell Rider 600QX419-6	Keepsake	Yr.Iss.	6.00	24.00
86-115-017	Heavenly Dreamer 575QX417-3	Keepsake	Yr.Iss.	5.75	32-35.00
86-115-018	Mouse in the Moon 550QX416-6	Keepsake	Yr.Iss.	5.50	20-28.00
86-115-019	Merry Koala 500QX415-3	Keepsake	Yr.Iss.	5.00	22.50
86-115-020	Chatty Penguin 575QX417-6	Keepsake	Yr.Iss.	5.75	19.00
86-115-021	Special Delivery 500QX415-6	Keepsake	Yr.Iss.	5.00	24.50
86-115-022	Jolly Hiker 500QX483-2	Keepsake	Yr.Iss.	5.00	20-30.00
86-115-023	Cookies for Santa 450QX414-6	Keepsake	Yr.Iss.	4.50	15-25.00
86-115-024	Merry Mouse 450QX403-2	Keepsake	Yr.Iss.	4.50	22.00
86-115-025	Skateboard Raccoon 650QX473-2	Keepsake	Yr.Iss.	6.50	39.50
86-115-026	Beary Smooth Ride 650QX480-5	Keepsake	Yr.Iss.	6.50	19.50
86-115-027	Snow-Pitching Snowman 450QX470-2	Keepsake	Yr.Iss.	4.50	22.50
86-115-028	Kitty Mischief 500QX474-5	Keepsake	Yr.Iss.	5.00	24.50
86-115-029	Soccer Beaver 650QX477-5	Keepsake	Yr.Iss.	6.50	24.50
86-115-030	Do Not Disturb Bear 775QX481-2	Keepsake	Yr.Iss.	7.75	24.50
Hallmark Keepsake Ornaments		**1986 Special Edition**			
86-116-001	Jolly St. Nick 2250QX429-6	Keepsake	Yr.Iss.	22.50	55-73.00
Hallmark Keepsake Ornaments		**1986 Limited Edition**			
86-117-001	Magical Unicorn 2750QX429-3	Keepsake	Yr.Iss.	27.50	125-135.
Hallmark Keepsake Ornaments		**1986 Christmas Medley Collection**			
86-118-001	Joyful Carolers 975QX513-6	Keepsake	Yr.Iss.	9.75	30-40.00
86-118-002	Festive Treble Clef 875QX513-3	Keepsake	Yr.Iss.	8.75	27.50
86-118-003	Favorite Tin Drum 850QX514-3	Keepsake	Yr.Iss.	8.50	30.00
86-118-004	Christmas Guitar 700QX512-6	Keepsake	Yr.Iss.	7.00	18-25.00
86-118-005	Holiday Horn 800QX514-6	Keepsake	Yr.Iss.	8.00	29.50
Hallmark Keepsake Ornaments		**1986 Country Treasures Collection**			
86-119-001	Country Sleigh 1000QX511-3	Keepsake	Yr.Iss.	10.00	23-30.00
86-119-002	Remembering Christmas 865QX510-6	Keepsake	Yr.Iss.	8.75	25-30.00
86-119-003	Little Drummers 1250QX511-6	Keepsake	Yr.Iss.	12.50	28-35.00
86-119-004	Nutcracker Santa 1000QX512-3	Keepsake	Yr.Iss.	10.00	38-45.00
86-119-005	Welcome, Christmas 825QX510-3	Keepsake	Yr.Iss.	8.25	30-35.00
Hallmark Keepsake Ornaments		**1986 Traditional Ornaments**			
86-120-001	Holiday Jingle Bell 1600QX404-6	Keepsake	Yr.Iss.	16.00	35-45.00
86-120-002	Memories to Cherish 750QX427-6	Keepsake	Yr.Iss.	7.50	24.50
86-120-003	Bluebird 725QX428-3	Keepsake	Yr.Iss.	7.25	49.50
86-120-004	Glowing Christmas Tree 700QX428-6	Keepsake	Yr.Iss.	7.00	12.75
86-120-005	Heirloom Snowflake 675QX515-3	Keepsake	Yr.Iss.	6.75	19-22.00
86-120-006	Christmas Beauty 600QX322-3	Keepsake	Yr.Iss.	6.00	10.00
86-120-007	Star Brighteners 600QX322-6	Keepsake	Yr.Iss.	6.00	16.50
86-120-008	The Magi 475QX272-6	Keepsake	Yr.Iss.	4.75	12.75
86-120-009	Mary Emmerling: American Country Collection 795QX275-2	Keepsake	Yr.Iss.	7.95	25.00
Hallmark Keepsake Ornaments		**1986 Collectible Series**			
86-121-001	Mr. and Mrs. Claus-1st Edition1300QX402-6	Keepsake	Yr.Iss.	13.00	80-85.00
86-121-002	Reindeer Champs-1st Edition750QX422-3	Keepsake	Yr.Iss.	7.50	100-125.
86-121-003	Betsey Clark: Home for Christmas-1st Edition 500QX277-6	Keepsake	Yr.Iss.	5.00	25-35.00
86-121-004	Windows of the World-2nd Ed.1000QX408-3	Keepsake	Yr.Iss.	10.00	40-50.00
86-121-005	Miniature Creche-2nd Edition900QX407-6	Keepsake	Yr.Iss.	9.00	48-60.00
86-121-006	Nostalgic Houses and Shops-3rd Edition 1375QX403-3	Keepsake	Yr.Iss.	13.75	125-200.
86-121-007	Wood Childhood Ornaments-3rd Edition 750QX407-3	Keepsake	Yr.Iss.	7.50	29.50
86-121-008	Twelve Days of Christmas-3rd Edition 650QX378-6	Keepsake	Yr.Iss.	6.50	47-50.00
86-121-009	Art Masterpiece-3rd & Final Ed. 675QX350-6	Keepsake	Yr.Iss.	6.75	13-24.50
86-121-010	Porcelain Bear-4th Edition 775QX405-6	Keepsake	Yr.Iss.	7.75	25-41.00
86-121-011	Tin Locomotive-5th Edition 1475QX403-6	Keepsake	Yr.Iss.	14.75	60-75.00
86-121-012	Holiday Wildlife-5th Edition 750QX321-6	Keepsake	Yr.Iss.	7.50	25-30.00
86-121-013	Clothespin Soldier-5th Edition 550QX406-3	Keepsake	Yr.Iss.	5.50	23-29.50
86-121-014	Rocking Horse-6th Edition 1075QX401-6	Keepsake	Yr.Iss.	10.75	40-53.00
86-121-015	Norman Rockwell-7th Edition 775QX321-3	Keepsake	Yr.Iss.	7.75	18-26.00
86-121-016	Frosty Friends-7th Edition 850QX405-3	Keepsake	Yr.Iss.	8.50	30-60.00
86-121-017	Here Comes Santa-8th Edition 1400QX404-3	Keepsake	Yr.Iss.	14.00	54.50
86-121-018	Thimble-9th Edition 575QX406-6	Keepsake	Yr.Iss.	5.75	20-33.00
Hallmark Keepsake Ornaments		**1986 Lighted Ornament Collection**			
86-122-001	Baby's First Christmas1950QLX710-3	Keepsake	Yr.Iss.	19.50	35-50.00
86-122-002	First Christmas Together2200QLX707-3	Keepsake	Yr.Iss.	14.00	39.50
86-122-003	Santa and Sparky-1st Edition2200QLX703-3	Keepsake	Yr.Iss.	22.00	75-125.00
86-122-004	Christmas Classics-1st Edition1750QLX704-3	Keepsake	Yr.Iss.	17.50	60-85.00
86-122-005	Chris Mouse-2nd Edition1300QLX705-6	Keepsake	Yr.Iss.	13.00	50-70.00
86-122-006	Village Express 2450QLX707-2	Keepsake	Yr.Iss.	24.50	95-110.00
86-122-007	Christmas Sleigh Ride 2450QLX701-2	Keepsake	Yr.Iss.	24.50	115.00
86-122-008	Santa's On His Way 1500QLX711-5	Keepsake	Yr.Iss.	15.00	69.50
86-122-009	General Store 1575QLX705-3	Keepsake	Yr.Iss.	15.75	58-60.00
86-122-010	Gentle Blessings 1500QLX708-3	Keepsake	Yr.Iss.	15.00	150-175.
86-122-011	Keep on Glowin' 1000QLX707-6	Keepsake	Yr.Iss.	10.00	49.50
86-122-012	Santa's Snack 1000QLX706-6	Keepsake	Yr.Iss.	10.00	45-56.00
86-122-013	Merry Christmas Bell 850QLX709-3	Keepsake	Yr.Iss.	8.50	25.00
86-122-014	Sharing Friendship 850QLX706-3	Keepsake	Yr.Iss.	8.50	22-25.00
86-122-015	Mr. and Mrs. Santa 1450QLX705-2	Keepsake	Yr.Iss.	14.50	95.00
86-122-016	Sugarplum Cottage 1100QLX701-1	Keepsake	Yr.Iss.	11.00	45.00
Hallmark Keepsake Ornaments		**1987 Commermoratives**			
87-123-001	Baby's First Christmas 975QX411-3	Keepsake	Yr.Iss.	9.75	25.00
87-123-002	Baby's First Christmas Photoholder 750QX4661-9	Keepsake	Yr.Iss.	7.50	29.50
87-123-003	Baby's First Christmas 600QX372-9	Keepsake	Yr.Iss.	6.00	15-17.00
87-123-004	Baby's First Christmas-Baby Girl 475QX274-7	Keepsake	Yr.Iss.	4.75	20.00
87-123-005	Baby's First Christmas-Baby Boy475QX274-9	Keepsake	Yr.Iss.	4.75	20-25.00
87-123-006	Grandchild's First Christmas900QX460-9	Keepsake	Yr.Iss.	9.00	24.50
87-123-007	Baby's Second Christmas 575QX460-7	Keepsake	Yr.Iss.	5.75	20-30.00

Company / Number	Name	Series / Artist	Edition Limit	Issue Price	Quote
87-123-008	Child's Third Christmas 575QX459-9	Keepsake	Yr.Iss.	5.75	25-28.00
87-123-009	Baby Locket 1500QX461-7	Keepsake	Yr.Iss.	15.00	29.50
87-123-010	Mother and Dad 700QX462-7	Keepsake	Yr.Iss.	7.00	18.00
87-123-011	Mother 650QX373-7	Keepsake	Yr.Iss.	6.50	15.00
87-123-012	Dad 600QX462-9	Keepsake	Yr.Iss.	6.00	40-46.00
87-123-013	Husband 700QX373-9	Keepsake	Yr.Iss.	7.00	12.00
87-123-014	Sister 600QX474-7	Keepsake	Yr.Iss.	6.00	15.00
87-123-015	Daughter 575QX463-7	Keepsake	Yr.Iss.	5.75	18-39.00
87-123-016	Son 575QX463-9	Keepsake	Yr.Iss.	5.75	19.50
87-123-017	Niece 475QX275-9	Keepsake	Yr.Iss.	4.75	12.50
87-123-018	Grandmother 475QX277-9	Keepsake	Yr.Iss.	4.75	12.50
87-123-019	Grandparents 475QX277-7	Keepsake	Yr.Iss.	4.75	15-17.50
87-123-020	Grandson 475QX276-9	Keepsake	Yr.Iss.	4.75	15.00
87-123-021	Granddaughter 600QX374-7	Keepsake	Yr.Iss.	6.00	7-15.00
87-123-022	Godchild 475QX276-7	Keepsake	Yr.Iss.	4.75	10-15.00
87-123-023	First Christmas Together 1500QX446-9	Keepsake	Yr.Iss.	15.00	20-30.00
87-123-024	First Christmas Together 950QX446-7	Keepsake	Yr.Iss.	9.50	25-30.00
87-123-025	First Christmas Together 800QX445-9	Keepsake	Yr.Iss.	8.00	21-27.50
87-123-026	First Christmas Together 650QX371-9	Keepsake	Yr.Iss.	6.50	15.50
87-123-027	First Christmas Together 475QX272-9	Keepsake	Yr.Iss.	4.75	15-25.00
87-123-028	Ten Years Together 700QX444-7	Keepsake	Yr.Iss.	7.00	24.50
87-123-029	Twenty-Five Years Together750QX443-9	Keepsake	Yr.Iss.	7.50	24.50
87-123-030	Fifty Years Together 800QX443-7	Keepsake	Yr.Iss.	8.00	22.50
87-123-031	Word of Love 800QX447-7	Keepsake	Yr.Iss.	8.00	20-30.00
87-123-032	Heart in Blossom 600QX372-7	Keepsake	Yr.Iss.	6.00	24.50
87-123-033	Sweetheart 1100QX447-9	Keepsake	Yr.Iss.	11.00	25-30.00
87-123-034	Love is Everywhere 475QX278-7	Keepsake	Yr.Iss.	4.75	19.50
87-123-035	Holiday Greetings 600QX375-7	Keepsake	Yr.Iss.	6.00	12.75
87-123-036	Warmth of Friendship 600QX375-9	Keepsake	Yr.Iss.	6.00	12.00
87-123-037	Time for Friends 475QX280-7	Keepsake	Yr.Iss.	4.75	17.00
87-123-038	From Our Home to Yours 475QX279-9	Keepsake	Yr.Iss.	4.75	12.00
87-123-039	New Home 600QX376-7	Keepsake	Yr.Iss.	6.00	29.50
87-123-040	Babysitter 475QX279-7	Keepsake	Yr.Iss.	4.75	12.00
87-123-041	Teacher 575QX466-7	Keepsake	Yr.Iss.	5.75	19.50
Hallmark Keepsake Ornaments		**1987 Holiday Humor**			
87-124-001	Snoopy and Woodstock 725QX472-9	Keepsake	Yr.Iss.	7.25	20-38.00
87-124-002	Bright Christmas Dreams 725QX440-7	Keepsake	Yr.Iss.	7.25	45-70.00
87-124-003	Joy Ride 1150QX440-7	Keepsake	Yr.Iss.	11.50	38-50.00
87-124-004	Pretty Kitten 1100QX448-9	Keepsake	Yr.Iss.	11.00	34.50
87-124-005	Santa at the Bat 775QX457-9	Keepsake	Yr.Iss.	7.75	16-30.00
87-124-006	Jogging Through the Snow725QX457-7	Keepsake	Yr.Iss.	7.25	29.50
87-124-007	Jack Frosting 700QX449-9	Keepsake	Yr.Iss.	7.00	36.50
87-124-008	Raccoon Biker 700QX458-7	Keepsake	Yr.Iss.	7.00	25.00
87-124-009	Treetop Dreams 675QX459-7	Keepsake	Yr.Iss.	6.75	15-25.00
87-124-010	Night Before Christmas 650QX451-7	Keepsake	Yr.Iss.	6.50	22-33.00
87-124-011	"Owliday" Wish 650QX455-9	Keepsake	Yr.Iss.	6.50	20-25.00
87-124-012	Let It Snow 650QX458-9	Keepsake	Yr.Iss.	6.50	22.00
87-124-013	Hot Dogger 650QX471-9	Keepsake	Yr.Iss.	6.50	24.00
87-124-014	Spots 'n Stripes 550QX452-9	Keepsake	Yr.Iss.	5.50	20-27.00
87-124-015	Seasoned Greetings 625QX454-9	Keepsake	Yr.Iss.	6.25	10-25.00
87-124-016	Chocolate Chipmunk 600QX456-7	Keepsake	Yr.Iss.	6.00	35-40.00
87-124-017	Fudge Forever 500QX449-7	Keepsake	Yr.Iss.	5.00	30-35.00
87-124-018	Sleepy Santa 625QX450-7	Keepsake	Yr.Iss.	6.25	30-33.00
87-124-019	Reindoggy 575QX452-7	Keepsake	Yr.Iss.	5.75	25-30.00
87-124-020	Christmas Cuddle 575QX453-7	Keepsake	Yr.Iss.	5.75	25-35.00
87-124-021	Paddington Bear 550QX472-7	Keepsake	Yr.Iss.	5.50	30-35.00
87-124-022	Nature's Decorations 475QX273-9	Keepsake	Yr.Iss.	4.75	25-33.00
87-124-023	Dr. Seuss: The Grinch's Christmas 475QX278-3	Keepsake	Yr.Iss.	4.75	30.00
87-124-024	Jammie Pies 475QX283-9	Keepsake	Yr.Iss.	4.75	14.50
87-124-025	Peanuts 475QX281-9	Keepsake	Yr.Iss.	4.75	29.50
87-124-026	Happy Santa 475QX456-9	Keepsake	Yr.Iss.	4.75	29.50
87-124-027	Icy Treat 450QX450-9	Keepsake	Yr.Iss.	4.50	20-25.00
87-124-028	Mouse in the Moon 550QX416-6	Keepsake	Yr.Iss.	5.50	21.00
87-124-029	L'il Jingler 675QX419-3	Keepsake	Yr.Iss.	6.75	27.50
87-124-030	Walnut Shell Rider 600QX419-6	Keepsake	Yr.Iss.	6.00	18.00
87-124-031	Treetop Trio 1100QX425-6	Keepsake	Yr.Iss.	11.00	29.50
87-124-032	Jolly Hiker 500QX483-2	Keepsake	Yr.Iss.	5.00	17.50
87-124-033	Merry Koala 500QX415-3	Keepsake	Yr.Iss.	5.00	15-17.00
Hallmark Keepsake Ornaments		**1987 Old-Fashioned Christmas Collection**			
87-125-001	Nostalgic Rocker 650QX468-9	Keepsake	Yr.Iss.	6.50	29.50
87-125-002	Little Whittler 600QX469-9	Keepsake	Yr.Iss.	6.00	25-33.00
87-125-003	Country Wreath 575QX470-9	Keepsake	Yr.Iss.	5.75	29.50
87-125-004	In a Nutshell 550QX469-7	Keepsake	Yr.Iss.	5.50	32.50
87-125-005	Folk Art Santa 525QX474-9	Keepsake	Yr.Iss.	5.25	25-33.00
Hallmark Keepsake Ornaments		**1987 Christmas Pizzazz Collection**			
87-126-001	Doc Holiday 800QX467-7	Keepsake	Yr.Iss.	8.00	30-46.00
87-126-002	Christmas Fun Puzzle 800QX467-9	Keepsake	Yr.Iss.	8.00	24.50
87-126-003	Jolly Follies 850QX466-9	Keepsake	Yr.Iss.	8.50	20-30.00
87-126-004	St. Louie Nick 775QX453-9	Keepsake	Yr.Iss.	7.75	24.50
87-126-005	Holiday Hourglass 800QX470-7	Keepsake	Yr.Iss.	8.00	20-23.00
87-126-006	Mistletoad 700QX468-7	Keepsake	Yr.Iss.	7.00	25-30.00
87-126-007	Happy Holidata 650QX471-7	Keepsake	Yr.Iss.	6.50	29.50
Hallmark Keepsake Ornaments		**1987 Traditional Ornaments**			
87-127-001	Goldfinch 700QX464-9	Keepsake	Yr.Iss.	7.00	65-80.00
87-127-002	Heavenly Harmony 1500QX465-9	Keepsake	Yr.Iss.	15.00	33-35.00
87-127-003	Special Memories Photoholder675QX 464-7	Keepsake	Yr.Iss.	6.75	22.50
87-127-004	Joyous Angels 775QX465-7	Keepsake	Yr.Iss.	7.75	25-30.00
87-127-005	Promise of Peace 650QX374-9	Keepsake	Yr.Iss.	6.50	24.50
87-127-006	Christmas Keys 575QX473-9	Keepsake	Yr.Iss.	5.75	29.50
87-127-007	I Remember Santa 475QX278-9	Keepsake	Yr.Iss.	4.75	22-25.00
87-127-008	Norman Rockwell: Christmas Scenes 475QX282-7	Keepsake	Yr.Iss.	4.75	23-25.00
87-127-009	Currier & Ives: American Farm Scene 475QX282-9	Keepsake	Yr.Iss.	4.75	15-22.50
Hallmark Keepsake Ornaments		**1987 Limited Edition**			
87-128-001	Christmas Time Mime 2750QX442-9	Keepsake	Yr.Iss.	27.50	40-60.00
87-128-002	Christmas is Gentle 1750QX444-9	Keepsake	Yr.Iss.	17.50	40-75.00
Hallmark Keepsake Ornaments		**1987 Special Edition**			
87-129-001	Favorite Santa 2250QX445-7	Keepsake	Yr.Iss.	22.50	45-47.00
Hallmark Keepsake Ornaments		**1987 Artists' Favorites**			
87-130-001	Three Men in a Tub 800QX454-7	Keepsake	Yr.Iss.	8.00	20-30.00
87-130-002	Wee Chimney Sweep 625QX451-9	Keepsake	Yr.Iss.	6.25	25-30.00
87-130-003	December Showers 550QX448-7	Keepsake	Yr.Iss.	5.50	30-35.00
87-130-004	Beary Special 475QX455-7	Keepsake	Yr.Iss.	4.75	28.00

Company / Number	Name	Series / Artist	Edition Limit	Issue Price	Quote
Hallmark Keepsake Ornaments		**1987 Collectible Series**			
87-131-001	Holiday Heirloom-1st Ed./limited ed. 2500QX485-7	Keepsake	Yr.Iss.	25.00	35-50.00
87-131-002	Collector's Plate-1st Edition 800QX481-7	Keepsake	Yr.Iss.	8.00	50-78.00
87-131-003	Mr. and Mrs. Claus-2nd Edition 2nd Edition 132QX483-7	Keepsake	Yr.Iss.	13.25	35-53.00
87-131-004	Reindeer Champs-2nd Edition 750QX480-9	Keepsake	Yr.Iss.	7.50	30-48.00
87-131-005	Betsey Clark: Home for Christmas-2nd edition 500QX272-7	Keepsake	Yr.Iss.	5.00	15-25.00
87-131-006	Windows of the World-3rd Edition 1000QX482-7	Keepsake	Yr.Iss.	10.00	20-46.00
87-131-007	Miniature Creche -3rd Edition 900QX481-9	Keepsake	Yr.Iss.	9.00	32-35.00
87-131-008	Nostalgic Houses and Shops-4th Edition 483QX483-9	Keepsake	Yr.Iss.	14.00	55-65.00
87-131-009	Twelve Days of Christmas-4th Edition 650QX370-9	Keepsake	Yr.Iss.	6.50	25-38.00
87-131-010	Wood Childhood Ornaments-4th Edition 750QX441-7	Keepsake	Yr.Iss.	7.50	24.50
87-131-011	Porcelain Bear-5th Edition 775QX442-7	Keepsake	Yr.Iss.	7.75	30-35.00
87-131-012	Tin Locomotive-6th Edition 1475QX484-9	Keepsake	Yr.Iss.	14.75	57-63.00
87-131-013	Holiday Wildlife -6th Edition 750QX371-7	Keepsake	Yr.Iss.	7.50	23-30.00
87-131-014	Clothespin Soldier-6th & Final Ed. 550QX480-7	Keepsake	Yr.Iss.	5.50	25-30.00
87-131-015	Frosty Friends -8th Edition 850QX440-9	Keepsake	Yr.Iss.	8.50	40-55.00
87-131-016	Rocking Horse-7th Edition1075QX482-9	Keepsake	Yr.Iss.	10.75	45-53.00
87-131-017	Norman Rockwell-8th Edition775QX370-7	Keepsake	Yr.Iss.	7.75	15-30.00
87-131-018	Here Comes Santa-9th Edition 1400QX484-7	Keepsake	Yr.Iss.	14.00	45-53.00
87-131-019	Thimble-10th Edition 575QX441-9	Keepsake	Yr.Iss.	5.75	29.50
Hallmark Keepsake Ornaments		**1987 Keepsake Magic Ornaments**			
87-132-001	Baby's First Christmas 1350QLX704-9	Keepsake	Yr.Iss.	13.50	30-41.00
87-132-002	First Christmas Together 1150QLX708-7	Keepsake	Yr.Iss.	11.50	42.50
87-132-003	Santa and Sparky-2nd Edition1950QLX701-9	Keepsake	Yr.Iss.	19.50	75.00
87-132-004	Christmas Classics-2nd Ed.1600ZLX702-9	Keepsake	Yr.Iss.	16.00	75.00
87-132-005	Chris Mouse-3rd Edition1100QLX705-7	Keepsake	Yr.Iss.	11.00	40-53.00
87-132-006	Christmas Morning 2450QLX701-3	Keepsake	Yr.Iss.	24.50	40-50.00
87-132-007	Loving Holiday 2200QLX701-6	Keepsake	Yr.Iss.	22.00	52.50
87-132-008	Angelic Messengers 1875QLX711-3	Keepsake	Yr.Iss.	18.75	45-68.00
87-132-009	Good Cheer Blimp 1600QLX704-6	Keepsake	Yr.Iss.	16.00	49-51.00
87-132-010	Train Station 1275QLX703-9	Keepsake	Yr.Iss.	12.75	50-60.00
87-132-011	Keeping Cozy 1175QLX704-7	Keepsake	Yr.Iss.	11.75	34.50
87-132-012	Lacy Brass Snowflake 1150QLX709-7	Keepsake	Yr.Iss.	11.50	25.00
87-132-013	Meowy Christmas I 1000QLX708-9	Keepsake	Yr.Iss.	10.00	62.50
87-132-014	Memories are Forever Photoholder 850QLX706-7	Keepsake	Yr.Iss.	8.50	27.50
87-132-015	Season for Friendship 850QLX706-9	Keepsake	Yr.Iss.	8.50	19.50
87-132-016	Bright Noel 700QLX705-9	Keepsake	Yr.Iss.	7.00	29.50
Hallmark Keepsake Ornaments		**1987 Keepsake Collector's Club**			
87-133-001	Wreath of Memories QXC580-9	Keepsake	Yr.Iss.	Unkn.	58-75.00
87-133-002	Carrousel Reindeer QXC580-7	Keepsake	Yr.Iss.	Unkn.	65-85.00
Hallmark Keepsake Ornaments		**1988 Commemoratives**			
88-134-001	Baby's First Christmas 975QX470-1	Keepsake	Yr.Iss.	9.75	24.50
88-134-002	Baby's First Christmas 750QX470-4	Keepsake	Yr.Iss.	7.50	20.00
88-134-003	Baby's First Christmas 600QX372-1	Keepsake	Yr.Iss.	6.00	20.00
88-134-004	Baby's Second Christmas 600QX471-1	Keepsake	Yr.Iss.	6.00	20-30.00
88-134-005	Child's Third Christmas 600QX471-4	Keepsake	Yr.Iss.	6.00	27.50
88-134-006	Baby's First Christmas (Boy)475QX272-1	Keepsake	Yr.Iss.	4.75	15-26.00
88-134-007	Baby's First Christmas (Girl)475QX272-4	Keepsake	Yr.Iss.	4.75	15-26.00
88-134-008	Mother and Dad 800QX414-4	Keepsake	Yr.Iss.	8.00	20.00
88-134-009	Sister 800QX499-4	Keepsake	Yr.Iss.	8.00	17.50
88-134-010	Dad 700QX414-1	Keepsake	Yr.Iss.	7.00	15-26.00
88-134-011	Mother 650QX375-1	Keepsake	Yr.Iss.	6.50	10-13.00
88-134-012	Daughter 575QX415-1	Keepsake	Yr.Iss.	5.75	40-45.50
88-134-013	Son 575QX415-4	Keepsake	Yr.Iss.	5.75	37-40.00
88-134-014	Grandmother 475QX276-4	Keepsake	Yr.Iss.	4.75	13-15.00
88-134-015	Grandparents 475QX277-1	Keepsake	Yr.Iss.	4.75	15-17.50
88-134-016	Granddaughter 475QX277-4	Keepsake	Yr.Iss.	4.75	10-20.00
88-134-017	Grandson 475QX278-1	Keepsake	Yr.Iss.	4.75	19.50
88-134-018	Godchild 475QX278-4	Keepsake	Yr.Iss.	4.75	6-22.50
88-134-019	Sweetheart 975QX490-1	Keepsake	Yr.Iss.	9.75	20-27.00
88-134-020	First Christmas Together 900QX489-4	Keepsake	Yr.Iss.	9.00	20-25.00
88-134-021	First Christmas Together 675QX373-1	Keepsake	Yr.Iss.	6.75	20-25.00
88-134-022	Twenty-Five Years Together 675QX373-4	Keepsake	Yr.Iss.	6.75	13.50
88-134-023	Fifty Years Together 675QX374-1	Keepsake	Yr.Iss.	6.75	19.00
88-134-024	Love Fills the Heart 600QX374-4	Keepsake	Yr.Iss.	6.00	19.50
88-134-025	First Christmas Together 475QX274-1	Keepsake	Yr.Iss.	4.75	25.00
88-134-026	Five Years Together 475QX274-4	Keepsake	Yr.Iss.	4.75	19.50
88-134-027	Ten Years Together 475QX275-1	Keepsake	Yr.Iss.	4.75	15-25.00
88-134-028	Love Grows 475QX275-4	Keepsake	Yr.Iss.	4.75	19.00
88-134-029	Spirit of Christmas 475QX276-1	Keepsake	Yr.Iss.	4.75	15.50
88-134-030	Year to Remember 700QX416-4	Keepsake	Yr.Iss.	7.00	14.50
88-134-031	Teacher 625QX417-1	Keepsake	Yr.Iss.	6.25	16.50
88-134-032	Gratitude 600QX375-4	Keepsake	Yr.Iss.	6.00	12.00
88-134-033	New Home 600QX376-1	Keepsake	Yr.Iss.	6.00	19.50
88-134-034	Babysitter 475QX279-1	Keepsake	Yr.Iss.	4.75	10.50
88-134-035	From Our Home to Yours 475QX279-4	Keepsake	Yr.Iss.	4.75	12.00
Hallmark Keepsake Ornaments		**1988 Hallmark Handcrafted Ornaments**			
88-135-001	Peanuts 475QX280-1	Keepsake	Yr.Iss.	4.75	24.50
88-135-002	Jingle Bell Clown 1500QX477-4	Keepsake	Yr.Iss.	15.00	34.50
88-135-003	Travels with Santa 1000QX477-1	Keepsake	Yr.Iss.	10.00	30-32.50
88-135-004	Goin' Cross-Country 850QX476-4	Keepsake	Yr.Iss.	8.50	24.00
88-135-005	Winter Fun 850QX478-1	Keepsake	Yr.Iss.	8.50	25.00
88-135-006	Go For The Gold 800QX417-4	Keepsake	Yr.Iss.	8.00	20-26.50
88-135-007	Party Line 875QX476-1	Keepsake	Yr.Iss.	8.75	20-27.00
88-135-008	Soft Landing 700QX475-1	Keepsake	Yr.Iss.	7.00	18.00
88-135-009	Feliz Navidad 675QX416-1	Keepsake	Yr.Iss.	6.75	28-30.00
88-135-010	Squeaky Clean 675QX475-4	Keepsake	Yr.Iss.	6.75	25-27.00
88-135-011	Christmas Memories 650QX372-4	Keepsake	Yr.Iss.	6.50	19.50
88-135-012	Purrfect Snuggle 625QX474-4	Keepsake	Yr.Iss.	6.25	25.00
88-135-013	Snoopy and Woodstock 600QX474-1	Keepsake	Yr.Iss.	6.00	25-30.00
88-135-014	The Town Crier 550QX473-4	Keepsake	Yr.Iss.	5.50	17-25.00
88-135-015	Christmas Scenes 475QX273-1	Keepsake	Yr.Iss.	4.75	17.50
88-135-016	Jolly Walrus 450QX473-1	Keepsake	Yr.Iss.	4.50	22.50
88-135-017	Slipper Spaniel 450QX472-4	Keepsake	Yr.Iss.	4.50	15-20.00
88-135-018	Arctic Tenor 400QX472-1	Keepsake	Yr.Iss.	4.00	15-17.00
88-135-019	Christmas Cuckoo 800QX480-1	Keepsake	Yr.Iss.	8.00	22.50
88-135-020	Peek-a-boo Kittens 750QX487-1	Keepsake	Yr.Iss.	7.50	15-20.00

CHRISTMAS ORNAMENTS

Company / Number	Series / Name	Artist	Edition Limit	Issue Price	Quote
88-135-021	Cool Juggler 650QX487-4	Keepsake	Yr.Iss.	6.50	17.00
88-135-022	Sweet Star 500QX418-4	Keepsake	Yr.Iss.	5.00	15-27.00
88-135-023	Hoe-Hoe-Hoel 500QX422-1	Keepsake	Yr.Iss.	5.00	15-23.00
88-135-024	Nick the Kick 500QX422-4	Keepsake	Yr.Iss.	5.00	18.00
88-135-025	Holiday Hero 500QX423-1	Keepsake	Yr.Iss.	5.00	15.50
88-135-026	Polar Bowler 500QX478-1	Keepsake	Yr.Iss.	5.00	17.00
88-135-027	Par for Santa 500QX479-1	Keepsake	Yr.Iss.	5.00	17.00
88-135-028	Gone Fishing 500QX479-4	Keepsake	Yr.Iss.	5.00	14.00
88-135-029	Kiss the Claus 500QX486-1	Keepsake	Yr.Iss.	5.00	17.00
88-135-030	Love Santa 500QX486-4	Keepsake	Yr.Iss.	5.00	17.00
88-135-031	Teeny Taster 475QX418-1	Keepsake	Yr.Iss.	4.75	20-35.00
88-135-032	Filled with Fudge 475QX419-1	Keepsake	Yr.Iss.	4.75	25-28.00
88-135-033	Santa Flamingo 475QX483-4	Keepsake	Yr.Iss.	4.75	25-30.00
88-135-034	Kiss from Santa 450QX482-1	Keepsake	Yr.Iss.	4.50	15-25.00
88-135-035	Oreo 400QX481-4	Keepsake	Yr.Iss.	4.00	20-25.00
88-135-036	Noah's Ark 850QX490-4	Keepsake	Yr.Iss.	8.50	25-35.00
88-135-037	Sailing! Sailing! 850QX491-1	Keepsake	Yr.Iss.	8.50	30-35.00
88-135-038	Americana Drum 775QX488-1	Keepsake	Yr.Iss.	7.75	25-35.00
88-135-039	Kringle Portrait 750QX496-1	Keepsake	Yr.Iss.	7.50	23-30.00
88-135-040	Uncle Sam Nutcracker 700QX488-4	Keepsake	Yr.Iss.	7.00	15-30.00
88-135-041	Kringle Tree 650QX495-4	Keepsake	Yr.Iss.	6.50	32-37.00
88-135-042	Glowing Wreath 600QX492-1	Keepsake	Yr.Iss.	6.00	14.50
88-135-043	Sparkling Tree 600QX483-1	Keepsake	Yr.Iss.	6.00	8-15.00
88-135-044	Shiny Sleigh 575QX492-4	Keepsake	Yr.Iss.	5.75	15.00
88-135-045	Kringle Moon 550QX495-1	Keepsake	Yr.Iss.	5.00	17-27.50
88-135-046	Loving Bear 475QX493-4	Keepsake	Yr.Iss.	4.75	19.50
88-135-047	Christmas Cardinal 475QX494-1	Keepsake	Yr.Iss.	4.75	20.00
88-135-048	Starry Angel 475494-4	Keepsake	Yr.Iss.	4.75	14.50
88-135-049	Old-Fashioned School House 400QX497-1	Keepsake	Yr.Iss.	4.00	16.50
88-135-050	Old-Fashioned Church 400QX498-1	Keepsake	Yr.Iss.	4.00	16.50
Hallmark Keepsake Ornaments	**1988 Special Edition**				
88-136-001	The Wonderful Santacycle 2250QX411-4	Keepsake	Yr.Iss.	22.50	48-50.00
Hallmark Keepsake Ornaments	**1988 Artist Favorites**				
88-137-001	Little Jack Horner 800QX408-1	Keepsake	Yr.Iss.	8.00	25-28.00
88-137-002	Merry-Mint Unicorn 850QX423-4	Keepsake	Yr.Iss.	8.50	15-20.00
88-137-003	Midnight Snack 600QX410-4	Keepsake	Yr.Iss.	6.00	20-26.00
88-137-004	Cymbals of Christmas 550QX411-1	Keepsake	Yr.Iss.	5.50	25-28.00
88-137-005	Baby Redbird 500QX410-1	Keepsake	Yr.Iss.	5.00	15-20.00
88-137-006	Very Strawbeary 475QX409-1	Keepsake	Yr.Iss.	4.75	17-25.00
Hallmark Keepsake Ornaments	**1988 Collectible Series**				
88-138-001	Holiday Heirloom-Second Ed.2500QX406-4	Keepsake	Yr.Iss.	25.00	30-50.00
88-138-002	Tin Locomotive-Seventh Ed.1475QX400-4	Keepsake	Yr.Iss.	14.75	25-50.00
88-138-003	Nostalgic Houses and Shops-Fifth Edition -1450QX401-4	Keepsake	Yr.Iss.	14.50	40-50.00
88-138-004	Here Comes Santa-Tenth Ed.1400QX400-1	Keepsake	Yr.Iss.	14.00	33-43.00
88-138-005	Mr. and Mrs. Claus-Third Ed.1300QX401-1	Keepsake	Yr.Iss.	13.00	30-46.00
88-138-006	Rocking Horse-Eighth Ed.1075QX402-4	Keepsake	Yr.Iss.	10.75	30-40.00
88-138-007	Windows of the World-Fourth Edition 1000QX402 1	Keepsake	Yr.Iss.	10.00	20-36.00
88-138-008	Frosty Friends-Ninth Ed.875QX403-1	Keepsake	Yr.Iss.	8.75	40-53.00
88-138-009	Miniature Creche-Fourth Ed.850QX403-4	Keepsake	Yr.Iss.	8.50	12-24.50
88-138-010	Porcelain Bear-Sixth Ed.800QX404-4	Keepsake	Yr.Iss.	8.00	37-48.00
88-138-011	Collector's Plate-Second Ed.800QX406-1	Keepsake	Yr.Iss.	8.00	28-51.00
88-138-012	Norman Rockwell-Ninth Ed.775QX370-4	Keepsake	Yr.Iss.	7.75	18-24.00
88-138-013	Holiday Wildlife-Seventh Ed.775QX371-1	Keepsake	Yr.Iss.	7.75	17-23.00
88-138-014	Wood Childhood-Fifth Ed.750QX404-1	Keepsake	Yr.Iss.	7.50	24.50
88-138-015	Reindeer Champs-Third Ed.750QX405-1	Keepsake	Yr.Iss.	7.50	25-35.00
88-138-016	Five Golden Rings-Fifth Ed.650QX371-4	Keepsake	Yr.Iss.	6.50	20-23.00
88-138-017	Thimble-Eleventh Ed.575QX405-4	Keepsake	Yr.Iss.	5.75	25-27.00
88-138-018	Mary's Angels-First Ed.500QX407-4	Keepsake	Yr.Iss.	5.00	30-45.00
88-138-019	Betsey Clark: Home for Christmas-Third Edition 500QX271-4	Keepsake	Yr.Iss.	5.00	20-23.00
Hallmark Keepsake Ornaments	**1988 Keepsake Magic Ornaments**				
88-139-001	Baby's First Christmas 2400QLX718-4	Keepsake	Yr.Iss.	24.00	50-55.00
88-139-002	First Christmas Together 1200QLX702-7	Keepsake	Yr.Iss.	12.00	32.50
88-139-003	Santa and Sparky-Third Ed.1950QLX719-1	Keepsake	Yr.Iss.	19.50	30-50.00
88-139-004	Christmas Classics-Third Ed.1500QLX716-1	Keepsake	Yr.Iss.	15.00	30-50.00
88-139-005	Chris Mouse-Fourth Ed.875QLX715-4	Keepsake	Yr.Iss.	8.75	35-42.50
88-139-006	Country Express 2450QLX721-1	Keepsake	Yr.Iss.	24.50	35-77.00
88-139-007	Kringle's Toy Shop 2450QLX701-7	Keepsake	Yr.Iss.	24.50	45-55.00
88-139-008	Parade of the Toys 2200QLX719-4	Keepsake	Yr.Iss.	22.00	30-49.50
88-139-009	Last-Minute Hug 1950QLX718-1	Keepsake	Yr.Iss.	19.50	35-58.00
88-139-010	Skater's Waltz 1950QLX720-1	Keepsake	Yr.Iss.	19.50	49.50
88-139-011	Kitty Capers 1300QLX716-4	Keepsake	Yr.Iss.	13.00	35-38.00
88-139-012	Christmas is Magic 1200QLX717-1	Keepsake	Yr.Iss.	12.00	49.50
88-139-013	Heavenly Glow 1175QLX711-4	Keepsake	Yr.Iss.	11.75	16-29.00
88-139-014	Radiant Tree 1175QLX712-1	Keepsake	Yr.Iss.	11.75	22-25.00
88-139-015	Festive Feeder 1150QLX720-4	Keepsake	Yr.Iss.	11.50	44.50
88-139-016	Circling the Globe 1050QLX712-4	Keepsake	Yr.Iss.	10.50	28-37.00
88-139-017	Bearly Reaching 950QLX715-1	Keepsake	Yr.Iss.	9.50	30-33.00
88-139-018	Moonlit Nap 875QLX713-4	Keepsake	Yr.Iss.	8.75	24.50
88-139-019	Tree of Friendship 850QLX710-4	Keepsake	Yr.Iss.	8.50	22.50
88-139-020	Song of Christmas 850QLX711-1	Keepsake	Yr.Iss.	8.50	20-23.00
Hallmark Keepsake Ornaments	**1988 Keepsake Miniature Ornaments**				
88-140-001	Baby's First Christmas	Keepsake	Yr.Iss.	6.00	15.00
88-140-002	First Christmas Together	Keepsake	Yr.Iss.	4.00	20.00
88-140-003	Mother	Keepsake	Yr.Iss.	3.00	12.50
88-140-004	Friends Share Joy	Keepsake	Yr.Iss.	2.00	15.00
88-140-005	Love is Forever	Keepsake	Yr.Iss.	2.00	15.00
88-140-006	Holy Family	Keepsake	Yr.Iss.	8.50	15-21.00
88-140-007	Sweet Dreams	Keepsake	Yr.Iss.	7.00	23-26.00
88-140-008	Skater's Waltz	Keepsake	Yr.Iss.	7.00	10-22.00
88-140-009	Little Drummer Boy	Keepsake	Yr.Iss.	4.50	20-26.50
88-140-010	Three Little Kitties	Keepsake	Yr.Iss.	6.00	18.50
88-140-011	Snuggly Skater	Keepsake	Yr.Iss.	4.50	20-27.50
88-140-012	Happy Santa	Keepsake	Yr.Iss.	4.50	15-20.00
88-140-013	Sneaker Mouse	Keepsake	Yr.Iss.	4.00	20-22.00
88-140-014	Country Wreath	Keepsake	Yr.Iss.	4.00	12.00
88-140-015	Joyous Heart	Keepsake	Yr.Iss.	3.50	25-30.00
88-140-016	Candy Cane Elf	Keepsake	Yr.Iss.	3.00	20-22.00
88-140-017	Folk Art Lamb	Keepsake	Yr.Iss.	2.50	19.50
88-140-018	Folk Art Reindeer	Keepsake	Yr.Iss.	2.50	19.50
88-140-019	Gentle Angel	Keepsake	Yr.Iss.	2.00	19.50
88-140-020	Brass Star	Keepsake	Yr.Iss.	1.50	20-28.00
88-140-021	Brass Angel	Keepsake	Yr.Iss.	1.50	19.50
88-140-022	Brass Tree	Keepsake	Yr.Iss.	1.50	19.50
88-140-023	Jolly St. Nick	Keepsake	Yr.Iss.	8.00	28-37.00
88-140-024	Family Home-First Edition	Keepsake	Yr.Iss.	8.50	30-45.00
88-140-025	Kittens in Toyland-First Edition	Keepsake	Yr.Iss.	5.00	20-30.00
88-140-026	Rocking Horse-First Edition	Keepsake	Yr.Iss.	4.50	30-50.00
88-140-027	Penguin Pal-First Edition	Keepsake	Yr.Iss.	3.75	25-30.00
Hallmark Keepsake Ornaments	**1988 Hallmark Keepsake Ornament Collector's Club**				
88-141-001	Our Clubhouse QXC580-4	Keepsake	Yr.Iss.	Unkn.	42-50.00
88-141-002	Sleighful of Dreams 800QC580-1	Keepsake	Yr.Iss.	8.00	55-75.00
88-141-003	Holiday Heirloom-Second Edition 2500QXC406-4	Keepsake	Yr.Iss.	25.00	30-65.00
88-141-004	Christmas is Sharing 1750QXC407-1	Keepsake	Yr.Iss.	17.50	25-40.00
88-141-005	Angelic Minstrel 2750QXC408-4	Keepsake	Yr.Iss.	27.50	36-40.00
88-141-006	Hold on Tight QXC570-4	Keepsake	Yr.Iss.	Unkn.	60-80.00
Hallmark Keepsake Ornaments	**1989 Commemoratives**				
89-142-001	Baby's First Christmas Photoholder 625QX468-2	Keepsake	Yr.Iss.	6.25	25.00
89-142-002	Baby's First Christmas-Baby Girl475QX272-2	Keepsake	Yr.Iss.	4.75	10-18.00
89-142-003	Baby's First Christmas-Baby Boy475QX272-5	Keepsake	Yr.Iss.	4.75	15-18.00
89-142-004	Baby's First Christmas 675QX381-5	Keepsake	Yr.Iss.	6.75	10-20.00
89-142-005	Granddaughter's First Christmas 675QX382-2	Keepsake	Yr.Iss.	6.75	15.00
89-142-006	Grandson's First Christmas 675QX382-5	Keepsake	Yr.Iss.	6.75	15.00
89-142-007	Baby's First Christmas 725QX449-2	Keepsake	Yr.Iss.	7.25	30-45.00
89-142-008	Baby's Second Christmas 675QX449-5	Keepsake	Yr.Iss.	6.75	25-28.00
89-142-009	Baby's Third Christmas 675QX469-5	Keepsake	Yr.Iss.	6.75	18-20.00
89-142-010	Baby's Fourth Christmas 675QX543-2	Keepsake	Yr.Iss.	6.75	16.50
89-142-011	Baby's Fifth Christmas 675QX543-5	Keepsake	Yr.Iss.	6.75	16.50
89-142-012	Mother 975QX440-5	Keepsake	Yr.Iss.	9.75	22.50
89-142-013	Mom and Dad 975QX442-5	Keepsake	Yr.Iss.	9.75	20.00
89-142-014	Dad 725QX442-5	Keepsake	Yr.Iss.	7.25	15-21.00
89-142-015	Sister 475QX279-2	Keepsake	Yr.Iss.	4.75	15-22.00
89-142-016	Grandparents 475QX277-2	Keepsake	Yr.Iss.	4.75	15.00
89-142-017	Grandmother 475QX277-5	Keepsake	Yr.Iss.	4.75	19.50
89-142-018	Granddaughter 475QX278	Keepsake	Yr.Iss.	4.75	19.50
89-142-019	Grandson 475QX278-5	Keepsake	Yr.Iss.	4.75	14-24.00
89-142-020	Godchild 625QX311-2	Keepsake	Yr.Iss.	6.25	12.50
89-142-021	Sweetheart 975QX486-5	Keepsake	Yr.Iss.	9.75	22.00
89-142-022	First Christmas Together 675QX485-2	Keepsake	Yr.Iss.	9.75	19.50
89-142-023	First Christmas Together 675QX383-2	Keepsake	Yr.Iss.	6.75	20.00
89-142-024	First Christmas Together 475QX273-2	Keepsake	Yr.Iss.	4.75	19.50
89-142-025	Five Years Together 475QX273-5	Keepsake	Yr.Iss.	4.75	19.50
89-142-026	Ten Years Together 475QX274-2	Keepsake	Yr.Iss.	4.75	19.50
89-142-027	Twenty-five Years Together Photoholder 875QX485-5	Keepsake	Yr.Iss.	8.75	12-17.50
89-142-028	Forty Years Together Photoholder 875QX545-2	Keepsake	Yr.Iss.	8.75	9-17.50
89-142-029	Fifty Years Together Photoholder 875QX486-2	Keepsake	Yr.Iss.	8.75	17.50
89-142-030	Language of Love 625QX383-5	Keepsake	Yr.Iss.	6.25	16.50
89-142-031	World of Love 475QX274-5	Keepsake	Yr.Iss.	4.75	16.50
89-142-032	Friendship Time 975QX413-2	Keepsake	Yr.Iss.	9.75	32.50
89-142-033	Teacher 575QX412-5	Keepsake	Yr.Iss.	5.75	24.50
89-142-034	New Home 475QX275-5	Keepsake	Yr.Iss.	4.75	19.50
89-142-035	Festive Year 775QX384-2	Keepsake	Yr.Iss.	7.75	15.00
89-142-036	Gratitude 675QX385-2	Keepsake	Yr.Iss.	6.75	13.50
89-142-037	From Our Home to Yours 625QX384-5	Keepsake	Yr.Iss.	6.25	12.50
89-142-038	Daughter 625QX443-2	Keepsake	Yr.Iss.	6.25	10-15.00
89-142-039	Son 625QX444-5	Keepsake	Yr.Iss.	6.25	15.00
Hallmark Keepsake Ornaments	**1989 Holiday Traditions**				
89-143-001	Joyful Trio 975QX437-2	Keepsake	Yr.Iss.	9.75	20-26.00
89-143-002	Old-World Gnome 775QX434-5	Keepsake	Yr.Iss.	7.75	20-30.00
89-143-003	Hoppy Holidays 775QX469-2	Keepsake	Yr.Iss.	7.75	17.50
89-143-004	The First Christmas 775QX547-5	Keepsake	Yr.Iss.	7.75	15.50
89-143-005	Gentle Fawn 775QX548-5	Keepsake	Yr.Iss.	7.75	15-20.00
89-143-006	Spencer Sparrow, Esq. 675QX431-2	Keepsake	Yr.Iss.	6.75	20.00
89-143-007	Snoopy and Woodstock 675QX433-2	Keepsake	Yr.Iss.	6.75	16-25.00
89-143-008	Sweet Memories Photoholder 675QX438-5	Keepsake	Yr.Iss.	6.75	19.00
89-143-009	Stocking Kitten 675QX456-5	Keepsake	Yr.Iss.	6.75	11-15.00
89-143-010	George Washington Bicentennial 625QX386-2	Keepsake	Yr.Iss.	6.25	12-15.00
89-143-011	Feliz Navidad 675QX439-2	Keepsake	Yr.Iss.	6.75	19.50
89-143-012	Cranberry Bunny 575QX426-2	Keepsake	Yr.Iss.	5.75	14.50
89-143-013	Deer Disguise 575QX426-5	Keepsake	Yr.Iss.	5.75	24.50
89-143-014	Paddington Bear 575QX429-2	Keepsake	Yr.Iss.	5.75	20-28.00
89-143-015	Snowplow Santa 575QX420-5	Keepsake	Yr.Iss.	5.75	15.50
89-143-016	Kristy Claus 575QX424-5	Keepsake	Yr.Iss.	5.75	11.50
89-143-017	Here's the Pitch 575QX545-5	Keepsake	Yr.Iss.	5.75	13.50
89-143-018	North Pole Jogger 575QX546-2	Keepsake	Yr.Iss.	5.75	13.50
89-143-019	Camera Claus 575QX546-5	Keepsake	Yr.Iss.	5.75	15.50
89-143-020	Sea Santa 575QX415-2	Keepsake	Yr.Iss.	5.75	13.50
89-143-021	Gym Dandy 575QX418-5	Keepsake	Yr.Iss.	5.75	15.50
89-143-022	On the Links 575QX419-2	Keepsake	Yr.Iss.	5.75	14.50
89-143-023	Special Delivery 525QX432-5	Keepsake	Yr.Iss.	5.25	15.00
89-143-024	Hang in There 525QX430-5	Keepsake	Yr.Iss.	5.25	25-34.50
89-143-025	Owliday Greetings 400QX436-5	Keepsake	Yr.Iss.	4.00	15.00
89-143-026	Norman Rockwell 475QX276-2	Keepsake	Yr.Iss.	4.75	19.50
89-143-027	A Charlie Brown Christmas 475QX276-5	Keepsake	Yr.Iss.	4.75	25-30.00
89-143-028	Party Line 875QX476-1	Keepsake	Yr.Iss.	8.75	26.50
89-143-029	Peek-a-Boo Kitties 750QX487-1	Keepsake	Yr.Iss.	7.50	17-22.00
89-143-030	Polar Bowler 575QX478-4	Keepsake	Yr.Iss.	5.75	17.00
89-143-031	Gone Fishing 575QX479-4	Keepsake	Yr.Iss.	5.75	17.00
89-143-032	Teeny Taster 475QX418-1	Keepsake	Yr.Iss.	4.75	17.00
89-143-033	A Kiss™ From Santa 450QX482-1	Keepsake	Yr.Iss.	4.50	19.50
89-143-034	Oreo® Chocolate Sandwich Cookies 400QX481-4	Keepsake	Yr.Iss.	4.00	15.00
Hallmark Keepsake Ornaments	**1989 New Attractions**				
89-144-001	Sparkling Snowflake 775QX547-2	Keepsake	Yr.Iss.	7.75	22-25.00
89-144-002	Festive Angel 675QX463-5	Keepsake	Yr.Iss.	6.75	18-22.00
89-144-003	Graceful Swan 675QX464-2	Keepsake	Yr.Iss.	6.75	18-22.00
89-144-004	Nostalgic Lamb 675QX466-5	Keepsake	Yr.Iss.	6.75	13.50
89-144-005	Horse Weathervane 575QX463-2	Keepsake	Yr.Iss.	5.75	14.50
89-144-006	Rooster Weathervane 575QX467-5	Keepsake	Yr.Iss.	5.75	10-14.00
89-144-007	Country Cat 625QX467-2	Keepsake	Yr.Iss.	6.25	15-17.00
89-144-008	Nutshell Holiday 575QX465-2	Keepsake	Yr.Iss.	5.75	20-27.50
89-144-009	Nutshell Dreams 575QX465-5	Keepsake	Yr.Iss.	5.75	20-27.50
89-144-010	Nutshell Workshop 575QX487-2	Keepsake	Yr.Iss.	5.75	20-27.50
89-144-011	Claus Construction 775QX488-5	Keepsake	Yr.Iss.	7.75	15-20.00
89-144-012	Cactus Cowboy 675QX411-2	Keepsake	Yr.Iss.	6.75	32-40.00
89-144-013	Rodney Reindeer 675QX407-2	Keepsake	Yr.Iss.	6.75	13.50
89-144-014	Let's Play 725QX488-2	Keepsake	Yr.Iss.	7.25	25-40.00

Company Number	Name	Series Artist	Edition Limit	Issue Price	Quote
89-144-015	TV Break 625QX409-2	Keepsake	Yr.Iss.	6.25	15.50
89-144-016	Balancing Elf 675QX489-5	Keepsake	Yr.Iss.	6.75	22.50
89-144-017	Wiggly Snowman 675QX489-2	Keepsake	Yr.Iss.	6.75	24.50
89-144-018	Cool Swing 625QX487-5	Keepsake	Yr.Iss.	6.25	35.00
89-144-019	Goin' South 425QX410-5	Keepsake	Yr.Iss.	4.25	24.50-30.00
89-144-020	Peppermint Clown 2475QX450-5	Keepsake	Yr.Iss.	24.75	28-35.00
Hallmark Keepsake Ornaments		**1989 Artists' Favorites**			
89-145-001	Merry-Go-Round Unicorn 1075QX447-2	Keepsake	Yr.Iss.	10.75	20.00
89-145-002	Carousel Zebra 925QX451-5	Keepsake	Yr.Iss.	9.25	19.50
89-145-003	Mail Call 875QX452-2	Keepsake	Yr.Iss.	8.75	20-30.00
89-145-004	Baby Partridge 675QX452-5	Keepsake	Yr.Iss.	6.75	15-18.00
89-145-005	Playful Angel 675QX453-5	Keepsake	Yr.Iss.	6.75	15-22.00
89-145-006	Cherry Jubilee 500QX453-2	Keepsake	Yr.Iss.	5.00	35.00
89-145-007	Bear-i-Tone 475QX454-2	Keepsake	Yr.Iss.	4.75	14.50
Hallmark Keepsake Ornaments		**1989 Special Edition**			
89-146-001	The Ornament Express 2200QX580-5	Keepsake	Yr.Iss.	22.00	35-53.00
Hallmark Keepsake Ornaments		**1989 Collectible Series**			
89-147-001	Christmas Kitty-First Ed.1475QX544-5	Keepsake	Yr.Iss.	14.75	15-29.00
89-147-002	Winter Surprise-First Ed.1075QX427-2	Keepsake	Yr.Iss.	10.75	25.00
89-147-003	Hark! It's Herald-First Ed.675QX455-5	Keepsake	Yr.Iss.	6.75	15-20.00
89-147-004	Crayola Crayon-First Ed.875QX435-2	Keepsake	Yr.Iss.	8.75	30-49.00
89-147-005	The Gift Bringers-First Ed.500QX279-5	Keepsake	Yr.Iss.	5.00	20-30.00
89-147-006	Mary's Angels-Second Ed.575QX454-5	Keepsake	Yr.Iss.	5.75	23-30.00
89-147-007	Collector's Plate-Third Ed.825QX461-2	Keepsake	Yr.Iss.	8.25	15-35.00
89-147-008	Mr. and Mrs. Claus-Fourth Ed.1325QX457-5	Keepsake	Yr.Iss.	13.25	32-35.00
89-147-009	Reindeer Champs-Fourth Ed.775QX456-2	Keepsake	Yr.Iss.	7.75	30.00
89-147-010	Betsey Clark: Home for Christmas-Fourth Edition 500QX230-2	Keepsake	Yr.Iss.	5.00	15-27.00
89-147-011	Windows of the World-Fifth Ed.1075QX462-5	Keepsake	Yr.Iss.	10.75	20-25.00
89-147-012	Miniature Creche-Fifth Ed.925QX459-2	Keepsake	Yr.Iss.	9.25	16-20.00
89-147-013	Nostalgic Houses and Shops-Sixth Edition 1425QX458-2	Keepsake	Yr.Iss.	14.25	35-45.00
89-147-014	Wood Childhood Ornaments-Sixth Edition 775QX459-5	Keepsake	Yr.Iss.	7.75	20-22.00
89-147-015	Twelve Days of Christmas-Sixth Ed. 675QX381-2	Keepsake	Yr.Iss.	6.75	17.50
89-147-016	Porcelain Bear-Seventh Ed.875QX461-5	Keepsake	Yr.Iss.	8.75	15-27.00
89-147-017	Tin Locomotive-Eighth Ed.1475QX460-2	Keepsake	Yr.Iss.	14.75	34.50
89-147-018	Rocking Horse-Ninth Ed.1075QX462-2	Keepsake	Yr.Iss.	10.75	41.00
89-147-019	Frosty Friends-Tenth Ed.925QX457-2	Keepsake	Yr.Iss.	9.25	27-30.00
89-147-020	Here Comes Santa-Eleventh Ed.1475QX458-5	Keepsake	Yr.Iss.	14.75	30-44.00
89-147-021	Thimble-Twelfth Edition 575QX455-2	Keepsake	Yr.Iss.	5.75	12-18.00
Hallmark Keepsake Ornaments		**1989 Keepsake Magic Collection**			
89-148-001	Baby's First Christmas 3000QLX727-2	Keepsake	Yr.Iss.	30.00	45-60.00
89-148-002	First Christmas Together1750QLX734-2	Keepsake	Yr.Iss.	17.50	45.00
89-148-003	Forest Frolics-First Edition2450QLX728-2	Keepsake	Yr.Iss.	24.50	60-65.00
89-148-004	Christmas Classics-Fourth Ed.1350QLX724-2	Keepsake	Yr.Iss.	13.50	25-30.00
89-148-005	Chris Mouse-Fifth Edition 950QLX722-5	Keepsake	Yr.Iss.	9.50	35-40.00
89-148-006	Joyous Carolers 3000QLX729-5	Keepsake	Yr.Iss.	30.00	60.00
89-148-007	Tiny Tinker 1950QLX717-4	Keepsake	Yr.Iss.	19.50	40.00
89-148-008	Rudolph the Red-Nosed Reindeer 1950QLX725-2	Keepsake	Yr.Iss.	19.50	40-50.00
89-148-009	Loving Spoonful 1950QLX726-2	Keepsake	Yr.Iss.	19.50	33-38.00
89-148-010	Holiday Bell 1750QLX722-2	Keepsake	Yr.Iss.	17.50	35.00
89-148-011	Busy Beaver 1750QLX724-5	Keepsake	Yr.Iss.	17.50	40-50.00
89-148-012	Backstage Bear 1350QLX721-5	Keepsake	Yr.Iss.	13.50	30-38.00
89-148-013	The Animals Speak 1350QLX723-2	Keepsake	Yr.Iss.	13.50	50.00
89-148-014	Angel Melody 950QLX720-2	Keepsake	Yr.Iss.	9.50	15-17.00
89-148-015	Unicorn Fantasy 950QLX723-5	Keepsake	Yr.Iss.	9.50	19.00
89-148-016	Moonlit Nap 875QLX713-4	Keepsake	Yr.Iss.	8.75	22.50
89-148-017	Kringle's Toy Shop 2450QLX701-7	Keepsake	Yr.Iss.	24.50	40-60.00
89-148-018	Metro Express 2800QLX727-5	Keepsake	Yr.Iss.	28.00	70-75.00
89-148-019	Spirit of St. Nick 2450QLX728-5	Keepsake	Yr.Iss.	24.50	65.00
Hallmark Keepsake Ornaments		**1989 Keepsake Miniature Ornaments**			
89-149-001	Baby's First Christmas 600QXM573-2	Keepsake	Yr.Iss.	6.00	15.00
89-149-002	Mother 600QXM564-5	Keepsake	Yr.Iss.	6.00	14.50
89-149-003	First Christmas Together 850QXM564-2	Keepsake	Yr.Iss.	8.50	15.00
89-149-004	Lovebirds 600QXM563-5	Keepsake	Yr.Iss.	6.00	14.50
89-149-005	Special Friend 450QXM565-2	Keepsake	Yr.Iss.	4.50	14.00
89-149-006	Sharing a Ride 850QXM576-5	Keepsake	Yr.Iss.	8.50	15.00
89-149-007	Little Star Bringer 600QXM562-2	Keepsake	Yr.Iss.	6.00	18-32.00
89-149-008	Santa's Roadster 600QXM566-5	Keepsake	Yr.Iss.	6.00	15-25.00
89-149-009	Load of Cheer 600QXM574-5	Keepsake	Yr.Iss.	6.00	18-20.00
89-149-010	Slow Motion 600QXM575-2	Keepsake	Yr.Iss.	6.00	16.50
89-149-011	Merry Seal 600QXM575-5	Keepsake	Yr.Iss.	6.00	15.00
89-149-012	Starlit Mouse 450QXM565-5	Keepsake	Yr.Iss.	4.50	22.00
89-149-013	Little Soldier 450QXM567-5	Keepsake	Yr.Iss.	4.50	10.00
89-149-014	Acorn Squirrel 450QXM568-2	Keepsake	Yr.Iss.	4.50	9.00
89-149-015	Happy Bluebird 450QXM566-2	Keepsake	Yr.Iss.	4.50	10-21.00
89-149-016	Stocking Pal 450QXM567-2	Keepsake	Yr.Iss.	4.50	10-15.00
89-149-017	Scrimshaw Reindeer 450QXM568-5	Keepsake	Yr.Iss.	4.50	8-10.00
89-149-018	Folk Art Bunny 450QXM569-2	Keepsake	Yr.Iss.	4.50	9.00
89-149-019	Brass Snowflake 450QXM570-2	Keepsake	Yr.Iss.	4.50	8-14.00
89-149-020	Pinecone Basket 450QXM573-4	Keepsake	Yr.Iss.	4.50	8-40.00
89-149-021	Strollin' Snowman 450QXM574-2	Keepsake	Yr.Iss.	4.50	9.00
89-149-022	Brass Partridge 300QXM572-5	Keepsake	Yr.Iss.	3.00	5-12.00
89-149-023	Cozy Skater 450QXM573-5	Keepsake	Yr.Iss.	4.50	15-20.00
89-149-024	Old-World Santa 300QXM569-5	Keepsake	Yr.Iss.	3.00	6.00
89-149-025	Roly-Poly Ram 300QXM570-5	Keepsake	Yr.Iss.	3.00	10-15.00
89-149-026	Roly-Poly Pig 300QXM571-2	Keepsake	Yr.Iss.	3.00	8-10.00
89-149-027	Puppy Cart 300QXM571-5	Keepsake	Yr.Iss.	3.00	15.00
89-149-028	Kitty Cart 300QXM572-2	Keepsake	Yr.Iss.	3.00	8-15.00
89-149-029	Holiday Deer 300QXM577-2	Keepsake	Yr.Iss.	3.00	12.00
89-149-030	Bunny Hug 300QXM577-5	Keepsake	Yr.Iss.	3.00	11.00
89-149-031	Rejoice 300QXM578-2	Keepsake	Yr.Iss.	3.00	10.00
89-149-032	Holy Family 850QXM561-1	Keepsake	Yr.Iss.	8.50	14.50
89-149-033	Three Little Kitties 600QXM569-4	Keepsake	Yr.Iss.	6.00	18.50
89-149-034	Country Wreath 450QXM573-1	Keepsake	Yr.Iss.	4.50	12.00
89-149-035	Noel R.R.-First Edition 850QXM576-2	Keepsake	Yr.Iss.	8.50	30-35.00
89-149-036	The Kringles-First Edition600QXM562-2	Keepsake	Yr.Iss.	6.00	25-35.00
89-149-037	Old English Village-Second Ed.850QXM561-5	Keepsake	Yr.Iss.	8.50	15-30.00
89-149-038	Penguin Pal-Second Ed.450QXM560-2	Keepsake	Yr.Iss.	4.50	20-37.00
89-149-039	Rocking Horse-Second Ed. 450QXM560-5	Keepsake	Yr.Iss.	4.50	18-30.00
89-149-040	Kittens in Toyland-Second Ed.450QXM561-2	Keepsake	Yr.Iss.	4.50	15-20.00
89-149-041	Santa's Magic Ride 850QXM563-2	Keepsake	Yr.Iss.	8.50	15-20.00
Hallmark Keepsake Ornaments		**1989 Hallmark Keepsake Ornament Collector's Club**			
89-150-001	Visit from Santa QXC580-2	Keepsake	Yr.Iss.	Unkn.	50.00

Company Number	Name	Series Artist	Edition Limit	Issue Price	Quote
89-150-002	Collect a Dream 900QXC428-5	Keepsake	Yr.Iss.	9.00	52-65.00
89-150-003	Christmas is Peaceful 1850QXC451-2	Keepsake	Yr.Iss.	18.50	45.00
89-150-004	Noelle 1975QXC448-3	Keepsake	Yr.Iss.	19.75	40.00
89-150-005	Holiday Heirloom-Third Ed.2500QXC460-5	Keepsake	Yr.Iss.	25.00	35-44.00
89-150-006	Sitting Purrty QXC581-2	Keepsake	Yr.Iss.	Unkn.	45-54.00
Hallmark Keepsake Ornaments		**1990 Commemoratives**			
90-151-001	Baby's First Christmas 975QX4853	Keepsake	Yr.Iss.	9.75	20-33.00
90-151-002	Baby's First Christmas 675QX3036	Keepsake	Yr.Iss.	6.75	23.00
90-151-003	Baby's First Christmas-Baby Boy475QX2063	Keepsake	Yr.Iss.	4.75	15-24.00
90-151-004	Baby's First Christmas-Baby Girl475QX2066	Keepsake	Yr.Iss.	4.75	15.00
90-151-005	Baby's First Christmas-Photo Holder 775QX4843	Keepsake	Yr.Iss.	7.75	16-20.00
90-151-006	Granddaughter's First Christmas675QX3106	Keepsake	Yr.Iss.	6.75	13.50
90-151-007	Mom-to-Be 575QX4916	Keepsake	Yr.Iss.	5.75	20-25.00
90-151-008	Grandson's First Christmas 675QX3063	Keepsake	Yr.Iss.	6.75	13.50
90-151-009	Dad-to-Be 575QX4913	Keepsake	Yr.Iss.	5.75	20-22.00
90-151-010	Baby's First Christmas 775QX4856	Keepsake	Yr.Iss.	7.75	20-25.00
90-151-011	Baby's Second Christmas 675QX4683	Keepsake	Yr.Iss.	6.75	20.00
90-151-012	Child's Third Christmas 675QX4866	Keepsake	Yr.Iss.	6.75	15-20.00
90-151-013	Child's Fourth Christmas 675QX4873	Keepsake	Yr.Iss.	6.75	15.00
90-151-014	Child's Fifth Christmas 675QX4876	Keepsake	Yr.Iss.	6.75	15.00
90-151-015	Sweetheart 1175QX4893	Keepsake	Yr.Iss.	11.75	20-23.00
90-151-016	Our First Christmas Together 975QX4883	Keepsake	Yr.Iss.	9.75	15-20.00
90-151-017	Our First Christmas Together -Photo Holder Ornament 775QX4886	Keepsake	Yr.Iss.	7.75	15.50
90-151-018	Our First Christmas Together 675QX3146	Keepsake	Yr.Iss.	6.75	16-20.00
90-151-019	Our First Christmas Together 475QX2136	Keepsake	Yr.Iss.	4.75	12-15.00
90-151-020	Time for Love 475QX2133	Keepsake	Yr.Iss.	4.75	16.00
90-151-021	Peaceful Kingdom 475QX2106	Keepsake	Yr.Iss.	4.75	12.00
90-151-022	Jesus Loves Me 675QX3156	Keepsake	Yr.Iss.	6.75	13.50
90-151-023	Five Years Together 475QX2103	Keepsake	Yr.Iss.	4.75	15.00
90-151-024	Ten Years Together 475QX2153	Keepsake	Yr.Iss.	4.75	13-15.00
90-151-025	Twenty-Five Years Together 975QX4896	Keepsake	Yr.Iss.	9.75	19.50
90-151-026	Forty Years Together 975QX4903	Keepsake	Yr.Iss.	9.75	19.50
90-151-027	Fifty Years Together 975QX4906	Keepsake	Yr.Iss.	9.75	19.50
90-151-028	Mother 875QX4536	Keepsake	Yr.Iss.	8.75	15.50
90-151-029	Dad 675QX4533	Keepsake	Yr.Iss.	6.75	13.50
90-151-030	Mom and Dad 875QX4593	Keepsake	Yr.Iss.	8.75	20.00
90-151-031	Grandmother 475QX2236	Keepsake	Yr.Iss.	4.75	15.00
90-151-032	Grandparents 475QX2253	Keepsake	Yr.Iss.	4.75	15.00
90-151-033	Godchild 675QX3167	Keepsake	Yr.Iss.	6.75	14-21.00
90-151-034	Son 575QX4516	Keepsake	Yr.Iss.	5.75	12.50
90-151-035	Daughter 575QX4496	Keepsake	Yr.Iss.	5.75	12.50
90-151-036	Brother 575QX4493	Keepsake	Yr.Iss.	5.75	15-20.00
90-151-037	Sister 475QX2273	Keepsake	Yr.Iss.	4.75	17.50
90-151-038	Grandson 475QX2293	Keepsake	Yr.Iss.	4.75	12-18.00
90-151-039	Granddaughter 475QX2286	Keepsake	Yr.Iss.	4.75	15-29.00
90-151-040	Friendship Kitten 675QX4142	Keepsake	Yr.Iss.	6.75	20-22.00
90-151-041	New Home 675QX4343	Keepsake	Yr.Iss.	6.75	20-22.00
90-151-042	Across The Miles 675QX3173	Keepsake	Yr.Iss.	6.75	13.50-17.50
90-151-043	From Our Home to Yours 475QX2166	Keepsake	Yr.Iss.	4.75	9.50
90-151-044	Teacher 775QX4483	Keepsake	Yr.Iss.	7.75	15.50
90-151-045	Copy of Cheer 775QX4486	Keepsake	Yr.Iss.	7.75	15.50
90-151-046	Child Care Giver 675QX3166	Keepsake	Yr.Iss.	6.75	13.50
Hallmark Keepsake Ornaments		**1990 New Attractions**			
90-152-001	S. Claus Taxi 1175QX4686	Keepsake	Yr.Iss.	11.75	25-30.00
90-152-002	Coyote Carols 875QX4993	Keepsake	Yr.Iss.	8.75	19.50
90-152-003	King Klaus 775QX4106	Keepsake	Yr.Iss.	7.75	18-28.00
90-152-004	Hot Dogger 775QX4976	Keepsake	Yr.Iss.	7.75	18-29.00
90-152-005	Poolside Walrus 775QX4986	Keepsake	Yr.Iss.	7.75	15.50
90-152-006	Three Little Piggies 775QX4996	Keepsake	Yr.Iss.	7.75	16-28.00
90-152-007	Billboard Bunny 775QX5196	Keepsake	Yr.Iss.	7.75	10-15.50
90-152-008	Mooy Christmas 675QX4933	Keepsake	Yr.Iss.	6.75	20-25.00
90-152-009	Pepperoni Mouse 675QX4973	Keepsake	Yr.Iss.	6.75	20.00
90-152-010	Santa Schnoz 675QX4983	Keepsake	Yr.Iss.	6.75	20-28.00
90-152-011	Cozy Goose 575QX4966	Keepsake	Yr.Iss.	5.75	12.25
90-152-012	Two Peas in a Pod 475QX4926	Keepsake	Yr.Iss.	4.75	22-30.00
90-152-013	Chiming In 975QX4366	Keepsake	Yr.Iss.	9.75	23-30.00
90-152-014	Christmas Croc 775QX4373	Keepsake	Yr.Iss.	7.75	15.50
90-152-015	Born to Dance 775QX5043	Keepsake	Yr.Iss.	7.75	15-24.00
90-152-016	Stocking Pals 1075QX5493	Keepsake	Yr.Iss.	10.75	22.00
90-152-017	Home for the Owlidays 675QX5183	Keepsake	Yr.Iss.	6.75	14-21.00
90-152-018	Baby Unicorn 975QX5486	Keepsake	Yr.Iss.	9.75	19.50
90-152-019	Spoon Rider 975QX5496	Keepsake	Yr.Iss.	9.75	20-24.00
90-152-020	Lovable Dears 875QX5476	Keepsake	Yr.Iss.	8.75	17.50
90-152-021	Meow Mart 775QX4446	Keepsake	Yr.Iss.	7.75	20.00
90-152-022	Perfect Catch 775QX4693	Keepsake	Yr.Iss.	7.75	16-26.00
90-152-023	Nutshell Chat 675QX5193	Keepsake	Yr.Iss.	6.75	13-21.00
90-152-024	Gingerbread Elf 575QX5033	Keepsake	Yr.Iss.	5.75	20.00
90-152-025	Stitches of Joy 775QX5186	Keepsake	Yr.Iss.	7.75	20-25.00
90-152-026	Little Drummer Boy 775QX5233	Keepsake	Yr.Iss.	7.75	20-29.00
90-152-027	Goose Cart 775QX5236	Keepsake	Yr.Iss.	7.75	16-23.00
90-152-028	Holiday Cardinals 775QX5243	Keepsake	Yr.Iss.	7.75	15-18.00
90-152-029	Christmas Partridge 775QX5246	Keepsake	Yr.Iss.	7.75	15.50
90-152-030	Joy is in the Air 775QX5503	Keepsake	Yr.Iss.	7.75	18-30.00
90-152-031	Happy Voices 675QX4645	Keepsake	Yr.Iss.	6.75	14.50
90-152-032	Jolly Dolphin 675QX4683	Keepsake	Yr.Iss.	6.75	28-35.00
90-152-033	Long Winter's Nap 675QX4703	Keepsake	Yr.Iss.	6.75	17.50
90-152-034	Hang in There 675QX4713	Keepsake	Yr.Iss.	6.75	14-24.00
90-152-035	Kitty's Best Pal 675QX4716	Keepsake	Yr.Iss.	6.75	20-22.50
90-152-036	SNOOPY and WOODSTOCK 675QX4723	Keepsake	Yr.Iss.	6.75	25-28.00
90-152-037	Beary Good Deal 675QX4733	Keepsake	Yr.Iss.	6.75	13.50
90-152-038	Country Angel 675QX5046	Keepsake	Yr.Iss.	6.75	65-85.00
90-152-039	Feliz Navidad 675QX5173	Keepsake	Yr.Iss.	6.75	15-32.00
90-152-040	Bearback Rider 975QX5483	Keepsake	Yr.Iss.	9.75	20-27.00
90-152-041	Polar Sport 775QX5156	Keepsake	Yr.Iss.	7.75	15.50
90-152-042	Polar Pair 575QX4626	Keepsake	Yr.Iss.	5.75	15.00
90-152-043	Polar Video 575QX4633	Keepsake	Yr.Iss.	5.75	12-19.00
90-152-044	Polar V.I.P. 575QX4663	Keepsake	Yr.Iss.	5.75	11.50
90-152-045	Polar TV 775QX5166	Keepsake	Yr.Iss.	7.75	15.00
90-152-046	Polar Jogger 575QX4666	Keepsake	Yr.Iss.	5.75	12-19.00
90-152-047	Garfield 475QX2303	Keepsake	Yr.Iss.	4.75	18-20.00
90-152-048	Peanuts 475QX2233	Keepsake	Yr.Iss.	4.75	20.00
90-152-049	Norman Rockwell Art 475QX2296	Keepsake	Yr.Iss.	4.75	15.00
Hallmark Keepsake Ornaments		**1990 Artists' Favorites**			
90-153-001	Donder's Diner 1375QX4823	Keepsake	Yr.Iss.	13.75	18-39.00
90-153-002	Welcome, Santa 1175QX4773	Keepsake	Yr.Iss.	11.75	19-23.00
90-153-003	Happy Woodcutter 975QX4763	Keepsake	Yr.Iss.	9.75	20-26.00
90-153-004	Angel Kitty 875QX4746	Keepsake	Yr.Iss.	8.75	15-20.00
90-153-005	Gentle Dreamers 875QX4756	Keepsake	Yr.Iss.	8.75	20-32.00

Company / Number	Name	Series / Artist	Edition Limit	Issue Price	Quote
90-153-006	Mouseboat 775QX4753	Keepsake	Yr.Iss.	7.75	15-23.00
Hallmark Keepsake Ornaments		**1990 Special Edition**			
90-154-001	Dickens Caroler Bell-Mr. Ashbourne 2175QX5056	Keepsake	Yr.Iss.	21.75	35-45.00
Hallmark Keepsake Ornaments		**1990 Collectible Series**			
90-155-001	Merry Olde Santa-First Edition 1475QX4736	Keepsake	Yr.Iss.	14.75	42-65.00
90-155-002	Greatest Story-First Edition 1275QX4656	Keepsake	Yr.Iss.	12.75	15-25.50
90-155-003	Heart of Christmas-First Edition 1375QX4726	Keepsake	Yr.Iss.	13.75	38-67.00
90-155-004	Fabulous Decade-First Edition 775QX4466	Keepsake	Yr.Iss.	7.75	15-30.00
90-155-005	Christmas Kitty-Second Edition 1475QX4506	Keepsake	Yr.Iss.	14.75	20-35.00
90-155-006	Winter Surprise-Second Edition 1075QX4443	Keepsake	Yr.Iss.	10.75	25-33.00
90-155-007	CRAYOLA Crayon-Bright Moving Colors-Second Edition 875QX4586	Keepsake	Yr.Iss.	8.75	25-35.00
90-155-008	Hark! It's Herald-Second Edition 675QX4463	Keepsake	Yr.Iss.	6.75	11-20.00
90-155-009	The Gift Bringers-St. Lucia-Second Edition 500QX2803	Keepsake	Yr.Iss.	5.00	8-20.00
90-155-010	Mary's Angels-Rosebud-Third Edition 575QX4423	Keepsake	Yr.Iss.	5.75	15-20.00
90-155-011	Cookies for Santa-Fourth Edition 875QX4436	Keepsake	Yr.Iss.	8.75	20.00
90-155-012	Popcorn Party-Fifth Edition 1375QX4393	Keepsake	Yr.Iss.	13.75	30-35.00
90-155-013	Reindeer Champs-Comet-Fifth Edition 775QX4433	Keepsake	Yr.Iss.	7.75	9-18.00
90-155-014	Betsey Clark: Home forChristmas-Fifth Edition 500QX2033	Keepsake	Yr.Iss.	5.00	10-17.50
90-155-015	Holiday Home-Seventh Edition 1475QX4696	Keepsake	Yr.Iss.	14.75	35-38.00
90-155-016	Seven Swans A-Swimming-Seventh Edition 675QX3033	Keepsake	Yr.Iss.	6.75	10-18.00
90-155-017	Rocking Horse-Tenth Edition 1075QX4646	Keepsake	Yr.Iss.	10.75	50-75.00
90-155-018	Frosty Friends-Eleventh Edition 975QX4396	Keepsake	Yr.Iss.	9.75	20-25.00
90-155-019	Festive Surrey-Twelfth Edition 1475QX4923	Keepsake	Yr.Iss.	14.75	30-34.50
90-155-020	Irish-Sixth Edition 1075QX4636	Keepsake	Yr.Iss.	10.75	15-22.00
90-155-021	Cinnamon Bear-Eighth Edition 875QX4426	Keepsake	Yr.Iss.	8.75	15-32.00
Hallmark Keepsake Ornaments		**1990 Keepsake Magic Ornaments**			
90-156-001	Children's Express 2800QLX7243	Keepsake	Yr.Iss.	28.00	55-76.00
90-156-002	Hop 'N Pop Popper 2000QLX7353	Keepsake	Yr.Iss.	20.00	45-50.00
90-156-003	Baby's First Christmas 2800QLX7246	Keepsake	Yr.Iss.	28.00	35 58.00
90-156-004	Christmas Memories 2500QLX7276	Keepsake	Yr.Iss.	25.00	40-55.00
90-156-005	Forest Frolics 2500QLX7236	Keepsake	Yr.Iss.	25.00	50-60.00
90-156-006	Santa's Ho-Ho-Hoedown 2500QLX7256	Keepsake	Yr.Iss.	25.00	50-65.00
90-156-007	Mrs. Santa's Kitchen 2500QLX7263	Keepsake	Yr.Iss.	25.00	55-60.00
90-156-008	Song and Dance 2000QLX7253	Keepsake	Yr.Iss.	20.00	65.00
90-156-009	Elfin Whittler 2000QLX7265	Keepsake	Yr.Iss.	20.00	25-45.00
90-156-010	Deer Crossing 1800QLX7213	Keepsake	Yr.Iss.	18.00	40-45.00
90-156-011	Our First Christmas Together 1800QLX7255	Keepsake	Yr.Iss.	18.00	40-45.00
90-156-012	Holiday Flash 1800QLX7333	Keepsake	Yr.Iss.	18.00	36.00
90-156-013	Starship Christmas 1800QLX7336	Keepsake	Yr.Iss.	18.00	30-45.00
90-156-014	Partridges in a Pear 1400QLX7212	Keepsake	Yr.Iss.	14.00	28.00
90-156-015	Letter to Santa 1400QLX7226	Keepsake	Yr.Iss.	14.00	28.00
90-156-016	Starlight Angel 1400QLX7306	Keepsake	Yr.Iss.	14.00	19-28.00
90-156-017	The Littlest Angel 1400QLX7303	Keepsake	Yr.Iss.	14.00	28.00
90-156-018	Blessings of Love 1400QLX7363	Keepsake	Yr.Iss.	14.00	35-54.00
90-156-019	Chris Mouse Wreath 1000QLX7296	Keepsake	Yr.Iss.	10.00	20-33.00
90-156-020	Beary Short Nap 1000QLX7326	Keepsake	Yr.Iss.	10.00	20-23.00
90-156-021	Elf of the Year 1000QLX7356	Keepsake	Yr.Iss.	10.00	20-26.00
Hallmark Keepsake Ornaments		**1990 Keepsake Miniature Ornaments**			
90-157-001	Thimble Bells 600QXM5543	Keepsake	Yr.Iss.	6.00	15-20.00
90-157-002	Nature's Angels 450QMX5733	Keepsake	Yr.Iss.	4.50	15-28.00
90-157-003	Cloisonne Poinsettia 1050QMX5533	Keepsake	Yr.Iss.	10.50	20-24.50
90-157-004	Coal Car 850QXM5756	Keepsake	Yr.Iss.	8.50	18-20.00
90-157-005	School 850QXM5763	Keepsake	Yr.Iss.	8.50	20.00
90-157-006	The Kringles 600QXM5753	Keepsake	Yr.Iss.	6.00	15-20.00
90-157-007	Kittens in Toyland 450QXM5736	Keepsake	Yr.Iss.	4.50	15-20.00
90-157-008	Rocking Horse 450QXM5743	Keepsake	Yr.Iss.	4.50	15-20.00
90-157-009	Penguin Pal 450QXM5746	Keepsake	Yr.Iss.	4.50	13-15.00
90-157-010	Santa's Streetcar 850QQXM5766	Keepsake	Yr.Iss.	8.50	17.00
90-157-011	Snow Angel 600QXM5773	Keepsake	Yr.Iss.	6.00	10-12.00
90-157-012	Baby's First Christmas 850QXM5703	Keepsake	Yr.Iss.	8.50	17.00
90-157-013	Grandchild's First Christmas 600QXM5723	Keepsake	Yr.Iss.	6.00	12.00
90-157-014	Special Friends 600QXM5726	Keepsake	Yr.Iss.	6.00	10-14.00
90-157-015	Mother 450QXM5716	Keepsake	Yr.Iss.	4.50	12-19.00
90-157-016	Warm Memories 450QXM5713	Keepsake	Yr.Iss.	4.50	10-19.00
90-157-017	First Christmas Together 600QXM5536	Keepsake	Yr.Iss.	6.00	13.50
90-157-018	Loving Hearts 300QXM5523	Keepsake	Yr.Iss.	3.00	6-14.00
90-157-019	Stringing Along 850QXM5606	Keepsake	Yr.Iss.	8.50	17.00
90-157-020	Santa's Journey 850QXM5826	Keepsake	Yr.Iss.	8.50	25.00
90-157-021	Wee Nutcracker 850QXM5843	Keepsake	Yr.Iss.	8.50	20.00
90-157-022	Bear Hug 600QXM5633	Keepsake	Yr.Iss.	6.00	12-20.00
90-157-023	Acorn Wreath 600QXM5686	Keepsake	Yr.Iss.	6.00	12.00
90-157-024	Puppy Love 600QXM5666	Keepsake	Yr.Iss.	6.00	12.00
90-157-025	Madonna and Child 600QXM5643	Keepsake	Yr.Iss.	6.00	12.00
90-157-026	Basket Buddy 600QXM5696	Keepsake	Yr.Iss.	6.00	12.00
90-157-027	Ruby Reindeer 600QXM5816	Keepsake	Yr.Iss.	6.00	12.00
90-157-028	Perfect Fit 450QXM5516	Keepsake	Yr.Iss.	4.50	13-18.00
90-157-029	Panda's Surprise 450QXM5616	Keepsake	Yr.Iss.	4.50	13.50
90-157-030	Stamp Collector 450QXM5623	Keepsake	Yr.Iss.	4.50	9.50
90-157-031	Christmas Dove 450QXM5636	Keepsake	Yr.Iss.	4.50	12-19.00
90-157-032	Type of Joy 450QXM5646	Keepsake	Yr.Iss.	4.50	12-17.00
90-157-033	Teacher 450QXM5653	Keepsake	Yr.Iss.	4.50	10-17.00
90-157-034	Air Santa 450QXM5656	Keepsake	Yr.Iss.	4.50	12.50
90-157-035	Sweet Slumber 450QXM5663	Keepsake	Yr.Iss.	4.50	12-15.00
90-157-036	Busy Carver 450QXM5673	Keepsake	Yr.Iss.	4.50	10.00
90-157-037	Lion and Lamb 450QXM5676	Keepsake	Yr.Iss.	4.50	15-19.00
90-157-038	Going Sledding 450QXM5683	Keepsake	Yr.Iss.	4.50	9.50
90-157-039	Country Heart 450QXM5693	Keepsake	Yr.Iss.	4.50	10-19.00
90-157-040	Nativity 450QXM5706	Keepsake	Yr.Iss.	4.50	10-13.00
90-157-041	Holiday Cardinal 300QXM5526	Keepsake	Yr.Iss.	3.00	9-12.00
90-157-042	Brass Bouquet 600QMX5776	Keepsake	Yr.Iss.	6.00	6.50
90-157-043	Brass Santa 300QXM5786	Keepsake	Yr.Iss.	3.00	7-15.00
90-157-044	Brass Horn 300QXM5793	Keepsake	Yr.Iss.	3.00	6.50
90-157-045	Brass Peace 300QXM5796	Keepsake	Yr.Iss.	3.00	7.00
90-157-046	Brass Year 300QXM5833	Keepsake	Yr.Iss.	3.00	7.00
Hallmark Keepsake Ornaments		**1990 Limited Edition**			
90-158-001	Dove of Peace 2475QXC447-6	Keepsake	25,400	24.75	60-70.00
90-158-002	Christmas Limited1975 QXC476-6	Keepsake	38,700	19.75	75-85.00
90-158-003	Sugar Plum Fairy 2775QXC447-3	Keepsake	25,400	27.75	55-60.00
Hallmark Keepsake Ornaments		**1990 Keepsake Collector's Club**			
90-159-001	Club Hollow QXC445-6	Keepsake	Yr.Iss.	Unkn.	30-46.00
90-159-002	Crown Prince QXC560-3	Keepsake	Yr.Iss.	Unkn.	40.00
90-159-003	Armful of Joy 800QXC445-3	Keepsake	Yr.Iss.	8.00	45-50.00
Hallmark Keepsake Ornaments		**1991 Commemoratives**			
91-160-001	Baby's First Christmas 1775QX5107	Keepsake	Yr.Iss.	17.75	40-50.00
91-160-002	Baby's First Christmas-Baby Boy475QX2217	Keepsake	Yr.Iss.	4.75	10-18.00
91-160-003	Baby's First Christmas-Baby Girl475QX2227	Keepsake	Yr.Iss.	4.75	15-18.00
91-160-004	Baby's First Christmas-Photo Holder 775QX4869	Keepsake	Yr.Iss.	7.75	19.50
91-160-005	Mom-to-Be 575QX4877	Keepsake	Yr.Iss.	5.75	20.00
91-160-006	Dad-to-Be 575QX4879	Keepsake	Yr.Iss.	5.75	20.00
91-160-007	Grandson's First Christmas 675QX5117	Keepsake	Yr.Iss.	6.75	15.00
91-160-008	Granddaughter's First Christmas 675QX5119	Keepsake	Yr.Iss.	6.75	15.00
91-160-009	A Child's Christmas 975QX4887	Keepsake	Yr.Iss.	9.75	15.50
91-160-010	Baby's First Christmas 775QX4889	Keepsake	Yr.Iss.	7.75	15-25.00
91-160-011	Baby's Second Christmas 675QX4897	Keepsake	Yr.Iss.	6.75	20-25.00
91-160-012	Child's Third Christmas 675QX4899	Keepsake	Yr.Iss.	6.75	20-30.00
91-160-013	Child's Fourth Christmas 675QX4907	Keepsake	Yr.Iss.	6.75	15.50
91-160-014	Child's Fifth Christmas 675QX4909	Keepsake	Yr.Iss.	6.75	15.50
91-160-015	Sweetheart 975QX4957	Keepsake	Yr.Iss.	9.75	17.50
91-160-016	Our First Christmas Together-Photo Holder 875QX4917	Keepsake	Yr.Iss.	8.75	20.00
91-160-017	Our First Christmas Together 875QX4919	Keepsake	Yr.Iss.	8.75	10-20.00
91-160-018	Our First Christmas Together 675QX3139	Keepsake	Yr.Iss.	6.75	20.00
91-160-019	Our First Christmas Together 475QX2229	Keepsake	Yr.Iss.	4.75	15-20.00
91-160-020	Under the Mistletoe 875QX4949	Keepsake	Yr.Iss.	8.75	20.00
91-160-021	Jesus Loves Me 775QX3147	Keepsake	Yr.Iss.	7.75	15.50
91-160-022	Five Years Together 775QX4927	Keepsake	Yr.Iss.	7.75	15.50
91-160-023	Ten Years Together 775QX4929	Keepsake	Yr.Iss.	7.75	15.50
91-160-024	Twenty -Five Years Together 875QX4937	Keepsake	Yr.Iss.	8.75	19.50
91-160-025	Forty Years Together 775QX4939	Keepsake	Yr.Iss.	7.75	19.50
91-160-026	Fifty Years Together 875QX4947	Keepsake	Yr.Iss.	8.75	16-20.00
91-160-027	Mother 975QX5457	Keepsake	Yr.Iss.	9.75	22.50
91-160-028	Dad 775QX5127	Keepsake	Yr.Iss.	7.75	19.50
91-160-029	Mom and Dad 975QX5467	Keepsake	Yr.Iss.	9.75	20.00
91-160-030	Grandmother 475QX2307	Keepsake	Yr.Iss.	4.75	15.50
91-160-031	Grandparents 475QX2309	Keepsake	Yr.Iss.	4.75	15.50
91-160-032	Godchild 675QX5489	Keepsake	Yr.Iss.	6.75	15.50
91-160-033	Son 575QX5469	Keepsake	Yr.Iss.	5.75	10-16.00
91-160-034	Daughter 575QX5477	Keepsake	Yr.Iss.	5.75	10-24.00
91-160-035	Brother 675QX5479	Keepsake	Yr.Iss.	6.75	14-20.00
91-160-036	Sister 675QX5487	Keepsake	Yr.Iss.	6.75	19.50
91-160-037	Grandson 475QX2297	Keepsake	Yr.Iss.	4.75	15.50
91-160-038	Granddaughter 475QX2299	Keepsake	Yr.Iss.	4.75	16-22.00
91-160-039	Friends Are Fun 975QX5289	Keepsake	Yr.Iss.	9.75	17-20.00
91-160-040	Extra-Special Friends 475QX2279	Keepsake	Yr.Iss.	4.75	15.50
91-160-041	New Home 675QX5449	Keepsake	Yr.Iss.	6.75	13-20.00
91-160-042	Across the Miles 675QX3157	Keepsake	Yr.Iss.	6.75	15.50
91-160-043	From Our Home to Yours 475QX2287	Keepsake	Yr.Iss.	4.75	12.50
91-160-044	Terrific Teacher 675QX5309	Keepsake	Yr.Iss.	6.75	13.50
91-160-045	Teacher 475QX2289	Keepsake	Yr.Iss.	4.75	14-25.00
91-160-046	Gift of Joy 875QX5319	Keepsake	Yr.Iss.	8.75	19.50
91-160-047	The Big Cheese 675QX5327	Keepsake	Yr.Iss.	6.75	13-18.00
Hallmark Keepsake Ornaments		**1991 New Attractions**			
91-161-001	Winnie-the Pooh 975QX5569	Keepsake	Yr.Iss.	9.75	33-55.00
91-161-002	Piglet and Eeyore 975QX5577	Keepsake	Yr.Iss.	9.75	40-55.00
91-161-003	Christopher Robin 975QX5579	Keepsake	Yr.Iss.	9.75	25-45.00
91-161-004	Rabbit 975QX5607	Keepsake	Yr.Iss.	9.75	20-30.00
91-161-005	Tigger 975QX5609	Keepsake	Yr.Iss.	9.75	75-125.00
91-161-006	Kanga and Roo 975QX5617	Keepsake	Yr.Iss.	9.75	30-50.00
91-161-007	Look Out Below 875QX4959	Keepsake	Yr.Iss.	8.75	15-20.00
91-161-008	Yule Logger 875QX4967	Keepsake	Yr.Iss.	8.75	19.50
91-161-009	Glee Club Bears 87566QX4969	Keepsake	Yr.Iss.	8.75	18-20.00
91-161-010	Plum Delightful 875QX4977	Keepsake	Yr.Iss.	8.75	19.50
91-161-011	Snow Twins 875QX4979	Keepsake	Yr.Iss.	8.75	18-23.00
91-161-012	Loving Stitches 875QX4987	Keepsake	Yr.Iss.	8.75	25-30.00
91-161-013	Fanfare Bear 875QX5337	Keepsake	Yr.Iss.	8.75	19.50
91-161-014	Mrs. Cratchit 1375QX4999	Keepsake	Yr.Iss.	13.75	23-38.00
91-161-015	Merry Carolers 2975QX4799	Keepsake	Yr.Iss.	29.75	49.50
91-161-016	Ebenezer Scrooge 1375QX4989	Keepsake	Yr.Iss.	13.75	27.50
91-161-017	Bob Cratchit 1375QX4997	Keepsake	Yr.Iss.	13.75	22.50
91-161-018	Tiny Tim 1075QX5037	Keepsake	Yr.Iss.	10.75	23-33.00
91-161-019	Evergreen Inn 875QX5389	Keepsake	Yr.Iss.	8.75	15.50
91-161-020	Santa's Studio 875QX5397	Keepsake	Yr.Iss.	8.75	15.50
91-161-021	Holiday Cafe 875QX5399	Keepsake	Yr.Iss.	8.75	15.50
91-161-022	Jolly Wolly Santa 775QX5419	Keepsake	Yr.Iss.	7.75	28.00
91-161-023	Jolly Wolly Snowman 775QX5427	Keepsake	Yr.Iss.	7.75	23-28.00
91-161-024	Jolly Wolly Soldier 775QX5429	Keepsake	Yr.Iss.	7.75	20-28.00
91-161-025	Partridge in a Pear Tree 975QX5297	Keepsake	Yr.Iss.	9.75	19.50
91-161-026	Christmas Welcome 975QX5299	Keepsake	Yr.Iss.	9.75	19.50
91-161-027	Night Before Christmas 975QX5307	Keepsake	Yr.Iss.	9.75	18-25.00
91-161-028	SNOOPY and WOODSTOCK 675QX5197	Keepsake	Yr.Iss.	6.75	20-31.00
91-161-029	PEANUTS 500QX2257	Keepsake	Yr.Iss.	5.00	15-25.00
91-161-030	GARFIELD 775QX5177	Keepsake	Yr.Iss.	7.75	20.00
91-161-031	Norman Rockwell Art 500QX2259	Keepsake	Yr.Iss.	5.00	16.00
91-161-032	Mary Engelbreit 475QX2237	Keepsake	Yr.Iss.	4.75	19.50
91-161-033	Up 'N'Down Journey 975QX5047	Keepsake	Yr.Iss.	9.75	23-25.00
91-161-034	Old-Fashioned Sled 875QX4317	Keepsake	Yr.Iss.	8.75	20-26.00
91-161-035	Folk Art Reindeer 875QX5359	Keepsake	Yr.Iss.	8.75	15.50
91-161-036	Sweet Talk 875QX5367	Keepsake	Yr.Iss.	8.75	18-26.00
91-161-037	Snowy Owl 775QX5269	Keepsake	Yr.Iss.	7.75	20.00
91-161-038	Dinoclaus 775QX5277	Keepsake	Yr.Iss.	7.75	19.50
91-161-039	Basket Bell Players 775QX5377	Keepsake	Yr.Iss.	7.75	16-25.00
91-161-040	Nutshell Nativity 675QX5176	Keepsake	Yr.Iss.	6.75	20-28.00
91-161-041	Cuddly Lamb 675QX5199	Keepsake	Yr.Iss.	6.75	19.50
91-161-042	Feliz Navidad 675QX5279	Keepsake	Yr.Iss.	6.75	13.50
91-161-043	Polar Classic 675QX5287	Keepsake	Yr.Iss.	6.75	17.50
91-161-044	All-Star 675QX5329	Keepsake	Yr.Iss.	6.75	18-26.00
91-161-045	Chilly Chap 675QX5339	Keepsake	Yr.Iss.	6.75	15-20.00
91-161-046	On a Roll 675QX5347	Keepsake	Yr.Iss.	6.75	20-26.00
91-161-047	Joyous Memories-Photoholder 675QX5369	Keepsake	Yr.Iss.	6.75	17.50
91-161-048	Ski Lift Bunny 675QX5447	Keepsake	Yr.Iss.	6.75	15.50
91-161-049	Nutty Squirrel 575QX4833	Keepsake	Yr.Iss.	5.75	15.50
91-161-050	Notes of Cheer 575QX5357	Keepsake	Yr.Iss.	5.75	15.50
Hallmark Keepsake Ornaments		**1991 Artists' Favorites**			
91-162-001	Polar Circus Wagon 1375QX4399	Keepsake	Yr.Iss.	13.75	30-35.00
91-162-002	Noah's Ark 1375QX4867	Keepsake	Yr.Iss.	13.75	30-37.00
91-162-003	Santa Sailor 975QX4389	Keepsake	Yr.Iss.	9.75	15-22.00
91-162-004	Hooked on Santa 775QX4109	Keepsake	Yr.Iss.	7.75	15-28.00
91-162-005	Fiddlin' Around 775QX4387	Keepsake	Yr.Iss.	7.75	15-18.00
91-162-006	Tramp and Laddie 775QX4397	Keepsake	Yr.Iss.	7.75	22-25.00

Company Number	Name	Series Artist	Edition Limit	Issue Price	Quote
Hallmark Keepsake Ornaments		**1991 Special Edition**			
91-163-001	Dickens Caroler Bell-Mrs. Beaumont -2175QX5039	Keepsake	Yr.Iss.	21.75	35-51.00
Hallmark Keepsake Ornaments		**1991 Collectible Series**			
91-164-001	1957 Corvette-First Edition1275QX4319	Keepsake	Yr.Iss.	12.75	75-125.00
91-164-002	Peace on Earth-Italy First Ed. 1175QX5129	Keepsake	Yr.Iss.	11.75	25-30.00
91-164-003	Heavenly Angels-First Edition 775QX4367	Keepsake	Yr.Iss.	7.75	20.00
91-164-004	Puppy Love-First Edition 775QX5379	Keepsake	Yr.Iss.	7.75	30-40.00
91-164-005	Merry Olde Santa-Second Ed. 1475QX4359	Keepsake	Yr.Iss.	14.75	40-50.00
91-164-006	Heart of Christmas-Second Ed. 1375QX4357	Keepsake	Yr.Iss.	13.75	20-25.00
91-164-007	Greatest Story-Second Edition 1275QX4129	Keepsake	Yr.Iss.	12.75	25.50
91-164-008	Fabulous Decade-Second Ed. 775QX4119	Keepsake	Yr.Iss.	7.75	15-33.00
91-164-009	Winter Surprise-Third Ed. 1075QX4277	Keepsake	Yr.Iss.	10.75	22-25.00
91-164-010	CRAYOLA CRAYON-Bright Vibrant Carols-Third Edition 975QX4219	Keepsake	Yr.Iss.	9.75	20-30.00
91-164-011	Hark! It's Herald Third Edition 675QX4379	Keepsake	Yr.Iss.	6.75	12-32.00
91-164-012	The Gift Bringers-Christkind Third Edition 500QX2117	Keepsake	Yr.Iss.	5.00	15.00
91-164-013	Mary's Angels-Iris Fourth Ed. 675QX4279	Keepsake	Yr.Iss.	6.75	15-31.00
91-164-014	Let It Snow! Fifth Ediiton 875QX4369	Keepsake	Yr.Iss.	8.75	15-20.00
91-164-015	Checking His List Sixth Edition 1375QX4339	Keepsake	Yr.Iss.	13.75	25-30.00
91-164-016	Reindeer Champ-Cupid Sixth Ed. 775QX4347	Keepsake	Yr.Iss.	7.75	15-33.00
91-164-017	Fire Station-Eigth Edition 1475QX4139	Keepsake	Yr.Iss.	14.75	30-35.00
91-164-018	Eight Maids A-Milking-Eigth Ed. 675QX3089	Keepsake	Yr.Iss.	6.75	15.50
91-164-019	Rocking Horse-11th Ed. 1075QX4147	Keepsake	Yr.Iss.	10.75	20-25.50
91-164-020	Frosty Friends-Twelfth Edition 975QX4327	Keepsake	Yr.Iss.	9.75	20-28.00
91-164-021	Santa's Antique Car-13th Ed. 1475QX4349	Keepsake	Yr.Iss.	14.75	28-33.00
91-164-022	Christmas Kitty-Third Edition 1475QX4377	Keepsake	Yr.Iss.	14.75	20-30.00
91-164-023	Betsey Clark: Home for Christmas Sixth Edition 500QX2109	Keepsake	Yr.Iss.	5.00	10.00
Hallmark Keepsake Ornaments		**1991 Keepsake Magic Ornaments**			
91-165-001	PEANUTS 1800QLX7229	Keepsake	Yr.Iss.	18.00	35-50.00
91-165-002	Santa Special 4000QLX7167	Keepsake	Yr.Iss.	40.00	60.00
91-165-003	Salvation Army Band 3000QLX7273	Keepsake	Yr.Iss.	30.00	50-60.00
91-165-004	Forest Frolics 2500QLX7219	Keepsake	Yr.Iss.	25.00	50.00
91-165-005	Chris Mouse Mail 1000QLX7207	Keepsake	Yr.Iss.	10.00	25-32.00
91-165-006	Arctic Dome 2500QLX7117	Keepsake	Yr.Iss.	25.00	49.50
91-165-007	Baby's First Christmas 3000QLX7247	Keepsake	Yr.Iss.	30.00	56-64.00
91-165-008	Bringing Home the Tree-2800QLX7249	Keepsake	Yr.Iss.	28.00	55.50
91-165-009	Ski Trip 2800QLX7266	Keepsake	Yr.Iss.	28.00	45-60.00
91-165-010	Kringles's Bumper Cars-2500QLX7119	Keepsake	Yr.Iss.	25.00	49.50
91-165-011	Our First Christmas Together-2500QXL7137	Keepsake	Yr.Iss.	25.00	49.50
91-165-012	Jingle Bears 2500QLX7323	Keepsake	Yr.Iss.	25.00	49.50
91-165-013	Toyland Tower 2000QLX7129	Keepsake	Yr.Iss.	20.00	36-40.00
91-165-014	Mole Family Home 2000QLX7149	Keepsake	Yr.Iss.	20.00	40-46.00
91-165-015	Starship Enterprise 2000QLX7199	Keepsake	Yr.Iss.	20.00	150-300.
91-165-016	It's A Wonderful Life 2000QLX7237	Keepsake	Yr.Iss.	20.00	40-50.00
91-165-017	Sparkling Angel 1800QLX7157	Keepsake	Yr.Iss.	18.00	29.50
91-165-018	Santa's Hot Line 1800QLX7159	Keepsake	Yr.Iss.	18.00	35.50
91-165-019	Father Christmas 1400QLX7147	Keepsake	Yr.Iss.	14.00	30.00
91-165-020	Holiday Glow 1400QLX7177	Keepsake	Yr.Iss.	14.00	30-35.00
91-165-021	Festive Brass Church 1400QLX7179	Keepsake	Yr.Iss.	14.00	24.50
91-165-022	Friendship Tree 1000QLX7169	Keepsake	Yr.Iss.	10.00	25-33.00
91-165-023	Elfin Engineer 1000QLX7209	Keepsake	Yr.Iss.	10.00	19.50
91-165-024	Angel of Light 3000QLT7239	Keepsake	Yr.Iss.	30.00	59.50
Hallmark Keepsake Ornaments		**1991 Keepsake Miniature Ornaments**			
91-166-001	Woodland Babies 600QXM5667	Keepsake	Yr.Iss.	6.00	20-30.00
91-166-002	Thimble Bells-Second Edition 600QXM5659	Keepsake	Yr.Iss.	6.00	10-18.00
91-166-003	Nature's Angels-Second Ed. 450QXM5657	Keepsake	Yr.Iss.	4.50	15-27.00
91-166-004	Passenger Car-Third Ed. 850QXM5649	Keepsake	Yr.Iss.	8.50	19.50
91-166-005	The Kringles-Third Edition 6000QXM5647	Keepsake	Yr.Iss.	6.00	15-20.00
91-166-006	Inn-Fourth Edition 850QXM5627	Keepsake	Yr.Iss.	8.50	19.50
91-166-007	Rocking Horse-Fourth Ed. 450QXM5637	Keepsake	Yr.Iss.	4.50	15-30.00
91-166-008	Kittens in Toyland-Fourth Ed. 450QXM5639	Keepsake	Yr.Iss.	4.50	18-24.00
91-166-009	Penquin Pal-Fourth Ed. 450QXM5629	Keepsake	Yr.Iss.	4.50	17.50
91-166-010	Ring-A-Ding Elf 850QXM5669	Keepsake	Yr.Iss.	8.50	18-28.00
91-166-011	Lulu & Family 600QXM5677	Keepsake	Yr.Iss.	6.00	20.00
91-166-012	Silvery Santa 975QXM5679	Keepsake	Yr.Iss.	9.75	20-23.00
91-166-013	Heavenly Minstrel 975QXM5687	Keepsake	Yr.Iss.	9.75	20-31.00
91-166-014	Tiny Tea Party Set of 6 2900QXM5827	Keepsake	Yr.Iss.	29.00	100-125.
91-166-015	Special Friends 850QXM5797	Keepsake	Yr.Iss.	8.50	19.50
91-166-016	Mom 600QXM5699	Keepsake	Yr.Iss.	6.00	20-27.00
91-166-017	Baby's First Christmas 600QXM5799	Keepsake	Yr.Iss.	6.00	14.50
91-166-018	Our First Christmas Together 600QXM5819	Keepsake	Yr.Iss.	6.00	19.50
91-166-019	Key to Love 450QXM5689	Keepsake	Yr.Iss.	4.50	19.50
91-166-020	Grandchild's First Christmas 450QXM5697	Keepsake	Yr.Iss.	4.50	17.50
91-166-021	Treeland Trio 850QXM5899	Keepsake	Yr.Iss.	8.50	19.50
91-166-022	Wee Toymaker 850QXM5967	Keepsake	Yr.Iss.	8.50	17.50
91-166-023	Feliz Navidad 600QXM5887	Keepsake	Yr.Iss.	6.00	18-23.00
91-166-024	Top Hatter 600QXM5889	Keepsake	Yr.Iss.	6.00	20-26.00
91-166-025	Upbeat Bear 600QXM5907	Keepsake	Yr.Iss.	6.00	15-20.00
91-166-026	Friendly Fawn 600QXM5947	Keepsake	Yr.Iss.	6.00	19.50
91-166-027	Caring Shepherd 600QXM5949	Keepsake	Yr.Iss.	6.00	19.50
91-166-028	Cardinal Cameo 600QXM5957	Keepsake	Yr.Iss.	6.00	18-26.00
91-166-029	Courier Turtle 450QXM5857	Keepsake	Yr.Iss.	4.50	17.50
91-166-030	Fly By 450QXM5859	Keepsake	Yr.Iss.	4.50	19.50
91-166-031	Love Is Born 600QXM5959	Keepsake	Yr.Iss.	6.00	19.50
91-166-032	Cool 'n' Sweet 450QXM5867	Keepsake	Yr.Iss.	4.50	15-23.00
91-166-033	All Aboard 450QXM5869	Keepsake	Yr.Iss.	4.50	19.50
91-166-034	Bright Boxers 450QXM5877	Keepsake	Yr.Iss.	4.50	17.50
91-166-035	Li'l Popper 450QXM5897	Keepsake	Yr.Iss.	4.50	20.00
91-166-036	Kitty in a Mitty 450QXM5879	Keepsake	Yr.Iss.	4.50	14.50
91-166-037	Seaside Otter 450QXM5909	Keepsake	Yr.Iss.	4.50	14.50
91-166-038	Fancy Wreath 450QXM5917	Keepsake	Yr.Iss.	4.50	17.50
91-166-039	N. Pole Buddy 450QXM5927	Keepsake	Yr.Iss.	4.50	22.50
91-166-040	Vision of Santa 450QXM5937	Keepsake	Yr.Iss.	4.50	18-23.00
91-166-041	Busy Bear 450QXM5939	Keepsake	Yr.Iss.	4.50	12.50
91-166-042	Country Sleigh 450QXM5999	Keepsake	Yr.Iss.	4.50	10-15.00
91-166-043	Brass Church 300QXM5979	Keepsake	Yr.Iss.	3.00	10-19.00
91-166-044	Brass Soldier 300QXM5987	Keepsake	Yr.Iss.	3.00	9.50
91-166-045	Noel 300QXM5989	Keepsake	Yr.Iss.	3.00	12.50
91-166-046	Holiday Snowflake 300QXM5997	Keepsake	Yr.Iss.	3.00	12.50
Hallmark Keepsake Ornaments		**1991 Club Limited Editions**			
91-167-001	Secrets for Santa 2375QXC4797	Keepsake	28,700	23.75	50.00
91-167-002	Galloping Into Christmas 1975QXC4779	Keepsake	28,400	19.75	55-63.00
Hallmark Keepsake Ornaments		**1991 Keepsake Collector's Club**			
91-168-001	Hidden Treasure/Li'l Keeper 1500QXC4769	Keepsake	Yr.Iss.	15.00	30-35.00
91-168-002	Beary Artistic 1000QXC7259	Keepsake	Yr.Iss.	10.00	40-45.00
Hallmark Keepsake Ornaments		**1992 Collectible Series**			
92-169-001	Tobin Fraley Carousel-First Ed. 2800QX4891	Keepsake	Yr.Iss.	28.00	45-85.00
92-169-002	Owliver-First Ed. 775QX4544	Keepsake	Yr.Iss.	7.75	15.00
92-169-003	Betsey's Country Christmas-First Ed. 500QX2104	Keepsake	Yr.Iss.	5.00	5 .00
92-169-004	1966 Mustang-Second Ed. 1275QX4284	Keepsake	Yr.Iss.	12.75	28-35.00
92-169-005	Peace On Earth-Spain Second Ed. 1175QX5174	Keepsake	Yr.Iss.	11.75	11.75
92-169-006	Heavenly Angels-Second Ed.775QX4454	Keepsake	Yr.Iss.	7.75	15.00
92-169-007	Puppy Love-Second Ed. 775QX4484	Keepsake	Yr.Iss.	7.75	20-25.00
92-169-008	Merry Olde Santa-Third Ed. 1475QX4414	Keepsake	Yr.Iss.	14.75	18-20.00
92-169-009	Heart of Christmas-Third Ed. 1375QX4411	Keepsake	Yr.Iss.	13.75	16-18.00
92-169-010	Fabulous Decade-Third Ed. 775QX4244	Keepsake	Yr.Iss.	7.75	15-30.00
92-169-011	CRAYOLA CRAYON-Bright Colors Fourth Ed. 975QX4264	Keepsake	Yr.Iss.	9.75	18.00
92-169-012	The Gift Bringers-Kolyada Fourth Ed. 500QX2124	Keepsake	Yr.Iss.	5.00	5.00
92-169-013	Mary's Angels-Lily Fifth Ed. 675QX4274	Keepsake	Yr.Iss.	6.75	25-55.00
92-169-014	Gift Exchange Seventh Ed. 1475QX4294	Keepsake	Yr.Iss.	14.75	20-25.00
92-169-015	Reindeer Champs-Donder Seventh Ed. 875QX5284	Keepsake	Yr.Iss.	8.75	23.00
92-169-016	Five-and-Ten-Cent Store Ninth Ed. 1475QX4254	Keepsake	Yr.Iss.	14.75	20-25.00
92-169-017	Nine Ladies Dancing Ninth Ed. 675QX3031	Keepsake	Yr.Iss.	6.75	6.75
92-169-018	Rocking Horse Twelfth Ed. 1075QX4261	Keepsake	Yr.Iss.	10.75	20.00
92-169-019	Frosty Friends 13th Ed. 975QX4291	Keepsake	Yr.Iss.	9.75	15.00
92-169-020	Kringle Tours 14th Ed. 1475QX4341	Keepsake	Yr.Iss.	14.75	17-20.00
92-169-021	Greatest Story Third Ed. 1275QX4251	Keepsake	Yr.Iss.	12.75	20.00
92-169-022	Winter Surprise Fourth Ed. 1175QX4271	Keepsake	Yr.Iss.	11.75	12-15.00
92-169-023	Hark! It's Herald Fourth Ed. 775QX4464	Keepsake	Yr.Iss.	7.75	7.75
92-169-024	Sweet Holiday Harmony Sixth Ed. 875QX4461	Keepsake	Yr.Iss.	8.75	13-15.00
Hallmark Keepsake Ornaments		**1992 Artists' Favorites**			
92-170-001	Mother Goose 1375QX4984	Keepsake	Yr.Iss.	13.75	30.00
92-170-002	Elfin Marionette1175QX5931	Keepsake	Yr.Iss.	11.75	11.75
92-170-003	Polar Post 875QX4914	Keepsake	Yr.Iss.	8.75	8.75
92-170-004	Turtle Dreams 875QX4991	Keepsake	Yr.Iss.	8.75	8.75
92-170-005	Uncle Art's Ice Cream 875QX5001	Keepsake	Yr.Iss.	8.75	8.75
92-170-006	Stocked With Joy 775QX5934	Keepsake	Yr.Iss.	7.75	7.75
Hallmark Keepsake Ornaments		**1992 Special Edition**			
92-171-001	Dickens Caroler Bell-Lord Chadwick Third Ed. 2175QX4554	Keepsake	Yr.Iss.	21.75	21.75
Hallmark Keepsake Ornaments		**1992 Commemoratives**			
92-172-001	Baby's First Christmas1875QX4581	Keepsake	Yr.Iss.	18.75	20.00
92-172-002	Baby's First Christmas 775QX4641	Keepsake	Yr.Iss.	7.75	12.00
92-172-003	Baby's First Christmas-Baby Girl 475QX2204	Keepsake	Yr.Iss.	4.75	4.75
92-172-004	Baby's First Christmas-Baby Boy 475QX2191	Keepsake	Yr.Iss.	4.75	4.75
92-172-005	For My Grandma 775QX5184	Keepsake	Yr.Iss.	7.75	7.75
92-172-006	A Child's Christmas 975QX4574	Keepsake	Yr.Iss.	9.75	20.00
92-172-007	Grandson's First Christmas 675QX4621	Keepsake	Yr.Iss.	6.75	6.75
92-172-008	Grandaughter's First Christmas 675QX4634	Keepsake	Yr.Iss.	6.75	6.75
92-172-009	Mom-to-Be 675QX4614	Keepsake	Yr.Iss.	6.75	6.75
92-172-010	Dad-to-Be 675QX4611	Keepsake	Yr.Iss.	6.75	6.75
92-172-011	Baby's First Christmas 775QX4644	Keepsake	Yr.Iss.	7.75	15.00
92-172-012	Baby's Second Christmas 675QX4651	Keepsake	Yr.Iss.	6.75	15.00
92-172-013	Child's Third Christmas 675QX4654	Keepsake	Yr.Iss.	6.75	6.75
92-172-014	Child's Fourth Christmas 675QX4661	Keepsake	Yr.Iss.	6.75	15.00
92-172-015	Child's Fifth Christmas 675QX4664	Keepsake	Yr.Iss.	6.75	6.75
92-172-016	For The One I Love 975QX4884	Keepsake	Yr.Iss.	9.75	9.75
92-172-017	Our First Christmas Together 975QX5061	Keepsake	Yr.Iss.	9.75	9.75
92-172-018	Out First Christmas Together 875QX4694	Keepsake	Yr.Iss.	8.75	8.75
92-172-019	Our First Christmas Together 675QX3011	Keepsake	Yr.Iss.	6.75	6.75
92-172-020	Love To Skate 875QX4841	Keepsake	Yr.Iss.	8.75	8.75
92-172-021	Anniversary Year 975QX4851	Keepsake	Yr.Iss.	9.75	9.75
92-172-022	Dad 775QX4674	Keepsake	Yr.Iss.	7.75	7.75
92-172-023	Mom 775QX5164	Keepsake	Yr.Iss.	7.75	7.75
92-172-024	Brother 675QX4684	Keepsake	Yr.Iss.	6.75	6.75
92-172-025	Sister 675QX4681	Keepsake	Yr.Iss.	6.75	6.75
92-172-026	Son 675QX5024	Keepsake	Yr.Iss.	6.75	6.75
92-172-027	Daughter 675QX5031	Keepsake	Yr.Iss.	6.75	6.75
92-172-028	Mom and Dad 975QX4671	Keepsake	Yr.Iss.	9.75	20-25.00
92-172-029	Grandparents 475QX2004	Keepsake	Yr.Iss.	4.75	4.75
92-172-030	Grandmother 475QX2011	Keepsake	Yr.Iss.	4.75	4.75
92-172-031	Godchild 675QX5941	Keepsake	Yr.Iss.	6.75	6.75
92-172-032	Grandaughter 675QX5604	Keepsake	Yr.Iss.	6.75	6.75
92-172-033	Grandson 675QX5611	Keepsake	Yr.Iss.	6.75	12.00
92-172-034	Friendship Line 975QX5034	Keepsake	Yr.Iss.	9.75	20.00
92-172-035	Friendly Greetings 775QX5041	Keepsake	Yr.Iss.	7.75	7.75
92-172-036	New Home 875QX5191	Keepsake	Yr.Iss.	8.75	8.75
92-172-037	Across the Miles 675QX3044	Keepsake	Yr.Iss.	6.75	6.75
92-172-038	From Our Home To yours 475QX2131	Keepsake	Yr.Iss.	4.75	4.75
92-172-039	Secret Pal 775QX5424	Keepsake	Yr.Iss.	7.75	7.75
92-172-040	Teacher 475QX2264	Keepsake	Yr.Iss.	4.75	4.75
92-172-041	World-Class Teacher 775QX5054	Keepsake	Yr.Iss.	7.75	7.75
92-172-042	V. P. of Important Stuff 675QX5051	Keepsake	Yr.Iss.	6.75	6.75
92-172-043	Holiday Memo 775QX5044	Keepsake	Yr.Iss.	7.75	7.75
92-172-044	Special Dog 775QX5421	Keepsake	Yr.Iss.	7.75	30.00
92-172-045	Special Cat 775QX5414	Keepsake	Yr.Iss.	7.75	7.75
Hallmark Keepsake Ornaments		**1992 New Attractions**			
92-173-001	Eric the Baker 875QX5244	Keepsake	Yr.Iss.	8.75	8.75
92-173-002	Otto the Carpenter 875QX5254	Keepsake	Yr.Iss.	8.75	8.75
92-173-003	Max the Tailor 875QX5251	Keepsake	Yr.Iss.	8.75	8.75
92-173-004	Franz the Artist 875QX5261	Keepsake	Yr.Iss.	8.75	8.75
92-173-005	Freida the Animals' Friend 875QX5264	Keepsake	Yr.Iss.	8.75	8.75
92-173-006	Ludwig the Musician 875QX5281	Keepsake	Yr.Iss.	8.75	8.75
92-173-007	Silver Star 2800QX5324	Keepsake	Yr.Iss.	28.00	45.00
92-173-008	Locomotive 975QX5311	Keepsake	Yr.Iss.	9.75	25.00
92-173-009	Coal Car 975QX5401	Keepsake	Yr.Iss.	9.75	15.00
92-173-010	Stock Car 975QX5314	Keepsake	Yr.Iss.	9.75	15.00
92-173-011	Caboose 975QX5321	Keepsake	Yr.Iss.	9.75	20.00
92-173-012	Gone Wishin' 875QX5171	Keepsake	Yr.Iss.	8.75	8.75
92-173-013	Skiing 'Round 875QX5214	Keepsake	Yr.Iss.	8.75	8.75
92-173-014	North Pole Fire Fighter 975QX5104	Keepsake	Yr.Iss.	9.75	30.00
92-173-015	Rapid Delivery 875QX5094	Keepsake	Yr.Iss.	8.75	8.75
92-173-016	Green Thumb Santa 775QX5101	Keepsake	Yr.Iss.	7.75	7.75
92-173-017	Golf's a Ball 675QX5984	Keepsake	Yr.Iss.	6.75	15.00
92-173-018	A Santa-Full! 975QX5991	Keepsake	Yr.Iss.	9.75	20.00
92-173-019	Tasty Christmas 975QX5994	Keepsake	Yr.Iss.	9.75	9.75
92-173-020	Santa's Roundup 875QX5084	Keepsake	Yr.Iss.	8.75	8.75
92-173-021	Deck the Hogs 875QX5204	Keepsake	Yr.Iss.	8.75	20.00

Company / Number	Name	Series / Artist	Edition Limit	Issue Price	Quote
92-173-022	Patridge In a Pear Tree 875QX5234	Keepsake	Yr.Iss.	8.75	8.75
92-173-023	Spirit of Christmas Stress 875QX5231	Keepsake	Yr.Iss.	8.75	20.00
92-173-024	Please Pause Here 1475QX5291	Keepsake	Yr.Iss.	14.75	23-25.00
92-173-025	SNOOPY® and WOODSTOCK 875QX5954	Keepsake	Yr.Iss.	8.75	8.75
92-173-026	Mary Engelbreit Santa Jolly Wolly 775QX5224	Keepsake	Yr.Iss.	7.75	7.75
92-173-027	GARFIELD 775QX5374	Keepsake	Yr.Iss.	7.75	7.75
92-173-028	Norman Rockwell Art 500QX2224	Keepsake	Yr.Iss.	5.00	5.00
92-173-029	PEANUTS® 500QX2244	Keepsake	Yr.Iss.	5.00	5.00
92-173-030	Owl 975QX5614	Keepsake	Yr.Iss.	9.75	20.00
92-173-031	Santa Maria 1275QX5074	Keepsake	Yr.Iss.	12.75	12.75
92-173-032	Fun on a Big Scale 1075QX5134	Keepsake	Yr.Iss.	10.75	16.00
92-173-033	Genius at Work 1075QX5371	Keepsake	Yr.Iss.	10.75	20.00
92-173-034	Hello-Ho-Ho 975QX5141	Keepsake	Yr.Iss.	9.75	9.75
92-173-035	Cheerful Santa 975QX5154	Keepsake	Yr.Iss.	9.75	25-35.00
92-173-036	Memories to Cherish 1075QX5161	Keepsake	Yr.Iss.	10.75	10.75
92-173-037	Tread Bear 875QX5091	Keepsake	Yr.Iss.	8.75	8.75
92-173-038	Merry "Swiss" Mouse 775QX5114	Keepsake	Yr.Iss.	7.75	7.75
92-173-039	Honest George 775QX5064	Keepsake	Yr.Iss.	7.75	7.75
92-173-040	Bear Bell Champ 775QX5071	Keepsake	Yr.Iss.	7.75	7.75
92-173-041	Egg Nog Nest 775QX5121	Keepsake	Yr.Iss.	7.75	7.75
92-173-042	Jesus Loves Me 775QX3024	Keepsake	Yr.Iss.	7.75	7.75
92-173-043	Loving Shepherd 775QX5151	Keepsake	Yr.Iss.	7.75	7.75
92-173-044	Toboggan Tail 775QX5459	Keepsake	Yr.Iss.	7.75	7.75
92-173-045	Down-Under Holiday 775QX5144	Keepsake	Yr.Iss.	7.75	7.75
92-173-046	Holiday Wishes 775QX5131	Keepsake	Yr.Iss.	7.75	7.75
92-173-047	Feliz Navidad 675QX5181	Keepsake	Yr.Iss.	6.75	6.75
92-173-048	Holiday Teatime 1475QX5431	Keepsake	Yr.Iss.	14.75	14.75
92-173-049	Santa's Hook Shot 1275QX5434	Keepsake	Yr.Iss.	12.75	12.75
92-173-050	Cool Fliers 1075QX5474	Keepsake	Yr.Iss.	10.75	10.75
92-173-051	Elvis 1495QX562-4	Keepsake	Yr.Iss.	14.95	14.95
Hallmark Keepsake Ornaments		**1992 Magic Ornaments**			
92-174-001	PEANUTS-Second Ed. 1800QLX7214	Keepsake	Yr.Iss.	18.00	18.00
92-174-002	Forest Frolics-Fourth Ed. 2800QLX7254	Keepsake	Yr.Iss.	28.00	28.00
92-174-003	Chris Mouse Tales-Eighth Ed. 1200QLX7074	Keepsake	Yr.Iss.	12.00	12.00
92-174-004	Santa Special 4000QLX7167	Keepsake	Yr.Iss.	40.00	40.00
92-174-005	Continental Express 3200QLX7264	Keepsake	Yr.Iss.	32.00	32.00
92-174-006	Look! It's Santa 1400QLX7094	Keepsake	Yr.Iss.	14.00	14.00
92-174-007	The Dancing Nutcracker 3000QLX7261	Keepsake	Yr.Iss.	30.00	30.00
92-174-008	EnchantedClock 3000QLX7274	Keepsake	Yr.Iss.	30.00	30.00
92-174-009	Christmas Parade 3000QLX7271	Keepsake	Yr.Iss.	30.00	30.00
92-174-010	Good Sledding Ahead 2800QLX7244	Keepsake	Yr.Iss.	28.00	28.00
92-174-011	Yuletide Rider 2800QLX7314	Keepsake	Yr.Iss.	28.00	28.00
92-174-012	Santa's Answering Machine 2200QLX7241	Keepsake	Yr.Iss.	22.00	22.00
92-174-013	Baby's First Christmas 2200QLX7281	Keepsake	Yr.Iss.	22.00	60-65.00
92-174-014	Out First Christmas Together 2000QLX7221	Keepsake	Yr.Iss.	20.00	20.00
92-174-015	Santa Sub 1800QLX7321	Keepsake	Yr.Iss.	18.00	18.00
92-174-016	Lighting the Way 1800QLX7231	Keepsake	Yr.Iss.	18.00	18.00
92-174-017	Under Construction 1800QLX7324	Keepsake	Yr.Iss.	18.00	18.00
92-174-018	Feathered Friends 1400QLX7091	Keepsake	Yr.Iss.	14.00	14.00
92-174-019	Watch Owls 1200QLX7084	Keepsake	Yr.Iss.	12.00	12.00
92-174-020	Nut Sweet Nut 1000QLX7081	Keepsake	Yr.Iss.	10.00	10.00
92-174-021	Angel Of Light 3000QLT7239	Keepsake	Yr.Iss.	30.00	30.00
Hallmark Keepsake Ornaments		**1992 Miniature Ornaments**			
92-175-001	The Night Before Christmas 1375QXM5541	Keepsake	Yr.Iss.	13.75	25-90.00
92-175-002	The Bearymores-First Ed. 575QXM5544	Keepsake	Yr.Iss.	5.75	10.00
92-175-003	Woodland Babies-Second Ed. 600QXM5444	Keepsake	Yr.Iss.	6.00	6.00
92-175-004	Thimble Bells-Third Ed. 600QXM5461	Keepsake	Yr.Iss.	6.00	6.00
92-175-005	Nature's Angels-Third Ed. 450QXM5451	Keepsake	Yr.Iss.	4.50	4.50
92-175-006	Box Car-Fourth Ed/Noel R.R. 700QXM5441	Keepsake	Yr.Iss.	7.00	15-20.00
92-175-007	The Kringles-Fourth Ed. 600QXM5381	Keepsake	Yr.Iss.	6.00	6.00
92-175-008	Church-Fifth Ed./Old English V. 700QXM5384	Keepsake	Yr.Iss.	7.00	7.00
92-175-009	Rocking Horse-Fifth Ed. 450QXM5454	Keepsake	Yr.Iss.	4.50	4.50
92-175-010	Kittens in Toyland-Fifth Ed. 450QXM5391	Keepsake	Yr.Iss.	4.50	4.50
92-175-011	Feeding Time 575QXM5481	Keepsake	Yr.Iss.	5.75	8.00
92-175-012	Black-Capped Chickadee 300QXM5484	Keepsake	Yr.Iss.	3.00	3.00
92-175-013	Holiday Holly 975QXM5364	Keepsake	Yr.Iss.	9.75	9.75
92-175-014	Harmony Trio-Set of Three 1175QXM5471	Keepsake	Yr.Iss.	11.75	11.75
92-175-015	Grandchild's First Christmas 575QXM5501	Keepsake	Yr.Iss.	5.75	5.75
92-175-016	Baby's First Christmas 450QXM5494	Keepsake	Yr.Iss.	4.50	4.50
92-175-017	Mom 450QXM5504	Keepsake	Yr.Iss.	4.50	4.50
92-175-018	Grandma 450QXM5514	Keepsake	Yr.Iss.	4.50	4.50
92-175-019	Friends Are Tops 450QXM5521	Keepsake	Yr.Iss.	4.50	4.50
92-175-020	A+ Teacher 375QXM5511	Keepsake	Yr.Iss.	3.75	3.75
92-175-021	Inside Story 725QXM5881	Keepsake	Yr.Iss.	7.25	7.25
92-175-022	Holiday Splash 575QXM5834	Keepsake	Yr.Iss.	5.75	5.75
92-175-023	Christmas Copter 575QXM5844	Keepsake	Yr.Iss.	5.75	5.75
92-175-024	"Coca-Cola" Santa 575QXM5884	Keepsake	Yr.Iss.	5.75	12.00
92-175-025	Wee Three Kings 575QXM5531	Keepsake	Yr.Iss.	5.75	5.75
92-175-026	Angelic Harpist 450QXM5524	Keepsake	Yr.Iss.	4.50	4.50
92-175-027	Polar Polka 450QXM5534	Keepsake	Yr.Iss.	4.50	4.50
92-175-028	Buck-A-Roo 450QXM5814	Keepsake	Yr.Iss.	4.50	4.50
92-175-029	Ski For Two 450QXM5821	Keepsake	Yr.Iss.	4.50	4.50
92-175-030	Hoop It Up 450QXM5831	Keepsake	Yr.Iss.	4.50	4.50
92-175-031	Visions Of Acorns 450QXM5851	Keepsake	Yr.Iss.	4.50	4.50
92-175-032	Friendly Tin Soldier 450QXM5874	Keepsake	Yr.Iss.	4.50	10.00
92-175-033	Bright Stringers 375QXM5841	Keepsake	Yr.Iss.	3.75	3.75
92-175-034	Fast Finish 375QXM5301	Keepsake	Yr.Iss.	3.75	3.75
92-175-035	Cozy Kayak 375QXM5551	Keepsake	Yr.Iss.	3.75	3.75
92-175-036	Snug Kitty 375QXM5554	Keepsake	Yr.Iss.	3.75	3.75
92-175-037	Snowshoe Bunny 375QXM5564	Keepsake	Yr.Iss.	3.75	3.75
92-175-038	Gerbil Inc. 375QXM5924	Keepsake	Yr.Iss.	3.75	3.75
92-175-039	Hickory, Dickory, Dock 375QXM5861	Keepsake	Yr.Iss.	3.75	3.75
92-175-040	Going Places 375QXM5871	Keepsake	Yr.Iss.	3.75	3.75
92-175-041	Minted For Santa 375QXM5854	Keepsake	Yr.Iss.	3.75	3.75
92-175-042	Cool Uncle Sam 300QXM5561	Keepsake	Yr.Iss.	3.00	3.00
92-175-043	Perfect Balance 300QXM5571	Keepsake	Yr.Iss.	3.00	3.00
92-175-044	Puppet Show 300QXM5574	Keepsake	Yr.Iss.	3.00	3.00
92-175-045	Christmas Bonus 300QXM5811	Keepsake	Yr.Iss.	3.00	3.00
92-175-046	Spunky Monkey 300QXM5921	Keepsake	Yr.Iss.	3.00	3.00
92-175-047	Little Town of Bethlehem 300QXM5864	Keepsake	Yr.Iss.	3.00	3.00
92-175-048	Sew Sew Tiny (set of 6) 2900QXM5794	Keepsake	Yr.Iss.	29.00	29.00
Hallmark Keepsake Ornaments		**1992 Collectors' Club**			
92-176-001	Santa's Club List	Keepsake	Yr.Iss.	15.00	15.00
Hallmark Keepsake Ornaments		**1992 Limited Edition Ornaments**			
92-177-001	Victorian Skater (w/ base)	Keepsake	14,700	25.00	35.00
Hamilton Gifts/Enesco		**Maud Humphrey Bogart Ornaments**			
89-01-001	Sarah H1367	M. Humphrey	19,500	35.00	38.00
90-01-002	Victoria H1365	M. Humphrey	19,500	35.00	38.00
90-01-003	Michelle H1370	M. Humphrey	19,500	35.00	38.00
90-01-004	Catherine H1366	M. Humphrey	19,500	35.00	38.00
90-01-005	Gretchen H1369	M. Humphrey	19,500	35.00	38.00
90-01-006	Rebecca H5513	M. Humphrey	19,500	35.00	38.00
91-01-007	Cleaning House-915084	M. Humphrey	Open	24.00	24.00
91-01-008	Gift of Love-915092	M. Humphrey	Open	24.00	24.00
91-01-009	My First Dance-915106	M. Humphrey	Open	24.00	24.00
91-01-010	Special Friends-915114	M. Humphrey	Open	24.00	24.00
91-01-011	Susanna-915122	M. Humphrey	Open	24.00	24.00
91-01-012	Sarah-915165	M. Humphrey	Open	24.00	24.00
92-01-013	Hollies For You-915726	M. Humphrey	Closed	24.00	24.00
Hamilton Gifts/Enesco		**Cherished Teddies**			
89-02-001	Bear In Stocking, dated	P. Hillman	Yr.Iss.	16.00	30-50.00
Hand & Hammer		**Hand & Hammer Ornaments**			
80-01-001	Icicle-009	De Matteo	490	25.00	30.00
81-01-002	Roundel -109	De Matteo	220	25.00	45.00
81-01-003	Gabriel with Liberty Cap-301	De Matteo	275	25.00	50.00
81-01-004	Gabriel -320	De Matteo	Suspd.	25.00	32.00
82-01-005	Fleur de Lys Angel-343	De Matteo	320	28.00	35.00
82-01-006	Madonna & Child-388	De Matteo	175	28.00	50.00
84-01-007	Beardsley Angel-398	De Matteo	Open	28.00	48.00
82-01-008	Carved Heart -425	De Matteo	Suspd.	29.00	48.00
82-01-009	Straw Star -448	De Matteo	590	25.00	40.00
83-01-010	Fire Angel -473	De Matteo	315	25.00	28-36.00
83-01-011	Indian-494	De Matteo	190	29.00	50.00
83-01-012	Pollock Angel-502	De Matteo	Suspd.	35.00	50.00
83-01-013	Calligraphic Deer-511	De Matteo	Suspd.	25.00	29.00
83-01-014	Egyptian Cat-521	De Matteo	Unkn.	13.00	13.00
83-01-015	Dove-522	De Matteo	Unkn.	13.00	13.00
83-01-016	Sargent Angel-523	De Matteo	690	29.00	34.00
83-01-017	Cherub-528	De Matteo	295	29.00	50.00
83-01-018	Japanese Snowflake-534	De Matteo	350	29.00	35.00
83-01-019	Sunburst-543	De Matteo	Unkn.	13.00	50.00
83-01-020	Wise Man-549	De Matteo	Suspd.	29.00	36.00
84-01-021	Freer Star-553	De Matteo	Unkn.	13.00	30.00
84-01-022	Pineapple-558	De Matteo	Suspd.	30.00	38.00
84-01-023	Crescent Angel-559	De Matteo	Suspd.	30.00	32.00
84-01-024	Rosette-571	De Matteo	220	32.00	50.00
84-01-025	Nine Hearts-572	De Matteo	275	34.00	50.00
84-01-026	USHS 1984 Angel-574	De Matteo	Suspd.	35.00	50.00
84-01-027	Wreath-575	De Matteo	Unkn.	13.00	30.00
84-01-028	Praying Angel-576	De Matteo	Suspd.	29.00	30.00
84-01-029	Rocking Horse-581	De Matteo	Unkn.	13.00	13.00
84-01-030	Bunny-582	De Matteo	Unkn.	13.00	30.00
84-01-031	Ibex-584	De Matteo	400	29.00	50.00
84-01-032	Bird & Cherub-588	De Matteo	Unkn.	13.00	30.00
84-01-033	Wild Swan-592	De Matteo	Suspd.	35.00	50.00
84-01-034	Moravian Star-595	De Matteo	Open	38.00	50.00
84-01-035	Manger-601	De Matteo	Suspd.	29.00	32.00
84-01-036	Mt. Vernon Weathervane-602	De Matteo	Suspd.	32.00	39.00
85-01-037	Peacock-603	De Matteo	470	34.00	37.00
85-01-038	Model A Ford-604	De Matteo	Unkn.	13.00	30.00
85-01-039	Crane-606	De Matteo	150	39.00	50.00
85-01-040	Angel-607	De Matteo	225	36.00	50.00
85-01-041	Militiaman-608	De Matteo	460	25.00	30.00
85-01-042	Nutcracker-609	De Matteo	510	30.00	50.00
85-01-043	Liberty Bell-611	De Matteo	Suspd.	32.00	40.00
85-01-044	Angel-612	De Matteo	217	32.00	50.00
85-01-045	Abigail-613	De Matteo	500	32.00	50.00
85-01-046	Audubon Swallow-614	De Matteo	Suspd.	48.00	60.00
85-01-047	Audubon Bluebird-615	De Matteo	Suspd.	48.00	60.00
85-01-048	Guardian Angel-616	De Matteo	1,340	35.00	39.00
85-01-049	Shepherd-617	De Matteo	1,770	35.00	39.00
85-01-050	Carousel Pony-618	De Matteo	Unkn.	13.00	13.00
85-01-051	Art Deco Deer-620	De Matteo	Suspd.	34.00	38.00
85-01-052	Halley's Comet-621	De Matteo	432	35.00	50.00
85-01-053	Mermaid-622	De Matteo	Suspd.	35.00	39.00
85-01-054	George Washington-629	De Matteo	Suspd.	35.00	39.00
85-01-055	USHS Madonna-630	De Matteo	Suspd.	35.00	50.00
85-01-056	USHS Bluebird-631	De Matteo	Suspd.	29.00	50.00
85-01-057	USHS Swallow-632	De Matteo	Suspd.	29.00	50.00
85-01-058	Grasshopper-634	De Matteo	Open	32.00	39.00
85-01-059	Hosanna-635	De Matteo	715	32.00	50.00
85-01-060	Teddy-637	De Matteo	Suspd.	37.00	40.00
85-01-061	Herald Angel-641	De Matteo	Suspd.	36.00	40.00
85-01-062	Cherub-642	De Matteo	815	37.00	37.00
85-01-063	Butterfly-646	De Matteo	Suspd.	39.00	39.00
85-01-064	French Quarter Heart-647	De Matteo	Open	37.00	36.00
85-01-065	Samantha-648	De Matteo	Suspd.	35.00	36.00
85-01-066	Eagle-652	De Matteo	375	30.00	50.00
85-01-067	Piazza-653	De Matteo	Suspd.	32.00	50.00
85-01-068	Camel-655	De Matteo	Unkn.	13.00	30.00
85-01-069	Reindeer-656	De Matteo	Unkn.	13.00	30.00
85-01-070	Lafarge Angel-658	De Matteo	Suspd.	32.00	50.00
85-01-071	Family-659	De Matteo	915	32.00	40.00
85-01-072	Unicorn-660	De Matteo	Suspd.	37.00	37.00
85-01-073	Old North Church-661	De Matteo	Open	35.00	39.00
85-01-074	Madonna-666	De Matteo	227	35.00	50.00
85-01-075	Bicycle-669	De Matteo	Unkn.	13.00	30.00
85-01-076	St. Nicholas-670	De Matteo	Unkn.	13.00	30.00
86-01-077	Nativity-679	De Matteo	Suspd.	36.00	38.00
86-01-078	Winged Dove-680	De Matteo	Suspd.	35.00	36.00
86-01-079	Nutcracker-681	De Matteo	1,356	37.00	37.00
86-01-080	Phaeton-683	De Matteo	Unkn.	13.00	13.00
86-01-081	Archangel-684	De Matteo	Suspd.	29.00	30.00
86-01-082	Teddy Bear-685	De Matteo	Suspd.	38.00	40.00
86-01-083	Hallelujah-686	De Matteo	Unkn.	38.00	38.00
86-01-084	Bear Claus-692	De Matteo	Unkn.	13.00	13.00
86-01-085	Prancer-698	De Matteo	Open	38.00	38.00
86-01-086	USHS Angel-703	De Matteo	Suspd.	35.00	50.00
86-01-087	Teddy-707	De Matteo	Unkn.	13.00	30.00
86-01-088	Christmas Tree-708	De Matteo	Unkn.	13.00	13.00
86-01-089	Lafarge Angel-710	De Matteo	Suspd.	31.00	50.00
86-01-090	Salem Lamb-712	De Matteo	Suspd.	32.00	40.00
86-01-091	Snowflake-713	De Matteo	Suspd.	36.00	40.00
86-01-092	Wreath-714	De Matteo	Suspd.	36.00	38.00
86-01-093	Santa Skates-715	De Matteo	Suspd.	36.00	36.00
86-01-094	Nightingale-716	De Matteo	Suspd.	35.00	50.00
86-01-095	Mother Goose-719	De Matteo	Open	34.00	40.00
86-01-096	Kringle Bear-723	De Matteo	Unkn.	13.00	30.00

Company Number	Name	Series Artist	Edition Limit	Issue Price	Quote
86-01-097	Victorian Santa-724	De Matteo	250	32.00	35.00
87-01-098	Noel-731	De Matteo	Open	38.00	38.00
87-01-099	Naptime-732	J. Walpole	Suspd.	32.00	32.00
87-01-100	Hunting Horn-738	De Matteo	Open	37.00	37.00
87-01-101	Santa Star-739	J. Walpole	Suspd.	32.00	32.00
87-01-102	Sweetheart Star-740	De Matteo	Suspd.	39.50	39.50
87-01-103	Santa-741	De Matteo	Unkn.	13.00	13.00
87-01-104	Pegasus-745	De Matteo	Unkn.	13.00	13.00
87-01-105	Snow Queen-746	De Matteo	Suspd.	35.00	39.00
87-01-106	Dove-747	De Matteo	Unkn.	13.00	13.00
87-01-107	USHS Gloria Angel-748	De Matteo	Suspd.	39.00	50.00
87-01-108	Angel with Lyre-750	De Matteo	Suspd.	32.00	40.00
87-01-109	Santa and Sleigh-751	De Matteo	Suspd.	32.00	40.00
87-01-110	Reindeer-752	De Matteo	Open	38.00	38.00
87-01-111	Snowman-753	De Matteo	825	38.00	38.00
87-01-112	Cat-754	De Matteo	Open	37.00	37.00
87-01-113	Clipper Ship-756	De Matteo	Suspd.	35.00	35.00
87-01-114	Ride a Cock Horse-757	De Matteo	Suspd.	34.00	39.00
87-01-115	Art Deco Angel-765	De Matteo	Suspd.	38.00	40.00
87-01-116	Old Ironsides-767	De Matteo	Open	35.00	39.00
87-01-117	First Christmas-771	De Matteo	Unkn.	13.00	13.00
87-01-118	Stocking-772	De Matteo	Unkn.	13.00	13.00
88-01-119	Drummer Bear-773	De Matteo	Unkn.	13.00	13.00
88-01-120	Stocking-774	De Matteo	Unkn.	13.00	13.00
88-01-121	Minuteman-776	De Matteo	Suspd.	35.00	40.00
87-01-122	Buffalo-777	De Matteo	Suspd.	36.00	36.00
88-01-123	Star of the East-785	De Matteo	Suspd.	35.00	35.00
88-01-124	Dove-786	De Matteo	112	36.00	50.00
88-01-125	Madonna-787	De Matteo	600	35.00	35.00
88-01-126	Magi-788	De Matteo	Suspd.	39.50	39.50
88-01-127	Jack in the Box-789	De Matteo	Suspd.	39.50	39.50
88-01-128	Skaters-790	De Matteo	Suspd.	39.50	39.50
88-01-129	Angel-797	De Matteo	Unkn.	13.00	13.00
88-01-130	Christmas Tree-798	De Matteo	Unkn.	13.00	13.00
88-01-131	Thumbelina-803	De Matteo	Suspd.	35.00	40.00
88-01-132	Star-806	De Matteo	311	50.00	150.00
88-01-133	Madonna-809	De Matteo	15	39.00	50.00
89-01-134	Carousel Horse-811	De Matteo	2,150	34.00	34.00
88-01-135	Bank-812	De Matteo	400	40.00	40.00
88-01-136	Santa with Scroll-814	De Matteo	250	34.00	37.00
88-01-137	Madonna-815	De Matteo	Suspd.	39.00	50.00
88-01-138	Rabbit-816	De Matteo	Unkn.	13.00	13.00
88-01-139	Buggy-817	De Matteo	Unkn.	13.00	13.00
88-01-140	Angel-818	De Matteo	Suspd.	32.00	40.00
88-01-141	Boston State House-819	De Matteo	Open	34.00	40.00
88-01-142	US Capitol-820	De Matteo	Open	38.00	40.00
88-01-143	Nativity-821	De Matteo	Suspd.	32.00	39.00
88-01-144	Old King Cole-824	De Matteo	Suspd.	34.00	39.00
88-01-145	Stocking-827	De Matteo	Unkn.	13.00	13.00
88-01-146	Conn. State House-833	De Matteo	Open	38.00	38.00
88-01-147	Sleigh-834	De Matteo	Open	34.00	38.00
89-01-148	Stocking Bear-835	De Matteo	Unkn.	13.00	13.00
88-01-149	Night Before Xmas Col.-841	De Matteo	10,000	160.00	160.00
89-01-150	First Christmas-842	De Matteo	Unkn.	13.00	13.00
89-01-151	Locket Bear-844	De Matteo	Unkn.	25.00	25.00
88-01-152	Cable Car-848	De Matteo	Open	38.00	38.00
88-01-153	Star-854	De Matteo	275	32.00	35.00
89-01-154	Santa 1989-856	De Matteo	1,715	35.00	35.00
89-01-155	Goose-857	De Matteo	650	37.00	37.00
89-01-156	Presidential Seal-858	De Matteo	500	39.00	39.00
88-01-157	Eiffel Tower-861	De Matteo	225	38.00	40.00
88-01-158	Coronado-864	De Matteo	Suspd.	38.00	38.00
90-01-159	Carousel Horse -866	De Matteo	1,915	38.00	38.00
90-01-160	Joy-867	De Matteo	1,140	36.00	36.00
90-01-161	Goose & Wreath-868	De Matteo	Open	37.00	37.00
90-01-162	1990 Santa-869	De Matteo	2,250	38.00	38.00
90-01-163	Cardinals-870	De Matteo	Open	39.00	39.00
90-01-164	Angel with Star-871	De Matteo	Open	38.00	38.00
89-01-165	Nutcracker 1989-872	De Matteo	1,790	38.00	38.00
89-01-166	USHS Angel 1989-901	De Matteo	Suspd.	38.00	38.00
89-01-167	Swan Boat-904	De Matteo	Open	38.00	38.00
89-01-168	MFA Noel-905	De Matteo	Suspd.	36.00	42.00
89-01-169	MFA Angel w/Tree-906	De Matteo	Suspd.	36.00	42.00
89-01-170	MFA Durer Snowflake-907	De Matteo	2,000	36.00	42.00
89-01-171	Independence Hall-908	De Matteo	Open	38.00	38.00
90-01-172	Cat on Pillow-915	De Matteo	Unkn.	13.00	13.00
90-01-173	Mouse w/Candy Cane-916	De Matteo	Unkn.	13.00	13.00
89-01-174	L&T Ugly Duckling-917	De Matteo	Suspd.	38.00	38.00
90-01-175	Farmhouse-919	De Matteo	Suspd.	37.00	37.00
90-01-176	Covered Bridge-920	De Matteo	Suspd.	37.00	37.00
90-01-177	Church-921	De Matteo	Suspd.	37.00	37.00
90-01-178	Mill-922	De Matteo	Suspd.	37.00	37.00
90-01-179	Currier & Ives Set -Victorian Village-923	De Matteo	2,000	140.00	140.00
90-01-180	Santa & Reindeer-929	De Matteo	395	39.00	43.00
90-01-181	Christmas Seal-931	De Matteo	Unkn.	25.00	25.00
89-01-182	Bugle Bear-935	De Matteo	Unkn.	12.00	12.00
89-01-183	Jack in the Box Bear-936	De Matteo	Unkn.	12.00	12.00
89-01-184	MFA LaFarge Angel set-937	De Matteo	Suspd.	98.00	98.00
90-01-185	First Christmas Bear-940	De Matteo	Suspd.	35.00	35.00
90-01-186	Santa in the Moon-941	De Matteo	Suspd.	38.00	38.00
90-01-187	Mole & Rat Wind in Will-944	De Matteo	Open	36.00	36.00
90-01-188	Toad Wind in Willows-945	De Matteo	Open	38.00	38.00
90-01-189	Merry Christmas Locket-948	De Matteo	Unkn.	25.00	25.00
90-01-190	Teddy Bear Locket-949	De Matteo	Unkn.	25.00	25.00
89-01-191	Barnesville Buggy 1989-950	De Matteo	Unkn.	13.00	13.00
89-01-192	Victorian Heart-954	De Matteo	Unkn.	13.00	13.00
89-01-193	Stocking Bear-955	De Matteo	Unkn.	12.00	12.00
89-01-194	Stocking w/Toys-956	De Matteo	Unkn.	12.00	12.00
90-01-195	Teddy Bear w/Heart-957	De Matteo	Unkn.	13.00	13.00
90-01-196	Clown w/Dog-958	De Matteo	Unkn.	13.00	13.00
90-01-197	Heart Angel-959	De Matteo	Suspd.	39.00	39.00
90-01-198	Carriage-960	De Matteo	Unkn.	13.00	13.00
90-01-199	Blake Angel-961	De Matteo	Unkn.	36.00	36.00
90-01-200	Colonial Capitol-965	De Matteo	Open	39.00	39.00
90-01-201	Governor's Palace-966	De Matteo	Open	39.00	39.00
90-01-202	Cockatoo-969	De Matteo	Unkn.	13.00	13.00
90-01-203	Father Christmas-970	De Matteo	Suspd.	36.00	36.00
90-01-204	Old Fashioned Santa-971	De Matteo	Suspd.	36.00	36.00
90-01-205	Patriotic Santa-972	De Matteo	Suspd.	36.00	36.00
90-01-206	Santa in Balloon-973	De Matteo	Suspd.	36.00	36.00
90-01-207	Santa on Reindeer-974	De Matteo	Suspd.	36.00	36.00
90-01-208	Santa UpTo Date-975	De Matteo	Suspd.	36.00	36.00
90-01-209	Presidential Homes-990	De Matteo	Open	350.00	350.00
90-01-210	Mrs. Rabbit-991	De Matteo	Open	39.50	39.50
90-01-211	Jeremy Fisher-992	De Matteo	Open	39.50	39.50
90-01-212	Peter Rabbit-993	De Matteo	Open	39.50	39.50
90-01-213	Peter's First Christmas-994	De Matteo	Suspd.	39.50	39.50
90-01-214	Flopsy Bunnies-995	De Matteo	Suspd.	39.50	39.50
90-01-215	First Baptist Angel-997	De Matteo	200	35.00	35.00
91-01-216	I Love Santa-998	De Matteo	Open	36.00	36.00
90-01-217	1990 Peter Rabbit-1018	De Matteo	4,315	39.50	39.50
90-01-218	Peter Rabbit Locket Ornament-1019	De Matteo	Unkn.	30.00	30.00
90-01-219	Jemima Puddleduck-1020	De Matteo	Unkn.	30.00	30.00
90-01-220	Landing Duck-1021	De Matteo	Unkn.	13.00	13.00
90-01-221	White Tail Deer-1022	De Matteo	Unkn.	13.00	13.00
90-01-222	Elk-1023	De Matteo	Unkn.	13.00	13.00
90-01-223	Angel With Violin-1024	De Matteo	Suspd.	39.00	39.00
91-01-224	Carousel Horse-1025	De Matteo	Open	38.00	38.00
91-01-225	Angel With Horn-1026	De Matteo	Open	32.00	32.00
90-01-226	Conestoga Wagon-1027	De Matteo	Open	38.00	38.00
90-01-227	Liberty Bell-1028	De Matteo	Open	38.00	38.00
90-01-228	The Boston Light-1032	De Matteo	Open	39.50	39.50
90-01-229	1990 Snowflake-1033	De Matteo	1,415	36.00	38.00
90-01-230	Pegasus-1037	De Matteo	Suspd.	35.00	35.00
90-01-231	Angels-1039	De Matteo	Suspd.	36.00	36.00
90-01-232	Beardsley Angel-1040	De Matteo	Suspd.	34.00	34.00
90-01-233	Georgia State Capitol-1042	De Matteo	2,000	39.50	39.50
90-01-234	N. Carolina State Capitol-1043	De Matteo	2,000	39.50	39.50
90-01-235	Florida State Capitol-1044	De Matteo	2,000	39.50	39.50
90-01-236	S. Carolina State Capitol-1045	De Matteo	2,000	39.50	39.50
90-01-237	Joy-1047	De Matteo	Suspd.	39.00	39.00
90-01-238	Steadfast Tin Soldier-1050	De Matteo	Suspd.	36.00	36.00
91-01-239	Cow Jumped Over The Moon-1055	De Matteo	Suspd.	38.00	38.00
91-01-240	1991 Santa-1056	De Matteo	3,750	38.00	38.00
90-01-241	USHS Angel 1990-1061	De Matteo	Suspd.	39.00	39.00
90-01-242	San Francisco Row House-1071	De Matteo	Open	39.50	39.50
91-01-243	Mommy & Baby Seal-1075	De Matteo	Suspd.	36.00	36.00
91-01-244	Mommy & Baby Wolves-1076	De Matteo	Suspd.	36.00	36.00
91-01-245	Mommy & Baby Koala Bear-1077	De Matteo	Suspd.	36.00	36.00
91-01-246	Mommy & Baby Kangaroo-1078	De Matteo	Suspd.	36.00	36.00
91-01-247	Mommy & Baby Panda Bear-1079	De Matteo	Suspd.	36.00	36.00
91-01-248	Large Jemima Puddleduck-1083	De Matteo	Open	49.50	49.50
90-01-249	Ferrel's Angel 1990-1084	De Matteo	Unkn.	15.00	15.00
91-01-250	Olivers Rocking Horse-1085	De Matteo	Open	37.00	37.00
91-01-251	Mrs. Rabbit 1991-1086	De Matteo	Suspd.	39.50	39.50
91-01-252	Tailor of Gloucester-1087	De Matteo	Open	39.50	39.50
91-01-253	Pig Robinson-1090	De Matteo	Open	39.50	39.50
91-01-254	Appley Dapply-1091	De Matteo	Open	39.50	39.50
91-01-255	Peter Rabbit With Book-1093	De Matteo	Open	39.50	39.50
90-01-256	Koala San Diego Zoo-1095	De Matteo	Open	36.00	36.00
90-01-257	Locomotive-1100	De Matteo	Suspd.	39.00	39.00
90-01-258	Montpelier-1113	De Matteo	Open	36.00	36.00
90-01-259	Ducklings-1114	De Matteo	Open	38.00	38.00
91-01-260	Large Peter Rabbit-1116	De Matteo	Open	49.50	49.50
91-01-261	Large Tailor of Gloucester-1117	De Matteo	Open	49.50	49.50
91-01-262	Nativity-1118	De Matteo	Open	38.00	38.00
91-01-263	Alice-1119	De Matteo	Open	39.00	39.00
91-01-264	Mad Tea Party-1120	De Matteo	Open	39.00	39.00
91-01-265	White Rabbit-1121	De Matteo	Open	39.00	39.00
91-01-266	Queen of Hearts-1122	De Matteo	Open	39.00	39.00
91-01-267	Waiting For Santa-1123	De Matteo	Open	38.00	38.00
90-01-268	Ember-1124	De Matteo	120	N/A	N/A
91-01-269	USHS Angel 1991-1139	De Matteo	Suspd.	38.00	38.00
91-01-270	Columbus-1140	De Matteo	1,500	39.00	39.00
91-01-271	The Voyages Of Columbus-1141	De Matteo	1,500	39.00	39.00
91-01-272	Precious Planet-1142	De Matteo	2,000	120.00	120.00
91-01-273	MFA Snowflake 1991-1143	De Matteo	Suspd.	36.00	36.00
91-01-274	Fir Tree-1145	De Matteo	Open	39.00	39.00
91-01-275	Nutcracker-1151	De Matteo	Open	49.50	49.50
91-01-276	Paul Revere-1158	De Matteo	Open	39.00	39.00
91-01-277	Alice in Wonderland-1159	De Matteo	Open	140.00	140.00
91-01-278	Nutcracker-1183	De Matteo	Open	38.00	38.00
91-01-279	Nutrcracker Suite-1184	De Matteo	Open	38.00	38.00
91-01-280	Gus-1195	De Matteo	200	N/A	N/A
91-01-281	San Francisco Heart-1196	De Matteo	Open	39.00	39.00
92-01-282	Xmas Tree & Heart-1162	De Matteo	Suspd.	36.00	36.00
92-01-283	Andrea-1163	De Matteo	Suspd.	36.00	36.00
92-01-284	Joy-1164	De Matteo	Open	39.50	39.50
92-01-285	Unicorn-1165	De Matteo	Suspd.	36.00	36.00
92-01-286	Noah's Ark-1166	De Matteo	Open	36.00	36.00
92-01-287	Jemima Puddleduck 1992-1167	De Matteo	Suspd.	39.50	39.50
92-01-288	Mrs. Rabbit-1181	De Matteo	Open	39.50	39.50
92-01-289	Round Teapot-1206	De Matteo	Open	49.50	49.50
92-01-290	Revere Teapot-1207	De Matteo	Open	49.50	49.50
92-01-291	Chocolate Pot-1208	De Matteo	Open	49.50	49.50
92-01-292	Angel W/ Double Horn-1212	De Matteo	2,000	49.50	49.50
92-01-293	Angel-1213	De Matteo	2,000	39.00	39.00
92-01-294	Della Robbia Ornament-1219	De Matteo	Open	39.00	39.00
92-01-295	Fairy Tale Angel-1222	De Matteo	Open	36.00	36.00
92-01-296	Parrot-1233	De Matteo	Open	37.00	37.00
92-01-297	St. John Lion-1235	De Matteo	10,000	39.00	39.00
92-01-298	St. John Angel-1236	De Matteo	10,000	39.00	39.00
92-01-299	Scrooge-1241	De Matteo	Open	36.00	36.00
92-01-300	Bob & Tiny Tim-1242	De Matteo	Open	36.00	36.00
92-01-301	Marley's Ghost-1243	De Matteo	Open	36.00	36.00
92-01-302	Mrs. Cratchit-1244	De Matteo	Open	36.00	36.00
92-01-303	America At Peace-1245	De Matteo	2,000	85.00	85.00
92-01-304	MFA Snowflake-1246	De Matteo	Open	39.00	39.00
92-01-305	Princess & The Pea-1247	De Matteo	Open	39.00	39.00
92-01-306	Dorothy-1284	De Matteo	Open	36.00	36.00
92-01-307	Tin Man-1285	De Matteo	Open	36.00	36.00
92-01-308	Scarecrow-1286	De Matteo	Open	36.00	36.00
92-01-309	Cowardly Lion-1287	De Matteo	Open	36.00	36.00
92-01-310	Heart of Christmas-1301	De Matteo	Open	39.00	39.00
93-01-311	Angel Bell-1312	De Matteo	Open	38.00	38.00
93-01-312	Clara with Nutcracker-1316	De Matteo	Open	38.00	38.00
93-01-313	Carousel Horse 1993-1321	De Matteo	Yr.Iss.	38.00	38.00
93-01-314	Lion and Lamb-1322	De Matteo	Open	38.00	38.00
93-01-315	Mrs. Rabbit 1993-1325	De Matteo	Yr.Iss	39.50	39.50
93-01-316	Peace-1327	De Matteo	Open	36.00	36.00
93-01-317	Partridge & Pear-1328	De Matteo	Open	38.00	38.00
93-01-318	Violin-1340	De Matteo	Open	39.50	39.50
93-01-319	Angel-1342	De Matteo	Open	38.00	38.00
93-01-320	Zig Zag Tree-1343	De Matteo	Open	39.00	39.00
93-01-321	Beantown-1344	De Matteo	Open	38.00	38.00
93-01-322	Creche-1351	De Matteo	Open	38.00	38.00
93-01-323	Celebrate America-1352	De Matteo	Open	38.00	38.00
93-01-324	Cheer Mouse-1359	De Matteo	Open	39.00	39.00

Company / Number	Name	Series / Artist	Edition Limit	Issue Price	Quote
93-01-325	Window-1360	De Matteo	Open	38.00	38.00
93-01-326	Cable Car to the Stars-1363	De Matteo	Open	39.00	39.00
93-01-327	Public Garden-1370	De Matteo	Open	38.00	38.00
Hand & Hammer		**Annual Ornaments**			
87-02-001	Silver Bells-737	De Matteo	2,700	38.00	50.00
88-02-002	Silver Bells-792	De Matteo	3,150	39.50	39.50
89-02-003	Silver Bells-843	De Matteo	3,150	39.50	39.50
90-02-004	Silver Bells-865	De Matteo	3,615	39.00	39.00
90-02-005	Silver Bells Rev.-964	De Matteo	4,490	39.00	39.00
91-02-006	Silver Bells-1080	De Matteo	4,100	39.50	39.50
92-02-007	Silver Bells-1148	De Matteo	4,100	39.50	39.50
93-02-008	Silver Bells-1311	De Matteo	Yr.Iss.	39.50	39.50
John Hine N.A. Ltd.		**David Winter Ornaments**			
92-01-001	Scrooge's Counting House	D. Winter	Closed	15.00	23-30.00
92-01-002	Hogmanay	D. Winter	Closed	15.00	23-30.00
92-01-003	A Christmas Carol	D. Winter	Closed	15.00	23-30.00
92-01-004	Mister Fezziwig's Emporium	D. Winter	Closed	15.00	23-30.00
92-01-005	Set	D. Winter	Closed	60.00	72-125.00
92-01-006	Fairytale Castle	D. Winter	Closed	15.00	15-23.00
92-01-007	Fred's Home	D. Winter	Closed	15.00	15-23.00
92-01-008	Suffolk House	D. Winter	Closed	15.00	15-23.00
92-01-009	Tudor Manor	D. Winter	Closed	15.00	15-23.00
Iris Arc Crystal		**Christmas Ornaments**			
84-01-001	1984 Merry Christmas Ornament	P. Hale	Retrd.	28.00	28.00
85-01-001	1985 Noel Ornament	P. Hale	Retrd.	28.00	28.00
86-01-001	1986 Noel Christmas Ornament	P. Hale	Retrd.	30.00	30.00
87-01-001	1987 Angel Christmas Ornament	P. Hale	Retrd.	30.00	30.00
89-01-001	1989 Christmas Ornament	P. Hale	Retrd.	30.00	30.00
92-01-001	1992 Angel Christmas Ornament	M. Goena	Retrd.	30.00	30.00
93-01-001	1993 Dove Christmas Ornament	M. Goena	Open	35.00	35.00
Kirk Stieff		**Colonial Williamsburg**			
87-01-001	Rocking Horse, silverplate	D. Bacorn	Closed	19.95	30.00
87-01-002	Tin Drum, silverplate	D. Bacorn	Closed	19.95	30.00
88-01-003	Lamb, silverplate	D. Bacorn	Closed	19.95	22.00
83-01-004	Tree Top Star, silverplate	D. Dacorn	Open	29.50	29.50
89-01-005	Doll ornament, silverplate	D. Bacorn	Closed	22.00	22.00
88-01-006	Unicorn, silverplate	D. Bacorn	Closed	22.00	22.00
Kirk Stieff		**Twelve Days of Christmas**			
85-02-001	Partridge in a Pear Tree	J. Barata	Closed	9.95	10.95
85-02-002	Two Turtle Doves	J. Barata	Closed	9.95	10.95
86-02-003	Three French Hens	J. Barata	Closed	9.95	10.95
86-02-004	Four Calling Birds	J. Barata	Closed	9.95	10.95
87-02-005	Five Golden Rings	J. Barata	Closed	9.95	10.95
87-02-006	Six Geese-A-Laying	J. Barata	Closed	9.95	10.95
88-02-007	Seven Swans-A-Swimming	J. Barata	Closed	9.95	10.95
88-02-008	Eight Maids-A-Milking	J. Barata	Closed	9.95	10.95
89-02-009	Nine Ladies Dancing	J. Barata	Closed	10.95	10.95
89-02-010	Ten Lords-a-Leaping	J. Barata	Closed	10.95	10.95
Kirk Stieff		**The Nutcracker Stained Glass Ornaments**			
86-03-001	Clara's Gift	Kirk Stieff	Closed	17.50	17.50
86-03-002	The Battle	Kirk Stieff	Closed	17.50	17.50
86-03-003	The Nutcracker Prince	Kirk Stieff	Closed	17.50	17.50
86-03-004	The Sugar Plum Fairy	Kirk Stieff	Closed	17.50	17.50
86-03-005	Set of Four	Kirk Stieff	Closed	69.95	69.95
Kirk Stieff		**Kirk Stieff Ornaments**			
84-04-001	Unicorn	D. Bacorn	Closed	17.50	19.95
83-04-002	Charleston Locomotive	D. Bacorn	Closed	17.50	19.95
86-04-003	Icicle, sterling silver	D. Bacorn	Closed	35.00	50.00
89-04-004	Smithsonian Carousel Horse	Kirk Stieff	Closed	50.00	50.00
89-04-005	Smithsonian Carousel Seahorse	Kirk Stieff	Closed	50.00	50.00
90-04-006	Toy Ship	Kirk Stieff	Closed	23.00	23.00
Lance Corporation		**Sebastian Christmas Ornaments**			
43-01-001	Madonna of the Chair	P.W. Baston	Closed	2.00	150-200.
81-01-002	Santa Claus	P.W. Baston	Open	28.50	30.00
82-01-003	Madonna of the Chair (Reissue of '43)	P.W. Baston	Closed	15.00	30-45.00
85-01-004	Home for the Holidays	P.W. Baston Jr.	Open	10.00	12.50
86-01-005	Holiday Sleigh Ride	P.W. Baston Jr.	Open	10.00	12.50
87-01-006	Santa	P.W. Baston Jr.	Open	10.00	12.50
88-01-007	Decorating the Tree	P.W. Baston Jr.	Open	12.50	12.50
89-01-008	Final Preparations for Christmas	P.W. Baston Jr.	Open	13.90	13.90
90-01-009	Stuffing the Stockings	P.W. Baston Jr.	Open	14.00	14.00
91-01-010	Merry Christmas	P.W. Baston Jr.	Open	14.50	14.50
92-01-011	Final Check	P.W. Baston Jr.	Open	14.50	14.50
93-01-012	Ethnic Santa	P.W. Baston Jr.	Open	12.50	12.50
Lenox China		**Annual Ornaments**			
82-01-001	1982 Ornament	Lenox	Yr.Iss.	30.00	50-90.00
83-01-002	1983 Ornament	Lenox	Yr.Iss.	35.00	75.00
84-01-003	1984 Ornament	Lenox	Yr.Iss.	38.00	65.00
85-01-004	1985 Ornament	Lenox	Yr.Iss.	37.50	60.00
86-01-005	1986 Ornament	Lenox	Yr.Iss.	38.50	50.00
87-01-006	1987 Ornament	Lenox	Yr.Iss.	39.00	45.00
88-01-007	1988 Ornament	Lenox	Yr.Iss.	39.00	45.00
89-01-008	1989 Ornament	Lenox	Yr.Iss.	39.00	39.00
90-01-009	1990 Ornament	Lenox	Yr.Iss.	42.00	42.00
91-01-010	1991 Ornament	Lenox	Yr.Iss.	39.00	39.00
92-01-011	1992 Ornament	Lenox	Yr.Iss.	39.00	39.00
Lenox China		**Days of Christmas**			
87-02-001	Partridge	Lenox	Open	22.50	22.50
88-02-002	Two Turtle Doves	Lenox	Open	22.50	22.50
89-02-003	Three French Hens	Lenox	Open	22.50	22.50
90-02-004	Four Calling Birds	Lenox	Open	25.00	25.00
91-02-005	Five Golden Rings	Lenox	Open	25.00	25.00
92-02-006	Six Geese-a-Laying	Lenox	Open	25.00	25.00
Lenox China		**Yuletide**			
85-03-001	Teddy Bear	Lenox	Closed	18.00	18.00
85-03-002	Christmas Tree	Lenox	Open	18.00	18.00
89-03-003	Santa with Tree	Lenox	Closed	18.00	18.00
89-03-004	Angel with Horn	Lenox	Open	18.00	18.00
90-03-005	Dove	Lenox	Open	19.50	19.50
91-03-006	Snowman	Lenox	Open	19.50	19.50
92-03-007	Goose	Lenox	Open	20.00	20.00
Lenox China		**Carved**			
87-04-001	Portrait Wreath	Lenox	Closed	21.00	21.00
89-04-002	Georgian Frame	Lenox	Open	25.00	25.00
Lenox China		**Renaissance Angels**			
87-05-001	Angel with Trumpet	Lenox	Closed	21.00	21.00
87-05-002	Angel with Violin	Lenox	Closed	21.00	21.00
87-05-003	Angel with Mandolin	Lenox	Closed	21.00	21.00
Lenox China		**Golden Renaissance Angels**			
91-06-001	Angel with Trumpet	Lenox	Open	25.00	25.00
91-06-002	Angel with Violin	Lenox	Open	25.00	25.00
91-06-003	Angel with Mandolin	Lenox	Open	25.00	25.00
Lenox China		**Nativity**			
89-07-001	Mary & Child	Lenox	Closed	21.00	21.00
89-07-002	Joseph	Lenox	Closed	21.00	21.00
90-07-003	Melchior	Lenox	Closed	22.00	22.00
90-07-004	Gaspar	Lenox	Closed	22.00	22.00
90-07-005	Balthazar	Lenox	Closed	22.00	22.00
Lenox China		**Commemoratives**			
89-08-001	First Christmas Together (Dated)	Lenox	Yr.Iss.	22.50	25.00
89-08-002	Baby's First Christmas (Dated)	Lenox	Yr.Iss.	22.50	25.00
Lenox China		**Holiday Homecoming**			
88-09-001	Hearth	Lenox	Closed	22.50	22.50
89-09-002	Door (Dated)	Lenox	Closed	22.50	22.50
90-09-003	Hutch	Lenox	Open	25.00	25.00
91-09-004	Window (Dated)	Lenox	Yr.Iss.	25.00	25.00
92-09-005	Stove (Dated)	Lenox	Yr.Iss.	25.00	25.00
Lenox China		**Santa's Portraits**			
89-10-001	Santa's Visit	Lenox	Open	27.00	27.00
90-10-002	Santa With Garland	Lenox	Open	29.00	29.00
90-10-003	Santa's Ride	Lenox	Open	29.00	29.00
91-10-004	Santa And Child	Lenox	Open	29.00	29.00
92-10-005	Santa in Chimney	Lenox	Open	29.00	29.00
Lenox China		**Lenox Christmas Village**			
89-11-001	Village Church	Lenox	Open	39.00	39.00
90-11-002	Village Inn	Lenox	Open	39.00	39.00
91-11-003	Village Town Hall (Dated)	Lenox	Yr.Iss.	39.00	39.00
92-11-004	Sweet Shop (Dated)	Lenox	Yr.Iss.	39.00	39.00
Lenox China		**Yuletide Express**			
88-12-001	Locomotive	Lenox	Open	39.00	39.00
89-12-002	Caboose	Lenox	Open	39.00	90.00
90-12-003	Passenger Car	Lenox	Open	39.00	39.00
91-12-004	Dining Car (Dated)	Lenox	Yr.Iss.	39.00	39.00
92-12-005	Tender Car (Dated)	Lenox	Yr.Iss.	39.00	39.00
Lenox China		**Renaissance Angel Treetopper**			
89-13-001	Angel Treetopper	Lenox	Closed	100.00	100.00
Lenox China		**Victorian Homes**			
90-14-001	Sheffield Manor	Lenox	Open	25.00	25.00
91-14-002	Cambridge Manor	Lenox	Open	25.00	25.00
Lenox China		**Lenox Christmas Keepsakes**			
90-15-001	Swan	Lenox	Open	42.00	42.00
90-15-002	Rocking Horse	Lenox	Open	42.00	42.00
91-15-003	Sleigh	Lenox	Open	42.00	42.00
92-15-004	Fire Engine	Lenox	Open	42.00	42.00
Lenox China		**Victorian Lace**			
91-16-001	Christmas Tree	Lenox	Open	25.00	25.00
91-16-002	Fan	Lenox	Open	25.00	25.00
Lenox China		**Cathedral Portraits**			
91-17-001	15th Century Madonna & Child	Botticelli	Open	29.00	29.00
91-17-002	16th Century Madonna & Child	Raphael	Open	29.00	29.00
Lenox Collections		**The Christmas Carousel**			
89-01-001	White Horse	Lenox	Open	19.50	19.50
89-01-002	Zebra	Lenox	Open	19.50	19.50
89-01-003	Lion	Lenox	Open	19.50	19.50
89-01-004	Sea Horse	Lenox	Open	19.50	19.50
89-01-005	Pinto	Lenox	Open	19.50	19.50
89-01-006	Goat	Lenox	Open	19.50	19.50
89-01-007	Reindeer	Lenox	Open	19.50	19.50
89-01-008	Polar Bear	Lenox	Open	19.50	19.50
89-01-009	Hare	Lenox	Open	19.50	19.50
89-01-010	Elephant	Lenox	Open	19.50	19.50
89-01-011	Swan	Lenox	Open	19.50	19.50
89-01-012	Unicorn	Lenox	Open	19.50	19.50
89-01-013	Palomino	Lenox	Open	19.50	19.50
89-01-014	Black Horse	Lenox	Open	19.50	19.50
89-01-015	Cat	Lenox	Open	19.50	19.50
89-01-016	Tiger	Lenox	Open	19.50	19.50
90-01-017	Camel	Lenox	Open	19.50	19.50
90-01-018	Rooster	Lenox	Open	19.50	19.50
90-01-019	Giraffe	Lenox	Open	19.50	19.50
90-01-020	Panda	Lenox	Open	19.50	19.50
90-01-021	Frog	Lenox	Open	19.50	19.50
90-01-022	Pig	Lenox	Open	19.50	19.50
90-01-023	St. Bernard	Lenox	Open	19.50	19.50
90-01-024	Medieval Horse	Lenox	Open	19.50	19.50
90-01-025	Set of 24	Lenox	Open	468.00	468.00
Lenox Crystal		**Crystal Ball Ornaments**			
84-01-001	Deep Cut Ball	Lenox	Yr.Iss.	35.00	50.00
85-01-002	Cut Ball	Lenox	Yr.Iss.	35.00	50.00
86-01-003	Cut Ball	Lenox	Yr.Iss.	35.00	45.00
87-01-004	Cut Ball	Lenox	Yr.Iss.	29.00	29.00
88-01-005	Christmas Lights Ball	Lenox	Yr.Iss.	30.00	30.00
89-01-006	Starlight Ornament	Lenox	Open	34.00	34.00
89-01-007	Crystal Lights Ornaments	Lenox	Open	30.00	30.00
91-01-008	Crystal Abbey Ball	Lenox	Open	45.00	45.00
91-01-009	Crystal Starlight Ball-Blue	Lenox	Open	45.00	45.00
91-01-010	Crystal Starlight Ball-Red	Lenox	Open	45.00	45.00
91-01-011	Crystal Starlight Ball-Green	Lenox	Open	45.00	45.00
92-01-012	Crystal Optika	Lenox	Open	37.00	37.00

Company / Number	Name	Series / Artist	Edition Limit	Issue Price	Quote
Lenox Crystal		**Annual Bell Series**			
87-02-001	Partridge Bell	Lenox	Yr.Iss.	45.00	45.00
88-02-002	Angel Bell	Lenox	Open	45.00	45.00
89-02-003	St. Nicholas Bell	Lenox	Open	45.00	45.00
90-02-004	Christmas Tree Bell	Lenox	Open	49.00	49.00
91-02-005	Teddy Bear Bell	Lenox	Yr.Iss.	49.00	49.00
92-02-006	Snowman Bell	Lenox	Yr.Iss.	49.00	49.00
Lenox Crystal		**Crystal Ornaments**			
89-03-001	Candlelight Bell	Lenox	Open	38.00	38.00
89-03-002	Annual Christmas Tree	Lenox	Yr.Iss.	26.00	26.00
89-03-003	Crystal Icicle	Lenox	Open	30.00	30.00
89-03-004	Our First Christmas	Lenox	Yr.Iss.	26.00	26.00
89-03-005	Baby's First Christmas	Lenox	Yr.Iss	26.00	26.00
89-03-006	Nativity	Lenox	Open	26.00	26.00
89-03-007	Snowflake	Lenox	Open	32.00	32.00
89-03-008	Christmas Lights Tree Top Ornament	Lenox	Open	55.00	55.00
90-03-009	Our First Christmas-1990	Lenox	Yr.Iss.	32.00	32.00
90-03-010	Baby's First Christmas-1990	Lenox	Yr.Iss.	30.00	30.00
90-03-011	Candy Cane	Lenox	Open	30.00	30.00
90-03-012	Christmas Tree-1990	Lenox	Yr.Iss.	30.00	30.00
90-03-013	Christmas Goose	Lenox	Open	29.00	29.00
91-03-014	Our First Christmas-1991	Lenox	Yr.Iss.	29.00	29.00
91-03-015	Baby's First Christmas-1991	Lenox	Yr.Iss.	29.00	29.00
91-03-016	Christmas Tree-1991	Lenox	Yr.Iss.	29.00	29.00
91-03-017	Christmas Stocking	Lenox	Open	29.00	29.00
91-03-018	Angel Pendent	Lenox	Open	29.00	29.00
91-03-019	Bird-Clear	Lenox	Open	29.00	29.00
91-03-020	Bird-Blue	Lenox	Open	29.00	29.00
91-03-021	Bird-Red	Lenox	Open	29.00	29.00
91-03-022	Bird-Green	Lenox	Open	29.00	29.00
91-03-023	Herald Angel-Clear	Lenox	Open	29.00	29.00
91-03-024	Herald Angel-Blue	Lenox	Open	29.00	29.00
91-03-025	Herald Angel-Red	Lenox	Open	29.00	29.00
91-03-026	Herald Angel-Green	Lenox	Open	29.00	29.00
91-03-027	Dove	Lenox	Open	32.00	32.00
91-03-028	Snowman	Lenox	Open	32.00	32.00
91-03-029	Abbey Treetopper	Lenox	Open	54.00	54.00
Lilliput Lane Ltd.		**Christmas Ornaments**			
92-01-001	Mistletoe Cottage	Lilliput Lane	Closed	27.50	27.50
93-01-002	Robin Cottage	Lilliput Lane	Yr.Iss.	35.00	35.00
Lladro		**Miniature Ornaments**			
88-01-001	Miniature Angels-L1604G (Set of 3)	Lladro	Yr.Iss.	75.00	150-200.
89-01-002	Holy Family-L5657G (Set of 3)	Lladro	Yr.Iss.	79.50	175.00
90-01-003	Three Kings-L5729G (Set of 3)	Lladro	Yr Iss.	87.50	150.00
91-01-004	Holy Shepherds-L5809G	Lladro	Yr.Iss.	97.50	175.00
Lladro		**Annual Ornaments**			
88-02-001	Christmas Ball-L1603M	Lladro	Yr.Iss.	60.00	110-150.
89-02-002	Christmas Ball-L5656M	Lladro	Yr.Iss.	65.00	85-100.00
90-02-003	Christmas Ball-L5730M	Lladro	Yr Iss.	70.00	75-90.00
91-02-004	Christmas Ball-L5829M	Lladro	Yr.Iss.	52.00	52-90.00
92-02-005	Christmas Ball-L5914M	Lladro	Yr.Iss.	52.00	52-90.00
Lladro		**Tree Topper Ornaments**			
90-03-001	Angel Tree Topper-L5719G-Blue	Lladro	Yr.Iss.	115.00	250.00
91-03-002	Angel Tree Topper-L5831G-Pink	Lladro	Yr.Iss.	115.00	225.00
92-03-003	Angel Tree Topper-L5875G-Green	Lladro	Yr.Iss.	120.00	120.00
Lladro		**Ornaments**			
92-04-001	Snowman-L5841G	Lladro	Yr.Iss.	50.00	50.00
92-04-002	Santa-L5842G	Lladro	Yr.Iss.	55.00	55.00
92-04-003	Baby's First-1992-L5922G	Lladro	Yr.Iss.	55.00	55.00
92-04-004	Our First-1992-L5923G	Lladro	Yr.Iss.	50.00	50.00
92-04-005	Elf Ornament-L5938G	Lladro	Yr.Iss.	50.00	50.00
92-04-006	Mrs. Claus-L5939G	Lladro	Yr.Iss.	55.00	55.00
92-04-007	Christmas Morning-L5940G	Lladro	Yr.Iss.	97.50	97.50
Lladro		**Angel Orchestra**			
91-05-001	Heavenly Harpist 15830	Lladro	Yr.Iss.	135.00	135.00
92-05-002	Angelic Cymbalist 5876	Lladro	Yr.Iss.	140.00	140.00
Seymour Mann Inc.		**Christmas Collection**			
85-01-001	Angel Wall XMAS-523	J. White	Open	12.00	12.00
86-01-002	Cupid Head XMAS-53	J. White	Open	25.00	25.00
86-01-003	Santa XMAS-384	J. White	Closed	7.50	7.50
89-01-004	Christmas Cat in Teacup XMAS-660	J. White	Open	13.50	13.50
91-01-005	Floral Plaque XMAS-911	J. White	Open	10.00	10.00
91-01-006	Flower Basket XMAS-912	J. White	Open	10.00	10.00
90-01-007	Cupid CPD-5	J. White	Open	13.50	13.50
90-01-008	Cupid CPD-6	J. White	Open	13.50	13.50
90-01-009	Doll Tree Topper OM-124	J. White	Open	85.00	85.00
90-01-010	Hat w/ Streamers OM-116	J. White	Open	20.00	20.00
90-01-011	Heartlace OM-119	J. White	Open	12.00	12.00
90-01-012	Lace Ball OM-120	J. White	Open	10.00	10.00
90-01-013	Tassel OM-118	J. White	Open	7.50	7.50
91-01-014	Elf w/ Reindeer CJ-422	Jaimy	Open	9.00	9.00
91-01-015	Elves w/ Mail CJ-464	J. White	Open	30.00	30.00
91-01-016	Flat Red Santa CJ-115R	Jaimy	Open	2.88	2.88
91-01-017	Flat Santa CJ-115	Jaimy	Open	7.50	7.50
91-01-018	Santas, set of 6 CJ-12	Jaimy	Open	60.00	60.00
Seymour Mann Inc.		**Gingerbread Christmas Collection**			
91-02-001	Gingerbread Angel CJ-411	J. Sauerbrey	Open	7.50	7.50
91-02-002	Gingerbread House CJ-416	J. Sauerbrey	Open	7.50	7.50
91-02-003	Gingerbread Man CJ-415	J. Sauerbrey	Open	7.50	7.50
91-02-004	Gingerbread Mouse/Boot CJ-409	J. Sauerbrey	Open	7.50	7.50
91-02-005	Gingerbread Mrs. Claus CJ-414	J. Sauerbrey	Open	7.50	7.50
91-02-006	Gingerbread Reindeer CJ-410	J. Sauerbrey	Open	7.50	7.50
91-02-007	Gingerbread Santa CJ-408	J. Sauerbrey	Open	7.50	7.50
91-02-008	Gingerbread Sleigh CJ-406	J. Sauerbrey	Open	7.50	7.50
91-02-009	Gingerbread Snowman CJ-412	J. Sauerbrey	Open	7.50	7.50
91-02-010	Gingerbread Tree CJ-407	J. Sauerbrey	Open	7.50	7.50
Seymour Mann Inc.		**Victorian Christmas Collection**			
91-03-001	Couple Against Wind CJ-420	Jaimy	Open	15.00	15.00
June McKenna Collectibles, Inc.		**Flatback Ornaments**			
82-01-001	Santa With Toys	J. McKenna	Closed	14.00	50-80.00
82-01-002	Mama Bear, Blue Cape	J. McKenna	Closed	12.00	75-125.00
82-01-003	Papa Bear, Red Cape	J. McKenna	Closed	12.00	100-275.
82-01-004	Baby Bear, Teeshirt	J. McKenna	Closed	11.00	75-200.00
82-01-005	Candy Cane	J. McKenna	Closed	10.00	250.00
82-01-006	Colonial Man, available in 2 colors	J. McKenna	Closed	12.00	100-125.
82-01-007	Colonial Woman, available in 2 colors	J. McKenna	Closed	12.00	85-100.00
82-01-008	Kate Greenaway Boy	J. McKenna	Closed	12.00	300-500.
82-01-009	Kate Greenaway Girl	J. McKenna	Closed	12.00	350-500.
82-01-010	Angel With Toys	J. McKenna	Closed	14.00	65-75.00
83-01-011	Grandma, available in 4 colors	J. McKenna	Closed	12.00	60-75.00
83-01-012	Grandpa, available in 4 colors	J. McKenna	Closed	12.00	60-85.00
83-01-013	Mother Bear in Dress, available in 2 colors	J. McKenna	Closed	12.00	65-95.00
83-01-014	Father Bear in Suit, available in 2 colors	J. McKenna	Closed	12.00	65-75.00
83-01-015	Baby Bear in Vest, available in 2 colors	J. McKenna	Closed	11.00	55-65.00
83-01-016	Raggedy Ann	J. McKenna	Closed	12.00	175.00
83-01-017	Raggedy Andy	J. McKenna	Closed	12.00	175.00
83-01-018	St. Nick With Lantern	J. McKenna	Closed	14.00	50-75.00
83-01-019	Gloria Angel	J. McKenna	Closed	14.00	350-500.
83-01-020	Baby, available in 2 colors	J. McKenna	Closed	11.00	85.00
84-01-021	Angel with Horn	J. McKenna	Closed	14.00	125-225.
84-01-022	Mr. Claus	J. McKenna	Closed	14.00	85-95.00
84-01-023	Mrs. Claus	J. McKenna	Closed	14.00	85-95.00
84-01-024	Country Boy, available in 2 colors	J. McKenna	Closed	12.00	60-85.00
84-01-025	Country Girl, available in 2 colors	J. McKenna	Closed	12.00	60-85.00
84-01-026	Old World Santa, available in 3 colors	J. McKenna	Closed	14.00	50-95.00
85-01-027	Bride	J. McKenna	Closed	25.00	200.00
85-01-028	Groom	J. McKenna	Closed	25.00	200.00
85-01-029	Baby Pig	J. McKenna	Closed	11.00	95.00
85-01-030	Father Pig	J. McKenna	Closed	12.00	150.00
85-01-031	Mother Pig	J. McKenna	Closed	12.00	150.00
85-01-032	Amish Man	J. McKenna	Closed	13.00	50-275.00
85-01-033	Amish Woman	J. McKenna	Closed	13.00	50-275.00
85-01-034	Primitive Santa	J. McKenna	Closed	17.00	75-150.00
86-01-035	Amish Boy	J. McKenna	Closed	13.00	65-275.00
86-01-036	Amish Girl	J. McKenna	Closed	13.00	65-275.00
86-01-037	Santa with Bells, green	J. McKenna	Closed	14.00	200-400.
86-01-038	Santa with Bells, blue	J. McKenna	Closed	14.00	50-75.00
86-01-039	Santa with Bear	J. McKenna	Closed	14.00	40.00
86-01-040	Santa with Bag	J. McKenna	Closed	16.00	30-40.00
88-01-041	Elizabeth, sill sitter	J. McKenna	Closed	20.00	200-300.
88-01-042	Guardian Angel	J. McKenna	Closed	16.00	40.00
88-01-043	1776 Santa	J. McKenna	Closed	17.00	40.00
88-01-044	Santa With Book (blue & red)	J. McKenna	Closed	17.00	40-110.00
88-01-045	Santa With Toys	J. McKenna	Closed	17.00	40.00
88-01-046	Santa With Wreath	J. McKenna	Closed	17.00	40.00
89-01-047	Glorious Angel	J. McKenna	Open	17.00	17.00
89-01-048	Santa With Staff	J. McKenna	Closed	17.00	40.00
89-01-049	Santa WithTree	J. McKenna	Closed	17.00	40.00
89-01-050	Winking Santa	J. McKenna	Closed	17.00	40.00
90-01-051	Ho Ho Ho	J. McKenna	Closed	17.00	40.00
90-01-052	Elf Jeffrey	J. McKenna	Closed	17.00	40.00
90-01-053	Harvest Santa	J. McKenna	Closed	17.00	40.00
91-01-054	Santa With Lights, black or white	J. McKenna	Closed	20.00	20.00
91-01-055	Santa With Banner	J. McKenna	Closed	20.00	20.00
91-01-056	Elf Joey	J. McKenna	Closed	20.00	20.00
91-01-057	Boy Angel	J. McKenna	Closed	20.00	20.00
91-01-058	Girl Angel	J. McKenna	Open	20.00	30.00
92-01-059	Santa With Basket	J. McKenna	Open	25.00	30.00
92-01-060	Santa With Sack	J. McKenna	Open	25.00	30.00
92-01-061	Northpole News	J. McKenna	Open	25.00	30.00
92-01-062	Elf Scotty	J. McKenna	Open	25.00	30.00
92-01-063	Praying Angel	J. McKenna	Open	25.00	30.00
93-01-064	Old Lamplighter	J. McKenna	Open	30.00	30.00
93-01-065	Christmas Treat	J. McKenna	Open	30.00	30.00
93-01-066	Final Notes	J. McKenna	Open	30.00	30.00
93-01-067	Elf Bernie	J. McKenna	Open	30.00	30.00
93-01-068	Angel of Peace- white or pink	J. McKenna	Open	30.00	30.00
Midwest Importers		**Wendt und Kuhn Ornaments**			
78-01-001	Angel Clip-on Ornament 07296	Wendt/Kuhn	Open	20.00	21.00
89-01-002	Trumpeting Angel Ornament,2 asst. 94029	Wendt/Kuhn	Open	14.00	15.00
91-01-003	Angel in Ring Ornament 12089	Wendt/Kuhn	Open	12.00	12.50
Midwest Importers		**Heritage Santa Collection Ornaments**			
90-02-001	Scanda Klaus Fabric Mache 05208	Midwest Importers	Retrd.	18.00	18.00
90-02-002	Herr Kristmas Fabric Mache 05216	Midwest Importers	Retrd.	18.00	18.00
90-02-003	MacNicholas Fabric Mache 05224	Midwest Importers	Retrd.	18.00	18.00
90-02-004	Papa Frost Fabric Mache 05232	Midwest Importers	Retrd.	18.00	18.00
91-02-005	Scanda Klaus Dimensional 29414	Midwest Importers	Open	11.50	11.50
91-02-006	Herr Kristmas Dimensional 29422	Midwest Importers	Open	11.50	11.50
91-02-007	MacNicholas Dimensional 29430	Midwest Importers	Open	11.50	11.50
91-02-008	Papa Frost Dimensional 29448	Midwest Importers	Retrd.	11.50	11.50
91-02-009	Father Christmas Dimensional 29456	Midwest Importers	Open	11.50	11.50
91-02-010	Santa Niccolo Dimensional 29464	Midwest Importers	Open	11.50	11.50
92-02-011	Santa Nykolai Dimensional 67745	Midwest Importers	Open	11.50	11.50
92-02-012	Pere Noel Dimensional 67739	Midwest Importers	Open	11.50	11.50
93-02-013	Santa España Dimensional 73766	Midwest Importers	Open	11.50	11.50
93-02-014	Santa O'Nicholas Dimensional 73773	Midwest Importers	Open	11.50	11.50
Orrefors		**Christmas Ornaments**			
84-01-001	Dove	O. Alberius	Yr.Iss.	30.00	45.00
85-01-002	Angel	O. Alberius	Yr.Iss.	30.00	40.00
86-01-003	Reindeer	O. Alberius	Yr.Iss.	30.00	40.00
87-01-004	Snowman	O. Alberius	Yr.Iss.	30.00	40.00
88-01-005	Sleigh	O. Alberius	Yr.Iss.	30.00	40.00
89-01-006	Christmas Tree "1989"	O. Alberius	Yr.Iss.	35.00	40.00
90-01-007	Holly Leaves And Berries	O. Alberius	Yr.Iss.	35.00	40.00
91-01-008	Stocking	O. Alberius	Yr.Iss.	40.00	40.00
92-01-009	Star	O. Alberius	Yr.Iss.	35.00	40.00
93-01-010	Bell	O. Alberius	Open	35.00	40.00
93-01-011	Baby's1st Christmas	O. Alberius	Open	40.00	40.00
Reco International		**The Reco Angel Collection Hang-Ups**			
87-01-001	Innocence	J. McClelland	Open	7.50	7.50
87-01-002	Harmony	J. McClelland	Open	7.50	7.50
87-01-003	Love	J. McClelland	Open	7.50	7.50
87-01-004	Gloria	J. McClelland	Open	7.50	7.50
87-01-005	Devotion	J. McClelland	Open	7.50	7.50
87-01-006	Joy	J. McClelland	Open	7.50	7.50
87-01-007	Adoration	J. McClelland	Open	10.00	10.00
87-01-008	Peace	J. McClelland	Open	10.00	10.00
87-01-009	Serenity	J. McClelland	Open	10.00	10.00
87-01-010	Hope	J. McClelland	Open	10.00	10.00

Company Number	Name	Series Artist	Edition Limit	Issue Price	Quote
Reco International		**The Reco Ornament Collection**			
88-02-001	Billy	S. Kuck	Yr.Iss.	15.00	15.00
88-02-002	Lisa	S. Kuck	Yr.Iss.	15.00	15.00
89-02-003	Heather	S. Kuck	Yr.Iss.	15.00	15.00
89-02-004	Timothy	S. Kuck	Yr.Iss.	15.00	15.00
90-02-005	Amy	S. Kuck	Yr.Iss.	15.00	15.00
90-02-006	Johnny	S. Kuck	Yr.Iss.	15.00	15.00
90-02-007	Peace On Earth	S. Kuck	17,500	17.50	17.50
Reed & Barton		**Christmas Cross**			
71-01-001	Sterling Silver-1971	Reed & Barton	Closed	10.00	140-300.
71-01-002	24Kt. Gold over Sterling-V1971	Reed & Barton	Closed	17.50	225.00
72-01-003	Sterling Silver-1972	Reed & Barton	Closed	10.00	60-125.00
72-01-004	24Kt. Gold over Sterling-V1972	Reed & Barton	Closed	17.50	65-105.
73-01-005	Sterling Silver-1973	Reed & Barton	Closed	10.00	60-75.00
73-01-006	24Kt. Gold over Sterling-V1973	Reed & Barton	Closed	17.50	55-65.00
74-01-007	Sterling Silver-1974	Reed & Barton	Closed	12.95	40-60.00
74-01-008	24Kt. Gold over Sterling-V1974	Reed & Barton	Closed	20.00	50-60.00
75-01-009	Sterling Silver-1975	Reed & Barton	Closed	12.95	35-55.00
75-01-010	24Kt. Gold over Sterling-V1975	Reed & Barton	Closed	20.00	45-50.00
76-01-011	Sterling Silver-1976	Reed & Barton	Closed	13.95	55.00
76-01-012	24Kt. Gold over Sterling-V1976	Reed & Barton	Closed	19.95	45-50.00
77-01-013	Sterling Silver-1977	Reed & Barton	Closed	15.00	35-55.00
77-01-014	24Kt. Gold over Sterling-V1977	Reed & Barton	Closed	18.50	45-50.00
78-01-015	Sterling Silver-1978	Reed & Barton	Closed	16.00	40-60.00
78-01-016	24Kt. Gold over Sterling-V1978	Reed & Barton	Closed	20.00	45-55.00
79-01-017	Sterling Silver-1979	Reed & Barton	Closed	20.00	45-60.00
79-01-018	24Kt. Gold over Sterling-V1979	Reed & Barton	Closed	24.00	32-57.00
80-01-019	Sterling Silver-1980	Reed & Barton	Closed	35.00	45-60.00
80-01-020	24Kt. Gold over Sterling-V1980	Reed & Barton	Closed	40.00	45-50.00
81-01-021	Sterling Silver-1981	Reed & Barton	Closed	35.00	45.00
81-01-022	24Kt. Gold over Sterling-V1981	Reed & Barton	Closed	40.00	45.00
82-01-023	Sterling Silver-1982	Reed & Barton	Closed	35.00	45-53.00
82-01-024	24Kt. Gold over Sterling-V1982	Reed & Barton	Closed	40.00	45.00
83-01-025	Sterling Silver-1983	Reed & Barton	Closed	35.00	50.00
83-01-026	24Kt. Gold over Sterling-V1983	Reed & Barton	Closed	40.00	40-45.00
84-01-027	Sterling Silver-1984	Reed & Barton	Closed	35.00	45.00
84-01-028	24Kt. Gold over Sterling-V1984	Reed & Barton	Closed	45.00	45.00
85-01-029	Sterling Silver-1985	Reed & Barton	Closed	35.00	30-40.00
85-01-030	24Kt. Gold over Sterling-V1985	Reed & Barton	Closed	40.00	40.00
86-01-031	Sterling Silver-1986	Reed & Barton	Closed	38.50	38.50
86-01-032	24Kt. Gold over Sterling-V1986	Reed & Barton	Closed	40.00	40.00
87-01-033	Sterling Silver-1987	Reed & Barton	Closed	35.00	35.00
87-01-034	24Kt. Gold over Sterling-V1987	Reed & Barton	Closed	40.00	40.00
88-01-035	Sterling Silver-1988	Reed & Barton	Closed	35.00	35.00
88-01-036	24Kt. Gold over Sterling-V1988	Reed & Barton	Closed	40.00	40.00
89-01-037	Sterling Silver-1989	Reed & Barton	Closed	35.00	35.00
89-01-038	24Kt. Gold over Sterling-V1989	Reed & Barton	Closed	40.00	40.00
90-01-039	Sterling Silver-1990	Reed & Barton	Closed	40.00	40.00
90-01-040	24Kt. Gold over Sterling-1990	Reed & Barton	Closed	45.00	45.00
91-01-041	Sterling Silver-1991	Reed & Barton	Closed	40.00	40.00
91-01-042	24Kt Gold over Sterling-1991	Reed & Barton	Closed	45.00	45.00
92-01-043	Sterling Silver-1992	Reed & Barton	Closed	40.00	40.00
92-01-044	24Kt Gold over Sterling-1992	Reed & Barton	Closed	45.00	45.00
93-01-045	Sterling Silver-1993	Reed & Barton	Yr.Iss.	40.00	40.00
93-01-046	24Kt Gold over Sterling-1993	Reed & Barton	Yr.Iss.	45.00	45.00
Reed & Barton		**Holly Ball**			
76-02-001	1976 Silver plated	Reed & Barton	Closed	13.95	50.00
77-02-002	1977 Silver plated	Reed & Barton	Closed	15.00	35.00
78-02-003	1978 Silver plated	Reed & Barton	Closed	15.00	35.00
79-02-004	1979 Silver plated	Reed & Barton	Closed	15.00	35.00
Reed & Barton		**Holly Bell**			
80-03-001	1980 Bell	Reed & Barton	Closed	22.50	40.00
80-03-002	Bell, gold plate, V1980	Reed & Barton	Closed	25.00	45.00
81-03-003	1981 Bell	Reed & Barton	Closed	22.50	35.00
81-03-004	Bell, gold plate, V1981	Reed & Barton	Closed	27.50	35.00
82-03-005	1982 Bell	Reed & Barton	Closed	22.50	35.00
82-03-006	Bell, gold plate, V1982	Reed & Barton	Closed	27.50	35.00
83-03-007	1983 Bell	Reed & Barton	Closed	23.50	40.00
83-03-008	Bell, gold plate, V1983	Reed & Barton	Closed	30.00	35.00
84-03-009	1984 Bell	Reed & Barton	Closed	25.00	30.00
84-03-010	Bell, gold plate, V1984	Reed & Barton	Closed	28.50	35.00
85-03-011	1985 Bell	Reed & Barton	Closed	25.00	35.00
85-03-012	Bell, gold plate, V1985	Reed & Barton	Closed	28.50	28.50
86-03-013	1986 Bell	Reed & Barton	Closed	25.00	35.00
86-03-014	Bell, gold plate, V1986	Reed & Barton	Closed	28.50	32.50
87-03-015	1987 Bell	Reed & Barton	Closed	27.50	30.00
87-03-016	Bell, gold plate, V1987	Reed & Barton	Closed	30.00	30.00
88-03-017	1988 Bell	Reed & Barton	Closed	27.50	30.00
88-03-018	Bell, gold plate, V1988	Reed & Barton	Closed	30.00	30.00
89-03-019	1989 Bell	Reed & Barton	Closed	27.50	27.50
89-03-020	Bell, gold plate, V1989	Reed & Barton	Closed	30.00	30.00
90-03-021	Bell, gold plate, V1990	Reed & Barton	Closed	30.00	30.00
90-03-022	1990 Bell	Reed & Barton	Closed	27.50	27.50
91-03-023	Bell, gold plate, V1991	Reed & Barton	Closed	30.00	30.00
91-03-024	1991 Bell	Reed & Barton	Closed	27.50	27.50
92-03-025	Bell, gold plate, V1992	Reed & Barton	Closed	30.00	30.00
92-03-026	Bell, silver plate, 1992	Reed & Barton	Closed	27.50	27.50
93-03-027	Bell, gold plate, V1993	Reed & Barton	Yr.Iss.	27.50	27.50
93-03-028	Bell, silver plate, 1993	Reed & Barton	Yr.Iss.	30.00	30.00
Reed & Barton		**12 Days of Christmas**			
83-04-001	Partridge in a Pear Tree	Reed & Barton	Closed	16.50	20.00
83-04-002	Turtle Doves	Reed & Barton	Closed	16.50	20.00
84-04-003	French Hens	Reed & Barton	Closed	18.50	20.00
84-04-004	Calling Birds	Reed & Barton	Closed	18.50	20.00
85-04-005	Gold Rings	Reed & Barton	Closed	20.00	20.00
85-04-006	Geese A'Laying	Reed & Barton	Closed	20.00	20.00
86-04-007	Swans A'Swimming	Reed & Barton	Closed	20.00	20.00
86-04-008	Maids A'Milking	Reed & Barton	Closed	20.00	20.00
87-04-009	Ladies Dancing	Reed & Barton	Closed	20.00	20.00
87-04-010	Lords A'Leaping	Reed & Barton	Closed	20.00	20.00
88-04-011	Pipers Piping	Reed & Barton	Closed	20.00	20.00
88-04-012	Drummers Drumming	Reed & Barton	Closed	20.00	20.00
Reed & Barton		**12 Days of Christmas Sterling and Lead Crystal**			
88-05-001	Partridge in a Pear Tree	Reed & Barton	Closed	25.00	27.50
89-05-002	Two Turtle Doves	Reed & Barton	Closed	25.00	27.50
90-05-003	French Hens	Reed & Barton	Closed	27.50	27.50
91-05-004	Colly birds	Reed & Barton	Closed	27.50	27.50
92-05-005	Five Golden Rings	Reed & Barton	Closed	27.50	27.50
93-05-006	Six French Hens	Reed & Barton	Yr.Iss.	27.50	27.50
Reed & Barton		**Carousel Horse**			
88-06-001	Silverplate-1988	Reed & Barton	Closed	13.50	13.50
88-06-002	Gold-covered-1988	Reed & Barton	Closed	15.00	15.00
89-06-003	Silverplate-1989	Reed & Barton	Closed	13.50	13.50
89-06-004	Gold-covered-1989	Reed & Barton	Closed	15.00	15.00
90-06-005	Silverplate-1990	Reed & Barton	Closed	13.50	13.50
90-06-006	Gold-covered-1990	Reed & Barton	Closed	15.00	15.00
91-06-007	Silverplate-1991	Reed & Barton	Closed	13.50	13.50
91-06-008	Gold-covered-1991	Reed & Barton	Closed	15.00	15.00
92-06-009	Silverplate-1992	Reed & Barton	Closed	13.50	13.50
92-06-010	Gold-covered-1992	Reed & Barton	Closed	15.00	15.00
93-06-011	Silverplate-1993	Reed & Barton	Yr.Iss.	13.50	13.50
93-06-012	Gold-covered-1993	Reed & Barton	Yr.Iss.	15.00	15.00
Norman Rockwell Gallery		**Ornaments**			
91-01-001	Rockwell's Legends of Santa(Set of 4)	Rockwell-Inspired	N/A	49.95	49.95
92-01-002	Rockwell's Classic Santas(Set of 3)	Rockwell-Inspired	N/A	39.95	39.95
Royal Orleans		**Ornaments**			
84-01-001	Jimmy	J. Hagara	2-Yr.	10.00	225.00
84-01-002	Jenny	J. Hagara	2-Yr.	10.00	125.00
84-01-003	Lisa	J. Hagara	2-Yr.	10.00	35-60.00
84-01-004	Anne	J. Hagara	2-Yr.	10.00	60-125.00
Roman, Inc.		**The Discovery of America**			
91-01-001	Kitstopher Kolumbus	I. Spencer	1,992	15.00	15.00
91-01-002	Queen Kitsabella	I. Spencer	1,992	15.00	15.00
Roman, Inc.		**Fontanini Annual Christmas Ornaments**			
91-02-001	1991 Annual (Girl)	E. Simonetti	Yr.Iss.	8.50	8.50
91-02-002	1991 Annual (Boy)	E. Simonetti	Yr.Iss.	8.50	8.50
92-02-003	1992 Annual (Girl)	E. Simonetti	Yr.Iss.	8.50	8.50
92-02-004	1992 Annual (Boy)	E. Simonetti	Yr.Iss.	8.50	8.50
93-02-005	1993 Annual (Girl)	E. Simonetti	Yr.Iss.	8.50	8.50
93-02-006	1993 Annual (Boy)	E. Simonetti	Yr.Iss.	8.50	8.50
Roman, Inc.		**Catnippers**			
88-03-001	Christmas Mourning	I. Spencer	Open	15.00	15.00
88-03-002	Ring A Ding-Ding	I. Spencer	Open	15.00	15.00
88-03-003	Puss in Berries	I. Spencer	Open	15.00	15.00
89-03-004	Bow Brummel	I. Spencer	Open	15.00	15.00
89-03-005	Happy Holidaze	I. Spencer	Open	15.00	15.00
89-03-006	Sandy Claws	I. Spencer	Open	15.00	15.00
90-03-007	Sock It to Me Santa	I. Spencer	Open	15.00	15.00
90-03-008	Stuck on Christmas	I. Spencer	Open	15.00	15.00
90-03-009	Felix Navidad	I. Spencer	Open	15.00	15.00
91-03-010	Meowy Christmas	I. Spencer	Open	15.00	15.00
91-03-011	Christmas Knight	I. Spencer	Open	15.00	15.00
91-03-012	Faux Paw	I. Spencer	Open	15.00	15.00
91-03-013	Snow Biz	I. Spencer	Open	15.00	15.00
91-03-014	Holly Days Are Happy Days	I. Spencer	Open	15.00	15.00
91-03-015	Pawtridge in a Purr Tree	I. Spencer	Open	15.00	15.00
Sarah's Attic, Inc.		**Santas Of The Month Ornaments**			
88-01-001	Jan. Mini Santa	Sarah's Attic	Closed	14.00	21.00
88-01-002	Feb. Mini Santa	Sarah's Attic	Closed	14.00	21.00
88-01-003	March Mini Santa	Sarah's Attic	Closed	14.00	21.00
88-01-004	April Mini Santa	Sarah's Attic	Closed	14.00	21.00
88-01-005	May Mini Santa	Sarah's Attic	Closed	14.00	21.00
88-01-006	June Mini Santa	Sarah's Attic	Closed	14.00	21.00
88-01-007	July Mini Santa	Sarah's Attic	Closed	14.00	21.00
88-01-008	Aug. Mini Santa	Sarah's Attic	Closed	14.00	21.00
88-01-009	Sept. Mini Santa	Sarah's Attic	Closed	14.00	21.00
88-01-010	Oct. Mini Santa	Sarah's Attic	Closed	14.00	21.00
88-01-011	Nov. Mini Santa	Sarah's Attic	Closed	14.00	21.00
88-01-012	Dec.Mini Santa	Sarah's Attic	Closed	14.00	21.00
Schmid		**Lowell Davis Country Christmas**			
83-01-001	Mailbox	L. Davis	Yr.Iss.	17.50	52-75.00
84-01-002	Cat in Boot	L. Davis	Yr.Iss.	17.50	60-65.00
85-01-003	Pig in Trough	L. Davis	Yr.Iss.	17.50	50-75.00
86-01-004	Church	L. Davis	Yr.Iss.	17.50	35-55.00
87-01-005	Blossom	L. Davis	Yr.Iss.	19.50	25-60.00
88-01-006	Wisteria	L. Davis	Yr.Iss.	19.50	25-50.00
89-01-007	Wren	L. Davis	Yr.Iss.	19.50	30-47.50
90-01-008	Wintering Deer	L. Davis	Yr.Iss.	19.50	30.00
91-01-009	Church at Red Oak II	L. Davis	Yr.Iss.	25.00	25.00
92-01-010	Born On A Starry Night	L. Davis	Yr.Iss.	25.00	25.00
93-01-011	Waiting for Mr. Lowell	L. Davis	Yr.Iss.	20.00	20.00
Schmid		**Lowell Davis Glass Ornaments**			
86-02-001	Christmas at Red Oak	L. Davis	Yr.Iss.	5.00	7-10.00
87-02-002	Blossom's Gift	L. Davis	Yr.Iss.	5.50	12.00
88-02-003	Hope Mom Likes It	L. Davis	Yr.Iss.	5.00	10.00
89-02-004	Peter and the Wren	L. Davis	Yr.Iss.	6.50	8.00
90-02-005	Wintering Deer	L. Davis	Yr.Iss.	6.50	6.50
91-02-006	Christmas at Red Oak II	L. Davis	Yr.Iss.	7.50	7.50
92-02-007	Born On A Starry Night Ball	L. Davis	Yr.Iss.	7.50	7.50
93-02-008	Waiting for Mr. Lowell	L. Davis	Yr.Iss.	7.50	7.50
Schmid		**Kitty Cucumber Annual**			
89-03-001	Ring Around the Rosie	M. Lillemoe	Yr.Iss.	25.00	25.00
90-03-002	Swan Lake	M. Lillemoe	Yr.Iss.	12.00	12.00
91-03-003	Tea Party	M. Lillemoe	Yr.Iss.	12.00	24.00
92-03-004	Dance 'Round the Maypole	M. Lillemoe	Yr.Iss.	10.00	10.00
Schmid		**Disney Annual**			
85-04-001	Snow Biz	Disney Studios	Yr.Iss.	8.50	20.00
86-04-002	Tree for Two	Disney Studios	Yr.Iss.	8.50	15.00
87-04-003	Merry Mouse Medley	Disney Studios	Yr.Iss.	8.50	10.00
88-04-004	Warm Winter Ride	Disney Studios	Yr.Iss.	11.00	45.00
89-04-005	Merry Mickey Claus	Disney Studios	Yr.Iss.	11.00	11.00
90-04-006	Holly Jolly Christmas	Disney Studios	Yr.Iss.	13.50	30.00
91-04-007	Mickey & Minnie's Rockin' Christmas	Disney Studios	Yr.Iss.	13.50	13.50
Schmid		**Friends of Mine**			
89-05-001	Sun Worshippers	L. Davis	Yr.Iss.	32.50	32.50
90-05-002	Sunday Afternoon Treat	L. Davis	Yr.Iss.	37.50	37.50
91-05-003	Warm Milk	L. Davis	Yr.Iss.	37.50	37.50

CHRISTMAS ORNAMENTS

Company / Number	Name	Series / Artist	Edition Limit	Issue Price	Quote
92-05-004	Cat and Jenny Wren	L. Davis	Yr.Iss.	35.00	35.00
Schmid		**Pen Pals**			
93-06-001	The Old Home Place	L. Davis	Yr.Iss.	24.00	24.00
Schmid/B.F.A.		**The Littlest Night**			
93-01-001	"The Littlest Night" Ornament-2D	B. Hummel	Open	15.00	15.00
Sculpture Workshop Designs		**Annual**			
85-01-001	The Return of the Christmas Comet	F. Kreitchet	7,500	39.00	100.00
86-01-002	Liberty/Peace	F. Kreitchet	7,500	49.00	150.00
87-01-003	Christmas at Home	F. Kreitchet	2,500	57.00	90.00
88-01-004	Christmas Doves	F. Kreitchet	2,500	57.00	80.00
89-01-005	Santa's Reindeer	F. Kreitchet	2,500	60.00	75.00
90-01-006	Joyful Angels	F. Kreitchet	2,500	75.00	75.00
91-01-007	Angel & Shepherds	F. Krietchet	2,500	75.00	75.00
Sculpture Workshop Designs		**Annual-Special Commemorative**			
87-02-001	The Bicentennial of the U.S. Constitution	F. Kreitchet	200	95.00	250.00
89-02-002	The Presidential Signatures	F. Kreitchet	200	95.00	125.00
91-02-003	The U.S. Bill of Rights	F. Kreitchet	200	150.00	150.00
Sculpture Workshop Designs		**Santa Series**			
92-03-001	Forever Santa	F. Kreitchet	2,500	68.00	68.00
Swarovski America Ltd.		**Holiday Ornaments**			
86-01-001	Small Angel/Noel	Unknown	Yr.Iss.	18.00	18.00
86-01-002	Small Bell/Merry Christmas	Unknown	Yr.Iss.	18.00	18.00
86-01-003	Small Dove/Peace	Unknown	Yr.Iss.	18.00	18.00
86-01-004	Small Holly/Merry Christmas	Unknown	Yr.Iss.	18.00	18.00
86-01-005	Small Snowflake	Unknown	Yr.Iss.	18.00	18.00
86-01-006	Medium Snowflake	Unknown	Yr.Iss.	22.50	22.50
86-01-007	Medium Bell/Merry Christmas	Unknown	Yr.Iss.	22.50	22.50
86-01-008	Medium Angel/Joyeux Noel	Unknown	Yr.Iss.	22.50	22.50
86-01-009	Large Angel/Noel	Unknown	Yr.Iss.	35.00	35.00
86-01-010	Large Partridge/Merry Christmas	Unknown	Yr.Iss.	35.00	35.00
87-01-011	1987 Holiday Etching-Candle	Unknown	Yr.Iss.	20.00	85-100.00
88-01-012	1988 Holiday Etching-Wreath	Unknown	Yr.Iss.	25.00	36-75.00
89-01-013	1989 Holiday Etching-Dove	Unknown	Yr.Iss.	35.00	75-90.00
90-01-014	1990 Holiday Etching	Unknown	Yr.Iss.	25.00	100.00
91-01-015	1991 Holiday Ornament	Unknown	Yr.Iss.	35.00	40-60.00
92-01-016	1992 Holiday Ornament	Unknown	Yr.Iss.	37.50	37.50
Towle Silversmiths		**Sterling Twelve Days of Christmas Medallions**			
71-01-001	Partridge in Pear Tree	Towle	15,000	20.00	700.00
72-01-001	Two Turtle Doves	Towle	45,000	20.00	75-250.00
73-01-003	Three French Hens	Towle	75,000	20.00	150.00
74-01-004	Four Mockingbirds	Towle	60,000	30.00	100.00
75-01-005	Five Golden Rings	Towle	60,000	30.00	65.00
76-01-006	Six Geese-a-Laying	Towle	60,000	30.00	40-90.00
77-01-007	Seven Swans-a-Swimming	Towle	60,000	35.00	50.00
78-01-008	Eight Maids-a-Milking	Towle	60,000	37.00	50.00
79-01-009	Nine Ladies Dancing	Towle	40,000	Unkn.	50.00
80-01-010	Ten Lords-a-Leaping	Towle	25,000	76.00	50.00
81-01-011	Eleven Pipers Piping	Towle	25,000	50.00	50.00
82-01-012	Twelve Drummers Drumming	Towle	20,000	35.00	40.00
Towle Silversmiths		**Songs of Christmas Medallions**			
78-02-001	Silent Night Medallion	Towle	25,000	35.00	60.00
79-02-002	Deck The Halls	Towle	5,000	Unkn.	50.00
80-02-003	Jingle Bells	Towle	5,000	52.50	60.00
81-02-004	Hark the Hearld Angels Sing	Towle	5,000	52.50	60.00
82-02-005	O Christmas Tree	Towle	2,000	35.00	50.00
83-02-006	Silver Bells	Towle	2,500	40.00	60.00
84-02-007	Let It Snow	Towle	6,500	30.00	50.00
85-02-008	Chestnuts Roasting on Open Fire	Towle	3,000	35.00	50.00
86-02-009	It Came Upon a Midnight Clear	Towle	3,500	35.00	45.00
87-02-010	White Christmas	Towle	3,500	35.00	45.00
Towle Silversmiths		**Sterling Floral Medallions**			
83-03-001	Christmas Rose	Towle	20,000	40.00	50.00
84-03-002	Hawthorne/Glastonbury Thorn	Towle	20,000	40.00	50.00
85-03-003	Poinsettia	Towle	14,000	35.00	50.00
86-03-004	Laurel Bay	Towle	12,000	35.00	40.00
87-03-005	Mistletoe	Towle	10,000	35.00	45.00
88-03-006	Holly	Towle	10,000	40.00	40.00
89-03-007	Ivy	Towle	10,000	35.00	45.00
90-03-008	Christmas Cactus	Towle	10,000	40.00	40.00
91-03-009	Chrysanthemum	Towle	N/A	40.00	40.00
92-03-010	Star of Bethlehem	Towle	N/A	40.00	40.00
Towle Silversmiths		**Sterling Nativity Medallion**			
88-04-001	Angel Gabriel	Towle	7,500	40.00	50-60.00
89-04-002	The Journey	Towle	7,500	40.00	55.00
90-04-003	No Room at the Inn	Towle	7,500	40.00	40.00
91-04-004	Tidings of Joy	Towle	N/A	40.00	40.00
92-04-005	Star of Bethlehem	Towle	N/A	40.00	40.00
Towle Silversmiths		**Twelve Days of Christmas**			
79-05-001	Silverplate Etched	Towle	1,000	3.60	10.00
79-05-002	Silverplate Etched	Towle	1,000	3.60	10.00
79-05-003	Silverplate Etched	Towle	1,000	3.60	10.00
79-05-004	Silverplate Etched	Towle	1,000	3.60	10.00
79-05-005	Silverplate Etched	Towle	1,000	3.60	10.00
79-05-006	Silverplate Etched	Towle	1,000	3.60	10.00
79-05-007	Silverplate Etched	Towle	1,000	3.60	10.00
79-05-008	Silverplate Etched	Towle	1,000	3.60	10.00
79-05-009	Silverplate Etched	Towle	1,000	3.60	10.00
79-05-010	Silverplate Etched	Towle	1,000	3.60	10.00
79-05-011	Silverplate Etched	Towle	1,000	3.60	10.00
79-05-012	Silverplate Etched	Towle	1,000	3.60	10.00
Towle Silversmiths		**Twelve Days of Christmas**			
88-06-001	Goldplate Etched	Towle	2,500	7.00	7.00
88-06-002	Goldplate Etched	Towle	2,500	7.00	7.00
88-06-003	Goldplate Etched	Towle	2,500	7.00	7.00
88-06-004	Goldplate Etched	Towle	2,500	7.00	7.00
88-06-005	Goldplate Etched	Towle	2,500	7.00	7.00
88-06-006	Goldplate Etched	Towle	2,500	7.00	7.00
88-06-007	Goldplate Etched	Towle	2,500	7.00	7.00
88-06-008	Goldplate Etched	Towle	2,500	7.00	7.00
88-06-009	Goldplate Etched	Towle	2,500	7.00	7.00
88-06-010	Goldplate Etched	Towle	2,500	7.00	7.00
88-06-011	Goldplate Etched	Towle	2,500	7.00	7.00
88-06-012	Goldplate Etched	Towle	2,500	7.00	7.00
Towle Silversmiths		**Sterling Christmas Ornaments**			
89-07-001	Faceted Ball	Towle	Open	38.00	38.00
89-07-002	Plain Ball	Towle	Open	38.00	38.00
89-07-003	Fluted Ball	Towle	Open	38.00	38.00
89-07-004	Pomander Ball	Towle	Open	33.00	33.00
Towle Silversmiths		**Remembrance Collection**			
90-08-001	Old Master Snowflake-1990	Towle	N/A	45.00	45.00
91-08-002	Old Master Snowflake-1991	Towle	N/A	45.00	45.00
92-08-003	Old Master Snowflake-1992	Towle	N/A	45.00	45.00
Towle Silversmiths		**Twelve Days of Christmas**			
91-09-001	Partridge in Wreath	Towle	N/A	45.00	45.00
92-09-002	Two Turtledoves in Wreath	Towle	N/A	45.00	45.00
Towle Silversmiths		**Christmas Angel**			
91-10-001	1991 Angel	Towle	N/A	45.00	45.00
92-10-002	1992 Angel	Towle	N/A	45.00	45.00
United Design Corporation		**Angels Collection-Tree Ornaments™**			
90-01-001	Crystal Angel IBO-401	P.J. Jonas	Open	20.00	20.00
90-01-002	Rose of Sharon IBO-402	P.J. Jonas	Open	20.00	20.00
90-01-003	Star Glory IBO-403	P.J. Jonas	Open	15.00	15.00
90-01-004	Victorian Angel IBO-404	P.J. Jonas	Open	15.00	15.00
90-01-005	Crystal Angel, ivory IBO-405	P.J. Jonas	Open	20.00	20.00
90-01-006	Rose of Sharon, ivory IBO-406	P.J. Jonas	Open	20.00	20.00
90-01-007	Star Glory, ivory IBO-407	P.J. Jonas	Open	15.00	15.00
90-01-008	Victorian Angel, ivory IBO-408	P.J. Jonas	Open	15.00	15.00
91-01-009	Victorian Cupid, ivory IBO-409	P.J. Jonas	Open	15.00	15.00
91-01-010	Rosetti Angel, ivory IBO-410	P.J. Jonas	Open	20.00	20.00
91-01-011	Angel Waif, ivory IBO-411	P.J. Jonas	Open	15.00	15.00
91-01-012	Peace Descending, ivory IBO-412	P.J. Jonas	Open	20.00	20.00
91-01-013	Girl Cupid w/Rose, ivory IBO-413	S. Bradford	Open	15.00	15.00
91-01-014	Fra Angelico Drummer, blue IBO-414	S. Bradford	Open	20.00	20.00
91-01-015	Victorian Cupid IBO-415	S. Bradford	Open	15.00	15.00
91-01-016	Rosetti Angel IBO-416	P.J. Jonas	Open	20.00	20.00
91-01-017	Angel Waif IBO-417	P.J. Jonas	Open	15.00	15.00
91-01-018	Peace Descending IBO-418	P.J. Jonas	Open	20.00	20.00
91-01-019	Fra Angelico Drummer, ivory IBO-420	S. Bradford	Open	20.00	20.00
92-01-020	Angel and Tambourine IBO-422	S. Bradford	Open	20.00	20.00
92-01-021	St. Francis and Critters IBO-423	S. Bradford	Open	20.00	20.00
92-01-022	Mary and Dove IBO-424	S. Bradford	Open	20.00	20.00
92-01-023	Angel and Tambourine, ivory IBO-425	S. Bradford	Open	20.00	20.00
93-01-024	Angel Baby w/ Bunny IBO-426	D. Newburn	Open	22.50	22.50
93-01-025	Stars & Lace IBO-427	P.J. Jonas	Open	18.00	18.00
93-01-026	Heavenly Harmony IBO-428	P.J. Jonas	Open	25.00	25.00
93-01-027	Renaissance Angel IBO-429	P.J. Jonas	Open	24.00	24.00
93-01-028	Little Angel IBO-430	D. Newburn	Open	18.00	18.00
93-01-029	Renaissance Angel, crimson IBO-431	P.J. Jonas	Open	24.00	24.00
93-01-030	Stars & Lace, Emerald IBO-432	P.J. Jonas	Open	18.00	18.00
93-01-031	Heavenly Harmony, crimson IBO-433	P.J. Jonas	Open	22.00	22.00
93-01-032	Rosetti Angel, crimson IBO-434	P.J. Jonas	Open	20.00	20.00
93-01-033	Victorian Angel, plum IBO-435	P.J. Jonas	Open	18.00	18.00
93-01-034	Peace Descending, crimson IBO-436	P.J. Jonas	Open	20.00	20.00
93-01-035	Angle Waif, plum IBO-437	P.J. Jonas	Open	20.00	20.00
93-01-036	Star Glory, crimson IBO-438	P.J. Jonas	Open	20.00	20.00
93-01-037	Rose of Sharon, crimson IBO-439	P.J. Jonas	Open	20.00	20.00
93-01-038	Victorian Cupid, crimson IBO-440	P.J. Jonas	Open	15.00	15.00
93-01-039	Little Angel, crimson IBO-445	D. Newburn	Open	18.00	18.00
93-01-040	Crystal Angel, emerald IBO-446	P.J. Jonas	Open	25.00	25.00
Wallace Silversmiths		**Annual Silverplated Bells**			
71-01-001	1st Edition Sleigh Bell	Wallace	Closed	12.95	500-1050.
72-01-002	2nd Edition Sleigh Bell	Wallace	Closed	12.95	150-400.
73-01-003	3rd Edition Sleigh Bell	Wallace	Closed	12.95	150-400.
74-01-004	4th Edition Sleigh Bell	Wallace	Closed	13.95	100-300.
75-01-005	5th Edition Sleigh Bell	Wallace	Closed	13.95	250.00
76-01-006	6th Edition Sleigh Bell	Wallace	Closed	13.95	300.00
77-01-007	7th Edition Sleigh Bell	Wallace	Closed	14.95	150.00
78-01-008	8th Edition Sleigh Bell	Wallace	Closed	14.95	85.00
79-01-009	9th Edition Sleigh Bell	Wallace	Closed	15.95	100.00
80-01-010	10th Edition Sleigh Bell	Wallace	Closed	18.95	50.00
81-01-011	11th Edition Sleigh Bell	Wallace	Closed	18.95	60.00
82-01-012	12th Edition Sleigh Bell	Wallace	Closed	19.95	80.00
83-01-013	13th Edition Sleigh Bell	Wallace	Closed	19.95	80.00
84-01-014	14th Edition Sleigh Bell	Wallace	Closed	21.95	75.00
85-01-015	15th Edition Sleigh Bell	Wallace	Closed	21.95	75.00
86-01-016	16th Edition Sleigh Bell	Wallace	Closed	21.95	35.00
87-01-017	17th Edition Sleigh Bell	Wallace	Closed	21.99	25.00
88-01-018	18th Edition Sleigh Bell	Wallace	Closed	21.99	25.00
89-01-019	19th Edition Sleigh Bell	Wallace	Closed	24.99	25.00
90-01-020	20th Edition Sleigh Bell	Wallace	Yr.Iss.	25.00	25.00
90-01-021	Special Edition Sleigh Bell, gold	Wallace	Yr.Iss.	35.00	35.00
92-01-022	22th Edition Sleigh Bell	Wallace	Yr.Iss.	25.00	25.00
Wallace Silversmiths		**24K Goldplate Sculptures**			
88-02-001	Dove	Wallace	Open	15.99	15.99
88-02-002	Candy Cane	Wallace	Open	15.99	15.99
88-02-003	Christmas Tree	Wallace	Open	15.99	15.99
88-02-004	Angel	Wallace	Open	15.99	15.99
88-02-005	Nativity Scene	Wallace	Open	15.99	15.99
88-02-006	Snowflake	Wallace	Open	15.99	15.99
Wallace Silversmiths		**Christmas Cookie Ornaments**			
88-03-001	Angel	Wallace	Open	8.99	10.00
88-03-002	Dragon	Wallace	Open	8.99	10.00
88-03-003	Goose	Wallace	Open	8.99	10.00
88-03-004	Teddy Bear	Wallace	Open	8.99	10.00
88-03-005	Elephant	Wallace	Open	8.99	10.00
88-03-006	Christmas Village	Wallace	Open	8.99	10.00
88-03-007	The Night Before	Wallace	Open	8.99	10.00
88-03-008	Polar Bear	Wallace	Open	8.99	10.00
88-03-009	Baby Bear	Wallace	Open	8.99	10.00
85-03-010	Clown	Wallace	Closed	6.95	10.00
85-03-011	Unicorn	Wallace	Closed	6.95	10.00
85-03-012	Teddy Bear	Wallace	Open	6.95	10.00
84-03-013	Horn	Wallace	Closed	6.95	10.00
84-03-014	Puppy in Boot	Wallace	Closed	6.95	10.00
83-03-015	Rocking Horse	Wallace	Closed	5.95	10.00
83-03-016	Mrs. Claus	Wallace	Closed	5.95	10.00

CHRISTMAS ORNAMENTS/DOLLS

Number	Name	Artist	Edition Limit	Issue Price	Quote
83-03-017	Toy Soldier	Wallace	Closed	5.95	10.00
83-03-018	Jack-In-The-Box	Wallace	Closed	5.95	10.00
83-03-019	Gingerbread House	Wallace	Closed	5.95	10.00
80-03-020	Santa	Wallace	Closed	5.95	10.00
86-03-021	Panda	Wallace	Closed	5.95	10.00
86-03-022	Santa Head	Wallace	Closed	6.95	10.00
86-03-023	Penguin	Wallace	Closed	6.95	10.00
86-03-024	Girl Honey Bear	Wallace	Closed	6.95	10.00
86-03-025	Dressed Kitten	Wallace	Closed	6.95	15.00
86-03-026	Tugboat	Wallace	Closed	6.95	10.00
87-03-027	Giraffe	Wallace	Closed	7.95	10.00
87-03-028	Angel with Heart	Wallace	Open	7.95	10.00
87-03-029	Polar Bear	Wallace	Open	7.95	10.00
87-03-030	Ski Cabin	Wallace	Closed	7.95	10.00
85-03-031	Boy Skater	Wallace	Closed	10.95	10.00
85-03-032	Hot-Air Balloon	Wallace	Closed	10.95	10.00
87-03-033	Snowbird	Wallace	Closed	7.95	10.00
81-03-034	Drum	Wallace	Closed	5.95	15.00
80-03-035	Tree	Wallace	Closed	5.95	15.00
80-03-036	Snowman	Wallace	Closed	5.95	15.00
81-03-037	Reindeer	Wallace	Closed	5.95	15.00
81-03-038	Bell	Wallace	Closed	5.95	15.00
82-03-039	Mouse	Wallace	Closed	5.95	15.00
82-03-040	Train	Wallace	Closed	5.95	15.00
83-03-041	Boy Caroler	Wallace	Closed	5.95	15.00
84-03-042	Mother and Child	Wallace	Closed	6.95	15.00
84-03-043	Carol Singer	Wallace	Closed	6.95	15.00
86-03-044	Goose	Wallace	Closed	6.95	15.00
80-03-045	Angel	Wallace	Closed	5.95	20.00
82-03-046	Dove	Wallace	Closed	5.95	20.00
83-03-047	Husky	Wallace	Closed	5.95	20.00
86-03-048	Carrousel Horse	Wallace	Closed	6.95	20.00
86-03-049	Dog on Sled	Wallace	Closed	6.95	20.00
86-03-050	New Design Snowman	Wallace	Closed	6.95	20.00
89-03-051	Snowbird	Wallace	Open	9.99	10.00
89-03-052	Santa	Wallace	Open	9.99	10.00
89-03-053	Rocking Horse	Wallace	Open	9.99	10.00
Wallace Silversmiths		**Antique Pewter Ornaments**			
XX-04-001	Toy Soldier	Wallace	Open	9.99	9.99
XX-04-002	Gingerbread House	Wallace	Open	9.99	9.99
XX-04-003	Teddy Bear	Wallace	Open	9.99	9.99
XX-04-004	Rocking Horse	Wallace	Open	9.99	9.99
XX-04-005	Dove	Wallace	Open	9.99	9.99
XX-04-006	Candy Cane	Wallace	Open	9.99	9.99
89-04-007	Wreath	Wallace	Open	9.99	9.99
89-04-008	Angel with Candles	Wallace	Open	9.99	9.99
89-04-009	Teddy Bear	Wallace	Open	9.99	9.99
89-04-010	Cherub with Horn	Wallace	Open	9.99	9.99
89-04-011	Santa	Wallace	Open	9.99	9.99
Wallace Silversmiths		**Candy Canes**			
81-05-001	Peppermint	Wallace	Closed	8.95	225.00
82-05-002	Wintergreen	Wallace	Closed	9.95	60.00
83-05-003	Cinnamon	Wallace	Closed	10.95	50.00
84-05-004	Clove	Wallace	Closed	10.95	50.00
85-05-005	Dove Motif	Wallace	Closed	11.95	50.00
86-05-006	Bell Motif	Wallace	Closed	11.95	80.00
87-05-007	Teddy Bear Motif	Wallace	Closed	12.95	50.00
88-05-008	Christmas Rose	Wallace	Closed	13.99	40.00
89-05-009	Christmas Candle	Wallace	Closed	14.99	35.00
90-05-010	Reindeer	Wallace	Closed	16.00	20.00
Wallace Silversmiths		**Grande Baroque 12 Day Series**			
88-06-001	Partridge	Wallace	Closed	39.99	55.00
89-06-002	Two Turtle Doves	Wallace	Closed	39.99	50.00
90-06-003	Three French Hens	Wallace	Closed	40.00	40.00
Wallace Silversmiths		**Cathedral Ornaments**			
88-07-001	1988-1st Edition	Wallace	Closed	24.99	35.00
89-07-002	1989-2nd Edition	Wallace	Closed	24.99	24.99
90-07-003	1990-3rd Edition	Wallace	Closed	25.00	25.00
Wallace Silversmiths		**Sterling Memories**			
89-08-001	Church	Wallace	Open	34.99	34.99
89-08-002	Mother & Child	Wallace	Open	34.99	34.99
89-08-003	Drummer Boy	Wallace	Open	34.99	34.99
89-08-004	Sleigh	Wallace	Open	34.99	34.99
89-08-005	Rocking Horse	Wallace	Open	34.99	34.99
89-08-006	Snowflake	Wallace	Open	34.99	34.99
89-08-007	Dove	Wallace	Open	34.99	34.99
89-08-008	Nativity Angel	Wallace	Open	34.99	34.99
89-08-009	Carolers	Wallace	Open	34.99	34.99
89-08-010	Reindeer	Wallace	Open	34.99	34.99
89-08-011	Bear with Blocks	Wallace	Open	34.99	34.99
89-08-012	Snowman	Wallace	Open	34.99	34.99
Wallace Silversmiths		**Sterling Memories - Hand Enameled with Color**			
89-09-001	Elf with Gift	Wallace	Open	34.99	34.99
89-09-002	Santa	Wallace	Open	34.99	34.99
89-09-003	Train	Wallace	Open	34.99	34.99
89-09-004	Kneeling Angel	Wallace	Open	34.99	34.99
89-09-005	Skater	Wallace	Open	34.99	34.99
89-09-006	Single Candle	Wallace	Open	34.99	34.99
89-09-007	Fireplace	Wallace	Open	34.99	34.99
89-09-008	Candy Cane	Wallace	Open	34.99	34.99
89-09-009	Church	Wallace	Open	34.99	34.99
89-09-010	Toy Soldier	Wallace	Open	34.99	34.99
Wallace Silversmiths		**Antique Pewter Bells**			
89-10-001	Reindeer	Wallace	Open	15.99	15.99
89-10-002	Teddy Bear	Wallace	Open	15.99	15.99
89-10-003	Toy Soldier	Wallace	Open	15.99	15.99
90-10-004	Carousel Horse	Wallace	Open	16.00	16.00
90-10-005	Santa Claus	Wallace	Open	16.00	16.00
Wallace Silversmiths		**Cameo Frame Ornaments**			
89-11-001	Christmas Ball	Wallace	Open	14.99	14.99
89-11-002	Snowman	Wallace	Open	14.99	14.99
89-11-003	Wreath	Wallace	Open	14.99	14.99
89-11-004	Dino	Wallace	Open	14.99	14.99
89-11-005	Angel	Wallace	Open	14.99	14.99
89-11-006	Kitten	Wallace	Open	14.99	14.99
89-11-007	Santa	Wallace	Open	14.99	14.99
89-11-008	Soldier	Wallace	Open	14.99	14.99
89-11-009	Elephant	Wallace	Open	14.99	14.99
Waterford Wedgwood U.S.A.		**Waterford Crystal Christmas Ornaments**			
78-01-001	1978 Ornament	Waterford	Annual	25.00	60.00
79-01-002	1979 Ornament	Waterford	Annual	28.00	50.00
80-01-003	1980 Ornament	Waterford	Annual	28.00	44.50
81-01-004	1981 Ornament	Waterford	Annual	28.00	44.50
82-01-005	1982 Ornament	Waterford	Annual	28.00	44.50
83-01-006	1983 Ornament	Waterford	Annual	28.00	39.00
84-01-007	1984 Ornament	Waterford	Annual	28.00	39.00
85-01-008	1985 Ornament	Waterford	Annual	28.00	39.00
86-01-009	1986 Ornament	Waterford	Annual	28.00	31.00
87-01-010	1987 Ornament	Waterford	Annual	29.00	29.00
88-01-011	1988 Ornament	Waterford	Annual	30.00	30.00
89-01-012	1989 Ornament	Waterford	Annual	32.00	32.00
Waterford Wedgwood U.S.A.		**Wedgwood Christmas Ornaments**			
88-02-001	Jasper Christmas Tree Ornament	Wedgwood	Open	20.00	28.00
89-02-002	Jasper Angel Ornament	Wedgwood	Open	25.00	28.00
90-02-003	Jasper Santa Claus Ornament	Wedgwood	Open	28.00	28.00
91-02-004	Jasper Wreath Ornament	Wedgwood	Open	28.00	28.00
92-02-005	Jasper Stocking Ornament	Wedgwood	Open	25.00	25.00

DOLLS

Number	Name	Artist	Edition Limit	Issue Price	Quote
Kurt S. Adler/Santa's World		**Christmas In Chelsea Collection**			
92-01-001	Amy W2729	J. Mostrom	Open	21.00	21.00
92-01-001	Allison W2729	J. Mostrom	Open	21.00	21.00
Kurt S. Adler/Santa's World		**Royal Heritage Collection**			
93-02-001	Anastasia J5746	J. Mostrom	3,000	125.00	125.00
93-02-002	Medieval King of Christmas W2981	J. Mostrom	2,000	390.00	390.00
93-02-003	Good King Wenceslas W2928	J. Mostrom	2,000	130.00	130.00
Annalee Mobilitee Dolls		**Santas**			
72-01-001	7" Santa With Mushroom	A. Thorndike	540	Unkn.	275.00
82-01-002	7" Santa Wreath Centerpiece	A. Thorndike	1,150	Unkn.	150.00
74-01-003	7" Black Santa	A. Thorndike	1,157	5.50	225.00
81-01-004	7" Santa With Mistletoe	A. Thorndike	Unkn.	10.50	40.00
79-01-005	7" Santa With Mistletoe	A. Thorndike	Unkn.	7.95	50.00
81-01-006	7" Santa With Pot Belly Stove	A. Thorndike	Unkn.	11.95	75.00
73-01-007	18" Mrs.Santa With Cardholder	A. Thorndike	3,900	14.95	150.00
65-01-008	18" Santa	A. Thorndike	Unkn.	9.00	150.00
73-01-009	18" Mrs. Santa	A. Thorndike	3,700	7.00	150.00
65-01-010	12" Santa	A. Thorndike	Unkn.	5.00	125.00
74-01-011	29" Mrs. Santa With Cardholder	A. Thorndike	Unkn.	28.95	200.00
54-01-112	26" Bean Nose Santa	A. Thorndike	Unkn.	19.95	700.00
78-01-013	7" Santa With Deer And Tree	A. Thorndike	5,813	18.50	400.00
75-01-014	18" Mrs. Santa With Plum Pudding	A. Thorndike	N/A	12.00	300.00
87-01-015	18" Workshop Santa	A. Thorndike	980	N/A	600.00
81-01-016	10" Ballooning Santa	A. Thorndike	1,737	39.95	325.00
74-01-017	7" Santa In Ski Bob	A. Thorndike	704	4.95	450.00
72-01-018	29" Santa With Cardholder Sack	A. Thorndike	686	24.95	150.00
82-01-019	5" Santa With Deer	A. Thorndike	3,072	20.00	235.00
72-01-020	18" Mr. Santa With Sack	A. Thorndike	850	N/A	150.00
88-01-021	30" Victorian Mrs. Santa With Tray	A. Thorndike	N/A	119.95	360.00
56-01-022	12" Santa With Bean Nose	A. Thorndike	N/A	20.00	1000.00
65-01-023	7" Mr. & Mrs. Santa	A. Thorndike	N/A	5.95	325.00
59-01-024	7" Santa With Fur Trim Suit	A. Thorndike	N/A	2.95	225.00
71-01-025	7" Mr. & Mrs. Santa With Basket	A. Thorndike	3,403	5.95	150.00
89-01-026	10" Collector Mrs. Santa, proof	A. Thorndike	1	N/A	300.00
80-01-027	7" Santa With Stocking	A. Thorndike	17,665	9.95	75.00
81-01-028	7" X-Country Ski Santa	A. Thorndike	5,180	10.95	100.00
72-01-029	7" Mr. & Mrs. Tuckered	A. Thorndike	1,187	6.50	375.00
87-01-030	7" Victorian Mr. & Mrs. Santa	A. Thorndike	N/A	23.95	200.00
84-01-031	7" Santa on a Moon	A. Thorndike	N/A	N/A	150.00
82-01-032	5" Mrs. Santa With Gift Box	A. Thorndike	7,566	10.95	75.00
71-01-033	18" Mrs. Santa With Cardholder	A. Thorndike	1,563	8.00	200.00
79-01-034	18" Mr. Santa With Cardholder	A. Thorndike	N/A	N/A	75.00
86-01-035	18" Mrs. Victorian Santa	A. Thorndike	2,000	N/A	200.00
87-01-036	18" Mr. Victorian Santa	A. Thorndike	2,150	57.50	200.00
70-01-037	7" Santa With 10" X-mas Mushroom	A. Thorndike	N/A	7.00	125.00
72-01-038	7" Mrs. Santa With Apron And Cap	A. Thorndike	8,867	5.50	50.00
70-01-039	10" Christmas Mushroom With 7" Santa On Top And 7" Deer Hugging Stem	A. Thorndike	N/A	11.00	600.00
87-01-040	10" Collector Santa Trimming Lighted Tree	A. Thorndike	N/A	130.00	250.00
67-01-041	7" Santa With Toy Bag	A. Thorndike	N/A	3.95	275.00
60-01-042	7" Mr. & Mrs. Tuckered	A. Thorndike	N/A	N/A	500.00
91-01-043	10" Summer Santa, proof	A. Thorndike	1	None	1050.00
73-01-044	7" Santa Mailman	A. Thorndike	3,276	5.00	200.00
73-01-045	7" Mr. & Mrs. Santa in Wicker Loveseat	A. Thorndike	3,973	10.95	250.00
77-01-046	7" Mr. & Mrs. Santa W/ Wicker Loveseat	A. Thorndike	4,935	11.95	175.00
66-01-047	29" Mr. Outdoor Santa	A. Thorndike	N/A	17.00	350.00
68-01-048	18" Mrs. Indoor Santa	A. Thorndike	N/A	7.50	250.00
68-01-049	18" Mr. Indoor Santa	A. Thorndike	N/A	7.50	225.00
86-01-050	7" Victorian Santa W/Sleigh & Deer	A. Thorndike	6,820	44.00	200.00
68-01-051	7" Mr. &Mrs. Santa Tuckered	A. Thorndike	N/A	3.00	200.00
65-01-052	26" Mrs. Santa W/Apron	A. Thorndike	N/A	14.95	1000.00
68-01-053	29" Mr. Santa W/Vest & Sack	A. Thorndike	N/A	16.00	500.00
87-01-054	30" Mrs. Victorian Santa	A. Thorndike	425	150.00	350.00
87-01-055	30" Mr. Victorian Santa	A. Thorndike	450	150.00	350.00
79-01-056	7" C.B. Santa	A. Thorndike	2,206	7.95	75.00
79-01-057	29" Motorized Mr. & Mrs. Santa In Rocking Chair	A. Thorndike	136	400.00	1600.00
92-01-058	10" Santa At Workbench, proof	A. Thorndike	1	N/A	750.00
92-01-059	10" Tennis Santa , proof	A. Thorndike	1	N/A	600.00
92-01-060	10" Santa W/Bank, proof	A. Thorndike	1	N/A	925.00
92-01-061	10" Fishing Mr. & Mrs. Santa, proof	A. Thorndike	1	N/A	1100.00
86-01-062	7" Mr. & Mrs. Victorian Santa	A. Thorndike	N/A	19.95	450.00
70-01-063	18" Mr. & Mrs. All Tuckered Out	A. Thorndike	215	16.00	400.00
78-01-064	29" Animated Santa & Deer	A. Thorndike	10	280.00	1300.00
70-01-065	10" Christmas Mushroom w/7" Santa and Deer	A. Thorndike	424	10.90	375.00
69-01-066	7" Mr. & Mrs. Santa on Ski Bob	A. Thorndike	N/A	7.95	350.00
93-01-067	10" Santa w/Toboggan, Proof	A. Thorndike	1	N/A	375.00
93-01-068	10" Mr. & Mrs. Santa Skating, proof	A. Thorndike	1	N/A	700.00
93-01-069	7" Victorian Santa w/ Sleigh, proof	A. Thorndike	1	N/A	500.00
50-01-070	20" Santa w/ Corkscrew Nose	A. Thorndike	N/A	N/A	3300.00
93-01-071	10" Gardening Santa, proof	A. Thorndike	1	N/A	550.00
93-01-072	10" Santa w/ Fireplace, proof	A. Thorndike	1	N/A	500.00
77-01-073	4" Mrs. Santa	A. Thorndike	147	150.00	500.00

Company Number	Name	Series Artist	Edition Limit	Issue Price	Quote
77-01-074	4" Mr .Santa	A. Thorndike	185	150.00	300.00
87-01-075	18" Workshop Santa Animated	A. Thorndike	N/A	119.50	240.00
88-01-076	18" Mr. & Mrs. Fireside Santa	A. Thorndike	2,786	68.95	150.00
93-01-077	7" Santa w/Lights	A. Thorndike	N/A	29.95	29.95
93-01-078	7" Santa Skiing	A. Thorndike	N/A	27.95	27.95
93-01-079	10" Skating Santa	A. Thorndike	N/A	49.95	49.95
93-01-080	10" Mrs. Skating Santa	A. Thorndike	N/A	49.95	49.95
93-01-081	10" Gardening Summer Santa	A. Thorndike	N/A	69.95	69.95
93-01-082	10" Santa w/Fireplace and 3" Child	A. Thorndike	N/A	89.95	89.95
93-01-083	10" Toboggan Santa	A. Thorndike	N/A	59.95	59.95
93-01-084	12" Santa in Chimney	A. Thorndike	N/A	69.95	69.95
93-01-085	18" Santa on Toboggan	A. Thorndike	N/A	69.95	69.95
93-01-086	18" Santa w/Lights	A. Thorndike	N/A	54.95	54.95
93-01-087	18" Santa in Sleigh	A. Thorndike	N/A	74.95	74.95
93-01-088	18" Mrs. Outdoor Santa	A. Thorndike	N/A	49.95	49.95
93-01-089	7" Victorian Santa	A. Thorndike	N/A	29.95	29.95
93-01-090	7" Victorian Mrs. Santa	A. Thorndike	N/A	29.95	29.95
93-01-091	7" Victorian Santa in Sleigh	A. Thorndike	N/A	49.95	49.95
93-01-092	18" Victorian Mrs. Santa	A. Thorndike	N/A	64.95	64.95
93-01-093	18" Victorian Santa	A. Thorndike	N/A	64.95	64.95
93-01-094	3" Fishing Santa in Boat	A. Thorndike	N/A	24.95	24.95
93-01-095	3" Santa Pin in Card	A. Thorndike	N/A	16.95	16.95
Annalee Mobilitee Dolls		**Christmas Animals**			
81-02-001	7" Santa Monkey	A. Thorndike	4,606	10.00	200.00
81-02-002	12" Santa Monkey	A. Thorndike	1,800	24.00	250.00
82-02-003	7" Santa Fox	A. Thorndike	3,726	12.95	250.00
82-02-004	18" Santa Fox	A. Thorndike	1,499	29.95	575.00
80-02-005	10" Santa Frog	A. Thorndike	7,631	9.95	125.00
82-02-006	22" Christmas Giraffe With Elf	A. Thorndike	448	44.00	500.00
85-02-007	18" Christmas Panda	A. Thorndike	2,207	43.95	100.00
84-02-008	5" Duck In Santa Hat	A. Thorndike	2,371	12.95	75.00
73-02-009	7" Christmas Panda	A. Thorndike	1,094	8.95	350.00
85-02-010	10" Panda With Toy Bag	A. Thorndike	1,904	20.00	100.00
81-02-011	18" Cat With 7" Mouse And Mistletoe	A. Thorndike	10,999	46.95	140.00
80-02-012	18" Santa Frog	A. Thorndike	2,126	25.00	145.00
93-02-013	7" Angel Mouse	A. Thorndike	N/A	21.95	21.95
93-02-014	7" White Mouse in Slipper	A. Thorndike	N/A	24.95	24.95
93-02-015	7" White Mouse w/Present	A. Thorndike	N/A	21.95	21.95
93-02-016	5" Black Christmas Lamb	A. Thorndike	N/A	19.95	19.95
93-02-017	Small Christmas Dove	A. Thorndike	N/A	25.95	25.95
93-02-018	Christmas Chicken	A. Thorndike	N/A	34.95	34.95
93-02-019	10" Kitten w/Ornament	A. Thorndike	N/A	33.95	33.95
93-02-020	10" Santa's Helper Bear	A. Thorndike	N/A	33.95	33.95
Annalee Mobilitee Dolls		**Reindeer**			
85-03-001	10" Reindeer With Bell	A. Thorndike	6,398	13.95	55.00
78-03-002	18" Reindeer	A. Thorndike	Unkn.	18.00	125.00
78-03-003	36" Reindeer With Saddlebags	A. Thorndike	594	58.00	175.00
81-03-004	18" Reindeer With Saddlebags	A. Thorndike	7,121	27.95	75.00
83-03-005	18" Fawn	A. Thorndike	1,444	32.95	225.00
78-03-006	18" Reindeer	A. Thorndike	5,134	9.00	125.00
70-03-007	10" Reindeer With Hat	A. Thorndike	144	5.00	175.00
83-03-008	18" Fawn	A. Thorndike	N/A	33.00	200.00
84-03-009	18" Fawn With Wreath	A. Thorndike	1,444	32.95	225.00
69-03-010	10" Reindeer With Red Nose	A. Thorndike	N/A	4.95	350.00
65-03-011	10" Reindeer	A. Thorndike	N/A	4.95	550.00
71-03-012	36" Reindeer With Two 18" Gnomes	A. Thorndike	624	38.00	700.00
81-03-013	5" Miniature Reindeer	A. Thorndike	9,080	11.50	120.00
72-03-014	18" Reindeer With 12" Gnome	A. Thorndike	1,617	21.00	400.00
71-03-015	10" Red Nosed Reindeer	A. Thorndike	1,588	4.95	225.00
75-03-016	10" Red Nosed Reindeer	A. Thorndike	4,854	N/A	100.00
68-03-017	36" Red Nosed Reindeer	A. Thorndike	N/A	N/A	300.00
78-03-018	10" Red Nosed Reindeer	A. Thorndike	6,698	N/A	160.00
69-03-019	10" Reindeer w/ Red Nose	A. Thorndike	N/A	4.95	250.00
Annalee Mobilitee Dolls		**Mice**			
82-04-001	12" Nightshirt Mouse	A. Thorndike	2,319	25.95	125.00
69-04-002	12" Nightshirt Mouse	A. Thorndike	Unkn.	Unkn.	225.00
79-04-003	12" Santa Mouse	A. Thorndike	Unkn.	Unkn.	125.00
79-04-004	12" Mrs. Santa Mouse	A. Thorndike	7,210	Unkn.	125.00
79-04-005	7" Santa Mouse	A. Thorndike	12,649	7.95	100.00
84-04-006	7" Nightshirt Mouse	A. Thorndike	Unkn.	11.95	150.00
66-04-007	7" Mouse With Candle	A. Thorndike	Unkn.	Unkn.	225.00
80-04-008	7" Mouse With Chimney	A. Thorndike	4,452	Unkn.	75.00
84-04-009	7" Mouse With Wreath	A. Thorndike	Unkn.	12.95	55.00
64-04-010	7" Christmas Mouse	A. Thorndike	Unkn.	3.95	450.00
78-04-011	29" Caroler Mouse	A. Thorndike	658	50.00	750.00
83-04-012	7" Equestrine Mouse	A. Thorndike	Unkn.	12.95	200.00
81-04-013	7" Woodchopper Mouse	A. Thorndike	2,121	11.00	100.00
82-04-014	7" Woodchopper Mouse	A. Thorndike	1,910	11.95	75.00
80-04-015	7" Pilot Mouse	A. Thorndike	2,011	9.95	100.00
71-04-016	7" Chef Mouse	A. Thorndike	Unkn.	Unkn.	75.00
81-04-017	7" Airplane Pilot Mouse	A. Thorndike	1,910	9.95	325.00
71-04-018	7" Mouse With Inner Tube	A. Thorndike	267	4.00	200.00
75-04-019	7" Fisherman Mouse	A. Thorndike	1,343	5.50	200.00
80-04-020	7" Fishing Mouse	A. Thorndike	Unkn.	7.50	150.00
81-04-021	7" Iceskater Mouse	A. Thorndike	1,429	9.95	150.00
80-04-022	7" Card Playing Girl Mouse	A. Thorndike	1,826	9.50	125.00
81-04-023	7" Card Playing Girl Mouse	A. Thorndike	863	9.95	125.00
84-04-024	7" Bowling Mouse	A. Thorndike	1,472	13.95	75.00
85-04-025	7" Girl Tennis Mouse	A. Thorndike	1,947	14.95	75.00
86-04-026	7" Boating Mouse	A. Thorndike	2,320	16.95	55.00
73-04-027	7' Football Mouse	A. Thorndike	944	4.50	150.00
82-04-028	7" Football Mouse	A. Thorndike	2,164	10.50	200.00
81-04-029	7" Jogger Mouse	A. Thorndike	1,783	9.95	75.00
81-04-030	7" Backpacker Mouse	A. Thorndike	1,008	9.95	100.00
80-04-031	7" Girl Disco Mouse	A. Thorndike	915	9.50	150.00
80-04-032	7" Boy Disco Mouse	A. Thorndike	363	9.50	150.00
80-04-033	7" Volleyball Mouse	A. Thorndike	915	9.50	75.00
84-04-034	7" Hockeyplayer Mouse	A. Thorndike	1,525	5.50	200.00
74-04-035	7" Hunter Mouse With 10" Deer	A. Thorndike	1,282	11.50	175.00
83-04-036	7" Quilting Mouse	A. Thorndike	2,786	11.95	75.00
85-04-037	7" Get-Well Mouse	A. Thorndike	1,425	14.95	75.00
82-04-038	7" Graduate Boy Mouse	A. Thorndike	4,971	12.00	100.00
85-04-039	7" Graduate Girl Mouse	A. Thorndike	2,884	13.95	100.00
78-04-040	7" Gardener Mouse	A. Thorndike	Unkn.	7.00	75.00
80-04-041	7" Greenthumb Mouse	A. Thorndike	1,869	9.50	75.00
77-04-042	7" Groom Mouse	A. Thorndike	1,211	6.95	50.00
87-04-043	7" Groom Mouse	A. Thorndike	1,800	14.50	55.00
82-04-044	7" Groom Mouse	A.Thorndike	3,406	10.95	50.00
87-04-045	7" Bride Mouse	A. Thorndike	1,801	14.50	55.00
82-04-046	7" Bride Mouse	A. Thorndike	3,681	10.95	50.00
85-04-047	7" Bride & Groom Mice	A. Thorndike	2,963	13.95	170.00
80-04-048	7" Bride & Groom Mice	A. Thorndike	2,418	9.50	175.00
64-04-049	7" Bride & Groom Mice	A. Thorndike	Unkn.	2.75	750.00
83-04-050	7" Cheerleader Mouse	A. Thorndike	2,025	11.95	200.00
75-04-051	7" Bicyclist Mouse	A. Thorndike	1,561	5.50	125.00
79-04-052	7" C.B. Mouse	A. Thorndike	1,039	6.95	75.00
78-04-053	7" C.B. Mouse	A. Thorndike	2,396	6.95	75.00
74-04-054	7" Painter Mouse	A. Thorndike	Unkn.	4.00	175.00
81-04-055	7" Baseball Mouse	A. Thorndike	2,380	Unkn.	100.00
74-04-056	7" Cowboy Mouse	A. Thorndike	394	5.50	150.00
83-04-057	7" Cowboy Mouse	A. Thorndike	1,794	12.95	150.00
83-04-058	7" Cowgirl Mouse	A. Thorndike	1,517	12.95	150.00
79-04-059	7" Carpenter Mouse	A. Thorndike	2,024	6.95	175.00
86-04-060	7" Mouse With Wheelborrow	A. Thorndike	2,037	16.95	75.00
73-04-061	7" Waiter Mouse	A. Thorndike	Unkn.	4.00	250.00
79-04-062	7" Fireman Mouse	A. Thorndike	1,773	6.95	200.00
78-04-063	7" Fireman Mouse	A. Thorndike	Unkn.	6.95	200.00
73-04-064	7" Skiing Mouse	A. Thorndike	2,774	4.00	175.00
84-04-065	7" Mrs. Retired Mouse	A. Thorndike	1,356	13.95	95.00
74-04-066	7" Pregnant Mouse	A. Thorndike	820	Unkn.	200.00
84-04-067	7" Devil Mouse	A. Thorndike	3,571	13.95	100.00
75-04-068	7" Beautician Mouse	A. Thorndike	1,349	4.00	300.00
77-04-069	7" Beautician Mouse	A. Thorndike	1,521	5.50	250.00
74-04-070	7" Vacation Mouse	A. Thorndike	Unkn.	Unkn.	175.00
82-04-071	7" Mrs. A.M. Mouse	A. Thorndike	2,184	11.95	80.00
74-04-072	7" Secretary Mouse	A. Thorndike	364	4.00	150.00
79-04-073	7" Skateboard Mouse	A. Thorndike	1,821	6.00	300.00
77-04-074	7" Sweetheart Mouse	A. Thorndike	3,323	5.50	100.00
86-04-075	7" Sweetheart Mouse	A. Thorndike	6,271	12.95	100.00
78-04-076	7" Teacher Mouse	A. Thorndike	2,249	5.50	100.00
84-04-077	7" Teacher Mouse	A. Thorndike	3,150	13.95	75.00
81-04-078	7" Nurse Mouse	A. Thorndike	3,222	11.95	50.00
73-04-079	7" Golfer Mouse	A. Thorndike	Unkn.	5.00	100.00
74-04-080	7" Seamstress Mouse	A. Thorndike	387	4.00	175.00
83-04-081	7" Windsurfer Mouse	A. Thorndike	2,352	13.95	125.00
86-04-082	7" Birthday Girl Mouse	A. Thorndike	3,724	14.95	125.00
78-04-083	7" Policeman Mouse	A. Thorndike	1,189	7.00	150.00
74-04-084	7" Artist Mouse	A. Thorndike	397	5.50	110.00
85-04-085	7" Hiker Mouse	A. Thorndike	1,781	13.95	275.00
77-04-086	7" Bingo Mouse	A. Thorndike	1,221	6.00	150.00
84-04-087	7" Mouse With Strawberry	A. Thorndike	1,776	11.95	75.00
77-04-088	7" Vacationer Mouse	A. Thorndike	1,040	6.00	175.00
84-04-089	12" Devil Mouse	A. Thorndike	1,118	29.95	145.00
83-04-090	12" Bride Mouse	A. Thorndike	854	31.95	200.00
83-04-091	12" Groom Mouse	A. Thorndike	826	31.95	200.00
76-04-092	12" Colonial Boy Mouse	A. Thorndike	838	13.50	400.00
76-04-093	12" Colonial Girl Mouse	A. Thorndike	691	13.50	350.00
70-04-094	7" Architect Mouse	A. Thorndike	2,051	3.95	375.00
79-04-095	7" Chimney Sweep Mouse	A. Thorndike	6,331	7.95	275.00
78-04-096	7" Policeman Mouse	A. Thorndike	1,189	6.95	350.00
80-04-097	7" Backpacker Mouse	A. Thorndike	1,008	9.95	375.00
73-04-098	7" Painter Mouse	A. Thorndike	N/A	4.50	275.00
80-04-099	7" Disco Boy Mouse	A. Thorndike	363	9.50	150.00
80-04-100	7" Disco Girl Mouse	A. Thorndike	N/A	9.50	325.00
67-04-101	7" Santa Mouse	A. Thorndike	N/A	2.00	250.00
73-04-102	12" Nightshirt Mouse	A. Thorndike	122	7.50	350.00
79-04-103	7" Pregnant Mouse	A. Thorndike	1,856	7.95	225.00
79-04-104	7" Gardener Mouse	A. Thorndike	1,939	7.95	375.00
84-04-105	7" Teacher Mouse	A. Thorndike	3,023	13.95	225.00
77-04-106	29" Mrs. Santa Mouse	A. Thorndike	571	49.95	450.00
78-04-107	7" Nightshirt Mouse	A. Thorndike	6,444	7.95	75.00
71-04-108	7" Baseball Mouse	A. Thorndike	553	4.00	150.00
84-04-109	7" Devil Mouse	A. Thorndike	3,571	12.95	100.00
74-04-110	7" Hockey Mouse	A. Thorndike	687	7.95	200.00
82-04-111	7" Witch Mouse On Broom	A. Thorndike	2,798	12.95	75.00
82-04-112	7" Sweetheart Mouse	A. Thorndike	4,110	11.00	75.00
76-04-113	7" Mr. Holly Mouse	A. Thorndike	2,774	5.50	125.00
76-04-114	7" Mrs. Holly Mouse	A. Thorndike	3,078	5.50	125.00
77-04-115	7" Baseball Mouse	A. Thorndike	1,634	6.00	100.00
85-04-116	7" Graduation Mouse	A. Thorndike	1,999	14.00	75.00
78-04-117	7" Doctor Mouse	A. Thorndike	816	6.95	75.00
68-04-118	7" Nightshirt Boy Mouse	A. Thorndike	N/A	3.95	200.00
76-04-119	12" Girl Mouse With Plum Pudding	A. Thorndike	1,482	13.50	400.00
64-04-120	12" George & Sheila, Bride & Groom Mice	A. Thorndike	N/A	12.95	600.00
65-04-121	7" Lawyer Mouse	A. Thorndike	N/A	6.95	425.00
73-04-122	7" Fireman Mouse	A. Thorndike	557	4.50	200.00
72-04-123	7" Pregnant Mouse	A. Thorndike	820	5.50	100.00
89-04-124	7" Sweetheart Mouse	A. Thorndike	N/A	16.95	35.00
86-04-125	7" Tennis Mouse	A. Thorndike	1,947	15.95	80.00
82-04-126	7" Mouse With Strawberry	A. Thorndike	N/A	11.95	75.00
79-04-127	7" Mrs. Santa Mouse With Holly	A. Thorndike	N/A	7.95	50.00
82-04-128	12" Pilgrim Boy Mouse	A. Thorndike	2,151	27.95	175.00
82-04-129	12" Pilgrim Girl Mouse	A. Thorndike	2,017	27.95	175.00
71-04-130	7" Artist Mouse	A. Thorndike	422	3.95	175.00
72-04-131	7" Yachtsman Mouse	A. Thorndike	1,130	3.95	250.00
72-04-132	7" Housewife Mouse	A. Thorndike	1,768	3.95	250.00
79-04-133	7" Boy Golfer Mouse	A. Thorndike	2,743	7.95	100.00
75-04-134	7" Pregnant Mouse	A. Thorndike	879	5.50	150.00
71-04-135	7" Ski Mouse	A. Thorndike	1,326	3.95	175.00
79-04-136	7" Fishing Mouse	A. Thorndike	3,053	7.95	150.00
74-04-137	7" Carpenter Mouse	A. Thorndike	551	5.50	175.00
77-04-138	7" Diet Time Mouse	A. Thorndike	1,478	6.00	200.00
79-04-139	12" Nightshirt Mouse With Candle	A. Thorndike	5,739	16.00	225.00
86-04-140	7" Tennis Mouse	A. Thorndike	1,947	15.95	100.00
82-04-141	7" Girl Tennis Mouse	A. Thorndike	2,443	10.95	135.00
79-04-142	7" Girl Golfer Mouse	A. Thorndike	2,316	7.95	90.00
87-04-143	7" Graduation Boy Mouse	A. Thorndike	N/A	19.95	100.00
78-04-144	7" Girl Golfer Mouse	A. Thorndike	2,215	6.95	100.00
78-04-145	7" Doctor Mouse	A. Thorndike	2,028	6.95	100.00
85-04-146	7" Boy Golfer Mouse	A. Thorndike	2,099	14.95	75.00
72-04-147	7" Girl Golfer Mouse	A. Thorndike	N/A	3.95	100.00
84-04-148	7" Teacher Mouse, Girl	A. Thorndike	5,064	13.95	200.00
89-04-149	7" Tacky Tourist Mouse, proof	A. Thorndike	1	N/A	400.00
89-04-150	7" Business Man Mouse, proof	A. Thorndike	1	N/A	375.00
89-04-151	7" Knitting Mouse, proof	A. Thorndike	1	N/A	550.00
79-04-152	7" C.B. Mouse	A. Thorndike	1,039	7.95	100.00
81-04-153	7" Witch Mouse On Broom With Moon	A. Thorndike	1,585+	24.95	200.00
79-04-154	7" Quilting Mouse	A. Thorndike	213	N/A	150.00
86-04-155	7" Witch Mouse In Pumpkin Balloon	A. Thorndike	868	77.95	275.00
81-04-156	12" Witch Mouse On Broom	A. Thorndike	1,049	34.95	160.00
78-04-157	7" Groom Mouse	A. Thorndike	2,952	9.50	85.00
78-04-158	7" Groom Mouse	A. Thorndike	N/A	14.50	125.00
74-04-159	12" Retired Grandma Mouse	A. Thorndike	1,135	13.50	300.00

Company		Series			
Number	Name	Artist	Edition Limit	Issue Price	Quote
74-04-160	12" Retired Grandpa Mouse	A. Thorndike	1,103	13.50	pair
82-04-161	7" Cheerleader Mouse	A. Thorndike	3,441	10.95	150.00
75-04-162	7" Two In Tent Mice	A. Thorndike	914	N/A	85.00
75-04-163	7" Goin' Fishin' Mouse	A. Thorndike	4,507	5.95	125.00
76-04-164	7" Colonial Boy Mouse	A. Thorndike	5,457	N/A	200.00
75-04-165	7" Christmas Mouse In Santa's Mitten	A. Thorndike	3,959	5.95	150.00
76-04-166	7" Birthday Girl Mouse	A. Thorndike	732	5.50	250.00
77-04-167	29" Mr. Niteshirt Mouse	A. Thorndike	309	49.95	650.00
72-04-168	7" Diaper Mouse, It's A Girl	A. Thorndike	2,293	4.50	225.00
72-04-169	7" Diaper Mouse, It's A Boy	A. Thorndike	2,293	4.50	175.00
79-04-170	7" Swimmer Mouse	A. Thorndike	3,640	9.50	225.00
77-04-171	29" Mrs. Santa Mouse With Muff	A. Thorndike	571	49.95	500.00
82-04-172	7" Windsurfer Mouse	A. Thorndike	4,114	13.95	250.00
72-04-173	7" Bar-Be-Que Mouse	A. Thorndike	907	3.95	225.00
86-04-174	7" Indian Girl Mouse With Papoose	A. Thorndike	6,992	24.95	115.00
65-04-175	7" Singing Christmas Mouse	A. Thorndike	N/A	4.95	275.00
86-04-176	7" Ballerina Mouse	A. Thorndike	N/A	N/A	200.00
90-04-177	7" Artist Mouse, Proof	A. Thorndike	1	N/A	750.00
67-04-178	7" Miguel The Mouse	A. Thorndike	N/A	3.95	400.00
90-04-179	7" Maui Mouse, Proof	A. Thorndike	1	N/A	600.00
90-04-180	7" Sailor Mouse, Proof	A. Thorndike	1	N/A	675.00
76-04-181	7" Card Playing Girl Mouse	A. Thorndike	2,878	5.95	175.00
78-04-182	7" Skateboard Mouse	A. Thorndike	3,733	7.95	300.00
87-04-183	7" Baby Mouse	A. Thorndike	2,500	13.95	80.00
70-04-184	7" Plumber Mouse	A. Thorndike	196	3.95	350.00
72-04-185	7" Christmas Mouse	A. Thorndike	2,793	3.95	425.00
84-04-186	7" Angel Mouse	A. Thorndike	2,093	14.95	150.00
75-04-187	7" Retired Grandpa Mouse	A. Thorndike	793	5.50	95.00
87-04-188	7" Bicyclist Boy Mouse	A. Thorndike	1,507	19.95	175.00
78-04-189	7" Policeman Mouse	A. Thorndike	1,189	6.95	200.00
77-04-190	7" Hobo Mouse	A. Thorndike	1,004	5.95	250.00
70-04-191	7" Nightshirt Girl Mouse	A. Thorndike	N/A	3.95	175.00
70-04-192	7" Carpenter Mouse	A. Thorndike	307	3.95	300.00
70-04-193	7" Architect Mouse	A. Thorndike	205	3.95	350.00
75-04-194	7" Ski Mouse	A. Thorndike	5,219	5.50	200.00
76-04-195	7" Colonial Girl Mouse	A. Thorndike	5,457	5.50	225.00
74-04-196	7" Hunter Mouse W/Bird	A. Thorndike	690	5.50	300.00
90-04-197	7" Sailor Mouse	A. Thorndike	6,838	23.95	118.00
75-04-198	7" Bouquet Girl Mouse	A. Thorndike	N/A	3.95	300.00
76-04-199	7" Gardener Mouse	A. Thorndike	1,255	5.50	225.00
67-04-200	7" Conductor Mouse	A. Thorndike	N/A	3.95	300.00
91-04-201	7" Red Cross Nurse Mouse, proof	A. Thorndike	1	N/A	525.00
68-04-202	7" Mr. Holly Mouse	A. Thorndike	N/A	3.95	250.00
91-04-203	7" Desert Storm Mouse	A. Thorndike	1	N/A	800.00
87-04-204	7" Barbeque Mouse	A. Thorndike	1,798	17.95	85.00
89-04-205	7" Knitting Mouse	A. Thorndike	N/A	19.95	75.00
78-04-206	7" Airplane Pilot Mouse	A. Thorndike	2,308	6.95	375.00
74-04-207	7" Doctor Mouse	A. Thorndike	720	5.50	200.00
76-04-208	7" Nurse Mouse	A. Thorndike	5,164	5.95	250.00
67-04-209	7" Mrs. Holly Mouse	A. Thorndike	N/A	3.95	150.00
85-04-210	12" Indian Boy Mouse	A. Thorndike	N/A	34.50	100.00
89-04-211	12" Trick or Treat Mouse	A. Thorndike	N/A	39.95	225.00
93-04-212	7" Baseball Mouse, proof	A. Thorndike	1	N/A	525.00
93-04-213	7" Fireman Mouse, proof	A. Thorndike	1	N/A	425.00
93-04-214	7" Factory in the Woods Mouse, proof	A. Thorndike	1	N/A	550.00
65-04-215	7" Eek, Peek, Squeek Mouse	A. Thorndike	N/A	3.95	500.00
67-04-216	7" Mr. Santa Mouse	A. Thorndike	N/A	3.95	300.00
89-04-217	7" Business Man Mouse	A. Thorndike	5,085	21.95	150.00
82-04-218	7" Cowboy Mouse	A. Thorndike	3,776	28.95	75.00
80-04-219	7" Skating Mouse	A. Thorndike	3,369	10.95	100.00
82-04-220	7" Graduate Girl Mouse	A. Thorndike	3,563	10.95	85.00
75-04-221	7" Housewife Mouse	A. Thorndike	1,632	5.50	250.00
70-04-222	7" Boxing Mouse	A. Thorndike	321	3.95	400.00
70-04-223	7" Professor Mouse	A. Thorndike	248	3.95	225.00
70-04-224	7" Sheriff Mouse	A. Thorndike	11	3.95	500.00
76-04-225	12" Colonial Boy & Girl Mouse	A. Thorndike	N/A	26.90	900.00
93-04-225	7" Baseball Mouse	A. Thorndike	N/A	25.95	25.95
93-04-226	7" Fireman Mouse	A. Thorndike	N/A	25.95	25.95
93-04-227	7" Factory in the Woods Mouse	A. Thorndike	N/A	29.95	29.95
93-04-228	7" St. Patrick's Day Mouse	A. Thorndike	N/A	25.95	25.95
93-04-229	7" Ghost Mouse	A. Thorndike	N/A	25.95	25.95
93-04-230	7" Wizard Mouse	A. Thorndike	N/A	27.95	27.95
93-04-231	7" Witch Mouse	A. Thorndike	N/A	25.95	25.95
93-04-232	7" White Skating Mouse	A. Thorndike	N/A	21.95	21.95
93-04-233	7" White Mouse on Toboggan with Present	A. Thorndike	N/A	29.95	29.95
Annalee Mobilitee Dolls		**Snowmen**			
84-05-001	4" Snowman	A. Thorndike	Unkn.	169.95	350.00
84-05-002	30" Snowgirl & Boy	A. Thorndike	685	79.95	475.00
78-05-003	18" Snowman	A. Thorndike	3,971	79.95	250.00
83-05-004	7" Snowman	A. Thorndike	15,980	12.95	75.00
71-05-005	29" Snowman With Broom	A. Thorndike	1,075	19.95	200.00
84-05-006	30" Snowman	A. Thorndike	956	79.50	475.00
84-05-007	30" Snowgirl	A. Thorndike	685	79.50	475.00
79-05-008	10" Snowman	A. Thorndike	12,888	7.95	100.00
79-05-009	29" Snowman	A. Thorndike	917	42.95	400.00
78-05-010	10" Snowman	A. Thorndike	9,701	6.95	175.00
71-05-011	7" Snowman	A. Thorndike	1,917	3.95	275.00
93-05-012	7" Snow Woman	A. Thorndike	N/A	25.95	25.95
93-05-013	7" Snowman on Toboggan	A. Thorndike	N/A	29.95	29.95
Annalee Mobilitee Dolls		**Clowns**			
81-06-001	18" Clown	A. Thorndike	2,742	24.95	200.00
78-06-002	10" Clown	A. Thorndike	4,020	6.50	175.00
80-06-003	18" Clown	A. Thorndike	3,192	24.95	125.00
85-06-004	18" Clown	A. Thorndike	2,275	36.95	200.00
86-06-005	Ballooning Clown	A. Thorndike	2,700	16.95	110.00
85-06-006	18" Clown with Balloon	A. Thorndike	1,485	36.95	200.00
86-06-007	10" Clown	A. Thorndike	3,897	15.50	75.00
80-06-008	10" Clown	A. Thorndike	8,136	12.50	75.00
81-06-009	10" Clown	A. Thorndike	6,479	12.95	100.00
77-06-010	10" Clown	A. Thorndike	4,784	6.00	125.00
71-06-011	10" Clown	A. Thorndike	708	2.00	200.00
87-06-012	10" Clown	A. Thorndike	Unkn.	17.95	55.00
76-06-013	30" Clown	A. Thorndike	466	30.00	650.00
84-06-014	30" Clown	A. Thorndike	387	69.95	400.00
70-06-015	10" Clown	A. Thorndike	2,362	4.00	125.00
76-06-016	18" Clown	A. Thorndike	916	13.50	200.00
77-06-017	18" Clown	A. Thorndike	2,343	13.50	475.00
80-06-018	4' Clown	A. Thorndike	224	150.00	900.00
84-06-019	10" Clown	A. Thorndike	6,383	13.95	95.00
84-06-020	18" Clown	A. Thorndike	N/A	32.95	150.00
70-06-021	18" Clown	A. Thorndike	542	5.00	250.00
80-06-022	18" Clown With Balloon	A. Thorndike	3,192	24.95	100.00

Company		Series			
Number	Name	Artist	Edition Limit	Issue Price	Quote
76-06-023	10" Clown	A. Thorndike	2,285	5.50	100.00
81-06-024	10" Clown	A. Thorndike	6,479	9.95	125.00
84-06-025	30" Clown	A. Thorndike	381	165.00	325.00
78-06-026	18" Clown	A. Thorndike	4,000	13.95	225.00
80-06-027	42" Clown w/ Stand	A. Thorndike	224	84.95	600.00
90-06-028	30" Clown w/ Stand	A. Thorndike	530	99.95	150.00
93-06-029	18" Halloween Clown	A. Thorndike	1	N/A	2600.00
90-06-030	10" Yellow Clown	A. Thorndike	3,100	25.95	75.00
90-06-031	10" Clown w/ Base	A. Thorndike	2,750	27.95	75.00
84-06-032	18" Clown	A. Thorndike	1,828	32.95	250.00
Annalee Mobilitee Dolls		**Kids/Babies**			
82-07-001	7" I'm a 10" Baby	A. Thorndike	2,159	12.95	125.00
60-07-002	7" Baby With Bow	A. Thorndike	Unkn.	1.50	125.00
68-07-003	5" Baby In Santa Cap	A. Thorndike	Unkn.	2.00	150.00
63-07-004	5" Baby With Santa Hat	A. Thorndike	Unkn.	2.50	175.00
84-07-005	7" Country Girl With Basket	A. Thorndike	715	16.95	250.00
63-07-006	5" Baby	A. Thorndike	Unkn.	Unkn.	300.00
80-07-007	7" Baby In Bassinette	A. Thorndike	Unkn.	Unkn.	125.00
85-07-008	7" Dressup Girl	A. Thorndike	1,536	18.95	425.00
85-07-009	7" Dressup Boy	A. Thorndike	1,174	18.95	225.00
85-07-010	7" Baseball Kid	A. Thorndike	1,225	Unkn.	75.00
84-07-011	7" Boy With Firecracker	A. Thorndike	1,893	19.95	140.00
85-07-012	7" Kid With Kite	A. Thorndike	1,084	17.95	75.00
84-07-013	7" Jogger Kid	A. Thorndike	Unkn.	17.95	85.00
85-07-014	7" Hockey Player Kid	A. Thorndike	1,578	18.95	125.00
85-07-015	7" Happy Birthday Boy	A. Thorndike	937	19.00	100.00
84-07-016	7" Cupid in Heart	A. Thorndike	2,445	32.95	150.00
84-07-017	7" Cupid Kid	A. Thorndike	6,808	14.95	150.00
83-07-018	7" Fishing Boy	A. Thorndike	Unkn.	12.95	125.00
84-07-019	18" Candy Girl	A. Thorndike	1,333	29.95	125.00
84-07-020	18" Candy Boy	A. Thorndike	1,350	29.95	300.00
82-07-021	18" Girl P.J. Kid	A. Thorndike	5,389	25.50	125.00
84-07-022	18" Girl On Sled	A. Thorndike	2,328	29.95	150.00
84-07-023	18" Boy On Sled	A. Thorndike	2,205	29.95	150.00
87-07-024	3" Baby Witch	A. Thorndike	Unkn.	13.95	55.00
57-07-025	10" Boy Skier	A. Thorndike	N/A	16.00	800.00
57-07-026	10" Girl & Boy in Boat	A. Thorndike	N/A	17.50	900.00
71-07-027	18" Choir Girl	A. Thorndike	424	7.95	400.00
85-07-028	7" Baseball Kid	A. Thorndike	1,221	16.95	425.00
78-07-029	18" Candy Girl	A. Thorndike	1,333	14.95	375.00
68-07-030	5" Baby in Santa Hat	A. Thorndike	N/A	3.00	225.00
85-07-031	7" Birthday Girl	A. Thorndike	1,017	18.95	75.00
75-07-032	10" Lass	A. Thorndike	558	6.00	300.00
84-07-033	7" Baseball Kid	A. Thorndike	2,079	13.00	200.00
75-07-034	18" Lad & Lass On Bike	A. Thorndike	206	24.00	275.00
64-07-035	18" P.J. Boy & Girl	A. Thorndike	N/A	7.00	525.00
65-07-036	7" Dresden China Babies, 2	A. Thorndike	N/A	N/A	525.00
69-07-037	7" X-mas Baby On 3 Hot Boxes	A. Thorndike	N/A	3.00	400.00
87-07-038	7" Indian Boy	A. Thorndike	N/A	19.95	60.00
81-07-039	18" Boy On Sled	A. Thorndike	N/A	12.50	200.00
75-07-040	10" Lad On Bicycle	A. Thorndike	453	6.00	300.00
85-07-041	7" Jogger Kid	A. Thorndike	654	17.95	85.00
86-07-042	7" Cupid In Hot Air Balloon	A. Thorndike	391	54.95	175.00
50-07-043	9" Choir Boy	A. Thorndike	N/A	N/A	400.00
75-07-044	10" Lad & Lass	A. Thorndike	162	12.00	249.00
87-07-045	3" Cupid In Heart Balloon	A. Thorndike	1,715	38.95	175.00
54-07-046	5" Sno Bunny, (Kid)	A. Thorndike	N/A	N/A	300.00
69-07-047	18" Santa Kid	A. Thorndike	N/A	7.45	250.00
87-07-048	7" Girl Graduate	A. Thorndike	2,438	19.95	80.00
87-07-049	7" Boy Graduate	A. Thorndike	2,034	N/A	80.00
69-07-050	25" Country Boy	A. Thorndike	70	7.00	500.00
69-07-051	25" Country Girl	A. Thorndike	69	7.00	pair
86-07-052	7" Skiing Kid	A. Thorndike	8,057	18.45	75.00
60-07-053	7" Baby With Pink Bow	A. Thorndike	N/A	N/A	450.00
63-07-054	7" Saturday Night Baby	A. Thorndike	N/A	2.95	350.00
60-07-055	7" Baby In Stocking	A. Thorndike	N/A	N/A	275.00
68-07-056	7" Baby I'm Reading	A. Thorndike	N/A	N/A	375.00
68-07-057	7" Baby Vain Jane	A. Thorndike	N/A	2.50	300.00
70-07-058	18" Patchwork Kid	A. Thorndike	496	7.50	250.00
70-07-059	10" Choir Boy	A. Thorndike	3,517	4.50	150.00
76-07-060	10" Girl in Tire Swing	A. Thorndike	357	6.95	225.00
76-07-061	10" Boy In Tire Swing	A. Thorndike	358	6.95	200.00
75-07-062	25" Lass With Basket Of Flowers	A. Thorndike	92	28.95	450.00
71-07-063	18" Santa Fur Kid	A. Thorndike	1,191	7.95	400.00
70-07-064	10" Choir Girl	A. Thorndike	7,245	5.50	225.00
71-07-065	10" Choir Boy	A. Thorndike	904	3.95	175.00
87-07-066	7" Baby W/Blanket & Sweater	A. Thorndike	7,836	21.95	60.00
80-07-067	10" Boy on Raft	A. Thorndike	1,087	28.95	300.00
85-07-068	12" Kid W/Sled	A. Thorndike	4,707	31.50	115.00
65-07-069	10" Fishing Boy	A. Thorndike	N/A	7.95	300.00
54-07-070	8" Boy Skier	A. Thorndike	N/A	N/A	550.00
62-07-071	10" Skeeple (Boy)	A. Thorndike	N/A	9.00	425.00
70-07-072	7" Treasure Baby	A. Thorndike	N/A	3.95	200.00
71-07-073	7" Baby Bunting In Basket	A. Thorndike	195	3.95	350.00
76-07-074	10" Lass w/Planter Basket	A. Thorndike	313	6.95	200.00
67-07-075	10" Surfer Boy	A. Thorndike	N/A	4.95	300.00
57-07-076	10" Easter Holiday Doll	A. Thorndike	N/A	10.00	800.00
65-07-077	10" Fishing Girl	A. Thorndike	N/A	9.95	400.00
67-07-078	7" Garden Club Baby	A. Thorndike	N/A	2.95	350.00
54-07-079	5" Sno-Bunny Child	A. Thorndike	N/A	2.95	350.00
81-07-080	7" Naughty Angel	A. Thorndike	12,359	10.95	75.00
56-07-081	7" Baby Angel With Feather Hair	A. Thorndike	Unkn.	3.95	325.00
84-07-082	7" Baseball Player	A. Thorndike	937	15.95	75.00
84-07-083	7" Cupid Kid	A. Thorndike	6,808	15.50	200.00
93-07-084	7" Fishing Boy, Proof	A. Thorndike	1	N/A	500.00
93-07-085	7" Girl Eating Turkey, Proof	A. Thorndike	1	N/A	525.00
93-07-086	7" Boy Building Snowman, Proof	A. Thorndike	1	N/A	450.00
93-07-087	7" Hot Shot Business Man Kid, Proof	A. Thorndike	1	N/A	600.00
93-07-088	18" P.J. Kid	A. Thorndike	1	N/A	875.00
93-07-089	7" Bedtime Kid, Proof	A. Thorndike	1	N/A	450.00
93-07-090	7" Jump Rope Kid, Proof	A. Thorndike	1	N/A	500.00
93-07-091	7" Basketball Kid, Proof	A. Thorndike	1	N/A	550.00
88-07-092	10" Shepherd Boy w/ Lamb	A. Thorndike	1,300	89.95	175.00
83-07-093	7" Fishing Boy	A. Thorndike	3,927	16.95	175.00
72-07-094	18" P.J. Kid	A. Thorndike	N/A	N/A	125.00
93-07-095	7" Court Jester	A. Thorndike	N/A	3.95	325.00
93-07-096	7" Jump Rope Girl	A. Thorndike	N/A	25.95	25.95
93-07-097	7" Fishing Boy	A. Thorndike	N/A	29.95	29.95
93-07-098	7" Basketball Boy	A. Thorndike	N/A	25.95	25.95
93-07-099	7" Bar Mitzvah Boy	A. Thorndike	N/A	27.95	27.95
93-07-100	7" Hot Shot Business Man Kid	A. Thorndike	N/A	27.95	27.95
93-07-101	7" Bed Time Kid	A. Thorndike	N/A	25.95	25.95
93-07-102	7" Arab Boy	A. Thorndike	N/A	35.95	35.95

Company Number	Name	Series Artist	Edition Limit	Issue Price	Quote
93-07-103	7" Pink Flower Kid	A. Thorndike	N/A	25.95	25.95
93-07-104	7" Yellow Flower Kid	A. Thorndike	N/A	25.95	25.95
93-07-105	7" Butterfly Kid	A. Thorndike	N/A	27.95	27.95
93-07-106	7" Flower Kid (Yellow)	A. Thorndike	N/A	27.95	27.95
93-07-107	30" Witch Kid	A. Thorndike	N/A	149.95	149.95
93-07-108	12" Boy Pilgrim w/Basket	A. Thorndike	N/A	44.95	44.95
93-07-109	12" Girl Pilgrim w/Pie	A. Thorndike	N/A	44.95	44.95
93-07-110	12" Indian Boy	A. Thorndike	N/A	35.95	35.95
93-07-111	7" Pilgrim Boy Hugging Fawn	A. Thorndike	N/A	40.95	40.95
93-07-112	7" Pilgrim Girl w/Pie	A. Thorndike	N/A	25.95	25.95
93-07-113	5" Baby Jesus in Manger w/Hay	A. Thorndike	N/A	25.95	25.95
93-07-114	3" Baby Jesus in Manger	A. Thorndike	N/A	16.95	16.95
93-07-115	7" Choir Girl	A. Thorndike	N/A	25.95	25.95
93-07-116	7" Choir Boy	A. Thorndike	N/A	25.95	25.95
93 07 117	7" Boy Building Snowman	A. Thorndike	N/A	21.95	21.95
Annalee Mobilitee Dolls		**Angels**			
85-08-001	12" Naughty Angel	A. Thorndike	1,393	Unkn.	125.00
63-08-002	5" Baby Angel With Halo	A. Thorndike	Unkn.	2.00	300.00
82-08-003	7" Angel With Teardrop	A. Thorndike	3,092	12.95	200.00
84-08-004	7" Naughty Angel	A. Thorndike	4,258	Unkn.	75.00
78-08-005	7" Tree Top Angel With Wreath	A. Thorndike	Unkn.	Unkn.	100.00
68-08-006	5" Baby Angel On Cloud	A. Thorndike	N/A	3.00	300.00
78-08-007	7" Tree Top Angel With Wreath	A. Thorndike	8,613	6.50	100.00
66-08-008	7" Angel, White Wings	A. Thorndike	N/A	N/A	225.00
86-08-009	12" Naughty Angel With Slingshot	A. Thorndike	N/A	36.95	225.00
71-08-010	7" Angel With Paper Wings	A. Thorndike	608	3.00	325.00
64-08-011	7" Angel in A Blanket	A. Thorndike	N/A	2.50	300.00
56-08-012	10" Baby Angel	A. Thorndike	N/A	5.50	550.00
91-08-013	10" Nativity Angel, Proof	A. Thorndike	1	N/A	1200.00
60-08-014	12" Big Angel On Cloud	A. Thorndike	N/A	9.95	350.00
60-08-015	7" Baby Angel	A. Thorndike	N/A	N/A	300.00
60-08-016	7" Baby Angel With Star On Leg	A. Thorndike	N/A	N/A	300.00
76-08-017	7" Mistletoe Angel	A. Thorndike	17,540	6.00	80.00
84-08-018	7" Angel On Star	A. Thorndike	772	32.95	200.00
60-08-019	7" Baby Angel w/Blue Wings	A. Thorndike	N/A	N/A	300.00
63-08-020	7" Baby Angel On Cloud	A. Thorndike	N/A	N/A	300.00
69-08-021	7" Angel w/Blue Wings	A. Thorndike	N/A	2.95	225.00
64-08-022	7" Sat. Nite Angel w/Blanket	A. Thorndike	N/A	2.95	250.00
93-08-022	7" Angel (Black Hair)	A. Thorndike	N/A	22.95	22.95
93-08-023	7" Angel (Blonde Hair)	A. Thorndike	N/A	22.95	22.95
93-08-024	7" Angel (Brown Hair)	A. Thorndike	N/A	22.95	22.95
Annalee Mobilitee Dolls		**Bunnies**			
64-09-001	5" Brown Bunny	A. Thorndike	N/A	N/A	540.00
71-09-002	30" White Bunny With Carrot	A. Thorndike	172	Unkn.	165.00
71-09-003	7" White Bunny With Candlewreath	A. Thorndike	227	4.95.	350.00
86-09-004	30" Boy Bunny With Wheelbarrow	A. Thorndike	252	119.50	200.00
72-09-005	30" Boy Bunny	A. Thorndike	237	25.00	225.00
72-09-006	18" Boy Bunny With Burlap Sack Cardholder	A. Thorndike	326	10.95	450.00
72-09-007	30" Girl Bunny	A. Thorndike	223	25.00	225.00
79-09-008	29" E.P. Mom Bunny	A. Thorndike	662	42.95	200.00
70-09-009	29" Girl Bunny	A. Thorndike	Unkn.	22.00	250.00
70-09-010	18" White Bunny With Butterfly	A. Thorndike	258	10.95	500.00
70-09-011	18" Bunny With Butterfly	A. Thorndike	258	10.95	500.00
73-09-012	7" White Bunny	A. Thorndike	1,600	5.50	125.00
72-09-013	7" Ballerina Bunny	A. Thorndike	4,700	4.00	100.00
79-09-014	7" Ballerina Bunny	A. Thorndike	4,700	7.50	100.00
80-09-015	7" Ballerina Bunny	A. Thorndike	Unkn.	8.95	175.00
82-09-016	7" Ballerina Bunny	A. Thorndike	4,179	9.95	100.00
78-09-017	7" Artist Bunny	A. Thorndike	4,217	7.50	250.00
86-09-018	7" Valentine Bunny	A. Thorndike	Unkn.	14.50	125.00
81-09-019	7" Country Bunnies	A. Thorndike	7,940	Unkn.	185.00
78-09-020	7" Bunnies With Basket	A. Thorndike	2,253	Unkn.	150.00
84-09-021	7" Country Bunnies With Basket	A. Thorndike	2,345	25.95	75.00
87-09-022	18" E.P. Girl Sample Bunny	A. Thorndike	1	Unkn.	300.00
87-09-023	18" E.P. Boy Sample Bunny	A. Thorndike	1	Unkn.	300.00
79-09-024	18" Artist Bunny	A. Thorndike	1,064	15.95	275.00
70-09-025	18" Girl Bunny With Egg	A. Thorndike	1,727	15.95	150.00
82-09-026	4' Boy Bunny	A. Thorndike	186	190.00	450.00
84-09-027	7" E.P. Boy Bunny	A. Thorndike	5,989	12.95	35.00
83-09-028	7" E.P. Girl Bunny	A. Thorndike	Unkn.	12.50	50.00
83-09-029	7" E.P. Boy Bunny	A. Thorndike	Unkn.	12.50	50.00
83-09-030	7" Country Boy Bunny With Butterfly	A. Thorndike	N/A	12.50	100.00
85-09-031	7" Boy Bunny With Carrot	A. Thorndike	3,273	14.95	55.00
86-09-032	7" Boy Bunny With Carrot	A. Thorndike	2,949	15.50	95.00
83-09-033	5" Country Girl Bunny	A. Thorndike	5,163	Unkn.	50.00
83-09-034	5" Floppy-ear Boy Bunny With Basket	A. Thorndike	Unkn.	11.50	55.00
84-09-035	5" Country Bunnies With Basket	A. Thorndike	1,110	Unkn.	150.00
77-09-036	29" Mechanical See Saw Bunny	A. Thorndike	N/A	300.00	900.00
83-09-037	5" Bunny On Music Box	A. Thorndike	N/A	29.95	375.00
70-09-038	7" Bunny On Box	A. Thorndike	N/A	N/A	250.00
73-09-039	7" Bunny On Box	A. Thorndike	795	5.50	125.00
77-09-040	7" Bunny With Butterfly	A. Thorndike	2,721	6.00	125.00
82-09-041	7" Easter Parade Boy Bunny	A. Thorndike	7,108	11.95	50.00
86-09-042	7" Bunny With Egg	A. Thorndike	2,233	16.95	55.00
77-09-043	18" Easter Parade Boy Bunny	A. Thorndike	1,567	13.50	150.00
77-09-044	29" Easter Parade Pop Bunny	A. Thorndike	477	35.00	250.00
72-09-045	29" Easter Parade Mom Bunny	A. Thorndike	508	35.00	250.00
84-09-046	5" Girl Bunny	A. Thorndike	2,594	11.50	65.00
66-09-047	7" Yum Yum Bunny	A. Thorndike	N/A	3.95	525.00
71-09-048	18" Peter Bunny	A. Thorndike	219	10.95	425.00
77-09-049	29" Pop Bunny With Basket	A. Thorndike	N/A	11.50	400.00
65-09-050	7" Dumb Bunny	A. Thorndike	N/A	3.95	400.00
83-09-051	29" Easter Parade Girl Bunny	A. Thorndike	N/A	71.95	200.00
81-09-052	18" Country Boy Bunny With Carrot	A. Thorndike	1,998	23.95	275.00
88-09-053	7" Bunny With Sled	A. Thorndike	3,050	21.95	45.00
88-09-054	7" Set of Three Bunnies On Revolving Music Box Maypole	A. Thorndike	610	69.95	150.00
85-09-055	7" Valentine Bunny	A. Thorndike	5,602	13.95	75.00
84-09-056	7" Two Bunnies With Bushel Basket	A. Thorndike	2,339	25.95	75.00
66-09-057	7" Yum Yum Bunny	A. Thorndike	N/A	3.95	400.00
67-09-058	12" Yum Yum Bunny	A. Thorndike	N/A	9.95	550.00
85-09-059	18" Country Boy Bunny With Watering Can	A. Thorndike	2,355	46.95	N/A
87-09-060	18" Victorian Country Boy Bunny	A. Thorndike	1,394	49.95	350.00
87-09-061	18" Victorian Country Girl Bunny	A. Thorndike	1,492	49.95	pair
72-09-062	7" Bunny, (With Bandana)	A. Thorndike	1,615	3.95	150.00
84-09-063	18" Country Girl Bunny With Basket	A. Thorndike	1,481	31.95	300.00
88-09-064	18" Country Mom Bunny w/Baby	A. Thorndike	1,800	68.95	140.00
70-09-065	7" Bunny w/Butterfly	A. Thorndike	1,264	4.95	150.00
84-09-066	5" Floppy Ear Girl Bunny	A. Thorndike	2,594	11.50	75.00
90-09-067	18" Strawberry Bunny	A. Thorndike	2,365	59.95	200.00
90-09-068	30" Strawberry Bunny	A. Thorndike	582	135.95	300.00
86-09-069	18" C.B. Bunny w/Wheelbarrow	A. Thorndike	1,224	46.95	75.00

Company Number	Name	Series Artist	Edition Limit	Issue Price	Quote
86-09-070	18" C.G. Bunny w/Flowers	A. Thorndike	1,205	41.50	75.00
80-09-071	18" C.G. Bunny w/Basket	A. Thorndike	3,964	19.95	150.00
78-09-072	29" E.P. Mom & Pop Bunnies (pair)	A. Thorndike	529	36.95	400.00
77-09-073	7" Bunny w/Egg	A. Thorndike	2,442	5.95	125.00
70-09-074	7" Yellow Bunny	A. Thorndike	N/A	3.95	300.00
77-09-074	7" Yellow Bunny	A. Thorndike	N/A	N/A	275.00
65-09-075	12" Nipsy-Tipsy Hare	A. Thorndike	N/A	7.50	700.00
69-09-076	7" Bunny w/Oversized Carrot	A. Thorndike	N/A	4.95	400.00
84-09-077	7" Valentine Bunny	A. Thorndike	5,603	13.95	125.00
84-09-078	7" Valentine Bunny	A. Thorndike	5,602	13.95	125.00
76-09-079	18" Girl Bunny With Egg	A. Thorndike	789	13.50	375.00
76-09-080	18" Easter Parade Boy Bunny	A. Thorndike	791	13.50	300.00
Annalee Mobilitee Dolls		**Pigs**			
82-10-001	8" Boy BBQ Pig	A. Thorndike	1,044	11.95	55.00
81-10-002	8" Boy BBQ Pig	A. Thorndike	1,159	11.95	100.00
81-10-003	8" Girl BBQ Pig	A. Thorndike	2,596	9.95	250.00
80-10-004	4" Pig	A. Thorndike	1,615	8.50	100.00
81-10-005	4" Pig	A. Thorndike	3,194	7.95	100.00
82-10-006	8" Ballerina Pig	A. Thorndike	1,058	12.95	250.00
81-10-007	3" Pig	A. Thorndike	3,435	7.95	100.00
79-10-008	14" Father Pig	A. Thorndike	1,500	18.95	150.00
79-10-009	14" Mom Pig	A. Thorndike	1,807	18.95	150.00
81-10-010	8" Boy B-B-Q Pig	A. Thorndike	4,072	10.50	200.00
81-10-011	8" Girl B-B-Q Pig	A. Thorndike	3,854	10.50	pair
88-10-012	10" Easter Parade Boy Pig	A. Thorndike	3,005	24.50	180.00
88-10-013	10" Easter Parade Girl Pig	A. Thorndike	3,400	24.50	pair
69-10-014	4" Pig-Bubble Time w/Champagne Glass	A. Thorndike	N/A	4.95	275.00
Annalee Mobilitee Dolls		**Frogs**			
69-11-001	10" Bride & Groom Frogs Courtin'	A. Thorndike	N/A	7.95	550.00
74-11-002	42" Willie Wog Frog	A. Thorndike	223	51.95	700.00
74-11-003	10" Wille Wog Goin' Fishing	A. Thorndike	Unkn.	5.50	200.00
79-11-004	10" Girl Frog	A. Thorndike	5,970	8.50	90.00
79-11-005	18" Girl Frog	A. Thorndike	2,338	18.95	225.00
87-11-006	10" Leap Frogs	A. Thorndike	1,800	31.95	80.00
71-11-007	10" Bride & Groom Frogs On Bike	A. Thorndike	13	17.50	625.00
81-11-008	18" Girl Frog	A. Thorndike	666	24.00	225.00
80-11-009	10" Boy Frog	A. Thorndike	4,185	9.50	125.00
80-11-010	10" Girl Frog	A. Thorndike	421	9.50	125.00
80-11-011	42" Frog	A. Thorndike	202	89.95	500.00
80-11-012	10" Bride Frog	A. Thorndike	1,653	14.95	150.00
80-11-013	10" Groom Frog	A. Thorndike	1,611	14.95	150.00
80-11-014	18" Boy Frog	A. Thorndike	1,285	23.00	150.00
81-11-015	10" Groom Frog	A. Thorndike	2,061	14.95	150.00
81-11-016	10" Bride Frog	A. Thorndike	1,239	14.95	150.00
69-11-017	42" Frog	A. Thorndike	30	29.95	700.00
69-11-018	10" Croaker Frog Band	A. Thorndike	N/A	24.95	3700.00
69-11-019	18" Croaker Crosby Frog With Instrument	A. Thorndike	N/A	10.95	300.00
71-11-020	18" Frog w/Bass Viola	A. Thorndike	224	11.95	1350.00
71-11-021	10" Frog w/Instrument	A. Thorndike	233	3.95	200.00
79-11-022	10" Boy Frog	A. Thorndike	5,642	8.50	90.00
80-11-023	42" Santa Frog	A. Thorndike	206	100.00	700.00
80-11-024	18" Santa Frog	A. Thorndike	2,126	25.00	225.00
92-11-025	10" Frog In Boat, proof	A. Thorndike	1	N/A	900.00
Annalee Mobilitee Dolls		**Assorted Animals**			
81-12-001	18" Escort Fox*	A. Thorndike	Unkn.	28.50	350.00
81-12-002	18" Foxy Lady*	A. Thorndike	Unkn.	28.50	350.00
81-12-003	7" Escort Fox	A. Thorndike	Unkn.	12.50	250.00
81-12-004	7" Foxy Lady	A. Thorndike	Unkn.	12.50	250.00
72-12-005	36" Election Elephant	A. Thorndike	113	Unkn.	550.00
76-12-006	8" Election Elephant	A. Thorndike	1,223	Unkn.	175.00
72-12-007	30" Election Donkey	A. Thorndike	120	23.95	350.00
83-12-008	5" Dragon With Wings & Baby	A. Thorndike	199	22.50	900.00
82-12-009	5" Dragon With Bushboy	A. Thorndike	1,066	17.95	475.00
81-12-010	14" Dragon With Bushboy	A. Thorndike	1,257	28.95	650.00
81-12-011	29" Dragon With Bushboy	A. Thorndike	76	69.95	1050.00
85-12-012	12" Jazz Cat	A. Thorndike	2,622	Unkn.	250.00
87-12-013	10" Bride & Groom Cat	A. Thorndike	727	Unkn.	200.00
76-12-014	36" Election Donkey	A. Thorndike	119	Unkn.	650.00
76-12-015	10" Vote Donkey	A. Thorndike	1,202	5.95	225.00
82-12-016	12" Girl Skunk	A. Thorndike	936	27.95	225.00
82-12-017	12" Boy Skunk	A. Thorndike	935	27.95	225.00
82-12-018	12" Skunk With Snowball	A. Thorndike	1,304	Unkn.	225.00
76-12-019	8" Rooster	A. Thorndike	1,094	5.50	250.00
77-12-020	15" Purple Rooster	A. Thorndike	548	5.48	450.00
70-12-021	7" Blue Monkey	A. Thorndike	293	Unkn.	250.00
81-12-022	7" Monkey With Banana Trapeze	A. Thorndike	3,075	Unkn.	125.00
81 12 023	12" Boy Monkey With Trapeze	A. Thorndike	1,800	23.95	300.00
81-12-024	12" Girl Monkey With Trapeze	A. Thorndike	857	23.95	200.00
73-12-025	12" Girl Nightshirt Monkey	A. Thorndike	Unkn.	7.50	300.00
75-12-026	18" Horse	A. Thorndike	221	17.00	200.00
86-12-027	18" Valentine Cat	A. Thorndike	Unkn.	Unkn.	125.00
72-12-028	12" Cat With Mouse	A. Thorndike	N/A	13.00	450.00
83-12-029	5" Dragon With Wings & Baby	A. Thorndike	199	22.50	300.00
76-12-030	15" Rooster	A. Thorndike	485	13.50	1050.00
76-12-031	36" Horse	A. Thorndike	27	48.00	500.00
76-12-032	18" Elephant	A. Thorndike	285	16.95	425.00
72-12-033	10" Donkey	A. Thorndike	861	5.95	175.00
77-12-034	8" Rooster	A. Thorndike	1,642	6.00	400.00
68-12-035	12" Ice Pack Cat	A. Thorndike	N/A	6.95	500.00
71-12-036	7" Yellow Kitten	A. Thorndike	103	4.50	575.00
68-12-037	12" Tessie Tar Cat	A. Thorndike	N/A	6.95	450.00
85-12-038	15" Jazz Cat	A. Thorndike	2,622	31.95	250.00
76-12-039	10" Donkey	A. Thorndike	1,202	5.95	150.00
76-12-040	10" Elephant	A. Thorndike	1,223	5.95	225.00
83-12-041	24" Stork With Baby	A. Thorndike	858	36.95	175.00
77-12-042	8" Rooster	A. Thorndike	1,642	5.95	300.00
81-12-043	29" Dragon With Bushboy	A. Thorndike	75	63.95	1050.00
73-12-044	7" Girl Niteshirt Mouse	A. Thorndike	1,740	5.50	105.00
87-12-045	10" Bride Cat	A. Thorndike	727	35.95	250.00
87-12-046	10" Groom Cat	A. Thorndike	762	35.95	pair
85-12-047	18" Valentine Cat With Heart	A. Thorndike	2,129	34.95	225.00
65-12-048	8" Elephant-Republican	A. Thorndike	N/A	4.95	225.00
70-12-049	7" Monkey	A. Thorndike	293	4.95	525.00
87-12-050	24" Christmas Goose With Basket	A. Thorndike	N/A	54.95	150.00
67-12-051	36" Christmas Cat	A. Thorndike	N/A	12.00	350.00
67-12-052	12" Laura May Cat	A. Thorndike	N/A	6.95	850.00
68-12-053	6" Myrtle Turtle	A. Thorndike	N/A	3.95	700.00
86-12-054	10" Christmas Panda w/Toybag	A. Thorndike	4,397	18.95	150.00
76-12-055	18" Vote 76 Donkey	A. Thorndike	285	16.95	300.00
72-12-056	16" Elephant	A. Thorndike	230	12.95	285.00
81-12-057	18" Cat w/Mouse & Mistletoe	A. Thorndike	18,995	46.95	150.00

DOLLS

Company Number	Name	Series / Artist	Edition Limit	Issue Price	Quote
88-12-058	10" Stork w/3" Baby	A. Thorndike	500	49.95	145.00
86-12-059	10" Kitten w/Yarn & Basket	A. Thorndike	3,917	27.95	125.00
67-12-060	12" Fancy Nancy Cat Christmas	A. Thorndike	N/A	6.95	700.00
82-12-061	7" Santa Fox w/Bag	A. Thorndike	3,622	12.95	400.00
92-12-062	10" Spring Chicken, proof	A. Thorndike	1	N/A	800.00
66-12-063	12" Sneaky Cat	A. Thorndike	Unkn.	6.95	525.00
70-12-064	7" Monkey (Bristol Blue)	A. Thorndike	293	4.95	300.00
70-12-065	22" Monkey (Hot Pink)	A. Thorndike	70	10.95	1650.00
70-12-066	10" Nightshirt Monkey With Candle	A. Thorndike	71	4.95	500.00
73-12-067	12" Nightshirt Monkey	A. Thorndike	835	7.50	225.00
84-12-068	18" Christmas Panda With Toybag	A. Thorndike	4,144	39.95	275.00
72-12-069	8" Elephant	A. Thorndike	966	7.00	200.00
72-12-070	16" Elephant (Republican)	A. Thorndike	230	12.95	600.00
72-12-071	16" Democratic Donkey	A. Thorndike	219	12.95	600.00
73-12-072	7" Bear With Bumblebee	A. Thorndike	694	4.50	250.00
76-12-073	15" Duck	A. Thorndike	1,895	13.50	175.00
81-12-074	18" Cat With 7" Mouse & Mistletoe	A. Thorndike	5,685	31.95	275.00
81-12-075	7" Escort & Lady Fox	A. Thorndike	N/A	N/A	475.00
82-12-076	18" Boy Skunk	A. Thorndike	935	N/A	250.00
85-12-077	12" Jazz Cat With Instrument	A. Thorndike	2,622	31.95	225.00
85-12-078	18" Be My Honey Bear	A. Thorndike	705	39.95	130.00
87-12-079	10" Girl Bear	A. Thorndike	2,200	20.95	225.00
86-12-080	15" Hobo Cat	A. Thorndike	4,130	35.95	250.00
88-12-081	10" Easter Parade Boy Pig	A. Thorndike	N/A	24.50	75.00
88-12-082	10" Easter Parade Girl Pig	A. Thorndike	N/A	24.50	75.00
88-12-083	10" Easter Parade Goose	A. Thorndike	2,450	29.95	60.00
87-12-084	10" Frog In Top Hat & Tails	A. Thorndike	1,325	23.95	95.00
89-12-085	10" Christmas Goose	A. Thorndike	3,007	30.95	55.00
89-12-086	24" Christmas Goose With Basket	A. Thorndike	2,036	57.95	75.00
89-12-087	10" Bear On Sled	A. Thorndike	3,563	28.95	60.00
89-12-088	10" Country Boy Goose	A. Thorndike	N/A	N/A	65.00
89-12-089	10" Country Girl Goose	A. Thorndike	N/A	N/A	65.00
90-12-090	24" Spring Swan	A. Thorndike	671	62.95	150.00
93-12-091	10" Cooking Bear	A. Thorndike	1	N/A	900.00
93-12-092	10" Skating Penguin	A. Thorndike	1	N/A	525.00
93-12-094	10" Doctor Bear	A. Thorndike	1	N/A	600.00
93-12-095	10" Beach Bear	A. Thorndike	1	N/A	850.00
88-12-096	10" Eskimo Bear	A. Thorndike	7,500	31.95	100.00
93-12-097	10" Doctor Bear	A. Thorndike	N/A	35.95	35.95
93-12-098	8" Girl Turkey	A. Thorndike	N/A	34.95	34.95
93-12-099	8" Boy Turkey	A. Thorndike	N/A	34.95	34.95
93-12-100	10" Angel Bear	A. Thorndike	N/A	32.95	32.95
93-12-101	10" Skating Penguin	A. Thorndike	N/A	34.95	34.95
Annalee Mobilitee Dolls		**Ducks**			
83-13-001	5" Sweetheart Duck	A. Thorndike	1,530	Unkn.	40.00
83-13-002	5" E.P. Boy Duck	A. Thorndike	5,133	Unkn.	50.00
83-13-003	5" E.P. Girl Duck	A. Thorndike	5,577	Unkn.	50.00
84-13-004	5" Pilot Duckling	A. Thorndike	4,396	14.95	150.00
86-13-005	5" Duck with Raincoat	A. Thorndike	5,029	Unkn.	200.00
85-13-006	12" Duck with Raincoat	A. Thorndike	Unkn.	Unkn.	275.00
82-13-007	12" Duck with Kerchief	A. Thorndike	5,861	26.95	125.00
75-13-008	5" Baby Duck	A. Thorndike	1,333	4.00	135.00
76-13-009	8" White Duck	A. Thorndike	3,265	4.95	225.00
87-13-010	12" Duck On Sled	A. Thorndike	300	N/A	500.00
Annalee Mobilitee Dolls		**Elves/Gnomes/Woodsprites/Leprechauns**			
74-14-001	22" Workshop Elf With Apron	A. Thorndike	1,404	10.95	882.00
82-14-002	10" Elf On Butterfly	A. Thorndike	882	Unkn.	275.00
81-14-003	10" Elf On Butterfly	A. Thorndike	1,625	24.95	300.00
60-14-004	5" Elf	A. Thorndike	Unkn.	Unkn.	200.00
54-14-005	10" Elf	A. Thorndike	Unkn.	Unkn.	275.00
70-14-006	10" Elf Skier	A. Thorndike	597	Unkn.	200.00
69-14-007	10" White Elf With Presents	A. Thorndike	Unkn.	Unkn.	180.00
67-14-008	10" Elf with Skis	A. Thorndike	48	3.00	350.00
77-14-009	18" White Elf	A. Thorndike	2,600	Unkn.	150.00
78-14-010	12" Christmas Gnome	A. Thorndike	10,140	Unkn.	125.00
63-14-011	10" Yellow Woodsprite	A. Thorndike	Unkn.	Unkn.	275.00
63-14-012	10" White Woodsprite	A. Thorndike	Unkn.	Unkn.	325.00
63-14-013	10" Elf Skier	A. Thorndike	Unkn.	Unkn.	350.00
83-14-014	10" Workshop Elf	A. Thorndike	Unkn.	Unkn.	75.00
65-14-015	5" Green Gnome	A. Thorndike	Unkn.	Unkn.	125.00
80-14-016	7" Gnome	A. Thorndike	13,238	9.50	150.00
79-14-017	18" Gnome	A. Thorndike	9,048	16.95	350.00
63-14-018	5" Christmas Elf	A. Thorndike	Unkn.	3.00	200.00
81-14-019	10" Jack Frost with Snowflake	A. Thorndike	5,950	31.95	175.00
72-14-020	18" Leprechaun	A. Thorndike	1,372	Unkn.	200.00
81-14-021	12" Elf With Butterfly	A. Thorndike	N/A	27.95	475.00
70-14-022	10" Casualty Elf	A. Thorndike	991	225	300.00
71-14-023	5" Gnome With Candle	A. Thorndike	N/A	3.00	300.00
64-14-024	18" Woodsprite	A. Thorndike	N/A	6.00	325.00
72-14-025	10" Robin Hood Elf	A. Thorndike	N/A	2.50	175.00
82-14-026	10" Jackfrost With Snowflake	A. Thorndike	2,289	13.50	250.00
67-14-027	10" Workshop Elf	A. Thorndike	N/A	N/A	175.00
57-14-028	9" Elf With Musical instrument	A. Thorndike	N/A	3.50	550.00
57-14-029	10" Mr. Holly Elf	A. Thorndike	N/A	N/A	1600.00
64-14-030	10" Imp Skier	A. Thorndike	N/A	4.00	350.00
64-14-031	22" Woodsprite	A. Thorndike	N/A	5.95	325.00
79-14-032	29" Gnome	A. Thorndike	1,762	47.95	400.00
83-14-033	10" Ballooning Elves	A. Thorndike	7,395	59.95	200.00
74-14-034	22" Workshop Elf	A. Thorndike	1,404	10.45	125.00
63-14-035	18" Friar Bottle Cover	A. Thorndike	N/A	3.00	350.00
71-14-036	10" Elf Skier	A. Thorndike	N/A	N/A	100.00
63-14-037	24" Woodsprite	A. Thorndike	N/A	5.45	125.00
67-14-038	10" Elf With Round Box	A. Thorndike	N/A	2.50	350.00
59-14-039	10" Elf With Instrument	A. Thorndike	N/A	3.50	400.00
57-14-040	10" Holly Elf	A. Thorndike	N/A	N/A	500.00
71-14-041	7" Three Gnomes w/Large Candle	A. Thorndike	80	11.95	700.00
63-14-042	10" Christmas Elf w/Tinsel	A. Thorndike	N/A	N/A	250.00
62-14-043	5" Elf w/Feather Hair	A. Thorndike	N/A	9.00	300.00
77-14-044	22" Jack Frost Elf	A. Thorndike	2,600	11.95	400.00
78-14-045	12" Gnome	A. Thorndike	10,140	9.50	175.00
59-14-046	10" Green Woodsprite	A. Thorndike	N/A	6.95	350.00
67-14-047	12" Gnome w/PJ Suit	A. Thorndike	N/A	N/A	425.00
67-14-048	7" Gnome w/PJ Suit	A. Thorndike	N/A	2.50	250.00
93-14-049	10" Winter Elf	A. Thorndike	N/A	16.95	16.95
Annalee Mobilitee Dolls		**Humans**			
87-15-001	3" Bride & Groom	A. Thorndike	1,250	38.95	135.00
68-15-002	7" Fat Fanny	A. Thorndike	Unkn.	6.00	375.00
84-15-003	10" Aerobic Dancer	A. Thorndike	4,785	Unkn.	75.00
85-15-004	10" Bride	A. Thorndike	318	Unkn.	125.00
85-15-005	10" Groom	A. Thorndike	264	Unkn.	125.00

Company Number	Name	Series / Artist	Edition Limit	Issue Price	Quote
57-15-006	10" Boy With Straw Hat	A. Thorndike	Unkn.	Unkn.	500.00
59-15-007	10" Boy & Girl On Bike	A. Thorndike	Unkn.	Unkn.	575.00
56-15-008	10" Fishing Girl	A. Thorndike	Unkn.	Unkn.	425.00
57-15-009	10" Boy Building Boat	A. Thorndike	Unkn.	Unkn.	925.00
59-15-010	10" Girl Swimmer	A. Thorndike	Unkn.	Unkn.	550.00
55-15-011	10" Boy Swimmer	A. Thorndike	Unkn.	Unkn.	550.00
63-15-012	10" Girl Waterskier	A. Thorndike	Unkn.	7.50	450.00
59-15-013	10" Boy Golfer	A. Thorndike	Unkn.	Unkn.	475.00
50-15-014	10" Girl Golfer	A. Thorndike	Unkn.	Unkn.	475.00
81-15-015	10" Boy on Raft	A. Thorndike	Unkn.	Unkn.	200.00
57-15-016	10" Valentine Doll	A. Thorndike	Unkn.	Unkn.	925.00
57-15-017	10" Thanksgiving Doll	A. Thorndike	Unkn.	Unkn.	600.00
76-15-018	10" Country Girl In Tire Swing	A. Thorndike	357	Unkn.	200.00
74-15-019	10" Ladd & Lass	A. Thorndike	453	Unkn.	300.00
84-15-020	18" Bob Cratchet	A. Thorndike	1,819	49.95	250.00
84-15-021	18" Martha Cratchet	A. Thorndike	1,751	35.95	350.00
84-15-022	18" Aerobic Dancer	A. Thorndike	622	35.95	175.00
75-15-023	18" Lass	A. Thorndike	224	11.95	95.00
75-15-024	18" Ladd	A. Thorndike	206	11.95	175.00
76-15-025	18" Uncle Sam	A. Thorndike	345	17.00	425.00
57-15-026	10" Girl Skier	A. Thorndike	Unkn.	Unkn.	1000.00
57-15-027	10" Girl Skier	A. Thorndike	Unkn.	Unkn.	825.00
59-15-028	10" Boy Skier	A. Thorndike	Unkn.	Unkn.	800.00
85-15-029	10" Cross Country Skier	A. Thorndike	1,150	Unkn.	75.00
59-15-030	7" Girl Skier	A. Thorndike	Unkn.	Unkn.	675.00
60-15-031	10" Girl Skier	A. Thorndike	Unkn.	Unkn.	400.00
55-15-032	7" Boy Skier	A. Thorndike	Unkn.	Unkn.	1250.00
75-15-033	10" Caroler Boy	A. Thorndike	Unkn.	Unkn.	275.00
76-15-034	18" Choir Boy	A. Thorndike	Unkn.	Unkn.	500.00
76-15-035	10" Drummer Boy	A. Thorndike	Unkn.	6.00	200.00
76-15-036	18" Drummer Boy	A. Thorndike	402	13.50	400.00
87-15-037	5" Monk	A. Thorndike	Unkn.	13.95	50.00
67-15-038	10" Monk	A. Thorndike	Unkn.	Unkn.	200.00
82-15-039	10" Monk	A. Thorndike	6,968	12.95	130.00
83-15-040	16" Monk With Jug	A. Thorndike	Unkn.	27.95	200.00
84-15-041	30" Monk	A. Thorndike	432	78.50	300.00
63-15-042	18" Friar	A. Thorndike	Unkn.	Unkn.	400.00
87-15-043	18" Bottlecover Monk	A. Thorndike	718	29.95	105.00
84-15-044	18" Monk With Jug	A. Thorndike	1,821	34.95	295.00
76-15-045	18" Yankee Doodle Dandy	A. Thorndike	153	Unkn.	425.00
78-15-046	10" Boy Pilgrim	A. Thorndike	3,461	7.00	325.00
78-15-047	10" Boy Pilgrim	A. Thorndike	3,465	7.00	325.00
59-15-048	10" Boy Golfer	A. Thorndike	N/A	10.00	325.00
57-15-049	10" Girl Skier	A. Thorndike	N/A	15.00	1500.00
68-15-050	7" Fat Fanny	A. Thorndike	N/A	5.95	375.00
57-15-051	10" Casualty Ski Group	A. Thorndike	N/A	35.00	3100.00
68-15-052	10" Boy With Beachball	A. Thorndike	N/A	5.95	375.00
59-15-053	10" Boy Square Dancer	A. Thorndike	N/A	10.00	475.00
69-15-054	10" Nun On Skis	A. Thorndike	1,551	4.50	300.00
59-15-055	10" Girl Square Dancer	A. Thorndike	N/A	10.00	475.00
66-15-056	10" Boy Go-Go Dancer	A. Thorndike	N/A	10.00	275.00
57-15-057	10" Casualty Toboggan Group	A. Thorndike	N/A	35.00	900.00
58-15-058	10" Spring Doll	A. Thorndike	N/A	10.00	3500.00
59-15-059	10" Football Player	A. Thorndike	N/A	10.00	600.00
70-15-060	10" Monk With Skis	A. Thorndike	406	4.00	350.00
84-15-061	10" Aerobic Dancer	A. Thorndike	4,875	17.95	150.00
59-15-062	10" Boy & Girl in Fishing Boat	A. Thorndike	N/A	17.00	1000.00
69-15-063	22" Girl Go-Go Dancer	A. Thorndike	N/A	10.00	300.00
71-15-064	10" Nun On Skis	A. Thorndike	617	4.00	300.00
84-15-065	16" Monk With Jug	A. Thorndike	1,767	34.95	200.00
50-15-066	20" Boy & Girl Calypso Dancers	A. Thorndike	N/A	N/A	800.00
59-15-067	10" Dentist	A. Thorndike	N/A	10.00	600.00
59-15-068	10" Texas Oil Man	A. Thorndike	N/A	16.00	1550.00
60-15-069	33" Boy & Girl On Tandem Bike	A. Thorndike	N/A	N/A	3500.00
64-15-070	10" Gendarme	A. Thorndike	N/A	4.00	450.00
65-15-071	10" Back To School, Boy &Girl	A. Thorndike	N/A	19.90	525.00
66-15-072	10" Go-Go Boy &Girl	A. Thorndike	N/A	3.95	500.00
76-15-073	25" Yankee Doodle Dandy On 30" Horse	A. Thorndike	41	77.50	1600.00
89-15-074	10" Two Wisemen, Proof	A. Thorndike	1	N/A	350.00
89-15-075	10" Bob Cratchet &Tiny Tim, Proof	A. Thorndike	1	N/A	450.00
89-15-076	10" Pilgrim Couple, Proof	A. Thorndike	1	N/A	575.00
89-15-077	10" Merlin The Magician, Proof	A. Thorndike	1	N/A	500.00
89-15-078	10" Americana Couple, Proof	A. Thorndike	1	N/A	450.00
89-15-079	10" Wiseman With Camel, Proof	A. Thorndike	1	N/A	600.00
89-15-080	10" Jacob Marley, Proof	A. Thorndike	1	N/A	550.00
84-15-081	10" Downhill Skier	A. Thorndike	3,535	31.95	75.00
84-15-082	8" Monk With Jug	A. Thorndike	3,502	17.95	95.00
65-15-083	10"Monk With Christmas Tree Planting	A. Thorndike	N/A	3.00	275.00
59-15-084	10" Architect	A. Thorndike	N/A	N/A	700.00
57-15-085	10" Fourth Of July Doll	A. Thorndike	N/A	10.00	1600.00
91-15-086	10" Martha Cratchet, Proof	A. Thorndike	1	N/A	650.00
60-15-087	10" Girl Ski Doll	A. Thorndike	N/A	N/A	450.00
64-15-088	10" Monk With Cap	A. Thorndike	N/A	3.00	275.00
57-15-089	10" Skier With Leg In Cast Held By Two Skiers	A. Thorndike	N/A	35.00	1950.00
50-15-090	10" Boy & Girl Skiers	A. Thorndike	N/A	15.00	1250.00
57-15-091	10" Girl Square Dancer	A. Thorndike	N/A	9.95	475.00
57-15-092	10" Boy Square Dancer	A. Thorndike	N/A	9.95	475.00
54-15-093	10" Country Girl	A. Thorndike	N/A	8.95	1000.00
67-15-094	18" Nun	A. Thorndike	296	8.00	525.00
56-15-095	10" Water Skier Girl	A. Thorndike	N/A	9.95	800.00
84-15-096	32" Monk With Holly Garland	A. Thorndike	416	78.50	600.00
57-15-097	10" Valentine Doll	A. Thorndike	N/A	10.00	900.00
87-15-098	10" Huck Fin, #690	A. Thorndike	1,200	102.95	400.00
81-15-099	18" Monk w/Jug	A. Thorndike	494	N/A	290.00
67-15-100	10" Surfer Boy	A. Thorndike	N/A	9.95	400.00
67-15-101	10" Surfer Girl	A. Thorndike	N/A	9.95	400.00
60-15-102	10" Bathing Girl	A. Thorndike	N/A	3.95	300.00
67-15-103	18" Monk w/Plant	A. Thorndike	N/A	7.50	400.00
92-15-104	10" Father Time, proof	A. Thorndike	1	N/A	550.00
89-15-105	10" Merlin	A. Thorndike	3,565	69.95	300.00
71-15-106	10" Choir Girl	A. Thorndike	925	3.95	250.00
77-15-107	8" Drummer Boy	A. Thorndike	6,522	6.00	100.00
76-15-108	10" Uncle Sam	A. Thorndike	1,095	5.95	325.00
63-15-109	22" Bellhop (red)	A. Thorndike	N/A	N/A	700.00
64-15-110	10" Monk (green)	A. Thorndike	N/A	3.00	275.00
50-15-111	10" Frogman (girl diver)	A. Thorndike	N/A	9.95	3800.00
92-15-112	10" Bob Cratchet, proof	A. Thorndike	1	N/A	700.00
92-15-113	10" Scrooge, proof	A. Thorndike	1	N/A	650.00
92-15-114	10" Snow Queen, proof	A. Thorndike	1	N/A	925.00
54-15-115	10" Saks Fifth Ave. Skier	A. Thorndike	50	9.95	1500.00
53-15-116	Girl Water Skier	A. Thorndike	Unkn.	10.00	200.00
93-15-117	7" Girl Eating Turkey	A. Thorndike	N/A	38.95	38.95

Company Number	Name	Series Artist	Edition Limit	Issue Price	Quote
93-15-118	18" Man Skater	A. Thorndike	N/A	44.95	44.95
93-15-119	18" Woman Skater	A. Thorndike	N/A	44.95	44.95
Annalee Mobilitee Dolls		**Miscellaneous**			
84-16-001	10" Gingerbread Man	A. Thorndike	4,615	15.95	200.00
83-16-002	18" Gingerbread Man	A. Thorndike	5,027	28.95	250.00
82-16-003	22" Sun	A. Thorndike	838	Unkn.	200.00
83-16-004	22" Sun	A. Thorndike	Unkn.	Unkn.	75.00
76-16-005	42" Scarecrow	A. Thorndike	134	62.00	375.00
83-16-006	18" Scarecrow	A. Thorndike	3,150	32.95	175.00
84-16-007	10" Scarecrow	A. Thorndike	3,008	15.95	125.00
76-16-008	10" Scarecrow	A. Thorndike	2,341	6.00	200.00
83-16-009	18" Scarecrow	A. Thorndike	2,300	28.95	150.00
77-16-010	18" Scarecrow	A. Thorndike	Unkn.	13.50	175.00
85-16-011	10" Scarecrow	A. Thorndike	2,930	15.95	325.00
83-16-012	18" Scarecrow	A. Thorndike	3,896	32.95	200.00
76-16-013	10" Scarecrow	A. Thorndike	2,341	5.95	120.00
77-16-014	10" Scarecrow	A. Thorndike	4,879	5.95	225.00
81-16-015	18" Butterfly w/10" Elf	A. Thorndike	2,517	27.95	400.00
86-16-016	Large Pumpkin w/7" Witch M.	A. Thorndike	668	77.95	250.00
76-16-017	18" Scarecrow	A. Thorndike	916	13.50	250.00
70-16-018	14" Spring Mushroom	A. Thorndike	N/A	N/A	450.00
85-16-019	Christmas Tree Skirt	A. Thorndike	1,332	24.95	110.00
87-16-020	Carrot	A. Thorndike	2,503	9.95	300.00
93-16-021	Large Flower w/Face	A. Thorndike	N/A	20.95	20.95
93-16-022	Headless Horseman w/Pumpkin on Horse	A. Thorndike	N/A	56.95	56.95
93-16-023	Large Usable Pumpkin w/Removable Top	A. Thorndike	N/A	49.95	49.95
93-16-024	10" Snow Queen Tree Top	A. Thorndike	N/A	29.95	29.95
Annalee Mobilitee Dolls		**Doll Society-Folk Heroes**			
84-17-001	Robin Hood, Proof	A. Thorndike	1	N/A	1200.00
84-17-002	Johnny Appleseed, Proof	A. Thorndike	1	N/A	1000.00
85-17-003	Annie Oakley, Proof	A. Thorndike	1	N/A	1000.00
86-17-004	Mark Twain, Proof	A. Thorndike	1	N/A	1500.00
87-17-005	Ben Franklin, Proof	A. Thorndike	1	N/A	2100.00
88-17-006	Sherlock Holmes, Proof	A. Thorndike	1	N/A	1000.00
89-17-007	Abraham Lincoln, Proof	A. Thorndike	1	N/A	1350.00
90-17-008	Betsy Ross, Proof	A. Thorndike	1	N/A	1500.00
84-17-009	Robin Hood	A. Thorndike	1,500	80.00	N/A
84-17-010	Johnny Appleseed, #627	A. Thorndike	1,500	80.00	900.00
85-17-011	Annie Oakley, #185	A. Thorndike	1,500	95.00	700.00
86-17-012	Mark Twain, #467	A. Thorndike	2,500	119.50	500.00
87-17-013	Ben Franklin, #1776	A. Thorndike	2,500	119.50	525.00
88-17-014	Sherlock Holmes, #391	A. Thorndike	2,500	119.50	500.00
89-17-015	Abraham Lincoln, Current Item	A. Thorndike	2,500	119.50	119.50
90 17 016	Betsy Ross, Current Item	A. Thorndike	2,500	119.50	119.50
91-17-017	10" Christopher Columbus, Proof	A. Thorndike	1	N/A	1600.00
92-17-018	Uncle Sam	A. Thorndike	2,500	87.50	87.50
Annalee Mobilitee Dolls		**Doll Society-Logo Kids**			
85-18-001	7" Logo Kid, Proof	A. Thorndike	1	N/A	500.00
86-18-002	7" Logo Kid, Proof	A. Thorndike	1	N/A	575.00
87-18-003	7" Logo Kid, Proof	A. Thorndike	1	N/A	500.00
88-18-004	7" Logo Kid, Proof	A. Thorndike	1	N/A	400.00
89-18-005	7" Logo Kid, Proof	A. Thorndike	1	N/A	550.00
90-18-006	7" Logo Kid, Proof	A. Thorndike	1	N/A	850.00
85-18-007	7" Logo Kid	A. Thorndike	3,562	N/A	250.00
86-18-008	7" Logo Kid	A. Thorndike	6,271	N/A	175.00
87-18-009	7" Logo Kid	A. Thorndike	11,000	N/A	150.00
88-18-010	7" Logo Kid	A. Thorndike	N/A	N/A	100.00
89-18-011	7" Logo Kid	A. Thorndike	N/A	N/A	N/A
90-18-012	7" Logo Kid, Current Item	A. Thorndike	N/A	N/A	N/A
91-18-013	7" Logo Kid, Proof	A. Thorndike	1	N/A	775.00
92-18-014	Back to School Girl	A. Thorndike	N/A	24.95	24.95
Annalee Mobilitee Dolls		**Doll Society-Animals**			
85-19-001	10" Penguin With Chick, Proof	A. Thorndike	1	N/A	650.00
86-19-002	10" Unicorn, Proof	A. Thorndike	1	N/A	1050.00
87-19-003	10" Kangaroo, Proof	A. Thorndike	1	N/A	375.00
88-19-004	10" Owl, Proof	A. Thorndike	1	N/A	900.00
89-19-005	10" Polar Bear, Proof	A. Thorndike	1	N/A	1100.00
90-19-006	10" Chicken, Proof	A. Thorndike	1	N/A	1150.00
85-19-007	10" Penguin With Chick, #178	A. Thorndike	3,000	30.00	225.00
86-19-008	10" Unicorn, #268	A. Thorndike	3,000	36.50	350.00
87-19-009	7" Kangaroo	A. Thorndike	3,000	37.50	N/A
88-19-010	5" Owl	A. Thorndike	3,000	37.50	N/A
89-19-011	7" Polar Bear Cub, Current Item	A. Thorndike	3,000	37.50	N/A
90-19-012	7" Chicken, Current Item	A. Thorndike	3,000	37.50	N/A
91-19-013	10" World War II Aviator Frog, Proof	A. Thorndike	1	N/A	775.00
91-19-014	7" Sherrif Mouse, Proof	A. Thorndike	1	N/A	675.00
Annalee Mobilitee Dolls		**Commemoratives**			
66-20-001	10" Central Gas Co. Elf	A. Thorndike	N/A	N/A	350.00
61-20-002	10" Human Red Devil One-Of-A-Kind	A. Thorndike	1	N/A	450.00
81-20-003	7" "I'm Late Bunny"	A. Thorndike	N/A	N/A	575.00
66-20-004	5" New Hampton School Baby (Winter Carnival)	A. Thorndike	300	N/A	200.00
91-20-005	10" Victory Ski Doll, Proof	A. Thorndike	1	N/A	600.00
63-20-006	10" Bamboo Shop Girl	A. Thorndike	1	N/A	650.00
62-20-007	10" Two Realtor Dolls w/Land	A. Thorndike	1	N/A	875.00
ANRI		**Disney Dolls**			
89-01-001	Mickey Mouse, 14"	Disney Studios	Closed	850.00	895.00
89-01-002	Minnie Mouse, 14"	Disney Studios	Closed	850.00	895.00
89-01-003	Pinocchio, 14"	Disney Studios	Closed	850.00	895.00
90-01-004	Donald Duck, 14"	Disney Studios	Closed	895.00	895.00
90-01-005	Daisy Duck, 14"	Disney Studios	Closed	895.00	895.00
ANRI		**Sarah Kay Dolls**			
88-02-001	Jennifer, 14"	S. Kay	Closed	500.00	500.00
88-02-002	Rebecca, 14"	S. Kay	Closed	500.00	500.00
88-02-003	Sarah, 14"	S. Kay	Closed	500.00	500.00
88-02-004	Katherine, 14"	S. Kay	Closed	500.00	500.00
88-02-005	Martha, 14"	S. Kay	Closed	500.00	500.00
88-02-006	Emily, 14"	S. Kay	Closed	500.00	500.00
88-02-007	Rachael, 14"	S. Kay	Closed	500.00	500.00
88-02-008	Victoria, 14"	S. Kay	Closed	500.00	500.00
89-02-009	Bride to Love And To Cherish	S. Kay	750	750.00	775.00
89-02-010	Groom With This Ring Doll	S. Kay	750	550.00	575.00
89-02-011	Charlotte (Blue)	S. Kay	Closed	550.00	575.00
89-02-012	Henry	S. Kay	Closed	550.00	575.00
89-02-013	Elizabeth (Patchwork)	S. Kay	Closed	550.00	575.00
89-02-014	Helen (Brown)	S. Kay	Closed	550.00	575.00

Company Number	Name	Series Artist	Edition Limit	Issue Price	Quote
89-02-015	Eleanor (Floral)	S. Kay	Closed	550.00	575.00
89-02-016	Mary (Red)	S. Kay	Closed	550.00	575.00
90-02-017	Polly, 14"	S. Kay	1,000	575.00	680.00
90-02-018	Christina, 14"	S. Kay	1,000	575.00	730.00
90-02-019	Faith, 14"	S. Kay	1,000	575.00	685.00
90-02-020	Sophie, 14"	S. Kay	1,000	575.00	660.00
91-02-021	Jessica, 7"	S. Kay	1,500	300.00	300.00
91-02-022	Michelle, 7"	S. Kay	1,500	300.00	300.00
91-02-023	Peggy, 7"	S. Kay	1,500	300.00	300.00
91-02-024	Annie, 7"	S. Kay	1,500	300.00	300.00
91-02-025	Susan, 7"	S. Kay	1,500	300.00	300.00
91-02-026	Julie, 7"	S. Kay	1,500	300.00	300.00
91-02-027	Janine, 14"	S. Kay	1,500	750.00	750.00
91-02-028	Patricia, 14"	S. Kay	1,500	730.00	730.00
ANRI		**Ferrandiz Dolls**			
89-03-001	Gabriel, 14"	J. Ferrandiz	Closed	550.00	575.00
89-03-002	Maria, 14"	J. Ferrandiz	Closed	550.00	575.00
90-03-003	Margarite, 14"	J. Ferrandiz	1,000	575.00	730.00
90-03-004	Philipe, 14"	J. Ferrandiz	1,000	575.00	680.00
91-03-005	Carmen, 14"	J. Ferrandiz	1,000	730.00	730.00
91-03-006	Fernando, 14"	J. Ferrandiz	1,000	730.00	730.00
91-03-007	Miguel, 7"	J. Ferrandiz	1,500	300.00	300.00
91-03-008	Juanita, 7"	J. Ferrandiz	1,500	300.00	300.00
Artaffects		**Perillo Doll Collection**			
86-01-001	Morning Star (17-1/2")	G. Perillo	1,000	250.00	250.00
88-01-002	Sunflower (12")	G. Perillo	2,500	175.00	175.00
Artaffects		**Art Doll Collection**			
90-02-001	Little Dove (12")	G. Perillo	5,000	175.00	175.00
90-02-002	Straight Arrow (12")	G. Perillo	5,000	175.00	175.00
Artaffects		**Children of the Plains**			
92-03-001	Brave and Free (10" seated)	G. Perillo	Open	111.00	111.00
93-03-002	Song of Sioux (10" seated)	G. Perillo	Open	111.00	111.00
Ashton-Drake Galleries		**Yolanda's Picture - Perfect Babies**			
85-01-001	Jason	Y. Bello	Closed	48.00	750-1000.
86-01-002	Heather	Y. Bello	Closed	48.00	350-400.
87-01-003	Jennifer	Y. Bello	Closed	58.00	300-450.
87-01-004	Matthew	Y. Bello	Closed	58.00	225-350.
87-01-005	Sarah	Y. Bello	Closed	58.00	100-200.
88-01-006	Amanda	Y. Bello	Closed	63.00	125-225.
89-01-007	Jessica	Y. Bello	Closed	63.00	70-85.00
90-01-008	Michael	Y. Bello	Closed	63.00	100-150.
90-01-009	Lisa	Y. Bello	Closed	63.00	75-125.
91-01-010	Emily	Y. Bello	Closed	63.00	75-125.00
91-01-011	Danielle	Y. Bello	Closed	69.00	69.00
Ashton-Drake Galleries		**Children of Mother Goose**			
87-02-001	Little Bo Peep	Y. Bello	Closed	58.00	250-300.
87-02-002	Mary Had a Little Lamb	Y. Bello	Closed	58.00	175-225.
88-02-003	Little Jack Horner	Y. Bello	Closed	63.00	125-175.
89-02-004	Miss Muffet	Y. Bello	Closed	63.00	85-125.00
Ashton-Drake Galleries		**Yolanda's Lullaby Babies**			
91-03-001	Christy (Rock-a-Bye)	Y. Bello	Closed	69.00	69.00
92-03-002	Joey (Twinkle, Twinkle)	Y. Bello	12/93	69.00	69.00
93-03-003	Amy (Brahms Lullaby)	Y. Bello	12/93	75.00	75.00
93-03-004	Eddie (Teddy Bear Lullaby)	Y. Bello	12/93	75.00	75.00
93-03-005	Jacob (Silent Night)	Y. Bello	12/93	75.00	75.00
Ashton-Drake Galleries		**Moments To Remember**			
91-04-001	Justin	Y. Bello	Closed	75.00	75.00
92-04-002	Jill	Y. Bello	12/93	75.00	75.00
93-04-003	Brandon (Ring Bearer)	Y. Bello	12/93	79.95	79.95
93-04-004	Suzanne (Flower Girl)	Y. Bello	12/93	79.95	79.95
Ashton-Drake Galleries		**Yolanda's Precious Playmates**			
92-05-001	David	Y. Bello	Closed	69.95	69.95
93-05-002	Paul	Y. Bello	12/93	69.95	69.95
Ashton-Drake Galleries		**Parade of American Fashion**			
87-06-001	The Glamour of the Gibson Girl	Stevens/Siegel	Closed	77.00	225-300.
88-06-002	The Southern Belle	Stevens/Siegel	Closed	77.00	150-225.
90-06-003	Victorian Lady	Stevens/Siegel	Closed	82.00	125.00
91-06-004	Romantic Lady	Stevens/Siegel	Closed	85.00	85.00
Ashton-Drake Galleries		**Heroines from the Fairy Tale Forests**			
88-07-001	Little Red Riding Hood	D. Effner	Closed	68.00	150-295.
89-07-002	Goldilocks	D. Effner	Closed	68.00	78-150.00
90-07-003	Snow White	D. Effner	Closed	73.00	80-150.00
91-07-004	Rapunzel	D. Effner	Closed	79.00	100.00
92-07-005	Cinderella	D. Effner	Closed	79.00	79.00
93-07-006	Cinderella (Ballgown)	D. Effner	12/93	79.95	79.95
Ashton-Drake Galleries		**International Festival of Toys and Tots**			
89-08-001	Chen, a Little Boy of China	K. Hippensteel	Closed	78.00	150-300.
89-08-002	Natasha	K. Hippensteel	Closed	78.00	100.00
90-08-003	Molly	K. Hippensteel	Closed	83.00	83.00
91-08-004	Hans	K. Hippensteel	Closed	88.00	100.00
92-08-005	Miki, Eskimo	K. Hippensteel	Closed	88.00	88.00
Ashton-Drake Galleries		**Born To Be Famous**			
89-09-001	Little Sherlock	K. Hippensteel	Closed	87.00	110-125.
90-09-002	Little Florence Nightingale	K. Hippensteel	Closed	87.00	100.00
91-09-003	Little Davey Crockett	K. Hippensteel	Closed	92.00	92.00
92-09-004	Little Christopher Columbus	K. Hippensteel	12/93	95.00	110-145.
Ashton-Drake Galleries		**Baby Book Treasures**			
90-10-001	Elizabeth's Homecoming	K. Hippensteel	Closed	58.00	80.00
91-10-002	Catherine's Christening	K. Hippensteel	Closed	58.00	58.00
91-10-003	Christopher's First Smile	K. Hippensteel	Closed	63.00	63.00
Ashton-Drake Galleries		**Growing Young Minds**			
91-11-001	Alex	K. Hippensteel	12/93	79.00	79.00
Ashton-Drake Galleries		**Happiness Is...**			
91-12-001	Patricia (My First Tooth)	K. Hippensteel	Closed	69.00	69.00
92-12-002	Crystal	K. Hippensteel	12/93	69.95	69.95
93-12-003	Brittany (Blowing Kisses)	K. Hippensteel	12/93	69.95	69.95
93-12-004	Joy (My First Christmas)	K. Hippensteel	12/93	69.95	69.95

Company / Number	Name	Series / Artist	Edition Limit	Issue Price	Quote
Ashton-Drake Galleries		**Cindy's Playhouse Pals**			
89-13-001	Meagan	C. McClure	Closed	87.00	100-150.
89-13-002	Shelly	C. McClure	Closed	87.00	87-110.00
90-13-003	Ryan	C. McClure	Closed	89.00	89.00
91-13-004	Samantha	C. McClure	Closed	89.00	89.00
Ashton-Drake Galleries		**A Children's Circus**			
90-14-001	Tommy The Clown	J. McClelland	Closed	78.00	78-95.00
91-14-002	Katie The Tightrope Walker	J. McClelland	Closed	78.00	78.00
91-14-003	Johnnie The Strongman	J. McClelland	Closed	83.00	83.00
92-14-004	Maggie The Animal Trainer	J. McClelland	Closed	83.00	83.00
Ashton-Drake Galleries		**Maude Fangel's Cover Babies**			
90-15-001	Peek-A-Boo Peter	Fangel-Inspired	Closed	73.00	73.00
90-15-002	Benjamin's Ball	Fangel-Inspired	Closed	73.00	73.00
Ashton-Drake Galleries		**Amish Blessings**			
90-16-001	Rebeccah	J. Good-Kruger	Closed	68.00	68.00
91-16-002	Rachel	J. Good-Kruger	Closed	69.00	69.00
91-16-003	Adam	J. Good-Kruger	Closed	75.00	75.00
92-16-004	Ruth	J. Good-Kruger	12/93	75.00	75.00
92-16-005	Eli	J. Good-Kruger	12/93	79.95	79.95
Ashton-Drake Galleries		**Polly's Tea Party**			
90-17-001	Polly	S. Krey	Closed	78.00	90-125.00
91-17-002	Lizzie	S. Krey	Closed	79.00	79.00
92-17-003	Annie	S. Krey	12/93	83.00	83.00
Ashton-Drake Galleries		**Yesterday's Dreams**			
90-18-001	Andy	M. Oldenburg	Closed	68.00	68.00
91-18-002	Janey	M. Oldenburg	Closed	69.00	69.00
Ashton-Drake Galleries		**My Closest Friend**			
91-19-001	Boo Bear 'N Me	J. Goodyear	Closed	78.00	100-150.
91-19-002	Me and My Blankie	J. Goodyear	Closed	79.00	79.00
93-19-003	My Secret Pal (Robbie)	J. Goodyear	12/93	85.00	85.00
93-19-004	My Beary Best Friend	J. Goodyear	12/93	79.95	79.95
Ashton-Drake Galleries		**The Littlest Clowns**			
91-20-001	Sparkles	M. Tretter	Closed	63.00	63.00
91-20-002	Bubbles	M. Tretter	Closed	65.00	65.00
91-20-003	Smooch	M. Tretter	Closed	69.00	69.00
92-20-004	Daisy	M. Tretter	12/93	69.95	69.95
Ashton Drake Galleries		**Romantic Flower Maidens**			
88-21-001	Rose, Who is Love	M. Roderick	Closed	87.00	135-195.
89-21-002	Daisy	M. Roderick	Closed	87.00	87-150.00
90-21-003	Violet	M. Roderick	Closed	92.00	92.00
90-21-004	Lily	M. Roderick	Closed	92.00	105-175.
Ashton-Drake Galleries		**Precious Memories of Motherhood**			
90-22-001	Loving Steps	S. Kuck	Closed	125.00	150-195.
90-22-002	Lullaby	S. Kuck	Closed	125.00	125.00
91-22-003	Expectant Moments	S. Kuck	Closed	149.00	149.00
92-22-004	Bedtime	S. Kuck	12/93	149.95	149.95
Ashton-Drake Galleries		**Brides of The Century**			
90-23-001	Flora, The 1900s Bride	E. Williams	Closed	145.00	145.00
91-23-002	Jennifer, The 1980s Bride	E. Williams	Closed	149.00	149.00
92-23-003	Cathleen, The 1990s Bride	E. Williams	12/93	149.95	149.95
Ashton-Drake Galleries		**My Fair Lady**			
91-24-001	Eliza at Ascot	P. Ryan Brooks	Closed	125.00	225-400.
Ashton-Drake Galleries		**The King & I**			
91-25-001	Shall We Dance?	P. Ryan Brooks	Closed	175.00	285-450.
Ashton-Drake Galleries		**Stepping Out**			
91-26-001	Millie	Akers/Girardi	Closed	99.00	99-225.00
Ashton-Drake Galleries		**Year Book Memories**			
91-27-001	Peggy Sue	Akers/Girardi	Closed	87.00	87.00
93-27-002	Going Steady	Akers/Girardi	12/93	89.95	89.95
Ashton-Drake Galleries		**Winterfest**			
91-28-001	Brian	S. Sherwood	Closed	89.00	125.00
92-28-002	Michelle	S. Sherwood	12/93	89.95	89.95
93-28-003	Bradley	S. Sherwood	12/93	89.95	89.95
Ashton-Drake Galleries		**Dianna Effner's Mother Goose**			
90-29-001	Mary, Mary, Quite Contrary	D. Effner	Closed	78.00	110-250.
91-29-002	The Little Girl With The Curl (Horrid)	D. Effner	Closed	79.00	100-150.
91-29-003	The Little Girl With The Curl (Good)	D. Effner	Closed	79.00	79-110.00
93-29-004	Little Boy Blue	D. Effner	12/93	85.00	85.00
93-29-005	Snips & Snails	D. Effner	12/93	85.00	85.00
93-29-006	Sugar & Spice	D. Effner	12/93	89.95	89.95
Ashton-Drake Galleries		**A Child's Garden of Verses**			
91-30-001	Nathan (The Land of Nod)	J. Singer	Closed	79.00	79.00
93-30-002	My Toy Soldiers	J. Singer	12/93	79.95	79.95
93-30-003	Picture Books in Winter	J. Singer	12/93	85.00	85.00
93-30-004	My Ship & I	J. Singer	12/93	85.00	85.00
Ashton-Drake Galleries		**Down The Garden Path**			
91-31-001	Rosemary	P. Coffer	Closed	79.00	79.00
91-31-002	Angelica	P. Coffer	12/93	85.00	85.00
93-31-003	Amanda by the Shore	P. Coffer	12/93	89.95	89.95
Ashton-Drake Galleries		**Beautiful Dreamers**			
92-32-001	Katrina	G. Rademann	Closed	89.00	89.00
92-32-002	Nicolette	G. Rademann	12/93	89.95	89.95
93-32-003	Brigitte	G. Rademann	12/93	94.00	94.00
93-32-004	Isabella	G. Rademann	12/93	94.00	94.00
Ashton-Drake Galleries		**Great Moments From Hollywood**			
91-33-001	Shall We Dance?	P. Brooks	Closed	175.00	175.00
Ashton-Drake Galleries		**International Spirit Of Christmas**			
89-34-001	American Santa	F. Wick	Closed	125.00	125.00
Ashton-Drake Galleries		**From The Heart**			
92-35-001	Carolin	T. Menzenbach	Closed	79.95	79.95
92-35-002	Erik	T. Menzenbach	12/93	79.95	79.95
Ashton-Drake Galleries		**Little House On The Prarie**			
92-36-001	Laura	J. Ibarolle	12/93	79.95	79.95
93-36-002	Mary Ingalls	J. Ibarolle	12/93	79.95	79.95
93-36-003	Nellie Olson	J. Ibarolle	12/93	85.00	85.00
93-36-004	Almanzo	J. Ibarolle	12/93	85.00	85.00
Ashton-Drake Galleries		**Rockwell Christmas**			
90-37-001	Scotty Plays Santa	Rockwell-Inspired	Closed	48.00	48.00
91-37-002	Scotty Gets His Tree	Rockwell-Inspired	Closed	59.00	59.00
93-37-003	Merry Christmas Grandma	Rockwell-Inspired	12/93	59.95	59.95
Ashton-Drake Galleries		**Holy Hunt's Bonnet Babies**			
91-38-001	Missy (Grandma's Little Girl)	H. Hunt	Closed	69.00	69.00
92-38-002	Susie (Somebody Loves Me)	H. Hunt	12/93	69.00	69.00
Ashton-Drake Galleries		**Heavenly Inspirations**			
92-39-001	Every Cloud Has a Silver Lining	C. MC Clure	12/93	59.95	59.95
93-39-002	Wish Upon A Star	C. MC Clure	12/93	59.95	59.95
Ashton-Drake Galleries		**Elvis: Lifetime Of A Legend**			
92-40-001	'68 Comeback	L. Di Leo	12/93	99.95	99.95
Ashton-Drake Galleries		**Caught In The Act**			
92-41-001	Stevie, Catch Me If You Can	M. Tretter	12/93	49.95	49.95
93-41-002	Kelly, Don't I Look Pretty?	M. Tretter	12/93	49.95	49.95
Ashton-Drake Galleries		**Your Heart's Desire**			
91-42-001	Julia	M. Stauber	Closed	99.00	99.00
Ashton-Drake Galleries		**My Heart Belongs To Daddy**			
93-43-001	Peanut	J. Singer	12/93	49.95	49.95
93-43-002	Pumpkin	J. Singer	12/93	49.95	49.95
Ashton-Drake Galleries		**Yolanda's Playtime Babies**			
93-44-001	Todd	Y. Bello	12/93	59.95	59.95
Ashton-Drake Galleries		**Little Bits**			
93-45-001	Lil Bit of Sunshine	G. Rademann	12/94	39.95	39.95
93-45-002	Lil Bit of Love	G. Rademann	12/94	39.95	39.95
Ashton-Drake Galleries		**Victorian Lace**			
93-46-001	Alicia	C. Layton	12/94	89.95	89.95
Ashton-Drake Galleries		**Father's Touch**			
93-47-001	2 A.M. Feeding	L. Di Leo	12/94	99.95	99.95
Ashton-Drake Galleries		**Big Imaginations**			
93-48-001	Fire's Out	J. Singer	12/93	69.95	69.95
93-48-002	Call Me Tex	J. Singer	12/94	69.95	69.95
Ashton-Drake Galleries		**Lasting Traditions**			
93-49-001	Something Old	W. Hanson	12/94	69.95	69.95
Ashton-Drake Galleries		**Joys of Summer**			
93-50-001	Tickles	K. Hippensteel	12/93	49.95	49.95
93-50-002	Yummy	K. Hippensteel	12/93	49.95	49.95
Ashton-Drake Galleries		**A Sense of Discovery**			
93-51-001	Sweetie	K. Hippensteel	12/93	59.95	59.95
Ashton-Drake Galleries		**I Want Mommy**			
93-52-001	Timmy (Mommy I'm Sleepy)	K. Hippensteel	12/93	59.95	59.95
93-52-002	Tommy (Mommy I'm Sorry)	K. Hippensteel	12/93	59.95	59.95
Band Creations		**Pat Wilson's Original Santas**			
92-01-001	Victorian Father Christmas	P. Wilson	200	370.00	370.00
92-01-002	Victorian Long Beard	P. Wilson	200	370.00	370.00
92-01-003	Victorian, white	P. Wilson	200	370.00	370.00
92-01-004	Seaside Santa, large	P. Wilson	200	370.00	370.00
92-01-005	Long Beard, small	P. Wilson	200	170.00	170.00
92-01-006	Seaside Santa, small	P. Wilson	200	170.00	170.00
92-01-007	Victorian, small	P. Wilson	200	170.00	170.00
The Collectables Inc.		**The Collectibles Inc. Dolls**			
86-01-001	Tatiana	P. Parkins	1,000	270.00	800-1200.
87-01-002	Tasha	P. Parkins	1,000	290.00	1400.00
87-01-003	Storytime By Sarah Jane	P. Parkins	1,000	330.00	500.00
89-01-004	Michelle	P. Parkins	250	270.00	400-450.
89-01-005	Welcome Home	D. Effner	1,000	330.00	465.00
90-01-006	Lizbeth Ann	D. Effner	1,000	420.00	420.00
90-01-007	Bassinet Baby	P. Parkins	2,000	130.00	130.00
90-01-008	Danielle	P. Parkins	1,000	400.00	400.00
90-01-009	In Your Easter Bonnet	P. Parkins	1,000	350.00	350.00
91-01-010	Yvette	P. Parkins	300	580.00	580.00
91-01-011	Lauren	P. Parkins	S/O	490.00	490.00
91-01-012	Bethany	P. Parkins	Closed	450.00	450.00
91-01-013	Natasha	P. Parkins	Closed	510.00	510.00
91-01-014	Adrianna	P. Parkins	Closed	1350.00	1350.00
91-01-015	Kelsie	P. Parkins	500	320.00	320.00
92-01-016	Karlie	P. Parkins	500	380.00	380.00
92-01-017	Marissa	P. Parkins	300	350.00	350.00
92-01-018	Shelley	P. Parkins	300	450.00	450.00
92-01-019	Angel on My Shoulder (Lillianne w/CeCe)	P. Parkins	500	530.00	530.00
92-01-020	Molly	P. Parkins	450	350.00	350.00
92-01-021	Matia	P. Parkins	250	190.00	190.00
92-01-022	Marty	P. Parkins	250	190.00	190.00
92-01-023	Missy	P. Parkins	Open	59.00	59.00
The Collectables Inc.		**Mother's Little Treasures**			
85-02-001	1st Edition	D. Effner	1,000	380.00	700.00
90-02-002	2nd Edition	D. Effner	1,000	440.00	600.00
The Collectables Inc.		**Yesterday's Child**			
82-03-001	Jason And Jessica	D. Effner	1,000	150.00	300.00
82-03-002	Cleo	D. Effner	1,000	180.00	250.00
82-03-003	Columbine	D. Effner	1,000	180.00	250.00
83-03-004	Chad And Charity	D. Effner	1,000	190.00	190.00
83-03-005	Noel	D. Effner	1,000	190.00	240.00
84-03-006	Kevin And Karissa	D. Effner	1,000	190.00	250-300.
84-03-007	Rebecca	D. Effner	1,000	250.00	250-300.
86-03-008	Todd And Tiffany	D. Effner	1,000	220.00	250.00
86-03-009	Ashley	P. Parkins	1,000	220.00	275.00

Company / Number	Name	Series / Artist	Edition Limit	Issue Price	Quote
The Collectables Inc.		**Cherished Memories**			
86-04-001	Amy And Andrew	P. Parkins	1,000	220.00	325.00
88-04-002	Jennifer	P. Parkins	1,000	380.00	500-600.
88-04-003	Brittany	P. Parkins	1,000	240.00	300.00
88-04-004	Heather	P. Parkins	1,000	280.00	300-350.
88-04-005	Leigh Ann And Leland	P. Parkins	1,000	250.00	250-300.
88-04-006	Tea Time	D. Effner	1,000	380.00	450.00
90-04-007	Cassandra	P. Parkins	Closed	500.00	550.00
89-04-008	Generations	P. Parkins	1,000	480.00	500.00
90-04-009	Twinkles	P. Parkins	Closed	170.00	275.00
The Collectables Inc.		**Fairy**			
88-05-001	Tabatha	P. Parkins	1,500	370.00	400-450.
The Collectables Inc.		**Butterfly Babies**			
89-06-001	Belinda	P. Parkins	Closed	270.00	375.00
90-06-002	Willow	P. Parkins	Closed	240.00	240.00
92-06-003	Laticia	P. Parkins	500	320.00	320.00
The Collectables Inc.		**Enchanted Children**			
90-07-001	Kristin	P. Parkins	S/O	550.00	650.00
90-07-002	Tiffy	P. Parkins	S/O	370.00	500.00
90-07-003	Kara	P. Parkins	Closed	550.00	550.00
90-07-004	Katlin	P. Parkins	Closed	550.00	550.00
The Collectables Inc.		**Collector's Club Doll**			
90-08-001	Mandy	P. Parkins	Closed	360.00	360.00
91-08-002	Kallie	P. Parkins	Closed	410.00	410.00
92-08-003	Mommy and Me	P. Parkins	Yr.Iss.	810.00	810.00
The Collectables Inc.		**Tiny Treasures**			
91-09-001	Little Girl	P. Parkins	1,000	140.00	140.00
91-09-002	Toddler Girl	P. Parkins	1,000	130.00	130.00
91-09-003	Toddler Boy	P. Parkins	1,000	130.00	130.00
91-09-004	Victorian Girl	P. Parkins	1,000	150.00	150.00
91-09-005	Victorian Boy	P. Parkins	1,000	150.00	150.00
91-09-006	Holly	P. Parkins	1,000	150.00	150.00
92-09-007	Nicole	P. Parkins	500	180.00	180.00
92-09-008	Nicolaus	P. Parkins	500	160.00	160.00
92-09-009	Tori	P. Parkins	1,000	170.00	170.00
92-09-010	Tommie	P. Parkins	1,000	160.00	160.00
The Collectables Inc.		**Limited Edition Vinyl Dolls**			
92-10-001	Jessica	P. Parkins	2,500	190.00	190.00
92-10-002	Jenny and Jeremy (Puppy Love)	P. Parkins	2,500	180.00	180.00
92-10-003	Brent	P. Parkins	2,500	190.00	190.00
92-10-004	Annie	P. Parkins	2,500	190.00	190.00
92-10-005	Brenda (Blue Dress)	P. Parkins	2,500	180.00	180.00
92-10-006	Brenda (Spring)	P. Parkins	250	240.00	240.00
92-10-007	Brenda (Christmas)	P. Parkins	250	240.00	240.00
Department 56		**Heritage Village Doll Collection**			
87-01-001	Christmas Carol Dolls1000-6 4/set (Tiny Tim, Bob Crachet, Mrs. Crachet, Scrooge)	Department 56	250	1500.00	1500.00
87-01-002	Christmas Carol Dolls5907-2 4/set(Tiny Tim, Bob Crachet, Mrs. Crachet, Scrooge)	Department 56	Open	250.00	250.00
88-01-003	Christmas Carol Dolls1001-4 4/set(Tiny Tim, Bob Crachet, Mrs. Crachet, Scrooge)	Department 56	350	1600.00	1600.00
88-01-004	Mr. & Mrs. Fezziwig 5594-8-Set of 2	Department 56	Open	172.00	172.00
Department 56		**Snowbabies Dolls**			
88-02-001	Allison & Duncan- Set of 2, 7730-5	Department 56	Closed	200.00	200-500.
Dolls by Jerri		**Dolls by Jerri**			
84-01-001	Clara	J. McCloud	1,000	320.00	1500.00
84-01-002	Emily	J. McCloud	1,000	330.00	2400-3500.
85-01-003	Scotty	J. McCloud	1,000	340.00	1200-2000.
85-01-004	Uncle Joe	J. McCloud	1,000	160.00	250-300.
85-01-005	Miss Nanny	J. McCloud	1,000	160.00	250-300.
85-01-006	Bride	J. McCloud	1,000	350.00	350-400.
86-01-007	David-2 Years Old	J. McCloud	1,000	330.00	550.00
86-01-008	Princess and the Unicorn	J. McCloud	1,000	370.00	370.00
86-01-009	Charlotte	J. McCloud	1,000	330.00	450-500.
86-01-010	Cane	J. McCloud	1,000	350.00	1200.00
86-01-011	Clown-David 3 Yrs. Old	J. McCloud	1,000	340.00	450.00
86-01-012	Tammy	J. McCloud	1,000	350.00	900.00
86-01-013	Samantha	J. McCloud	1,000	350.00	500.00
86-01-014	Elizabeth	J. McCloud	1,000	340.00	340.00
86-01-015	Audrey	J. McCloud	300	550.00	550.00
86-01-016	Yvonne	J. McCloud	300	500.00	500.00
86-01-017	Annabelle	J. McCloud	300	600.00	600.00
86-01-018	Ashley	J. McCloud	1,000	350.00	450-500.
86-01-019	Allison	J. McCloud	1,000	350.00	450-500.
86-01-020	Nobody	J. McCloud	1,000	350.00	550.00
86-01-021	Somebody	J. McCloud	1,000	350.00	550.00
86-01-022	Danielle	J. McCloud	1,000	350.00	500.00
86-01-023	Helenjean	J. McCloud	1,000	350.00	500-550.
86-01-024	David-Magician	J. McCloud	1,000	350.00	350-500.
86-01-025	Amber	J. McCloud	1,000	350.00	875.00
86-01-026	Joy	J. McCloud	1,000	350.00	350.00
86-01-027	Mary Beth	J. McCloud	1,000	350.00	350.00
86-01-028	Jacqueline	J. McCloud	300	500.00	500.00
86-01-029	Lucianna	J. McCloud	300	500.00	500.00
86-01-030	Bridgette	J. McCloud	300	500.00	500.00
86-01-031	The Fool	J. McCloud	1,000	350.00	350.00
86-01-032	Alfalfa	J. McCloud	1,000	350.00	350.00
85-01-033	Candy	J. McCloud	1,000	340.00	1000-2000.
82-01-034	Baby David	J. McCloud	538	290.00	2000.00
88-01-035	Holly	J. McCloud	1,000	370.00	750-825.
89-01-036	Laura Lee	J. McCloud	1,000	370.00	575.00
XX-01-037	Boy	J. McCloud	1,000	350.00	425.00
XX-01-038	Uncle Remus	J. McCloud	500	290.00	400-450.
XX-01-039	Gina	J. McCloud	1,000	350.00	475.00
XX-01-040	Laura	J. McCloud	1,000	350.00	425-500.
89-01-041	Goose Girl, Guild	J. McCloud	Closed	300.00	700-875.
XX-01-042	Little Bo Peep	J. McCloud	1,000	340.00	395-450.
XX-01-043	Little Miss Muffet	J. McCloud	1,000	340.00	395-450.
XX-01-044	Megan	J. McCloud	750	420.00	550.00
XX-01-045	Denise	J. McCloud	1,000	380.00	550.00
XX-01-046	Meredith	J. McCloud	750	430.00	600.00
XX-01-047	Goldilocks	J. McCloud	1,000	370.00	450-600.
XX-01-048	Jamie	J. McCloud	800	380.00	450.00
Dynasty Doll		**Annual**			
89-01-001	Amber	Unknown	Yr.Iss.	90.00	90.00
90-01-002	Marcella	Unknown	Yr.Iss.	90.00	90.00
91-01-003	Butterfly Princess	Unknown	Yr.Iss.	110.00	110.00
93-01-004	Annual Bride	H. Tertsakian	Yr.Iss.	190.00	190.00
Dynasty Doll		**Christmas**			
87-02-001	Merrie	Unknown	3,500	60.00	60.00
88-02-002	Noel	Unknown	3,500	80.00	80.00
90-02-003	Faith	Unknown	5,000	110.00	110.00
91-02-004	Joy	Unknown	5,000	125.00	125.00
Dynasty Doll		**Ballerina Series**			
91-03-001	Masha-Nutcracker	Lee Po Nan	7,500	190.00	190.00
93-03-002	Tina Ballerina	K. Henderson	Open	175.00	175.00
Dynasty Doll		**Anna Collection**			
92-04-001	Pocahontas	Unknown	3,500	95.00	95.00
92-04-002	Communion Girl	G. Hoyt	Yr.Iss.	125.00	125.00
Dynasty Doll		**Dynasty Collection**			
91-05-001	Lana	Unknown	Open	85.00	85.00
93-05-002	Tami	M. Cohen	7,500	190.00	190.00
93-05-003	Tory	M. Cohen	7,500	190.00	190.00
93-05-004	Juliet	G. Tepper	2,500	160.00	160.00
93-05-005	Heather	G. Tepper	2,500	160.00	160.00
Elke's Originals, Ltd.		**Elke Hutchens**			
89-01-001	Annabelle	E. Hutchens	250	575.00	1295.00
90-01-002	Aubra	E. Hutchens	250	575.00	1295.00
90-01-003	Aurora	E. Hutchens	250	595.00	1295.00
91-01-004	Alicia	E. Hutchens	250	595.00	1295.00
91-01-005	Braelyn	E. Hutchens	400	595.00	1150-1500.
91-01-006	Bellinda	E. Hutchens	400	595.00	800-1000.
91-01-007	Brianna	E. Hutchens	400	595.00	1000.00
92-01-008	Bethany	E. Hutchens	400	595.00	1000.00
92-01-009	Cecilia	E. Hutchens	435	635.00	950.00
92-01-010	Cherie	E. Hutchens	435	635.00	N/A
90-01-011	Little Liebchen	E. Hutchens	250	475.00	1000.00
90-01-012	Victoria	E. Hutchens	500	645.00	N/A
90-01-013	Kricket	E. Hutchens	500	575.00	1000.00
Enesco Corporation		**Precious Moments Dolls**			
81-01-001	Mikey, 18"- E-6214B	S. Butcher	Suspd.	150.00	225.00
81-01-002	Debbie, 18"- E-6214G	S. Butcher	Suspd.	150.00	235.00
82-01-003	Cubby, 18"- E-7267B	S. Butcher	5,000	200.00	450.00
82-01-004	Tammy, 18"- E-7267G	S. Butcher	5,000	300.00	675-700.
83-01-005	Katie Lynne, 16"- E-0539	S. Butcher	Suspd.	165.00	175-185.
84-01-006	Mother Sew Dear, 18"- E-2850	S. Butcher	Retrd.	350.00	350-375.
84-01-007	Kristy, 12"- E-2851	S. Butcher	Suspd.	150.00	185.00
84-01-008	Timmy, 12"- E-5397	S. Butcher	Open	125.00	150-175.
85-01-009	Aaron, 12"- 12424	S. Butcher	Suspd.	135.00	150.00
85-01-010	Bethany, 12"- 12432	S. Butcher	Suspd.	135.00	150.00
85-01-011	P.D., 7"- 12475	S. Butcher	Suspd.	50.00	75.00
85-01-012	Trish, 7" - 12483	S. Butcher	Suspd.	50.00	95.00
86-01-013	Bong Bong, 13" - 100455	S. Butcher	12,000	150.00	225.00
86-01-014	Candy, 13" - 100463	S. Butcher	12,000	150.00	250.00
86-01-015	Connie, 12" - 102253	S. Butcher	7,500	160.00	225.00
87-01-016	Angie, The Angel of Mercy - 12491	S. Butcher	12,500	160.00	200.00
90-01-017	The Voice of Spring-408786	S. Butcher	2 Yr.	150.00	150.00
90-01-018	Summer's Joy-408794	S. Butcher	2 Yr.	150.00	150.00
90-01-019	Autumn's Praise-408808	S. Butcher	2 Yr.	150.00	150.00
90-01-020	Winter's Song-408816	S. Butcher	2 Yr.	150.00	150.00
91-01-021	You HaveTouched So Many Hearts-427527	S. Butcher	2 Yr.	90.00	90.00
91-01-022	May You Have An Old Fashioned Christmas-417785	S. Butcher	2 Yr.	150.00	150.00
91-01-023	The Eyes Of The Lord Are Upon You (Boy, Action Musical)-429570	S. Butcher	Open	65.00	65.00
91-01-024	The Eyes Of The Lord Are Upon You (Girl, Action Musical)-429589	S. Butcher	Open	65.00	65.00
Enesco Corporation		**Precious Moments-Jack-In-The-Boxes**			
91-02-001	You Have Touched So Many Hearts-422282	S. Butcher	2 Yr.	175.00	175.00
91-02-002	May You Have An Old Fashioned Christmas-417777	S. Butcher	2 Yr.	200.00	200.00
Enesco Corporation		**Jack-In-The-Boxes-4 Seasons**			
90-03-001	Voice of Spring-408735	S. Butcher	2 Yr.	200.00	200.00
90-03-002	Summer's Joy-408743	S. Butcher	2 Yr.	200.00	200.00
90-03-003	Autumn's Praise-408751	S. Butcher	2 Yr.	200.00	200.00
90-03-004	Winter's Song-408778	S. Butcher	2 Yr.	200.00	200.00
Fitz and Floyd, Inc.		**Wonderland Floppy Folks™**			
93-01-001	The Mad Hatter	R. Havins	3,000	60.00	60.00
93-01-002	The Cheshire Cat	R. Havins	3,000	60.00	60.00
93-01-003	The White Rabbit	R. Havins	3,000	60.00	60.00
Fitz and Floyd, Inc.		**Bloomers Floppy Folks™**			
93-01-001	Peony	M. Collins	Open	50.00	50.00
93-01-002	Bloomer	M. Collins	Open	50.00	50.00
Ganz/Little Cheesers		**Cheeserville Picnic Collection**			
92-01-001	Sweet Cicely Musical Doll In Basket	G.D.A. Group	Open	85.00	85.00
Georgetown Collection, Inc.		**Nursery Babies**			
90-01-001	Baby Bunting	T. DeHetre	Closed	118.20	225.00
90-01-002	Patty Cake	T. DeHetre	Closed	118.20	118.20
91-01-003	Diddle, Diddle	T. DeHetre	Closed	118.20	118.20
91-01-004	Little Girl	T. DeHetre	100-day	118.20	118.20
91-01-005	This Little Piggy	T. DeHetre	100-day	118.20	118.20
Georgetown Collection, Inc.		**Baby Kisses**			
92-02-001	Michelle	T. DeHetre	100-day	118.60	118.60
Georgetown Collection, Inc.		**Let's Play**			
92-03-001	Peek-A-Boo Beckie	T. DeHetre	100-day	118.60	118.60
92-03-002	Eentsy Weentsy Willie	T. DeHetre	100-day	118.60	118.60
Georgetown Collection, Inc.		**Sugar & Spice**			
91-04-001	Little Sweetheart	L. Mason	100-day	118.25	118.25
91-04-002	Red Hot Pepper	L. Mason	100-day	118.25	118.25
92-04-003	Little Sunshine	L. Mason	100-day	141.10	141.10

Company Number	Name	Series Artist	Edition Limit	Issue Price	Quote
Georgetown Collection, Inc.		**American Diary Dolls**			
90-05-001	Jennie Cooper	L. Mason	100-day	129.25	129.25
91-05-002	Bridget Quinn	L. Mason	100-day	129.25	129.25
91-05-003	Christina Merovina	L. Mason	100-day	129.25	129.25
91-05-004	Many Stars	L. Mason	100-day	129.25	129.25
92-05-005	Rachel Williams	L. Mason	100-day	129.25	129.25
92-05-006	Tulu	L. Mason	100-day	129.25	129.25
Georgetown Collection, Inc.		**Little Loves**			
90-06-001	Laura	B. Deval	Closed	139.20	139.20
89-06-002	Katie	B. Deval	Closed	139.20	139.20
88-06-003	Emma	B. Deval	Closed	139.20	139.20
89-06-004	Megan	B. Deval	Closed	138.00	160.00
Georgetown Collection, Inc.		**Small Wonders**			
90-07-001	Corey	B. Deval	100-day	97.60	97.60
91-07-002	Abbey	B. Deval	100-day	97.60	97.60
92-07-003	Sarah	B. Deval	100-day	97.60	97.60
Georgetown Collection, Inc.		**Faerie Princess**			
89-08-001	Faerie Princess	B. Deval	Closed	248.00	248.00
Georgetown Collection, Inc.		**Miss Ashley**			
89-09-001	Miss Ashley	P. Thompson	Closed	228.00	228.00
Georgetown Collection, Inc.		**Tansie**			
88-10-001	Tansie	P. Coffer	Closed	81.00	81.00
Georgetown Collection, Inc.		**Kindergarten Kids**			
92-11-001	Nikki	V. Walker	100-day	129.60	129.60
Georgetown Collection, Inc.		**Portraits of Perfection**			
93-12-001	Peaches & Cream	A. Timmerman	100-day	149.60	149.60
Georgetown Collection, Inc.		**Hearts in Song**			
92-13-002	Grace	J. Galperin	100-day	149.60	149.60
Goebel, Inc.		**Victoria Ashlea Originals**			
88-01-001	Campbell Kid-Girl-758700	B. Ball	Closed	13.80	13.80
88-01-002	Campbell Kid-Boy-758701	B. Ball	Closed	13.80	13.80
84-01-003	Claude-901032	B. Ball	Closed	110.00	225.00
84-01-004	Claudette-901033	B. Ball	Closed	110.00	225.00
84-01-005	Henri-901035	B. Ball	Closed	100.00	200.00
84-01-006	Henrietta-901036	B. Ball	Closed	100.00	200.00
84-01-007	Jeannie-901062	B. Ball	Closed	200.00	550.00
84-01-008	Victoria-901068	B. Ball	Closed	200.00	1500.00
84-01-009	Laura-901106	B. Ball	Closed	300.00	575.00
83-01-010	Deborah-901107	B. Ball	Closed	220.00	400.00
84-01-011	Barbara-901108	B. Ball	Closed	57.00	110.00
84-01-012	Diana-901119	B. Ball	Closed	55.00	135.00
84-01-013	Clown-901136	B. Ball	Closed	90.00	120.00
84-01-014	Sabina-901155	B. Ball	Closed	75.00	N/A
85-01-015	Dorothy-901157	B. Ball	Closed	130.00	275.00
85-01-016	Claire-901158	B. Ball	Closed	115.00	160.00
85-01-017	Adele-901172	B. Ball	Closed	145.00	275.00
85-01-018	Roxanne-901174	B. Ball	Closed	155.00	275.00
86-01-019	Gina-901176	B. Ball	Closed	300.00	300.00
86-01-020	Cat/Kitty Cheerful Gr Dr-901179	B. Ball	Closed	60.00	60.00
85-01-021	Garnet-901183	B. Ball	Closed	160.00	295.00
86-01-022	Pepper Rust Dr/Appr-901184	B. Ball	Closed	125.00	200.00
86-01-023	Patty Artic Flower Print-901185	B. Ball	Closed	140.00	140.00
87-01-024	Lillian-901199	B. Ball	Closed	85.00	100.00
87-01-025	Suzanne-901200	B. Ball	Closed	85.00	100.00
87-01-026	Kitty Cuddles-901201	B. Ball	Closed	65.00	65.00
87-01-027	Bonnie Pouty-901207	B. Ball	Closed	100.00	100.00
87-01-028	Amanda Pouty-901209	B. Ball	Closed	150.00	215.00
87-01-029	Tiffany Pouty-901211	B. Ball	Closed	120.00	160.00
87-01-030	Alice-901212	B. Ball	Closed	95.00	135.00
88-01-031	Elizabeth-901214	B. Ball	Closed	90.00	90.00
87-01-032	Bride Allison-901218	B. Ball	Closed	180.00	180.00
87-01-033	Dominique-901219	B. Ball	Closed	170.00	225.00
87-01-034	Sarah-901220	B. Ball	Closed	350.00	350.00
87-01-035	Tasha-901221	B. Ball	Closed	115.00	130.00
87-01-036	Michelle-901222	B. Ball	Closed	90.00	90.00
87-01-037	Nicole-901225	B. Ball	Closed	575.00	575.00
87-01-038	Clementine-901226	B. Ball	Closed	75.00	75.00
87-01-039	Catanova-901227	B. Ball	Closed	75.00	75.00
87-01-040	Caitlin-901228	B. Ball	Closed	260.00	260.00
88-01-041	Christina-901229	B. Ball	Closed	350.00	400.00
88-01-042	Melissa-901230	B. Ball	Closed	110.00	110.00
82-01-043	Marie-901231	B. Ball	Closed	95.00	95.00
82-01-044	Trudy-901232	B. Ball	Closed	100.00	100.00
82-01-045	Holly-901233	B. Ball	Closed	160.00	200.00
88-01-046	Brandon-901234	B. Ball	Closed	90.00	90.00
88-01-047	Ashley-901235	B. Ball	Closed	110.00	110.00
88-01-048	April-901239	B. Ball	Closed	225.00	225.00
88-01-049	Sandy-901240	K. Kennedy	Closed	115.00	115.00
88-01-050	Erin-901241	B. Ball	Closed	170.00	170.00
88-01-051	Catherine-901242	B. Ball	Closed	240.00	240.00
88-01-052	Susan-901243	B. Ball	Closed	100.00	100.00
88-01-053	Paulette-901244	B. Ball	Closed	90.00	90.00
88-01-054	Bernice-901245	B. Ball	Closed	90.00	90.00
88-01-055	Ellen-901246	B. Ball	Closed	100.00	100.00
88-01-056	Cat Maude-901247	B. Ball	Closed	85.00	85.00
88-01-057	Jennifer-901248	B. Ball	Closed	150.00	150.00
90-01-058	Helene-901249	K. Kennedy	Closed	160.00	160.00
89-01-059	Ashlea-901250	B. Ball	Closed	550.00	550.00
90-01-060	Matthew-901251	B. Ball	Closed	100.00	100.00
89-01-061	Marissa-901252	K. Kennedy	Closed	225.00	225.00
89-01-062	Holly-901254	B. Ball	Closed	180.00	180.00
89-01-063	Valerie-901255	B. Ball	Closed	175.00	175.00
90-01-064	Justine-901256	B. Ball	Closed	200.00	200.00
89-01-065	Claudia-901257	K. Kennedy	1,000	225.00	225.00
90-01-066	Rebecca-901258	B. Ball	Closed	250.00	250.00
89-01-067	Megan-901260	B. Ball	Closed	120.00	120.00
90-01-068	Carolyn-901261	K. Kennedy	1,000	200.00	200.00
90-01-069	Amy-901262	B. Ball	Closed	110.00	110.00
89-01-070	Lindsey-901263	B. Ball	Closed	100.00	100.00
90-01-071	Heidi-901266	B. Ball	2,000	150.00	150.00
84-01-072	Tobie-912023	B. Ball	Closed	30.00	30.00
84-01-073	Sheila-912060	B. Ball	Closed	75.00	135.00
84-01-074	Jamie-912061	B. Ball	Closed	65.00	100.00
85-01-075	Michelle-912066	B. Ball	Closed	100.00	225.00
85-01-076	Phyllis-912067	B. Ball	Closed	60.00	60.00
85-01-077	Clown Casey-912078	B. Ball	Closed	40.00	40.00
85-01-078	Clown Jody-912079	B. Ball	Closed	100.00	150.00
85-01-079	Clown Christie-912084	B. Ball	Closed	60.00	90.00
85-01-080	Chauncey-912085	B. Ball	Closed	75.00	110.00
86-01-081	Baby Lauren Pink-912086	B. Ball	Closed	120.00	120.00
85-01-082	Rosalind-912087	B. Ball	Closed	145.00	225.00
86-01-083	Clown Cyd-912093	B. Ball	Closed	70.00	70.00
82-01-084	Charleen-912094	B. Ball	Closed	65.00	65.00
86-01-085	Clown Christabel-912095	B. Ball	Closed	100.00	150.00
86-01-086	Clown Clarabella-912096	B. Ball	Closed	80.00	80.00
86-01-087	Baby Brock Beige Dress-912103	B. Ball	Closed	60.00	60.00
86-01-088	Clown Calypso-912104	B. Ball	Closed	70.00	70.00
86-01-089	Girl Frog Freda-912105	B. Ball	Closed	20.00	20.00
86-01-090	Googley German Astrid-912109	B. Ball	Closed	60.00	60.00
86-01-091	Clown Clarissa-912123	B. Ball	Closed	75.00	110.00
86-01-092	Baby Courtney-912124	B. Ball	Closed	120.00	120.00
85-01-093	Mary-912126	B. Ball	Closed	60.00	90.00
86-01-094	Clown Lollipop-912127	B. Ball	Closed	125.00	225.00
86-01-095	Clown Cat Cadwalader-912132	B. Ball	Closed	55.00	55.00
86-01-096	Clown Kitten-Cleo-912133	B. Ball	Closed	50.00	50.00
85-01-097	Millie-912135	B. Ball	Closed	70.00	125.00
85-01-098	Lynn-912144	B. Ball	Closed	90.00	135.00
86-01-099	Ashley-912147	B. Ball	Closed	125.00	125.00
87-01-100	Megan-912148	B. Ball	Closed	70.00	70.00
87-01-101	Joy-912155	B. Ball	Closed	50.00	50.00
87-01-102	Kittle Cat-912167	B. Ball	Closed	55.00	55.00
87-01-103	Christine-912168	B. Ball	Closed	75.00	75.00
87-01-104	Noel-912170	B. Ball	Closed	125.00	125.00
87-01-105	Sophia-912173	B. Ball	Closed	40.00	40.00
87-01-106	Julia-912174	B. Ball	Closed	80.00	80.00
87-01-107	Clown Champagne-912180	B. Ball	Closed	95.00	95.00
82-01-108	Clown Jolly-912181	B. Ball	Closed	70.00	70.00
87-01-109	Baby Doll-912184	B. Ball	Closed	75.00	75.00
87-01-110	Baby Lindsay-912190	B. Ball	Closed	80.00	80.00
87-01-111	Caroline-912191	B. Ball	Closed	80.00	80.00
87-01-112	Jacqueline-912192	B. Ball	Closed	80.00	80.00
87-01-113	Jessica-912195	B. Ball	Closed	120.00	135.00
87-01-114	Doreen-912198	B. Ball	Closed	75.00	75.00
88-01-115	Clown Cotton Candy-912199	B. Ball	Closed	67.00	67.00
88-01-116	Baby Daryl-912200	B. Ball	Closed	85.00	85.00
88-01-117	Angelica-912204	B. Ball	Closed	150.00	150.00
88-01-118	Karen-912205	B. Ball	Closed	200.00	250.00
88-01-119	Polly-912206	B. Ball	Closed	100.00	125.00
88-01-120	Brittany-912207	B. Ball	Closed	130.00	145.00
88-01-121	Melissa-912208	B. Ball	Closed	125.00	125.00
88-01-122	Baby Jennifer-912210	B. Ball	Closed	75.00	75.00
88-01-123	Molly-912211	K. Kennedy	Closed	75.00	75.00
88-01-124	Lauren-912212	B. Ball	Closed	110.00	110.00
88-01-125	Anne-912213	B. Ball	Closed	130.00	150.00
89-01-126	Alexa-912214	B. Ball	Closed	195.00	195.00
88-01-127	Diana-912218	B. Ball	Closed	270.00	270.00
88-01-128	Sarah w/Pillow-912219	B. Ball	Closed	105.00	105.00
88-01-129	Betty Doll-912220	B. Ball	Closed	90.00	90.00
88-01-130	Jennifer-912221	B. Ball	Closed	80.00	80.00
88-01-131	Baby Katie-912222	B. Ball	Closed	70.00	70.00
88-01-132	Maritta Spanish-912224	B. Ball	Closed	140.00	140.00
88-01-133	Laura-912225	B. Ball	Closed	135.00	135.00
88-01-134	Crystal-912226	B. Ball	Closed	75.00	75.00
88-01-135	Jesse-912231	B. Ball	1,000	110.00	110.00
88-01-136	Whitney Blk-912232	B. Ball	1,000	62.50	62.50
88-01-137	Goldilocks-912234	K. Kennedy	Closed	65.00	65.00
88-01-138	Snow White-912235	K. Kennedy	Closed	65.00	65.00
88-01-139	Stephanie-912238	B. Ball	Closed	200.00	200.00
88-01-140	Morgan-912239	K. Kennedy	Closed	75.00	75.00
XX-01-141	Charity-912244	B. Ball	Closed	70.00	70.00
88-01-142	Renae-912245	B. Ball	Closed	120.00	120.00
88-01-143	Amanda-912246	B. Ball	Closed	180.00	180.00
88-01-144	Heather-912247	B. Ball	Closed	135.00	135.00
89-01-145	Merry-912249	B. Ball	Closed	200.00	200.00
90-01-146	January Birthstone Doll-912250	K. Kennedy	Closed	25.00	25.00
90-01-147	February Birthstone Doll-912251	K. Kennedy	Closed	25.00	25.00
90-01-148	March Birthstone Doll-912252	K. Kennedy	Closed	25.00	25.00
90-01-149	April Birthstone Doll-912253	K. Kennedy	Closed	25.00	25.00
90-01-150	May Birthstone Doll-912254	K. Kennedy	Closed	25.00	25.00
90-01-151	June Birthstone Doll-912255	K. Kennedy	Closed	25.00	25.00
90-01-152	July Birthstone Doll-912256	K. Kennedy	Closed	25.00	25.00
90-01-153	August Birthstone Doll-912257	K. Kennedy	Closed	25.00	25.00
90-01-154	September Birthstone Doll-912258	K. Kennedy	Closed	25.00	25.00
90-01-155	October Birthstone Doll-912259	K. Kennedy	Closed	25.00	25.00
90-01-156	November Birthstone Doll-912260	K. Kennedy	Closed	25.00	25.00
90-01-157	December Birthstone Doll-912261	K. Kennedy	Closed	25.00	25.00
89-01-158	Tammy-912264	B. Ball	Closed	110.00	110.00
89-01-159	Maria-912265	B. Ball	Closed	90.00	90.00
89-01-160	Nancy-912266	B. Ball	Closed	110.00	110.00
89-01-161	Pinky Clown-912268	K. Kennedy	1,000	70.00	70.00
89-01-162	Margot-912269	B. Ball	Closed	110.00	110.00
89-01-163	Jingles-912271	B. Ball	Closed	60.00	60.00
89-01-164	Vanessa-912272	B. Ball	Closed	110.00	110.00
89-01-165	Alexandria-912273	B. Ball	Closed	275.00	275.00
89-01-166	Lisa-912275	B. Ball	Closed	160.00	160.00
89-01-167	Loni-912276	B. Ball	1,200	125.00	125.00
89-01-168	Diana Bride-912277	B. Ball	Closed	180.00	180.00
90-01-169	Annabelle-912278	B. Ball	Closed	200.00	200.00
89-01-170	Sara-912279	B. Ball	Closed	175.00	175.00
89-01-171	Terry-912281	B. Ball	2,000	125.00	125.00
89-01-172	Sigrid-912282	B. Ball	Closed	145.00	145.00
89-01-173	Missy-912283	B. Ball	1,000	110.00	110.00
89-01-174	Melanie-912284	K. Kennedy	Closed	135.00	135.00
89-01-175	Kristin-912285	K. Kennedy	Closed	90.00	90.00
89-01-176	Suzanne-912286	B. Ball	Closed	120.00	120.00
90-01-177	Ginny-912287	K. Kennedy	Closed	140.00	140.00
89-01-178	Candace-912288	K. Kennedy	Closed	70.00	70.00
89-01-179	Joy-912289	K. Kennedy	Closed	110.00	110.00
90-01-180	Licorice-912290	B. Ball	Closed	75.00	75.00
89-01-181	Jimmy Baby w/ Pillow-912291	K. Kennedy	Closed	165.00	165.00
89-01-182	Hope Baby w/ Pillow-912292	B. Ball	Closed	110.00	110.00
90-01-183	Fluffer-912293	B. Ball	1,000	135.00	135.00
90-01-184	Marshmallow-912294	K. Kennedy	Closed	75.00	75.00
89-01-185	Suzy-912295	B. Ball	Closed	110.00	110.00
90-01-186	Alice-912296	K. Kennedy	Closed	65.00	65.00
90-01-187	Baryshnicat-912298	K. Kennedy	Closed	25.00	25.00
90-01-188	Tasha-912299	K. Kennedy	Closed	25.00	25.00

Number	Name	Artist	Edition Limit	Issue Price	Quote
Company		**Series**			
90-01-189	Priscilla-912300	B. Ball	1,000	185.00	185.00
90-01-190	Mrs. Katz-912301	B. Ball	1,000	140.00	140.00
89-01-200	Pamela-912302	B. Ball	Closed	95.00	95.00
89-01-201	Emily-912303	B. Ball	Closed	150.00	150.00
90-01-202	Brandy-912304	K. Kennedy	Closed	150.00	150.00
90-01-203	Sheri-912305	K. Kennedy	Closed	115.00	115.00
90-01-204	Gigi-912306	K. Kennedy	1,000	150.00	150.00
90-01-205	Joanne-912307	K. Kennedy	Closed	165.00	165.00
89-01-206	Melinda-912309	K. Kennedy	Closed	70.00	70.00
90-01-207	Bettina-912310	B. Ball	1,000	100.00	100.00
90-01-208	Stephanie-912312	B. Ball	Closed	150.00	150.00
90-01-209	Amie-912313	K. Kennedy	Closed	150.00	150.00
90-01-210	Samantha-912314	B. Ball	2,000	185.00	185.00
90-01-211	Tracie-912315	B. Ball	Closed	125.00	125.00
90-01-212	Paula-912316	B. Ball	Closed	100.00	100.00
90-01-213	Debra-912319	K. Kennedy	Closed	120.00	120.00
90-01-214	Robin-912321	B. Ball	2,000	160.00	160.00
90-01-215	Heather-912322	B. Ball	Closed	150.00	150.00
90-01-216	Jillian-912323	B. Ball	2,000	150.00	150.00
90-01-217	Angela-912324	K. Kennedy	2,000	130.00	130.00
90-01-218	Penny-912325	K. Kennedy	Closed	130.00	130.00
90-01-219	Tiffany-912326	K. Kennedy	Closed	180.00	180.00
90-01-220	Susie-912328	B. Ball	2,000	115.00	115.00
90-01-221	Jacqueline-912329	K. Kennedy	2,000	136.00	136.00
90-01-222	Kelly-912331	B. Ball	Closed	95.00	95.00
90-01-223	Annette-912333	K. Kennedy	Closed	85.00	85.00
90-01-224	Julia-912334	K. Kennedy	Closed	85.00	85.00
90-01-225	Monique-912335	K. Kennedy	Closed	85.00	85.00
90-01-226	Monica-912336	K. Kennedy	1,000	100.00	100.00
90-01-227	Helga-912337	B. Ball	Closed	325.00	325.00
90-01-228	Sheena-912338	B. Ball	Closed	115.00	115.00
90-01-229	Kimberly-912341	B. Ball	1,000	140.00	140.00
84-01-230	Amelia-933006	B. Ball	Closed	100.00	100.00
84-01-231	Stephanie-933012	B. Ball	Closed	115.00	115.00
92-01-232	Wendy-912330	K. Kennedy	1,000	125.00	125.00
92-01-233	Margaret-912354	K. Kennedy	Closed	150.00	150.00
92-01-234	Cassandra-912355	K. Kennedy	1,000	165.00	165.00
92-01-235	Noelle-912360	K. Kennedy	1,000	165.00	165.00
92-01-236	Kelly-912361	B. Ball	1,000	160.00	160.00
92-01-237	Ashley-911004	B. Ball	2,000	99.00	99.00
92-01-238	Lauren-912363	K. Kennedy	1,000	190.00	190.00
92-01-239	Denise-912362	K. Kennedy	1,000	145.00	145.00
92-01-240	Kris-912345	K. Kennedy	Closed	160.00	160.00
92-01-241	Hilary-912353	B. Ball	1,000	130.00	130.00
92-01-242	Toni-912367	K. Kennedy	Closed	120.00	120.00
92-01-243	Angelica-912339	B. Ball	1,000	145.00	145.00
92-01-244	Marjorie-912357	B. Ball	1,000	180.00	180.00
92-01-245	Brittany-912365	K. Kennedy	1,000	140.00	140.00
92-01-246	Allison-912358	B. Ball	1,000	160.00	160.00
92-01-247	Jenny-912374	K. Kennedy	Closed	150.00	150.00
92-01-248	Holly Belle-912380	B. Ball	500	125.00	125.00
92-01-249	Michelle-912381	K. Kennedy	500	175.00	175.00
92-01-250	Tamika-912382	B. Ball	500	185.00	185.00
92-01-251	Sherise-912383	K. Kennedy	500	145.00	145.00
92-01-252	Cindy-912384	B. Ball	1,000	185.00	185.00
92-01-253	Tulip-912385	K. Kennedy	500	145.00	145.00
92-01-254	Carol-912387	K. Kennedy	1,000	140.00	140.00
92-01-255	Alicia-912388	B. Ball	500	135.00	135.00
92-01-256	Iris-912389	K. Kennedy	500	165.00	165.00
92-01-257	Betsy-912390	B. Ball	500	150.00	150.00
92-01-258	Trudie-912391	B. Ball	500	135.00	135.00
92-01-259	Dottie-912393	K. Kennedy	1,000	160.00	160.00
Goebel/Schmid		**M. I. Hummel Collectibles Dolls**			
64-01-001	Gretel 1901	M. I. Hummel	Closed	55.00	125.00
64-01-002	Hansel 1902	M. I. Hummel	Closed	55.00	110.00
64-01-003	Rosa-Blue Baby 1904/B	M. I. Hummel	Closed	45.00	85.00
64-01-004	Rosa-Pink Baby 1904/P	M. I. Hummel	Closed	45.00	75.00
64-01-005	Little Knitter 1905	M. I. Hummel	Closed	55.00	75.00
64-01-006	Merry Wanderer 1906	M. I. Hummel	Closed	55.00	90.00
64-01-007	Chimney Sweep 1908	M. I. Hummel	Closed	55.00	110.00
64-01-008	School Girl 1909	M. I. Hummel	Closed	55.00	75.00
64-01-009	School Boy 1910	M. I. Hummel	Closed	55.00	80.00
64-01-010	Goose Girl 1914	M. I. Hummel	Closed	55.00	80.00
64-01-011	For Father 1917	M. I. Hummel	Closed	55.00	90.00
64-01-012	Merry Wanderer 1925	M. I. Hummel	Closed	55.00	110.00
64-01-013	Lost Stocking 1926	M. I. Hummel	Closed	55.00	75.00
64-01-014	Visiting and Invalid 1927	M. I. Hummel	Closed	55.00	75.00
64-01-015	On Secret Path 1928	M. I. Hummel	Closed	55.00	80.00
Goebel/Schmid		**M. I. Hummel Porcelain Dolls**			
84-02-001	Birthday Serenade/Boy	M. I. Hummel	Closed	225.00	250-300.
84-02-002	Birthday Serenade/Girl	M. I. Hummel	Closed	225.00	250-300.
84-02-003	On Holiday	M. I. Hummel	Closed	225.00	250-300.
84-02-004	Postman	M. I. Hummel	Closed	225.00	250-300.
85-02-005	Carnival	M. I. Hummel	Closed	225.00	250-300.
85-02-006	Easter Greetings	M. I. Hummel	Closed	225.00	250-300.
85-02-007	Lost Sheep	M. I. Hummel	Closed	225.00	250-300.
85-02-008	Signs of Spring	M. I. Hummel	Closed	225.00	250-300.
Gorham		**Gorham Dolls**			
81-01-001	Jillian, 16"	S. Stone Aiken	Closed	200.00	350-475.
81-01-002	Alexandria, 18"	S. Stone Aiken	Closed	250.00	550-575.
81-01-003	Christopher, 19"	S. Stone Aiken	Closed	250.00	750-950.
81-01-004	Stephanie, 18"	S. Stone Aiken	Closed	250.00	1650-2100.
81-01-005	Cecile, 16"	S. Stone Aiken	Closed	200.00	700-950.
81-01-006	Christina, 16"	S. Stone Aiken	Closed	200.00	400-475.
81-01-007	Danielle, 14"	S. Stone Aiken	Closed	150.00	300-375.
81-01-008	Melinda, 14"	S. Stone Aiken	Closed	150.00	300-375.
81-01-009	Elena, 14"	S. Stone Aiken	Closed	150.00	600-750.
81-01-010	Rosemond, 18"	S. Stone Aiken	Closed	250.00	650-750.
82-01-011	Mlle. Monique, 12"	S. Stone Aiken	Closed	125.00	300.00
82-01-012	Mlle. Jeanette, 12"	S. Stone Aiken	Closed	125.00	175-225.
82-01-013	Mlle. Lucille, 12"	S. Stone Aiken	Closed	125.00	275-475.
82-01-014	Benjamin, 18"	S. Stone Aiken	Closed	200.00	550-600.
82-01-015	Ellice, 18"	S. Stone Aiken	Closed	200.00	550-600.
82-01-016	Corrine, 21"	S. Stone Aiken	Closed	250.00	400-600.
82-01-017	Baby in Blue Dress, 12"	S. Stone Aiken	Closed	150.00	350-375.
82-01-018	Baby in Apricot Dress, 16"	S. Stone Aiken	Closed	175.00	375.00
82-01-019	Baby in White Dress, 18"	Gorham	Closed	250.00	395.00
82-01-020	Melanie, 23"	S. Stone Aiken	Closed	300.00	650-725.
82-01-021	Jeremy, 23"	S. Stone Aiken	Closed	300.00	750-800.
82-01-022	Mlle. Yvonne, 12"	Unknown	Closed	125.00	275-450.

Number	Name	Artist	Edition Limit	Issue Price	Quote
Company		**Series**			
82-01-023	M. Anton, 12"	Unknown	Closed	125.00	195.00
82-01-024	Mlle. Marsella, 12"	Unknown	Closed	125.00	295.00
82-01-025	Kristin, 23"	S. Stone Aiken	Closed	300.00	550-700.
83-01-026	Jennifer, 19" Bridal Doll	S. Stone Aiken	Closed	325.00	700-825.
85-01-027	Linda, 19"	S. Stone Aiken	Closed	275.00	400-475.
85-01-028	Odette, 19"	S. Stone Aiken	Closed	250.00	450-475.
85-01-029	Amelia, 19"	S. Stone Aiken	Closed	275.00	325-400.
85-01-030	Nanette, 19"	S. Stone Aiken	Closed	275.00	325-400.
85-01-031	Alexander, 19"	S. Stone Aiken	Closed	275.00	400-500.
85-01-032	Gabrielle, 19"	S. Stone Aiken	Closed	225.00	400-450.
86-01-033	Julia, 16"	S. Stone Aiken	Closed	225.00	375-425.
86-01-034	Lauren, 14"	S. Stone Aiken	Closed	175.00	375-450.
86-01-035	Emily, 14"	S. Stone Aiken	Closed	175.00	375-450.
86-01-036	Fleur, 19"	S. Stone Aiken	Closed	300.00	400-500.
87-01-037	Juliet	S. Stone Aiken	Closed	325.00	400-450.
86-01-038	Meredith	S. Stone Aiken	Closed	295.00	350-400.
86-01-039	Alissa	S. Stone Aiken	Closed	245.00	300-375.
86-01-040	Jessica	S. Stone Aiken	Closed	195.00	275-350.
Gorham		**Limited Edition Dolls**			
82-02-001	Allison, 19"	S. Stone Aiken	Closed	300.00	4800.00
83-02-002	Ashley, 19"	S. Stone Aiken	Closed	350.00	1200.00
84-02-003	Nicole, 19"	S. Stone Aiken	Closed	350.00	1000.00
84-02-004	Holly (Christmas), 19"	S. Stone Aiken	Closed	300.00	750-900.
85-02-005	Lydia,19"	S. Stone Aiken	Closed	550.00	1800.00
85-02-006	Joy (Christmas), 19"	S. Stone Aiken	Closed	350.00	500-725.
86-02-007	Noel (Christmas), 19"	S. Stone Aiken	Closed	400.00	700-800.
87-02-008	Jacqueline, 19"	S. Stone Aiken	Closed	500.00	600-850.
87-02-009	Merrie (Christmas), 19"	S. Stone Aiken	Closed	500.00	795.00
88-02-010	Andrew, 19"	S. Stone Aiken	Closed	475.00	625-850.
88-02-011	Christa (Christmas), 19"	S. Stone Aiken	Closed	550.00	1500.00
90-02-012	Amey (10th Anniversary Edition)	S. Stone Aiken	Closed	650.00	750-1100.
Gorham		**Gorham Holly Hobbie Childhood Memories**			
85-03-001	Mother's Helper	Holly Hobbie	Closed	45.00	125.00
85-03-002	Best Friends	Holly Hobbie	Closed	45.00	125.00
85-03-003	First Day of School	Holly Hobbie	Closed	45.00	125.00
85-03-004	Christmas Wishes	Holly Hobbie	Closed	45.00	125.00
Gorham		**Gorham Holly Hobbie For All Seasons**			
84-04-001	Summer Holly 12"	Holly Hobbie	Closed	42.50	195.00
84-04-002	Fall Holly 12"	Holly Hobbie	Closed	42.50	195.00
84-04-003	Winter Holly 12"	Holly Hobbie	Closed	42.50	195.00
84-04-004	Spring Holly 12"	Holly Hobbie	Closed	42.50	195.00
Gorham		**Holly Hobbie**			
83-05-001	Blue Girl, 14"	Holly Hobbie	Closed	80.00	325.00
83-05-002	Christmas Morning, 14"	Holly Hobbie	Closed	80.00	275.00
83-05-003	Heather, 14"	Holly Hobbie	Closed	80.00	275.00
83-05-004	Little Amy, 14"	Holly Hobbie	Closed	80.00	275.00
83-05-005	Robbie, 14"	Holly Hobbie	Closed	80.00	275.00
83-05-006	Sweet Valentine, 16"	Holly Hobbie	Closed	100.00	350.00
83-05-007	Yesterday's Memories, 18"	Holly Hobbie	Closed	125.00	450.00
83-05-008	Sunday Best, 18"	Holly Hobbie	Closed	115.00	350.00
83-05-009	Blue Girl, 18"	Holly Hobbie	Closed	115.00	395.00
Gorham		**Little Women**			
83-06-001	Beth, 16"	S. Stone Aiken	Closed	225.00	575.00
83-06-002	Amy, 16"	S. Stone Aiken	Closed	225.00	575.00
83-06-003	Meg, 19"	S. Stone Aiken	Closed	275.00	695.00
83-06-004	Jo, 19"	S. Stone Aiken	Closed	275.00	675.00
Gorham		**Kezi Doll For All Seasons**			
85-07-001	Ariel 16"	Kezi	Closed	135.00	500.00
85-07-002	Aubrey 16"	Kezi	Closed	135.00	500.00
85-07-003	Amber 16"	Kezi	Closed	135.00	500.00
85-07-004	Adrienne 16"	Kezi	Closed	135.00	500-525.
Gorham		**Kezi Golden Gifts**			
84-08-001	Faith 18"	Kezi	Closed	95.00	195-225.
84-08-002	Felicity 18"	Kezi	Closed	95.00	195.00
84-08-003	Patience 18"	Kezi	Closed	95.00	195.00
84-08-004	Prudence 18"	Kezi	Closed	85.00	195.00
84-08-005	Hope 16"	Kezi	Closed	85.00	175-225.
84-08-006	Grace 16"	Kezi	Closed	85.00	175.00
84-08-007	Charity 16"	Kezi	Closed	85.00	175-195.
84-08-008	Merrie 16"	Kezi	Closed	85.00	175-195.
Gorham		**Limited Edition Sister Set**			
88 09 001	Kathleen	S. Stone Aiken	Closed	550.00	750 850.
88-09-002	Katelin	S. Stone Aiken	Set	Set	Set
Gorham		**Southern Belles**			
85-10-001	Amanda, 19"	S. Stone Aiken	Closed	300.00	850.00
86-10-002	Veronica, 19"	S. Stone Aiken	Closed	325.00	750.00
87-10-003	Rachel, 19"	S. Stone Aiken	Closed	375.00	825.00
88-10-004	Cassie, 19"	S. Stone Aiken	Closed	500.00	700.00
Gorham		**Valentine Ladies**			
87-11-001	Jane	P. Valentine	Closed	145.00	350-400.
87-11-002	Lee Ann	P. Valentine	Closed	145.00	325.00
87-11-003	Elizabeth	P. Valentine	Closed	145.00	450.00
87-11-004	Rebecca	P. Valentine	Closed	145.00	325.00
87-11-005	Patrice	P. Valentine	Closed	145.00	325.00
87-11-006	Anabella	P. Valentine	Closed	145.00	395-425.
87-11-007	Sylvia	P. Valentine	Closed	160.00	395.00
87-11-008	Rosanne	P. Valentine	Closed	145.00	325.00
87-11-009	Marianna	P. Valentine	Closed	160.00	400.00
88-11-010	Maria Theresa	P. Valentine	Closed	225.00	425.00
88-11-011	Priscilla	P. Valentine	Closed	195.00	325.00
88-11-012	Judith Anne	P. Valentine	Closed	195.00	325.00
88-11-013	Felicia	P. Valentine	Closed	225.00	395.00
89-11-014	Julianna	P. Valentine	Closed	225.00	275-325.
89-11-015	Rose	P. Valentine	Closed	225.00	275-325.
Gorham		**Precious as Pearls**			
86-12-001	Colette	S. Stone Aiken	Closed	400.00	1500-1650.
87-12-002	Charlotte	S. Stone Aiken	Closed	425.00	795-895.
88-12-003	Chloe	S. Stone Aiken	Closed	525.00	925.00
89-12-004	Cassandra	S. Stone Aiken	Closed	525.00	1300-1500.
XX-12-005	Set	S. Stone Aiken	Closed	1875.00	4200.00

DOLLS

Number	Name	Artist	Edition Limit	Issue Price	Quote
Gorham		**Gorham Baby Doll Collection**			
87-13-001	Christening Day	Aiken/Matthews	Closed	245.00	295.00
87-13-002	Leslie	Aiken/Matthews	Closed	245.00	325.00
87-13-003	Matthew	Aiken/Matthews	Closed	245.00	285.00
Gorham		**Beverly Port Designer Collection**			
87-14-001	Silver Bell 17"	B. Port	Closed	175.00	295.00
87-14-002	Kristobear Kringle 17"	B. Port	Closed	200.00	325.00
87-14-003	Tedwina Kimelina Bearkin 10"	B. Port	Closed	95.00	150.00
87-14-004	Christopher Paul Bearkin 10"	B. Port	Closed	95.00	150.00
87-14-005	Molly Melinda Bearkin 10"	B. Port	Closed	95.00	150.00
87-14-006	Tedward Jonathan Bearkin 10"	B. Port	Closed	95.00	150.00
88-14-007	Baery Mab 9-1/2"	B. Port	Closed	110.00	150.00
88-14-008	Miss Emily 18"	B. Port	Closed	350.00	450.00
88-14-009	T.R. 28-1/2"	B. Port	Closed	400.00	600.00
88-14-010	The Amazing Calliope Merriweather 17"	B. Port	Closed	275.00	425.00
88-14-011	Hollybeary Kringle 15"	B. Port	Closed	350.00	395.00
88-14-012	Theodore B. Bear 14"	B. Port	Closed	175.00	195.00
Gorham		**Bonnets & Bows**			
88-15-001	Belinda	B. Gerardi	Closed	195.00	395.00
88-15-002	Annemarie	B. Gerardi	Closed	195.00	395.00
88-15-003	Allessandra	B. Gerardi	Closed	195.00	395.00
88-15-004	Lisette	B. Gerardi	Closed	285.00	495.00
88-15-005	Bettina	B. Gerardi	Closed	285.00	495.00
88-15-006	Ellie	B. Gerardi	Closed	285.00	495.00
88-15-007	Alicia	B. Gerardi	Closed	385.00	800.00
88-15-008	Bethany	B. Gerardi	Closed	385.00	1350-1500.
88-15-009	Jesse	B. Gerardi	Closed	525.00	800-850.
88-15-010	Francie	B. Gerardi	Closed	625.00	895.00
Gorham		**Small Wonders**			
88-16-001	Patina	B. Gerardi	Closed	265.00	265.00
88-16-002	Madeline	B. Gerardi	Closed	365.00	365.00
88-16-003	Marguerite	B. Gerardi	Closed	425.00	425.00
Gorham		**Joyful Years**			
89-17-001	William	B. Gerardi	Closed	295.00	295.00
89-17-002	Katrina	B. Gerardi	Closed	295.00	295.00
Gorham		**Victorian Cameo Collection**			
90-18-001	Victoria	B. Gerardi	1,500	375.00	375.00
91-18-002	Alexandra	B. Gerardi	Closed	375.00	375.00
Gorham		**Children Of Christmas**			
89-19-001	Clara, 16"	S. Stone Aiken	Closed	325.00	675-850.
90-19-002	Natalie, 16"	S. Stone Aiken	1,500	350.00	395-450.
91-19-003	Emily	S. Stone Aiken	1,500	375.00	375.00
92-19-004	Virginia	S. Stone Aiken	1,500	375.00	375.00
Gorham		**Les Belles Bebes Collection**			
91-20-001	Cherie	S. Stone Aiken	Closed	375.00	375-600.
91-20-002	Desiree	S. Stone Aiken	1,500	375.00	375.00
93-20-003	Camille	S. Stone Aiken	1,500	375.00	375.00
Gorham		**Childhood Memories**			
91-21-001	Amanda	D. Valenza	Open	98.00	98.00
91-21-002	Kimberly	D. Valenza	Closed	98.00	98.00
91-21-003	Jessica Anne's Playtime	D. Valenza	Open	98.00	98.00
91-21-004	Jennifer	D. Valenza	Closed	98.00	98.00
Gorham		**Gifts of the Garden**			
91-22-001	Priscilla	S. Stone Aiken	Closed	125.00	125.00
91-22-002	Lauren	S. Stone Aiken	Closed	125.00	125.00
91-22-003	Irene	S. Stone Aiken	Closed	125.00	125.00
91-22-004	Valerie	S. Stone Aiken	Closed	125.00	125.00
91-22-005	Deborah	S. Stone Aiken	Closed	125.00	125.00
91-22-006	Alisa	S. Stone Aiken	Closed	125.00	125.00
91-22-007	Maria	S. Stone Aiken	Closed	125.00	125.00
91-22-008	Joelle (Christmas)	S. Stone Aiken	Closed	150.00	195.00
91-22-009	Holly (Christmas)	S. Stone Aiken	Closed	150.00	150.00
Gorham		**Dolls of the Month**			
91-23-001	Miss January	Gorham	Closed	79.00	79.00
91-23-002	Miss February	Gorham	Closed	79.00	79.00
91-23-003	Miss March	Gorham	Closed	79.00	79.00
91-23-004	Miss April	Gorham	Closed	79.00	79.00
91-23-005	Miss May	Gorham	Closed	79.00	79.00
91-23-006	Miss June	Gorham	Closed	79.00	79.00
91-23-007	Miss July	Gorham	Closed	79.00	79.00
91-23-008	Miss August	Gorham	Closed	79.00	79.00
91-23-009	Miss September	Gorham	Closed	79.00	79.00
91-23-010	Miss October	Gorham	Closed	79.00	79.00
91-23-011	Miss November	Gorham	Closed	79.00	79.00
91-23-012	Miss December	Gorham	Closed	79.00	79.00
Gorham		**Legendary Heroines**			
91-24-001	Jane Eyre	S. Stone Aiken	1,500	245.00	245.00
91-24-002	Guinevere	S. Stone Aiken	1,500	245.00	245.00
91-24-003	Juliet	S. Stone Aiken	1,500	245.00	245.00
91-24-004	Lara	S. Stone Aiken	1,500	245.00	245.00
Gorham		**Gift of Dreams**			
91-25-001	Samantha	Young/Gerardi	Closed	495.00	495.00
91-25-002	Katherine	Young/Gerardi	Closed	495.00	495.00
91-25-003	Melissa	Young/Gerardi	Closed	495.00	495.00
91-25-004	Elizabeth	Young/Gerardi	Closed	495.00	495.00
91-25-005	Christina (Christmas)	Young/Gerardi	Closed	695.00	695.00
Gorham		**The Friendship Dolls**			
91-26-001	Peggy-The American Traveler	P. Seaman	Open	98.00	98.00
91-26-002	Meagan-The Irish Traveler	L. O'Connor	Open	98.00	98.00
91-26-003	Angela-The Italian Traveler	S. Nappo	Open	98.00	98.00
91-26-004	Kinuko-The Japanese Traveler	S. Ueki	Open	98.00	98.00
Gorham		**Special Moments**			
91-27-001	Baby's First Christmas	E. Worrell	Open	135.00	135.00
92-27-002	Baby's Christening	E. Worrell	Closed	135.00	135.00
92-27-003	Baby's First Birthday	E. Worrell	Open	135.00	135.00
92-27-004	Baby's First Steps	E. Worrell	Open	135.00	135.00
Gorham		**Dollie And Me**			
91-28-001	Dollie's First Steps	J. Pilallis	Open	160.00	160.00
Gorham		**The Victorian Collection**			
92-29-001	Victoria's Jubilee	E. Woodhouse	Yr.Iss.	295.00	295.00
Gorham		**Days Of The Week**			
92-30-001	Monday's Child	R./L. Schrubbe	Open	98.00	98.00
92-30-002	Tuesday's Child	R./L. Schrubbe	Open	98.00	98.00
92-30-003	Wednesday's Child	R./L. Schrubbe	Open	98.00	98.00
92-30-004	Thurday's Child	R./L. Schrubbe	Open	98.00	98.00
92-30-005	Friday's Child	R./L. Schrubbe	Open	98.00	98.00
92-30-006	Saturday's Child	R./L. Schrubbe	Open	98.00	98.00
92-30-007	Sunday's Child	R./L. Schrubbe	Open	98.00	98.00
Gorham		**Times To Treasure**			
90-31-001	Storytime	L. Di Leo	Open	195.00	195.00
91-31-002	Bedtime	L. Di Leo	Open	195.00	195.00
93-31-003	Playtime	L. Di Leo	Open	195.00	195.00
93-31-004	Cradletime	L. Di Leo	Open	195.00	195.00
Gorham		**Victorian Children**			
92-32-001	Sara's Tea Time	S. Stone Aiken	1,000	495.00	495.00
93-32-002	Catching Butterflies	S. Stone Aiken	1,000	495.00	495.00
Gorham		**Bride Dolls**			
93-33-001	Susannah's Wedding Day	D. Valenza	9,500	295.00	295.00
Gorham		**Carousel Dolls**			
93-34-001	Ribbons And Roses	C. Shafer	Open	119.00	119.00
Gorham		**Pillow Baby Dolls**			
93-35-001	Sitting Pretty	L. Gordon	Open	39.00	39.00
93-35-002	Tickling Toes	L. Gordon	Open	39.00	39.00
93-35-002	On the Move	L. Gordon	Open	39.00	39.00
Gorham		**Victorian Flower Girls**			
93-36-001	Rose	J. Pillalis	Open	95.00	95.00
Gorham		**Celebrations Of Childhood**			
92-37-003	Happy Birthday Amy	L. Di Leo	Open	160.00	160.00
Gorham		**Littlest Angel Dolls**			
92-38-001	Merriel	L. Di Leo	Open	49.50	49.50
Gorham		**Puppy Love Dolls**			
92-39-001	Katie And Kyle	R./ L. Schrubbe	Open	119.00	119.00
Gorham		**Daydreamer Dolls**			
92-40-001	Heather's Daydream	S. Stone Aiken	Open	119.00	119.00
Gorham		**Cuddly Companions**			
93-41-001	Tara And Teddy	R./ L. Schrubbe	Open	119.00	119.00
Gorham		**Raggedy Ann And Andy**			
93-42-001	Raggedy Ann & Andy	Unknown	9,500	195.00	195.00
Gorham		**Bonnet Babies**			
93-43-001	Chelsea's Bonnet	M. Sirko	Open	95.00	95.00
Gorham		**Imaginary People**			
93-44-001	Melinda, The Tooth Fairy	R. Tonner	2,900	95.00	95.00
Gorham		**International Babies**			
93-45-001	Natalia's Matrioshka	R. Tonner	Open	95.00	95.00
Gorham		**Nature's Bounty**			
93-46-001	Jamie's Fruitful Harvest	R. Tonner	Open	95.00	95.00
Gorham		**Portrait Perfect Victorian Dolls**			
93-47-001	Pretty in Peach	R. Tonner	2,900	119.00	119.00
Gorham		**Sporting Kids**			
93-48-001	Up At Bat	R. Schrubbe	Open	49.50	49.50
Gorham		**Tender Hearts**			
93-49-001	Saying Grace	M. Murphy	Open	119.00	119.00
Gorham		**Christmas Traditions**			
93-50-001	Trimming the Tree	S. Stone Aiken	2,500	295.00	295.00
Gorham		**CHristmas Treasures**			
93-51-001	Chrissy	S. Stone Aiken	Open	150.00	150.00
Green Valley World		**Norman Rockwell Character Doll**			
XX-01-001	Mimi	M. Moline	Closed	200.00	200.00
XX-01-002	Anne	M. Moline	Closed	200.00	200.00
XX-01-003	Davey	M. Moline	Closed	200.00	200.00
XX-01-004	Susie	M. Moline	Closed	200.00	200.00
XX-01-005	Willma	M. Moline	20,000	200.00	200.00
XX-01-006	Nell	M. Moline	Closed	200.00	200.00
XX-01-007	Tina	M. Moline	Closed	200.00	200.00
XX-01-008	Junior	M. Moline	Closed	200.00	200.00
XX-01-009	Polly	M. Moline	20,000	200.00	200.00
XX-01-010	Dr. Chrisfield	M. Moline	Closed	200.00	200.00
XX-01-011	Jane	M. Moline	Closed	200.00	200.00
XX-01-012	Beth	M. Moline	20,000	200.00	200.00
XX-01-013	Amy	M. Moline	20,000	200.00	200.00
XX-01-014	John	M. Moline	Closed	200.00	200.00
XX-01-015	Mary	M. Moline	Closed	200.00	200.00
XX-01-016	Sally	M. Moline	20,000	200.00	200.00
XX-01-017	Laura	M. Moline	20,000	200.00	200.00
XX-01-018	Santa	M. Moline	Closed	200.00	200.00
XX-01-019	Molly	M. Moline	Closed	200.00	200.00
XX-01-020	Rockwell	M. Moline	Closed	200.00	200.00
H & G Studios, Inc.		**Brenda Burke Dolls**			
89-01-001	Arabelle	B. Burke	500	695.00	1400.00
89-01-002	Angelica	B. Burke	50	1495.00	3000.00
89-01-003	Adelaine	B. Burke	25	1795.00	3600.00
89-01-004	Amanda	B. Burke	25	1995.00	6000.00
89-01-005	Alicia	B. Burke	125	895.00	1800.00
89-01-006	Alexandra	B. Burke	125	995.00	2000.00
89-01-007	Bethany	B. Burke	45	2995.00	2995.00
89-01-008	Beatrice	B. Burke	85	2395.00	2395.00
89-01-009	Brittany	B. Burke	75	2695.00	2695.00

Number	Name	Artist	Edition Limit	Issue Price	Quote
90-01-010	Belinda	B. Burke	12	3695.00	3695.00
91-01-011	Tender Love	B. Burke	25	3295.00	3295.00
91-01-012	Sleigh Ride	B. Burke	20	3695.00	3695.00
91-01-013	Charlotte	B. Burke	20	2395.00	2395.00
91-01-014	Clarissa	B. Burke	15	3595.00	3595.00
92-01-015	Dorothea	B. Burke	500	395.00	395.00
H & G Studios, Inc.		**Childhood Memories**			
89-02-001	Early Days	B. Burke	95	2595.00	2595.00
91-02-002	Playtime	B. Burke	35	2795.00	2795.00
H & G Studios, Inc.		**The Four Seasons**			
90-03-001	Spring	B. Burke	125	1995.00	1995.00
H & G Studios, Inc.		**Dancing Through The Ages**			
90-04-001	Minuet	B. Burke	95	2495.00	2495.00
H & G Studios, Inc.		**Birthday Party**			
90-05-001	Suzie	B. Burke	500	695.00	695.00
Hallmark Galleries		**Victorian Memories**			
92-01-001	Daisy -plush bear	J. Greene	2,500	85.00	85.00
92-01-002	Bear-plush bear	J. Greene	9,500	35.00	35.00
92-01-003	Abner	J. Greene	4,500	110.00	110.00
92-01-004	Seth-plush bear	J. Greene	9,500	40.00	40.00
92-01-005	Katherine	J. Greene	1,200	150.00	150.00
92-01-006	Abigail	J. Greene	4,500	125.00	125.00
92-01-007	Olivia	J. Greene	4,500	125.00	125.00
92-01-008	Teddy -plush bear	J. Greene	9,500	45.00	45.00
92-01-009	Alice	J. Greene	4,500	125.00	125.00
92-01-010	Bunny B-plush rabbit	J. Greene	9,500	35.00	35.00
92-01-011	Emma/miniature doll	J. Greene	9,500	25.00	25.00
Hamilton Collection		**Songs of the Seasons Hakata Doll Collection**			
85-01-001	Winter Song Maiden	T. Murakami	9,800	75.00	75.00
85-01-002	Spring Song Maiden	T. Murakami	9,800	75.00	75.00
85-01-003	Summer Song Maiden	T. Murakami	9,800	75.00	75.00
85-01-004	Autumn Song Maiden	T. Murakami	9,800	75.00	75.00
Hamilton Collection		**Dolls of America's Colonial Heritage**			
86-02-001	Katrina	A. Elekfy	Open	55.00	55.00
86-02-002	Nicole	A. Elekfy	Open	55.00	55.00
87-02-003	Maria	A. Elekfy	Open	55.00	55.00
87-02-004	Priscilla	A. Elekfy	Open	55.00	55.00
87-02-005	Colleen	A. Elekfy	Open	55.00	55.00
88-02-006	Gretchen	A. Elekfy	Open	55.00	55.00
Hamilton Collection		**Star Trek Doll Collection**			
88-03-001	Mr. Spock	E. Daub	Closed	75.00	150.00
88-03-002	Captain Kirk	E. Daub	Closed	75.00	175.00
89-03-003	Dr. Mc Coy	E. Daub	Closed	75.00	120.00
89-03-004	Scotty	E. Daub	Closed	75.00	120.00
90-03-005	Sulu	E. Daub	Closed	75.00	120.00
90-03-006	Chekov	E. Daub	Closed	75.00	120.00
91-03-007	Uhura	E. Daub	Closed	75.00	120.00
Hamilton Collection		**The Antique Doll Collection**			
89-04-001	Nicole	Unknown	Open	195.00	195-325.
90-04-002	Colette	Unknown	Open	195.00	195.00
91-04-003	Lisette	Unknown	Open	195.00	195.00
91-04-004	Katrina	Unknown	Open	195.00	195.00
Hamilton Collection		**The Bessie Pease Gutmann Doll Collection**			
89-05-001	Love is Blind	B.P. Gutmann	Open	135.00	135.00
89-05-002	He Won't Bite	B.P. Gutmann	Open	135.00	135.00
91-05-003	Virginia	B.P. Gutmann	Open	135.00	135.00
91-05-004	First Dancing Lesson	B.P. Gutmann	Open	195.00	195.00
91-05-005	Good Morning	B.P. Gutmann	Open	195.00	195.00
91-05-006	Love At First Sight	B.P. Gutmann	Open	195.00	195.00
Hamilton Collection		**The Maud Humphrey Bogart Doll Collection**			
89-06-001	Playing Bride	M.H. Bogart	Open	135.00	135.00
90-06-002	First Party	M.H. Bogart	Open	135.00	135.00
90-06-003	The First Lesson	M.H. Bogart	Open	135.00	135.00
91-06-004	Seamstress	M.H. Bogart	Open	135.00	135.00
91-06-005	Little Captive	M.H. Bogart	Open	135.00	135.00
Hamilton Collection		**Connie Walser Derek Baby Doll**			
90-07-001	Jessica	C.W. Derek	Closed	155.00	250-300.
91-07-002	Sara	C.W. Derek	Open	155.00	155.00
91-07-003	Andrew	C.W. Derek	Open	155.00	155.00
91-07-004	Amanda	C.W. Derek	Open	155.00	155.00
Hamilton Collection		**I Love Lucy**			
90-08-001	Lucy	Unknown	Open	95.00	95.00
91-08-002	Ricky	Unknown	Open	95.00	95.00
92-08-003	Queen of the Gypsies	Unknown	Open	95.00	95.00
92-08-004	Vitameatavegamin	Unknown	Open	95.00	95.00
Hamilton Collection		**Russian Czarra Dolls**			
91-09-001	Alexandra	Unknown	4,950	295.00	295.00
Hamilton Collection		**Storyboook Dolls**			
91-10-001	Alice in Wonderland	L. Di Leo	Open	75.00	75.00
Hamilton Collection		**International Children**			
91-11-001	Miko	C. Woodie	Closed	49.50	80.00
91-11-002	Anastasia	C. Woodie	Open	49.50	49.50
91-11-003	Angelina	C. Woodie	Open	49.50	49.50
92-11-004	Lian	C. Woodie	Open	49.50	49.50
92-11-005	Monique	C. Woodie	Open	49.50	49.50
92-11-006	Lisa	C. Woodie	Open	49.50	49.50
Hamilton Collection		**Central Park Skaters**			
91-12-001	Central Park Skaters	Unknown	Open	245.00	245.00
Hamilton Collection		**Jane Zidjunas Toddler Dolls**			
91-13-001	Jennifer	J. Zidjunas	Open	135.00	135.00
91-13-002	Megan	J. Zidjunas	Open	135.00	135.00
92-13-003	Kimberly	J. Zidjunas	Open	135.00	135.00
92-13-004	Amy	J. Zidjunas	Open	135.00	135.00
Hamilton Collection		**Jane Zidjunas Party Dolls**			
91-14-001	Kelly	J. Zidjunas	Open	135.00	135.00
92-14-002	Katie	J. Zidjunas	Open	135.00	135.00
93-14-003	Meredith	J. Zidjunas	Open	135.00	135.00
Hamilton Collection		**The Royal Beauty Dolls**			
91-15-001	Chen Mai	Unknown	Open	195.00	195.00
Hamilton Collection		**Abbie Williams Doll Collection**			
92-16-001	Molly	A. Williams	2,500	155.00	155.00
Hamilton Collection		**Zolan Dolls**			
91-17-001	A Christmas Prayer	D. Zolan	Open	95.00	95.00
92-17-002	Winter Angel	D. Zolan	Open	95.00	95.00
92-17-003	Rainy Day Pals	D. Zolan	Open	95.00	95.00
Hamilton Collection		**Baby Portrait Dolls**			
91-18-001	Melissa	B. Parker	Open	135.00	135.00
92-18-002	Jenna	B. Parker	Open	135.00	135.00
92-18-003	Bethany	B. Parker	Open	135.00	135.00
93-18-004	Mindy	B. Parker	Open	135.00	135.00
Hamilton Collection		**Helen Kish Dolls**			
91-19-001	Ashley	H. Kish	Open	135.00	135.00
92-19-002	Elizabeth	H. Kish	Open	135.00	135.00
92-19-003	Hannah	H. Kish	Open	135.00	135.00
93-19-004	Margaret	H. Kish	Open	135.00	135.00
Hamilton Collection		**Picnic In The Park**			
91-20-001	Rebecca	J. Esteban	Open	155.00	155.00
92-20-002	Emily	J. Esteban	Open	155.00	155.00
92-20-003	Victoria	J. Esteban	Open	155.00	155.00
93-20-004	Benjamin	J. Esteban	Open	155.00	155.00
Hamilton Collection		**Bride Dolls**			
91-21-001	Portrait of Innocence	Unknown	Open	195.00	195.00
92-21-002	Portrait of Loveliness	Unknown	Open	195.00	195.00
Hamilton Collection		**Maud Humphrey Bogart Dolls**			
92-22-001	Playing Bridesmaid	Unknown	Closed	195.00	195.00
Hamilton Collection		**Year Round Fun**			
92-23-001	Allison	D. Schurig	Open	95.00	95.00
93-23-002	Christy	D. Schurig	Open	95.00	95.00
Hamilton Collection		**Laura Cobabe Dolls**			
92-24-001	Amber	L. Cobabe	Open	195.00	195.00
92-24-002	Brook	L. Cobabe	Open	195.00	195.00
Hamilton Collection		**Belles of the Countryside**			
92-25-001	Erin	C. Heath Orange	Open	135.00	135.00
92-25-002	Rose	C. Heath Orange	Open	135.00	135.00
Hamilton Collection		**Dolls By Kay McKee**			
92-26-001	Shy Violet	K. McKee	Open	135.00	135.00
92-26-002	Robin	K. McKee	Open	135.00	135.00
93-26-003	Katy Did It!	K. McKee	Open	135.00	135.00
Hamilton Collection		**Parker-Levi Toddlers**			
92-27-001	Courtney	B. Parker	Open	135.00	135.00
92-27-002	Melody	B. Parker	Open	135.00	135.00
Hamilton Collection		**Parkins Treasures**			
92-28-001	Tiffany	P. Parkins	Open	55.00	55.00
92-28-002	Dorothy	P. Parkins	Open	55.00	55.00
93-28-003	Charlotte	P. Parkins	Open	55.00	55.00
Hamilton Collection		**I'm So Proud Doll Collection**			
92-29-001	Christina	L. Cobabe	Open	95.00	95.00
Hamilton Collection		**Through The Eyes of Virginia Turner**			
92-30-001	Michelle	V. Turner	Open	95.00	95.00
92-30-002	Danielle	V. Turner	Open	95.00	95.00
93-30-003	Wendy	V. Turner	Open	95.00	95.00
Hamilton Collection		**Santa's Little Helpers**			
92-31-001	Nicholas	C.W. Derek	Open	155.00	155.00
93-31-002	Hope	C.W. Derek	Open	155.00	155.00
Hamilton Collection		**Victorian Treasures**			
92-32-001	Katherine	C.W. Derek	Open	155.00	155.00
93-32-002	Madeline	C.W. Derek	Open	155.00	155.00
Hamilton Collection		**Daddy's Little Girls**			
92-33-001	Lindsay	M. Snyder	Open	95.00	95.00
Hamilton Collection		**Proud Indian Nation**			
92-34-001	Navaho Little One	N/A	Open	95.00	95.00
Hamilton Collection		**Holiday Carollers**			
92-35-001	Joy	U. Lepp	Open	155.00	155.00
Hamilton Collection		**Joke Grobben Dolls**			
92-36-001	Heather	J. Grobben	Open	69.00	69.00
Hamilton Collection		**Treasured Toddlers**			
92-37-001	Whitney	V. Turner	Open	95.00	95.00
92-37-002	Lara	N/A	7,450	295.00	295.00
Hamilton Collection		**Children To Cherish**			
91-38-001	A Gift of Innocence	N/A	Yr.Iss.	135.00	135.00
91-38-002	A Gift of Beauty	N/A	Open	135.00	135.00
Hamilton Collection		**Wooden Dolls**			
91-39-001	Gretchen	N/A	9,850	225.00	225.00
91-39-002	Heidi	N/A	9,850	225.00	225.00
Hamilton Collection		**Little Rascals™**			
92-40-001	Spanky	S./J. Hoffman	Open	69.00	69.00
Hamilton Gifts/Enesco		**Maud Humphrey Bogart Porcelain Dolls**			
91-01-001	Sarah H5617	M. Humphrey	Open	37.00	37.00
91-01-002	Susanna H5648	M. Humphrey	Open	37.00	37.00

DOLLS

Company		Series			
Number	Name	Artist	Edition Limit	Issue Price	Quote
91-01-003	My First Party H5686	M. Humphrey	Open	135.00	135.00
91-01-004	Playing Bride H5618	M. Humphrey	Open	135.00	135.00
Edna Hibel Studios		**Child's Fancy**			
85-01-001	Jenny's Lady Jennifer	E. Hibel	800	395.00	700-1000.
Edna Hibel Studios		**Wax Doll Collection**			
86-02-001	Wax Doll	E. Hibel	12	2500.00	3000-3400.
Annette Himstedt		**Barefoot Children**			
87-01-001	Fatou	A. Himstedt	Closed	329.00	900-1500.
87-01-002	Bastian	A. Himstedt	Closed	329.00	650-850.
87-01-003	Ellen	A. Himstedt	Closed	329.00	700-950.
87-01-004	Paula	A. Himstedt	Closed	329.00	800-950.
87-01-005	Lisa	A. Himstedt	Closed	329.00	900-950.
87-01-006	Kathe	A. Himstedt	Closed	329.00	900-950.
Annette Himstedt		**Heartland Series**			
88-02-001	Timi	A. Himstedt	Closed	329.00	525-550.
88-02-002	Toni	A. Himstedt	Closed	329.00	525-550.
Annette Himstedt		**Blessed Are The Children**			
88-03-001	Friederike	A. Himstedt	Closed	499.00	800-950.
88-03-002	Makimura	A. Himstedt	Closed	499.00	750-850.
88-03-003	Kasimir	A. Himstedt	Closed	499.00	900-1200.
88-03-004	Michiko	A. Himstedt	Closed	499.00	850-950.
88-03-005	Malin	A. Himstedt	Closed	499.00	950-1000.
Annette Himstedt		**Reflection of Youth**			
89-04-001	Adrienne (France)	A. Himstedt	Closed	558.00	700-850.
89-04-002	Kai (German)	A. Himstedt	Closed	558.00	600-750.
89-04-003	Janka (Hungry)	A. Himstedt	Closed	558.00	700-750.
89-04-004	Ayoka (Africa)	A. Himstedt	Closed	558.00	825-950.
Annette Himstedt		**Fiene And The Barefoot Babies**			
90-05-001	Annchen-German Baby Girl	A. Himstedt	2 Yr.	498.00	498.00
90-05-002	Taki-Japanese Baby Girl	A. Himstedt	2 Yr.	498.00	498.00
90-05-003	Mo-American Baby Boy	A. Himstedt	2 Yr.	498.00	498.00
90-05-004	Fiene-Belgian Girl	A. Himstedt	2 Yr.	598.00	695.00
Annette Himstedt		**Faces of Friendship**			
91-06-001	Liliane (Netherlands)	A. Himstedt	2 Yr.	598.00	598.00
91-06-002	Shireem (Bali)	A. Himstedt	2 Yr.	598.00	598.00
91-06-003	Neblina (Switzerland)	A. Himstedt	2 Yr.	598.00	598.00
Annette Himstedt		**Summer Dreams**			
92-07-001	Sanga	A. Himstedt	2 Yr.	599.00	599.00
92-07-002	Pemba	A. Himstedt	2 Yr.	599.00	599.00
92-07-003	Jule	A. Himstedt	2 Yr.	599.00	599.00
92-07-004	Enzo	A. Himstedt	2 Yr.	599.00	599.00
Annette Himstedt		**Summer Dreams**			
93-08-001	Lona	A. Himstedt	2 Yr.	N/A	N/A
93-08-002	Tara	A. Himstedt	2 Yr.	N/A	N/A
93-08-003	Kima	A. Himstedt	2 Yr.	N/A	N/A
Ladie and Friends™		**The Family and Friends of Lizzie High®**			
85-01-001	Lizzie High®-1100	B.K. Wisber	Open	36.00	37.00
85-01-002	Sabina Valentine (First Edition)-1101	B.K. Wisber	Closed	32.00	48.00
88-01-003	Sabina Valentine (Second Edition)-1101	B.K. Wisber	Open	41.00	42.00
85-01-004	Nettie Brown (First Edition)-1102	B.K. Wisber	Closed	32.00	43.00
88-01-005	Nettie Brown (Second Edition)-1102	B.K. Wisber	Open	37.00	38.00
85-01-006	Emma High-1103	B.K. Wisber	Closed	32.00	42.00
85-01-007	Rebecca Bowman (First Edition)-1104	B.K. Wisber	Closed	32.00	42.00
89-01-008	Rebecca Bowman (Second Edition)-1104	B.K. Wisber	Open	58.00	59.00
85-01-009	Mary Valentine-1105	B.K. Wisber	Closed	32.00	42.00
85-01-010	Wendel Bowman (First Edition)-1106	B.K. Wisber	Closed	32.00	42.00
92-01-011	Wendel Bowman (Second Edition)-1106	B.K. Wisber	Open	60.00	61.00
85-01-012	Russell Dunn-1107	B.K. Wisber	Closed	32.00	42.00
85-01-013	Luther Bowman-1108	B.K. Wisber	Closed	32.00	42.00
85-01-014	Elizabeth Sweetland (First Edition)-1109	B.K. Wisber	Closed	32.00	42.00
91-01-015	Elizabeth Sweetland (Second Edition)-1109	B.K. Wisber	Open	56.00	57.00
85-01-016	Christian Bowman-1110	B.K. Wisber	Closed	32.00	42.00
85-01-017	Amanda High (First Edition)-1111	B.K. Wisber	Closed	32.00	42.00
90-01-018	Amanda High (Second Edition)-1111	B.K. Wisber	Open	56.00	57.00
85-01-019	Louella Valentine-1112	B.K. Wisber	Closed	35.00	42.00
85-01-020	Peter Valentine-1113	B.K. Wisber	Closed	36.00	43.00
85-01-021	Nettie Brown (Christmas)-1114	B.K. Wisber	Closed	32.00	42.00
85-01-022	Cora High-1115	B.K. Wisber	Closed	32.00	42.00
85-01-023	Ida Valentine-1116	B.K. Wisber	Closed	32.00	42.00
85-01-024	Martin Bowman-1117	B.K. Wisber	Closed	36.00	43.00
85-01-025	Esther Dunn (First Edition)-1127	B.K. Wisber	Closed	45.00	60.00
91-01-026	Esther Dunn (SecondEdition)-1127	B.K. Wisber	Open	60.00	61.00
91-01-027	Cynthia High-1127A	B.K. Wisber	Open	60.00	61.00
85-01-028	Benjamin Bowman-1129	B.K. Wisber	Closed	32.00	40.00
85-01-029	Flossie High (First Edition)-1128	B.K. Wisber	Closed	45.00	62.00
89-01-030	Flossie High (Second Edition)-1128	B.K. Wisber	Open	55.00	56.00
85-01-031	Hannah Brown-1131	B.K. Wisber	Closed	45.00	60.00
85-01-032	Benjamin Bowman (Santa)-1134	B.K. Wisber	Open	39.00	40.00
85-01-033	Katrina Valentine-1135	B.K. Wisber	Closed	32.00	42.00
86-01-034	Grace Valentine (First Edition)-1146	B.K. Wisber	Closed	33.00	42.00
90-01-035	Grace Valentine (Second Edition)-1146	B.K. Wisber	Open	48.00	49.00
86-01-036	Juliet Valentine (First Edition)-1147	B.K. Wisber	Closed	33.00	42.00
90-01-037	Juliet Valentine (Second Edition)-1147	B.K. Wisber	Open	49.00	50.00
86-01-038	Alice Valentine-1148	B.K. Wisber	Closed	33.00	42.00
86-01-039	Susanna Bowman-1149	B.K. Wisber	Closed	45.00	58.00
86-01-040	Annie Bowman (First Edition)-1150	B.K. Wisber	Closed	33.00	42.00
93-01-041	Annie Bowman (Second Edition)-1150	B.K. Wisber	Open	68.00	68.00
86-01-042	Martha High-1151	B.K. Wisber	Closed	33.00	42.00
86-01-043	Dora High (First Edition)-1152	B.K. Wisber	Closed	32.00	41.00
92-01-044	Dora High (Second Edition)-1152	B.K. Wisber	Closed	48.00	48.00
86-01-045	Delia Valentine-1153	B.K. Wisber	Closed	33.00	42.00
86-01-046	Sarah Valentine-1154	B.K. Wisber	Open	37.00	38.00
86-01-047	Sally Bowman-1155	B.K. Wisber	Closed	35.00	42.00
86-01-048	Tillie Brown-1156	B.K. Wisber	Closed	34.00	42.00
86-01-049	Andrew Brown-1157	B.K. Wisber	Closed	45.00	58.00
86-01-050	Edward Bowman-1158	B.K. Wisber	Closed	45.00	58.00
86-01-051	Thomas Bowman-1159	B.K. Wisber	Closed	32.00	41.00
86-01-052	Maggie High-1160	B.K. Wisber	Closed	32.00	41.00
86-01-053	Karl Valentine-1161	B.K. Wisber	Closed	32.00	41.00
86-01-054	Willie Bowman-1162	B.K. Wisber	Closed	35.00	41.00
86-01-055	Sadie Valentine-1163	B.K. Wisber	Open	47.00	48.00
86-01-056	Sophie Valentine-1164	B.K. Wisber	Closed	47.00	58.00

Company		Series			
Number	Name	Artist	Edition Limit	Issue Price	Quote
86-01-057	Katie Bowman-1178	B.K. Wisber	Open	38.00	39.00
86-01-058	Cassie Yocum (First Edition)-1179	B.K. Wisber	Closed	37.00	42.00
92-01-059	Cassie Yocum (Second Edition)-1179	B.K. Wisber	Open	79.00	80.00
86-01-060	Jillian Bowman-1180	B.K. Wisber	Closed	34.00	42.00
86-01-061	Jenny Valentine-1181	B.K. Wisber	Closed	34.00	42.00
86-01-062	Christopher High-1182	B.K. Wisber	Closed	35.00	42.00
86-01-063	Marland Valentine-1183	B.K. Wisber	Closed	33.00	42.00
86-01-064	Marie Valentine (First Edition)-1184	B.K. Wisber	Closed	48.00	58.00
92-01-065	Marie Valentine (Second Edition)-1184	B.K. Wisber	Open	68.00	69.00
86-01-066	Emily Bowman (First Edition)-1185	B.K. Wisber	Closed	34.00	34.00
90-01-067	Emily Bowman (Second Edition)-1185	B.K. Wisber	Open	48.00	49.00
86-01-068	Matthew Yocum-1186	B.K. Wisber	Closed	33.00	42.00
86-01-069	Madaleine Valentine (First Edition)-1187	B.K. Wisber	Closed	34.00	42.00
89-01-070	Madaleine Valentine (Second Edition)-1187	B.K. Wisber	Open	38.00	39.00
86-01-071	Rachel Bowman (First Edition)-1188	B.K. Wisber	Closed	34.00	42.00
89-01-072	Rachel Bowman (Second Edition)-1188	B.K. Wisber	Open	36.00	37.00
86-01-073	Molly Yocum (First Edition)-1189	B.K. Wisber	Closed	34.00	43.00
89-01-074	Molly Yocum(Second Edition)-1189	B.K. Wisber	Open	40.00	41.00
86-01-075	Carrie High (First Edition)-1190	B.K. Wisber	Closed	45.00	43.00
89-01-076	Carrie High (Second Edition)-1190	B.K. Wisber	Open	47.00	48.00
86-01-077	William Valentine-1191	B.K. Wisber	Closed	37.00	44.00
86-01-078	Jeremy Bowman-1192	B.K. Wisber	Closed	37.00	44.00
86-01-079	Marisa Valentine (w/ Brother Petey)-1194	B.K. Wisber	Open	48.00	49.00
86-01-080	Marisa Valentine (alone)-1194A	B.K. Wisber	Open	37.00	38.00
86-01-081	David Yocum-1195	B.K. Wisber	Open	35.00	36.00
86-01-082	Little Ghosts-1197	B.K. Wisber	Open	17.00	18.00
87-01-083	Johanna Valentine-1198	B.K. Wisber	Closed	37.00	42.00
87-01-084	Abigail Bowman-1199	B.K. Wisber	Open	44.00	45.00
87-01-085	Naomi Valentine-1200	B.K. Wisber	Open	43.00	44.00
87-01-086	Amy Bowman-1201	B.K. Wisber	Open	40.00	41.00
87-01-087	Addie High-1202	B.K. Wisber	Open	40.00	41.00
87-01-088	The Wedding (Bride)-1203	B.K. Wisber	Open	39.00	40.00
87-01-089	The Wedding (Groom)-1203A	B.K. Wisber	Open	35.00	36.00
87-01-090	The Flower Girl-1204	B.K. Wisber	Open	22.00	23.00
87-01-091	Olivia High-1205	B.K. Wisber	Open	40.00	41.00
87-01-092	Imogene Bowman-1206	B.K. Wisber	Open	39.00	40.00
87-01-093	Rebecca's Mother-1207	B.K. Wisber	Open	42.00	42.00
87-01-094	Penelope High-1208	B.K. Wisber	Closed	41.00	49.00
87-01-095	Margaret Bowman-1213	B.K. Wisber	Open	40.00	41.00
87-01-096	Patsy Bowman-1214	B.K. Wisber	Open	51.00	52.00
87-01-097	Ramona Brown-1215	B.K. Wisber	Closed	40.00	50.00
87-01-098	Gretchen High-1216	B.K. Wisber	Open	43.00	44.00
87-01-099	Cat on Chair-1217	B.K. Wisber	Closed	17.00	20.00
87-01-100	Katie and Barney-1219	B.K. Wisber	Open	40.00	41.00
87-01-101	Melanie Bowman (First Edition)-1220	B.K. Wisber	Closed	36.00	36.00
92-01-102	Melanie Bowman (Second Edition)-1220	B.K. Wisber	Open	46.00	47.00
87-01-103	Charles Bowman (First Edition)-1221	B.K. Wisber	Closed	34.00	42.00
92-01-104	Charles Bowman (Second Edition)-1221	B.K. Wisber	Open	46.00	47.00
87-01-105	Bridget Bowman-1222	B.K. Wisber	Open	45.00	46.00
87-01-106	Laura Valentine-1223	B.K. Wisber	Open	38.00	39.00
87-01-107	Santa Claus (sitting)-1224	B.K. Wisber	Closed	51.00	61.00
87-01-108	Little Witch-1225	B.K. Wisber	Open	21.00	22.00
87-01-109	Priscilla High-1226	B.K. Wisber	Open	60.00	61.00
88-01-110	Megan Valentine-1227	B.K. Wisber	Open	47.00	48.00
87-01-111	Pauline Bowman-1228	B.K. Wisber	Open	47.00	48.00
88-01-112	Allison Bowman-1229	B.K. Wisber	Open	58.00	59.00
88-01-113	Jacob High-1230	B.K. Wisber	Open	45.00	46.00
88-01-114	Janie Valentine-1231	B.K. Wisber	Open	40.00	41.00
88-01-115	Ruth Anne Bowman-1232	B.K. Wisber	Open	45.00	46.00
88-01-116	Daphne Bowman-1235	B.K. Wisber	Open	39.00	40.00
88-01-117	Mary Ellen Valentine-1236	B.K. Wisber	Open	42.00	43.00
88-01-118	Kinch Bowman-1237	B.K. Wisber	Open	48.00	49.00
88-01-119	Samantha Bowman-1238	B.K. Wisber	Open	48.00	49.00
88-01-120	Hattie Bowman-1239	B.K. Wisber	Open	43.00	44.00
88-01-121	Eunice High-1240	B.K. Wisber	Open	57.00	58.00
88-01-122	Bess High-1241	B.K. Wisber	Open	47.00	48.00
88-01-123	Bessie Valentine-1245	B.K. Wisber	Open	43.00	43.00
88-01-124	Phoebe High-1246	B.K. Wisber	Closed	49.00	59.00
89-01-125	Vanessa High-1247	B.K. Wisber	Open	47.00	48.00
89-01-126	Amelia High-1248	B.K. Wisber	Open	47.00	48.00
89-01-127	Victoria Bowman-1249	B.K. Wisber	Open	41.00	42.00
89-01-128	Johann Bowman-1250	B.K. Wisber	Open	41.00	42.00
89-01-129	Emmy Lou Valentine-1251	B.K. Wisber	Open	46.00	47.00
89-01-130	Peggy Bowman-1252	B.K. Wisber	Open	59.00	60.00
89-01-131	Jessica High (with Mother)-1253	B.K. Wisber	Open	59.00	60.00
89-01-132	Jessica High (alone)-1253A	B.K. Wisber	Open	22.00	23.00
89-01-133	Jason High (with Mother)-1254	B.K. Wisber	Open	59.00	60.00
89-01-134	Jason High (alone)-1254A	B.K. Wisber	Open	22.00	23.00
89-01-135	Lucy Bowman-1255	B.K. Wisber	Open	46.00	47.00
89-01-136	Miriam High-1256	B.K. Wisber	Open	47.00	48.00
89-01-137	Santa (with Tub)-1257	B.K. Wisber	Open	60.00	61.00
89-01-138	Mrs. Claus-1258	B.K. Wisber	Open	43.00	44.00
90-01-139	Marlene Valentine-1259	B.K. Wisber	Open	49.00	50.00
90-01-140	Albert Valentine-1260	B.K. Wisber	Open	43.00	44.00
90-01-141	Nancy Bowman-1261	B.K. Wisber	Open	49.00	50.00
91-01-142	Annabelle Bowman-1267	B.K. Wisber	Open	68.00	69.00
91-01-143	Michael Bowman-1268	B.K. Wisber	Open	52.00	53.00
91-01-144	Trudy Valentine-1269	B.K. Wisber	Open	64.00	65.00
91-01-145	The Department Store Santa-1270	B.K. Wisber	Open	76.00	77.00
91-01-146	Santa's Helper-1271	B.K. Wisber	Open	52.00	53.00
91-01-147	Barbara Helen-1274	B.K. Wisber	Open	58.00	59.00
92-01-148	Edwin Bowman-1281	B.K. Wisber	Open	70.00	71.00
92-01-149	Carol Anne Bowman-1282	B.K. Wisber	Open	70.00	71.00
92-01-150	Joseph Valentine-1283	B.K. Wisber	Open	62.00	63.00
92-01-151	Natalie Valentine-1284	B.K. Wisber	Open	62.00	63.00
92-01-152	Kathryn Bowman (Limited Edition)-1285	B.K. Wisber	3,000	140.00	140.00
92-01-153	Wendy Bowman-1293	B.K. Wisber	Open	78.00	79.00
92-01-154	Timothy Bowman-1294	B.K. Wisber	Open	56.00	57.00
92-01-155	Joanie Valentine-1295	B.K. Wisber	Open	48.00	49.00
93-01-156	Justine Valentine-1302	B.K. Wisber	Open	84.00	84.00
93-01-157	Pearl Bowman-1303	B.K. Wisber	Open	56.00	56.00
92-01-158	Ashley Bowman-1304	B.K. Wisber	Open	48.00	48.00
92-01-159	Francis Bowman-1305	B.K. Wisber	Open	48.00	48.00
Ladie and Friends™		**The Little Ones**			
85-02-001	White Girl (First Edition)-1130	B.K. Wisber	Closed	15.00	26.00
85-02-002	Black Girl (First Edition)-1130	B.K. Wisber	Closed	15.00	26.00
85-02-003	White Boy (First Edition)-1130	B.K. Wisber	Closed	15.00	26.00
85-02-004	Black Boy (First Edition)-1130	B.K. Wisber	Closed	15.00	26.00
89-02-005	White Girl-pastels (Second Edition)-1130D	B.K. Wisber	Open	22.00	23.00
89-02-006	Black Girl-pastels (Second Edition)-1130E	B.K. Wisber	Open	22.00	23.00
89-02-007	White Girl-country color (2nd Edition)-1130F	B.K. Wisber	Open	22.00	23.00
89-02-008	Black Girl-country color(2nd Edition)-1130G	B.K. Wisber	Open	22.00	23.00

Number	Name	Artist	Edition Limit	Issue Price	Quote
89-02-009	White Boy (Second Edition)-1130H	B.K. Wisber	Open	22.00	23.00
89-02-010	Black Boy (Second Edition)-1130I	B.K. Wisber	Open	22.00	23.00
92-02-011	Little One w/Beach Bucket-1275	B.K. Wisber	Open	26.00	27.00
92-02-012	Little One w/Easter Eggs-1276	B.K. Wisber	Open	26.00	27.00
92-02-013	Little One wApples-1277	B.K. Wisber	Open	26.00	27.00
92-02-014	Little One w/Kitten and Yarn-1278	B.K. Wisber	Open	34.00	35.00
92-02-015	Little One w/Birthday Gift-1279	B.K. Wisber	Open	26.00	27.00
92-02-016	Little One w/Kitten and Milk-1280	B.K. Wisber	Open	32.00	33.00
92-02-017	Little One Reading-1286	B.K. Wisber	Open	36.00	37.00
92-02-018	Little One w/Christmas Lights-1287	B.K. Wisber	Open	34.00	35.00
92-02-019	Little One w/Snowman-1288	B.K. Wisber	Open	36.00	37.00
92-02-020	Little One w/Sled-1289	B.K. Wisber	Open	30.00	31.00
92-02-021	Little One Clown-1290	B.K. Wisber	Open	32.00	33.00
92-02-022	Little One w/Valentine-1291	B.K. Wisber	Open	30.00	31.00
92-02-023	Little One Girl w/Easter Flowers-1296	B.K. Wisber	Open	34.00	34.00
93-02-024	Little One Bunny-1297	B.K. Wisber	Open	36.00	36.00
93-02-025	Little One 4th of July Girl-1298	B.K. Wisber	Open	30.00	30.00
93-02-026	Little One w/Spinning Wheel-1299	B.K. Wisber	Open	36.00	36.00
93-02-027	Little One w/Mop-1300	B.K. Wisber	Open	36.00	36.00
92-02-028	Little One Boy w/Easter Flowers-1306	B.K. Wisber	Open	30.00	30.00
93-02-029	Little One 4th of July Boy-1307	B.K. Wisber	Open	28.00	28.00
Ladie and Friends™		**The Little Ones at Christmas**			
90-03-001	Little One w/Basket of Greens-1263	B.K. Wisber	Open	24.00	25.00
90-03-002	Little One w/Cookie-1264	B.K. Wisber	Open	24.00	25.00
90-03-003	Little One w/Tree Garland-1265	B.K. Wisber	Open	24.00	25.00
90-03-004	Little One w/Gift-1266	B.K. Wisber	Open	24.00	25.00
91-03-005	White Girl w/Santa Photo-1272	B.K. Wisber	Open	26.00	27.00
91-03-006	Black Girl w/Santa Photo-1272A	B.K. Wisber	Open	26.00	27.00
91-03-007	White Boy w/Santa Photo-1273	B.K. Wisber	Open	26.00	27.00
91-03-008	Black Boy w/Santa Photo-1273A	B.K. Wisber	Open	26.00	27.00
Ladie and Friends™		**The Pawtuckets™ of Sweet Briar Lane**			
86-04-001	Aunt Minnie Pawtucket™-1136	B.K. Wisber	Closed	45.00	60.00
86-04-002	Grammy Pawtucket™-1137	B.K. Wisber	Closed	34.00	43.00
86-04-003	Uncle Harley Pawtucket™-1138	B.K. Wisber	Closed	34.00	43.00
86-04-004	Sister Flora Pawtucket™-1139	B.K. Wisber	Closed	34.00	43.00
86-04-005	Brother Noah Pawtucket™-1140	B.K. Wisber	Closed	34.00	43.00
86-04-006	Aunt Lillian Pawtucket™-1141	B.K. Wisber	Closed	34.00	43.00
86-04-007	Mama Pawtucket™-1142	B.K. Wisber	Closed	36.00	44.00
86-04-008	Pappy Pawtucket™-1143	B.K. Wisber	Closed	34.00	42.00
86-04-009	Cousin Clara Pawtucket™-1144	B.K. Wisber	Closed	34.00	42.00
86-04-010	The Little One Bunnies-girl-1145	B.K. Wisber	Closed	15.00	20.00
86-04-011	The Little One Bunnies-boy-1145	B.K. Wisber	Closed	15.00	20.00
87-04-012	Cousin Isabel Pawtucket™-1209	B.K. Wisber	Closed	36.00	43.00
87-04-013	Cousin Alberta Pawtucket™-1210	B.K. Wisber	Closed	36.00	43.00
87-04-014	Sister Clemmie Pawtucket™-1211	B.K. Wisber	Closed	34.00	42.00
87-04-015	Aunt Mabel Pawtucket™-1212	B.K. Wisber	Closed	45.00	54.00
87-04-016	Bunny Bed-1218	B.K. Wisber	Closed	16.00	20.00
88-04-017	Cousin Winnie Pawtucket™-1233	B.K. Wisber	Closed	49.00	59.00
88-04-018	Cousin Jed Pawtucket™-1234	B.K. Wisber	Closed	34.00	42.00
Ladie and Friends™		**The Grummels™ of Log Hollow**			
86-05-001	Cousin Miranda Grummel™-1165	B.K. Wisber	Closed	47.00	60.00
86-05-002	Uncle Hollis Grummel™-1166	B.K. Wisber	Closed	34.00	42.00
86-05-003	Ma Grummel™-1167	B.K. Wisber	Closed	36.00	43.00
86-05-004	Teddy Bear Bed-1168	B.K. Wisber	Closed	15.00	18.00
86-05-005	Aunt Polly Grummel™-1169	B.K. Wisber	Closed	34.00	42.00
86-05-006	Cousin Lottie Grummel™-1170	B.K. Wisber	Closed	36.00	42.00
86-05-007	Aunt Gertie Grummel™-1171	B.K. Wisber	Closed	34.00	42.00
86-05-008	Pa Grummel™-1172	B.K. Wisber	Closed	34.00	42.00
86-05-009	Grandma Grummel™-1173	B.K. Wisber	Closed	45.00	45.00
86-05-010	Aunt Hilda Grummel™-1174	B.K. Wisber	Closed	34.00	42.00
86-05-011	Washline-1175	B.K. Wisber	Closed	15.00	20.00
86-05-012	Grandpa Grummel™-1176	B.K. Wisber	Closed	36.00	42.00
86-05-013	Sister Nora Grummel™-1177	B.K. Wisber	Closed	34.00	42.00
86-05-014	The Little Ones-Grummels™ (boy/girl)-1196	B.K. Wisber	Closed	15.00	20.00
Ladie and Friends™		**The Thanksgiving Play**			
88-06-001	Pilgrim Boy-1242	B.K. Wisber	Open	41.00	42.00
88-06-002	Pilgrim Girl-1243	B.K. Wisber	Open	49.00	50.00
88-06-003	Indian Squaw-1244	B.K. Wisber	Open	37.00	38.00
Ladie and Friends™		**The Christmas Pageant**			
85-07-001	Mary and Baby Jesus-1118	B.K. Wisber	Open	36.00	37.00
85-07-002	Joseph and Donkey-1119	B.K. Wisber	Open	36.00	37.00
85-07-003	"Peace" Angel-1120	B.K. Wisber	Closed	32.00	42.00
85-07-004	"On" Angel-1121	B.K. Wisber	Closed	32.00	42.00
85-07-005	"Earth" Angel-1122	B.K. Wisber	Closed	32.00	42.00
89-07-006	"Peace" Angel (Second Edition)-1120	B.K. Wisber	Open	49.00	50.00
85-07-007	"Noel" Angel (First Edition)-1126	B.K. Wisber	Closed	32.00	32.00
89-07-008	"Noel" Angel (Second Edition)-1126	B.K. Wisber	Open	49.00	50.00
85-07-009	Wiseman #1-1123	B.K. Wisber	Open	36.00	37.00
85-07-010	Wiseman #2-1124	B.K. Wisber	Open	36.00	37.00
85-07-011	Wiseman #3-1125	B.K. Wisber	Open	36.00	37.00
85-07-012	Wooden Creche-1132	B.K. Wisber	Open	30.00	31.00
85-07-013	Christmas Wooly Lamb-1133	B.K. Wisber	Closed	12.00	14.00
86-07-014	Shepherd-1193	B.K. Wisber	Open	36.00	37.00
Ladie and Friends™		**The Christmas Concert**			
90-08-001	Claire Valentine-1262	B.K. Wisber	Open	56.00	57.00
92-08-002	Judith High-1292	B.K. Wisber	Open	70.00	71.00
Ladie and Friends™		**Lizzie High Society Members Only Club**			
93-09-001	Audrey High-1301	B.K. Wisber	Yr. Iss.	59.00	59.00
Lawtons		**Childhood Classics**			
83-01-001	Alice In Wonderland	W. Lawton	Closed	225.00	2000-3000.
84-01-002	Heidi	W. Lawton	Closed	325.00	650-850.00
85-01-003	Hans Brinker	W. Lawton	Closed	325.00	1000-1800.
86-01-004	Anne Of Green Gables	W. Lawton	Closed	325.00	2000-2400.
86-01-005	Pollyanna	W. Lawton	Closed	325.00	1000-1600.
86-01-006	Laura Ingals	W. Lawton	Closed	325.00	500-900.
87-01-007	Mary Lennox	W. Lawton	Closed	325.00	500-950.
87-01-008	Just David	W. Lawton	Closed	325.00	700-1100.
87-01-009	Polly Pepper	W. Lawton	Closed	325.00	450-700.
88-01-010	Rebecca	W. Lawton	Closed	350.00	500-850.
88-01-011	Eva	W. Lawton	Closed	350.00	500-1000.
88-01-012	Topsy	W. Lawton	Closed	350.00	750-1200.
89-01-013	Little Princess	W. Lawton	Closed	395.00	650-950.
89-01-014	Honey Bunch	W. Lawton	Closed	350.00	550-800.
90-01-015	Mary Frances	W. Lawton	Closed	350.00	425.00
90-01-016	Poor Little Match Girl	W. Lawton	Closed	350.00	475.00
91-01-017	The Bobbsey Twins	W. Lawton	Closed	725.00	795.00
91-01-018	Hiawatha	W. Lawton	Closed	395.00	500.00
91-01-019	Little Black Sambo	W. Lawton	Closed	395.00	595.00
Lawtons		**Childhood Classics II**			
92-02-001	Peter And The Wolf	W. Lawton	750	495.00	495.00
92-02-002	Marigold Garden	W. Lawton	750	450.00	450.00
92-02-003	Oliver Twist	W. Lawton	750	450.00	450.00
Lawtons		**Sugar 'n' Spice**			
86-03-001	Kimberly	W. Lawton	Closed	250.00	550-800.
86-03-002	Kersten	W. Lawton	Closed	250.00	550-800.
86-03-003	Jason	W. Lawton	Closed	250.00	800-1700.
86-03-004	Jessica	W. Lawton	Closed	250.00	800-1700.
87-03-005	Marie	W. Lawton	Closed	275.00	450.00
87-03-006	Ginger	W. Lawton	Closed	275.00	395-550.
Lawtons		**Newcomer Collection**			
87-04-001	Ellin Elizabeth	W. Lawton	Closed	335.00	900-1200.
87-04-002	Ellin Elizabeth, Eyes Closed	W. Lawton	Closed	335.00	750-1000.
Lawtons		**Timeless Ballads**			
87-05-001	Highland Mary	W. Lawton	Closed	550.00	600-875.
87-05-002	Annabel Lee	W. Lawton	Closed	550.00	600-695.
87-05-003	Young Charlotte	W. Lawton	Closed	550.00	850-900.
85-05-004	She Walks In Beauty	W. Lawton	Closed	550.00	600.00
Lawtons		**One-Of-A Kind Issues**			
89-06-001	Amelia	W. Lawton	1	N/A	N/A
90-06-002	Goldilocks And Baby Bear	W. Lawton	1	N/A	4250.00
91-06-003	Felicity Minds The Quints	W. Lawton	1	N/A	N/A
Lawtons		**Special Edition**			
88-07-001	Marcella And Raggedy Ann	W. Lawton	Closed	395.00	650.00
Lawtons		**Christmas Dolls**			
88-08-001	Christmas Joy	W. Lawton	Closed	325.00	750-1200.
89-08-002	Noel	W. Lawton	Closed	325.00	325-750.
90-08-003	Christmas Angel	W. Lawton	Closed	325.00	325.00
91-08-004	Yuletide Carole	W. Lawton	Closed	395.00	395.00
Lawtons		**Special Occasion**			
88-09-001	Nanthy	W. Lawton	Closed	325.00	450-525.
88-09-002	First Day Of School	W. Lawton	Closed	325.00	450-550.
90-09-003	First Birthday	W. Lawton	Closed	295.00	350.00
Lawtons		**Seasons**			
88-10-001	Amber Autumn	W. Lawton	Closed	325.00	400-525.
89-10-002	Summer Rose	W. Lawton	Closed	325.00	375-475.
90-10-003	Crystal Winter	W. Lawton	Closed	325.00	325.00
91-10-004	Spring Blossom	W. Lawton	Closed	350.00	350.00
Lawtons		**Wee Bits**			
88-11-001	Wee Bit O'Heaven	W. Lawton	Closed	295.00	450-600.
88-11-002	Wee Bit O'Woe	W. Lawton	Closed	295.00	450-700.
88-11-003	Wee Bit O'Sunshine	W. Lawton	Closed	295.00	450-600.
89-11-004	Wee Bit O'Bliss	W. Lawton	Closed	295.00	350.00
89-11-005	Wee Bit O'Wonder	W. Lawton	Closed	295.00	395.00
Lawtons		**Playthings Past**			
89-12-001	Victoria And Teddy	W .Lawton	Closed	395.00	395.00
89-12-002	Edward And Dobbin	W. Lawton	Closed	395.00	495-600.
89-12-003	Elizabeth And Baby	W. Lawton	Closed	395.00	495-650.
Lawtons		**Cherished Customs**			
90-13-001	The Blessing/Mexico	W. Lawton	Closed	395.00	800-1200.
90-13-002	Midsommar/Sweden	W. Lawton	Closed	395.00	395.00
90-13-003	Girls Day/Japan	W. Lawton	Closed	395.00	450-600.
90-13-004	High Tea/Great Britain	W. Lawton	Closed	395.00	450-550.
91-13-005	Ndeko/Zaire	W. Lawton	Closed	395.00	550-750.
91-13-006	Frolic/Amish	W. Lawton	Closed	395.00	395.00
92-13-007	Pascha/Ukraine	W. Lawton	750	495.00	495.00
92-13-008	Carnival/Brazil	W. Lawton	750	425.00	425.00
92-13-009	Cradleboard/Navajo	W. Lawton	750	425.00	425.00
Lawtons		**Guild Dolls**			
89-14-001	Baa Baa Black Sheep	W. Lawton	Closed	395.00	750-1000.
90-14-002	Lavender Blue	W. Lawton	Closed	395.00	450-600.
91-14-003	To Market, To Market	W. Lawton	Closed	495.00	495.00
92-14-004	Little Boy Blue	W. Lawton	Closed	395.00	395.00
93-14-005	Lawton Logo Doll	W. Lawton	Yr.Iss.	350.00	350.00
Lawtons		**The Children's Hour**			
91-15-001	Grave Alice	W. Lawton	Closed	395.00	395.00
91-15-002	Laughing Allegra	W. Lawton	Closed	395.00	395.00
91-15-003	Edith With Golden Hair	W. Lawton	Closed	395.00	395.00
Lawtons		**Store Exclusives**			
91-16-001	Main Street, USA	W. Lawton	Closed	350.00	350.00
91-16-002	Liberty Square	W. Lawton	Closed	350.00	395.00
91-16-003	Little Colonel	W. Lawton	Closed	395.00	395.00
91-16-004	Garden Song Marta	W. Lawton	Closed	335.00	335.00
91-16-005	Tish	W. Lawton	Closed	395.00	395.00
Lawtons		**Christmas Legends**			
91-17-001	The Legend Of The Poinsettia	W. Lawton	750	395.00	395.00
Lawtons		**Folk Tales And Fairy Stories**			
92-18-001	Little Red Riding Hood	W. Lawton	750	450.00	450.00
92-18-002	The Little Emperor's Nightingale	W. Lawton	750	425.00	425.00
92-18-003	William Tell, The Younger	W. Lawton	750	395.00	395.00
92-18-004	Swan Princess	W. Lawton	750	495.00	495.00
Lenox Collections		**Lenox China Dolls**			
84-01-001	Maryanne, 20"	J. Grammer	Unkn.	425.00	2000.00
84-01-002	Abigail, 20"	J. Grammer	Unkn.	425.00	2000.00
84-01-003	Jessica, 20"	J. Grammer	Unkn.	450.00	1900.00
84-01-004	Rebecca, 16"	J. Grammer	Unkn.	375.00	1700.00
84-01-005	Amanda, 16"	J. Grammer	Unkn.	385.00	1700.00
84-01-006	Maggie, 16"	J. Grammer	Unkn.	375.00	1700.00
84-01-007	Melissa, 16"	J. Grammer	Unkn.	450.00	3100.00
84-01-008	Samantha, 16"	J. Grammer	500	500.00	2800.00

DOLLS

Number	Name	Artist	Edition Limit	Issue Price	Quote
Lenox Collections		**China Dolls -Cloth Bodies**			
85-02-001	Amy, 14"	J. Grammer	Unkn.	250.00	995.00
85-02-002	Elizabeth, 14"	J. Grammer	Unkn.	250.00	995.00
85-02-003	Sarah, 14"	J. Grammer	Unkn.	250.00	995.00
85-02-004	Annabelle, 14"	J. Grammer	Unkn.	250.00	995.00
85-02-005	Miranda, 14"	J. Grammer	Unkn.	250.00	995.00
85-02-006	Jennifer, 14"	J. Grammer	Unkn.	250.00	995.00
Lenox Collections		**Lenox Victorian Dolls**			
89-03-001	The Victorian Bride	Unknown	Open	295.00	295.00
90-03-002	Christmas Doll, Elizabeth	Unknown	Open	195.00	195.00
91-03-003	Victorian Christening Doll	Unknown	Open	295.00	295.00
92-03-004	Lady at Gala	Unknown	Open	295.00	295.00
Lenox Collections		**Children of the World**			
89-04-001	Hannah, The Little Dutch Maiden	Unknown	Open	119.00	119.00
90-04-002	Heather, Little Highlander	Unknown	Open	119.00	119.00
91-04-003	Amma-The African Girl	Unknown	Open	119.00	119.00
91-04-004	Sakura-The Japanese Girl	Unknown	Open	119.00	119.00
92-04-005	Gretchen, German Doll	Unknown	Open	119.00	119.00
Lenox Collections		**Sibling Dolls**			
91-05-001	Skating Lesson	A. Lester	Open	195.00	195.00
Lenox Collections		**Ellis Island Dolls**			
91-06-001	Megan	P. Thompson	Closed	150.00	150.00
91-06-002	Stefan	P. Thompson	Closed	150.00	150.00
92-06-003	Angelina	P. Thompson	Closed	150.00	150.00
92-06-004	Catherine	P. Thompson	Closed	152.00	152.00
92-06-005	Anna	P. Thompson	Closed	152.00	152.00
Lenox Collections		**Musical Baby Dolls**			
91-07-001	Patrick's Lullabye	Unknown	Open	95.00	95.00
Lenox Collections		**Bolshoi Nutcracker Dolls**			
91-08-001	Clara	Unknown	Open	195.00	195.00
Lenox Collections		**Country Decor Dolls**			
91-09-001	Molly	Unknown	Open	150.00	150.00
Lenox Collections		**Children With Toys Dolls**			
91-10-001	Tea For Teddy	Unknown	Open	136.00	136.00
Lenox Collections		**Little Women**			
92-11-001	Amy	Unknown	Open	150.00	150.00
92-11-002	Amy, The Inspiring Artist	Unknown	Open	152.00	152.00
Lenox Collections		**Bonnet Baby Dolls**			
92-12-001	Easter Bonnet	Unknown	Open	95.00	95.00
Lenox Collections		**First Collector Doll**			
92-13-001	Lauren	Unknown	Open	152.00	152.00
Lenox Collections		**Inspirational Doll**			
92-14-001	Blessed Are The Peacemakers	Unknown	Open	119.00	119.00
Lenox Collections		**International Baby Doll**			
92-15-001	Natalia, Russian Baby	Unknown	Open	119.00	119.00
Lenox Collections		**Nutcracker Dolls**			
92-16-001	Sugarplum	Unknown	Open	195.00	195.00
93-16-002	Nutcracker	Unknown	Open	195.00	195.00
Lenox Collections		**Prima Ballerina Collection**			
92-17-001	Odette, Queen of the Swans	Unknown	Open	195.00	195.00
93-17-002	Sleeping Beauty	Unknown	Open	195.00	195.00
Seymour Mann Inc.		**Connossieur Doll Collection**			
84-01-001	Miss Debutante Debi	E. Mann	Closed	75.00	180.00
85-01-002	Christmas Cheer-124	E. Mann	Closed	40.00	100.00
85-01-003	Wendy-C120	E. Mann	Closed	45.00	150.00
86-01-004	Camelot Fairy-C-84	E. Mann	Closed	75.00	225.00
87-01-005	Audrina-YK-200	E. Mann	Closed	85.00	140.00
87-01-006	Cynthia-DOM-211	E. Mann	Closed	85.00	85.00
87-01-006	Dawn-C185	E. Mann	Closed	75.00	175.00
87-01-007	Linda-C190	E. Mann	Closed	60.00	120.00
87-01-008	Marcy-YK122	E. Mann	Closed	55.00	100.00
87-01-009	Nirmala-YK-210	E. Mann	Closed	50.00	50.00
87-01-010	Rapunzel-C158	E. Mann	Closed	95.00	165.00
87-01-011	Sabrina-C208	E. Mann	Closed	65.00	95.00
87-01-012	Sailorette-DOM217	E. Mann	Closed	70.00	150.00
87-01-013	Vivian-C-201P	E. Mann	Closed	80.00	80.00
88-01-014	Ashley-C-278	E. Mann	Closed	80.00	80.00
88-01-015	Brittany-TK-5	E. Mann	2,500	120.00	120.00
88-01-016	Cissie-DOM263	E. Mann	Closed	65.00	135.00
88-01-017	Crying Courtney-PS75	E. Mann	Closed	115.00	115.00
88-01-018	Cynthia-DOM-211	E. Mann	3,500	85.00	85.00
88-01-019	Doll Oliver-FH392	E. Mann	2,500	100.00	100.00
88-01-020	Giselle on Goose-FH176	E. Mann	Closed	105.00	225.00
88-01-021	Emily-YK-243V	E. Mann	Closed	70.00	70.00
88-01-022	Frances-C-233	E. Mann	Closed	80.00	125.00
88-01-023	Jessica-DOM-267	E. Mann	Closed	90.00	90.00
88-01-024	Joanne Cry Baby-PS50	E. Mann	25,000	100.00	100.00
88-01-025	Jolie-C231	E. Mann	Closed	65.00	150.00
88-01-026	Julie-C245A	E. Mann	Closed	65.00	160.00
88-01-027	Juliette Bride Musical-C246LTM	E. Mann	Closed	150.00	150.00
88-01-028	Kirsten-PS-40G	E. Mann	2,500	70.00	70.00
88-01-029	Lionel-FH206B	E. Mann	Closed	50.00	120.00
88-01-030	Lucinda-DOM-293	E. Mann	2,500	90.00	90.00
88-01-031	Michelle & Marcel-YK176	E. Mann	Closed	70.00	150.00
88-01-032	Pauline-YK-230	E. Mann	Closed	90.00	90.00
88-01-033	Sabrina -C-208	E. Mann	Closed	65.00	95.00
88-01-034	Sister Agnes 14"-C250	E. Mann	2,500	75.00	75.00
88-01-035	Sister Ignatius Notre Dame-FH184	E. Mann	2,500	75.00	75.00
88-01-036	Sister Teresa-FH187	E. Mann	2,500	80.00	80.00
88-01-037	Tracy-C-3006	E. Mann	Closed	95.00	150.00
88-01-038	Vivian-C201P	E. Mann	3,500	80.00	80.00
89-01-039	Ashley-C-278	E. Mann	3,500	80.00	80.00
89-01-040	Amber-DOM-281A	E. Mann	Closed	85.00	85.00
89-01-041	Betty-PS27G	E. Mann	Closed	65.00	125.00
89-01-042	Brett-PS27B	E. Mann	Closed	65.00	125.00
89-01-043	Brittany-TK-4	E. Mann	Closed	150.00	150.00
89-01-044	Baby John-PS-49B	E. Mann	2,500	85.00	85.00
89-01-045	Crying Courtney-PS-75	E. Mann	Closed	115.00	115.00
89-01-046	Daphne Ecru/Mint Green-C3025	E. Mann	2,500	85.00	85.00
89-01-047	Elisabeth-OM-32	E. Mann	2,500	120.00	120.00
89-01-048	Elizabeth-C-246P	E. Mann	Closed	150.00	200.00
89-01-049	Emily-PS-48	E. Mann	Closed	110.00	110.00
89-01-050	Frances-C233	E. Mann	Closed	80.00	125.00
89-01-051	Happy Birthday-C3012	E. Mann	Closed	80.00	125.00
89-01-052	Heidi-260	E. Mann	Closed	50.00	95.00
89-01-053	Jaqueline-DOLL-254M	E. Mann	Closed	85.00	85.00
89-01-054	Joanne Cry Baby-PS-50	E. Mann	2,500	100.00	100.00
89-01-055	Kayoko-PS-24	E. Mann	Closed	75.00	175.00
89-01-056	Kirsten-PS-40G	E. Mann	Closed	70.00	70.00
89-01-057	Ling-Ling-PS-87G	E. Mann	2,500	90.00	90.00
89-01-058	Liz -YK-269	E. Mann	Closed	70.00	100.00
89-01-059	Lucinda -DOM-293	E. Mann	Closed	90.00	90.00
89-01-060	Mai-Ling-PS-79	E. Mann	2,500	100.00	100.00
89-01-061	Marcey-YK-4005	E. Mann	3,500	90.00	90.00
89-01-062	Margaret-245	E. Mann	Closed	100.00	150.00
89-01-063	Maureen-PS-84	E. Mann	Closed	90.00	90.00
89-01-064	Meimei-PS22	E. Mann	Closed	75.00	225.00
89-01-065	Melissa-LL-794	E. Mann	Closed	95.00	95.00
89-01-066	Miss Kim-PS-25	E. Mann	Closed	75.00	175.00
89-01-067	Patricia/Patrick-215GBB	E. Mann	3,500	105.00	135.00
89-01-068	Paula-PS-56	E. Mann	2,500	75.00	75.00
89-01-069	Pauline Bonaparte-OM68	E. Mann	2,500	120.00	120.00
89-01-070	Ramona-PS-31B	E. Mann	2,500	80.00	80.00
89-01-071	Rebecca-PS-34V	E. Mann	2,500	45.00	45.00
89-01-072	Rosie-290M	E. Mann	Closed	55.00	85.00
89-01-073	Sister Mary-C-249	E. Mann	3,500	75.00	125.00
89-01-074	Sunny-PS-59V	E. Mann	2,500	71.00	71.00
89-01-075	Suzie-PS-32	E. Mann	2,500	80.00	80.00
89-01-076	Tatiana Pink Ballerina-OM-60	E. Mann	Closed	120.00	120.00
89-01-077	Terri-PS-104	E. Mann	2,500	85.00	85.00
89-01-078	Wendy-PS-51	E. Mann	2,500	105.00	105.00
90-01-079	Anabelle-C-3080	E. Mann	Closed	85.00	85.00
90-01-080	Angel-DOM-335	E. Mann	2,500	105.00	105.00
90-01-081	Angela-C-3084	E. Mann	2,500	105.00	105.00
90-01-082	Angela-C-3084M	E. Mann	2,500	115.00	115.00
90-01-083	Anita-FH-277G	E. Mann	Closed	65.00	65.00
90-01-084	Ashley-FH-325	E. Mann	Closed	75.00	75.00
90-01-085	Audrey-YK-4089	E. Mann	3,500	125.00	125.00
90-01-086	Baby Betty-YK-4087	E. Mann	3,500	125.00	125.00
90-01-087	Baby Bonnie-SP-341	E. Mann	2,500	55.00	55.00
90-01-088	Baby Brent-EP-15	E. Mann	2,500	85.00	85.00
90-01-089	Baby Ecru-WB-17	E. Mann	2,500	65.00	65.00
90-01-090	Baby Kate-WB-19	E. Mann	2,500	85.00	85.00
90-01-091	Baby Nelly-PS-163	E. Mann	Closed	95.00	95.00
90-01-092	Baby Sue-DOLL-402B	E. Mann	2,500	27.50	27.50
90-01-093	Baby Sunshine-C-3055	E. Mann	Closed	90.00	90.00
90-01-094	Beth-YK-4099A/B	E. Mann	2,500	125.00	125.00
90-01-095	Bettina-TR-4	E. Mann	2,500	125.00	125.00
90-01-096	Beverly-DOLL-335	E. Mann	2,500	110.00	110.00
90-01-097	Billie-YK-4056V	E. Mann	3,500	65.00	65.00
90-01-098	Caillin-DOLL-11PH	E. Mann	Closed	60.00	60.00
90-01-099	Caitlin-YK-4051V	E. Mann	3,500	90.00	90.00
90-01-100	Carole-YK-4085W	E. Mann	3,500	125.00	125.00
90-01-101	Charlene-YK-4112	E. Mann	Closed	90.00	90.00
90-01-102	Chin Fa-C-3061	E. Mann	Closed	95.00	95.00
90-01-103	Chinook-WB-24	E. Mann	2,500	85.00	85.00
90-01-104	Chrissie-WB-2	E. Mann	Closed	75.00	75.00
90-01-105	Daisy-EP-6	E. Mann	Closed	90.00	90.00
90-01-106	Daphne Ecru-C-3025	E. Mann	Closed	85.00	85.00
90-01-107	Dianna-TK-31	E. Mann	Closed	175.00	175.00
90-01-108	Diane-FH-275	E. Mann	Closed	90.00	90.00
90-01-109	Domino-C-3050	E. Mann	Closed	145.00	145.00
90-01-110	Dorri-DOLL-16PH	E. Mann	Closed	85.00	85.00
90-01-111	Dorothy-TR-10	E. Mann	2,500	135.00	135.00
90-01-112	Eileen-FH-367	E. Mann	Closed	100.00	100.00
90-01-113	Felicia-TR-9	E. Mann	2,500	115.00	115.00
90-01-114	Francesca-C-3021	E. Mann	Closed	100.00	175.00
90-01-115	Gerri Beige-YK4094	E. Mann	2,500	95.00	95.00
90-01-116	Ginny-YK-4119	E. Mann	3,500	100.00	100.00
90-01-117	Hope-YK-4118	E. Mann	3,500	90.00	90.00
90-01-118	Hyacinth-DOLL-15PH	E. Mann	2,500	85.00	85.00
90-01-119	Indian Doll-FH-295	E. Mann	Closed	60.00	60.00
90-01-120	Janette-DOLL-385	E. Mann	Closed	85.00	85.00
90-01-121	Jillian-DOLL-41PH	E. Mann	Closed	90.00	90.00
90-01-122	Joanne-TR-12	E. Mann	2,500	175.00	175.00
90-01-123	Julie-WB-35	E. Mann	2,500	70.00	70.00
90-01-124	Karen-PS-198	E. Mann	2,500	150.00	150.00
90-01-125	Kate-C-3060	E. Mann	Closed	95.00	95.00
90-01-126	Kathy w/Bear-TE1	E. Mann	2,500	70.00	70.00
90-01-127	Kiku-EP-4	E. Mann	2,500	100.00	100.00
90-01-128	Laura-DOLL-25PH	E. Mann	Closed	55.00	55.00
90-01-129	Lauren-SP-300	E. Mann	2,500	85.00	85.00
90-01-130	Lavender Blue-YK-4024	E. Mann	3,500	95.00	135.00
90-01-131	Lien Wha-YK-4092	E. Mann	3,500	100.00	100.00
90-01-132	Ling-Ling-DOLL	E. Mann	2,500	50.00	50.00
90-01-133	Lisa-FH-379	E. Mann	Closed	100.00	100.00
90-01-134	Lisa Beige Accordion Pleat-YK4093	E. Mann	2,500	125.00	125.00
90-01-135	Liza-C-3053	E. Mann	Closed	100.00	100.00
90-01-136	Lola-SP-79	E. Mann	2,500	105.00	105.00
90-01-137	Loretta-FH-321	E. Mann	Closed	90.00	90.00
90-01-138	Lori-WB-72BM	E. Mann	2,500	75.00	75.00
90-01-139	Madame De Pompadour-C-3088	E. Mann	2,500	250.00	250.00
90-01-140	Maggie-PS-151P	E. Mann	Closed	90.00	90.00
90-01-141	Maggie-WB-51	E. Mann	2,500	105.00	105.00
90-01-142	Maria-YK-4116	E. Mann	3,500	85.00	85.00
90-01-143	Melanie-YK-4115	E. Mann	Closed	80.00	80.00
90-01-144	Melissa-DOLL-390	E. Mann	Closed	75.00	75.00
90-01-145	Merry Widow-C-3040	E. Mann	3,500	145.00	145.00
90-01-146	Merry Widow 20"-C-3040M	E. Mann	2,500	140.00	140.00
90-01-147	Nanook-WB-23	E. Mann	2,500	75.00	75.00
90-01-148	Natasha-PS-102	E. Mann	Closed	100.00	100.00
90-01-149	Odessa-FH-362	E. Mann	Closed	65.00	65.00
90-01-150	Ping-Ling-DOLL-363RV	E. Mann	2,500	50.00	50.00
90-01-151	Polly-DOLL-22PH	E. Mann	Closed	90.00	90.00
90-01-152	Princess Fair Skies-FH-268B	E. Mann	2,500	75.00	75.00
90-01-153	Princess Red Feather-PS-189	E. Mann	2,500	90.00	90.00
90-01-154	Priscilla-WB-50	E. Mann	2,500	105.00	105.00
90-01-155	Sabrina-C3050	E. Mann	Closed	105.00	105.00
90-01-156	Sally-WB-20	E. Mann	Closed	95.00	95.00
90-01-157	Shirley-WB-37	E. Mann	2,500	65.00	65.00

DOLLS

Company Number	Name	Series Artist	Edition Limit	Issue Price	Quote
90-01-158	Sister Mary-WB-15	E. Mann	Closed	70.00	70.00
90-01-159	Sophie-OM-1	E. Mann	Open	65.00	65.00
90-01-160	Stacy-TR-5	E. Mann	2,500	105.00	105.00
90-01-161	Sue Chuen-C-3061G	E. Mann	Closed	95.00	95.00
90-01-162	Sunny-FH-331	E. Mann	Closed	70.00	70.00
90-01-163	Susan-DOLL-364MC	E. Mann	Closed	75.00	75.00
90-01-164	Tania-DOLL-376P	E. Mann	2,500	65.00	65.00
90-01-165	Tina-DOLL-371	E. Mann	Closed	85.00	85.00
90-01-166	Tina-WB-32	E. Mann	Closed	65.00	65.00
90-01-167	Tommy-C-3064	E. Mann	Closed	75.00	75.00
90-01-168	Wendy-TE-3	E. Mann	Closed	75.00	75.00
90-01-169	Wilma-PS-174	E. Mann	Closed	75.00	75.00
90-01-170	Yen Yen-YK-4091	E. Mann	3,500	95.00	95.00
91-01-171	Abigail-EP-3	E. Mann	2,500	100.00	100.00
91-01-172	Abigal-WB-72WM	E. Mann	2,500	75.00	75.00
91-01-173	Abby 16" Pink Dress-C3145	E. Mann	2,500	100.00	100.00
91-01-174	Alexis 24" Beige Lace-EP32	E. Mann	2,500	220.00	220.00
91-01-175	Alicia-YK-4215	E. Mann	3,500	90.00	90.00
91-01-176	Amanda Toast-OM-182	E. Mann	2,500	260.00	260.00
91-01-177	Amelia-TR-47	E. Mann	2,500	105.00	105.00
91-01-178	Amy-C-3147	E. Mann	2,500	135.00	135.00
91-01-179	Ann-TR-52	E. Mann	2,500	135.00	135.00
91-01-180	Annette-TR-59	E. Mann	2,500	130.00	130.00
91-01-181	Annie-YK-4214	E. Mann	3,500	145.00	145.00
91-01-182	Antoinette-FH-452	E. Mann	2,500	100.00	100.00
91-01-183	Arabella-C-3163	E. Mann	2,500	135.00	135.00
91-01-184	Ariel 34" Blue/White-EP-33	E. Mann	2,500	175.00	175.00
91-01-185	Audrey-FH-455	E. Mann	2,500	125.00	125.00
91-01-186	Aurora Gold 22"-OM-181	E. Mann	2,500	260.00	260.00
91-01-187	Azure-AM-15	E. Mann	2,500	175.00	175.00
91-01-188	Baby Beth-DOLL-406P	E. Mann	2,500	27.50	27.50
91-01-189	Baby Bonnie w/Walker Music-DOLL-409	E. Mann	2,500	40.00	40.00
91-01-190	Baby Bonnie-SP-341	E. Mann	2,500	55.00	55.00
91-01-191	Baby Brent-EP-15	E. Mann	Closed	85.00	85.00
91-01-192	Baby Carrie-DOLL-402P	E. Mann	2,500	27.50	27.50
91-01-193	Baby Ecru-WB-17	E. Mann	2,500	65.00	65.00
91-01-194	Baby Ellie Ecru Musical-DOLL-402E	E. Mann	2,500	27.50	27.50
91-01-195	Baby Gloria Black Baby-PS-289	E. Mann	2,500	75.00	75.00
91-01-196	Baby John-PS-498	E. Mann	2,500	85.00	85.00
91-01-197	Baby Linda-DOLL-406E	E. Mann	2,500	27.50	27.50
91-01-198	Baby Sue-DOLL-402B	E. Mann	2,500	27.50	27.50
91-01-199	Belinda-C-3164	E. Mann	2,500	150.00	150.00
91-01-200	Bernetta-EP-40	E. Mann	2,500	115.00	115.00
91-01-201	Betsy-AM-6	E. Mann	2,500	105.00	105.00
91-01-202	Bettina-YK-4144	E. Mann	3,500	105.00	105.00
91-01-203	Blaine-TR-61	E. Mann	2,500	115.00	115.00
91-01-204	Blythe-CH-15V	E. Mann	2,500	135.00	135.00
91-01-205	Bo-Peep w/Lamb-C-3128	E. Mann	2,500	105.00	105.00
91-01-206	Bridget-SP-379	E. Mann	2,500	105.00	105.00
91-01-207	Brooke-FH-461	E. Mann	2,500	115.00	115.00
91-01-208	Bryna-AM-100B	E. Mann	2,500	70.00	70.00
91-01-209	Camellia-FH-457	E. Mann	2,500	100.00	100.00
91-01-210	Caroline-LL-838	E. Mann	2,500	110.00	110.00
91-01-211	Caroline-LL-905	E. Mann	2,500	110.00	110.00
91-01-212	Cheryl-TR-49	E. Mann	2,500	120.00	120.00
91-01-213	Chin Chin-YK-4211	E. Mann	3,500	85.00	85.00
91-01-214	Christina-PS-261	E. Mann	2,500	115.00	115.00
91-01-215	Cindy Lou-FH-464	E. Mann	2,500	85.00	85.00
91-01-216	Cissy-EP-56	E. Mann	2,500	95.00	95.00
91-01-217	Clare-DOLL-465	E. Mann	Open	100.00	100.00
91-01-218	Claudine-C-3146	E. Mann	2,500	95.00	95.00
91-01-219	Colette-WB-7	E. Mann	2,500	65.00	65.00
91-01-220	Colleen-YK-4163	E. Mann	3,500	120.00	120.00
91-01-221	Cookie-GU-6	E. Mann	2,500	110.00	110.00
91-01-222	Courtney-LL-859	E. Mann	2,500	150.00	150.00
91-01-223	Creole-AM-17	E. Mann	2,500	160.00	160.00
91-01-224	Crystal-YK-4237	E. Mann	3,500	125.00	125.00
91-01-225	Danielle-AM-5	E. Mann	2,500	125.00	125.00
91-01-226	Darcy-EP-47	E. Mann	2,500	110.00	110.00
91-01-227	Darcy-FH-451	E. Mann	2,500	105.00	105.00
91-01-228	Daria-C-3122	E. Mann	2,500	110.00	110.00
91-01-229	Darlene-DOLL-444	E. Mann	2,500	75.00	75.00
91-01-230	Dawn-C-3135	E. Mann	Closed	130.00	130.00
91-01-231	Denise-LL-852	E. Mann	2,500	105.00	105.00
91-01-232	Dephine-SP-308	E. Mann	2,500	135.00	135.00
91-01-233	Desiree-LL-898	E. Mann	2,500	120.00	120.00
91-01-234	Duanane-SP-366	E. Mann	Closed	85.00	85.00
91-01-235	Dulcie-YK-4131V	E. Mann	3,500	100.00	100.00
91-01-236	Dwayne-C-3123	E. Mann	2,500	120.00	120.00
91-01-237	Edie -YK-4177	E. Mann	3,500	115.00	115.00
91-01-238	Elisabeth and Lisa-C-3095	E. Mann	2,500	195.00	195.00
91-01-239	Elise -PS-259	E. Mann	2,500	105.00	105.00
91-01-240	Elizabeth-AM-32	E. Mann	2,500	105.00	105.00
91-01-241	Emmaline-OM-191	E. Mann	2,500	300.00	300.00
91-01-242	Emmaline Beige/Lilac-OM-197	E. Mann	Closed	300.00	300.00
91-01-243	Emmy-C-3099	E. Mann	2,500	125.00	125.00
91-01-244	Erin-DOLL-4PH	E. Mann	Closed	60.00	60.00
91-01-245	Evelina-C-3124	E. Mann	2,500	135.00	135.00
91-01-246	Fifi-AM-100F	E. Mann	2,500	70.00	70.00
91-01-247	Fleurette-PS-286	E. Mann	2,500	75.00	75.00
91-01-248	Flora-TR-46	E. Mann	2,500	125.00	125.00
91-01-249	Francesca-AM-14	E. Mann	2,500	175.00	175.00
91-01-250	Georgia-YK-4131	E. Mann	3,500	100.00	100.00
91-01-251	Georgia-YK-4143	E. Mann	3,500	150.00	150.00
91-01-252	Gigi-C-3107	E. Mann	2,500	135.00	135.00
91-01-253	Ginger-LL-907	E. Mann	2,500	115.00	115.00
91-01-254	Gloria-AM-100G	E. Mann	2,500	70.00	70.00
91-01-255	Gloria-YK-4166	E. Mann	3,500	105.00	105.00
91-01-256	Gretchen-DOLL-446	E. Mann	Open	45.00	45.00
91-01-257	Gretel-DOLL-434	E. Mann	Open	60.00	60.00
91-01-258	Hansel and Gretel-DOLL-448V	E. Mann	Open	60.00	60.00
91-01-259	Helene-AM-29	E. Mann	2,500	150.00	150.00
91-01-260	Holly-CH-6	E. Mann	2,500	100.00	100.00
91-01-261	Honey-FH-401	E. Mann	2,500	100.00	100.00
91-01-262	Honey Bunny-WB-9	E. Mann	Closed	70.00	70.00
91-01-263	Hope-FH-434	E. Mann	2,500	90.00	90.00
91-01-264	Indira-AM-4	E. Mann	2,500	125.00	125.00
91-01-265	Iris-TR-58	E. Mann	2,500	120.00	120.00
91-01-266	Ivy-PS-307	E. Mann	2,500	75.00	75.00
91-01-267	Jane-PS-243L	E. Mann	Closed	115.00	115.00
91-01-268	Janice-OM-194	E. Mann	2,500	300.00	300.00
91-01-269	Jessica-FH-423	E. Mann	2,500	95.00	95.00
91-01-270	Joy-EP-23V	E. Mann	2,500	130.00	130.00
91-01-271	Joyce-AM-100J	E. Mann	2,500	35.00	35.00
91-01-272	Julia-C-3102	E. Mann	Closed	135.00	135.00
91-01-273	Juliette-OM-192	E. Mann	2,500	300.00	300.00
91-01-274	Karen-EP-24	E. Mann	2,500	115.00	115.00
91-01-275	Karmela-EP-57	E. Mann	2,500	120.00	120.00
91-01-276	Kelly-AM-8	E. Mann	2,500	125.00	125.00
91-01-277	Kerry-FH-396	E. Mann	2,500	100.00	100.00
91-01-278	Kim-AM-100K	E. Mann	2,500	70.00	70.00
91-01-279	Kinesha-SP-402	E. Mann	2,500	110.00	110.00
91-01-280	Kristi-FH-402	E. Mann	2,500	100.00	100.00
91-01-281	Kyla-YK-4137	E. Mann	3,500	95.00	95.00
91-01-282	Laura-WB-110P	E. Mann	2,500	85.00	85.00
91-01-283	Leigh-DOLL-457	E. Mann	2,500	95.00	95.00
91-01-284	Leila-AM-2	E. Mann	2,500	125.00	125.00
91-01-285	Lenore-LL-911	E. Mann	2,500	105.00	105.00
91-01-286	Lenore-YK-4218	E. Mann	3,500	135.00	135.00
91-01-287	Libby-EP-18	E. Mann	2,500	85.00	85.00
91-01-288	Lila-AM-10	E. Mann	2,500	125.00	125.00
91-01-289	Lila-FH-404	E. Mann	2,500	100.00	100.00
91-01-290	Lindsey-C-3127	E. Mann	2,500	135.00	135.00
91-01-291	Linetta-C-3166	E. Mann	2,500	135.00	135.00
91-01-292	Lisa-AM-100L	E. Mann	2,500	70.00	70.00
91-01-293	Little Boy Blue-C-3159	E. Mann	2,500	100.00	100.00
91-01-294	Liz-C-3150	E. Mann	2,500	100.00	100.00
91-01-295	Liza-YK-4226	E. Mann	3,500	35.00	35.00
91-01-296	Lola-SP-363	E. Mann	2,500	90.00	90.00
91-01-297	Loni-FH-448	E. Mann	2,500	100.00	100.00
91-01-298	Lori-EP-52	E. Mann	2,500	95.00	95.00
91-01-299	Louise-LL-908	E. Mann	2,500	105.00	105.00
91-01-300	Lucy-LL-853	E. Mann	2,500	80.00	80.00
91-01-301	Madeleine-C-3106	E. Mann	2,500	95.00	95.00
91-01-302	Marcy-TR-55	E. Mann	2,500	135.00	135.00
91-01-303	Mariel 18" Ivory-C-3119	E. Mann	2,500	125.00	125.00
91-01-304	Maude-AM-100M	E. Mann	2,500	70.00	70.00
91-01-305	Melissa-AM-9	E. Mann	2,500	120.00	120.00
91-01-306	Melissa-CH-3	E. Mann	2,500	110.00	110.00
91-01-307	Melissa-LL-901	E. Mann	2,500	135.00	135.00
91-01-308	Meredith-FH-391-P	E. Mann	2,500	95.00	95.00
91-01-309	Meryl-FH-463	E. Mann	2,500	95.00	95.00
91-01-310	Michael w/School Books-FH-439B	E. Mann	2,500	95.00	95.00
91-01-311	Michelle Lilac/Green-EP36	E. Mann	2,500	95.00	95.00
91-01-312	Michelle w/School Books-FH-439G	E. Mann	2,500	95.00	95.00
91-01-313	Miranda-DOLL-9PH	E. Mann	Closed	75.00	75.00
91-01-314	Missy-DOLL-464	E. Mann	2,500	70.00	70.00
91-01-315	Missy-PS-258	E. Mann	2,500	90.00	90.00
91-01-316	Mon Yun w/Parasol-TR33	E. Mann	2,500	115.00	115.00
91-01-317	Nancy 21" Pink w/Rabbit-EP-31	E. Mann	2,500	165.00	165.00
91-01-318	Nancy -WB-73	E. Mann	2,500	65.00	65.00
91-01-319	Nellie-EP-1B	E. Mann	2,500	75.00	75.00
91-01-320	Nicole-AM-12	E. Mann	Closed	135.00	135.00
91-01-321	Noelle-PS-239V	E. Mann	Closed	95.00	95.00
91-01-322	Patti-DOLL-440	E. Mann	2,500	65.00	65.00
91-01-323	Patty-YK-4221	E. Mann	3,500	125.00	125.00
91-01-324	Pepper-PS-277	E. Mann	2,500	130.00	130.00
91-01-325	Pia-PS-246L	E. Mann	Closed	115.00	115.00
91-01-326	Princess Summer Winds-FH-427	E. Mann	2,500	120.00	120.00
91-01-327	Prissy White/Blue-C-3140	E. Mann	2,500	100.00	100.00
91-01-328	Rapunzel-C-3157	E. Mann	2,500	150.00	150.00
91-01-329	Red Wing-AM-30	E. Mann	2,500	165.00	165.00
91-01-330	Robin-AM-22	E. Mann	2,500	120.00	120.00
91-01-331	Rosalind-C-3090	E. Mann	2,500	150.00	150.00
91-01-332	Samantha-GU-3	E. Mann	2,500	100.00	100.00
91-01-333	Sandra-DOLL-6-PHE	E. Mann	2,500	65.00	65.00
91-01-334	Scarlett-FH-399	E. Mann	2,500	100.00	100.00
91-01-335	Scarlett-FH-436	E. Mann	2,500	135.00	135.00
91-01-336	Shaka-SP-401	E. Mann	2,500	110.00	110.00
91-01-337	Sharon 21" Blue-EP-34	E. Mann	2,500	120.00	120.00
91-01-338	Shau Chen-GU-2	E. Mann	2,500	85.00	85.00
91-01-339	Shelley-CH-1	E. Mann	2,500	110.00	110.00
91-01-340	Sophie-TR-53	E. Mann	2,500	135.00	135.00
91-01-341	Stacy-DOLL-6PH	E. Mann	2,500	65.00	65.00
91-01-342	Stephanie-AM-11	E. Mann	2,500	105.00	105.00
91-01-343	Stephanie-FH-467	E. Mann	2,500	95.00	95.00
91-01-344	Stephanie Pink & White-OM-196	E. Mann	2,500	300.00	300.00
91-01-345	Summer-AM-33	E. Mann	2,500	200.00	200.00
91-01-346	Sybil 20" Beige-C-3131	E. Mann	2,500	135.00	135.00
91-01-347	Sybil Pink-DOLL-12PHMC	E. Mann	2,500	75.00	75.00
91-01-348	Tamara-OM-187	E. Mann	2,500	135.00	135.00
91-01-349	Terri-TR-62	E. Mann	2,500	75.00	75.00
91-01-350	Tessa-AM-19	E. Mann	2,500	135.00	135.00
91-01-351	Tina-AM-16	E. Mann	2,500	130.00	130.00
91-01-352	Vanessa-AM-34	E. Mann	2,500	90.00	90.00
91-01-353	Vicki-C-3101	E. Mann	2,500	200.00	200.00
91-01-345	Violet-EP-41	E. Mann	2,500	135.00	135.00
91-01-355	Violet-OM-186	E. Mann	2,500	270.00	270.00
91-01-356	Virginia-SP-359	E. Mann	2,500	120.00	120.00
91-01-357	Wah-Ching Watching Oriental Toddler-YK-4175	E. Mann	2,500	110.00	110.00
92-01-358	Alice-JNC-4013	E. Mann	Open	90.00	90.00
92-01-359	Amy-OM-06	E. Mann	2,500	150.00	150.00
92-01-360	Beth-OM-05	E. Mann	2,500	135.00	135.00
92-01-361	Bette-OM-01	E. Mann	9,200	115.00	115.00
92-01-362	Charlotte-FH-484	E. Mann	2,500	115.00	115.00
92-01-363	Chelsea-IND-397	E. Mann	Open	85.00	85.00
92-01-364	Cordelia-OM-009	E. Mann	9,200	250.00	250.00
92-01-365	Cordelia-OM-09	E. Mann	2,500	250.00	250.00
92-01-366	Debbie-JNC-4006	E. Mann	Open	90.00	90.00
92-01-367	Deidre-FH-473	E. Mann	2,500	115.00	115.00
92-01-368	Deidre-YK-4083	E. Mann	3,500	95.00	95.00
92-01-369	Dona-FH-494	E. Mann	2,500	100.00	100.00
92-01-370	Eugenie-OM-225	E. Mann	2,500	300.00	300.00
92-01-371	Giselle-OM-02	E. Mann	9,200	90.00	90.00
92-01-372	Jan-OM-012	E. Mann	9,200	135.00	135.00
92-01-373	Janet-FH-496	E. Mann	2,500	120.00	120.00
92-01-374	Jet-FH-478	E. Mann	2,500	115.00	115.00
92-01-375	Jodie-FH-495	E. Mann	2,500	115.00	115.00
92-01-376	Juliette-OM-08	E. Mann	2,500	175.00	175.00
92-01-377	Laura-OM-010	E. Mann	2,500	250.00	250.00
92-01-378	Laurie-JNC-4004	E. Mann	Open	90.00	90.00
92-01-379	Lydia-OM-226	E. Mann	2,.500	250.00	250.00
92-01-380	Maggie-FH-505	E. Mann	2,500	125.00	125.00
92-01-381	Melissa-OM-03	E. Mann	2,500	135.00	135.00
92-01-382	Nancy-JNC-4001	E. Mann	Open	90.00	90.00

Company / Number	Name	Series / Artist	Edition Limit	Issue Price	Quote
92-01-383	Sally-FH-492	E. Mann	2,500	105.00	105.00
92-01-384	Sapphires-OM-223	E. Mann	2,500	250.00	250.00
92-01-385	Sara Ann-FH-474	E. Mann	2,500	115.00	115.00
92-01-386	Scarlett-FH-471	E. Mann	2,500	120.00	120.00
92-01-387	Sonja-FH-486	E. Mann	2,500	125.00	125.00
92-01-388	Sue-JNC-4003	E. Mann	Open	90.00	90.00
92-01-389	Tiffany-OM-014	E. Mann	2,500	150.00	150.00
92-01-390	Trina-OM-011	E. Mann	9,200	165.00	165.00
92-01-391	Violette-FH-503	E. Mann	2,500	120.00	120.00
92-01-392	Yvette-OM-015	E. Mann	9,200	150.00	150.00
Seymour Mann Inc.		**Signature Doll Series**			
91-02-001	Amber-MS-1	M. Severino	5,000	95.00	95.00
91-02-002	Becky-MS-2	M. Severino	5,000	95.00	95.00
91-02-003	Bianca-PK-101	M. Severino	5,000	120.00	120.00
91-02-004	Bridgette-PK-104	P. Kolesar	5,000	120.00	120.00
91-02-005	Clair-Ann-PK-252	P. Kolesar	5,000	100.00	100.00
91-02-006	Daddy's Little Darling-MS-8	M. Severino	5,000	165.00	165.00
91-02-007	Dozy Elf w/ Featherbed-MAB-100	M.A. Byerly	5,000	110.00	110.00
91-02-008	Duby Elf w/ Featherbed-MAB-103	M.A. Byerly	5,000	110.00	110.00
91-02-009	Dudley Elf w/ Featherbed-MAB-101	M.A. Byerly	5,000	110.00	110.00
91-02-010	Duffy Elf w/ Featherbed-MAB-102	M.A. Byerly	5,000	110.00	110.00
91-02-011	Enoc-PK-100	P. Kolesar	5,000	100.00	100.00
91-02-012	Mikey-MS-3	M. Severino	5,000	95.00	95.00
91-02-013	Mommy's Rays of Sunshine-MS-9	M. Severino	5,000	165.00	165.00
91-02-014	Paulette-PAC-2	P. Aprile	5,000	250.00	250.00
91-02-015	Paulette-PAC-4	P. Aprile	5,000	250.00	250.00
91-02-016	Precious Baby-SB-100	S. Bilotto	5,000	250.00	250.00
91-02-017	Precious Pary Time-SB-102	S. Bilotto	5,000	250.00	250.00
91-02-018	Precious Spring Time-SB-104	S. Bilotto	5,000	250.00	250.00
91-02-019	Shun Lee-PK-102	P. Kolesar	5,000	120.00	120.00
91-02-020	Sparkle-PK-250	P. Kolesar	5,000	100.00	100.00
91-02-021	Stephie-MS-6	M. Severino	5,000	125.00	125.00
91-02-022	Alice-MS-7	M. Severino	5,000	120.00	120.00
91-02-023	Su Lin-MS-5	M. Severino	5,000	105.00	105.00
91-02-024	Susan Marie-PK-103	P. Kolesar	5,000	120.00	120.00
91-02-025	Sweet Pea-PK-251	P. Kolesar	5,000	100.00	100.00
91-02-026	Yawning Kate-MS-4	M. Severino	5,000	105.00	105.00
92-02-027	Abigail-MS-11	M. Severino	5,000	125.00	125.00
92-02-028	Adora-MS-14	M. Severino	5,000	185.00	185.00
92-02-029	Alexandria-PAC-19	P. Aprile	5,000	300.00	300.00
92-02-030	Baby Cakes Crumbs-PK-CRUMBS	P. Kolesar	5,000	17.50	17.50
92-02-031	Baby Cakes Crumbs/Black-PK-CRUMBS/B	P. Kolesar	5,000	17.50	17.50
92-02-032	Bride & Flower Girl-PAC-6	P. Aprile	5,000	600.00	600.00
92-02-033	Cassandra-PAC-8	P. Aprile	5,000	450.00	450.00
92-02-034	Cassie Flower Girl-PAC-9	P. Aprile	5,000	175.00	175.00
92-02-035	Celine-PAC-11	P. Aprile	5,000	165.00	165.00
92-02-036	Clarissa-PAC-3	P. Aprile	5,000	165.00	165.00
92-02-037	Cody-MS-19	M. Severino	5,000	120.00	120.00
92-02-038	Creole Black-HP-202	H. Payne	5,000	250.00	250.00
92-02-039	Cynthia-PAC-10	P. Aprile	5,000	165.00	165.00
92-02-040	Darla-HP-204	H. Payne	5,000	250.00	250.00
92-02-041	Dulcie-HP-200	H. Payne	5,000	250.00	250.00
92-02-042	Dustin-HP-201	H. Payne	5,000	250.00	250.00
92-02-043	Eugenie Bride-PAC-1	P. Aprile	5,000	165.00	165.00
92-02-044	Evening Star-PAC-5	P. Aprile	5,000	500.00	500.00
92-02-045	Kate-MS-15	M. Severino	5,000	190.00	190.00
92-02-046	Little Match Girl-HP-205	H. Payne	5,000	150.00	150.00
92-02-047	"Little Turtle" Indian-PK-110	P. Kolesar	5,000	150.00	150.00
92-02-048	Megan-MS-12	M. Severino	5,000	125.00	125.00
92-02-049	Melanie-PAC-14	P. Aprile	5,000	300.00	300.00
92-02-050	Nadia-PAC-18	P. Aprile	5,000	175.00	175.00
92-02-051	Olivia-PAC-12	P. Aprile	5,000	300.00	300.00
92-02-052	Pavlova-PAC-17	P. Aprile	5,000	145.00	145.00
92-02-053	Polly-HP-206	H. Payne	5,000	120.00	120.00
92-02-054	Raven Eskimo-PK-106	P. Kolesar	5,000	130.00	130.00
92-02-055	Rebecca Beige Bonnet-MS-17B	M. Severino	5,000	175.00	175.00
92-02-056	Ruby-MS-18	M. Severino	5,000	135.00	135.00
92-02-057	Sally-MS-25	M. Severino	5,000	110.00	110.00
92-02-058	Spanky-HP-25	H. Payne	5,000	250.00	250.00
92-02-059	Stacy-MS-24	M. Severino	5,000	110.00	110.00
92-02-060	Vanessa-PAC-15	P. Aprile	5,000	300.00	300.00
92-02-061	Victoria w/Blanket-MS-10	M. Severino	5,000	110.00	110.00
92-02-062	Violetta-PAC-16	P. Aprile	5,000	165.00	165.00
Jan McLean Originals		**Flowers of the Heart Collection**			
90-01-001	Pansy	J. McLean	100	2200.00	2800-3200.
90-01-002	Poppy	J. McLean	100	2200.00	2400-2800.
91-01-003	Primrose	J. McLean	100	2500.00	2500.00
91-01-004	Marigold	J. McLean	100	2400.00	2400.00
Jan McLean Originals		**Jan McLean Originals**			
90-02-001	Phoebe I	J. McLean	25	2700.00	2700.00
91-02-00	Lucrezia	J. McLean	15	6000.00	6000.00
Middleton Doll Company		**Porcelain Limited Edition Series**			
88-01-001	Cherish-1st Edition	L. Middleton	750	350.00	500.00
88-01-002	Sincerity -1st Edition-Nettie/Simplicity	L. Middleton	750	330.00	350-475.
89-01-003	My Lee	L. Middleton	629	500.00	500.00
89-01-004	Devan	L. Middleton	525	500.00	500.00
90-01-005	Baby Grace	L. Middleton	500	500.00	500.00
90-01-006	Johanna	L. Middleton	500	500.00	500.00
91-01-007	Molly Rose	L. Middleton	500	500.00	500.00
Middleton Doll Company		**Limited Edition Vinyl**			
81-02-001	Little Angel-Kingdom (Hand Painted)	L. Middleton	800	40.00	300.00
85-02-002	Little Angel-King-2 (Hand Painted)	L. Middleton	400	40.00	200.00
87-02-003	Christmas Angel 1987	L. Middleton	4,174	130.00	200.00
88-02-004	Christmas Angel 1988	L. Middleton	6,385	130.00	160.00
89-02-005	Christmas Angel 1989	L. Middleton	7,500	150.00	160.00
89-02-006	Angel Fancy	L. Middleton	10,000	120.00	130.00
90-02-007	Baby Grace	L. Middleton	5,000	190.00	190.00
90-02-008	Christmas Angel 1990	L. Middleton	5,000	150.00	150.00
90-02-009	Sincerity-Apricots n' Cream	L. Middleton	5,000	250.00	250.00
90-02-010	Sincerity-Apples n' Spice	L. Middleton	5,000	250.00	250.00
90-02-011	Forever Cherish	L. Middleton	5,000	170.00	170.00
90-02-012	First Moments-Twin Boy	L. Middleton	5,000	180.00	180.00
90-02-013	First Moments-Twin Girl	L. Middleton	5,000	180.00	180.00
90-02-014	Angel Locks	L. Middleton	10,000	140.00	150.00
90-02-015	Missy- Buttercup	L. Middleton	5,000	160.00	170.00
90-02-016	Dear One-Sunday Best	L. Middleton	5,000	140.00	140.00
91-02-017	Bubba Batboy	L. Middleton	5,000	190.00	190.00
91-02-018	My Lee Candy Cane	L. Middleton	2,500	170.00	170.00
91-02-019	Devan Delightful	L. Middleton	5,000	170.00	170.00
91-02-020	Gracie Mae	L. Middleton	5,000	250.00	250.00
91-02-021	Christmas Angel 1991	L. Middleton	5,000	180.00	180.00
91-02-022	Johanna	L. Middleton	5,000	190.00	190.00
Middleton Doll Company		**First Moments Series**			
84-03-001	First Moments (Sleeping)	L. Middleton	41,000	69.00	150.00
86-03-002	First Moments Blue Eyes	L. Middleton	15,000	120.00	150.00
86-03-003	First Moments Brown Eyes	L. Middleton	5,490	120.00	150.00
87-03-004	First Moments Boy	L. Middleton	6,075	130.00	160.00
87-03-005	First Moments Christening (Asleep)	L. Middleton	Open	160.00	180.00
87-03-006	First Moments Christening (Awake)	L. Middleton	Open	160.00	180.00
90-03-007	First Moments Sweetness	L. Middleton	Open	180.00	180.00
Middleton Doll Company		**Vinyl Collectors Series**			
86-04-001	Bubba Chubbs	L. Middleton	5,600	100.00	150-200.
88-04-002	Bubba Chubbs Railroader	L. Middleton	Open	140.00	170.00
86-04-003	Little Angel - 3rd Edition	L. Middleton	Open	90.00	110.00
85-04-004	Angel Face	L. Middleton	20,200	90.00	150.00
87-04-005	Missy	L. Middleton	Open	100.00	120.00
87-04-006	Amanda - 1st Edition	L. Middleton	4,200	140.00	160.00
86-04-007	Dear One - 1st Edition	L. Middleton	4,935	90.00	200.00
88-04-008	Cherish	L. Middleton	Open	160.00	160.00
88-04-009	Sincerity - Limited 1st Ed. -Nettie/Simplicity	L. Middleton	4,380	160.00	160.00
89-04-010	My Lee	L. Middleton	Open	170.00	170.00
89-04-011	Devan	L. Middleton	Open	170.00	170.00
89-04-012	Sincerity-Schoolgirl	L. Middleton	Open	180.00	180.00
Middleton Doll Company		**Littlest Ballet Company**			
88-05-001	April (Dressed in Pink)	S. Wakeen	7,500	100.00	110.00
88-05-002	Melanie (Dressed in Blue)	S. Wakeen	7,500	100.00	110.00
88-05-003	Jeanne (Dressed in White)	S. Wakeen	7,500	100.00	110.00
88-05-004	Lisa (Black Leotards)	S. Wakeen	7,500	100.00	110.00
89-05-005	April (In Leotard)	S. Wakeen	7,500	100.00	110.00
89-05-006	Melanie (In Leotard)	S. Wakeen	7,500	100.00	110.00
89-05-007	Jeannie (In Leotard)	S. Wakeen	7,500	100.00	110.00
Middleton Doll Company		**First Collectibles**			
90-06-001	Sweetest Little Dreamer (Asleep)	L. Middleton	Open	40.00	40.00
90-06-002	Day Dreamer (Awake)	L. Middleton	Open	42.00	42.00
91-06-003	Day Dreamer Sunshine	L. Middleton	Open	49.00	49.00
91-06-004	Teenie	L. Middleton	Open	59.00	59.00
Nahrgang Collection		**Porcelain Doll Series**			
89-01-001	Palmer	J. Nahrgang	250	270.00	270.00
90-01-002	Grant (Take Me Out To The Ball Game)	J. Nahrgang	500	390.00	390.00
90-01-003	Maggie	J. Nahrgang	500	295.00	295.00
90-01-004	Kelsey	J. Nahrgang	250	350.00	350.00
90-01-005	Kasey	J. Nahrgang	250	450.00	450.00
90-01-006	Alicia	J. Nahrgang	250	330.00	330.00
90-01-007	Karman (Gypsy)	J. Nahrgang	250	350.00	350.00
90-01-008	Karissa	J. Nahrgang	500	350.00	395.00
91-01-009	McKinsey	J. Nahrgang	250	350.00	350.00
91-01-010	Rae	J. Nahrgang	250	350.00	350.00
91-01-011	Aubry	J. Nahrgang	250	390.00	390.00
91-01-012	Laura	J. Nahrgang	250	450.00	450.00
91-01-013	Sophie	J. Nahrgang	250	450.00	450.00
91-01-014	Carson	J. Nahrgang	250	350.00	350.00
91-01-015	Erin	J. Nahrgang	250	295.00	295.00
91-01-016	Ana Marie	J. Nahrgang	250	390.00	390.00
91-01-017	Holly	J. Nahrgang	175	295.00	295.00
92-01-018	Brooke	J. Nahrgang	250	390.00	390.00
92-01-019	Alexis	J. Nahrgang	250	390.00	390.00
92-01-020	Katie	J. Nahrgang	250	295.00	295.00
92-01-021	Pocahontas	J. Nahrgang	100	395.00	395.00
92-01-022	Molly Pitcher	J. Nahrgang	100	395.00	395.00
92-01-023	Harriet Tubman	J. Nahrgang	100	395.00	395.00
92-01-024	Florence Nightingale	J. Nahrgang	100	395.00	395.00
92-01-025	Dolly Madison	J. Nahrgang	100	395.00	395.00
92-01-026	Annie Sullivan	J. Nahrgang	25	895.00	895.00
92-01-027	Taylor	J. Nahrgang	250	295.00	295.00
Nahrgang Collection		**Vinyl Doll Series**			
90-02-001	Karman (Gypsy)	J. Nahrgang	2,000	190.00	190.00
91-02-002	Aubry	J. Nahrgang	1,000	225.00	225.00
91-02-003	Laura	J. Nahrgang	1,000	250.00	250.00
91-02-004	Ann Marie	J. Nahrgang	500	225.00	225.00
91-02-005	Molly	J. Nahrgang	500	190.00	190.00
91-02-006	Alexis	J. Nahrgang	500	250.00	250.00
91-02-007	Brooke	J. Nahrgang	500	250.00	250.00
91-02-008	Beatrix	J. Nahrgang	500	250.00	250.00
91-02-009	Angela	J. Nahrgang	500	190.00	190.00
91-02-010	Vanessa	J. Nahrgang	250	250.00	250.00
91-02-011	Chelsea	J. Nahrgang	250	190.00	190.00
91-02-012	Polly	J. Nahrgang	250	270.00	270.00
92-02-013	Pocahontas	J. Nahrgang	500	199.00	199.00
92-02-014	Molly Pitcher	J. Nahrgang	500	199.00	199.00
92-02-015	Harriet Tubman	J. Nahrgang	500	199.00	199.00
92-02-016	Florence Nightingale	J. Nahrgang	500	199.00	199.00
92-02-017	Dolly Madison	J. Nahrgang	500	199.00	199.00
Original Appalachian Artworks		**Little People**			
78-01-001	Helen, Blue	X. Roberts	Closed	150.00	3000-7600.
80-01-002	SP, Preemie	X. Roberts	Closed	100.00	400-700.
80-01-003	Celebrity	X. Roberts	Closed	200.00	400-800.
80-01-004	Nicholas	X. Roberts	Closed	200.00	1500-2000.
80-01-005	Noel	X. Roberts	Closed	200.00	700.00
82-01-006	Baby Rudy	X. Roberts	Closed	200.00	800-900.
82-01-007	Christy Nicole	X. Roberts	Closed	200.00	800.00
82-01-008	Amy	X. Roberts	Closed	125.00	700-800.
82-01-009	Bobbie	X. Roberts	Closed	125.00	700-800.
82-01-010	Billie	X. Roberts	Closed	125.00	700-800.
82-01-011	Gilda	X. Roberts	Closed	125.00	1400-1600.
82-01-012	Tyler	X. Roberts	Closed	125.00	1700-2500.
82-01-013	Sybil	X. Roberts	Closed	125.00	700-1000.
82-01-014	Marilyn	X. Roberts	Closed	125.00	700-800.
82-01-015	Otis	X. Roberts	Closed	125.00	800-1000.
82-01-016	Rebecca	X. Roberts	Closed	125.00	700-900.
82-01-017	Dorothy	X. Roberts	Closed	125.00	700-900.
82-01-018	PE, New 'ears Preemie	X. Roberts	Closed	140.00	300-450.
Original Appalachian Artworks		**Cabbage Patch Kids International**			
83-02-001	Oriental	X. Roberts	Closed	150.00	1200-1500.

Company / Number	Name	Series / Artist	Edition Limit	Issue Price	Quote
83-02-002	American Indian	X. Roberts	Closed	150.00	800-1800.
Original Appalachian Artworks		**Cabbage Patch Kids**			
83-03-002	Andre / Madeira	X. Roberts	Closed	250.00	1500-2000.
84-03-003	Daddy's Darlins'-Pun'kin	X. Roberts	Closed	300.00	500-700.
84-03-004	Daddy's Darlins'-Tootsie	X. Roberts	Closed	300.00	500-700.
84-03-005	Daddys Darlins'-Princess	X. Roberts	Closed	300.00	500-700.
84-03-006	Daddy's Darlins'-Kitten	X. Roberts	Closed	300.00	500-700.
88-03-007	Tiger's Eye-Valentine's Day	X. Roberts	Closed	150.00	200-400.
89-03-008	Tiger's Eye-Mother's Day	X. Roberts	Closed	150.00	150-400.
90-03-009	Joy	X. Roberts	Closed	250.00	400-750.
91-03-010	Nick	X. Roberts	700	275.00	275.00
92-03-011	Christy Claus	X. Roberts	700	285.00	285.00
93-03-012	Unicoi Edition	X. Roberts	1,500	210.00	210.00
Original Appalachian Artworks		**Cabbage Patch Kids Circus Parade**			
87-04-001	Big Top Clown-Baby Cakes	X. Roberts	2,000	180.00	425-550.
89-04-002	Happy Hobo-Bashful Billy	X. Roberts	1,000	180.00	225-400.
91-04-003	Mitzi	X. Roberts	1,000	220.00	220.00
Original Appalachian Artworks		**Collectors Club Editions**			
89-05-001	Anna Ruby	X. Roberts	Closed	250.00	400.00
90-05-002	Lee Ann	X. Roberts	Closed	250.00	250.00
91-05-003	Richard Russell	X. Roberts	Closed	250.00	250.00
92-05-004	Baby Dodd	X. Roberts	Open	250.00	250.00
Original Appalachian Artworks		**Convention Baby**			
89-06-001	Ashley	X. Roberts	Closed	150.00	1000.00
90-06-002	Bradley	X. Roberts	Closed	175.00	600.00
91-06-003	Caroline	X. Roberts	Closed	200.00	200.00
92-06-004	Duke	X. Roberts	Closed	225.00	225.00
Princeton Gallery		**Little Ladies of Victorian England**			
90-01-001	Victoria Anne	Unknown	Open	59.00	59.00
91-01-002	Abigail	Unknown	Open	59.00	59.00
91-01-003	Valerie	Unknown	Open	58.50	58.50
92-01-004	Caroline	Unknown	Open	58.50	58.50
92-01-005	Heather	Unknown	Open	58.50	58.50
93-01-006	Beverly	Unknown	Open	58.50	58.50
Princeton Gallery		**Best Friend Dolls**			
91-02-001	Sharing Secrets	Unknown	Open	78.00	78.00
Princeton Gallery		**Childhood Songs Dolls**			
91-03-001	It's Raining, It's Pouring	Unknown	Open	78.00	78.00
Princeton Gallery		**Dress Up Dolls**			
91-04-001	Grandma's Attic	Unknown	Open	95.00	95.00
Princeton Gallery		**Fabrique Santa**			
91-05-001	Christmas Dream	Unknown	Open	76.00	76.00
Princeton Gallery		**Santa Doll**			
91-06-001	Checking His List	Unknown	Open	119.00	119.00
Princeton Gallery		**Rock-N-Roll Dolls**			
91-07-001	Cindy at the Hop	M. Sirko	Open	95.00	95.00
92-07-002	Chantilly Lace	M. Sirko	Open	95.00	95.00
93-07-003	Yellow Dot Bikini	Unknown	Open	95.00	95.00
Princeton Gallery		**Terrible Twos Dolls**			
91-08-001	One Man Band	M. Sirko	Open	95.00	95.00
Princeton Gallery		**Imaginary People**			
92-09-001	Melinda, Tooth Fairy	Unknown	Open	95.00	95.00
Reco International		**Precious Memories of Motherhood**			
90-01-001	Loving Steps	S. Kuck	Yr.Iss.	125.00	150-195.
91-01-002	Lullaby	S. Kuck	Yr.Iss.	125.00	125.00
92-01-003	Expectant Moments	S. Kuck	Yr.Iss.	149.00	149.00
93-01-004	Bedtime	S. Kuck	Yr.Iss.	149.00	149.00
Reco International		**Children's Circus Doll Collection**			
91-02-001	Tommy The Clown	J. McClelland	Yr.Iss.	78.00	78.00
91-02-002	Katie The Tightrope Walker	J. McClelland	Yr.Iss.	78.00	78.00
91-02-003	Johnny The Strongman	J. McClelland	Yr.Iss.	83.00	83.00
92-02-004	Maggie The Animal Trainer	J. McClelland	Yr.Iss.	83.00	83.00
Rhodes Studio		**A Norman Rockwell Christmas**			
90-01-001	Scotty Plays Santa	Rockwell-Inspired	Yr.Iss.	48.00	48.00
91-01-002	Scotty Gets His Tree	Rockwell-Inspired	Yr.Iss.	59.00	59.00
Roman, Inc.		**Ellen Williams Doll**			
89-01-001	Noelle	E. Williams	5,000	125.00	125.00
89-01-002	Rebecca 999	E. Williams	7,500	195.00	195.00
Roman, Inc.		**A Christmas Dream**			
90-02-001	Chelsea	E. Williams	5,000	125.00	125.00
90-02-002	Carole	E. Williams	5,000	125.00	125.00
Roman, Inc.		**Tyrolean Treasures: Wood Body, Moveable Joint**			
90-03-001	Nadia	Unkn.	2,000	650.00	650.00
90-03-002	Susie	Unkn.	2,000	650.00	650.00
90-03-003	Verena	Unkn.	2,000	650.00	650.00
90-03-004	Monica	Unkn.	2,000	650.00	650.00
90-03-005	Melissa	Unkn.	2,000	650.00	650.00
90-03-006	Karin	Unkn.	2,000	650.00	650.00
90-03-007	Tina	Unkn.	2,000	650.00	650.00
90-03-008	Ann	Unkn.	2,000	650.00	650.00
90-03-009	Lisa	Unkn.	2,000	650.00	650.00
90-03-010	David	Unkn.	2,000	650.00	650.00
Roman, Inc.		**Tyrolean Treasures: Soft Body, Human Hair**			
90-04-001	Erika	Unkn.	2,000	575.00	575.00
90-04-002	Ellan	Unkn.	2,000	575.00	575.00
90-04-003	Marisa	Unkn.	2,000	575.00	575.00
90-04-004	Sarah	Unkn.	2,000	575.00	575.00
90-04-005	Andrew	Unkn.	2,000	575.00	575.00
90-04-006	Matthew	Unkn.	2,000	575.00	575.00
Roman, Inc.		**Classic Brides of the Century**			
90-05-001	Flora	E. Williams	Open	145.00	145.00
91-05-002	Jennifer	E. Williams	Open	149.00	149.00
Roman, Inc.		**Abbie Williams Collection**			
91-06-001	Molly	E. Williams	5,000	155.00	155.00
Sally-Lynne Dolls		**French Replicas**			
85-01-001	Victoria, 30"	S. Beatty	100	1050.00	3100.00
85-01-002	Charles, 30"	S. Beatty	100	1050.00	2500.00
85-01-003	Annabelle, 28"	S. Beatty	Closed	950.00	3100.00
85-01-004	Candice	S. Beatty	100	950.00	2500.00
86-01-005	Victoria at Christmas, 30"	S. Beatty	Closed	2500.00	4100.00
Sarah's Attic, Inc.		**Angels in The Attic Collection**			
89-01-001	Joy Angel	Sarah's Attic	Closed	50.00	50.00
89-01-002	Holly Angel	Sarah's Attic	Closed	50.00	50.00
89-01-003	Liberty Angel	Sarah's Attic	Closed	50.00	50.00
89-01-004	Glory Angel	Sarah's Attic	Closed	50.00	50.00
89-01-005	Hope Angel	Sarah's Attic	Closed	50.00	50.00
89-01-006	Peace Angel	Sarah's Attic	Closed	50.00	50.00
Sarah's Attic Inc.		**Beary Adorables Collection**			
90-02-001	Betty Bear Sunday	Sarah's Attic	Closed	160.00	160.00
90-02-002	Teddy Bear Sunday	Sarah's Attic	Closed	160.00	160.00
90-02-003	Teddy School Bear	Sarah's Attic	Closed	160.00	160.00
90-02-004	Americana Bear	Sarah's Attic	Closed	160.00	160.00
91-02-005	Christmas Betty Bear	Sarah's Attic	Closed	160.00	160.00
91-02-006	Christmas Teddy Bear	Sarah's Attic	Closed	160.00	160.00
91-02-007	Springtime Betty Bear	Sarah's Attic	Closed	160.00	160.00
91-02-008	Springtime Teddy Bear	Sarah's Attic	Closed	160.00	160.00
Sarah's Attic Inc.		**Black Heritage Collection**			
90-03-001	School Days Sassafras	Sarah's Attic	2,000	140.00	150-175.
90-03-002	Sweet Dreams Sassafras	Sarah's Attic	2,000	140.00	150-175.
90-03-003	Playtime Sassafras	Sarah's Attic	2,000	140.00	150-175.
90-03-004	Beachtime Sassafras	Sarah's Attic	2,000	140.00	150-175.
90-03-005	Sunday's Best Sassafras	Sarah's Attic	2,000	150.00	150-175.
90-03-006	Americana Sassafras	Sarah's Attic	2,000	150.00	150-175.
90-03-007	School Days Hickory	Sarah's Attic	2,000	140.00	150-175.
90-03-008	Sweet Dreams Hickory	Sarah's Attic	2,000	140.00	150-175.
90-03-009	Playtime Hickory	Sarah's Attic	2,000	140.00	150-175.
90-03-010	Beachtime Hickory	Sarah's Attic	2,000	140.00	150-175.
90-03-011	Sunday's Best Hickory	Sarah's Attic	2,000	150.00	150-175.
90-03-012	Americana Hickory	Sarah's Attic	2,000	150.00	150-175.
91-03-013	Christmas Sassafras	Sarah's Attic	2,000	150.00	150-175.
91-03-014	Christmas Hickory	Sarah's Attic	2,000	150.00	150-175.
91-03-015	Springtime Sassafras	Sarah's Attic	2,000	150.00	150-175.
91-03-016	Springtime Hickory	Sarah's Attic	2,000	150.00	150-175.
Sarah's Attic, Inc.		**Happy Collection**			
89-04-001	Harmony Clown	Sarah's Attic	Closed	150.00	150.00
89-04-002	X-Mas Clown Noel	Sarah's Attic	Closed	150.00	150.00
89-04-003	Freedom Clown	Sarah's Attic	Closed	150.00	150.00
88-04-004	Smiley Clown	Sarah's Attic	Closed	118.00	118.00
Sarah's Attic, Inc.		**Little Charmers Collection**			
89-05-001	Beverly Jane Black	Sarah's Attic	Closed	160.00	160.00
89-05-002	Becky	Sarah's Attic	Closed	120.00	120.00
89-05-003	Bobby	Sarah's Attic	Closed	120.00	120.00
89-05-004	Sunday's a Best-Bevie Jane	Sarah's Attic	Closed	160.00	160.00
89-05-005	Green Beverly Jane	Sarah's Attic	Closed	160.00	160.00
89-05-006	Red Beverly Jane	Sarah's Attic	Closed	160.00	160.00
90-05-007	Megan Doll	Sarah's Attic	Closed	70.00	100.00
90-05-008	Scott Doll	Sarah's Attic	Closed	70.00	100.00
87-05-009	Molly Small 5 Piece Doll	Sarah's Attic	Closed	36.00	36.00
87-05-010	Sunshine 5 Piece Doll	Sarah's Attic	Closed	79.00	79.00
88-05-011	Michael 5 Piece Doll	Sarah's Attic	Closed	44.00	44.00
91-05-012	Victorian Emily	Sarah's Attic	500	250.00	250.00
91-05-013	Country Emily	Sarah's Attic	500	250.00	250.00
91-05-014	Victorian Hilary	Sarah's Attic	500	200.00	200.00
91-05-015	Country Hilary	Sarah's Attic	500	200.00	200.00
91-05-016	Victorian Edie	Sarah's Attic	500	170.00	170.00
91-05-017	Country Edie	Sarah's Attic	500	170.00	170.00
91-05-018	Playtime Edie	Sarah's Attic	500	170.00	170.00
91-05-019	Victorian Emma	Sarah's Attic	500	160.00	160.00
91-05-020	Country Emma	Sarah's Attic	500	160.00	160.00
91-05-021	Playtime Emma	Sarah's Attic	500	160.00	160.00
Sarah's Attic, Inc.		**Spirit Of Christmas**			
89-06-001	Spirit of America Santa	Sarah's Attic	500	150.00	150.00
88-06-002	Mrs. Claus 5 Piece Doll	Sarah's Attic	Closed	120.00	120.00
88-06-003	Santa 5 Piece Doll	Sarah's Attic	Closed	120.00	120.00
Sarah's Attic, Inc.		**Tattered 'N Torn**			
91-07-001	All Cloth Opie White Doll	Sarah's Attic	Closed	90.00	90.00
91-07-002	All Cloth Polly White Doll	Sarah's Attic	Closed	90.00	90.00
91-07-003	All Cloth Puffin Black Doll	Sarah's Attic	Closed	90.00	90.00
91-07-004	All Cloth Muffin Black Doll	Sarah's Attic	Closed	90.00	90.00
Sarah's Attic, Inc.		**Heavenly Wings**			
91-08-001	All Cloth Enos Angel	Sarah's Attic	Closed	90.00	90.00
91-08-002	All Cloth Adora Angel	Sarah's Attic	Closed	90.00	90.00
Schmid		**June Amos Grammer**			
88-01-001	Rosamund	J. Amos Grammer	750	225.00	225.00
89-01-002	Katie	J. Amos Grammer	1,000	180.00	180.00
89-01-003	Vanessa	J. Amos Grammer	1,000	180.00	210.00
90-01-004	Lauren	J. Amos Grammer	1,000	279.00	280.00
90-01-005	Jester Love	J. Amos Grammer	1,000	195.00	210.00
90-01-006	Leigh Ann	J. Amos Grammer	1,000	195.00	210.00
90-01-007	Megan	J. Amos Grammer	750	380.00	380.00
91-01-008	Lauren	J. Amos Grammer	1,000	280.00	280.00
91-01-009	Mitsuko	J. Amos Grammer	1,000	210.00	210.00
91-01-010	Heather	J. Amos Grammer	1,000	210.00	210.00
Sports Impressions/Enesco		**Porcelain Dolls**			
90-01-001	Mickey Mantle	Sports Impressions	1,956	150.00	150.00
90-01-002	Don Mattingly	Sports Impressions	1,990	150.00	150.00
Turner Dolls Inc.		**Turner Dolls**			
83-01-001	Kristi	J. Turner	Closed	1000.00	1000.00
83-01-002	Baby Nell	J. Turner	Closed	970.00	970.00
84-01-003	Mindy	J. Turner	Closed	720.00	720.00
84-01-004	Petunia	J. Turner	Closed	720.00	720.00
84-01-005	Winston	J. Turner	Closed	900.00	900.00
84-01-006	Sonny	J. Turner	Closed	640.00	640.00

Company Number	Name	Series Artist	Edition Limit	Issue Price	Quote
84-01-007	Leslie	J. Turner	Closed	970.00	970.00
85-01-008	Sun Hee	J. Turner	Closed	720.00	720.00
85-01-009	Yong Mi	J. Turner	Closed	720.00	720.00
85-01-010	Cassandra (open)	J. Turner	Closed	900.00	900.00
85-01-011	Cassandra (closed)	J. Turner	Closed	900.00	900.00
85-01-012	Baby Teri	J. Turner	Closed	390.00	390.00
86-01-013	Chelsea	J. Turner	Closed	1000.00	1000.00
86-01-014	Concha	J. Turner	Closed	390.00	390.00
86-01-015	Carrie	J. Turner	Closed	390.00	390.00
86-01-016	Darci	J. Turner	Closed	390.00	390.00
86-01-017	Tressy	J. Turner	Closed	390.00	390.00
86-01-018	Amelia	J. Turner	Closed	640.00	640.00
86-01-019	Timothy/Tabitha	J. Turner	Closed	390.00	390.00
87-01-020	Freddie	J. Turner	Closed	500.00	500.00
87-01-021	Phoebe	J. Turner	Closed	500.00	500.00
87-01-022	Keisha	J. Turner	Closed	410.00	410.00
87-01-023	Senji	J. Turner	Closed	450.00	450.00
87-01-024	Shizuko	J. Turner	Closed	450.00	450.00
87-01-025	Lollie	J. Turner	Closed	450.00	450.00
88-01-026	Jena	J. Turner	Closed	410.00	410.00
88-01-027	Julie D	J. Turner	Closed	450.00	450.00
88-01-028	Susan Jayne	J. Turner	Closed	450.00	450.00
88-01-029	Seth	J. Turner	Closed	450.00	450.00
88-01-030	Tara Renee Baby	J. Turner	Closed	570.00	570.00
88-01-031	Tara Renee Toddler	J. Turner	Closed	570.00	570.00
88-01-032	Melinda	J. Turner	Closed	820.00	1100.00
89-01-033	Bretta	J. Turner	Closed	450.00	450.00
89-01-034	Cami	J. Turner	Closed	450.00	450.00
89-01-035	Cameron	J. Turner	Closed	450.00	450.00
89-01-036	Gabaree	J. Turner	Closed	1000.00	1000.00
89-01-037	Jilli	J. Turner	Closed	640.00	640.00
89-01-038	Lindsey	J. Turner	Closed	450.00	450.00
89-01-039	Selena	J. Turner	Closed	1050.00	1050.00
89-01-040	Jeannie	V.. Turner	Closed	420.00	420.00
89-01-041	Molly	V. Turner	Closed	420.00	420.00
90-01-042	Chad w/sled	J. Turner	Closed	590.00	590.00
90-01-043	Chad w/airplane	J. Turner	Closed	500.00	500.00
90-01-044	Lynette	J. Turner	Closed	900.00	900.00
90-01-045	Marci	J. Turner	Closed	570.00	570.00
90-01-046	Rudy	J. Turner	Closed	700.00	700.00
90-01-047	Whitney	J. Turner	Closed	770.00	770.00
90-01-048	Rudy	J. Turner	Closed	700.00	700.00
90-01-049	Alli	V. Turner	Closed	570.00	570.00
90-01-050	Christina	V. Turner	Closed	570.00	570.00
90-01-051	Tori	V. Turner	Closed	570.00	570.00
90-01-052	Katrina	V. Turner	Closed	620.00	620.00
90-01-053	Melodie	V. Turner	Closed	470.00	470.00
90-01-054	Jenalee	V. Turner	Closed	620.00	620.00
90-01-055	Cymbre	V. Turner	Closed	620.00	620.00
91-01-056	Christmas Marta	J. Turner	Closed	1100.00	1100.00
91-01-057	Marta	J. Turner	Closed	900.00	900.00
91-01-058	Mei Chun	J. Turner	Closed	900.00	900.00
91-01-059	Heather	V. Turner	Closed	700.00	700.00
91-01-060	Kitty Kay	V. Turner	Closed	450.00	450.00
91-01-061	Suzette (small)	V. Turner	Closed	700.00	700.00
91-01-062	Suzette (large)	V. Turner	Closed	1300.00	1300.00
91-01-063	Christmas Hannah	V. Turner	Closed	1100.00	1100.00
91-01-064	Hannah	V. Turner	Closed	900.00	900.00
92-01-065	Baby Joe Michael	V. Turner	Open	470.00	470.00
92-01-066	Nikkeya	V. Turner	350	800.00	800.00
92-01-067	Terrace	V. Turner	350	750.00	750.00
92-01-068	Sarah Chang	V. Turner	150	600.00	600.00
92-01-069	Sarah Chang (Ballerina)	V. Turner	50	1200.00	1200.00
92-01-070	Bucky the Newsboy	V. Turner	200	650.00	650.00
92-01-071	Christmas Bucky	V. Turner	50	900.00	900.00
92-01-072	Christmas Raven	V. Turner	50	1100.00	1100.00
92-01-073	Spring Raven	V. Turner	250	900.00	900.00
92-01-074	Autumn Raven	V. Turner	150	900.00	900.00
92-01-075	Makenzie	V. Turner	250	600.00	600.00

Susan Wakeen Doll Co. Inc. — The Littlest Ballet Company

Number	Name	Artist	Edition Limit	Issue Price	Quote
85-01-001	Jeanne	S. Wakeen	375	198.00	800.00
85-01-002	Patty	S. Wakeen	375	198.00	500.00
85-01-003	Cynthia	S. Wakeen	375	198.00	350.00
87-01-004	Elizabeth	S. Wakeen	250	425.00	1000.00

FIGURINES

Kurt S. Adler/Santa's World — Camelot Steinbach Nutcracker Series

Number	Name	Artist	Edition Limit	Issue Price	Quote
91-01-001	Merlin The Magician ES610	K.S. Adler	Retrd.	185.00	1000-1500.
92-01-002	King Arthur ES621	K.S. Adler	Retrd.	195.00	195.00
93-01-003	Sir Lancelot ES638	Steinbach	12,000	225.00	225.00

Kurt S. Adler/Santa's World — American Presidents Steinbach Nutcracker Series

Number	Name	Artist	Edition Limit	Issue Price	Quote
92-02-001	Abraham Lincoln ES622	Steinbach	12,000	195.00	225.00
92-02-002	George Washington ES623	Steinbach	12,000	195.00	225.00
93-02-003	Teddy Roosevelt ES644	Steinbach	10,000	225.00	225.00

Kurt S. Adler/Santa's World — American Inventors Steinbach Nutcracker Series

Number	Name	Artist	Edition Limit	Issue Price	Quote
93-03-001	Ben Franklin ES622	Steinbach	12,000	225.00	225.00

Kurt S. Adler/Santa's World — Famous Chieftans Steinbach Nutcracker Series

Number	Name	Artist	Edition Limit	Issue Price	Quote
93-04-001	Chief Sitting Bull ES637	Steinbach	8,500	225.00	225.00

Kurt S. Adler/Santa's World — Christmas Legends Steinbach Nutcracker Series

Number	Name	Artist	Edition Limit	Issue Price	Quote
93-05-001	Father Christmas ES645	Steinbach	7,500	225.00	225.00

Kurt S. Adler/Santa's World — Camelot Steinbach Smoking Figure Series

Number	Name	Artist	Edition Limit	Issue Price	Quote
92-06-001	Merlin The Magician ES830	Steinbach	7,500	150.00	150.00
93-06-004	King Arthur ES832	Steinbach	7,500	175.00	175.00

Kurt S. Adler/Santa's World — Zuber Nutcracker Series

Number	Name	Artist	Edition Limit	Issue Price	Quote
92-07-001	The Pilgrim EK14	K.S. Adler	5,000	125.00	125.00
92-07-002	The Indian EK15	K.S. Adler	5,000	135.00	135.00
92-07-003	The Bavarian EK16	K.S. Adler	5,000	130.00	130.00
92-07-004	The Fisherman EK17	K.S. Adler	5,000	125.00	125.00
92-07-005	The Gold Prospector EK18	K.S. Adler	5,000	125.00	125.00
92-07-006	The Country Singer EK19	K.S. Adler	5,000	125.00	125.00
92-07-007	Gepetto, The Toymaker EK9	K.S. Adler	5,000	125.00	125.00
92-07-008	The West Point Cadet With Canon EK8	K.S. Adler	5,000	130.00	130.00
92-07-009	The Chimney Sweep EK6	K.S. Adler	5,000	125.00	125.00
92-07-010	The Annapolis Midshipman EK7	K.S. Adler	5,000	125.00	125.00
92-07-011	The Golfer EK5	K.S. Adler	5,000	125.00	125.00
92-07-012	Bronco Billy The Cowboy EK1	K.S. Adler	5,000	125.00	125.00
92-07-013	The Nor' Easter Sea Captain EK3	K.S. Adler	5,000	125.00	125.00
92-07-014	TheTyrolean EK4	K.S. Adler	5,000	125.00	125.00
92-07-015	Paul Bunyan The Lumberjack EK2	K.S. Adler	5,000	125.00	125.00
93-07-016	The Drosselmeir EK21	Zuber	5,000	150.00	150.00
93-07-017	The Pizzamaker EK22	Zuber	5,000	150.00	150.00
93-07-018	Napoleon Bonaparte EK23	Zuber	5,000	150.00	150.00
93-07-019	The Ice Cream Vendor EK24	Zuber	5,000	150.00	150.00

Kurt S. Adler/Santa's World — Steinbach Nutcracker Collection

Number	Name	Artist	Edition Limit	Issue Price	Quote
92-08-001	Happy Santa ES601	K.S. Adler	Open	190.00	220.00

Kurt S. Adler/Santa's World — Disney Nutcracker Series

Number	Name	Artist	Edition Limit	Issue Price	Quote
92-09-001	Goofy H1216	K.S. Adler	Open	78.00	78.00
92-09-002	Mickey Mouse Sorcerer H1221	K.S. Adler	Open	100.00	100.00
92-09-003	Mickey Mouse Soldier H1194	K.S. Adler	Open	72.00	72.00
93-09-004	Pinnochio H1222	K.S. Adler	Open	110.00	110.00
93-09-005	Donald Duck H1235	K.S. Adler	Open	90.00	90.00

Kurt S. Adler/Santa's World — Fabriché™ Holiday Figures

Number	Name	Artist	Edition Limit	Issue Price	Quote
91-10-001	Santa Fiddler W1549	K.S. Adler	Open	100.00	100.00
91-10-002	Hello! Little One W1552	K.S. Adler	12,000	90.00	90.00
92-10-003	Bringin in the Yule Log W1589	M. Rothenberg	5,000	200.00	200.00
92-10-004	Santa's Ice Capades W1588	M. Rothenberg	Open	110.00	110.00
92-10-005	Santa Steals A Kiss & A Cookie W1581	M. Rothenberg	Open	150.00	150.00
92-10-006	An Apron Full of Love W1582	M. Rothenberg	Open	75.00	75.00
92-10-007	Christmas is in the Air W1590	K.S. Adler	Open	110.00	110.00
92-10-008	Bundles of Joy W1578	K.S. Adler	Open	78.00	78.00
92-10-009	Homeward Bound W1568	K.S. Adler	Open	61.00	61.00
92-10-010	Merry Kissmas W1548	M. Rothenberg	Open	140.00	140.00
92-10-011	Santa's Cat Nap W1504	M .Rothenberg	Open	98.00	98.00
92-10-012	St. Nicholas The Bishop W1532	K.S. Adler	Open	78.00	78.00
92-10-013	Hugs and Kisses W1531	K.S. Adler	Open	67.00	67.00
92-18-014	I'm Late, I'm Late J7947	T. Rubel	Open	100.00	100.00
92-18-015	It's Time To Go J7943	T. Rubel	Open	150.00	150.00
92-18-016	He Did It Again J7944	T. Rubel	Open	160.00	160.00
93-10-017	Par For The Claus W1603	K.S. Adler	Open	60.00	60.00
93-10-018	Checking It Twice W1604	K.S. Adler	Open	56.00	56.00
93-10-019	Bringing the Gifts W1605	K.S. Adler	Open	60.00	60.00
93-10-020	Forever Green W1607	K.S. Adler	Open	56.00	56.00
93-10-021	With All The Trimmings W1616	K.S. Adler	Open	76.00	76.00
93-10-022	Playtime For Santa W1619	K.S. Adler	Open	67.00	67.00
93-10-023	All That Jazz W1620	K.S. Adler	Open	67.00	67.00
93-10-024	Here Kitty W1618	M. Rothenberg	Open	90.00	90.00
93-10-025	Grandpa Santa's Piggyback W1621	M. Rothenberg	7,500	138.00	138.00
93-10-026	Stocking Stuffer W1622	K.S. Adler	Open	56.00	56.00
93-10-027	Top Brass W1630	K.S. Adler	Open	67.00	67.00

Kurt S. Adler/Santa's World — Fabriché™ Thomas Nast Figurines

Number	Name	Artist	Edition Limit	Issue Price	Quote
92-11-001	Christmas Sing-A-Long W1576	K.S. Adler	12,000	110.00	110.00
92-11-002	Caught in the Act W1577	K.S. Adler	12,000	133.00	133.00
93-11-003	Letters to Santa W1602	K.S. Adler	7,500	110.00	110.00
93-11-004	Dear Santa W1602	K.S. Adler	7,500	110.00	110.00

Kurt S. Adler/Santa's World — Smithsonian Institution Fabriché™ Series

Number	Name	Artist	Edition Limit	Issue Price	Quote
91-12-001	Santa On A Bicycle W1527	K.S. Adler	Open	150.00	150.00
92-12-002	Holiday Drive W1556	K.S. Adler	Open	155.00	155.00
92-12-003	Peace on Earth Angel Treetop W1583	K.S. Adler	Open	52.00	52.00
92-12-004	Peace on Earth Flying Angel W1585	K.S. Adler	Open	49.00	49.00
93-12-005	Holiday Flight W1617	Smithsonian	Open	144.00	144.00

Kurt S. Adler/Santa's World — Fabriché™ Angel Series

Number	Name	Artist	Edition Limit	Issue Price	Quote
92-13-001	Heavenly Messenger W1584	K.S. Adler	Open	41.00	41.00

Kurt S. Adler/Santa's World — Camelot Fabriché™ Figure Series

Number	Name	Artist	Edition Limit	Issue Price	Quote
93-14-001	Merlin the Magician J7966	P. Mauk	7,500	120.00	120.00
93-14-002	Young Arthur J7967	P. Mauk	7,500	120.00	120.00

Kurt S. Adler/Santa's World — Fabriché™ Santa at Home Series

Number	Name	Artist	Edition Limit	Issue Price	Quote
93-15-001	Grandpa Santa's Piggyback Ride W1621	M. Rothenberg	7,500	84.00	84.00

Kurt S. Adler/Santa's World — Fabriché™ Santa's Helpers Series

Number	Name	Artist	Edition Limit	Issue Price	Quote
92-16-001	A Stitch in Time W1591	M. Rothenberg	5,000	135.00	135.00
93-16-002	A Friend in Need W1629	M. Rothenberg	5,000	134.00	134.00
93-16-003	Little Olde Clockmaker W1629	M. Rothenberg	5,000	134.00	134.00

Kurt S. Adler/Santa's World — Old World Santa Series

Number	Name	Artist	Edition Limit	Issue Price	Quote
92-17-001	Large Black Forest Santa W2717	J. Mostrom	3,000	110.00	110.00
92-17-002	Small Grandfather Frost W2718	J. Mostrom	3,000	106.00	106.00
92-17-003	Large Father Christmas W2719	J. Mostrom	3,000	106.00	106.00
92-17-004	Patriotic Santa W2720	J. Mostrom	3,000	128.00	128.00
92-17-005	Chelsea Garden Santa W2721	J. Mostrom	5,000	33.50	33.50
92-17-006	Small Father Christmas W2712	J. Mostrom	5,000	33.50	33.50
92-17-007	Pere Noel W2723	J. Mostrom	5,000	33.50	33.50
92-17-008	Small Black Forest Santa W2712	J. Mostrom	5,000	40.00	40.00
92-17-009	St. Nickolas W2713	J. Mostrom	5,000	30.00	30.00
92-17-010	Mrs. Claus W2714	J. Mostrom	5,000	37.00	37.00
92-17-011	Workshop Santa W2715	J. Mostrom	5,000	43.00	43.00
92-17-012	Small Grandfather Frost W2716	J. Mostrom	5,000	43.00	43.00

Kurt S. Adler/Santa's World — Smithsonian Institution Carousel Figure Series

Number	Name	Artist	Edition Limit	Issue Price	Quote
87-18-001	The Antique Carousel Goat S3027/1	K.S. Adler	Retrd.	14.50	14.50
87-18-002	The Antique Carousel Bunny S3027/2	K.S. Adler	Retrd.	14.50	14.50
88-18-003	The Antique Carousel Horse S3027/3	K.S. Adler	Retrd.	14.50	14.50
88-18-004	The Antique Carousel Giraffe S3027/4	K.S. Adler	Retrd.	14.50	14.50
89-18-005	The Antique Carousel Lion S3027/5	K.S. Adler	Open	14.50	15.00
89-18-006	The Antique Carousel Cat S3027/6	K.S. Adler	Open	14.50	15.00
90-18-007	The Antique Carousel Zebra S3027/7	K.S. Adler	Open	14.50	15.00
90-18-008	The Antique Carousel Seahorse S3027/8	K.S. Adler	Open	14.50	15.00
91-18-009	The Antique Carousel Rooster S3027/9	K.S. Adler	Open	14.50	15.00
91-18-010	The Antique Carousel Horse S3027/10	K.S. Adler	Open	14.50	15.00
92-18-011	The Antique Carousel Elephant S3027/11	K.S. Adler	Open	14.50	15.00
92-18-012	The Antique Carousel Camel S3027/12	K.S. Adler	Open	15.00	15.00
93-18-013	The Antique Carousel Tiger S3027/13	K.S. Adler	Open	15.00	15.00
93-18-014	The Antique Carousel Horse S3027/14	K.S. Adler	Open	15.00	15.00

Kurt S. Adler/Santa's World — Visions Of Santa Series

Number	Name	Artist	Edition Limit	Issue Price	Quote
92-19-001	Workshop Santa J825	K.S. Adler	7,500	27.00	27.00
92-19-002	Santa Holding Child J826	K.S. Adler	7,500	24.50	24.50
92-19-003	Santa With Sack Holding Toy J827	K.S. Adler	7,500	24.50	24.50
92-19-004	Santa Spilling Bag Of Toys J1022	K.S. Adler	7,500	25.50	25.50
92-19-005	Santa Coming Out Of Fireplace J1023	K.S. Adler	7,500	29.00	29.00
92-19-006	Santa With Little Girls On Lap J1024	K.S. Adler	7,500	24.50	24.50

Company		Series			
Number	**Name**	**Artist**	**Edition Limit**	**Issue Price**	**Quote**
Kurt S. Adler/Santa's World		**The Fabriche Bear & Friends Series**			
92-20-001	Laughing All The Way J1567	K.S. Adler	Open	83.00	83.00
92-20-002	Not A Creature Was Stirring W1534	K.S. Adler	Open	67.00	67.00
93-20-003	Teddy Bear Parade W1601	K.S. Adler	Open	73.00	73.00
Kurt S. Adler/Santa's World		**Disney Fabriché™ Series**			
93-21-001	Mickey Mouse With Gift Boxes W1608	K.S. Adler	Open	78.00	78.00
All God's Children		**All God's Children**			
85-01-001	Abe -1357	M. Holcombe	Retrd.	24.95	950-1250.
89-01-002	Adam - 1526	M. Holcombe	Open	36.00	36.00
87-01-003	Amy - 1405W	M. Holcombe	Open	22.00	26.00
87-01-004	Angel - 1401W	M. Holcombe	Open	19.99	26.00
86-01-005	Annie Mae 8 1/2" -1310	M. Holcombe	Retrd.	26.95	100-175.
86-01-006	Annie Mae 6" -1311	M. Holcombe	Retrd.	18.95	70-120.00
87-01-007	Aunt Sarah - blue -1440	M. Holcombe	Retrd.	45.00	90-175.00
87-01-008	Aunt Sarah - red-1440	M. Holcombe	Retrd.	45.00	225-340.
92-01-009	Barney - 1557	M. Holcombe	Open	32.00	32.00
88-01-010	Bean (Clear Water)-1521	M. Holcombe	Retrd.	36.00	90-350.00
92-01-011	Bean (Painted Water)-1521	M. Holcombe	Retrd.	36.00	72.00
87-01-012	Becky with Patch - 1402W	M. Holcombe	Retrd.	18.95	150-170.
87-01-013	Becky - 1402W	M. Holcombe	Open	22.00	26.00
87-01-014	Ben - 1504	M. Holcombe	Retrd.	21.95	200-350.
91-01-015	Bessie & Corkie - 1547	M. Holcombe	Open	70.00	70.00
92-01-016	Beth - 1558	M. Holcombe	Open	32.00	32.00
88-01-017	Betsy (Clear Water)- 1513	M. Holcombe	Retrd.	36.00	125.00
92-01-018	Betsy (Painted Water)- 1513	M. Holcombe	Retrd.	36.00	72.00
89-01-019	Beverly - 1525	M. Holcombe	Retrd.	50.00	200-450.
91-01-020	Billy - 1545	M. Holcombe	Retrd.	36.00	72.00
87-01-021	Blossom - blue - 1500	M. Holcombe	Retrd.	59.95	150-200.
87-01-022	Blossom - red- 1500	M. Holcombe	Retrd.	59.95	120-180.
89-01-023	Bo - 1530	M. Holcombe	Open	22.00	22.00
85-01-024	Booker T - 1320	M. Holcombe	Retrd.	18.95	850-1200.
88-01-025	Boone - 1510	M. Holcombe	Retrd.	16.00	65-80.00
89-01-026	Bootsie - 1529	M. Holcombe	Open	22.00	22.00
87-01-027	Bonnie & Buttons - 1502	M. Holcombe	Retrd.	24.00	48.00
92-01-028	Caitlin - 1554	M. Holcombe	Open	36.00	36.00
85-01-029	Callie 4 1/2" - 1361	M. Holcombe	Retrd.	18.95	250-400.
85-01-030	Callie 2 1/4" - 1362	M. Holcombe	Retrd.	12.00	225-325.
88-01-031	Calvin - 777	M. Holcombe	Retrd.	200.00	1000-1400.
87-01-032	Cassie - 1503	M. Holcombe	Retrd.	21.95	60-100.00
87-01-033	Charity - 1408	M. Holcombe	Open	28.00	28.00
89-01-034	David - 1528	M. Holcombe	Open	28.00	28.00
91-01-035	Dori (green dress) - 1544	M. Holcombe	Retrd.	30.00	100-300.
87-01-036	Eli - 1403W	M. Holcombe	Open	26.00	26.00
85-01-037	Emma - 1322	M. Holcombe	Retrd.	26.95	1000-1700.
92-01-038	Faith - 1555	M. Holcombe	Open	32.00	32.00
87-01-039	Ginnie - 1508	M. Holcombe	Retrd.	22.00	200-350.
86-01-040	Grandma - 1323	M. Holcombe	Retrd.	29.95	2500-3300.
88-01-041	Hannah - 1515	M. Holcombe	Open	36.00	36.00
88-01-042	Hope - 1519	M. Holcombe	Open	36.00	36.00
87-01-043	Jacob - 1407W	M. Holcombe	Open	26.00	26.00
90-01-044	Jerome - 1532	M. Holcombe	Open	30.00	30.00
89-01-045	Jessica and Jeremy -1522-1523	M. Holcombe	Retrd.	195.00	1300-1600.
89-01-046	Jessie - 1501	M. Holcombe	Open	30.00	30.00
87-01-047	Jessie (no base) -1501W	M. Holcombe	Retrd.	18.95	200-375.
88-01-048	John -1514	M. Holcombe	Retrd.	30.00	75-150.00
90-01-049	Joseph - 1537	M. Holcombe	Open	30.00	30.00
92-01-050	Joy - 1548	M. Holcombe	Open	30.00	30.00
90-01-051	Kacie - 1533	M. Holcombe	Open	38.00	38.00
88-01-052	Kezia - 1518	M. Holcombe	Open	36.00	36.00
86-01-053	Lil' Emmie 4 1/2" -1344	M. Holcombe	Retrd.	17.99	60-100.00
86-01-054	Lil' Emmie 3 1/2"-1345	M. Holcombe	Retrd.	13.99	45-75.00
90-01-055	Mary - 1536	M. Holcombe	Open	30.00	30.00
88-01-056	Maya - 1520	M. Holcombe	Open	36.00	36.00
88-01-057	Meg (blue dress, long hair) -1505	M. Holcombe	Retrd.	21.00	300-325.
88-01-058	Meg (blue dress, short hair) -1505	M. Holcombe	Retrd.	21.00	275-325.
88-01-059	Meg (beige dress) -1505	M. Holcombe	Retrd.	21.00	850-1000.
92-01-060	Melissa - 1556	M. Holcombe	Open	32.00	32.00
92-01-061	Merci - 1559	M. Holcombe	Open	36.00	36.00
88-01-062	Michael & Kim - 1517	M. Holcombe	Open	36.00	36.00
88-01-063	Moe & Pokey - 1552	M. Holcombe	Open	16.00	16.00
87-01-064	Moses - 1506	M. Holcombe	Retrd.	30.00	60.00
91-01-065	Nellie - 1546	M. Holcombe	Open	36.00	36.00
87-01-066	Paddy Paw & Luke - 1551	M. Holcombe	Open	24.00	24.00
87-01-067	Paddy Paw & Lucy - 1553	M. Holcombe	Open	24.00	24.00
88-01-068	Peanut -1509	M. Holcombe	Retrd.	16.00	50-100.00
90-01-069	Preshus - 1538	M. Holcombe	Open	24.00	24.00
87-01-070	Primas Jones -1377	M. Holcombe	Retrd.	39.95	400-600.
87-01-071	Primas Jones (w/base) -1377	M. Holcombe	Retrd.	39.95	575-675.
87-01-072	Prissy with Yarn Hair (6 strands) -1343	M. Holcombe	Retrd.	18.95	50-150.00
87-01-073	Prissy with Yarn Hair (9 strands) -1343	M. Holcombe	Retrd.	18.95	200-400.
87-01-074	Prissy with Basket -1346	M. Holcombe	Retrd.	16.00	70-100.00
86-01-075	Prissy (Moon Pie) - 1557	M. Holcombe	Open	19.99	30.00
86-01-076	Prissy (Bear) - 1558	M. Holcombe	Open	17.99	24.00
87-01-077	Pud- 1550	M. Holcombe	Retrd.	10.99	1000-1200.
87-01-078	Rachel - 1404W	M. Holcombe	Open	19.99	26.00
92-01-079	Rakiya - 1561	M. Holcombe	Open	36.00	36.00
88-01-080	Sally -1507	M. Holcombe	Retrd.	18.95	75-100.00
91-01-081	Samantha - 1542	M. Holcombe	Open	38.00	38.00
91-01-082	Samuel - 1541	M. Holcombe	Open	32.00	32.00
89-01-083	Sasha - 1531	M. Holcombe	Open	30.00	30.00
86-01-084	Selina Jane (6 strands) -1338	M. Holcombe	Retrd.	21.95	85-150.00
86-01-085	Selina Jane (9 strands) -1338	M. Holcombe	Retrd.	21.95	150-350.
86-01-086	St. Nicholas-W -1315	M. Holcombe	Retrd.	29.95	75-115.00
86-01-087	St. Nicholas-B -1316	M. Holcombe	Retrd.	29.95	75-115.00
92-01-088	Stephen (Nativity Shepherd) - 1563	M. Holcombe	Open	36.00	75-115.00
90-01-089	Sunshine - 1535	M. Holcombe	Open	38.00	38.00
88-01-090	Tansi & Tedi (green socks, collar, cuffs)-1516	M. Holcombe	Retrd.	30.00	125-150.
88-01-091	Tansy & Tedi - 1516	M. Holcombe	Open	N/A	36.00
89-01-092	Tara - 1527	M. Holcombe	Open	36.00	36.00
90-01-093	Tess - 1534	M. Holcombe	Open	30.00	30.00
90-01-094	Thaliyah- 778	M. Holcombe	Retrd.	150.00	1100-1200.
92-01-095	Thomas - 1549	M. Holcombe	Open	30.00	30.00
87-01-096	Tiffany - 1511	M. Holcombe	Open	32.00	32.00
86-01-097	Toby 4 1/2"- 1331	M. Holcombe	Retrd.	15.99	50-100.00
86-01-098	Toby 3 1/2"- 1332	M. Holcombe	Retrd.	12.99	40-75.00
85-01-099	Tom- 1353	M. Holcombe	Retrd.	15.95	225-265.
86-01-100	Uncle Bud 8 1/2"- 1303	M. Holcombe	Retrd.	26.95	80-175.00
86-01-101	Uncle Bud 6"- 1304	M. Holcombe	Retrd.	18.95	90-125.00
92-01-102	Valerie - 1560	M. Holcombe	Open	36.00	36.00
87-01-103	Willie - 1406	M. Holcombe	Open	21.95	26.00
87-01-104	Willie (no base)- 1406W	M. Holcombe	Retrd.	19.95	275-400.

Company		Series			
Number	**Name**	**Artist**	**Edition Limit**	**Issue Price**	**Quote**
All God's Children		**Christmas**			
87-02-001	1987 Father Christmas-W -1750	M. Holcombe	Retrd.	145.00	500-550.
87-02-002	1987 Father Christmas-B -1751	M. Holcombe	Retrd.	145.00	450-550.
88-02-003	1988 Father Christmas-W -1757	M. Holcombe	Retrd.	195.00	425-450.
88-02-004	1988 Father Christmas-B -1758	M. Holcombe	Retrd.	195.00	400-450.
88-02-005	Santa Claus-W -1767	M. Holcombe	Retrd.	185.00	400-450.
88-02-006	Santa Claus-B -1768	M. Holcombe	Retrd.	185.00	400-500.
89-02-007	1989 Father Christmas-W -1769	M. Holcombe	Retrd.	195.00	450-550.
89-02-008	1989 Father Christmas-B -1770	M. Holcombe	Retrd.	195.00	450-550.
91-02-009	1990-91 Father Christmas-W -1771	M. Holcombe	Retrd.	195.00	450-500.
91-02-010	1990-91 Father Christmas-B -1772	M. Holcombe	Retrd.	195.00	350-500.
92-02-011	1991-92 Father Christmas-W -1773	M. Holcombe	5,000	195.00	195.00
92-02-012	1991-92 Father Christmas-B -1774	M. Holcombe	5,000	195.00	195.00
92-02-013	Father Christmas Bust-W -1775	M. Holcombe	5,000	145.00	145.00.
92-02-014	Father Christmas Bust-B -1776	M. Holcombe	5,000	145.00	145.00.
All God's Children		**Sugar And Spice**			
87-03-001	God is Love (Angel) -1401	M. Holcombe	Retrd.	21.95	375-500.
87-03-002	Friend Show Love (Becky) -1402	M. Holcombe	Retrd.	21.95	375-500.
87-03-003	Blessed are the Peacemakers (Eli) -1403	M. Holcombe	Retrd.	21.95	375-500.
87-03-004	Old Friends are Best (Rachel) -1404	M. Holcombe	Retrd.	21.95	375-500.
87-03-005	Jesus Loves Me (Amy) -1405	M. Holcombe	Retrd.	21.95	375-500.
87-03-006	Sharing with Friends (Willie) -1406	M. Holcombe	Retrd.	21.95	375-500.
87-03-007	Friendship Warms the Heart (Jacob) -1407	M. Holcombe	Retrd.	21.95	375-500.
All God's Children		**International Series**			
88-04-001	Juan - 1807	M. Holcombe	Retrd.	26.00	52.00
87-04-002	Kameko - 1802	M. Holcombe	Open.	26.00	26.00
87-04-003	Karl - 1808	M. Holcombe	Open.	26.00	26.00
88-04-004	Katrina - 1803	M. Holcombe	Retrd.	26.00	52.00
87-04-005	Kelli - 1805	M. Holcombe	Open	30.00	30.00
87-04-006	Little Chief - 1804	M. Holcombe	Open	32.00	32.00
87-04-007	Pike - 1806	M. Holcombe	Open	30.00	30.00
87-04-008	Tat - 1801	M. Holcombe	Open	30.00	30.00
All God's Children		**Historical Series**			
89-05-001	Harriet Tubman - 1900	M. Holcombe	Open	65.00	65.00
90-05-002	Sojourner Truth - 1901	M. Holcombe	Open	65.00	65.00
91-05-003	Frederick Douglass - 1902	M. Holcombe	Open	70.00	70.00
92-05-004	Dr. Daniel Williams - 1903	M. Holcombe	Open	70.00	70.00
92-05-005	Mary Bethune - 1904	M. Holcombe	Open	70.00	70.00
92-05-006	Frances Harper - 1905	M. Holcombe	Open	70.00	70.00
92-05-007	Ida B. Wells - 1906	M. Holcombe	Open	70.00	70.00
92-05-008	George Washington Carver - 1907	M. Holcombe	Open	70.00	70.00
All God's Children		**Collectors' Club**			
89-06-001	Molly -1524	M. Holcombe	Retrd.	38.00	250-500.
90-06-002	Joey -1539	M. Holcombe	Retrd.	32.00	225-250.
91-06-003	Mandy-1540	M. Holcombe	Retrd.	36.00	125-175.
92-06-004	Olivia-1562	M. Holcombe	5/93	36.00	36.00
American Artists		**Fred Stone Figurines**			
85-01-001	The Black Stallion, porcelain	F. Stone	2,500	125.00	260.00
85-01-002	The Black Stallion, bronze	F. Stone	1,500	150.00	175.00
86-01-003	Arab Mare & Foal	F. Stone	2,500	150.00	225.00
86-01-004	Tranquility	F. Stone	2,500	175.00	275.00
87-01-005	Rearing Black Stallion (Porcelain)	F. Stone	3,500	150.00	175.00
87-01-006	Rearing Black Stallion (Bronze)	F. Stone	1,250	175.00	195.00
ANRI		**Ferrandiz Shepherds of the Year**			
77-01-001	Friendships, 6"	J. Ferrandiz	Annual	110.00	500-675.
77-01-002	Friendships, 3"	J. Ferrandiz	Annual	53.50	330.00
78-01-003	Spreading the Word, 6"	J. Ferrandiz	Annual	270.50	500.00
78-01-004	Spreading the Word, 3"	J. Ferrandiz	Annual	115.00	275.00
79-01-005	Drummer Boy, 6"	J. Ferrandiz	Annual	220.00	425.00
79-01-006	Drummer Boy, 3"	J. Ferrandiz	Annual	80.00	250.00
80-01-007	Freedom Bound, 6"	J. Ferrandiz	Annual	225.00	400.00
80-01-008	Freedom Bound, 3"	J. Ferrandiz	Annual	90.00	225.00
81-01-009	Jolly Piper, 6"	J. Ferrandiz	2,250	225.00	375.00
82-01-010	Companions, 6"	J. Ferrandiz	2,250	220.00	275-300.
83-01-011	Good Samaritan, 6"	J. Ferrandiz	2,250	220.00	320.00
84-01-012	Devotion, 6"	J. Ferrandiz	2,250	180.00	200-250.
84-01-013	Devotion, 3"	J. Ferrandiz	2,250	82.50	125.00
ANRI		**Ferrandiz Matching Number Woodcarvings**			
88-02-001	Dear Sweetheart, 6"	J. Ferrandiz	Closed	525.00	900.00
88-02-002	For My Sweetheart, 6"	J. Ferrandiz	Set	Set	Set
88-02-003	Dear Sweetheart, 3"	J. Ferrandiz	Closed	285.00	495.00
88-02-004	For My Sweetheart, 3"	J. Ferrandiz	Set	Set	Set
88-02-005	Extra, Extra!, 6"	J. Ferrandiz	100	665.00	665.00
88-02-006	Sunny Skies, 6"	J. Ferrandiz	Set	Set	Set
88-02-007	Extra, Extra!, 3"	J. Ferrandiz	100	315.00	315.00
88-02-008	Sunny Skies, 3"	J. Ferrandiz	Set	Set	Set
88-02-009	Picnic for Two, 6"	J. Ferrandiz	Closed	845.00	845.00
88-02-010	Bon Appetit, 6"	J. Ferrandiz	Set	Set	Set
88-02-011	Picnic for Two, 3"	J. Ferrandiz	Closed	390.00	390.00
88-02-012	Bon Appetit, 3"	J. Ferrandiz	Set	Set	Set
89-02-013	Baker / Pastry, 6"	J. Ferrandiz	100	680.00	680.00
89-02-014	Baker / Pastry, 3"	J. Ferrandiz	100	340.00	340.00
90-02-015	Alpine Music / Friend, 6"	J. Ferrandiz	100	900.00	900.00
90-02-016	Alpine Music / Friend, 3"	J. Ferrandiz	100	450.00	450.00
91-02-017	Catalonian Boy/Girl, 6"	J. Ferrandiz	100	1000.00	1000.00
91-02-018	Catalonian Boy/Girl, 3"	J. Ferrandiz	100	455.00	455.00
ANRI		**Ferrandiz Boy and Girl**			
76-03-001	Cowboy, 6"	J. Ferrandiz	Closed	75.00	500-600.
76-03-002	Harvest Girl, 6"	J. Ferrandiz	Closed	75.00	400-800.
77-03-003	Tracker, 6"	J. Ferrandiz	Closed	100.00	375.00
77-03-004	Leading the Way, 6"	J. Ferrandiz	Closed	100.00	300-375
78-03-005	Peace Pipe, 6"	J. Ferrandiz	Closed	140.00	325-450.
78-03-006	Basket of Joy, 6"	J. Ferrandiz	Closed	140.00	350-450.
79-03-007	Happy Strummer, 6"	J. Ferrandiz	Closed	160.00	395.00
79-03-008	First Blossom, 6"	J. Ferrandiz	Closed	135.00	375.00
80-03-009	Friends, 6"	J. Ferrandiz	Closed	200.00	300-350.
80-03-010	Melody for Two, 6"	J. Ferrandiz	Closed	200.00	350.00
81-03-011	Merry Melody, 6"	J. Ferrandiz	Closed	210.00	300-350.
81-03-012	Tiny Sounds, 6"	J. Ferrandiz	Closed	210.00	300-350.
82-03-013	Guiding Light, 6"	J. Ferrandiz	Closed	225.00	275-350.
82-03-014	To Market, 6"	J. Ferrandiz	Closed	220.00	250.00
83-03-015	Bewildered, 6"	J. Ferrandiz	Closed	196.00	250.00
83-03-016	Admiration, 6"	J. Ferrandiz	Closed	220.00	250.00
84-03-017	Wanderer's Return, 6"	J. Ferrandiz	Closed	196.00	250.00
84-03-018	Wanderer's Return, 3"	J. Ferrandiz	Closed	93.00	125.00

FIGURINES

Company Number	Name	Series Artist	Edition Limit	Issue Price	Quote
84-03-019	Friendly Faces, 6"	J. Ferrandiz	Closed	210.00	225.00
84-03-020	Friendly Faces, 3"	J. Ferrandiz	Closed	93.00	110.00
85-03-021	Tender Love, 6"	J. Ferrandiz	Closed	225.00	250.00
85-03-022	Tender Love, 3"	J. Ferrandiz	Closed	100.00	125.00
85-03-023	Peaceful Friends, 6"	J. Ferrandiz	Closed	250.00	250.00
85-03-024	Peaceful Friends, 3"	J. Ferrandiz	Closed	120.00	120.00
86-03-025	Season's Bounty, 6"	J. Ferrandiz	Closed	245.00	245.00
86-03-026	Season's Bounty, 3"	J. Ferrandiz	Closed	125.00	125.00
86-03-027	Golden Sheaves, 6"	J. Ferrandiz	Closed	245.00	245.00
86-03-028	Golden Sheaves, 3"	J. Ferrandiz	Closed	125.00	125.00
87-03-029	Dear Sweetheart, 6"	J. Ferrandiz	Closed	250.00	250.00
87-03-030	Dear Sweetheart, 3"	J. Ferrandiz	Closed	130.00	130.00
87-03-031	For My Sweetheart, 6"	J. Ferrandiz	Closed	250.00	250.00
87-03-032	For My Sweetheart, 3"	J. Ferrandiz	Closed	130.00	130.00
88-03-033	Extra, Extra!, 6"	J. Ferrandiz	2,250	320.00	320.00
88-03-034	Extra, Extra!, 3"	J. Ferrandiz	2,250	145.00	145.00
88-03-035	Sunny Skies, 6"	J. Ferrandiz	Closed	320.00	320.00
88-03-036	Sunny Skies, 3"	J. Ferrandiz	Closed	145.00	145.00
89-03-037	Baker Boy, 6"	J. Ferrandiz	1,500	340.00	340.00
89-03-038	Baker Boy, 3"	J. Ferrandiz	1,500	170.00	170.00
89-03-039	Pastry Girl, 6"	J. Ferrandiz	1,500	340.00	340.00
89-03-040	Pastry Girl, 3"	J. Ferrandiz	1,500	170.00	170.00
89-03-041	Swiss Girl, 6"	J. Ferrandiz	Open	470.00	470.00
89-03-042	Swiss Girl, 3"	J. Ferrandiz	Open	200.00	200.00
89-03-043	Swiss Boy, 6"	J. Ferrandiz	Open	380.00	380.00
89-03-044	Swiss Boy, 3"	J. Ferrandiz	Open	180.00	180.00
90-03-045	Alpine Music, 6"	J. Ferrandiz	1,500	450.00	450.00
90-03-046	Alpine Music, 3"	J. Ferrandiz	1,500	225.00	225.00
90-03-047	Alpine Friend, 6"	J. Ferrandiz	1,500	450.00	450.00
90-03-048	Alpine Friend, 3"	J. Ferrandiz	1,500	225.00	225.00
91-03-049	Catalonian Boy, 6"	J. Ferrandiz	1,500	500.00	500.00
91-03-050	Catalonian Boy, 3"	J. Ferrandiz	1,500	227.50	227.50
91-03-051	Catalonian Girl, 6"	J. Ferrandiz	1,500	500.00	500.00
91-03-052	Catalonian Girl, 3"	J. Ferrandiz	1,500	227.50	227.50
92-03-053	Waste Not, Want Not, 6"	J. Ferrandiz	1,000	430.00	430.00
92-03-054	Waste Not, Want Not, 3"	J. Ferrandiz	1,000	190.00	190.00
92-03-055	May I, Too?, 6"	J. Ferrandiz	1,000	440.00	440.00
92-03-056	May I, Too?, 3"	J. Ferrandiz	1,000	230.00	230.00
92-03-057	Madonna With Child, 6"	J. Ferrandiz	1,000	370.00	370.00
92-03-058	Madonna With Child, 3"	J. Ferrandiz	1,000	190.00	190.00
92-03-059	Pascal Lamb, 6"	J. Ferrandiz	1,000	460.00	460.00
92-03-060	Pascal Lamb, 3"	J. Ferrandiz	1,000	210.00	210.00
ANRI		**Ferrandiz Woodcarvings**			
69-04-001	Sugar Heart, 6"	J. Ferrandiz	Closed	25.00	525.00
69-04-002	Sugar Heart, 3"	J. Ferrandiz	Closed	12.50	450.00
69-04-003	Angel Sugar Heart, 6"	J. Ferrandiz	Closed	25.00	2500.00
69-04-004	Heavenly Quintet, 6"	J. Ferrandiz	Closed	25.00	2000.00
69-04-005	Heavenly Gardener, 6"	J. Ferrandiz	Closed	25.00	2000.00
69-04-006	Love's Messenger, 6"	J. Ferrandiz	Closed	25.00	2000.00
74-04-007	Greetings, 6"	J. Ferrandiz	Closed	55.00	475.00
74-04-008	Greetings, 3"	J. Ferrandiz	Closed	30.00	300.00
74-04-009	New Friends, 6"	J. Ferrandiz	Closed	55.00	550.00
74-04-010	New Friends, 3"	J. Ferrandiz	Closed	30.00	275.00
74-04-011	Tender Moments, 6"	J. Ferrandiz	Closed	55.00	575.00
74-04-012	Tender Moments, 3"	J. Ferrandiz	Closed	30.00	375.00
74-04-013	Helping Hands, 6"	J. Ferrandiz	Closed	55.00	700.00
74-04-014	Helping Hands, 3"	J. Ferrandiz	Closed	30.00	350.00
74-04-015	Spring Outing, 6"	J. Ferrandiz	Closed	55.00	900.00
74-04-016	Spring Outing, 3"	J. Ferrandiz	Closed	30.00	625.00
73-04-017	Sweeper, 6"	J. Ferrandiz	Closed	75.00	425.00
73-04-018	Sweeper, 3"	J. Ferrandiz	Closed	35.00	130.00
74-04-019	The Bouquet, 6"	J. Ferrandiz	Closed	75.00	325.00
74-04-020	The Bouquet, 3"	J. Ferrandiz	Closed	35.00	175.00
70-04-021	Artist, 6"	J. Ferrandiz	Closed	25.00	350.00
74-04-022	Artist, 3"	J. Ferrandiz	Closed	30.00	175.00
74-04-023	Little Mother, 6"	J. Ferrandiz	Closed	85.00	285.00
74-04-024	Little Mother, 3"	J. Ferrandiz	Closed	136.00	290.00
74-04-025	Romeo, 6"	J. Ferrandiz	Closed	85.00	375.00
74-04-026	Romeo, 3"	J. Ferrandiz	Closed	50.00	225.00
75-04-027	Inspector, 6"	J. Ferrandiz	Closed	80.00	350.00
75-04-028	Inspector, 3"	J. Ferrandiz	Closed	40.00	225.00
76-04-029	Girl with Rooster, 6"	J. Ferrandiz	Closed	60.00	275.00
76-04-030	Girl with Rooster, 3"	J. Ferrandiz	Closed	32.50	175.00
75-04-031	The Gift, 6"	J. Ferrandiz	Closed	70.00	250.00
75-04-032	The Gift, 3"	J. Ferrandiz	Closed	40.00	150.00
75-04-033	Love Gift, 6"	J. Ferrandiz	Closed	70.00	250.00
75-04-034	Love Gift, 3"	J. Ferrandiz	Closed	40.00	150.00
77-04-035	The Blessing, 6"	J. Ferrandiz	Closed	125.00	250.00
77-04-036	The Blessing, 3"	J. Ferrandiz	Closed	45.00	150.00
69-04-037	Love Letter, 6"	J. Ferrandiz	Closed	25.00	250.00
69-04-038	Love Letter, 3"	J. Ferrandiz	Closed	12.50	150.00
75-04-039	Courting, 6"	J. Ferrandiz	Closed	150.00	450.00
75-04-040	Courting, 3"	J. Ferrandiz	Closed	70.00	235.00
75-04-041	Wanderlust, 6"	J. Ferrandiz	Closed	70.00	450.00
76-04-042	Wanderlust, 3"	J. Ferrandiz	Closed	32.50	125.00
76-04-043	Catch a Falling Star, 6"	J. Ferrandiz	Closed	75.00	250.00
76-04-044	Catch a Falling Star, 3"	J. Ferrandiz	Closed	35.00	150.00
75-04-045	Mother and Child, 6"	J. Ferrandiz	Closed	90.00	250.00
75-04-046	Mother and Child, 3"	J. Ferrandiz	Closed	45.00	125.00
77-04-047	Journey, 6"	J. Ferrandiz	Closed	120.00	400.00
77-04-048	Journey, 3"	J. Ferrandiz	Closed	67.50	175.00
77-04-049	Night Night, 6"	J. Ferrandiz	Closed	67.50	250-315.
77-04-050	Night Night, 3"	J. Ferrandiz	Closed	45.00	120.00
76-04-051	Sharing, 6"	J. Ferrandiz	Closed	32.50	225-275.
76-04-052	Sharing, 3"	J. Ferrandiz	Closed	32.50	130.00
82-04-053	Clarinet, 6"	J. Ferrandiz	Closed	175.00	200.00
82-04-054	Clarinet, 3"	J. Ferrandiz	Closed	80.00	100.00
82-04-055	Violin, 6"	J. Ferrandiz	Closed	175.00	195.00
82-04-056	Violin, 3"	J. Ferrandiz	Closed	80.00	95.00
82-04-057	Bagpipe, 6"	J. Ferrandiz	Closed	175.00	190.00
82-04-058	Bagpipe, 3"	J. Ferrandiz	Closed	80.00	95.00
82-04-059	Flute, 6"	J. Ferrandiz	Closed	175.00	190.00
82-04-060	Flute, 3"	J. Ferrandiz	Closed	80.00	95.00
82-04-061	Guitar, 6"	J. Ferrandiz	Closed	175.00	190.00
82-04-062	Guitar, 3"	J. Ferrandiz	Closed	80.00	95.00
82-04-063	Harmonica, 6"	J. Ferrandiz	Closed	175.00	190.00
82-04-064	Harmonica, 3"	J. Ferrandiz	Closed	80.00	95.00
82-04-065	Harmonica, 3"	J. Ferrandiz	Closed	80.00	95.00
82-04-066	Lighting the Way, 6"	J. Ferrandiz	Closed	225.00	255.00
82-04-067	Lighting the Way, 3"	J. Ferrandiz	Closed	105.00	120.00
81-04-068	Musical Basket, 6"	J. Ferrandiz	Closed	200.00	225.00
81-04-069	Musical Basket, 3"	J. Ferrandiz	Closed	90.00	115.00
82-04-070	The Good Life, 6"	J. Ferrandiz	Closed	225.00	250.00
82-04-071	The Good Life, 3"	J. Ferrandiz	Closed	100.00	200.00
82-04-072	Star Bright, 6"	J. Ferrandiz	Closed	250.00	260.00
82-04-073	Star Bright, 3"	J. Ferrandiz	Closed	110.00	125.00
82-04-074	Encore, 6"	J. Ferrandiz	Closed	225.00	235.00
82-04-075	Encore, 3"	J. Ferrandiz	Closed	100.00	115.00
82-04-076	Play It Again, 6"	J. Ferrandiz	Closed	250.00	255.00
82-04-077	Play It Again, 3"	J. Ferrandiz	Closed	100.00	120.00
73-04-078	Girl with Dove, 6"	J. Ferrandiz	Closed	50.00	175-200.
73-04-079	Girl with Dove, 3"	J. Ferrandiz	Closed	30.00	110.00
79-04-080	Stitch in Time, 6"	J. Ferrandiz	Closed	150.00	235.00
79-04-081	Stitch in Time, 3"	J. Ferrandiz	Closed	75.00	125.00
79-04-082	He's My Brother, 6"	J. Ferrandiz	Closed	155.00	240.00
79-04-083	He's My Brother, 3"	J. Ferrandiz	Closed	70.00	130.00
81-04-084	Stepping Out, 6"	J. Ferrandiz	Closed	220.00	252.00
81-04-085	Stepping Out, 3"	J. Ferrandiz	Closed	95.00	110-140.
79-04-086	High Riding, 6"	J. Ferrandiz	Closed	340.00	475.00
79-04-087	High Riding, 3"	J. Ferrandiz	Closed	145.00	200.00
80-04-088	Umpapa, 4"	J. Ferrandiz	Closed	125.00	140.00
81-04-089	Jolly Piper, 3"	J. Ferrandiz	Closed	100.00	120.00
77-04-090	Tracker, 3"	J. Ferrandiz	Closed	70.00	120.00
81-04-091	Merry Melody, 3"	J. Ferrandiz	Closed	90.00	115.00
82-04-092	Guiding Light, 3"	J. Ferrandiz	Closed	100.00	115.00
82-04-093	Companions, 3"	J. Ferrandiz	Closed	95.00	115.00
77-04-094	Leading the Way, 3"	J. Ferrandiz	Closed	62.50	120.00
82-04-095	To Market, 3"	J. Ferrandiz	Closed	95.00	115.00
78-04-096	Basket of Joy, 3"	J. Ferrandiz	Closed	65.00	120.00
81-04-097	Tiny Sounds, 3"	J. Ferrandiz	Closed	90.00	105.00
78-04-098	Spring Dance, 12"	J. Ferrandiz	Closed	950.00	1750.00
78-04-099	Spring Dance, 24"	J. Ferrandiz	Closed	4750.00	6200.00
76-04-100	Gardener, 3"	J. Ferrandiz	Closed	32.00	195.00
76-04-101	Gardener, 6"	J. Ferrandiz	Closed	65.00	275.00
79-04-102	First Blossom, 3"	J. Ferrandiz	Closed	70.00	110.00
81-04-103	Sweet Arrival Pink, 6"	J. Ferrandiz	Closed	225.00	225.00
81-04-104	Sweet Arrival Pink, 3"	J. Ferrandiz	Closed	105.00	110.00
81-04-105	Sweet Arrival Blue, 6"	J. Ferrandiz	Closed	225.00	255.00
81-04-106	Sweet Arrival Blue, 3"	J. Ferrandiz	Closed	105.00	110.00
82-04-107	The Champion, 6"	J. Ferrandiz	Closed	225.00	225.00
82-04-108	The Champion, 3"	J. Ferrandiz	Closed	98.00	110.00
82-04-109	Sweet Melody, 6"	J. Ferrandiz	Closed	198.00	210.00
82-04-110	Sweet Melody, 3"	J. Ferrandiz	Closed	80.00	90.00
73-04-111	Trumpeter, 6"	J. Ferrandiz	Closed	120.00	240.00
73-04-112	Trumpeter, 3"	J. Ferrandiz	Closed	69.00	115.00
80-04-113	Trumpeter, 10"	J. Ferrandiz	Closed	500.00	500.00
84-04-114	Trumpeter, 20"	J. Ferrandiz	Closed	2350.00	3050.00
79-04-115	Peace Pipe, 3"	J. Ferrandiz	Closed	85.00	120.00
83-04-116	Peace Pipe, 10"	J. Ferrandiz	Closed	460.00	480.00
84-04-117	Peace Pipe, 20"	J. Ferrandiz	Closed	2200.00	3500.00
74-04-118	Happy Wanderer, 6"	J. Ferrandiz	Closed	70.00	200.00
74-04-119	Happy Wanderer, 3"	J. Ferrandiz	Closed	40.00	105.00
73-04-120	Happy Wanderer, 10"	J. Ferrandiz	Closed	120.00	500.00
74-04-121	Flight Into Egypt, 6"	J. Ferrandiz	Closed	70.00	500.00
74-04-122	Flight Into Egypt, 3"	J. Ferrandiz	Closed	35.00	125.00
77-04-123	Poor Boy, 6"	J. Ferrandiz	Closed	125.00	215.00
77-04-124	Poor Boy, 3"	J. Ferrandiz	Closed	50.00	110.00
79-04-125	Happy Strummer, 3"	J. Ferrandiz	Closed	75.00	110.00
78-04-126	Harvest Girl, 3"	J. Ferrandiz	Closed	75.00	110-140.
82-04-127	Hitchhiker, 6"	J. Ferrandiz	Closed	125.00	230.00
82-04-128	Hitchhiker, 3"	J. Ferrandiz	Closed	98.00	110.00
84-04-129	High Hopes, 6"	J. Ferrandiz	Closed	170.00	247.50
84-04-130	High Hopes, 3"	J. Ferrandiz	Closed	81.00	81.00
88-04-131	Abracadabra, 6"	J. Ferrandiz	Closed	315.00	345.00
88-04-132	Abracadabra, 3"	J. Ferrandiz	Closed	145.00	165.00
88-04-133	Peace Maker, 6"	J. Ferrandiz	Closed	360.00	395.00
88-04-134	Peace Maker, 3"	J. Ferrandiz	Closed	180.00	200.00
88-04-135	Picnic for Two, 6"	J. Ferrandiz	Closed	425.00	465.00
88-04-136	Picnic for Two, 3"	J. Ferrandiz	Closed	190.00	210.00
88-04-137	Bon Appetit, 6"	J. Ferrandiz	Closed	395.00	440.00
88-04-138	Bon Appetit, 3"	J. Ferrandiz	Closed	175.00	195.00
69-04-139	The Good Sheperd, 3"	J. Ferrandiz	Closed	12.50	120.50
69-04-140	The Good Shepherd, 6"	J. Ferrandiz	Closed	25.00	236.50
71-04-141	The Good Shepherd, 10"	J. Ferrandiz	Closed	90.00	90.00
75-04-142	Going Home, 3"	J. Ferrandiz	Closed	40.00	110.00
75-04-143	Going Home, 6"	J. Ferrandiz	Closed	70.00	240.00
75-04-144	Holy Family, 3"	J. Ferrandiz	Closed	75.00	250.00
75-04-145	Holy Family, 6"	J. Ferrandiz	Closed	200.00	670.00
73-04-146	Nature Girl, 3"	J. Ferrandiz	Closed	30.00	30.00
73-04-147	Nature Girl, 6"	J. Ferrandiz	Closed	60.00	272.00
73-04-148	Girl in the Egg, 3"	J. Ferrandiz	Closed	30.00	127.00
73-04-149	Girl in the Egg, 6"	J. Ferrandiz	Closed	60.00	272.00
76-04-150	Flower Girl, 3"	J. Ferrandiz	Closed	40.00	40.00
76-04-151	Flower Girl, 6"	J. Ferrandiz	Closed	90.00	310.00
76-04-152	The Letter, 3"	J. Ferrandiz	Closed	40.00	40.00
76-04-153	The Letter, 6"	J. Ferrandiz	Closed	90.00	600.00
69-04-154	Talking to the Animals, 3"	J. Ferrandiz	Closed	12.50	125.00
69-04-155	Talking to the Animals, 6"	J. Ferrandiz	Closed	45.00	45.00
71-04-156	Talking to the Animals, 10"	J. Ferrandiz	Closed	90.00	90.00
71-04-157	Talking to Animals, 20"	J. Ferrandiz	Closed	Unkn.	3000.00
70-04-158	Duet, 3"	J. Ferrandiz	Open	36.00	165.00
70-04-159	Duet, 6"	J. Ferrandiz	Open	Unkn.	355.00
73-04-160	Spring Arrivals, 3"	J. Ferrandiz	Open	30.00	130-145.
73-04-161	Spring Arrivals, 6"	J. Ferrandiz	Open	50.00	340.00
80-04-162	Spring Arrivals, 10"	J. Ferrandiz	Open	435.00	500.00
80-04-163	Spring Arrivals, 20"	J. Ferrandiz	250	2,000	3300.00
75-04-164	Summertime, 3"	J. Ferrandiz	Closed	35.00	35.00
75-04-165	Summertime, 6"	J. Ferrandiz	Closed	70.00	258.00
76-04-166	Cowboy, 3"	J. Ferrandiz	Closed	35.00	140-160.
84-04-167	Cowboy, 10"	J. Ferrandiz	Closed	370.00	500.00
83-04-168	Cowboy, 20"	J. Ferrandiz	Closed	2100.00	2100.00
87-04-169	Serenity, 3"	J. Ferrandiz	Closed	125.00	150.50
84-04-170	Bird's Eye View, 3"	J. Ferrandiz	Closed	88.00	129.00
84-04-171	Bird's Eye View, 6"	J. Ferrandiz	Closed	216.00	700.00
86-04-172	God's Little Helper, 2"	J. Ferrandiz	Closed	170.00	255.00
86-04-173	God's Little Helper, 4"	J. Ferrandiz	Closed	425.00	550.00
85-04-174	Butterfly Boy, 3"	J. Ferrandiz	Closed	95.00	140.00
85-04-175	Butterfly Boy, 6"	J. Ferrandiz	Closed	220.00	322.00
84-04-176	Shipmates, 3"	J. Ferrandiz	Closed	81.00	118.50
84-04-177	Shipmates, 6"	J. Ferrandiz	Closed	170.00	247.50
78-04-178	Spreading the Word, 3"	J. Ferrandiz	Closed	115.00	193.50
78-04-179	Spreading the Word, 6"	J. Ferrandiz	Closed	270.00	494.50
82-04-180	Bundle of Joy, 3"	J. Ferrandiz	Closed	100.00	300.00
82-04-181	Bundle of Joy, 6"	J. Ferrandiz	Closed	225.00	322.50
77-04-182	Riding Thru the Rain, 5"	J. Ferrandiz	Open	145.00	399.00

Company		Series			
Number	Name	Artist	Edition Limit	Issue Price	Quote
77-04-183	Riding Thru the Rain, 10"	J. Ferrandiz	Open	400.00	1000.00
81-04-184	Sweet Dreams, 3"	J. Ferrandiz	Closed	100.00	140.00
77-04-185	Hurdy Gurdy, 3"	J. Ferrandiz	Closed	53.00	150.00
77-04-186	Hurdy Gurdy, 6"	J. Ferrandiz	Closed	112.00	390.00
77-04-187	Proud Mother, 3"	J. Ferrandiz	Closed	52.50	150.00
77-04-188	Proud Mother, 6"	J. Ferrandiz	Closed	130.00	350.00
80-04-189	Drummer Boy, 3"	J. Ferrandiz	Closed	130.00	200.00
80-04-190	Drummer Boy, 6"	J. Ferrandiz	Closed	300.00	400.00
82-04-191	Circus Serenade, 3"	J. Ferrandiz	Closed	100.00	160.00
82-04-192	Circus Serenade, 6"	J. Ferrandiz	Closed	220.00	220.00
82-04-193	Surprise, 3"	J. Ferrandiz	Closed	100.00	150.00
82-04-194	Surprise, 6"	J. Ferrandiz	Closed	225.00	325.00
75-04-195	Cherub, 2"	J. Ferrandiz	Closed	32.00	90.00
75-04-196	Cherub, 4"	J. Ferrandiz	Closed	32.00	275.00
69-04-197	The Quintet, 3"	J. Ferrandiz	Closed	12.50	140.00
69-04-198	The Quintet, 6"	J. Ferrandiz	Closed	25.00	340.00
71-04-199	The Quintet, 10"	J. Ferrandiz	Closed	100.00	600.00
71-04-200	The Quintet, 20"	J. Ferrandiz	Closed	Unkn.	3000.00
87-04-201	Serenity, 6"	J. Ferrandiz	Closed	245.00	290.50
87-04-202	Nature's Wonder, 3"	J. Ferrandiz	Closed	125.00	150.50
87-04-203	Nature's Wonder, 6"	J. Ferrandiz	Closed	245.00	290.50
87-04-204	Black Forest Boy, 3"	J. Ferrandiz	Closed	125.00	150.50
87-04-205	Black Forest Boy, 6"	J. Ferrandiz	Closed	250.00	301.00
87-04-206	Black Forest Girl, 3"	J. Ferrandiz	Closed	125.00	150.50
87-04-207	Black Forest Girl, 6"	J. Ferrandiz	Closed	250.00	300-350.
87-04-208	Heavenly Concert, 2"	J. Ferrandiz	Closed	200.00	200.00
87-04-209	Heavenly Concert, 4"	J. Ferrandiz	Closed	450.00	550.00
86-04-210	Swiss Girl, 3"	J. Ferrandiz	Open	122.00	122.00
86-04-211	Swiss Girl, 6"	J. Ferrandiz	Open	245.00	303.50
86-04-212	Swiss Boy, 3"	J. Ferrandiz	Open	122.00	161.50
86-04-213	Swiss Boy, 6"	J. Ferrandiz	Open	245.00	323.50
86-04-214	A Musical Ride, 4"	J. Ferrandiz	Closed	165.00	236.50
86-04-215	A Musical Ride, 8"	J. Ferrandiz	Closed	395.00	559.00
82-04-216	Sweet Dreams, 6"	J. Ferrandiz	Closed	225.00	330.00
83-04-217	Love Message, 3"	J. Ferrandiz	Closed	105.00	150.50
83-04-218	Love Message, 6"	J. Ferrandiz	Closed	240.00	365.50
83-04-219	Edelweiss, 3"	J. Ferrandiz	Open	95.00	140.00
83-04-220	Edelweiss, 6"	J. Ferrandiz	Open	220.00	325.00
86-04-221	Edelweiss, 10"	J. Ferrandiz	Open	500.00	750.00
86-04-222	Edelweiss, 20"	J. Ferrandiz	250	3300.00	5160.00
83-04-223	Golden Blossom, 3"	J. Ferrandiz	Open	95.00	140.00
83-04-224	Golden Blossom, 6"	J. Ferrandiz	Open	220.00	325.00
86-04-225	Golden Blossom, 10"	J. Ferrandiz	Open	500.00	750.00
86-04-226	Golden Blossom, 20"	J. Ferrandiz	250	3300.00	5160.00
86-04-227	Golden Blossom, 40"	J. Ferrandiz	50	8300.00	12950.00
88-04-228	Winter Memories, 3"	J. Ferrandiz	Closed	180.00	195.00
88-04-229	Winter Memories, 6"	J. Ferrandiz	Closed	398.00	440.00
87-04-230	Among Friends, 3"	J. Ferrandiz	Closed	125.00	150.50
87-04-231	Among Friends, 6"	J. Ferrandiz	Closed	245.00	290.50
89-04-232	Mexican Girl, 3"	J. Ferrandiz	1,500	170.00	175.00
89-04-233	Mexican Girl, 6"	J. Ferrandiz	1,500	340.00	350.00
89-04-234	Mexican Boy, 3"	J. Ferrandiz	1,500	170.00	175.00
89-04-235	Mexican Boy, 6"	J. Ferrandiz	1,500	340.00	350.00
93-04-236	Santa and Teddy, 5"	J. Ferrandiz	750	395.00	395.00
93-04-237	Christmas Time, 5"	J. Ferrandiz	750	395.00	395.00
93-04-238	Holiday Greetings, 3"	J. Ferrandiz	1,000	230.00	230.00
93-04-239	Holiday Greetings, 6"	J. Ferrandiz	1,000	480.00	480.00
93-04-240	Lots of Gifts, 3"	J. Ferrandiz	1,000	230.00	230.00
93-04-241	Lots of Gifts, 6"	J. Ferrandiz	1,000	480.00	480.00
ANRI		**Ferrandiz Message Collection**			
89-05-001	He is the Light, 4 1/2"	J. Ferrandiz	5,000	300.00	300.00
89-05-002	Heaven Sent, 4 1/2"	J. Ferrandiz	5,000	300.00	300.00
89-05-003	God's Precious Gift, 4 1/2"	J. Ferrandiz	5,000	300.00	300.00
89-05-004	Love Knows No Bounds, 4 1/2"	J. Ferrandiz	5,000	300.00	300.00
89-05-005	Love So Powerful, 4 1/2"	J. Ferrandiz	5,000	300.00	300.00
89-05-006	Light From Within, 4 1/2"	J. Ferrandiz	5,000	300.00	300.00
89-05-007	He Guides Us, 4 1/2"	J. Ferrandiz	5,000	300.00	300.00
89-05-008	God's Miracle, 4 1/2"	J. Ferrandiz	5,000	300.00	300.00
89-05-009	He is the Light, 9"	J. Ferrandiz	5,000	600.00	600.00
90-05-010	God's Creation 4 1/2"	J. Ferrandiz	5,000	300.00	300.00
90-05-011	Count Your Blessings, 4 1/2"	J. Ferrandiz	5,000	300.00	300.00
90-05-012	Christmas Carillon, 4 1/2"	J. Ferrandiz	2,500	299.00	299.00
ANRI		**Ferrandiz Mini Nativity Set**			
84-06-001	Mary, 1 1/2"	J. Ferrandiz	Open	300.00	540.00
84-06-002	Joseph, 1 1/2"	J. Ferrandiz	Open	Set	Set
84-06-003	Infant, 1 1/2"	J. Ferrandiz	Open	Set	Set
84-06-004	Leading the Way, 1 1/2"	J. Ferrandiz	Open	Set	Set
84-06-005	Ox Donkey, 1 1/2"	J. Ferrandiz	Open	Set	Set
84-06-006	Sheep Standing, 1 1/2"	J. Ferrandiz	Open	Set	Set
84-06-007	Sheep Kneeling, 1 1/2"	J. Ferrandiz	Open	Set	Set
85-06-008	Reverence, 1 1/2"	J. Ferrandiz	Open	45.00	53.00
85-06-009	Harmony, 1 1/2"	J. Ferrandiz	Open	45.00	53.00
85-06-010	Rest, 1 1/2"	J. Ferrandiz	Open	45.00	53.00
85-06-011	Thanksgiving, 1 1/2"	J. Ferrandiz	Open	45.00	53.00
85-06-012	Small Talk, 1 1/2"	J. Ferrandiz	Open	45.00	53.00
85-06-013	Camel, 1 1/2"	J. Ferrandiz	Open	45.00	53.00
85-06-014	Camel Guide, 1 1/2"	J. Ferrandiz	Open	45.00	53.00
85-06-015	Baby Camel, 1 1/2"	J. Ferrandiz	Open	45.00	53.00
86-06-016	Mini Melchoir, 1 1/2"	J. Ferrandiz	Open	45.00	53.00
86-06-017	Mini Caspar, 1 1/2"	J. Ferrandiz	Open	45.00	53.00
86-06-018	Mini Balthasar, 1 1/2"	J. Ferrandiz	Open	45.00	53.00
86-06-019	Mini Angel, 1 1/2"	J. Ferrandiz	Open	45.00	53.00
86-06-020	Mini Free Ride, plus Mini Lamb, 1 1/2"	J. Ferrandiz	Open	45.00	53.00
86-06-021	Mini Weary Traveller, 1 1/2"	J. Ferrandiz	Open	45.00	53.00
86-06-022	Mini The Stray, 1 1/2"	J. Ferrandiz	Open	45.00	53.00
86-06-023	Mini The Hiker, 1 1/2"	J. Ferrandiz	Open	45.00	53.00
86-06-024	Mini Star Struck, 1 1/2"	J. Ferrandiz	Open	45.00	53.00
88-06-025	Jolly Gift, 1 1/2"	J. Ferrandiz	Open	53.00	53.00
88-06-026	Sweet Inspiration, 1 1/2"	J. Ferrandiz	Open	53.00	53.00
88-06-028	Sweet Dreams, 1 1/2"	J. Ferrandiz	Open	53.00	53.00
88-06-029	Long Journey, 1 1/2"	J. Ferrandiz	Open	53.00	53.00
88-06-030	Devotion, 1 1/2"	J. Ferrandiz	Open	53.00	53.00
ANRI		**Limited Edition Couples**			
85-07-001	Springtime Stroll, 8"	J. Ferrandiz	Closed	590.00	950.00
85-07-002	First Kiss, 8"	J. Ferrandiz	Closed	590.00	900.00
86-07-003	A Tender Touch, 8"	J. Ferrandiz	Closed	590.00	850.00
86-07-004	My Heart Is Yours, 8"	J. Ferrandiz	Closed	590.00	850.00
87-07-005	Heart to Heart, 8"	J. Ferrandiz	Closed	590.00	850.00
88-07-006	A Loving Hand, 8"	J. Ferrandiz	Closed	795.00	850.00

Company		Series			
Number	Name	Artist	Edition Limit	Issue Price	Quote
ANRI		**Sarah Kay Figurines**			
83-08-001	Morning Chores,6"	S. Kay	Closed	210.00	495.00
83-08-002	Morning Chores, 4"	S. Kay	Closed	95.00	300.00
83-08-003	Morning Chores, 1 1/2"	S. Kay	Closed	45.00	110.00
83-08-004	Helping Mother, 6"	S. Kay	Closed	210.00	495.00
83-08-005	Helping Mother, 4"	S. Kay	Closed	95.00	300.00
83-08-006	Helping Mother, 1 1/2"	S. Kay	Closed	45.00	110.00
83-08-007	Sweeping, 6"	S. Kay	Closed	195.00	435.00
83-08-008	Sweeping, 4"	S. Kay	Closed	95.00	230.00
83-08-009	Sweeping, 1 1/2"	S. Kay	Closed	45.00	110.00
83-08-010	Playtime, 6"	S. Kay	Closed	195.00	445.00
83-08-011	Playtime, 4"	S. Kay	Closed	95.00	230.00
83-08-012	Playtime, 1 1/2"	S. Kay	Closed	45.00	110.00
83-08-013	Feeding the Chickens, 6"	S. Kay	Closed	195.00	435.00
83-08-014	Feeding the Chickens, 4"	S. Kay	Closed	95.00	230.00
83-08-015	Feeding the Chickens, 1 1/2"	S. Kay	Closed	45.00	110.00
83-08-016	Waiting for Mother, 6"	S. Kay	Closed	195.00	445.00
83-08-017	Waiting for Mother, 4"	S. Kay	Closed	95.00	230.00
83-08-018	Waiting for Mother, 1 1/2"	S. Kay	Closed	45.00	110.00
83-08-019	Waiting for Mother, 11"	S. Kay	Closed	495.00	795.00
83-08-020	Bedtime, 6"	S. Kay	Closed	195.00	435.00
83-08-021	Bedtime, 4"	S. Kay	Closed	95.00	230.00
83-08-022	Bedtime, 1 1/2"	S. Kay	Closed	45.00	110.00
83-08-023	From the Garden, 6"	S. Kay	Closed	195.00	450.00
83-08-024	From the Garden, 4"	S. Kay	Closed	95.00	235.00
83-08-025	From the Garden, 1 1/2"	S. Kay	Closed	45.00	110.00
83-08-026	Wake Up Kiss, 6"	S. Kay	Closed	210.00	550.00
84-08-027	Wake Up Kiss, 4"	S. Kay	Closed	95.00	155.00
84-08-028	Wake Up Kiss, 1 1/2"	S. Kay	Closed	45.00	550.00
84-08-029	Finding R Way, 6"	S. Kay	Closed	210.00	495.00
84-08-030	Finding R Way, 4"	S. Kay	Closed	95.00	245.00
84-08-031	Finding R Way, 1 1/2"	S. Kay	Closed	45.00	135.00
84-08-032	Daydreaming, 6"	S. Kay	Closed	195.00	445.00
84-08-033	Daydreaming, 4"	S. Kay	Closed	95.00	235.00
84-08-034	Daydreaming,1 1/2"	S. Kay	Closed	45.00	125.00
84-08-035	Off to School, 6"	S. Kay	4,000	195.00	325.00
84-08-036	Off to School, 4"	S. Kay	4,000	95.00	185.00
84-08-037	Off to School,1 1/2"	S. Kay	Closed	45.00	125.00
84-08-038	Off to School, 11"	S. Kay	750	Unkn.	770.00
84-08-039	Off to School, 20"	S. Kay	100	Unkn.	4000.00
84-08-040	Flowers for You, 6"	S. Kay	Closed	195.00	430.00
84-08-041	Flowers for You, 4"	S. Kay	Closed	95.00	230.00
84-08-042	Flowers for You, 1 1/2"	S. Kay	Closed	45.00	125.00
84-08-043	Watchful Eye, 6"	S. Kay	Closed	195.00	445.00
84-08-044	Watchful Eye, 4"	S. Kay	Closed	95.00	235.00
84-08-045	Watchful Eye,1 1/2"	S. Kay	Closed	45.00	125.00
84-08-046	Special Delivery, 6"	S. Kay	Closed	195.00	312.00
84-08-047	Special Delivery, 4"	S. Kay	Closed	95.00	172.00
84-08-048	Special Delivery, 1 1/2"	S. Kay	Closed	45.00	125.00
84-08-049	Tag Along, 6"	S. Kay	4,000	195.00	290.00
84-08-050	Tag Along, 4"	S. Kay	4,000	95.00	225.00
84-08-051	Tag Along,1 1/2"	S. Kay	Closed	45.00	130.00
85-08-052	A Special Day, 6"	S. Kay	Closed	195.00	325.00
85-08-053	A Special Day, 4"	S. Kay	Closed	95.00	185.00
85-08-054	Afternoon Tea, 6"	S. Kay	Closed	195.00	325.00
85-08-055	Afternoon Tea, 4"	S. Kay	Closed	95.00	185.00
85-08-056	Afternoon Tea, 11"	S. Kay	Closed	Unkn.	770.00
85-08-057	Afternoon Tea, 20"	S. Kay	Closed	Unkn.	3500.00
85-08-058	Nightie Night, 6"	S. Kay	Closed	195.00	325.00
85-08-059	Nightie Night, 4"	S. Kay	Closed	95.00	185.00
85-08-060	Yuletide Cheer, 6"	S. Kay	Closed	210.00	435.00
85-08-061	Yuletide Cheer, 4"	S. Kay	4,000	95.00	185.00
85-08-062	'Tis the Season, 6"	S. Kay	Closed	210.00	425.00
85-08-063	'Tis the Season, 4"	S. Kay	4,000	95.00	185.00
85-08-064	Giddyap!, 6"	S. Kay	Closed	195.00	325.00
85-08-065	Giddyap!, 4"	S. Kay	Closed	95.00	185.00
86-08-066	Our Puppy, 6"	S. Kay	Closed	210.00	355.00
86-08-067	Our Puppy, 4"	S. Kay	Closed	95.00	185.00
86-08-068	Our Puppy, 1 1/2"	S. Kay	Closed	45.00	90.00
86-08-069	Always By My Side, 6"	S. Kay	Closed	195.00	375.00
86-08-070	Always By My Side, 4"	S. Kay	Closed	95.00	195.00
86-08-071	Always By My Side, 1 1/2"	S. Kay	Closed	45.00	95.00
86-08-072	Finishing Touch, 6"	S. Kay	Closed	195.00	312.00
86-08-073	Finishing Touch, 4"	S. Kay	Closed	95.00	172.00
86-08-074	Finishing Touch, 1 1/2"	S. Kay	Closed	45.00	85.00
86-08-075	Good As New, 6"	S. Kay	4,000	195.00	325.00
86-08-076	Good As New, 4"	S. Kay	4,000	95.00	185.00
86-08-077	Good As New, 1 1/2"	S. Kay	Closed	45.00	90.00
86-08-078	Bunny Hug, 6"	S. Kay	Closed	210.00	395.00
86-08-079	Bunny Hug, 4"	S. Kay	Closed	95.00	172.00
86-08-080	Bunny Hug, 1 1/2"	S. Kay	Closed	45.00	85.00
86-08-081	Sweet Treat, 6"	S. Kay	Closed	195.00	312.00
86-08-082	Sweet Treat, 4"	S. Kay	Closed	95.00	172.00
86-08-083	Sweet Treat, 1 1/2"	S. Kay	Closed	45.00	85.00
86-08-084	To Love And To Cherish, 6"	S. Kay	Closed	195.00	312.00
86-08-085	To Love And To Cherish, 4"	S. Kay	Closed	95.00	172.00
86-08-086	To Love And To Cherish, 1 1/2"	S. Kay	Closed	45.00	85.00
86-08-087	To Love and To Cherish, 11"	S. Kay	Closed	Unkn.	667.00
86-08-088	To Love and To Cherish, 20"	S. Kay	Closed	Unkn.	3600.00
86-08-089	With This Ring, 6"	S. Kay	Closed	195.00	312.00
86-08-090	With This Ring, 4"	S. Kay	Closed	95.00	172.00
86-08-091	With This Ring, 1 1/2"	S. Kay	Closed	45.00	85.00
86-08-092	With This Ring, 11"	S. Kay	Closed	Unkn.	667.50
86-08-093	With This Ring, 20"	S. Kay	Closed	Unkn.	3600.00
87-08-094	All Aboard, 6"	S. Kay	Closed	265.00	355.00
87-08-095	All Aboard, 4"	S. Kay	Closed	130.00	185.00
87-08-096	All Aboard, 1 1/2"	S. Kay	Closed	49.50	90.00
87-08-097	Let's Play, 6"	S. Kay	Closed	265.00	355.00
87-08-098	Let's Play, 4"	S. Kay	Closed	130.00	185.00
87-08-099	Let's Play, 1 1/2"	S. Kay	Closed	49.50	90.00
87-08-100	A Loving Spoonful, 6"	S. Kay	4,000	295.00	400.00
87-08-101	A Loving Spoonful, 4"	S. Kay	4,000	150.00	200.00
87-08-102	A Loving Spoonful, 1 1/2"	S. Kay	Closed	49.50	90.00
87-08-103	Little Nanny, 6"	S. Kay	Closed	295.00	400.00
87-08-104	Little Nanny, 4"	S. Kay	Closed	150.00	200.00
87-08-105	Little Nanny, 1 1/2"	S. Kay	Closed	49.50	90.00
87-08-106	All Mine, 6"	S. Kay	Closed	245.00	465.00
87-08-107	All Mine, 4"	S. Kay	Closed	130.00	225.00
87-08-108	All Mine, 1 1/2"	S. Kay	Closed	49.50	95.00
87-08-109	Cuddles, 6"	S. Kay	Closed	245.00	465.00
87-08-110	Cuddles, 4"	S. Kay	Closed	130.00	225.00
87-08-111	Cuddles, 1 1/2"	S. Kay	Closed	49.50	95.00
88-08-112	My Little Brother, 6"	S. Kay	Closed	375.00	450.00

Company Number	Name	Series Artist	Edition Limit	Issue Price	Quote
88-08-113	My Little Brother, 4"	S. Kay	Closed	195.00	225.00
88-08-114	My Little Brother, 1 1/2"	S. Kay	Closed	70.00	90.00
88-08-115	Purrfect Day, 6"	S. Kay	Closed	265.00	455.00
88-08-116	Purrfect Day, 4"	S. Kay	Closed	184.00	215.00
88-08-117	Purrfect Day, 1 1/2"	S. Kay	Closed	70.00	90.00
88-08-118	Penny for Your Thoughts, 6"	S. Kay	Closed	365.00	455.00
88-08-119	Penny for Your Thoughts, 4"	S. Kay	Closed	185.00	215.00
88-08-120	Penny for Your Thoughts, 1 1/2"	S. Kay	Closed	70.00	90.00
88-08-121	New Home, 6"	S. Kay	Closed	365.00	500.00
88-08-122	New Home, 4"	S. Kay	Closed	185.00	240.00
88-08-123	New Home, 1 1/2"	S. Kay	Closed	70.00	90.00
88-08-124	Ginger Snap, 6"	S. Kay	Closed	300.00	355.00
88-08-125	Ginger Snap, 4"	S. Kay	Closed	150.00	185.00
88-08-126	Ginger Snap, 1 1/2"	S. Kay	Closed	70.00	90.00
88-08-127	Hidden Treasures, 6"	S. Kay	Closed	300.00	355.00
88-08-128	Hidden Treasures, 4"	S. Kay	Closed	150.00	185.00
88-08-129	Hidden Treasures, 1 1/2"	S. Kay	Closed	70.00	90.00
89-08-130	First School Day, 6"	S. Kay	2,000	550.00	630.00
89-08-131	First School Day, 4"	S. Kay	2,000	290.00	295.00
89-08-132	First School Day, 1 1/2"	S. Kay	Closed	85.00	95.00
89-08-133	Yearly Check-Up, 6"	S. Kay	Closed	390.00	390.00
89-08-134	Yearly Check-Up, 4"	S. Kay	Closed	190.00	195.00
89-08-135	Yearly Check-Up, 1 1/2"	S. Kay	Closed	85.00	95.00
89-08-136	House Call, 6"	S. Kay	Closed	390.00	390.00
89-08-137	House Call, 4"	S. Kay	Closed	190.00	195.00
89-08-138	House Call, 1 1/2"	S. Kay	Closed	85.00	95.00
89-08-139	Take Me Along, 6"	S. Kay	1,000	440.00	475.00
89-08-140	Take Me Along, 4"	S. Kay	2,000	220.00	240.00
89-08-141	Take Me Along, 1 1/2"	S. Kay	Closed	85.00	95.00
89-08-142	Garden Party, 6"	S. Kay	2,000	440.00	475.00
89-08-143	Garden Party, 4"	S. Kay	2,000	220.00	240.00
89-08-144	Garden Party, 1 1/2"	S. Kay	Closed	85.00	95.00
89-08-145	Fisherboy, 6"	S. Kay	1,000	440.00	475.00
89-08-146	Fisherboy, 4"	S. Kay	2,000	220.00	240.00
89-08-147	Fisherboy, 1 1/2"	S. Kay	Closed	85.00	95.00
89-08-148	Cherish, 6"	S. Kay	2,000	398.00	450.00
89-08-149	Cherish, 4"	S. Kay	2,000	199.00	225.00
89-08-150	Cherish, 1 1/2"	S. Kay	Closed	80.00	95.00
90-08-151	Holiday Cheer, 6"	S. Kay	1,000	450.00	495.00
90-08-152	Holiday Cheer, 4"	S. Kay	2,000	225.00	240.00
90-08-153	Holiday Cheer, 1 1/2"	S. Kay	Closed	90.00	95.00
90-08-154	Tender Loving Care, 6"	S. Kay	2,000	440.00	475.00
90-08-155	Tender Loving Care, 4"	S. Kay	2,000	220.00	240.00
90-08-156	Tender Loving Care, 1 1/2"	S. Kay	Closed	90.00	95.00
90-08-157	Spring Fever, 6"	S. Kay	2,000	450.00	495.00
90-08-158	Spring Fever, 4"	S. Kay	2,000	225.00	240.00
90-08-159	Spring Fever, 1 1/2"	S. Kay	Closed	90.00	95.00
90-08-160	Batter Up, 6"	S. Kay	2,000	440.00	450.00
90-08-161	Batter Up, 4"	S. Kay	2,000	220.00	225.00
90-08-162	Batter Up, 1 1/2"	S. Kay	Closed	90.00	95.00
90-08-163	Seasons Greetings, 6"	S. Kay	1,000	450.00	495.00
90-08-164	Seasons Greetings, 4"	S. Kay	2,000	225.00	240.00
90-08-165	Seasons Greetings, 1 1/2"	S. Kay	Closed	90.00	95.00
90-08-166	Shootin' Hoops, 6"	S. Kay	2,000	440.00	450.00
90-08-167	Shootin' Hoops, 4"	S. Kay	2,000	220.00	225.00
90-08-168	Shootin' Hoops,1 1/2"	S. Kay	Closed	90.00	95.00
91-08-169	Figure Eight, 6"	S. Kay	2,000	550.00	550.00
91-08-170	Figure Eight, 4"	S. Kay	2,000	270.00	270.00
91-08-171	Figure Eight, 1 1/2"	S. Kay	3,750	110.00	110.00
91-08-172	Season's Joy, 6"	S. Kay	1,000	550.00	550.00
91-08-173	Season's Joy, 4"	S. Kay	2,000	270.00	270.00
91-08-174	Season's Joy, 1 1/2"	S. Kay	3,750	110.00	110.00
91-08-175	Winter Surprise, 6"	S. Kay	1,000	550.00	550.00
91-08-176	Winter Surprise, 4"	S. Kay	2,000	270.00	270.00
91-08-177	Winter Surprise, 1 1/2"	S. Kay	3,750	110.00	110.00
91-08-178	Dress Up, 6"	S. Kay	2,000	550.00	550.00
91-08-179	Dress Up, 4"	S. Kay	2,000	270.00	270.00
91-08-180	Dress Up, 1 1/2"	S. Kay	3,750	110.00	110.00
91-08-181	Touch Down, 6"	S. Kay	2,000	550.00	550.00
91-08-182	Touch Down, 4"	S. Kay	2,000	270.00	270.00
91-08-183	Touch Down, 1 1/2"	S. Kay	3,750	110.00	110.00
91-08-184	Fore!!, 6"	S. Kay	2,000	550.00	550.00
91-08-185	Fore!!, 4"	S. Kay	2,000	270.00	270.00
91-08-186	Fore!!, 1 1/2"	S. Kay	3,750	110.00	110.00
92-08-187	Raindrops, 6"	S. Kay	1,000	640.00	640.00
92-08-188	Raindrops, 4"	S. Kay	1,000	350.00	350.00
92-08-189	Raindrops, 1 1/2"	S. Kay	3,750	110.00	110.00
92-08-190	Free Skating, 6"	S. Kay	1,000	590.00	590.00
92-08-191	Free Skating, 4"	S. Kay	1,000	310.00	310.00
92-08-192	Free Skating, 1 1/2"	S. Kay	3,750	110.00	110.00
92-08-193	Merry Christmas, 6"	S. Kay	1,000	580.00	580.00
92-08-194	Merry Christmas, 4"	S. Kay	1,000	350.00	350.00
92-08-195	Merry Christmas, 1 1/2"	S. Kay	3,750	110.00	110.00
92-08-196	Tulips For Mother, 6"	S. Kay	1,000	590.00	590.00
92-08-197	Tulips For Mother, 4"	S. Kay	1,000	310.00	310.00
92-08-198	Tulips For Mother, 1 1/2"	S. Kay	3,750	110.00	110.00
92-08-199	Winter Cheer, 6"	S. Kay	1,000	580.00	580.00
92-08-200	Winter Cheer, 4"	S. Kay	2,000	300.00	300.00
ANRI		**Sarah Kay Santas**			
88-09-001	Jolly St. Nick, 6"	S. Kay	Closed	398.00	850.00
88-09-002	Jolly St. Nick, 4"	S. Kay	Closed	199.00	300-550.
88-09-003	Jolly Santa, 6"	S. Kay	Closed	480.00	600.00
88-09-004	Jolly Santa, 4"	S. Kay	Closed	235.00	300-350.
89-09-005	Jolly Santa, 12"	S. Kay	Closed	1300.00	1300.00
89-09-006	Santa, 6"	S. Kay	Closed	480.00	480.00
89-09-007	Santa, 4"	S. Kay	Closed	235.00	350.00
90-09-008	Kris Kringle Santa, 6"	S. Kay	Closed	550.00	550.00
90-09-009	Kris Kringle Santa, 4"	S. Kay	Closed	275.00	350.00
91-09-010	A Friend To All, 6"	S. Kay	750	590.00	590.00
91-09-011	A Friend To All, 4"	S. Kay	750	300.00	300.00
92-09-012	Father Christmas, 6"	S. Kay	750	590.00	590.00
92-09-013	Father Christmas, 4"	S. Kay	750	350.00	350.00
ANRI		**Sarah Kay Mini Santas**			
91-10-001	Jolly St. Nick, 1 1/2"	S. Kay	Closed	110.00	110.00
91-10-002	Jolly Santa, 1 1/2"	S. Kay	Closed	110.00	110.00
91-10-003	Sarah Kay Santa, 1 1/2"	S. Kay	Closed	110.00	110.00
91-10-004	Kris Kringle, 1 1/2"	S. Kay	Closed	110.00	110.00
ANRI		**Sarah Kay 10th Anniversary**			
93-11-001	Mr. Santa, 4"	S. Kay	750	375.00	375.00
93-11-002	Mr. Santa, 6"	S. Kay	750	695.00	695.00
93-11-003	Mrs. Santa, 4"	S. Kay	750	375.00	375.00
93-11-004	Mrs. Santa, 6"	S. Kay	750	695.00	695.00
93-11-005	Joy to the World, 4"	S. Kay	1,000	310.00	310.00
93-11-006	Joy to the World, 6"	S. Kay	1,000	600.00	600.00
93-11-007	Christmas Basket, 4"	S. Kay	1,000	310.00	310.00
93-11-008	Christmas Basket, 6"	S. Kay	1,000	600.00	600.00
93-11-009	Innocence, 4"	S. Kay	1,000	345.00	345.00
93-11-010	Innocence, 6"	S. Kay	1,000	650.00	650.00
93-11-011	My Favorite Doll, 4"	S. Kay	1,000	350.00	350.00
93-11-012	My Favorite Doll, 6"	S. Kay	1,000	650.00	650.00
ANRI		**Club ANRI**			
83-12-001	Welcome 4"	J. Ferrandiz	Closed	110.00	395.00
84-12-002	My Friend 4"	J. Ferrandiz	Closed	110.00	400.00
84-12-003	Apple of My Eye 4 1/2"	S. Kay	Closed	135.00	385.00
85-12-004	Harvest Time 4"	J. Ferrandiz	Closed	125.00	175-385.
85-12-005	Dad's Helper 4 1/2"	S. Kay	Closed	135.00	150-375.
86-12-006	Harvest's Helper 4"	J. Ferrandiz	Closed	135.00	175-335.
86-12-007	Romantic Notions 4"	S. Kay	Closed	135.00	175-310.
86-12-008	Celebration March 5"	J. Ferrandiz	Closed	165.00	225-295.
87-12-009	Will You Be Mine 4"	J. Ferrandiz	Closed	135.00	175-310.
86-12-010	Make A Wish 4"	S. Kay	Closed	165.00	215-325.
87-12-011	A Young Man's Fancy 4"	S. Kay	Closed	135.00	165-265.
88-12-012	Forever Yours 4"	J. Ferrandiz	Closed	170.00	250.00
88-12-013	I've Got a Secret 4"	S. Kay	Closed	170.00	205.00
88-12-014	Maestro Mickey 4 1/2"	Disney Studio	Closed	170.00	200-215.
89-12-015	Diva Minnie 4 1/2"	Disney Studio	Closed	190.00	190.00
89-12-016	I'll Never Tell 4"	S. Kay	Closed	190.00	190.00
89-12-017	Twenty Years of Love 4"	J. Ferrandiz	Closed	190.00	190.00
90-12-018	You Are My Sunshine 4"	J. Ferrandiz	Yr.Iss.	220.00	220.00
90-12-019	A Little Bashful 4"	S. Kay	Yr.Iss.	220.00	220.00
90-12-020	Dapper Donald 4"	Disney Studio	Closed	199.00	199.00
91-12-021	With All My Heart 4"	J. Ferrandiz	N/A	250.00	250.00
91-12-022	Kiss Me 4"	S.Kay	N/A	250.00	250.00
91-12-023	Daisy Duck 4 1/2"	Disney Studio	N/A	250.00	250.00
92-12-024	You Are My All 4"	J. Ferrandiz	N/A	260.00	260.00
92-12-025	My Present For You 4"	S. Kay	N/A	270.00	270.00
ANRI		**Disney Woodcarving**			
87-13-001	Mickey Mouse, 4"	Disney Studio	Closed	150.00	210.00
87-13-002	Minnie Mouse, 4"	Disney Studio	Closed	150.00	210.00
87-13-003	Pinocchio, 4"	Disney Studio	Closed	150.00	195.00
87-13-004	Donald Duck, 4"	Disney Studio	Closed	150.00	195.00
87-13-005	Goofy, 4"	Disney Studio	Closed	150.00	195.00
87-13-006	Mickey & Minnie, 6" (matching numbers)	Disney Studio	Closed	625.00	1650.00
88-13-007	Donald Duck, 6"	Disney Studio	Closed	350.00	700.00
88-13-008	Goofy, 6"	Disney Studio	Closed	380.00	700.00
88-13-009	Mickey Mouse, 4"	Disney Studio	Closed	180.00	199.00
88-13-010	Pluto, 4"	Disney Studio	Closed	180.00	199.00
88-13-011	Pinocchio, 4"	Disney Studio	Closed	180.00	199.00
88-13-012	Donald Duck, 4"	Disney Studio	Closed	180.00	199.00
88-13-013	Goofy, 4"	Disney Studio	Closed	180.00	199.00
88-13-014	Mickey Mouse, 1 3/4"	Disney Studio	Closed	80.00	100.00
88-13-015	Pluto, 1-3/4"	Disney Studio	Closed	80.00	100.00
88-13-016	Pinocchio, 1 3/4"	Disney Studio	Closed	80.00	100.00
88-13-017	Donald Duck, 1 3/4"	Disney Studio	Closed	80.00	100.00
88-13-018	Goofy, 1 3/4"	Disney Studio	Closed	80.00	100.00
89-13-019	Pluto, 4"	Disney Studio	Closed	190.00	205.00
88-13-020	Pluto, 6"	Disney Studio	Closed	350.00	350.00
88-13-021	Goofy, 6"	Disney Studio	Closed	350.00	350.00
89-13-022	Mickey, 4"	Disney Studio	Closed	190.00	205.00
89-13-023	Minnie, 4"	Disney Studio	Closed	190.00	205.00
89-13-024	Donald, 4"	Disney Studio	Closed	190.00	205.00
89-13-025	Daisy, 4"	Disney Studio	Closed	190.00	205.00
89-13-026	Goofy, 4"	Disney Studio	Closed	190.00	205.00
89-13-027	Mini Mickey, 2"	Disney Studio	Closed	85.00	100.00
89-13-028	Mini Minnie, 2"	Disney Studio	Closed	85.00	100.00
89-13-029	Mini Donald, 2"	Disney Studio	Closed	85.00	100.00
89-13-030	Minnie Daisy, 2"	Disney Studio	Closed	85.00	100.00
89-13-031	Mini Goofy, 2"	Disney Studio	Closed	85.00	100.00
89-13-032	Mini Pluto, 2"	Disney Studio	Closed	85.00	100.00
89-13-033	Mickey, 10"	Disney Studio	Closed	700.00	750.00
89-13-034	Minnie, 10"	Disney Studio	Closed	700.00	750.00
89-13-035	Mickey, 20"	Disney Studio	Closed	3500.00	3500.00
89-13-036	Minnie, 20"	Disney Studio	Closed	3500.00	3500.00
89-13-037	Mickey & Minnie, 20" matched set	Disney Studio	Closed	7000.00	7000.00
89-13-038	Mickey & Minnie Set, 6"	Disney Studio	Closed	700.00	700.00
88-13-039	Mickey Sorcerer's Apprentice, 6"	Disney Studio	Closed	350.00	700.00
88-13-040	Mickey Sorcerer's Apprentice, 4"	Disney Studio	Closed	180.00	199.00
88-13-041	Mickey Sorcerer's Apprentice, 2"	Disney Studio	Closed	80.00	100.00
89-13-042	Pinocchio, 6"	Disney Studio	Closed	350.00	350.00
89-13-043	Pinocchio, 4"	Disney Studio	Closed	190.00	199.00
89-13-044	Pinocchio, 2"	Disney Studio	Closed	85.00	100.00
89-13-045	Pinocchio, 10"	Disney Studio	Closed	700.00	700.00
89-13-046	Pinocchio, 20"	Disney Studio	Closed	3500.00	3500.00
90-13-047	Mickey Mouse, 4"	Disney Studio	Closed	199.00	205.00
90-13-045	Mickey Mouse, 2"	Disney Studio	Closed	100.00	100.00
90-13-049	Minnie Mouse, 4"	Disney Studio	Closed	199.00	205.00
90-13-050	Minnie Mouse, 2"	Disney Studio	Closed	100.00	100.00
90-13-051	Chef Goofy, 5"	Disney Studio	Closed	265.00	265.00
90-13-052	Chef Goofy, 2 1/2"	Disney Studio	Closed	125.00	125.00
90-13-053	Donald & Daisy, 6" (Matched Set)	Disney Studio	Closed	700.00	700.00
91-13-054	Mickey Skating, 4"	Disney Studio	Closed	250.00	250.00
91-13-055	Minnie Skating, 4"	Disney Studio	Closed	250.00	250.00
91-13-056	Mickey Skating, 2"	Disney Studio	Closed	120.00	120.00
91-13-057	Minnie Skating, 2"	Disney Studio	Closed	120.00	120.00
91-13-058	Bell Boy Donald, 6"	Disney Studio	Closed	400.00	400.00
91-13-059	Bell Boy Donald, 4"	Disney Studio	Closed	250.00	250.00
ANRI		**Mickey Mouse Thru The Ages**			
90-14-001	Steam Boat Willie, 4"	Disney Studio	Closed	295.00	295.00
91-14-002	The Mad Dog, 4"	Disney Studio	Closed	500.00	500.00
Armani		**Wildlife**			
83-01-001	Eagle 3213	G. Armani	Open	210.00	425.00
83-01-002	Royal Eagle with Babies 3553	G. Armani	Open	215.00	400.00
82-01-003	Snow Bird 5548	G. Armani	Open	100.00	180.00
88-01-004	Peacock 455S	G. Armani	5,000	600.00	675.00
88-01-005	Peacock 458S	G. Armani	5,000	630.00	700.00
88-01-006	Bird Of Paradise 454S	G. Armani	5,000	475.00	500.00
90-01-007	Three Doves 996S	G. Armani	5,000	670.00	750.00
90-01-008	Soaring Eagles 970S	G. Armani	5,000	620.00	700.00
90-01-009	Bird of Paradise 718S	G. Armani	5,000	550.00	575.00

FIGURINES

Company / Number	Name	Series / Artist	Edition Limit	Issue Price	Quote
Armani		**My Fair Ladies™**			
87-02-001	Lady With Peacock 385C	G. Armani	Retrd.	380.00	900-1850.
87-02-002	Lady with Compact 386C	G. Armani	Retrd.	300.00	400-700.
87-02-003	Lady with Muff 388C	G. Armani	5,000	250.00	450.00
87-02-004	Lady With Fan 387C	G. Armani	5,000	300.00	400.00
87-02-005	Flamenco Dancer 389C	G. Armani	5,000	400.00	500.00
87-02-006	Lady With Book 384C	G. Armani	5,000	300.00	450.00
87-02-007	Lady With Great Dane 429C	G. Armani	5,000	365.00	475.00
87-02-008	Mother & Child 405C	G. Armani	5,000	410.00	550.00
89-02-009	Lady With Parrot 616C	G. Armani	5,000	400.00	500.00
Armani		**Wedding**			
82-03-001	Wedding Couple 5132	G. Armani	Open	110.00	190.00
87-03-002	Wedding Couple 407C	G. Armani	Open	525.00	550.00
88-03-003	Bride & Groom Wedding 475P	G. Armani	Open	270.00	285.00
89-03-004	Just Married 827C	G. Armani	5,000	950.00	1000.00
91-03-005	Wedding Couple At Threshold 813C	G. Armani	7,500	400.00	400.00
91-03-006	Wedding Couple With Bicycle 814C	G. Armani	7,500	600.00	600.00
91-03-007	Wedding Couple Kissing 815C	G. Armani	7,500	500.00	500.00
92-03-008	Bride With Doves 885C	G. Armani	Open	280.00	280.00
92-03-009	Bride With Doves 885F	G. Armani	Open	220.00	220.00
93-03-010	Bride & Groom In Carriage 902C	G. Armani	2,500	1000.00	1000.00
Armani		**Special Times**			
82-04-001	Sledding 5111E	G. Armani	Retrd.	115.00	250.00
82-04-002	Girl with Sheep Dog 5117E	G. Armani	Retrd.	100.00	210.00
82-04-003	Girl with Chicks 5122E	G. Armani	Suspd.	95.00	165.00
82-04-004	Shy Kiss 5138E	G. Armani	Retrd.	125.00	285.00
82-04-005	Soccer Boy 5109	G. Armani	Open	75.00	180.00
82-04-006	Card Players (Cheaters) 3280	G. Armani	Open	400.00	1200.00
91-04-007	Couple in Car 862C	G. Armani	5,000	1000.00	1000.00
91-04-008	Lady with Car 861C	G. Armani	3,000	900.00	900.00
91-04-009	Doctor in Car 848C	G. Armani	2,000	800.00	800.00
Armani		**Premiere Ballerina**			
88-05-001	Ballerina Group in Flight 518C	G. Armani	Retrd.	810.00	900.00
88-05-002	Ballerina with Drape 504C	G. Armani	Retrd.	450.00	550.00
88-05-003	Ballerina 508C	G. Armani	Retrd.	430.00	530.00
88-05-004	Two Ballerinas 515C	G. Armani	Retrd.	620.00	775.00
88-05-005	Ballerina in Flight 503C	G. Armani	Retrd.	420.00	500.00
88-05-006	Ballerina 517C	G. Armani	Retrd.	325.00	530.00
Armani		**Religious**			
87-06-001	Choir Boys 900	G. Armani	5,000	350.00	620.00
88-06-002	Crucifix 1158C	G. Armani	10,000	155.00	350-375.
90-06-003	Crucifix Plaque 711C	G. Armani	15,000	265.00	265.00
91-06-004	Crucifix 790C	G. Armani	15,000	180.00	180.00
92-06-005	Madonna With Child 787C	G. Armani	Open	425.00	425.00
92-06-006	Madonna With Child 787F	G. Armani	Open	265.00	265.00
92-06-007	Madonna With Child 787B	G. Armani	Open	260.00	260.00
93-06-008	Crucifix 786C	G. Armani	7,500	250.00	250.00
Armani		**Pearls Of The Orient**			
89-07-001	Madame Butterfly 610C	G. Armani	10,000	450.00	500.00
89-07-002	Turnadot 611C	G. Armani	10,000	475.00	500.00
89-07-003	Chu Chu San 612C	G. Armani	10,000	500.00	550.00
89-07-004	Lotus Blossom 613C	G. Armani	10,000	450.00	475.00
Armani		**Moonlight Masquerade**			
90-08-001	Harlequin Lady 740C	G. Armani	7,500	450.00	450.00
90-08-002	Lady Pierrot 741C	G. Armani	7,500	390.00	390.00
90-08-003	Lady Clown with Cane 742C	G. Armani	7,500	390.00	390.00
90-08-004	Lady Clown with Doll 743C	G. Armani	7,500	410.00	410.00
90-08-005	Queen of Hearts 744C	G. Armani	7,500	450.00	450.00
Armani		**Renaissance**			
92-09-001	Abundance 870C	G. Armani	5,000	600.00	600.00
92-09-002	Vanity 871C	G. Armani	5,000	585.00	585.00
92-09-003	Twilight 872C	G. Armani	5,000	560.00	560.00
92-09-004	Dawn 874C	G. Armani	5,000	500.00	500.00
92-09-005	Lilac & Roses-Girl w/Flowers 882C	G. Armani	7,500	410.00	410.00
92-09-006	Lilac & Roses-Girl w/Flowers 882B	G. Armani	Open	220.00	220.00
92-09-007	Aurora-Girl With Doves 884C	G. Armani	7,500	370.00	370.00
92-09-008	Aurora-Girl With Doves 884B	G. Armani	Open	220.00	220.00
92-09-009	Liberty-Girl On Horse 903C	G. Armani	5,000	750.00	750.00
92-09-010	Liberty-Girl On Horse 903B	G. Armani	Open	450.00	450.00
93-09-011	Freedom-Man And Horse 906C	G. Armani	3,000	850.00	850.00
93-09-012	Wind Song-Girl With Sail 904C	G. Armani	5,000	520.00	520.00
93-09-013	Galloping Horse 905S	G. Armani	7,500	N/A	N/A
93-09-014	Rampant Horse 907S	G. Armani	7,500	N/A	N/A
93-09-015	Running Horse 909S	G. Armani	7,500	N/A	N/A
Armani		**Special Issues**			
91-10-001	Discovery of America Plaque 867C	G. Armani	2,500	400.00	400.00
93-10-002	Mother's Day Plaque 899C	G. Armani	Yr. Iss.	100.00	100.00
Armani		**G. Armani Society Members Only Figurine**			
90-11-001	Awakening 591C	G. Armani	Closed	137.50	650-1000.
91-11-002	Ruffles 745E	G. Armani	Closed	139.00	400-500.
92-11-003	Ascent 866C	G. Armani	Closed	195.00	195.00
93-11-004	Venus 881C	G. Armani	Yr.Iss.	225.00	225.00
Armani		**G. Armani Society Members Only Event**			
90-12-001	My Fine Feathered Friends (Bonus)122S	G. Armani	Closed	175.00	175.00
91-12-002	Peace & Harmony (Bonus) 824C	G. Armani	Closed	300.00	250-400.
91-12-003	Bust of Eve 590T	G. Armani	Closed	250.00	500-800.
92-12-004	Lady with Basket of Flowers 961C	G. Armani	Closed	250.00	250.00
92-12-005	Boy with Dog 409S	G. Armani	Closed	200.00	200.00
93-12-006	Loving Arms 880E	G. Armani	Yr.Iss.	250.00	250.00
Armani		**Garden Series**			
91-13-001	Lady with Cornucopie 870C	G. Armani	10,000	600.00	600.00
91-13-002	Lady with Peacock 871C	G. Armani	10,000	585.00	585.00
91-13-003	Lady with Violin 872C	G. Armani	10,000	560.00	560.00
91-13-004	Lady with Harp 874C	G. Armani	10,000	500.00	500.00
Armani		**Can-Can Dancers**			
89-14-001	Two Can-Can Dancers 516C	G. Armani	1,000	820.00	975.00
Armani		**Four Seasons**			
90-15-001	Lady With Bicycle (Spring) 539C	G. Armani	Open	550.00	550.00
90-15-002	Lady With Umbrella (Fall) 541C	G. Armani	Open	475.00	475.00
90-15-003	Lady With Ice Skates (Winter) 542C	G. Armani	Open	400.00	400.00
90-15-004	Lady on Seashore (Summer) 540C	G. Armani	Open	440.00	440.00
92-15-005	Lady With Roses (Spring)181C	G. Armani	Open	275.00	275.00
92-15-006	Lady With Roses (Spring)181B	G. Armani	Open	135.00	135.00
92-15-007	Lady With Fruit (Summer) 182C	G. Armani	Open	275.00	275.00
92-15-008	Lady With Fruit (Summer) 182B	G. Armani	Open	135.00	135.00
92-15-009	Lady With Grapes (Fall) 183C	G. Armani	Open	275.00	275.00
92-15-010	Lady With Grapes (Fall)182B	G. Armani	Open	135.00	135.00
92-15-011	Lady With Vegetables (Winter)183C	G. Armani	Open	275.00	275.00
92-15-012	Lady With Vegetables (Winter)183B	G. Armani	Open	135.00	135.00
Armani		**Special Walt Disney Production**			
92-16-001	Cinderella	G. Armani	Retrd.	390.00	2000-2400.
Armani		**Motherhood**			
92-17-001	Mother With Child (Mother's Day) 185C	G. Armani	Open	400.00	400.00
92-17-002	Mother With Child (Mother's Day) 185B	G. Armani	Open	235.00	235.00
Armani		**Sports**			
92-18-001	Lady Equestrian 910C	G. Armani	Open	315.00	315.00
92-18-002	Lady Equestrian 910F	G. Armani	Open	155.00	155.00
92-18-003	Lady Golfer 911C	G. Armani	Open	325.00	325.00
92-18-004	Lady Golfer 911F	G. Armani	Open	170.00	170.00
92-18-005	Lady Tennis 912C	G. Armani	Open	275.00	275.00
92-18-006	Lady Tennis 912F	G. Armani	Open	175.00	175.00
92-18-007	Lady Skater 913C	G. Armani	Open	300.00	300.00
92-18-008	Lady Skater 913F	G. Armani	Open	170.00	170.00
Armstrong's		**The Red Skelton Collection**			
81-01-001	Freddie in the Bathtub	R. Skelton	7,500	80.00	80.00
81-01-002	Freddie on the Green	R. Skelton	7,500	80.00	80.00
81-01-003	Freddie the Freeloader	R. Skelton	7,500	70.00	150.00
81-01-004	Sheriff Deadeye	R. Skelton	7,500	75.00	75.00
81-01-005	Clem Kadiddlehopper	R. Skelton	7,500	75.00	75.00
81-01-006	Jr., The Mean Widdle Kid	R. Skelton	7,500	75.00	150.00
81-01-007	San Fernando Red	R. Skelton	7,500	75.00	150.00
Armstrong's		**Armstrong's/Ron Lee**			
84-02-001	Captain Freddie	R. Skelton	7,500	85.00	150.00
84-02-002	Freddie the Torchbearer	R. Skelton	7,500	110.00	190.00
Armstrong's		**Happy Art**			
82-03-001	Woody's Triple Self-Portrait	W. Lantz	5,000	95.00	300.00
Armstrong's		**Ceramic Plaque**			
85-04-001	Flamborough Head	A. D'Estrehan	500	195.00	195.00
85-04-002	Flamborough Head (Artist's Proof)	A. D'Estrehan	50	295.00	295.00
88-04-003	Katrina	L. De Winne	500	195.00	195.00
Armstrong's		**Ceramic Plaque**			
85-05-001	The Stamp Collector	M. Paredes	400	195.00	195.00
85-05-002	The Stamp Collector (Artist's Proof)	M. Paredes	50	295.00	295.00
85-05-003	Mother's Pride	M. Paredes	400	195.00	195.00
85-05-004	Mother's Pride (Artist's Proof)	M. Paredes	50	295.00	295.00
Armstrong's		**Pro Autographed Ceramic Baseball Card Plaque**			
85-06-001	Brett, Garvey, Jackson, Rose, Seaver, auto, 3-1/4X5	Unknown	1,000	149.75	149.75
Armstrong's		**Pro Classic Ceramic Baseball Card Plaques**			
85-07-001	George Brett, 2-1/2" x 3-1/2"	Unknown	Open	9.95	9.95
85-07-002	Steve Garvey, 2-1/2" x 3-1/2"	Unknown	Open	9.95	9.95
85-07-003	Reggie Jackson, 2-1/2" x 3-1/2"	Unknown	Open	9.95	9.95
85-07-004	Pete Rose, 2-1/2" x 3-1/2"	Unknown	Open	9.95	9.95
85-07-005	Tom Seaver, 2-1/2" x 3-1/2"	Unknown	Open	9.95	9.95
Art-Line		**Traditions 'N Stone-Large Traditions**			
92-01-001	Letter to Santa (African)-7192	S. Class	1,500	25.00	25.00
92-01-002	Letter to Santa-7292	S. Class	1,500	25.00	25.00
92-01-003	Russian Santa (White)-7393	S. Class	1,500	25.00	25.00
92-01-004	Father Christmas-7492	S. Class	1,500	25.00	25.00
92-01-005	Merry Christmas-7592	S. Class	1,500	25.00	25.00
92-01-006	Santa Traditional-7692	S. Class	1,500	25.00	25.00
92-01-007	Workshop Santa-7792	S. Class	1,500	25.00	25.00
92-01-008	Kris Kringle-7892	S. Class	1,500	25.00	25.00
92-01-009	Swedish Santa (blue)-7992	S. Class	1,500	25.00	25.00
Art-Line		**Traditions 'N Stone-Grand Traditions**			
92-02-001	Traditional Santa-9092	S. Class	500	95.00	95.00
92-02-002	Santa with Bag of Toys-9192	S. Class	500	95.00	95.00
Artaffects		**Heavenly Blessings**			
85-01-001	First Step	Unknown	Open	15.00	19.00
85-01-002	Heaven Scent	Unknown	Open	15.00	19.00
85-01-003	Bubbles	Unknown	Open	15.00	19.00
85-01-004	So Soft	Unknown	Open	15.00	19.00
85-01-005	See!	Unknown	Open	15.00	19.00
85-01-006	Listen!	Unknown	Open	15.00	19.00
85-01-007	Happy Birthday	Unknown	Open	15.00	19.00
85-01-008	Day Dreams	Unknown	Open	15.00	19.00
85-01-009	Just Up	Unknown	Open	15.00	19.00
85-01-010	Beddy Bye	Unknown	Open	15.00	19.00
85-01-011	Race You!	Unknown	Open	15.00	19.00
85-01-012	Yum, Yum!	Unknown	Open	15.00	19.00
Artaffects		**Musical Figurines**			
84-02-001	The Wedding	R. Sauber	Open	65.00	70.00
86-02-002	The Anniversary	R. Sauber	Open	65.00	70.00
87-02-003	Home Sweet Home	R. Sauber	Open	65.00	70.00
87-02-004	Newborn	R. Sauber	Open	65.00	70.00
87-02-005	Motherhood	R. Sauber	Open	65.00	70.00
87-02-006	Fatherhood	R. Sauber	Open	65.00	70.00
87-02-007	Sweet Sixteen	R. Sauber	Open	65.00	70.00
Artaffects		**Christian Collection**			
87-03-001	Bring To Me the Children	A. Tobey	Open	65.00	100.00
88-03-002	The Healer	A. Tobey	Open	65.00	65.00
Artaffects		**Reflections of Youth**			
88-04-001	Julia	MaGo	N/A	29.50	70.00
89-04-002	Jessica	MaGo	14-day	29.50	60.00
89-04-003	Sebastian	MaGo	14-day	29.50	40.00

Company / Number	Name	Series / Artist	Edition Limit	Issue Price	Quote
Artaffects		**Single Issue**			
82-05-001	Babysitter Musical Fig.	G. Perillo	2,500	65.00	90.00
Artaffects		**The Professionals**			
80-06-001	The Big Leaguer	G. Perillo	10,000	65.00	150.00
80-06-002	Ballerina's Dilemma	G. Perillo	10,000	65.00	75.00
81-06-003	The Quarterback	G. Perillo	10,000	65.00	75.00
82-06-004	Rodeo Joe	G. Perillo	10,000	80.00	80.00
82-06-005	Major Leaguer	G. Perillo	10,000	65.00	175.00
83-06-006	Hockey Player	G. Perillo	10,000	65.00	125.00
Artaffects		**The Storybook Collection**			
80-07-001	Little Red Ridinghood	G. Perillo	10,000	65.00	95.00
81-07-002	Cinderella	G. Perillo	10,000	65.00	95.00
82-07-003	Hansel and Gretel	G. Perillo	10,000	80.00	110.00
82-07-004	Goldilocks & 3 Bears	G. Perillo	10,000	80.00	110.00
Artaffects		**The Princesses**			
84-08-001	Lily of the Mohawks	G. Perillo	1,500	65.00	155.00
84-08-002	Pocahontas	G. Perillo	1,500	65.00	125.00
84-08-003	Minnehaha	G. Perillo	1,500	65.00	125.00
84-08-004	Sacajawea	G. Perillo	1,500	65.00	125.00
Artaffects		**The Chieftains**			
83-09-001	Sitting Bull	G. Perillo	5,000	65.00	500.00
83-09-002	Joseph	G. Perillo	5,000	65.00	250.00
83-09-003	Red Cloud	G. Perillo	5,000	65.00	275.00
83-09-004	Geronimo	G. Perillo	5,000	65.00	135.00
83-09-005	Crazy Horse	G. Perillo	5,000	65.00	200.00
Artaffects		**Child Life**			
83-10-001	Siesta	G. Perillo	2,500	65.00	75.00
83-10-002	Sweet Dreams	G. Perillo	1,500	65.00	75.00
Artaffects		**Members Only Limited Edition Redemption Offerings**			
83-11-001	Apache Brave (Bust)	G. Perillo	Open	50.00	150.00
86-11-002	Painted Pony	G. Perillo	Open	125.00	125.00
91-11-003	Chief Crazy Horse	G. Perillo	Open	195.00	195.00
Artaffects		**Limited Edition Free Gifts to Members**			
86-12-001	Dolls	G. Perillo	Open	Gift	N/A
91-12-002	Sunbeam	G. Perillo	Open	Gift	N/A
93-12-003	Little Shadow	G. Perillo	Open	Gift	N/A
Artaffects		**The Little Indians**			
82-13-001	Blue Spruce	G. Perillo	10,000	50.00	75.00
82-13-002	White Rabbit	G. Perillo	10,000	50.00	75.00
82-13-003	Tender Love	G. Perillo	10,000	65.00	75-250.00
90-13-004	Babysitter	G. Perillo	10,000	65.00	65.00
Artaffects		**Special Issue**			
82-14-001	The Peaceable Kingdom	G. Perillo	950	750.00	1500.00
84-14-001	Papoose	G. Perillo	325	500.00	500-975.
84-14-001	Apache Boy Bust	G. Perillo	Open	40.00	75.00
84-14-002	Apache Girl Bust	G. Perillo	Open	40.00	75.00
85-14-001	Lovers	G. Perillo	Open	70.00	125.00
Artaffects		**The War Pony**			
83-15-001	Sioux War Pony	G. Perillo	495	150.00	250.00
83-15-002	Nez Perce War Pony	G. Perillo	495	150.00	250.00
83-15-003	Apache War Pony	G. Perillo	495	150.00	250.00
Artaffects		**The Tribal Ponies**			
84-16-001	Arapaho	G. Perillo	1,500	65.00	200.00
84-16-002	Comanche	G. Perillo	1,500	65.00	200.00
84-16-003	Crow	G. Perillo	1,500	65.00	250.00
Artaffects		**Pride of America's Indians**			
88-17-001	Brave and Free	G. Perillo	10-day	50.00	150.00
89-17-002	Dark Eyed Friends	G. Perillo	10-day	45.00	75.00
89-17-003	Noble Companions	G. Perillo	10-day	45.00	50.00
89-17-004	Kindred Spirits	G. Perillo	10-day	45.00	50.00
89-17-005	Loyal Alliance	G. Perillo	10-day	45.00	75.00
89-17-006	Small & Wise	G. Perillo	10-day	45.00	50.00
89-17-007	Winter Scouts	G. Perillo	10-day	45.00	50.00
89-17-008	Peaceful Comrades	G. Perillo	10-day	45.00	50.00
Artaffects		**Sagebrush Kids**			
85-18-001	Hail to the Chief	G. Perillo	Closed	19.50	52.00
85-18-002	Dressing Up	G. Perillo	Closed	19.50	52.00
85-18-003	Favorite Kachina	G. Perillo	Closed	19.50	52.00
85-18-004	Message of Joy	G. Perillo	Closed	19.50	52.00
85-18-005	Boots	G. Perillo	Closed	19.50	52.00
85-18-006	Stay Awhile	G. Perillo	Closed	19.50	52.00
85-18-007	Room for Two?	G. Perillo	Closed	19.50	52.00
85-18-008	Blue Bird	G. Perillo	Closed	19.50	52.00
85-18-009	Ouch!	G. Perillo	Closed	19.50	52.00
85-18-010	Take One	G. Perillo	Closed	19.50	52.00
86-18-011	The Long Wait	G. Perillo	Closed	19.50	52.00
86-18-012	Westward Ho!	G. Perillo	Closed	19.50	52.00
86-18-013	Finishing Touches	G. Perillo	Closed	19.50	52.00
86-18-014	Deputies	G. Perillo	Closed	19.50	52.00
86-18-015	Country Music	G. Perillo	Closed	19.50	52.00
86-18-016	Practice Makes Perfect	G. Perillo	Closed	19.50	52.00
86-18-017	The Hiding Place	G. Perillo	Closed	19.50	52.00
86-18-018	Prarie Prayers	G. Perillo	Closed	19.50	52.00
87-18-019	Just Picked	G. Perillo	Closed	19.50	52.00
87-18-020	Row, Row	G. Perillo	Closed	19.50	52.00
87-18-021	My Papoose	G. Perillo	Closed	19.50	52.00
87-18-022	Playing House	G. Perillo	Closed	19.50	52.00
87-18-023	Wagon Train	G. Perillo	Closed	19.50	52.00
87-18-024	Small Talk	G. Perillo	Closed	19.50	52.00
90-18-025	How! Do I Love Thee?	G. Perillo	Closed	39.50	50.00
90-18-026	Easter Offering	G. Perillo	Closed	27.50	50.00
90-18-027	Just Married	G. Perillo	Closed	45.00	45.00
91-18-028	Baby Bronc	G. Perillo	Closed	27.50	80.00
91-18-029	Little Warriors	G. Perillo	Closed	27.50	35.00
91-18-030	Toy Totem	G. Perillo	Closed	27.50	35.00
91-18-031	Just Baked	G. Perillo	Closed	27.50	35.00
91-18-032	Lovin Spoonful	G. Perillo	Closed	27.50	35.00
91-18-033	Teddy Too??	G. Perillo	Closed	27.50	35.00
Artaffects		**Sagebrush Kids-Christmas Caravan**			
87-19-001	Leading the Way	G. Perillo	Open	90.00	120.00
87-19-002	Sleepy Sentinels	G. Perillo	Open	45.00	50.00
87-19-003	Singing Praises	G. Perillo	Open	45.00	50.00
87-19-004	Gold, Frankincense & Gifts	G. Perillo	Open	35.00	35.00
87-19-005	4-Piece Set (Above)	G. Perillo	Open	185.00	255.00
Artaffects		**Sagebrush Kids-Nativity**			
86-20-001	Christ Child	G. Perillo	Open	12.50	13.50
86-20-002	Mary	G. Perillo	Open	17.50	19.50
86-20-003	Joseph	G. Perillo	Open	17.50	19.50
86-20-004	Teepee	G. Perillo	Open	17.50	22.50
86-20-005	4-pc. Set (Above)	G. Perillo	Open	50.00	65.00
86-20-006	King with Corn	G. Perillo	Open	17.50	22.50
86-20-007	King with Pottery	G. Perillo	Open	17.50	22.50
86-20-008	King with Jewelry	G. Perillo	Open	17.50	22.50
86-20-009	Shepherd with Lamb	G. Perillo	Open	17.50	22.50
86-20-010	Shepherd Kneeling	G. Perillo	Open	17.50	22.50
86-20-011	Cow	G. Perillo	Open	12.00	13.50
86-20-012	Donkey	G. Perillo	Open	12.00	13.50
86-20-013	Lamb	G. Perillo	Open	6.00	8.00
86-20-014	Goat	G. Perillo	Open	8.00	9.50
86-20-015	Backdrop Dove	G. Perillo	Open	17.50	21.50
86-20-016	Backdrop Pottery	G. Perillo	Open	17.50	21.50
86-20-017	15 piece Set (Above)	G. Perillo	Open	225.00	245.00
89-20-018	Pig	G. Perillo	Open	15.00	15.00
89-20-019	Racoon	G. Perillo	Open	12.50	12.50
89-20-020	Cactus	G. Perillo	Open	24.50	24.50
89-20-021	Buffalo	G. Perillo	Open	17.50	17.50
90-20-022	Harmony Angel	G. Perillo	Open	37.50	37.50
90-20-023	Melody Angel	G. Perillo	Open	37.50	37.50
91-20-024	Peace Angel	G. Perillo	Open	27.50	27.50
91-20-025	Joy Angel	G. Perillo	Open	27.50	27.50
Artaffects		**Sagebrush Kids-Christmas Treasury**			
90-21-025	Santa's Lullaby	G. Perillo	Open	45.00	45.00
90-21-001	3/Set:Flight Into Egypt (Holy Family /Donkey)	G. Perillo	Open	65.00	65.00
Artaffects		**Sagebrush Kids-Banks**			
90-22-001	Perillo's Piggy Bank	G. Perillo	Open	39.50	39.50
90-22-002	Buckaroo Bank	G. Perillo	Open	39.50	39.50
90-22-003	Wampum Wig-Wam Bank	G. Perillo	Open	39.50	39.50
Artaffects		**Sagebrush Kids-Wedding Party**			
90-23-001	Bride	G. Perillo	Open	24.50	24.50
90-23-002	Groom	G. Perillo	Open	24.50	24.50
90-23-003	Flower Girl	G. Perillo	Open	22.50	22.50
90-23-004	Ring Bearer	G. Perillo	Open	22.50	22.50
90-23-005	Donkey	G. Perillo	Open	22.50	22.50
90-23-006	Chief	G. Perillo	Open	24.50	24.50
90-23-007	Wedding Backdrop	G. Perillo	Open	27.50	27.50
90-23-008	7 Piece Set (Above)	G. Perillo	Open	165.00	165.00
Artaffects		**Perillo Limited Edition Porcelain Figurines**			
91-24-001	One Nation Under God	G. Perillo	5,000	195.00	195.00
91-24-002	Safe And Dry (Umbrella Boy)	G. Perillo	5,000	95.00	95.00
91-24-003	Out Of The Rain (Umbrella Girl)	G. Perillo	5,000	95.00	95.00
91-24-004	Angel of the Plains	G. Perillo	5,000	75.00	75.00
91-24-005	The Sioux Carousel Horse	G. Perillo	5,000	95.00	95.00
91-24-006	The Cheyenne Carousel Horse	G. Perillo	5,000	95.00	95.00
Artaffects		**Musical Figurines**			
89-25-001	A Boy's Prayer	G. Perillo	Open	45.00	65.00
89-25-002	A Girl's Prayer	G. Perillo	Open	45.00	65.00
Artaffects		**Wildlife Figurines**			
90-26-001	Mustang	G. Perillo	Open	85.00	85.00
90-26-002	White-Tailed Deer	G. Perillo	Open	95.00	95.00
90-26-003	Mountain Lion	G. Perillo	Open	75.00	75.00
90-26-004	Bald Eagle	G. Perillo	Open	65.00	65.00
93-26-005	Buffalo	G. Perillo	Open	75.00	75.00
93-26-006	Timber Wolf	G. Perillo	Open	85.00	85.00
93-26-007	Polar Bear	G. Perillo	Open	65.00	65.00
93-26-008	Bighorn Sheep	G. Perillo	Open	75.00	75.00
Artaffects		**The Great Chieftains**			
91-27-001	Crazy Horse (Club Piece)	G. Perillo	Open	195.00	195.00
91-27-002	Sitting Bull	G. Perillo	5,000	195.00	195.00
91-27-003	Red Cloud	G. Perillo	5,000	195.00	195.00
91-27-004	Chief Joseph	G. Perillo	5,000	195.00	195.00
91-27-005	Cochise	G. Perillo	5,000	195.00	195.00
91-27-006	Geronimo	G. Perillo	5,000	195.00	195.00
Artaffects		**The Young Chieftains**			
85-28-001	Young Sitting Bull	G. Perillo	5,000	50.00	50.00
85-28-002	Young Joseph	G. Perillo	5,000	50.00	50.00
85-28-003	Young Red Cloud	G. Perillo	5,000	50.00	50.00
85-28-004	Young Geronimo	G. Perillo	5,000	50.00	50.00
85-28-005	Young Crazy Horse	G. Perillo	5,000	50.00	50.00
Artaffects		**Grand Bronze Collection**			
88-29-001	Free Spirit	G. Perillo	21-day	175.00	175.00
88-29-002	Fresh Waters	G. Perillo	21-day	350.00	350.00
88-29-003	Silhouette	G. Perillo	2,500	300.00	300.00
88-29-004	Partners	G. Perillo	2,500	200.00	200.00
88-29-005	Chief Red Cloud	G. Perillo	2,500	500.00	500.00
88-29-006	Discovery	G. Perillo	2,500	150.00	150.00
88-29-007	Peacemaker	G. Perillo	2,500	300.00	300.00
Artaffects		**American Indian Heritage**			
91-30-001	Cheyenne Nation (bust)	G. Perillo	10-day	55.00	55.00
Artaffects		**Village of the Sun**			
91-31-001	Sunbeam (Club Only)	G. Perillo	Open	Gift	N/A
92-31-002	Little Shadow (Club Renewal Only)	G. Perillo	Open	Gift	N/A
92-31-003	Rolling Thunder (Medicine Man)	G. Perillo	Open	24.00	24.00
92-31-004	Cloud Catcher (Boy with Dog)	G. Perillo	Open	24.00	24.00
92-31-005	Smiling Eyes (Baby with Lamb)	G. Perillo	Open	19.50	19.50
92-31-006	Many Bears (Farmer)	G. Perillo	Open	27.50	27.50
92-31-007	Cactus Flower (Weaver)	G. Perillo	Open	39.50	39.50
92-31-008	Dancing Waters (Tortilla Maker)	G. Perillo	Open	27.50	27.50
92-31-009	Red Bird (Jewelry Maker)	G. Perillo	Open	27.50	27.50
92-31-010	Bright Sky (Cook)	G. Perillo	Open	27.50	27.50

Number	Name	Artist	Edition Limit	Issue Price	Quote
92-31-011	Summer Breeze (Maiden)	G. Perillo	Open	24.00	24.00
92-31-012	Standing Deer (Brave)	G. Perillo	Open	27.50	27.50
92-31-013	Noble Guardian (Horse)	G. Perillo	Open	39.50	39.50
92-31-014	Lambs	G. Perillo	Open	10.00	10.00
92-31-015	Small Cactus (Yellow Flowers)	G. Perillo	Open	7.50	7.50
92-31-016	Small Cactus (Pink Flowers)	G. Perillo	Open	7.50	7.50
92-31-017	Medium Cactus	G. Perillo	Open	10.00	10.00
92-31-018	Large Cactus	G. Perillo	Open	15.00	15.00
92-31-019	Hogan	G. Perillo	Open	59.00	59.00
Artaffects		**Simple Wonders**			
91-32-001	Joseph	C. Roeda	N/A	45.00	45.00
91-32-002	Joseph (Black)	C. Roeda	N/A	45.00	45.00
91-32-003	Mary	C. Roeda	N/A	40.00	40.00
91-32-004	Mary (Black)	C. Roeda	N/A	40.00	40.00
91-32-005	Baby Jesus	C. Roeda	N/A	35.00	35.00
91-32-006	Baby Jesus (Black)	C. Roeda	N/A	35.00	35.00
91-32-007	Sheep Dog	C. Roeda	N/A	15.00	15.00
91-32-008	Off To School	C. Roeda	N/A	49.50	49.50
91-32-009	Playing Hookey	C. Roeda	N/A	49.50	49.50
91-32-010	Mommy's Best	C. Roeda	N/A	49.50	49.50
91-32-011	Made With Love	C. Roeda	N/A	49.50	49.50
91-32-012	Bride	C. Roeda	N/A	55.00	55.00
91-32-013	Groom	C. Roeda	N/A	45.00	45.00
91-32-014	The Littlest Angel	C. Roeda	N/A	29.50	29.50
91-32-015	Star Light, Star Bright	C. Roeda	N/A	35.00	35.00
91-32-016	Lighting the Way	C. Roeda	N/A	39.50	39.50
91-32-017	Forever Friends	C. Roeda	N/A	39.50	39.50
91-32-018	Song of Joy	C. Roeda	N/A	39.50	39.50
91-32-019	I Love Ewe	C. Roeda	N/A	37.50	37.50
91-32-020	The Littlest Angel (Black)	C. Roeda	N/A	29.50	29.50
92-32-021	Ten Penny Serenade	C. Roeda	N/A	45.00	45.00
92-32-022	Ten Penny Serenade (Black)	C. Roeda	N/A	45.00	45.00
92-32-023	Rainbow Patrol	C. Roeda	N/A	39.50	39.50
92-32-024	The Three Bears	C. Roeda	N/A	45.00	45.00
92-32-025	Trick or Treat	C. Roeda	N/A	39.50	39.50
92-32-026	A Perfect Fit	C. Roeda	N/A	45.00	45.00
92-32-027	Pocketful of Love	C. Roeda	N/A	35.00	35.00
92-32-028	Pocketful of Love (Black)	C. Roeda	N/A	35.00	35.00
92-32-029	This Too Shall Pass	C. Roeda	N/A	35.00	35.00
92-32-030	Fallen Angel	C. Roeda	N/A	35.00	35.00
92-32-031	Lil' Dumplin	C. Roeda	N/A	25.00	25.00
92-32-032	Lil' Dumplin (Black)	C. Roeda	N/A	25.00	25.00
92-32-033	Little Big Shot	C. Roeda	N/A	35.00	35.00
92-32-034	With Open Arms (Wisechild)	C. Roeda	N/A	39.50	39.50
92-32-035	Following the Star (Wisechild)	C. Roeda	N/A	45.00	45.00
92-32-036	Catch the Spirit (Wisechild)	C. Roeda	N/A	35.00	35.002
Artists of the World		**DeGrazia Figurine**			
84-01-001	Flower Girl	T. DeGrazia	Open	65.00	125.00
84-01-002	Flower Boy	T. DeGrazia	Closed	65.00	140.00
84-01-003	Sunflower Boy	T. DeGrazia	Closed	65.00	200-300.
84-01-004	My First Horse	T. DeGrazia	Closed	65.00	195.00
84-01-005	White Dove	T. DeGrazia	Open	45.00	110.00
84-01-006	Wondering	T. DeGrazia	Closed	85.00	135-175.
84-01-007	Flower Girl Plaque	T. DeGrazia	Closed	45.00	95.00
85-01-008	Little Madonna	T. DeGrazia	Open	80.00	145.00
85-01-009	Mary	T. DeGrazia	Open	55.00	90.00
85-01-010	Joseph	T. DeGrazia	Open	55.00	100.00
85-01-011	Jesus	T. DeGrazia	Open	25.00	55.00
85-01-012	Nativity Set-3 pieces	T. DeGrazia	Open	135.00	245.00
86-01-013	The Blue Boy	T. DeGrazia	Open	70.00	110.00
86-01-014	Festival Lights	T. DeGrazia	Open	75.00	110.00
86-01-015	Merry Little Indian	T. DeGrazia	12,500	175.00	275.00
85-01-016	Pima Drummer Boy	T. DeGrazia	Closed	65.00	150.00
87-01-017	Love Me	T. DeGrazia	Open	95.00	145-175.
87-01-018	Wee Three	T. DeGrazia	Closed	180.00	195.00
88-01-019	Christmas Prayer Angel	T. DeGrazia	Closed	70.00	125.00
88-01-020	Los Niños	T. DeGrazia	5,000	595.00	950.00
88-01-021	Beautiful Burden	T. DeGrazia	Closed	175.00	185-200.
88-01-022	Merrily, Merrily, Merrily	T. DeGrazia	Closed	95.00	110-150.
88-01-023	Flower Boy Plaque	T. DeGrazia	Closed	80.00	85.00
89-01-024	Two Little Lambs	T. DeGrazia	Open	70.00	150.00
89-01-025	My First Arrow	T. DeGrazia	Open	95.00	175.00
89-01-026	My Beautiful Rocking Horse	T. DeGrazia	Open	225.00	275.00
89-01-027	Los Ninos (Artist's Edition)	T. DeGrazia	48	695.00	1200.00
90-01-028	Alone	T. DeGrazia	Open	395.00	595.00
90-01-029	El Burrito	T. DeGrazia	Open	60.00	90.00
90-01-030	Sunflower Girl	T. DeGrazia	Open	95.00	125.00
90-01-031	Crucifixion	T. DeGrazia	Yr.Iss.	295.00	295.00
90-01-032	Navajo Boy	T. DeGrazia	Yr.Iss.	110.00	135.00
90-01-033	Desert Harvest	T. DeGrazia	5,000	135.00	145.00
90-01-034	Biggest Drum	T. DeGrazia	Yr.Iss.	110.00	135.00
90-01-035	Little Prayer	T. DeGrazia	Yr.Iss.	85.00	95.00
91-01-036	Navajo Mother	T. DeGrazia	3,500	295.00	325.00
91-01-037	Shepherd Boy	T. DeGrazia	Open	95.00	95.00
92-01-038	Sun Showers	T. DeGrazia	5,000	195.00	225.00
92-01-039	Navajo Madonna	T. DeGrazia	Open	135.00	145.00
92-01-040	Coming Home	T. DeGrazia	3,500	165.00	175.00
93-01-041	Feliz Navidad	T. DeGrazia	1,992	195.00	225.00
93-01-042	Saddle Up	T. DeGrazia	5,000	195.00	215.00
93-01-043	El Toro	T. DeGrazia	Open	95.00	97.50
93-01-044	Little Medicine Man	T. DeGrazia	Open	175.00	185.00
Artists of the World		**Goebel Miniatures: DeGrazia**			
85-02-001	Flower Girl 501-P	R. Olszewski	Suspd.	85.00	85-125.00
85-02-002	Flower Boy 502-P	R. Olszewski	Suspd.	85.00	85-125.00
85-02-003	My First Horse 503-P	R. Olszewski	Suspd.	85.00	85-125.00
85-02-004	Sunflower Boy 551- P	R. Olszewski	Suspd.	93.00	150.00
85-02-005	White Dove 504-P	R. Olszewski	Suspd.	80.00	80-125.00
85-02-006	Wondering 505-P	R. Olszewski	Suspd.	93.00	95-150.00
86-02-007	Little Madonna 552-P	R. Olszewski	Suspd.	93.00	150.00
86-02-008	Pima Drummer Boy 506-P	R. Olszewski	Suspd.	85.00	250-300.
86-02-009	Festival of Lights 507-P	R. Olszewski	Suspd.	85.00	225-250.
87-02-010	Merry Little Indian 508-P	R. Olszewski	Suspd.	95.00	295.00
88-02-011	Adobe Display 948D	R. Olszewski	Suspd.	45.00	59.00
89-02-013	Beautiful Burden 554-P	R. Olszewski	Suspd.	110.00	110.00
90-02-012	Adobe Hacienda (large) Display 958-D	R. Olszewski	Suspd.	85.00	95.00
90-02-015	Chapel Display 971-D	R. Olszewski	Suspd.	95.00	100.00
91-02-014	My Beautiful Rocking Horse 555-P	R. Olszewski	Suspd.	110.00	110.00
Artists of the World		**DeGrazia Pendants**			
85-03-001	Flower Girl Pendant 561-P	R. Olszewski	Open	125.00	150.00
87-03 -002	Festival of Lights 562-P	R. Olszewski	Open	90.00	195.00
Bing & Grondahl		**Loveable Babies of the Animal Kingdom**			
93-01-001	Koala Bear	A. Therkelsen	5,000	100.00	100.00
Boehm Studios		**Boehm**			
83-01-001	Great Egret	Boehm	Yr.Iss.	1200.00	2400.00
84-01-002	Whooping Crane	Boehm	Yr.Iss.	1800.00	2000.00
85-01-003	Trumpeter Swan	Boehm	Yr.Iss.	1500.00	1800.00
Boehm Studios		**Bird Sculptures**			
57-02-001	American Eagle, large	Boehm	31	225.00	1100.00
57-02-002	American Eagle, small	Boehm	76	225.00	19200.00
58-02-003	American Redstarts	Boehm	500	350.00	2000.00
80-02-004	Arctic Tern	Boehm	350	1400.00	2850.00
69-02-005	Black-headed Grosbeak	Boehm	675	1250.00	2000.00
56-02-006	Black-tailed Bantams, pair	Boehm	57	350.00	4700.00
58-02-007	Black-throated Blue Warbler	Boehm	500	400.00	1875.00
76-02-008	Black-throated Blue Warbler	Boehm	200	900.00	1100.00
67-02-009	Blue Grosbeak	Boehm	750	1050.00	1500.00
62-02-010	Blue Jays, pair	Boehm	250	2000.00	12750.00
64-02-011	Bobolink	Boehm	500	550.00	1550.00
53-02-012	Bob White Quail, pair	Boehm	750	400.00	2600.00
72-02-013	Brown Pelican	Boehm	100	10500.00	14500.00
73-02-014	Brown Thrasher	Boehm	260	1850.00	1875.00
72-02-015	Cactus Wren	Boehm	225	3000.00	3300.00
57-02-016	California Quail, pair	Boehm	500	400.00	2900.00
78-02-017	Canada Geese, pair	Boehm	100	4200.00	4200.00
77-02-018	Cape May Warbler	Boehm	400	825.00	950.00
55-02-019	Cardinals, pair	Boehm	500	550.00	3750.00
77-02-020	Cardinals	Boehm	200	3500.00	3850.00
57-02-021	Carolina Wrens	Boehm	100	750.00	5500.00
65-02-022	Catbird	Boehm	500	900.00	2135.00
56-02-023	Cedar Waxwings, pair	Boehm	100	600.00	7750.00
57-02-024	Cerulean Warblers	Boehm	100	800.00	4335.00
68-02-025	Common Tern	Boehm	500	1400.00	6200.00
67-02-026	Crested Flycatcher	Boehm	500	1650.00	2925.00
57-02-027	Downy Woodpeckers	Boehm	500	450.00	1775.00
76-02-028	Eagle of Freedom I	Boehm	15	35000.00	53000.00
59-02-029	Eastern Bluebirds, pair	Boehm	100	1800.00	12000.00
75-02-030	Eastern Kingbird	Boehm	100	3500.00	3900.00
73-02-031	Everglades Kites	Boehm	50	5800.00	7200.00
77-02-032	Fledgling Brown Thrashers	Boehm	400	500.00	655.00
67-02-033	Fledgling Canada Warbler	Boehm	750	550.00	2275.00
65-02-034	Fledgling Great Horned Owl	Boehm	750	350.00	1475.00
71-02-035	Flicker	Boehm	250	2400.00	2950.00
56-02-036	Golden-crowned Kinglets	Boehm	500	1400.00	2400.00
54-02-037	Golden Pheasant, decorated	Boehm	7	350.00	19000.00
54-02-038	Golden Pheasant, bisque	Boehm	7	200.00	11250.00
61-02-039	Goldfinches	Boehm	500	400.00	1800.00
66-02-040	Green Jays, pair	Boehm	400	1850.00	4200.00
74-02-041	Hooded Warbler	Boehm	100	2400.00	3150.00
73-02-042	Horned Larks	Boehm	200	3800.00	5000.00
68-02-043	Kestrels, pair	Boehm	460	2300.00	3000.00
64-02-044	Killdeer, pair	Boehm	300	1750.00	4500.00
74-02-045	Lark Sparrow	Boehm	150	,100.00	2200.00
73-02-046	Lazuli Buntings	Boehm	250	1800.00	2300.00
79-02-047	Least Tern	Boehm	350	1275.00	3100.00
62-02-048	Lesser Prairie Chickens, pair	Boehm	300	1200.00	2400.00
52-02-049	Mallards, pair	Boehm	500	650.00	1700.00
57-02-050	Meadowlark	Boehm	750	350.00	3100.00
63-02-051	Mearn's Quail, pair	Boehm	350	950.00	3450.00
68-02-052	Mergansers, pair	Boehm	440	2200.00	2825.00
61-02-053	Mockingbirds, pair	Boehm	500	650.00	3800.00
78-02-054	Mockingbirds	Boehm	Unkn.	2200.00	2800.00
63-02-055	Mountain Bluebirds	Boehm	300	1900.00	5850.00
58-02-056	Mourning Doves	Boehm	500	550.00	1250.00
71-02-057	Mute swans, life-size, pair	Boehm	3	Unkn.	Unkn.
71-02-058	Mute Swans, small size, pair	Boehm	400	4000.00	8200.00
74-02-059	Myrtle Warblers	Boehm	210	1850.00	2075.00
58-02-060	Nonpareil Buntings	Boehm	750	250.00	1075.00
67-02-061	Northern Water Thrush	Boehm	500	800.00	1400.00
70-02-062	Orchard Orioles	Boehm	550	1750.00	2200.00
70-02-063	Oven-bird	Boehm	450	1400.00	1800.00
65-02-064	Parula Warblers	Boehm	400	1500.00	3150.00
75-02-065	Pekin Robins	Boehm	100	7000.00	8550.00
62-02-066	Ptarmigan, pair	Boehm	350	800.00	3575.00
74-02-067	Purple Martins	Boehm	50	6700.00	8450.00
75-02-068	Red-billed Blue Magpie	Boehm	100	4600.00	5950.00
57-02-069	Red-winged Blackbirds, pair	Boehm	100	700.00	5250.00
54-02-070	Ringed-necked Pheasants, pair	Boehm	500	650.00	1825.00
68-02-071	Roadrunner	Boehm	500	2600.00	3700.00
64-02-072	Robin (Daffodils)	Boehm	500	600.00	5700.00
77-02-073	Robin (nest)	Boehm	350	1650.00	1840.00
60-02-074	Ruffed Grouse, pair	Boehm	250	950.00	4950.00
66-02-075	Rufous Hummingbirds	Boehm	500	850.00	1900.00
77-02-076	Scarlet Tanager	Boehm	4	1800.00	4000.00
77-02-077	Scissor-tailed Flycatcher	Boehm	100	3200.00	3200.00
79-02-078	Scops Owl	Boehm	300	975.00	1500.00
80-02-079	Screech Owl	Boehm	350	2100.00	3100.00
70-02-080	Slate-colored Junco	Boehm	NA	1600.00	2000.00
81-02-081	Snow Buntings	Boehm	350	2400.00	2950.00
56-02-082	Song Sparrows, pair	Boehm	50	2000.00	38000.00
61-02-083	Sugarbirds	Boehm	100	2500.00	13250.00
63-02-084	Towhee	Boehm	500	350.00	2600.00
65-02-085	Tufted Titmice	Boehm	500	600.00	2000.00
65-02-086	Varied Buntings	Boehm	300	2200.00	4500.00
74-02-087	Varied Thrush	Boehm	NA	2500.00	3000.00
69-02-088	Verdins	Boehm	575	1150.00	1525.00
69-02-089	Western Bluebirds	Boehm	300	5500.00	6600.00
71-02-090	Western Meadowlark	Boehm	350	1425.00	1675.00
54-02-091	Woodcock	Boehm	500	300.00	1950.00
51-02-092	Wood Thrush	Boehm	2	375.00	Unkn.
66-02-093	Wood Thrushes, pair	Boehm	400	4200.00	8400.00
72-02-094	Yellow-bellied Sapsucker	Boehm	NA	2700.00	3000.00
74-02-095	Yellow-bellied Cuckoo	Boehm	NA	2800.00	3000.00
74-02-096	Yellow-headed Blackbird	Boehm	75	3200.00	3600.00
73-02-097	Young American Eagle, Inaugural	Boehm	100	1500.00	2100.00
69-02-098	Young American Eagle	Boehm	850	700.00	1400.00
75-02-099	Young & Spirited 1976	Boehm	1,121	950.00	1800.00
79-02-100	Avocet	Boehm	175	1200.00	1200.00
72-02-101	Barn Owl	Boehm	350	3600.00	5600.00
73-02-102	Blackbirds, pair	Boehm	75	5400.00	6300.00

FIGURINES

Company		Series			
Number	**Name**	**Artist**	**Edition Limit**	**Issue Price**	**Quote**
72-02-103	Black Grouse	Boehm	175	2800.00	3025.00
73-02-104	Blue Tits	Boehm	300	3000.00	3000.00
74-02-105	Chaffinch	Boehm	125	2000.00	2200.00
74-02-106	Crested Tit	Boehm	400	1150.00	1250.00
75-02-107	European Goldfinch	Boehm	225	1150.00	1350.00
72-02-108	Goldcrest	Boehm	500	650.00	1200.00
73-02-109	Green Woodpeckers	Boehm	50	4200.00	4800.00
79-02-110	Grey Wagtail	Boehm	150	1050.00	1260.00
76-02-111	Kingfishers	Boehm	200	1900.00	2300.00
73-02-112	Lapwing	Boehm	100	2600.00	2975.00
71-02-113	Little Owl	Boehm	350	700.00	1325.00
73-02-114	Long Tail Tits	Boehm	200	2600.00	2900.00
71-02-115	Nuthatch	Boehm	350	650.00	1100.00
73-02-116	Peregrine Falcon	Boehm	350	4400.00	5450.00
76-02-117	Rivoli's Hummingbird	Boehm	350	950.00	1550.00
74-02-118	Ruby-throated Hummingbird	Boehm	200	1900.00	2650.00
73-02-119	Screech Owl	Boehm	50	850.00	1425.00
74-02-120	Song Thrushes	Boehm	100	2800.00	3350.00
74-02-121	Stonechats	Boehm	150	2200.00	2400.00
74-02-122	Swallows	Boehm	125	3400.00	4100.00
72-02-123	Tree Creepers	Boehm	200	3200.00	4200.00
71-02-124	Winter Robin	Boehm	225	1150.00	1440.00
73-02-125	Yellowhammers	Boehm	350	3300.00	4200.00
Boehm Studios		**Animal Sculptures**			
69-03-001	Adios	Boehm	130	1500.00	1800.00
52-03-002	Hunter	Boehm	250	600.00	1300.00
57-03-003	Polo Player	Boehm	100	850.00	4450.00
78-03-004	Thoroughbred with Jockey	Boehm	25	2600.00	2800.00
77-03-005	African Elephant	Boehm	50	9500.00	14400.00
76-03-006	American Mustangs	Boehm	75	3700.00	5700.00
80-03-007	Asian Lion	Boehm	100	1500.00	1500.00
78-03-008	Black Rhinoceros	Boehm	50	9500.00	11000.00
71-03-009	Bobcats	Boehm	200	1600.00	2000.00
78-03-010	Camel & Calf	Boehm	50	3600.00	3900.00
80-03-011	Cheetah	Boehm	100	2700.00	2900.00
79-03-012	Fallow Deer	Boehm	30	7500.00	7500.00
71-03-013	Foxes	Boehm	200	1800.00	2550.00
75-03-014	Giant Panda	Boehm	100	3800.00	6350.00
78-03-015	Gorilla	Boehm	50	3800.00	4400.00
79-03-016	Hunter Chase	Boehm	20	4000.00	4000.00
73-03-017	Nyala Antelope	Boehm	100	4700.00	6500.00
76-03-018	Otter	Boehm	75	1100.00	1450.00
75-03-019	Puma	Boehm	50	5700.00	6800.00
71-03-020	Raccoons	Boehm	200	1600.00	2250.00
72-03-021	Red Squirrels	Boehm	100	2600.00	2800.00
78-03-022	Snow Leopard	Boehm	75	3500.00	5500.00
79-03-023	Young & Free Fawns	Boehm	160	1875.00	1875.00
Boehm Studios		**Floral Sculptures**			
79-04-001	Cactus Dahlia	Boehm	300	800.00	960.00
72-04-002	Chrysanthemums	Boehm	350	1100.00	1950.00
71-04-003	Daisies	Boehm	350	600.00	975.00
74-04-004	Debutante Camellia	Boehm	500	625.00	800.00
73-04-005	Dogwood	Boehm	250	625.00	975.00
78-04-006	Double Clematis Centerpiece	Boehm	150	1500.00	1950.00
74-04-007	Double Peony	Boehm	275	575.00	1050.00
75-04-008	Emmett Barnes Camellia	Boehm	425	550.00	780.00
74-04-009	Gentians	Boehm	350	425.00	725.00
79-04-010	Grand Floral Centerpiece	Boehm	15	7500.00	8700.00
78-04-011	Helen Boehm Camellia	Boehm	500	600.00	1050.00
78-04-012	Helen Boehm Daylily	Boehm	175	975.00	1160.00
78-04-013	Helen Boehm Iris	Boehm	175	975.00	1175.00
79-04-014	Honeysuckle	Boehm	200	900.00	1080.00
75-04-015	Magnolia Grandiflora	Boehm	750	650.00	1350.00
76-04-016	Orchid Cactus	Boehm	100	650.00	975.00
76-04-017	Queen of the Night Cactus	Boehm	125	650.00	850.00
78-04-018	Rhododendron Centerpiece	Boehm	350	1150.00	1750.00
80-04-019	Rose, Alec's Red	Boehm	500	1050.00	1300.00
78-04-020	Rose, Blue Moon	Boehm	500	650.00	900.00
78-04-021	Rose, Pascali	Boehm	500	950.00	1375.00
76-04-022	Rose, Supreme Peace	Boehm	250	850.00	1575.00
76-04-023	Rose, Supreme Yellow	Boehm	250	850.00	1575.00
78-04-024	Rose, Tropicana	Boehm	500	475.00	1085.00
78-04-025	Spanish Iris	Boehm	500	600.00	600.00
73-04-026	Streptocalyx Poeppigii	Boehm	50	3400.00	4300.00
71-04-027	Swan Centerpiece	Boehm	135	1950.00	2725.00
76-04-028	Swan Lake Camellia	Boehm	750	825.00	1725.00
76-04-029	Sweet Viburnum	Boehm	35	650.00	1425.00
74-04-030	Waterlily	Boehm	350	400.00	660.00
78-04-031	Watsonii Magnolia	Boehm	250	575.00	690.00
Boehm Studios		**Figurines**			
77-05-001	Beverly Sills	Boehm	100	950.00	1500.00
77-05-002	Jerome Hines	Boehm	12	825.00	1000.00
Byers' Choice Ltd.		**Carolers**			
82-01-001	Victorian Adult Caroler (1st Version)	J. Byers	Closed	32.00	300.00
82-01-002	Victorian Child Caroler (1st Version)	J. Byers	Closed	32.00	300.00
83-01-003	Victorian Adult Caroler (2nd Version)	J. Byers	Open	35.00	46.00
83-01-004	Victorian Child Caroler (2nd Version)	J. Byers	Open	33.00	46.00
86-01-005	Traditional Grandparents	J. Byers	Open	35.00	42.00
86-01-006	Singing Dogs	J. Byers	Open	13.00	15.00
88-01-007	Victorian Grand Parent Carolers	J. Byers	Open	40.00	45.00
88-01-008	Children with Skates	J. Byers	Open	40.00	47.00
88-01-009	Singing Cats	J. Byers	Open	13.50	15.00
91-01-010	Toddler on Sled	J. Byers	Closed	30.00	30.00
Byers' Choice Ltd.		**Special Characters**			
81-02-001	Thanksgiving Man (Clay Hands)	J. Byers	Closed	Unkn.	2000.00
81-02-002	Thanksgiving Lady (Clay Hands)	J. Byers	Closed	Unkn.	2000.00
82-02-003	Icabod	J. Byers	Closed	32.00	1150.00
82-02-004	Choir Children, boy and girl	J. Byers	Closed	32.00	250.00
82-02-005	Valentine Boy	J. Byers	Closed	32.00	450.00
82-02-006	Valentine Girl	J. Byers	Closed	32.00	450.00
82-02-007	Easter Boy	J. Byers	Closed	32.00	450.00
82-02-008	Easter Girl	J. Byers	Closed	32.00	450.00
82-02-009	Leprechauns	J. Byers	Closed	34.00	1200.00
82-02-010	Conductor	J. Byers	Closed	32.00	42.00
82-02-011	Drummer Boy	J. Byers	Closed	34.00	46.00
83-02-012	Boy on Rocking Horse	J. Byers	300	85.00	1500.00
84-02-013	Chimney Sweep (Adult)	J. Byers	Closed	36.00	1200.00
85-02-014	Pajama Children	J. Byers	Closed	35.00	185.00
87-02-015	Boy on Sled	J. Byers	Closed	50.00	175.00
87-02-016	Caroler with Lamp	J. Byers	Closed	40.00	150.00
87-02-017	Mother's Day	J. Byers	225	125.00	350.00
88-02-018	Mother's Day (Son)	J. Byers`	Closed	125.00	225-275.
88-02-019	Mother's Day (Daughter)	J. Byers	Closed	125.00	225.00
88-02-020	Angel Tree Top	J. Byers	100	Unkn.	150.00
88-02-021	Mother Holding Baby	J. Byers	Open	40.00	47.00
89-02-022	Newsboy with Bike	J. Byers	Closed	78.00	90.00
89-02-023	Girl with Hoop	J. Byers	Closed	44.00	50.00
89-02-024	Mother's Day (with Carriage)	J. Byers	3,000	75.00	200.00
90-02-025	Postman	J. Byers	Open	45.00	47.00
90-02-026	Parson	J. Byers	Open	44.00	46.00
90-02-027	Victorian Girl On Rocking Horse	J. Byers	Closed	70.00	125.00
91-02-028	Chimney Sweep (Child)	J. Byers	Open	50.00	50.00
91-02-029	Boy W/Tree	J. Byers	Open	49.00	49.00
92-02-030	Schoolteacher	J. Byers	Open	48.00	48.00
92-02-031	Victorian Mother With Toddler (Spr/Sum)	J. Byers	Open	60.00	60.00
92-02-031	Victorian Mother With Toddler (Fall/Win)	J. Byers	Open	60.00	60.00
93-02-032	Choir Director	J. Byers	Open	56.00	56.00
93-02-033	School Kids	J. Byers	Open	48.00	48.00
Byers' Choice Ltd.		**Santas**			
78-03-001	Old World Santa	J. Byers	Closed	33.00	250.00
78-03-002	Velvet Santa	J. Byers	Open	Unkn.	46.00
82-03-003	Santa in a Sleigh (1st Version)	J. Byers	Closed	46.00	800.00
83-03-004	Working Santa	J. Byers	Closed	38.00	60.00
84-03-005	Santa in Sleigh (2nd Version)	J. Byers	Closed	70.00	500.00
84-03-006	Mrs. Claus	J. Byers	Closed	38.00	60.00
86-03-007	Mrs. Claus on Rocker	J. Byers	Closed	73.00	400.00
86-03-008	Victorian Santa	J. Byers	Closed	39.00	175.00
87-03-009	Velvet Mrs. Claus	J. Byers	Open	44.00	44.00
88-03-010	Saint Nicholas	J. Byers	Closed	44.00	60.00
88-03-011	Knecht Ruprecht (Black Peter)	J. Byers	Closed	38.00	80.00
89-03-012	Russian Santa	J. Byers	Closed	85.00	150.00
90-03-013	Weihnachtsmann (German Santa)	J. Byers	Closed	56.00	75-200.00
91-03-014	Father Christmas	J. Byers	Closed	48.00	50.00
92-03-015	Mrs. Claus (2nd Version)	J. Byers	Open	50.00	50.00
92-03-016	Working Santa (2nd Version)	J. Byers	Open	52.00	52.00
93-03-017	Skating Santa	J. Byers	Open	60.00	60.00
Byers' Choice Ltd.		**Dickens Series**			
83-04-001	Scrooge (1st Edition)	J. Byers	Closed	36.00	1000-2000.
84-04-002	Mrs. Cratchit (1st Edition)	J. Byers	Closed	38.00	1000-1700.
84-04-003	Scrooge (2nd Edition)	J. Byers	Open	38.00	38.00
85-04-004	Mrs. Fezziwig (1st Edition)	J. Byers	Closed	43.00	500-650.
85-04-005	Mr. Fezziwig (1st Edition)	J. Byers	Closed	43.00	500-780.
85-04-006	Mrs. Cratchit (2nd Edition)	J. Byers	Open	39.00	39.00
86-04-007	Marley's Ghost (1st Edition)	J. Byers	Closed	40.00	300-500.
86-04-008	Mrs. Fezziwig (2nd Edition)	J. Byers	Closed	43.00	150-300.
86-04-009	Mr. Fezziwig (2nd Edition)	J. Byers	Closed	43.00	150-300.
87-04-010	Spirit of Christmas Past (1st Edition)	J. Byers	Closed	42.00	250.00
87-04-011	Marley's Ghost (2nd Edition)	J. Byers	Closed	42.00	75.00
88-04-012	Spirit of Christmas Present (1st Edition)	J. Byers	Closed	44.00	150-175.
88-04-013	Spirit of Christmas Past (2nd Edition)	J. Byers	Closed	46.00	125.00
89-04-014	Spirit of Christmas Future (1st Edition)	J. Byers	Closed	46.00	150.00
89-04-015	Spirit of Christmas Present (2nd Edition)	J. Byers	Closed	48.00	125.00
90-04-016	Bob Cratchit & Tiny Tim (1st Edition)	J. Byers	Closed	84.00	125.00
90-04-017	Spirit of Christmas Future (2nd Edition)	J. Byers	Closed	48.00	125.00
91-04-018	Happy Scrooge (1st Edition)	J. Byers	Closed	50.00	125.00
91-04-019	Bob Cratchit & Tiny Tim (2nd Edition)	J. Byers	Open	86.00	86.00
92-04-020	Happy Scrooge (2nd Edition)	J. Byers	Closed	50.00	65.00
Byers' Choice Ltd.		**Musicians**			
83-05-001	Violin Player Man (1st Version)	J. Byers	Closed	38.00	800.00
84-05-002	Violin Player Man (2nd Version)	J. Byers	Closed	38.00	1500.00
85-05-003	Horn Player, chubby face	J. Byers	Closed	37.00	900.00
85-05-004	Horn Player	J. Byers	Closed	38.00	450.00
86-05-005	Victorian Girl with Violin	J. Byers	Closed	39.00	175.00
89-05-006	Musician with Clarinet	J. Byers	Closed	44.00	300-350.
90-05-007	Musician With Mandolin	J. Byers	Closed	46.00	125-200.
91-05-008	Musician with Accordian	J. Byers	Closed	48.00	125-150.
91-05-009	Boy W/Mandolin	J. Byers	Closed	48.00	185.00
92-05-010	Musician With French Horn	J. Byers	Closed	52.00	60.00
Byers' Choice Ltd.		**Nativity**			
87-06-001	Black Angel	J. Byers	Closed	36.00	125.00
87-06-002	Angel-Great Star (Blonde)	J. Byers	Closed	40.00	100.00
87-06-003	Angel-Great Star (Brunette)	J. Byers	Closed	40.00	75.00
87-06-004	Angel-Great Star (Red Head)	J. Byers	Closed	40.00	75.00
88-06-005	Shepherds	J. Byers	Closed	37.00	65.00
89-06-006	King Gasper	J. Byers	Closed	40.00	65.00
89-06-007	King Melchior	J. Byers	Closed	40.00	65.00
89-06-008	King Balthasar	J. Byers	Closed	40.00	65.00
90-06-009	Holy Family	J. Byers	Closed	90.00	145.00
Byers' Choice Ltd.		**Display Figures**			
81-07-001	Display Man	J. Byers	Closed	Unkn.	2000.00
81-07-002	Display Lady	J. Byers	Closed	Unkn.	2000.00
82-07-003	Display Drummer Boy-1st	J. Byers	Closed	96.00	600.00
85-07-004	Display Drummer Boy-2nd	J. Byers	Closed	160.00	300.00
82-07-005	Display Santa	J. Byers	Closed	96.00	600.00
83-07-006	Display Carolers	J. Byers	Closed	200.00	500.00
84-07-007	Display Working Santa	J. Byers	Closed	260.00	400.00
85-07-008	Display Old World Santa	J. Byers	Closed	260.00	500.00
85-07-009	Display Children	J. Byers	Closed	140.00	500.00
86-07-010	Display Adults	J. Byers	Closed	170.00	500.00
87-07-011	Mechanical Boy W/ Drum	J. Byers	Closed	N/A	N/A
90-07-012	Display Santa-red	J. Byers	Closed	250.00	300.00
90-07-013	Display Santa-bayberry	J. Byers	Closed	250.00	300.00
Byers' Choice Ltd.		**Cries Of London**			
91-08-001	Apple Lady	J. Byers	Closed	80.00	375-500.
92-08-002	Baker	J. Byers	Closed	62.00	62.00
93-08-003	Chestnut Roaster	J. Byers	Yr.Iss.	64.00	64.00
Byers' Choice Ltd.		**Skaters**			
91-09-001	Adult Skaters	J. Byers	Open	50.00	50.00
92-09-002	Children Skaters	J. Byers	Open	50.00	50.00
93-09-003	Grandparent Skaters	J. Byers	Open	50.00	50.00
93-09-004	Boy Skater on Log	J. Byers	Open	55.00	55.00
Byers' Choice Ltd.		**Lil' Dickens**			
92-10-001	Shovel	J. Byers	Open	17.00	19.00

Company		Series			
Number	**Name**	**Artist**	**Edition Limit**	**Issue Price**	**Quote**
92-10-002	Snowball (lg.)	J. Byers	Open	17.00	19.00
92-10-003	Sled	J. Byers	Open	17.00	19.00
93-10-004	Package	J. Byers	Open	18.50	18.50
93-10-005	Gingerbread Boy	J. Byers	Open	18.50	18.50
93-10-006	Teddy Bear	J. Byers	Open	18.50	18.50
Byers' Choice Ltd.		**Salvation Army Band**			
92-11-001	Woman With Kettle	J. Byers	Open	64.00	64.00
93-11-002	Man With Cornet	J. Byers	Open	54.00	54.00
Byers' Choice Ltd.		**The Nutcracker**			
93-12-001	Marie(1st Edition)	J. Byers	Yr.Iss.	52.00	52.00
Byers' Choice Ltd.		**Children of The World**			
92-13-001	Dutch Boy	J. Byers	Yr.Iss.	50.00	50.00
92-13-002	Dutch Girl	J. Byers	Yr.Iss.	50.00	50.00
93-13-003	Bavarian Boy	J. Byers	Yr.Iss.	50.00	50.00
Byers' Choice Ltd.		**Wayside Country Store Exclusives**			
86-14-001	Colonial Lamplighter s/n	J. Byers	600	46.00	500.00
87-14-002	Colonial Watchman s/n	J. Byers	600	49.00	400.00
88-14-003	Colonial Lady s/n	J. Byers	600	49.00	350.00
Byers' Choice Ltd.		**Snow Goose Exclusive**			
88-15-001	Man with Goose	J. Byers	600	60.00	350.00
Byers' Choice Ltd.		**Country Christmas Store Exclusive**			
88-16-001	Toymaker	J. Byers	600	59.00	500.00
Byers' Choice Ltd.		**Woodstock Inn Exclusives**			
87-17-001	Skier Boy	J. Byers	200	40.00	400.00
87-17-002	Skier Girl	J. Byers	200	40.00	400.00
88-17-003	Woodstock Lady	J. Byers	N/A	41.00	250.00
88-17-004	Woodstock Man	J. Byers	N/A	41.00	250.00
88-17-005	Sugarin Kids (Woodstock)	J. Byers	N/A	41.00	300.00
Byers' Choice Ltd.		**Stacy's Gifts & Collectibles Exclusives**			
87-18-001	Santa in Rocking Chair with Boy	J. Byers	100	130.00	550.00
87-18-002	Santa in Rocking Chair with Girl	J. Byers	100	130.00	450.00
Byers' Choice Ltd.		**Port-O-Call Exclusives**			
87-19-001	Cherub Angel-pink	J. Byers	Closed	N/A	N/A
87-19-001	Cherub Angel-rose	J. Byers	Closed	N/A	N/A
87-19-001	Cherub Angel-blue	J. Byers	Closed	N/A	N/A
Cast Art Industries		**Dreamsicles Cherubs**			
92-01-001	Logo Piece-pink-DC001	K. Haynes	Open	33.00	33.00
92-01-002	Logo Piece-blue-DC002	K. Haynes	Open	33.00	33.00
92-01-003	Cherub and Child-DC100	K. Haynes	Open	15.00	15.00
92-01-004	Sitting Pretty-DC101	K. Haynes	Open	10.00	10.00
92-01-005	Forever Friends-DC102	K. Haynes	Open	15.00	15.00
92-01-006	Best Pals-DC103	K. Haynes	Open	15.00	15.00
92-01-007	Mischief Maker-DC105	K. Haynes	Open	10.00	10.00
92-01-008	Heavenly Dreamer-DC106	K. Haynes	Open	11.00	11.00
92-01-009	Wildflower-DC107	K. Haynes	Open	11.00	11.00
92-01-010	Bright Eyes-DC108	K. Haynes	Open	10.00	10.00
92-01-011	Forever Yours-DC110	K. Haynes	10,000	50.00	50.00
92-01-012	Limited Edtion Cherub-DC111	K. Haynes	Retrd.	50.00	50.00
92-01-013	Cherub For All Seasons-DC114	K. Haynes	Open	50.00	50.00
92-01-014	Bluebird On My Shoulder-DC115	K. Haynes	Open	20.00	20.00
93-01-015	Me and My Shadow-DC116	K. Haynes	Open	20.00	20.00
92-01-016	Make A Wish-DC118	K. Haynes	Open	15.00	15.00
92-01-017	Life Is Good-DC119	K. Haynes	Open	11.00	11.00
93-01-018	Wishin' On A Star-DC120	K. Haynes	Open	11.00	11.00
92-01-019	My Prayer-DC121	K. Haynes	Open	15.00	15.00
92-01-020	Sleigh Ride-DC122	K. Haynes	Open	16.00	16.00
93-01-021	Teacher's Pet-DC124	K. Haynes	Open	12.00	12.00
93-01-022	Sweet Dreams-DC125	K. Haynes	Open	30.00	30.00
93-01-023	Long Fellow-DC126	K. Haynes	Open	25.00	25.00
93-01-024	Little Dickens-DC127	K. Haynes	Open	25.00	25.00
93-01-025	Bookends-DC128	K. Haynes	Open	48.00	48.00
93-01-026	Thinking Of You-DC129	K. Haynes	Open	45.00	45.00
92-01-027	Dance Ballerina Dance-DC140	K. Haynes	Open	39.00	39.00
92-01-028	Bundle Of Joy-DC142	K. Haynes	Open	7.50	7.50
92-01-029	Littlest Angel-DC143	K. Haynes	Open	7.50	7.50
92-01-030	Dream A Little Dream-DC144	K. Haynes	Open	7.50	7.50
92-01-031	A Child's Prayer-DC145	K. Haynes	Open	7.50	7.50
92-01-032	Little Darlin'-DC146	K. Haynes	Open	7.50	7.50
92-01-033	Baby Love-DC147	K. Haynes	Open	7.50	7.50
93-01-034	Tiny Dancer-DC165	K. Haynes	Open	15.00	15.00
93-01-035	Catch A Falling Star-DC166	K. Haynes	Open	13.00	13.00
92-01-036	My Funny Valentine-DC201	K. Haynes	Open	17.00	17.00
92-01-037	Cupid's Bow-DC202	K. Haynes	Open	27.00	27.00
93-01-038	P.S. I Love You-DC203	K. Haynes	Open	8.00	8.00
93-01-039	Handful of Hearts-DC204	K. Haynes	Open	8.00	8.00
92-01-040	Caroler-Center Scroll-DC216	K. Haynes	Open	19.00	19.00
92-01-041	Caroler-Right Scroll-DC217	K. Haynes	Open	19.00	19.00
92-01-042	Caroler-Left Scroll-DC218	K. Haynes	Open	19.00	19.00
93-01-043	Flying Lesson Limited Edition-DC251	K. Haynes	10,000	80.00	80.00
Cast Art Industries		**Dreamsicles Christmas**			
92-02-001	Cherub and Child-DX100	K. Haynes	Open	16.00	16.00
92-02-002	Sitting Pretty-DX101	K. Haynes	Open	11.00	11.00
92-02-003	Forever Friends-DX102	K. Haynes	Open	16.00	16.00
92-02-004	Best Pals-DX103	K. Haynes	Open	16.00	16.00
92-02-005	Mischief Maker-DX105	K. Haynes	Open	11.00	11.00
92-02-006	Heavenly Dreamer-DX106	K. Haynes	Open	12.00	12.00
92-02-007	Wildflower-DX107	K. Haynes	Open	12.00	12.00
92-02-008	Bright Eyes-DX108	K. Haynes	Open	11.00	11.00
92-02-009	Forever Yours-DX110	K. Haynes	10,000	50.00	50.00
92-02-010	Bluebird On My Shoulder-DX115	K. Haynes	Open	21.00	21.00
93-02-011	Me and My Shadow-DX116	K. Haynes	Open	21.00	21.00
92-02-012	Make a Wish-DX118	K. Haynes	Open	16.00	16.00
92-02-013	Life is Good-DX119	K. Haynes	Open	12.00	12.00
93-02-014	Wishin' On a Star-DX120	K. Haynes	Open	12.00	12.00
92-02-015	My Prayer-DX121	K. Haynes	Open	16.00	16.00
92-02-016	Sleigh Ride-DX122	K. Haynes	Open	17.00	17.00
93-02-017	Teacher's Pet-DX124	K. Haynes	Open	13.00	13.00
93-02-018	Sweet Dreams-DX125	K. Haynes	Open	31.00	31.00
93-02-019	Long Fellow-DX126	K. Haynes	Open	26.00	26.00
93-02-020	Little Dickens-DX127	K. Haynes	Open	26.00	26.00
93-02-021	Thinking of You-DX129	K. Haynes	Open	46.00	46.00
92-02-022	Prancer-DX202	K. Haynes	Open	39.00	39.00

Company		Series			
Number	**Name**	**Artist**	**Edition Limit**	**Issue Price**	**Quote**
92-02-023	Santa Bunny-DX203	K. Haynes	Open	33.00	33.00
92-02-024	Here Comes Trouble-DX214	K. Haynes	Open	39.00	39.00
92-02-025	Caroler-Center Scroll-DX216	K. Haynes	Open	20.00	20.00
92-02-026	Caroler-Right Scroll-DX217	K. Haynes	Open	20.00	20.00
92-02-027	Caroler-Left Scroll-DX218	K. Haynes	Open	20.00	20.00
92-02-028	Santa's Elf-DX240	K. Haynes	Open	20.00	20.00
92-02-029	Little Drummer Boy-DX241	K. Haynes	Open	33.00	33.00
92-02-030	Jolly Old Santa-DX244	K. Haynes	Open	28.00	28.00
92-02-031	Here Comes Santa Claus-DX245	K. Haynes	Open	70.00	70.00
92-02-032	Santa In Dreamsicle Land-DX247	K. Haynes	Open	85.00	85.00
92-02-033	Snowman-DX252	K. Haynes	Open	11.00	11.00
92-02-034	Gathering Flowers-DX320	K. Haynes	Open	20.00	20.00
Cast Art Industries		**Dreamsicles**			
91-03-001	Hanging Cherub on Ribbon-5104	K. Haynes	Retrd.	10.00	10.00
91-03-002	Xmas Cherub on Ribbon-5104C	K. Haynes	Retrd.	10.50	10.50
91-03-003	Cherub Wall Plaque-5130	K. Haynes	Retrd.	15.00	15.00
91-03-004	Cherub Wall Plaque-5131	K. Haynes	Retrd.	15.00	15.00
91-03-005	Musician w/Trumpet-5151	K. Haynes	Retrd.	22.00	22.00
91-03-006	Musician w/Drums-5152	K. Haynes	Retrd.	22.00	22.00
91-03-007	Musician w/Flute-5153	K. Haynes	Retrd.	22.00	22.00
91-03-008	Musician w/Cymbals-5154	K. Haynes	Retrd.	22.00	22.00
91-03-009	Ballerina Box-5700	K. Haynes	Retrd.	9.00	9.00
91-03-010	"I Love You" Box-5701	K. Haynes	Retrd.	9.00	9.00
91-03-011	Bunny Box-5750	K. Haynes	Retrd.	14.00	14.00
91-03-012	Heart Cherub Box-5751	K. Haynes	Retrd.	14.00	14.00
91-03-013	Queen Cherub Box-5804	K. Haynes	Retrd.	26.00	26.00
Cast Art Industries		**Dreamsicles Animals**			
92-04-001	Mr. Bunny-DA107	K. Haynes	Open	27.00	27.00
92-04-002	Mrs. Bunny-DA108	K. Haynes	Open	27.00	27.00
92-04-003	Sir Hareold-DA123	K. Haynes	Open	39.00	39.00
92-04-004	King Rabbit-DA124	K. Haynes	Open	66.00	66.00
92-04-005	Witch-DA660	K. Haynes	Open	17.00	17.00
Cast Art Industries		**Animal Attraction**			
93-05-001	The Flasher-AA001	S.&G. Hackett	Open	32.00	32.00
93-05-002	Udderly Ridiculous-AA002	S.&G. Hackett	Open	28.00	28.00
93-05-003	Pigs in a Blanket-AA003	S.&G. Hackett	Open	11.00	11.00
93-05-004	Barnyard Shuffle-AA004	S.&G. Hackett	Open	15.00	15.00
93-05-005	Bar-B-Cutie-AA005	S.&G. Hackett	Open	15.00	15.00
93-05-006	Hog Heaven-AA006	S.&G. Hackett	Open	28.00	28.00
93-05-007	Punker Pig-AA007	S.&G. Hackett	Open	11.00	11.00
93-05-008	V. I. Pig-AA008	S.&G. Hackett	Open	11.00	11.00
93-05-009	Bacon in the Sun-AA009	S.&G. Hackett	Open	15.00	15.00
93-05-010	Unexpected Guest-AA010	S.&G. Hackett	Open	17.00	17.00
93-05-011	Honey Bear Blues-AA011	S.&G. Hackett	Open	23.00	23.00
93-05-012	Bear Hug-AA012	S.&G. Hackett	Open	26.00	26.00
93-05-013	Expecting-AA013	S.&G. Hackett	Open	16.50	16.50
93-05-014	Papa's Turn-AA014	S.&G. Hackett	Open	28.00	28.00
93-05-015	Undelivered Mail-AA015	S.&G. Hackett	Open	15.00	15.00
93-05-016	Feeding Time-AA016	S.&G. Hackett	Open	10.00	10.00
93-05-017	Pigrobics-AA017	S.&G. Hackett	Open	15.00	15.00
Cast Art Industries		**Story Time Treasures**			
93-06-001	Three Little Pigs ST001	S.&G. Hackett	Open	28.00	28.00
93-06-002	Goldilocks and the Three Bears ST002	S.&G. Hackett	Open	36.00	36.00
93-06-003	Puff the Magic Dragon ST003	S.&G. Hackett	Open	50.00	50.00
93-06-004	Peter Rabbit ST004	S.&G. Hackett	Open	28.00	28.00
93-06-005	The Frog Prince ST005	S.&G. Hackett	Open	28.00	28.00
93-06-006	Little Red Riding Hood ST006	S.&G. Hackett	Open	28.00	28.00
Cast Art Industries		**Cuckoo Corners**			
93-07-001	Duck Soup CC001	K. Haynes	Open	33.00	33.00
93-07-002	Let's Play Doctor CC002	K. Haynes	Open	27.00	27.00
93-07-003	Impractical Nurse CC003	K. Haynes	Open	27.00	27.00
93-07-004	King of the Road CC004	K. Haynes	Open	33.00	33.00
93-07-005	Ground Stroke CC010	K. Haynes	Open	28.00	28.00
93-07-006	Double Fault CC011	K. Haynes	Open	28.00	28.00
93-07-007	Hooked Again CC021	K. Haynes	Open	33.00	33.00
93-07-008	Fore! CC031	K. Haynes	Open	33.00	33.00
93-07-009	Teed Off CC032	K. Haynes	Open	28.00	28.00
93-07-010	Laides' Day CC033	K. Haynes	Open	28.00	28.00
93-07-011	Mr. Bigtop CC041	K. Haynes	Open	40.00	40.00
93-07-012	Mr. Greasepaint CC042	K. Haynes	Open	40.00	40.00
93-07-013	Circus Left Town CC043	K. Haynes	Open	33.00	33.00
93-07-014	Merry Widow CC050	K. Haynes	Open	33.00	33.00
93-07-015	Hens' Teeth CC051	K. Haynes	Open	35.00	35.00
93-07-016	Sailor Boy CC060	K. Haynes	Open	22.00	22.00
93-07-017	Playmates CC061	K. Haynes	Open	22.00	22.00
93-07-018	Flower Child CC062	K. Haynes	Open	27.00	27.00
93-07-019	Sassy CC063	K. Haynes	Open	22.00	22.00
93-07-020	Lucky Duck CC064	K. Haynes	Open	27.00	27.00
93-07-021	Rug Rat CC070	K. Haynes	Open	16.50	16.50
93-07-022	Time for A Change CC071	K. Haynes	Open	16.50	16.50
93-07-023	Midnight Feeding CC072	K. Haynes	Open	16.50	16.50
93-07-024	Temper Tantrum CC073	K. Haynes	Open	16.50	16.50
93-07-025	Pacified CC074	K. Haynes	Open	16.50	16.50
93-07-026	Beddy Bye CC075	K. Haynes	Open	16.50	16.50
The Cat's Meow		**Series I**			
83-01-001	Federal House	F. Jones	Retrd.	8.00	75-100.00
83-01-002	Inn	F. Jones	Retrd.	8.00	56-200.00
83-01-003	Garrison House	F. Jones	Retrd.	8.00	60-95.00
83-01-004	Victorian House	F. Jones	Retrd.	8.00	35-75.00
83-01-005	School	F. Jones	Retrd.	8.00	50-100.00
83-01-006	Barbershop	F. Jones	Retrd.	8.00	50-130.00
83-01-007	Sweetshop	F. Jones	Retrd.	8.00	75-130.00
83-01-008	Book Store	F. Jones	Retrd.	8.00	50-130.00
83-01-009	Antique Shop	F. Jones	Retrd.	8.00	50-100.00
83-01-010	Florist Shop	F. Jones	Retrd.	8.00	75-130.00
83-01-011	Toy Shoppe	F. Jones	Retrd.	8.00	75-130.00
83-01-012	Apothecary	F. Jones	Retrd.	8.00	35-130.00
83-01-013	Set	F. Jones	Retrd.	96.00	850-3200.
The Cat's Meow		**Series II**			
84-02-001	Grandinere House	F. Jones	Retrd.	8.00	50-80.00
84-02-002	Brocke House	F. Jones	Retrd.	8.00	50-80.00
84-02-003	Eaton House	F. Jones	Retrd.	8.00	50-80.00
84-02-004	Church	F. Jones	Retrd.	8.00	50-150.00
84-02-005	Town Hall	F. Jones	Retrd.	8.00	50-150.00
84-02-006	Music Shop	F. Jones	Retrd.	8.00	50-150.00
84-02-007	Attorney/Bank	F. Jones	Retrd.	8.00	50-80.00

Company / Number	Name	Series / Artist	Edition Limit	Issue Price	Quote
84-02-008	S&T Clothiers	F. Jones	Retrd.	8.00	50-80.00
84-02-009	Millinery/Quilt	F. Jones	Retrd.	8.00	50-150.00
84-02-010	Tobacconist/Shoemaker	F. Jones	Retrd.	8.00	50-80.00
84-02-011	Set	F. Jones	Retrd.	96.00	600-2000.
The Cat's Meow		**Series III**			
85-03-001	Hobart-Harley House	F. Jones	Retrd.	8.00	20-56.00
85-03-002	Kalorama Guest House	F. Jones	Retrd.	8.00	20-56.00
85-03-003	Allen-Coe House	F. Jones	Retrd.	8.00	20-56.00
85-03-004	Opera House	F. Jones	Retrd.	8.00	20-56.00
85-03-005	Connecticut Ave. FireHouse	F. Jones	Retrd.	8.00	20-56.00
85-03-006	Dry Goods Store	F. Jones	Retrd.	8.00	20-56.00
85-03-007	Fine Jewelers	F. Jones	Retrd.	8.00	20-56.00
85-03-008	Edinburgh Times	F. Jones	Retrd.	8.00	20-56.00
85-03-009	Main St. Carriage Shop	F. Jones	Retrd.	8.00	20-56.00
85-03-010	Ristorante	F. Jones	Retrd.	8.00	20-56.00
85-03-011	Set	F. Jones	Retrd.	80.00	560.00
The Cat's Meow		**Series IV**			
86-04-001	John Belville House	F. Jones	Retrd.	8.00	14-27.00
86-04-002	Westbrook House	F. Jones	Retrd.	8.00	14-27.00
86-04-003	Bennington-Hull House	F. Jones	Retrd.	8.00	14-27.00
86-04-004	Vandenberg House	F. Jones	Retrd.	8.00	14-27.00
86-04-005	Chepachet Union Church	F. Jones	Retrd.	8.00	14-27.00
86-04-006	Chagrin Falls Popcorn Shop	F. Jones	Retrd.	8.00	14-27.00
86-04-007	O'Malley's Livery Stable	F. Jones	Retrd.	8.00	14-27.00
86-04-008	The Little House Giftables	F. Jones	Retrd.	8.00	14-27.00
86-04-009	Jones Bros. Tea Co.	F. Jones	Retrd.	8.00	14-27.00
86-04-010	Village Clock Shop	F. Jones	Retrd.	8.00	14-27.00
86-04-011	Set	F. Jones	Retrd.	80.00	270.00
The Cat's Meow		**Series V**			
87-05-001	Murray Hotel	F. Jones	Retrd.	8.00	16-18.00
87-05-002	Congruity Tavern	F. Jones	Retrd.	8.00	16-18.00
87-05-003	M. Washington House	F. Jones	Retrd.	8.00	16-18.00
87-05-004	Creole House	F. Jones	Retrd.	8.00	16-18.00
87-05-005	Police Department	F. Jones	Retrd.	8.00	16-18.00
87-05-006	Markethouse	F. Jones	Retrd.	8.00	16-18.00
87-05-007	Southport Bank	F. Jones	Retrd.	8.00	16-18.00
87-05-008	Amish Oak/Dixie Shoe	F. Jones	Retrd.	8.00	16-18.00
87-05-009	Dentist/Physician	F. Jones	Retrd.	8.00	16-18.00
87-05-010	Architect/Tailor	F. Jones	Retrd.	8.00	16-18.00
87-05-011	Set	F. Jones	Retrd.	80.00	180.00
The Cat's Meow		**Series VI**			
88-06-001	Burton Lancaster House	F. Jones	Open	8.00	9.00
88-06-002	Ohliger House	F. Jones	Open	8.00	9.00
88-06-003	Stiffenbody Funeral Home	F. Jones	Open	8.00	9.00
88-06-004	Pruyn House	F. Jones	Open	8.00	9.00
88-06-005	First Baptist Church	F. Jones	Open	8.00	9.00
88-06-006	City Hospital	F. Jones	Open	8.00	9.00
88-06-007	Lincoln School	F. Jones	Open	8.00	9.00
88-06-008	Fish/Meat Market	F. Jones	Open	8.00	9.00
88-06-009	New Masters Gallery	F. Jones	Open	8.00	9.00
88-06-010	Williams & Sons	F. Jones	Open	8.00	9.00
The Cat's Meow		**Series VII**			
89-07-001	Thorpe House Bed & Breakfast	F. Jones	Open	8.00	9.00
89-07-002	Justice of the Peace	F. Jones	Open	8.00	9.00
89-07-003	Old Franklin Book Shop	F. Jones	Open	8.00	9.00
89-07-004	Octagonal School	F. Jones	Open	8.00	9.00
89-07-005	Winkler Bakery	F. Jones	Open	8.00	9.00
89-07-006	Black Cat Antiques	F. Jones	Open	8.00	9.00
89-07-007	Village Tinsmith	F. Jones	Open	8.00	9.00
89-07-008	Williams Apothecary	F. Jones	Open	8.00	9.00
89-07-009	Handcrafted Toys	F. Jones	Open	8.00	9.00
89-07-010	Hairdressing Parlor	F. Jones	Open	8.00	9.00
The Cat's Meow		**Series VIII**			
90-08-001	Puritan House	F. Jones	Open	8.00	9.00
90-08-002	Haberdashers	F. Jones	Open	8.00	9.00
90-08-003	Walldorff Furniture	F. Jones	Open	8.00	9.00
90-08-004	Victoria's Parlour	F. Jones	Open	8.00	9.00
90-08-005	Globe Corner Bookstore	F. Jones	Open	8.00	9.00
90-08-006	Medina Fire Department	F. Jones	Open	8.00	9.00
90-08-007	Piccadilli Pipe & Tobacco	F. Jones	Open	8.00	9.00
90-08-008	Noah's Ark Veterinary	F. Jones	Open	8.00	9.00
90-08-009	F.J. Realty Company	F. Jones	Open	8.00	9.00
90-08-010	Nell's Stems & Stitches	F. Jones	Open	8.00	9.00
The Cat's Meow		**Series IX**			
91-09-001	Central City Opera House	F. Jones	Open	8.00	9.00
91-09-002	All Saints Chapel	F. Jones	Open	8.00	9.00
91-09-003	City Hall	F. Jones	Open	8.00	9.00
91-09-004	Gov. Snyder Mansion	F. Jones	Open	8.00	9.00
91-09-005	American Red Cross	F. Jones	Open	8.00	9.00
91-09-006	The Treble Clef	F. Jones	Open	8.00	9.00
91-09-007	Osbahr's Upholstery	F. Jones	Open	8.00	9.00
91-09-008	Spanky's Hardware Co.	F. Jones	Open	8.00	9.00
91-09-009	CPA/Law Office	F. Jones	Open	8.00	9.00
91-09-010	Jeweler/Optometrist	F. Jones	Open	8.00	9.00
The Cat's Meow		**Series X**			
92-10-001	Henyan's Athletic Shop	F. Jones	Open	8.50	9.00
92-10-002	Grand Haven	F. Jones	Open	8.50	9.00
92-10-003	Fudge Kitchen	F. Jones	Open	8.50	9.00
92-10-004	United Church of Acworth	F. Jones	Open	8.50	9.00
92-10-005	City News	F. Jones	Open	8.50	9.00
92-10-006	Pure Gas Station	F. Jones	Open	8.50	9.00
92-10-007	Pickles Pub	F. Jones	Open	8.50	9.00
92-10-008	Madeline's Dress Shop	F. Jones	Open	8.50	9.00
92-10-009	Owl And The Pussycat	F. Jones	Open	8.50	9.00
92-10-010	Leppert's 5 &10¢	F. Jones	Open	8.50	9.00
The Cat's Meow		**Series XI**			
93-11-001	Shrimplin & Jones Produce	F. Jones	Open	9.00	9.00
93-11-002	Johann Singer Boots & Shoes	F. Jones	Open	9.00	9.00
93-11-003	Haddonfield Bank	F. Jones	Open	9.00	9.00
93-11-004	Stone's Restaurant	F. Jones	Open	9.00	9.00
93-11-005	U.S. Post Office	F. Jones	Open	9.00	9.00
93-11-006	Police-Troop C	F. Jones	Open	9.00	9.00
93-11-007	Immanuel Church	F. Jones	Open	9.00	9.00
93-11-008	Barbershop/Gallery	F. Jones	Open	9.00	9.00

Company / Number	Name	Series / Artist	Edition Limit	Issue Price	Quote
93-11-009	U.S. Armed Forces	F. Jones	Open	9.00	9.00
93-11-010	Pet Shop/Gift Shop	F. Jones	Open	9.00	9.00
The Cat's Meow		**Roscoe Village**			
86-12-001	Roscoe General Store	F. Jones	Retrd.	8.00	16-33.00
86-12-002	Jackson Twp. Hall	F. Jones	Retrd.	8.00	16-33.00
86-12-003	Old Warehouse Rest.	F. Jones	Retrd.	8.00	16-33.00
86-12-004	Canal Company	F. Jones	Retrd.	8.00	16-33.00
The Cat's Meow		**Fall**			
86-13-001	Mail Pouch Barn	F. Jones	Retrd.	8.00	16-50.00
86-13-002	Vollant Mills	F. Jones	Retrd.	8.00	16-33.00
86-13-003	Grimm's Farmhouse	F. Jones	Retrd.	8.00	16-33.00
86-13-004	Golden Lamb Buttery	F. Jones	Retrd.	8.00	16-33.00
The Cat's Meow		**Nautical**			
87-14-001	Monhegan Boat Landing	F. Jones	Retrd.	8.00	16-19.00
87-14-002	Lorain Lighthouse	F. Jones	Retrd.	8.00	16-19.00
87-14-003	Yacht Club	F. Jones	Retrd.	8.00	16-19.00
87-14-004	H & E Ships Chandlery	F. Jones	Retrd.	8.00	16-19.00
The Cat's Meow		**Main St.**			
87-15-001	Historical Museum	F. Jones	Retrd.	8.00	16-19.00
87-15-002	Franklin Library	F. Jones	Retrd.	8.00	16-19.00
87-15-003	Garden Theatre	F. Jones	Retrd.	8.00	16-19.00
87-15-004	Telegraph/Post Office	F. Jones	Retrd.	8.00	16-19.00
The Cat's Meow		**Nantucket**			
87-16-001	Nantucket Atheneum	F. Jones	Retrd.	8.00	16-19.00
87-16-002	Unitarian Church	F. Jones	Retrd.	8.00	16-19.00
87-16-003	Maria Mitchell House	F. Jones	Retrd.	8.00	16-19.00
87-16-004	Jared Coffin House	F. Jones	Retrd.	8.00	16-19.00
The Cat's Meow		**Hagerstown**			
88-17-001	The Yule Cupboard	F. Jones	Open	8.00	9.00
88-17-002	J Hager House	F. Jones	Open	8.00	9.00
88-17-003	Miller House	F. Jones	Open	8.00	9.00
88-17-004	Woman's Club	F. Jones	Open	8.00	9.00
The Cat's Meow		**Tradesman**			
88-18-001	Hermannhof Winery	F. Jones	Open	8.00	9.00
88-18-002	Jenney Grist Mill	F. Jones	Open	8.00	9.00
88-18-003	Buckeye Candy & Tobacco	F. Jones	Open	8.00	9.00
88-18-004	C.O. Wheel Company	F. Jones	Open	8.00	9.00
The Cat's Meow		**Liberty St.**			
88-19-001	County Courthouse	F. Jones	Open	8.00	9.00
88-19-002	Wilton Railway Depot	F. Jones	Open	8.00	9.00
88-19-003	Graf Printing Co.	F. Jones	Open	8.00	9.00
88-19-004	Z. Jones Basketmaker	F. Jones	Open	8.00	9.00
The Cat's Meow		**Painted Ladies**			
88-20-001	Lady Elizabeth	F. Jones	Open	8.00	9.00
88-20-002	Lady Iris	F. Jones	Open	8.00	9.00
88-20-003	Lady Amanda	F. Jones	Open	8.00	9.00
88-20-004	Andrews Hotel	F. Jones	Open	8.00	9.00
The Cat's Meow		**Wild West**			
89-21-001	F.C. Zimmermann's Gun Shop	F. Jones	Open	8.00	9.00
89-21-002	Drink 'em up Saloon	F. Jones	Open	8.00	9.00
89-21-003	Wells, Fargo & Co.	F. Jones	Open	8.00	9.00
89-21-004	Marshal's Office	F. Jones	Open	8.00	9.00
The Cat's Meow		**Market St.**			
89-22-001	Schumacher Mills	F. Jones	Open	8.00	9.00
89-22-002	Seville Hardware Store	F. Jones	Open	8.00	9.00
89-22-003	West India Goods Store	F. Jones	Open	8.00	9.00
89-22-004	Yankee Candle Company	F. Jones	Open	8.00	9.00
The Cat's Meow		**Lighthouse**			
90-23-001	Split Rock Lighthouse	F. Jones	Open	8.00	9.00
90-23-002	Cape Hatteras Lighthouse	F. Jones	Open	8.00	9.00
90-23-003	Sandy Hook Lighthouse	F. Jones	Open	8.00	9.00
90-23-004	Admiralty Head	F. Jones	Open	8.00	9.00
The Cat's Meow		**Ohio Amish**			
91-24-001	Jonas Troyer Home	F. Jones	Open	8.00	9.00
91-24-002	Ada Mae's Quilt Barn	F. Jones	Open	8.00	9.00
91-24-003	Eli's Harness Shop	F. Jones	Open	8.00	9.00
91-24-004	Brown School	F. Jones	Open	8.00	9.00
The Cat's Meow		**Washington, D.C.**			
91-25-001	U.S. Capitol	F. Jones	Open	8.00	9.00
91-25-002	White House	F. Jones	Open	8.00	9.00
91-25-003	National Archives	F. Jones	Open	8.00	9.00
91-25-004	U.S. Supreme Court	F. Jones	Open	8.00	9.00
The Cat's Meow		**American Barns**			
92-26-001	Ohio Barn	F. Jones	Open	8.50	9.00
92-26-002	Bank Barn	F. Jones	Open	8.50	9.00
92-26-003	Crib Barn	F. Jones	Open	8.50	9.00
92-26-004	Vermont Barn	F. Jones	Open	8.50	9.00
The Cat's Meow		**Chippewa Amusement Park**			
93-27-001	Pavilion	F. Jones	Open	9.00	9.00
93-27-002	Midway	F. Jones	Open	9.00	9.00
93-27-003	Bath House	F. Jones	Open	9.00	9.00
93-27-004	Ballroom	F. Jones	Open	9.00	9.00
The Cat's Meow		**Accessories**			
83-28-001	Summer Tree	F. Jones	Retrd.	4.00	30-46.00
83-28-002	Fall Tree	F. Jones	Retrd.	4.00	27-46.00
83-28-003	Pine Tree	F. Jones	Retrd.	4.00	26-35.00
83-28-004	XMas Pine Tree	F. Jones	Retrd.	4.00	27-35.00
83-28-005	XMas Pine Tree w/Red Bows	F. Jones	Retrd.	3.00	100-175.
84-28-006	8" Picket Fence	F. Jones	Retrd.	3.25	35-50.00
84-28-007	5" Hedge	F. Jones	Retrd.	3.00	25-45.00
84-28-008	8" Hedge	F. Jones	Retrd.	3.25	35-50.00
84-28-009	Gas Light	F. Jones	Open	3.25	4.10
84-28-010	Dairy Wagon	F. Jones	Retrd.	4.00	9.00
84-28-011	Horse & Carriage	F. Jones	Retrd.	4.00	9.00
85-28-012	Lilac Bushes	F. Jones	Retrd.	3.00	125-200.
85-28-013	Telephone Booth	F. Jones	Open	3.00	4.10

Company Number	Name	Series Artist	Edition Limit	Issue Price	Quote
85-28-014	FJ Real Estate Sign	F. Jones	Retrd.	3.00	8-13.00
85-28-015	U.S. Flag	F. Jones	Open	3.25	4.10
85-28-016	Chickens	F. Jones	Retrd.	3.25	9-15.00
85-28-017	Ducks	F. Jones	Retrd.	3.25	9-12.00
85-28-018	Cows	F. Jones	Retrd.	4.00	11-15.00
85-28-019	Main St. Sign	F. Jones	Open	3.25	4.10
85-28-020	Flower Pots	F. Jones	Open	3.00	4.10
86-28-021	Carolers	F. Jones	Retrd.	4.00	8-12.00
86-28-022	5" Iron Fence	F. Jones	Retrd.	3.00	45-50.00
86-28-023	8" Iron Fence	F. Jones	Retrd.	3.25	46-50.00
86-28-024	Wishing Well	F. Jones	Retrd.	3.25	9.00
86-28-025	Skipjacks	F. Jones	Open	6.50	6.50
86-28-026	Ice Wagon	F. Jones	Retrd.	4.00	9.00
86-28-027	Mail Wagon	F. Jones	Open	4.00	4.10
86-28-028	Iron Gate	F. Jones	Retrd.	3.00	55-65.00
86-28-029	Poplar Tree	F. Jones	Retrd.	4.00	35-46.00
86-28-030	Street Clock	F. Jones	Open	3.25	4.10
86-28-031	Cherry Tree	F. Jones	Retrd.	4.00	35-100.00
87-28-032	Wooden Gate	F. Jones	Retrd.	3.00	35-40.00
87-28-033	Band Stand	F. Jones	Retrd.	6.50	14.00
87-28-034	Horse & Sleigh	F. Jones	Retrd.	4.00	9.00
87-28-035	5" Picket Fence	F. Jones	Retrd.	3.00	5-35.00
87-28-036	FJ Express	F. Jones	Retrd.	4.00	9.00
87-28-037	Liberty St. Sign	F. Jones	Retrd.	3.25	5.00-9.00
87-28-038	Railroad Sign	F. Jones	Retrd.	3.00	7.00
87-28-039	Windmill	F. Jones	Retrd.	3.25	7.00
87-28-040	Cable Car	F. Jones	Retrd.	4.00	9.00
87-28-041	Butch & T.J.	F. Jones	Retrd.	4.00	9.00
87-28-042	Charlie & Co.	F. Jones	Retrd.	4.00	9.00
87-28-043	Nanny	F. Jones	Retrd.	4.00	9.00
88-28-044	Ada Belle	F. Jones	Open	4.00	4.10
88-28-045	Colonial Bread Wagon	F. Jones	Open	4.00	4.10
89-28-046	Pony Express Rider	F. Jones	Open	4.00	4.10
89-28-047	Wells, Fargo Wagon	F. Jones	Retrd.	4.00	9.00-12.00
89-28-048	Market St. Sign	F. Jones	Retrd.	3.25	8.00-9.00
89-28-049	Passenger Train Car	F. Jones	Open	4.00	4.10
89-28-050	Harry's Hotdogs	F. Jones	Open	4.00	4.10
89-28-051	Clothesline	F. Jones	Open	4.00	4.10
89-28-052	Touring Car	F. Jones	Retrd.	4.00	9.00
89-28-053	Pumpkin Wagon	F. Jones	Open	3.25	4.10
89-28-054	Rudy & Aldine	F. Jones	Open	4.00	4.10
89-28-055	Tad & Toni	F. Jones	Open	4.00	4.10
89-28-056	Snowmen	F. Jones	Open	4.00	4.10
89-28-057	Rose Trellis	F. Jones	Open	3.25	4.10
89-28-058	Quaker Oats Train Car	F. Jones	Open	4.00	4.10
90-28-059	Gerstenslager Buggy	F. Jones	Open	4.00	4.10
90-28-060	1914 Fire Pumper	F. Jones	Open	4.00	4.10
90-28-061	1913 Peerless Touring Car	F. Jones	Open	4.00	4.10
90-28-062	1909 Franklin Limousine	F. Jones	Open	4.00	4.10
90-28-063	Watkins Wagon	F. Jones	Open	4.00	4.10
90-28-064	Veterinary Wagon	F. Jones	Open	4.00	4.10
90-28-065	Amish Buggy	F. Jones	Open	4.00	4.10
90-28-066	Victorian Outhouse	F. Jones	Open	4.00	4.10
90-28-067	Bus Stop	F. Jones	Open	4.00	4.10
90-28-068	Eugene	F. Jones	Open	4.00	4.10
90-28-069	Christmas Tree Lot	F. Jones	Open	4.00	4.10
90-28-070	Santa & Reindeer	F. Jones	Open	4.00	4.10
90-28-071	5" Wrought Iron Fence	F. Jones	Open	3.00	4.10
90-28-072	Little Red Caboose	F. Jones	Open	4.00	4.10
90-28-073	Red Maple Tree	F. Jones	Open	4.00	4.10
90-28-074	Tulip Tree	F. Jones	Open	4.00	4.10
90-28-075	Blue Spruce	F. Jones	Open	4.00	4.10
90-28-076	XMas Spruce	F. Jones	Open	4.00	4.10
91-28-077	School Bus	F. Jones	Open	4.00	4.10
91-28-078	Popcorn Wagon	F. Jones	Open	4.00	4.10
91-28-079	Scarey Harry (Scarecrow)	F. Jones	Open	4.00	4.10
91-28-080	Amish Garden	F. Jones	Open	4.00	4.10
91-28-081	Chessie Hopper Car	F. Jones	Open	4.00	4.10
91-28-082	USMC War Memorial	F. Jones	Open	6.50	6.50
91-28-083	Village Entrance Sigh	F. Jones	Open	6.50	6.50
91-28-084	Concert in the Park	F. Jones	Open	4.00	4.10
91-28-085	Martin House	F. Jones	Open	3.25	4.10
91-28-086	Marble Game	F. Jones	Open	4.00	4.10
91-28-087	Barnyard	F. Jones	Open	4.00	4.10
91-28-088	Ski Party	F. Jones	Open	4.00	4.10
91-28-089	On Vacation	F. Jones	Open	4.00	4.10
91-28-090	Jack The Postman	F. Jones	Open	3.25	4.10
92-28-091	Forsythia Bush	F. Jones	Open	3.98	4.10
92-28-092	Police Car	F. Jones	Open	3.98	4.10
92-28-093	Delivery Truck	F. Jones	Open	3.98	4.10
92-28-094	School Crossing	F. Jones	Open	3.98	4.10
92-28-095	Mr. Softee Truck	F. Jones	Open	3.98	4.10
92-28-096	Gasoline Truck	F. Jones	Open	3.98	4.10
92-28-097	Silo	F. Jones	Open	3.98	4.10
92-28-098	Springhouse	F. Jones	Open	3.25	4.10
92-28-099	Nutcracker Billboard	F. Jones	Open	3.98	4.10
93-28-100	Jennie & George's Wedding	F. Jones	Open	4.00	4.00
93-28-101	Market Wagon	F. Jones	Open	4.00	4.00
93-28-102	Chippewa Lake Billboard	F. Jones	Open	4.00	4.00
93-28-103	Garden House	F. Jones	Open	3.25	3.25
93-28-104	Johnny Appleseed Statue	F. Jones	Open	4.00	4.00
93-28-105	Getting Directions	F. Jones	Open	4.00	4.00
93-28-106	Grape Arbor	F. Jones	Open	4.00	4.00
93-28-107	Rustic Fence	F. Jones	Open	4.00	4.00
93-28-108	Cannonball Express	F. Jones	Open	4.00	4.00
93-28-109	Little Marine	F. Jones	Open	4.00	4.00
The Cat's Meow		**Williamsburg Christmas**			
83-29-001	Christmas Church	F. Jones	Retrd.	6.00	N/A
83-29-002	Garrison House	F. Jones	Retrd.	6.00	N/A
83-29-003	Federal House	F. Jones	Retrd.	6.00	N/A
83-29-004	Georgian House	F. Jones	Retrd.	6.00	N/A
83-29-005	Set	F. Jones	Retrd	24.00	N/A
The Cat's Meow		**Nantucket Christmas**			
84-30-001	Powell House	F. Jones	Retrd.	6.50	N/A
84-30-002	Shaw House	F. Jones	Retrd.	6.50	N/A
84-30-003	Wintrop House	F. Jones	Retrd.	6.50	N/A
84-30-004	Christmas Shop	F. Jones	Retrd.	6.50	N/A
84-30-005	Set	F. Jones	Retrd.	26.00	400-1350.
The Cat's Meow		**Ohio Western Reserve Christmas**			
85-31-001	Western Reserve Academy	F. Jones	Retrd.	7.00	35-175.00
85-31-002	Olmstead House	F. Jones	Retrd.	7.00	35-175.00
85-31-003	Bellevue House	F. Jones	Retrd.	7.00	35-175.00
85-31-004	Gates Mills Church	F. Jones	Retrd.	7.00	35-175.00
85-31-005	Set	F. Jones	Retrd.	27.00	400-700.
The Cat's Meow		**Savannah Christmas**			
86-32-001	J.J. Dale Row House	F. Jones	Retrd.	7.25	150.00
86-32-002	Liberty Inn	F. Jones	Retrd.	7.25	150.00
86-32-003	Lafayette Square House	F. Jones	Retrd.	7.25	150.00
86-32-004	Simon Mirault Cottage	F. Jones	Retrd.	7.25	150.00
86-32-005	Set	F. Jones	Retrd.	29.00	475-1050.
The Cat's Meow		**Maine Christmas**			
87-33-001	Damariscotta Church	F. Jones	Retrd.	7.75	125.00
87-33-002	Portland Head Lighthouse	F. Jones	Retrd.	7.75	125-200.
87-33-003	Cappy's Chowder House	F. Jones	Retrd.	7.75	125.00
87-33-004	Captain's House	F. Jones	Retrd.	7.75	125.00
87-33-005	Set	F. Jones	Retrd.	31.00	750-1350
The Cat's Meow		**Philadelphia Christmas**			
88-34-001	Graff House	F. Jones	Retrd.	7.75	50-175.00
88-34-002	Hill-Physick-Keith House	F. Jones	Retrd.	7.75	85-175.00
88-34-003	Elfreth's Alley	F. Jones	Retrd.	7.75	75-175.00
88-34-004	The Head House	F. Jones	Retrd.	7.75	75-175.00
88-34-005	Set	F. Jones	Retrd.	31.00	350-600.
The Cat's Meow		**Christmas In New England**			
89-35-001	The Old South Meeting House	F. Jones	Retrd.	8.00	75-125.00
89-35-002	Hunter House	F. Jones	Retrd.	8.00	50-125.00
89-35-003	Sheldon's Tavern	F. Jones	Retrd.	8.00	55-125.00
89-35-004	The Vermont Country Store	F. Jones	Retrd.	8.00	55-125.00
89-35-005	Set	F. Jones	Retrd.	32.00	200-400.
The Cat's Meow		**Colonial Virginia Christmas**			
90-36-001	Rising Sun Tavern	F. Jones	Retrd.	8.00	25-35.00
90-36-002	St. John's Church	F. Jones	Retrd.	8.00	15-25.00
90-36-003	Dulany House	F. Jones	Retrd.	8.00	35.00
90-36-004	Shirley Plantation	F. Jones	Retrd.	8.00	25-35.00
90-36-005	Set	F. Jones	Retrd.	32.00	100-250.
The Cat's Meow		**Rocky Mountain Christmas**			
91-37-001	First Presbyterian Church	F. Jones	Retrd.	8.20	17-35.00
91-37-002	Tabor House	F. Jones	Retrd.	8.20	17-35.00
91-37-003	Western Hotel	F. Jones	Retrd.	8.20	17-35.00
91-37-004	Wheller-Stallard House	F. Jones	Retrd.	8.20	17-35.00
91-37-005	Set	F. Jones	Retrd.	32.80	75-100.00
The Cat's Meow		**Hometown Christmas**			
92-38-001	Wayne Co. Courthouse	F. Jones	Retrd.	8.50	15-19.00
92-38-002	Overholt House	F. Jones	Retrd.	8.50	15-19.00
92-38-003	August Imgard House	F. Jones	Retrd.	8.50	15-19.00
92-38-004	Howey House	F. Jones	Retrd.	8.50	15-19.00
92-38-005	Set	F. Jones	Retrd.	34.00	50-80.00
The Cat's Meow		**St. Charles Christmas**			
93-39-001	Newbill-McElhiney House	F. Jones	Open	9.00	9.00
93-39-002	St. Peter's Catholic Church	F. Jones	Open	9.00	9.00
93-39-003	Lewis & Clark Center	F. Jones	Open	9.00	9.00
93-39-004	Stone Row	F. Jones	Open	9.00	9.00
The Cat's Meow		**Collector Club Gift - Houses**			
89-40-001	Betsy Ross House	F. Jones	Closed	Gift	150.00
90-40-002	Amelia Earhart	F. Jones	Closed	Gift	80.00
91-40-003	Limberlost Cabin	F. Jones	Closed	Gift	N/A
92-40-004	Abigail Adams Birthplace	F. Jones	Closed	Gift	N/A
93-40-005	Pearl S. Buck House	F. Jones	Yr.Iss.	Gift	N/A
The Cat's Meow		**Collector Club Pieces - Famous Authors**			
89-41-001	Harriet Beecher Stowe	F. Jones	Closed	8.75	85.00
89-41-002	Orchard House	F. Jones	Closed	8.75	85.00
89-41-003	Longfellow House	F. Jones	Closed	8.75	85.00
89-41-004	Herman Melville's Arrowhead	F. Jones	Closed	8.75	85.00
89-41-005	Set	F. Jones	Closed	35.00	750.00
The Cat's Meow		**Collector Club Pieces - Great Inventors**			
90-42-001	Thomas Edison	F. Jones	Closed	9.25	N/A
90-42-002	Ford Motor Co.	F. Jones	Closed	9.25	N/A
90-42-003	Seth Thomas Clock Co.	F. Jones	Closed	9.25	N/A
90-42-004	Wright Cycle Co.	F. Jones	Closed	9.25	N/A
90-42-005	Set	F. Jones	Closed	37.00	500-750.
The Cat's Meow		**Collector Club Pieces - American Songwriters**			
91-43-001	Benjamin R. Hanby House	F. Jones	Closed	9.25	N/A
91-43-002	Anna Warner House	F. Jones	Closed	9.25	N/A
91-43-003	Stephen Foster Home	F. Jones	Closed	9.25	N/A
91-43-004	Oscar Hammerstein House	F. Jones	Closed	9.25	N/A
91-42-005	Set	F. Jones	Closed	37.00	150-400.
The Cat's Meow		**Collector Club Pieces - Signers of the Declaration**			
92-44-001	Josiah Bartlett Home	F. Jones	Closed	9.75	9.75
92-44-002	George Clymer Home	F. Jones	Closed	9.75	9.75
92-44-003	Stephen Hopkins Home	F. Jones	Closed	9.75	9.75
92-44-004	John Witherspoon Home	F. Jones	Closed	9.75	9.75
The Cat's Meow		**Collector Club Pieces - 19th Century Master Builders**			
93-45-001	Henry Hobson Richardson	F. Jones	Yr.Iss.	10.25	10.25
93-45-002	Samuel Sloan	F. Jones	Yr.Iss.	10.25	10.25
93-45-003	Alexander Jackson Davis	F. Jones	Yr.Iss.	10.25	10.25
93-45-004	Andrew Jackson Downing	F. Jones	Yr.Iss.	10.25	10.25
The Cat's Meow		**Miscellaneous**			
85-46-001	Pencil Holder	F. Jones	Closed	3.95	210.00
85-46-002	Recipe Holder	F. Jones	Closed	3.95	210.00
Creart		**African Wildlife**			
86-01-001	Running Elephant -73	Perez	2,500	260.00	320.00
87-01-002	African Elephant -10	Perez	S/O	410.00	410.00
87-01-003	African Elephant With Leaf -22	Martinez	2,500	230.00	280.00
87-01-004	Giraffe -43	Perez	2,500	250.00	320.00
87-01-005	Cob Antelope -46	Perez	2,500	310.00	370.00
87-01-006	African Lion -61	Martinez	2,500	260.00	320.00
87-01-007	Zebra -67	Perez	2,500	305.00	380.00
87-01-008	White Rhinoceros -136	Perez	2,500	330.00	410.00

Company Number	Name	Series Artist	Edition Limit	Issue Price	Quote
90-01-009	Symbol of Power Lion -40	Quezada	2,500	450.00	470.00
90-01-010	Hippopotamus -55	Quezeda	2,500	420.00	420.00
91-01-011	Breaking Away Gazelles -256	Quezeda	1,500	650.00	650.00
91-01-012	Sound of Warning Elephant -268	Perez	2,500	500.00	500.00
92-01-013	Small African Elephant- 271	Perez	2,500	320.00	320.00
Creart		**American Wildlife**			
85-02-001	Pigeons- 64	Perez	Closed	265.00	265.00
86-02-002	Polar Bear- 58	Martinez	2,500	200.00	240.00
86-02-003	Bald Eagle- 70	Martinez	Susp.	730.00	730.00
86-02-004	American Bison- 121	Perez	Susp.	400.00	400.00
87-02-005	Grizzley Bear- 31	Perez	2,500	210.00	270.00
87-02-006	Royal Eagle- 49	Martinez	Closed	545.00	545.00
87-02-007	Puma- 130	Perez	2,500	370.00	470.00
88-02-008	Mammoth-112	Martinez	2,500	450.00	550.00
88-02-009	Flamingo Upright-169	Perez	2,500	230.00	294.00
88-02-010	Flamingo Head Down-172	Perez	2,500	230.00	294.00
88-02-011	Flamingo Flapping-175	Perez	2,500	230.00	298.00
89-02-012	Jaguar- 79	Gonzalez	500	700.00	750.00
89-02-013	Rooster- R40	Martinez	Closed	290.00	290.00
89-02-014	Penguins- R76	Del Valle	Closed	175.00	175.00
90-02-015	The Challenge, Rams- 82	Gonzalez	1,500	698.00	698.00
90-02-016	Over the Clouds Falcon- 85	Martinez	2,500	520.00	520.00
90-02-017	Gray Wolf- 88	Quezada	2,500	365.00	370.00
90-02-018	Dolphin, Front- 142	Perez	2,500	210.00	236.00
90-02-019	Dolphin, Middle- 145	Perez	2,500	210.00	236.00
90-02-020	Dolphin, Back- 148	Perez	2,500	210.00	236.00
90-02-021	White Tail Deer- 151	Martinez	2,500	380.00	460.00
90-02-022	White Tail Doe- 154	Martinez	2,500	330.00	400.00
90-02-023	White Tail Fawn- 157	Martinez	2,500	220.00	280.00
91-02-024	White Hunter Polar Bear- 250	Gonzalez	2,500	380.00	390.00
91-02-025	Royal Eagle With Snake- 259	Martinez	2,500	700.00	700.00
91-02-026	Mischievous Raccoon- 262	Quezada	2,500	370.00	370.00
91-02-027	Playmates Sparrows- 265	Martinez	2,500	500.00	500.00
92-02-028	Soaring Royal Eagle- 52	Martinez	2,500	580.00	580.00
92-02-029	Penguins- 76	Perez	2,500	100.00	100.00
92-02-030	Standing Whitetail Deer- 109	Martinez	2,500	364.00	364.00
92-02-031	California Grizzly- 238	Perez	2,500	270.00	270.00
93-02-032	The Red Fox- 220	Contreras	1,500	199.00	199.00
93-02-033	Howling Coyote- 217	Martinez	1,500	199.00	199.00
Creart		**Wild America Edition**			
92-03-001	Puma Head- 334	Perez	900	320.00	320.00
92-03-002	Twelve Pointer Deer- 337	Perez	900	472.00	472.00
93-03-003	White Blizzard- 331	Perez	1,500	275.00	275.00
93-03-004	American Symbol- 328	Contreras	1,500	N/A	N/A
Creart		**Horses And Cattle**			
85-04-001	Running Horse- 7	Martinez	2,500	360.00	420.00
85-04-002	Arabian Horse- 34	Martinez	2,500	230.00	280.00
85-04-003	Bull- 28	Martinez	Susp.	285.00	285.00
87-04-004	Horse In Passage- 127	Martinez	2,500	500.00	550.00
88-04-005	Horse Head- 139	Martinez	2,500	440.00	480.00
89-04-006	Quarter Horse Recoil- 1	Gonzalez	Closed	310.00	310.00
89-04-007	Brahma Bull- 13	Gonzalez	2,500	420.00	470.00
89-04-008	Arabian Horse- 91	Perez	2,500	260.00	260.00
89-04-009	Lippizzan Horse- 94	Perez	2,500	260.00	260.00
89-04-010	Thoroughbred Horse-97	Perez	2,500	260.00	260.00
89-04-011	Apaloosa Horse- 100	Martinez	2,500	260.00	260.00
89-04-012	Quarter Horse II- 103	Perez	2,500	260.00	260.00
92-04-013	Pegasus- 106	Perez	2,500	420.00	420.00
Creart		**From Asia & Europe**			
85-05-001	Indian Elephant Mother- 25	Perez	Susp.	485.00	485.00
85-05-002	Marco Polo Sheep- 37	Martinez	2,500	270.00	300.00
85-05-003	Tiger- R55	Martinez	Closed	200.00	200.00
86-05-004	Deer- 4	Martinez	Closed	560.00	560.00
86-05-005	Indian Elephant Baby- 16	Perez	Susp.	200.00	200.00
87-05-006	Drover of Camels- 124	Martinez	2,500	650.00	700.00
87-05-007	Royal Owl- 133	Perez	Closed	340.00	340.00
88-05-008	Bengal Tiger- 115	Perez	2,500	440.00	480.00
90-05-009	Giant Panda- 244	Martinez	2,500	280.00	290.00
Creart		**Pets**			
87-06-001	Labrador Retriever- 19	Martinez	2,500	300.00	350.00
89-06-002	Cocker Spaniel American- 184	Martinez	Susp.	100.00	100.00
89-06-003	Boxer- 187	Martinez	Susp.	135.00	135.00
89-06-004	Schnauzer Miniature- 190	Perez	Susp.	110.00	110.00
89-06-005	Great Dane, Brown- 193	Martinez	Susp.	140.00	140.00
89-06-006	Great Dane, Harlequi- 196	Martinez	Susp.	140.00	140.00
89-06-007	Pointer, Brown- 199	Perez	Susp.	132.00	132.00
89-06-008	Pointer, Black- 202	Perez	Susp.	132.00	132.00
89-06-009	Poodle- 205	Perez	Susp.	120.00	120.00
89-06-010	Saint Bernard- 208	Perez	Susp.	130.00	130.00
89-06-011	Labrador, Golden- 211	Martinez	Susp.	130.00	130.00
89-06-012	Labrador, Black- 214	Martinez	Susp.	130.00	130.00
91-06-013	German Shepherd Dog- 253	Martinez	2,500	360.00	360.00
Creart		**Nature's Care Collection**			
93-07-001	Penguin and Chicks- 76	A.Del Valle	2,000	99.00	99.00
93-07-002	Otters- 325	Estevez	2,000	99.00	99.00
93-07-003	Grizzly and Cubs- 340	Contreras	2,000	99.00	99.00
93-07-004	Jack Rabbit and Young- 343	Martinez	2,000	99.00	99.00
93-07-005	Lioness and Cubs- 346	Contreras	2,000	99.00	99.00
93-07-006	Wolf and Pups- 349	Contreras	2,000	99.00	99.00
93-07-007	Doe and Fawns- 355	Contreras	2,000	99.00	99.00
93-07-008	Gorilla and Baby- 394	Contreras	2,000	99.00	99.00
Crystal World		**Limited Edition Series**			
86-01-001	Eiffel Tower	T. Suzuki	2,000	1300.00	1300.00
86-01-002	Empire State Building- large	R. Nakai	2,000	700.00	700.00
86-01-003	Empire State Building- extra large	R. Nakai	Closed	1300.00	1300.00
88-01-004	Dream Castle	R. Nakai	500	10000.00	10000.00
88-01-005	Grand Castle	R. Nakai	1500	2500.00	2500.00
88-01-006	Manhattanscape	G. Vieth	Closed	1050.00	1050.00
88-01-007	Taj Mahal	T. Suzuki	1,000	2100.00	2100.00
88-01-008	U. S. Capitol Building-large	T. Suzuki	Closed	1050.00	1050.00
89-01-009	Eiffel Tower-Small	T. Suzuki	2,000	600.00	600.00
89-01-010	Tower Bridge	T. Suzuki	Closed	600.00	600.00
89-01-011	Space Shuttle Launch	T. Suzuki	Closed	1000.00	1000.00
90-01-012	Cruise Ship	T. Suzuki	1,000	2100.00	2100.00
90-01-013	Ellis Island	R. Nakai	Closed	450.00	450.00
90-01-014	The Whitehouse	R. Nakai	Closed	3000.00	3000.00

Company Number	Name	Series Artist	Edition Limit	Issue Price	Quote
93-01-015	Country Gristmill	T. Suzuki	1,250	320.00	320.00
93-01-016	Enchanted Castle	R. Nakai	750	800.00	800.00
93-01-017	Victorian House	N. Mulargia	2,000	190.00	190.00
C.U.I./Carolina Collection/Dram Tree		**Legends of Santa Claus**			
91-01-001	Checkin' it Twice	Christjohn	2,500	60.00	60.00
91-01-002	Have You Been a Good Little Boy	Christjohn	2,500	60.00	60.00
91-01-003	Have You Been a Good Little Girl	Christjohn	2,500	60.00	60.00
91-01-004	Mrs. Claus	Christjohn	2,500	60.00	60.00
91-01-005	Won't You Guide My Sleigh Tonight	Christjohn	2,500	60.00	60.00
91-01-006	With A Finger Aside His Nose	Christjohn	2,500	60.00	60.00
Cybis		**Animal Kingdom**			
71-01-001	American Bullfrog	Cybis	Closed	250.00	600.00
75-01-002	American White Buffalo	Cybis	250	1250.00	4000.00
71-01-003	Appaloosa Colt	Cybis	Closed	150.00	300.00
80-01-004	Arctic White Fox	Cybis	100	4500.00	4700.00
84-01-005	Australian Greater Sulpher Crested Cockatoo	Cybis	25	9850.00	9850.00
85-01-006	Baxter and Doyle	Cybis	400	450.00	450.00
68-01-007	Bear	Cybis	Closed	85.00	400.00
85-01-008	Beagles, Branigan and Clancy	Cybis	Open	375.00	625.00
81-01-009	Beavers, Egbert and Brewster	Cybis	400	285.00	335.00
68-01-010	Buffalo	Cybis	Closed	115.00	185.00
XX-01-011	Bull	Cybis	100	150.00	4500.00
76-01-012	Bunny, Muffet	Cybis	Closed	85.00	150.00
77-01-013	Bunny Pat-a-Cake	Cybis	Closed	90.00	150.00
85-01-014	Bunny, Snowflake	Cybis	Open	65.00	75.00
84-01-015	Chantilly, Kitten	Cybis	Open	175.00	210.00
76-01-016	Chipmunk w/Bloodroot	Cybis	225	625.00	675.00
69-01-017	Colts, Darby and Joan	Cybis	Closed	295.00	475.00
82-01-018	Dall Sheep	Cybis	50	Unkn.	4250.00
86-01-019	Dapple Grey Foal	Cybis	Open	195.00	250.00
70-01-020	Deer Mouse in Clover	Cybis	Closed	65.00	160.00
78-01-021	Dormouse, Maximillian	Cybis	Closed	250.00	285.00
78-01-022	Dormouse, Maxine	Cybis	Closed	195.00	225.00
68-01-023	Elephant	Cybis	100	600.00	5000.00
85-01-024	Elephant, Willoughby	Cybis	Open	195.00	245.00
61-01-025	Horse	Cybis	100	150.00	2000.00
86-01-026	Huey, the Harmonious Hare	Cybis	Open	175.00	275.00
67-01-027	Kitten, Blue Ribbon	Cybis	Closed	95.00	500.00
75-01-028	Kitten, Tabitha	Cybis	Closed	90.00	150.00
75-01-029	Kitten, Topaz	Cybis	Closed	90.00	150.00
86-01-030	Mick, The Melodious Mutt	Cybis	Open	175.00	275.00
85-01-031	Monday, Rhinoceros	Cybis	Open	85.00	150.00
71-01-032	Nashua	Cybis	100	2000.00	3000.00
78-01-033	Pinky Bunny/Carrot	Cybis	200	200.00	265.00
72-01-034	Pinto Colt	Cybis	Closed	175.00	250.00
76-01-035	Prairie Dog	Cybis	Closed	245.00	345.00
65-01-036	Raccoon, Raffles	Cybis	Closed	110.00	365.00
68-01-038	Snail, Sir Escargot	Cybis	Closed	50.00	300.00
65-01-039	Squirrel, Mr. Fluffy Tail	Cybis	Closed	90.00	350.00
80-01-040	Squirrel, Highrise	Cybis	400	475.00	525.00
68-01-041	Stallion	Cybis	350	475.00	850.00
66-01-042	Thoroughbred	Cybis	350	425.00	1500.00
86-01-043	White Tailed Deer	Cybis	50	9500.00	11500.00
Cybis		**Biblical**			
60-02-001	Exodus	Cybis	50	350.00	2600.00
60-02-002	Flight Into Egypt	Cybis	50	175.00	2500.00
56-02-003	Holy Child of Prague	Cybis	10	1500.00	75000.00
XX-02-004	Holywater Font "Holy Ghost"	Cybis	Closed	15.00	145.00
57-02-005	Madonna, House of Gold	Cybis	8	125.00	4000.00
60-02-006	Madonna Lace & Rose	Cybis	Open	15.00	295.00
63-02-007	Moses, The Great Lawgiver	Cybis	750	250.00	5500.00
84-02-008	Nativity, Mary	Cybis	Open	Unkn.	325.00
84-02-009	Nativity, Joseph	Cybis	Open	Unkn.	325.00
84-02-010	Christ Child with Lamb	Cybis	Open	Unkn.	290.00
84-02-011	Nativity, Angel, Color	Cybis	Open	395.00	575.00
84-02-012	Nativity, Camel, Color	Cybis	Open	625.00	825.00
85-02-013	Nativity, Cow, Color	Cybis	Open	175.00	195.00
85-02-014	Nativity, Cow, White	Cybis	Open	125.00	225.00
85-02-015	Nativity, Donkey, Color	Cybis	Open	195.00	225.00
85-02-016	Nativity, Donkey, White	Cybis	Open	130.00	150.00
85-02-017	Nativity, Lamb, Color	Cybis	Open	150.00	195.00
85-02-018	Nativity, Lamb, White	Cybis	Open	115.00	125.00
84-02-019	Nativity, Shepherd, Color	Cybis	Open	395.00	475.00
76-02-020	Noah	Cybis	500	975.00	2800.00
64-02-021	St. Peter	Cybis	500	Unkn.	1250.00
60-02-022	The Prophet	Cybis	50	250.00	3500.00
Cybis		**Birds & Flowers**			
85-03-001	American Bald Eagle	Cybis	300	2900.00	3595.00
72-03-002	American Crested Iris	Cybis	400	975.00	1150.00
76-03-003	American White Turkey	Cybis	75	1450.00	1600.00
76-03-004	American Wild Turkey	Cybis	75	1950.00	2200.00
77-03-005	Apple Blossoms	Cybis	400	350.00	550.00
72-03-006	Autumn Dogwood w/Chickadees	Cybis	350	1100.00	1200.00
XX-03-007	Birds & Flowers	Cybis	250	500.00	4500.00
61-03-008	Blue-Grey Gnatcatchers, pair	Cybis	200	400.00	2500.00
60-03-009	Blue Headed Virio Building Nest	Cybis	Closed	60.00	1100.00
60-03-010	Blue Headed Virio with Lilac	Cybis	275	1200.00	2200.00
XX-03-011	Butterfly w/Dogwood	Cybis	200	Unkn.	350.00
68-03-012	Calla Lily	Cybis	500	750.00	1750.00
65-03-013	Christmas Rose	Cybis	500	250.00	750.00
77-03-014	Clematis	Cybis	Closed	210.00	315.00
69-03-015	Clematis with House Wren	Cybis	350	1300.00	1400.00
76-03-016	Colonial Basket	Cybis	100	2750.00	5500.00
76-03-017	Constancy Flower Basket	Cybis	Closed	345.00	400.00
64-03-018	Dahlia, Yellow	Cybis	350	450.00	1800.00
76-03-019	Devotion Flower Basket	Cybis	Closed	345.00	400.00
62-03-020	Duckling "Baby Brother"	Cybis	Closed	35.00	140.00
77-03-021	Duckling "Buttercup & Daffodil"	Cybis	Closed	165.00	295.00
70-03-022	Dutch Crocus	Cybis	350	550.00	750.00
76-03-023	Felicity Flower Basket	Cybis	Closed	325.00	345.00
61-03-024	Golden Clarion Lily	Cybis	100	250.00	4500.00
74-03-025	Golden Winged Warbler	Cybis	200	1075.00	1150.00
75-03-026	Great Horned Owl, Color	Cybis	50	3250.00	7500.00
75-03-027	Great Horned Owl, White	Cybis	150	1950.00	4500.00
64-03-028	Great White Heron	Cybis	350	850.00	3750.00
77-03-029	Hermit Thrush	Cybis	150	1450.00	1450.00
59-03-030	Hummingbird	Cybis	Closed	95.00	950.00
63-03-031	Iris	Cybis	250	500.00	4500.00

Company Number	Name	Series Artist	Edition Limit	Issue Price	Quote
77-03-032	Krestrel	Cybis	175	1875.00	1925.00
78-03-033	Kinglets on Pyracantha	Cybis	175	900.00	1100.00
71-03-034	Little Blue Heron	Cybis	500	425.00	1500.00
63-03-035	Magnolia	Cybis	Closed	350.00	450-1500.
76-03-036	Majesty Flower Basket	Cybis	Closed	345.00	400.00
70-03-037	Mushroom with Butterfly	Cybis	Closed	225.00	450.00
68-03-038	Narcissus	Cybis	500	350.00	550.00
78-03-039	Nestling Bluebirds	Cybis	Closed	235.00	250.00
72-03-040	Pansies, China Maid	Cybis	1,000	275.00	350.00
75-03-041	Pansies, Chinolina Lady	Cybis	750	295.00	400.00
60-03-042	Pheasant	Cybis	150	750.00	5000.00
XX-03-043	Sandpipers	Cybis	400	700.00	1500.00
85-03-044	Screech Owl & Siblings	Cybis	100	3250.00	3925.00
XX-03-045	Skylarks	Cybis	350	330.00	1800.00
62-03-046	Sparrow on a Log	Cybis	Closed	35.00	450.00
82-03-047	Spring Bouquet	Cybis	200	750.00	750.00
57-03-048	Turtle Doves	Cybis	500	350.00	5000.00
68-03-049	Wood Duck	Cybis	500	325.00	800.00
80-03-050	Yellow Rose	Cybis	Closed	80.00	450.00
80-03-051	Yellow Condesa Rose	Cybis	Closed	Unkn.	255.00
Cybis		**Children to Cherish**			
64-04-001	Alice in Wonderland	Cybis	Closed	50.00	850.00
78-04-002	Alice (Seated)	Cybis	Closed	350.00	550.00
78-04-003	Allegra	Cybis	Closed	310.00	350.00
63-04-004	Ballerina on Cue	Cybis	Closed	150.00	700.00
68-04-005	Ballerina, Little Princess	Cybis	Closed	125.00	750.00
85-04-006	Ballerina, Recital	Cybis	Open	275.00	275.00
60-04-007	Ballerina Red Shoes	Cybis	Closed	75.00	1200.00
85-04-008	Ballerina, Swanilda	Cybis	Open	450.00	725.00
68-04-009	Baby Bust	Cybis	239	375.00	1000.00
85-04-010	Beth	Cybis	Open	235.00	275.00
77-04-011	Boys Playing Marbles	Cybis	Closed	285.00	425.00
84-04-012	The Choirboy	Cybis	Open	325.00	345.00
85-04-013	Clara	Cybis	Open	395.00	395.00
86-04-014	Clarissa	Cybis	Open	165.00	195.00
78-04-015	Edith	Cybis	Closed	310.00	325.00
76-04-016	Elizabeth Ann	Cybis	Closed	195.00	275.00
85-04-017	Felicia	Cybis	Open	425.00	525.00
86-04-018	"Encore" Figure Skater	Cybis	750	625.00	675.00
85-04-019	Figure Eight	Cybis	750	625.00	750.00
XX-04-020	First Bouquet	Cybis	250	150.00	300.00
66-04-021	First Flight	Cybis	Closed	50.00	475.00
81-04-022	Fleurette	Cybis	1,000	725.00	1075.00
73-04-023	Goldilocks	Cybis	Closed	145.00	525.00
74-04-024	Gretel	Cybis	Closed	260.00	425.00
74-04-025	Hansel	Cybis	Closed	270.00	550.00
62-04-026	Heide, White	Cybis	Closed	165.00	550.00
62-04-027	Heide, Color .	Cybis	Closed	165.00	550.00
84-04-028	Jack in the Beanstalk	Cybis	750	575.00	575.00
85-04-029	Jody	Cybis	Open	235.00	275.00
86-04-030	Kitri	Cybis	Open	450.00	550.00
78-04-031	Lisa and Lynette	Cybis	Closed	395.00	475.00
78-04-032	Little Boy Blue	Cybis	Closed	425.00	500.00
84-04-033	Little Champ	Cybis	Open	325.00	375.00
80-04-034	Little Miss Muffet	Cybis	Closed	335.00	365.00
73-04-035	Little Red Riding Hood	Cybis	Closed	110.00	475.00
86-04-036	Lullaby, Pink	Cybis	Open	125.00	160.00
86-04-037	Lullaby, Blue	Cybis	Open	125.00	160.00
86-04-038	Lullaby, Ivory	Cybis	Open	125.00	160.00
85-04-039	Marguerite	Cybis	Open	425.00	525.00
74-04-040	Mary, Mary	Cybis	500	475.00	750.00
76-04-041	Melissa	Cybis	Closed	285.00	425.00
84-04-042	Michael	Cybis	Open	235.00	350.00
67-04-043	Pandora Blue	Cybis	Closed	265.00	325.00
58-04-044	Peter Pan	Cybis	Closed	80.00	1000.00
71-04-045	Polyanna	Cybis	Closed	195.00	550.00
75-04-046	Rapunzel, Apricot	Cybis	1,500	475.00	1200.00
78-04-047	Rapunzel, Lilac	Cybis	1,000	675.00	1000.00
72-04-048	Rapunzel, Pink	Cybis	1,000	425.00	1100.00
64-04-049	Rebecca	Cybis	Closed	110.00	360.00
85-04-050	Recital	Cybis	Open	275.00	275.00
82-04-051	Robin	Cybis	1,000	475.00	850.00
82-04-052	Sleeping Beauty	Cybis	750	695.00	1475.00
63-04-053	Springtime	Cybis	Closed	45.00	775.00
57-04-054	Thumbelina	Cybis	Closed	45.00	525.00
59-04-055	Tinkerbell	Cybis	Closed	95.00	1500.00
85-04-056	Vanessa	Cybis	Open	425.00	525.00
75-04-057	Wendy with Flowers	Cybis	Unkn.	250.00	450.00
75-04-058	Yankee Doodle Dandy	Cybis	Closed	275.00	325.00
Cybis		**Commemoratives**			
81-05-001	Arion, Dolphin Rider	Cybis	1,000	575.00	1150.00
69-05-002	Apollo II Moon Mission	Cybis	111	1500.00	2500.00
72-05-003	Chess Set	Cybis	10	30000.00	60000.00
67-05-004	Columbia	Cybis	200	1000.00	2500.00
86-05-005	1986 Commemorative Egg	Cybis	Open	365.00	365.00
67-05-006	Conductor's Hands	Cybis	250	250.00	1500.00
71-05-007	Cree Indian	Cybis	100	2500.00	5500.00
84-05-008	Cree Indian "Magic Boy"	Cybis	200	4250.00	4995.00
75-05-009	George Washington Bust	Cybis	Closed	275.00	350.00
85-05-010	Holiday Ornament	Cybis	Open	75.00	75.00
81-05-011	Kateri Takakwitha	Cybis	100	2875.00	2975.00
86-05-012	Little Miss Liberty	Cybis	Open	295.00	350.00
77-05-013	Oceania	Cybis	200	1250.00	975-1550.
81-05-014	Phoenix	Cybis	100	950.00	950.00
80-05-015	The Bride	Cybis	100	6500.00	10500.00
84-05-016	1984 Cybis Holiday	Cybis	Open	145.00	145.00
85-05-017	Liberty	Cybis	100	1875.00	4000.00
Cybis		**Fantasia**			
74-06-001	Cybele	Cybis	500	675.00	800.00
81-06-002	Desiree, White Deer	Cybis	400	575.00	595.00
84-06-003	Flight and Fancy	Cybis	1,000	975.00	1175.00
80-06-004	Pegasus	Cybis	500	1450.00	3750.00
80-06-005	Pegaus, Free Spirit	Cybis	1,000	675.00	775.00
81-06-006	Prince Brocade Unicorn	Cybis	500	2200.00	2600.00
78-06-007	"Satin" Horse Head	Cybis	500	1100.00	2800.00
77-06-008	Sea King's Steed "Oceania"	Cybis	200	1250.00	1450.00
78-06-009	"Sharmaine" Sea Nymph	Cybis	250	1450.00	1650.00
82-06-010	Theron	Cybis	350	675.00	850.00
69-06-011	Unicorn	Cybis	500	1250.00	3750.00
77-06-012	Unicorns, Gambol and Frolic	Cybis	1,000	425.00	2300.00

Company Number	Name	Series Artist	Edition Limit	Issue Price	Quote
85-06-013	Dore'	Cybis	1,000	575.00	1075.00
Cybis		**Land of Chemeric**			
77-07-001	Marigold	Cybis	Closed	185.00	550.00
81-07-002	Melody	Cybis	1,000	725.00	800.00
79-07-003	Pip, Elfin Player	Cybis	1,000	450.00	665.00
77-07-004	Queen Titania	Cybis	750	725.00	2500.00
77-07-005	Tiffin	Cybis	Closed	175.00	550.00
85-07-006	Oberon	Cybis	750	825.00	825.00
Cybis		**North American Indian**			
74-08-001	Apache, "Chato"	Cybis	350	1950.00	3300.00
69-08-002	Blackfeet "Beaverhead Medicine Man"	Cybis	500	2000.00	2775.00
82-08-003	Choctaw "Tasculusa"	Cybis	200	2475.00	4050.00
77-08-004	Crow Dancer	Cybis	200	3875.00	8500.00
69-08-005	Dakota "Minnehaha Laughing Water"	Cybis	500	1500.00	2500.00
73-08-006	Eskimo Mother	Cybis	200	1875.00	2650.00
79-08-007	Great Spirit "Wankan Tanka"	Cybis	200	3500.00	4150.00
73-08-008	Iriquois "At the Council Fire"	Cybis	500	4250.00	4975.00
69-08-009	Onondaga "Haiwatha"	Cybis	500	1500.00	2450.00
71-08-010	Shoshone "Sacajawea"	Cybis	500	2250.00	2775.00
85-08-011	Yaqui "Deer Dancer"	Cybis	200	2095.00	2850.00
Cybis		**Portraits in Porcelain**			
76-09-001	Abigail Adams	Cybis	600	875.00	1300.00
73-09-002	Ballet-Princess Aurora	Cybis	200	1125.00	1500.00
73-09-003	Ballet-Prince Florimond	Cybis	200	975.00	1100.00
84-09-004	Bathsheba	Cybis	500	1975.00	3250.00
65-09-005	Beatrice	Cybis	700	225.00	1800.00
79-09-006	Berengaria	Cybis	500	1450.00	2000-4700.
86-09-007	Carmen	Cybis	500	1675.00	1975.00
82-09-008	Desdemona	Cybis	500	1850.00	4000.00
71-09-009	Eleanor of Aquitaine	Cybis	750	875.00	4250.00
67-09-010	Folk Singer	Cybis	283	300.00	850.00
78-09-011	Good Queen Anne	Cybis	350	975.00	1500.00
67-09-012	Guinevere	Cybis	800	250.00	2400.00
68-09-013	Hamlet	Cybis	500	350.00	2000.00
81-09-014	Jane Eyre	Cybis	500	975.00	1500.00
65-09-015	Juliet	Cybis	800	175.00	4000.00
85-09-016	King Arthur	Cybis	350	2350.00	3450.00
85-09-017	King David	Cybis	350	1475.00	2175.00
72-09-018	Kwan Yin	Cybis	350	1250.00	2000.00
82-09-019	Lady Godiva	Cybis	200	1875.00	3250.00
75-09-020	Lady Macbeth	Cybis	750	850.00	1350.00
79-09-021	Nefertiti	Cybis	500	2100.00	3000.00
69-09-022	Ophelia	Cybis	800	750.00	3500-4400.
85-09-023	Pagliacci	Cybis	Open	325.00	325.00
82-09-024	Persephone	Cybis	200	3250.00	5250.00
73-09-025	Portia	Cybis	750	825.00	3750.00
76-09-026	Priscilla	Cybis	500	825.00	1500.00
74-09-027	Queen Esther	Cybis	750	925.00	1800.00
85-09-028	Romeo and Juliet	Cybis	500	2200.00	3400.00
68-09-029	Scarlett	Cybis	500	450.00	3250-3500.
85-09-030	Tristan and Isolde	Cybis	200	2200.00	2200.00
Cybis		**Theatre of Porcelain**			
81-10-001	Columbine	Cybis	250	2250.00	2250.00
78-10-002	Court Jester	Cybis	250	1450.00	1750.00
80-10-003	Harlequin	Cybis	250	1575.00	1875.00
81-10-004	Puck	Cybis	250	2300.00	2450.00
Cybis		**Carousel-Circus**			
75-11-001	"Barnaby" Bear	Cybis	Closed	165.00	325.00
81-11-002	Bear, "Bernhard"	Cybis	325	1125.00	1150.00
75-11-003	Bicentennial Horse Ticonderoga	Cybis	350	925.00	4000.00
75-11-004	"Bosun" Monkey	Cybis	Closed	195.00	425.00
81-11-005	Bull, Plutus	Cybis	325	1125.00	2050.00
85-11-006	Carousel Unicorn	Cybis	325	1275.00	2750.00
79-11-007	Circus Rider "Equestrienne Extraordinaire"	Cybis	150	2275.00	3500.00
77-11-008	"Dandy" Dancing Dog	Cybis	Closed	145.00	295.00
81-11-009	Frollo	Cybis	1,000	750.00	825.00
76-11-010	"Funny Face" Child Head/Holly	Cybis	Closed	325.00	750.00
82-11-011	Giraffe	Cybis	750	Unkn.	1750.00
73-11-012	Carousel Goat	Cybis	325	875.00	1750.00
73-11-013	Carousel Horse	Cybis	325	925.00	7500.00
74-11-014	Lion	Cybis	325	1025.00	1350.00
76-11-015	Performing Pony "Poppy"	Cybis	1,000	325.00	1200.00
84-11-016	Phineas, Circus Elephant	Cybis	Open	325.00	425.00
86-11-017	Pierre, the Performing Poodle	Cybis	Open	225.00	275.00
81-11-018	Pony	Cybis	750	975.00	975.00
76-11-019	"Sebastian" Seal	Cybis	Closed	195.00	200.00
74-11-020	Tiger	Cybis	325	925.00	1500.00
85-11-021	Jumbles and Friend	Cybis	750	675.00	725.00
85-11-022	Valentine	Cybis	Open	335.00	375.00
Cybis		**Children of the World**			
72-12-001	Eskimo Child Head	Cybis	Closed	165.00	400.00
75-12-002	Indian Girl Head	Cybis	Closed	325.00	900.00
75-12-003	Indian Boy Head	Cybis	Closed	425.00	900.00
78-12-004	Jason	Cybis	Closed	285.00	375.00
78-12-005	Jennifer	Cybis	Closed	325.00	375.00
77-12-006	Jeremy	Cybis	Closed	315.00	475.00
79-12-007	Jessica	Cybis	Closed	325.00	475.00
Cybis		**Sport Scenes**			
80-13-001	Jogger, Female	Cybis	Closed	345.00	425.00
80-13-002	Jogger, Male	Cybis	Closed	395.00	475.00
Cybis		**Everyone's Fun Time (Limnettes)**			
72-14-001	Country Fair	Cybis	500	125.00	200.00
72-14-002	Windy Day	Cybis	500	125.00	200.00
72-14-003	The Pond	Cybis	500	125.00	200.00
72-14-004	The Seashore	Cybis	500	125.00	200.00
Cybis		**The Wonderful Seasons (Limnettes)**			
72-15-001	Autumn	Cybis	500	125.00	200.00
72-15-002	Spring	Cybis	500	125.00	200.00
72-15-003	Summer	Cybis	500	125.00	200.00
72-15-004	Winter	Cybis	500	125.00	200.00
Cybis		**When Bells are Ringing (Limnettes)**			
72-16-001	Easter Egg Hunt	Cybis	500	125.00	200.00
72-16-002	Independence Celebration	Cybis	500	125.00	200.00

Company Number	Name	Series Artist	Edition Limit	Issue Price	Quote
72-16-003	Merry Christmas	Cybis	500	125.00	200.00
72-16-004	Sabbath Morning	Cybis	500	125.00	200.00
Danbury Mint		**Rockwell Figurines**			
80-01-001	Trick or Treat	N. Rockwell	Closed	55.00	60.00
80-01-002	Gramps at the Reins	N. Rockwell	Closed	55.00	75.00
80-01-003	Grandpa Snowman	N. Rockwell	Closed	55.00	60.00
80-01-004	Caught in the Act	N. Rockwell	Closed	55.00	75.00
80-01-005	Boy on Stilts	N. Rockwell	Closed	55.00	60.00
80-01-006	Young Love	N. Rockwell	Closed	55.00	125.00
Department 56		**Dickens' Village Collection**			
84-01-001	The Original Shops of Dickens' Village 6515-3, Set of 7	Department 56	Closed	175.00	1100-1800.
84-01-002	Crowntree Inn 6515-3	Department 56	Closed	25.00	275-400.
84-01-003	Candle Shop 6515-3	Department 56	Closed	25.00	175-250.
84-01-004	Green Grocer 6515-3	Department 56	Closed	25.00	160-250.
84-01-005	Golden Swan Baker 6515-3	Department 56	Closed	25.00	125-190.
84-01-006	Bean And Son Smithy Shop 6515-3	Department 56	Closed	25.00	165-200.
84-01-007	Abel Beesley Butcher 6515-3	Department 56	Closed	25.00	120-150.
84-01-008	Jones & Co. Brush & Basket Shop 6515-3	Department 56	Closed	25.00	300-350.
84-01-009	Dickens' Village Church (cream) 6516-1	Department 56	Closed	35.00	200-375.
85-01-010	Dickens' Village Church(tan) 6516-1	Department 56	Closed	35.00	125-150.
85-01-011	Dickens' Village Church(green) 6516-1	Department 56	Closed	35.00	275-400.
85-01-012	Dickens' Cottages 6518-8 Set of 3	Department 56	Closed	75.00	950-1150.
85-01-013	Thatched Cottage 6518-8	Department 56	Closed	25.00	175-250.
85-01-014	Stone Cottage 6518-8	Department 56	Closed	25.00	400-500.
85-01-015	Tudor Cottage 6518-8	Department 56	Closed	25.00	375-475.
85-01-016	Dickens' Village Mill 6519-6	Department 56	2,500	35.00	5000-6000.
86-01-017	Christmas Carol Cottages 6500-5, Set of 3 (Fezziwig's Warehouse, Scrooge and Marley Counting House, The Cottage of Bob Cratchit & Tiny Tim)	Department 56	Open	75.00	90.00
86-01-018	Norman Church 6502-1	Department 56	3,500	40.00	3000-3800.
86-01-019	Dickens' Lane Shops 6507-2, Set of 3	Department 56	Closed	80.00	425-575.
86-01-020	Thomas Kersey Coffee House 6507-2	Department 56	Closed	27.00	135-175.
86-01-021	Cottage Toy Shop 6507-2	Department 56	Closed	27.00	200-250.
86-01-022	Tuttle's Pub 6507-2	Department 56	Closed	27.00	200-260.
86-01-023	Blythe Pond Mill House 6508-0	Department 56	Closed	37.00	200-250.
86-01-024	By The Pond Mill House 6508-0	Department 56	Closed	37.00	110-165.
86-01-025	Chadbury Station and Train 6528-5	Department 56	Closed	65.00	325-500.
87-01-026	Barley Bree 5900-5,Set of 2 (Farmhouse, Barn)	Department 56	Closed	60.00	300-400.
87-01-027	The Old Curiosity Shop 5905-6	Department 56	Open	32.00	37.50
87-01-028	Kenilworth Castle 5916-1	Department 56	Closed	70.00	400-500.
87-01-029	Brick Abbey 6549-8	Department 56	Closed	33.00	350-450.
87-01-030	Chesterton Manor House 6568-4	Department 56	7,500	45.00	1500-1900.
88-01-031	Counting House & Silas Thimbleton Barrister 5902-1	Department 56	Closed	32.00	80-150.00
88-01-032	C. Fletcher Public House 5904-8	Department 56	12,500	35.00	550-800.
88-01-033	Cobblestone Shops 5924-2, Set of 3	Department 56	Closed	95.00	250-350.
88-01-034	The Wool Shop 5924-2	Department 56	Closed	32.00	130-190.
88-01-035	Booter and Cobbler 5924-2	Department 56	Closed	32.00	80-140.00
88-01-036	T. Wells Fruit & Spice Shop 5924-2	Department 56	Closed	32.00	75-125.00
88-01-037	Nicholas Nickleby 5925-0, Set of 2	Department 56	Closed	72.00	140-225.
88-01-038	Nicholas Nickleby Cottage 5925-0	Department 56	Closed	36.00	75-100.00
88-01-039	Wackford Squeers Boarding School 5925-0	Department 56	Closed	36.00	75-100.00
88-01-040	Nickolas Nickleby Cottage 5925-0-misspelled	Department 56	Closed	36.00	95-125.00
88-01-041	Merchant Shops 5926-9, 5/set(Poulterer, Geo. Weeton Watchmaker, The Mermaid Fish Shoppe, White Horse Bakery,Walpole Tailors	Department 56	Open	150.00	175.00
88-01-042	Ivy Glen Church 5927-7	Department 56	Closed	35.00	75-125.00
89-01-043	David Copperfield 5550-6, Set of 3	Department 56	Closed	125.00	210-250.
89-01-044	Mr. Wickfield Solicitor 5550-6	Department 56	Closed	42.50	85-100.00
89-01-045	Betsy Trotwood's Cottage 5550-6	Department 56	Closed	42.50	70-100.00
89-01-046	Peggotty's Seaside Cottage 5550-6 (green boat)	Department 56	Closed	42.50	90-100.00
89-01-047	David Copperfield 5550-6, Set of 3 with tan boat	Department 56	Closed	125.00	175-250.
89-01-048	Peggotty's Seaside Cottage 5550-6 (tan boat)	Department 56	Closed	42.50	150-175.
89-01-049	Victoria Station 5574-3	Department 56	Open	100.00	100.00
89-01-050	Knottinghill Church 5582-4	Department 56	Open	50.00	50.00
89-01-051	Cobles Police Station 5583-2	Department 56	Closed	37.50	80-145.00
89-01-052	Theatre Royal 5584-0	Department 56	Closed	45.00	75-95.00
89-01-053	Ruth Marion Scotch Woolens 5585-9	Department 56	17,500	65.00	350-450.
89-01-054	Green Gate Cottage 5586-7	Department 56	22,500	65.00	275-450.
89-01-055	The Flat of Ebenezer Scrooge 5587-5	Department 56	Open	37.50	37.50
90-01-056	Bishops Oast House 5567-0	Department 56	Closed	45.00	75-100.00
90-01-057	Kings Road 5568-9, Set of 2 (Tutbury Printer, C.H. Watt Physician)	Department 56	Open	72.00	72.00
91-01-058	Fagin's Hide-A-Way 5552-2	Department 56	Open	68.00	68.00
91-01-059	Oliver Twist 5553-0 Set of 2, (Brownlow House, Maylie Cottage)	Department 56	Open	75.00	75.00
91-01-060	Ashbury Inn 5555-7	Department 56	Open	55.00	55.00
91-01-061	Nephew Fred's Flat 5557-3	Department 56	Open	35.00	35.00
92-01-062	Crown & Cricket Inn (Charles Dickens' Signature Series), 5750-9	Department 56	Closed	100.00	150-200.
92-01-063	Old Michaelchurch, 5562-0	Department 56	Open	42.00	42.00
92-01-064	Hembleton Pewterer, 5800-9	Department 56	Open	72.00	72.00
92-01-065	King's Road Post Office, 5801-7	Department 56	Open	45.00	45.00
92-01-066	The Pied Bull Inn (Charles Dickens' Signature Series), 5751-7	Department 56	Yr.Iss.	100.00	100.00
Department 56		**New England Village Collection**			
86-02-001	New England Village 6530-7, Set of 7	Department 56	Closed	170.00	800-1100.
86-02-002	Apothecary Shop 6530-7	Department 56	Closed	25.00	70-115.00
86-02-003	General Store 6530-7	Department 56	Closed	25.00	250-345.
86-02-004	Nathaniel Bingham Fabrics 6530-7	Department 56	Closed	25.00	90-160.00
86-02-005	Livery Stable & Boot Shop 6530-7	Department 56	Closed	25.00	85-130.00
86-02-006	Steeple Church 6530-7	Department 56	Closed	25.00	75-135.00
86-02-007	Brick Town Hall 6530-7	Department 56	Closed	25.00	175-245.
86-02-008	Red Schoolhouse 6530-7	Department 56	Closed	25.00	200-325.
86-02-009	Jacob Adams Farmhouse and Barn 6538-2	Department 56	Closed	65.00	360-475.
86-02-010	Steeple Church 6539-0	Department 56	Closed	30.00	75-135.00
87-02-011	Craggy Cove Lighthouse 5930-7	Department 56	Open	35.00	44.00
87-02-012	Weston Train Station 5931-5	Department 56	Closed	42.00	200-300.
87-02-013	Smythe Woolen Mill 6543-1	Department 56	7,500	42.00	900-1300.
87-02-014	Timber Knoll Log Cabin 6544-7	Department 56	Closed	28.00	90-150.00
88-02-015	Old North Church 5932-3	Department 56	Open	40.00	42.00
88-02-016	Cherry Lane Shops 5939-0, Set of 3	Department 56	Closed	80.00	190-275.
88-02-017	Ben's Barbershop 5939-0	Department 56	Closed	27.00	65-110.00
88-02-018	Otis Hayes Butcher Shop 5939-0	Department 56	Closed	27.00	60-110.00
88-02-019	Anne Shaw Toys 5939-0	Department 56	Closed	27.00	95-135.
88-02-020	Ada's Bed and Boarding House (lemon yellow) 5940-4	Department 56	Closed	36.00	125-275.
88-02-021	Ada's Bed and Boarding House (pale yellow) 5940-4	Department 56	Closed	36.00	85-140.
89-02-022	Berkshire House (medium blue) 5942-0	Department 56	Closed	40.00	95-150.00
89-02-023	Berkshire House (teal) 5942-0	Department 56	Closed	40.00	80-100.00
89-02-024	Jannes Mullet Amish Farm House 5943-9	Department 56	Closed	32.00	70-95.00
89-02-025	Jannes Mullet Amish Barn 5944-7	Department 56	Closed	48.00	75-100.00
90-02-026	Shingle Creek House 5946-3	Department 56	Open	37.50	37.50
90-02-027	Captain's Cottage 5947-1	Department 56	Open	40.00	40.00
90-02-028	Sleepy Hollow 5954-4, Set of 3 (Sleepy Hollow School, Van Tassel Manor Ichabod Crane's Cottage)	Department 56	Open	96.00	96.00
90-02-029	Sleepy Hollow Church 5955-2	Department 56	Open	36.00	36.00
91-02-030	McGrebe-Cutters & Sleighs 5640-5	Department 56	Open	45.00	45.00
92-02-031	Bluebird Seed and Bulb, 5642-1	Department 56	Open	48.00	48.00
92-02-032	Yankee Jud Bell Casting 5643-0	Department 56	Open	44.00	44.00
92-02-033	Stoney Brook Town Hall 5644-8	Department 56	Open	42.00	42.00
Department 56		**Alpine Village Collection**			
86-03-001	Alpine Village 6540-4, 5/set (Bessor Bierkeller, Gasthof Eisl, Apotheke, E. Staubr Backer, Milch-Kase)	Department 56	Open	150.00	185.00
87-03-002	Josef Engel Farmhouse 5952-8	Department 56	Closed	33.00	400-575.
87-03-003	Alpine Church 6541-2	Department 56	Closed	32.00	85-150.00
88-03-004	Grist Mill 5953-6	Department 56	Open	42.00	44.00
90-03-005	Bahnhof 5615-4	Department 56	Open	42.00	42.00
91-03-006	St. Nikolaus Kirche 5617-0	Department 56	Open	37.50	37.50
92-03-007	Alpine Shops 5618-9,2/set (Metterniche Wurst, Kukuck Uhren)	Department 56	Open	75.00	75.00
Department 56		**Christmas In the City Collection**			
87-04-001	Sutton Place Brownstones 5961-7	Department 56	Closed	80.00	700-950.
87-04-002	The Cathedral 5962-5	Department 56	Closed	60.00	275-400.
87-04-003	Palace Theatre 5963-3	Department 56	Closed	45.00	800-1200.
87-04-004	Christmas In The City 6512-9, Set of 3	Department 56	Closed	112.00	300-450.
87-04-005	Toy Shop and Pet Store 6512-9	Department 56	Closed	37.50	100-150.
87-04-006	Bakery 6512-9	Department 56	Closed	37.50	75-125.00
87-04-007	Tower Restaurant 6512-9	Department 56	Closed	37.50	125-185.
88-04-008	Chocolate Shoppe 5968-4	Department 56	Closed	40.00	70-125.00
88-04-009	City Hall (standard) 5969-2	Department 56	Closed	65.00	125-185.
88-04-010	City Hall (small) 5969-2	Department 56	Closed	65.00	200-250.
88-04-011	Hank's Market 5970-6	Department 56	Closed	40.00	75-95.00
88-04-012	Variety Store 5972-2	Department 56	Closed	45.00	100-160.
89-04-013	Ritz Hotel 5973-0	Department 56	Open	55.00	55.00
89-04-014	Dorothy's Dress Shop 5974-9	Department 56	12,500	70.00	325-475.
89-04-015	Dorothy's Dress Shop (proof) 5974-9	Department 56	12,500	70.00	250-300.
89-04-016	5607 Park Avenue Townhouse 5977-3	Department 56	Closed	48.00	75-100.00
89-04-017	5609 Park Avenue Townhouse 5978-1	Department 56	Closed	48.00	75-100.00
90-04-018	Red Brick Fire Station 5536-0	Department 56	Open	55.00	55.00
90-04-019	Wong's In Chinatown 5537-9	Department 56	Open	55.00	55.00
91-04-020	Hollydale's Department Store 5534-4	Department 56	Open	75.00	75.00
91-04-021	"Little Italy" Ristorante 5538-7	Department 56	Open	50.00	50.00
91-04-022	All Saints Corner Church 5542-5	Department 56	Open	96.00	96.00
91-04-023	Arts Academy 5543-3	Department 56	Open	45.00	45.00
90-04-024	The Doctor's Office 5544-1	Department 56	Open	60.00	60.00
92-04-025	Cathedral Church of St. Mark 5549-2	Department 56	17,500	120.00	3000-4500.
92-04-026	Uptown Shoppes 5531-0, Set of 3 (Haberdashery, City Clockworks, Music Emporium)	Department 56	Open	150.00	150.00
Department 56		**Little Town of Bethlehem Collection**			
87-05-001	Little Town of Bethlehem 5975-7, Set of 12	Department 56	Open	150.00	150.00
Department 56		**The Original Snow Village Collection**			
76-06-001	Mountain Lodge 5001-3	Department 56	Closed	20.00	385-600.
76-06-002	Gabled Cottage 5002-1	Department 56	Closed	20.00	350-400.
76-06-003	The Inn 5003-9	Department 56	Closed	20.00	440-500.
76-06-004	Country Church 5004-7	Department 56	Closed	18.00	300-380.
76-06-005	Steepled Church 5005-4	Department 56	Closed	25.00	450-750.
76-06-006	Small Chalet 5006-2	Department 56	Closed	15.00	300-375.
77-06-007	Victorian House 5007-0	Department 56	Closed	30.00	330-500.
77-06-008	Mansion 5008-8	Department 56	Closed	30.00	475-625.
77-06-009	Stone Church 5009-6 (10")	Department 56	Closed	35.00	400-650.
78-06-010	Homestead 5011-2	Department 56	Closed	30.00	225-350.
78-06-011	General Store 5012-0	Department 56	Closed	25.00	350-800.
78-06-012	Cape Cod 5013-8	Department 56	Closed	20.00	350-400.
78-06-013	Nantucket 5014-6	Department 56	Closed	25.00	200-300.
78-06-014	Skating Rink, Duck Pond (Set) 5015-3	Department 56	Closed	16.00	1150-1850.
78-06-016	Small Double Trees w/ red birds 5016-1	Department 56	Closed	13.50	35-75.00
79-06-017	Thatched Cottage 5050-0 Meadowland Series	Department 56	Closed	30.00	400-1400.
79-06-018	Countryside Church 5051-8 Meadowland Series	Department 56	Closed	25.00	275-1800.
79-06-019	Victorian 5054-2	Department 56	Closed	30.00	375-425.
79-06-020	Knob Hill 5055-9	Department 56	Closed	30.00	300-450.
79-06-021	Brownstone 5056-7	Department 56	Closed	36.00	425-600.
79-06-022	Log Cabin 5057-5	Department 56	Closed	22.00	425-500.
79-06-023	Countryside Church 5058-3	Department 56	Closed	27.50	250-400.
79-06-024	Stone Church 5059-1 (8")	Department 56	Closed	32.00	475-900.
79-06-025	School House 5060-9	Department 56	Closed	30.00	300-500.
79-06-026	Tudor House 5061-7	Department 56	Closed	25.00	300-400.
79-06-027	Mission Church 5062-5	Department 56	Closed	30.00	880-1500.
79-06-028	Mobile Home 5063-3	Department 56	Closed	18.00	1500-2500.
79-06-029	Giant Trees 5065-8	Department 56	Closed	20.00	300-400.
79-06-030	Adobe House 5066-6	Department 56	Closed	18.00	2000-2600.
80-06-031	Cathedral Church 5067-4	Department 56	Closed	36.00	1100-3000.
80-06-032	Stone Mill House 5068-2	Department 56	Closed	30.00	550-700.
80-06-033	Colonial Farm House 5070-9	Department 56	Closed	30.00	300-400.
80-06-034	Town Church 5071-7	Department 56	Closed	33.00	325-425.
80-06-035	Train Station with 3 Train Cars 5085-6	Department 56	Closed	100.00	350-450.
81-06-036	Wooden Clapboard 5072-5	Department 56	Closed	32.00	250-400.
81-06-037	English Cottage 5073-3	Department 56	Closed	25.00	275-325.
81-06-038	Barn 5074-1	Department 56	Closed	32.00	350-500.
81-06-039	Corner Store 5076-8	Department 56	Closed	30.00	225-350.
81-06-040	Bakery 5077-6	Department 56	Closed	30.00	225-340.
81-06-041	English Church 5078-4	Department 56	Closed	30.00	275-350.
81-06-042	Large Single Tree 5080-6	Department 56	Closed	17.00	42-60.00
82-06-043	Skating Pond 5017-2	Department 56	Closed	25.00	275-400.
82-06-044	Street Car 5019-9	Department 56	Closed	16.00	330-400.
82-06-045	Centennial House 5020-2	Department 56	Closed	32.00	300-400.
82-06-046	Carriage House 5021-0	Department 56	Closed	28.00	275-350.
82-06-047	Pioneer Church 5022-9	Department 56	Closed	30.00	300-450.
82-06-048	Swiss Chalet 5023-7	Department 56	Closed	28.00	350-400.

Company		Series			
Number	**Name**	**Artist**	**Edition Limit**	**Issue Price**	**Quote**
82-06-049	Bank 5024-5	Department 56	Closed	32.00	500-650.
82-06-050	Gabled House 5081-4	Department 56	Closed	30.00	350-500.
82-06-051	Flower Shop 5082-2	Department 56	Closed	25.00	375-475.
82-06-052	New Stone Church 5083-0	Department 56	Closed	32.00	200-275.
83-06-053	Town Hall 5000-8	Department 56	Closed	32.00	300-475.
83-06-054	Grocery 5001-6	Department 56	Closed	35.00	300-350.
83-06-055	Victorian Cottage 5002-4	Department 56	Closed	35.00	330-400.
83-06-056	Governor's Mansion 5003-2	Department 56	Closed	32.00	200-250.
83-06-057	Turn of the Century 5004-0	Department 56	Closed	36.00	200-325.
83-06-058	Gingerbread HouseBank(Non-lighted)5025-3	Department 56	Closed	24.00	300-700.
83-06-059	Village Church 5026-1	Department 56	Closed	30.00	275-350.
83-06-060	Gothic Church 5028-8	Department 56	Closed	36.00	200-275.
83-06-061	Parsonage 5029-6	Department 56	Closed	35.00	325-400.
83-06-062	Wooden Church 5031-8	Department 56	Closed	30.00	350-400.
83-06-063	Fire Station 5032-6	Department 56	Closed	32.00	500-700.
83-06-064	English Tudor 5033-4	Department 56	Closed	30.00	250-275.
83-06-065	Chateau 5084-9	Department 56	Closed	35.00	300-350.
84-06-066	Main Street House 5005-9	Department 56	Closed	27.00	200-350.
84-06-067	Stratford House 5007-5	Department 56	Closed	28.00	175-250.
84-06-068	Haversham House 5008-3	Department 56	Closed	37.00	225-375.
84-06-069	Galena House 5009-1	Department 56	Closed	32.00	285-450.
84-06-070	River Road House 5010-5	Department 56	Closed	36.00	150-300.
84-06-071	Delta House 5012-1	Department 56	Closed	32.00	275-375.
84-06-072	Bayport 5015-6	Department 56	Closed	30.00	200-300.
84-06-073	Congregational Church 5034-2	Department 45	Closed	28.00	300-375.
84-06-074	Trinity Church 5035-0	Department 56	Closed	32.00	220-350.
84-06-075	Summit House 5036-9	Department 56	Closed	28.00	300-400.
84-06-076	New School House 5037-7	Department 56	Closed	35.00	250-350.
84-06-077	Parish Church 5039-3	Department 56	Closed	32.00	300-475.
85-06-078	Stucco Bungalow 5045-8	Department 56	Closed	30.00	300-400.
85-06-079	Williamsburg House 5046-6	Department 56	Closed	37.00	100-125.
85-06-080	Plantation House 5047-4	Department 56	Closed	37.00	80-105.00
85-06-081	Church of the Open Door 5048-2	Department 56	Closed	34.00	100-150.
85-06-082	Spruce Place 5049-0	Department 56	Closed	33.00	250-325.
85-06-083	Duplex 5050-4	Department 56	Closed	35.00	100-150.
85-06-084	Depot and Train with 2 Train Cars 5051-2	Department 56	Closed	65.00	110-150.
85-06-085	Ridgewood 5052-0	Department 56	Closed	35.00	100-135.
86-06-086	Waverly Place 5041-5	Department 56	Closed	35.00	250-350.
86-06-087	Twin Peaks 5042-3	Department 56	Closed	32.00	275-330.
86-06-088	2101 Maple 5043-1	Department 56	Closed	32.00	325-400.
86-06-089	Lincoln Park Duplex 5060-1	Department 56	Closed	33.00	85-130.00
86-06-090	Sonoma House 5062-8	Department 56	Closed	33.00	88-140.00
86-06-091	Highland Park House 5063-6	Department 56	Closed	35.00	100-150.
86-06-092	Beacon Hill House 5065-2	Department 56	Closed	31.00	90-125.00
86-06-093	Pacific Heights House 5066-0	Department 56	Closed	33.00	90-120.00
86-06-094	Ramsey Hill House 5067-9	Department 56	Closed	36.00	95-150.00
86-06-095	Saint James Church 5068-7	Department 56	Closed	37.00	100-150.
86-06-096	All Saints Church 5070-9	Department 56	Open	38.00	45.00
86-06-097	Carriage House 5071-7	Department 56	Closed	29.00	75-150.00
86-06-098	Toy Shop 5073-3	Department 56	Closed	36.00	90-125.00
86-06-099	Apothecary 5076-8	Department 56	Closed	34.00	75-125.00
86-06-100	Bakery 5077-6	Department 56	Closed	35.00	75-100.00
86-06-101	Mickey's Diner 5078-4	Department 56	Closed	22.00	325-475.
87-06-102	St. Anthony Hotel & Post Office 5006-7	Department 56	Closed	40.00	85-150.00
87-06-103	Snow Village Factory 5013-0	Department 56	Closed	45.00	100-150.
87-06-104	Cathedral Church 5019-9	Department 56	Closed	50.00	90-120.00
87-06-105	Cumberland House 5024-5	Department 56	Open	42.00	44.00
87-06-106	Springfield House 5027-0	Department 56	Closed	40.00	85-110.00
87-06-107	Lighthouse 5030-0	Department 56	Closed	36.00	300-450.
87-06-108	Red Barn 5081-4	Department 56	Closed	38.00	65-85.00
87-06-109	Jefferson School 5082-2	Department 56	Closed	36.00	100-115.
87-06-110	Farm House 5089-0	Department 56	Closed	40.00	65-110.00
87-06-111	Fire Station No. 2 5091-1	Department 56	Closed	40.00	100-145.
87-06-112	Snow Village Resort Lodge 5092-0	Department 56	Closed	55.00	90-150.00
88-06-113	Village Market 5044-0	Department 56	Closed	39.00	75-100.00
88-06-114	Kenwood House 5054-7	Department 56	Closed	50.00	90-160.00
88-06-115	Maple Ridge Inn 5121-7	Department 56	Closed	55.00	85-115.
88-06-116	Village Station and Train 5122-5	Department 56	Closed	65.00	85-125.00
88-06-117	Cobblestone Antique Shop 5123-3	Department 56	Closed	36.00	60-85.00
88-06-118	Corner Cafe 5124-1	Department 56	Closed	37.00	75-95.00
88-06-119	Single Car Garage 5125-0	Department 56	Closed	22.00	50-90.00
88-06-120	Home Sweet Home/House & Windmill5126-8	Department 56	Closed	60.00	90-125.00
88-06-121	Redeemer Church 5127-6	Department 56	Closed	42.00	65-100.00
88-06-122	Service Station 5128-4	Department 56	Closed	37.50	85-135.00
88-06-123	Stonehurst House 5140-3	Department 56	Open	37.50	37.50
88-06-124	Palos Verdes 5141-1	Department 56	Closed	37.50	65-95.00
89-06-125	Jingle Belle Houseboat 5114-4	Department 56	Closed	42.00	85-100.00
89-06-126	Colonial Church 5119-5	Department 56	Closed	60.00	70-90.00
89-06-127	North Creek Cottage 5120-9	Department 56	Closed	45.00	60.00
89-06-128	Paramount Theater 5142-0	Department 56	Open	42.00	42.00
89-06-129	Doctor's House 5143-8	Department 56	Closed	56.00	85-110.00
89-06-130	Courthouse 5144-6	Department 56	Open	65.00	65.00
89-06-131	Village Warming House 5145-4	Department 56	Closed	42.00	50-77.00
89-06-132	J. Young's Granary 5149-7	Department 56	Closed	45.00	55-85.00
89-06-133	Pinewood Log Cabin 5150-0	Department 56	Open	37.50	37.50
90-06-134	56 Flavors Ice Cream Parlor 5151-9	Department 56	Closed	42.00	70-85.00
90-06-135	Morningside House 5152-7	Department 56	Closed	45.00	60-85.00
90-06-136	Mainstreet Hardware Store 5153-5	Department 56	Open	42.00	42.00
90-06-137	Village Realty 5154-3	Department 56	Open	42.00	42.00
90-06-138	Spanish Mission Church 5155-1	Department 56	Closed	42.00	75-95.00
90-06-139	Prairie House (American Architecture Series), 5156-0	Department 56	Open	42.00	42.00
90-06-140	Queen Anne Victorian (American Architecture Series), 5157-8	Department 56	Open	48.00	48.00
91-06-141	Oak Grove Tudor 5400-3	Department 56	Open	42.00	42.00
91-06-142	Honeymooner Motel 5401-1	Department 56	Open	42.00	42.00
91-06-143	The Christmas Shop 5097-0	Department 56	Open	37.50	37.50
91-06-144	Village Greenhouse 5402-0	Department 56	Open	35.00	35.00
91-06-145	Southern Colonial (American Architecture Series), 5403-8	Department 56	Open	48.00	48.00
91-06-146	Gothic Farmhouse (American Architecture Series), 5404-6	Department 56	Open	48.00	48.00
91-06-147	Finklea's Finery: Costume Shop 5405-4	Department 56	Open	45.00	45.00
91-06-148	Jack's Corner Barber Shop 5406-2	Department 56	Open	42.00	42.00
91-06-149	Double Bungalow, 5407-0	Department 56	Open	45.00	45.00
92-06-150	Post Office 5422-4	Department 56	Open	35.00	35.00
92-06-151	Grandma's Cottage 5420-8	Department 56	Open	45.00	45.00
92-06-152	St. Luke's Church 5421-6	Department 56	Open	45.00	45.00
92-06-153	Al's TV Shop 5423-2	Department 56	Open	40.00	40.00
92-06-154	Good Shepherd Chapel & Church School Set of 2 5424-0	Department 56	Open	72.00	72.00
92-06-155	Print Shop & Village News 5425-9	Department 56	Open	37.50	37.50
92-06-156	Hartford House 5426-7	Department 56	Open	55.00	55.00
92-06-157	Village Vet and Pet Shop 5427-5	Department 56	Open	32.00	32.00
92-06-158	Craftsman Cottage (American Architecture Series),5437-2	Department 56	Open	55.00	55.00
92-06-159	Village Station 5438-0	Department 56	Open	65.00	65.00
92-06-160	Airport 5439-9	Department 56	Open	60.00	60.00
Department 56		**North Pole Collection**			
90-07-001	Santa's Workshop 5600-6	Department 56	Open	72.00	72.00
90-07-002	North Pole 5601-4 Set of 2 (Reindeer Barn, Elf Bunkhouse)	Department 56	Open	70.00	70.00
91-07-003	Neenee's Dolls & Toys 5620-0	Department 56	Open	37.50	36.00
91-07-004	North Pole Shops, Set of 2 5621-9 (Orly's Bell & Harness Supply, Rimpy's Bakery)	Department 56	Open	75.00	75.00
91-07-005	Tassy's Mittens & Hassel's Woolies 5622-7	Department 56	Open	50.00	50.00
92-07-006	North Pole Post Office 5623-5	Department 56	Open	45.00	45.00
92-07-007	Obbie's Books & Letrinka's Candy 5624-3	Department 56	Open	70.00	70.00
92-07-008	Elfie's Sleds & Skates 5625-1	Department 56	Open	48.00	48.00
Department 56		**Event Piece - Heritage Village Collection Accessory**			
92-08-001	Gate House 5530-1	Department 56	Closed	22.50	65-80.00
Department 56		**Retired Heritage Village Collection Accessories**			
84-09-001	Carolers 6526-9, Set Of 3 w/ Lamppost(wh)	Department 56	Closed	10.00	100-170.
84-09-002	Carolers 6526-9, Set Of 3 w/ Lamppost(bl)	Department 56	Closed	10.00	25-60.00
85-09-003	Village Train Brighton 6527-7, Set Of 3	Department 56	Closed	12.00	330-450.
86-09-004	Christmas Carol Figures 6501-3, Set of 3	Department 56	Closed	12.50	30-55.00
86-09-005	Lighted Tree With Children & Ladder 6510-2	Department 56	Closed	35.00	275-435.
86-09-006	Sleighride 6511-0	Department 56	Closed	19.50	40-65.00
86-09-007	Covered Wooden Bridge 6531-5	Department 56	Closed	10.00	30-50.00
86-09-008	New England Winter Set 6532-3, Set of 5	Department 56	Closed	18.00	30-65.00
86-09-009	Porcelain Trees 6537-4, Set of 3	Department 56	Closed	14.00	33-50.00
86-09-010	Alpine Villagers 6542-0, Set of 3	Department 56	Closed	13.00	30-50.00
87-09-011	Farm People And Animals 5901-3, Set Of 5	Department 56	Closed	24.00	50-75.00
87-09-012	Blacksmith 5934-0, Set of 3	Department 56	Closed	20.00	40-65.00
87-09-013	City People 5965-0, Set of 5	Department 56	Closed	27.50	40-50.00
87-09-014	Silo And Hay Shed 5950-1	Department 56	Closed	18.00	90-125.00
87-09-015	Ox Sled 5951-0	Department 56	Closed	20.00	75-130.00
87-09-016	Shopkeepers 5966-8, Set Of 4	Department 56	Closed	15.00	25-45.00
87-09-017	City Workers 5967-6, Set Of 4	Department 56	Closed	15.00	30-45.00
87-09-018	Skating Pond 6545-5	Department 56	Closed	24.00	65-95.00
87-09-019	Stone Bridge 6546-3	Department 56	Closed	12.00	60-80.00
87-09-020	Village Well And Holy Cross 6547-1, Set Of 2	Department 56	Closed	13.00	90-135.00
87-09-021	Maple Sugaring Shed 6589-7, Set Of 3	Department 56	Closed	19.00	130-175.
87-09-022	Dover Coach 6590-0	Department 56	Closed	18.00	50-85.00
87-09-023	Dover Coach w/o Mustache 6590-0	Department 56	Closed	18.00	85-130.00
87-09-024	Village Express Train (electric, black),5997-8	Department 56	Closed	89.95	250-325.
88-09-025	Fezziwig and Friends 5928-5, Set Of 3	Department 56	Closed	12.50	30-50.00
88-09-026	Village Train Trestle 5981-1	Department 56	Closed	17.00	45-70.00
88-09-027	Woodcutter And Son 5986-2, Set Of 2	Department 56	Closed	10.00	25-48.00
88-09-028	Childe Pond and Skaters 5903-0, Set of 4	Department 56	Closed	30.00	65-100.00
88-09-029	Nicholas Nickleby Characters 5929-3,Set of 4	Department 56	Closed	20.00	35-75.00
88-09-030	Village Harvest People 5941-2 Set of4	Department 56	Closed	27.50	33-58.00
88-09-031	City Newsstand 5971-4, Set of 4	Department 56	Closed	25.00	40-65.00
88-09-032	City Bus & Milk Truck 5983-8, Set of 2	Department 56	Closed	15.00	30-45.00
88-09-033	Salvation Army Band 5985-4, Set of 6	Department 56	Closed	24.00	40-60.00
89-09-034	Constables 5579-4, Set Of 3	Department 56	Closed	17.50	40-60.00
89-09-035	Farm Animals 5945-5, Set of 4	Department 56	Closed	15.00	25-40.00
89-09-036	Organ Grinder 5957-9, Set of 3	Department 56	Closed	21.00	35-45.00
89-09-037	River Street Ice House Cart 5959-5	Department 56	Closed	20.00	35-55.00
89-09-038	David Copperfield Characters, Set of 5 5551-4	Department 56	Closed	32.50	40-65.00
89-09-039	Royal Coach 5578-6	Department 56	Closed	55.00	70-100.00
89-09-040	Violet Vendor/Carolers/Chestnut Vendor Set of 3 5580-8	Department 56	Closed	23.00	30-42.00
89-09-041	Popcorn Vendor, Set of 3 5958-7	Department 56	Closed	22.00	30-42.00
89-09-042	U.S. Mail Box and Fire Hydrant, 5517-4	Department 56	Closed	5.00	15-35.00
90-09-043	Busy Sidewalks, Set of 4 5535-2	Department 56	Closed	28.00	40-65.00
90-09-044	Amish Family, Set of 3 5948-0	Department 56	Closed	20.00	35-46.00
90-09-045	Amish Buggy 5949-8	Department 56	Closed	22.00	35-56.00
90-09-046	Sleepy Hollow Characters, Set of 3 5956-0	Department 56	Closed	27.50	40-48.00
XX-09-047	Heritage Village Sign, 9963-8	Department 56	Closed	10.00	16-20.00
Department 56		**The Original Snow Village Collection Accessories Retired**			
79-10-001	Aspen Trees 5052-6, Meadowland Series	Department 56	Closed	16.00	32.00
79-10-002	Sheep, 9 White, 3 Black 5053-4 Meadowland Series	Department 56	Closed	12.00	24.00
79-10-003	Carolers 5064-1	Department 56	Closed	12.00	100-150.
80-10-004	Ceramic Car 5069-0	Department 56	Closed	5.00	30-75.00
81-10-005	Ceramic Sleigh 5079-2	Department 56	Closed	5.00	40-70.00
82-10-006	Snowman With Broom 5018-0	Department 56	Closed	3.00	10-30.00
83-10-007	Monks-A-Caroling (butterscotch) 6459-9	Department 56	Closed	6.00	65-125.00
84-10-008	Scottie With Tree 5038-5	Department 56	Closed	3.00	100-125.
84-10-009	Monks-A-Caroling (brown) 5040-7	Department 56	Closed	6.00	30-40.00
85-10-010	Singing Nuns 5053-9	Department 56	Closed	6.00	75-85.00
85-10-011	Snow Kids Sled, Skis 5056-3	Department 56	Closed	11.00	30-55.00
85-10-012	Family Mom/Kids, Goose/Girl 5057-1	Department 56	Closed	11.00	35-55.00
85-10-013	Santa/Mailbox 5059-8	Department 56	Closed	11.00	30-50.00
86-10-014	Girl/Snowman, Boy 5095-4	Department 56	Closed	11.00	30-50.00
86-10-015	Shopping Girls With Packages 5096-2	Department 56	Closed	11.00	25-50.00
86-10-016	Kids Around The Tree 5094-6	Department 56	Closed	15.00	30-60.00
87-10-017	3 Nuns With Songbooks 5102-0	Department 56	Closed	6.00	50-75.00
87-10-018	Praying Monks 5103-9	Department 56	Closed	6.00	25-40.00
87-10-019	Children In Band 5104-7	Department 56	Closed	15.00	25-40.00
87-10-020	Caroling Family 5105-5, Set Of 3	Department 56	Closed	20.00	30-40.00
87-10-021	Christmas Children 5107-1, Set Of 4	Department 56	Closed	20.00	30-40.00
87-10-022	Snow Kids 5113-6, Set of 4	Department 56	Closed	20.00	30-60.00
88-10-023	Hayride 5117-9	Department 56	Closed	30.00	45-75.00
88-10-024	School Children 5118-7, Set of 3	Department 56	Closed	15.00	20-35.00
88-10-025	Apple Girl/Newspaper Boy 5129-2, Set of 2	Department 56	Closed	11.00	20-32.00
88-10-026	Woodsman and Boy 5130-6, Set of 2	Department 56	Closed	13.00	25-46.00
88-10-027	Woody Station Wagon 5136-5	Department 56	Closed	6.50	15-50.00
88-10-028	Water Tower 5133-0	Department 56	Closed	20.00	45-85.00
88-10-029	School Bus, Snow Plow 5137-3, Set of 2	Department 56	Closed	16.00	30-35.00
88-10-030	Sisal Tree Lot 8183-3	Department 56	Closed	45.00	50-85.00
88-10-031	Man On Ladder Hanging Garland 5116-0	Department 56	Closed	7.50	12-22.00
88-10-032	Doghouse/Cat In Garbage Can,set/2 5131-4	Department 56	Closed	15.00	20-33.00
89-10-033	US Special Delivery 5148-9 Set of 2	Department 56	Closed	16.00	50-75.00
89-10-034	US Mailbox 5179-9	Department 56	Closed	3.50	15-30.00
89-10-035	Kids Tree House 5168-3	Department 56	Closed	25.00	40-70.00
89-10-036	Skate Faster Mom 5170-5	Department 56	Closed	13.00	30-35.00
89-10-037	Through the Woods 5172-1, Set of 2	Department 56	Closed	18.00	30.00
89-10-038	Statue of Mark Twain 5173-0	Department 56	Closed	15.00	25-35.00
89-10-039	Calling All Cars 5174-8, Set of 2	Department 56	Closed	15.00	25-45.00

Number	Name	Artist	Edition Limit	Issue Price	Quote
Company		**Series**			
89-10-040	Choir Kids 5147-0	Department 56	Closed	15.00	18.00
89-10-041	Bringing Home The Tree 5169-1	Department 56	Closed	15.00	15.00
90-10-042	Sleighride 5160-8	Department 56	Closed	30.00	40-55.00
90-10-043	Here We Come A Caroling, set/3 5161-6	Department 56	Closed	18.00	20.00
90-10-044	Home Delivery, set of 2 5162-4	Department 56	Closed	16.00	18.00
90-10-045	SV Special Delivery, set of 2 5197-7	Department 56	Closed	16.00	30-40.00
91-10-046	Come Join The Parade 5411-9	Department 56	Closed	12.50	16.00
91-10-047	Village Marching Band, set of 3 5412-7	Department 56	Closed	30.00	40.00
Department 56		**Snowbabies**			
86-11-001	Give Me A Push 7955-3	Department 56	Closed	12.00	35-50.00
86-11-002	Hold On Tight 7956-1	Department 56	Open	12.00	12.00
86-11-003	Best Friends 7958-8	Department 56	Closed	12.00	65-100.00
86-11-004	Snowbaby Nite-Lite 7959-6	Department 56	Closed	15.00	300-350.
86-11-005	I'm Making Snowballs 7962-6	Department 56	Closed	12.00	25-35.00
86-11-006	Climbing on Snowball 7965-0	Department 56	Closed	15.00	50-100.00
86-11-007	Hanging Pair 7966-9	Department 56	Closed	15.00	45-85.00
86-11-008	Snowbaby Holding Picture Frame, Set of 2 7970-7	Department 56	Closed	15.00	330-400.
87-11-009	Tumbling In the Snow, Set of 5 7957-0	Department 56	Open	35.00	35.00
87-11-010	Down The Hill We Go 7960-0	Department 56	Open	20.00	20.00
87-11-011	Don't Fall Off 7968-5	Department 56	Closed	12.50	35-65.00
87-11-012	Climbing On Tree, Set Of 2 7971-5	Department 56	Closed	25.00	350-500.
87-11-013	Winter Surprise 7974-0	Department 56	Closed	15.00	25-35.00
88-11-014	Are All These Mine? 7977-4	Department 56	Open	10.00	10.00
88-11-015	Polar Express 7978-2	Department 56	Closed	22.00	45-65.00
88-11-016	Tiny Trio, Set Of 3 7979-0	Department 56	Closed	20.00	70-115.00
88-11-017	Frosty Frolic 7981-2	Department 56	4,800	35.00	550-800.
89-11-018	Helpful Friends 7982-0	Department 56	Open	30.00	30.00
89-11-019	Frosty Fun 7983-9	Department 56	Closed	27.50	50-75.00
89-11-020	All Fall Down, set Of 4 7984-7	Department 56	Closed	36.00	60-85.00
89-11-021	Finding Fallen Stars 7985-5	Department 56	6,000	32.50	135-175.
89-11-022	Penguin Parade 7986-3	Department 56	Closed	25.00	45-65.00
89-11-023	Icy Igloo 7987-1	Department 56	Open	37.50	37.50
90-11-024	Twinkle Little Stars 7942-1 set of 2	Department 56	Open	37.50	37.50
90-11-025	Wishing on a Star 7943-0	Department 56	Open	20.00	20.00
90-11-026	Read Me a Story 7945-6	Department 56	Open	25.00	25.00
90-11-027	We Will Make it Shine 7946-4	Department 56	Closed	45.00	70-85.00
90-11-028	Playing Games Is Fun 7947-2	Department 56	Open	30.00	30.00
90-11-029	A Special Delivery 7948-0	Department 56	Open	13.50	13.50
90-11-030	Who Are You? 7949-9	Department 56	12,500	32.50	100-175.
91-11-031	I Will Put Up The Tree 6800-4	Department 56	Open	24.00	24.00
91-11-032	Why Don't You Talk To Me 6801-2	Department 56	Open	24.00	24.00
91-11-033	I Made This Just For You 6802-0	Department 56	Open	15.00	15.00
91-11-034	Is That For Me 6803-9 Set of 2	Department 56	Open	32.50	32.50
91-11-035	Snowbaby Polar Sign 6804-7	Department 56	Open	20.00	20.00
91-11-036	This Is Where We Live 6805-5	Department 56	Open	60.00	60.00
91-11-037	Waiting For Christmas 6807-1	Department 56	Open	27.50	27.50
91-11-038	Dancing To a Tune 6808-0, set of 3	Department 56	Open	30.00	30.00
91-11-039	Fishing For Dreams 6809-8	Department 56	Open	28.00	28.00
92-11-040	Can I Help Too? 6806-3	Department 56	Closed	48.00	70-100.00
92-11-041	I Need A Hug 6813-6	Department 56	Open	20.00	20.00
92-11-042	Let's Go Skiing 6815-2	Department 56	Open	15.00	15.00
92-11-043	Wait For Me 6812-8	Department 56	Open	48.00	48.00
92-11-044	Winken, Blinken, and Nod 6814-4	Department 56	Open	60.00	60.00
92-11-045	This Willl Cheer You Up 6816-0	Department 56	Open	30.00	30.00
92-11-046	Help Me, I'm Stuck 6817-9	Department 56	Open	32.50	32.50
92-11-047	You Can't Find Me! 6818-7	Department 56	Open	45.00	45.00
92-11-048	Look What I Can Do! 6819-5	Department 56	Open	16.50	16.50
92-11-049	Shall I Play For You? 6820-9	Department 56	Open	16.50	16.50
92-11-050	You Didn't Forget Me 6821-7	Department 56	Open	32.50	32.50
92-11-051	Stars-In-A-Row, Tic-Tac-Toe 6822-5	Department 56	Open	32.50	32.50
92-11-052	Just One Little Candle 6823-3	Department 56	Open	15.00	15.00
92-11-053	Join The Parade 6824-1	Department 56	Open	37.50	37.50
92-11-054	Snowbabies Bridge "Over the Milky Way" 6828-4	Department 56	Open	32.00	32.00
92-11-055	Snowbabies Trees "Starry Pines" set of 2, 6829-2	Department 56	Open	17.50	17.50
Department 56		**Snowbabies Pewter Miniatures**			
89-12-001	Are All These Mine? 7605-8	Department 56	Closed	7.00	12.00
89-12-002	Helpful Friends, set of 4 7608-2	Department 56	Closed	13.50	18.00
89-12-003	Polar Express, set of 2 7609-0	Department 56	Closed	13.50	N/A
89-12-004	Icy Igloo, w/tree, set of 2 7610-4	Department 56	Closed	7.50	12.00
89-12-005	Tumbling in the Snow!, set of 5 7614-7	Department 56	Closed	30.00	N/A
89-12-006	Finding Fallen Stars, set of 2 7618-0	Department 56	Closed	12.50	N/A
Department 56		**Village CCP Miniatures**			
87-13-001	Dickens' Village Original, set of 7 6558-7	Department 56	Closed	72.00	125-250.
87-13-002	Crowntree Inn 6558-7	Department 56	Closed	12.00	25-40.00
87-13-003	Candle Shop 6558-7	Department 56	Closed	12.00	30-40.00
87-13-004	Green Grocer 6558-7	Department 56	Closed	12.00	30-40.00
87-13-005	Golden Swan Baker 6558-7	Department 56	Closed	12.00	25-40.00
87-13-006	Bean and Son Smithy Shop 6558-7	Department 56	Closed	12.00	25-34.00
87-13-007	Abel Beesley Butcher 6558-7	Department 56	Closed	12.00	33-60.00
87-13-008	Jones & Co. Brush & Basket Shop 6558-7	Department 56	Closed	12.00	33-40.00
87-13-009	Dickens' Cottages, set of 3 6559-5	Department 56	Closed	30.00	150-275.
87-13-010	Thatched Cottage 6559-5	Department 56	Closed	10.00	55-80.00
87-13-011	Stone Cottage 6559-5	Department 56	Closed	10.00	55-82.00
87-13-012	Tudor Cottage 6559-5	Department 56	Closed	10.00	100-150.
87-13-013	Dickens' Village Assorted, set of 3 6560-9	Department 56	Closed	48.00	N/A
87-13-014	Dickens Village Church 6560-9	Department 56	Closed	16.00	33-52.00
87-13-015	Norman Church 6560-9	Department 56	Closed	16.00	55-100.00
87-13-016	Blythe Pond Mill House 6560-9	Department 56	Closed	16.00	36-50.00
87-13-017	Christmas Carol Cottages, set of 3 6561-7	Department 56	Closed	30.00	45-77.00
87-13-018	Fezziwig's Warehouse 6561-7	Department 56	Closed	10.00	25-35.00
87-13-019	Scrooge & Marley Countinghouse 6561-7	Department 56	Closed	10.00	26-33.00
87-13-020	The Cottage of Bob Cratchit & Tiny Tim 6561-7	Department 56	Closed	10.00	26.00
87-13-021	Dickens' Village Assorted, set of 4 6562-5	Department 56	Closed	60.00	N/A
87-13-022	The Old Curiosity Shop 6562-5	Department 56	Closed	15.00	42-55.00
87-13-023	Brick Abbey 6562-5	Department 56	Closed	15.00	50-75.00
87-13-024	Chesterton Manor House 6562-5	Department 56	Closed	15.00	75-90.00
87-13-025	Barley Bree Farmhouse 6562-5	Department 56	Closed	15.00	35-40.00
88-13-026	Dickens' Kenilworth Castle 6565-0	Department 56	Closed	30.00	70-90.00
87-13-027	Dickens' Lane Shops, set of 3 6591-9	Department 56	Closed	30.00	75-125.00
87-13-028	Thomas Kersey Coffee House 6591-9	Department 56	Closed	10.00	26-50.00
87-13-029	Cottage Toy Shop 6591-9	Department 56	Closed	10.00	26-32.00
87-13-030	Tuttle's Pub 6591-9	Department 56	Closed	10.00	28-40.00
87-13-031	Dickens' Chadbury Station & Train 6592-7	Department 56	Closed	27.50	55-75.00
88-13-032	New England Village Original, set of 7 5935-8	Department 56	Closed	72.00	250-425.
88-13-033	Apothecary Shop 5935-8	Department 56	Closed	10.50	30-45.00

Number	Name	Artist	Edition Limit	Issue Price	Quote
Company		**Series**			
88-13-034	General Store 5935-8	Department 56	Closed	10.50	50-60.00
88-13-035	Nathaniel Bingham Fabrics 5935-8	Department 56	Closed	10.50	50.00
88-13-036	Livery Stable & Boot Shop 5935-8	Department 56	Closed	10.50	30-50.00
88-13-037	Steeple Church 5935-8	Department 56	Closed	10.50	40-125.00
88-13-038	Brick Town Hall 5935-8	Department 56	Closed	10.50	40-55.00
88-13-039	Red Schoolhouse 5935-8	Department 56	Closed	10.50	40-65.00
88-13-040	New England Village Assorted, set of 6 5937-4	Department 56	Closed	85.00	225.00
88-13-041	Timber Knoll Log Cabin 5937-4	Department 56	Closed	14.50	30-42.00
88-13-042	Smythe Wollen Mill 5937-4	Department 56	Closed	14.50	65-80.00
88-13-043	Jacob Adams Farmhouse 5937-4	Department 56	Closed	14.50	42-50.00
88-13-044	Jacob Adams Barn 5937-4	Department 56	Closed	14.50	30-60.00
88-13-045	Craggy Cove Lighthouse 5937-4	Department 56	Closed	14.50	100-125.
88-13-046	Maple Sugaring Shed 5937-4	Department 56	Closed	14.50	32-48.00
87-13-047	Little Town of Bethlehem, set of 12 5976-5	Department 56	Closed	85.00	140-200.
86-13-048	Victorian Miniatures, set of 5 6563-3	Department 56	Closed	65.00	N/A
86-13-049	Victorian Miniatures, set of 2 6564-1	Department 56	Closed	45.00	300.00
86-13-050	Estate 6564-1	Department 56	Closed	22.50	N/A
86-13-051	Church 6564-1	Department 56	Closed	22.50	N/A
86-13-052	Williamsburg Snowhouse Series, set of 6 6566-8	Department 56	Closed	60.00	500-575.
86-13-053	Williamsburg House, White 6566-8	Department 56	Closed	10.00	40.00
86-13-054	Williamsburg House, Blue 6566-8	Department 56	Closed	10.00	60.00
86-13-055	Williamsburg House, Brown Brick 6566-8	Department 56	Closed	10.00	40.00
86-13-056	Williamsburg House, Brown Clapboard 6566-8	Department 56	Closed	10.00	40.00
86-13-057	Williamsburg House, Red 6566-8	Department 56	Closed	10.00	60.00
86-13-059	Williamsburg House, White 6566-8	Department 56	Closed	10.00	75.00
Walt Disney		**Classics Collection**			
92-01-001	Cinderella 6" 41000	Disney Studios	Open	195.00	195.00
92-01-002	Lucifer 2 3/5" 41001	Disney Studios	Open	69.00	69.00
92-01-003	Bruno 4 2/5" 41002	Disney Studios	Open	69.00	69.00
92-01-004	Cinderella's Sewing Book 41003	Disney Studios	Open	69.00	69.00
92-01-005	Needle Mouse 5 4/5" 41004	Disney Studios	Open	69.00	69.00
92-01-006	Birds With Sash 6 2/5" 41005	Disney Studios	Open	149.00	149.00
92-01-007	Chalk Mouse 3 2/5" 41006	Disney Studios	Open	65.00	65.00
92-01-008	Gus 3 2/5" 41007	Disney Studios	Open	65.00	65.00
92-01-009	Jaq 4 1/5" 41008	Disney Studios	Open	65.00	65.00
92-01-010	Cinderella 41009	Disney Studios	Open	29.00	29.00
92-01-011	Bambi & Flower 6" 41010	Disney Studios	10,000	298.00	298.00
92-01-012	Friend Owl 8 3/5" 41011	Disney Studios	Open	195.00	195.00
92-01-013	Field Mouse 5 3/5" 41012	Disney Studios	7,500	195.00	195.00
92-01-014	Thumper 3" 41013	Disney Studios	Open	55.00	55.00
92-01-015	Thumper's Sisters 3 3/5" 41014	Disney Studios	Open	69.00	69.00
92-01-016	Bambi 41015	Disney Studios	Open	29.00	29.00
92-01-017	Sorcerer Mickey 5 1/5" 41016	Disney Studios	Open	195.00	195.00
92-01-018	Broom (Two) 5 4/5" 41017	Disney Studios	Open	150.00	150.00
92-01-019	Fantasia 41019	Disney Studios	Open	29.00	29.00
92-01-020	Mickey 6" 41020	Disney Studios	Open	125.00	125.00
92-01-021	Minnie 6" 41021	Disney Studios	Open	125.00	125.00
92-01-022	Pluto 3 3/5" 41022	Disney Studios	Open	65.00	65.00
Walt Disney		**Cinderella Dress 9"**			
93-02-001	A Lovely Dress For Cinderelly	Disney Studios	Closed	800.00	800.00
Walt Disney		**The Delivery Boy**			
93-03-001	Opening Title: "The Delivery Boy"	Disney Studios	Open	29.00	29.00
93-03-002	Mickey	Disney Studios	Open	125.00	125.00
93-03-003	Minnie	Disney Studios	Open	125.00	125.00
93-03-004	Pluto	Disney Studios	Open	65.00	65.00
Duncan Royale		**History of Santa Claus I**			
83-01-001	St. Nicholas	P. Apsit	Retrd.	175.00	650-1800.
83-01-002	Dedt Moroz	P. Apsit	Retrd.	145.00	375-600.
83-01-003	Black Peter	P. Apsit	Retrd.	145.00	225-500.
83-01-004	Victorian	P. Apsit	Retrd.	120.00	250-450.
83-01-005	Medieval	P. Apsit	Retrd.	220.00	1200-3500.
83-01-006	Russian	P. Apsit	Retrd.	145.00	450-1000.
83-01-007	Wassail	P. Apsit	Retrd.	90.00	250-600.
83-01-008	Kris Kringle	P. Apsit	Retrd.	165.00	1200-2500.
83-01-009	Soda Pop	P. Apsit	Retrd.	145.00	850-3500.
83-01-010	Pioneer	P. Apsit	Retrd.	145.00	300-825.
83-01-011	Civil War	P. Apsit	10,000	145.00	250-600.
83-01-012	Nast	P. Apsit	Retrd.	90.00	2500-6900.
Duncan Royale		**History of Santa Claus II**			
86-02-001	Odin	P. Apsit	10,000	200.00	250.00
86-02-002	Lord of Misrule	P. Apsit	10,000	160.00	200.00
86-02-003	Mongolian/Asian	P. Apsit	10,000	240.00	300.00
86-02-004	The Magi	P. Apsit	10,000	350.00	400.00
86-02-005	St. Lucia	P. Apsit	10,000	180.00	225.00
86-02-006	Befana	P. Apsit	10,000	200.00	250.00
86-02-007	Babouska	P. Apsit	10,000	170.00	200.00
86-02-008	Bavarian	P. Apsit	10,000	250.00	300.00
86-02-009	Alsace Angel	P. Apsit	10,000	250.00	300.00
86-02-010	Frau Holda	P. Apsit	10,000	160.00	180.00
86-02-011	Sir Christmas	P. Apsit	10,000	150.00	175.00
86-02-012	The Pixie	P. Apsit	10,000	140.00	175.00
Duncan Royale		**History of Santa Claus III**			
90-03-001	St. Basil	Duncan Royale	10,000	300.00	300.00
90-03-002	Star Man	Duncan Royale	10,000	300.00	300.00
90-03-003	Julenisse	Duncan Royale	10,000	200.00	200.00
90-03-004	Ukko	Duncan Royale	10,000	250.00	250.00
90-03-005	Druid	Duncan Royale	10,000	250.00	250.00
91-03-006	Saturnalia King	Duncan Royale	10,000	200.00	200.00
91-03-007	Judah Maccabee	Duncan Royale	10,000	300.00	300.00
91-03-008	King Wenceslas	Duncan Royale	10,000	300.00	300.00
91-03-009	Hoteisho	Duncan Royale	10,000	200.00	200.00
91-03-010	Knickerbocker	Duncan Royale	10,000	300.00	300.00
91-03-011	Samichlaus	Duncan Royale	10,000	350.00	350.00
91-03-012	Grandfather Frost & Snow Maiden	Duncan Royale	10,000	400.00	400.00
Duncan Royale		**History Of Santa Claus-Special Releases**			
91-04-001	Signature Piece	Duncan Royale	Open	50.00	50.00
92-04-002	Nast & Sleigh	Duncan Royale	5,000	500.00	500.00
Duncan Royale		**History of Santa Claus I -Wood**			
87-05-001	St. Nicholas-8" wood	P. Apsit	500	450.00	450.00
87-05-002	Dedt Moroz-8" wood	P. Apsit	Retrd.	450.00	450.00
87-05-003	Black Peter-8" wood	P. Apsit	Retrd.	450.00	450.00
87-05-004	Victorian-8" wood	P. Apsit	500	450.00	450.00

Company Number	Name	Series Artist	Edition Limit	Issue Price	Quote
87-05-005	Medieval-8" wood	P. Apsit	500	450.00	450.00
87-05-006	Russian-8" wood	P. Apsit	Retrd.	450.00	450.00
87-05-007	Wassail-8" wood	P. Apsit	500	450.00	450.00
87-05-008	Kris Kringle-8" wood	P. Apsit	500	450.00	450.00
87-05-009	Soda Pop-8" wood	P. Apsit	Retrd.	450.00	450.00
87-05-010	Pioneer-8" wood	P. Apsit	Retrd.	450.00	450.00
87-05-011	Civil War-8" wood	P. Apsit	500	450.00	450.00
87-05-012	Nast-8" wood	P. Apsit	Retrd.	450.00	450.00
Duncan Royale		**History of Santa Claus (18")**			
89-06-013	St. Nicholas-18"	P. Apsit	1,000	1500.00	1500.00
89-06-014	Medieval-18"	P. Apsit	1,000	1500.00	1500.00
89-06-015	Russian-18"	P. Apsit	1,000	1500.00	1500.00
89-06-016	Kris Kringle-18"	P. Apsit	1,000	1500.00	1500.00
89-06-017	Soda Pop-18"	P. Apsit	1,000	1500.00	1500.00
89-06-018	Nast-18"	P. Apsit	1,000	1500.00	1500.00
Duncan Royale		**History of Santa Claus I (6")**			
88-07-001	St. Nicholas-6" porcelain	P. Apsit	6,000/yr.	70.00	80.00
88-07-002	Dedt Moroz -6" porcelain	P. Apsit	6,000/yr.	70.00	80.00
88-07-003	Black Peter-6" porcelain	P. Apsit	6,000/yr.	70.00	80.00
88-07-004	Victorian-6" porcelain	P. Apsit	6,000/yr.	60.00	80.00
88-07-005	Medieval-6" porcelain	P. Apsit	6,000/yr.	70.00	80.00
88-07-006	Russian-6" porcelain	P. Apsit	6,000/yr.	70.00	80.00
88-07-007	Wassail-6" porcelain	P. Apsit	6,000/yr.	60.00	80.00
88-07-008	Kris Kringle-6" porcelain	P. Apsit	6,000/yr.	60.00	80.00
88-07-009	Soda Pop-6" porcelain	P. Apsit	6,000/yr.	60.00	80.00
88-07-010	Pioneer-6" porcelain	P. Apsit	6,000/yr.	60.00	80.00
88-07-011	Civil War-6" porcelain	P. Apsit	6,000/yr.	60.00	80.00
88-07-012	Nast-6" porcelain	P. Apsit	6,000/yr.	60.00	80.00
Duncan Royale		**History of Santa Claus II (6")**			
88-08-001	Odin-6" porcelain	P. Apsit	6,000/yr.	80.00	90.00
88-08-002	Lord of Misrule-6" porcelain	P. Apsit	6,000/yr.	60.00	80.00
88-08-003	Mongolian/Asian-6" porcelain	P. Apsit	6,000/yr.	80.00	90.00
88-08-004	Magi-6" porcelain	P. Apsit	6,000/yr.	130.00	150.00
88-08-005	St. Lucia-6" porcelain	P. Apsit	6,000/yr.	70.00	80.00
88-08-006	Befana-6" porcelain	P. Apsit	6,000/yr.	70.00	80.00
88-08-007	Babouska-6" porcelain	P. Apsit	6,000/yr.	70.00	80.00
88-08-008	Bavarian-6" porcelain	P. Apsit	6,000/yr.	90.00	100.00
88-08-009	Alsace Angel-6" porcelain	P. Apsit	6,000/yr.	80.00	90.00
88-08-010	Frau Holda-6" porcelain	P. Apsit	6,000/yr.	50.00	80.00
88-08-011	Sir Christmas-6" porcelain	P. Apsit	6,000/yr.	60.00	80.00
88-08-012	Pixie-6" porcelain	P. Apsit	6,000/yr.	50.00	80.00
90-08-013	Bob Hope-6" porcelain	P. Apsit	6,000/yr.	130.00	130.00
Duncan Royale		**History of Classic Entertainers**			
87-09-001	Greco-Roman	P. Apsit	Retrd.	180.00	200.00
87-09-002	Jester	P. Apsit	Retrd.	410.00	450.00
87-09-003	Pierrot	P. Apsit	Retrd.	180.00	200.00
87-09-004	Harlequin	P. Apsit	Retrd.	250.00	270.00
87-09-005	Grotesque	P. Apsit	Retrd.	230.00	250.00
87-09-006	Pantalone	P. Apsit	Retrd.	270.00	270.00
87-09-007	Pulcinella	P. Apsit	Retrd.	220.00	220.00
87-09-008	Russian	P. Apsit	Retrd.	190.00	200.00
87-09-009	Auguste	P. Apsit	Retrd.	220.00	240.00
87-09-010	Slapstick	P. Apsit	Retrd.	250.00	270.00
87-09-011	Uncle Sam	P. Apsit	Retrd.	160.00	160.00
87-09-012	American	P. Apsit	Retrd.	160.00	200.00
90-09-013	Mime-18"	P. Apsit	Retrd.	1500.00	1500.00
90-09-014	Bob Hope-18"	P. Aspit	Retrd.	1500.00	1500.00
Duncan Royale		**History of Classic Entertainers II**			
88-10-001	Goliard	P. Apsit	Retrd.	200.00	200.00
88-10-002	Touchstone	P. Apsit	Retrd.	200.00	200.00
88-10-003	Feste	P. Apsit	Retrd.	250.00	250.00
88-10-004	Tartaglia	P. Apsit	Retrd.	200.00	200.00
88-10-005	Zanni	P. Apsit	Retrd.	200.00	200.00
88-10-006	Mountebank	P. Apsit	Retrd.	270.00	270.00
88-10-007	Pedrolino	P. Apsit	Retrd.	200.00	200.00
88-10-008	Thomassi	P. Apsit	Retrd.	200.00	200.00
88-10-009	Tramp	P. Apsit	Retrd.	200.00	200.00
88-10-010	White Face	P. Apsit	Retrd.	250.00	250.00
88-10-011	Mime	P. Apsit	Retrd.	200.00	200.00
88-10-012	Bob Hope	P. Apsit	Retrd.	250.00	250.00
Duncan Royale		**History of Classic Entertainers-Special Releases**			
88-11-001	Signature Piece	P. Apsit	Retrd.	50.00	50.00
Duncan Royale		**Greatest Gift...Love**			
88-12-001	Annunciation, marble	P. Apsit	5,000	270.00	270.00
88-12-002	Annunciation, painted porcelain	P. Apsit	5,000	270.00	270.00
88-12-003	Nativity, marble	P. Apsit	5,000	500.00	500.00
88-12-004	Nativity, painted porcelain	P. Apsit	5,000	500.00	500.00
88-12-005	Crucifixion, marble	P. Apsit	5,000	300.00	300.00
88-12-006	Crucifixion, painted porcelain	P. Apsit	5,000	300.00	300.00
Duncan Royale		**Woodland Fairies**			
88-13-001	Cherry	Duncan Royale	10,000	70.00	70.00
88-13-002	Mulberry	Duncan Royale	10,000	70.00	70.00
88-13-003	Apple	Duncan Royale	10,000	70.00	70.00
88-13-004	Poplar	Duncan Royale	10,000	70.00	70.00
88-13-005	Elm	Duncan Royale	10,000	70.00	70.00
88-13-006	Chestnut	Duncan Royale	10,000	70.00	70.00
88-13-007	Calla Lily	Duncan Royale	10,000	70.00	70.00
88-13-008	Pear Blossom	Duncan Royale	10,000	70.00	70.00
88-13-010	Lime Tree	Duncan Royale	10,000	70.00	70.00
88-13-011	Christmas Tree	Duncan Royale	10,000	70.00	70.00
88-13-012	Sycamore	Duncan Royale	10,000	70.00	70.00
88-13-013	Pine Tree	Duncan Royale	10,000	70.00	70.00
88-13-014	Almond Blossom	Duncan Royale	10,000	70.00	70.00
Duncan Royale		**Calendar Secrets (12")**			
90-14-001	January	D. Aphessetche	5,000	260.00	260.00
90-14-002	February	D. Aphessetche	5,000	370.00	370.00
90-14-003	March	D. Aphessetche	5,000	350.00	350.00
90-14-004	April	D. Aphessetche	5,000	370.00	370.00
90-14-005	May	D. Aphessetche	5,000	390.00	390.00
90-14-006	June	D. Aphessetche	5,000	410.00	410.00
90-14-007	July	D. Aphessetche	5,000	280.00	280.00
90-14-008	August	D. Aphessetche	5,000	300.00	300.00
90-14-009	September	D. Aphessetche	5,000	300.00	300.00
90-14-010	October	D. Aphessetche	5,000	350.00	350.00
90-14-011	November	D. Aphessetche	5,000	410.00	410.00
90-14-012	December	D. Aphessetche	5,000	410.00	410.00
Duncan Royale		**Calendar Secrets (6")**			
93-15-001	January	D. Aphessetche	6,000	N/A	N/A
93-15-002	February	D. Aphessetche	6,000	N/A	N/A
93-15-003	March	D. Aphessetche	6,000	N/A	N/A
93-15-004	April	D. Aphessetche	6,000	N/A	N/A
93-15-005	May	D. Aphessetche	6,000	N/A	N/A
93-15-006	June	D. Aphessetche	6,000	N/A	N/A
93-15-007	July	D. Aphessetche	6,000	N/A	N/A
93-15-008	August	D. Aphessetche	6,000	N/A	N/A
93-15-009	September	D. Aphessetche	6,000	N/A	N/A
93-15-010	October	D. Aphessetche	6,000	N/A	N/A
93-15-011	November	D. Aphessetche	6,000	N/A	N/A
93-15-012	December	D. Aphessetche	6,000	N/A	N/A
Duncan Royale		**Ebony Collection**			
90-16-001	The Fiddler	Duncan Royale	5,000	90.00	90.00
90-16-002	Harmonica Man	Duncan Royale	5,000	80.00	80.00
90-16-003	Banjo Man	Duncan Royale	5,000	80.00	80.00
91-16-004	Spoons	Duncan Royale	5,000	90.00	90.00
91-16-005	Preacher	Duncan Royale	5,000	90.00	90.00
91-16-006	Female Gospel Singer	Duncan Royale	5,000	90.00	90.00
91-16-007	Male Gospel Singer	Duncan Royale	5,000	90.00	90.00
91-16-008	Jug Man	Duncan Royale	5,000	90.00	90.00
92-16-009	Jug Tooter	Duncan Royale	5,000	90.00	90.00
92-16-010	A Little Magic	Duncan Royale	5,000	80.00	80.00
92-16-011	Jazz Man Set	Duncan Royale	5,000	500.00	500.00
92-16-012	Sax	Duncan Royale	5,000	90.00	90.00
92-16-013	Trumpet	Duncan Royale	5,000	90.00	90.00
92-16-014	Bass	Duncan Royale	5,000	90.00	90.00
92-16-015	Piano	Duncan Royale	5,000	130.00	130.00
92-16-016	Bongo	Duncan Royale	5,000	90.00	90.00
93-16-017	Guitar Man	Duncan Royale	5,000	100.00	100.00
Duncan Royale		**Ebony Collection-Special Releases**			
91-17-001	Signature Piece	Duncan Royale	Open	50.00	50.00
Duncan Royale		**Buckwheat Collection**			
92-18-001	Petee & Friend	Duncan Royale	5,000	90.00	90.00
92-18-002	Painter	Duncan Royale	5,000	90.00	90.00
92-18-003	O'Tay	Duncan Royale	5,000	90.00	90.00
92-18-004	Smile For The Camera	Duncan Royale	5,000	90.00	90.00
Duncan Royale		**Early American (12")**			
91-19-001	Doctor	Duncan Royale	10,000	150.00	150.00
91-19-002	Accountant	Duncan Royale	10,000	170.00	170.00
91-19-003	Lawyer	Duncan Royale	10,000	170.00	170.00
91-19-004	Nurse	Duncan Royale	10,000	150.00	150.00
91-19-005	Fireman	Duncan Royale	10,000	150.00	150.00
91-19-006	Policeman	Duncan Royale	10,000	150.00	150.00
91-19-007	Salesman	Duncan Royale	10,000	150.00	150.00
91-19-008	Storekeeper	Duncan Royale	10,000	150.00	150.00
91-19-009	Dentist	Duncan Royale	10,000	150.00	150.00
91-19-010	Pharmacist	Duncan Royale	10,000	150.00	150.00
91-19-011	Teacher	Duncan Royale	10,000	150.00	150.00
91-19-012	Homemaker	Duncan Royale	10,000	150.00	150.00
91-19-013	Banker	Duncan Royale	10,000	150.00	150.00
91-19-014	Secretary	Duncan Royale	10,000	150.00	150.00
91-19-015	Chiropractor	Duncan Royale	10,000	150.00	150.00
91-19-016	Set of 15	Duncan Royale	10,000	2290.00	2290.00
Duncan Royale		**Early American (6")**			
92-20-001	Doctor	Duncan Royale	6,000	80.00	80.00
92-20-002	Accountant	Duncan Royale	6,000	80.00	80.00
92-20-003	Lawyer	Duncan Royale	6,000	80.00	80.00
92-20-004	Nurse	Duncan Royale	6,000	80.00	80.00
92-20-005	Fireman	Duncan Royale	6,000	80.00	80.00
92-20-006	Policeman	Duncan Royale	6,000	80.00	80.00
92-20-007	Salesman	Duncan Royale	6,000	80.00	80.00
92-20-008	Storekeeper	Duncan Royale	6,000	80.00	80.00
92-20-009	Dentist	Duncan Royale	6,000	80.00	80.00
92-20-010	Pharmacist	Duncan Royale	6,000	80.00	80.00
92-20-011	Teacher	Duncan Royale	6,000	80.00	80.00
92-20-012	Homemaker	Duncan Royale	6,000	80.00	80.00
92-20-013	Banker	Duncan Royale	6,000	80.00	80.00
92-20-014	Secretary	Duncan Royale	6,000	80.00	80.00
92-20-015	Chiropractor	Duncan Royale	6,000	80.00	80.00
92-20-016	Set of 15	Duncan Royale	6,000	1200.00	1200.00
Duncan Royale		**Christmas Images**			
91-21-001	The Carolers	Duncan Royale	10,000	120.00	120.00
91-21-002	The Christmas Pageant	Duncan Royale	10,000	175.00	175.00
92-21-003	Are You Really Santa?	Duncan Royale	10,000	N/A	N/A
92-21-004	The Midnight Watch	Duncan Royale	10,000	N/A	N/A
92-21-005	The Christmas Angel	Duncan Royale	10,000	110.00	110.00
92-21-006	Sneaking A Peek	Duncan Royale	10,000	N/A	N/A
Duncan Royale		**Painted Pewter Miniatures-Santa 1st Series**			
86-22-001	St. Nicholas	Duncan Royale	500	30.00	30.00
86-22-002	Dedt Moroz	Duncan Royale	500	30.00	30.00
86-22-003	Black Peter	Duncan Royale	500	30.00	30.00
86-22-004	Victorian	Duncan Royale	500	30.00	30.00
86-22-005	Medieval	Duncan Royale	500	30.00	30.00
86-22-006	Russian	Duncan Royale	500	30.00	30.00
86-22-007	Wassail	Duncan Royale	500	30.00	30.00
86-22-008	Kris Kringle	Duncan Royale	500	30.00	30.00
86-22-009	Soda Pop	Duncan Royale	500	30.00	30.00
86-22-010	Pioneer	Duncan Royale	500	30.00	30.00
86-22-011	Civil War	Duncan Royale	500	30.00	30.00
86-22-012	Nast	Duncan Royale	500	30.00	30.00
86-22-013	Set of 12	Duncan Royale	500	360.00	360-495.
Duncan Royale		**Painted Pewter Miniatures-Santa 2nd Series**			
88-23-001	Odin	Duncan Royale	500	30.00	30.00
88-23-002	Lord of Misrule	Duncan Royale	500	30.00	30.00
88-23-003	Mongolian	Duncan Royale	500	30.00	30.00
88-23-004	Magi	Duncan Royale	500	30.00	30.00
88-23-005	St. Lucia	Duncan Royale	500	30.00	30.00
88-23-006	Befana	Duncan Royale	500	30.00	30.00
88-23-007	Babouska	Duncan Royale	500	30.00	30.00
88-23-008	Bavarian	Duncan Royale	500	30.00	30.00

Company Number	Name	Series Artist	Edition Limit	Issue Price	Quote
88-23-009	Alsace Angel	Duncan Royale	500	30.00	30.00
88-23-010	Frau Holda	Duncan Royale	500	30.00	30.00
88-23-011	Sir Christmas	Duncan Royale	500	30.00	30.00
88-23-012	Pixie	Duncan Royale	500	30.00	30.00
88-23-013	Set of 12	Duncan Royale	500	360.00	360-495.

Duncan Royale — **Collector Club**

Number	Name	Artist	Edition Limit	Issue Price	Quote
91-24-001	Today's Nast	Duncan Royale	Retrd.	80.00	95.00

Duncan Royale — **1990 & 1991 Special Event Piece**

Number	Name	Artist	Edition Limit	Issue Price	Quote
XX-25-001	Nast & Music	Duncan Royale	Retrd.	79.95	79.95

Enesco Corporation — **Precious Moments Special Edition**

Number	Name	Artist	Edition Limit	Issue Price	Quote
81-01-001	Hello, Lord, It's Me Again-PM-811	S. Butcher	Closed	25.00	425-435.
82-01-002	Smile, God Loves You-PM-821	S. Butcher	Closed	25.00	250.00
83-01-003	Put on a Happy Face-PM-822	S. Butcher	Closed	25.00	190-250.
83-01-004	Dawn's Early Light-PM-831	S. Butcher	Closed	27.50	90.00
84-01-005	God's Ray of Mercy-PM-841	S. Butcher	Closed	25.00	70-85.00
84-01-006	Trust in the Lord to the Finish-PM-842	S. Butcher	Closed	25.00	65.00
85-01-007	The Lord is My Shepherd-PM-851	S. Butcher	Closed	25.00	75-88.00
85-01-008	I Love to Tell the Story-PM-852	S. Butcher	Closed	27.50	80-125.00
86-01-009	Grandma's Prayer-PM-861	S. Butcher	Closed	25.00	85-115.00
86-01-010	I'm Following Jesus-PM-862	S. Butcher	Closed	25.00	85-125.00
87-01-011	Feed My Sheep-PM-871	S. Butcher	Closed	25.00	75-95.00
87-01-012	In His Time-PM-872	S. Butcher	Closed	25.00	50-65.00
87-01-013	Loving You Dear Valentine-PM-873	S. Butcher	Closed	25.00	25.00
87-01-014	Loving You Dear Valentine-PM-874	S. Butcher	Closed	25.00	25.00
88-01-015	God Bless You for Touching My Life-PM-881	S. Butcher	Closed	27.50	50-85.00
88-01-016	You Just Can't Chuck A Good Friendship-PM-882	S. Butcher	Closed	27.50	45-65.00
89-01-017	You Will Always Be My Choice- PM-891	S. Butcher	Closed	27.50	35-55.00
89-01-018	Mow Power To Ya-PM-892	S. Butcher	Closed	27.50	35-80.00
90-01-019	Ten Years And Still Going Strong-PM-901	S. Butcher	Closed	30.00	56-65.00
90-01-020	You Are A Blessing To Me-PM-902	S. Butcher	Closed	27.50	60-75.00
91-01-021	One Step At A Time-PM-911	S. Butcher	Closed	33.00	45-50.00
91-01-022	Lord, Keep Me In TeePee Top Shape-PM-912	S. Butcher	Closed	27.50	65.00
92-01-023	Only Love Can Make A Home-PM-921	S. Butcher	Closed	30.00	60.00
92-01-024	Sowing The Seeds of Love-PM-922	S. Butcher	Closed	30.00	30.00
92-01-025	This Land Is Our Land-527386	S. Butcher	Yr.Iss.	350.00	400-500.

Enesco Corporation — **Precious Moments Collectors Club Welcome Gift**

Number	Name	Artist	Edition Limit	Issue Price	Quote
82-02-001	But Love Goes On Forever-Plaque-E-0202	S. Butcher	Yr.Iss.	Unkn.	70-85.00
83-02-002	Let Us Call the Club to Order-E-0303	S. Butcher	Yr.Iss.	Unkn.	55-60.00
84-02-003	Join in on the Blessings-E-0404	S. Butcher	Yr.Iss.	Unkn.	40-60.00
85-02-004	Seek and Ye Shall Find-E-0005	S. Butcher	Yr.Iss.	Unkn.	40-50.00
86-02-005	Birds of a Feather Collect Together-E-0006	S. Butcher	Yr.Iss.	Unkn.	30-45.00
87-02-006	Sharing Is Universal-E-0007	S. Butcher	Yr.Iss.	Unkn.	35-45.00
88-02-007	A Growing Love-E-0008	S. Butcher	Yr.Iss.	Unkn.	35-50.00
89-02-008	Always Room For One More-C-0009	S. Butcher	Yr.Iss.	Unkn.	35-50.00
90-02-009	My Happiness-C-0010	S. Butcher	Yr.Iss.	Unkn.	40-75.00
91-02-010	Sharing the Good News Together-C-0011	S. Butcher	Yr.Iss.	Unkn.	40-50.00
92-02-011	The Club That's Out Of This World-C-0012	S. Butcher	Yr.Iss.	Unkn.	40.00

Enesco Corporation — **Precious Moments Inscribed Charter Member Renewal Gift**

Number	Name	Artist	Edition Limit	Issue Price	Quote
81-03-001	But Love Goes on Forever-E-0001	S. Butcher	Yr.Iss.	Unkn.	175-225.
82-03-002	But Love Goes on Forever-Plaque-E-0102	S. Butcher	Yr.Iss.	Unkn.	80-100.00
83-03-003	Let Us Call the Club to Order-E-0103	S. Butcher	Yr.Iss.	25.00	65-75.00
84-03-004	Join in on the Blessings-E-0104	S. Butcher	Yr.Iss.	25.00	55-90.00
85-03-005	Seek and Ye Shall Find-E-0105	S. Butcher	Yr.Iss.	25.00	40-60.00
86-03-006	Birds of a Feather Collect Together-E-0106	S. Butcher	Yr.Iss.	25.00	45-65.00
87-03-007	Sharing Is Universal -E-0107	S. Butcher	Yr.Iss.	25.00	45-60.00
88-03-008	A Growing Love-E-0108	S. Butcher	Yr.Iss.	25.00	45-55.00
89-03-009	Always Room For One More-C-0109	S. Butcher	Yr.Iss.	35.00	45-60.00
90-03-010	My Happiness-C-0110	S. Butcher	Yr.Iss.	Unkn.	35-45.00
91-03-011	Sharing The Good News Together-C-0111	S. Butcher	Yr.Iss.	Unkn.	40.00
92-03-012	The Club That's Out Of This World-C-0012	S. Butcher	Yr.Iss.	Unkn.	40.00

Enesco Corporation — **Precious Moments Figurines**

Number	Name	Artist	Edition Limit	Issue Price	Quote
83-04-001	Sharing Our Season Together-E-0501	S. Butcher	Suspd.	50.00	110-145.
83-04-002	Jesus is the Light that Shines-E-0502	S. Butcher	Suspd.	23.00	50-60.00
83-04-003	Blessings from My House to Yours-E-0503	S. Butcher	Suspd.	27.00	60-80.00
83-04-004	God Sent His Son-E-0507	S. Butcher	Suspd.	32.50	65-90.00
83-04-005	Prepare Ye the Way of the Lord-E-0508	S. Butcher	Suspd.	75.00	95-125.00
83-04-006	Bringing God's Blessing to You-E-0509	S. Butcher	Suspd.	35.00	70-100.00
83-04-007	Tubby's First Christmas-E-0511	S. Butcher	Open	12.00	16.50-40.00
83-04-008	It's a Perfect Boy-E-0512	S. Butcher	Suspd.	18.50	40-60.00
83-04-009	Onward Christian Soldiers-E-0523	S. Butcher	Open	24.00	35-95.00
83-04-010	He Upholdeth Those Who Fall-E-0526	S. Butcher	Suspd.	35.00	65-115.00
79-04-011	Jesus Loves Me-E-1372B	S. Butcher	Open	7.00	27.50-99.00
79-04-012	Jesus Loves Me-E-1372G	S. Butcher	Open	7.00	25-115.00
79-04-013	Make a Joyful Noise-E-1374G	S. Butcher	Open	8.00	28-125.00
79-04-014	Love Lifted Me-E-1375A	S. Butcher	Open	11.00	35-115.00
79-04-015	Prayer Changes Things-E-1375B	S. Butcher	Suspd.	11.00	125-200.
79-04-016	Love One Another-E-1376	S. Butcher	Open	10.00	48-119.00
79-04-017	He Leadeth Me-E-1377A	S. Butcher	Suspd.	9.00	75-125.00
79-04-018	He Careth For You-E-1377B	S. Butcher	Suspd.	9.00	85-120.00
79-04-019	Love is Kind-E-1379A	S. Butcher	Suspd.	8.00	80-130.00
79-04-020	God Understands-E-1379B	S. Butcher	Suspd.	8.00	90-130.00
79-04-021	Jesus is the Answer-E-1381	S. Butcher	Suspd.	11.50	120-160.
79-04-022	We Have Seen His Star-E-2010	S. Butcher	Suspd.	8.00	80-115.00
79-04-023	Jesus is Born-E-2012	S. Butcher	Suspd.	12.00	90-125.00
79-04-024	Unto Us a Child is Born-E-2013	S. Butcher	Suspd.	12.00	85-130.00
82-04-025	May Your Christmas Be Cozy-E-2345	S. Butcher	Suspd.	23.00	60-80.00
82-04-026	May Your Christmas Be Warm-E-2348	S. Butcher	Suspd.	30.00	88-105.00
82-04-027	Tell Me the Story of Jesus-E-2349	S. Butcher	Suspd.	30.00	75-100.00
82-04-028	Dropping in for Christmas-E-2350	S. Butcher	Suspd.	18.00	70-85.00
82-04-029	I'll Play My Drum for Him-E-2356	S. Butcher	Suspd.	30.00	65-110.00
82-04-030	I'll Play My Drum for Him-E-2360	S. Butcher	Open	16.00	25-95.00
82-04-031	Christmas Joy from Head to Toe-E-2361	S. Butcher	Suspd.	25.00	55-80.00
82-04-032	Camel Figurine-E-2363	S. Butcher	Open	20.00	33-50.00
82-04-033	Goat Figurine-E-2364	S. Butcher	Suspd.	10.00	30-43.00
82-04-034	The First Noel-E-2365	S. Butcher	Suspd.	16.00	45-60.00
82-04-035	The First Noel-E-2366	S. Butcher	Suspd.	16.00	45-65.00
82-04-036	Bundles of Joy-E-2374	S. Butcher	Open	27.50	45-90.00
82-04-037	Our First Christmas Together-E-2377	S. Butcher	Suspd.	35.00	60-95.00
82-04-038	3 Mini Nativity Houses & Palm Tree-E-2387	S. Butcher	Open	45.00	75-110.00
82-04-039	Come Let Us Adore Him-E-2395(11pc. set)	S. Butcher	Open	80.00	130-175.
80-04-040	Come Let Us Adore Him-E2800(9 pc. set)	S. Butcher	Open	70.00	125-175.
80-04-041	Jesus is Born-E-2801	S. Butcher	Suspd.	37.00	225-350.
80-04-042	Christmas is a Time to Share-E-2802	S. Butcher	Suspd.	20.00	65-100.00
80-04-043	Crown Him Lord of All-E-2803	S. Butcher	Suspd.	20.00	60-95.00
80-04-044	Peace on Earth-E-2804	S. Butcher	Suspd.	20.00	115-135.
84-04-045	You Have Touched So Many Hearts-E-2821	S. Butcher	Open	25.00	35-50.00
84-04-046	To God Be the Glory-E-2823	S. Butcher	Suspd.	40.00	70-100.00
84-04-047	To a Very Special Mom-E-2824	S. Butcher	Open	27.50	37.50-55.00
84-04-048	To a Very Special Sister-E-2825	S. Butcher	Open	37.50	65.00
84-04-049	May Your Birthday Be a Blessing-E-2826	S. Butcher	Suspd.	37.50	70-99.00
84-04-050	I Get a Kick Out of You-E-2827	S. Butcher	Suspd.	50.00	85-120.00
84-04-051	Precious Memories-E-2828	S. Butcher	Open	45.00	60-75.00
84-04-052	I'm Sending You a White Christmas-E-2829	S. Butcher	Open	37.50	50-70.00
84-04-053	God Bless the Bride-E-2832	S. Butcher	Open	35.00	50-60.00
86-04-054	Sharing Our Joy Together-E-2834	S. Butcher	Suspd.	30.00	40-60.00
84-04-055	Baby Figurines (set of 6)-E-2852	S. Butcher	Open	12.00	99-168.00
80-04-056	Blessed Are the Pure in Heart-E-3104	S. Butcher	Suspd.	9.00	25-65.00
80-04-057	He Watches Over Us All-E-3105	S. Butcher	Suspd.	11.00	70-90.00
80-04-058	Mother Sew Dear-E-3106	S. Butcher	Open	13.00	27.50-80.00
80-04-059	The Hand that Rocks the Future-E-3108	S. Butcher	Suspd.	13.00	60-95.00
80-04-060	The Purr-fect Grandma-E-3109	S. Butcher	Open	13.00	27.50-79.00
80-04-061	Loving is Sharing-E-3110B	S. Butcher	Open	13.00	30-95.00
80-04-062	Loving is Sharing-E-3110G	S. Butcher	Open	13.00	30-95.00
80-04-063	Thou Art Mine-E-3113	S. Butcher	Open	16.00	35-90.00
80-04-064	The Lord Bless You and Keep You-E-3114	S. Butcher	Open	16.00	37.50-85.00
80-04-065	But Love Goes on Forever-E-3115	S. Butcher	Open	16.50	35-115.00
80-04-066	Thee I Love-E-3116	S. Butcher	Open	16.50	37.50-100.
80-04-067	Walking By Faith-E-3117	S. Butcher	Open	35.00	70-125.00
80-04-068	It's What's Inside that Counts-E-3119	S. Butcher	Suspd.	13.00	70-120.00
80-04-069	To Thee With Love-E-3120	S. Butcher	Suspd.	13.00	65-95.00
81-04-070	The Lord Bless You and Keep You-E-4720	S. Butcher	Suspd.	14.00	32-48.00
81-04-071	The Lord Bless You and Keep You-E-4721	S. Butcher	Open	14.00	30-80.00
81-04-072	Love Cannot Break a True Friendship-E-4722	S. Butcher	Suspd.	22.50	90-130.00
81-04-073	Peace Amid the Storm-E-4723	S. Butcher	Suspd.	22.50	60-80.00
81-04-074	Rejoicing with You-E-4724	S. Butcher	Open	25.00	45-99.00
81-04-075	Peace on Earth-E-4725	S. Butcher	Suspd.	25.00	60-89.00
81-04-076	Bear Ye One Another's Burdens-E-5200	S. Butcher	Suspd.	20.00	80-105.00
81-04-077	Love Lifted Me-E-5201	S. Butcher	Suspd.	25.00	70-110.00
81-04-078	Thank You for Coming to My Ade-E-5202	S. Butcher	Suspd.	22.50	80-120.00
81-04-079	Let Not the Sun Go Down Upon Your Wrath-E-5203	S. Butcher	Suspd.	22.50	100-160.
81-04-080	To A Special Dad-E-5212	S. Butcher	Open	20.00	35-79.00
81-04-081	God is Love-E-5213	S. Butcher	Suspd.	17.00	60-99.00
81-04-082	Prayer Changes Things-E-5214	S. Butcher	Suspd.	35.00	85-150.00
84-04-083	May Your Christmas Be Blessed-E-5376	S. Butcher	Suspd.	37.50	59-75.00
84-04-084	Joy to the World-E-5378	S. Butcher	Suspd.	18.00	37-45.00
84-04-085	Isn't He Precious?-E-5379	S. Butcher	Open	20.00	30-45.00
84-04-086	A Monarch is Born-E-5380	S. Butcher	Suspd.	33.00	60-75.00
84-04-087	His Name is Jesus-E-5381	S. Butcher	Suspd.	45.00	70-85.00
84-04-088	For God So Loved the World-E-5382	S. Butcher	Suspd.	70.00	110-135.
84-04-089	Wishing You a Merry Christmas-E-5383	S. Butcher	Yr.Iss.	17.00	45-55.00
84-04-090	I'll Play My Drum for Him-E-5384	S. Butcher	Open	10.00	15-30.00
84-04-091	Oh Worship the Lord-E-5385	S. Butcher	Suspd.	10.00	34-45.00
84-04-092	Oh Worship the Lord-E-5386	S. Butcher	Suspd.	10.00	34-45.00
81-04-093	Come Let Us Adore Him-E-5619	S. Butcher	Suspd.	10.00	30-50.00
81-04-094	Donkey Figurine-E-5621	S. Butcher	Open	6.00	13.50-35.00
81-04-095	They Followed the Star-E-5624	S. Butcher	Open	130.00	200-270.
81-04-096	Wee Three Kings-E-5635	S. Butcher	Open	40.00	75-125.00
81-04-097	Rejoice O Earth-E-5636	S. Butcher	Open	15.00	30-65.00
81-04-098	The Heavenly Light-E-5637	S. Butcher	Open	15.00	27.50-60.00
81-04-099	Cow with Bell Figurine-E-5638	S. Butcher	Open	16.00	30-50.00
81-04-100	Isn't He Wonderful-E-5639	S. Butcher	Suspd.	12.00	40-65.00
81-04-101	Isn't He Wonderful-E-5640	S. Butcher	Suspd.	12.00	40-65.00
81-04-102	They Followed the Star-E-5641	S. Butcher	Suspd.	75.00	165-185.
81-04-103	Nativity Wall (2 pc. set)-E-5644	S. Butcher	Open	60.00	120-145.
84-04-104	God Sends the Gift of His Love-E-6613	S. Butcher	Suspd.	22.50	65-90.00
82-04-105	God is Love, Dear Valentine-E-7153	S. Butcher	Suspd.	16.00	40-59.00
82-04-106	God is Love, Dear Valentine-E-7154	S. Butcher	Suspd.	16.00	40-65.00
82-04-107	Thanking Him for You-E-7155	S. Butcher	Suspd.	16.00	60-75.00
82-04-108	Love Beareth All Things-E-7158	S. Butcher	Open	25.00	37.50-64.00
82-04-109	Lord Give Me Patience-E-7159	S. Butcher	Suspd.	25.00	50-65.00
82-04-110	The Perfect Grandpa-E-7160	S. Butcher	Suspd.	25.00	45-65.00
82-04-111	His Sheep Am I-E-7161	S. Butcher	Suspd.	25.00	55-65.00
82-04-112	Love is Sharing-E-7162	S. Butcher	Suspd.	25.00	130-150.
82-04-113	God is Watching Over You-E-7163	S. Butcher	Suspd.	27.50	65-85.00
82-04-114	Bless This House-E-7164	S. Butcher	Suspd.	45.00	110-150.
82-04-115	Let the Whole World Know-E-7165	S. Butcher	Suspd.	45.00	80-150.00
83-04-116	Love is Patient-E-9251	S. Butcher	Suspd.	35.00	55-85.00
83-04-117	Forgiving is Forgetting-E-9252	S. Butcher	Suspd.	37.50	60-85.00
83-04-118	The End is in Sight-E-9253	S. Butcher	Suspd.	25.00	53-95.00
83-04-119	Praise the Lord Anyhow-E-9254	S. Butcher	Open	35.00	50-75.00
83-04-120	Bless You Two-E-9255	S. Butcher	Open	21.00	32.50-44.00
83-04-121	We are God's Workmanship-E-9258	S. Butcher	Open	19.00	27.50-53.00
83-04-122	We're In It Together-E-9259	S. Butcher	Suspd.	24.00	49-65.00
83-04-123	God's Promises are Sure-E-9260	S. Butcher	Suspd.	30.00	55-75.00
83-04-124	Seek Ye the Lord-E-9261	S. Butcher	Suspd.	21.00	37-54.00
83-04-125	Seek Ye the Lord-E-9262	S. Butcher	Suspd.	21.00	45-55.00
83-04-126	How Can Two Walk Together Except They Agree-E-9263	S. Butcher	Suspd.	35.00	90-139.00
83-04-127	Press On-E-9265	S. Butcher	Open	40.00	55-87.00
83-04-128	Animal Collection, Teddy Bear-E-9267A	S. Butcher	Suspd.	6.50	18-24.30
83-04-129	Animal Collection, Dog W/ Slippers-E-9267B	S. Butcher	Suspd.	6.50	18-24.30
83-04-130	Animal Collection, Bunny W/ Carrot-E-9267C	S. Butcher	Suspd.	6.50	18-24.30
83-04-131	Animal Collection, Kitty With Bow-E-9267D	S. Butcher	Suspd.	6.50	18-24.30
83-04-132	Animal Collection, Lamb With Bird-E-9267E	S. Butcher	Suspd.	6.50	18-24.30
83-04-133	Animal Collection, Pig W/ Patches-E-9267F	S. Butcher	Suspd.	6.50	18-24.30
83-04-134	Jesus Loves Me-E-9278	S. Butcher	Open	9.00	15-27.00
83-04-135	Jesus Loves Me-E-9279	S. Butcher	Open	9.00	15-32.00
83-04-136	To Some Bunny Special-E-9282A	S. Butcher	Suspd.	8.00	20-37.00
83-04-137	You're Worth Your Weight In Gold-E-9282B	S. Butcher	Suspd.	8.00	21-37.00
83-04-138	Especially For Ewe-E-9282C	S. Butcher	Suspd.	8.00	20-37.00
83-04-139	If God Be for Us, Who Can Be Against Us-E-9285	S. Butcher	Suspd.	27.50	55-65.00
83-04-140	Peace on Earth-E-9287	S. Butcher	Suspd.	37.50	60-80.00
83-04-141	Sending You a Rainbow-E-9288	S. Butcher	Suspd.	22.50	55-75.00
83-04-142	Trust in the Lord-E-9289	S. Butcher	Suspd.	21.00	50-65.00
85-04-143	Love Covers All-12009	S. Butcher	Suspd.	27.50	45-65.00
85-04-144	Part of Me Wants to be Good-12149	S. Butcher	Suspd.	19.00	40-65.00
87-04-145	This Is The Day Which The Lord Has Made-12157	S. Butcher	Suspd.	20.00	55-100.00
85-04-146	Get into the Habit of Prayer-12203	S. Butcher	Suspd.	19.00	35-45.00
85-04-147	Miniature Clown-12238A	S. Butcher	Open	13.50	19-29.00
85-04-148	Miniature Clown-12238B	S. Butcher	Open	13.50	19-29.00
85-04-149	Miniature Clown-12238C	S. Butcher	Open	13.50	19-29.00
85-04-150	Miniature Clown-12238D	S. Butcher	Open	13.50	19-29.00
85-04-151	It is Better to Give than to Receive-12297	S. Butcher	Suspd.	19.00	50-80.00
85-04-152	Love Never Fails-12300	S. Butcher	Open	25.00	35-49.00
85-04-153	God Bless Our Home-12319	S. Butcher	Open	40.00	55-65.00
86-04-154	You Can Fly-12335	S. Butcher	Suspd.	25.00	50-65.00

Company		Series			
Number	Name	Artist	Edition Limit	Issue Price	Quote
85-04-155	Jesus is Coming Soon-12343	S. Butcher	Suspd.	22.50	40-55.00
85-04-156	Halo, and Merry Christmas-12351	S. Butcher	Suspd.	40.00	90-120.00
85-04-157	May Your Christmas Be Delightful-15482	S. Butcher	Open	25.00	35-50.00
85-04-158	Honk if You Love Jesus-15490	S. Butcher	Open	13.00	19-35.00
85-04-159	Baby's First Christmas-15539	S. Butcher	Yr.Iss.	13.00	42-45.00
85-04-160	Baby's First Christmas-15547	S. Butcher	Yr.Iss.	13.00	45.00
85-04-161	God Sent His Love-15881	S. Butcher	Yr.Iss.	17.00	30-39.00
86-04-162	To My Favorite Paw-100021	S. Butcher	Suspd.	22.50	50-65.00
87-04-163	To My Deer Friend-100048	S. Butcher	Open	33.00	50-92.00
86-04-164	Sending My Love-100056	S. Butcher	Suspd.	22.50	35-60.00
86-04-165	O Worship the Lord-100064	S. Butcher	Open	24.00	35-49.00
86-04-166	To My Forever Friend-100072	S. Butcher	Open	33.00	50-90.00
87-04-167	He's The Healer Of Broken Hearts-100080	S. Butcher	Open	33.00	50-59.00
86-04-168	Lord I'm Coming Home-100110	S. Butcher	Open	22.50	32.50-72.00
86-04-169	The Joy of the Lord is My Strength-100137	S. Butcher	Open	35.00	50-89.00
86-04-170	God Bless the Day We Found You-100145	S. Butcher	Suspd.	37.50	70-85.00
86-04-171	God Bless the Day We Found You-100153	S. Butcher	Suspd.	37.50	62-100.00
86-04-172	Serving the Lord-100161	S. Butcher	Suspd.	19.00	39-55.00
86-04-173	I'm a Possibility-100188	S. Butcher	Open	21.00	32.50-40.00
87-04-174	The Lord Giveth & the Lord Taketh Away-100226	S. Butcher	Open	33.50	40-49.00
86-04-175	Friends Never Drift Apart-100250	S. Butcher	Open	35.00	50-69.00
86-04-176	He Cleansed My Soul-100277	S. Butcher	Open	24.00	35-42.00
86-04-177	Serving the Lord-100293	S. Butcher	Suspd.	19.00	27.50-47.00
86-04-178	Brotherly Love-100544	S. Butcher	Suspd.	37.00	59-75.00
87-04-179	No Tears Past The Gate-101826	S. Butcher	Open	40.00	60-67.00
86-04-180	O Worship the Lord-102229	S. Butcher	Open	24.00	35-42.00
86-04-181	Shepherd of Love-102261	S. Butcher	Open	10.00	15-24.00
86-04-182	Three Mini Animals-102296	S. Butcher	Open	13.50	19-30.00
86-04-183	Wishing You a Cozy Christmas-102342	S. Butcher	Yr.Iss.	17.00	39-45.00
86-04-184	Love Rescued Me-102393	S. Butcher	Open	21.00	32.50-44.00
86-04-185	Angel of Mercy-102482	S. Butcher	Open	19.00	30-39.00
86-04-186	Sharing our Christmas Together-102490	S. Butcher	Suspd.	35.00	65-70.00
87-04-187	We Are All Precious In His Sight-102903	S. Butcher	Yr.Iss.	30.00	80-120.00
86-04-188	God Bless America-102938	S. Butcher	Yr.Iss.	30.00	65-85.00
86-04-189	It's the Birthday of a King-102962	S. Butcher	Suspd.	18.50	35-47.00
87-04-190	I Would Be Sunk Without You-102970	S. Butcher	Open	15.00	19-29.00
87-04-191	My Love Will Never Let You Go-103497	S. Butcher	Open	25.00	35-45.00
86-04-192	I Believe in the Old Rugged Cross-103632	S. Butcher	Open	25.00	35-47.00
86-04-193	Come Let Us Adore Him-104000 (9 pc. set w/cassette)	S. Butcher	Open	95.00	110-115.
87-04-194	With this Ring I...-104019	S. Butcher	Open	40.00	55-65.00
87-04-195	Love Is The Glue That Mends-104027	S. Butcher	Suspd.	33.50	59-75.00
87-04-196	Cheers To The Leader-104035	S. Butcher	Open	22.50	30-39.00
87-04-197	Happy Days Are Here Again-104396	S. Butcher	Suspd.	25.00	43-70.00
87-04-198	A Tub Full of Love-104817	S. Butcher	Open	22.50	30-42.00
87-04-199	Sitting Pretty-104825	S. Butcher	Suspd.	22.50	43-60.00
87-04-200	Have I Got News For You-105635	S. Butcher	Suspd.	22.50	30-50.00
88-04-201	Something's Missing When You're Not Around -105643	S. Butcher	Suspd.	32.50	37.50
87-04-202	To Tell The Tooth You're Special-105813	S. Butcher	Suspd.	38.50	65-85.00
88-04-203	Hallelujah Country-105821	S. Butcher	Open	35.00	45-54.00
87-04-204	We're Pulling For You-106151	S. Butcher	Suspd.	40.00	60-75.00
87-04-205	God Bless You Graduate-106194	S. Butcher	Open	20.00	30-35.00
87-04-206	Congratulations Princess-106208	S. Butcher	Open	20.00	30-35.00
87-04-207	Lord Help Me Make the Grade-106216	S. Butcher	Suspd.	25.00	35-70.00
88-04-208	Heaven Bless Your Togetherness-106755	S. Butcher	Open	65.00	80-87.00
88-04-209	Precious Memories-106763	S. Butcher	Open	37.50	50-55.00
88-04-210	Puppy Love Is From Above-106798	S. Butcher	Open	45.00	55-63.00
88-04-211	Happy Birthday Poppy-106836	S. Butcher	Open	27.50	33.50-37.00
88-04-212	Sew In Love-106844	S. Butcher	Open	45.00	55-60.00
87-04-213	They Followed The Star-108243	S. Butcher	Open	75.00	100-115.00
87-04-214	The Greatest Gift Is A Friend-109231	S. Butcher	Open	30.00	37.50-49.00
88-04-215	Believe the Impossible-109487	S. Butcher	Suspd.	35.00	50-105.00
87-04-216	Wishing You A Yummy Christmas-109754	S. Butcher	Open	35.00	45-55.00
87-04-217	We Gather Together To Ask The Lord's Blessing-109762	S. Butcher	Open	130.00	150-169.
88-04-218	Meowie Christmas-109800	S. Butcher	Open	30.00	40-65.00
87-04-219	Oh What Fun It Is To Ride-109819	S. Butcher	Open	85.00	110-120.
88-04-220	Wishing You A Happy Easter-109886	S. Butcher	Open	23.00	27.50-34.00
88-04-221	Wishing You A Basket Full Of Blessings-109924	S. Butcher	Open	23.00	27.50-33.00
88-04-222	Sending You My Love-109967	S. Butcher	Open	35.00	45-57.00
88-04-223	Mommy, I Love You-109975	S. Butcher	Open	22.50	27.50-34.00
87-04-224	Love Is The Best Gift of All-110930	S. Butcher	Yr.Iss.	22.50	45-49.00
88-04-225	Faith Takes The Plunge-111155	S. Butcher	Open	27.50	33.50-125.00
88-04-226	Tis the Season-111163	S. Butcher	Open	27.50	35-45.00
87-04-227	O Come Let Us Adore Him (4 pc. 9" Nativity)-111333	S. Butcher	Suspd.	200.00	245-275.
88-04-228	Mommy, I Love You-112143	S. Butcher	Open	22.50	27.50-32.00
87-04-229	A Tub Full of Love-112313	S. Butcher	Open	22.50	30-33.00
88-04-230	This Too Shall Pass-114014	S. Butcher	Open	23.00	27.50-37.00
88-04-231	Some Bunny's Sleeping-115274	S. Butcher	Open	15.00	25-40.00
88-04-232	Our First Christmas Together-115290	S. Butcher	Suspd.	50.00	70-80.00
88-04-233	Time to Wish You a Merry Christmas-115339	S. Butcher	Yr.Iss.	24.00	35-48.00
88-04-234	Rejoice O Earth-520268	S. Butcher	Open	13.00	15-22.00
88-04-235	Jesus the Savior Is Born-520357	S. Butcher	Open	25.00	32.50-40.00
92-04-236	The Lord Turned My Life Around-520535	S. Butcher	Open	35.00	35.00
91-04-237	In The Spotlight Of His Grace-520543	S. Butcher	Open	35.00	35.00
90-04-238	Lord, Turn My Life Around-520551	S. Butcher	Open	35.00	35-49.00
92-04-239	You Deserve An Ovation-520578	S. Butcher	Open	35.00	35.00
89-04-240	My Heart Is Exposed With Love-520624	S. Butcher	Open	45.00	50-60.00
89-04-241	A Friend Is Someone Who Cares-520632	S. Butcher	Open	30.00	32.50-45.00
89-04-242	Eggspecially For You-520667	S. Butcher	Open	45.00	50-60.00
89-04-243	Your Love Is So Uplifting-520675	S. Butcher	Open	60.00	65-79.00
89-04-244	Just A LineTo Wish You A Happy Day-520721	S. Butcher	Open	65.00	70-79.00
89-04-245	Friendship Hits The Spot-520748	S. Butcher	Open	55.00	60-68.00
89-04-246	Jesus Is The Only Way-520756	S. Butcher	Open	40.00	45-50.00
89-04-247	Puppy Love-520764	S. Butcher	Open	12.50	13.50-22.00
89-04-248	Wishing You Roads Of Happiness-520780	S. Butcher	Open	60.00	65-73.00
89-04-249	My Days Are Blue Without You-520802	S. Butcher	Suspd.	65.00	75-125.00
89-04-250	We Need A Good Friend Through The Ruff Times-520810	S. Butcher	Suspd.	35.00	50-70.00
89-04-251	You Are My Number One-520829	S. Butcher	Open	25.00	27.50-30.00
89-04-252	The Lord Is Your Light To Happiness-520837	S. Bucher	Open	50.00	55-62.00
89-04-253	Wishing You A Perfect Choice-520845	S.Butcher	Open	55.00	60-67.00
89-04-254	I Belong To The Lord-520853	S. Butcher	Suspd.	25.00	35-50.00
90-04-255	Heaven Bless You-520934	S. Butcher	Open	35.00	35-150.00
93-04-256	There Is No Greater Treasure Than To Have A Friend Like You -521000	S. Butcher	Open	30.00	30.00
90-04-257	That's What Friends Are For-521183	S. Butcher	Open	45.00	45-49.00
90-04-258	Hope You're Up And OnThe Trail Again-521205	S. Butcher	Open	35.00	35-45.00

Company		Series			
Number	Name	Artist	Edition Limit	Issue Price	Quote
91-04-259	Take Heed When You Stand-521272	S. Butcher	Open	55.00	55.00
90-04-260	Happy Trip-521280	S. Butcher	Open	35.00	35-73.00
91-04-261	Hug One Another-521299	S. Butcher	Open	45.00	45-49.00
90-04-262	Yield Not To Temptation-521310	S. Butcher	Open	27.50	27.50-37.00
90-04-263	Faith Is A Victory-521396	S. Butcher	Open	25.00	25-34.00
90-04-264	I'll Never Stop Loving You-521418	S. Butcher	Open	37.50	37.50-49.00
91-04-265	To A Very Special Mom & Dad-521434	S. Butcher	Open	35.00	35.00
90-04-266	Lord, Help Me Stick To My Job-521450	S. Butcher	Open	30.00	30-40.00
89-04-267	Tell It To Jesus-521477	S. Butcher	Open	35.00	37.50-49.00
91-04-268	There's A Light At The End Of The Tunnel-521485	S. Butcher	Open	55.00	55.00
91-04-269	A Special Delivery-521493	S. Butcher	Open	30.00	30.00
91-04-270	Thumb-body Loves You-521698	S. Butcher	Open	55.00	55-59.00
90-04-271	Sweep All Your Worries Away-521779	S. Butcher	Open	40.00	40-130.00
90-04-272	Good Friends Are Forever-521817	S. Butcher	Open	50.00	50-57.00
90-04-273	Love Is From Above-521841	S. Butcher	Open	45.00	45-59.00
89-04-274	The Greatest of These Is Love-521868	S. Butcher	Suspd.	27.50	40-54.00
90-04-275	Easter's On Its Way-521892	S. Butcher	Open	60.00	60-75.00
91-04-276	Hoppy Easter Friend-521906	S. Butcher	Open	40.00	40-43.00
93-04-277	Safe In The Arms Of Jesus-521922	S. Butcher	Open	30.00	30.00
89-04-278	Wishing You A Cozy Season-521949	S. Butcher	Open	42.50	45-53.00
90-04-279	High Hopes-521957	S. Butcher	Open	30.00	30-40.00
91-04-280	To A Special Mum-521965	S. Butcher	Open	30.00	30-33.00
79-04-281	May Your Life Be Blessed With Touchdowns-522023	S. Butcher	Open	45.00	50-58.00
89-04-282	Thank You Lord For Everything-522031	S. Butcher	Open	55.00	60-70.00
91-04-283	May Your World Be Trimmed With Joy-522082	S. Butcher	Open	55.00	55.00
90-04-284	There Shall Be Showers Of Blessings-522090	S. Butcher	Open	60.00	60-69.00
92-04-285	It's No Yolk When I Say Love You-522104	S. Butcher	Open	60.00	60.00
89-04-286	Don't Let the Holidays Get You Down-522112	S. Butcher	Open	42.50	45-54.00
89-04-287	Wishing You A Very Successful Season-522120	S. Butcher	Open	60.00	65-70.00
89-04-288	Bon Voyage!-522201	S. Butcher	Open	75.00	80-99.00
89-04-289	He Is The Star Of The Morning-522252	S. Butcher	Open	55.00	60-65.00
89-04-290	To Be With You Is Uplifting-522260	S. Butcher	Open	20.00	22.50-30.00
91-04-291	A Reflection Of His Love-522279	S. Butcher	Open	50.00	50.00
90-04-292	Thinking Of You Is What I Really Like To Do-522287	S. Butcher	Open	30.00	30-35.00
89-04-293	Merry Christmas Deer-522317	S. Butcher	Open	50.00	55-65.00
89-04-294	Isn't He Precious-522988	S. Butcher	Open	15.00	16.50-20.00
90-04-295	Some Bunny's Sleeping-522996	S. Butcher	Open	12.00	12-19.00
89-04-296	Jesus Is The Sweetest Name I Know-523097	S. Butcher	Open	22.50	25-29.00
91-04-297	Joy On Arrival-523178	S. Butcher	Open	50.00	50.00
90-04-298	The Good Lord Always Delivers- 523453	S. Butcher	Open	27.50	27.50-35.00
90-04-299	This Day Has Been Made In Heaven-523496	S. Butcher	Open	30.00	30-45.00
90-04-300	God Is Love Dear Valentine-523518	S. Butcher	Open	27.50	27.50-32.00
91-04-301	I Will Cherish The Old Rugged Cross-523534	S. Butcher	Yr.Iss.	27.50	40-45.00
92-04-302	You Are The Type I Love-523542	S. Butcher	Open	40.00	40.00
93-04-303	The Lord Will Provide-523593	S. Butcher	Yr.Iss.	40.00	40.00
91-04-304	Good News Is So Uplifting-523615	S. Butcher	Open	60.00	60.00
90-04-305	Time Heals-523739	S. Butcher	Open	37.50	37.50-40.00
90-04-306	Blessings From Above-523747	S. Butcher	Open	45.00	45-50.00
91-04-307	I Can't Spell Success Without You-523763	S. Butcher	Open	40.00	40-45.00
90-04-308	Once Upon A Holy Night-523836	S. Butcher	Yr.Iss.	25.00	25-29.00
92-04-309	My Warmest Thoughts Are You-524085	S. Butcher	Open	55.00	55.00
91-04-310	Good Friends Are For Always-524123	S. Butcher	Open	27.50	27.50
91-04-311	May Your Christmas Be Merry-524166	S. Butcher	Yr.Iss.	27.50	27.50
91-04-312	He Loves Me -524263	S. Butcher	Yr.Iss.	35.00	35-40.00
92-04-313	Friendship Grows When You Plant A Seed-524271	S. Butcher	Open	40.00	40.00
93-04-314	May Your Every Wish Come True-524298	S. Butcher	Open	50.00	50.00
91-04-315	May Your Birthday Be A Blessing-524301	S. Butcher	Open	30.00	30-35.00
92-04-316	What The World Needs Now-524352	S. Butcher	Open	50.00	50.00
91-04-317	May Only Good Things Come Your Way-524425	S. Butcher	Open	30.00	30-35.00
93-04-318	Sealed With A Kiss-524441	S. Butcher	Open	50.00	50.00
90-04-319	Happy Birthday Dear Jesus-524875	S. Butcher	Open	13.50	13.50-16.00
92-04-320	It's So Uplifting To Have A Friend Like You-524905	S. Butcher	Open	40.00	40.00
90-04-321	We're Going To Miss You-524913	S. Butcher	Open	50.00	50-55.00
91-04-322	Angels We Have Heard On High-524921	S. Butcher	Open	60.00	60.00
92-04-323	Tubby's First Christmas-525278	S. Butcher	Open	10.00	10.00
91-04-324	It's A Perfect Boy-525286	S. Butcher	Open	16.50	16.50
93-04-325	May Your Future Be Blessed-525316	S. Butcher	Open	35.00	35.00
92-04-326	Going Home-525979	S. Butcher	Open	60.00	60.00
92-04-327	I Would Be Lost Without You-526142	S. Butcher	Open	27.50	27.50
92-04-328	You Are My Happiness-526185	S. Butcher	Yr.Iss.	37.50	37.50
91-04-329	We Have Come From Afar-526959	S. Butcher	Open	17.50	17.50
93-04-330	Bless-Um You-527335	S. Butcher	Open	35.00	35.00
92-04-331	You Are My Favorite Star-527378	S. Butcher	Open	55.00	55.00
92-04-332	Bring The Little Ones To Jesus-527556	S. Butcher	Open	90.00	90.00
92-04-333	God Bless The U.S.A.-527564	S. Butcher	Yr.Iss.	32.50	32.50
92-04-334	Wishing You A Ho Ho Ho-527629	S. Butcher	Open	40.00	40.00
92-04-335	But The Greatest of These Is Love-527688	S. Butcher	Yr.Iss.	27.50	27.50
92-04-336	Wishing You A Comfy Christmas-527750	S. Butcher	Open	30.00	30.00
93-04-327	I Only Have Arms For You-527769	S. Butcher	Open	15.00	15.00
92-04-338	This Land Is Our Land-527777	S. Butcher	Yr.Iss.	35.00	35.00
93-04-339	America You're Beautiful-528862	S. Butcher	Yr.Iss.	35.00	35.00
Enesco Corporation		**Precious Moments Bridal Party**			
84-05-001	Bridesmaid-E-2831	S. Butcher	Open	13.50	20-30.00
85-05-002	Ringbearer-E-2833	S. Butcher	Open	11.00	20-30.00
85-05-003	Flower Girl-E-2835	S. Butcher	Open	11.00	15-25.00
84-05-004	Groomsman-E-2836	S. Butcher	Open	13.50	20-30.00
86-05-005	Groom-E-2837	S. Butcher	Open	13.50	20-40.00
85-05-006	Junior Bridesmaid-E-2845	S. Butcher	Open	12.50	19-30.00
87-05-007	Bride-E-2846	S. Butcher	Open	18.00	25-30.00
87-05-008	God Bless Our Family (Parents of the Groom)-100498	S. Butcher	Open	35.00	50-55.00
87-05-009	God Bless Our Family (Parents of the Bride)-100501	S. Butcher	Open	35.00	50-55.00
87-05-010	Wedding Arch-102369	S. Butcher	Suspd.	22.50	35.00
Enesco Corporation		**Precious Moments Baby's First**			
84-06-001	Baby's First Step-E-2840	S. Butcher	Suspd.	35.00	60-89.00
84-06-002	Baby's First Picture-E-2841	S. Butcher	Retrd.	45.00	115-165.
85-06-003	Baby's First Haircut-12211	S. Butcher	Suspd.	32.50	65-75.00
86-06-004	Baby's First Trip-16012	S. Butcher	Suspd.	32.50	70-95.00
89-06-005	Baby's First Pet-520705	S. Butcher	Open	45.00	50-60.00
90-06-006	Baby's First Meal-524077	S. Butcher	Open	35.00	35.00

Number	Name	Artist	Edition Limit	Issue Price	Quote
Company	**Series**				
90-06-007	Baby's First Word-527238	S. Butcher	Open	24.00	24.00
93-06-008	Baby's First Birthday-524069	S. Butcher	Open	25.00	25.00
Enesco Corporation	**Precious Moments Anniversary Figurines**				
84-07-001	God Blessed Our Years Together With So Much Love And Happiness-E-2853	S. Butcher	Open	35.00	50-60.00
84-07-002	God Blessed Our Year Together With So Much Love And Happiness (1st)-E-2854	S. Butcher	Open	35.00	50-60.00
84-07-003	God Blessed Our Years Together With So Much Love And Happiness (5th)-E-2855	S. Butcher	Open	35.00	50-55.00
84-07-004	God Blessed Our Years Together With So Much Love And Happiness (10th)-E-2856	S. Butcher	Open	35.00	50-55.00
84-07-005	God Blessed Our Years Together With So Much Love And Happiness (25th)-E-2857	S. Butcher	Open	35.00	50-65.00
84-07-006	God Blessed Our Years Together With So Much Love And Happiness (40th)-E-2859	S. Butcher	Open	35.00	50-65.00
84-07-007	God Blessed Our Years Together With So Much Love And Happiness (50th)-E-2860	S. Butcher	Open	35.00	50-65.00
Enesco Corporation	**Precious Moments The Four Seasons**				
85-08-001	The Voice of Spring-12068	S. Butcher	Yr.Iss.	30.00	250-325.
85-08-002	Summer's Joy-12076	S. Butcher	Yr.Iss.	30.00	95-110.00
86-08-003	Autumn's Praise-12084	S. Butcher	Yr.Iss.	30.00	60-95.00
86-08-004	Winter's Song-12092	S. Butcher	Yr.Iss.	30.00	70-120.00
86-08-005	Set	S. Butcher	Yr.Iss.	120.00	485-585.
Enesco Corporation	**Precious Moments Rejoice in the Lord**				
87-09-001	Lord Keep My Life In Tune - 12165	S. Butcher	Suspd.	37.50	70-100.00
85-09-002	There's a Song in My Heart-12173	S. Butcher	Suspd.	11.00	25-45.00
85-09-003	Happiness is the Lord-12378	S. Butcher	Suspd.	15.00	35-60.00
85-09-004	Lord Give Me a Song-12386	S. Butcher	Suspd.	15.00	30-50.00
85-09-005	He is My Song-12394	S. Butcher	Suspd.	17.50	35-60.00
Enesco Corporation	**Precious Moments Clown**				
XX-10-001	I Get a Bang Out of You-12262	S. Butcher	Open	30.00	45-55.00
86-10-002	Lord Keep Me On the Ball-12270	S. Butcher	Open	30.00	45-55.00
85-10-003	Waddle I Do Without You-12459	S. Butcher	Retrd.	30.00	65-110.00
86-10-004	The Lord Will Carry You Through-12467	S. Butcher	Retrd.	30.00	75-105.00
Enesco Corporation	**Precious Moments Club Fifth Anniversary Commemorative Edition**				
85-11-001	God Bless Our Years Together-12440	S. Butcher	Closed	175.00	300-325.
Enesco Corporation	**Precious Moments Family Christmas Scene**				
85-12-001	May You Have the Sweetest Christmas-15776	S. Butcher	Suspd.	17.00	35-55.00
85-12-002	The Story of God's Love-15784	S. Butcher	Suspd.	22.50	35-90.00
85-12-003	Tell Me a Story-15792	S. Butcher	Suspd.	10.00	20-75.00
85-12-004	God Gave His Best-15806	S. Butcher	Suspd.	13.00	22-85.00
85-12-005	Silent Night-15814	S. Butcher	Suspd.	37.50	69-120.00
86-12-006	Sharing Our Christmas Together-102490	S. Butcher	Suspd.	40.00	55-80.00
89-12-007	Have A Beary Merry Christmas-522856	S. Butcher	Suspd.	15.00	30-45.00
90-12-008	Christmas Fireplace-524883	S. Butcher	Suspd.	37.50	100-125.
Enesco Corporation	**Retired Precious Moments Figurines**				
79-13-001	Smile, God Loves You-E-1373B	S. Butcher	Retrd.	7.00	65-95.00
79-13-002	Praise the Lord Anyhow-E-1374B	S. Butcher	Retrd.	8.00	75-105.00
79-13-003	God Loveth a Cheerful Giver-E-1378	S. Butcher	Retrd.	11.00	750-1000.
79-13-004	O, How I Love Jesus-E-1380B	S. Butcher	Retrd.	8.00	105-125.
79-13-005	His Burden Is Light-E-1380G	S. Butcher	Retrd.	8.00	90-130.00
79-13-006	Come Let Us Adore Him-E-2011	S. Butcher	Retrd.	10.00	325-350.
80-13-007	Wishing you a Season Filled w/ Joy-E-2805	S. Butcher	Retrd.	20.00	95-125.00
80-13-008	Blessed are the Peacemakers-E-3107	S. Butcher	Retrd.	13.00	85-115.00
80-13-009	Be Not Weary In Well Doing-E-3111	S. Butcher	Retrd.	14.00	75-130.00
80-13-010	God's Speed-E-3112	S. Butcher	Retrd.	14.00	70-120.00
80-13-011	Eggs Over Easy-E-3118	S. Butcher	Retrd.	12.00	75-125.00
82-13-012	O Come All Ye Faithful-E-2353	S. Butcher	Retrd.	27.50	70-100.00
82-13-013	There is Joy in Serving Jesus-E-7157	S. Butcher	Retrd.	17.00	50-80.00
83-13-014	Taste and See that the Lord is Good-E-9274	S. Butcher	Retrd.	22.50	60-80.00
87-13-015	His Eye Is On The Sparrow-E-0530	S. Butcher	Retrd.	28.50	85-110.00
87-13-016	Holy Smokes-E-2351	S. Butcher	Retrd.	27.00	80-115.00
87-13-017	Love is Kind-E-5377	S. Butcher	Retrd.	27.50	80-100.00
87-13-018	Let Love Reign-E-9273	S. Butcher	Retrd.	27.50	65-85.00
79-13-019	Jesus is the Light-E-1373G	S. Butcher	Retrd.	7.00	55-125.00
84-13-020	This is Your Day to Shine-E-2822	S. Butcher	Retrd.	37.50	50-100.00
83-13-021	Surrounded with Joy-E-0506	S. Butcher	Retrd.	21.00	50-80.00
83-13-022	You Can't Run Away from God-E-0525	S. Butcher	Retrd.	28.50	80-100.00
86-13-023	Lord, Keep Me On My Toes-100129	S. Butcher	Retrd.	22.50	75-85.00
86-13-024	Help, Lord, I'm In a Spot-100269	S. Butcher	Retrd.	18.50	55-65.00
83-13-025	Christmastime Is for Sharing-E-0504	S. Butcher	Retrd.	37.00	85-95.00
83-13-026	Nobody's Perfect-E-9268	S. Butcher	Retrd.	21.00	65-75.00
87-13-027	Make Me A Blessing-100102	S. Butcher	Retrd.	35.00	70-135.00
89-13-028	Many Moons In Same Canoe, Blessum You-520772	S. Butcher	Retrd.	50.00	145-250.
82-13-029	Dropping Over for Christmas-E-2375	S. Butcher	Retrd.	30.00	70-110.00
87-13-030	Smile Along The Way-101842	S. Butcher	Retrd.	30.00	135-190.
87-13-031	Scent From Above-100528	S. Butcher	Retrd.	19.00	50-80.00
87-13-032	The Spirit Is Willing But The Flesh Is Weak-100196	S. Butcher	Retrd.	19.00	50-75.00
89-13-033	I'm So Glad You Fluttered Into My Life-520640	S. Butcher	Retrd.	40.00	250-300.
82-13-034	I Believe in Miracles-E-7156	S. Butcher	Retrd.	17.00	100-175.
87-13-035	I Believe In Miracles-E-7156R	S. Butcher	Retrd.	22.50	65-90.00
87-13-036	Lord, Help Us Keep Our Act Together-101850	S. Butcher	Retrd.	35.00	115-175.
88-13-037	Happiness Divine-109584	S. Butcher	Retrd.	25.00	50-75.00
89-13-038	Sending You Showers Of Blessings-520683	S. Butcher	Retrd.	32.50	65-100.00
89-13-039	Someday My Love-520799	S. Butcher	Retrd.	40.00	55-80.00
Enesco Corporation	**Precious Moments Collection 10th Anniv. Commemorative Edition**				
88-14-001	The Good Lord has Blessed Us Tenfold-114022	S. Butcher	Yr.Iss.	90.00	135-195.
Enesco Corporation	**Precious Moments Birthday Train Figurines**				
88-15-001	Isn't Eight Just Great-109460	S. Butcher	Open	18.50	22.50-30.00
88-15-002	Wishing You Grr-eatness-109479	S. Butcher	Open	18.50	22.50-30.00
86-15-003	May Your Birthday Be Warm-15938	S. Butcher	Open	10.00	15-40.00
86-15-004	Happy Birthday Little Lamb-15946	S. Butcher	Open	10.00	15-39.00
86-15-005	Heaven Bless Your Special Day-15954	S. Butcher	Open	11.00	16.50-30.00
86-15-006	God Bless You On Your Birthday-15962	S. Butcher	Open	11.00	16.50-40.00
86-15-007	May Your Birthday Be Gigantic -15970	S. Butcher	Open	12.50	18.50-40.00
86-15-008	This Day Is Something To Roar About-15989	S. Butcher	Open	13.50	20-40.00
86-15-009	Keep Looking Up-15997	S. Butcher	Open	13.50	20-43.00
86-15-010	Bless The Days Of Our Youth-16004	S. Butcher	Open	15.00	22.50-45.00
92-15-011	May Your Birthday Be Mammoth-521825	S. Butcher	Open	25.00	25-40.00
92-15-012	Being Nine Is Just Divine-521833	S. Butcher	Open	25.00	25-40.00
Enesco Corporation	**Precious Moments Birthday Club Figurines**				
86-16-001	Fishing For Friends-BC-861	S. Butcher	Yr.Iss.	10.00	120-140.
87-16-002	Hi Sugar-BC-871	S. Butcher	Yr.Iss.	11.00	85-100.00
88-16-003	Somebunny Cares-BC-881	S. Butcher	Yr.Iss.	13.50	50-85.00
89-16-004	Can't Bee Hive Myself Without You-BC-891	S. Butcher	Yr.Iss.	13.50	35-75.00
90-16-005	Collecting Makes Good Scents-BC-901	S. Butcher	Yr.Iss.	15.00	35-40.00
90-16-006	I'm Nuts Over My Collection-BC-902	S. Butcher	Yr.Iss.	15.00	35-40.00
91-16-007	Love Pacifies-BC-911	S. Butcher	Yr.Iss.	15.00	15.00
91-16-008	True Blue Friends-BC-912	S. Butcher	Yr.Iss.	15.00	15.00
92-16-009	Every Man's House Is His Castle-BC-921	S. Butcher	Yr.Iss.	16.50	16.50
Enesco Corporation	**Precious Moments Birthday Club Welcome Gift**				
86-17-001	Our Club Can't Be Beat-B-0001	S. Butcher	Yr.Iss.	Unkn.	75-95.00
87-17-002	A Smile's The Cymbal of Joy-B-0002	S. Butcher	Yr.Iss.	Unkn.	50-65.00
88-17-003	The Sweetest Club Around-B-0003	S. Butcher	Yr.Iss.	Unkn.	35-65.00
89-17-004	Have A Beary Special Birthday- B-0004	S. Butcher	Yr.Iss.	Unkn.	35-55.00
90-17-005	Our Club Is A Tough Act To Follow-B-0005	S. Butcher	Yr.Iss.	Unkn.	25-45.00
91-17-006	Jest To Let You Know You're Tops-B-0006	S. Butcher	Yr.Iss.	Unkn.	45.00
92-17-007	All Aboard For Birthday Club Fun-B-0007	S. Butcher	Yr.Iss.	Unkn.	25.00
Enesco Corporation	**Birthday Club Inscribed Charter Member Renewal Gift**				
87-18-001	A Smile's the Cymbal of Joy-B-0102	S. Butcher	Yr.Iss.	Unkn.	60-70.00
88-18-002	The Sweetest Club Around-B-0103	S. Butcher	Yr.Iss.	Unkn.	35-65.00
89-18-003	Have A Beary Special Birthday- B-0104	S. Butcher	Yr.Iss.	Unkn.	30-55.00
90-18-004	Our Club Is A Tough Act To Follow-B-0105	S. Butcher	Yr.Iss.	Unkn.	25-40.00
91-18-005	Jest To Let You Know You're Tops-B-0106	S. Butcher	Yr.Iss.	Unkn.	25-40.00
92-18-006	All Aboard For Birthday Club Fun-B-0107	S. Butcher	Yr.Iss.	Unkn.	25.00
Enesco Corporation	**Birthday Series**				
88-19-001	Friends To The End-104418	S. Butcher	Open	15.00	18.50-35.00
87-19-002	Showers Of Blessings-105945	S. Butcher	Open	16.00	30-35.00
88-19-003	Brighten Someone's Day-105953	S. Butcher	Open	12.50	15-30.00
90-19-005	To My Favorite Fan-521043	S. Butcher	Open	16.00	16-50.00
89-19-004	Hello World!-521175	S. Butcher	Open	13.50	15-30.00
90-19-006	Not A Creature Was Stirring-524484	S. Butcher	Open	17.00	17-25.00
91-19-007	Can't Be Without You-524492	S. Butcher	Open	16.00	16-29.00
91-19-008	How Can I Ever Forget You-526924	S. Butcher	Open	15.00	15.00
92-19-009	Let's Be Friends-527270	S. Butcher	Open	15.00	15.00
92-19-010	Happy Birdie-527343	S. Butcher	Open	8.00	8.00
Enesco Corporation	**Precious Moments Events Figurines**				
88-20-001	You Are My Main Event-115231	S. Butcher	Yr.Iss.	30.00	50-95.00
89-20-002	Sharing Begins In The Heart-520861	S. Butcher	Yr.Iss.	25.00	45-80.00
90-20-003	I'm A Precious Moments Fan-523526	S. Butcher	Yr.Iss.	25.00	45-65.00
90-20-004	Good Friends Are Forever-525049	S. Butcher	Yr.Iss.	25.00	25.00
91-20-005	You Can Always Bring A Friend-527122	S. Butcher	Yr.Iss.	27.50	45.00
92-20-006	An Event Worth Wading For-527319	S. Butcher	Yr.Iss.	32.50	32.50
93-20-007	An Event For All Seasons-530158	S. Butcher	Yr.Iss.	30.00	30.00
Enesco Corporation	**Precious Moments Commemorative Easter Seal Figurines**				
88-21-001	Jesus Loves Me-9" Fig.-104531	S. Butcher	1,000	N/A	1500-1700.
87-21-002	He Walks With Me-107999	S. Butcher	Yr.Iss.	25.00	38-50.00
88-21-003	Blessed Are They That Overcome-115479	S. Butcher	Yr.Iss.	27.50	35-40.00
89-21-004	Make A Joyful Noise-9" Fig.-520322	S. Butcher	1,500	N/A	1000-1300.
89-21-005	His Love Will Shine On You-522376	S. Butcher	Yr.Iss.	30.00	40-50.00
90-21-006	Always In His Care-524522	S. Butcher	Yr.Iss.	30.00	40.00
90-21-007	You Have Touched So Many Hearts-9" fig.-523283	S. Butcher	2,000	N/A	650-1000.
91-21-008	Sharing A Gift Of Love-527114	S. Butcher	Yr.Iss.	30.00	40-50.00
91-21-009	We Are God's Workmanship-9" fig.-523879	S. Butcher	2,000	N/A	650-1000.
92-21-010	A Universal Love-527173	S. Butcher	Yr.Iss.	32.50	32.50
92-21-011	You Are Such A Purr-fect Friend9" fig.-526010	S. Butcher	2,000	N/A	N/A
93-21-012	Gather Your Dreams-9" fig.-529680	S. Butcher	2,000	N/A	N/A
93-21-013	You're My Number One Friend-530026	S. Butcher	Yr.Iss.	30.00	30.00
Enesco Corporation	**Precious Moments Musical Figurines**				
83-22-001	Sharing Our Season Together-E-0519	S. Butcher	Retrd.	70.00	100-150.
83-22-002	Wee Three Kings-E-0520	S. Butcher	Suspd.	60.00	90-110.00
83-22-003	Let Heaven And Nature Sing-E-2346	S. Butcher	Suspd.	55.00	115-130.
93-22-004	O Come All Ye Faithful-E-2352	S. Butcher	Open	50.00	50.00
82-22-005	I'll Play My Drum For Him-E-2355	S. Butcher	Suspd.	45.00	110-140.
79-22-006	Christmas Is A Time To Share-E-2806	S. Butcher	Retrd.	35.00	140-170.
79-22-007	Crown Him Lord Of All-E-2807	S. Butcher	Suspd.	35.00	75-110.00
79-22-008	Unto Us A Child Is Born-E-2808	S. Butcher	Suspd.	35.00	65-115.00
80-22-009	Jesus Is Born-E-2809	S. Butcher	Suspd.	35.00	90-120.00
80-22-010	Come Let Us Adore Him-E-2810	S. Butcher	Open	45.00	85-125.00
80-22-011	Peace On Earth-E-4726	S. Butcher	Suspd.	45.00	95-120.00
80-22-012	The Hand That Rocks The Future-E-5204	S. Butcher	Open	30.00	55-85.00
80-22-013	My Guardian Angel-E-5205	S. Butcher	Suspd.	22.50	65-75.00
81-22-014	My Guardian Angel-E-5206	S. Butcher	Suspd.	22.50	55-85.00
84-22-015	Wishing You A Merry Christmas-E-5394	S. Butcher	Suspd.	55.00	80-100.00
80-22-016	Silent Knight-E-5642	S. Butcher	Suspd.	45.00	125-150.
81-22-017	Rejoice O Earth-E-5645	S. Butcher	Retrd.	35.00	80-110.00
81-22-018	The Lord Bless You And Keep You-E-7180	S. Butcher	Open	55.00	80-100.00
81-22-019	Mother Sew Dear-E-7182	S. Butcher	Open	35.00	55-75.00
81-22-020	The Purr-fect Grandma-E-7184	S. Butcher	Open	35.00	55-80.00
81-22-021	Love Is Sharing-E-7185	S. Butcher	Retrd.	40.00	125-165.
81-22-022	Let the Whole World Know-E-7186	S. Butcher	Suspd.	60.00	135.00
93-22-023	Lord Keep My Life In Tune (2/set)-12165	S. Butcher	Open	50.00	50.00
84-22-024	We Saw A Star-12408	S. Butcher	Suspd.	50.00	65-80.00
93-22-025	Lord Keep My Life In Tune (2/set)-12580	S. Butcher	Open	50.00	50.00
93-22-026	God Sent You Just In Time-15504	S. Butcher	Retrd.	60.00	60.00
93-22-027	Silent Night-15814	S. Butcher	Open	55.00	55.00
85-22-028	Heaven Bless You-100285	S. Butcher	Open	45.00	60-75.00
86-22-029	Our 1st Christmas Together-101702	S. Butcher	Retrd.	50.00	85-150.00
93-22-030	Let's Keep In Touch-102520	S. Butcher	Open	85.00	85.00
93-22-031	Peace On Earth-109796	S. Butcher	Open	120.00	120.00
87-22-032	I'm Sending You A White Christmas-112402	S. Butcher	Open	55.00	70-75.00
87-22-033	You Have Touched So Many Hearts-112577	S. Butcher	Open	50.00	50-60.00
91 22 034	Lord Keep My Life In Balance-520691	S. Butcher	Open	60.00	68.00
93-22-035	The Light Of The World Is Jesus-521507	S. Butcher	Open	65.00	65.00
92-22-036	Do Not Open Till Christmas-522244	S. Butcher	Open	75.00	75.00
92-22-037	This Day Has Been Made In Heaven-523682	S. Butcher	Open	60.00	60.00
93-22-038	Wishing You Were Here-526916	S. Butcher	Open	100.00	100.00
Enesco Corporation	**Precious Moments Calendar Girl**				
88-23-001	January-109983	S. Butcher	Open	37.50	45-67.00
88-23-002	February-109991	S. Butcher	Open	27.50	33.50-67.00
88-23-003	March-110019	S. Butcher	Open	27.50	33.50-64.00
88-23-004	April-110027	S. Butcher	Open	30.00	35-113.00

Company / Number	Series / Name	Artist	Edition Limit	Issue Price	Quote
88-23-005	May -110035	S. Butcher	Open	25.00	30-150.00
88-23-006	June-110043	S. Butcher	Open	40.00	50-112.00
88-23-007	July-110051	S. Butcher	Open	35.00	45-58.00
88-23-008	August-110078	S. Butcher	Open	40.00	50-57.00
88-23-009	September-110086	S. Butcher	Open	27.50	33.50-49.00
88-23-010	October-110094	S. Butcher	Open	35.00	45-59.00
88-23-011	November-110108	S. Butcher	Open	32.50	37.50-50.00
88-23-012	December-110116	S. Butcher	Open	27.50	35-75.00
Enesco Corporation	**Bless Those Who Serve Their Country**				
91-24-001	Bless Those Who Serve Their Country (Navy) 526568	S. Butcher	Suspd.	32.50	32.50
91-24-002	Bless Those Who Serve Their Country (Army) 526576	S. Butcher	Suspd.	32.50	32.50
91-24-003	Bless Those Who Serve Their Country (Air Force) 526584	S. Butcher	Suspd.	32.50	35.00
91-24-004	Bless Those Who Serve Their Country (Girl Soldier) 527289	S. Butcher	Suspd.	32.50	35.00
91-24-005	Bless Those Who Serve Their Country (Soldier) 527297	S. Butcher	Suspd.	32.50	32.50
91-24-006	Bless Those Who Serve Their Country (Marine) 527521	S. Butcher	Suspd.	32.50	45.00
Enesco Corporation	**Sugartown**				
92-25-001	Christmas Tree-528684	S. Butcher	Open	15.00	15.00
92-25-002	Chapel-529621	S. Butcher	Open	85.00	85.00
92-25-003	Nativity-529508	S. Butcher	Open	20.00	20.00
92-25-004	Grandfather-529516	S. Butcher	Open	15.00	15.00
92-25-005	Sam Butcher-529567	S. Butcher	Yr. Iss.	22.50	22.50
92-25-006	Aunt Ruth & Aunt Dorothy-529486	S. Butcher	Open	20.00	20.00
92-25-007	Philip-529494	S. Butcher	Open	17.00	17.00
Enesco Corporation	**Spring Catalog Figurine**				
93-26-001	Happiness Is At Our Fingertips-529931	S. Butcher	Yr.Iss.	35.00	35.00
Enesco Corporation	**Two By Two**				
93-27-001	Noah, Noah's Wife, & Noah's Ark (lighted)-530042	S. Butcher	Open	125.00	125.00
93-27-002	Sheep (mini double fig.) -530077	S. Butcher	Open	10.00	10.00
93-27-003	Pigs (mini double fig.) -530085	S. Butcher	Open	12.00	12.00
93-27-004	Giraffes (mini double fig.) -530115	S. Butcher	Open	16.00	16.00
93-27-005	Bunnies (mini double fig.) -530123	S. Butcher	Open	9.00	9.00
93-27-006	Elephants (mini double fig.) -530131	S. Butcher	Open	18.00	18.00
93-27-007	Eight Piece Collector's Set -530948	S. Butcher	Open	190.00	190.00
Enesco Corporation	**Memories of Yesterday Special Edition**				
88-28-001	Mommy, I Teared It-523488	M. Attwell	10,000	25.00	175-325.
89-28-002	As Good As His Mother Ever Made-522392	M. Attwell	9,600	32.50	114-150.
90-28-003	A Lapful of Luck -525014	M. Attwell	5,000	30.00	114-180.
Enesco Corporation	**Memories of Yesterday -Charter 1988**				
88-29-001	Mommy, I Teared It-114480	M. Attwell	Open	25.00	32-64.00
88-29-002	Now I Lay Me Down To Sleep-114499	M. Attwell	Open	20.00	25-40.00
88-29-003	We's Happy! How's Yourself?-114502	M. Attwell	Open	40.00	45-60.00
88-29-004	Hang On To Your Luck!-114510	M. Attwell	Open	25.00	27.50-50.00
88-29-005	How Do You Spell S-O-R-R-Y?-114529	M. Attwell	Retrd.	25.00	35-70.00
88-29-006	What Will I Grow Up To Be?-114537	M. Attwell	Open	40.00	45-72.00
88-29-007	Can I Keep Her Mommy?-114545	M. Attwell	Open	25.00	27-50.00
88-29-008	Hush!-114553	M. Attwell	Retrd.	45.00	60-100.00
88-29-009	It Hurts When Fido Hurts-114561	M. Attwell	Retrd.	30.00	32.50-52.00
88-29-010	Anyway, Fido Loves Me-114588	M. Attwell	Open	30.00	32.50-45.00
88-29-011	If You Can't Be Good, Be Careful-114596	M. Attwell	Open	50.00	55-80.00
88-29-012	Mommy, I Teared It, 9"-115924	M. Attwell	Closed	85.00	140-200.
88-29-013	Welcome Santa-114960	M. Attwell	Open	45.00	50-75.00
88-29-014	Special Delivery-114979	M. Attwell	Retrd.	30.00	32.50-50.00
88-29-015	How 'bout A Little Kiss?-114987	M. Attwell	Open	25.00	27.50-50.00
88-29-016	Waiting For Santa-114995	M. Attwell	Open	40.00	45-60.00
88-29-017	Dear Santa. . .-115002	M. Attwell	Open	50.00	55-75.00
88-29-018	I Hope Santa Is Home . . .-115010	M. Attwell	Open	30.00	32.50-40.00
88-29-019	It's The Thought That Counts-115029	M. Attwell	Open	25.00	27.50-45.00
88-29-020	Is It Really Santa?-115347	M. Attwell	Open	50.00	55-65.00
88-29-021	He Knows IF You've Been Bad Or Good-115355	M. Attwell	Open	40.00	45-60.00
88-29-022	Now He Can Be Your Friend, Too!-115363	M. Attwell	Open	45.00	50-65.00
88-29-023	We Wish You A Merry Christmas-115371	M. Attwell	Open	70.00	75-125.00
88-29-024	Good Morning Mr. Snowman-115401	M. Attwell	Retrd.	75.00	80-170.00
Enesco Corporation	**Memories of Yesterday Figurines**				
89-30-001	Blow Wind, Blow-520012	M. Attwell	Open	40.00	40.00
89-30-002	Let's Be Nice Like We Was Before-520047	M. Attwell	Open	50.00	50.00
89-30-003	I'se Spoken For-520071	M. Attwell	Retrd.	30.00	30-45.00
89-30-004	Daddy, I Can Never Fill Your Shoes-520187	M. Attwell	Open	30.00	30.00
89-30-005	This One's For You, Dear-520195	M. Attwell	Open	50.00	50.00
89-30-006	Should I . . . ?-520209	M. Attwell	Open	50.00	50.00
89-30-007	Here Comes The Bride-God Bless Her! -9"-5205272	M. Attwell	Closed	95.00	100-125.
89-30-008	We's Happy! How's Yourself?-520616	M. Attwell	Retrd.	70.00	85-100.00
89-30-009	Here Comes The Bride & Groom God Bless 'Em-520896	M. Attwell	Open	50.00	50.00
89-30-010	The Long and Short of It-522384	M. Attwell	Open	32.50	32.50
89-30-011	As Good As His Mother Ever Made-522392	M. Attwell	Open	32.50	32.50
89-30-012	Must Feed Them Over Christmas-522406	M. Attwell	Open	38.50	38.50
89-30-013	Knitting You A Warm & Cozy Winter-522414	M. Attwell	Open	37.50	37.50
89-30-014	Joy To You At Christmas-522449	M. Attwell	Open	45.00	45.00
89-30-015	For Fido And Me-522457	M. Attwell	Open	70.00	70.00
90-30-016	Hold It! You're Just Swell-520020	M. Attwell	Open	50.00	50.00
90-30-017	Kiss The Place And Make It Well-520039	M. Attwell	Open	50.00	50.00
90-30-018	Where's Muvver?-520101	M. Attwell	Open	30.00	30.00
90-30-019	Here Comes The Bride And Groom God Bless 'Em!-520136	M. Attwell	Open	80.00	80.00
90-30-020	Luck At Last! He Loves Me-520217	M. Attwell	Retrd.	35.00	35.00
90-30-021	I'm Not As Backwards As I Looks-523240	M. Attwell	Open	32.50	32.50
90-30-022	I Pray The Lord My Soul To Keep-523259	M. Attwell	Open	25.00	25.00
90-30-023	He Hasn't Forgotten Me-523267	M. Attwell	Open	30.00	30.00
90-30-024	Time For Bed 9"-523275	M. Attwell	Closed	95.00	95-125.00
90-30-025	Got To Get Home For The Holidays-524751	M. Attwell	Open	100.00	100.00
90-30-026	Hush-A-Bye Baby-524778	M. Attwell	Open	80.00	80.00
90-30-027	Let Me Be Your Guardian Angel-524670	M. Attwell	Open	32.50	32.50
90-30-028	I'se Been Painting-524700	M. Attwell	Open	37.50	37.50
90-30-029	A Lapful Of Luck-524689	M. Attwell	Open	15.00	15.00
90-30-030	The Greatest Treasure The World Can Hold-524808	M. Attwell	Open	50.00	50.00
90-30-031	Hoping To See You Soon-524824	M. Attwell	Open	30.00	30.00
90-30-032	A Dash of Something With Something For the Pot-524727	M. Attwell	Open	55.00	55.00
90-30-033	Not A Creature Was Stirrin'-524697	M. Attwell	Open	45.00	45.00
90-30-034	Collection Sign-513156	M. Attwell	Open	7.00	7.00
91-30-035	He Loves Me -9" -525022	M. Attwell	Closed	100.00	100.00
91-30-036	Give It Your Best Shot-525561	M. Attwell	Open	35.00	35.00
91-30-037	Wishful Thinking-522597	M. Attwell	Open	45.00	45.00
91-30-038	Them Dishes Nearly Done-524611	M. Attwell	Open	50.00	50.00
91-30-039	Just Thinking 'bout You-523461	M. Attwell	Open	70.00	70.00
91-30-040	Who Ever Told Mother To Order Twins?-520063	M. Attwell	Open	33.50	33.50
91-30-041	Tying The Knot-522678	M. Attwell	Open	60.00	60.00
91-30-042	Pull Yourselves Together Girls, Waists Are In-522783	M. Attwell	Open	30.00	30.00
91-30-043	I Must Be Somebody's Darling-524832	M. Attwell	Open	30.00	30.00
91-30-044	We All Loves A Cuddle-524832	M. Attwell	Retrd.	30.00	30.00
91-30-045	Sitting Pretty-522708	M. Attwell	Open	40.00	40.00
91-30-046	Why Don't You Sing Along?-522600	M. Attwell	Open	55.00	55.00
91-30-047	Wherever I Am, I'm Dreaming of You-522686	M. Attwell	Open	40.00	40.00
91-30-048	Opening Presents Is Much Fun!-524735	M. Attwell	Open	37.50	37.50
91-30-049	I'm As Comfy As Can Be-525480	M. Attwell	Open	50.00	50.00
91-30-050	Friendship Has No Boundaries (Special Understamp)-525545	M. Attwell	Yr.Iss.	30.00	30-40.00
91-30-051	Could You Love Me For Myself Alone?-525618	M. Attwell	Open	30.00	30.00
91-30-052	Good Morning, Little Boo-Boo-525766	M. Attwell	Open	40.00	40.00
91-30-053	S'no Use Lookin' Back Now!-527203	M. Attwell	Open	75.00	75.00
92-30-054	I Pray the Lord My Soul To Keep (Musical)-525596	M. Attwell	Open	65.00	65.00
92-30-055	Time For Bed-527076	M. Attwell	Open	30.00	30.00
92-30-056	Now Be A Good Dog Fido-524581	M. Attwell	Open	45.00	45.00
92-30-057	A Kiss From Fido-523119	M. Attwell	Open	35.00	35.00
92-30-058	I'se Such A Good Little Girl Sometimes-522759	M. Attwell	Open	30.00	30.00
92-30-059	Send All Life's Little Worries Skipping-527505	M. Attwell	Open	30.00	30.00
92-30-060	A Whole Bunch of Love For You-522732	M. Attwell	Open	40.00	40.00
92-30-061	Hurry Up For the Last Train to Fairyland-525863	M. Attwell	Open	40.00	40.00
92-30-062	I'se So Happy You Called-526401	M. Attwell	2 Yr.	100.00	100.00
92-30-063	I'm Hopin' You're Missing Me Too-525499	M. Attwell	Open	55.00	55.00
92-30-064	You'll Always Be My Hero-524743	M. Attwell	Open	50.00	50.00
92-30-065	Things Are Rather Upside Down-522775	M. Attwell	Open	30.00	30.00
92-30-066	The Future-God Bless 'Em!-524719	M. Attwell	Open	37.50	37.50
92-30-067	Making Something Special For You-525472	M. Attwell	Open	45.00	45.00
92-30-068	Home's A Grand Place To Get Back To Musical-525553	M. Attwell	Open	100.00	100.00
92-30-069	Five Years Of Memories-525669 (Five Year Anniversary Figurine)	M. Attwell	Yr.Iss.	50.00	50.00
92-30-070	Good Night and God Bless You In Every Way!-525634	M. Attwell	Open	50.00	50.00
92-30-071	Collection Sign-527300	M. Attwell	Open	30.00	30.00
92-30-072	Merry Christmas, Little Boo-Boo-528803	M. Attwell	Open	37.50	37.50
92-30-073	Five Years Of Memories. Celebrating Our Five Years1992-525669A	M. Attwell	500	N/A	N/A
93-30-074	You Do Make Me Happy-520098	M. Attwell	Open	27.50	27.50
93-30-075	Will You Be Mine?-522694	M. Attwell	Open	30.00	30.00
93-30-076	Now I Lay Me Down To Sleep-525413 (musical)	M. Attwell	Open	65.00	65.00
93-30-077	The Jolly Ole Sun Will Shine Again-525502	M. Attwell	Open	55.00	55.00
93-30-078	May Your Flowers Be Even Better Than The Pictures On The Packets-525685	M. Attwell	Open	37.50	37.50
93-30-079	You Won't Catch Me Being A Golf Widow -525715	M. Attwell	Open	30.00	30.00
93-30-080	Having A Wash And Brush Up-527424	M. Attwell	Open	35.00	35.00
93-30-081	Hullo! Did You Come By Underground? -527653	M. Attwell	Yr.Iss.	40.00	40.00
93-30-082	Strikes Me, I'm Your Match-529656	M. Attwell	Open	27.50	27.50
93-30-083	Wot's All This Talk About Love?-529737	M. Attwell	2 Yr.	100.00	100.00
Enesco Corporation	**Memories of Yesterday Once Upon A Fairy Tale™...**				
92-31-001	Mother Goose-526428	M. Attwell	18,000	50.00	50.00
92-31-002	Mary Had A Little Lamb-526479	M. Attwell	18,000	45.00	45.00
92-31-003	Simple Simon-526452	M. Attwell	18,000	35.00	35.00
Enesco Corporation	**Memories of Yesterday-Exclusive Membership Figurine**				
91-32-001	We Belong Together-S0001	M. Attwell	Yr.Iss.	Gift	54.00
92-32-002	Waiting For The Sunshine-S0002	M. Attwell	Yr.Iss.	Gift	N/A
Enesco Corporation	**Memories of Yesterday-Exclusive Charter Membership Figurine**				
92-33-001	Waiting For The Sunshine-S0102	M. Attwell	Yr.Iss.	Gift	N/A
Enesco Corporation	**Memories of Yesterday-Society Figurines**				
91-34-001	Welcome To Your New Home-M4911	M. Attwell	Yr.Iss.	30.00	85.00
91-34-002	I Love My Friends-MY921	M. Attwell	Yr.Iss.	32.50	32.50
Enesco Corporation	**Memories of Yesterday-Exclusive Heritage Dealer Figurine**				
91-35-001	A Friendly Chat and a Cup of Tea-525510	M. Attwell	Yr.Iss.	50.00	50.00
Fitz And Floyd, Inc.	**Figures From History**				
92-01-001	Christopher Columbus, teapot	T. Kerr	7,500	60.00	60.00
93-01-002	George Washington, teapot	T. Kerr	5,000	75.00	75.00
Fitz And Floyd, Inc.	**Famous Landmarks Around the World**				
93-02-001	The White House, teapot	T. Kerr	5,000	75.00	75.00
Fitz And Floyd, Inc.	**Musical Maestros**				
93-03-001	Wolfgang Amadeus Mozart, teapot	T. Kerr	5,000	75.00	75.00
Fitz And Floyd, Inc.	**Important Women**				
93-04-001	Betsy Ross, teapot	T. Kerr	1,777	75.00	75.00
Fitz And Floyd, Inc.	**Fables and Fairytales**				
93-05-001	Bremen Town Musicians, teapot	T. Kerr	1,500	75.00	75.00
Fitz And Floyd, Inc.	**Realm of Camelot**				
93-06-001	Realm of Camelot, teapot	V. Balcou	2,000	75.00	75.00
93-06-002	Unicorn figurines, set of 3	V. Balcou	1,000	45.00	45.00
93-06-003	Realm of Camelot, waterball	V. Balcou	1,500	45.00	45.00
Fitz And Floyd, Inc.	**Wonderland**				
93-07-001	Wonderland Characters, set of 6	R. Havins	3,000	100.00	100.00

Company / Number	Name	Series / Artist	Edition Limit	Issue Price	Quote
93-07-002	A Mad Tea Party, waterball	R. Havins	2,000	75.00	75.00
Flambro Imports		**Emmett Kelly, Jr. Figurines**			
81-01-001	Looking Out To See	Undis.	12,000	75.00	1500-3000.
81-01-002	Sweeping Up	Undis.	12,000	75.00	600-1600.
82-01-003	Wet Paint	Undis.	15,000	80.00	600-1000.
82-01-004	The Thinker	Undis.	15,000	60.00	900-1700.
82-01-005	Why Me?	Undis.	15,000	65.00	400-900.
83-01-006	The Balancing Act	Undis.	10,000	75.00	700-950.
83-01-007	Wishful Thinking	Undis.	10,000	65.00	500-700.
83-01-008	Hole In The Sole	Undis.	10,000	75.00	300-600.
83-01-009	Balloons For Sale	Undis.	10,000	75.00	500-700.
83-01-010	Spirit of Christmas I	Undis.	3,500	125.00	1400-3500.
84-01-011	Eating Cabbage	Undis.	12,000	75.00	275-600.
84-01-012	Big Business	Undis.	9,500	110.00	600-950.
84-01-013	Piano Player	Undis.	9,500	160.00	300-750.
84-01-014	Spirit of Christmas II	Undis.	3,500	270.00	250-685.
85-01-015	Man's Best Friend	Undis.	9,500	98.00	325-600.
85-01-016	No Strings Attached	Undis.	9,500	98.00	125-375.
85-01-017	In The Spotlight	Undis.	12,000	103.00	150-375.
85-01-018	Emmett's Fan	Undis.	12,000	80.00	250-650.
85-01-019	Spirit of Christmas III	Undis.	3,500	220.00	240-700.
86-01-020	The Entertainers	Undis.	12,000	120.00	140-200.
86-01-021	Cotton Candy	Undis.	12,000	98.00	300-500.
86-01-022	Bedtime	Undis.	12,000	98.00	150-325.
86-01-023	Making New Friends	Undis.	9,500	140.00	160-450.
86-01-024	Fair Game	Undis.	2,500	450.00	900-1800.
86-01-025	Spirit of Christmas IV	Undis.	3,500	150.00	250-600.
87-01-026	On The Road Again	Undis.	9,500	109.00	175-400.
87-01-027	My Favorite Things	Undis.	9,500	109.00	350-700.
87-01-028	Saturday Night	Undis.	7,500	153.00	400-750.
87-01-029	Toothache	Undis.	12,000	98.00	170-199.
87-01-030	Spirit of Christmas V	Undis.	2,400	170.00	500-750.
88-01-031	Over a Barrel	Undis.	9,500	130.00	115-300.
88-01-032	Wheeler Dealer	Undis.	7,500	160.00	200-250.
88-01-033	Dining Out	Undis.	12,000	120.00	150-300.
88-01-034	Amen	Undis.	12,000	120.00	175-400.
88-01-035	Spirit of Christmas VI	Undis.	2,400	194.00	200-700.
89-01-036	Making Up	Undis.	7,500	200.00	264.00
89-01-037	No Loitering	Undis	7,500	200.00	264.00
89-01-038	Hurdy-Gurdy Man	Undis.	9,500	150.00	175-250.
89-01-039	65th Birthday Commemorative	Undis.	1,989	275.00	840-2500.
90-01-040	Watch the Birdie	Undis.	9,500	200.00	210.00
90-01-041	Convention-Bound	Undis.	7,500	225.00	230.00
90-01-042	Balloons for Sale II	Undis.	7,500	250.00	250.00
90-01-043	Misfortune?	Undis.	3,500	400.00	350-700.
90-01-044	Spirit Of Christmas VII	Undis.	3,500	275.00	350-700.
91-01-045	Finishing Touch	Undis.	7,500	245.00	245.00
91-01-046	Artist At Work	Undis.	7,500	295.00	295.00
91-01-047	Follow The Leader	Undis.	7,500	200.00	200.00
91-01-048	Spirit Of Christmas VIII	Undis.	3,500	250.00	250-500.
92-01-049	No Use Crying	Undis.	7,500	200.00	200.00
92-01-050	Ready-Set-Go	Undis.	7,500	200.00	200.00
92-01-051	Peanut Butter?	Undis.	7,500	200.00	200.00
93-01-052	Kittens For Sale	Undis.	7,500	190.00	190.00
93-01-053	World Traveler	Undis.	7,500	190.00	190.00
93-01-054	After The Parade	Undis.	7,500	190.00	190.00
93-01-055	Spirit of Christmas IX	Undis.	3,500	200.00	200.00
Flambro Imports		**Circus World Museum Clowns**			
85-02-001	Paul Jerome (Hobo)	Undis.	9,500	80.00	80-150.00
85-02-002	Paul Jung (Neat)	Undis.	9,500	80.00	110-120.
85-02-003	Felix Adler (Grotesque)	Undis.	9,500	80.00	80-110.00
87-02-004	Paul Jerome with Dog	Undis.	7,500	90.00	90.00
87-02-005	Paul Jung, Sitting	Undis.	7,500	90.00	90.00
87-02-006	Felix Adler with Balloon	Undis.	7,500	90.00	90.00
87-02-007	Abe Goldstein, Keystone Kop	Undis.	7,500	90.00	90.00
Flambro Imports		**Emmett Kelly, Jr, Miniatures**			
86-03-001	Looking Out To See	Undis.	Retrd.	25.00	90-175.00
86-03-002	Sweeping Up	Undis.	Retrd.	25.00	75-175.00
86-03-003	Wet Paint	Undis.	Retrd.	25.00	50-75.00
86-03-004	Why Me?	Undis.	Retrd.	25.00	45-100.00
86-03-005	The Thinker	Undis.	Retrd.	25.00	35-70.00
86-03-006	Balancing Act	Undis.	Retrd.	25.00	48-65.00
86-03-007	Hole in the Sole	Undis.	Retrd.	25.00	50-125.00
86-03-008	Balloons for Sale	Undis.	Retrd.	25.00	50-55.00
86-03-009	Wishful Thinking	Undis.	Retrd.	25.00	35-75.00
87-03-010	Emmett's Fan	Undis.	Retrd.	30.00	40-50.00
87-03-011	Eating Cabbage	Undis.	Retrd.	30.00	40-65.00
88-03-012	Spirit of Christmas I	Undis.	Retrd.	40.00	70-150.00
88-03-013	Big Business	Undis.	Numbrd.	35.00	38.50
90-03-014	Saturday Night	Undis.	Numbrd.	50.00	50.00
90-03-015	My Favorite Things	Undis.	Numbrd.	45.00	45.00
90-03-016	Spirit Of Christmas III	Undis.	Retrd.	50.00	50.00
89-03-017	Man's Best Friend?	Undis.	Numbrd.	35.00	35.00
89-03-018	Cotton Candy	Undis.	Retrd.	30.00	50.00
91-03-019	In The Spotlight	Undis.	Numbrd.	35.00	35.00
91-03-020	No Strings Attached	Undis.	Numbrd.	35.00	35.00
92-03-021	Spirit of Christmas II	Undis.	Numbrd.	50.00	50.00
92-03-022	Making New Friends	Undis.	Numbrd.	40.00	40.00
92-03-023	Piano Player	Undis.	Numbrd.	50.00	50.00
92-03-024	On the Road Again	Undis.	Numbrd.	35.00	35.00
93-03-025	Spirit of Christmas IV	Undis.	Numbrd.	40.00	40.00
Flambro Imports		**Annual Emmett Kelly Jr. Nutcracker**			
90-04-001	1990 Nutcracker	Undis.	Yr.Iss.	50.00	75.00
Flambro Imports		**Emmett Kelly Jr. Metal Sculptures**			
91-05-001	Carousel Rider	Undis.	5,000	125.00	125.00
91-05-002	The Magician	Undis.	5,000	125.00	125.00
91-05-003	Emmett's Pooches	Undis.	5,000	125.00	125.00
91 05 004	Balancing Act, Too	Undis.	5,000	125.00	125.00
Flambro Imports		**Emmett Kelly Jr. A Day At The Fair**			
90-06-001	Step Right Up	Undis.	Numbrd.	65.00	65.00
90-06-002	Three For A Dime	Undis.	Numbrd.	65.00	65.00
90-06-003	Look At You	Undis.	Retrd.	65.00	65.00
90-06-004	75 Please	Undis.	Numbrd.	65.00	65.00
90-06-005	The Stilt Man	Undis.	Retrd.	65.00	65.00
90-06-006	Ride The Wild Mouse	Undis.	Numbrd.	65.00	65.00
90-06-007	You Can Do It, Emmett	Undis.	Retrd.	65.00	65.00
90-06-008	Thanks Emmett	Undis.	Numbrd.	65.00	65.00
90-06-009	You Go First, Emmett	Undis.	Retrd.	65.00	65.00
91-06-010	The Trouble With Hot Dogs	Undis.	N/A	65.00	65.00
91-06-011	Popcorn!	Undis.	N/A	65.00	65.00
91-06-012	Coin Toss	Undis.	N/A	65.00	65.00
92-06-013	Stilt Man	Undis.	N/A	65.00	65.00
Flambro Imports		**Emmett Kelly Jr. Appearance Figurine**			
92-07-001	Now Appearing	Undis.	N/A	100.00	100.00
93-07-002	The Vigilante	Undis.	N/A	75.00	75.00
Flambro Imports		**Emmett Kelly Jr. Members Only Figurine**			
90-08-001	Merry-Go-Round	Undis.	Closed	125.00	200-550.
91-08-002	10 Years Of Collecting	Undis.	N/A	100.00	100-180.
92-08-003	All Aboard	Undis.	N/A	75.00	75.00
93-08-004	Ringmaster	Undis.	N/A	125.00	125.00
Flambro Imports		**Emmett Kelly Jr. Real Rags Collection**			
93-09-001	Checking His List	Undis.	Open	100.00	100.00
93-09-002	Thinker II	Undis.	Open	120.00	120.00
93-09-003	Sweeping Up II	Undis.	Open	100.00	100.00
93-09-004	Looking Out To See II	Undis.	Open	100.00	100.00
93-09-005	Big Business II	Undis.	Open	140.00	140.00
Flambro Imports		**Raggedy Ann & Andy**			
88-10-001	70 Years Young	C. Beylon	2,500	95.00	110.00
88-10-002	Giddy Up	C. Beylon	3,500	95.00	110.00
88-10-003	Wet Paint	C. Beylon	3,500	70.00	80.00
88-10-004	Oops!	C. Beylon	3,500	80.00	90.00
Flambro Imports		**Pleasantville 1893**			
90-11-001	Sweet Shoppe & Bakery	J. Berg Victor	Open	40.00	40.00
90-11-002	Toy Store	J. Berg Victor	Open	30.00	30.00
90-11-003	1st Church Of Pleasantville	J. Berg Victor	Open	35.00	35.00
90-11-004	Department Store	J. Berg Victor	Open	25.00	25.00
90-11-005	Pleasantville Library	J. Berg Victor	Open	32.00	32.00
90-11-006	The Band Stand	J. Berg Victor	Open	12.00	12.00
90-11-007	The Gerber House	J. Berg Victor	Open	30.00	30.00
90-11-008	Reverend Littlefield's House	J. Berg Victor	Open	34.00	34.00
90-11-009	Mason's Hotel and Saloon	J. Berg Victor	Open	35.00	35.00
91-11-010	Methodist Church	J. Berg Victor	Open	40.00	40.00
91-11-011	Fire House	J. Berg Victor	Open	40.00	40.00
91-11-012	Court House	J. Berg Victor	Open	36.00	36.00
91-11-013	School Houe	J. Berg Victor	Open	36.00	36.00
92-11-014	Railroad Station	J. Berg Victor	Open	N/A	N/A
92-11-015	Blacksmith/Livery	J. Berg Victor	Open	N/A	N/A
92-11-016	Bank/Real Estate Office	J. Berg Victor	Open	N/A	N/A
92-11-017	Apothecary/Ice Cream Shop	J. Berg Victor	Open	N/A	N/A
92-11-018	Tubbs, Jr. House	J. Berg Victor	Open	N/A	N/A
92-11-019	Miss Fountains	J. Berg Victor	Open	N/A	N/A
92-11-021	Covered Bridge	J. Berg Victor	Open	N/A	N/A
93-11-022	Balcombs Farm	J. Berg Victor	Open	N/A	N/A
93-11-023	Blacksmith Shop	J. Berg Victor	Open	N/A	N/A
93-11-024	Blacksmith/Livery Stable	J. Berg Victor	Open	N/A	N/A
93-11-025	New Sculpted Bandstand/Gazebo	J. Berg Victor	Open	N/A	N/A
93-11-026	Catholic Church	J. Berg Victor	Open	N/A	N/A
93-11-027	Sacred Heart Catholic Church	J. Berg Victor	Open	N/A	N/A
93-11-028	Sacred Heart Rectory	J. Berg Victor	Open	N/A	N/A
93-11-029	Pleasantville Gazette Building	J. Berg Victor	Open	N/A	N/A
Flambro Imports		**Daddy Loves You**			
91-12-001	Make You....Giggle!	C. Pracht	2,500	100.00	100.00
91-12-002	You're Sooo....Sweet	C. Pracht	2,500	100.00	100.00
91-12-003	C'mon, Daddy!	C. Pracht	2,500	100.00	100.00
91-12-004	Soo....You Like It?	C. Pracht	2,500	100.00	100.00
Flambro Imports		**Gnomes Limited Edition**			
92-13-001	Welcome Home Gnome	Poortvliet	1,500	55.00	55.00
92-13-002	The Garden Gnome	Poortvliet	1,500	100.00	100.00
92-13-003	The Farm Gnome	Poortvliet	1,500	100.00	100.00
Flambro Imports		**Gnome Miniatures**			
92-14-001	Bill & Bella	Poortvliet	Open	27.00	27.00
92-14-002	Harold	Poortvliet	Open	25.00	25.00
92-14-003	Daniel & Dede	Poortvliet	Open	27.00	27.00
92-14-004	Al Jo	Poortvliet	Open	27.00	27.00
92-14-005	Patrick	Poortvliet	Open	23.00	23.00
92-14-006	George	Poortvliet	Open	22.00	22.00
92-14-007	Julius	Poortvliet	Open	23.00	23.00
92-14-008	Tilly	Poortvliet	Open	19.00	19.00
92-14-009	Wilbur	Poortvliet	Open	25.00	25.00
92-14-010	Mary & Michael	Poortvliet	Open	30.00	30.00
92-14-011	Oscar	Poortvliet	Open	20.00	20.00
92-14-012	Benjamin	Poortvliet	Open	23.00	23.00
92-14-013	Catrina & Charles	Poortvliet	Open	30.00	30.00
92-14-014	Henry	Poortvliet	Open	23.00	23.00
Flambro Imports		**Gnomes**			
92-15-001	Snorri	Poortvliet	Open	51.00	51.00
92-15-002	Genevieve	Poortvliet	Open	49.00	49.00
92-15-003	Abram	Poortvliet	Open	55.00	55.00
92-15-004	Ritkig	Poortvliet	Open	27.00	27.00
92-15-005	Pieter & Hattie	Poortvliet	Open	47.00	47.00
92-15-006	Marta with Bunny	Poortvliet	Open	50.00	50.00
92-15-007	David	Poortvliet	Open	46.00	46.00
92-15-008	Theodor	Poortvliet	Open	40.00	40.00
92-15-009	Tobias	Poortvliet	Open	38.00	40.00
92-15-010	Jacob	Poortvliet	Open	37.00	37.00
92-15-011	Gabriel	Poortvliet	Open	20.00	20.00
92-15-012	Quentin	Poortvliet	Open	30.00	30.00
92-15-013	Hannah & Josh	Poortvliet	Open	27.00	27.00
92-15-014	Franz with Christoph & Katya	Poortvliet	Open	45.00	45.00
92-15-015	Claire	Poortvliet	Open	36.00	36.00
92-15-016	Slumber Chief	Poortvliet	Open	40.00	40.00
92-15-017	Ollie	Poortvliet	Open	27.00	27.00
92-15-018	Purdy & Pippin	Poortvliet	Open	39.00	39.00
92-15-019	Columbine	Poortvliet	Open	25.00	25.00
92-15-020	Sigfried	Poortvliet	Open	52.00	52.00
92-15-021	Sophia	Poortvliet	Open	52.00	52.00
92-15-022	Brina & Borg	Poortvliet	Open	45.00	45.00
92-15-023	Ahni with Max & Molly	Poortvliet	Open	55.00	55.00
92-15-024	Stephie & Stoffie	Poortvliet	Open	19.00	19.00
92-15-025	Trudy & Frederick	Poortvliet	Open	50.00	50.00
92-15-026	Richard & Rosemary	Poortvliet	Open	53.00	53.00

Company / Number	Name	Series / Artist	Edition Limit	Issue Price	Quote
92-15-027	Otto	Poortvliet	Open	40.00	40.00
92-15-028	Willie	Poortvliet	Open	37.00	37.00
92-15-029	Gideon	Poortvliet	Open	40.00	40.00
92-15-030	Nicolas (Siberian)	Poortvliet	Open	35.00	35.00
92-15-031	Jonathan (Snowman)	Poortvliet	Open	40.00	40.00
92-15-032	Pepi (Skiing)	Poortvliet	Open	42.00	42.00
92-15-033	Gobby & Lou (Goblin)	Poortvliet	Open	39.00	39.00
Kevin Francis		**Political Series-Toby Jugs**			
89-01-001	Winston Churchill (9")	P. Davies	5,000	250.00	250.00
90-01-002	Mrs. Thatcher (9")	D. Tootle	Retrd.	250.00	250.00
90-01-003	Gorbachev (9")	A. Moss	Retrd.	250.00	250.00
90-01-004	Helmut Kohl (9")	A. Moss	999	250.00	250.00
92-01-005	Boris Yeltsin (9")	A. Moss	250	450.00	450.00
92-01-006	John F. Kennedy (9")	A. Moss	750	250.00	250.00
Kevin Francis		**Artists And Potters-Toby Jugs**			
90-02-001	David Winter (9")	D.Tootle	950	450.00	450.00
92-02-002	Ralph Wood (9")	D.Tootle	350	450.00	450.00
92-02-003	Josiah Wedgewood (9")	D.Tootle	350	450.00	450.00
92-02-004	William Moorcroft (9")	D.Tootle	350	450.00	450.00
92-02-005	Sir Henry Doulton (9")	D.Tootle	350	450.00	450.00
92-02-006	Sandra Kuck (9")	D.Tootle	600	450.00	450.00
92-02-007	Bernard Leach (9")	D.Tootle	200	500.00	500.00
92-02-008	George Tinworth (9")	D.Tootle	350	450.00	450.00
Kevin Francis		**Royalty-Toby Jugs**			
92-03-001	Queen Mother (9")	D.Tootle	900	250.00	250.00
92-03-002	Princess Di (9")	D.Tootle	Retrd.	250.00	250.00
92-03-003	Queen Elizabeth II (9")	D.Tootle	400	250.00	250.00
Kevin Francis		**Great Artists-Toby Jugs**			
92-04-001	Picasso (9")	A. Moss	350	450.00	450.00
92-04-002	Salvador Dali (9")	A. Moss	350	450.00	450.00
Kevin Francis		**Military Leaders-Toby Jugs**			
90-05-008	Churchill Standing Toby (9")	D.Tootle	750	220.00	400-450.
91-05-001	Montgomery (9")	D.Tootle	750	250.00	250.00
91-05-002	Rommel (9")	D.Tootle	750	250.00	250.00
91-05-003	General Patton (9")	D.Tootle	750	250.00	250.00
91-05-004	Admiral Churchill (9")	D.Tootle	750	250.00	250.00
92-05-005	General Eisenhower (9")	A. Moss	750	250.00	250.00
92-05-006	Napoleon (9")	A. Moss	750	250.00	250.00
93-05-007	Wellington (9")	R. Noble	750	250.00	250.00
93-05-007	Stonewall Jackson (9")	A. Moss	750	250.00	250.00
Kevin Francis		**USA Series-Toby Jugs**			
92-06-001	Moe Wideman (9")	A. Moss	350	450.00	450.00
92-06-002	Mark Clause (9")	A. Moss	750	300.00	300.00
Kevin Francis		**Historical-Toby Jugs**			
90-07-001	Shakespeare (9")	G. Blower	1,000	250.00	250.00
91-07-002	Henry VIII (9")	G. Blower	750	250.00	250.00
92-07-003	Christopher Columbus (9")	G. Blower	Retrd.	250.00	250.00
Kevin Francis		**Traditional Tobies**			
92-08-001	Toby Fillpot (9")	A. Moss	750	250.00	250.00
Kevin Francis		**Miscellaneous Toby Jugs**			
89-09-001	The Golfer (9")	A. Moss	1,000	250.00	250.00
89-09-002	Santa (9")	A. Moss	1,500	250.00	250.00
90-09-003	Pershore Miller (9")	R. Noble	1,500	300.00	300.00
92-09-004	Sherlock Holmes (9")	G. Blower	750	400.00	400.00
Kevin Francis		**Small Toby Jugs**			
90-10-001	Little Vic (6")	A. Moss	2,500	120.00	120.00
90-10-001	Little Teddy (6")	A. Moss	2,500	120.00	120.00
90-10-001	Little Gorbachev (6")	A. Moss	2,500	120.00	120.00
90-10-001	Little Clarice (6")	A. Moss	2,500	120.00	120.00
90-10-001	Little Winston (6")	A. Moss	2,500	120.00	120.00
90-10-001	Little Golfer (6")	A. Moss	2,500	120.00	120.00
Kevin Francis		**Miniature Toby Jugs**			
92-11-001	Mini Teddy (4")	A. Moss	2,500	50.00	50.00
92-11-002	Mini Cat (4")	A. Moss	1,000	50.00	50.00
92-11-003	Mini Dog (4")	A. Moss	1,000	50.00	50.00
92-11-004	Mini Lion Club (4")	A. Moss	1,000	50.00	50.00
92-11-005	Mini Rabbit (4")	A. Moss	1,000	50.00	50.00
92-11-006	Mini Duck (4")	A. Moss	1,000	50.00	50.00
92-11-007	Mini Chicken (4")	A. Moss	1,000	50.00	50.00
92-11-008	Mini Monkey (4")	A. Moss	1,000	50.00	50.00
92-11-009	Mini Elephant (4")	A. Moss	1,000	50.00	50.00
92-11-010	Mini Alligator (4")	A. Moss	1,000	50.00	50.00
92-11-011	Mini Frog (4")	A. Moss	1,000	50.00	50.00
Kevin Francis		**Kevin Francis Character Jugs**			
89-12-001	Ian Botham	G. Blower	1,000	90.00	90.00
92-12-002	John Major P. M.	R. Noble	500	125.00	125.00
Kevin Francis		**Spitting Image Series-Toby Jugs**			
92-13-001	Margaret Thatcher	R. Law	650	125.00	125.00
92-13-002	John Major	R. Law	650	125.00	125.00
92-13-003	Neil Kinnock	R. Law	650	125.00	125.00
92-13-004	Charles & Di	R. Law	650	175.00	175.00
Kevin Francis		**John Hine Studios Commissions**			
92-14-001	The Toby Inn	H. Macdonald	950	199.00	199.00
93-14-002	The Village Idiots House	H. Macdonald	750	250.00	250.00
Kevin Francis		**Figures**			
92-15-001	Last of the Reindeer	A. Moss	50	950.00	950.00
92-15-002	Lady With Fan	G. Blower	500	300.00	300.00
92-15-003	Dancing Nymph	G. Blower	500	300.00	300.00
93-15-004	Charlotte Rhead	A. Moss	175	450.00	450.00
Franklin Mint		**Joys of Childhood**			
76-01-001	Hopscotch	N. Rockwell	3,700	120.00	175.00
76-01-002	The Fishing Hole	N. Rockwell	3,700	120.00	175.00
76-01-003	Dressing Up	N. Rockwell	3,700	120.00	175.00
76-01-004	The Stilt Walker	N. Rockwell	3,700	120.00	175.00
76-01-005	Trick or Treat	N. Rockwell	3,700	120.00	175.00
76-01-006	Time Out	N. Rockwell	3,700	120.00	175.00
76-01-007	The Marble Champ	N. Rockwell	3,700	120.00	175.00
76-01-008	The Nurse	N. Rockwell	3,700	120.00	175.00
76-01-009	Ride 'Em Cowboy	N. Rockwell	3,700	120.00	175.00
76-01-010	Coasting Along	N. Rockwell	3,700	120.00	175.00
Ganz/Little Cheesers		**Cheeserville Picnic Collection**			
91-01-001	Papa Woodsworth	G.D.A. Group	Open	13.00	13.00
91-01-002	Auntie Marigold Eating Cookie	G.D.A. Group	Open	13.00	13.00
91-01-003	Baby Cicely	G.D.A. Group	Open	8.00	8.00
91-01-004	Medley Meadowmouse With Bouquet	G.D.A. Group	Open	13.00	13.00
91-01-005	Violet With Peaches	G.D.A. Group	Open	13.00	13.00
91-01-006	Baby Truffle	G.D.A. Group	Open	8.00	8.00
91-01-007	Harriet Harvestmouse	G.D.A. Group	Open	13.00	13.00
91-01-008	Grandpapa Thistledown Carrying Basket	G.D.A. Group	Open	13.00	13.00
91-01-009	Jenny Butterfield Kneeling	G.D.A. Group	Open	13.00	13.00
91-01-010	Mama With Rolling Pin	G.D.A. Group	Open	13.00	13.00
91-01-011	Grandmama Thistledown Holding Bread	G.D.A. Group	Open	13.00	13.00
91-01-012	Harley Harvestmouse Waving	G.D.A. Group	Open	13.00	13.00
91-01-013	Cousin Woody With Bread and Fruit	G.D.A. Group	Open	14.00	14.00
91-01-014	Marigold Thistledown Picking Up Jar	G.D.A. Group	Open	14.00	14.00
91-01-015	Little Truffle Eating Grapes	G.D.A. Group	Open	8.00	8.00
91-01-016	Jeremy Butterfield	G.D.A. Group	Open	13.00	13.00
91-01-017	Mama Fixing Sweet Cicely's Hair	G.D.A. Group	Open	16.50	16.50
91-01-018	Picnic Buddies	G.D.A. Group	Open	19.00	19.00
91-01-019	Blossom & Hickory In Love	G.D.A. Group	Open	19.00	19.00
91-01-020	Little Truffle Smelling Flowers	G.D.A. Group	Open	16.50	16.50
91-01-021	Fellow With Picnic Hamper	G.D.A. Group	Retrd.	13.00	13.00
91-01-022	Fellow With Plate Of Cookies	G.D.A. Group	Retrd.	13.00	13.00
91-01-023	Lady With Grapes	G.D.A. Group	Retrd.	14.00	14.00
91-01-024	Mama Woodsworth With Crate	G.D.A. Group	Retrd.	14.00	14.00
93-01-025	Sunday Drive	C.Thammavongsa	Open	40.00	40.00
93-01-026	Sweet Dreams	C.Thammavongsa	Open	27.50	27.50
93-01-027	Willy's Toe-Tappin' Tunes	C.Thammavongsa	Open	15.00	15.00
93-01-028	The Storyteller	C.Thammavongsa	10,000	25.00	25.00
93-01-029	For Someone Special	C.Thammavongsa	Open	13.50	13.50
93-01-030	Words Of Wisdom	C.Thammavongsa	Open	14.00	14.00
93-01-031	Clownin' Around	C.Thammavongsa	Open	10.50	10.50
93-01-032	Chuckles The Clown	C.Thammavongsa	Open	16.00	16.00
93-01-033	Little Cheesers Display Plaque	C.Thammavongsa	Open	24.00	24.00
Ganz/Little Cheesers		**Cheeserville Picnic Collection Mini-Food Accessories**			
91-02-001	Food Trolley	G.D.A. Group	Retrd.	12.00	12.00
91-02-002	Set Of Four Bottles	G.D.A. Group	Retrd.	10.00	10.00
91-02-003	Napkin In Can	G.D.A. Group	Retrd.	2.00	2.00
91-02-004	Honey Jar	G.D.A. Group	Retrd.	2.00	2.00
91-02-005	Wine Glass	G.D.A. Group	Open	1.25	1.25
91-02-006	Ice Cream	G.D.A. Group	Open	2.00	2.00
91-02-007	Candy	G.D.A. Group	Open	2.00	2.00
91-02-008	Sundae	G.D.A. Group	Open	2.00	2.00
91-02-009	Egg Tart	G.D.A. Group	Open	1.00	1.00
91-02-010	Hot Dog	G.D.A. Group	Open	2.00	2.00
91-02-011	Basket Of Peaches	G.D.A. Group	Open	2.00	2.00
91-02-012	Cherry Mousse	G.D.A. Group	Open	2.00	2.00
91-02-013	Blueberry Cake	G.D.A. Group	Open	2.50	2.50
91-02-014	Chocolate Topped Cake	G.D.A. Group	Open	2.50	2.50
91-02-015	Chocolate Cheesecake	G.D.A. Group	Open	2.00	2.00
91-02-016	Strawberry Cake	G.D.A. Group	Open	2.00	2.00
91-02-017	Doughnut Basket	G.D.A. Group	Open	2.50	2.50
91-02-018	Bread Basket	G.D.A. Group	Open	2.50	2.50
91-02-019	Basket Of Apples	G.D.A. Group	Open	2.25	2.25
91-02-020	Hazelnut Roll	G.D.A. Group	Retrd.	2.00	2.00
91-02-021	Lemon Cake	G.D.A. Group	Retrd.	2.00	2.00
91-02-022	Cherry Pie	G.D.A. Group	Retrd.	2.00	2.00
91-02-023	Food Basket With Blue Cloth	G.D.A. Group	Open	6.50	6.50
91-02-024	Food Basket With Pink Cloth	G.D.A. Group	Open	6.00	6.00
91-02-025	Food Basket With Green Cloth	G.D.A. Group	Open	7.50	7.50
91-02-026	Food Basket With Purple Cloth	G.D.A. Group	Open	5.00	5.00
Ganz/Little Cheesers		**Cheeserville Picnic Collection Musicals**			
91-03-001	Musical Sunflower Base	G.D.A. Group	Open	65.00	65.00
91-03-002	Musical Picnic Base	G.D.A. Group	Open	60.00	60.00
91-03-003	Musical Violet Woodsworth Cookie Jar	G.D.A. Group	Retrd.	75.00	75.00
91-03-004	Musical Medley Meadowmouse Cookie Jar	G.D.A. Group	Retrd.	75.00	75.00
91-03-005	Mama & Sweet Cicely Waterglobe	G.D.A. Group	Retrd.	55.00	55.00
91-03-006	Medley Meadowmouse Waterglobe	G.D.A. Group	Open	45.00	45.00
92-03-007	Sweet Cicely Musical Doll Basket	G.D.A. Group	Open	85.00	85.00
91-03-008	Blossom & Hickory Musical Jewelry Box	G.D.A. Group	Retrd.	65.00	65.00
91-03-009	Musical Basket Trinket Box	G.D.A. Group	Open	30.00	30.00
91-03-010	Musical Floral Trinket Box	G.D.A. Group	Open	32.00	32.00
93-03-011	Musical "Secret Treasures" Trinket Box	C.Thammavongsa	Open	36.00	36.00
93-03-012	Wishing Well Musical	C.Thammavongsa	Open	50.00	50.00
Ganz/Little Cheesers		**The Wedding Collection**			
92-04-001	Harley & Harriet Harvestmouse	GDA/Thammavongsa	Open	20.00	20.00
92-04-002	Jenny Butterfield/Sweet Cicely (bridesmaids)	GDA/Thammavongsa	Open	20.00	20.00
92-04-003	Blossom Thistledown (bride)	GDA/Thammavongsa	Open	16.00	16.00
92-04-004	Hickory Harvestmouse (groom)	GDA/Thammavongsa	Open	16.00	16.00
92-04-005	Cousin Woody & Little Truffle	GDA/Thammavongsa	Open	20.00	20.00
92-04-006	Grandmama & Grandpapa Thistledown	GDA/Thammavongsa	Open	20.00	20.00
92-04-007	Pastor Smallwood	GDA/Thammavongsa	Open	16.00	16.00
92-04-008	Little Truffle (ringbearer)	GDA/Thammavongsa	Open	10.00	10.00
92-04-009	Myrtle Meadowmouse With Medley	GDA/Thammavongsa	Retrd.	20.00	20.00
92-04-010	Frowzy Roquefort III With Gramophone	GDA/Thammavongsa	Open	20.00	20.00
92-04-011	Marigold Thistledown & Oscar Bobbins	GDA/Thammavongsa	Open	20.00	20.00
92-04-012	Great Aunt Rose Beside Table	GDA/Thammavongsa	Open	20.00	20.00
92-04-013	Mama & Papa Woodsworth Dancing	GDA/Thammavongsa	Open	20.00	20.00
92-04-014	Wedding Procession	GDA/Thammavongsa	Open	40.00	40.00
Ganz/Little Cheesers		**The Wedding Collection Mini-Food Accessories**			
92-05-001	Flour Bag	G.D.A. Group	Retrd.	2.00	2.00
92-05-002	Salt Can	G.D.A. Group	Retrd.	2.00	2.00
92-05-003	Chocolate Pastry	G.D.A. Group	Retrd.	2.00	2.00
92-05-004	Souffle	G.D.A. Group	Retrd.	2.50	2.50
92-05-005	Teddy Mouse	G.D.A. Group	Open	2.00	2.00
92-05-006	Chocolate Pudding	G.D.A. Group	Open	2.50	2.50
92-05-007	Tea Pot Set	G.D.A. Group	Open	3.00	3.00
92-05-008	Honey Pot	G.D.A. Group	Open	2.00	2.00
92-05-009	Candles	G.D.A. Group	Open	3.00	3.00
92-05-010	Big Chocolate Cake	G.D.A. Group	Open	4.50	4.50
92-05-011	Fruit Salad	G.D.A. Group	Open	3.00	300
92-05-012	Cherry Jello	G.D.A. Group	Open	3.00	3.00
92-05-013	Ring Cake	G.D.A. Group	Open	3.00	3.00
92-05-014	Soup Pot	G.D.A. Group	Open	3.00	3.00
92-05-015	Flower Vase	G.D.A. Group	Open	3.00	3.00

Number	Name	Artist	Edition Limit	Issue Price	Quote
92-05-016	Groom Candleholder	GDA/Thammavongsa	Open	20.00	20.00
92-05-017	Bride Candleholder	GDA/Thammavongsa	Open	20.00	20.00
92-05-018	Cake Trinket Box	GDA/Thammavongsa	Open	14.00	14.00
92-05-019	Bible Trinket Box	GDA/Thammavongsa	Open	16.50	16.50
92-05-020	Grass Base	GDA/Thammavongsa	Open	3.50	3.50
Ganz/Little Cheesers	**The Wedding Collection Musicals**				
92-06-001	Musical Wooden Base For Wedding Processional	G.D.A. Group	Open	25.00	25.00
92-06-002	Musical Wedding Base	GDA/Thammavongsa	Open	32.00	32.00
92-06-003	Musical Blossom & Hickory Wedding Waterglobe	GDA/Thammavongsa	Open	55.00	55.00
Ganz/Little Cheesers	**The Christmas Collection**				
91-07-001	Cheeser Snowman	G.D.A. Group	Open	7.50	7.50
91-07-002	Violet With Snowball	G.D.A. Group	Open	8.00	8.00
91-07-003	Medley Playing Drum	G.D.A. Group	Open	8.00	8.00
91-07-004	Little Truffle With Stocking	G.D.A. Group	Open	8.00	8.00
91-07-005	Jeremy With Teddy Bear	G.D.A. Group	Open	12.00	12.00
91-07-006	Santa Cheeser	G.D.A. Group	Open	13.00	13.00
91-07-007	Frowzy Roquefort III Skating	G.D.A. Group	Open	14.00	14.00
91-07-008	Jenny On Sleigh	G.D.A. Group	Open	16.00	16.00
91-07-009	Auntie Blossom With Ornaments	G.D.A. Group	Open	14.00	14.00
91-07-010	Mama Pouring Tea	G.D.A. Group	Open	14.00	14.00
91-07-011	Great Aunt Rose With Tray	G.D.A. Group	Open	14.00	14.00
91-07-012	Abner Appleton Ringing Bell	G.D.A. Group	Open	14.00	14.00
91-07-013	Grandpapa Blowing Horn	G.D.A. Group	Open	14.00	14.00
91-07-014	Hickory Playing Cello	G.D.A. Group	Open	14.00	14.00
91-07-015	Myrtle Meadowmouse With Book	G.D.A. Group	Open	14.00	14.00
91-07-016	Cousin Woody Playing Flute	G.D.A. Group	Open	14.00	14.00
91-07-017	Harley & Harriet Dancing	G.D.A. Group	Open	19.00	19.00
91-07-018	Grandpapa & Sweet Cicely	G.D.A. Group	Open	19.00	19.00
91-07-019	Grandmama & Little Truffle	G.D.A.Group	Open	19.00	19.00
91-07-020	Marigold & Oscar Stealing A Christmas Kiss	G.D.A. Group	Open	19.00	19.00
Ganz/Little Cheesers	**The Christmas Collection Accessories**				
91-08-001	Christmas Tree	G.D.A. Group	Open	9.00	9.00
91-08-002	Lamp Post	G.D.A. Group	Open	8.50	8.50
91-08-003	Parlor Scene Base	G.D.A. Group	Open	37.50	37.50
91-08-004	Outdoor Scene Base	G.D.A. Group	Open	35.00	35.00
Ganz/Little Cheesers	**The Christmas Collection Musicals**				
92-09-001	Musical Santa Cheeser Roly-Poly	G.D.A. Group	Open	55.00	55.00
92-09-002	Little Truffle Christmas Waterglobe	G.D.A. Group	Open	40.00	40.00
92-09-003	Jenny Butterfield Christmas Waterglobe	GDA/Thammavongsa	Retrd.	55.00	55.00
Ganz/Little Cheesers	**Springtime In Cheeserville Collection**				
92-10-001	Hippity-Hop. It's Eastertime!	C.Thammavongsa	Open	16.00	16.00
92-10-002	A Wheelbarrow Of Sunshine	C.Thammavongsa	Open	17.00	17.00
92-10-003	Springtime Delights	C.Thammavongsa	Open	12.00	12.00
92-10-004	A Basket Full Of Joy	C.Thammavongsa	Open	16.00	16.00
Ganz/Little Cheesers	**Springtime In Cheeserville Collection Accessories**				
92-11-001	Decorated With Love	C.Thammavongsa	Open	7.50	7.50
92-11-002	April Showers Bring May Flowers	C.Thammavongsa	Open	7.50	7.50
92-11-003	For Somebunny Special	C.Thammavongsa	Open	7.50	7.50
Ganz/Little Cheesers	**Springtime In Cheeserville Collection Musicals**				
92-12-001	Tulips & Ribbons Musical Trinket Box	GDA/Thammavongsa	Open	28.00	28.00
Gartlan USA, Inc.	**Plaques**				
85-01-001	Pete Rose-"Desire to Win", signed	T. Sizemore	4,192	75.00	75.00
86-01-002	George Brett-"Royalty in Motion", signed	J. Martin	2,000	85.00	250-275.
86-01-003	Reggie Jackson-"The Roundtripper", signed	J. Martin	500	150.00	200-375.
86-01-004	Reggie Jackson Artist Proof-"The Roundtripper", signed	J. Martin	44	175.00	250-475.
87-01-005	Roger Staubach, signed	C. Soileau	1,979	85.00	150-250.
Gartlan USA, Inc.	**Baseball/Football/Hockey Card Series**				
85-02-001	Pete Rose Ceramic Baseball Card	T. Sizemore	Open	9.95	18.00
85-02-002	Pete Rose Ceramic Baseball Card, signed	T. Sizemore	4,192	39.00	50-100.00
86-02-003	George Brett Baseball Rounder	J. Martin	Open	9.95	14.00
86-02-004	George Brett Baseball Rounder, signed	J. Martin	2,000	30.00	50-60.00
86-02-005	George Brett Ceramic Baseball	J. Martin	Open	20.00	20.00
86-02-006	Geroge Brett Ceramic Baseball, signed	J. Martin	2,000	39.75	95-125.00
87-02-007	Roger Staubach Ceramic Football Card	C. Soileau	Open	9.95	18.00
87-02-008	Roger Staubach Ceramic Football Card, signed	C. Soileau	1,979	39.00	39.00
90-02-009	Wayne Gretzky Ceramic Hockey Card	M. Taylor	Open	16.00	18.00
91-02-010	Joe Montana CeramicFootball Card	M. Taylor	Open	18.00	18.00
92-02-011	Carlton Fisk Ceramic Baseball Card	M. Taylor	Open	18.00	18.00
92-02-012	Tom Seaver	M. Taylor	Open	18.00	18.00
92-02-013	Gordon Howe	M. Taylor	Open	18.00	18.00
92-02-014	Phil Esposito	M. Taylor	Open	18.00	18.00
Gartlan USA, Inc.	**Magic Johnson Gold Rim Collection**				
88-03-001	Magic Johnson Artist Proof-"Magic in Motion", signed	Roger	250	175.00	2900-3900.
88-03-002	Magic Johnson-"Magic in Motion"	Roger	1,737	125.00	325-700.
88-03-003	Magic Johnson Commemorative	Roger	32	275.00	4000-6500.
Gartlan USA, Inc.	**Mike Schmidt "500th" Home Run Edition**				
87-04-001	Figurine-signed	Roger	1,987	150.00	725-950.
87-04-002	Figurine-signed, Artist Proof	Roger	20	275.00	1200-1700.
87-04-003	Plaque-"Only Perfect"-signed	Paluso	500	150.00	350-450.
87-04-004	Plaque-"Only Perfect", Artist Proof	Paluso	20	200.00	550.00
Gartlan USA, Inc.	**Pete Rose Diamond Collection**				
88-05-001	Farewell Ceramic Baseball Card-signed	Forbes	4,256	39.00	50-100.00
88-05-002	Farewell Ceramic Baseball Card	Forbes	Open	9.95	18.00
Gartlan USA, Inc.	**Reggie Jackson "500th" Home Run Edition**				
86-06-001	Ceramic Baseball Card, signed	J. Martin	1,986	39.00	60-75.00
86-06-002	Ceramic Baseball Card	J. Martin	Open	9.95	18.00
Gartlan USA, Inc.	**Kareem Abdul-Jabbar Sky-Hook Collection**				
89-07-001	Kareem Abdul-Jabbar "The Captain"-signed	L. Heyda	1,989	175.00	300-400.
89-07-002	Kareem Abdul-Jabbar, Artist Proof	L. Heyda	100	200.00	650-1750.
89-07-003	Kareem Abdul-Jabbar, Commemorative	L. Heyda	33	275.00	1000-6000.
Gartlan USA, Inc.	**Signed Figurines**				
85-08-001	Pete Rose-"For the Record", signed	H. Reed	4,192	125.00	850-1200.
89-08-002	Carl Yastrzemski-"Yaz"	L. Heyda	1,989	150.00	300-375.
89-08-003	Carl Yastrzemski-"Yaz" , Artist Proof	L. Heyda	250	150.00	400-450.
89-08-004	Johnny Bench	L. Heyda	1,989	150.00	325-375.
89-08-005	Johnny Bench, Artist Proof	L. Heyda	250	150.00	425-450.
89-08-006	Joe DiMaggio	L. Heyda	2,214	275.00	750-1150.
90-08-007	Joe DiMaggio- Pinstripe Yankee Clipper	L. Heyda	325	695.00	1200-2500.
89-08-008	John Wooden-Coaching Classics	L. Heyda	1,975	175.00	175.00
89-08-009	John Wooden-Coaching Classics, Artist Pr.	L. Heyda	250	350.00	350.00
89-08-010	Ted Williams	L. Heyda	2,654	295.00	400-650.
89-08-011	Ted Williams, Artist Proof	L. Heyda	250	650.00	800.00
89-08-012	Wayne Gretzky	L. Heyda	1,851	225.00	500-950.
89-08-013	Wayne Gretzky, Artist Proof	L. Heyda	300	695.00	1000-1850.
89-08-014	Yogi Berra	F. Barnum	2,150	225.00	225-250.
89-08-015	Yogi Berra, Artist Proof	F. Barnum	250	350.00	350.00
89-08-016	Steve Carlton	L. Heyda	3,290	175.00	175-350.
89-08-017	Steve Carlton, Artist Proof	L. Heyda	300	350.00	350.00
90-08-018	Whitey Ford	S. Barnum	2,360	225.00	225.00
90-08-019	Whitey Ford, Artist Proof	S. Barnum	250	350.00	350.00
90-08-020	Luis Aparicio	J. Slockbower	1,984	225.00	225.00
90-08-021	Darryl Strawberry	L. Heyda	2,500	225.00	225.00
90-08-022	George Brett	F. Barnum	2,250	225.00	225.00
91-08-023	Ken Griffey, Jr	J. Slockbower	1,989	225.00	225.00
91-08-024	Warren Spahn	J. Slockbower	1,973	225.00	225.00
91-08-025	Rod Carew - Hitting Splendor	J. Slockbower	1,991	225.00	225.00
91-08-026	Brett Hull - The Golden Brett	L. Heyda	1,986	250.00	250.00
92-08-027	Brett Hull, Artist Proof	L. Heyda	300	350.00	350.00
91-08-028	Bobby Hull - The Golden Jet	L. Heyda	1,983	250.00	250.00
92-08-029	Bobby Hull, Artist Proof	L. Heyda	300	350.00	350.00
91-08-030	Hull Matched Figurines	L. Heyda	950	500.00	500.00
91-08-031	Al Barlick	V. Bova	1,989	175.00	175.00
91-08-032	Monte Irvin	V. Bova	1,973	225.00	225.00
91-08-033	Joe Montana	F. Barnum	2,250	325.00	325-425.
91-08-034	Joe Montana, Artist Proof	F. Barnum	250	500.00	650-700.
92-08-035	Isiah Thomas	J. Slockbower	1,990	225.00	225.00
92-08-036	Hank Aaron	F. Barnum	1,982	225.00	225.00
92-08-037	Carlton Fisk	J. Slockbower	1,972	225.00	225.00
92-08-038	Carlton Fisk, Artist Proof	J. Slockbower	300	350.00	350.00
92-08-039	Gordie Howe	L. Heyda	2,358	225.00	225.00
92-08-040	Gordie Howe, Artist Proof	L. Heyda	250	500.00	500.00
92-08-041	Phil Esposito	L. Heyda	1, 984	225.00	225.00
92-08-042	Phil Esposito, Artist Proof	L. Heyda	250	500.00	500.00
92-08-043	Hank Aaron Commemorative w/display case	F. Barnum	755	275.00	275.00
92-08-044	Hank Aaron, Artist Proof	F. Barnum	300	325.00	325.00
92-08-045	Stan Musial	J. Slockbower	1,969	325.00	325.00
92-08-046	Stan Musial, Artist Proof	J. Slockbower	300	500.00	500.00
92-08-047	Ralph Kiner	J. Slockbower	1,975	225.00	225.00
92-08-048	Tom Seaver	J. Slockbower	1,992	225.00	225.00
Gartlan USA, Inc.	**All-Star Gems Miniature Figurines**				
89-09-001	Carl Yastrzemski	L. Heyda	10,000	75.00	79.00
89-09-002	Johnny Bench	L. Heyda	10,000	75.00	75.00
89-09-003	Ted Williams	L. Heyda	10,000	75.00	79.00
89-09-004	Steve Carlton	L. Heyda	10,000	75.00	79.00
90-09-005	John Wooden	L. Heyda	10,000	75.00	79.00
90-09-006	Wayne Gretzky	L. Heyda	10,000	75.00	79.00
90-09-007	Pete Rose	F. Barnum	10,000	75.00	79.00
90-09-008	Mike Schmidt	Roger	10,000	75.00	79.00
90-09-009	Yogi Berra	F. Barnum	10,000	75.00	79.00
90-09-010	George Brett	F. Barnum	10,000	75.00	79.00
90-09-011	Whitey Ford	F. Barnum	10,000	75.00	79.00
90-09-012	Luis Aparicio	J. Slockbower	10,000	75.00	79.00
90-09-013	Darryl Strawberry	L. Heyda	10,000	75.00	79.00
90-09-014	Kareem Abdul-Jabbar	L. Heyda	10,000	75.00	75.00
91-09-015	Ken Griffey, Jr.	J. Slockbower	10,000	75.00	79.00
91-09-016	Warren Spahn	J. Slockbower	10,000	75.00	79.00
91-09-017	Rod Carew	J. Slockbower	10,000	75.00	79.00
91-09-018	Brett Hull	L. Heyda	10,000	75.00	79.00
91-09-019	Bobby Hull	L. Heyda	10,000	75.00	79.00
91-09-020	Monte Irvin	V. Bova	10,000	75.00	79.00
91-09-021	Joe Montana	F. Barnum	10,000	79.00	95.00
92-09-022	Isiah Thomas	J. Slockbower	10,000	79.00	79.00
92-09-023	Hank Aaron	F. Barnum	10,000	79.00	79.00
92-09-024	Carlton Fisk	J. Slockbower	10,000	79.00	79.00
92-09-025	Phil Esposito	L. Heyda	10,000	79.00	79.00
92-09-026	Stan Musial	J. Slockbower	2, 269	99.00	99.00
92-09-027	Tom Seaver	J. Slockbower	10,000	79.00	79.00
92-09-028	Ralph Kiner	J. Slockbower	10,000	79.00	79.00
92-09-029	Gordie Howe	L. Heyda	10,000	79.00	79.00
Gartlan USA, Inc.	**Members Only Figurine**				
90-10-001	Wayne Gretzky-Home Uniform	L. Heyda	N/A	75.00	250.00
91-10-002	Joe Montana-Road Uniform	F. Barnum	N/A	75.00	125-150.
91-10-003	Kareem Abdul-Jabbar	L. Heyda	N/A	75.00	100-200.
92-10-004	Mike Schmidt	J. Slockbower	N/A	79.00	100-200.
93-10-005	Hank Aaron	J. Slockbower	N/A	79.00	79.00
Gartlan USA, Inc.	**Club Gift**				
89-11-001	Pete Rose, Plate (8 1/2")	B. Forbes	Closed	Gift	100-295.
90-11-002	Al Barlick, Plate (8 1/2")	M. Taylor	Closed	Gift	30-75.00
91-11-003	Joe Montana (8 1/2")	M. Taylor	Closed	Gift	50-95.00
92-11-004	Ken Griffey Jr., Plate (8 1/2")	M. Taylor	Closed	30.00	30.00
93-11-005	Gordie Howe, Plate (8 1/2")	M. Taylor	Yr.Iss.	30.00	30.00
Gartlan USA, Inc.	**Master's Museum Collection**				
91-12-001	Kareem Abdul-Jabbar	L. Heyda	500	3000.00	3000-3200.
91-12-002	Wayne Gretzky	L. Heyda	500	set	set
91-12-003	Joe Montana	F. Barnum	500	set	set
91-12-004	Ted Williams	L. Heyda	500	set	set
93-12-005	Stan Muscial	J. Slockbower	500	850	850
Gartlan USA, Inc.	**Negro League Series**				
91-13-001	James "Cool Papa" Bell	V. Bova	1,499	195.00	195.00
91-13-002	Ray Dandridge	V. Bova	1,987	195.00	195.00
91-13-003	Buck Leonard	V. Bova	1,972	195.00	195.00
91-13-004	Matched-Number set #1-950	V. Bova	950	500.00	500.00
Goebel Inc.	**Goebel Figurines**				
63-01-001	Little Veterinarian (Mysterious Malady)	N. Rockwell	Closed	15.00	400.00
63-01-002	Boyhood Dreams (Adventurers between Adventures)	N. Rockwell	Closed	12.00	400.00
63-01-003	Mother's Helper (Pride of Parenthood)	N. Rockwell	Closed	15.00	400.00
63-01-004	His First Smoke	N. Rockwell	Closed	9.00	400.00

Number	Name	Artist	Edition Limit	Issue Price	Quote
63-01-005	My New Pal (A Boy Meets His Dog)	N. Rockwell	Closed	12.00	400.00
63-01-006	Home Cure	N. Rockwell	Closed	16.00	400.00
63-01-007	Timely Assistance (Love Aid)	N. Rockwell	Closed	16.00	400.00
63-01-008	She Loves Me (Day Dreamer)	N. Rockwell	Closed	8.00	400.00
63-01-009	Buttercup Test (Beguiling Buttercup)	N. Rockwell	Closed	10.00	400.00
63-01-010	First Love (A Scholarly Pace)	N. Rockwell	Closed	30.00	400.00
63-01-012	Patient Anglers (Fisherman's Paradise)	N. Rockwell	Closed	18.00	400.00
63-01-013	Advertising Plaque	N. Rockwell	Closed	Unkn.	600.00
Goebel Inc.		**Betsey Clark Figurines**			
72-02-001	Bless You	G. Bochmann	Closed	18.00	275.00
72-02-002	Friends	G. Bochmann	Closed	21.00	400.00
72-02-003	So Much Beauty	G. Bochmann	Closed	24.50	350.00
72-02-004	Little Miracle	G. Bochmann	Closed	24.50	350.00
Goebel Miniatures		**Goebel Miniatures: Children's Series**			
80-01-001	Blumenkinder-Courting 630-P	R. Olszewski	Closed	55.00	265-400.
81-01-002	Summer Days 631-P	R. Olszewski	Closed	65.00	265.00
82-01-003	Out and About 632-P	R. Olszewski	Closed	85.00	385.00
83-01-004	Backyard Frolic 633-P	R. Olszewski	Closed	65.00	125-250.
85-01-005	Snow Holiday 635-P	R. Olszewski	Closed	75.00	100-125.
86-01-006	Clowning Around 636-P	R. Olszewski	Closed	85.00	175.00
87-01-007	Carrousel Days 637-P	R. Olszewski	Closed	85.00	150-165.
88-01-008	Little Ballerina 638-P	R. Olszewski	Closed	85.00	110-150.
88-01-009	Children's Display (small)	R. Olszewski	Closed	45.00	50.00
84-01-010	Grandpa 634-P	R. Olszewski	Closed	75.00	125-165.
90-01-011	Building Blocks Castle (large) 968-D	R. Olszewski	Closed	75.00	90.00
Goebel Miniatures		**Goebel Miniatures: Wildlife Series**			
80-02-001	Chipping Sparrow 620-P	R. Olszewski	Open	55.00	270-525.
81-02-002	Owl-Daylight Encounter 621-P	R. Olszewski	Closed	65.00	250-365.
82-02-003	Western Bluebird 622-P	R. Olszewski	Closed	65.00	195.00
83-02-004	Red-Winged Blackbird 623-P	R. Olszewski	Closed	65.00	150-225.
84-02-005	Winter Cardinal 624-P	R. Olszewski	Closed	65.00	150-225.
85-02-006	American Goldfinch 625-P	R. Olszewski	Open	65.00	120.00
86-02-007	Autumn Blue Jay 626-P	R. Olszewski	Open	65.00	150-205.
87-02-008	Mallard Duck 627-P	R. Olszewski	Open	75.00	195.00
88-02-009	Spring Robin 628-P	R. Olszewski	Closed	75.00	165-195.
87-02-010	Country Display (small) 940-D	R. Olszewski	Open	45.00	55.00
90-02-011	Wildlife Display (large) 957-D	R. Olszewski	Open	85.00	95.00
89-02-012	Hooded Oriole 629-P	R. Olszewski	Open	80.00	115-175.
90-02-013	Hummingbird 696-P	R. Olszewski	Closed	85.00	125-150.
Goebel Miniatures		**Goebel Miniatures: Women's Series**			
80-03-001	Dresden Dancer 610-P	R. Olszewski	Closed	55.00	400-550.
81-03-002	The Hunt With Hounds 611-P	R. Olszewski	Closed	75.00	200-445.
82-03-003	Precious Years 612-P	R. Olszewski	Closed	65.00	315.00
83-03-004	On The Avenue 613-P	R. Olszewski	Closed	65.00	100-150.
84-03-005	Roses 614-P	R. Olszewski	Closed	65.00	105-150.
86-03-006	I Do 615-P	R. Olszewski	Closed	85.00	195.00
89-03-007	Women's Display (small) 950-D	R. Olszewski	Closed	40.00	59.00
Goebel Miniatures		**Goebel Miniatures: Historical Series**			
80-04-001	Capodimonte 600-P	R. Olszewski	Closed	90.00	565.00
81-04-002	Masquerade-St. Petersburg 601-P	R. Olszewski	Closed	65.00	150-325.
83-04-003	The Cherry Pickers 602-P	R. Olszewski	Closed	85.00	285.00
84-04-004	Moor With Spanish Horse 603-P	R. Olszewski	Open	85.00	100-200.
85-04-005	Floral Bouquet Pompadour 604-P	R. Olszewski	Open	85.00	130.00
87-04-006	Meissen Parrot 605-P	R. Olszewski	Open	85.00	100-150.
88-04-007	Minton Rooster 606-P	R. Olszewski	7,500	85.00	95-195.00
89-04-008	Farmer w/Doves 607-P	R. Olszewski	Open	85.00	95-150.00
90-04-009	Gentleman Fox Hunt 616-P	R. Olszewski	Open	145.00	145.00
88-04-010	Historical Display 943-D	R. Olszewski	Suspd.	45.00	50.00
90-04-011	English Country Garden 970-D	R. Olszewski	Open	85.00	110.00
92-04-012	Poultry Seller 608-G	R. Olszewski	Open	200.00	200.00
Goebel Miniatures		**Goebel Miniatures: Oriental Series**			
80-05-001	Kuan Yin 640-W	R. Olszewski	Closed	40.00	150-225.
82-05-002	The Geisha 641-P	R. Olszewski	Closed	65.00	150-195.
85-05-003	Tang Horse 642-P	R. Olszewski	Open	65.00	100-175.
86-05-004	The Blind Men and the Elephant 643-P	R. Olszewski	Open	70.00	100-175.
87-05-005	Chinese Water Dragon 644-P	R. Olszewski	Closed	70.00	175.00
87-05-006	Oriental Display (small) 945-D	R. Olszewski	Suspd.	45.00	59.00
89-05-007	Tiger Hunt 645-P	R. Olszewski	Open	85.00	105.00
90-05-008	Chinese Temple Lion 646-P	R. Olszewski	Open	90.00	90.00
90-05-009	Empress' Garden 967-D	R. Olszewski	Open	95.00	110.00
Goebel Miniatures		**Goebel Miniatures: Americana Series**			
81-06-001	The Plainsman 660-B	R. Olszewski	Closed	45.00	265.00
82-06-002	American Bald Eagle 661-B	R. Olszewski	Closed	45.00	345.00
83-06-003	She Sounds the Deep 662-B	R. Olszewski	Closed	45.00	145.00
84-06-004	Eyes on the Horizon 663-B	R. Olszewski	Closed	45.00	125.00
85-06-005	Central Park Sunday 664-B	R. Olszewski	Closed	45.00	115.00
86-06-006	Carrousel Ride 665-B	R. Olszewski	Closed	45.00	115.00
87-06-007	To The Bandstand 666-B	R. Olszewski	Closed	45.00	110.00
89-06-008	Blacksmith 676-B	R. Olszewski	Closed	55.00	145.00
86-06-009	Americana Display 951-D	R. Olszewski	Suspd.	80.00	95.00
Goebel Miniatures		**Goebel Miniatures: The American Frontier Collection**			
87-07-001	The End of the Trail 340-B	Frazier	Open	80.00	80-90.00
87-07-002	The First Ride 330-B	Rogers	Open	85.00	85.00
87-07-003	Eight Count 310-B	Pounder	Open	75.00	75.00
87-07-004	Grizzly's Last Stand 320-B	Jonas	Open	65.00	65.00
87-07-005	Indian Scout and Buffalo 300-B	Bonheur	Open	95.00	95.00
87-07-006	The Bronco Buster 350-B	Remington	Open	80.00	80.00
87-07-006	American Frontier-947-D Display	R. Olszewski	Open	80.00	95.00
Goebel Miniatures		**Goebel Miniatures: Portrait of America**			
88-08-001	The Doctor and the Doll 361-P	N. Rockwell	Open	85.00	95.00
88-08-002	No Swimming 360-P	N. Rockwell	Open	85.00	95.00
88-08-003	Marbles Champion 362-P	N. Rockwell	Open	85.00	95.00
88-08-004	Check-Up 363-P	N. Rockwell	Open	85.00	105.00
88-08-005	Triple Self-Portrait 364-P	N. Rockwell	Open	85.00	175.00
88-08-006	Bottom of the Sixth 365-P	N. Rockwell	Open	85.00	95.00
89-08-007	Bottom Drawer 366-P	N. Rockwell	7,500	85.00	95.00
88-08-008	Rockwell Display-952-D	N. Rockwell	Open	80.00	93.00
Goebel Miniatures		**Disney-Snow White**			
87-09-001	Sneezy 161-P	R. Olszewski	19,500	60.00	85.00
87-09-002	Doc 162-P	R. Olszewski	19,500	60.00	85.00
87-09-003	Sleepy 163-P	R. Olszewski	19,500	60.00	85.00
87-09-004	Happy 164-P	R. Olszewski	19,500	60.00	85.00
87-09-005	Bashful 165-P	R. Olszewski	19,500	60.00	85.00
87-09-006	Grumpy 166-P	R. Olszewski	19,500	60.00	85.00
87-09-007	Dopey 167-P	R. Olszewski	19,500	60.00	85.00
87-09-008	Snow White 168-P	R. Olszewski	19,500	60.00	90.00
90-09-009	Snow White's Prince 170-P	R. Olszewski	19,500	80.00	85.00
87-09-010	Cozy Cottage Display 941-D	R. Olszewski	Closed	35.00	185.00
88-09-011	House In The Woods Display 944-D	R. Olszewski	Open	60.00	105.00
90-09-012	The Wishing Well Display 969-D	R. Olszewski	Open	65.00	70.00
91-09-013	Castle Courtyard Display 981-D	R. Olszewski	Open	105.00	105.00
92-09-014	Snow White's Witch 183-P	R. Olszewski	Open	100.00	100.00
92-09-015	Snow White's Queen 182-P	R. Olszewski	Open	100.00	100.00
92-09-016	Path In The Woods 996-D	R. Olszewski	Open	140.00	140.00
Goebel Miniatures		**Disney-Pinocchio**			
90-10-001	Geppetto/Figaro 682-P	R. Olszewski	Open	90.00	95.00
90-10-002	Gideon 683-P	R. Olszewski	Open	75.00	85.00
90-10-003	J. Worthington Foulfellow 684-P	R. Olszewski	Open	95.00	95.00
90-10-004	Jiminy Cricket 685-P	R. Olszewski	Open	75.00	85.00
90-10-005	Pinocchio 686-P	R. Olszewski	Open	75.00	85.00
91-10-006	Little Street Lamp Display 964-D	R. Olszewski	Open	65.00	65.00
90-10-007	Geppetto's Toy Shop Display 965-D	R. Olszewski	Open	95.00	105.00
91-10-008	Stromboli 694-P	R. Olszewski	Open	95.00	95.00
91-10-009	Blue Fairy 693-P	R. Olszewski	Open	95.00	95.00
91-10-010	Stromboli's Street Wagon 979-D	R. Olszewski	Open	105.00	105.00
92-10-011	Monstro The Whale 985-D	R. Olszewski	Open	120.00	120.00
Goebel Miniatures		**Disney-Cinderella**			
91-11-001	Anastasia 172-P	R.Olszewski	Open	85.00	85.00
91-11-002	Jaq 173-P	R.Olszewski	Open	80.00	80.00
91-11-003	Drizella 174-P	R.Olszewski	Open	85.00	85.00
91-11-004	Lucifer 175-P	R.Olszewski	Open	80.00	80.00
91-11-005	Cinderella 176-P	R.Olszewski	Open	85.00	85.00
91-11-006	Gus 177-P	R.Olszewski	Open	80.00	80.00
91-11-007	Stepmother 178-P	R.Olszewski	Open	85.00	85.00
91-11-008	Prince Charming 179-P	R.Olszewski	Open	85.00	85.00
91-11-009	Fairy Godmother 180-P	R.Olszewski	Open	85.00	85.00
91-11-010	Footman 181-P	R.Olszewski	Open	85.00	85.00
91-11-011	Cinderella's Dream Castle 976-D	R.Olszewski	Open	95.00	95.00
91-11-012	Cinderella's Coach Display 978-D	R.Olszewski	Open	95.00	95.00
Goebel Miniatures		**Mickey Mouse**			
90-12-001	The Sorcerer's Apprentice 171-P	R. Olszewski	Open	80.00	80.00
90-12-002	Fantasia Living Brooms 972-D	R. Olszweski	Open	85.00	85.00
Goebel Miniatures		**Night Before Christmas (1st Edition)**			
90-13-001	Sugar Plum Boy 687-P	R. Olszewski	5,000	70.00	85.00
90-13-002	Yule Tree 688-P	R. Olszewski	5,000	90.00	95.00
90-13-003	Sugar Plum Girl 689-P	R. Olszewski	5,000	70.00	85.00
90-13-004	St. Nicholas 690-P	R. Olszewski	5,000	95.00	105.00
90-13-005	Eight Tiny Reindeer 691-P	R. Olszewski	5,000	110.00	110.00
90-13-006	Mama & Papa 692-P	R. Olszewski	5,000	110.00	120.00
91-13-007	Up To The Housetop 966-D	R. Olszewski	5,000	95.00	95.00
Goebel Miniatures		**Special Release-Alice in Wonderland**			
82-14-001	Alice In the Garden 670-P	R. Olszewski	Closed	60.00	485-785.
83-14-002	Down the Rabbit Hole 671-P	R. Olszewski	Closed	75.00	450-480.
84-14-003	The Cheshire Cat 672-P	R. Olszewski	Closed	75.00	500.00
Goebel Miniatures		**Special Release-Wizard of Oz**			
84-15-001	Scarecrow 673-P	R. Olszewski	Closed	75.00	425.00
85-15-002	Tinman 674-P	R. Olszewski	Closed	80.00	285.00
86-15-003	The Cowardly Lion 675-P	R. Olszewski	Closed	85.00	180-240.
87-15-004	The Wicked Witch 676-P	R. Olszewski	5,000	85.00	110-170.
88-15-005	The Munchkins 677-P	R. Olszewski	5,000	85.00	100-200.
87-15-006	Oz Display 942-D	R. Olszewski	Closed	45.00	210.00
92-15-007	Dorothy/Glinda 695-P	R. Olszewski	5,000	135.00	135.00
92-15-008	Good-Bye to Oz Display 980-D	R. Olszewski	5,000	110.00	120.00
92-15-009	Set	R. Olszewski	5,000	730.00	1275-1400.
Goebel Miniatures		**Three Little Pigs**			
89-16-001	Little Sticks Pig 678-P	R. Olszewski	7,500	75.00	85.00
90-16-002	Little Straw Pig 679-P	R. Olszewski	7,500	75.00	85.00
91-16-003	Little Bricks Pig 680-P	R. Olszewski	Closed	75.00	75.00
91-16-004	The Hungry Wolf 681-P	R. Olszewski	Closed	80.00	80.00
89-16-005	Three Little Pigs House 956-D	R. Olszewski	7,500	50.00	55.00
Goebel Miniatures		**Pendants**			
88-17-001	Mickey Mouse 169-P	R. Olszewski	5,000	92.00	185.00
90-17-002	Hummingbird 697-P	R. Olszewski	Open	125.00	135.00
86-17-003	Camper Bialosky 151-P	R. Olszewski	Open	95.00	145.00
91-17-004	Rose Pendant 220-P	R. Olszewski	Open	135.00	135.00
91-17-005	Daffodil Pendant 221-P	R. Olszewski	Open	135.00	135.00
91-17-006	Chrysanthemum Pendant 222-P	R. Olszewski	Open	135.00	135.00
91-17-007	Poinsettia Pendant 223-P	R. Olszewski	Open	135.00	135.00
Goebel Miniatures		**Nativity Collection**			
91-18-001	Mother/Child 440-P	R. Olszewski	10,000	120.00	120.00
91-18-002	Joseph 401-P	R. Olszewski	10,000	95.00	95.00
91-18-003	Joyful Cherubs 403-P	R. Olszewski	10,000	130.00	130.00
91-18-004	The Stable Donkey 402-P	R. Olszewski	10,000	95.00	95.00
91-18-005	Holy Family Display 982-D	R. Olszewski	10,000	85.00	85.00
92-18-006	Balthazar 405-P	R. Olszewski	10,000	135.00	135.00
92-18-007	Melchoir 404-P	R. Olszewski	10,000	135.00	135.00
92-18-008	Gaspar 406-P	R. Olszewski	10,000	135.00	135.00
92-18-009	3 Kings Display 987-D	R. Olszewski	10,000	85.00	85.00
Goebel Miniatures		**Special Releases**			
91-19-001	Portrait Of The Artist 658-P	R. Olszewski	Open	195.00	195.00
92-19-002	Summer Days Collector Plaque 659-P	R. Olszewski	Open	130.00	130.00
Goebel Miniatures		**Saturday Evening Post**			
91-20-001	Soldier 368-P	N. Rockwell	Open	85.00	85.00
91-20-002	Mother 369-P	N. Rockwell	Open	85.00	85.00
91-20-003	Home Coming Vignette 990-D	N. Rockwell	Open	85.00	85.00
Goebel Miniatures		**Disney-Peter Pan**			
92-21-001	Peter Pan 184-P	R. Olszewski	Open	90.00	90.00
92-21-002	Wendy 185-P	R. Olszewski	Open	90.00	90.00
92-21-003	John 186-P	R. Olszewski	Open	90.00	90.00
92-21-004	Michael 187-P	R. Olszewski	Open	90.00	90.00
92-21-005	Nana 189-P	R. Olszewski	Open	95.00	95.00
92-21-006	Peter Pan's London 986-D	R. Olszewski	Open	125.00	125.00.

Company / Number	Name	Series / Artist	Edition Limit	Issue Price	Quote
Goebel Miniatures		**Archive Releases**			
92-22-001	Autumn Blue Jay 626-P	R. Olszewski	Open	125.00	125.00
93-22-002	Cherry Pickers 602-P	R. Olszewski	Open	175.00	175.00
93-22-003	Kuan Yin 640-W	R. Olszewski	Open	100.00	100.00
Goebel United States		**Blumenkinder- First Edition**			
66-01-001	Her First Bouquet	Lore	Closed	30.00	Unkn.
66-01-002	A Butterfly's Kiss	Lore	Closed	27.50	Unkn.
66-01-003	St. Valentine's Messenger	Lore	Closed	30.00	Unkn.
66-01-004	Nature's Treasures	Lore	Closed	25.00	Unkn.
66-01-005	Flute Recital	Lore	Closed	25.00	Unkn.
66-01-006	Bearer of Gifts	Lore	Closed	27.50	Unkn.
66-01-007	Apronful of Flowers	Lore	Closed	25.00	Unkn.
66-01-008	The Flower Farmer	Lore	Closed	30.00	Unkn.
66-01-009	Tender Loving Care	Lore	Closed	30.00	Unkn.
66-01-010	Garden Romance	Lore	Closed	50.00	Unkn.
66-01-011	Barefoot Lad	Lore	Closed	27.50	Unkn.
66-01-012	Her Kitten	Lore	Closed	27.50	Unkn.
66-01-013	Display Plaque	Lore	Closed	4.00	Unkn.
Goebel United States		**Blumenkinder-Second Edition**			
69-02-001	Summer Magic	Lore	Closed	50.00	Unkn.
69-02-002	Garden Princes	Lore	Closed	50.00	Unkn.
69-02-003	First Journey	Lore	Closed	25.00	Unkn.
69-02-004	First Love	Lore	Closed	25.00	Unkn.
71-02-005	Country Lad	Lore	Closed	35.00	Unkn.
71-02-006	Country Maiden	Lore	Closed	35.00	Unkn.
71-02-007	The Boy Friend	Lore	Closed	65.00	Unkn.
71-02-008	Bird Song	Lore	Closed	65.00	Unkn.
71-02-009	Cello Recital	Lore	Closed	80.00	Unkn.
71-02-010	Courting Country Style	Lore	Closed	80.00	Unkn.
Goebel United States		**Blumenkinder-Third Edition**			
72-03-001	Party Guest	Lore	Closed	95.00	Unkn.
72-03-002	First Date	Lore	Closed	95.00	Unkn.
73-03-003	The Patient	Lore	Closed	95.00	Unkn.
73-03-004	The Hitchhiker	Lore	Closed	80.00	Unkn.
73-03-005	The Accompanist	Lore	Closed	95.00	Unkn.
73-03-006	By A Garden Pond	Lore	Closed	75.00	Unkn.
73-03-007	Kittens	Lore	Closed	75.00	Unkn.
73-03-008	Easter Time	Lore	Closed	80.00	Unkn.
Goebel United States		**Blumenkinder-Fourth Edition**			
75-04-001	The Lucky One	Lore	Closed	150.00	Unkn.
75-04-002	With Love	Lore	Closed	150.00	Unkn.
75-04-003	Both in Harmony	Lore	Closed	95.00	Unkn.
75-04-004	Happy Minstrel	Lore	Closed	95.00	Unkn.
75-04-005	Springtime	Lore	Closed	95.00	Unkn.
75-04-006	For You-With Love	Lore	Closed	95.00	Unkn.
75-04-007	Companions	Lore	Closed	85.00	Unkn.
75-04-008	Loyal Friend	Lore	Closed	85.00	Unkn.
Goebel United States		**Blumenkinder-Fifth Edition**			
79-05-001	Garden Friends	Lore	Closed	175.00	Unkn.
79-05-002	Farmhouse Companions	Lore	Closed	175.00	Unkn.
79-05-003	Harvest Treat	Lore	Closed	149.00	Unkn.
79-05-004	Sweet Treat	Lore	Closed	149.00	Unkn.
79-05-005	Loving Touch	Lore	Closed	201.00	Unkn.
79-05-006	Birthday Morning	Lore	Closed	201.00	Unkn.
Goebel United States		**Blumenkinder-Sixth Edition**			
80-06-001	Flutist	Lore	Closed	175.00	Unkn.
80-06-002	Drummer Boy	Lore	Closed	180.00	Unkn.
80-06-003	Violinist	Lore	Closed	180.00	Unkn.
80-06-004	Spring Song	Lore	Closed	180.00	Unkn.
80-06-005	Dancing Song	Lore	Closed	175.00	Unkn.
80-06-006	Romance	Lore	Closed	175.00	Unkn.
Goebel United States		**Blumenkinder-Seventh Edition**			
82-07-001	Happy Sailing	Lore	Closed	150.00	Unkn.
82-07-002	The Spinning Top	Lore	Closed	150.00	Unkn.
82-07-003	Mail Call	Lore	Closed	165.00	Unkn.
82-07-004	Little Mommy	Lore	Closed	165.00	Unkn.
82-07-005	Autumn Delight	Lore	Closed	165.00	Unkn.
82-07-006	Play Bell	Lore	Closed	165.00	Unkn.
Goebel United States		**Co-Boy**			
71-08-001	Robby the Vegetarian	G. Skrobek	Closed	16.00	80.00
71-08-002	Mike the Jam Maker	G. Skrobek	Closed	16.00	72.00
71-08-003	Bit the Bachelor	G. Skrobek	Closed	16.00	28-80.00
71-08-004	Tom the Honey Lover	G. Skrobek	Closed	16.00	28.00
71-08-005	Sam the Gourmet	G. Skrobek	Closed	16.00	28.00
71-08-006	Plum the Pastry Chef	G. Skrobek	Closed	16.00	28-60.00
71-08-007	Wim the Court Supplier	G. Skrobek	Closed	16.00	28.00
71-08-008	Fips the Foxy Fisherman	G. Skrobek	Closed	16.00	72.00
72-08-009	Porz the Mushroom Muncher	G. Skrobek	Closed	20.00	28.00
72-08-010	Sepp the Beer Buddy	G. Skrobek	Closed	20.00	72.00
72-08-011	Kuni the Big Dipper	G. Skrobek	Closed	20.00	28-50.00
71-08-012	Fritz the Happy Boozer	G. Skrobek	Closed	16.00	42-50.00
72-08-013	Bob the Bookworm	G. Skrobek	Closed	20.00	42-50.00
72-08-014	Brum the Lawyer	G. Skrobek	Closed	20.00	72.00
72-08-015	Utz the Banker	G. Skrobek	Closed	20.00	42-50.00
72-08-016	Co-Boy Plaque	G. Skrobek	Closed	20.00	42-50.00
XX-08-017	Jack the Village Pharmacist	G. Skrobek	Closed	Unkn.	42-50.00
XX-08-018	John the Hawkeye Hunter	G. Skrobek	Closed	Unkn.	72.00
XX-08-019	Petrl the Village Angler	G. Skrobek	Closed	Unkn.	72.00
XX-08-020	Conny the Night Watchman	G. Skrobek	Closed	Unkn.	42-50.00
XX-08-021	Ed the Wine Cellar Steward	G. Skrobek	Closed	Unkn.	42-50.00
XX-08-022	Toni the Skier	G. Skrobek	Closed	Unkn.	72.00
XX-08-023	Candy the Baker's Delight	G. Skrobek	Closed	Unkn.	42-50.00
XX-08-024	Mark-Safety First	G. Skrobek	Closed	Unkn.	42-50.00
XX-08-025	Bert the Soccer Star	G. Skrobek	Closed	Unkn.	50.00
XX-08-026	Jim the Bowler	G. Skrobek	Closed	Unkn.	50.00
XX-08-027	Max the Boxing Champ	G. Skrobek	Closed	Unkn.	50.00
78-08-028	Gil the Goalie	G. Skrobek	Closed	34.00	50.00
78-08-029	Pat the Pitcher	G. Skrobek	Closed	34.00	50.00
78-08-030	Tommy Touchdown	G. Skrobek	Closed	34.00	50.00
80-08-031	Ted the Tennis Player	G. Skrobek	Closed	49.00	50.00
80-08-032	Herb the Horseman	G. Skrobek	Closed	49.00	85.00
80-08-033	Monty the Mountain Climber	G. Skrobek	Closed	49.00	72.00
80-08-034	Carl the Chef	G. Skrobek	Closed	49.00	72-80.00
80-08-035	Doc the Doctor	G. Skrobek	Closed	49.00	72.00
80-08-036	Gerd the Diver	G. Skrobek	Closed	49.00	50.00
81-08-037	George the Gourmand	G. Skrobek	Closed	45.00	72.00

Company / Number	Name	Series / Artist	Edition Limit	Issue Price	Quote
81-08-038	Greg the Gourmet	G. Skrobek	Closed	45.00	50.00
81-08-039	Ben the Blacksmith	G. Skrobek	Closed	45.00	50.00
81-08-040	Al the Trumpet Player	G. Skrobek	Closed	45.00	50.00
81-08-041	Peter the Accordionist	G. Skrobek	Closed	45.00	50.00
81-08-042	Niels the Strummer	G. Skrobek	Closed	45.00	50.00
81-08-043	Greta the Happy Housewife	G. Skrobek	Closed	45.00	50.00
81-08-044	Nick the Nightclub Singer	G. Skrobek	Closed	45.00	50.00
81-08-045	Walter the Jogger	G. Skrobek	Closed	45.00	50.00
84-08-046	Rudy the World Traveler	G. Skrobek	Closed	45.00	80.00
84-08-047	Sid the Vintner	G. Skrobek	Closed	45.00	50.00
84-08-048	Herman the Butcher	G. Skrobek	Closed	45.00	50.00
84-08-049	Rick the Fireman	G. Skrobek	Closed	45.00	50-80.00
84-08-050	Chuck the Chimney Sweep	G. Skrobek	Closed	45.00	50.00
84-08-051	Chris the Shoemaker	G. Skrobek	Closed	45.00	50.00
84-08-052	Felix the Baker	G. Skrobek	Closed	45.00	85.00
84-08-053	Marthe the Nurse	G. Skrobek	Closed	45.00	50.00
84-08-054	Paul the Dentist	G. Skrobek	Closed	45.00	50.00
84-08-055	Homer the Driver	G. Skrobek	Closed	45.00	50-80.00
84-08-056	Brad the Clockmaker	G. Skrobek	Closed	75.00	95.00
87-08-057	Clock-Cony the Watchman	G. Skrobek	Closed	125.00	125.00
87-08-058	Clock-Sepp and the Beer Keg	G. Skrobek	Closed	125.00	125.00
87-08-059	Bank-Pete the Pirate	G. Skrobek	Closed	80.00	80.00
87-08-060	Bank-Utz the Money Bags	G. Skrobek	Closed	80.00	80.00
87-08-061	Chuck on His Pig	G. Skrobek	Closed	75.00	75.00
Goebel United States		**Fashions on Parade**			
82-09-001	The Garden Fancier	G. Bochmann	Open	30.00	50.00
82-09-002	The Visitor	G. Bochmann	Open	30.00	50.00
82-09-003	The Cosmopolitan	G. Bochmann	Open	30.00	50.00
82-09-004	At The Tea Dance	G. Bochmann	Open	30.00	50.00
82-09-005	Strolling On The Avenue	G. Bochmann	Open	30.00	50.00
82-09-006	Edwardian Grace	G. Bochmann	Open	30.00	50.00
83-09-007	Gentle Thoughts	G. Bochmann	Open	32.50	50.00
83-09-008	Demure Elegance	G. Bochmann	Open	32.50	50.00
83-09-009	Reflections	G. Bochmann	Open	32.50	50.00
83-09-010	Impatience	G. Bochmann	Closed	32.50	50.00
83-09-011	Waiting For His Love-Groom	G. Bochmann	Open	32.50	50.00
83-09-012	Her Treasured Day-Bride	G. Bochmann	Open	32..50	50.00
83-09-013	Bride and Groom	G. Bochmann	Open	65.00	100.00
84-09-014	On The Fairway	G. Bochmann	Closed	32.50	45.00
84-09-015	Center Court	G. Bochmann	Closed	32.50	45.00
84-09-016	Skimming Gently	G. Bochmann	Closed	32.50	45.00
85-09-017	A Lazy Day	G. Bochmann	Closed	22.50	35.00
85-09-018	A Gentle Moment	G. Bochmann	Closed	22.50	35.00
85-09-019	Afternoon Tea	G. Bochmann	Open	32.50	50.00
85-09-020	River Outing	G. Bochmann	Open	32.50	50.00
85-09-021	To The Hunt	G. Bochmann	Open	32.50	50.00
85-09-022	Gentle Breezes	G. Bochmann	Open	32.50	50.00
86-09-023	Equestrian	G. Bochmann	Open	36.00	50.00
86-09-024	Southern Belle	G. Bochmann	Open	36.00	50.00
86-09-025	Fashions on Parade Plaque	G. Bochmann	Open	10.00	12.50
87-09-026	Say Please	G. Bochmann	Open	55.00	55.00
87-09-027	The Viscountess Diana	G. Bochmann	Open	55.00	55.00
87-09-028	The Shepherdess	G. Bochmann	Open	55.00	55.00
87-09-029	Paris In Fall	G. Bochmann	Open	55.00	55.00
87-09-030	Promenade in Nice	G. Bochmann	Open	55.00	55.00
87-09-031	Silver Lace and Rhinestones	G. Bochmann	Open	55.00	55.00
88-09-032	The Promise-Groom	G. Bochmann	Open	55.00	55.00
88-09-033	Forever and Always-Bride	G. Bochmann	Open	55.00	55.00
88-09-034	Bride and Groom-2nd Set	G. Bochmann	Open	110.00	110.00
Goebel/Schmid		**M.I. Hummel Collectibles Figurines**			
88-01-001	A Budding Maestro 477	M.I. Hummel	Open	Unkn.	95.00
XX-01-002	A Fair Measure 345	M.I. Hummel	Open	Unkn.	260.00
93-01-003	A Free Flight 569	M.I. Hummel	Open	Unkn.	185.00
XX-01-004	A Gentle Glow 439	M.I. Hummel	Open	Unkn.	190.00
91-01-005	A Nap 534	M.I. Hummel	Open	Unkn.	110.00
XX-01-006	Accordion Boy 185	M.I. Hummel	Open	Unkn.	180.00
XX-01-007	Adoration 23/I	M.I. Hummel	Open	Unkn.	325.00
XX-01-008	Adoration 23/III	M.I. Hummel	Open	Unkn.	510.00
XX-01-009	Adventure Bound 347	M.I. Hummel	Open	Unkn.	3500.00
89-01-010	An Apple A Day 403	M.I. Hummel	Open	Unkn.	260.00
XX-01-011	Angel Duet 261	M.I. Hummel	Open	Unkn.	195.00
XX-01-012	Angel Serenade 214/0	M.I. Hummel	Open	Unkn.	80.00
XX-01-013	Angel Serenade with Lamb 83	M.I. Hummel	Open	Unkn.	195.00
XX-01-014	Angel with Accordion 238/B	M.I. Hummel	Open	Unkn.	50.00
XX-01-015	Angel with Lute 238/A	M.I. Hummel	Open	Unkn.	50.00
XX-01-016	Angel With Trumpet 238/C	M.I. Hummel	Open	Unkn.	50.00
XX-01-017	Angelic Song 144	M.I. Hummel	Open	Unkn.	135.00
XX-01-018	Apple Tree Boy 142/3/0	M.I. Hummel	Open	Unkn.	130.00
XX-01-019	Apple Tree Boy 142/I	M.I. Hummel	Open	Unkn.	245.00
XX-01-020	Apple Tree Boy 142/V	M.I. Hummel	Open	Unkn.	1080.00
XX-01-021	Apple Tree Girl 141/3/0	M.I. Hummel	Open	Unkn.	174.00
XX-01-022	Apple Tree Girl 141/I	M.I. Hummel	Open	Unkn.	245.00
XX-01-023	Apple Tree Girl 141/V	M.I. Hummel	Open	Unkn.	1080.00
91-01-024	Art Critic 318	M.I. Hummel	Open	Unkn.	260.00
XX-01-025	Artist, The 304	M.I. Hummel	Open	Unkn.	220.00
XX-01-026	Auf Wiedersehen 153/0	M.I. Hummel	Open	Unkn.	220.00
XX-01-027	Auf Wiedersehen 153/I	M.I. Hummel	Open	Unkn.	270.00
XX-01-028	Autumn Harvest 355	M.I. Hummel	Open	Unkn.	195.00
XX-01-029	Baker 128	M.I. Hummel	Open	Unkn.	175.00
XX-01-030	Baking Day 330	M.I. Hummel	Open	Unkn.	240.00
XX-01-031	Band Leader 129	M.I. Hummel	Open	Unkn.	180.00
XX-01-032	Band Leader 129/4/0	M.I. Hummel	Open	Unkn.	90.00
XX-01-033	Barnyard Hero 195/2/0	M.I. Hummel	Open	Unkn.	150.00
XX-01-034	Barnyard Hero 195/I	M.I. Hummel	Open	Unkn.	290.00
XX-01-035	Bashful 377	M.I. Hummel	Open	Unkn.	180.00
90-01-036	Bath Time 412	M.I. Hummel	Open	Unkn.	350.00
XX-01-037	Begging His Share 9	M.I. Hummel	Open	Unkn.	220.00
XX-01-038	Be Patient 197/2/0	M.I. Hummel	Open	Unkn.	175.00
XX-01-039	Be Patient 197/I	M.I. Hummel	Open	Unkn.	260.00
XX-01-040	Big Housecleaning 363	M.I. Hummel	Open	Unkn.	260.00
XX-01-041	Bird Duet 169	M.I. Hummel	Open	Unkn.	130.00
XX-01-042	Bird Watcher 300	M.I. Hummel	Open	Unkn.	205.00
89-01-043	Birthday Cake 338	M.I. Hummel	Open	Unkn.	130.00
XX-01-044	Birthday Serenade 218/2/0	M.I. Hummel	Open	Unkn.	160.00
XX-01-045	Birthday Serenade 218/0	M.I. Hummel	Open	Unkn.	270.00
XX-01-046	Blessed Event 333	M.I. Hummel	Open	Unkn.	300.00
XX-01-047	Bookworm 8	M.I. Hummel	Open	Unkn.	195.00
XK-01-048	Bookworm 3/I	M.I. Hummel	Open	Unkn.	270.00
XX-01-049	Boots 143/0	M.I. Hummel	Open	Unkn.	180.00
XX-01-050	Boots 143/I	M.I. Hummel	Open	Unkn.	300.00
XX-01-051	Botanist, The 351	M.I. Hummel	Open	Unkn.	195.00
XX-01-052	Boy with Accordion 390	M.I. Hummel	Open	Unkn.	75.00

Company Number	Series Name	Artist	Edition Limit	Issue Price	Quote
XX-01-053	Boy with Horse 239C	M.I. Hummel	Open	Unkn.	50.00
XX-01-054	Boy with Toothache 217	M.I. Hummel	Open	Unkn.	200.00
XX-01-055	Brother 95	M.I. Hummel	Open	Unkn.	180.00
XX-01-056	Builder, The 305	M.I. Hummel	Open	Unkn.	220.00
XX-01-057	Busy Student 367	M.I. Hummel	Open	Unkn.	150.00
XX-01-058	Carnival 328	M.I. Hummel	Open	Unkn.	205.00
XX-01-059	Celestial Musician 188/0	M.I. Hummel	Open	Unkn.	195.00
XX-01-060	Celestial Musician 188/I	M.I. Hummel	Open	Unkn.	230.00
93-01-061	Celestial Musician (mini) 188/4/0	M.I. Hummel	Open	Unkn.	90.00
XX-01-062	Chick Girl 57/2/0	M.I. Hummel	Open	Unkn.	135.00
XX-01-063	Chick Girl 57/0	M.I. Hummel	Open	Unkn.	155.00
XX-01-064	Chick Girl 57/I	M.I. Hummel	Open	Unkn.	250.00
XX-01-065	Chicken-Licken 385	M.I. Hummel	Open	Unkn.	260.00
XX-01-066	Chicken-Licken 385/4	M.I. Hummel	Open	Unkn.	90.00
XX-01-067	Chimney Sweep 12/2/0	M.I. Hummel	Open	Unkn.	110.00
XX-01-068	Chimney Sweep 12/I	M.I. Hummel	Open	Unkn.	195.00
89-01-069	Christmas Angel 301	M.I. Hummel	Open	Unkn.	230.00
XX-01-070	Christmas Song 343	M.I. Hummel	Open	Unkn.	195.00
XX-01-071	Cinderella 337	M.I. Hummel	Open	Unkn.	260.00
XX-01-072	Close Harmony 336	M.I. Hummel	Open	Unkn.	260.00
XX-01-073	Confidentially 314	M.I. Hummel	Open	Unkn.	260.00
XX-01-074	Congratulations 17/0	M.I. Hummel	Open	Unkn.	180.00
XX-01-075	Coquettes 179	M.I. Hummel	Open	Unkn.	260.00
XX-01-076	Crossroads (Original) 331	M.I. Hummel	Open	Unkn.	380.00
XX-01-077	Crossroads (Commemorative) 331	M.I. Hummel	10,000	Unkn.	650-1250.
XX-01-078	Culprits 56/A	M.I. Hummel	Open	Unkn.	265.00
89-01-079	Daddy's Girls 371	M.I. Hummel	Open	Unkn.	220.00
XX-01-080	Doctor 127	M.I. Hummel	Open	Unkn.	145.00
XX-01-081	Doll Bath 319	M.I. Hummel	Open	Unkn.	260.00
XX-01-082	Doll Mother 67	M.I. Hummel	Open	Unkn.	190.00
XX-01-083	Duet 130	M.I. Hummel	Open	Unkn.	250.00
XX-01-084	Easter Greetings 378	M.I. Hummel	Open	Unkn.	195.00
XX-01-085	Easter Time 384	M.I. Hummel	Open	Unkn.	240.00
92-01-086	Evening Prayer 495	M.I. Hummel	Open	Unkn.	105.00
XX-01-087	Eventide 99	M.I. Hummel	Open	Unkn.	315.00
XX-01-088	Farewell 65	M.I. Hummel	Open	Unkn.	240.00
XX-01-089	Farm Boy 66	M.I. Hummel	Open	Unkn.	205.00
XX-01-090	Favorite Pet 361	M.I. Hummel	Open	Unkn.	260.00
XX-01-091	Feathered Friends 344	M.I. Hummel	Open	Unkn.	240.00
XX-01-092	Feeding Time 199/0	M.I. Hummel	Open	Unkn.	175.00
XX-01-093	Feeding Time 199/I	M.I. Hummel	Open	Unkn.	240.00
XX-01-094	Festival Harmony, with Mandolin 172/0	M.I. Hummel	Open	Unkn.	280.00
XX-01-095	Festival Harmony, with Flute 173/0	M.I. Hummel	Open	Unkn.	280.00
XX-01-096	Flower Vendor 381	M.I. Hummel	Open	Unkn.	220.00
XX-01-097	Follow the Leader 369	M.I. Hummel	Open	Unkn.	1100.00
XX-01-098	For Father 87	M.I. Hummel	Open	Unkn.	195.00
XX-01-099	For Mother 257/2/0	M.I. Hummel	Open	Unkn.	110.00
XX-01-100	For Mother 257	M.I. Hummel	Open	Unkn.	185.00
XX-01-101	Forest Shrine 183	M.I. Hummel	Open	Unkn.	495.00
91-01-102	Friend Or Foe 434	M.I. Hummel	Open	Unkn.	195.00
XX-01-103	Friends 136/I	M.I. Hummel	Open	Unkn.	195.00
XX-01-104	Friends 136/V	M.I. Hummel	Open	Unkn.	1080.00
XX-01-105	Gay Adventure 356	M.I. Hummel	Open	Unkn.	175.00
XX-01-106	Girl with Doll 239/B	M.I. Hummel	Open	Unkn.	50.00
XX-01-107	Girl with Nosegay 239/A	M.I. Hummel	Open	Unkn.	50.00
XX-01-108	Girl with Sheet Music 389	M.I. Hummel	Open	Unkn.	75.00
XX-01-109	Girl with Trumpet 391	M.I. Hummel	Open	Unkn.	75.00
XX-01-110	Going Home 383	M.I. Hummel	Open	Unkn.	280.00
XX-01-111	Going to Grandma's 52/0	M.I. Hummel	Open	Unkn.	250.00
XX-01-112	Good Friends 182	M.I. Hummel	Open	Unkn.	175.00
XX-01-113	Good Hunting 307	M.I. Hummel	Open	Unkn.	220.00
XX-01-114	Good Night 214/C	M.I. Hummel	Open	Unkn.	80.00
XX-01-115	Good Shepherd 42/0	M.I. Hummel	Open	Unkn.	220.00
XX-01-116	Goose Girl 47/3/0	M.I. Hummel	Open	Unkn.	155.00
XX-01-117	Goose Girl 47/0	M.I. Hummel	Open	Unkn.	205.00
XX-01-118	Goose Girl 47/II	M.I. Hummel	Open	Unkn.	380.00
XX-01-119	Grandma's Girl 561	M.I. Hummel	Open	Unkn.	135.00
XX-01-120	Grandpa's Boy 562	M.I. Hummel	Open	Unkn.	135.00
XX-01-121	Guiding Angel 357	M.I. Hummel	Open	Unkn.	80.00
XX-01-122	Happiness 86	M.I. Hummel	Open	Unkn.	120.00
XX-01-123	Happy Birthday 176/0	M.I. Hummel	Open	Unkn.	195.00
XX-01-124	Happy Birthday 176/I	M.I. Hummel	Open	Unkn.	270.00
XX-01-125	Happy Days 150/2/0	M.I. Hummel	Open	Unkn.	160.00
XX-01-126	Happy Days 150/0	M.I. Hummel	Open	Unkn.	270.00
XX-01-127	Happy Days 150/I	M.I. Hummel	Open	Unkn.	430.00
XX-01-128	Happy Pastime 69	M.I. Hummel	Open	Unkn.	145.00
XX-01-129	Happy Traveller 109/0	M.I. Hummel	Open	Unkn.	130.00
XX-01-130	Hear Ye! Hear Ye! 15/0	M.I. Hummel	Open	Unkn.	180.00
XX-01-131	Hear Ye! Hear Ye! 15/I	M.I. Hummel	Open	Unkn.	225.00
XX-01-132	Hear Ye! Hear Ye! 15/II	M.I. Hummel	Open	Unkn.	400.00
XX-01-133	Hear Ye! Hear Ye! 15/2/0	M.I. Hummel	Open	Unkn.	135.00
XX-01-134	Heavenly Angel 21/0	M.I. Hummel	Open	Unkn.	110.00
XX-01-135	Heavenly Angel 21/0/1/2	M.I. Hummel	Open	Unkn.	190.00
XX-01-136	Heavenly Angel 21/I	M.I. Hummel	Open	Unkn.	230.00
XX-01-137	Heavenly Angel 21/II	M.I. Hummel	Open	Unkn.	390.00
XX-01-138	Heavenly Lullaby 262	M.I. Hummel	Open	Unkn.	170.00
XX-01-139	Heavenly Protection 88/I	M.I. Hummel	Open	Unkn.	395.00
XX-01-140	Heavenly Protection 88/II	M.I. Hummel	Open	Unkn.	590.00
XX-01-141	Hello 124/0	M.I. Hummel	Open	Unkn.	195.00
XX-01-142	Home from Market 198/2/0	M.I. Hummel	Open	Unkn.	130.00
XX-01-143	Home from Market 198/I	M.I. Hummel	Open	Unkn.	195.00
XX-01-144	Homeward Bound 334	M.I. Hummel	Open	Unkn.	320.00
90-01-145	Horse Trainer 423	M.I. Hummel	Open	Unkn.	200.00
89-01-146	Hosanna 480	M.I. Hummel	Open	Unkn.	90.00
89-01-147	I'll Protect Him 483	M.I. Hummel	Open	Unkn.	75.00
89-01-148	I'm Here 478	M.I. Hummel	Open	Unkn.	95.00
89-01-149	In D Major 430	M.I. Hummel	Open	Unkn.	180.00
XX-01-150	In The Meadow 459	M.I. Hummel	Open	Unkn.	180.00
XX-01-151	In Tune 414	M.I. Hummel	Open	Unkn.	250.00
XX-01-152	Is It Raining? 420	M.I. Hummel	Open	Unkn.	240.00
XX-01-153	Joyful 53	M.I. Hummel	Open	Unkn.	110.00
XX-01-154	Joyous News 27/III	M.I. Hummel	Open	Unkn.	195.00
XX-01-155	Just Fishing 373	M.I. Hummel	Open	Unkn.	205.00
XX-01-156	Just Resting 112/3/0	M.I. Hummel	Open	Unkn.	135.00
XX-01-157	Just Resting 112/I	M.I. Hummel	Open	Unkn.	250.00
XX-01-158	Kindergartner 467	M.I. Hummel	Open	Unkn.	180.00
XX-01-159	Kiss Me 311	M.I. Hummel	Open	Unkn.	260.00
XX-01-160	Knitting Lesson 256	M.I. Hummel	Open	Unkn.	475.00
XX-01-161	Knit One, Purl One 432	M.I. Hummel	Open	Unkn.	105.00
92-01-162	Land in Sight 530	M.I. Hummel	30,000	Unkn.	1600.00
XX-01-163	Latest News 184/0	M.I. Hummel	Open	Unkn.	260.00
XX-01-164	Let's Sing 110/0	M.I. Hummel	Open	Unkn.	115.00
XX-01-165	Let's Sing 110/I	M.I. Hummel	Open	Unkn.	155.00
XX-01-166	Letter to Santa Claus 340	M.I. Hummel	Open	Unkn.	305.00
93-01-167	Little Architect 410/I	M.I. Hummel	Open	Unkn.	290.00
XX-01-168	Little Bookkeeper 306	M.I. Hummel	Open	Unkn.	260.00
XX-01-169	Little Cellist 89/I	M.I. Hummel	Open	Unkn.	195.00
XX-01-170	Little Cellist 89/II	M.I. Hummel	Open	Unkn.	380.00
XX-01-171	Little Drummer 240	M.I. Hummel	Open	Unkn.	135.00
XX-01-172	Little Fiddler 2/4/0	M.I. Hummel	Open	Unkn.	90.00
XX-01-173	Little Fiddler 4	M.I. Hummel	Open	Unkn.	185.00
XX-01-174	Little Fiddler 2/0	M.I. Hummel	Open	Unkn.	205.00
XX-01-175	Little Fiddler 2/I	M.I. Hummel	Open	Unkn.	370.00
XX-01-176	Little Gabriel 32	M.I. Hummel	Open	Unkn.	125.00
XX-01-177	Little Gardener 74	M.I. Hummel	Open	Unkn.	110.00
XX-01-178	Little Goat Herder 200/0	M.I. Hummel	Open	Unkn.	175.00
XX-01-179	Little Goat Herder 200/I	M.I. Hummel	Open	Unkn.	220.00
XX-01-180	Little Guardian 145	M.I. Hummel	Open	Unkn.	135.00
XX-01-181	Little Helper 73	M.I. Hummel	Open	Unkn.	110.00
XX-01-182	Little Hiker 16/2/0	M.I. Hummel	Open	Unkn.	110.00
XX-01-183	Little Hiker 16/I	M.I. Hummel	Open	Unkn.	200.00
XX-01-184	Little Nurse 376	M.I. Hummel	Open	Unkn.	225.00
XX-01-185	Little Pharmacist 322	M.I. Hummel	Open	Unkn.	220.00
XX-01-186	Little Scholar 80	M.I. Hummel	Open	Unkn.	195.00
XX-01-187	Little Shopper 96	M.I. Hummel	Open	Unkn.	130.00
XX-01-188	Little Sweeper 171/4/0	M.I. Hummel	Open	Unkn.	90.00
88-01-189	Little Sweeper 171	M.I. Hummel	Open	Unkn.	120.00
XX-01-190	Little Tailor 308	M.I. Hummel	Open	Unkn.	220.00
XX-01-191	Little Thrifty 118	M.I. Hummel	Open	Unkn.	130.00
XX-01-192	Little Tooter 214/H	M.I. Hummel	Open	Unkn.	95.00
XX-01-193	Little Tooter 214/H	M.I. Hummel	Open	Unkn.	110.00
XX-01-194	Lost Sheep 68/2/0	M.I. Hummel	Open	Unkn.	125.00
XX-01-195	Lost Sheep 68/0	M.I. Hummel	Open	Unkn.	180.00
XX-01-196	Lost Stocking 374	M.I. Hummel	Open	Unkn.	130.00
XX-01-197	Mail is Here 226	M.I. Hummel	Open	Unkn.	505.00
89-01-198	Make A Wish 475	M.I. Hummel	Open	Unkn.	175.00
XX-01-199	March Winds 43	M.I. Hummel	Open	Unkn.	145.00
XX-01-200	Max and Moritz 123	M.I. Hummel	Open	Unkn.	205.00
XX-01-201	Meditation 13/2/0	M.I. Hummel	Open	Unkn.	130.00
XX-01-202	Meditation 13/0	M.I. Hummel	Open	Unkn.	205.00
XX-01-203	Merry Wanderer 11/2/0	M.I. Hummel	Open	Unkn.	125.00
XX-01-204	Merry Wanderer 11/0	M.I. Hummel	Open	Unkn.	175.00
XX-01-205	Merry Wanderer 7/0	M.I. Hummel	Open	Unkn.	245.00
XX-01-206	Merry Wanderer 7/I	M.I. Hummel	Open	Unkn.	360.00
XX-01-207	Merry Wanderer 7/II	M.I. Hummel	Open	Unkn.	1100.00
XX-01-208	Mischief Maker 342	M.I. Hummel	Open	Unkn.	240.00
XX-01-209	Mother's Darling 175	M.I. Hummel	Open	Unkn.	195.00
XX-01-210	Mother's Helper 133	M.I. Hummel	Open	Unkn.	175.00
XX-01-211	Mountaineer 315	M.I. Hummel	Open	Unkn.	195.00
XX-01-212	Not For You 317	M.I. Hummel	Open	Unkn.	220.00
89-01-213	One For You, One For Me 482	M.I. Hummel	Open	Unkn.	95.00
93-01-214	One Plus One 556	M.I. Hummel	Open	Unkn.	115.00
XX-01-215	On Holiday 350	M.I. Hummel	Open	Unkn.	160.00
XX-01-216	On Secret Path 386	M.I. Hummel	Open	Unkn.	225.00
XX-01-217	Out of Danger 56/B	M.I. Hummel	Open	Unkn.	265.00
93-01-218	Parade Of Lights 616	M.I. Hummel	Open	Unkn.	235.00
XX-01-219	Photographer 178	M.I. Hummel	Open	Unkn.	260.00
XX-01-220	Playmates 58/2/0	M.I. Hummel	Open	Unkn.	135.00
XX-01-221	Playmates 58/0	M.I. Hummel	Open	Unkn.	155.00
XX-01-222	Playmates 58/I	M.I. Hummel	Open	Unkn.	250.00
XX-01-223	Postman 119	M.I. Hummel	Open	Unkn.	180.00
89-01-224	Postman 119/2/0	M.I. Hummel	Open	Unkn.	125.00
XX-01-225	Prayer Before Battle 20	M.I. Hummel	Open	Unkn.	155.00
XX-01-226	Retreat to Safety 201/2/0	M.I. Hummel	Open	Unkn.	150.00
XX-01-227	Retreat to Safety 201/I	M.I. Hummel	Open	Unkn.	275.00
XX-01-228	Ride into Christmas 396/2/0	M.I. Hummel	Open	Unkn.	220.00
XX-01-229	Ride into Christmas 396/I	M.I. Hummel	Open	Unkn.	390.00
XX-01-230	Ring Around the Rosie 348	M.I. Hummel	Open	Unkn.	2500.00
XX-01-231	Run-A-Way 327	M.I. Hummel	Open	Unkn.	225.00
XX-01-232	St. George 55	M.I. Hummel	Open	Unkn.	300.00
92-01-233	Scamp 553	M.I. Hummel	Open	Unkn.	105.00
XX-01-234	School Boy 82/2/0	M.I. Hummel	Open	Unkn.	130.00
XX-01-235	School Boy 82/0	M.I. Hummel	Open	Unkn.	175.00
XX-01-236	School Boy 82/II	M.I. Hummel	Open	Unkn.	415.00
XX-01-237	School Boys 170/I	M.I. Hummel	Open	Unkn.	1100.00
XX-01-238	School Girl 81/2/0	M.I. Hummel	Open	Unkn.	130.00
XX-01-239	School Girl 81/0	M.I. Hummel	Open	Unkn.	175.00
XX-01-240	School Girls 177/I	M.I. Hummel	Open	Unkn.	1100.00
XX-01-241	Sensitive Hunter 6/0	M.I. Hummel	Open	Unkn.	175.00
XX-01-242	Sensitive Hunter 6/I	M.I. Hummel	Open	Unkn.	230.00
XX-01-243	Sensitive Hunter 6/2/0	M.I. Hummel	Open	Unkn.	135.00
XX-01-244	Serenade 85/0	M.I. Hummel	Open	Unkn.	120.00
XX-01-245	Serenade 85/4/0	M.I. Hummel	Open	Unkn.	90.00
XX-01-246	Serenade 85/II	M.I. Hummel	Open	Unkn.	410.00
XX-01-247	She Loves Me, She Loves Me Not 174	M.I. Hummel	Open	Unkn.	170.00
XX-01-248	Shepherd's Boy 214/G/II	M.I. Hummel	Open	Unkn.	120.00
XX-01-249	Shepherd's Boy 64	M.I. Hummel	Open	Unkn.	200.00
XX-01-250	Shining Light 358	M.I. Hummel	Open	Unkn.	80.00
XX-01-251	Sing Along 433	M.I. Hummel	Open	Unkn.	260.00
XX-01-252	Singing Lesson 63	M.I. Hummel	Open	Unkn.	110.00
XX-01-253	Sing With Me 405	M.I. Hummel	Open	Unkn.	280.00
XX-01-254	Sister 98/2/0	M.I. Hummel	Open	Unkn.	130.00
XX-01-255	Sister 98/0	M.I. Hummel	Open	Unkn.	180.00
XX-01-256	Skier 59	M.I. Hummel	Open	Unkn.	195.00
90-01-257	Sleep Tight 424	M.I. Hummel	Open	Unkn.	200.00
XX-01-258	Smart Little Sister 346	M.I. Hummel	Open	Unkn.	225.00
XX-01-259	Soldier Boy 332	M.I. Hummel	Open	Unkn.	195.00
XX-01-260	Soloist 135/4/0	M.I. Hummel	Open	Unkn.	90.00
XX-01-261	Soloist 135	M.I. Hummel	Open	Unkn.	120.00
88-01-262	Song of Praise 454	M.I. Hummel	Open	Unkn.	90.00
88-01-263	Sound the Trumpet 457	M.I. Hummel	Open	Unkn.	90.00
88-01-264	Sounds of the Mandolin 438	M.I. Hummel	Open	Unkn.	110.00
XX-01-265	Spring Dance 353/0	M.I. Hummel	Open	Unkn.	280.00
XX-01-266	Star Gazer 132	M.I. Hummel	Open	Unkn.	195.00
XX-01-267	Stitch in Time 255	M.I. Hummel	Open	Unkn.	260.00
XX-01-268	Stitch in Time 255	M.I. Hummel	Open	Unkn.	85.00
XX-01-269	Stormy Weather 71/I	M.I. Hummel	Open	Unkn.	415.00
XX-01-270	Stormy Weather 71/2/0	M.I. Hummel	Open	Unkn.	270.00
92-01-271	Storybook Time 458	M.I. Hummel	Open	Unkn.	360.00
XX-01-272	Street Singer 131	M.I. Hummel	Open	Unkn.	170.00
XX-01-273	Surprise 94/3/0	M.I. Hummel	Open	Unkn.	140.00
XX-01-274	Surprise 94/I	M.I. Hummel	Open	Unkn.	260.00
XX-01-275	Sweet Greetings 352	M.I. Hummel	Open	Unkn.	195.00
XX-01-276	Sweet Music 186	M.I. Hummel	Open	Unkn.	180.00
XX-01-277	Telling Her Secret 196/0	M.I. Hummel	Open	Unkn.	270.00
88-01-278	The Accompanist 453	M.I. Hummel	Open	Unkn.	90.00

Company / Number	Name	Series / Artist	Edition Limit	Issue Price	Quote
91-01-279	The Guardian 455	M.I. Hummel	Open	Unkn.	155.00
92-01-280	The Professor 320/0	M.I. Hummel	Open	Unkn.	195.00
XX-01-281	Thoughtful 415	M.I. Hummel	Open	Unkn.	205.00
XX-01-282	Timid Little Sister 394	M.I. Hummel	Open	Unkn.	390.00
XX-01-283	To Market 49/3/0	M.I. Hummel	Open	Unkn.	150.00
XX-01-284	To Market 49/0	M.I. Hummel	Open	Unkn.	250.00
XX-01-285	Trumpet Boy 97	M.I. Hummel	Open	Unkn.	120.00
89-01-286	Tuba Player 437	M.I. Hummel	Open	Unkn.	240.00
XX-01-287	Tuneful Angel 359	M.I. Hummel	Open	Unkn.	80.00
XX-01-288	Umbrella Boy 152/0/A	M.I. Hummel	Open	Unkn.	530.00
XX-01-289	Umbrella Boy 152/II/A	M.I. Hummel	Open	Unkn.	1300.00
XX-01-290	Umbrella Girl 152/0/B	M.I. Hummel	Open	Unkn.	530.00
XX-01-291	Umbrella Girl 152/II/B	M.I. Hummel	Open	Unkn.	1300.00
XX-01-292	Village Boy 51/3/0	M.I. Hummel	Open	Unkn.	110.00
XX-01-293	Village Boy 51/2/0	M.I. Hummel	Open	Unkn.	125.00
XX-01-294	Village Boy 51/0	M.I. Hummel	Open	Unkn.	220.00
XX-01-295	Visiting an Invalid 382	M.I. Hummel	Open	Unkn.	195.00
XX-01-296	Volunteers 50/2/0	M.I. Hummel	Open	Unkn.	205.00
XX-01-297	Volunteers 50/0	M.I. Hummel	Open	Unkn.	270.00
XX-01-298	Waiter 154/0	M.I. Hummel	Open	Unkn.	195.00
XX-01-299	Waiter 154/I	M.I. Hummel	Open	Unkn.	260.00
XX-01-300	Wash Day 321	M.I. Hummel	Open	Unkn.	260.00
89-01-301	Wash Day 321/4/0	M.I. Hummel	Open	Unkn.	90.00
XX-01-302	Watchful Angel 194	M.I. Hummel	Open	Unkn.	290.00
XX-01-303	Wayside Devotion 28/II	M.I. Hummel	Open	Unkn.	395.00
XX-01-304	Wayside Devotion 28/III	M.I. Hummel	Open	Unkn.	520.00
XX-01-305	Wayside Harmony 111/3/0	M.I. Hummel	Open	Unkn.	135.00
XX-01-306	Wayside Harmony 111/I	M.I. Hummel	Open	Unkn.	245.00
XX-01-307	Weary Wanderer 204	M.I. Hummel	Open	Unkn.	225.00
XX-01-308	We Congratulate 214/E/II	M.I. Hummel	Open	Unkn.	150.00
XX-01-309	We Congratulate 220	M.I. Hummel	Open	Unkn.	145.00
90-01-310	What's New? 418	M.I. Hummel	Open	Unkn.	260.00
XX-01-311	Which Hand? 258	M.I. Hummel	Open	Unkn.	180.00
92-01-312	Whistler's Duet 413	M.I. Hummel	Open	Unkn.	250.00
XX-01-313	Whitsuntide 163	M.I. Hummel	Open	Unkn.	290.00
88-01-314	Winter Song 476	M.I. Hummel	Open	Unkn.	100.00
XX-01-315	With Loving Greetings 309	M.I. Hummel	Open	Unkn.	175.00
XX-01-316	Worship 84/0	M.I. Hummel	Open	Unkn.	145.00
Goebel/Schmid		**M.I. Hummel's Temp. Out of Production**			
XX-02-001	Angel Serenade 260/E	M.I. Hummel	Suspd.	Unkn.	N/A
XX-02-002	Apple Tree Boy 142/X	M.I. Hummel	Suspd.	Unkn.	17000.00
XX-02-003	Apple Tree Girl 141/X	M.I. Hummel	Suspd.	Unkn.	17000.00
XX-02-004	Blessed Child 78/I/83	M.I. Hummel	Suspd.	Unkn.	35.00
XX-02-005	Blessed Child 78/II/83	M.I. Hummel	Suspd.	Unkn.	40.00
XX-02-006	Blessed Child 78/III/83	M.I. Hummel	Suspd.	Unkn.	50.00
XX-02-007	Bookworm 3/II	M.I. Hummel	Suspd.	Unkn.	900-1200.
XX-02-008	Bookworm 3/III	M.I. Hummel	Suspd.	Unkn.	975-1300.
XX-02-009	Christ Child 18	M.I. Hummel	Suspd.	Unkn.	120-300.
XX-02-010	Donkey 260/L	M.I. Hummel	Suspd.	Unkn.	115.00
XX-02-011	Festival Harmony, with Mandolin 172/II	M.I. Hummel	Suspd.	Unkn.	325-400.
XX-02-012	Festival Harmony ,with Flute 173/II	M.I. Hummel	Suspd.	Unkn.	325-400.
XX-02-013	Flower Madonna, color 10/III/II	M.I. Hummel	Suspd.	Unkn.	375-475.
XX-02-014	Flower Madonna, white 10/III/W	M.I. Hummel	Suspd.	Unkn.	250-310.
XX-02-015	Going to Grandma's 52/I	M.I. Hummel	Suspd.	Unkn.	325-390.
XX-02-016	Good Night 260/D	M.I. Hummel	Suspd.	Unkn.	120.00
XX-02-017	Happy Traveler 109/II	M.I. Hummel	Suspd.	Unkn.	350-750.
XX-02-018	Hello 124/I	M.I. Hummel	Suspd.	Unkn.	160-230.
XX-02-019	Holy Child 70	M.I. Hummel	Suspd.	Unkn.	135-160.
XX-02-020	"Hummel" Display Plaque 187	M.I. Hummel	Suspd.	Unkn.	150-200.
XX-02-021	King, Kneeling 260/P	M.I. Hummel	Suspd.	Unkn.	430.00
XX-02-022	King, Moorish 260/N	M.I. Hummel	Suspd.	Unkn.	450.00
XX-02-023	King, Standing 260/O	M.I. Hummel	Suspd.	Unkn.	450.00
XX-02-024	Little Band 392	M.I. Hummel	Suspd.	Unkn.	132-225.
XX-02-025	Little Fiddler 2/II	M.I. Hummel	Suspd.	Unkn.	900-1200.
XX-02-026	Little Fiddler 2/III	M.I. Hummel	Suspd.	Unkn.	975-1300.
XX-02-027	Little Tooter 260/K	M.I. Hummel	Suspd.	Unkn.	140.00
XX-02-028	Lullaby 24/III	M.I. Hummel	Suspd.	Unkn.	285-450.
XX-02-029	Madonna w/o Halo, color 46/I/6	M.I. Hummel	Suspd.	Unkn.	N/A
XX-02-030	Madonna w/o Halo,white 46/I/W	M.I. Hummel	Suspd.	Unkn.	N/A
XX-02-031	Madonna Praying, color 46/III/6	M.I. Hummel	Suspd.	Unkn.	155.00
XX-02-032	Madonna Praying, white 46/0/W	M.I. Hummel	Suspd.	Unkn.	45.00
XX-02-033	Madonna Praying, white 46/I/W	M.I. Hummel	Suspd.	Unkn.	75-95.00
XX-02-034	Meditation 13/II	M.I. Hummel	Suspd.	Unkn.	275-360.
XX-02-035	Meditation 13/V	M.I. Hummel	Suspd.	Unkn.	975-1250.
XX-02-036	Merry Wanderer 7/III	M.I. Hummel	Suspd.	Unkn.	975-1200.
XX-02-037	Merry Wanderer 7/X	M.I. Hummel	Suspd.	Unkn.	17000.00
XX-02-038	Ox 260/M	M.I. Hummel	Suspd.	Unkn.	130.00
XX-02-039	School Boys 170/III	M.I. Hummel	Suspd.	Unkn.	1850-5000.
XX-02-040	School Girls 177/III	M.I. Hummel	Suspd.	Unkn.	1850-5000.
XX-02-041	Sensitive Hunter 6/II	M.I. Hummel	Suspd.	Unkn.	300-400.
XX-02-042	Sheep (Lying) 260/R	M.I. Hummel	Suspd.	Unkn.	40.00
XX-02-043	Sheep (Standing) w/ Lamb 260/H	M.I. Hummel	Suspd.	Unkn.	80.00
XX-02-044	Shepherd, Standing 260/G	M.I. Hummel	Suspd.	Unkn.	475.00
XX-02-045	Shepherd Boy, Kneeling 260/J	M.I. Hummel	Suspd.	Unkn.	270.00
XX-02-046	Spring Cheer 72	M.I. Hummel	Suspd.	Unkn.	150-200.
XX-02-047	Spring Dance 353/I	M.I. Hummel	Suspd.	Unkn.	265-500.
XX-02-048	Telling Her Secret 196/I	M.I. Hummel	Suspd.	Unkn.	240-375.
XX-02-049	To Market 49/I	M.I. Hummel	Suspd.	Unkn.	240-420.
XX-02-050	Volunteers 50/I	M.I. Hummel	Suspd.	Unkn.	240-425.
XX-02-051	Village Boy 51/I	M.I. Hummel	Suspd.	Unkn.	110-250.
XX-02-052	We Congratulate 260/F	M.I. Hummel	Suspd.	Unkn.	330.00
XX-02-053	Worship 84/V	M.I. Hummel	Suspd.	Unkn.	925-1050.
XX-02-054	16-Pc. Set Figs. only, Color, 214/A/M/I, B/I, A/K/I, C/I, D/I, E/I, F/I, G/I, H/I, J/I, K/I, L/I, M/I, N/I, O/I, 366/I	M.I. Hummel	Suspd.	Unkn.	1820.00
XX-02-055	17-Pc. Set large color 16 Figs.& Wooden Stable 260 A-R	M.I. Hummel	Suspd.	Unkn.	4540.00
Goebel/Schmid		**M.I. Hummel Collectibles Figurines Retired**			
XX-03-001	Jubilee 416	M.I. Hummel	Closed	200.00	300-375.
XX-03-002	Supreme Protection 364	M.I. Hummel	Closed	150.00	300-400.
XX-03-003	Puppy Love I	M.I. Hummel	Closed	125.00	300-750.
XX-03-004	Strolling Along 5	M.I. Hummel	Closed	115.00	225-625.
XX-03-005	Signs Of Spring 203/2/0	M.I. Hummel	Closed	120.00	150-400.
XX-03-006	Signs Of Spring 203/I	M.I. Hummel	Closed	155.00	200-900.
XX-03-007	Globe Trotter 79	M.I. Hummel	Closed	Unkn.	200-400.
Goebel/Schmid		**M.I. Hummel Collectibles-Century Collection**			
86-04-001	Chapel Time 442	M.I. Hummel	Closed	500.00	1200-2000.
87-04-002	Pleasant Journey 406	M.I. Hummel	Closed	500.00	1200-2000.
88-04-003	Call to Worship 441	M.I. Hummel	Closed	600.00	750-1000.
89-04-004	Harmony in Four Parts 471	M.I. Hummel	Closed	850.00	900-1250.

Company / Number	Name	Series / Artist	Edition Limit	Issue Price	Quote
90-04-005	Let's Tell the World 487	M.I. Hummel	Closed	875.00	1000-1500.
91-04-006	We Wish You The Best 600	M.I. Hummel	Closed	1300.00	900-1500.
92-04-007	On Our Way 472	M.I. Hummel	Closed	950.00	1200.00
93-04-008	Welcome Spring 635	M.I. Hummel	Yr.Iss.	1085.00	1085.00
Goebel/Schmid		**M.I. Hummel Collectibles Nativity Components**			
XX-05-001	Madonna 214/A/M/0	M.I. Hummel	Open	Unkn.	120.00
XX-05-002	Infant Jesus 214/A/K/0	M.I. Hummel	Open	Unkn.	40.00
XX-05-003	St. Joseph 214/B/0	M.I. Hummel	Open	Unkn.	120.00
XX-05-004	Shepherd Standing 214/F/0	M.I. Hummel	Open	Unkn.	145.00
XX-05-005	Shepherd Kneeling 214/G/0	M.I. Hummel	Open	Unkn.	110.00
XX-05-006	Donkey 214/J/0	M.I. Hummel	Open	Unkn.	50.00
XX-05-007	Ox,214/K/0	M.I. Hummel	Open	Unkn.	50.00
XX-05-008	King, Moorish 214/L/0	M.I. Hummel	Open	Unkn.	140.00
XX-05-009	King, Kneeling 214M/0	M.I. Hummel	Open	Unkn.	130.00
XX-05-010	King, Kneeling w/ Box 214/N/0	M.I. Hummel	Open	Unkn.	131.00
XX-05-011	Lamb 214/O/0	M.I. Hummel	Open	Unkn.	17.00
XX-05-012	Flying Angel 366/0	M.I. Hummel	Open	Unkn.	85.00
XX-05-013	Little Tooter 214/14/0	M.I. Hummel	Open	Unkn.	95.00
XX-05-014	Small Camel Standing	Goebel	Open	Unkn.	160.00
XX-05-015	Small Camel Lying	Goebel	Open	Unkn.	160.00
XX-05-016	Small Camel Kneeling	Goebel	Open	Unkn.	160.00
XX-05-017	Madonna 214/A/M/I	M.I. Hummel	Open	Unkn.	160.00
XX-05-018	Infant Jesus 214/A/K/I	M.I. Hummel	Open	Unkn.	60.00
XX-05-019	St. Joseph color 214/B/I	M.I. Hummel	Open	Unkn.	160.00
XX-05-020	Good Night 214/C/I	M.I. Hummel	Open	Unkn.	80.00
XX-05-021	Angel Serenade 214/D/I	M.I. Hummel	Open	Unkn.	80.00
XX-05-022	We Congratulate 214/E/I	M.I. Hummel	Open	Unkn.	150.00
XX-05-023	Shepherd with Sheep-1 piece 214/F/I	M.I. Hummel	Open	Unkn.	165.00
XX-05-024	Shepherd Boy 214/G/I	M.I. Hummel	Open	Unkn.	120.00
XX-05-025	Little Tooter 214/H/I	M.I. Hummel	Open	Unkn.	110.00
XX-05-026	Donkey 214/J/I	M.I. Hummel	Open	Unkn.	65.00
XX-05-027	Ox 214/K/I	M.I. Hummel	Open	Unkn.	65.00
XX-05-028	King, Moorish 214/L/I	M.I. Hummel	Open	Unkn.	170.00
XX-05-029	King, Kneeling 214/M/I	M.I. Hummel	Open	Unkn.	160.00
XX-05-030	King, Kneeling w/Box 214/N/I	M.I. Hummel	Open	Unkn.	150.00
XX-05-031	Lamb 214/0/I	M.I. Hummel	Open	Unkn.	20.00
XX-05-032	Flying Angel/color 366/I	M.I. Hummel	Open	Unkn.	115.00
XX-05-033	Camel Standing	Goebel	Open	Unkn.	205.00
XX-05-034	Camel Lying	Goebel	Open	Unkn.	205.00
XX-05-035	Camel Kneeling	Goebel	Open	Unkn.	205.00
XX-05-036	Madonna-260/A	M.I. Hummel	Open	Unkn.	590.00
XX-05-037	St. Joseph 260/B	M.I. Hummel	Open	Unkn.	590.00
XX-05-038	Infant Jesus 260/C	M.I. Hummel	Open	Unkn.	120.00
XX-05-039	Good Night 260/D	M.I. Hummel	Suspd.	Unkn.	120.00
XX-05-040	Angel Serenade 260/E	M.I. Hummel	Suspd.	Unkn.	115.00
XX-05-041	We Congratulate 260/F	M.I. Hummel	Suspd.	Unkn.	330.00
XX-05-042	Shepherd, Standing 260/G	M.I. Hummel	Suspd.	Unkn.	475.00
XX-05-043	Sheep (Standing) w/ Lamb 260/H	M.I. Hummel	Suspd.	Unkn.	80.00
XX-05-044	Shepherd Boy, Kneeling 260/J	M.I. Hummel	Suspd.	Unkn.	270.00
XX-05-045	Little Tooter 260/K	M.I. Hummel	Suspd.	Unkn.	140.00
XX-05-046	Donkey 260/L	M.I. Hummel	Suspd.	Unkn.	115.00
XX-05-047	Ox 260/M	M.I. Hummel	Suspd.	Unkn.	130.00
XX-05-048	King, Moorish 260/N	M.I. Hummel	Suspd.	Unkn.	450.00
XX-05-049	King, Standing 260/O	M.I. Hummel	Suspd.	Unkn.	450.00
XX-05-050	King, Kneeling 260/P	M.I. Hummel	Suspd.	Unkn.	430.00
XX-05-051	Sheep (Lying) 260/R	M.I. Hummel	Suspd.	Unkn.	40.00
XX-05-052	Holy Family,3 Pcs., Color 214/A/M/0, B/0, A/K/0	M.I. Hummel	Open	Unkn.	270.00
XX-05-053	Holy Family 3 Pcs.,Color 214/A/M/I, B/I, A/K/I	M.I. Hummel	Open	Unkn.	380.00
XX-05-054	12-Pc. Set Figs. only, Color, 214/A/M/I, B/I, A/K/I, F/I,G/I,J/I K/I, L/I, M/I, N/I, O/I, 366/I	M.I. Hummel	Open	Unkn.	1350.00
XX-05-055	16-Pc. Set Figs. only, Color, 214/A/M/I, B/I, A/K/I, C/I, D/I, E/I, F/I, G/I, H/I, J/I, K/I, L/I, M/I, N/I, O/I, 366/I	M.I. Hummel	Suspd.	Unkn.	1820.00
XX-05-056	17-Pc. Set Large Color 16 Figs.& Wooden Stable 260 A-R	M.I. Hummel	Suspd.	Unkn.	4540.00
XX-05-057	Stable only, fits 3-pc. HUM214 Set	M.I. Hummel	Open	Unkn.	45.00
XX-05-058	Stable only, fits12 or16-pc. HUM 214/II Set	M.I. Hummel	Open	Unkn.	100.00
XX-05-059	Stable only, fits 16-piece HUM260 Set	M.I. Hummel	Open	Unkn.	400.00
Goebel/Schmid		**M.I. Hummel Collectibles-Madonna Figurines**			
XX-06-001	Flower Madonna, color 10/I/II	M.I. Hummel	Open	Unkn.	390.00
XX-06-002	Flower Madonna, white 10/I/W	M.I. Hummel	Open	Unkn.	165.00
XX-06-003	Madonna Holding Child, color 151/II	M.I. Hummel	Open	Unkn.	115.00
XX-06-004	Madonna Holding Child, white 151/W	M.I. Hummel	Open	Unkn.	320.00
XX-06-005	Madonna with Halo, color 45/I/6	M.I. Hummel	Open	Unkn.	115.00
XX-06-006	Madonna with Halo, white 45/I/W	M.I. Hummel	Open	Unkn.	70.00
XX-06-007	Madonna without Halo, color 46/I/6	M.I. Hummel	Suspd.	Unkn.	75.00
XX-06-008	Madonna without Halo, white 46/I/W	M.I. Hummel	Suspd.	Unkn.	50.00
Goebel/Schmid		**M.I. Hummel Collectibles-Christmas Angels**			
93-07-001	Angel in Cloud 585	M.I. Hummel	Open	25.00	25.00
93-07-002	Angel with Lute 580	M.I. Hummel	Open	25.00	25.00
93-07-003	Angel with Trumpet 586	M.I. Hummel	Open	25.00	25.00
93-07-004	Celestial Musician 578	M.I. Hummel	Open	25.00	25.00
93-07-005	Festival Harmony with Flute 577	M.I. Hummel	Open	25.00	25.00
93-07-006	Festival Harmony with Mandolin 576	M.I. Hummel	Open	25.00	25.00
93-07-007	Gentle Song 582	M.I. Hummel	Open	25.00	25.00
93-07-008	Heavenly Angel 575	M.I. Hummel	Open	25.00	25.00
93-07-009	Prayer of Thanks 581	M.I. Hummel	Open	25.00	25.00
93-07-010	Song of Praise 579	M.I. Hummel	Open	25.00	25.00
Goebel/Schmid		**First Edition M.I. Hummel Miniatures**			
91-08-001	Accordion Boy -37225	M.I. Hummel	Suspd.	105.00	105.00
89-08-002	Apple Tree Boy -37219	M.I. Hummel	Suspd.	115.00	125-250.
90-08-003	Baker -37222	M.I. Hummel	Suspd.	100.00	105-125.
92-08-004	Bavarian Church (Display) -37370	M.I. Hummel	Retrd.	60.00	60.00
88-08-005	Bavarian Cottage (Display) -37355	M.I. Hummel	Retrd.	60.00	64.00
90-08-006	Bavarian Marketsquare Bridge(Dsply) -37358	M.I. Hummel	Retrd.	110.00	110.00
88-08-007	Bavarian Village (Display) -37356	M.I. Hummel	Retrd.	100.00	100.00
91-08-008	Busy Student -37226	M.I. Hummel	Suspd.	105.00	105.00
91-08-009	Countryside School (Display) -37365	M.I. Hummel	Retrd.	100.00	100.00
90-08-010	Cinderella -37223	M.I. Hummel	Suspd.	115.00	115.00
89-08-011	Doll Bath -37214	M.I. Hummel	Suspd.	95.00	115-175.
92-08-012	Goose Girl -37238	M.I. Hummel	Suspd.	130.00	130.00
89-08-013	Little Fiddler -37211	M.I. Hummel	Suspd.	90.00	120-200.
89-08-014	Little Sweeper -37212	M.I. Hummel	Suspd.	90.00	125-250.
90-08-015	Marketsquare Hotel (Display)-37359	M.I. Hummel	Retrd.	70.00	70.00
90-08-016	Marketsquare Flower Stand (Display) -37360	M.I. Hummel	Retrd.	35.00	35.00
89-08-017	Merry Wanderer -37213	M.I. Hummel	Suspd.	95.00	120-200.

Company / Number	Name	Series / Artist	Edition Limit	Issue Price	Quote
91-08-018	Merry Wanderer Dealer Plaque -37229	M.I. Hummel	Retrd.	130.00	130.00
89-08-019	Postman -37217	M.I. Hummel	Suspd.	95.00	100-200.
91-08-020	Roadside Shrine (Display)-37366	M.I. Hummel	Retrd.	60.00	60.00
92-08-021	School Boy -37236	M.I. Hummel	Suspd.	120.00	120.00
91-08-022	Serenade -37228	M.I. Hummel	Suspd.	105.00	105.00
92-08-023	Snow-Covered Mountain (Display)-37371	M.I. Hummel	Retrd.	100.00	100.00
89-08-024	Stormy Weather -37215	M.I. Hummel	Suspd.	115.00	175-250.
92-08-025	Trees (Display)-37369	M.I. Hummel	Retrd.	40.00	40.00
89-08-026	Visiting an Invalid -37218	M.I. Hummel	Suspd.	105.00	115-130.
90-08-027	Waiter -37221	M.I. Hummel	Suspd.	100.00	125-250.
92-08-028	Wayside Harmony -37237	M.I. Hummel	Suspd.	140.00	140.00
91-08-029	We Congratulate -37227	M.I. Hummel	Suspd.	130.00	130.00
Goebel/Schmid		**M.I. Hummel Collectors Club Exclusives**			
77-09-001	Valentine Gift 387	M.I. Hummel	Closed	45.00	250-700.
78-09-002	Smiling Through Plaque 690	M.I. Hummel	Closed	50.00	175-250.
79-09-003	Bust of Sister-M.I.Hummel HU-3	G. Skrobek	Closed	75.00	165-300.
80-09-004	Valentine Joy 399	M.I. Hummel	Closed	95.00	200-300.
81-09-005	Daisies Don't Tell 380	M.I. Hummel	Closed	80.00	180-250.
82-09-005	It's Cold 421	M.I. Hummel	Closed	80.00	200-300.
83-09-007	What Now? 422	M.I. Hummel	Closed	90.00	200-300.
83-09-008	Valentine Gift Mini Pendant	R. Olszewski	Closed	85.00	175-300.
84-09-009	Coffee Break 409	M.I. Hummel	Closed	90.00	250-350.
85-09-010	Smiling Through 408/0	M.I. Hummel	Closed	125.00	300-325.
86-09-011	Birthday Candle 440	M.I. Hummel	Closed	95.00	150-300.
86-09-012	What Now? Mini Pendant	R. Olszewski	Closed	125.00	225-250.
87-09-013	Morning Concert 447	M.I. Hummel	Closed	98.00	175-250.
87-09-014	Little Cocopah Indian Girl	T. DeGrazia	Closed	140.00	175-300.
88-09-015	The Surprise 431	M.I. Hummel	Closed	125.00	275.00
89-09-016	Mickey and Minnie	H. Fischer	Closed	275.00	350-500.
89-09-017	Hello World 429	M.I. Hummel	Closed	130.00	250.00
90-09-018	I Wonder 486	M.I. Hummel	Closed	140.00	175.00
91-09-019	Gift From A Friend 485	M.I. Hummel	Open	160.00	160.00
91-09-020	Miniature Morning Concert w/ Display	R. Olszewski	Open	175.00	190.00
92-09-021	My Wish Is Small 463/0	M.I. Hummel	Open	170.00	170.00
92-09-022	Cheeky Fellow 554	M.I. Hummel	Open	120.00	120.00
93-09-023	I Didn't Do It 623	M.I. Hummel	Open	175.00	175.00
93-09-024	Sweet As Can Be 541	M.I. Hummel	Open	127.00	127.00
Goebel/Schmid		**Special Edition M.I. Hummel Anniversary Figurine For 5 & 10 & 15 Year Club Members**			
90-10-001	Flower Girl 548 (5 year)	M.I. Hummel	Open	105.00	120.00
90-10-002	The Little Pair 449 (10 year)	M.I. Hummel	Open	170.00	190.00
91-10-003	Honey Lover 312 (15 year)	M.I. Hummel	Open	190.00	196.00
Gorham		**A Boy And His Dog (Four Seasons)**			
72-01-001	A Boy Meets His Dog	N. Rockwell	2,500	200.00	1575.00
72-01-002	Adventurers Between Adventures	N. Rockwell	2,500	Set	Set
72-01-003	The Mysterious Malady	N. Rockwell	2,500	Set	Set
72-01-004	Pride of Parenthood	N. Rockwell	2,500	Set	Set
Gorham		**Young Love (Four Seasons)**			
73-02-001	Downhill Daring	N. Rockwell	2,500	250.00	1100.00
73-02-002	Beguiling Buttercup	N. Rockwell	2,500	Set	Set
73-02-003	Flying High	N. Rockwell	2,500	Set	Set
73-02-004	A Scholarly Pace	N. Rockwell	2,500	Set	Set
Gorham		**Four Ages of Love (Four Seasons)**			
74-03-001	Gaily Sharing Vintage Times	N. Rockwell	2,500	300.00	1250.00
74-03-002	Sweet Song So Young	N. Rockwell	2,500	Set	Set
74-03-003	Flowers In Tender Bloom	N. Rockwell	2,500	Set	Set
74-03-004	Fondly Do We Remember	N. Rockwell	2,500	Set	Set
Gorham		**Grandpa and Me (Four Seasons)**			
75-04-001	Gay Blades	N. Rockwell	2,500	300.00	900.00
75-04-002	Day Dreamers	N. Rockwell	2,500	Set	Set
75-04-003	Goin' Fishing	N. Rockwell	2,500	Set	Set
75-04-004	Pensive Pals	N. Rockwell	2,500	Set	Set
Gorham		**Me and My Pal (Four Seasons)**			
76-05-001	A Licking Good Bath	N. Rockwell	2,500	300.00	900.00
76-05-002	Young Man's Fancy	N. Rockwell	2,500	Set	Set
76-05-003	Fisherman's Paradise	N. Rockwell	2,500	Set	Set
76-05-004	Disastrous Daring	N. Rockwell	2,500	Set	Set
Gorham		**Grand Pals (Four Seasons)**			
77-06-001	Snow Sculpturing	N. Rockwell	2,500	350.00	675.00
77-06-002	Soaring Spirits	N. Rockwell	2,500	Set	Set
77-06-003	Fish Finders	N. Rockwell	2,500	Set	Set
77-06-004	Ghostly Gourds	N. Rockwell	2,500	Set	Set
Gorham		**Going On Sixteen (Four Seasons)**			
78-07-001	Chilling Chore	N. Rockwell	2,500	400.00	675.00
78-07-002	Sweet Serenade	N. Rockwell	2,500	Set	Set
78-07-003	Shear Agony	N. Rockwell	2,500	Set	Set
78-07-004	Pilgrimage	N. Rockwell	2,500	Set	Set
Gorham		**Tender Years (Four Seasons)**			
79-08-001	New Year Look	N. Rockwell	2,500	500.00	550.00
79-08-002	Spring Tonic	N. Rockwell	2,500	Set	Set
79 08 003	Cool Aid	N. Rockwell	2,500	Set	Set
79-08-004	Chilly Reception	N. Rockwell	2,500	Set	Set
Gorham		**A Helping Hand (Four Seasons)**			
80-09-001	Year End Court	N. Rockwell	2,500	650.00	700.00
80-09-002	Closed For Business	N. Rockwell	2,500	Set	Set
80-09-003	Swatter's Right	N. Rockwell	2,500	Set	Set
80-09-004	Coal Seasons Coming	N. Rockwell	2,500	Set	Set
Gorham		**Dad's Boy (Four Seasons)**			
81-10-001	Ski Skills	N. Rockwell	2,500	750.00	800.00
81-10-002	In His Spirit	N. Rockwell	2,500	Set	Set
81-10-003	Trout Dinner	N. Rockwell	2,500	Set	Set
81-10-004	Careful Aim	N. Rockwell	2,500	Set	Set
Gorham		**Rockwell**			
74-11-001	Weighing In	N. Rockwell	Closed	40.00	125.00
74-11-002	Missing Tooth	N. Rockwell	Closed	30.00	75.00
74-11-003	Tiny Tim	N. Rockwell	Closed	30.00	75.00
74-11-004	At The Vets	N. Rockwell	Closed	25.00	65.00
74-11-005	Fishing	N. Rockwell	Closed	50.00	100.00
74-11-006	Batter Up	N. Rockwell	Closed	40.00	90.00
74-11-007	Skating	N. Rockwell	Closed	37.50	85.00
74-11-008	Captain	N. Rockwell	Closed	45.00	95.00
75-11-009	Boy And His Dog	N. Rockwell	Closed	37.50	85.00
75-11-010	No Swimming	N. Rockwell	Closed	35.00	80.00
75-11-011	Old Mill Pond	N. Rockwell	Closed	45.00	95.00
76-11-012	Saying Grace	N. Rockwell	Closed	75.00	120.00
76-11-013	God Rest Ye Merry Gentlemen	N. Rockwell	Closed	50.00	800.00
76-11-014	Tackled (Ad Stand)	N. Rockwell	Closed	35.00	85.00
76-11-015	Independence	N. Rockwell	Closed	40.00	150.00
76-11-016	Marriage License	N. Rockwell	Closed	50.00	175.00
76-11-017	The Occultist	N. Rockwell	Closed	50.00	145-175.00
81-11-018	Day in the Life Boy II	N. Rockwell	Closed	75.00	85.00
81-11-019	Wet Sport	N. Rockwell	Closed	85.00	85.00
82-11-020	April Fool's (At The Curiosity Shop)	N. Rockwell	Closed	55.00	110.00
82-11-021	Tackled (Rockwell Name Signed)	N. Rockwell	Closed	45.00	70.00
82-11-022	A Day in the Life Boy III	N. Rockwell	Closed	85.00	85.00
82-11-023	A Day in the Life Girl III	N. Rockwell	Closed	85.00	85.00
81-11-024	Christmas Dancers	N. Rockwell	7,500	130.00	130.00
82-11-025	Marriage License	N. Rockwell	5,000	110.00	400.00
82-11-026	Saying Grace	N. Rockwell	5,000	110.00	450.00
82-11-027	Triple Self Portrait	N. Rockwell	5,000	300.00	500.00
80-11-028	Jolly Coachman	N. Rockwell	7,500	75.00	125.00
82-11-029	Merrie Christmas	N. Rockwell	7,500	75.00	75.00
83-11-030	Facts of Life	N. Rockwell	7,500	110.00	120.00
83-11-031	Antique Dealer	N. Rockwell	7,500	130.00	130.00
83-11-032	Christmas Goose	N. Rockwell	7,500	75.00	75.00
84-11-033	Serenade	N. Rockwell	7,500	95.00	95.00
84-11-034	Card Tricks	N. Rockwell	7,500	110.00	110.00
84-11-035	Santa's Friend	N. Rockwell	7,500	75.00	75.00
85-11-036	Puppet Maker	N. Rockwell	7,500	130.00	130.00
85-11-037	The Old Sign Painter	N. Rockwell	7,500	130.00	130.00
86-11-038	Drum For Tommy	N. Rockwell	Annual	90.00	90.00
87-11-039	Santa Planning His Annual Visit	N. Rockwell	7,500	95.00	95.00
88-11-040	Home for the Holidays	N. Rockwell	7,500	100.00	100.00
88-11-041	Gary Cooper in Hollywood	N. Rockwell	15,000	90.00	90.00
88-11-042	Cramming	N. Rockwell	15,000	80.00	80.00
88-11-043	Dolores & Eddie	N. Rockwell	15,000	75.00	75.00
88-11-044	Confrontation	N. Rockwell	15,000	75.00	75.00
88-11-045	The Diary	N. Rockwell	15,000	80.00	80.00
Gorham		**Miniature Christmas Figurines**			
79-12-001	Tiny Tim	N. Rockwell	Yr.Iss.	15.00	20.00
80-12-002	Santa Plans His Trip	N. Rockwell	Yr.Iss.	15.00	15.00
81-12-003	Yuletide Reckoning	N. Rockwell	Yr.Iss.	20.00	20.00
82-12-004	Checking Good Deeds	N. Rockwell	Yr.Iss.	20.00	20.00
83-12-005	Santa's Friend	N. Rockwell	Yr.Iss.	20.00	20.00
84-12-006	Downhill Daring	N. Rockwell	Yr.Iss.	20.00	20.00
85-12-007	Christmas Santa	T. Nast	Yr.Iss.	20.00	20.00
86-12-008	Christmas Santa	T. Nast	Yr.Iss.	25.00	25.00
87-12-009	Annual Thomas Nast Santa	T. Nast	Yr.Iss.	25.00	25.00
Gorham		**Miniatures**			
81-13-001	Young Man's Fancy	N. Rockwell	Closed	55.00	55.00
81-13-002	Beguiling Buttercup	N. Rockwell	Closed	45.00	45.00
81-13-003	Gay Blades	N. Rockwell	Closed	45.00	70.00
81-13-004	Sweet Song So Young	N. Rockwell	Closed	55.00	55.00
81-13-005	Snow Sculpture	N. Rockwell	Closed	45.00	70.00
81-13-006	Sweet Serenade	N. Rockwell	Closed	45.00	45.00
81-13-007	At the Vets	N. Rockwell	Closed	27.50	39.50
81-13-008	Boy Meets His Dog	N. Rockwell	Closed	37.50	37.50
81-13-009	Downhill Daring	N. Rockwell	Closed	45.00	70.00
81-13-010	Flowers in Tender Bloom	N. Rockwell	Closed	60.00	60.00
82-13-011	Triple Self Portrait	N. Rockwell	Closed	60.00	175.00
82-13-012	Marriage License	N. Rockwell	Closed	60.00	75.00
82-13-013	The Runaway	N. Rockwell	Closed	50.00	50.00
82-13-014	Vintage Times	N. Rockwell	Closed	50.00	50.00
82-13-015	The Annual Visit	N. Rockwell	Closed	50.00	75.00
83-13-016	Trout Dinner	N. Rockwell	15,000	60.00	60.00
84-13-017	Ghostly Gourds	N. Rockwell	Closed	60.00	60.00
84-13-018	Years End Court	N. Rockwell	Closed	60.00	60.00
84-13-019	Shear Agony	N. Rockwell	Closed	60.00	60.00
84-13-020	Pride of Parenthood	N. Rockwell	Closed	50.00	50.00
84-13-021	Goin Fishing	N. Rockwell	Closed	60.00	60.00
84-13-022	Careful Aims	N. Rockwell	Closed	55.00	55.00
84-13-023	In His Spirit	N. Rockwell	Closed	60.00	60.00
85-13-024	To Love & Cherish	N. Rockwell	Closed	32.50	32.50
85-13-025	Spring Checkup	N. Rockwell	Closed	60.00	60.00
85-13-026	Engineer	N. Rockwell	Closed	55.00	55.00
85-13-027	Best Friends	N. Rockwell	Closed	27.50	27.50
85-13-028	Muscle Bound	N. Rockwell	Closed	30.00	30.00
85-13-029	New Arrival	N. Rockwell	Closed	32.50	32.50
85-13-030	Little Red Truck	N. Rockwell	Closed	25.00	25.00
86-13-031	The Old Sign Painter	N. Rockwell	Closed	70.00	75.00
86-13-032	The Graduate	N. Rockwell	Closed	30.00	30.00
86-13-033	Football Season	N. Rockwell	Closed	60.00	60.00
86-13-034	Lemonade Stand	N. Rockwell	Closed	60.00	60.00
86-13-035	Welcome Mat	N. Rockwell	Closed	70.00	70.00
86-13-036	Shoulder Ride	N. Rockwell	Closed	50.00	60.00
86-13-037	Morning Walk	N. Rockwell	Closed	60.00	60.00
86-13-038	Little Angel	N. Rockwell	Closed	50.00	60.00
87-13-039	Starstruck	N. Rockwell	15,000	75.00	75.00
87-13-040	The Prom Dress	N. Rockwell	15,000	75.00	75.00
87-13-041	The Milkmaid	N. Rockwell	15,000	80.00	85.00
87-13-042	Cinderella	N. Rockwell	15,000	70.00	75.00
87-13-043	Springtime	N. Rockwell	15,000	65.00	65.00
87-13-044	Babysitter	N. Rockwell	15,000	75.00	75.00
87-13-045	Between The Acts	N. Rockwell	15,000	60.00	60.00
Gorham		**Old Timers (Four Seasons Miniatures)**			
82-14-001	Canine Solo	N. Rockwell	2,500	250.00	250.00
82-14-002	Sweet Surprise	N. Rockwell	2,500	Set	Set
82-14-003	Lazy Days	N. Rockwell	2,500	Set	Set
82-14-004	Fancy Footwork	N. Rockwell	2,500	Set	Set
Gorham		**Life With Father (Four Seasons Miniatures)**			
83-15-001	Big Decision	N. Rockwell	2,500	250.00	250.00
83-15-002	Blasting Out	N. Rockwell	2,500	Set	Set
83-15-003	Cheering The Champs	N. Rockwell	2,500	Set	Set
83-15-004	A Tough One	N. Rockwell	2,500	Set	Set
Gorham		**Old Buddies (Four Seasons)**			
84-16-001	Shared Success	N. Rockwell	2,500	250.00	250.00
84-16-002	Hasty Retreat	N. Rockwell	2,500	Set	Set
84-16-003	Final Speech	N. Rockwell	2,500	Set	Set

Company / Number	Name	Series / Artist	Edition Limit	Issue Price	Quote
84-16-004	Endless Debate	N. Rockwell	2,500	Set	Set
Gorham		**Traveling Salesman (Four Seasons)**			
85-17-001	Horse Trader	N. Rockwell	2,500	275.00	275.00
85-17-002	Expert Salesman	N. Rockwell	2,500	Set	Set
85-17-003	Traveling Salesman	N. Rockwell	2,500	Set	Set
85-17-004	Country Pedlar	N. Rockwell	2,500	Set	Set
Gorham		**Vasari Figurines**			
71-18-001	Mercenary Warrior	Vasari	250	250.00	500.00
71-18-002	Ming Warrior	Vasari	250	200.00	400.00
71-18-003	Swiss Warrior	Vasari	250	250.00	1000.00
73-18-004	Austrian Hussar	Vasari	250	300.00	600.00
73-18-005	D'Artagnan	Vasari	250	250.00	800.00
73-18-006	English Crusader	Vasari	250	250.00	500.00
73-18-007	French Crusader	Vasari	250	250.00	500.00
73-18-008	German Hussar	Vasari	250	250.00	500.00
73-18-009	German Mercenary	Vasari	250	250.00	500.00
73-18-010	Italian Crusader	Vasari	250	250.00	500.00
73-18-011	Pirate	Vasari	250	200.00	400.00
73-18-012	Porthos	Vasari	250	250.00	500.00
73-18-013	Roman Centurion	Vasari	250	200.00	400.00
73-18-014	Spanish Grandee	Vasari	250	200.00	400.00
73-18-015	The Cossack	Vasari	250	250.00	500.00
73-18-016	Venetian Nobleman	Vasari	250	200.00	400.00
73-18-017	Viking	Vasari	250	200.00	400.00
73-18-018	Cellini	Vasari	250	400.00	800.00
73-18-019	Christ	Vasari	250	250.00	500.00
73-18-020	Creche	Vasari	250	500.00	1000.00
73-18-021	Leonardo Da Vinci	Vasari	200	250.00	500.00
73-18-022	Michelangelo	Vasari	200	250.00	500.00
73-18-023	Three Kings, (Set of 3)	Vasari	200	750.00	1500.00
73-18-024	Three Musketeers, (Set of 3)	Vasari	200	750.00	1500.00
Gorham		**Leyendecker Annual Christmas Figurines**			
88-19-001	Christmas Hug	J.C. Leyendecker	7,500	95.00	95.00
Granget		**Granget Wood Carvings**			
XX-01-001	Barn Owl, 20 inches	G. Granget	250	2000.00	7000.00
73-01-002	Black Grouse, large	G. Granget	250	2800.00	8600.00
73-01-003	Golden Eagle, large	G. Granget	250	2000.00	8000.00
73-01-004	Lynx, large	G. Granget	250	1600.00	6000.00
73-01-005	Mallard, large	G. Granget	250	2000.00	6500.00
XX-01-006	Peregrine Falcon, large	G. Granget	250	2250.00	6500.00
73-01-007	Rooster, large	G. Granget	250	2400.00	6000.00
73-01-008	Black Grouse, small	G. Granget	1,000	700.00	1500.00
73-01-009	Fox, small	G. Granget	1,000	650.00	1500.00
73-01-010	Golden Eagle, small	G. Granget	1,000	550.00	1500.00
73-01-011	Lynx, small	G. Granget	1,000	400.00	700.00
73-01-012	Mallard, small	G. Granget	1,000	500.00	700.00
73-01-013	Partridge, small	G. Granget	1,000	550.00	1200.00
XX-01-014	Peregrine Falcon, small	G. Granget	1,000	500.00	600.00
73-01-015	Rooster, small	G. Granget	1,000	600.00	1000.00
73-01-016	Wild Boar, small	G. Granget	1,000	275.00	1200.00
XX-01-017	Wild Sow with Young, large	G. Granget	1,000	2800.00	8000.00
73-01-018	Fox, large	G. Granget	200	2800.00	9000.00
73-01-019	Partridge. large	G. Granget	200	2400.00	8000.00
73-01-020	Wild Boar, large	G. Granget	200	2400.00	8000.00
XX-01-021	Wild Sow with Young, small	G. Granget	200	600.00	1500.00
XX-01-022	Barn Owl, 10 inches	G. Granget	2,500	600.00	700.00
XX-01-023	Barn Owl, 12.5 inches	G. Granget	1,500	700.00	1200.00
XX-01-024	Peregrine Falcon, medium	G. Granget	1,500	700.00	1200.00
XX-01-025	Ring-necked Pheasant, large	G. Granget	Unkn.	2250.00	8000.00
XX-01-026	Ring-necked Pheasant, small	G. Granget	Unkn.	500.00	1000.00
Dave Grossman Creations		**Saturday Evening Post**			
90-01-001	No Swimming NRP-901	Rockwell-Inspired	Open	50.00	50.00
90-01-002	Daydreamer NRP-902	Rockwell-Inspired	Open	55.00	55.00
90-01-003	Prom Dress NRP-903	Rockwell-Inspired	Open	60.00	60.00
90-01-004	Bedside Manner NRP-904	Rockwell-Inspired	Open	65.00	65.00
90-01-005	Runaway NRP-905	Rockwell-Inspired	Open	130.00	130.00
90-01-006	Big Moment NRP-906	Rockwell-Inspired	Retrd.	100.00	100.00
90-01-007	Doctor and Doll NRP-907	Rockwell-Inspired	Retrd.	110.00	110.00
90-01-008	Bottom of the Sixth NRP-908	Rockwell-Inspired	Open	165.00	165.00
91-01-009	Catching The Big One NRP-909	Rockwell-Inspired	Open	75.00	75.00
91-01-010	Gramps NRP-910	Rockwell-Inspired	Open	85.00	85.00
91-01-011	The Pharmacist NRP-911	Rockwell-Inspired	Open	70.00	70.00
92-01-012	Choosin Up NRP-912	Rockwell-Inspired	7,500	110.00	110.00
Dave Grossman Creations		**Saturday Evening Post-Miniatures**			
91-02-001	A Boy Meets His Dog BMR-01	Rockwell-Inspired	Retrd.	35.00	35.00
91-02-002	Downhill Daring BMR-02	Rockwell-Inspired	Retrd.	40.00	40.00
91-02-003	Flowers in Tender Bloom BMR-03	Rockwell-Inspired	Retrd.	32.00	32.00
91-02-004	Fondly Do We Remember BMR-04	Rockwell-Inspired	Retrd.	30.00	30.00
91-02-005	In His Spirit BMR-05	Rockwell-Inspired	Retrd.	30.00	30.00
91-02-006	Pride of Parenthood BMR-06	Rockwell-Inspired	Retrd.	35.00	35.00
91-02-007	Sweet Serenade BMR-07	Rockwell-Inspired	Retrd.	32.00	32.00
91-02-008	Sweet Song So Young BMR-08	Rockwell-Inspired	Retrd.	30.00	30.00
Dave Grossman Creations		**Norman Rockwell America Collection-Large Limited Edition**			
89-03-001	Doctor and Doll NRP-300	Rockwell-Inspired	Retrd.	150.00	150.00
89-03-002	Bottom of the Sixth NRP-307	Rockwell-Inspired	Retrd.	190.00	190.00
89-03-003	Runaway NRP-310	Rockwell-Inspired	Retrd.	190.00	190.00
89-03-004	Weigh-In NRP-311	Rockwell-Inspired	Retrd.	160.00	160.00
Dave Grossman Creations		**Norman Rockwell America Collection**			
89-04-001	Doctor and Doll NRP-600	Rockwell-Inspired	Retrd.	90.00'	90.00
89-04-002	Locomotive NRC-603	Rockwell-Inspired	Retrd.	110.00	110.00
89-04-003	First Haircut NRC-604	Rockwell-Inspired	Retrd.	75.00	75.00
89-04-004	First Visit NRC-605	Rockwell-Inspired	Retrd.	110.00	110.00
89-04-005	First Day Home NRC-606	Rockwell-Inspired	Retrd.	80.00	80.00
89-04-006	Bottom of the Sixth NRC-607	Rockwell-Inspired	Retrd.	140.00	140.00
89-04-007	Runaway NRC-610	Rockwell-Inspired	Retrd.	140.00	140.00
89-04-008	Weigh-In NRC-611	Rockwell-Inspired	Retrd.	120.00	120.00
Dave Grossman Creations		**Norman Rockwell America Collection-Miniatures**			
89-05-001	First Haircut MRC-904	Rockwell-Inspired	Retrd.	45.00	45.00
89-05-002	First Day Home MRC-906	Rockwell-Inspired	Retrd.	45.00	45.00
Dave Grossman Creations		**Emmett Kelly-Circus Collection**			
92-06-001	Christmas Tunes	B. Leighton-Jones	15,000	40.00	40.00
92-06-002	Emmett The Caddy	B. Leighton-Jones	15,000	45.00	45.00
92-06-003	Emmett At The Organ	B. Leighton-Jones	15,000	50.00	50.00

Company / Number	Name	Series / Artist	Edition Limit	Issue Price	Quote
92-06-004	Emmett At Work	B. Leighton-Jones	15,000	45.00	45.00
92-06-005	Look At The Birdie	B. Leighton-Jones	15,000	40.00	40.00
Dave Grossman Creations		**Native American Series**			
91-07-001	Lone Wolf	E. Roberts	7,500	55.00	55.00
92-07-002	Tortoise Lady	E. Roberts	7,500	60.00	60.00
Dave Grossman Creations		**Gone With The Wind Series**			
92-08-001	Scarlett in Green Dress	Unknown	2 Yr.	70.00	70.00
Dave Grossman Designs		**Norman Rockwell Collection**			
73-01-001	Redhead NR-01	Rockwell-Inspired	Retrd.	20.00	200.00
73-01-002	Back To School NR-02	Rockwell-Inspired	Retrd.	20.00	35.00
73-01-003	Caroller NR-03	Rockwell-Inspired	Retrd.	22.50	35.00
73-01-004	Daydreamer NR-04	Rockwell-Inspired	Retrd.	22.50	50.00
73-01-005	No Swimming NR-05	Rockwell-Inspired	Retrd.	25.00	50.00
73-01-006	Love Letter NR-06	Rockwell-Inspired	Retrd.	25.00	60.00
73-01-007	Lovers NR-07	Rockwell-Inspired	Retrd.	45.00	66.00
73-01-008	Lazybones NR-08	Rockwell-Inspired	Retrd.	30.00	300.00
73-01-009	Leapfrog NR-09	Rockwell-Inspired	Retrd.	50.00	550.00
73-01-010	Schoolmaster NR-10	Rockwell-Inspired	Retrd.	55.00	225.00
73-01-011	Marble Players NR-11	Rockwell-Inspired	Retrd.	60.00	450.00
73-01-012	Doctor & Doll NR-12	Rockwell-Inspired	Retrd.	65.00	150.00
74-01-013	Friends In Need NR-13	Rockwell-Inspired	Retrd.	45.00	96.00
74-01-014	Springtime '33 NR-14	Rockwell-Inspired	Retrd.	30.00	45.00
74-01-015	Summertime '33 NR-15	Rockwell-Inspired	Retrd.	45.00	45.00
74-01-016	Baseball NR-16	Rockwell-Inspired	Retrd.	45.00	125.00
74-01-017	See America First NR-17	Rockwell-Inspired	Retrd.	50.00	85.00
74-01-018	Take Your Medicine NR-18	Rockwell-Inspired	Retrd.	50.00	95.00
75-01-019	Discovery NR-20	Rockwell-Inspired	Retrd.	55.00	160.00
75-01-020	Big Moment NR-21	Rockwell-Inspired	Retrd.	60.00	120.00
75-01-021	Circus NR-22	Rockwell-Inspired	Retrd.	55.00	100.00
75-01-022	Barbershop Quartet NR-23	Rockwell-Inspired	Retrd.	100.00	1400.00
76-01-023	Drum For Tommy NRC-24	Rockwell-Inspired	Retrd.	40.00	80.00
77-01-024	Springtime '35 NR-19	Rockwell-Inspired	Retrd.	50.00	55.00
77-01-025	Pals NR-25	Rockwell-Inspired	Retrd.	60.00	75.00
78-01-026	Young Doctor NRD-26	Rockwell-Inspired	Retrd.	100.00	100.00
78-01-027	First Day of School NR-27	Rockwell-Inspired	Retrd.	100.00	135.00
78-01-028	Magic Potion NR-28	Rockwell-Inspired	Retrd.	84.00	100.00
78-01-029	At the Doctor NR-29	Rockwell-Inspired	Retrd.	108.00	160.00
79-01-030	Teacher's Pet NRA-30	Rockwell-Inspired	Retrd.	35.00	80.00
79-01-031	Dreams of Long Ago NR-31	Rockwell-Inspired	Retrd.	100.00	160.00
79-01-032	Grandpa's Ballerina NR-32	Rockwell-Inspired	Retrd.	100.00	110.00
79-01-033	Back From Camp NR-33	Rockwell-Inspired	Retrd.	96.00	110.00
80-01-034	The Toss NR-34	Rockwell-Inspired	Retrd.	110.00	110.00
80-01-035	Exasperated Nanny NR-35	Rockwell-Inspired	Retrd.	96.00	96.00
80-01-036	Hankerchief NR-36	Rockwell-Inspired	Retrd.	110.00	110.00
80-01-037	Santa's Good Boys NR-37	Rockwell-Inspired	Retrd.	90.00	90.00
81-01-038	Spirit of Education NR-38	Rockwell-Inspired	Retrd.	96.00	110.00
82-01-039	A Visit With Rockwell NR-40	Rockwell-Inspired	Retrd.	120.00	120.00
82-01-040	Croquet NR-41	Rockwell-Inspired	Retrd.	100.00	110.00
82-01-041	American Mother NRG-42	Rockwell-Inspired	Retrd.	100.00	110.00
83-01-042	Country Critic NR-43	Rockwell-Inspired	Retrd.	75.00	75.00
83-01-043	Graduate NR-44	Rockwell-Inspired	Retrd.	30.00	35.00
83-01-044	Scotty's Surprise NRS-20	Rockwell-Inspired	Retrd.	25.00	25.00
84-01-045	Scotty's Home Plate NR-46	Rockwell-Inspired	Retrd.	30.00	40.00
86-01-046	Red Cross NR-47	Rockwell-Inspired	Retrd.	67.00	75.00
87-01-047	Young Love NR-48	Rockwell-Inspired	Retrd.	70.00	70.00
88-01-048	Wedding March NR-49	Rockwell-Inspired	Retrd.	110.00	110.00
Dave Grossman Designs		**Norman Rockwell Collection Miniatures**			
79-02-001	Redhead NR-201	Rockwell-Inspired	Retrd.	18.00	48.00
79-02-002	Back To School NR-202	Rockwell-Inspired	Retrd.	18.00	25.00
79-02-003	Caroller NR-203	Rockwell-Inspired	Retrd.	20.00	25.00
79-02-004	Daydreamer NR-204	Rockwell-Inspired	Retrd.	20.00	30.00
79-02-005	No Swimming NR-205	Rockwell-Inspired	Retrd.	22.00	30.00
79-02-006	Love Letter NR-206	Rockwell-Inspired	Retrd.	26.00	30.00
79-02-007	Lovers NR-207	Rockwell-Inspired	Retrd.	28.00	30.00
79-02-008	Lazybones NR-208	Rockwell-Inspired	Retrd.	22.00	30.00
79-02-009	Leapfrog NR-209	Rockwell-Inspired	Retrd.	32.00	32.00
79-02-010	Schoolmaster NR-210	Rockwell-Inspired	Retrd.	34.00	40.00
79-02-011	Marble Players NR-211	Rockwell-Inspired	Retrd.	36.00	38.00
79-02-012	Doctor and Doll NR-212	Rockwell-Inspired	Retrd.	40.00	40.00
80-02-013	Friends In Need NR-213	Rockwell-Inspired	Retrd.	30.00	40.00
80-02-014	Springtime '33 NR-214	Rockwell-Inspired	Retrd.	24.00	80.00
80-02-015	Summertime '33 NR-215	Rockwell-Inspired	Retrd.	22.00	25.00
80-02-016	Baseball NR-216	Rockwell-Inspired	Retrd.	40.00	50.00
80-02-017	See America First NR-217	Rockwell-Inspired	Retrd.	28.00	35.00
80-02-018	Take Your Medicine NR-218	Rockwell-Inspired	Retrd.	36.00	40.00
82-02-019	Springtime '35 NR-219	Rockwell-Inspired	Retrd.	24.00	30.00
82-02-020	Discovery NR-220	Rockwell-Inspired	Retrd.	35.00	45.00
82-02-021	Big Moment NR-221	Rockwell-Inspired	Retrd.	36.00	40.00
82-02-022	Circus NR-222	Rockwell-Inspired	Retrd.	35.00	40.00
82-02-023	Barbershop Quartet NR-223	Rockwell-Inspired	Retrd.	40.00	50.00
82-02-024	Drum For Tommy NRC-224	Rockwell-Inspired	Retrd.	25.00	30.00
83-02-025	Santa On the Train NR-245	Rockwell-Inspired	Retrd.	35.00	55.00
84-02-026	Pals NR-225	Rockwell-Inspired	Retrd.	25.00	25.00
84-02-027	Young Doctor NRD-226	Rockwell-Inspired	Retrd.	30.00	50.00
84-02-028	First Day of School NR-227	Rockwell-Inspired	Retrd.	35.00	35.00
84-02-029	Magic Potion NR-228	Rockwell-Inspired	Retrd.	30.00	40.00
84-02-030	At the Doctor's NR-229	Rockwell-Inspired	Retrd.	35.00	35.00
84-02-031	Dreams of Long Ago NR-231	Rockwell-Inspired	Retrd.	30.00	30.00
Dave Grossman Designs		**Norman Rockwell Collection-Large Limited Editions**			
74-03-001	Doctor and Doll NR-100	Rockwell-Inspired	Retrd.	300.00	1600.00
74-03-002	See America First NR-103	Rockwell-Inspired	Retrd.	100.00	300.00
75-03-003	No Swimming NR-101	Rockwell-Inspired	Retrd.	150.00	450.00
75-03-004	Baseball NR-102	Rockwell-Inspired	Retrd.	125.00	450.00
79-03-005	Leapfrog NR-104	Rockwell-Inspired	Retrd.	440.00	750.00
81-03-006	Dreams of Long Ago NR-105	Rockwell-Inspired	Retrd.	500.00	750.00
82-03-007	Circus NR-106	Rockwell-Inspired	Retrd.	500.00	550.00
84-03-008	Marble Players NR-107	Rockwell-Inspired	Retrd.	500.00	500.00
Dave Grossman Designs		**Norman Rockwell Collection-American Rockwell Series**			
81-04-001	Breaking Home Ties NRV-300	Rockwell-Inspired	Retrd.	2000.00	2300.00
82-04-002	Lincoln NRV-301	Rockwell-Inspired	Retrd.	300.00	375.00
82-04-003	Thanksgiving NRV-302	Rockwell-Inspired	Retrd.	2500.00	2650.00
Dave Grossman Designs		**Norman Rockwell Collection-Lladro Series**			
82-05-001	Lladro Love Letter RL-400	Rockwell-Inspired	Retrd.	650.00	925-1200.
82-05-002	Summer Stock RL-401	Rockwell-Inspired	Retrd.	750.00	775-950.
82-05-003	Practice Makes Perfect RL-402	Rockwell-Inspired	Retrd.	725.00	800-900.
82-05-004	Young Love RL-403	Rockwell-Inspired	Retrd.	450.00	975.00

Number	Name	Artist	Edition Limit	Issue Price	Quote
82-05-005	Daydreamer RL-404	Rockwell-Inspired	Retrd.	450.00	1500.00
82-05-006	Court Jester RL-405	Rockwell-Inspired	Retrd.	600.00	1100-1500.
82-05-007	Springtime RL-406	Rockwell-Inspired	Retrd.	450.00	1050-1800.
Dave Grossman Designs	**Norman Rockwell Collection-Rockwell Club Series**				
81-06-001	Young Artist RCC-01	Rockwell-Inspired	Retrd.	96.00	105.00
82-06-002	Diary RCC-02	Rockwell-Inspired	Retrd.	35.00	50.00
83-06-003	Runaway Pants RCC-03	Rockwell-Inspired	Retrd.	65.00	75.00
84-06-004	Gone Fishing RCC-04	Rockwell-Inspired	Retrd.	30.00	55.00
Dave Grossman Designs	**Norman Rockwell Collection-Tom Sawyer Series**				
75-07-001	Whitewashing the Fence TS-01	Rockwell-Inspired	Retrd.	60.00	200.00
76-07-002	First Smoke TS-02	Rockwell-Inspired	Retrd.	60.00	200.00
77-07-003	Take Your Medicine TS-03	Rockwell-Inspired	Retrd.	63.00	170.00
78-07-004	Lost In Cave TS-04	Rockwell-Inspired	Retrd.	70.00	145.00
Dave Grossman Designs	**Norman Rockwell Collection-Tom Sawyer Miniatures**				
83-08-001	Whitewashing the Fence TSM-01	Rockwell-Inspired	Retrd.	40.00	50.00
83-08-002	First Smoke TSM-02	Rockwell-Inspired	Retrd.	40.00	45.00
83-08-003	Take Your Medicine TSM-04	Rockwell-Inspired	Retrd.	40.00	45.00
83-08-004	Lost In Cave TSM-05	Rockwell-Inspired	Retrd.	40.00	45.00
Dave Grossman Designs	**Norman Rockwell Collection-Huck Finn Series**				
79-09-001	The Secret HF-01	Rockwell-Inspired	Retrd.	110.00	130.00
80-09-002	Listening HF-02	Rockwell-Inspired	Retrd.	110.00	120.00
80-09-003	No Kings HF-03	Rockwell-Inspired	Retrd.	110.00	110.00
80-09-004	Snake Escapes HF-04	Rockwell-Inspired	Retrd.	110.00	120.00
Dave Grossman Designs	**Norman Rockwell Collection-Boy Scout Series**				
81-10-001	Can't Wait BSA-01	Rockwell-Inspired	Retrd.	30.00	50.00
81-10-002	Scout Is Helpful BSA-02	Rockwell-Inspired	Retrd.	38.00	45.00
81-10-003	Physically Strong BSA-03	Rockwell-Inspired	Retrd.	56.00	60.00
81-10-004	Good Friends BSA-04	Rockwell-Inspired	Retrd.	58.00	65.00
81-10-005	Good Turn BSA-05	Rockwell-Inspired	Retrd.	65.00	100.00
81-10-006	Scout Memories BSA-06	Rockwell-Inspired	Retrd.	65.00	70.00
82-10-007	Guiding Hand BSA-07	Rockwell-Inspired	Retrd.	58.00	60.00
83-10-008	Tomorrow's Leader BSA-08	Rockwell-Inspired	Retrd.	45.00	55.00
Dave Grossman Designs	**Norman Rockwell Collection-Country Gentlemen Series**				
82-11-001	Turkey Dinner CG-01	Rockwell-Inspired	Retrd.	85.00	N/A
82-11-002	Bringing Home the Tree CG-02	Rockwell-Inspired	Retrd.	60.00	N/A
82-11-003	Pals CG-03	Rockwell-Inspired	Retrd.	36.00	45.00
82-11-004	The Catch CG-04	Rockwell-Inspired	Retrd.	50.00	60.00
82-11-005	On the Ice CG-05	Rockwell-Inspired	Retrd.	50.00	N/A
82-11-006	Thin Ice CG-06	Rockwell-Inspired	Retrd.	50.00	60.00
Dave Grossman Designs	**Norman Rockwell Collection-Select Collection, Ltd.**				
82-12-001	Boy & Mother With Puppies SC-1001	Rockwell-Inspired	Retrd.	27.50	N/A
82-12-002	Girl With Dolls In Crib SC-1002	Rockwell-Inspired	Retrd.	26.50	N/A
82-12-003	Young Couple SC-1003	Rockwell-Inspired	Retrd.	27.50	N/A
82-12-004	Football Player SC-1004	Rockwell-Inspired	Retrd.	22.00	N/A
82-12-005	Father With Child SC-1005	Rockwell-Inspired	Retrd.	22.00	N/A
82-12-006	Girl Bathing Dog SC-1006	Rockwell-Inspired	Retrd.	26.50	N/A
82-12-007	Helping Hand SC-1007	Rockwell-Inspired	Retrd.	32.00	N/A
82-12-008	Lemonade Stand SC-1008	Rockwell-Inspired	Retrd.	32.00	N/A
82-12-009	Shaving Lesson SC-1009	Rockwell-Inspired	Retrd.	30.00	N/A
82-12-010	Save Me SC-1010	Rockwell-Inspired	Retrd.	35.00	N/A
Dave Grossman Designs	**Norman Rockwell Collection-Pewter Figurines**				
80-13-001	Back to School FP-02	Rockwell-Inspired	Retrd.	25.00	N/A
80-13-002	Caroller FP-03	Rockwell-Inspired	Retrd.	25.00	N/A
80-13-003	No Swimming FP-05	Rockwell-Inspired	Retrd.	25.00	N/A
80-13-004	Lovers FP-07	Rockwell-Inspired	Retrd.	25.00	N/A
80-13-005	Doctor and Doll FP-12	Rockwell-Inspired	Retrd.	25.00	N/A
80-13-006	See America First FP-17	Rockwell-Inspired	Retrd.	25.00	N/A
80-13-007	Take Your Medicine FP-18	Rockwell-Inspired	Retrd.	25.00	N/A
80-13-008	Big Moment FP-21	Rockwell-Inspired	Retrd.	25.00	N/A
80-13-009	Circus FP-22	Rockwell-Inspired	Retrd.	25.00	N/A
80-13-010	Barbershop Quartet FP-23	Rockwell-Inspired	Retrd.	25.00	N/A
80-13-011	Magic Potion FP-28	Rockwell-Inspired	Retrd.	25.00	N/A
80-13-012	Grandpa's Ballerina FP-32	Rockwell-Inspired	Retrd.	25.00	N/A
80-13-013	Figurine Display Rack FDR-01	Rockwell-Inspired	Retrd.	60.00	N/A
Hallmark Galleries	**Moustershire**				
92-01-001	Andrew Allsgood- Honorable Citizen	D. Rhodus	Open	10.00	10.00
92-01-002	Chelsea Goforth- Ingenue	D. Rhodus	Open	10.00	10.00
92-01-003	Miles Fielding- Farmer	D. Rhodus	Open	10.00	10.00
92-01-004	Colin Tuneman- Musician of Note	D. Rhodus	Open	10.00	10.00
92-01-005	Olivia Puddingsby- Baker	D. Rhodus	Open	10.00	10.00
92-01-006	Hillary Hemstitch- Seamstress	D. Rhodus	Open	10.00	10.00
92-01-007	L.E. Hosten- Innkeeper	D. Rhodus	Open	10.00	10.00
92-01-008	Malcolm Cramwell- Mouserly Scholar	D. Rhodus	Open	10.00	10.00
92-01-009	Acorn Inn/Timothy Duzmuch	D. Rhodus	9,500	65.00	65.00
92-01-010	Bakery/Dunne Eaton	D. Rhodus	9,500	55.00	55.00
92-01-011	Bandstand/Cyrus & Cecilia Sunnyside	D. Rhodus	9,500	50.00	50.00
92-01-012	Nigel Puffmore- Talented Tubist	D. Rhodus	19,500	10.00	10.00
92-01-013	Robin Ripengood- Grocer	D. Rhodus	19,500	28.00	28.00
92-01-014	Claire Lovencare- Nanny	D. Rhodus	19,500	18.00	18.00
92-01-015	Hattie Chapeau- Milliner	D. Rhodus	19,500	15.00	15.00
92-01-016	Trio	D. Rhodus	19,500	23.00	23.00
92-01-017	The Picnic/Tree	D. Rhodus	9,500	50.00	50.00
92-01-018	The Park Gate	D. Rhodus	9,500	60.00	60.00
92-01-019	Acorn Inn Customers	D. Rhodus	9,500	28.00	28.00
92-01-020	Hyacinth House	D. Rhodus	9,500	65.00	65.00
92-01-021	Peter Philpott- Gardener	D. Rhodus	19,500	12.00	12.00
92-01-022	Village/Bay Crossroads Sign	D. Rhodus	19,500	10.00	10.00
92-01-023	Tess Tellingtale/Well	D. Rhodus	19,500	28.00	28.00
92-01-024	Michael McFogg/Lighthouse	D. Rhodus	9,500	55.00	55.00
92-01-025	Henrietta Seaworthy	D. Rhodus	19,500	15.00	15.00
Hallmark Galleries	**Times to Cherish**				
92-02-001	The Joys of Fatherhood	T. Andrews	4,500	60.00	60.00
92-02-002	Dancer's Dream	T. Andrews	4,500	50.00	50.00
92-02-003	Daily Devotion	T. Andrews	4,500	40.00	40.00
92-02-004	Beautiful Dreamer	T. Andrews	4,500	65.00	65.00
92-02-005	Sister Time	T. Andrews	4,500	55.00	55.00
92-02-006	Mother's Blessing	T. Andrews	4,500	65.00	65.00
92-02-007	The Embrace	T. Andrews	4,500	60.00	60.00
92-02-008	A Child's Prayer	T. Andrews	4,500	35.00	35.00
92-02-009	A Mother's Touch	T. Andrews	4,500	60.00	60.00
Hallmark Galleries	**Birds of North America**				
92-03-001	House Wren	G.&G. Dooly	2,500	85.00	85.00
92-03-002	Ovenbird	G.&G. Dooly	2,500	95.00	95.00
92-03-003	American Goldfinch	G.&G. Dooly	2,500	85.00	85.00
92-03-004	American Robins	G.&G. Dooly	2,500	175.00	175.00
92-03-005	Dark-eyed Junco	G.&G. Dooly	2,500	85.00	85.00
92-03-006	Cedar Waxwing	G.&G. Dooly	2,500	120.00	120.00
92-03-007	Cardinal	G.&G. Dooly	2,500	110.00	110.00
92-03-008	Red-breasted Nuthatch	G.&G. Dooly	2,500	95.00	95.00
Hallmark Galleries	**Lou Rankin's Creations**				
92-04-001	Orangutan -The Thinker	L. Rankin	19,500	38.00	38.00
92-04-002	Seated Rabbit	L. Rankin	19,500	30.00	30.00
92-04-003	Squirrel I -Satisfied	L. Rankin	19,500	25.00	25.00
92-04-004	Squirrel II -Sassy	L. Rankin	19,500	20.00	20.00
92-04-005	Happy Frog -Feelin' Fine	L. Rankin	19,500	35.00	35.00
92-04-006	Two Otters -Two's Company	L. Rankin	9,500	45.00	45.00
92-04-007	Seated Bear	L. Rankin	19,500	30.00	30.00
92-04-008	Reclining Bear	L. Rankin	19,500	35.00	35.00
92-04-009	Basset Hound -Faithful Friend	L. Rankin	19,500	38.00	38.00
92-04-010	Shih Tzu -The Sophisticate	L. Rankin	19,500	30.00	30.00
92-04-011	Bulldog and Beagle -Best Buddies	L. Rankin	9,500	48.00	48.00
92-04-012	Reclining Cat -Feline Fatale	L. Rankin	19,500	30.00	30.00
92-04-013	Pair of Pigs -Happy Hogs	L. Rankin	19,500	38.00	38.00
92-04-014	Pig with Head Raised - Little Porker	L. Rankin	19,500	35.00	35.00
Hallmark Galleries	**Enchanted Garden**				
92-05-001	Enchanted Garden (vase)	E. Richardson	1,200	115.00	115.00
92-05-002	Bunny Abundance (vase)	E. Richardson	9,500	75.00	75.00
92-05-003	Milk Bath (vase)	E. Richardson	9,500	80.00	80.00
92-05-004	Everybunny Can Fly (vase)	E. Richardson	9,500	70.00	70.00
92-05-005	Baby Bunny Hop (bowl)	E. Richardson	9,500	85.00	85.00
92-05-006	Promenade (bowl)	E. Richardson	9,500	65.00	65.00
92-05-007	Let Them Eat Carrots (pitcher)	E. Richardson	9,500	70.00	70.00
Hallmark Galleries	**Days to Remember-The Art of Norman Rockwell**				
92-06-001	Saying Grace	D. Unruh	1,500	375.00	375.00
92-06-002	Sleeping Children	D. Unruh	7,500	105.00	105.00
92-06-003	The Truth About Santa	D. Unruh	7,500	85.00	85.00
92-06-004	Santa and His Helpers	D. Unruh	7,500	95.00	95.00
92-06-005	The Fiddler	D. Unruh	4,500	95.00	95.00
92-06-006	Marbles Champion	D. Unruh	4,500	75.00	75.00
92-06-007	Low and Outside	D. Unruh	4,500	95.00	95.00
92-06-008	Springtime 1927	D. Unruh	4,500	95.00	95.00
92-06-009	Little Spooners	D. Unruh	4,500	70.00	70.00
Hallmark Galleries	**Innocent Wonders**				
92-07-001	Pockets	T. Blackshear	4,500	125.00	125.00
92-07-002	Dinky Toot	T. Blackshear	4,500	125.00	125.00
92-07-003	Bobo Bipps	T. Blackshear	2,500	150.00	150.00
92-07-004	Pippy Lou	T. Blackshear	4,500	150.00	150.00
92-07-005	Pinkie Poo	T. Blackshear	2,500	135.00	135.00
92-07-006	Zip Doodle	T. Blackshear	4,500	125.00	125.00
92-07-007	Waggletag	T. Blackshear	4,500	125.00	125.00
Hallmark Galleries	**Tobin Fraley Carousels**				
92-08-001	Musical Premier Horse	T. Fraley	1,200	275.00	275.00
92-08-002	Charles Carmel, circa 1914/musical	T. Fraley	4,500	40.00	40.00
92-08-003	Philadelphia Toboggan Co/1910/musical	T. Fraley	4,500	40.00	40.00
92-08-004	Stein & Goldstein/1914/musical	T. Fraley	2,500	60.00	60.00
92-08-005	Philadelphia Toboggan Co/1928/musical	T. Fraley	2,500	60.00	60.00
92-08-006	Playland Carousel/musical	T. Fraley	1,200	195.00	195.00
92-08-007	Revolving Brass/Wood Display	T. Fraley	4,500	40.00	40.00
92-08-008	M.C. Illions & Sons/1910/musical	T. Fraley	2,500	60.00	60.00
92-08-009	Charles Looff/1915/musical	T. Fraley	2,500	60.00	60.00
92-08-010	M.C. Illions & Sons/1910/musical	T. Fraley	4,500	40.00	40.00
92-08-011	C.W. Parker/1922/musical	T. Fraley	4,500	40.00	40.00
92-08-012	C.W. Parker/1922	T. Fraley	4,500	30.00	30.00
92-08-013	Charles Looff/1915	T. Fraley	4,500	50.00	50.00
92-08-014	M.C. Illions & Sons/1910	T. Fraley	4,500	50.00	50.00
92-08-015	Charles Carmel/1914	T. Fraley	4,500	30.00	30.00
92-08-016	Philadelphia Toboggan Co/1928	T. Fraley	4,500	50.00	50.00
92-08-017	Philadelphia Toboggan Co/1910	T. Fraley	4,500	30.00	30.00
92-08-018	Stein & Goldstein/1914	T. Fraley	4,500	50.00	50.00
92-08-019	M.C. Illions & Sons/1910	T. Fraley	4,500	30.00	30.00
Hallmark Galleries	**Majestic Wilderness**				
92-09-001	Bison	M. Newman	4,500	120.00	120.00
92-09-002	Red Fox	M. Newman	4,500	75.00	75.00
92-09-003	American Bald Eagle	M. Newman	4,500	195.00	195.00
92-09-004	Mountain Lion	M. Newman	4,500	75.00	75.00
92-09-005	Grizzly Mother with Cub	M. Newman	2,500	135.00	135.00
92-09-006	White-tailed Doe with Fawn	M. Newman	2,500	135.00	135.00
92-09-007	White-tailed Buck	M. Newman	2,500	135.00	135.00
92-09-008	Male Grizzly	M. Newman	2,500	145.00	145.00
92-09-009	Bighorn Sheep	M. Newman	4,500	125.00	125.00
92-09-010	Timber Wolves	M. Newman	2,500	135.00	135.00
Hallmark Cards, Inc.	**Tender Touches**				
88-10-001	Rabbits with Cake	E.Seale	Retrd.	20.00	40.00
88-10-002	Baby Raccoon	E.Seale	Retrd.	20.00	40.00
88-10-003	Raccoon with Cake	E.Seale	Retrd.	18.00	36.00
88-10-004	Raccoons Playing Ball	E.Seale	Retrd.	18.00	36.00
88-10-005	Squirrels with Bandage	E.Seale	6/93	18.00	18.00
88-10-006	Mouse with Heart	E.Seale	6/93	18.00	18.00
88-10-007	Mice at Tea Party	E.Seale	Open	23.00	23.00
88-10-008	Rabbits at Juice Stand	E.Seale	Open	23.00	23.00
88-10-009	Teacher with Student	E.Seale	Open	18.00	18.00
88-10-010	Mice in Rocking Chair	E.Seale	Open	18.00	18.00
88-10-011	Raccoons Fishing	E.Seale	Open	18.00	18.00
88-10-012	Bear with Umbrella	E.Seale	Open	16.00	16.00
88-10-013	Rabbit with Ribbon	E.Seale	Open	15.00	15.00
89-10-014	Bunny in Flowers	E.Seale	Retrd.	16.00	26.00
89-10-015	Chipmunk With Roses	E.Seale	Retrd.	16.00	26.00
89-10-016	Mouse with Violin	E.Seale	Retrd.	16.00	28.00
89-10-017	Halloween Trio	E.Seale	Retrd.	18.00	26.00
89-10-018	Pilgrim Mouse	E.Seale	Retrd.	16.00	30.00
89-10-019	Santa Mouse in Chair	E.Seale	Retrd.	20.00	28.00
89-10-020	Mouse at Desk	E.Seale	Retrd.	18.00	28.00
89-10-021	Rabbits Ice Skating	E.Seale	Retrd.	18.00	28.00
89-10-022	Chipmunk Praying	E.Seale	Retrd.	18.00	28.00
89-10-023	Bride & Groom	E.Seale	Open	20.00	20.00
89-10-024	Birthday Mouse	E.Seale	Open	16.00	16.00
89-10-025	Bear Decorating Tree	E.Seale	Open	18.00	18.00
89-10-026	Rabbit Painting Egg	E.Seale	Open	18.00	18.00

Number	Name	Artist	Edition Limit	Issue Price	Quote
Company		**Series**			
90-10-027	Dad and Son Bears	E.Seale	Retrd.	23.00	33.00
90-10-028	Teacher and Student Chipmunks	E.Seale	Retrd.	20.00	30.00
90-10-029	Bunny With Stocking	E.Seale	Retrd.	15.00	25.00
90-10-030	Mice With Mistletoe	E.Seale	Retrd.	20.00	30.00
90-10-031	Mouse in Pumpkin	E.Seale	Retrd.	18.00	28.00
90-10-032	Bears WIth Gift	E.Seale	Retrd.	18.00	28.00
90-10-033	Bear Praying	E.Seale	Retrd.	18.00	28.00
90-10-034	Baby Bear in Backpack	E.Seale	Retrd.	16.00	26.00
90-10-035	Mice in Red Car	E.Seale	Retrd.	20.00	30.00
90-10-036	Easter Egg Hunt	E.Seale	Retrd.	18.00	28.00
90-10-037	Romeo and Julie Mice	E.Seale	Retrd.	25.00	35.00
90-10-038	Tucking Baby in Bed	E.Seale	6/93	18.00	18.00
90-10-039	Bunnies with Slide	E.Seale	Open	20.00	20.00
90-10-040	Mice with Quilt	E.Seale	Open	20.00	20.00
90-10-041	Raccoon Watering Roses	E.Seale	Open	20.00	20.00
90-10-042	Bears Playing Baseball	E.Seale	Open	20.00	20.00
90-10-043	Bunnies Eating Ice Cream	E.Seale	Open	20.00	20.00
90-10-044	Bunny Pulling Wagon	E.Seale	Open	23.00	23.00
90-10-045	Raccoons with Wagon	E.Seale	Open	23.00	23.00
90-10-046	Raccoons with Flag	E.Seale	Open	23.00	23.00
90-10-047	Bunny in Boat	E.Seale	Open	18.00	18.00
90-10-048	Raccoon Mail Carrier	E.Seale	Open	16.00	16.00
90-10-049	Mouse Nurse	E.Seale	Open	15.00	15.00
90-10-050	Bear Graduate	E.Seale	Open	15.00	15.00
90-10-051	Bunny Hiding Valentine	E.Seale	Open	16.00	16.00
90-10-052	Beavers with Tree	E.Seale	Open	23.00	23.00
90-10-053	Santa in Chimney	E.Seale	Open	18.00	18.00
90-10-054	Bunny Cheerleader	E.Seale	Open	16.00	16.00
90-10-055	Bunny with Ice Cream	E.Seale	Open	15.00	15.00
90-10-056	Bear's Easter Parade	E.Seale	Open	23.00	23.00
91-10-057	Mouse Couple Sharing Soda	E.Seale	Retrd.	23.00	23.00
91-10-058	Bunny in High Chair	E.Seale	Retrd.	16.00	16.00
91-10-059	Bunny with Large Eggs	E.Seale	Retrd.	16.00	16.00
91-10-060	Mice Couple Slow Waltzing	E.Seale	Retrd.	20.00	20.00
91-10-061	First Christmas Mice @ Piano	E.Seale	Retrd.	23.00	23.00
91-10-062	Baby's 1st Bear Riding Rocking Bear	E.Seale	Retrd.	16.00	16.00
91-10-063	Father Bear Barbequing	E.Seale	Open	23.00	23.00
91-10-064	Foxes in Rowboat	E.Seale	Open	23.00	23.00
91-10-065	Mother Raccoon Reading Bible Stories	E.Seale	Open	20.00	20.00
91-10-066	Love-American Gothic-Farmer Raccoons	E.Seale	Open	20.00	20.00
91-10-067	Christmas Bunny Skiing	E.Seale	Open	18.00	18.00
91-10-068	Raccoon Witch	E.Seale	Open	16.00	16.00
92-10-069	Building a Pumpkin Man	E.Seale	Open	18.00	18.00
92-10-070	Sweet Sharing	E.Seale	Open	20.00	20.00
92-10-071	Waiting for Santa	E.Seale	Open	20.00	20.00
92-10-072	Stealing a Kiss	E.Seale	19,500	23.00	23.00
92-10-073	Fitting Gift	E.Seale	Open	23.00	23.00
92-10-074	Delightful Fright	E.Seale	19,500	23.00	23.00
92-10-075	New World, Ahoy!	E.Seale	Open	55.00	55.00
92-10-076	Tender Touches Tree House	E.Seale	9,500	55.00	55.00
92-10-077	Raccoons on Bridge	E.Seale	19,500	25.00	25.00
92-10-078	Thanksgiving Family Around Table	E.Seale	Open	25.00	25.00
92-10-079	Chatting Mice	E.Seale	19,500	23.00	23.00
92-10-080	Soapbox Racer	E.Seale	19,500	23.00	23.00
92-10-081	Beaver Growth Chart	E.Seale	19,500	20.00	20.00
92-10-082	Bunny with Kite	E.Seale	19,500	19.00	19.00
92-10-083	Newsboy Bear	E.Seale	Open	16.00	16.00
92-10-084	Chipmunks with Album	E.Seale	Open	23.00	23.00
92-10-085	Beaver with Double Bass	E.Seale	Open	18.00	18.00
92-10-086	Breakfast in Bed	E.Seale	Open	18.00	18.00
92-10-087	Bear Family Christmas	E.Seale	Open	45.00	45.00
Hallmark Galleries		**Kiddie Car Classics**			
92-11-001	Murray Airplane	E. Weirick	14,500	50.00	50.00
92-11-002	Murray Champion	E. Weirick	14,500	45.00	45.00
92-11-003	Murray Fire Truck	E. Weirick	14,500	50.00	50.00
92-11-004	Murray Dump Truck	E. Weirick	14,500	48.00	48.00
92-11-005	Murray Tractor and Trailer	E. Weirick	14,500	55.00	55.00
Hallmark Galleries		**Victorian Memories**			
92-12-001	Tea Set	J. Greene	9,500	35.00	35.00
92-12-002	Rebecca-cold cast	J. Lyle	9,500	60.00	60.00
92-12-003	Rabbit (on wheels)	J. Greene	4,500	65.00	65.00
92-12-004	Wooden Rocking Horse	J. Greene	4,500	75.00	75.00
92-12-005	Wicker Rocker	J. Greene	4,500	45.00	45.00
92-12-006	Sarah-cold cast	J. Lyle	9,500	60.00	60.00
92-12-007	Lillian-cold cast	J. Lyle	9,500	55.00	55.00
92-12-008	Wooden Horse Pull Toy-miniature	J. Greene	9,500	18.00	18.00
92-12-009	Wooden Train-miniature	J. Greene	9,500	15.00	15.00
92-12-010	Wooden Noah's Ark-miniature	J. Greene	9,500	15.00	15.00
92-12-011	Wooden Doll Carriage-miniature	J. Greene	9,500	20.00	20.00
Hamilton/Boehm		**Roses of Distinction**			
83-01-001	Peace Rose	Boehm	9,800	135.00	195.00
83-01-002	White Masterpiece Rose	Boehm	9,800	135.00	180.00
83-01-003	Angel Face Rose	Boehm	9,800	135.00	175.00
83-01-004	Queen Elizabeth Rose	Boehm	9,800	135.00	175.00
83-01-005	Elegance Rose	Boehm	9,800	135.00	175.00
83-01-006	Royal Highness Rose	Boehm	9,800	135.00	175.00
83-01-007	Tropicana Rose	Boehm	9,800	135.00	175.00
83-01-008	Mr. Lincoln Rose	Boehm	9,800	135.00	175.00
Hamilton/Boehm		**Favorite Garden Flowers**			
85-02-001	Morning Glory	Boehm	9,800	195.00	225.00
85-02-002	Hibiscus	Boehm	9,800	195.00	225.00
85-02-003	Tulip	Boehm	9,800	195.00	225.00
85-02-004	Sweet Pea	Boehm	9,800	195.00	225.00
85-02-005	Rose	Boehm	9,800	195.00	225.00
85-02-006	Carnation	Boehm	9,800	195.00	225.00
85-02-007	California Poppy	Boehm	9,800	195.00	225.00
85-02-008	Daffodil	Boehm	9,800	195.00	225.00
Hamilton Collection		**American Wildlife Bronze Collection**			
79-01-001	Cougar	H./N. Deaton	7,500	60.00	125.00
79-01-002	White-Tailed Deer	H./N. Deaton	7,500	60.00	105.00
79-01-003	Bobcat	H./N. Deaton	7,500	60.00	75.00
80-01-004	Beaver	H./N. Deaton	7,500	60.00	65.00
80-01-005	Polar Bear	H./N. Deaton	7,500	60.00	65.00
80-01-006	Sea Otter	H./N. Deaton	7,500	60.00	65.00
Hamilton Collection		**Rockwell Home of The Brave**			
82-02-001	Reminiscing	N. Rockwell	7,500	75.00	75.00
82-02-002	Hero's Welcome	N. Rockwell	7,500	75.00	75.00
82-02-003	Uncle Sam Takes Wings	N. Rockwell	7,500	75.00	75.00
82-02-004	Back to His Old Job	N. Rockwell	7,500	75.00	75.00
82-02-005	Willie Gillis in Church	N. Rockwell	7,500	75.00	75.00
82-02-006	Taking Mother over the Top	N. Rockwell	7,500	75.00	75.00
Hamilton Collection		**Ringling Bros. Circus Animals**			
83-03-001	Miniature Show Horse	P. Cozzolino	9,800	49.50	68.00
83-03-002	Baby Elephant	P. Cozzolino	9,800	49.50	55.00
83-03-003	Acrobatic Seal	P. Cozzolino	9,800	49.50	49.50
83-03-004	Skating Bear	P. Cozzolino	9,800	49.50	49.50
83-03-005	Mr. Chimpanzee	P. Cozzolino	9,800	49.50	49.50
83-03-006	Performing Poodles	P. Cozzolino	9,800	49.50	49.50
84-03-007	Roaring Lion	P. Cozzolino	9,800	49.50	49.60
84-03-008	Parade Camel	P. Cozzolino	9,800	49.50	49.50
Hamilton Collection		**Great Animals of the American Wilderness**			
83-04-001	Mountain Lion	H. Deaton	7,500	75.00	75.00
83-04-002	Grizzly Bear	H. Deaton	7,500	75.00	75.00
83-04-003	Timber Wolf	H. Deaton	7,500	75.00	75.00
83-04-004	Pronghorn Antelope	H. Deaton	7,500	75.00	75.00
83-04-005	Plains Bison	H. Deaton	7,500	75.00	75.00
83-04-006	Elk	H. Deaton	7,500	75.00	75.00
83-04-007	Mustang	H. Deaton	7,500	75.00	75.00
83-04-008	Bighorn Sheep	H. Deaton	7,500	75.00	75.00
Hamilton Collection		**American Garden Flowers**			
87-05-001	Camelia	D. Fryer	9,800	55.00	75.00
87-05-002	Gardenia	D. Fryer	15,000	75.00	75.00
87-05-003	Azalea	D. Fryer	15,000	75.00	75.00
87-05-004	Rose	D. Fryer	15,000	75.00	75.00
88-05-005	Day Lily	D. Fryer	15,000	75.00	75.00
88-05-006	Petunia	D. Fryer	15,000	75.00	75.00
88-05-007	Calla Lilly	D. Fryer	15,000	75.00	75.00
89-05-008	Pansy	D. Fryer	15,000	75.00	75.00
Hamilton Collection		**Celebration of Opera**			
86-06-001	Cio-Cio-San	J. Villena	7,500	95.00	95.00
86-06-002	Carmen	J. Villena	7,500	95.00	95.00
87-06-003	Figaro	J. Villena	7,500	95.00	95.00
88-06-004	Mimi	J. Villena	7,500	95.00	95.00
88-06-005	Aida	J. Villena	7,500	95.00	95.00
88-06-006	Canio	J. Villena	7,500	95.00	95.00
Hamilton Collection		**Exotic Birds of the World**			
84-07-001	The Cockatoo	Francesco	7,500	75.00	115.00
84-07-002	The Budgerigar	Francesco	7,500	75.00	105.00
84-07-003	The Rubenio Parakeet	Francesco	7,500	75.00	95.00
84-07-004	The Quetzal	Francesco	7,500	75.00	95.00
84-07-005	The Red Lorg	Francesco	7,500	75.00	95.00
84-07-006	The Fisher's Whydah	Francesco	7,500	75.00	95.00
84-07-007	The Diamond Dove	Francesco	7,500	75.00	95.00
84-07-008	The Peach-faced Lovebird	Francesco	7,500	75.00	95.00
Hamilton Collection		**Majestic Wildlife of North America**			
85-08-001	White-tailed Deer	H. Deaton	7,500	75.00	75.00
85-08-002	Ocelot	H. Deaton	7,500	75.00	75.00
85-08-003	Alaskan Moose	H. Deaton	7,500	75.00	75.00
85-08-004	Black Bear	H. Deaton	7,500	75.00	75.00
85-08-005	Mountain Goat	H. Deaton	7,500	75.00	75.00
85-08-006	Coyote	H. Deaton	7,500	75.00	75.00
85-08-007	Barren Ground Caribou	H. Deaton	7,500	75.00	75.00
85-08-008	Harbour Seal	H. Deaton	7,500	75.00	75.00
Hamilton Collection		**Magnificent Birds of Paradise**			
85-09-001	Emperor of Germany	Francesco	12,500	75.00	95.00
85-09-002	Greater Bird of Paradise	Francesco	12,500	75.00	95.00
85-09-003	Magnificent Bird of Paradise	Francesco	12,500	75.00	95.00
85-09-004	Raggiana Bird of Paradise	Francesco	12,500	75.00	95.00
85-09-005	Princess Stephanie Bird of Paradise	Francesco	12,500	75.00	95.00
85-09-006	Goldie's Bird of Paradise	Francesco	12,500	75.00	95.00
85-09-007	Blue Bird of Paradise	Francesco	12,500	75.00	95.00
85-09-008	Black Sickle-Billed Bird of Paradise	Francesco	12,500	75.00	95.00
Hamilton Collection		**Legendary Flowers of the Orient**			
85-10-001	Iris	Ito	15,000	55.00	55.00
85-10-002	Lotus	Ito	15,000	55.00	55.00
85-10-003	Chinese Peony	Ito	15,000	55.00	55.00
85-10-004	Gold Band Lily	Ito	15,000	55.00	55.00
85-10-005	Chrysanthemum	Ito	15,000	55.00	55.00
85-10-006	Cherry Blossom	Ito	15,000	55.00	55.00
85-10-007	Japanese Orchid	Ito	15,000	55.00	55.00
85-10-008	Wisteria	Ito	15,000	55.00	55.00
Hamilton Collection		**The Splendor of Ballet**			
87-11-001	Juliet	E. Daub	15,000	95.00	95.00
87-11-002	Odette	E. Daub	15,000	95.00	95.00
87-11-003	Giselle	E. Daub	15,000	95.00	95.00
87-11-004	Kitri	E. Daub	15,000	95.00	95.00
88-11-005	Aurora	E. Daub	15,000	95.00	95.00
89-11-006	Swanilda	E. Daub	15,000	95.00	95.00
89-11-007	Firebird	E. Daub	15,000	95.00	95.00
89-11-008	Clara	E. Daub	15,000	95.00	95.00
Hamilton Collection		**The Noble Swan**			
85-12-001	The Noble Swan	G. Granget	5,000	295.00	295.00
Hamilton Collection		**The Gibson Girls**			
86-13-001	The Actress	Unknown	Open	75.00	75.00
87-13-002	The Career Girl	Unknown	Open	75.00	75.00
87-13-003	The College Girl	Unknown	Open	75.00	75.00
87-13-004	The Bride	Unknown	Open	75.00	75.00
87-13-005	The Sportswoman	Unknown	Open	75.00	75.00
88-13-006	The Debutante	Unknown	Open	75.00	75.00
88-13-007	The Artist	Unknown	Open	75.00	75.00
88-13-008	The Society Girl	Unknown	Open	75.00	75.00
Hamilton Collection		**The Romance of Flowers**			
87-14-001	Springtime Bouquet	Maruri	15,000	95.00	95.00
87-14-002	Summer Bouquet	Maruri	15,000	95.00	95.00
88-14-003	Autumn Bouquet	Maruri	15,000	95.00	95.00
88-14-004	Winter Bouquet	Maruri	15,000	95.00	95.00

Number	Name	Artist	Edition Limit	Issue Price	Quote
Hamilton Collection		**Wild Ducks of North America**			
87-15-001	Common Mallard	C. Burgess	15,000	95.00	95.00
87-15-002	Wood Duck	C. Burgess	15,000	95.00	95.00
87-15-003	Green Winged Teal	C. Burgess	15,000	95.00	95.00
87-15-004	Hooded Merganser	C. Burgess	15,000	95.00	95.00
88-15-005	Northern Pintail	C. Burgess	15,000	95.00	95.00
88-15-006	Ruddy Duck Drake	C. Burgess	15,000	95.00	95.00
88-15-007	Bufflehead	C. Burgess	15,000	95.00	95.00
88-15-008	American Widgeon	C. Burgess	15,000	95.00	95.00
Hamilton Collection		**Snuggle Babies**			
88-16-001	Baby Bunnies	Jacqueline B.	Open	35.00	35.00
88-16-002	Baby Bears	Jacqueline B.	Open	35.00	35.00
88-16-003	Baby Skunks	Jacqueline B.	Open	35.00	35.00
88-16-004	Baby Foxes	Jacqueline B.	Open	35.00	35.00
89-16-005	Baby Chipmunks	Jacqueline B.	Open	35.00	35.00
89-16-006	Baby Raccoons	Jacqueline B.	Open	35.00	35.00
89-16-007	Baby Squirrels	Jacqueline B.	Open	35.00	35.00
89-16-008	Baby Fawns	Jacqueline B.	Open	35.00	35.00
Hamilton Collection		**Tropical Treasures**			
89-17-001	Sail-finned Surgeonfish	M. Wald	Open	37.50	37.50
89-17-002	Flag-tail Surgeonfish	M. Wald	Open	37.50	37.50
89-17-003	Pennant Butterfly Fish	M. Wald	Open	37.50	37.50
89-17-004	Sea Horse	M. Wald	Open	37.50	37.50
90-17-005	Zebra Turkey Fish	M. Wald	Open	37.50	37.50
90-17-006	Spotted Angel Fish	M. Wald	Open	37.50	37.50
90-17-007	Blue Girdled Angel Fish	M. Wald	Open	37.50	37.50
90-17-008	Beaked Coral Butterfly Fish	M. Wald	Open	37.50	37.50
Hamilton Collection		**A Celebration of Roses**			
89-18-001	Tiffany	N/A	Open	55.00	55.00
89-18-002	Color Magic	N/A	Open	55.00	55.00
89-18-003	Honor	N/A	Open	55.00	55.00
89-18-004	Brandy	N/A	Open	55.00	55.00
89-18-005	Miss All-American Beauty	N/A	Open	55.00	55.00
90-18-006	Oregold	N/A	Open	55.00	55.00
91-18-007	Paradise	N/A	Open	55.00	55.00
91-18-008	Ole'	N/A	Open	55.00	55.00
Hamilton Collection		**Heroes of Baseball-Porcelain Baseball Cards**			
90-19-001	Brooks Robinson	N/A	Open	19.50	19.50
90-19-002	Roberto Clemente	N/A	Open	19.50	19.50
90-19-003	Willie Mays	N/A	Open	19.50	19.50
90-19-004	Duke Snider	N/A	Open	19.50	19.50
91-19-005	Whitey Ford	N/A	Open	19.50	19.50
91-19-006	Gil Hodges	N/A	Open	19.50	19.50
91-19-007	Mickey Mantle	N/A	Open	19.50	19.50
91-19-008	Casey Stengel	N/A	Open	19.50	19.50
91-19-009	Jackie Robinson	N/A	Open	19.50	19.50
91-19-010	Ernie Banks	N/A	Open	19.50	19.50
91-19-011	Yogi Berra	N/A	Open	19.50	19.50
91-19-012	Satchel Page	N/A	Open	19.50	19.50
Hamilton Collection		**Little Night Owls**			
90-20-001	Tawny Owl	D.T. Lyttleton	Open	45.00	45.00
90-20-002	Barn Owl	D.T. Lyttleton	Open	45.00	45.00
90-20-003	Snowy Owl	D.T. Lyttleton	Open	45.00	45.00
91-20-004	Barred Owl	D.T. Lyttleton	Open	45.00	45.00
91-20-005	Great Horned Owl	D.T. Lyttleton	Open	45.00	45.00
91-20-006	White-Faced Owl	D.T. Lyttleton	Open	45.00	45.00
91-20-007	Great Grey Owl	D.T. Lyttleton	Open	45.00	45.00
91-20-008	Short-Eared Owl	D.T. Lyttleton	Open	45.00	45.00
Hamilton Collection		**Puppy Playtime Sculpture Collection**			
90-21-001	Double Take	J. Lamb	Open	29.50	29.50
91-21-002	Catch of the Day	J. Lamb	Open	29.50	29.50
91-21-003	Cabin Fever	J. Lamb	Open	29.50	29.50
91-21-004	Weekend Gardner	J. Lamb	Open	29.50	29.50
91-21-005	Hanging Out	J. Lamb	Open	29.50	29.50
91-21-006	Getting Acquainted	J. Lamb	Open	29.50	29.50
91-21-007	A New Leash on Life	J. Lamb	Open	29.50	29.50
91-21-008	Fun and Games	J. Lamb	Open	29.50	29.50
Hamilton Collection		**Freshwater Challenge**			
91-22-001	The Strike	M. Wald	Open	75.00	75.00
91-22-002	Rainbow Lure	M. Wald	Open	75.00	75.00
91-22-003	Sun Catcher	M. Wald	Open	75.00	75.00
92-22-004	Prized Catch	M. Wald	Open	75.00	75.00
Hamilton Collection		**Puss in Boots**			
92-23-001	Caught Napping	P. Cooper	Open	35.00	35.00
92-23-002	Sweet Dreams	P. Cooper	Open	35.00	35.00
93-23-003	Hide'n Go Seek	P. Cooper	Open	35.00	35.00
Hamilton Collection		**International Santa**			
92-24-001	Father Christmas	N/A	Open	55.00	55.00
92-24-002	Santa Claus	N/A	Open	55.00	55.00
92-24-003	Grandfather Frost	N/A	Open	55.00	55.00
93-24-004	Belsnickel	N/A	Open	55.00	55.00
93-24-005	Kris Kringle	N/A	Open	55.00	55.00
Hamilton Gifts/Enesco		**Maud Humphrey Bogart Figurines**			
88-01-001	Tea And Gossip H1301	M. Humphrey	Retrd.	65.00	85-120.00
88-01-002	Cleaning House H1303	M. Humphrey	Retrd.	60.00	70-100.00
88-01-003	Susanna H 1305	M. Humphrey	Retrd.	60.00	150-275.
88-01-004	Little Chickadees H1306	M. Humphrey	Retrd.	65.00	75-100.00
88-01-005	The Magic Kitten H1308	M. Humphrey	Retrd.	66.00	85-115.00
88-01-006	Seamstress H1309	M. Humphrey	Retrd.	66.00	125-150.
88-01-007	A Pleasure To Meet You H1310	M. Humphrey	15,000	65.00	75-100.00
88-01-008	My First Dance H1311	M. Humphrey	Retrd.	60.00	175-300.
88-01-009	Sarah H1312	M. Humphrey	Retrd.	60.00	275-425.
89-01-010	The Bride H1313	M. Humphrey	19,500	90.00	90.00
89-01-011	Sealed With A Kiss H1316	M. Humphrey	Retrd.	45.00	55-105.00
88-01-012	Special Friends H1317	M. Humphrey	Retrd.	66.00	100-140.
89-01-013	School Days H1318	M. Humphrey	Retrd.	42.50	60-100.00
89-01-014	Gift Of Love H1319	M. Humphrey	Retrd.	65.00	68.00
89-01-015	My 1st Birthday H1320	M. Humphrey	Retrd.	47.00	55.00
90-01-016	A Little Robin H1347	M. Humphrey	19,500	55.00	58.00
90-01-017	Autumn Days H1348	M. Humphrey	24,500	45.00	49.00
90-01-018	Little Playmates H1349	M. Humphrey	19,500	48.00	53.00
89-01-019	No More Tears H1351	M. Humphrey	24,500	44.00	49.00
89-01-020	Winter Fun H1354	M. Humphrey	Retired	46.00	54.00
89-01-021	Kitty's Lunch H1355	M. Humphrey	19,500	60.00	66.00
90-01-022	School Lesson H1356	M. Humphrey	19,500	77.00	79.00
89-01-023	In The Orchard H1373	M. Humphrey	24,500	33.00	36.00
89-01-024	The Little Captive H1374	M. Humphrey	19,500	55.00	58.00
89-01-025	Little Red Riding Hood H1381	M. Humphrey	24,500	42.50	46.00
89-01-026	Little Bo Peep H1382	M. Humphrey	24,500	45.00	49.00
90-01-027	Playtime H1383	M. Humphrey	19,500	60.00	66.00
90-01-028	Kitty's Bath H1384	M. Humphrey	19,500	103.00	109.00
89-01-029	Springtime Gathering H1385	M. Humphrey	7,500	295.00	299.00
89-01-030	A Sunday Outing H1386	M. Humphrey	15,000	135.00	139.50
89-01-031	Spring Beauties H1387	M. Humphrey	15,000	135.00	139.50
89-01-032	The Bride-Porcelain H1388	M. Humphrey	15,000	125.00	128.00
89-01-033	Little Chickadees-Porcelain H1389	M. Humphrey	15,000	125.00	128.00
89-01-034	Special Friends-Porcelain H1390	M. Humphrey	15,000	125.00	128.00
89-01-035	Playing Bridesmaid H5500	M. Humphrey	19,500	125.00	135.00
89-01-036	The Magic Kitten-Porcelain H5543	M. Humphrey	15,000	125.00	125.00
90-01-037	A Special Gift H5550	M. Humphrey	19,500	70.00	99.00
90-01-038	Holiday Surprise H5551	M. Humphrey	24,500	50.00	55.00
90-01-039	Winter Friends H5552	M. Humphrey	19,500	64.00	69.00
90-01-040	Winter Days H5553	M. Humphrey	24,500	50.00	55.00
90-01-041	My Winter Hat H5554	M. Humphrey	24,500	40.00	46.00
91-01-042	The Graduate H5559	M. Humphrey	19,500	75.00	75.00
90-01-043	A Chance Acquaintance H5589	M. Humphrey	19,500	70.00	135.00
91-01-044	Spring Frolic H5590	M. Humphrey	15,000	170.00	170.00
90-01-045	Sarah (Waterball) H5594	M. Humphrey	19,500	75.00	79.00
90-01-046	Susanna (Waterball) H5595	M. Humphrey	19,500	75.00	79.00
91-01-047	Spring Bouquet H5598	M. Humphrey	24,500	44.00	44.00
91-01-048	The Pinwheel H5600	M. Humphrey	24,500	45.00	45.00
91-01-049	Little Boy Blue H5612	M. Humphrey	19,500	55.00	55.00
91-01-050	Little Miss Muffet H5621	M. Humphrey	24,500	75.00	75.00
91-01-051	My First Dance-Porcelain H5650	M. Humphrey	15,000	110.00	110.00
91-01-052	Sarah-Porcelain H5651	M. Humphrey	15,000	110.00	110.00
91-01-053	Susanna-Porcelain H5652	M. Humphrey	15,000	110.00	110.00
91-01-054	Tea And Gossip-Porcelain H5653	M. Humphrey	15,000	132.00	132.00
91-01-055	Cleaning House (Waterball) H5654	M. Humphrey	19,500	75.00	75.00
91-01-056	My First Dance (Waterball) H5655	M. Humphrey	19,500	75.00	75.00
91-01-057	Hush A Bye Baby H5695	M. Humphrey	19,500	62.00	62.00
91-01-058	All Bundled Up -910015	M. Humphrey	19,500	85.00	85.00
91-01-059	Doubles -910023	M. Humphrey	19,500	70.00	70.00
91-01-060	Melissa -910031	M. Humphrey	24,500	55.00	55.00
91-01-061	My Snow Shovel -910058	M. Humphrey	19,500	7000	70.00
91-01-062	Winter Ride -910066	M. Humphrey	19,500	60.00	60.00
91-01-063	Melissa (Waterball) -910074	M. Humphrey	19,500	40.00	40.00
91-01-064	Winter Days (Waterball) -915130	M. Humphrey	19,500	75.00	75.00
91-01-065	Winter Friends (Waterball) -915149	M. Humphrey	19,500	75.00	75.00
91-01-066	My Winter Hat -921017	M. Humphrey	15,000	80.00	80.00
91-01-067	Winter Fun -921025	M. Humphrey	15,000	90.00	90.00
92-01-068	Spring's Child 910244	M. Humphrey	24,500	50.00	50.00
92-01-069	Summer's Child 910252	M. Humphrey	24,500	50.00	50.00
92-01-070	Autumn's Child 910260	M. Humphrey	24,500	50.00	50.00
92-01-071	Winter's Child 910279	M. Humphrey	24,500	50.00	50.00
92-01-072	Jack and Jill 910155	M. Humphrey	19,500	75.00	75.00
92-01-073	The Young Artist 910228	M. Humphrey	19,500	75.00	75.00
92-01-074	Stars and Stripes Forever 910201	M. Humphrey	Open	75.00	75.00
92-01-075	New Friends 910171	M. Humphrey	15,000	125.00	125.00
92-01-076	Under The Mistletoe 910309	M. Humphrey	19,500	75.00	75.00
92-01-077	Hollies For You 910317	M. Humphrey	24,500	55.00	55.00
92-01-078	Hush! Santa's Coming 915378	M. Humphrey	19,500	50.00	50.00
92-01-079	A Melody For You 915432	M. Humphrey	Open	60.00	60.00
92-01-080	The Christmas Carol 915823	M. Humphrey	24,500	75.00	75.00
92-01-081	Susanna (Musical) 921084	M. Humphrey	7,500	125.00	125.00
92-01-082	Sarah (Musical) 921076	M. Humphrey	7,500	125.00	125.00
92-01-083	Hollies For You (Musical) 921092	M. Humphrey	5,000	125.00	125.00
93-01-084	Tee Time 915386	M. Humphrey	10,000	50.00	50.00
93-01-085	The Entertainer 910562	M. Humphrey	19,500	60.00	60.00
93-01-086	A Basket Full of Blessings 910147	M. Humphrey	15,000	55.00	55.00
93-01-087	Love's First Bloom 910120	M. Humphrey	15,000	50.00	50.00
93-01-088	Bedtime Blessings 910236	M. Humphrey	10,000	60.00	60.00
93-01-089	Flying Lessons 910139	M. Humphrey	15,000	50.00	50.00
93-01-090	Playing Mama 5th Anniv. Figurine 915963	M. Humphrey	Yr.Iss.	80.00	80.00
93-01-091	Playing Mama Event Figurine 915963R	M. Humphrey	Yr.Iss.	80.00	80.00
Hamilton Gifts/Enesco		**Maud Humphrey Bogart Gallery Figurines**			
91-02-001	Mother's Treasures H5619	M. Humphrey	15,000	118.00	118.00
91-02-002	Sharing Secrets-910007	M. Humphrey	15,000	120.00	120.00
92-02-003	New Friends-910171	M. Humphrey	15,000	125.00	125.00
92-02-004	A Little Bird Told Me So-910570	M. Humphrey	7,500	120.00	120.00
93-02-005	May I Have This Dance?-915750	M. Humphrey	Yr.Iss.	Unkn.	Unkn.
Hamilton Gifts/Enesco		**Maud Humphrey Bogart Symbol Of Membership Figurines**			
91-03-001	A Flower For You H5596	M. Humphrey	Closed	Unkn.	48.00
92-03-002	Sunday Best M0002	M. Humphrey	Closed	Unkn.	Unkn.
93-03-003	Playful Companions M0003	M. Humphrey	Yr.Iss.	Unkn.	Unkn.
Hamilton Gifts/Enesco		**Maud Humphrey Bogart Collectors' Club Members Only**			
91-04-001	Friends For Life MH911	M. Humphrey	Closed	60.00	120-180.
92-04-002	Nature's Little Helper MH921	M. Humphrey	Open	65.00	65.00
Hamilton Gifts/Enesco		**Maud Humphrey Bogart Victorian Village Mini Figurines**			
93-05-001	No.5 Greenwood-911569	M. Humphrey	18,840	50.00	50.00
93-05-002	Village Sign-911542	M. Humphrey	Open	12.00	12.00
93-05-003	No.5 Greenwood Accessories-911534	M. Humphrey	Open	20.00	20.00
93-05-004	A.J. Warner-911518	M. Humphrey	Open	12.00	12.00
93-05-005	Maud Humphrey-911496	M. Humphrey	Open	12.00	12.00
93-05-006	Mabel Humphrey-911933	M. Humphrey	Open	12.00	12.00
93-05-007	No.5 Greenwood Collectors' Proof Set -913804	M. Humphrey	1,868	120.00	120.00
Harbour Lights		**Original Collection**			
91-01-001	Admiralty Head 101	Harbor Lights	5,500	60.00	60.00
91-01-002	Cape Hatteras 102	Harbor Lights	Retrd.	60.00	60.00
92-01-003	Cape Hatteras 102R	Harbor Lights	5,500	60.00	60.00
91-01-004	West Quoddy Head 103	Harbor Lights	5,500	60.00	60.00
91-01-005	Sandy Hook 104	Harbor Lights	5,500	60.00	60.00
91-01-006	Point Loma 105	Harbor Lights	5,500	60.00	60.00
91-01-007	North Head 106	Harbor Lights	5,500	60.00	60.00
91-01-008	Umpqua River 107	Harbor Lights	5,500	60.00	60.00
91-01-009	Burrows Island 108	Harbor Lights	5,500	60.00	60.00
91-01-010	Cape Blanco 109	Harbor Lights	5,500	60.00	60.00
91-01-011	Yaquina Head 110	Harbor Lights	5,500	60.00	60.00
91-01-012	Coquille River 111	Harbor Lights	Retrd.	60.00	60.00
91-01-013	Sand Island 112	Harbor Lights	5,500	60.00	60.00
91-01-014	Port Niagara 113	Harbor Lights	5,500	60.00	60.00

Company		Series			
Number	**Name**	**Artist**	**Edition Limit**	**Issue Price**	**Quote**
91-01-015	Gt. Captain's Island 114	Harbor Lights	5,500	60.00	60.00
91-01-016	St. George's Reef 115	Harbor Lights	5,500	60.00	60.00
91-01-017	Castle Hill 116	Harbor Lights	5,500	60.00	60.00
91-01-018	Boston Harbor 117	Harbor Lights	5,500	60.00	60.00
Harbour Lights		**Great Lakes Series**			
92-02-001	Old Mackinac Point 118	Harbor Lights	5,500	65.00	65.00
92-02-002	Cana Island 119	Harbor Lights	5,500	60.00	60.00
92-02-003	Grosse Point 120	Harbor Lights	5,500	60.00	60.00
92-02-004	Marblehead 121	Harbor Lights	5,500	50.00	50.00
92-02-005	Buffalo 122	Harbor Lights	5,500	60.00	60.00
92-02-006	Michigan City123	Harbor Lights	5,500	60.00	60.00
92-02-007	Split Rock 124	Harbor Lights	5,500	60.00	60.00
Harbour Lights		**New England Series**			
92-03-001	Portland Head 125	Harbor Lights	5,500	65.00	65.00
92-03-002	Nauset 126	Harbor Lights	5,500	65.00	65.00
92-03-003	Whaleback127	Harbor Lights	5,500	60.00	60.00
92-03-004	Southeast Block Island128	Harbor Lights	5,500	70.00	70.00
92-03-005	New London Ledge 129	Harbor Lights	5,500	65.00	65.00
92-03-006	Portland Breakwater 130	Harbor Lights	5,500	60.00	60.00
92-03-007	Minot's Ledge131	Harbor Lights	5,500	60.00	60.00
Harbour Lights		**Southern Belles**			
93-04-001	Ponce de Leon, FL 132	Harbor Lights	5,500	60.00	60.00
93-04-002	Tybee, GA 133	Harbor Lights	5,500	60.00	60.00
93-04-003	Key West, FL 134	Harbor Lights	5,500	60.00	60.00
93-04-004	Ocracoke, NC 135	Harbor Lights	5,500	60.00	60.00
93-04-005	Hilton Head, SC 136	Harbor Lights	5,500	60.00	60.00
93-04-006	St. Simons, GA 137	Harbor Lights	5,500	65.00	65.00
93-04-007	St. Augustine, FL 138	Harbor Lights	5,500	65.00	65.00
Hawthorne		**Concord: The Hometown of American Literature Victoria Grove Collection**			
92-01-001	Hawthorne's Wayside Retreat	K.&H. LeVan	12/93	39.90	39.90
92-01-002	Emerson's Old Manse	K.&H. LeVan	7/94	39.90	39.90
92-01-003	Lilac Cottage	K.&H. LeVan	12/93	34.90	34.90
92-01-004	Rose Haven	K.&H. LeVan	9/94	34.90	34.90
Hawthorne		**Stonefield Valley**			
92-02-001	Springbridge Cottage	K.&H. LeVan	12/93	34.90	34.90
92-02-002	Meadowbrook School	K.&H. LeVan	5/94	34.90	34.90
92-02-003	Weaver's Cottage	K.&H. LeVan	9/94	37.90	37.90
Hawthorne		**Strolling Through Colonial America**			
91-03-001	Jefferson's Ordinance	K.&H. LeVan	Closed	34.90	34.90
92-03-002	Millrace Store	K.&H. LeVan	Closed	34.90	34.90
92-03-003	Higgins' Grist Mill	K.&H. LeVan	Closed	37.90	37.90
92-03-004	Eastbrook Church	K.&H. LeVan	Closed	37.90	37.90
92-03-005	Court House on the Green	K.&H. LeVan	8/93	37.90	37.90
92-03-006	Captain Lee's Grammar School	K.&H. LeVan	12/93	37.90	37.90
92-03-007	The Village Smithy	K.&H. LeVan	2/94	39.90	39.90
Hawthorne		**Lost Victorians of Old San Francisco**			
92-04-001	The Grande Dame of Nob Hill	R. Bronillette	12/93	34.90	34.90
92-04-002	The Empress of Russian Hill	R. Bronillette	9/94	34.90	34.90
Hawthorne		**Rockwell's Home for the Holidays**			
92-05-001	Christmas Eve at the Studio	Unkn.	12/93	34.90	34.90
92-05-002	Bringing Home the Tree	Unkn.	8/94	34.90	34.90
Hawthorne		**Gone With theWInd Collection**			
92-06-001	Tara . . .Scarlett's Pride	K.&H. LeVan	12/94	39.90	39.90
92-06-002	Twelve Oaks: The Romance Begins	K.&H. LeVan	3/95	39.90	39.90
John Hine N.A. Ltd.		**David Winter Cottages**			
80-01-001	The Wine Merchant	D. Winter	Open	28.90	50.00
80-01-002	Little Market	D. Winter	Open	28.90	50.00
80-01-003	Rose Cottage	D. Winter	Open	28.90	50.00
80-01-004	Market Street	D. Winter	Open	48.80	80.00
81-01-005	Single Oast	D. Winter	Open	22.00	50-130.00
81-01-006	Triple Oast	D. Winter	Open	59.90	106.00
81-01-007	Stratford House	D. Winter	Open	74.80	118.00
81-01-008	The Village	D. Winter	Open	362.00	550.00
82-01-009	Drover's Cottage	D. Winter	Open	22.00	30.00
82-01-010	Sussex Cottage	D. Winter	Open	22.00	38.00
82-01-011	The Village Shop	D. Winter	Open	22.00	30.00
82-01-012	The Dower House	D. Winter	Open	22.00	30.00
82-01-013	Cotswold Cottage	D. Winter	Open	22.00	30.00
82-01-014	The Old Distillery	D. Winter	Open	312.20	530.00
83-01-015	The Bakehouse	D. Winter	Open	31.40	54.00
83-01-016	The Bothy	D. Winter	Open	31.40	54.00
83-01-017	Fisherman's Wharf	D. Winter	Open	31.40	54.00
83-01-018	The Green Dragon Inn	D. Winter	Open	31.40	54.00
83-01-019	Pilgrim's Rest	D. Winter	Open	48.80	80.00
84-01-020	The Parsonage	D. Winter	Open	390.00	530.00
85-01-021	The Cooper's Cottage	D. Winter	Open	57.90	78.00
85-01-022	Kent Cottage	D. Winter	Open	48.80	94.00
85-01-023	The Schoolhouse	D. Winter	Open	24.10	42.00
85-01-024	Craftsmen's Cottages	D. Winter	Open	24.10	38.00
85-01-025	The Vicarage	D. Winter	Open	24.10	38.00
85-01-026	The Hogs Head Tavern	D. Winter	Open	24.10	42.00
85-01-027	Blackfriars Grange	D. Winter	Open	24.10	38.00
85-01-028	Shirehall	D. Winter	Open	24.10	42.00
85-01-029	The Apothecary Shop	D. Winter	Open	24.10	42.00
85-01-030	Yeoman's Farmhouse	D. Winter	Open	24.10	38.00
85-01-031	Meadowbank Cottages	D. Winter	Open	24.10	38.00
85-01-032	St. George's Church	D. Winter	Open	24.10	42.00
87-01-033	Smuggler's Creek	D. Winter	Open	390.00	490.00
87-01-034	Devoncombe	D. Winter	Open	73.00	106.00
87-01-035	Tamar Cottage	D. Winter	Open	45.30	70.00
87-01-036	There was a Crooked House	D. Winter	Open	96.90	144.00
87-01-037	Devon Creamery	D. Winter	Open	62.90	94.00
88 01 038	Windmill	D. Winter	Open	37.50	50.00
88-01-039	Lock-keepers Cottage	D. Winter	Open	65.00	80.00
88-01-040	Derbyshire Cotton Mill	D. Winter	Open	65.00	80.00
88-01-041	Gunsmiths	D. Winter	Open	78.00	94.00
88-01-042	John Benbow's Farmhouse	D. Winter	Open	78.00	92.00
88-01-043	Coal Miner's Row	D. Winter	Open	90.00	106.00
88-01-044	Lacemaker's Cottage	D. Winter	Open	120.00	144.00
88-01-045	Cornish Harbour	D. Winter	Open	120.00	144.00
88-01-046	Cornish Engine House	D. Winter	Open	120.00	144.00
91-01-047	Inglenook Cottage	D. Winter	Open	60.00	66.00
91-01-048	The Weaver's Lodgings	D. Winter	Open	65.00	72.00

Company		Series			
Number	**Name**	**Artist**	**Edition Limit**	**Issue Price**	**Quote**
91-01-049	The Printers and The Bookbinders	D. Winter	Open	120.00	132.00
91-01-050	Moonlight Haven	D. Winter	Open	120.00	132.00
91-01-051	Castle in the Air	D. Winter	Open	675.00	675.00
John Hine N.A. Ltd.		**David Winter Retired Cottages**			
80-02-001	Mill House	D. Winter	Closed	50.00	2000-2800.
80-02-002	Little Mill	D. Winter	Closed	40.00	1700-2300.
80-02-003	Three Ducks Inn	D. Winter	Closed	60.00	2000-2500.
80-02-004	Dove Cottage	D. Winter	Closed	60.00	1700-2300.
80-02-005	The Forge	D. Winter	Closed	60.00	1800-2500.
80-02-006	Little Forge	D. Winter	Closed	40.00	5625.00.
80-02-007	Mill House-remodeled	D. Winter	Closed	Unkn.	Unkn.
80-02-008	Little Mill-remodeled	D. Winter	Closed	Unkn.	Unkn.
80-02-009	The Coaching Inn	D. Winter	Closed	165.00	4500-7000.
80-02-010	Quayside	D. Winter	Closed	60.00	1800-2600.
81-02-011	St. Paul's Cathedral	D. Winter	Closed	40.00	2000-2800.
81-02-012	Castle Keep	D. Winter	Closed	30.00	1800-2400.
81-02-013	Chichester Cross	D. Winter	Closed	50.00	3400-3600.
81-02-014	Double Oast	D. Winter	Closed	60.00	2800.00
81-02-015	The Old Curiosity Shop	D. Winter	Closed	40.00	1200-2500.
81-02-016	Tythe Barn	D. Winter	Closed	39.30	2250-4000.
82-02-017	Sabrina's Cottage	D. Winter	Closed	30.00	2000-3000.
82-02-018	William Shakespeare's Birthplace(large)	D. Winter	Closed	60.00	600-1650.
82-02-019	Cornish Cottage	D. Winter	Closed	30.00	1000-2800.
82-02-020	Blacksmith's Cottage	D. Winter	Closed	22.00	350-600.
82-02-021	Moorland Cottage	D. Winter	Closed	22.00	250-450.
82-02-022	The Haybarn	D. Winter	Closed	22.00	350-600.
82-02-023	Miner's Cottage	D. Winter	Closed	22.00	250-375.
83-02-024	The Alms Houses	D. Winter	Closed	59.90	450-750.
82-02-025	The House on Top	D. Winter	Closed	92.30	275-400.
84-02-026	House of the Master Mason	D. Winter	Closed	74.80	275-325.
83-02-027	Woodcutter's Cottage	D. Winter	Closed	87.00	250-500.
85-02-028	Hermit's Humble Home	D. Winter	Closed	87.00	250-375.
83-02-029	The Cotton Mill	D. Winter	Closed	41.30	600-800.
83-02-030	Cornish Tin Mine	D. Winter	Closed	22.00	75-150.00
87-02-031	Ebenezer Scrooge's Counting House	D. Winter	Closed	96.90	200-300.
88-02-032	Jim'll Fixit	D. Winter	Closed	350.00	2100-3500.
82-02-033	Fairytale Castle	D. Winter	Closed	115.40	225-500.
85-02-034	Suffolk House	D. Winter	Closed	48.80	70-145.00
86-02-035	Crofter's Cottage	D. Winter	Closed	51.00	60-125.00
88-02-036	Hogmanay	D. Winter	Closed	100.00	150-300.
89-02-037	A Christmas Carol	D. Winter	Closed	135.00	150-400.
88-02-038	The Grange	D. Winter	Closed	120.00	1100-1500.
86-02-039	Falstaff's Manor	D. Winter	Closed	242.00	325-400.
82-02-040	Cotswold Village	D. Winter	Closed	59.90	100-150.
85-02-041	Squires Hall	D. Winter	Closed	92.30	130-230.
90-02-042	Mr. Fezziwig's Emporium	D. Winter	Closed	135.00	100-200.
81-02-043	Tudor Manor House	D. Winter	Closed	48.80	135-275.
82-02-044	Brookside Hamlet	D. Winter	Closed	74.80	100-200.
84-02-045	Spinner's Cottage	D. Winter	Closed	28.90	75-125.00
87-02-046	Orchard Cottage	D. Winter	Closed	91.30	150-225.
88-02-047	Bottle Kilns	D. Winter	Closed	78.00	100-175.
91-02-048	Fred's Home:"A Merry Christmas, Uncle Ebeneezer," said Scrooge's nephew Fred, "and a Happy New Year."	D. Winter	Closed	145.00	125-185.
92-02-049	Audrey's Tea Room	D. Winter	Closed	90.00	175-350.
84-02-050	Tollkeeper's Cottage	D. Winter	Closed	87.00	150-250.
84-02-051	Castle Gate	D. Winter	Closed	154.90	200-275.
92-02-052	Diorama-Bright	D. Winter	Closed	50.00	N/A
82-02-053	Ivy Cottage	D. Winter	Closed	22.00	50-88.00
83-02-054	Hertford Court	D. Winter	Closed	87.00	165-188.
84-02-055	The Chapel	D. Winter	Closed	48.80	125.00
84-02-056	Snow Cottage	D. Winter	Closed	74.80	140-200.
92-02-057	Scrooge's School	D. Winter	Closed	160.00	160.00
92-02-058	Mad Baron Fourthrite's Folly	D. Winter	Closed	275.00	500.00
John Hine N.A. Ltd.		**David Winter Retired Cottages-Tiny Series**			
80-03-001	William Shakespeare's Birthplace	D. Winter	Closed	Unkn.	1000-1200.
80-03-002	Ann Hathaway's Cottage	D. Winter	Closed	Unkn.	1200.00
80-03-003	Sulgrave Manor	D. Winter	Closed	Unkn.	1000-1200.
80-03-004	Cotswold Farmhouse	D. Winter	Closed	Unkn.	1000-1200.
80-03-005	Crown Inn	D. Winter	Closed	Unkn.	1000-1200.
80-03-006	St. Nicholas' Church	D. Winter	Closed	Unkn.	1000-1500.
John Hine N.A. Ltd.		**Collectors Guild Exclusives**			
87-04-001	Robin Hood's Hideaway	D. Winter	Closed	54.00	300-600.
87-04-002	The Village Scene	D. Winter	Closed	Gift	200-400.
88-04-003	Queen Elizabeth Slept Here	D. Winter	Closed	183.00	325-500.
88-04-004	Black Bess Inn	D. Winter	Closed	60.00	200-300.
88-04-005	The Pavillion	D. Winter	Closed	52.00	250-300.
89-04-007	Homeguard	D. Winter	Closed	105.00	200-300.
89-04-008	Coal Shed	D. Winter	Closed	112.00	225-400.
89-04-009	Street Scene	D. Winter	Closed	Gift	150-250.
90-04-010	The Cobblers	D. Winter	Closed	40.00	75-125.00
90-04-011	The Pottery	D. Winter	Closed	40.00	75-150.00
90-04-012	Cartwrights Cottage	D. Winter	Closed	45.00	90-125.00
90-04-013	Plucked Duck	D. Winter	Closed	Gift	100-200.
91-04-014	Pershore Mill	D. Winter	Closed	Gift	85-125.
91-04-015	Tomfool's Cottage	D. Winter	Closed	100.00	100-120.
91-04-016	Will O' The Wisp	D. Winter	Closed	120.00	120.00
92-04-017	Candle Maker's	D. Winter	Closed	65.00	65.00
92-04-018	Bee Keeper's	D. Winter	Closed	65.00	65.00
92-04-019	Irish Water Mill	D. Winter	Closed	Gift	80.00
93-04-020	Thameside	D. Winter	Yr.Iss.	79.00	79.00
93-04-021	Swan Upping Cottage	D. Winter	Yr.Iss.	69.00	69.00
93-04-022	On The River Bank	D. Winter	Yr.Iss.	Gift	N/A
John Hine N.A. Ltd.		**Scottish Collection**			
89-05-001	Scottish Crofter	D. Winter	Open	42.00	54.00
89-05-002	House on the Loch	D. Winter	Open	65.00	80.00
89-05-003	Gillie's Cottage	D. Winter	Open	65.00	80.00
89-05-004	Gatekeeper's	D. Winter	Open	65.00	80.00
89-05-005	MacBeth's Castle	D. Winter	Open	200.00	244.00
89-05-006	Old Distillery	D. Winter	Open	450.00	530.00
John Hine N.A. Ltd.		**Irish Collection**			
92-06-001	Irish Round Tower	D. Winter	Open	65.00	65.00
92-06-002	Secret Shebeen	D. Winter	Open	70.00	70.00
92-06-003	Fogartys	D. Winter	Open	75.00	75.00
92-06-004	Only A Span Apart	D. Winter	Open	80.00	80.00
92-06-005	Murphys	D. Winter	Open	100.00	100.00
92-06-006	O'Donovan's Castle	D. Winter	Open	145.00	145.00

FIGURINES

Company		Series			
Number	**Name**	**Artist**	**Edition Limit**	**Issue Price**	**Quote**
John Hine N.A. Ltd.		**British Traditions**			
90-07-001	Burns' Reading Room	D. Winter	Open	31.00	34.00
90-07-002	Stonecutters Cottage	D. Winter	Open	48.00	52.00
90-07-003	The Boat House	D. Winter	Open	37.50	42.00
90-07-004	Pudding Cottage	D. Winter	Open	78.00	86.00
90-07-005	Blossom Cottage	D. Winter	Open	59.00	64.00
90-07-006	Knight's Castle	D. Winter	Open	59.00	64.00
90-07-007	St. Anne's Well	D. Winter	Open	48.00	52.00
90-07-008	Grouse Moor Lodge	D. Winter	Open	48.00	52.00
90-07-009	Staffordshire Vicarage	D. Winter	Open	48.00	52.00
90-07-010	Harvest Barn	D. Winter	Open	31.00	34.00
90-07-011	Guy Fawkes	D. Winter	Open	31.00	34.00
90-07-012	Bull & Bush	D. Winter	Open	37.50	42.00
John Hine N.A. Ltd.		**David Winter Cameos**			
92-08-001	Brooklet Bridge	D. Winter	Open	12.50	12.50
92-08-002	Poultry Ark	D. Winter	Open	12.50	12.50
92-08-003	The Potting Shed	D. Winter	Open	12.50	12.50
92-08-004	Lych Gate	D. Winter	Open	12.50	12.50
92-08-005	One Man Jail	D. Winter	Open	12.50	12.50
92-08-006	Market Day	D. Winter	Open	12.50	12.50
92-08-007	Welsh Pig Pen	D. Winter	Open	12.50	12.50
92-08-008	The Privy	D. Winter	Open	12.50	12.50
92-08-009	Greenwood Wagon	D. Winter	Open	12.50	12.50
92-08-010	Saddle Steps	D. Winter	Open	12.50	12.50
92-08-011	Barley Malt Kilns	D. Winter	Open	12.50	12.50
92-08-012	Penny Wishing Well	D. Winter	Open	12.50	12.50
92-08-013	Diorama-Light	D. Winter	Open	30.00	30.00
John Hine N.A. Ltd.		**Shires Collection**			
93-09-001	Oxfordshire Goat Yard	D. Winter	Open	32.00	32.00
93-09-002	Shropshire Pig Shelter	D. Winter	Open	32.00	32.00
93-09-003	Hampshire Hutches	D. Winter	Open	34.00	34.00
93-09-004	Wiltshire Waterwheel	D. Winter	Open	34.00	34.00
93-09-005	Cheshire Kennels	D. Winter	Open	36.00	36.00
93-09-006	Derbyshire Dovecote	D. Winter	Open	36.00	36.00
93-09-007	Staffordshire Stable	D. Winter	Open	36.00	36.00
93-09-008	Berkshire Milking Byre	D. Winter	Open	38.00	38.00
93-09-009	Buckinghamshire Bull Pen	D. Winter	Open	38.00	38.00
93-09-010	Lancashire Donkey Shed	D. Winter	Open	38.00	38.00
93-09-011	Yorkshire Sheep Fold	D. Winter	Open	38.00	38.00
93-09-012	Gloucestershire Greenhouse	D. Winter	Open	40.00	40.00
John Hine N.A. Ltd.		**American Collection**			
89-10-001	The Out House	M. Wideman	Open	15.00	16.00
89-10-002	Colonial Wellhouse	M. Wideman	Open	15.00	16.00
89-10-003	Wisteria	M. Wideman	Open	15.00	22.00
89-10-004	The Blockhouse	M. Wideman	Closed	25.00	25.00
89-10-005	Garconniere	M. Wideman	Open	25.00	28.00
89-10-006	The Log Cabin	M. Wideman	Open	45.00	56.00
89-10-007	Cherry Hill School	M. Wideman	Open	45.00	56.00
89-10-008	The Maple Sugar Shack	M. Wideman	Open	50.00	56.00
89-10-009	The Kissing Bridge	M. Wideman	Closed	50.00	56.00
89-10-010	The Gingerbread House	M. Wideman	Open	60.00	72.00
89-10-011	The New England Church	M. Wideman	Open	79.00	100.00
89-10-012	The Opera House	M. Wideman	Closed	89.00	100.00
89-10-013	The Pacific Lighthouse	M. Wideman	Open	89.00	110.00
89-10-014	King William Tavern	M. Wideman	Closed	99.00	100-200.
89-10-015	The Mission	M. Wideman	Open	99.00	110.00
89-10-016	New England Lighthouse	M. Wideman	Open	99.00	110.00
89-10-017	The River Bell	M. Wideman	Open	99.00	120.00
89-10-018	Plantation House	M. Wideman	Closed	119.00	185.00
89-10-019	Town Hall	M. Wideman	Open	129.00	144.00
89-10-020	Dog House	M. Wideman	Open	10.00	12.00
89-10-021	Star Cottage	M. Wideman	Open	30.00	34.00
89-10-022	Sod House	M. Wideman	Closed	40.00	62.00
89-10-023	Barber Shop	M. Wideman	Open	40.00	44.00
89-10-024	Octagonal House	M. Wideman	Open	40.00	44.00
89-10-025	Cajun Cottage	M. Wideman	Open	50.00	56.00
89-10-026	Prairie Forge	M. Wideman	Open	65.00	72.00
89-10-027	Oxbow Saloon	M. Wideman	Open	90.00	100.00
89-10-028	Sierra Mine	M. Wideman	Closed	120.00	149.00
89-10-029	California Winery	M. Wideman	Open	180.00	198.00
89-10-030	Railhead Inn	M. Wideman	Open	250.00	276.00
89-10-031	Haunted House	M. Wideman	Open	100.00	110.00
89-10-032	Tobacconist	M. Wideman	Open	45.00	50.00
89-10-033	Hawaiian Grass Hut	M. Wideman	Closed	45.00	50.00
89-10-034	The Old Mill	M. Wideman	Open	100.00	110.00
89-10-035	Band Stand	M. Wideman	Open	90.00	100.00
89-10-036	Seaside Cottage	M. Wideman	Closed	225.00	248.00
89-10-037	Tree House	M. Wideman	Open	45.00	50.00
89-10-038	Hacienda	M. Wideman	Open	51.00	56.00
89-10-039	Sweetheart Cottage	M. Wideman	Open	45.00	50.00
89-10-040	Forty-Niner Cabin	M. Wideman	Open	50.00	56.00
91-10-041	Desert Storm Tent	M. Wideman	Closed	75.00	75.00
91-10-042	Paul Revere's House	M. Wideman	Closed	90.00	100.00
91-10-043	Mo At Work	M. Wideman	Closed	35.00	35-70.00
91-10-044	Church in the Dale	M. Wideman	Open	130.00	144.00
91-10-045	Milk House	M. Wideman	Open	20.00	22.00
91-10-046	Moe's Diner	M. Wideman	Open	100.00	110.00
91-10-047	Fire Station	M. Wideman	Open	160.00	176.00
91-10-048	Joe's Service Station	M. Wideman	Open	90.00	100.00
92-10-049	News Stand	M. Wideman	Open	30.00	30.00
92-10-050	Village Mercantile	M. Wideman	Open	60.00	60.00
92-10-051	Grain Elevator	M. Wideman	Open	110.00	110.00
92-10-052	Telephone Booth	M. Wideman	Open	15.00	15.00
92-10-053	Topper's Drive-In	M. Wideman	Open	120.00	120.00
93-10-054	West Coast Longhouse	M. Wideman	Open	100.00	100.00
93-10-055	Mandan Earth Lodge	M. Wideman	Open	56.00	56.00
93-10-056	Plains Tipee	M. Wideman	Open	68.00	68.00
93-10-057	Sweat Lodge	M. Wideman	Open	34.00	34.00
93-10-058	Elm Bark Longhouse	M. Wideman	Open	56.00	56.00
93-10-059	Igloo	M. Wideman	Open	60.00	60.00
John Hine N.A. Ltd.		**Mushrooms**			
89-11-001	Royal Bank of Mushland	C. Lawrence	2,500	235.00	235.00
89-11-002	The Elders Mushroom	C. Lawrence	2,500	175.00	175.00.
89-11-003	The Cobblers	C. Lawrence	2,500	265.00	265.00
89-11-004	The Mush Hospital for Malingerers	C. Lawrence	2,500	250.00	250.00
89-11-005	The Ministry	C. Lawrence	2,500	185.00	185.00
89-11-006	The Gift Shop	C. Lawrence	1,200	350.00	420.00
89-11-007	The Constables	C. Lawrence	2,500	200.00	200.00
89-11-008	The Princess Palace	C. Lawrence	750	600.00	730.00
John Hine N.A. Ltd.		**Bugaboos**			
89-12-001	Arnold	John Hine Studio	Closed	45.00	45.00
89-12-002	Edna	John Hine Studio	Closed	45.00	45.00
89-12-003	Wilbur	John Hine Studio	Closed	45.00	45.00
89-12-004	Beryl	John Hine Studio	Closed	45.00	45.00
89-12-005	Gerald	John Hine Studio	Closed	45.00	45.00
89-12-006	Wesley	John Hine Studio	Closed	45.00	45.00
89-12-007	Oscar	John Hine Studio	Closed	45.00	45.00
89-12-008	Lizzie	John Hine Studio	Closed	45.00	45.00
89-12-009	Enid	John Hine Studio	Closed	45.00	45.00
John Hine N.A. Ltd.		**Great British Pubs**			
89-13-001	Smith's Arms	M. Cooper	Open	28.00	28.00
89-13-002	The Plough	M. Cooper	Open	28.00	28.00
89-13-003	King's Arms	M. Cooper	Closed	28.00	28.00
89-13-004	White Tower	M. Cooper	Open	35.00	35.00
89-13-005	Old Bridge House	M. Cooper	Open	37.50	37.50
89-13-006	White Horse	M. Cooper	Open	39.50	39.50
89-13-007	Jamaica Inn	M. Cooper	Open	39.50	39.50
89-13-008	The George	M. Cooper	Open	57.50	57.50
89-13-009	Montague Arms	M. Cooper	Open	57.50	57.50
89-13-010	Blue Bell	M. Cooper	Open	57.50	57.50
89-13-011	The Lion	M. Cooper	Open	57.50	57.50
89-13-012	Coach & Horses	M. Cooper	Open	79.50	79.50
89-13-013	Ye Olde Spotted Horse	M. Cooper	Open	79.50	79.50
89-13-014	The Crown Inn	M. Cooper	Open	79.50	79.50
89-13-015	The Bell	M. Cooper	Closed	79.50	100-350.
89-13-016	Black Swan	M. Cooper	Closed	79.50	100-350.
89-13-017	Ye Grapes	M. Cooper	Open	87.50	87.50
89-13-018	Old Bull Inn	M. Cooper	Open	87.50	87.50
89-13-019	Dickens Inn	M. Cooper	Open	100.00	100.00
89-13-020	Sherlock Holmes	M. Cooper	Closed	100.00	200.00
89-13-021	George Somerset	M. Cooper	Open	100.00	100.00
89-13-022	The Feathers	M. Cooper	Open	200.00	200.00
89-13-023	Hawkeshead	M. Cooper	Open	Unkn.	900.00
John Hine N.A. Ltd.		**Great British Pubs-Yard of Pubs**			
89-14-001	Grenadier	M. Cooper	Closed	25.00	25.00
89-14-002	Black Friars	M. Cooper	Closed	25.00	25.00
89-14-003	Falkland Arms	M. Cooper	Closed	25.00	25.00
89-14-004	George & Pilgrims	M. Cooper	Closed	25.00	25.00
89-14-005	Dirty Duck	M. Cooper	Closed	25.00	25.00
89-14-006	Wheatsheaf	M. Cooper	Closed	35.00	35.00
89-14-007	Lygon Arms	M. Cooper	Closed	35.00	35.00
89-14-008	Suffolk Bull	M. Cooper	Closed	35.00	35.00
89-14-009	The Swan	M. Cooper	Closed	35.00	35.00
89-14-010	The Falstaff	M. Cooper	Closed	35.00	35.00
89-14-011	The Eagle	M. Cooper	Closed	35.00	35.00
89-14-012	The Green Man	M. Cooper	Closed	Unkn.	75.00
John Hine N.A. Ltd.		**Father Christmas**			
88-15-001	Standing	J. King	Closed	70.00	70.00
88-15-002	Feet	J. King	Closed	70.00	70.00
88-15-003	Falling	J. King	Closed	70.00	70.00
John Hine N.A. Ltd.		**The Shoemaker's Dream**			
91-16-001	The Jester Boot	J. Herbert	Open	29.00	29.00
91-16-002	The Crooked Boot	J. Herbert	Open	35.00	35.00
91-16-003	Rosie's Cottage	J. Herbert	Open	40.00	40.00
91-16-004	Baby Booty (pink)	J. Herbert	Open	45.00	45.00
91-16-005	Baby Booty (blue)	J. Herbert	Open	45.00	45.00
91-16-006	Shoemaker's Palace	J. Herbert	Open	50.00	50.00
91-16-007	Tavern Boot	J. Herbert	Open	55.00	55.00
91-16-008	River Shoe Cottage	J. Herbert	Open	55.00	55.00
91-16-009	The Chapel	J. Herbert	Open	55.00	55.00
91-16-010	Castle Boot	J. Herbert	Open	55.00	55.00
91-16-011	The Clocktower Boot	J. Herbert	Open	60.00	60.00
91-16-012	Watermill Boot	J. Herbert	Open	60.00	60.00
91-16-013	Windmill Boot	J. Herbert	Open	65.00	65.00
91-16-014	The Gate Lodge	J. Herbert	Open	65.00	65.00
92-16-015	Wishing Well Shoe	J. Herbert	Open	32.00	32.00
92-16-016	The Golf Shoe	J. Herbert	Open	35.00	35.00
92-16-017	The Sports Shoe	J. Herbert	Open	35.00	35.00
92-16-018	Clown Boot	J. Herbert	Open	45.00	45.00
92-16-019	Upside Down Boot	J. Herbert	Open	45.00	45.00
92-16-020	Christmas Boot	J. Herbert	Open	55.00	55.00
93-16-021	Wedding Bells	J. Herbert	Open	45.00	45.00
93-16-022	Shiver me Timbers	J. Herbert	Open	45.00	45.00
93-16-023	The Woodcutter's Shoe	J. Herbert	Open	40.00	40.00
John Hine N.A. Ltd.		**Animal Antics**			
93-17-001	Sir Mouse	J. Herbert	Open	30.00	30.00
93-17-002	Lady Mouse	J. Herbert	Open	30.00	30.00
93-17-003	You're Bone Idle	J. Herbert	Open	45.00	45.00
93-17-004	Real Cool Carrot	J. Herbert	Open	55.00	55.00
93-17-005	Tabby Tabitha	J. Herbert	Open	55.00	55.00
93-17-006	Lucky Dragon	J. Herbert	Open	60.00	60.00
John Hine N.A. Ltd.		**Heartstrings**			
92-18-001	Hush, It's Sleepytime	S. Kuck	15,000	97.50	97.50
92-18-002	Taking Tea	S. Kuck	15,000	92.50	92.50
92-18-003	Day Dreaming	S. Kuck	15,000	92.50	92.50
92-18-004	Watch Me Waltz	S. Kuck	15,000	97.50	97.50
John Hine N.A. Ltd.		**Sandra Kuck Collectors Club**			
92-19-001	Friends For Keeps	S. Kuck	Yr.Iss.	Gift	N/A
92-19-002	Friends For Keeps Lithograph	S. Kuck	Yr.Iss.	Gift	N/A
92-19-003	La Belle	S. Kuck	Yr Iss.	Gift	N/A
John Hine N.A. Ltd.		**Santa's Big Day**			
92-20-001	Booting Up	J. King	Open	40.00	40.00
92-20-002	Home Rudolph	J. King	Open	50.00	50.00
92-20-003	Reindeer Breakfast	J. King	Open	50.00	50.00
92-20-004	Feet First	J. King	Open	55.00	55.00
92-20-005	Santa's Night Ride	J. King	Open	55.00	55.00
92-20-006	Tight Fit!	J. King	Open	55.00	55.00
92-20-007	Wakey, Wakey!	J. King	Open	55.00	55.00
92-20-008	Rest-a-while	J. King	Open	60.00	60.00
92-20-009	Whoops!	J. King	Open	60.00	60.00
92-20-010	Heave Ho!	J. King	Open	70.00	70.00
92-20-011	Ready Boys?	J. King	Open	80.00	80.00
92-20-012	Zzzzz...	J. King	Open	85.00	85.00

FIGURINES

Company / Number	Name / Series	Artist	Edition Limit	Issue Price	Quote
John Hine N.A. Ltd.	**London By Gaslight**				
92-21-001	Starter Packet (Knightsbridge Mansion, Banker's House in the City, end pieces, and transformer)	B. Russell	Open	150.00	150.00
92-21-002	Piccadilly Chambers	B. Russell	Open	65.00	65.00
92-21-003	St. Bartholomew's Church Gate	B. Russell	Open	75.00	75.00
92-21-004	Chelsea Townhouse	B. Russell	Open	60.00	60.00
92-21-005	Streatham South of Thames	B. Russell	Open	55.00	55.00
92-21-006	Belgravia Mews Cottage	B. Russell	Open	50.00	50.00
92-21-007	Cockney's Corner Shop and The Iron Duke, Blackfriars	B. Russell	Open	100.00	100.00
92-21-008	Weaver's Warehouse, Holborn	B. Russell	Open	50.00	50.00
92-21-009	Clothfriar Road, Smithfield	B. Russell	Open	55.00	55.00
92-21-010	Thameside Walk	B. Russell	Open	60.00	60.00
92-21-011	Regency House in St. James	B. Russell	Open	70.00	70.00
92-21-012	Birdcage Walk, Westminster	B. Russell	Open	70.00	70.00
John Hine N.A. Ltd.	**London By Gaslight- Accessories**				
92-22-001	Fire Engine	A. Stadden	Open	15.00	15.00
92-22-002	Hanson Cab (empty)	A. Stadden	Open	12.00	12.00
92-22-003	Hanson Cab	A. Stadden	Open	12.00	12.00
92-22-004	Organ Grinder	A. Stadden	Open	9.00	9.00
92-22-005	Goods Wagon	A. Stadden	Open	12.00	12.00
92-22-006	Five Men; Four Men	A. Stadden	Open	13.50	13.50
92-22-007	Police w/Two Children/Children Playing	A. Stadden	Open	9.00	9.00
92-22-008	Woman w/Baby/Three Drunks	A. Stadden	Open	9.00	9.00
92-22-009	Couple Walking/Two Couples Walking	A. Stadden	Open	11.00	11.00
92-22-010	Three Trees	A. Stadden	Open	20.00	20.00
92-22-011	Three Lampposts	A. Stadden	Open	15.00	15.00
92-22-012	Jack the Ripper/Victim/Holmes/Watson	A. Stadden	Open	15.00	15.00
92-22-013	Borrowman/Woman/Milk Float/Man/Trolley	A. Stadden	Open	15.00	15.00
92-22-014	Flower Seller/Gas Lamp Lighter/Post Box	A. Stadden	Open	9.00	9.00
92-22-015	Dog Cart/Stick Up Man/Wheelbarrow	A. Stadden	Open	11.00	11.00
Hoyle Products	**Various**				
80-01-001	The Country Pedlar	N. Rockwell	1,500	160.00	N/A
81-01-002	The Traveling Salesman	N. Rockwell	1,500	175.00	175.00
82-01-003	The Horsetrader	N. Rockwell	1,500	180.00	N/A
Hutschenreuther	**Portrait Figurines**				
77-01-001	Catherine The Great	D. Valenza	500	500.00	1100.00
77-01-002	Helen of Troy	D. Valenza	500	500.00	1050.00
77-01-003	Jennie Churchhill	D. Valenza	500	500.00	925.00
77-01-004	Queen Isabelle	D. Valenza	500	500.00	925.00
77-01-005	Judith	D. Valenza	500	500.00	1575.00
77-01-006	Isolde	D. Valenza	500	500.00	2650.00
77-01-007	Lillian Russell	D. Valenza	500	500.00	1825.00
Hutschenreuther	**American Limited Edition Collection**				
XX-02-001	A Family Affair	Granget	200	Unkn.	3700.00
XX-02-002	Take Cover	Granget	125	Unkn.	14000.00
XX-02-003	The Challenge	Granget	150	Unkn.	14000.00
XX-02-004	Heading South	Granget	150	Unkn.	14000.00
XX-02-005	First Lesson	Granget	175	Unkn.	3550.00
XX-02-006	Safe at Home	Granget	350	Unkn.	9000.00
XX-02-007	Off Season	Granget	125	Unkn.	4125.00
XX-02-008	Disdain-Owl	Granget	175	Unkn.	5200.00
XX-02-009	Friendly Enemies-Woodpecker	Granget	175	Unkn.	5200.00
XX-02-010	Engaged	Granget	250	Unkn.	1750.00
XX-02-011	Spring is Here	Granget	175	Unkn.	4500.00
XX-02-012	Anxious Moment	Granget	175	Unkn.	5225.00
XX-02-013	It's Spring Again	Granget	250	Unkn.	3475.00
XX-02-014	Freedom in Flight	Granget	200	Unkn.	9000.00
XX-02-015	Reluctant Fledgling	Granget	350	Unkn.	3475.00
XX-02-016	Proud Parent	Granget	250	Unkn.	13750.00
XX-02-017	Joe-Stag	Granget	150	Unkn.	12000.00
XX-02-018	Olympic Champion	Granget	500	Unkn.	3650.00
XX-02-019	The Sentinel-Springbok	Granget	150	Unkn.	5200.00
XX-02-020	Sea Frolic-Sea Lion	Granget	500	Unkn.	3500.00
XX-02-021	The Dance-Crowncrested Crane	Granget	25	Unkn.	30000.00
XX-02-022	The Contest	Granget	100	Unkn.	14000.00
XX-02-023	The Fish Hawk	Granget	500	Unkn.	12000.00
XX-02-024	To Ride the Wind	Granget	500	Unkn.	8650.00
XX-02-025	Decorated Sea Lions	Granget	100	Unkn.	6000.00
XX-02-026	Dolphin Group	Granget	500	Unkn.	4000.00
XX-02-027	Silver Heron	Netzsch	500	Unkn.	5000.00
XX-02-028	Sparrowhawk w/Kingbird	Granget	500	Unkn.	8250.00
XX-02-029	Saw Whet Owl	Granget	750	Unkn.	3575.00
XX-02-030	Pygmy Owls	Granget	650	Unkn.	6225.00
XX-02-031	Arabian Stallion	Achtziger	300	Unkn.	8525.00
XX-02-032	Whooping Cranes	Netzsch	300	Unkn.	8000.00
XX-02-033	Wren on Wild Rose	Netzsch	250	Unkn.	1675.00
XX-02-034	Redstart on Quince Branch	Netzsch	250	Unkn.	1300.00
XX-02-035	Linnet on Ear of Rye	Netzsch	250	Unkn.	1175.00
XX-02-036	Quince	Netzsch	375	Unkn.	2850.00
XX-02-037	Water Lily	O'Hara	375	Unkn.	4150.00
XX-02-038	Christmas Rose	O'Hara	375	Unkn.	3050.00
XX-02-039	Blue Dolphins	Granget	100	Unkn.	10000.00
Iris Arc Crystal	**1981 Introductions**				
81-01-001	Octopus	P. Hale	Open	32.00	48.00
81-01-002	Kitten	T. Holliman	Retrd.	40.00	48.00
81-01-003	Dachshund	P. Hale	Retrd.	48.00	58.00
81-01-004	Mushrooms	T. Holliman	Retrd.	50.00	60.00
81-01-005	Miniature Snail (Silver)	P. Hale	Retrd.	20.00	24.00
81-01-006	Miniature Snail (Rainbow)	P. Hale	Open	20.00	27.00
81-01-007	Miniature Koala	T. Holliman	Retrd.	24.00	29.00
81-01-008	Miniature Dragonfly	T. Holliman	Retrd.	20.00	24.00
81-01-009	Miniature Bunny	T. Holliman	Retrd.	28.00	33.75
81-01-010	Miniature Frog	P. Hale	Retrd.	20.00	24.00
81-01-011	Miniature Firefly (Silver)	T. Holliman	Retrd.	20.00	24.00
81-01-012	Miniature Firefly (Rainbow)	T. Holliman	Retrd.	20.00	24.00
81-01-013	MiniatureAngel	T. Holliman	Retrd.	24.00	29.00
Iris Arc Crystal	**1982 Introductions**				
82-02-001	Seal (Silver)	P. Hale	Retrd.	32.00	38.00
82-02-002	Seal (Rainbow)	P. Hale	Open	32.00	35.00
82-02-003	Hippo	P. Hale	Retrd.	64.00	77.00
82-02-004	Small Teddy Bear w/Heart (Silver)	P. Hale	Retrd.	36.00	43.00
82-02-005	Small Teddy Bear w/Heart (Rose)	P. Hale	Open	36.00	45.00
82-02-006	Polar Bear	P. Hale	Retrd.	32.00	39.00
82-02-007	Koala	T. Holliman	Retrd.	44.00	53.00
82-02-008	Squirrel	P. Hale	Retrd.	36.00	43.00
82-02-009	Small Mouse	Iris Arc	Retrd.	38.00	46.00
82-02-010	Large Mouse	Iris Arc	Retrd.	48.00	58.00
82-02-011	Swan Lake	P. Hale	Retrd.	40.00	48.00
82-02-012	Small Elephant	P. Hale	Retrd.	70.00	84.00
82-02-013	Arc Angel	Iris Arc	Retrd.	40.00	48.00
82-02-014	Birdbath	T. Holliman	Open	60.00	90.00
82-02-015	Snowman	P. Hale	Retrd.	42.00	51.00
82-02-016	Siamese Cat	T. Holliman	Retrd.	48.00	58.00
82-02-017	Unicorn	P. Hale	Retrd.	76.00	91.00
82-02-018	Small Butterfly	T. Holliman	Retrd.	44.00	53.00
82-02-019	Large Butterfly	T. Holliman	Retrd.	56.00	67.00
82-02-020	Miniature Swan	T. Holliman	Open	20.00	27.00
Iris Arc Crystal	**1983 Introductions**				
83-03-001	Panda	P. Hale	Retrd.	56.00	67.00
83-03-002	Kangaroo	P. Hale	Retrd.	36.00	43.00
83-03-003	Otter (Silver)	P. Hale	Retrd.	36.00	43.00
83-03-004	Otter (Rainbow)	P. Hale	Retrd.	36.00	43.00
83-03-005	Turtle	Iris Arc	Retrd.	48.00	58.00
83-03-006	Crab	P. Hale	Retrd.	32.00	38.00
83-03-007	Camel	T. Holliman	Retrd.	136.00	163.00
83-03-008	Miniature Turtle	P. Hale	Open	20.00	27.00
83-03-009	Miniature Dove	P. Hale	Retrd.	20.00	24.00
83-03-010	Miniature Owl	P. Patruno	Retrd.	24.00	29.00
83-03-011	Miniature Frog	P. Hale	Retrd.	20.00	24.00
Iris Arc Crystal	**1984 Introductions**				
84-04-001	Enchanted Castle	T. Holliman	Retrd.	1200.00	1440.00
84-04-002	Dragon Slayer	P. Hale	Retrd.	120.00	144.00
84-04-003	Dragon	P. Hale	Retrd.	190.00	228.00
84-04-004	Pegasus	P. Hale	Retrd.	100.00	120.00
84-04-005	Knight	P. Hale	Retrd.	56.00	67.00
84-04-006	Jester	P. Hale	Retrd.	50.00	60.00
84-04-007	Fairy	P. Hale	Retrd.	32.00	39.00
84-04-008	Maiden	P. Hale	Retrd.	56.00	67.00
84-04-009	Wizard	P. Hale	Retrd.	64.00	77.00
84-04-010	Med. Teddy Bear w/Heart (Silver)	P. Hale	Retrd.	56.00	67.00
84-04-011	Med. Teddy Bear w/Heart (Rose)	P. Hale	Open	56.00	70.00
84-04-012	Mini Teddy Bear w/Heart (Silver)	P. Hale	Retrd.	18.00	22.00
84-04-013	Mini Teddy Bear w/Heart (Rose)	P. Hale	Open	18.00	22.00
84-04-014	Panda w/Heart	P. Hale	Retrd.	58.00	70.00
84-04-015	Miniature Panda	P. Hale	Retrd.	18.00	22.00
84-04-016	Mini Panda w/Heart	P. Hale	Open	20.00	27.00
84-04-017	Koala w/Heart	P. Hale	Retrd.	46.00	55.00
84-04-018	Mini Koala w/Heart	P. Hale	Retrd.	13.00	16.00
84-04-019	Large Giraffe	P. Hale	Retrd.	240.00	288.00
84-04-020	Small Giraffe	P. Hale	Retrd.	100.00	120.00
84-04-021	Medium Elephant	P. Hale	Retrd.	150.00	180.00
84-04-022	Kangaroo	P. Hale	Retrd.	48.00	58.00
84-04-023	Rhino	P. Hale	Retrd.	56.00	67.00
84-04-024	Lion w/Heart	P. Hale	Retrd.	70.00	84.00
84-04-025	Peacock	P. Hale	Retrd.	140.00	168.00
84-04-026	Dog w/Bone	P. Hale	Retrd.	50.00	60.00
84-04-027	Kitten w/Ball	P. Hale	Retrd.	50.00	60.00
84-04-028	Dolphin	P. Hale	Retrd.	48.00	58.00
84-04-029	Whale	P. Hale	Retrd.	44.00	53.00
84-04-030	Penguin	P. Hale	Retrd.	32.00	39.00
84-04-031	Miniature Rabbit	P. Hale	Retrd.	18.00	22.00
84-04-032	Miniature Kitten	P. Hale	Open	18.00	27.00
84-04-033	Miniature Puppy	P. Hale	Retrd.	18.00	22.00
84-04-034	Miniature Robin	P. Hale	Retrd.	18.00	21.00
Iris Arc Crystal	**1985 Introductions**				
85-05-001	Rainbow Juggler	P. Hale	Retrd.	100.00	120.00
85-05-002	Small Rainbow Juggler	P. Hale	Retrd.	50.00	60.00
85-05-003	Nativity Scene	P. Hale	Retrd.	130.00	156.00
85-05-004	Baby Bunny with Carrot	P. Hale	Open	45.00	60.00
85-05-005	Small Unicorn	P. Hale	Retrd.	45.00	54.00
85-05-006	Ballerina	P. Hale	Retrd.	70.00	84.00
85-05-007	Rudolph the Rednose Reindeer®	P. Hale	Retrd.	100.00	120.00
85-05-008	Christmas Tree	P. Hale	Retrd.	150.00	180.00
85-05-009	Small Camel	P. Hale	Retrd.	88.00	106.00
85-05-010	Small Lion with Heart	P. Hale	Retrd.	45.00	54.00
85-05-011	Small Peacock	P. Hale	Retrd.	50.00	60.00
85-05-012	Small AB Peacock	P. Hale	Open	60.00	120.00
85-05-013	Medium AB Peacock	P. Hale	Open	160.00	200.00
85-05-014	Large Peacock	P. Hale	Retrd.	700.00	840.00
85-05-015	Large Swan Lake	P. Hale	Retrd.	170.00	204.00
85-05-016	Poodle	P. Hale	Retrd.	150.00	180.00
85-05-017	Bunny with Carrot	P. Hale	Retrd.	65.00	78.00
85-05-018	Medium Turtle	P. Hale	Retrd.	55.00	66.00
85-05-019	Medium Swan	P. Hale	Retrd.	60.00	72.00
85-05-020	Large Swan	P. Hale	Retrd.	350.00	420.00
85-05-021	Feeding Time	P. Hale	Retrd.	120.00	144.00
85-05-022	Wildflower with Hummingbird	P. Hale	Open	240.00	390.00
85-05-023	Wildflower	P. Hale	Retrd.	190.00	228.00
85-05-024	Large Owl	P. Hale	Retrd.	140.00	168.00
85-05-025	Small Owl	P. Hale	Retrd.	55.00	66.00
Iris Arc Crystal	**1986 Introductions**				
86-06-001	Rainbow Cloud Castle	P. Hale	Open	350.00	400.00
86-06-002	Lovebirds	P. Hale	Retrd.	150.00	180.00
86-06-003	Caprice Carousel Horse	P. Hale	Open	100.00	130.00
86-06-004	Angel with Cymbals	P. Hale	Open	30.00	35.00
86-06-005	Angel with Flute	P. Hale	Open	30.00	35.00
86-06-006	Angel with Guitar	P. Hale	Open	30.00	35.00
86-06-007	Angel with Harp	P. Hale	Open	30.00	35.00
86-06-008	Angel Singing	P. Hale	Open	30.00	35.00
86-06-009	Angel Gabriel	P. Hale	Open	30.00	35.00
86-06-010	Santa	P. Hale	Retrd.	90.00	108.00
86-06-011	Small Snowman	P. Hale	Open	36.00	45.00
86-06-012	Large Snowman	J. Mulroy	Retrd.	56.00	67.25
86-06-013	Guardian Angel	P. Hale	Open	50.00	65.00
86-06-014	Moose	P. Hale	Open	60.00	90.00
86-06-015	Large Parrot	P. Hale	Retrd.	350.00	420.00
86-06-016	Parrot	P. Hale	Retrd.	120.00	144.00
86-06-017	Baby Elephant	P. Hale	Open	52.00	65.00
86-06-018	Beaver	P. Hale	Retrd.	48.00	58.00
86-06-019	Small Swan	P. Hale	Open	30.00	40.00
86-06-020	U.S. Space Shuttle	P. Hale	Retrd.	250.00	300.00
86-06-021	Pig	P. Hale	Retrd.	65.00	78.00
86-06-022	Baby Butterfly	P. Hale	Retrd.	40.00	48.00
86-06-023	Small Butterfly	P. Hale	Retrd.	90.00	108.00

Company Number	Name	Series Artist	Edition Limit	Issue Price	Quote
86-06-024	Medium Butterfly	P. Hale	Retrd.	130.00	156.00
86-06-025	Large Butterfly	P. Hale	Retrd.	170.00	204.00
86-06-026	Small Sailboat	P. Hale	Open	65.00	85.00
86-06-027	Medium Sailboat	P. Hale	Retrd.	170.00	204.00
86-06-028	Large Sailboat	P. Hale	Retrd.	230.00	276.00
Iris Arc Crystal		**1987 Introductions**			
87-07-001	Calliope Carousel Horse	P. Hale	Retrd.	110.00	132.00
87-07-002	Cleanup Clown	P. Hale	Retrd.	72.00	87.00
87-07-003	"Happy Birthday" Clown	P. Hale	Retrd.	50.00	60.00
87-07-004	"Have a Happy Day" Clown	P. Hale	Retrd.	50.00	60.00
87-07-005	"Congratulations" Clown	P. Hale	Retrd.	50.00	60.00
87-07-006	"I Love You" Clown	P. Hale	Retrd.	50.00	60.00
87-07-007	"Merry Christmas" Clown	P. Hale	Retrd.	50.00	60.00
87-07-008	Flower Clown	M. Goena	Retrd.	80.00	96.00
87-07-009	Airplane	P. Hale	Open	48.00	55.00
87-07-010	Horse and Rider	P. Hale	Retrd.	130.00	156.00
87-07-011	Bison/Buffalo	M. Goena	Retrd.	50.00	60.00
87-07-012	Mother and Baby Bear	P. Hale	Retrd.	60.00	72.00
87-07-013	Small Santa	P. Hale	Retrd.	30.00	36.00
87-07-014	Sweetie Bear Couple	T. Holliman	Retrd.	140.00	168.00
87-07-015	Sweetie Bear Dancer	T. Holliman	Retrd.	72.00	87.00
87-07-016	Medium AB Swan	P. Hale	Open	100.00	100.00
87-07-017	Carousel Reindeer	P. Hale	Retrd.	120.00	144.00
87-07-018	Grand Duckling	P. Hale	Retrd.	300.00	360.00
87-07-019	Ram	M. Goena	Retrd.	60.00	72.00
87-07-020	Gazelle	M. Goena	Retrd.	130.00	156.00
87-07-021	Allegro Caousel Horse	P. Hale	Retrd.	170.00	204.00
87-07-022	Golf Cart	P. Hale	Retrd.	75.00	90.00
87-07-023	Roadster	P. Hale	Retrd.	60.00	72.00
87-07-024	Pickup Truck	P. Hale	Retrd.	60.00	72.00
87-07-025	Locomotive	P. Hale	Retrd.	90.00	108.00
87-07-026	Passenger Car	P. Hale	Retrd.	80.00	96.00
87-07-027	Coal Car	P. Hale	Retrd.	80.00	96.00
87-07-028	Semi Truck	P. Hale	Retrd.	100.00	120.00
87-07-029	Miniature Duckling	P. Hale	Retrd.	20.00	24.00
Iris Arc Crystal		**1988 Introductions**			
88-08-001	Bullfrog	M. Goena	Retrd.	30.00	36.00
88-08-002	Tambourine Gator	M. Goena	Retrd.	120.00	144.00
88-08-003	Drummer Gator	M. Goena	Retrd.	140.00	168.00
88-08-004	Banjo Gator	M. Goena	Retrd.	120.00	144.00
88-08-005	Lighthouse	P. Hale	Open	150.00	150.00
88-08-006	Rocking Horse	P. Hale	Open	120.00	135.00
88-08-007	Bunny with Flowers	P. Hale	Open	55.00	60.00
88-08-008	Basket of Violets	M. Goena	Open	50.00	60.00
88-08-009	Bear with Honey	M. Goena	Retrd.	80.00	96.00
88-08-010	Bear with Milk and Cookies	M. Goena	Retrd.	80.00	96.00
88-08-011	Bear with Candle	M. Goena	Retrd.	80.00	96.00
88-08-012	Miniature Frog	M. Goena	Open	23.00	27.00
88-08-013	Small Enchanted Castle®	P. Hale	Open	50.00	75.00
88-08-014	Medium Enchanted Castle®	P. Hale	Open	100.00	150.00
88-08-015	Large Enchanted Castle®	P. Hale	Open	180.00	250.00
88-08-016	Clown with Dog	M. Goena	Retrd.	90.00	108.00
88-08-017	Computer Bear	M. Goena	Open	80.00	95.00
88-08-018	Angel Bear	M. Goena	Retrd.	60.00	72.00
88-08-019	Golf Bag	M. Goena/P. Hale	Open	100.00	125.00
88-08-020	Cable Car	M. Goena/P. Hale	Retrd.	70.00	84.00
Iris Arc Crystal		**1989 Introductions**			
89-09-001	Small Mouse	P. Hale	Open	45.00	50.00
89-09-002	Blue Whale	M. Goena	Retrd.	32.00	39.00
89-09-003	Magic Bunny	P. Hale	Retrd.	48.00	58.00
89-09-004	Flower Cart	P. Hale	Open	90.00	95.00
89-09-005	Big Hearted Bunny	M. Goena	Open	55.00	60.00
89-09-006	Golfing Bear	P. Hale	Open	70.00	75.00
89-09-007	Basket of Bunnies	P. Hale	Open	100.00	120.00
89-09-008	Gingerbread Cottage	M. Goena	Open	130.00	170.00
89-09-009	Miniature Clown	M. Goena	Open	23.00	27.00
89-09-010	Miniature Lion	M. Goena	Open	23.00	27.00
89-09-011	Miniature Mouse	M. Goena	Open	23.00	27.00
89-09-012	Miniature Angel	M. Goena	Open	23.00	27.00
89-09-014	Miniature Sailboat	M. Goena	Open	23.00	27.00
89-09-015	Miniature Bunny with Carrot	P. Hale	Open	23.00	27.00
89-09-016	Rudolph the Red Nosed Reindeer®	M. Goena	Retrd.	80.00	96.00
89-09-017	Santa Claus	M. Goena	Open	55.00	60.00
89-09-018	Ski Bunny	M. Goena	Open	55.00	70.00
89-09-019	Train Set	M. Goena	Open	100.00	120.00
89-09-020	Dragon	M. Goena	Open	70.00	95.00
89-09-021	Wizard	M. Goena	Retrd.	80.00	96.00
89-09-022	Miniature Dog	M. Goena	Open	23.00	27.00
89-09-023	Miniature Pig	M. Goena	Open	23.00	27.00
89-09-024	Miniature Moose	M. Goena	Open	23.00	27.00
89-09-025	Miniature Butterfly AB	M. Goena	Open	23.00	27.00
89-09-026	Miniature Butterfly MV	M. Goena	Open	23.00	27.00
89-09-027	Miniature Oyster with Pearl	M. Goena	Open	23.00	27.00
Iris Arc Crystal		**1990 Introductions**			
90-10-001	Snuggle Bunnies	M. Goena	Open	40.00	45.00
90-10-002	Lovebirds	M. Goena	Open	90.00	100.00
90-10-003	Wishing Well	M. Goena	Open	130.00	150.00
90-10-004	Toy Chest	P. Hale	Open	60.00	60.00
90-10-005	Tennis Bear	P. Hale	Open	70.00	75.00
90-10-006	Large Rainbow Butterfly	M. Goena	Retrd.	80.00	96.00
90-10-007	Legendary Castle	P. Hale	Open	200.00	220.00
90-10-008	American Beauty Rose	P. Hale	Open	90.00	95.00
90-10-009	Baby Carriage	M. Goena	Open	50.00	50.00
90-10-010	Miniature Koala with Heart	M. Goena	Open	23.00	27.00
90-10-011	Miniature Castle	M. Goena	Open	23.00	27.00
90-10-012	Vase of Red Roses	M. Goena	Open	20.00	25.00
90-10-013	Small Flower Cart	P. Hale	Open	40.00	45.00
90-10-014	Lotus	P. Hale	Open	60.00	60.00
90-10-015	Crab	P. Hale	Open	40.00	45.00
90-10-016	Dog	M. Goena	Open	70.00	75.00
90-10-017	Cat	M. Goena	Open	70.00	75.00
90-10-018	Hummingbird	M. Goena	Open	85.00	90.00
90-10-019	Loveboat	P. Hale	Open	55.00	60.00
90-10-020	Carousel	C. Hughes	Retrd.	100.00	120.00
90-10-021	Medium Legendary Castle	P. Hale	Open	140.00	150.00
90-10-022	Mushroom Cottage	C. Hughes	Retrd.	130.00	156.00
90-10-023	Space Shuttle	M. Goena	Retrd.	140.00	168.00
90-10-024	Jazz Piano	C. Hughes	Open	150.00	160.00
90-10-025	Miniature Vase of Flowers	P. Hale	Open	25.00	27.00

Company Number	Name	Series Artist	Edition Limit	Issue Price	Quote
Iris Arc Crystal		**1991 Introductions**			
91-11-001	Snuggle Bears	M. Goena	Open	40.00	45.00
91-11-002	Bride and Groom	P. Hale	Open	130.00	150.00
91-11-003	Honeymoon Cottage	P. Hale	Open	120.00	130.00
91-11-004	Courting Bears	M. Goena	Open	90.00	90.00
91-11-005	Mouse Mobile	M. Goena	Retrd.	120.00	144.00
91-11-006	Beach Bunnies	M. Goena	Open	120.00	125.00
91-11-007	Red Wagon	P. Hale	Open	70.00	75.00
91-11-008	Jack inthe Box	C. Hughes	Open	40.00	40.00
91-11-009	Mother and Baby Bunny	C. Hughes	Retrd.	65.00	78.00
91-11-010	Oyster with Pearl RB	M. Goena	Open	40.00	40.00
91-11-011	Pelican	P. Hale	Retrd.	75.00	90.00
91-11-012	Otter	P. Hale	Open	35.00	40.00
91-11-013	Small Legendary Castle	P. Hale	Open	90.00	95.00
91-11-014	Basebsll Bear	M. Goena	Open	75.00	75.00
91-11-015	Speedboat Bunnies	P. Hale	Open	90.00	100.00
91-11-016	Miniature Whale	M. Goena	Open	25.00	27.00
91-11-017	Miniature Mushrooms	C. Hughes	Open	25.00	27.00
91-11-018	Miniature Bunny with Heart	M. Goena	Open	25.00	27.00
91-11-019	Miniature Elephant	M. Goena	Open	25.00	27.00
91-11-020	Miniature Bud Vase	M. Goena	Open	25.00	27.00
91-11-021	Miniature Penguin	M. Goena	Open	25.00	27.00
91-11-022	Miniature Bluebird	M. Goena	Open	25.00	27.00
91-11-023	Miniature Chistmas Tree	C. Hughes	Open	25.00	27.00
91-11-024	Miniature School of Fish	M. Goena	Open	125.00	135.00
91-11-025	Storybook Cottage	P. Hale	Open	80.00	80.00
91-11-026	Teeter Totter	C. Hughes	Retrd.	80.00	96.00
91-11-027	Cat and Fishbowl	P. Hale	Open	70.00	70.00
91-11-028	Mice and C heese	P. Hale	Open	70.00	75.00
91-11-029	Turtle Grotto	C. Hughes	Open	130.00	135.00
91-11-030	Happy Campers	C. Hughes	Open	110.00	120.00
91-11-031	Country Church	M. Goena	Open	150.00	170.00
91-11-032	Small Mushroom Cottage	C. Hughes	Open	80.00	85.00
91-11-033	Tea for Two	C. Hughes	Open	85.00	90.00
91-11-034	Christmas Morning	C. Hughes	Open	80.00	90.00
91-11-035	Small Gingerbread Cottage	M. Goena	Open	55.00	55.00
91-11-036	Basket of Roses	P. Hale	Open	60.00	60.00
91-11-037	Bouquet Basket	P. Hale	Open	80.00	85.00
91-11-038	Fishing Bear	C. Hughes	Open	50.00	50.00
Iris Arc Crystal		**1992 Introductions**			
92-12-001	Tunnel of Love	C. Hughes	Open	150.00	150.00
92-12-002	Love Doves	M. Goena	Open	40.00	45.00
92-12-003	Video Bear	C. Hughes	Open	75.00	80.00
92-12-004	Bible Bear	C. Hughes	Open	100.00	100.00
92-12-005	Rainbow Apple	M. Goena	Open	45.00	50.00
92-12-006	School House	M. Goena	Open	180.00	180.00
92-12-007	Windmill	C. Hughes	Open	100.00	100.00
92-12-008	Guitar with Stand	C. Hughes	Open	100.00	100.00
92-12-009	Grand Piano	C. Hughes	Open	150.00	150.00
92-12-010	Baby Grand Piano	C. Hughes	Open	50.00	50.00
92-12-011	Small Bouquet Basket	M. Goena	Open	50.00	50.00
92-12-012	Kitty in a Basket	M. Goena	Open	60.00	60.00
92-12-013	Birdhouse	M. Goena	Open	180.00	180.00
92-12-014	Kitten with Ball	M. Goena	Open	55.00	55.00
92-12-015	Treasure Chest	C. Hughes	Open	55.00	55.00
92-12-016	Golf Cart	M. Goena	Open	80.00	85.00
92-12-017	Basketball Bears	C. Hughes	Open	100.00	100.00
92-12-018	Teddy Bear with Blocks	C. Hughes	Open	55.00	60.00
92-12-019	Miniature Baby Carriage	M. Goena	Open	25.00	27.00
92-12-020	Miniature Vase of Pink Flowers	M. Goena	Open	25.00	27.00
92-12-021	Miniature Vase of Violets	M. Goena	Open	25.00	27.00
92-12-022	Miniature Oyster with Pearl AB	M. Goena	Open	25.00	27.00
92-12-023	Snuggle Kittens	M. Goena	Open	40.00	45.00
92-12-024	Romeo and Juliet	C. Hughes	Open	130.00	130.00
92-12-025	Home Sweet Home	C. Hughes	Open	150.00	150.00
92-12-026	Mouse House	C. Hughes	Open	170.00	170.00
92-12-027	Billiards Bunny	C. Hughes	Open	75.00	75.00
92-12-028	Surfin' USA	M. Goena	Open	100.00	100.00
92-12-029	Cruise Ship	M. Goena	Open	100.00	100.00
92-12-030	Miniature Flock of Butterflies	M. Goena	Open	125.00	135.00
92-12-031	Miniature Owl	M. Goena	Open	25.00	27.00
92-12-032	Miniature Bumblebee	M. Goena	Open	25.00	27.00
92-12-033	Nativity Scene	C. Hughes	Open	130.00	130.00
Iris Arc Crystal		**1993 Introductions**			
93-13-001	Balloon Bears	M. Goena	Open	130.00	130.00
93-13-002	Mountain Chapel	C. Hughes	Open	135.00	135.00
93-13-003	Business Bear	C. Hughes	Open	75.00	75.00
93-13-004	Antique Telephone	C. Hughes	Open	40.00	40.00
93-13-005	Dice	M. Goena	Open	45.00	45.00
93-13-006	Slot Machine	M. Goena	Open	100.00	100.00
93-13-007	Basket of Mice	C. Hughes	Open	55.00	55.00
93-13-008	Hide-N-Seek	C. Hughes	Open	70.00	70.00
93-13-009	Hockey Bear	C. Hughes	Open	90.00	90.00
93-13-010	Pacifier	M. Goena	Open	45.00	45.00
93-13-011	Kitty Cariage	C. Hughes	Open	70.00	70.00
93-13-012	Baby Seal	C. Hughes	Open	35.00	35.00
Iris Arc Crystal		**Limited Editions**			
83-14-001	Teddy Bear with Heart (Silver)	P. Hale	Retrd.	170.00	204.00
83-14-002	Teddy Bear with Heart (Rose)	P. Hale	Retrd.	170.00	204.00
83-14-003	Elephant	P. Hale	Retrd.	190.00	228.00
83-14-004	Peacock	P. Hale	Retrd.	140.00	168.00
86-14-005	Classic Car	T. Holliman	Retrd.	500.00	600.00
87-14-006	Carousel	T. Holliman	Retrd.	600.00	720.00
87-14-007	Eagle	P. Hale	Retrd.	700.00	840.00
88-14-008	Horse and Foal	M. Goena	Retrd.	1000.00	1200.00
89-14-009	Angel	M. Goena	2,500	180.00	240.00
90-14-010	Rainbow Enchanted Castle®	C. Hughes	500	1500.00	1500.00
91-14-011	Vase of Flowers	P. Hale	750	250.00	250.00
91-14-012	Country Cottage	M. Goena	300	1500.00	1500.00
91-14-013	Basket of Flowers	M. Goena	Retrd.	250.00	300.00
92-14-014	Victorian House	C. Hughes	750	270.00	290.00
92-14-015	Water Mill	M. Goena	350	900.00	950.00
92-14-016	Rainbow Cathedral	M. Goena	150	2500.00	2500.00
93-14-017	Country Church	M. Goena	350	590.00	590.00
Iris Arc Crystal		**Collector's Society Edition**			
92-15-001	Gramophone	C. Hughes	Open	100.00	100.00
Kaiser		**Birds of America Collection**			
72-01-001	Blue Bird-496, color/base	W. Gawantka	2,500	120.00	480.00

Number	Name	Artist	Edition Limit	Issue Price	Quote
73-01-002	Blue Jay-503, color/base	W. Gawantka	1,500	475.00	1198.00
76-01-003	Baltimore Oriole-536, color/base	G. Tagliariol	1,000	280.00	746.00
73-01-004	Cardinal-504, color/base	W. Gawantka	1,500	60.00	600.00
75-01-005	Sparrow-516, color/base	G. Tagliariol	1,500	300.00	596.00
70-01-006	Scarlet Tanager, color/base	Kaiser	Closed	60.00	90.00
XX-01-007	Sparrow Hawk-749, color/base	Kaiser	3,000	575.00	906.00
82-01-008	Hummingbird Group-660, color/base	G. Tagliariol	3,000	650.00	1232.00
81-01-009	Kingfisher-639, color/base	G. Tagliariol	Closed	45.00	60.00
73-01-010	Robin-502, color/base	W. Gawantka	1,500	340.00	718.00
XX-01-011	Robin II-537, color/base	Kaiser	1,000	260.00	888.00
XX-01-012	Robin & Worm, color/base	Kaiser	Closed	60.00	90.00
XX-01-013	Baby Titmice-501, white/base	W. Gawantka	1,200	200.00	754.00
XX-01-014	Baby Titmice-501, color/base	W. Gawantka	Closed	400.00	500.00
78-01-015	Baby Titmice-601, color/base	G. Tagliariol	2,000	Unkn.	956.00
78-01-016	Baby Titmice-601, white/base	G. Tagliariol	2,000	Unkn.	562.00
68-01-017	Pidgeon Group-475, white/base	U. Netzsch	2,000	60.00	412.00
68-01-018	Pidgeon Group-475, color/base	U. Netzsch	1,500	150.00	812.00
76-01-019	Pheasant-556, color/base	G. Tagliariol	1,500	3200.00	6020.00
84-01-020	Pheasant-715, color/base	G. Tagliariol	1,500	1000.00	1962.00
76-01-021	Pelican-534, color/base	G. Tagliariol	1,200	925.00	1768.00
XX-01-022	Pelican-534, white/base	G. Tagliariol	Closed	Unkn.	625.00
84-01-023	Peregrine Falcon-723, color/base	M. Tandy	1,500	850.00	4946.00
72-01-024	Goshawk-491, white/base	W. Gawantka	1,500	850.00	1992.00
72-01-025	Goshawk-491, color/base	W. Gawantka	1,500	2400.00	4326.00
XX-01-026	Roadrunner-492, color/base	Kaiser	Closed	350.00	900.00
72-01-027	Seagull-498, white/base	W. Gawantka	700	550.00	1586.00
72-01-028	Seagull-498, color/base	W. Gawantka	Closed	850.00	1150.00
73-01-028	Seagull-498, color bisque	W. Gawantka	Closed	Unkn.	1150.00
75-01-029	Woodpeckers-515, color/base	G. Tagliariol	800	900.00	1762.00
76-01-030	Screech Owl-532, white/base	W. Gawantka	Closed	175.00	199.00
76-01-031	Screech Owl-532, color bisque	W. Gawantka	Closed	Unkn.	175.00
XX-01-032	Horned Owl II-524, white/base	G. Tagliariol	1,000	Unkn.	918.00
XX-01-033	Horned Owl II- 524, color/base	G. Tagliariol	1,000	650.00	2170.00
69-01-034	Owl-476, color bisque	W. Gawantka	Closed	Unkn.	550.00
69-01-035	Owl -476, white bisque	W. Gawantka	Closed	Unkn.	180.00
77-01-036	Owl IV-559, color/base	G. Tagliariol	1,000	Unkn.	1270.00
XX-01-037	Snowy Owl -776, white/base	Kaiser	1,500	Unkn.	668.00
XX-01-038	Snowy Owl -776, color/base	Kaiser	1,500	Unkn.	1146.00
68-01-039	Pair of Mallards-456, white/base	U. Netzsch	2,000	75.00	518.00
68-01-040	Pair of Mallards-456, color/base	U. Netzsch	Closed	150.00	500.00
78-01-041	Pair of Mallards II-572, color/base	G. Tagliariol	1,500	Unkn.	1156.00
78-01-042	Pair of Mallards II-572, white/base	G. Tagliariol	1,500	Unkn.	2366.00
75-01-043	Wood Ducks-514, color/base	G. Tagliariol	800	Unkn.	2804.00
85-01-044	Pintails-747, white/base	Kaiser	1,500	Unkn.	364.00
85-01-045	Pintails-747, color/base	Kaiser	1,500	Unkn.	838.00
76-01-046	Canadian Geese-550, white/base	G. Tagliariol	1,500	1500.00	3490.00
81-01-047	Quails-640, color/base	G. Tagliariol	1,500	Unkn.	2366.00
79-01-048	Swan-602, color/base	G. Tagliariol	2,000	Unkn.	1370.00
69-01-049	Bald Eagle I -464, color	U. Netzsch	Closed	Unkn.	650.00
69-01-050	Bald Eagle I -464, white	U. Netzsch	Closed	Unkn.	250.00
73-01-051	Bald Eagle II -497, color bisque	G. Tagliariol	Closed	Unkn.	1300.00
74-01-052	Bald Eagle III -513, color bisque	W. Gawantka	Closed	Unkn.	850.00
74-01-053	Bald Eagle III -513,white bisque	W. Gawantka	Closed	Unkn.	378.00
76-01-054	Bald Eagle IV-552, white/base	W. Gawantka	1,500	210.00	572.00
76-01-055	Bald Eagle IV-552, color/base	W. Gawantka	1,500	450.00	998.00
78-01-056	Bald Eagle V-600, color/base	G. Tagliariol	1,500	Unkn.	3848.00
80-01-057	Bald Eagle VI-634, white/base	W. Gawantka	3,000	Unkn.	672.00
XX-01-058	Bald Eagle VII-637, color/base	G. Tagliariol	200	Unkn.	20694.00
82-01-059	Bald Eagle VIII-656, color/base	G. Tagliariol	Closed	800.00	880.00
82-01-060	Bald Eagle VIII-656, white/base	G. Tagliariol	1,000	400.00	904.00
84-01-061	Bald Eagle IX-714, white/base	W. Gawantka	4,000	190.00	374.00
84-01-062	Bald Eagle IX-714, color/base	W. Gawantka	3,500	500.00	850.00
85-01-063	Bald Eagle X-746, white/base	W. Gawantka	1,500	375.00	672.00
85-01-064	Bald Eagle X-746, color/base	W. Gawantka	1,500	Unkn.	1198.00
85-01-065	Bald Eagle XI-751, white/base	W. Gawantka	1,000	Unkn.	902.00
85-01-066	Bald Eagle XI-751, color/base	W. Gawantka	1,000	880.00	1422.00
81-01-067	Rooster-642, white/base	G. Tagliariol	1,500	380.00	688.00
81-01-068	Rooster-642, color/base	G. Tagliariol	1,500	860.00	1304.00
74-01-069	Falcon-507, color/base	W. Gawantka	1,500	820.00	1928.00
86-01-070	Sparrow Hawk-777, white bisque	M. Tandy	1,000	440.00	716.00
86-01-071	Sparrow Hawk-777, colored bisque	M. Tandy	10,000	950.00	1336.00
XX-01-072	Bald Eagle II-497, Colored	Kaiser	Closed	Unkn.	1300.00
XX-01-073	Paradise Bird-318, white bisque	Kaiser	Closed	Unkn.	135.00
XX-01-074	Fighting Peacocks -337, color glaze	G. Bochman	Closed	Unkn.	340.00
XX-01-075	Wild Ducks-456, color bisque	Kaiser	Closed	Unkn.	500.00
68-01-076	Wild Ducks-456, white bisque	Kaiser	2,000	Unkn.	175.00
72-01-077	Roadrunner-492, color bisque	W. Gawantka	1,000	175.00	199.00

Kaiser — **Horse Sculpture**

Number	Name	Artist	Edition Limit	Issue Price	Quote
69-02-001	Arabian Stallion-Comet, color/bisque	W. Gawantka	Closed	Unkn.	850.00
76-02-002	Hassan/Arabian-553, white/base	W. Gawantka	Closed	250.00	600.00
76-02-003	Hassan/Arabian-553, color/base	W. Gawantka	1,500	600.00	1100-1200.
80-02-004	Orion/Arabian-629, color/base	W. Gawantka	2,000	600.00	1038.00
80-02-005	Orion/Arabian-629, white/base	W. Gawantka	2,000	250.00	442.00
78-02-006	Capitano/Lipizzaner- 597, white	W. Gawantka	Closed	275.00	574.00
78-02-007	Capitano/Lipizzaner- 597, color	W. Gawantka	1,500	625.00	1496.00
75-02-008	Mare & Foal II-510, color/base	W. Gawantka	Closed	650.00	775.00
75-02-009	Mare & Foal II-510, white/bisque	W. Gawantka	Closed	Unkn.	775.00
80-02-010	Mare & Foal III-636, white/base	W. Gawantka	1,500	300.00	646.00
80-02-011	Mare & Foal III-636, color/base	W. Gawantka	1,500	950.00	1632.00
71-02-012	Pony Group-488, white/base	W. Gawantka	2,500	50.00	418.00
71-02-013	Pony Group-488, color/base	W. Gawantka	Closed	Unkn.	350.00
71-02-014	Pony Group-488, color bisque	W. Gawantka	Closed	Unkn.	350.00
87-02-015	Trotter-780, white/base	W. Gawantka	1,500	574.00	652.00
87-02-016	Trotter-780, color/base	W. Gawantka	1,500	1217.00	1350.00
87-02-017	Pacer-792, white/base	W. Gawantka	1,500	574.00	652.00
87-02-018	Pacer-792, color/base	W. Gawantka	1,500	1217.00	1350.00
90-02-019	Argos-633101/wht. bisq./base	W. Gawantka	1,000	578.00	672.00
90-02-020	Argos-633103/lt. color/base	W. Gawantka	1,000	1194.00	1388.00
90-02-021	Argos-633143/color/base	W. Gawantka	1,000	1194.00	1388.00
75-02-022	Lipizzaner/Maestoso-517/color bisque	W. Gawantka	Closed	Unkn.	1150.00
75-02-023	Lipizzaner/Maestoso-517white bisque	W. Gawantka	Closed	Unkn.	750.00

Kaiser — **Animals**

Number	Name	Artist	Edition Limit	Issue Price	Quote
75-03-001	German Shepherd-528, white bisque	W. Gawantka	Closed	185.00	420.00
75-03-002	German Shepherd-528, color bisque	W. Gawantka	Closed	250.00	652.00
76-03-003	Irish Setter-535, color bisque	W. Gawantka	1,000	290.00	652.00
76-03-004	Irish Setter-535, white/base	W. Gawantka	1,500	Unkn.	424.00
79-03-005	Bear & Cub-521, white bisque	W. Gawantka	Closed	125.00	378.00
79-03-006	Bear & Cub-521, color bisque	W. Gawantka	900	400.00	1072.00
85-03-007	Trout-739, color bisque	W. Gawantka	Open	95.00	488.00
85-03-008	Rainbow Trout-739, color bisque	W. Gawantka	Open	250.00	488.00
85-03-009	Brook Trout-739, color bisque	W. Gawantka	Open	250.00	488.00
85-03-010	Pike-737, color bisque	W. Gawantka	Open	350.00	682.00
69-03-011	Porpoise Group (3)-478, white bisque	W. Gawantka	Closed	85.00	375.00
78-03-012	Dolphin Group (4)-596/4, white bisque	W. Gawantka	4,500	75.00	956.00
75-03-013	Dolphin Group (4)-508, white bisque	W. Gawantka	Closed	Unkn.	575.00
75-03-014	Dolphin Group (5)-520/5, white bisque	W. Gawantka	800	850.00	3002.00
78-03-015	Killer Whale-579, color/bisque	W. Gawantka	2,000	420.00	798.00
78-03-016	Killer Whale-579, white/bisque	W. Gawantka	2,000	85.00	404.00
78-03-017	Killer Whales (2)-594, color	W. Gawantka	2,000	925.00	2008.00
78-03-018	Killer Whales (2)-594, white	W. Gawantka	2,000	425.00	1024.00
82-03-019	Two wild Boars-664, color bisque	H. Liederly	1,000	650.00	890.00
80-03-020	Bison-630, color bisque	G. Tagliariol	2,000	620.00	1044.00
80-03-021	Bison-690, white bisque	G. Tagliariol	2,000	350.00	488.00
91-03-022	Lion-701203, color bisque	W. Gawantka	1,500	1300.00	1300.00
91-03-023	Lion-701201, white bisque	W. Gawantka	1,500	650.00	650.00

Kaiser — **Human Figures**

Number	Name	Artist	Edition Limit	Issue Price	Quote
82-04-001	Father & Son-659, white/base	W. Gawantka	2,500	100.00	384.00
82-04-002	Father & Son-659, color/base	W. Gawantka	2,500	400.00	712.00
83-04-003	Mother & Child/bust-696, white	W. Gawantka	4,000	225.00	428.00
83-04-004	Mother & Child/bust-696, color	W. Gawantka	3,500	500.00	1066.00
XX-04-005	Father & Daughter-752, white	Kaiser	2,500	175.00	362.00
XX-04-006	Father & Daughter-752, color	Kaiser	2,500	390.00	710.00
82-04-007	Swan Lake Ballet-641, white	W. Gawantka	2,500	200.00	974.00
82-04-008	Swan Lake Ballet-641, color	W. Gawantka	2,500	650.00	1276.00
82-04-009	Ice Princess-667, white	W. Gawantka	5,000	200.00	416.00
82-04-010	Ice Princess-667, color	W. Gawantka	5,000	375.00	732.00
XX-04-011	Mother & Child-757, white	Kaiser	4,000	300.00	430.00
XX-04-012	Mother & Child-757, color	Kaiser	3,500	600.00	864.00
XX-04-013	Mother & Child-775, white	Kaiser	4,000	300.00	430.00
XX-04-014	Mother & Child-775, color	Kaiser	3,500	600.00	864.00
60-04-015	Mother & Child-398, white bisque	G. Bochmann	Open	Unkn.	312.00

Lance Corporation — **Chilmark Pewter American West**

Number	Name	Artist	Edition Limit	Issue Price	Quote
74-01-001	Cheyenne	D. Polland	S/O	200.00	2700-3000.
74-01-002	Counting Coup	D. Polland	S/O	225.00	1600-2000.
74-01-003	Crow Scout	D. Polland	S/O	250.00	1400-1700.
75-01-004	Maverick Calf	D. Polland	S/O	250.00	1300-1700.
76-01-005	Cold Saddles, Mean Horses	D. Polland	S/O	200.00	1100-1600.
75-01-006	The Outlaws	D. Polland	S/O	450.00	900-1180.
76-01-007	Buffalo Hunt	D. Polland	S/O	300.00	1200-2200.
76-01-008	Rescue	D. Polland	S/O	275.00	1300-2700.
76-01-009	Painting the Town	D. Polland	S/O	300.00	1550-1700.
76-01-010	Monday Morning Wash	D. Polland	S/O	200.00	1300-1800.
78-01-011	Dangerous Encounter	B. Rodden	Retrd.	475.00	600-950.
79-01-012	Border Rustlers	D. Polland	S/O	1295.00	1500.00
79-01-013	Mandan Hunter	D. Polland	S/O	65.00	780-900.
79-01-014	Getting Acquainted	D. Polland	S/O	215.00	500-1100.
79-01-015	Cavalry Officer	D. LaRocca	S/O	125.00	400-650.
79-01-016	Cowboy	D. LaRocca	S/O	125.00	500-750.
79-01-017	Mountain Man	D. LaRocca	Retrd.	95.00	500-650.
79-01-018	Indian Warrior	D. LaRocca	Retrd.	95.00	400.00
79-01-019	Running Battle	B. Rodden	Retrd.	400.00	750-900.
81-01-020	Buffalo Robe	D. Polland	2,500	235.00	315-600.
81-01-021	When War Chiefs Meet	D. Polland	S/O	300.00	850-900.
81-01-022	War Party	D. Polland	Retrd.	550.00	975-1150.
81-01-023	Dog Soldier	D. Polland	2,500	235.00	350.00
81-01-024	Enemy Tracks	D. Polland	S/O	225.00	700-725.
81-01-025	Ambushed	D. Polland	Retrd.	2370.00	2700.00
81-01-026	U.S. Marshal	D. Polland	S/O	95.00	450-600.
81-01-027	Plight of the Huntsman	M. Boyette	S/O	495.00	1100-1300.
82-01-028	Last Arrow	D. Polland	S/O	95.00	370-400.
82-01-029	Sioux War Chief	D. Polland	S/O	95.00	375-480.
82-01-030	Navajo Kachina Dancer	D. Polland	2,500	95.00	110.00
82-01-031	Arapaho Drummer	D. Polland	2,500	95.00	110.00
82-01-032	Apache Hostile	D. Polland	2,500	95.00	110.00
82-01-033	Buffalo Prayer	D. Polland	S/O	95.00	245-400.
82-01-034	Jemez Eagle Dancer	D. Polland	S/O	95.00	250-450.
82-01-035	Flathead War Dancer	D. Polland	2,500	95.00	110.00
82-01-036	Hopi Kachina Dancer	D. Polland	2,500	95.00	110.00
82-01-037	Apache Gan Dancer	D. Polland	2,500	95.00	110.00
82-01-038	Crow Medicine Dancer	D. Polland	2,500	95.00	110.00
82-01-039	Comanche Plaines Drummer	D. Polland	2,500	95.00	110.00
82-01-040	Yakima Salmon Fisherman	D. Polland	S/O	200.00	900.00
82-01-041	Mustanger	D. Polland	2,500	425.00	550.00
82-01-042	Blood Brothers	M. Boyett	Retrd.	250.00	610-995.
83-01-043	Line Rider	D. Polland	S/O	195.00	1000-1100.
83-01-044	Bounty Hunter	D. Polland	S/O	250.00	300-600.
83-01-045	The Wild Bunch	D. Polland	S/O	200.00	225-400.
83-01-046	Too Many Aces	D. Polland	Retrd.	400.00	495.00
83-01-047	Eye to Eye	D. Polland	2,500	350.00	475.00
83-01-048	Now or Never	D. Polland	Retrd.	265.00	800.00
84-01-049	Flat Out for Red River Station	M. Boyett	S/O	3000.00	5000-6500.
85-01-050	Postal Exchange	S. York	Retrd.	300.00	400-600.
85-01-051	Bear Meet	S. York	Retrd.	500.00	600-800.
85-01-052	Horse of A Different Color	S. York	Retrd.	500.00	600-800.
87-01-053	Cool Waters	F. Barnum	Suspd.	350.00	395.00
87-01-054	Treed	F. Barnum	Suspd.	300.00	345.00
88-01-055	Custer's Last Stand	F. Barnum	Suspd.	350.00	395.00
90-01-056	Pequot Wars	D. Polland	S/O	395.00	450-800.
90-01-057	Tecumseh's Rebellion	D. Polland	S/O	350.00	700.00
90-01-058	Red River Wars	D. Polland	S/O	425.00	700-850.

Lance Corporation — **Chilmark Pewter American West Annual Specials**

Number	Name	Artist	Edition Limit	Issue Price	Quote
83-02-001	The Chief	D. Polland	Yr.Iss.	275.00	1650-2050.
84-02-002	Unit Colors	D. Polland	Yr.Iss.	250.00	1250-1350.
85-02-003	Oh Great Spirit	D. Polland	Yr.Iss.	300.00	1000-1300.
86-02-004	Eagle Catcher	M. Boyett	Yr.Iss.	300.00	850-1200.
87-02-005	Surprise Encounter	F. Barnum	Yr.Iss.	250.00	600-750.
88-02-005	I Will Fight No More Forever	D. Polland	Yr.Iss.	350.00	600-750.
89-02-007	Geronimo	D. Polland	Yr.Iss.	375.00	700-785.
90-02-008	Cochise	D. Polland	Yr.Iss.	400.00	600-750.
91-02-009	Crazy Horse	D. Polland	Yr.Iss.	295.00	600.00
92-02-010	Strong Hearts to the Front	D. Polland	Yr.Iss.	425.00	425.00

Lance Corporation — **Chilmark Pewter American West Christmas Special**

Number	Name	Artist	Edition Limit	Issue Price	Quote
91-03-001	Merry Christmas Neighbor	D. Polland	Annual	395.00	550-600.
92-03-002	Merry Christmas My Love	D. Polland	Annual	350.00	350.00

Lance Corporation — **Chilmark Pewter American West Event Specials**

Number	Name	Artist	Edition Limit	Issue Price	Quote
91-04-001	Uneasy Truce	D. Polland	Annual	125.00	215.00
92-04-002	Irons In The Fire	D. Polland	Annual	125.00	125.00

Lance Corporation — **Chilmark Pewter Civil War Annual Specials**

Number	Name	Artist	Edition Limit	Issue Price	Quote
Company		**Series**			
89-05-001	Lee To The Rear	F. Barnum	Yr.Iss.	300.00	600-900.
90-05-002	Lee And Jackson	F. Barnum	Yr.Iss.	375.00	450-700.
91-05-003	Stonewall Jackson	F. Barnum	Yr.Iss.	295.00	500.00
92-05-004	Zouaves 1st Manassas	F. Barnum	Yr.Iss.	375.00	375.00
Lance Corporation		**Chilmark Pewter Civil War Event Specials**			
91-06-001	Boots and Saddles	F. Barnum	Annual	95.00	250.00
92-06-002	140th NY Zouave	F. Barnum	Annual	95.00	95.00
Lance Corporation		**Chilmark Pewter Civil War Christmas Specials**			
92-07-001	Merry Christmas Yank	F. Barnum	Annual	350.00	350.00
Lance Corporation		**Chilmark Pewter Wildlife**			
78-08-001	Buffalo	B. Rodden	S/O	170.00	375-400.
79-08-002	Elephant	D. Polland	S/O	315.00	450-550.
79-08-003	Giraffe	D. Polland	S/O	145.00	145.00
79-08-004	Kudu	D. Polland	S/O	160.00	160.00
79-08-005	Rhino	D. Polland	S/O	135.00	135-550.
80-08-006	Ruby-Throated Hummingbird	V. Hayton	S/O	275.00	350.00
80-08-007	Prairie Sovereign	M. Boyett	Retrd.	550.00	800.00
80-08-008	Duel of the Bighorns	M. Boyett	Retrd.	650.00	1200.00
80-08-009	Lead Can't Catch Him	M. Boyett	Retrd.	645.00	845.00
80-08-010	Voice of Experience	M. Boyett	Retrd.	645.00	850.00
88-08-011	The Patriarch	F. Barnum	Suspd.	350.00	395.00
88-08-012	Fishing Lesson	F. Barnum	Suspd.	325.00	365.00
89-08-013	Summit	F. Barnum	Suspd.	250.00	265.00
Lance Corporation		**Chilmark Pewter Horses**			
76-09-001	Stallion	B. Rodden	S/O	75.00	260.00
76-09-002	Running Free	B. Rodden	S/O	75.00	300.00
77-09-003	Rise and Shine	B. Rodden	S/O	135.00	200.00
77-09-004	The Challenge	B. Rodden	S/O	175.00	250-300.
78-09-005	Paddock Walk	A. Petito	Retrd.	85.00	215.00
80-09-006	Born Free	B. Rodden	S/O	250.00	500-680.
80-09-007	Affirmed	M. Jovine	Retrd.	850.00	1275.00
81-09-008	Clydesdale Wheel Horse	C. Keim	Retrd.	120.00	430.00
82-09-009	Tender Persuasion	J. Mootry	Retrd.	950.00	1250.00
85-09-010	Fighting Stallions	D. Polland	2,500	225.00	300.00
85-09-011	Wild Stallion	D. Polland	Retrd.	145.00	350.00
Lance Corporation		**Chilmark Pewter Rodeo**			
85-10-001	Saddle Bronc Rider	D. Polland	2,500	250.00	300.00
85-10-002	Bareback Rider	D. Polland	2,500	225.00	300.00
85-10-003	Bull Rider	D. Polland	2,500	265.00	335.00
85-10-004	Steer Wrestling	D. Polland	2,500	500.00	600.00
85-10-005	Team Roping	D. Polland	2,500	500.00	625.00
85-10-006	Calf Roper	D. Polland	2,500	300.00	375.00
85-10-007	Barrel Racer	D. Polland	2,500	275.00	325.00
Lance Corporation		**Chilmark Pewter Legacy of Courage**			
81-11-001	Apache Signals	M. Boyett	Retrd.	175.00	550-575.
81-11-002	Iroquois Warfare	M. Boyett	Retrd.	125.00	600.00
81-11-003	Victor Cheyenne	M. Boyett	Retrd.	175.00	500.00
81-11-004	Buffalo Stalker	M. Boyett	Retrd.	175.00	560.00
81-11-005	Comanche	M. Boyett	Retrd.	175.00	530-670.
81-11-006	Unconquered Seminole	M. Boyett	Retrd.	175.00	540.00
81-11-007	Blackfoot Snow Hunter	M. Boyett	Retrd.	175.00	650.00
82-11-008	Shoshone Eagle Catcher	M. Boyett	S/O	225.00	1650-2040.
82-11-009	Plains Talk-Pawnee	M. Boyett	Retrd.	195.00	625.00
82-11-010	Kiowa Scout	M. Boyett	Retrd.	195.00	525.00
82-11-011	Mandan Buffalo Dancer	M. Boyett	Retrd.	195.00	450-600.
82-11-012	Listening For Hooves	M. Boyett	Retrd.	150.00	400.00
82-11-013	Arapaho Sentinel	M. Boyett	Retrd.	195.00	500.00
82-11-014	Dance of the Eagles	M. Boyett	Retrd.	150.00	215.00
82-11-015	The Tracker Nez Perce	M. Boyett	Retrd.	150.00	575.00
83-11-016	Moment of Truth	M. Boyett	Retrd.	295.00	550-620.
83-11-017	Winter Hunt	M. Boyett	Retrd.	295.00	370.00
83-11-018	Along the Cherokee Trace	M. Boyett	Retrd.	295.00	720.00
83-11-019	Forest Watcher	M. Boyett	Retrd.	215.00	540.00
83-11-020	Rite of the Whitetail	M. Boyett	Retrd.	295.00	400.00
83-11-021	Circling the Enemy	M. Boyett	Retrd.	295.00	395.00
83-11-022	A Warrior's Tribute	M. Boyett	Retrd.	335.00	635.00
Lance Corporation		**Chilmark Pewter Off Canvas**			
90-12-001	Smoke Signal	A. T. McGrory	S/O	345.00	550-700.
90-12-002	Vigil	A. T. McGrory	S/O	345.00	500-700.
90-12-003	Warrior	A. T. McGrory	S/O	300.00	350-600.
Lance Corporation		**Chilmark Pewter Sculptures**			
79-13-001	Unicorn	R. Sylvan	S/O	115.00	550.00
79-13-002	Carousel	R. Sylvan	S/O	115.00	115.00
79-13-003	Moses	B. Rodden	S/O	140.00	235.00
79-13-004	Pegasus	R. Sylvan	Retrd.	95.00	175.00
80-13-005	Charge of the 7th Cavalry	B. Rodden	Retrd.	600.00	950.00
81-13-006	Budweiser Wagon	C. Keim	Retrd.	2000.00	3000.00
83-13-007	Dragon Slayer	D. LaRocca	Retrd.	385.00	500.00
84-13-008	Garden Unicorn	J. Royce	Retrd.	160.00	200.00
86-13-009	Camelot Chess Set	P. Jackson	Retrd.	2250.00	2250.00
Lance Corporation		**Chilmark Pewter The Sorcerer's Apprentice Collectors Series**			
90-14-001	The Sorcerer's Apprentice	Disney Studios	2,500	225.00	225.00
90-14-002	The Incantation	Disney Studios	2,500	150.00	150.00
90-14-003	The Dream	Disney Studios	2,500	225.00	225.00
90-14-004	The Whirlpool	Disney Studios	2,500	225.00	225.00
90-14-005	The Repentant Apprentice	Disney Studios	2,500	195.00	195.00
Lance Corporation		**Chilmark Pewter Disney Figurines**			
89-15-001	Hollywood Mickey	Disney Studios	Suspd.	165.00	170.00
89-15-002	"Gold Edition" Hollywood Mickey	Disney Studios	Retrd.	200.00	200.00
91-15-003	Mickey's Carousel Ride	Disney Studios	2,500	150.00	150.00
92-15-004	Minnie's Carousel Ride	Disney Studios	2,500	150.00	150.00
92-15-005	Cruising (Metal Art™)	Disney Studios	350	275.00	275.00
Lance Corporation		**Chilmark Pewter Generations of Mickey**			
87-16-001	Antique Mickey	Disney Studios	S/O	130.00	350.00
89-16-002	Steam Boat Willie	Disney Studios	2,500	165.00	175.00
89-16-003	Sorcerer's Apprentice	Disney Studios	2,500	150.00	160.00
89-16-004	Mickey's Gala Premiere	Disney Studios	2,500	150.00	150.00
90-16-005	Disneyland Mickey	Disney Studios	2,500	150.00	150.00
90-16-006	The Band Concert	Disney Studios	2,000	185.00	185.00
90-16-007	The Band Concert (Painted)	Disney Studios	500	215.00	215.00
91-16-008	Plane Crazy-1928	Disney Studios	2,500	175.00	175.00
91-16-009	The Mouse-1935	Disney Studios	1,200	185.00	185.00

Number	Name	Artist	Edition Limit	Issue Price	Quote
Company		**Series**			
Lance Corporation		**Chilmark Pewter The Adversaries**			
91-17-001	Robert E. Lee	F. Barnum	S/O	350.00	600-750.
92-17-002	Ulysses S. Grant	F. Barnum	S/O	350.00	500.00
92-17-003	Stonewall Jackson	F. Barnum	S/O	375.00	375.00
93-17-004	Wm. Tecumseh Sherman	F. Barnum	S/O	375.00	375.00
Lance Corporation		**Chilmark Pewter Civil War**			
87-18-001	Saving The Colors	F. Barnum	Retrd.	350.00	700.00
88-18-002	Johnny Shiloh	F. Barnum	S/O	100.00	220.00
92-18-003	Kennesaw Mountain	F. Barnum	S/O	650.00	850-1300.
92-18-004	Parson's Battery	F. Barnum	S/O	495.00	495.00
Lance Corporation		**Chilmark Pewter Eagles**			
81-19-001	Freedom Eagle	G. deLodzia	S/O	195.00	750-900.
82-19-002	Wings of Liberty	M. Boyett	S/O	625.00	1565.00
87-19-003	Winged Victory	J. Mullican	Suspd.	275.00	315.00
89-19-004	High and Mighty	A. McGrory	Suspd.	185.00	200.00
91-19-005	Cry of Freedom	S. Knight	Suspd.	395.00	395.00
Lance Corporation		**Chilmark Pewter Masters of the American West**			
84-20-001	Cheyenne (Remington)	C. Rousell	Retrd.	400.00	600.00
85-20-002	Bronco Buster (Large)	C. Rousell	Retrd.	400.00	400.00
88-20-003	End of the Trail (Mini)	A. McGrory	S/O	225.00	250.00
89-20-004	Trooper of the Plains	A. McGrory	Suspd.	250.00	265.00
89-20-005	The Triumph	A. McGrory	Suspd.	275.00	290.00
90-20-006	Remington Self Portrait	A. McGrory	Suspd.	275.00	275.00
Lance Corporation		**Chilmark Pewter The Cavalry Generals**			
92-21-001	J.E.B. Stuart	F. Barnum	S/O	375.00	375.00
Lance Corporation		**Chilmark Pewter World War II**			
90-22-001	NAVY Pearl Harbor	D. LaRocca	Suspd.	425.00	450.00
90-22-002	Army Corregidor	D. LaRocca	Suspd.	315.00	325.00
90-22-003	Air Corps Hickam Field	D. LaRocca	Suspd.	200.00	210.00
90-22-004	Marines Wake Island	D. LaRocca	Suspd.	200.00	210.00
91-22-005	Marines In Solomons	D. LaRocca	Suspd.	275.00	275.00
91-22-006	Army North Africa	D. LaRocca	Suspd.	375.00	375.00
91-22-007	Navy North Atlantic	D. LaRocca	Suspd.	375.00	375.00
91-22-008	Air Corps Tokyo Raid	D. LaRocca	Suspd.	350.00	350.00
Lance Corporation		**Chilmark Pewter Beautiful Women**			
84-23-001	Sibyl	A. Kann	Suspd.	150.00	165.00
84-23-002	Adrienne	A. Kann	Suspd.	175.00	195.00
84-23-003	Clarisse	A. Kann	Suspd.	195.00	200.00
84-23-004	Desiree	A. Kann	Suspd.	195.00	200.00
85-23-005	Giselle	A. Kann	Suspd.	225.00	225.00
89-23-006	Michelle	A. Kann	Suspd.	350.00	365.00
Lance Corporation		**Chilmark Pewter The Ballet**			
89-24-001	Nadia	S. Feldman	Suspd.	250.00	275.00
89-24-002	The Pair	S. Feldman	Suspd.	300.00	315.00
89-24-003	Anna	S. Feldman	Suspd.	350.00	375.00
Lance Corporation		**Chilmark Metal Art™ The Great Chiefs**			
92-25-001	Chief Joseph	J. Slockbower	S/O	975.00	975-1500.
92-25-002	Geronimo	J. Slockbower	S/O	975.00	975.00
Lance Corporation		**Chilmark Pewter/Metal Art™ The Warriors**			
92-26-001	Spirit of the Wolf (pewter)	D. Polland	S/O	350.00	500.00
Lance Corporation		**Chilmark Pewter/Metal Art™ The Medicine Men**			
92-27-001	False Face (pewter)	D. Polland	S/O	375.00	375.00
Lance Corporation		**Chilmark Pewter/Metal Art™ DISNEY**			
92-28-001	Cruising	Disney Studios	S/O	275.00	275.00
Lance Corporation		**Chilmark Pewter/Metal Art™ The Seekers**			
92-29-001	Buffalo Vision	A. McGrory	S/O	1075.00	1075.00
Lance Corporation		**Sebastian Miniature Figurines**			
80-30-001	S.M.C. Society Plaque ('80 Charter)	P.W. Baston	Yr.Iss.	Unkn.	20-30.00
83-30-002	Harry Hood	P.W. Baston, Jr.	S/O	Unkn.	200-250.
85-30-003	It's Hoods (Wagon)	P.W. Baston, Jr.	S/O	Unkn.	150-175.
86-30-004	Statue of Liberty (AT & T)	P.W. Baston, Jr.	S/O	Unkn.	175-200.
87-30-005	White House (Gold, Oval Base)	P.W. Baston, Jr.	S/O	17.00	75-100.00
91-30-006	America Salutes Desert Storm-painted	P.W. Baston, Jr.	S/O	49.50	49.50
91-30-007	America Salutes Desert Storm-bronze	P.W. Baston, Jr.	1,641	26.50	26.50
91-30-008	Happy Hood Holidays	P.W. Baston, Jr.	2,000	32.50	32.50
92-30-009	Firefighter	P.W. Baston, Jr.	S/O	28.00	28.00
92-30-010	I Know I Left It Here Somewhere	P.W. Baston, Jr.	1,000	28.50	28.50
Lance Corporation		**Sebastian Miniatures Children At Play**			
78-31-001	Sidewalk Days Boy	P.W. Baston	S/O	19.50	35-50.00
78-31-002	Sidewalk Days Girl	P.W. Baston	S/O	19.50	30-50.00
79-31-003	Building Days Boy	P.W. Baston	S/O	19.50	20-40.00
79-31-004	Building Days Girl	P.W. Baston	S/O	19.50	20-40.00
80-31-005	Snow Days Boy	P.W. Baston	S/O	19.50	20-40.00
80-31-006	Snow Days Girl	P.W. Baston	S/O	19.50	20-40.00
81-31-007	Sailing Days Boy	P.W. Baston	S/O	19.50	20-30.00
81-31-008	Sailing Days Girl	P.W. Baston	S/O	19.50	20-30.00
82-31-009	School Days Boy	P.W. Baston	S/O	19.50	20-30.00
82-31-010	School Days Girl	P.W. Baston	S/O	19.50	20-30.00
Lance Corporation		**Sebastian Miniatures America Remembers**			
79-32-001	Family Sing	P.W. Baston	Yr.Iss.	29.50	90-125.00
80-32-002	Family Picnic	P.W. Baston	Yr.Iss.	29.50	45-60.00
81-32-003	Family Reads Aloud	P.W. Baston	Yr.Iss.	34.50	34.50
82-32-004	Family Fishing	P.W. Baston	Yr.Iss.	34.50	34.50
83-32-005	Family Feast	P.W. Baston	Yr.Iss.	37.50	100-150.
Lance Corporation		**Sebastian Miniatures Jimmy Fund**			
83-33-001	Schoolboy	P.W. Baston	Yr.Iss.	24.50	50-75.00
84-33-002	Catcher	P.W. Baston	Yr.Iss.	24.50	50-75.00
85-33-003	Hockey Player	P.W. Baston,Jr.	Yr.Iss.	24.50	25-50.00
86-33-004	Soccer Player	P.W. Baston,Jr.	Yr.Iss.	25.00	25.00
87-33-005	Football Player	P.W. Baston,Jr.	Yr.Iss.	26.50	26.50
88-33-006	Santa	P.W. Baston,Jr.	Closed	32.50	32.50
Lance Corporation		**Sebastian Miniatures Exchange Figurines**			
83-34-001	Newspaper Boy	P.W. Baston	Yr.Iss.	28.50	45-60.00
84-34-002	First Things First	P.W. Baston,Jr.	Yr.Iss.	30.00	45.00
85-34-003	Newstand	P.W. Baston,Jr.	Yr.Iss.	30.00	40.00
86-34-004	News Wagon	P.W. Baston,Jr.	Yr.Iss.	35.00	40.00

Company / Number	Name / Series	Artist	Edition Limit	Issue Price	Quote
87-34-005	It's About Time	P.W. Baston,Jr.	Yr.Iss.	25.00	35.00
Lance Corporation	**Sebastian Miniatures Washington Irving-Member Only**				
80-35-001	Rip Van Winkle	P.W. Baston	Closed	19.50	19.50
81-35-002	Dame Van Winkle	P.W. Baston	Closed	19.50	19.50
81-35-003	Ichabod Crane	P.W. Baston	Closed	19.50	19.50
82-35-004	Katrina Van Tassel	P.W. Baston	Closed	19.50	19.50
82-35-005	Brom Bones(Headless Horseman)	P.W. Baston	Closed	22.50	22.50
83-35-006	Diedrich Knickerbocker	P.W. Baston	Closed	22.50	22.50
Lance Corporation	**Sebastian Miniatures Shakespearean-Member Only**				
84-36-001	Henry VIII	P.W. Baston	Yr.Iss.	19.50	19.50
84-36-002	Anne Boyeln	P.W. Baston	6 month	17.50	17.50
85-36-003	Falstaff	P.W. Baston	Yr.Iss.	19.50	19.50
85-36-004	Mistress Ford	P.W. Baston	6 month	17.50	17.50
86-36-005	Romeo	P.W. Baston	Yr.Iss.	19.50	19.50
86-36-006	Juliet	P.W. Baston	6 month	17.50	17.50
87-36-007	Malvolio	P.W. Baston	Yr.Iss.	21.50	21.50
87-36-008	Countess Olivia	P.W. Baston	6 month	19.50	19.50
88-36-009	Touchstone	P.W. Baston	Yr.Iss.	22.50	22.50
88-36-010	Audrey	P.W. Baston	6 month	22.50	22.50
89-36-011	Mark Anthony	P.W. Baston	Yr.Iss.	27.00	27.00
89-36-012	Cleopatra	P.W. Baston	6 month	27.00	27.00
88-36-013	Shakespeare	P.W. Baston,Jr.	Yr.Iss.	23.50	23.50
Lance Corporation	**Sebastian Miniatures Member Only**				
89-37-001	The Collectors	P.W. Baston,Jr.	Yr.Iss.	39.50	39.50
Lance Corporation	**Sebastian Miniatures Holiday Memories-Member Only**				
90-38-001	Thanksgiving Helper	P.W. Baston,Jr.	Yr.Iss.	39.50	39.50
90-38-002	Leprechaun	P.W. Baston,Jr.	Yr.Iss.	27.50	27.50
91-38-003	Trick or Treat	P.W. Baston,Jr.	Yr.Iss.	25.50	25.50
92-38-004	Christopher Columbus	P.W. Baston,Jr.	Yr.Iss.	28.50	28.50
Also see Sebastian Studios					
Lance Corporation	**Hudson Pewter Figures**				
69-39-001	George Washington (Cannon)	P.W. Baston	Closed	35.00	75-100.00
69-39-002	John Hancock	P.W. Baston	Closed	15.00	100-125.
69-39-003	Colonial Blacksmith	P.W. Baston	Closed	30.00	100-125.
69-39-004	Betsy Ross	P.W. Baston	Closed	30.00	100-125.
72-39-005	Benjamin Franklin	P.W. Baston	Closed	15.00	75-100.00
72-39-006	Thomas Jefferson	P.W. Baston	Closed	15.00	75-100.00
72-39-007	George Washington	P.W. Baston	Closed	15.00	75-100.00
72-39-008	John Adams	P.W. Baston	Closed	15.00	75-100.00
72-39-009	James Madison	P.W. Baston	Closed	15.00	50-75.00
75-39-010	Declaration Wall Plaque	P.W. Baston	Closed	Unkn.	300-500.
75-39-011	Washington's Letter of Acceptance	P.W. Baston	Closed	Unkn.	300-400.
75-39-012	Lincoln's Gettysburg Address	P.W. Baston	Closed	Unkn.	300-400.
75-39-013	Lee's Ninth General Order	P.W. Baston	Closed	Unkn.	300-400.
75-39-014	The Favored Scholar	P.W. Baston	Closed	Unkn.	600-1000.
75-39-015	Neighboring Pews	P.W. Baston	Closed	Unkn.	600-1000.
75-39-016	Weighing the Baby	P.W. Baston	Closed	Unkn.	600-1000.
75-39-017	Spirit of '76	P.W. Baston	Closed	Unkn.	750-1500.
76-39-018	Great Horned Owl	H. Wilson	Closed	Unkn.	41.50
76-39-019	Bald Eagle	H. Wilson	Closed	100.00	112.50
Lance Corporation	**Hudson Pewter Crystals of Zorn**				
88-40-001	Guarding the Crystal	D. Liberty	950	450.00	460.00
88-40-002	Charging the Stone	D. Liberty	950	375.00	395.00
88-40-003	USS Strikes Back	D. Liberty	500	650.00	675.00
88-40-004	Response of Ornic Force	D. Liberty	950	275.00	285.00
88-40-005	Battle on the Plains of Xenon	D. Liberty	950	250.00	265.00
88-40-006	Restoration	D. Liberty	950	425.00	435.00
90-40-007	Struggle For Supremacy	D. Liberty	950	395.00	400.00
90-40-008	Asmund's Workshop	D. Liberty	950	275.00	275.00
90-40-009	Vesting The Grail	D. Liberty	950	200.00	200.00
Lance Corporation	**Military Commemoratives**				
91-41-001	Desert Liberator (Pewter)	D. LaRocca	Retrd.	295.00	295.00
91-41-002	Desert Liberator (Painted Porcelain)	D. LaRocca	5,000	125.00	125.00
Lance Corporation	**Hudson Pewter The Villagers**				
87-42-001	Mr. Bosworth	Hudson Studios	Retrd.	35.00	35.00
87-42-002	Emily	Hudson Studios	Retrd.	23.00	23.00
87-42-003	Reginald	Hudson Studios	Retrd.	23.00	23.00
87-42-004	Oliver	Hudson Studios	Retrd.	20.00	20.00
87-42-005	Jenny	Hudson Studios	Retrd.	20.00	20.00
87-42-006	Thomas	Hudson Studios	Retrd.	20.00	20.00
88-42-007	Melissa	Hudson Studios	Retrd.	18.00	18.00
88-42-008	Tully's Pond	Hudson Studios	Retrd.	49.00	49.00
88-42-009	Main Street	Hudson Studios	Retrd.	47.00	47.00
88-42-010	Bosworth Manor	Hudson Studios	Retrd.	57.00	57.00
88-42-011	Santa	Hudson Studios	Retrd.	28.00	28.00
89-42-012	Grandpa Todd	Hudson Studios	Retrd.	23.00	23.00
89-42-013	Grandma Todd & Sarah	Hudson Studios	Retrd.	29.00	29.00
89-42-014	Rascal	Hudson Studios	Retrd.	25.00	25.00
89-42-015	Seated Santa	Hudson Studios	Yr.Iss.	25.00	25.00
89-42-016	Creche	Hudson Studios	Retrd.	15.00	15.00
89-42-017	Ben Torpey	Hudson Studios	Retrd.	28.00	28.00
89-42-018	Villagers Plaque	Hudson Studios	Retrd.	27.00	27.00
90-42-019	Santa & Holly	Hudson Studios	Yr.Iss.	32.00	32.00
91-42-020	Santa and Matthew	Hudson Studios	Yr.Iss.	35.00	35.00
92-42-021	Crack the Whip	Hudson Studios	1,500	95.00	95.00
92-42-022	1992 Annual Santa	Hudson Studios	Yr.Iss.	32.00	32.00
Lance Corporation	**Hudson Pewter Noah's Ark**				
82-43-001	Toucan Pair	Hudson Studios	Retrd.	18.00	18.00
83-43-002	Male Rhino	Hudson Studios	Retrd.	13.00	13.00
83-43-003	Female Rhino	Hudson Studios	Retrd.	13.00	13.00
83-43-004	Panda Pair	Hudson Studios	Retrd.	18.00	18.00
84-43-005	Male Tiger	Hudson Studios	Retrd.	13.00	13.00
84-43-006	Female Tiger	Hudson Studios	Retrd.	13.00	13.00
84-43-007	Male Deer	Hudson Studios	Retrd.	13.00	13.00
84-43-008	Female Deer	Hudson Studios	Retrd.	13.00	13.00
84-43-009	Mice Pair	Hudson Studios	Retrd.	14.00	14.00
84-43-010	Raccoon Pair	Hudson Studios	Retrd.	14.00	14.00
87-43-011	Cat Pair	Hudson Studios	Retrd.	18.00	18.00
87-43-012	Female Dog	Hudson Studios	Retrd.	13.00	13.00
87-43-013	Male Dog	Hudson Studios	Retrd.	16.00	16.00
87-43-014	Ram	Hudson Studios	Retrd.	16.00	16.00
87-43-015	Ewe	Hudson Studios	Retrd.	16.00	16.00
88-43-016	Geese Pair	Hudson Studios	Retrd.	18.00	18.00

Company / Number	Name / Series	Artist	Edition Limit	Issue Price	Quote
Ron Lee's World of Clowns	**The Original Ron Lee Collection-1976**				
76-01-001	Pinky Upside Down 111	R. Lee	Closed	25.00	150.00
76-01-002	Pinky Lying Down 112	R. Lee	Closed	25.00	150.00
76-01-003	Hobo Joe Hitchiking 116	R. Lee	Closed	55.00	65.00
76-01-004	Hobo Joe with Umbrella 117	R. Lee	Closed	58.00	65-160.00
76-01-005	Pinky Sitting 119	R. Lee	Closed	25.00	150.00
76-01-006	Hobo Joe with Balloons 120	R. Lee	Closed	63.00	90.00
76-01-007	Hobo Joe with Pal 115	R. Lee	Closed	63.00	85-170.00
76-01-008	Clown and Dog Act 101	R. Lee	Closed	48.00	78-140.00
76-01-009	Clown Tightrope Walker 104	R. Lee	Closed	50.00	82-155.00
76-01-010	Clown and Elephant Act 107	R. Lee	Closed	56.00	85-140.00
76-01-011	Pinky Standing 118	R. Lee	Closed	25.00	45-100.00
76-01-012	Owl With Guitar 500	R. Lee	Closed	15.00	35-78.00
76-01-013	Turtle On Skateboard 501	R. Lee	Closed	15.00	35-78.00
76-01-014	Frog Surfing 502	R. Lee	Closed	15.00	35-78.00
76-01-015	Penguin on Snowskis 503	R. Lee	Closed	15.00	35-78.00
76-01-016	Alligator Bowling 504	R. Lee	Closed	15.00	35-78.00
76-01-017	Hippo on Scooter 505	R. Lee	Closed	15.00	35-78.00
76-01-018	Rabbit Playing Tennis 507	R. Lee	Closed	15.00	35-78.00
76-01-019	Kangaroos Boxing 508	R. Lee	Closed	15.00	35-78.00
76-01-020	Pig Playing Violin 510	R. Lee	Closed	15.00	35-78.00
76-01-021	Bear Fishing 511	R. Lee	Closed	15.00	35-78.00
76-01-022	Dog Fishing 512	R. Lee	Closed	15.00	35-78.00
Ron Lee's World of Clowns	**The Original Ron Lee Collection-1977**				
77-02-001	Koala Bear In Tree 514	R. Lee	Closed	15.00	35-78.00
77-02-002	Koala Bear With Baby 515	R. Lee	Closed	15.00	35-78.00
77-02-003	Koala Bear On Log 516	R. Lee	Closed	15.00	35-78.00
77-02-004	Mr. Penguin 518	R. Lee	Closed	18.00	39-85.00
77-02-005	Owl Graduate 519	R. Lee	Closed	22.00	44-90.00
77-02-006	Mouse and Cheese 520	R. Lee	Closed	18.00	30-80.00
77-02-007	Monkey With Banana 521	R. Lee	Closed	18.00	30-80.00
77-02-008	Pelican and Python 522	R. Lee	Closed	18.00	30-80.00
77-02-009	Bear On Rock 523	R. Lee	Closed	18.00	30-80.00
Ron Lee's World of Clowns	**The Original Ron Lee Collection-1978**				
78-03-001	Polly, the Parrot & Crackers 201	R. Lee	Closed	63.00	100-170.
78-03-002	Corky, the Drummer Boy 202	R. Lee	Closed	53.00	85-130.00
78-03-003	Tinker Bowing 203	R. Lee	Closed	37.00	55-110.00
78-03-004	Bobbi on Unicyle 204	R. Lee	Closed	45.00	65-98.00
78-03-005	Clara-Bow 205	R. Lee	Closed	52.00	70-120.00
78-03-006	Sparky Skating 206	R. Lee	Closed	55.00	72-260.00
78-03-007	Pierrot Painting 207	R. Lee	Closed	50.00	80-170.00
78-03-008	Cuddles 208	R. Lee	Closed	37.00	55-110.00
78-03-009	Poppy with Puppet 209	R. Lee	Closed	60.00	75-140.00
78-03-010	Clancy, the Cop 210	R. Lee	Closed	55.00	72-130.00
78-03-011	Driver the Golfer 211	R. Lee	Closed	55.00	200-275.
78-03-012	Sad Sack 212	R. Lee	Closed	48.00	62-210.00
78-03-013	Elephant on Stand 213	R. Lee	Closed	26.00	42-80.00
78-03-014	Elephant on Ball 214	R. Lee	Closed	26.00	42-80.00
78-03-015	Elephant Sitting 215	R. Lee	Closed	26.00	42-80.00
78-03-016	Fireman with Hose 216	R. Lee	Closed	62.00	85-140.00
78-03-017	Tobi-Hands Outstretched 217	R. Lee	Closed	70.00	98-260.00
78-03-018	Coco-Hands on Hips 218	R. Lee	Closed	70.00	95-150.00
78-03-019	Jeri In a Barrel 219	R. Lee	Closed	75.00	110-180.
78-03-020	Hey Rube 220	R. Lee	Closed	35.00	53-92.00
78-03-021	Jocko with Lollipop 221	R. Lee	Closed	67.50	93-215.00
78-03-022	Bow Tie 222	R. Lee	Closed	67.50	93-215.00
78-03-023	Oscar On Stilts 223	R. Lee	Closed	55.00	90-120.00
78-03-024	Fancy Pants 224	R. Lee	Closed	55.00	90-120.00
78-03-025	Skippy Swinging 239	R. Lee	Closed	52.00	65-85.00
78-03-026	Sailfish 524	R. Lee	Closed	18.00	40-95.00
78-03-027	Dolphins 525	R. Lee	Closed	22.00	40-85.00
78-03-028	Prince Frog 526	R. Lee	Closed	22.00	40-85.00
78-03-029	Seagull 527	R. Lee	Closed	22.00	40-85.00
78-03-030	Hummingbird 528	R. Lee	Closed	22.00	40-85.00
78-03-031	Butterfly and Flower 529	R. Lee	Closed	22.00	40-85.00
78-03-032	Turtle on Rock 530	R. Lee	Closed	22.00	40-85.00
78-03-033	Sea Otter on Back 531	R. Lee	Closed	22.00	40-85.00
78-03-034	Sea Otter on Rock 532	R. Lee	Closed	22.00	40-85.00
Ron Lee's World of Clowns	**The Original Ron Lee Collection-1979**				
79-04-001	Timmy Tooting 225	R. Lee	Closed	35.00	52-85.00
79-04-002	Tubby Tuba 226	R. Lee	Closed	35.00	55-90.00
79-04-003	Lilli 227	R. Lee	Closed	75.00	105-145.
79-04-004	Doctor Sawbones 228	R. Lee	Closed	75.00	110-150.
79-04-005	Buttons Bicycling 229	R. Lee	Closed	75.00	110-150.
79-04-006	Kelly in Kar 230	R. Lee	Closed	164.00	210-380.
79-04-007	Kelly's Kar 231	R. Lee	Closed	75.00	90-230.00
79-04-008	Carousel Horse 232	R. Lee	Closed	119.00	130-195.
79-04-009	Harry and the Hare 233	R. Lee	Closed	69.00	102-180.
79-04-010	Fearless Fred in Cannon 234	R. Lee	Closed	80.00	105-300.
79-04-011	Darby with Flower 235	R. Lee	Closed	35.00	60-140.00
79-04-012	Darby with Umbrella 236	R. Lee	Closed	35.00	60-140.00
79-04-013	Darby With Violin 237	R. Lee	Closed	35.00	60-140.00
79-04-014	Darby Tipping Hat 238	R. Lee	Closed	35.00	60-140.00
79-04-015	Kelly at the Piano 241	R. Lee	Closed	185.00	280-510.
Ron Lee's World of Clowns	**The Original Ron Lee Collection-1980**				
80-05-001	Cubby Holding Balloon 240	R. Lee	Closed	50.00	65-70.00
80-05-002	Jingles Telling Time 242	R. Lee	Closed	75.00	90-190.00
80-05-003	Donkey What 243	R. Lee	Closed	60.00	92-250.00
80-05-004	Chuckles Juggling 244	R. Lee	Closed	98.00	105-150
80-05-005	P. T. Dinghy 245	R. Lee	Closed	65.00	80-190.00
80-05-006	Roni Riding Horse 246	R. Lee	Closed	115.00	180-290.
80-05-007	Peanuts Playing Concertina 247	R. Lee	Closed	65.00	150-285.
80-05-008	Carousel Horse 248	R. Lee	Closed	88.00	115-285.
80-05-009	Carousel Horse 249	R. Lee	Closed	88.00	115-285.
80-05-010	Jo-Jo at Make-up Mirror 250	R. Lee	Closed	86.00	125-185
80-05-011	Monkey 251	R. Lee	Closed	60.00	85-210.00
80-05-012	Dennis Playing Tennis 252	R. Lee	Closed	74.00	95-185.00
80-05-013	Jaque Downhill Racer 253	R. Lee	Closed	74.00	90-210.00
80-05-014	Ruford 254	R. Lee	Closed	43.00	82-190.00
80-05-015	Happy Waving 255	R. Lee	Closed	43.00	82-190.00
80-05-016	Zach 256	R. Lee	Closed	43.00	82-190.00
80-05-017	Emile 257	R. Lee	Closed	43.00	82-190.00
80-05-018	Banjo Willie 258	R. Lee	Closed	68.00	85-195.00
80-05-019	Hobo Joe in Tub 259	R. Lee	Closed	96.00	105-125
80-05-020	Doctor Jawbones 260	R. Lee	Closed	85.00	110-305.
80-05-021	Alexander's One Man Band 261	R. Lee	Closed	N/A	N/A
80-05-022	The Menagerie 262	R. Lee	Closed	N/A	N/A
80-05-023	Horse Drawn Chariot 263	R. Lee	Closed	N/A	N/A

Company Number	Name	Series Artist	Edition Limit	Issue Price	Quote
Ron Lee's World of Clowns		**The Original Ron Lee Collection-1981**			
81-06-001	Executive Reading 264	R. Lee	Closed	23.00	45-110.00
81-06-002	Executive with Umbrella 265	R. Lee	Closed	23.00	45-110.00
81-06-003	Executive Resting 266	R. Lee	Closed	23.00	45-110.00
81-06-004	Executive Hitchiking 267	R. Lee	Closed	23.00	45-110.00
81-06-005	Louie on Park Bench 268	R. Lee	Closed	56.00	85-160.00
81-06-006	Louie Hitching A Ride 269	R. Lee	Closed	47.00	58-135.00
81-06-007	Louie On Railroad Car 270	R. Lee	Closed	77.00	95-180.00
81-06-008	Elephant Reading 271	R. Lee	Closed	N/A	N/A
81-06-009	Pistol Pete 272	R. Lee	Closed	76.00	85-180.00
81-06-010	Barbella 273	R. Lee	Closed	N/A	N/A
81-06-011	Larry and His Hotdogs 274	R. Lee	Closed	76.00	90-200.00
81-06-012	Cashew On One Knee 275	R. Lee	Closed	N/A	N/A
81-06-013	Bojangles 276	R. Lee	Closed	N/A	N/A
81-06-014	Bozo Playing Cymbols 277	R. Lee	Closed	28.00	49-185.00
81-06-015	Bozo Riding Car 278	R. Lee	Closed	28.00	49-185.00
81-06-016	Bozo On Unicycle 279	R. Lee	Closed	28.00	49-185.00
81-06-017	Carousel Horse 280	R. Lee	Closed	88.00	125-240.
81-06-018	Carousel Horse 281	R. Lee	Closed	88.00	125-240.
81-06-019	Ron Lee Trio 282	R. Lee	Closed	144.00	280-435.
81-06-020	Kevin at the Drums 283	R. Lee	Closed	50.00	92-150.00
81-06-021	Al at the Bass 284	R. Lee	Closed	48.00	52-112.00
81-06-022	Ron at the Piano 285	R. Lee	Closed	46.00	55-110.00
81-06-023	Timothy In Big Shoes 286	R. Lee	Closed	37.00	50-95.00
81-06-024	Perry Sitting With Balloon 287	R. Lee	Closed	37.00	50-95.00
81-06-025	Perry Standing With Balloon 288	R. Lee	Closed	37.00	50-95.00
81-06-026	Nicky Sitting on Ball 289	R. Lee	Closed	39.00	48-92.00
81-06-027	Nicky Standing on Ball 290	R. Lee	Closed	39.00	48-92.00
81-06-028	Mickey With Umbrella 291	R. Lee	Closed	50.00	75-140.00
81-06-029	Mickey Tightrope Walker 292	R. Lee	Closed	50.00	75-140.00
81-06-030	Mickey Upside Down 293	R. Lee	Closed	50.00	75-140.00
81-06-031	Rocketman 294	R. Lee	Closed	77.00	92-180.00
81-06-032	My Son Darren 295	R. Lee	Closed	57.00	72-140.00
81-06-033	Harpo 296	R. Lee	Closed	120.00	190-350.
81-06-034	Pickles and Pooch 297	R. Lee	Closed	90.00	140-240.
81-06-035	Hobo Joe Praying 298	R. Lee	Closed	57.00	65-85.00
81-06-036	Bosom Buddies 299	R. Lee	Closed	135.00	90-280.00
81-06-037	Carney and Seal Act 300	R. Lee	Closed	63.00	75-140.00
Ron Lee's World of Clowns		**The Original Ron Lee Collection-1982**			
82-07-001	Ron Lee Carousel	R. Lee	Closed	10000.00	12500.00
82-07-002	Carney and Dog Act 301	R. Lee	Closed	63.00	75-149.00
82-07-003	Georgie Going Anywhere 302	R. Lee	Closed	95.00	125-256.
82-07-004	Fireman Watering House 303	R. Lee	Closed	99.00	99-180.00
82-07-005	Quincy Lying Down 304	R. Lee	Closed	80.00	92-210.00
82-07-006	Denny Eating Ice Cream 305	R. Lee	Closed	39.00	50-170.00
82-07-007	Denny Holding Gift Box 306	R. Lee	Closed	39.00	50-170.00
82-07-008	Denny Juggling Ball 307	R. Lee	Closed	39.00	50-170.00
82-07-009	Buster in Barrel 308	R. Lee	Closed	85.00	90-120.00
82-07-110	Sammy Riding Elephant 309	R. Lee	Closed	90.00	102-182.
82-07-111	Benny Pulling Car 310	R. Lee	Closed	190.00	235-360.
82-07-112	Dr. Painless and Patient 311	R. Lee	Closed	195.00	240-385.
82-07-113	Too Loose-L'Artiste 312	R. Lee	Closed	150.00	180-290.
82-07-114	Slim Charging Bull 313	R. Lee	Closed	195.00	265-410.
82-07-115	Norman Painting Dumbo 314	R. Lee	Closed	126.00	150-210.
82-07-116	Barnum Feeding Bacon 315	R. Lee	Closed	120.00	160-270.
82-07-117	Kukla and Friend 316	R. Lee	Closed	100.00	140-210.
82-07-118	Marion With Marrionette 317	R. Lee	Closed	105.00	135-225.
82-07-119	Two Man Valentinos 318	R. Lee	Closed	45.00	60-130.00
82-07-120	Three Man Valentinos 319	R. Lee	Closed	55.00	70-120.00
82-07-121	Captain Cranberry 320	R. Lee	Closed	115.00	145-180.
82-07-122	Charlie in the Rain 321	R. Lee	Closed	80.00	90-160.00
82-07-123	Hobo Joe on Cycle 322	R. Lee	Closed	125.00	170-280.
82-07-124	Tou Tou 323	R. Lee	Closed	70.00	90-190.00
82-07-125	Toy Soldier 324	R. Lee	Closed	95.00	140-270.
82-07-126	Herbie Dancing 325	R. Lee	Closed	26.00	40-110.00
82-07-127	Herbie Hands Outstretched 326	R. Lee	Closed	26.00	40-110.00
82-07-128	Herbie Balancing Hat 327	R. Lee	Closed	26.00	40-110.00
82-07-129	Herbie Lying Down 328	R. Lee	Closed	26.00	40-110.00
82-07-130	Herbie Legs in Air 329	R. Lee	Closed	26.00	40-110.00
82-07-131	Herbie Touching Ground 330	R. Lee	Closed	26.00	40-110.00
82-07-132	Clarence - The Lawyer 331	R. Lee	Closed	100.00	140-230.
82-07-133	Pinball Pal 332	R. Lee	Closed	150.00	195-287.
82-07-134	Clancy, the Cop and Dog 333	R. Lee	Closed	115.00	140-250.
82-07-135	Burrito Bandito 334	R. Lee	Closed	150.00	190-260.
82-07-136	Ali on His Magic Carpet 335	R. Lee	Closed	105.00	150-210.
82-07-137	Chico Playing Guitar 336	R. Lee	Closed	70.00	95-180.00
82-07-138	Murphy On Unicycle 337	R. Lee	Closed	115.00	160-288.
82-07-139	Robin Resting 338	R. Lee	Closed	110.00	125-210.
82-07-140	Nappy Snoozing 346	R. Lee	Closed	110.00	125-210.
82-07-141	Laurel & Hardy 700	R. Lee	Closed	225.00	290-500.
82-07-142	Charlie Chaplain 701	R. Lee	Closed	230.00	285-650.
82-07-144	Self Portrait 702	R. Lee	Closed	355.00	550-816.
82-07-145	Captain Mis-Adventure 703	R. Lee	Closed	250.00	300-550.
82-07-146	Steppin' Out 704	R. Lee	Closed	325.00	390-700.
82-07-147	Limousine Service 705	R. Lee	Closed	330.00	375-750.
82-07-148	Pig Brick Layer 800	R. Lee	Closed	23.00	35-92.00
82-07-149	Rabbit With Egg 801	R. Lee	Closed	23.00	35-92.00
82-07-150	Smokey, the Bear 802	R. Lee	Closed	23.00	35-92.00
82-07-151	Fish With Shoe 803	R. Lee	Closed	23.00	35-92.00
82-07-152	Seal Blowing His Horns 804	R. Lee	Closed	23.00	35-92.00
82-07-153	Dog Playing Guitar 805	R. Lee	Closed	23.00	35-92.00
82-07-154	Fox In An Airplane 806	R. Lee	Closed	23.00	35-92.00
82-07-155	Beaver Playing Accordian 807	R. Lee	Closed	23.00	35-92.00
82-07-156	Rooster With Barbell 808	R. Lee	Closed	23.00	35-92.00
82-07-157	Parrot Rollerskating 809	R. Lee	Closed	23.00	35-92.00
82-07-158	Walrus With Umbrella 810	R. Lee	Closed	23.00	35-92.00
82-07-159	Turtle With Gun 811	R. Lee	Closed	57.00	75-150.00
82-07-160	Reindeer 812	R. Lee	Closed	57.00	75-150.00
82-07-161	Ostrich 813	R. Lee	Closed	57.00	75-150.00
82-07-162	Tiger 814	R. Lee	Closed	57.00	75-150.00
82-07-163	Rooster 815	R. Lee	Closed	57.00	75-150.00
82-07-164	Giraffe 816	R. Lee	Closed	57.00	75-150.00
82-07-165	Lion 817	R. Lee	Closed	57.00	75-150.00
82-07-166	Camel 818	R. Lee	Closed	57.00	75-150.00
82-07-167	Horse 819	R. Lee	Closed	57.00	75-150.00
Ron Lee's World of Clowns		**The Original Ron Lee Collection-1983**			
83-08-001	Clyde Juggling 339	R. Lee	Closed	39.00	100-115.
83-08-002	Clyde Upside Down 340	R. Lee	Closed	39.00	105-115.
83-08-003	Little Horse - Head Up 341	R. Lee	Closed	29.00	72.00
83-08-004	Little Horse - Head Down 342	R. Lee	Closed	29.00	72.00
83-08-005	Rufus and His Refuse 343	R. Lee	Closed	65.00	160.00
83-08-006	Hobi in His Hammock 344	R. Lee	Closed	85.00	175-250.
83-08-007	Flipper Diving 345	R. Lee	Closed	115.00	200-350.
83-08-008	Ride 'em Roni 347	R. Lee	Closed	125.00	200-375.
83-08-009	Little Saturday Night 348	R. Lee	Closed	53.00	140-160.
83-08-010	Tottie Scottie 349	R. Lee	Closed	39.00	75-115.00
83-08-011	Teeter Tottie Scottie 350	R. Lee	Closed	55.00	105-165.
83-08-012	Casey Cruising 351	R. Lee	Closed	57.00	95-170.00
83-08-013	Tatters and Balloons 352	R. Lee	Closed	65.00	125-200.
83-08-014	Bumbles Selling Balloons 353	R. Lee	Closed	80.00	170-240.
83-08-015	Cecil and Sausage 354	R. Lee	Closed	90.00	200-270.
83-08-016	On The Road Again 355	R. Lee	Closed	220.00	300-650.
83-08-017	Engineer Billie 356	R. Lee	Closed	190.00	275-550.
83-08-018	My Daughter Deborah 357	R. Lee	Closed	63.00	125-185.
83-08-019	Beethoven's Fourth Paws 358	R. Lee	Closed	59.00	110-165.
83-08-020	Say It With Flowers 359	R. Lee	Closed	35.00	95-110.00
83-08-021	I Love You From My Heart 360	R. Lee	Closed	35.00	95-105.00
83-08-022	Chef's Cuisine 361	R. Lee	Closed	57.00	100-170.
83-08-023	Singin' In The Rain 362	R. Lee	Closed	105.00	225-300.
83-08-024	Buster and His Balloons 363	R. Lee	Closed	47.00	90-125.00
83-08-025	Up, Up and Away 364	R. Lee	Closed	50.00	100-150.
83-08-026	Lou Proposing 365	R. Lee	Closed	57.00	120-170.
83-08-027	Knickers Balancing Feather 366	R. Lee	Closed	47.00	120-135.
83-08-028	Daring Dudley 367	R. Lee	Closed	65.00	100-200.
83-08-029	Wilt the Stilt 368	R. Lee	Closed	49.00	100-155.
83-08-030	Coco and His Compact 369	R. Lee	Closed	55.00	145-175.
83-08-031	Josephine 370	R. Lee	Closed	55.00	145-175.
83-08-032	The Jogger 372	R. Lee	Closed	75.00	120-220.
83-08-033	Door to Door Dabney 373	R. Lee	Closed	100.00	200-285.
83-08-034	Riches to Rags 374	R. Lee	Closed	55.00	200-265.
83-08-035	Captain Freddy 375	R. Lee	Closed	85.00	200-425.
83-08-036	Gilbert Tee'd Off 376	R. Lee	Closed	60.00	100-200.
83-08-037	Cotton Candy 377	R. Lee	Closed	150.00	200-400.
83-08-038	Matinee Jitters 378	R. Lee	Closed	175.00	200-450.
83-08-039	The Last Scoop 379	R. Lee	Closed	175.00	300-475.
83-08-040	Cimba the Elephant 706	R. Lee	Closed	225.00	300-550.
83-08-041	The Bandwagon 707	R. Lee	Closed	900.00	1500-2700.
83-08-042	Catch the Brass Ring 708	R. Lee	Closed	510.00	900-1350.
83-08-043	The Last Scoop 900	R. Lee	Closed	325.00	300-725.
83-08-044	Matinee Jitters 901	R. Lee	Closed	325.00	350-500.
83-08-045	No Camping or Fishing 902	R. Lee	Closed	325.00	350-600.
83-08-046	Black Carousel Horse 1001	R. Lee	Closed	450.00	450-600.
83-08-047	Chestnut Carousel Horse 1002	R. Lee	Closed	450.00	700-1100.
83-08-048	White Carousel Horse 1003	R. Lee	Closed	450.00	700-1100.
83-08-049	Gazebo 1004	R. Lee	Closed	750.00	1300-1750.
Ron Lee's World of Clowns		**The Original Ron Lee Collection-1984**			
84-09-001	No Camping or Fishing 380	R. Lee	Closed	175.00	275-450.
84-09-002	Wheeler Sheila 381	R. Lee	Closed	75.00	175-225.
84-09-003	Mortimer Fishing 382	R. Lee	Closed	N/A	N/A
84-09-004	Give a Dog a Bone 383	R. Lee	Closed	95.00	95-182.00
84-09-005	The Peppermints 384	R. Lee	Closed	150.00	180-250.
84-09-006	T.K. and OH!! 385	R. Lee	Closed	85.00	200-325.
84-09-007	Just For You 386	R. Lee	Closed	110.00	150-250.
84-09-008	Baggy Pants 387	R. Lee	Closed	98.00	250-300.
84-09-009	Look at the Birdy 388	R. Lee	Closed	138.00	200-300.
84-09-010	Bozo's Seal of Approval 389	R. Lee	Closed	138.00	200-350.
84-09-011	A Bozo Lunch 390	R. Lee	Closed	148.00	250-400.
84-09-012	My Fellow Americans 391	R. Lee	Closed	138.00	250-425.
84-09-013	No Loitering 392	R. Lee	Closed	113.00	150-250.
84-09-014	Tisket and Tasket 393	R. Lee	Closed	93.00	150-250.
84-09-015	White Circus Horse 709	R. Lee	Closed	305.00	350-520.
84-09-016	Chestnut Circus Horse 710A	R. Lee	Closed	305.00	350-520.
84-09-017	Black Circus Horse 711A	R. Lee	Closed	305.00	350-520.
84-09-018	Rudy Holding Balloons 713	R. Lee	Closed	230.00	300-550.
84-09-019	Saturday Night 714	R. Lee	Closed	250.00	600-825.
Ron Lee's World of Clowns		**The Original Ron Lee Collection-1985**			
85-10-001	Giraffe Getting a Bath 428	R. Lee	Closed	160.00	235-450.
85-10-002	Whiskers Sweeping 744	R. Lee	Closed	240.00	500-800.
85-10-003	Whiskers Hitchhiking 745	R. Lee	Closed	240.00	500-800.
85-10-004	Whiskers Holding Balloons 746	R. Lee	Closed	265.00	500-800.
85-10-005	Whiskers Holding Umbrella 747	R. Lee	Closed	265.00	500-800.
85-10-006	Whiskers Bathing 749	R. Lee	Closed	305.00	500-800.
85-10-007	Whiskers On The Beach 750	R. Lee	Closed	230.00	500-800.
85-10-008	Clowns of the Caribbean PS101	R. Lee	Closed	1250.00	2000-2800.
Ron Lee's World of Clowns		**The Original Ron Lee Collection-1986**			
86-11-001	Wet Paint 436	R. Lee	Closed	80.00	100-200.
86-11-002	Bathing Buddies 450	R. Lee	Closed	145.00	250-375.
86-11-003	Hari and Hare 454	R. Lee	Closed	57.00	85-135.00
86-11-004	Ride 'Em Peanuts 463	R. Lee	Closed	55.00	70-135.00
86-11-005	Captain Cranberry 469	R. Lee	Closed	140.00	175-335.
86-11-006	Getting Even 485	R. Lee	Closed	85.00	125-225.00
86-11-007	Bums Day at the Beach L105	R. Lee	Closed	97.00	N/A
86-11-008	The Last Stop L106	R. Lee	Closed	99.00	N/A
86-11-009	Christmas Morning Magic L107	R. Lee	Closed	99.00	N/A
86-11-010	Most Requested Toy L108	R. Lee	Closed	264.00	N/A
86-11-011	High Above the Big Top L112	R. Lee	Closed	162.00	N/A
86-11-012	Puppy Love's Portrait L113	R. Lee	Closed	168.00	N/A
Ron Lee's World of Clowns		**The Original Ron Lee Collection-1987**			
87-12-001	Heartbroken Harry L101	R. Lee	Closed	63.00	125-225.
87-12-002	Lovable Luke L102	R. Lee	8,500	70.00	70.00
87-12-003	Puppy Love L103	R. Lee	8,500	71.00	71.00
87-12-004	Would You Like To Ride? L104	R. Lee	Closed	246.00	300-475.
87-12-005	Sugarland Express L109	R. Lee	Closed	342.00	400-600.
87-12-006	First & Main L110	R. Lee	Closed	368.00	500-725.
87-12-007	Show of Shows L115	R. Lee	Closed	175.00	N/A
87-12-008	Happines Is L116	R. Lee	Closed	155.00	N/A
Ron Lee's World of Clowns		**The Original Ron Lee Collection-1988**			
88-13-001	New Ron Lee Carousel	R. Lee	Closed	7000.00	9500.00
88-13-002	The Fifth Wheel L117	R. Lee	Closed	250.00	375.00
88-13-003	Bozorina L118	R. Lee	Closed	95.00	N/A
88-13-004	Dinner for Two L119	R. Lee	Closed	140.00	N/A
88-13-005	Anchors-A-Way L120	R. Lee	Closed	195.00	N/A
88-13-006	Pumpkuns Galore L121	R. Lee	Closed	135.00	N/A
88-13-007	Fore! L122	R. Lee	Closed	135.00	N/A
88-13-008	Tunnel of Love L123	R. Lee	Closed	490.00	600-800.
88-13-009	Boulder Bay L124	R. Lee	Closed	700.00	N/A
88-13-010	Cactus Pete L125	R. Lee	Closed	495.00	N/A
88-13-011	Together Again L126	R. Lee	Closed	130.00	N/A
88-13-012	To The Rescue L127	R. Lee	Closed	130.00	160-550.

Company Number	Name	Series Artist	Edition Limit	Issue Price	Quote
88-13-013	When You're Hot, You're Hot! L128	R. Lee	Closed	221.00	250-800.
Ron Lee's World of Clowns	**The Original Ron Lee Collection-1989**				
89-14-001	Be It Ever So Humble L111	R. Lee	Closed	900.00	950-1250.
89-14-002	Wishful Thinking L114	R. Lee	Closed	230.00	250-500.
89-14-003	No Fishing L130	R. Lee	Closed	247.00	N/A
89-14-004	Get Well L131	R. Lee	Closed	79.00	N/A
89-14-005	Maestro L132	R. Lee	Closed	173.00	N/A
89-14-006	If I Were A Rich Man L133	R. Lee	Closed	315.00	400-600.
89-14-007	I Pledge Allegiance L134	R. Lee	3,750	131.00	150-250.
89-14-008	In Over My Head L135	R. Lee	Closed	95.00	125-190.
89-14-009	Eye Love You L136	R. Lee	Closed	68.00	N/A
89-14-010	My Heart Beats For You L137	R. Lee	Closed	74.00	N/A
89-14-011	Just Carried Away L138	R. Lee	Closed	135.00	N/A
89-14-012	O' Solo Mia L139	R. Lee	Closed	85.00	90-150.00
89-14-013	Beauty Is In The Eye Of L140	R. Lee	Closed	190.00	N/A
89-14-014	Tee for Two L141	R. Lee	Closed	125.00	150.00
89-14-015	My Money's OnThe Bull L142	R. Lee	Closed	187.00	N/A
89-14-016	Circus Little L143	R. Lee	Closed	990.00	1250.00
89-14-017	Hughie Mungus L144	R. Lee	Closed	250.00	300-825.
89-14-018	Not A Ghost Of A Chance L145	R. Lee	Closed	195.00	N/A
89-14-019	Sh-h-h-h! L146	R. Lee	Closed	210.00	400-1000.
89-14-020	Today's Catch L147	R. Lee	Closed	230.00	245-325.
89-14-021	Catch A Falling Star L148	R. Lee	Closed	57.00	N/A
89-14-022	Rest Stop L149	R. Lee	Closed	47.00	N/A
89-14-023	Marcelle L150	R. Lee	Closed	47.00	N/A
89-14-024	Butt-R-Fly L151	R. Lee	Closed	47.00	N/A
89-14-025	Stormy Weathers L152	R. Lee	Closed	47.00	N/A
89-14-026	I Just Called! L153	R. Lee	Closed	47.00	N/A
89-14-027	Sunflower L154	R. Lee	Closed	47.00	N/A
89-14-028	Candy Apple L155	R. Lee	Closed	47.00	N/A
89-14-029	Just Go! L156	R. Lee	Closed	47.00	N/A
89-14-030	My Affections L157	R. Lee	Closed	47.00	N/A
89-14-031	Wintertime Pals L158	R. Lee	Closed	90.00	N/A
89-14-032	Merry Xmas L159	R. Lee	Closed	94.00	N/A
89-14-033	Santa's Dilemma L160	R. Lee	Closed	97.00	N/A
89-14-034	My First Tree L161	R. Lee	Closed	92.00	N/A
89-14-035	Happy Chanakah L162	R. Lee	Closed	106.00	N/A
89-14-036	Snowdrifter L163	R. Lee	Closed	230.00	275-450.
89-14-037	If That's Your Drive How's Your Putts L164	R. Lee	Closed	260.00	N/A
89-14-038	The Policeman L165	R. Lee	Closed	68.00	100-200.
89-14-039	The Pharmacist L166	R. Lee	Closed	65.00	N/A
89-14-040	The Salesman L167	R. Lee	Closed	68.00	N/A
89-14-041	The Nurse L168	R. Lee	Closed	65.00	N/A
89-14-042	The Fireman L169	R. Lee	Closed	68.00	150-200.
89-14-043	The Doctor L170	R. Lee	Closed	65.00	150-200.
89-14-044	The Lawyer 171	R. Lee	Closed	68.00	150-200.
89-14-045	The Photographer L172	R. Lee	Closed	68.00	150-200.
89-14-046	The Accountant L173	R. Lee	Closed	68.00	150-200.
89-14-047	The Optometrist L174	R. Lee	Closed	65.00	150-200.
89-14-048	The Dentist L175	R. Lee	Closed	65.00	150-200.
89-14-049	The Plumber L176	R. Lee	Closed	65.00	150-200.
89-14-050	The Real Estate Man L177	R. Lee	Closed	65.00	150-200.
89-14-051	The Chef L178	R. Lee	Closed	65.00	150-200.
89-14-052	The Secretary L179	R. Lee	Closed	65.00	150-200.
89-14-053	The Chiropractor L180	R. Lee	Closed	68.00	150-200.
89-14-054	The Housewife L181	R. Lee	Closed	75.00	150-200.
89-14-055	The Veterinarian L182	R. Lee	Closed	72.00	150-200.
89-14-056	The Beautician L183	R. Lee	Closed	68.00	150-200.
89-14-057	The Mechanic L184	R. Lee	Closed	68.00	150-200.
89-14-058	The Real Estate Lady L185	R. Lee	Closed	70.00	150-200.
89-14-059	The Football Player L186	R. Lee	Closed	65.00	150-200.
89-14-060	The Basketball Player L187	R. Lee	Closed	68.00	150-200.
89-14-061	The Golfer L188	R. Lee	Closed	72.00	150-200.
89-14-062	The Baseball Player L189	R. Lee	Closed	72.00	150-200.
89-14-063	The Tennis Player L190	R. Lee	Closed	72.00	150-200.
89-14-064	The Bowler L191	R. Lee	Closed	68.00	150-200.
89-14-065	The Surfer L192	R. Lee	Closed	72.00	150-200.
89-14-066	The Skier L193	R. Lee	Closed	75.00	150-200.
89-14-067	The Fisherman L194	R. Lee	7,500	72.00	150-200.
89-14-068	I Ain't Got No Money L195	R. Lee	Closed	325.00	N/A
89-14-069	I Should've When I Could've L196	R. Lee	Closed	325.00	N/A
89-14-070	Memories L197	R. Lee	Closed	325.00	N/A
89-14-071	Be Happy L198	R. Lee	Closed	160.00	N/A
89-14-072	Two a.m. Blues L199	R. Lee	Closed	125.00	N/A
89-14-073	Dang It L200	R. Lee	Closed	47.00	N/A
89-14-074	Hot Diggity Dog L201	R. Lee	Closed	47.00	N/A
89-14-075	The Serenade L202	R. Lee	Closed	47.00	N/A
89-14-076	Rain Bugs Me L203	R. Lee	Closed	225.00	N/A
89-14-077	Butterflies Are Free L204	R. Lee	Closed	225.00	N/A
89-14-078	She Loves Me Not L205	R. Lee	Closed	225.00	N/A
89-14-079	Birdbrain L206	R. Lee	Closed	110.00	N/A
89-14-080	Jingles With Umbrella L207	R. Lee	Closed	90.00	N/A
89-14-081	Jingles Holding Balloon L208	R. Lee	Closed	90.00	N/A
89-14-082	Jingles Hitchhiking L209	R. Lee	Closed	90.00	N/A
89-14-083	The Greatest Little Shoe On Earth L210	R. Lee	Closed	165.00	200-300.
89-14-084	Slots Of Luck L211	R. Lee	Closed	90.00	N/A
89-14-085	Craps L212	R. Lee	Closed	530.00	N/A
89-14-086	My Last Chip L213	R. Lee	Closed	550.00	N/A
89-14-087	Over 21 L214	R. Lee	Closed	550.00	N/A
89-14-088	I-D-D-D-Do! L215	R. Lee	Closed	180.00	N/A
89-14-089	You Must Be Kidding L216	R. Lee	Closed	N/A	N/A
89-14-090	Candy Man L217	R. Lee	2,750	350.00	350.00
89-14-091	The New Self Portrait L218	R. Lee	Closed	800.00	950.00
Ron Lee's World of Clowns	**The Original Ron Lee Collection-1990**				
90-15-001	Carousel Horse L219	R. Lee	Closed	150.00	N/A
90-15-002	Carousel Horse L220	R. Lee	Closed	150.00	N/A
90-15-003	Carousel Horse L221	R. Lee	Closed	150.00	N/A
90-15-004	Carousel Horse L222	R. Lee	Closed	150.00	N/A
90-15-005	Flapper Riding Carousel L223	R. Lee	Closed	190.00	N/A
90-15-006	Peaches Riding Carousel L224	R. Lee	Closed	190.00	N/A
90-15-007	Rascal Riding Carousel L225	R. Lee	Closed	190.00	N/A
90-15-008	Jo-Jo Riding Carousel L226	R. Lee	Closed	190.00	N/A
90-15-009	Me Too!! L231	R. Lee	3,500	70.00	70-80.00
90-15-010	Heartbroken Hobo L233	R. Lee	Closed	116.00	160.00
90-15-011	Scooter L234	R. Lee	2,750	240.00	275.00
90-15-012	Tandem Mania L235	R. Lee	2,750	360.00	360.00
90-15-013	The Big Wheel L236	R. Lee	2,750	240.00	240.00
90-15-014	Uni-Cycle L237	R. Lee	2,750	240.00	240.00
90-15-015	Fill'er Up L248	R. Lee	2,250	280.00	280.00
90-15-016	Push and Pull L249	R. Lee	2,250	260.00	260.00
90-15-017	Snowdrifter II L250	R. Lee	1,250	340.00	340-350.

Company Number	Name	Series Artist	Edition Limit	Issue Price	Quote
90-15-018	Kiss! Kiss! L251	R. Lee	2,750	37.00	37.00
90-15-019	Na! Na! L252	R. Lee	2,750	33.00	33.00
90-15-020	Henry 8-3/4 L260	R. Lee	2,750	37.00	37.00
90-15-021	Horsin' Around L262	R. Lee	2,750	37.00	37-50.00
Ron Lee's World of Clowns	**The Original Ron Lee Collection-1991**				
91-16-001	Cruising L265	R. Lee	1,500	170.00	170-175.
91-16-002	Business is Business L266	R. Lee	1,500	110.00	110.00
91-16-003	I'm Singin' In The Rain L268	R. Lee	1,500	135.00	135.00
91-16-004	Anywhere? L269	R. Lee	1,500	125.00	125-145.
91-16-005	Gilbert's Dilemma L270	R. Lee	1,750	90.00	90.00
91-16-006	Puppy Love Scootin' L275	R. Lee	1,750	73.00	73-80.00
91-16-007	Puppy Love's Free Ride L276	R. Lee	1,750	73.00	73-80.00
91-16-008	Puppy Love's Treat L277	R. Lee	1,750	73.00	73-80.00
91-16-009	Happy Birthday Puppy Love L278	R. Lee	1,750	73.00	73-80.00
91-16-010	Winter L279	R. Lee	1,500	115.00	115-125.
91-16-011	Spring L280	R. Lee	1,500	95.00	95-100.00
91-16-012	Summer L281	R. Lee	1,500	95.00	95-110.00
91-16-013	Fall L282	R. Lee	1,500	120.00	120-125.
91-16-014	TA DA L294	R. Lee	1,500	220.00	220-225.
91-16-015	Lit'l Snowdrifter L298	R. Lee	1,750	70.00	115.00
91-16-016	Our Nation's Pride L312	R. Lee	1,776	150.00	150.00
91-16-017	Give Me Liberty L313	R. Lee	1,776	155.00	155-165.
91-16-018	United We Stand L314	R. Lee	1,776	150.00	150.00
Ron Lee's World of Clowns	**The Ron Lee Disney Collection Exclusives**				
90-17-001	The Bandleader MM100	R. Lee	2,750	75.00	75.00
90-17-002	The Sorcerer MM200	R. Lee	Closed	85.00	120.00
90-17-003	Steamboat Willie MM300	R. Lee	2,750	95.00	95.00
90-17-004	Mickey's Christmas MM400	R. Lee	2,750	95.00	95.00
90-17-005	Pinocchio MM500	R. Lee	2,750	85.00	85.00
90-17-006	Dumbo MM600	R. Lee	2,750	110.00	110.00
90-17-007	Uncle Scrooge MM700	R. Lee	2,750	110.00	110.00
90-17-008	Snow White & Grumpy MM800	R. Lee	2,750	140.00	140.00
91-17-009	Goofy MM110	R. Lee	2,750	115.00	115.00
91-17-010	Dopey MM120	R. Lee	2,750	80.00	80.00
91-17-011	The Witch MM130	R. Lee	2,750	115.00	115.00
91-17-012	Two Gun Mickey MM140	R. Lee	2,750	115.00	115.00
91-17-013	Mickey's Adventure MM150	R. Lee	2,750	195.00	195.00
91-17-014	Mt. Mickey MM900	R. Lee	2,750	175.00	175.00
91-17-015	Tugboat Mickey MM160	R. Lee	2,750	180.00	180.00
91-17-016	Minnie Mouse MM170	R. Lee	2,750	80.00	80.00
91-17-017	Mickey & Minnie at the Piano MM180	R. Lee	2,750	195.00	195.00
91-17-018	Decorating Donald MM210	R. Lee	2,750	60.00	60.00
91-17-019	Mickey's Delivery MM220	R. Lee	2,750	70.00	70.00
91-17-020	Goofy's Gift MM230	R. Lee	2,750	70.00	70.00
91-17-021	Pluto's Treat MM240	R. Lee	2,750	60.00	60.00
91-17-022	Jimminy's List MM250	R. Lee	2,750	60.00	60.00
91-17-023	Lady and the Tramp MM280	R. Lee	1,500	295.00	295.00
91-17-024	Lion Around MM270	R. Lee	2,750	140.00	140.00
91-17-025	The Tea Cup Ride (Disneyland Exclusive) MM260	R. Lee	1,250	225.00	225.00
Ron Lee's World of Clowns	**The Ron Lee Emmett Kelly, Sr. Collection**				
91-18-001	That-A-Way EK201	R. Lee	1,750	125.00	125.00
91-18-002	Help Yourself EK202	R. Lee	1,750	145.00	145.00
91-18-003	Spike's Uninvited Guest EK203	R. Lee	1,750	165.00	165.00
91-18-004	Love at First Sight EK204	R. Lee	1,750	197.00	197.00
91-18-005	Time for a Change EK205	R. Lee	1,750	190.00	190.00
91-18-006	God Bless America EK206	R. Lee	1,750	130.00	130.00
91-18-007	My Protege EK207	R. Lee	1,750	160.00	160.00
91-18-008	Emmett Kelly, Sr. Sign E208	R. Lee	1,750	110.00	110.00
Ron Lee's World of Clowns	**The Ron Lee Looney Tunes Collection**				
91-19-001	Western Daffy Duck LT105	R. Lee	2,750	87.00	87-90.00
91-19-002	Michigan J. Frog LT110	R. Lee	2,750	115.00	115.00
91-19-003	Porky Pig LT115	R. Lee	2,750	97.00	97-100.00
91-19-004	Tasmanian Devil LT120	R. Lee	2,750	105.00	105.00
91-19-005	Elmer Fudd LT125	R. Lee	2,750	87.00	87-90.00
91-19-006	Yosemite Sam LT130	R. Lee	2,750	110.00	110.00
91-19-007	Sylvester & Tweety LT135	R. Lee	2,750	110.00	110-115.
91-19-008	Daffy Duck LT140	R. Lee	2,750	80.00	80-85.00
91-19-009	Pepe LePew & Penelope LT145	R. Lee	2,750	115.00	115.00
91-19-010	Bugs Bunny LT150	R. Lee	2,750	123.00	123.00
91-19-011	Tweety LT155	R. Lee	2,750	110.00	110-115.
91-19-012	Foghorn Leghorn & Henry Hawk LT160	R. Lee	2,750	115.00	115.00
91-19-013	1940 Bugs Bunny LT165	R. Lee	2,750	85.00	85.00
91-19-014	Marvin the Martian LT170	R. Lee	2,750	75.00	75.00
91-19-015	Wile E. Coyote & Roadrunner LT175	R. Lee	2,750	165.00	165-175.
91-19-016	Mt. Yosemite LT180	R. Lee	850	160.00	160-300.
Ron Lee's World of Clowns	**The Ron Lee Warner Bros. Collection**				
91-20-001	The Maltese Falcon WB100	R. Lee	1,250	175.00	175.00
91-20-002	Robin Hood Bugs WB200	R. Lee	1,000	190.00	190.00
Ron Lee's World of Clowns	**The Flintstones**				
91-21-001	The Flintstones HB100	R. Lee	2,750	410.00	410.00
91-21-002	Yabba-Dabba-Doo HB110	R. Lee	2,750	230.00	230.00
91-21-003	Saturday Blues HB120	R. Lee	2,750	105.00	105.00
91-21-004	Bedrock Serenade HB130	R. Lee	2,750	250.00	250.00
91-21-005	Joyride-A-Saurus HB140	R. Lee	2,750	107.00	107.00
91-21-006	Bogey Buddies HB150	R. Lee	2,750	143.00	143.00
91-21-007	Vac-A-Saurus HB160	R. Lee	2,750	105.00	105.00
91-21-008	Buffalo Brothers HB170	R. Lee	2,750	134.00	134.0
Ron Lee's World of Clowns	**The Jetsons**				
91-22-001	The Jetsons HB500	R. Lee	2,750	500.00	500.00
91-22-002	The Cosmic Couple HB510	R. Lee	2,750	105.00	105.00
91-22-003	Astro: Cosmic Canine HB520	R. Lee	2,750	275.00	275.00
91-22-004	I Rove Roo HB530	R. Lee	2,750	105.00	105.00
91-22-005	Scare-D-Dog HB540	R. Lee	2,750	160.00	160.00
91-22-006	4 O'Clock Tea HB550	R. Lee	2,750	203.00	203.00
Ron Lee's World of Clowns	**The Classics**				
91-23-001	Yogi Bear & Boo Boo HB800	R. Lee	2,750	95.00	95.00
91-23-002	Quick Draw McGraw HB805	R. Lee	2,750	90.00	90.00
91-23-003	Scooby Doo & Shaggy HB810	R. Lee	2,750	114.00	114.00
91-23-004	Huckleberry Hound HB815	R. Lee	2,750	90.00	90.00
Ron Lee's World of Clowns	**The Ron Lee Collector's Club Gifts**				
87-24-001	Hooping It Up CCG1	R. Lee	Closed	Gift	N/A
88-24-002	Pudge CCG2	R. Lee	Closed	Gift	N/A
89-24-003	Pals CCG3	R. Lee	Closed	Gift	N/A

Company Number	Name	Series Artist	Edition Limit	Issue Price	Quote
90-24-004	Potsie CCG4	R. Lee	Closed	Gift	N/A
91-24-005	Hi! Ya! CCG5	R. Lee	Closed	Gift	N/A
92-24-005	Bashful Beau CCG6	R. Lee	Yr.Iss.	Gift	N/A
Ron Lee's World of Clowns	**The Ron Lee Collector's Club Renewal Sculptures**				
87-25-001	Doggin' Along CC1	R. Lee	Yr.Iss.	75.00	115.00
88-25-002	Midsummer's Dream CC2	R. Lee	Yr.Iss.	97.00	140.00
89-25-003	Peek-A-Boo Charlie CC3	R. Lee	Yr.Iss.	65.00	100.00
90-25-004	Get The Message CC4	R. Lee	Yr.Iss.	65.00	N/A
91-25-005	I'm So Pretty CC5	R. Lee	Yr Iss.	65.00	N/A
92-25-006	It's For You CC6	R. Lee	Yr.Iss.	65.00	N/A
Ron Lee's World of Clowns	**Rocky & Bullwinkle And Friends Collection**				
92-26-001	Rocky & Bullwinkle RB600	R. Lee	1,750	120.00	120.00
92-26-002	The Swami RB605	R. Lee	1,750	175.00	175.00
92-26-003	Dudley Do-Right RB610	R. Lee	1,750	175.00	175.00
92-26-004	My Hero RB615	R. Lee	1,750	275.00	275.00
92-26-005	KA-BOOM! RB620	R. Lee	1,750	175.00	175.00
Ron Lee's World of Clowns	**The Wizard Of Oz Collection**				
92-27-001	Kansas WZ400	R. Lee	750	550.00	550.00
92-27-002	The Munchkins WZ405	R. Lee	750	620.00	620.00
92-27-003	The Ruby Slippers WZ410	R. Lee	750	620.00	620.00
92-27-004	The Scarecrow WZ415	R. Lee	750	510.00	510.00
92-27-005	The Tin Man WZ420	R. Lee	750	530.00	530.00
92-27-006	The Cowardly Lion WZ425	R. Lee	750	620.00	620.00
Ron Lee's World of Clowns	**The Woody Woodpecker And Friends Collection**				
92-28-001	Birdy for Woody WL005	R. Lee	1,750	117.00	117.00
92-28-002	Peck of My Heart WL010	R. Lee	1,750	370.00	370.00
92-28-003	Woody Woodpecker WL015	R. Lee	1,750	73.00	73.00
92-28-004	1940 Woody Woodpecker WL020	R. Lee	1,750	73.00	73.00
92-28-005	Andy and Miranda Panda WL025	R. Lee	1,750	140.00	140.00
92-28-006	Pals WL030	R. Lee	1,750	179.00	179.00
Ron Lee's World of Clowns	**The Popeye Collection**				
92-29-001	Liberty P001	R. Lee	1,750	184.00	184.00
92-29-002	Men!!! P002	R. Lee	1,750	230.00	230.00
92-29-003	Strong to The Finish P003	R. Lee	1,750	95.00	95.00
92-29-004	That's My Boy P004	R. Lee	1,750	145.00	145.00
92-29-005	Oh Popeye P005	R. Lee	1,750	230.00	230.00
92-29-006	Par Excellence P006	R. Lee	1,750	220.00	220.00
Ron Lee's World of Clowns	**The Ron Lee Looney Tunes II Collection**				
92-30-001	Speedy Gonzales LT185	R. Lee	2,750	73.00	73.00
92-30-002	For Better or Worse LT190	R. Lee	1,500	285.00	285.00
92-30-003	What The ...? LT195	R. Lee	1,500	240.00	240.00
92-30-004	Ditty Up LT200	R. Lee	2,750	110.00	110.00
92-30-005	Leopold & Giovanni LT205	R. Lee	1,500	225.00	225.00
92-30-006	No Pain No Gain LT210	R. Lee	950	270.00	270.00
92-30-007	What's up Doc? LT215	R. Lee	950	950.00	950.00
92-30-008	Beep Beep LT220	R. Lee	1,500	115.00	115.00
92-30-009	Rackin' Frackin' Varmint LT225	R. Lee	950	260.00	260.00
92-30-010	Van Duck LT230	R. Lee	950	335.00	335.00
92-30-011	The Virtuosos LT235	R. Lee	950	350.00	350.00
Geo. Zoltan Lefton Company	**Colonial Village**				
87-01-001	Church of the Golden Rule 05820	Lefton	Open	35.00	47.00
87-01-002	Li'l Red Schoolhouse 05821	Lefton	Open	35.00	47.00
87-01-003	Train Station 05822	Lefton	Closed	35.00	180.00
87-01-004	General Store 05823	Lefton	Closed	35.00	35.00
87-01-005	The Welcome Home 05824	Lefton	Open	35.00	45.00
87-01-006	Old Stone Church 05825	Lefton	Open	35.00	45.00
87-01-007	King's Cottage 05890	Lefton	Open	35.00	47.00
87-01-008	Nelson House 05891	Lefton	Closed	35.00	35.00
87-01-009	McCauley House 05892	Lefton	Closed	35.00	35.00
87-01-010	Penny House 05893	Lefton	Closed	35.00	35.00
87-01-011	Ritter House 05894	Lefton	Closed	35.00	102.00
87-01-012	Charity Chapel 05895	Lefton	Closed	35.00	35.00
88-01-013	Faith Church 06333	Lefton	Closed	40.00	40.00
88-01-014	Friendship Chapel 06334	Lefton	Open	40.00	45.00
88-01-015	Old Time Station 06335	Lefton	Open	40.00	47.00
88-01-016	Trader Tom's Gen'l Store 06336	Lefton	Open	40.00	45.00
88-01-017	House of Blue Gables 06337	Lefton	Open	40.00	45.00
88-01-018	The Stone House 06338	Lefton	Open	40.00	45.00
88-01-019	Greystone House 06339	Lefton	Open	40.00	45.00
88-01-020	City Hall 06340	Lefton	Open	40.00	45.00
88-01-021	The Ritz Hotel 06341	Lefton	Open	40.00	45.00
88-01-022	Engine Co. No. 5 Firehouse 06342	Lefton	Open	40.00	47.00
88-01-023	Post Office 06343	Lefton	Open	40.00	47.00
88-01-024	Village Police Station 06344	Lefton	Open	40.00	47.00
88-01-025	The State Bank 06345	Lefton	Open	40.00	47.00
88-01-026	Johnson's Antiques 06346	Lefton	Closed	40.00	40.00
88-01-027	New Hope Church (Musical) 06470	Lefton	Closed	40.00	40.00
89-01-028	Gull's Nest Lighthouse 06747	Lefton	Open	40.00	45.00
89-01-029	Maple St. Church 06748	Lefton	Closed	40.00	40.00
89-01-030	Village School 06749	Lefton	Closed	40.00	40.00
89-01-031	Cole's Barn 06750	Lefton	Open	40.00	45.00
89-01-032	Sweetheart's Bridge 06751	Lefton	Open	40.00	45.00
89-01-033	Village Library 06752	Lefton	Open	40.00	45.00
89-01-034	Bijou Theatre 06897	Lefton	Closed	40.00	60.00
89-01-035	The Village Bakery 06898	Lefton	Open	40.00	45.00
89-01-036	Quincy's Clock Shop 06899	Lefton	Open	40.00	45.00
89-01-037	Victorian Apothecary 06900	Lefton	Closed	40.00	40.00
89-01-038	Village Barber Shop 06901	Lefton	Open	40.00	45.00
89-01-039	The Major's Manor 06902	Lefton	Open	40.00	45.00
89-01-040	Cobb's Bootery 06903	Lefton	Open	40.00	45.00
89-01-041	Capper's Millinery 06904	Lefton	Open	40.00	45.00
89-01-042	Miller Bros. Silversmiths 06905	Lefton	Open	40.00	45.00
90-01-043	The First Church 07333	Lefton	Open	45.00	45.00
90-01-044	Fellowship Church 07334	Lefton	Open	45.00	45.00
90-01-045	The Victorian House 07335	Lefton	Closed	45.00	45.00
90-01-046	Hampshire House 07336	Lefton	Open	45.00	50.00
90-01-047	The Nob Hill 07337	Lefton	Open	45.00	47.00
90-01-048	The Ardmore 07338	Lefton	Open	45.00	45.00
90-01-049	Ship's Chandler's Shop 07339	Lefton	Open	45.00	45.00
90-01-050	Village Hardware 07340	Lefton	Open	45.00	47.00
90-01-051	Country Post Office 07341	Lefton	Open	45.00	45.00
90-01-052	Coffee & Tea Shoppe 07342	Lefton	Open	45.00	45.00
90-01-053	Pierpont-Smithe's Curios 07343	Lefton	Closed	45.00	45.00
90-01-054	Mulberry Station 07344	Lefton	Open	50.00	65.00
90-01-055	Ryman Auditorium-Special Edition 08010	Lefton	Open	50.00	55.00
90-01-056	Hillside Church 11991	Lefton	Closed	60.00	140-180.

Company Number	Name	Series Artist	Edition Limit	Issue Price	Quote
91-01-057	Smith's Smithy 07476	Lefton	Closed	45.00	45.00
91-01-058	The Toy Maker's Shop 07477	Lefton	Open	45.00	45.00
91-01-059	Daisy's Flower Shop 07478	Lefton	Open	45.00	45.00
91-01-060	Watt's Candle Shop 07479	Lefton	Open	45.00	45.00
91-01-061	Wig Shop 07480	Lefton	Open	45.00	45.00
91-01-062	Sweet Shop 07481	Lefton	Open	45.00	45.00
91-01-063	Belle-Union Saloon 07482	Lefton	Open	25.00	25.00
91-01-064	Victorian Gazebo 07925	Lefton	Open	45.00	45.00
91-01-065	Sanderson's Mill 07927	Lefton	Open	45.00	45.00
92-01-066	Northpoint School 07960	Lefton	Open	45.00	50.00
92-01-067	Brenner's Apothecary 07961	Lefton	Open	45.00	50.00
92-01-068	The Village Inn 07962	Lefton	Open	45.00	50.00
92-01-069	Village Green Gazebo 00227	Lefton	Open	22.00	22.00
92-01-070	Stearn's Stable 00228	Lefton	Open	45.00	50.00
92-01-071	Vanderspeck's Mill 00229	Lefton	Open	55.00	55.00
92-01-072	Main St. Church 00230	Lefton	Open	45.00	50.00
92-01-073	San Sebastian Mission 00231	Lefton	Open	45.00	50.00
92-01-074	Elegant Lady Dress Shop 00232	Lefton	Open	45.00	47.00
92-01-075	County Courthouse 00233	Lefton	Open	45.00	50.00
92-01-076	Lakehurst 11992	Lefton	Closed	55.00	55.00
93-01-077	St. Peter's Church w/Speaker 00715	Lefton	Open	60.00	60.00
93-01-078	Kirby House-CVRA Exclusive 00716	Lefton	Open	50.00	50.00
93-01-079	Burnside 00717	Lefton	Open	50.00	50.00
93-01-080	Joseph House 00718	Lefton	Open	50.00	50.00
93-01-081	Mark Hall 00719	Lefton	Open	50.00	50.00
93-01-082	Blacksmith 00720	Lefton	Open	47.00	47.00
93-01-083	Doctor's Office 00721	Lefton	Open	50.00	50.00
93-01-084	Baldwin's Fine Jewelry 00722	Lefton	Open	50.00	50.00
93-01-085	Antiques & Curiosities 00723	Lefton	Open	50.00	50.00
93-01-086	Dentist's Office 00724	Lefton	Open	50.00	50.00
93-01-087	Green's Grocery 00725	Lefton	Open	50.00	50.00
93-01-088	St. James Cathedral 11993	Lefton	5,000	75.00	75.00
Legends	**The Legendary West Premier Edition**				
88-01-001	Red Cloud's Coup	C. Pardell	S/O	480.00	4000-5500.
89-01-002	Pursued	C. Pardell	S/O	750.00	3000-4000.
89-01-003	Songs of Glory	C. Pardell	S/O	850.00	2600-3500.
90-01-004	Crow Warrior	C. Pardell	S/O	1225.00	3000-4500.
91-01-005	Triumphant	C. Pardell	S/O	1150.00	2500.00
92-01-006	The Final Charge	C. Pardell	S/O	1250.00	2000.00
Legends	**The Legacies Of The West Premier Edition**				
90-02-001	Mystic Vision	C. Pardell	S/O	990.00	2500-3500.
90-02-002	Victorious	C. Pardell	S/O	1275.00	2500-3800.
91-02-003	Defiant Comanche	C. Pardell	S/O	1300.00	1600-2100.
91-02-004	No More, Forever	C. Pardell	S/O	1500.00	1750-2500.
92-02-005	Esteemed Warrior	C. Pardell	S/O	1750.00	2000-2800.
Legends	**The Legendary West Collection**				
87-03-001	White Feather's Vision	C. Pardell	S/O	310.00	600-1100.
87-03-002	Pony Express (Bronze)	C. Pardell	S/O	320.00	450.00
87-03-003	Pony Express (Pewter)	C. Pardell	S/O	320.00	450.00
87-03-004	Johnson's Last Fight	C. Pardell	S/O	590.00	850-1000.
92-03-005	Crazy Horse	C. Pardell	S/O	390.00	500-750.
Legends	**American West Premier Edition**				
91-04-001	Unexpected Rescuer	C. Pardell	S/O	990.00	1400-2100.
91-04-002	First Coup	C. Pardell	S/O	1150.00	1300-1700.
92-04-003	American Horse Takes His Name	C. Pardell	950	1300.00	1300.00
Legends	**The Endangered Wildlife Collection**				
90-05-001	Forest Spirit	K. Cantrell	S/O	290.00	750-850.
92-05-002	Spirit Song	K. Cantrell	S/O	350.00	400-700.
Legends	**Annual Collectors Edition**				
90-06-001	The Night Before	C. Pardell	S/O	990.00	1500-1900.
91-06-002	Medicine Gift of Manhood	C. Pardell	S/O	990.00	1400-2300.
92-06-003	Spirit of the Wolf	C. Pardell	S/O	950.00	1400-1750.
Legends	**The Great Outdoorsman**				
88-07-001	Both Are Hooked (Bronze)	C. Pardell	Retrd.	320.00	320.00
88-07-002	Both Are Hooked (Pewter)	C. Pardell	Retrd.	320.00	320.00
Legends	**Classic Equestrian Collection**				
88-08-001	Lippizzaner (Bronze)	C. Pardell	Retrd.	200.00	200.00
Legends	**Wild Realm Collection**				
88-09-001	Fly Fisher (Bronze)	C. Pardell	Retrd.	330.00	330.00
88-09-002	Fly Fisher (Pewter)	C. Pardell	Retrd.	330.00	330.00
88-09-003	Alpha Pair (Bronze)	C. Pardell	Retrd.	330.00	330.00
88-09-004	Alpha Pair (Pewter)	C. Pardell	Retrd.	330.00	330.00
88-09-005	Alpha Pair (Mixed Media)	C. Pardell	S/O	390.00	500-1000.
Legends	**Oceanic World**				
89-10-001	Freedom's Beauty (Bronze)	D. Medina	Retrd.	330.00	330.00
89-10-002	Freedom's Beauty (Pewter)	D. Medina	Retrd.	130.00	130.00
89-10-003	Together (Bronze)	D. Medina	Retrd.	140.00	140.00
89-10-004	Together (Pewter)	D. Medina	Retrd.	130.00	130.00
Legends	**North American Wildlife**				
88-11-001	Double Trouble (Bronze)	D. Edwards	Retrd.	300.00	300.00
88-11-002	Double Trouble (Pewter)	D. Edwards	Retrd.	320.00	320.00
88-11-003	Grizzly Solitude (Bronze)	D. Edwards	Retrd.	310.00	310.00
88-11-004	Grizzly Solitude (Pewter)	D. Edwards	Retrd.	330.00	330.00
88-11-005	Defenders of Freedom (Bronze)	D. Edwards	Retrd.	340.00	340.00
88-11-006	Defenders of Freedom (Pewter)	D. Edwards	Retrd.	370.00	370.00
88-11-007	The Proud American (Bronze)	D. Edwards	Retrd.	330.00	330.00
88-11-008	The Proud American (Pewter)	D. Edwards	Retrd.	340.00	340.00
88-11-009	Downhill Run (Bronze)	D. Edwards	Retrd.	330.00	330.00
88-11-010	Downhill Run (Pewter)	D. Edwards	Retrd.	340.00	340.00
88-11-011	Sudden Alert (Bronze)	D. Edwards	Retrd.	300.00	300.00
88-11-012	Sudden Alert (Pewter)	D. Edwards	Retrd.	320.00	320.00
88-11-013	Ridge Runners (Bronze)	D. Edwards	Retrd.	300.00	300.00
88-11-014	Ridge Runners (Pewter)	D. Edwards	Retrd.	310.00	310.00
88-11-014	Last Glance (Bronze)	D. Edwards	Retrd.	300.00	300.00
88-11-015	Last Glance (Pewter)	D. Edwards	Retrd.	320.00	320.00
Legends	**American Heritage**				
87-12-001	Grizz Country (Bronze)	D. Edwards	Retrd.	350.00	350.00
87-12-002	Grizz Country (Pewter)	D. Edwards	Retrd.	370.00	370.00
87-12-003	Winter Provisions (Bronze)	D. Edwards	Retrd.	340.00	340.00
87-12-004	Winter Provisions (Pewter)	D. Edwards	Retrd.	370.00	370.00
87-12-005	Wrangler's Dare (Bronze)	D. Edwards	Retrd.	630.00	630.00

Company / Number	Name	Series / Artist	Edition Limit	Issue Price	Quote
87-12-006	Wrangler's Dare (Pewter)	D. Edwards	Retrd.	660.00	660.00
Legends		**Special Commissions**			
87-13-001	Mama's Joy (Bronze)	D. Edwards	Retrd.	200.00	200.00
87-13-002	Mama's Joy (Pewter)	D. Edwards	Retrd.	250.00	250.00
87-13-003	Wild Freedom (Bronze)	D. Edwards	Retrd.	320.00	320.00
87-13-004	Wild Freedom (Pewter)	D. Edwards	Retrd.	330.00	330.00
Legends		**Indian Arts Collection**			
89-14-001	Chief's Blanket	C. Pardell	S/O	350.00	500-1000.
Legends		**Gallery Editions**			
92-15-001	Resolute	C. Pardell	S/O	7950.00	10000-15000
Lenox Collections		**American Fashion**			
83-01-001	Springtime Promenade	Unknown	Open	95.00	95.00
84-01-002	Tea at the Ritz	Unknown	Open	95.00	95.00
84-01-003	First Waltz	Unknown	Open	95.00	95.00
85-01-004	Governor's Garden Party	Unknown	Open	95.00	95.00
86-01-005	Grand Tour	Unknown	Open	95.00	95.00
86-01-006	Belle of the Ball	Unknown	Open	95.00	95.00
87-01-007	Centennial Bride	Unknown	Open	95.00	95.00
87-01-008	Gala at the Whitehouse	Unknown	Open	95.00	95.00
92-01-009	Royal Reception	Unknown	Open	95.00	95.00
Lenox Collections		**Wildlife of the Seven Continents**			
84-02-001	North American Bighorn Sheep	Unknown	Open	120.00	120.00
85-02-002	Australian Koala	Unknown	Open	120.00	120.00
85-02-003	Asian Elephant	Unknown	Open	120.00	120.00
86-02-004	South American Puma	Unknown	Open	120.00	120.00
87-02-005	European Red Deer	Unknown	Open	136.00	136.00
87-02-006	Antarctic Seals	Unknown	Open	136.00	136.00
88-02-007	African Lion	Unknown	Open	136.00	136.00
Lenox Collections		**Legendary Princesses**			
85-03-001	Rapunzel	Unknown	Open	119.00	136.00
86-03-002	Sleeping Beauty	Unknown	Open	119.00	136.00
87-03-003	Snow Queen	Unknown	Open	119.00	136.00
88-03-004	Cinderella	Unknown	Open	136.00	136.00
89-03-005	Swan Princess	Unknown	Open	136.00	136.00
89-03-006	Snow White	Unknown	Open	136.00	136.00
90-03-007	Juliet	Unknown	Open	136.00	136.00
90-03-008	Guinevere	Unknown	Open	136.00	136.00
90-03-009	Cleopatra	Unknown	Open	136.00	136.00
91-03-010	Peacock Maiden	Unknown	Open	136.00	136.00
91-03-011	Pocohontas	Unknown	9,500	136.00	136.00
92-03-012	Firebird	Unknown	Open	156.00	156.00
92-03-013	Sheherezade	Unknown	Open	156.00	156.00
93-03-014	Little Mermaid	Unknown	Open	156.00	156.00
Lenox Collections		**Carousel Animals**			
87-04-001	Carousel Horse	Unknown	Open	136.00	152.00
88-04-002	Carousel Unicorn	Unknown	Open	136.00	152.00
89-04-003	Carousel Circus Horse	Unknown	Open	136.00	152.00
89-04-004	Carousel Reindeer	Unknown	Open	136.00	152.00
90-04-005	Carousel Elephant	Unknown	Open	136.00	152.00
90-04-006	Carousel Lion	Unknown	Open	136.00	152.00
90-04-007	Carousel Charger	Unknown	Open	136.00	152.00
91-04-008	Carousel Polar Bear	Unknown	Open	152.00	152.00
91-04-009	Pride of America	Unknown	12/92	152.00	152.00
91-04-010	Western Horse	Unknown	Open	152.00	152.00
92-04-011	Camelot Horse	Unknown	Open	152.00	152.00
92-04-012	Statement Piece	Unknown	Open	395.00	395.00
92-04-013	Victorian Romance Horse	Unknown	Open	156.00	156.00
92-04-014	Tropical Horse	Unknown	Open	156.00	156.00
92-04-015	Christmas Horse	Unknown	Open	156.00	156.00
93-04-016	Nautical Horse	Unknown	Open	156.00	156.00
Lenox Collections		**Nativity**			
86-05-001	Holy Family	Unknown	Open	119.00	136.00
87-05-002	Three Kings	Unknown	Open	119.00	152.00
88-05-003	Shepherds	Unknown	Open	119.00	152.00
88-05-004	Animals of the Nativity	Unknown	Open	119.00	152.00
89-05-005	Angels of Adoration	Unknown	Open	136.00	152.00
90-05-006	Children of Bethlehem	Unknown	Open	136.00	152.00
91-05-007	Townspeople of Bethlehem	Unknown	Open	136.00	152.00
91-05-008	Standing Camel & Driver	Unknown	9,500	152.00	152.00
Lenox Collections		**Garden Birds**			
85-06-001	Chickadee	Unknown	Open	39.00	45.00
86-06-002	Blue Jay	Unknown	Open	39.00	45.00
86-06-003	Eastern Bluebird	Unknown	Open	39.00	45.00
86-06-004	Tufted Titmouse	Unknown	Open	39.00	45.00
87-06-005	Red-Breasted Nuthatch	Unknown	Open	39.00	45.00
87-06-006	Cardinal	Unknown	Open	39.00	45.00
87-06-007	Turtle Dove	Unknown	Open	39.00	45.00
87-06-008	American Goldfinch	Unknown	Open	39.00	45.00
88-06-009	Hummingbird	Unknown	Open	39.00	45.00
88-06-010	Cedar Waxwing	Unknown	Open	39.00	45.00
89-06-011	Robin	Unknown	Open	39.00	45.00
89-06-012	Downy Woodpecker	Unknown	Open	39.00	45.00
89-06-013	Saw Whet Owl	Unknown	Open	45.00	45.00
90-06-014	Baltimore Oriole	Unknown	Open	45.00	45.00
90-06-015	Wren	Unknown	Open	45.00	45.00
90-06-016	Chipping Sparrow	Unknown	Open	45.00	45.00
90-06-017	Wood Duck	Unknown	Open	45.00	45.00
91-06-018	Purple Finch	Unknown	Open	45.00	45.00
91-06-019	Golden Crowned Kinglet	Unknown	Open	45.00	45.00
91-06-020	Dark Eyed Junco	Unknown	Open	45.00	45.00
91-06-021	Broadbilled Hummingbird	Unknown	Open	45.00	45.00
91-06-022	Rose Grosbeak	Unknown	Open	45.00	45.00
92-06-023	Scarlet Tanger	Unknown	Open	45.00	45.00
92 06 024	Magnificent Hummingbird	Unknown	Open	45.00	45.00
92-06-025	Western Meadowlark	Unknown	Open	45.00	45.00
93-06-026	Statement Piece	Unknown	Open	345.00	345.00
93-06-027	Mockingbird	Unknown	Open	45.00	45.00
93-06-028	Barn Swallow	Unknown	Open	45.00	45.00
93-06-029	Indigo Bunting	Unknown	Open	45.00	45.00
93-06-030	Sparrow	Unknown	Open	45.00	45.00
Lenox Collections		**Floral Sculptures**			
86-07-001	Rubrum Lily	Unknown	Open	119.00	136.00
87-07-002	Iris	Unknown	Open	119.00	136.00
88-07-003	Magnolia	Unknown	Open	119.00	136.00
88-07-004	Peace Rose	Unknown	Open	119.00	136.00
Lenox Collections		**Garden Flowers**			
88-08-001	Tea Rose	Unknown	Open	39.00	45.00
88-08-002	Cattleya Orchid	Unknown	Open	39.00	45.00
88-08-003	Parrot Tulip	Unknown	Open	39.00	39.00
89-08-004	Iris	Unknown	Open	45.00	45.00
90-08-005	Day Lily	Unknown	Open	45.00	45.00
90-08-006	Carnation	Unknown	Open	45.00	45.00
90-08-007	Daffodil	Unknown	Open	45.00	45.00
91-08-008	Morning Glory	Unknown	Open	45.00	45.00
91-08-009	Magnolia	Unknown	Open	45.00	45.00
91-08-010	Calla Lily	Unknown	Open	45.00	45.00
91-08-011	Camelia	Unknown	Open	45.00	45.00
91-08-012	Poinsettia	Unknown	Open	39.00	39.00
Lenox Collections		**Mother & Child**			
86-09-001	Cherished Moment	Unknown	Open	119.00	119.00
86-09-002	Sunday in the Park	Unknown	Open	119.00	119.00
87-09-003	Storytime	Unknown	Open	119.00	119.00
88-09-004	The Present	Unknown	Open	119.00	119.00
89-09-005	Christening	Unknown	Open	119.00	119.00
90-09-006	Bedtime Prayers	Unknown	Open	119.00	119.00
91-09-007	Afternoon Stroll	Unknown	7,500	136.00	136.00
91-09-008	Evening Lullaby	Unknown	7,500	136.00	136.00
92-09-009	Morning Playtime	Unknown	Open	136.00	136.00
Lenox Collections		**Owls of America**			
88-10-001	Snowy Owl	Unknown	Open	136.00	136.00
89-10-002	Barn Owl	Unknown	Open	136.00	136.00
90-10-003	Screech Owl	Unknown	Open	136.00	136.00
91-10-004	Great Horned Owl	Unknown	9,500	136.00	136.00
Lenox Collections		**International Horse Sculptures**			
88-11-001	Arabian Knight	Unknown	Open	136.00	136.00
89-11-002	Thoroughbred	Unknown	Open	136.00	136.00
90-11-003	Lippizan	Unknown	Open	136.00	136.00
90-11-004	Appaloosa	Unknown	Open	136.00	136.00
Lenox Collections		**Nature's Beautiful Butterflies**			
89-12-001	Blue Temora	Unknown	Open	39.00	45.00
90-12-002	Yellow Swallowtail	Unknown	Open	39.00	45.00
90-12-003	Monarch	Unknown	Open	39.00	45.00
90-12-004	Purple Emperor	Unknown	Open	45.00	45.00
91-12-005	Malachite	Unknown	Open	45.00	45.00
91-12-006	Adonis	Unknown	Open	45.00	45.00
93-12-007	Black Swallowtail	Unknown	Open	45.00	45.00
93-12-008	Great Orange Wingtip	Unknown	Open	45.00	45.00
Lenox Collections		**Kings of the Sky**			
89-13-001	American Bald Eagle	Unknown	Open	195.00	195.00
91-13-002	Golden Eagle	Unknown	Open	234.00	234.00
91-13-003	Defender of Freedom	Unknown	12/92	234.00	234.00
92-13-004	Take Off	Unknown	Open	234.00	234.00
Lenox Collections		**Endangered Baby Animals**			
90-14-001	Panda	Unknown	Open	39.00	39.00
91-14-002	Elephant	Unknown	Open	57.00	57.00
91-14-003	Baby Florida Panther	Unknown	Open	57.00	57.00
91-14-004	Baby Grey Wolf	Unknown	Open	57.00	57.00
92-14-005	Baby Rhinocerous	Unknown	Open	57.00	57.00
93-14-006	Indian Elephant Calf	Unknown	Open	57.00	57.00
Lenox Collections		**Lenox Baby Book**			
90-15-001	Baby's First Shoes	Unknown	Open	57.00	57.00
91-15-002	Baby's First Steps	Unknown	Open	57.00	57.00
91-15-003	Baby's First Christmas	Unknown	Open	57.00	57.00
92-15-004	Baby's First Portrait	Unknown	Open	57.00	57.00
Lenox Collections		**Lenox Puppy Collection**			
90-16-001	Beagle	Unknown	Open	76.00	76.00
91-16-002	Cocker Spaniel	Unknown	Open	76.00	76.00
92-16-003	Poodle	Unknown	Open	76.00	76.00
Lenox Collections		**International Brides**			
90-17-001	Russian Bride	Unknown	Open	136.00	136.00
92-17-002	Japanese Bride, Kiyoshi	Unknown	Open	136.00	136.00
Lenox Collections		**Life of Christ**			
90-18-001	The Children's Blessing	Unknown	Open	95.00	95.00
90-18-002	Madonna And Child	Unknown	Open	95.00	95.00
90-18-003	The Good Shepherd	Unknown	Open	95.00	95.00
91-18-004	The Savior	Unknown	Open	95.00	95.00
91-18-005	Jesus, The Teacher	Unknown	9,500	95.00	95.00
92-18-006	A Child's Prayer	Unknown	Open	95.00	95.00
92-18-007	Childrens's Devotion (Painted)	Unknown	Open	195.00	195.00
92-18-008	Mary & Christ Child (Painted)	Unknown	Open	195.00	195.00
92-18-009	A Child's Comfort	Unknown	Open	95.00	95.00
93-18-010	Jesus, The Carpenter	Unknown	Open	95.00	95.00
Lenox Collections		**North American Bird Pairs**			
90-19-001	Hummingbirds	Unknown	Open	119.00	119.00
91-19-002	Chickadees	Unknown	Open	119.00	119.00
91-19-003	Blue Jay Pairs	Unknown	Open	119.00	119.00
92-19-004	Cardinal	Unknown	Open	119.00	119.00
Lenox Collections		**Santa Claus Collections**			
90-20-001	Father Christmas	Unknown	Open	136.00	136.00
91-20-002	Americana Santa	Unknown	Open	136.00	136.00
91-20-003	Kris Kringle	Unknown	Open	136.00	136.00
92-20-004	Grandfather Frost	Unknown	Open	136.00	136.00
92-20-005	Pere Noel	Unknown	Open	136.00	136.00
93-20-006	St. Nick	Unknown	Open	136.00	136.00
Lenox Collections		**Woodland Animals**			
90-21-001	Red Squirrel	Unknown	Open	39.00	39.00
90-21-002	Raccoon	Unknown	Open	39.00	39.00
91-21-003	Chipmunk	Unknown	Open	39.00	39.00
92-21-004	Rabbit	Unknown	Open	39.00	39.00
93-21-005	Fawn	Unknown	Open	39.00	39.00

Company		Series			
Number	**Name**	**Artist**	**Edition Limit**	**Issue Price**	**Quote**
Lenox Collections		**Gentle Majesty**			
90-22-001	Bear Hug Polar Bear	Unknown	Open	76.00	76.00
90-22-002	Penguins	Unknown	Open	76.00	76.00
91-22-003	Keeping Warm (Foxes)	Unknown	Open	76.00	76.00
Lenox Collections		**Street Crier Collection**			
90-23-001	French Flower Maiden	Unknown	Open	136.00	136.00
91-23-002	Belgian Lace Maker	Unknown	Open	136.00	136.00
Lenox Collections		**Country Kids**			
91-24-001	Goose Girl	Unknown	Open	75.00	75.00
Lenox Collections		**Doves & Roses**			
91-25-001	Love's Promise	Unknown	Open	95.00	95.00
91-25-002	Dove's of Peace	Unknown	Open	95.00	95.00
92-25-003	Dove's of Honor	Unknown	Open	119.00	119.00
Lenox Collections		**Exotic Birds**			
91-26-001	Cockatoo	Unknown	Open	45.00	45.00
93-26-002	Parakeet	Unknown	Open	49.50	49.50
Lenox Collections		**Jessie Willcox Smith**			
91-27-001	Rosebuds	J.W.Smith	Open	60.00	60.00
91-27-002	Feeding Kitty	J.W.Smith	Open	60.00	60.00
Lenox Collections		**Baby Bears**			
91-28-001	Polar Bear	Unknown	Open	45.00	45.00
Lenox Collections		**Baby Bird Pairs**			
91-29-001	Robins	Unknown	Open	64.00	64.00
92-29-002	Orioles	Unknown	Open	64.00	64.00
92-29-003	Chickadee	Unknown	Open	64.00	64.00
Lenox Collections		**Lenox Sea Animals**			
91-30-001	Dance of the Dolphins	Unknown	Open	119.00	119.00
93-30-002	Flight of the Dolphins	Unknown	Open	119.00	119.00
Lenox Collections		**North American Wildlife**			
91-31-001	White Tailed Deer	Unknown	Open	195.00	195.00
Lenox Collections		**Porcelain Duck Collection**			
91-32-001	Wood Duck	Unknown	Open	45.00	45.00
91-32-002	Mallard Duck	Unknown	Open	45.00	45.00
92-32-003	Blue Winged Teal Duck	Unknown	Open	45.00	45.00
93-32-004	Pintail Duck	Unknown	Open	45.00	45.00
Lenox Collections		**Biblical Characters**			
92-33-001	Moses, The Lawgiver	Unknown	Open	95.00	95.00
Lenox Collections		**Parent & Child Bird Pairs**			
92-34-001	Blue Jay Pairs	Unknown	Open	119.00	119.00
Lenox Collections		**Renaissance Nativity**			
91-35-001	Holy Family	Unknown	Open	195.00	195.00
91-35-002	Shepherds of Bethlehem	Unknown	Open	195.00	195.00
91-35-003	Three Kings	Unknown	Open	195.00	195.00
91-35-004	Animals of the Nativity	Unknown	Open	195.00	195.00
91-35-005	Angels	Unknown	Open	195.00	195.00
Lenox Collections		**International Songbirds**			
92-36-001	European Goldfinch	Unknown	Open	152.00	152.00
92-36-002	American Goldfinch	Unknown	Open	152.00	152.00
Lenox Collections		**Challenge of the Eagles**			
93-37-001	Double Eagle	Unknown	Open	275.00	275.00
Lenox Collections		**Classical Goddesses**			
92-38-001	Aphrodite, Painted	Unknown	Open	136.00	136.00
92-38-002	Aphrodite	Unknown	Open	95.00	95.00
Lilliput Lane Ltd.		**Lilliput Lane Cottage Collection-English Cottages**			
82-01-001	Old Mine	D. Tate	Retrd.	15.95	3900-4800.
82-01-002	Drapers	D. Tate	Retrd.	15.95	3400-4000.
82-01-003	Dale House	D. Tate	Retrd.	25.00	1100.
82-01-004	Sussex Mill	D. Tate	Retrd.	25.00	325-500.
82-01-005	Lakeside House	D. Tate	Retrd.	40.00	995.00
82-01-006	Stone Cottage	D. Tate	Retrd.	40.00	350.00
82-01-007	Acorn Cottage-Mold 1	D. Tate	Retrd.	30.00	80-400.
83-01-008	Acorn Cottage-Mold 2	D. Tate	Retrd.	30.00	75-150.
82-01-009	Bridge House	D. Tate	Retrd.	15.95	50-200.00
82-01-010	April Cottage	D. Tate	Retrd.	Unkn.	50-75.00
82-01-011	Honeysuckle	D. Tate	Retrd.	45.00	120-150.
82-01-012	Oak Lodge	D. Tate	Retrd.	40.00	100-200.
82-01-013	Dale Farm	D. Tate	Retrd.	30.00	400-1100.
82-01-014	The Old Post Office	D. Tate	Retrd.	35.00	600-800.
82-01-015	Coach House	D. Tate	Retrd.	100.00	1000-1875.
82-01-016	Castle Street	D. Tate	Retrd.	130.00	460-910.
82-01-017	Holly Cottage	D. Tate	Retrd.	42.50	90-175.00
82-01-018	Burnside	D. Tate	Retrd.	30.00	400-600.
83-01-019	Coopers	D. Tate	Retrd.	15.00	300-500.
83-01-020	Millers	D. Tate	Retrd.	15.00	125-150.
83-01-021	Miners	D. Tate	Retrd.	15.00	350-750.
83-01-022	Toll House	D. Tate	Retrd.	15.00	115-200.
83-01-023	Woodcutters	D. Tate	Retrd.	15.00	125-250.
83-01-024	Tuck Shop	D. Tate	Retrd.	35.00	500-900.
83-01-025	Warwick Hall-Mold 1	D. Tate	Retrd.	185.00	3000-4000.
83-01-026	Warwick Hall-Mold 2	D. Tate	Retrd.	185.00	1200-1800.
82-01-027	Anne Hathaway's-Mold 1	D. Tate	Retrd.	40.00	1400.00
83-01-028	Anne Hathaway's-Mold 2	D. Tate	Retrd.	40.00	400-600.
84-01-029	Anne Hathaway's-Mold 3	D. Tate	Retrd.	40.00	400-600.
89-01-030	Anne Hathaway's-Mold 4	D. Tate	Open	130.00	150.00
82-01-031	William Shakespeare-Mold 1	D. Tate	Retrd.	55.00	3000.00
83-01-032	William Shakespeare-Mold 2	D. Tate	Retrd.	55.00	200-300.
86-01-033	William Shakespeare-Mold 3	D. Tate	Retrd.	55.00	200-300.
89-01-034	William Shakespeare-Mold 4	D. Tate	Retrd.	130.00	150.00
83-01-035	Red Lion	D. Tate	Retrd.	125.00	350-400.
83-01-036	Thatcher's Rest	D. Tate	Retrd.	185.00	225-375.
83-01-037	Troutbeck Farm	D. Tate	Retrd.	125.00	250-400.
83-01-038	Dove Cottage-Mold 1	D. Tate	Retrd.	35.00	1800.00
84-01-039	Dove Cottage-Mold 2	D. Tate	Retrd.	35.00	100-275.
84-01-040	Old School House	D. Tate	Retrd.	Unkn.	1000-1440.
84-01-041	Tintagel	D. Tate	Retrd.	39.50	150-250.
85-01-042	Old Curiosity Shop	D. Tate	Retrd.	62.50	250.00
85-01-043	St. Mary's Church	D. Tate	Retrd.	40.00	100-300.
85-01-044	Clare Cottage	D. Tate	Open	30.00	45.00
85-01-045	Fisherman's Cottage	D. Tate	Retrd.	30.00	45-100.00
85-01-046	Sawrey Gill	D. Tate	Retrd.	30.00	50.00
85-01-047	Ostlers Keep	D. Tate	Retrd.	55.00	100-200.
85-01-048	Moreton Manor	D. Tate	Retrd.	55.00	100-175.
85-01-049	Kentish Oast	D. Tate	Retrd.	55.00	75-175.
85-01-050	Watermill	D. Tate	Open	40.00	60.00
85-01-051	Bronte Parsonage	D. Tate	Retrd.	72.00	150-200.
85-01-052	Farriers	D. Tate	Retrd.	40.00	85-125.00
86-01-053	Dale Head	D. Tate	Retrd.	75.00	125-300.
86-01-054	Bay View	D. Tate	Retrd.	39.50	60-125.
86-01-055	Cobblers Cottage	D. Hall	Open	42.00	65.00
86-01-056	Gulliver	Unknown	Retrd.	65.00	200-275.
86-01-057	Three Feathers	D. Tate	Retrd.	115.00	175-275.
86-01-058	Spring Bank	D. Tate	Retrd.	42.00	50-95.00
86-01-059	Scroll on the Wall	D. Tate	Retrd.	55.00	175-275.
86-01-060	Tudor Court	Lilliput Lane	Retrd.	260.00	250-350.
87-01-061	Beacon Heights	Lilliput Lane	Retrd.	125.00	175-210.
87-01-062	Wealden House	D. Tate	Retrd.	125.00	200-500.
87-01-063	The Gables	Lilliput Lane	Retrd.	145.00	200-210.
87-01-064	Secret Garden	M. Adkinson	Open	145.00	220.00
87-01-065	Rydal View	D. Tate	Retrd.	220.00	275-400.
87-01-066	Stoneybeck	D. Tate	Retrd.	45.00	50-60.00
87-01-067	Riverview	D. Tate	Open	27.50	40.00
87-01-068	Clover Cottage	D. Tate	Open	27.50	40.00
87-01-069	Inglewood	D. Tate	Open	27.50	40.00
87-01-070	Tanners Cottage	D. Tate	Retrd.	27.50	34.00
87-01-071	Holme Dyke	D. Tate	Retrd.	50.00	150-250.
87-01-072	Saddlers Inn	M. Adkinson	Retrd.	50.00	95-125.00
87-01-073	Four Seasons	M. Adkinson	Retrd.	70.00	100-200.
87-01-074	Magpie Cottage	D. Tate	Retrd.	70.00	150-300.
87-01-074	Izaak Waltons Cottage	D. Tate	Retrd.	75.00	100-200.
87-01-076	Keepers Lodge	D. Tate	Retrd.	75.00	120-175.
87-01-077	Summer Haze	D. Tate	Open	90.00	130.00
87-01-078	Street Scene No. 1	Unknown	Retrd.	40.00	125-200.
87-01-079	Street Scene No. 2	Unknown	Retrd.	45.00	125-200.
87-01-080	Street Scene No. 3	Unknown	Retrd.	45.00	125-200.
87-01-081	Street Scene No. 4	Unknown	Retrd.	45.00	125-200.
87-01-082	Street Scene No. 5	Unknown	Retrd.	40.00	125-200.
87-01-083	Street Scene No. 6	Unknown	Retrd.	40.00	125-200.
87-01-084	Street Scene No. 7	Unknown	Retrd.	40.00	125-200.
87-01-085	Street Scene No. 8	Unknown	Retrd.	40.00	125-200.
87-01-086	Street Scene No. 9	Unknown	Retrd.	45.00	125-200.
87-01-087	Street Scene No. 10	Unknown	Retrd.	45.00	125-200.
88-01-088	Brockbank	D. Tate	Open	58.00	80.00
88-01-089	St. Marks	D. Tate	Retrd.	75.00	150.00
88-01-090	Swift Hollow	D. Tate	Retrd.	75.00	160-250.
88-01-091	Pargetters Retreat	D. Tate	Retrd.	75.00	165-250.
88-01-092	Swan Inn	D. Tate	Retrd.	120.00	150.00
88-01-093	Ship Inn	Lilliput Lane	Retrd.	210.00	250.00
88-01-094	Saxon Cottage	D. Tate	Retrd.	245.00	350-500.
88-01-095	Smallest Inn	D. Tate	Retrd.	42.50	95-150.00
88-01-096	Rising Sun	D. Tate	Retrd.	58.00	72.50
88-01-097	Crown Inn	D. Tate	Retrd.	120.00	140-225.
88-01-098	Royal Oak	D. Tate	Retrd.	145.00	175-250.
88-01-099	Bredon House	D. Tate	Retrd.	145.00	175-450.
89-01-100	Chine Cot	D. Tate	Open	36.00	50.00
89-01-101	Fiveways	D. Tate	Open	42.50	55.00
89-01-102	Ash Nook	D. Tate	Open	47.50	60.00
89-01-103	The Briary	D. Tate	Open	47.50	60.00
89-01-104	Victoria Cottage	D. Tate	Open	52.50	65.00
89-01-105	Butterwick	D. Tate	Open	52.50	70.00
89-01-106	Greensted Church	D. Tate	Open	72.50	95.00
89-01-107	Beehive Cottage	D. Tate	Open	72.50	95.00
89-01-108	Tanglewood Lodge	D. Tate	Retrd.	97.00	120-200.
89-01-109	St. Peter's Cove	D. Tate	Retrd.	1375.00	2000-3600.
89-01-110	Wight Cottage	D. Tate	Open	52.50	65.00
89-01-111	Helmere	D. Tate	Open	65.00	80.00
89-01-112	Titmouse Cottage	D. Tate	Open	92.50	120.00
89-01-113	St. Lawrence Church	D. Tate	Open	110.00	140.00
89-01-114	Olde York Toll	D. Tate	Retrd.	95.00	95.00
89-01-115	Mayflower House	D. Tate	Retrd.	79.50	79.50
90-01-116	Strawberry Cottage	D. Tate	Open	36.00	45.00
90-01-117	Buttercup Cottage	D. Tate	Retrd.	40.00	46.50
90-01-118	Bramble Cottage	D. Tate	Open	55.00	70.00
90-01-119	Mrs. Pinkerton's Post Office	D. Tate	Open	72.50	85.00
90-01-120	Sulgrave Manor	D. Tate	Retrd.	120.00	140.00
90-01-121	Periwinkle Cottage	D. Tate	Open	165.00	220.00
90-01-122	Robin's Gate	D. Tate	Open	33.50	45.00
90-01-123	Cherry Cottage	D. Tate	Open	33.50	45.00
90-01-124	Otter Reach	D. Tate	Open	33.50	45.00
90-01-125	Runswick House	D. Tate	Open	62.50	80.00
90-01-126	The King's Arms	D. Tate	Open	450.00	550.00
90-01-127	Convent in The Woods	D. Tate	Open	175.00	220.00
91-01-128	Armada House	D. Tate	Open	175.00	185.00
91-01-129	Moonlight Cove	D. Tate	Open	82.50	85.00
91-01-130	Pear Tree House	D. Tate	Open	82.50	85.00
91-01-131	Lapworth Lock	D. Tate	Open	82.50	85.00
91-01-132	Micklegate Antiques	D. Tate	Open	90.00	95.00
91-01-133	Bridge House 1991	D. Tate	Open	25.00	30.00
91-01-134	Tillers Green	D. Tate	Open	60.00	65.00
91-01-135	Wellington Lodge	D. Tate	Open	55.00	60.00
91-01-136	Primrose Hill	D. Tate	Open	46.50	50.00
91-01-137	Daisy Cottage	D. Tate	Open	37.50	40.00
91-01-138	Farthing Lodge	D. Tate	Open	37.50	40.00
91-01-139	Dovetails	D. Tate	Open	90.00	95.00
91-01-140	Lace Lane	D. Tate	Open	90.00	95.00
91-01-141	The Flower Sellers	D. Tate	Open	110.00	120.00
91-01-142	Witham Delph	D. Tate	Open	110.00	120.00
91-01-143	Village School	D. Tate	Open	120.00	130.00
91-01-144	Hopcroft Cottage	D. Tate	Open	120.00	130.00
91-01-145	John Barleycorn Cottage	D. Tate	Open	130.00	140.00
91-01-146	Paradise Lodge	D. Tate	Open	130.00	140.00
91-01-147	The Priest's House	D. Tate	Open	180.00	195.00
91-01-148	Old Shop at Bignor	D. Tate	Open	215.00	220.00
91-01-149	Chatsworth View	D. Tate	Open	250.00	275.00
91-01-150	Anne of Cleves	D. Tate	Open	360.00	395.00
91-01-151	Saxham St. Edmunds	D. Tate	4,500	1550.00	1650.00
92-01-152	Bow Cottage	D. Tate	Open	127.50	135.50
92-01-153	Granny Smiths	D. Tate	Open	60.00	65.00
92-01-154	Oakwood Smithy	D. Tate	Open	450.00	475.00
92-01-155	Pixie House	D. Tate	Open	55.00	60.00

Number	Name	Artist	Edition Limit	Issue Price	Quote
92-01-156	Puffin Row	D. Tate	Open	127.50	135.00
92-01-157	Rustic Root House	D. Tate	Open	110.00	120.00
92-01-158	Wheyside Cottage	Lilliput Lane	Open	46.50	50.00
92-01-159	Wedding Bells	Lilliput Lane	Open	75.00	80.00
92-01-160	Derwent-le-Dale	Lilliput Lane	Open	75.00	80.00
92-01-161	The Nutshell	Lilliput Lane	Open	75.00	80.00
92-01-162	Finchingfields	Lilliput Lane	Open	82.50	95.00
92-01-163	The Chocolate House	Lilliput Lane	Open	130.00	140.00
92-01-164	Grantchester Meadows	Lilliput Lane	Open	275.00	275.00
92-01-165	High Ghyll Farm	Lilliput Lane	Open	360.00	395.00
93-01-166	Cat's Coombe Cottage	Lilliput Lane	Open	95.00	95.00
93-01-167	Cley-next-the-sea	Lilliput Lane	2,500	725.00	725.00
93-01-168	Foxglove Fields	Lilliput Lane	Open	130.00	130.00
93-01-169	Junk and Disorderly	Lilliput Lane	Open	150.00	150.00
93-01-170	Purbeck Stores	Lilliput Lane	Open	55.00	55.00
93-01-171	Stocklebeck Mill	Lilliput Lane	Open	325.00	325.00
93-01-172	Stradling Priory	Lilliput Lane	Open	130.00	130.00
Lilliput Lane Ltd.		**Collectors Club Specials**			
86-02-001	Packhorse Bridge	D. Tate	Retrd.	Unkn.	600-950.
86-02-002	Crendon Manor	D. Tate	Retrd.	285.00	600-1000.
87-02-003	Little Lost Dog	D. Tate	Retrd.	Unkn.	200-300.
87-02-004	Yew Tree Farm	D. Tate	Retrd.	160.00	225-350.
88-02-005	Wishing Well	D. Tate	Retrd.	Unkn.	100-175.
89-02-006	Wenlock Rise	D. Tate	Retrd.	175.00	225-300.
89-02-007	Dovecot	D. Tate	Retrd.	Unkn.	100-175.
90-02-008	Lavender Cottage	D. Tate	Retrd.	50.00	100-175.
90-02-009	Bridle Way	D. Tate	Retrd.	100.00	175-300.
90-02-010	Cosy Corner	D. Tate	Retrd.	Unkn.	75-150.00
91-02-011	Puddlebronk	D. Tate	Retrd.	Unkn.	85-125.00
91-02-012	Gardeners Cottage	D. Tate	Retrd.	120.00	150-200.
91-02-013	Wren Cottage	D. Tate	Retrd.	13.95	150-200.
92-02-014	Pussy Willow	D. Tate	Retrd.	Unkn.	60.00
92-02-015	Forget-Me-Not	D. Tate	4/93	130.00	130.00
Lilliput Lane Ltd.		**German Collection**			
87-03-001	Meersburger Weinstube	D. Tate	Open	82.50	95.00
87-03-002	Jaghutte	D. Tate	Open	82.50	95.00
87-03-003	Das Gebirgskirchlein	D. Tate	Open	120.00	140.00
87-03-004	Nurnberger Burgerhaus	D. Tate	Open	140.00	160.00
87-03-005	Schwarzwaldhaus	D. Tate	Open	140.00	160.00
87-03-006	Moselhaus	D. Tate	Open	140.00	160.00
87-03-007	Haus Im Rheinland	D. Tate	Open	220.00	250.00
88-03-008	Der Familienschrein	D. Tate	Retrd.	52.50	78.00
88-03-009	Das Rathaus	D. Tate	Open	140.00	160.00
88-03-010	Die Kleine Backerei	D. Tate	Open	68.00	80.00
92-03-011	Alte Schmiede	D. Tate	Open	175.00	185.00
92-03-012	Der Bücherwurm	D. Tate	Open	140.00	160.00
92-03-013	Rosengartenhaus	D. Tate	Open	120.00	130.00
92-03-014	Strandvogthaus	D. Tate	Open	120.00	130.00
Lilliput Lane Ltd.		**Christmas Collection**			
88-04-001	Deer Park Hall	D. Tate	Retrd.	120.00	175-350.
89-04-002	St. Nicholas Church	D. Tate	Retrd.	130.00	175-250.
90-04-003	Yuletide Inn	D. Tate	Retrd.	145.00	175-300.
91-04-004	The Old Vicarage at Christmas	D. Tate	Retrd.	180.00	200-300.
92-04-005	Chestnut Cottage	Lilliput Lane	Open	46.50	50.00
92-04-006	Cranberry Cottage	Lilliput Lane	Open	46.50	50.00
92-04-007	Hollytree House	Lilliput Lane	Open	46.50	50.00
93-04-008	The Gingerbread Shop	Lilliput Lane	Yr.Iss.	50.00	50.00
93-04-009	Partridge Cottage	Lilliput Lane	Yr.Iss.	50.00	50.00
93-04-010	St. Joseph's Church	Lilliput Lane	Yr.Iss.	70.00	70.00
Lilliput Lane Ltd.		**Christmas Lodge Collection**			
92-05-001	Highland Lodge	Lilliput Lane	Retrd.	180.00	250.00
93-05-002	Eamont Lodge	Lilliput Lane	Yr.Iss.	185.00	185.00
Lilliput Lane Ltd.		**Blaise Hamlet Collection**			
89-06-001	Diamond Cottage	D. Tate	Open	110.00	135.00
89-06-002	Oak Cottage	D. Tate	Open	110.00	135.00
89-06-003	Circular Cottage	D. Tate	Open	110.00	135.00
90-06-004	Dial Cottage	D. Tate	Open	110.00	135.00
90-06-005	Vine Cottage	D. Tate	Open	110.00	135.00
90-06-006	Sweetbriar Cottage	D. Tate	Open	110.00	135.00
91-06-007	Double Cottage	D. Tate	Open	200.00	220.00
91-06-008	Jasmine Cottage	D. Tate	Open	140.00	150.00
91-06-009	Rose Cottage	D. Tate	Open	140.00	150.00
Lilliput Lane Ltd.		**Irish Cottages**			
87-07-001	Donegal Cottage	D. Tate	Retrd.	29.00	34.00
89-07-002	Kennedy Homestead	D. Tate	Open	33.50	45.00
89-07-003	Magilligans	D. Tate	Open	33.50	45.00
89-07-004	St. Columba's School	D. Tate	Open	47.50	60.00
89-07-005	St. Kevin's Church	D. Tate	Open	55.00	70.00
89-07-006	O'Lacey's Store	D. Tate	Open	68.00	85.00
89-07-007	Hegarty's Home	D. Tate	Retrd.	68.00	79.00
89-07-008	Kilmore Quay	D. Tate	Retrd.	68.00	85.00
89-07-009	Quiet Cottage	D. Tate	Retrd.	72.50	85.00
89-07-010	Thoor Ballylee	D. Tate	Retrd.	105.00	135.00
89-07-011	Pat Cohan's Bar	D. Tate	Open	110.00	140.00
89-07-012	Limerick House	D. Tate	Retrd.	110.00	130.00
89-07-013	St. Patrick's Church	D. Tate	Open	185.00	220.00
89-07-014	Ballykerne Croft	D. Tate	Open	75.00	95.00
Lilliput Lane Ltd.		**Scottish Collection**			
82-08-001	The Croft (without sheep)	D. Tate	Retrd.	29.00	800-1250.
84-08-002	The Croft (renovated)	D. Tate	Retrd.	36.00	50-100.00
85-08-003	Preston Mill	D. Tate	Retrd.	45.00	150.00
85-08-004	Burns Cottage	D. Tate	Retrd.	35.00	100-150.
85-08-005	7 St. Andrews Square	A. Yarrington	Retrd.	15.95	100-150.
87-08-006	East Neuk	D. Tate	Retrd.	29.00	60.00
87-08-007	Preston Mill (renovated)	D. Tate	Retrd.	62.50	72.50
89-08-008	Culloden Cottage	D. Tate	Open	36.00	45.00
89-08-009	Inverlochie Hame	D. Tate	Open	47.50	60.00
89-08-010	Carrick House	D. Tate	Open	47.50	60.00
89-08-011	Stockwell Tenement	D. Tate	Open	62.50	80.00
89-08-012	John Knox House	D. Tate	Retrd.	68.00	79.00
89-08-013	Claypotts Castle	D. Tate	Open	72.50	95.00
89-08-014	Kenmore Cottage	D. Tate	Open	87.00	110.00
89-08-015	Craigievar Castle	D. Tate	Retrd.	185.00	225-300.
89-08-016	Blair Atholl	D. Tate	Retrd.	275.00	400-500.
90-08-017	Fishermans Bothy	D. Tate	Open	36.00	45.00
90-08-018	Hebridean Hame	D. Tate	Retrd.	55.00	65.00
90-08-019	Kirkbrae Cottage	D. Tate	Open	55.00	70.00
90-08-020	Kinlochness	D. Tate	Open	79.00	85.00
90-08-021	Glenlochie Lodge	D. Tate	Open	110.00	120.00
90-08-022	Eilean Donan	D. Tate	Open	145.00	185.00
90-08-023	Cawdor Castle	D. Tate	Retrd.	295.00	550-800.
92-08-024	Culross House	D. Tate	Open	90.00	95.00
92-08-025	Duart Castle	D. Tate	3,000	450.00	475.00
92-08-026	Eriskay Croft	D. Tate	Open	50.00	55.00
92-08-027	Mair Haven	D. Tate	Open	46.50	50.00
Lilliput Lane Ltd.		**Lakeland Bridge Plaques**			
89-09-001	Aira Force	D. Simpson	Retrd.	35.00	35.00
89-09-002	Birks Bridge	D. Simpson	Retrd.	35.00	35.00
89-09-003	Stockley Bridge	D. Simpson	Retrd.	35.00	35.00
89-09-004	Hartsop Packhorse	D. Simpson	Retrd.	35.00	35.00
89-09-005	Bridge House	D. Simpson	Retrd.	35.00	35.00
89-09-006	Ashness Bridge	D. Simpson	Retrd.	35.00	35.00
Lilliput Lane Ltd.		**Countryside Scene Plaques**			
89-10-001	Country Inn	D. Simpson	Retrd.	49.50	49.50
89-10-002	Norfolk Windmill	D. Simpson	Retrd.	49.50	49.50
89-10-003	Watermill	D. Simpson	Retrd.	49.50	49.50
89-10-004	Parish Church	D. Simpson	Retrd.	49.50	49.50
89-10-005	Bottle Kiln	D. Simpson	Retrd.	49.50	49.50
89-10-006	Cornish Tin Mine	D. Simpson	Retrd.	49.50	49.50
89-10-007	Lighthouse	D. Simpson	Retrd.	49.50	49.50
89-10-008	Cumbrian Farmhouse	D. Simpson	Retrd.	49.50	49.50
89-10-009	Post Office	D. Simpson	Retrd.	49.50	49.50
89-10-010	Village School	D. Simpson	Retrd.	49.50	49.50
89-10-011	Old Smithy	D. Simpson	Retrd.	49.50	49.50
89-10-012	Oasthouse	D. Simpson	Retrd.	49.50	49.50
Lilliput Lane Ltd.		**Framed Scottish Plaques**			
90-11-001	Preston Oat Mill	D. Tate	Retrd.	59.50	59.50
90-11-002	Barra Black House	D. Tate	Retrd.	59.50	59.50
90-11-003	Kyle Point	D. Tate	Retrd.	59.50	59.50
90-11-004	Fife Ness	D. Tate	Retrd.	59.50	59.50
Lilliput Lane Ltd.		**Unframed Plaques**			
89-12-001	Small Stoney Wall Lea	D. Tate	Retrd.	47.50	47.50
89-12-002	Small Woodside Farm	D. Tate	Retrd.	47.50	47.50
89-12-003	Medium Cobble Combe Cottage	D. Tate	Retrd.	68.00	68.00
89-12-004	Medium Wishing Well	D. Tate	Retrd.	75.00	75.00
89-12-005	Large Lower Brockhampton	D. Tate	Retrd.	120.00	120.00
89-12-006	Large Somerset Springtime	D. Tate	Retrd.	130.00	130.00
Lilliput Lane Ltd.		**London Plaques**			
89-13-001	Buckingham Palace	D. Simpson	Retrd.	39.50	39.50
89-13-002	Trafalgar Square	D. Simpson	Retrd.	39.50	39.50
89-13-003	Tower Bridge	D. Simpson	Retrd.	39.50	39.50
89-13-004	Tower of London	D. Simpson	Retrd.	39.50	39.50
89-13-005	Big Ben	D. Simpson	Retrd.	39.50	39.50
89-13-006	Piccadilly Circus	D. Simpson	Retrd.	39.50	39.50
Lilliput Lane Ltd.		**Framed Irish Plaques**			
90-14-001	Ballyteag House	D. Tate	Retrd.	59.50	59.50
90-14-002	Shannons Bank	D. Tate	Retrd.	59.50	59.50
90-14-003	Pearses Cottages	D. Tate	Retrd.	59.50	59.50
90-14-004	Crockuna Croft	D. Tate	Retrd.	59.50	59.50
Lilliput Lane Ltd.		**Framed English Plaques**			
90-15-001	Huntingdon House	D. Tate	Retrd.	59.50	59.50
90-15-002	Coombe Cot	D. Tate	Retrd.	59.50	59.50
90-15-003	Ashdown Hall	D. Tate	Retrd.	59.50	59.50
90-15-004	Flint Fields	D. Tate	Retrd.	59.50	59.50
90-15-005	Fell View	D. Tate	Retrd.	59.50	59.50
90-15-006	Cat Slide Cottage	D. Tate	Retrd.	59.50	59.50
90-15-007	Battleview	D. Tate	Retrd.	59.50	59.50
90-15-008	Stowside	D. Tate	Retrd.	59.50	59.50
90-15-009	Jubilee Lodge	D. Tate	Retrd.	59.50	59.50
90-15-010	Trevan Cove	D. Tate	Retrd.	59.50	59.50
Lilliput Lane Ltd.		**Special Event Collection**			
89-16-001	Commemorative Medallion-1989 South Bend	D. Tate	Closed	Unkn.	95-220.00
90-16-002	Rowan Lodge-1990 South Bend	D. Tate	Closed	Unkn.	200-450.
91-16-003	Gamekeepers Cottage-1991 South Bend	D. Tate	Closed	Unkn.	200-425.
92-16-004	Ashberry Cottage-1992 South Bend	D. Tate	Closed	Unkn.	110.00
Lilliput Lane Ltd.		**Specials**			
83-17-001	Cliburn School	D. Tate	Retrd.	22.50	6000-7200.
83-17-002	Bridge House Dealer Sign	D. Tate	Retrd.	Unkn.	900.00
85-17-003	Bermuda Cottage (3 Colors)	D. Tate	Open	29.00	29-49.00
86-17-004	Seven Dwarf's Cottage	D. Tate	Retrd.	Unkn.	275-450.
87-17-005	Clockmaker's Cottage	D. Tate	Retrd.	40.00	200-250.
87-17-006	Guildhall	D. Tate	Retrd.	Unkn.	175-275.
88-17-007	Chantry Chapel	D. Tate	Retrd.	Unkn.	200-325.
89-17-008	Chiltern Mill	D. Tate	Open	87.50	110.00
89-17-009	Mayflower House	D. Tate	Retdr.	87.50	125-300.
89-17-010	Olde York Toll	D. Tate	Retrd.	82.50	95.00
90-17-011	Rowan Lodge	D. Tate	Retrd.	50.00	150-200.
91-17-012	Gamekeeper's Cottage	Lilliput Lane	Retrd.	75.00	120-140.
Lilliput Lane Ltd.		**American Landmark Series**			
89-18-001	Countryside Barn	R. Day	Retrd.	75.00	115-150.
89-18-002	Mail Pouch Barn	R. Day	Open	75.00	110.00
89-18-003	Falls Mill	R. Day	Retrd.	130.00	150-200.
90-18-004	Sign Of The Times	R. Day	Open	27.50	35.00
90-18-005	Pioneer Barn	R. Day	Retrd.	30.00	75-100.00
90-18-006	Great Point Light	R. Day	Open	39.50	55.00
90-18-007	Hometown Depot	R. Day	Open	68.00	95.00
90-18-008	Country Church	R. Day	Retrd.	82.50	120-150.
90-18-009	Riverside Chapel	R. Day	Open	82.50	130.00
90-18-010	Pepsi Cola Barn	R. Day	Retrd.	87.00	150-200.
90-18-011	Roadside Coolers	R. Day	Open	75.00	110.00
90-18-012	Covered Memories	R. Day	Open	110.00	160.00
91-18-013	Rambling Rose	R. Day	Open	60.00	65.00
91-18-014	School Days	R. Day	Open	60.00	80.00
91-18-015	Fire House 1	R. Day	Open	87.50	110.00
91-18-016	Victoriana	R. Day	Retrd.	295.00	300-500.
92-18-017	Home Seet Home	R. Day	Open	120.00	130.00
92-18-018	Small Town Library	R. Day	Open	130.00	140.00
92-18-019	16.9 Cents Per Gallon	R. Day	Open	150.00	160.00
92-18-020	Gold Miners' Claim	R. Day	Open	110.00	120.00

FIGURINES

Company		Series			
Number	**Name**	**Artist**	**Edition Limit**	**Issue Price**	**Quote**
92-18-021	Winnie's Place	R. Day	2,000	395.00	435.00
93-18-022	Simply Amish	R. Day	Open	160.00	160.00
Lilliput Lane Ltd.		**American Collection**			
84-19-001	Adobe Church	D. Tate	Retrd.	22.50	450-650.
84-19-002	Adobe Village	D. Tate	Retrd.	60.00	700-1000.
84-19-003	Cape Cod	D. Tate	Retrd.	22.50	400-600.
84-19-004	Covered Bridge	D. Tate	Retrd.	22.50	500-1000.
84-19-005	Country Church	D. Tate	Retrd.	22.50	500-800.
84-19-006	Forge Barn	D. Tate	Retrd.	22.50	550-660.
84-19-007	Grist Mill	D. Tate	Retrd.	22.50	500-785.
84-19-008	Log Cabin	D. Tate	Retrd.	22.50	500-650.
84-19-009	General Store	D. Tate	Retrd.	22.50	650-750.
84-19-010	Light House	D. Tate	Retrd.	22.50	700-1000.
84-19-011	Midwest Barn	D. Tate	Retrd.	22.50	250-450.
84-19-012	Wallace Station	D. Tate	Retrd.	22.50	350-1000.
84-19-013	San Francisco House	D. Tate	Retrd.	22.50	500-1000.
Lilliput Lane Ltd.		**Welsh Collection**			
85-20-001	Hermitage	D. Tate	Retrd.	30.00	150-200.
87-20-002	Hermitage Renovated	D. Tate	Retrd.	42.50	65-85.00
86-20-003	Brecon Bach	D. Tate	Open	42.00	65.00
91-20-004	Tudor Merchant	D. Tate	Open	90.00	95.00
91-20-005	Ugly House	D. Tate	Open	55.00	60.00
91-20-006	Bro Dawel	D. Tate	Open	37.50	40.00
92-20-007	St. Govan's Chapel	Lilliput Lane	Open	75.00	80.00
Lilliput Lane Ltd.		**Dutch Collection**			
91-21-001	Aan de Amstel	D. Tate	Open	79.00	85.00
91-21-002	Begijnhof	D. Tate	Open	55.00	60.00
91-21-003	Bloemenmarkt	D. Tate	Open	79.00	85.00
91-21-004	De Branderij	D. Tate	Open	72.50	80.00
91-21-005	De Diamantair	D. Tate	Open	79.00	85.00
91-21-006	De Pepermolen	D. Tate	Open	55.00	60.00
91-21-007	De Wolhandelaar	D. Tate	Open	72.50	80.00
91-21-008	De Zijdewever	D. Tate	Open	79.00	85.00
91-21-009	Rembrant van Rijn	D. Tate	Open	120.00	130.00
91-21-010	Rozengracht	D. Tate	Open	72.50	80.00
Lilliput Lane Ltd.		**French Collection**			
91-22-001	L' Auberge d'Armorique	D. Tate	Open	220.00	250.00
91-22-002	La Bergerie du Perigord	D. Tate	Open	230.00	250.00
91-22-003	La Cabane du Gardian	D. Tate	Open	55.00	60.00
91-22-004	La Chaumiere du Verger	D. Tate	Open	120.00	130.00
91-22-005	La Maselle de Nadaillac	D. Tate	Open	130.00	140.00
91-22-006	La Porte Schoenenberg	D. Tate	Open	75.00	85.00
91-22-007	Le Manoir de Champfleuri	D. Tate	Open	265.00	295.00
91-22-008	Le Mas du Vigneron	D. Tate	Open	120.00	130.00
91-22-009	Le Petite Montmartre	D. Tate	Open	130.00	140.00
91-22-010	Locmaria	D. Tate	Open	65.00	80.00
Lilliput Lane Ltd.		**Village Shop Collection**			
92-23-001	The Greengrocers	D. Tate	Open	120.00	130.00
92-23-002	Penny Sweets	Lilliput Lane	Open	N/A	130.00
Lilliput Lane Ltd.		**Blaise Hamlet Classics**			
93-24-001	Jasmine Cottage	Lilliput Lane	Open	95.00	95.00
93-24-002	Double Cottage	Lilliput Lane	Open	95.00	95.00
93-24-003	Vine Cottage	Lilliput Lane	Open	95.00	95.00
93-24-004	Circular Cottage	Lilliput Lane	Open	95.00	95.00
93-24-005	Diamond Cottage	Lilliput Lane	Open	95.00	95.00
93-24-006	Dial Cottage	Lilliput Lane	Open	95.00	95.00
93-24-007	Rose Cottage	Lilliput Lane	Open	95.00	95.00
93-24-008	Sweet Briar Cottage	Lilliput Lane	Open	95.00	95.00
93-24-009	Oak Cottage	Lilliput Lane	Open	95.00	95.00
Lladro		**Capricho**			
87-01-001	Orchid Arrangement C1541	Lladro	Closed	500.00	1700-1925.
87-01-002	Iris Basket C1542	Lladro	Closed	800.00	1250.00
87-01-003	Fan C1546	Lladro	Closed	650.00	900-1600.
87-01-004	Fan C1546.3	Lladro	Closed	650.00	900-1600.
87-01-005	Iris with Vase C1551	Lladro	Closed	110.00	375.00
Lladro		**Lladro**			
69-02-001	Shepherdess with Goats L1001	Lladro	Closed	80.00	460.00
69-02-002	Girl With Lamb L1010G	Lladro	Open	26.00	180.00
69-02-003	Girl With Pig L1011G	Lladro	Open	13.00	85.00
69-02-004	Centaur Girl L1012	Lladro	Closed	45.00	250.00
69-02-005	Centaur Boy L1013	Lladro	Closed	45.00	375.00
69-02-006	Dove L1015 G	Lladro	Open	21.00	105.00
69-02-007	Dove L1016 G	Lladro	Open	36.00	180.00
69-02-008	Idyl L1017G/M	Lladro	Closed	115.00	615.00
69-02-009	King Gaspar L1018 M	Lladro	Open	345.00	1895.00
69-02-010	King Melchior L1019 M	Lladro	Open	345.00	1850.00
69-02-011	King Balthasar L1020 M	Lladro	Open	345.00	1850.00
69-02-012	King Gaspar L1018	Lladro	Open	345.00	1895.00
69-02-013	King Melchior L1019	Lladro	Open	345.00	1850.00
69-02-014	King Baltasar L1020	Lladro	Open	345.00	1850.00
69-02-015	Horse Group L1021	Lladro	Closed	950.00	1950.00
69-02-016	Horse Group/All White L1022M	Lladro	Open	465.00	2100.00
69-02-017	Flute Player L1025	Lladro	Closed	73.00	575-870.
69-02-018	Clown with Concertina L1027G	Lladro	Open	95.00	735.00
69-02-019	Don Quixote w/Stand L1030G	Lladro	Open	225.00	1450.00
69-02-020	Sancho Panza L1031	Lladro	Closed	65.00	525.00
69-02-021	Old Folks L1033	Lladro	Closed	140.00	1100.00
69-02-022	Girl with Basket L1034	Lladro	Closed	30.00	225.00
69-02-023	Girl with Geese L1035G	Lladro	Open	37.50	180.00
69-02-024	Girl Geese L1036 G/M	Lladro	Open	Unkn.	155.00
69-02-025	Violinist and Girl L1039	Lladro	Closed	120.00	1000.00
69-02-026	Girl with Duck L1052G	Lladro	Open	30.00	205.00
69-02-027	Beagle Puppy L1071 G/M	Lladro	Open	17.50	135.00
69-02-028	Girl With Brush L1081	Lladro	Closed	14.50	100-295.
69-02-029	Girl Manicuring L1082	Lladro	Closed	14.50	100-295.
69-02-030	Girl With Doll L1083	Lladro	Closed	14.50	100.00
69-02-031	Girl Seated with Flowers L1088	Lladro	Closed	45.00	650.00
71-02-032	Pelusa Clown L1125	Lladro	Closed	70.00	875-1150.
71-02-033	Clown with Violin L1126	Lladro	Closed	71.00	1200-1400.
71-02-034	Puppy Love L1127G	Lladro	Open	50.00	285.00
71-02-035	Elephants (3) L1150G	Lladro	Open	100.00	795.00
71-02-036	Elephants (2) L1151G	Lladro	Open	45.00	390.00
71-02-037	Dog w/Microphone L1155	Lladro	Closed	35.00	325-475.
71-02-038	Kissing Doves L1169 G	Lladro	Open	32.00	140.00
71-02-039	Girl With Flowers L1172 G	Lladro	Open	27.00	295.00
71-02-040	Boy with Donkey L1181	Lladro	Closed	50.00	260.00
72-02-041	Little Girl with Cat L1187	Lladro	Closed	37.00	N/A
72-02-042	Boy Meets Girl L1188	Lladro	Closed	310.00	310.00
72-02-043	Eskimo L1195 G	Lladro	Open	30.00	135.00
72-02-044	Bear, White L1207 G	Lladro	Open	16.00	75.00
72-02-045	Bear, White L1208 G	Lladro	Open	16.00	75.00
72-02-046	Bear, White L1209 G	Lladro	Open	16.00	75.00
72-02-047	Girl With Doll L1211 G	Lladro	Open	72.00	440.00
72-02-048	Young Harlequin L1229G	Lladro	Open	70.00	520.00
72-02-049	Friendship L1230G/M	Lladro	Closed	68.00	325.00
72-02-050	Angel with Lute L1231	Lladro	Closed	60.00	375.00
72-02-051	Angel with Clarinet L1232	Lladro	Closed	60.00	375.00
72-02-052	Angel with Flute L1233	Lladro	Closed	60.00	375.00
72-02-053	Caress L1246	Lladro	Closed	50.00	300.00
74-02-054	Honey Lickers L1248	Lladro	Closed	100.00	525-600.
74-02-055	The Race L1249	Lladro	Closed	450.00	1800-2250.
74-02-056	Lovers from Verona L 1250	Lladro	Closed	330.00	1250.00
74-02-057	Hamlet and Yorick L1254	Lladro	Closed	325.00	1050.00
74-02-058	Seesaw L1255G	Lladro	Open	110.00	550.00
74-02-059	Flying Duck L1263 G	Lladro	Open	20.00	90.00
74-02-060	Flying Duck L1264 G	Lladro	Open	20.00	90.00
74-02-061	Flying Duck L1265 G	Lladro	Open	20.00	90.00
74-02-062	Girl with Ducks L1267G	Lladro	Open	55.00	260.00
74-02-063	Reminiscing L1270	Lladro	Closed	975.00	1375.00
74-02-064	Thoughts L1272G	Lladro	Open	87.50	3200.00
74-02-065	Lovers in the Park L1274G	Lladro	Open	450.00	1365.00
74-02-066	Feeding Time L1277G	Lladro	Closed	120.00	380.00
74-02-067	Devotion L1278	Lladro	Closed	140.00	400-450.
74-02-068	The Wind L1279M	Lladro	Open	250.00	795.00
74-02-069	Playtime L1280	Lladro	Closed	160.00	475-725.
74-02-070	Little Gardener L1283G	Lladro	Open	250.00	785.00
74-02-071	"My Flowers" L1284G	Lladro	Open	200.00	550.00
74-02-072	"My Goodness" L1285G	Lladro	Open	190.00	415.00
74-02-073	Flower Harvest L1286G	Lladro	Open	200.00	495.00
74-02-074	Picking Flowers L1287G	Lladro	Open	170.00	440.00
74-02-075	Aggressive Duck L1288G	Lladro	Open	170.00	475.00
74-02-076	Victorian Girl on Swing L1297	Lladro	Closed	520.00	2100.00
74-02-077	Valencian Lady with Flowers L1304G	Lladro	Open	200.00	625.00
74-02-078	"On the Farm" L1306	Lladro	Closed	130.00	240.00
74-02-079	Ducklings L1307G	Lladro	Open	47.50	150.00
74-02-080	Girl with Cats L1309G	Lladro	Open	120.00	310.00
74-02-081	Girl with Puppies in Basket L1311G	Lladro	Open	120.00	345.00
74-02-082	Schoolgirl L1313	Lladro	Closed	200.50	575-650.
76-02-083	IBIS L1319G	Lladro	Open	1550.00	2625.00
76-02-084	The Helmsman L1325M	Lladro	Closed	600.00	6400.00
76-02-086	Playing Cards L1327 M, numbered	Lladro	Open	3800.00	6600.00
77-02-087	Dove Group L1335	Lladro	Closed	950.00	1100.00
77-02-088	Blooming Roses L1339	Lladro	Closed	325.00	425.00
77-02-089	Wrath of Don Quixote L1343	Lladro	Closed	250.00	850.00
77-02-090	Derby L1344	Lladro	Closed	N/A	N/A
78-02-091	Under the Willow L1346	Lladro	Closed	1600.00	2000.00
78-02-092	Nautical Vision L1349	Lladro	Closed	Unkn.	3000.00
78-02-093	In the Gondola L1350G, numbered	Lladro	Open	1850.00	3250.00
78-02-094	Growing Roses L1354	Lladro	Closed	485.00	635.00
78-02-095	Phyllis L1356 G	Lladro	Open	75.00	170.00
78-02-096	Shelley L1357 G	Lladro	Open	75.00	170.00
78-02-097	Beth L1358 G	Lladro	Open	75.00	170.00
78-02-098	Heather L1359 G	Lladro	Open	75.00	170.00
78-02-099	Laura L1360 G	Lladro	Open	75.00	170.00
78-02-100	Julia L1361 G	Lladro	Open	75.00	170.00
78-02-101	Swinging L1366	Lladro	Closed	825.00	1375.00
78-02-102	Spring Birds L1368	Lladro	Closed	1600.00	2500.00
78-02-103	Anniversary Waltz L1372G	Lladro	Open	260.00	545.00
78-02-104	Waiting in the Park L1374G	Lladro	Open	235.00	450.00
78-02-105	Watering Flowers L1376	Lladro	Closed	400.00	700-1000.
78-02-106	A Rickshaw Ride L1383G	Lladro	Open	1500.00	2150.00
78-02-107	The Brave Knight L1385	Lladro	Closed	350.00	500.00
81-02-108	St. Joseph L1386G	Lladro	Open	250.00	385.00
81-02-109	Mary L1387G	Lladro	Open	240.00	385.00
81-02-110	Baby Jesus L1388G	Lladro	Open	85.00	140.00
81-02-111	Donkey L1389G	Lladro	Open	95.00	200.00
81-02-112	Cow L1390G	Lladro	Open	95.00	180.00
82-02-113	Holy Mary, numbered L1394G	Lladro	Open	1000.00	1450.00
82-02-114	Full of Mischief L1395G	Lladro	Open	420.00	765.00
82-02-115	Appreciation L1396G	Lladro	Open	420.00	765.00
82-02-116	Second Thoughts L1397G	Lladro	Open	420.00	750.00
82-02-117	Reverie L1398G	Lladro	Open	490.00	895.00
82-02-118	Dutch Woman with Tulips L1399	Lladro	Closed	Unkn.	700.00
82-02-119	Valencian Boy L1400	Lladro	Closed	297.50	400.00
82-02-120	Sleeping Nymph L1401	Lladro	Closed	210.00	525-750.
82-02-121	Daydreaming Nymph L1402	Lladro	Closed	210.00	525-625.
82-02-122	Pondering Nymph L1403	Lladro	Closed	210.00	525-625.
82-02-123	Matrimony L1404G	Lladro	Open	320.00	585.00
82-02-124	Illusion L1413G	Lladro	Open	115.00	245.00
82-02-125	Fantasy L1414G	Lladro	Open	115.00	240.00
82-02-126	Mirage L1415G	Lladro	Open	115.00	240.00
82-02-127	From My Garden L1416G	Lladro	Open	140.00	275.00
82-02-128	Nature's Bounty L1417G	Lladro	Open	160.00	310.00
82-02-129	Flower Harmony L1418G	Lladro	Open	130.00	245.00
82-02-130	A Barrow of Blossoms L1419G	Lladro	Open	390.00	675.00
82-02-131	Born Free w/base L1420G	Lladro	Open	1520.00	2850.00
82-02-132	Mariko w/base L1421G	Lladro	Open	860.00	1575.00
82-02-133	Miss Valencia L1422G	Lladro	Open	175.00	350.00
82-02-134	King Melchor L1423G	Lladro	Open	225.00	440.00
82-02-135	King Gaspar L1424G	Lladro	Open	265.00	475.00
82-02-136	King Baltasar L1425G	Lladro	Open	315.00	585.00
82-02-137	Male Tennis Player L1426	Lladro	Closed	200.00	275-325.
82-02-138	Female Tennis Player L1427	Lladro	Closed	200.00	375-425.
82-02-139	Afternoon Tea L1428G/M	Lladro	Open	115.00	250.00
82-02-140	Winter Wonderland w/base L1429G	Lladro	Open	1025.00	1925.00
82-02-141	High Society L1430G	Lladro	Open	305.00	595.00
82-02-142	The Debutante L1431G/M	Lladro	Open	115.00	245.00
83-02-143	Vows L1434	Lladro	Closed	600.00	950.00
83-02-144	Blue Moon L1435	Lladro	Closed	98.00	375.00
83-02-145	Moon Glow L1436	Lladro	Closed	98.00	375.00
83-02-146	Moon Light L1437	Lladro	Closed	98.00	375.00
83-02-147	Full Moon L1438	Lladro	Closed	115.00	500.00
83-02-148	"How Do You Do!" L1439G	Lladro	Open	185.00	295.00
83-02-149	Pleasantries L1440	Lladro	Closed	960.00	1900.00
83-02-150	A Litter of Love L1441G	Lladro	Open	385.00	645.00
83-02-151	Kitty Confrontation L1442G	Lladro	Open	155.00	285.00
83-02-152	Bearly Love L1443G	Lladro	Open	55.00	98.00
83-02-153	Purr-Fect L1444G	Lladro	Open	350.00	615.00

Company		Series			
Number	Name	Artist	Edition Limit	Issue Price	Quote
83-02-154	Springtime in Japan L1445G	Lladro	Open	965.00	1800.00
83-02-155	"Here Comes the Bride" L1446G	Lladro	Open	517.50	965.00
83-02-156	Michiko L1447G	Lladro	Open	235.00	460.00
83-02-157	Yuki L1448G	Lladro	Open	285.00	550.00
83-02-158	Mayumi L1449G	Lladro	Open	235.00	460.00
83-02-159	Kiyoko L1450G	Lladro	Open	235.00	460.00
83-02-160	Teruko L1451G	Lladro	Open	235.00	460.00
83-02-161	On the Town L1452G	Lladro	Open	220.00	440.00
83-02-162	Golfing Couple L1453G	Lladro	Open	248.00	485.00
83-02-163	Flowers of the Season L1454G	Lladro	Open	1460.00	2550.00
83-02-164	Reflections of Hamlet L1455	Lladro	Closed	1000.00	1260.00
83-02-165	Cranes w/base L1456G	Lladro	Open	1000.00	1950.00
85-02-166	Carefree Angel with Flute L1463	Lladro	Closed	220.00	575-650.
85-02-167	Carefree Angel with Lyre L1464	Lladro	Closed	220.00	575.00
85-02-168	Girl on Carousel Horse L1469G	Lladro	Open	470.00	835.00
85-02-169	Boy on Carousel Horse L1470G	Lladro	Open	470.00	850.00
85-02-170	Wishing On A Star L1475	Lladro	Closed	130.00	325-380.
85-02-171	Star Light Star Bright L1476	Lladro	Closed	130.00	325-380.
85-02-172	Star Gazing L1477	Lladro	Closed	130.00	325-350.
85-02-173	Hawaiian Dancer/Aloha L1478G	Lladro	Open	230.00	440.00
85-02-174	In a Tropical Garden L1479G	Lladro	Open	230.00	440.00
85-02-175	Aroma of the Islands L1480G	Lladro	Open	260.00	480.00
85-02-176	Eve L1482	Lladro	Closed	145.00	650.00
86-02-177	Lady of the East L1488G	Lladro	Open	625.00	1100.00
86-02-178	Valencian Children L1489G	Lladro	Open	700.00	1225.00
86-02-179	My Wedding Day L1494G	Lladro	Open	800.00	1450.00
86-02-180	A Lady of Taste L1495G	Lladro	Open	575.00	1025.00
86-02-181	Don Quixote & The Windmill L1497G	Lladro	Open	1100.00	2050.00
86-02-182	Tahitian Dancing Girls L1498G	Lladro	Open	750.00	1325.00
86-02-183	Blessed Family L1499G	Lladro	Open	200.00	360.00
86-02-184	Ragamuffin L1500G/M	Lladro	Closed	125.00	200.00
86-02-185	Rag Doll L1501G/M	Lladro	Closed	125.00	200.00
86-02-186	Forgotten L1502G/M	Lladro	Closed	125.00	200.00
86-02-187	Neglected L1503G/M	Lladro	Closed	125.00	200.00
86-02-188	The Reception L1504	Lladro	Closed	625.00	650.00
86-02-189	Nature Boy L1505G/M	Lladro	Closed	100.00	180.00
86-02-190	A New Friend L1506G/M	Lladro	Closed	110.00	180.00
86-02-191	Boy & His Bunny L1507G/M	Lladro	Closed	90.00	160.00
86-02-192	In the Meadow L1508G/M	Lladro	Closed	100.00	180.00
86-02-193	Spring Flowers L1509G/M	Lladro	Closed	100.00	185.00
87-02-194	Cafe De Paris L1511G	Lladro	Open	1900.00	2950.00
87-02-195	Hawaiian Beauty L1512	Lladro	Closed	575.00	725-1100.
87-02-196	A Flower for My Lady L1513	Lladro	Closed	1150.00	1375.00
87-02-197	Gaspar 's Page L1514	Lladro	Closed	275.00	450.00
87-02-198	Melchior's Page L1515	Lladro	Closed	290.00	450.00
87-02-199	Balthasar's Page L1516	Lladro	Closed	275.00	475-600.
87-02-200	Circus Train L1517G	Lladro	Open	2900.00	4350.00
87-02-201	Valencian Garden L1518G	Lladro	Closed	1100.00	1650.00
87-02-202	Stroll in the Park L1519G	Lladro	Open	1600.00	2600.00
87-02-203	The Landau Carriage L1521G	Lladro	Open	2500.00	3850.00
87-02-204	I am Don Quixote L1522G	Lladro	Open	2600.00	3950.00
87-02-205	Valencian Bouquet L1524G	Lladro	Closed	250.00	375.00
87-02-206	Valencian Dreams L1525G	Lladro	Closed	240.00	360.00
87-02-207	Valencian Flowers L1526G	Lladro	Closed	375.00	550.00
87-02-208	Tenderness L1527G	Lladro	Open	260.00	415.00
87-02-209	I Love You Truly L1528G	Lladro	Open	375.00	575.00
87-02-210	Momi L1529	Lladro	Closed	275.00	340.00
87-02-211	Leilani L1530	Lladro	Closed	275.00	500.00
87-02-212	Malia L1531	Lladro	Closed	275.00	340.00
87-02-213	Lehua L1532	Lladro	Closed	275.00	575.00
87-02-214	Not So Fast! L1533G	Lladro	Open	175.00	245.00
88-02-215	Little Sister L1534G	Lladro	Open	180.00	240.00
88-02-216	Sweet Dreams L1535G	Lladro	Open	150.00	195.00
88-02-217	Stepping Out L1537G	Lladro	Open	230.00	310.00
87-02-218	Wild Stallions w/Base L1566G	Lladro	Open	1100.00	1465.00
87-02-219	Running Free w/Base L1567G	Lladro	Open	1500.00	1525.00
87-02-220	Grand Dame L1568G	Lladro	Open	290.00	395.00
89-02-221	Fluttering Crane L1598G	Lladro	Open	115.00	145.00
89-02-222	Nesting Crane L1599G	Lladro	Open	95.00	115.00
89-02-223	Landing Crane L1600G	Lladro	Open	115.00	145.00
89-02-224	Rock Nymph L1601G	Lladro	Open	665.00	795.00
89-02-225	Spring Nymph L1602G	Lladro	Open	665.00	825.00
89-02-226	Latest Addition L1606G	Lladro	Open	385.00	480.00
89-02-227	Flight Into Egypt w/Base L1610G	Lladro	Open	885.00	1150.00
89-02-228	Courting Cranes L1611G	Lladro	Open	565.00	695.00
89-02-229	Preening Crane L1612G	Lladro	Open	385.00	485.00
89-02-230	Bowing Crane L1613G	Lladro	Open	385.00	485.00
89-02-231	Dancing Crane L1614G	Lladro	Open	385.00	485.00
90-02-232	Sprite w/Base L1720	Lladro	Open	1200.00	1400.00
90-02-233	Leprechaun w/Base L1721	Lladro	Open	1200.00	1395.00
70-02-234	Shepherdess with Lamb L2005	Lladro	Closed	100.00	710.00
70-02-235	Water Carrier Girl Lamp L2006	Lladro	Closed	N/A	600.00
71-02-236	Boy/Girl Eskimo L2038M	Lladro	Closed	100.00	275-455.
74-02-237	Oriental L2056M	Lladro	Open	35.00	100.00
74-02-238	Oriental L2057M	Lladro	Open	30.00	100.00
74-02-239	Thailandia L2058M	Lladro	Open	650.00	1725.00
77-02-240	Monk L2060M	Lladro	Open	60.00	130.00
77-02-241	Thai Dancers L2069M	Lladro	Open	300.00	725.00
77-02-242	A New Hairdo L2070	Lladro	Closed	1060.00	1430.00
77-02-243	Graceful Duo L2073M	Lladro	Open	775.00	1650.00
77-02-244	Nuns L2075M	Lladro	Open	90.00	230.00
78-02-245	Lonely L2076M	Lladro	Open	72.50	185.00
78-02-246	Rain in Spain L2077	Lladro	Closed	190.00	550.00
78-02-247	Girl Waiting L2093M	Lladro	Open	90.00	185.00
78-02-248	Tenderness L2094M	Lladro	Open	100.00	205.00
78-02-249	Duck Pulling Pigtail L2095M	Lladro	Open	110.00	275.00
78-02-250	Nosy Puppy L2096M	Lladro	Open	190.00	410.00
78-02-251	Laundress L2109	Lladro	Closed	325.00	325-650.
80-02-252	The Whaler L2121	Lladro	Closed	820.00	1050.00
81-02-253	Lost in Thought L2125	Lladro	Closed	210.00	250.00
83-02-254	American Heritage L2127	Lladro	Closed	525.00	650-950.
83-02-255	Venus L2128M	Lladro	Closed	650.00	1200.00
83-02-256	Mother & Son L2131M, numbered	Lladro	Open	850.00	1350.00
84-02-257	Nautical Watch L2134	Lladro	Closed	450.00	750.00
84-02-258	Mystical Joseph L2135	Lladro	Closed	427.50	700.00
84-02-259	The King L2136	Lladro	Closed	510.00	710.00
84-02-260	Fairy Ballerina L2137	Lladro	Closed	500.00	625.00
84-02-261	Friar Juniper L2138M	Lladro	Open	160.00	275.00
84-02-262	Aztec Indian L2139	Lladro	Closed	552.50	600.00
84-02-263	Pepita with Sombrero L2140M	Lladro	Open	N/A	185.00
84-02-264	Pedro with Jug L2141M	Lladro	Open	N/A	185.00
84-02-265	Sea Harvest L2142	Lladro	Closed	535.00	700.00
84-02-266	Aztec Dancer L2143	Lladro	Closed	462.50	650.00
84-02-267	Leticia L2144M	Lladro	Open	100.00	170.00
84-02-268	Gabriela L2145M	Lladro	Open	100.00	170.00
84-02-269	Desiree L2146M	Lladro	Open	100.00	170.00
84-02-270	Alida L2147M	Lladro	Open	100.00	170.00
84-02-271	Head of Congolese Woman L2148	Lladro	Closed	55.00	190.00
85-02-272	Young Madonna L2149	Lladro	Closed	400.00	675.00
85-02-273	A Tribute to Peace L2150M	Lladro	Open	470.00	850.00
85-02-274	A Bird on Hand L2151M	Lladro	Open	117.50	230.00
85-02-275	Hawaiian Flower Vendor L2154M	Lladro	Open	245.00	420.00
85-02-276	Arctic Winter L2156M	Lladro	Open	75.00	140.00
85-02-277	Eskimo Girl with Cold Feet L2157M	Lladro	Open	140.00	260.00
85-02-278	Pensive Eskimo Girl L2158M	Lladro	Open	100.00	190.00
85-02-279	Pensive Eskimo Boy L2159M	Lladro	Open	100.00	190.00
85-02-280	Flower Vendor L2160M	Lladro	Open	110.00	200.00
85-02-281	Fruit Vendor L2161M	Lladro	Open	120.00	230.00
85-02-282	Fish Vendor L2162M	Lladro	Open	110.00	205.00
87-02-283	Mountain Shepherd L2163M	Lladro	Open	120.00	190.00
87-02-284	My Lost Lamb L2164M	Lladro	Open	100.00	165.00
87-02-285	Chiquita L2165M	Lladro	Open	100.00	170.00
87-02-286	Paco L2166M	Lladro	Open	100.00	170.00
87-02-287	Fernando L2167M	Lladro	Open	100.00	170.00
87-02-288	Julio L2168M	Lladro	Open	100.00	170.00
87-02-289	Repose L2169M	Lladro	Open	120.00	175.00
87-02-290	Spanish Dancer L2170M	Lladro	Open	190.00	315.00
87-02-291	Ahoy There L2173M	Lladro	Open	190.00	295.00
88-02-292	Harvest Helpers L2178M	Lladro	Open	190.00	250.00
88-02-293	Sharing the Harvest L2179M	Lladro	Open	190.00	250.00
88-02-294	Dreams of Peace L2180M	Lladro	Open	880.00	1025.00
88-02-295	Bathing Nymph L2181M	Lladro	Open	560.00	760.00
88-02-296	Daydreamer L2182M	Lladro	Open	560.00	760.00
89-02-297	Wakeup Kitty L2183M	Lladro	Open	225.00	285.00
89-02-298	Angel and Friend L2184M	Lladro	Open	150.00	185.00
89-02-299	Devoted Reader L2185M	Lladro	Open	125.00	160.00
89-02-301	The Greatest Love L2186M	Lladro	Open	235.00	290.00
89-02-302	Jealous Friend L2187M	Lladro	Open	275.00	340.00
90-02-303	Mother's Pride L2189 M	Lladro	Open	300.00	350.00
80-02-304	To The Well L2190 M	Lladro	Open	250.00	295.00
90-02-305	Forest Born L2191 M	Lladro	Closed	230.00	250.00
80-02-306	King Of The Forest L2192 M	Lladro	Closed	290.00	310.00
80-02-307	Heavenly Strings L2194 M	Lladro	Open	170.00	195.00
90-02-308	Heavenly Sounds L2195 M	Lladro	Open	170.00	195.00
90-02-309	Heavenly Solo L2196 M	Lladro	Open	170.00	195.00
90-02-310	Heavenly Song L2197 M	Lladro	Open	175.00	185.00
90-02-311	A King is Born w/base L2198 M	Lladro	Open	750.00	880.00
90-02-312	Devoted Friends w/base L2199 M	Lladro	Open	700.00	825.00
90-02-313	A Big Hug! L2200 M	Lladro	Open	250.00	295.00
90-02-314	Our Daily Bread L2201 M	Lladro	Open	150.00	185.00
90-02-315	A Helping Hand L2202 M	Lladro	Open	150.00	185.00
90-02-316	Afternoon Chores L2203 M	Lladro	Open	150.00	185.00
90-02-317	Farmyard Grace L2204 M	Lladro	Open	180.00	210.00
90-02-318	Prayerful Stitch L2205 M	Lladro	Open	160.00	190.00
90-02-319	Sisterly Love L2206 M	Lladro	Open	300.00	350.00
90-02-320	What A Day! L2207 M	Lladro	Open	550.00	630.00
90-02-321	Let's Rest L2208 M	Lladro	Open	550.00	630.00
91-02-322	Long Day L2209M	Lladro	Open	295.00	315.00
91-02-323	Lazy Day L2210M	Lladro	Open	240.00	260.00
91-02-324	Patrol Leader L2212M	Lladro	Open	390.00	420.00
91-02-325	Nature's Friend L2213M	Lladro	Open	390.00	420.00
91-02-326	Seaside Angel L2214M	Lladro	Open	150.00	165.00
91-02-327	Friends in Flight L2215M	Lladro	Open	165.00	180.00
91-02-328	Laundry Day L2216M	Lladro	Open	350.00	385.00
91-02-329	Gentle Play L2217M	Lladro	Open	380.00	415.00
91-02-330	Costumed Couple L2218M	Lladro	Open	680.00	750.00
92-02-331	Underfoot L2219M	Lladro	Open	360.00	375.00
92-02-332	Free Spirit L2220M	Lladro	Open	235.00	245.00
92-02-333	Spring Beauty L2221M	Lladro	Open	285.00	295.00
92-02-334	Tender Moment L2222M	Lladro	Open	400.00	420.00
92-02-335	New Lamb L2223M	Lladro	Open	365.00	385.00
92-02-336	Cherish L2224M	Lladro	Open	1750.00	1850.00
92-02-337	Friendly Sparrow L2225M	Lladro	Open	295.00	310.00
92-02-338	Boy's Best Friend L2226M	Lladro	Open	390.00	410.00
92-02-339	Artic Allies L2227M	Lladro	Open	585.00	615.00
92-02-340	Snowy Sunday L2228M	Lladro	Open	550.00	575.00
92-02-341	Seasonal Gifts L2229M	Lladro	Open	450.00	475.00
92-02-342	Mary's Child L2230M	Lladro	Open	525.00	550.00
92-02-343	Afternoon Verse L2231M	Lladro	Open	580.00	595.00
92-02-344	Poor Little Bear L2232M	Lladro	Open	250.00	265.00
92-02-345	Guess What I Have L2233M	Lladro	Open	340.00	360.00
92-02-346	Playful Push L2234M	Lladro	Open	850.00	875.00
93-02-347	Adoring Mother L2235M	Lladro	Open	405.00	405.00
93-02-348	Frosty Outing L2236M	Lladro	Open	375.00	375.00
93-02-349	The Old Fishing Hole L2237M	Lladro	Open	625.00	625.00
93-02-350	Learning Together L2238M	Lladro	Open	500.00	500.00
93-02-351	Valencian Courtship L2239M	Lladro	Open	880.00	880.00
93-02-352	Winged Love L2240M	Lladro	Open	285.00	285.00
93-02-353	Winged Harmony L2241M	Lladro	Open	285.00	285.00
93-02-354	Away to School L2242M	Lladro	Open	465.00	465.00
93-02-355	Lion Tamer L2246M	Lladro	Open	375.00	375.00
93-02-356	Just Us L2247M	Lladro	Open	650.00	650.00
93-02-357	Noella L2251M	Lladro	Open	405.00	405.00
93-02-358	Waiting For Father L2252M	Lladro	Open	660.00	660.00
93-02-359	Noisy Friend L2253M	Lladro	Open	280.00	280.00
93-02-360	Step Aside L2254M	Lladro	Open	280.00	280.00
78-02-361	Native L3502	Lladro	Open	700.00	2450.00
78-02-362	Letters to Dulcinea L3509M	Lladro	Open	875.00	2050.00
78-02-364	Horse Heads L3511	Lladro	Closed	260.00	700.00
78-02-365	Girl With Pails L3512M	Lladro	Open	140.00	285.00
78-02-366	A Wintry Day L3513	Lladro	Closed	525.00	750.00
78-02-367	Pensive L3514M	Lladro	Open	500.00	1050.00
78-02-368	Nude with Rose L3517M	Lladro	Open	225.00	760.00
80-02-369	Lady Macbeth L3518	Lladro	Closed	N/A	425-1000.
80-02-370	Mother's Love L3521	Lladro	Closed	1000.00	1100.00
81-02-371	Weary L3525M	Lladro	Open	360.00	625.00
82-02-372	Contemplation L3526M	Lladro	Open	265.00	540.00
82-02-373	Stormy Sea L3554M	Lladro	Open	675.00	1325.00
84-02-374	Innocence with base/green L3558M	Lladro	Closed	960.00	1650.00
84-02-375	Innocence with base/red L3558.3	Lladro	Closed	960.00	1200.00
85-02-376	Peace Offering L3559M	Lladro	Open	397.00	665.00
69-02-377	Girl with Lamb L4505G	Lladro	Open	20.00	110.00
69-02-378	Boy with Kid L4506	Lladro	Closed	22.50	250.00
69-02-379	Girl with Parasol and Geese L4510G	Lladro	Open	40.00	245.00
69-02-380	Female Equestrian L4516G	Lladro	Open	170.00	695.00
69-02-381	Flamenco Dancers L4519G	Lladro	Open	495.00	1100.00

FIGURINES

Company		Series			
Number	Name	Artist	Edition Limit	Issue Price	Quote
70-02-382	Boy With Dog L4522G	Lladro	Open	25.00	155.00
69-02-383	Girl With Slippers L4523G/M	Lladro	Open	17.00	100.00
69-02-384	Donkey in Love L4524M	Lladro	Closed	15.00	275-500.
69-02-385	Joseph L4533G/M	Lladro	Open	60.00	100.00
69-02-386	Mary L4534G/M	Lladro	Open	60.00	85.00
69-02-387	Baby Jesus L4535G/M	Lladro	Open	60.00	70.00
69-02-388	Angel, Chinese L4536G/M	Lladro	Open	45.00	90.00
69-02-389	Angel, Black L4537G/M	Lladro	Open	13.00	90.00
69-02-390	Angel, Praying L4538G/M	Lladro	Open	13.00	90.00
69-02-391	Angel, Thinking L4539G/M	Lladro	Open	13.00	90.00
69-02-392	Angel with Horn L4540G/M	Lladro	Open	13.00	90.00
69-02-393	Angel Reclining L4541G/M	Lladro	Open	13.00	90.00
69-02-394	Group of Angels L4542G/M	Lladro	Open	31.00	185.00
69-02-395	Geese Group L4549G	Lladro	Open	28.50	210.00
69-02-396	Flying Dove L4550G	Lladro	Open	47.50	245.00
69-02-397	Ducks, Set of 3 Asst. L4551-3G	Lladro	Open	18.00	140.00
69-02-398	Shepherd L4554	Lladro	Closed	N/A	N/A
69-02-399	Sad Harlequin L4558G	Lladro	Open	110.00	510.00
69-02-400	Waiting Backstage L4559G	Lladro	Open	110.00	440.00
69-02-401	Girl with Geese L4568G	Lladro	Open	45.00	220.00
69-02-402	Mother & Child L4575G	Lladro	Open	50.00	265.00
69-02-403	Girl with Sheep L4584G	Lladro	Open	27.00	170.00
69-02-404	Holy Family L4585G	Lladro	Open	18.00	135.00
69-02-405	Shepherdess with Basket and Rooster L4591G	Lladro	Open	20.00	140.00
69-02-406	Fairy L4595G	Lladro	Open	27.50	140.00
69-02-407	Playfull Horses L4597	Lladro	Closed	240.00	925-1000.
69-02-408	Doctor L4602.3G	Lladro	Open	33.00	185.00
69-02-409	Nurse-L4603.3G	Lladro	Open	35.00	190.00
69-02-410	Nuns L4611G/M	Lladro	Open	37.50	155.00
69-02-411	Clown L4618G	Lladro	Open	70.00	415.00
69-02-412	Sea Captain L4621G	Lladro	Open	45.00	265.00
69-02-413	Angel with Child L4635G	Lladro	Open	15.00	95.00
69-02-414	Flamenco Dancers on Horseback L4647	Lladro	Closed	412.00	1000-1250.
69-02-415	Valencian Couple on Horseback L4648	Lladro	Closed	900.00	1200.00
69-02-416	Madonna Head L4649G	Lladro	Open	25.00	145.00
69-02-417	Madonna Head L4649M	Lladro	Open	25.00	150.00
69-02-418	Girl with Calla Lillies L4650G	Lladro	Open	18.00	135.00
69-02-419	Horses L4655G	Lladro	Open	110.00	760.00
69-02-420	Shepherdess L4660G	Lladro	Open	21.00	175.00
69-02-421	Baby Jesus L4670BG	Lladro	Open	18.00	50.00
69-02-422	Mary L4671G	Lladro	Open	33.00	75.00
69-02-423	St. Joseph L4672G	Lladro	Open	33.00	90.00
69-02-424	King Melchior L4673G	Lladro	Open	35.00	95.00
69-02-425	King Gaspar L4674G	Lladro	Open	35.00	95.00
69-02-426	King Balthasar L4675G	Lladro	Open	35.00	95.00
69-02-427	Shepherd with Lamb L4676G	Lladro	Open	14.00	95.00
69-02-428	Girl with Rooster L4677G	Lladro	Open	14.00	90.00
69-02-429	Girl with Basket L4678G	Lladro	Open	13.00	90.00
69-02-430	Donkey L4679G	Lladro	Open	36.50	100.00
69-02-431	Cow L4680G	Lladro	Open	36.50	90.00
70-02-432	Girl with Milkpail L4682	Lladro	Closed	28.00	350.00
70-02-433	Dressmaker L4700G	Lladro	Open	45.00	360.00
70-02-434	Mother & Child L4701G	Lladro	Open	45.00	295.00
70-02-435	Bird Watcher L4730	Lladro	Closed	35.00	375.00
71-02-436	Romeo and Juliet L4750G	Lladro	Open	150.00	1250.00
74-02-437	Lady with Dog L4761G	Lladro	Open	60.00	260.00
71-02-438	Dentist L4762	Lladro	Closed	36.00	475-500.
71-02-439	Obstetrician L4763-3G	Lladro	Open	40.00	235.00
71-02-440	Rabbit L4772G	Lladro	Open	17.50	135.00
71-02-441	Rabbit L4773G	Lladro	Open	17.50	130.00
71-02-442	Children, Praying L4779G	Lladro	Closed	36.00	180.00
71-02-443	Boy with Goat L4780	Lladro	Closed	80.00	475.00
72-02-444	Girl with Dog L4806	Lladro	Closed	N/A	N/A
72-02-445	Geisha L4807G	Lladro	Open	190.00	440.00
72-02-446	Wedding L4808G/M	Lladro	Open	50.00	175.00
72-02-447	Going Fishing L4809G	Lladro	Open	33.00	160.00
72-02-448	Young Sailor L4810G	Lladro	Open	33.00	165.00
72-02-449	Boy with Pails L4811	Lladro	Closed	30.00	275-425.
72-02-450	Getting Her Goat L4812	Lladro	Closed	55.00	275.00
72-02-451	Girl with Geese L4815G/M	Lladro	Closed	72.00	295.00
72-02-452	Male Golfer L4824G	Lladro	Open	66.00	285.00
72-02-453	Veterinarian L4825	Lladro	Closed	48.00	360-400.
72-02-454	Girl Feeding Rabbit L4826G	Lladro	Open	40.00	185.00
72-02-455	Cinderella L4828G	Lladro	Open	47.00	225.00
73-02-456	Clean Up Time L4838G	Lladro	Open	36.00	170.00
72-02-457	Shepherdess L4835G	Lladro	Closed	42.00	225.00
73-02-458	Oriental Flower Arranger/Girl L4840G/M	Lladro	Open	90.00	515.00
74-02-459	Girl from Valencia L4841G	Lladro	Open	35.00	205.00
73-02-460	Pharmacist L4844	Lladro	Closed	70.00	1000-2000.
73-02-461	Feeding The Ducks L4849G	Lladro	Open	60.00	250.00
73-02-462	Lady Golfer L4851M	Lladro	Closed	70.00	900.00
73-02-463	Don Quixote L4854G	Lladro	Open	40.00	205.00
73-02-464	Ballerina L4855G	Lladro	Open	45.00	330.00
83-02-465	Ballerina, white L4855.3	Lladro	Closed	110.00	250.00
74-02-466	Embroiderer L4865G	Lladro	Open	115.00	645.00
74-02-467	Girl with Swan and Dog L4866G	Lladro	Open	26.00	205.00
74-02-468	Seesaw L4867G	Lladro	Open	55.00	350.00
74-02-469	Girl with Candle L4868G	Lladro	Open	13.00	90.00
74-02-470	Boy Kissing L4869G	Lladro	Open	13.00	90.00
74-02-471	Boy Yawning L4870M	Lladro	Closed	13.00	200.00
74-02-472	Girl with Guitar L4871G	Lladro	Open	13.00	90.00
74-02-473	Girl Stretching L4872G	Lladro	Open	13.00	90.00
74-02-474	Girl Kissing L4873G	Lladro	Open	13.00	90.00
74-02-475	Boy & Girl L4874G	Lladro	Open	25.00	150.00
74-02-476	Boy Thinking L4876G	Lladro	Open	20.00	135.00
74-02-477	Lady with Parasol L4879G	Lladro	Open	48.00	300.00
74-02-478	Carnival Couple L4882G	Lladro	Open	60.00	300.00
79-02-479	Spanish Policeman L4889	Lladro	Open	N/A	360.00
76-02-480	"My Dog" L4893G	Lladro	Open	85.00	210.00
74-02-481	Ducks L4895G	Lladro	Open	45.00	90.00
74-02-482	Boy From Madrid L4898G	Lladro	Open	55.00	145.00
75-02-483	Lady with Shawl L4914G	Lladro	Open	220.00	685.00
75-02-484	Girl with Pigeons L4915	Lladro	Closed	110.00	215.00
74-02-485	Country Lass with Dog L4920G	Lladro	Open	185.00	495.00
74-02-486	Windblown Girl L4922G	Lladro	Open	150.00	375.00
74-02-487	Sad Clown L4924	Lladro	Closed	200.00	675.00
74-02-488	"Closing Scene" L4935G	Lladro	Open	180.00	520.00
83-02-489	"Closing Scene"/white L4935.3	Lladro	Closed	202.50	265.00
74-02-490	Spring Breeze L4936G	Lladro	Open	145.00	410.00
76-02-491	Baby's Outing L4938G	Lladro	Open	250.00	725.00
77-02-492	Cherub, Puzzled L4959G	Lladro	Open	40.00	98.00
77-02-493	Cherub, Smiling L4960G	Lladro	Open	40.00	98.00
77-02-494	Cherub, Dreaming L4961G	Lladro	Open	40.00	98.00
77-02-495	Cherub, Wondering L4962G	Lladro	Open	40.00	98.00
77-02-496	Cowboy & Sheriff Puppet L4969G	Lladro	Closed	85.00	575-600.
77-02-497	Girl with Calla Lillies sitting L4972G	Lladro	Open	65.00	170.00
77-02-498	Choir Lesson L4973	Lladro	Closed	N/A	1175.00.
77-02-499	Augustina of Aragon L4976	Lladro	Closed	N/A	1500-1800.
78-02-500	Naughty Dog L4982G	Lladro	Open	130.00	250.00
78-02-501	Gossip L4984	Lladro	Closed	260.00	525-575.00
78-02-502	Oriental Spring L4988G	Lladro	Open	125.00	325.00
78-02-503	Sayonara L4989G	Lladro	Open	125.00	300.00
78-02-504	Chrysanthemum L4990G	Lladro	Open	125.00	310.00
78-02-505	Butterfly L4991G	Lladro	Open	125.00	295.00
78-02-506	Don Quijote & Sancho L4998	Lladro	Closed	875.00	2800.00
78-02-507	Reading L5000G	Lladro	Open	150.00	255.00
78-02-508	Sunny Day L5005	Lladro	Open	192.50	360.00
78-02-509	Naughty L5006G	Lladro	Open	55.00	140.00
78-02-510	Bashful L5007G	Lladro	Open	55.00	140.00
78-02-511	Static-Girl w/Straw Hat L5008G	Lladro	Open	55.00	140.00
78-02-512	Curious-Girl w/Straw Hat L5009G	Lladro	Open	55.00	140.00
78-02-513	Coiffure-Girl w/Straw Hat L5010G	Lladro	Open	55.00	140.00
78-02-514	Trying on a Straw Hat L5011G	Lladro	Open	55.00	140.00
78-02-515	Daughters L5013	Lladro	Closed	425.00	1250.00
79-02-516	Flower Curtsy L5027G	Lladro	Open	230.00	470.00
80-02-517	Wildflower L5030G	Lladro	Open	360.00	695.00
79-02-518	Little Friskies L5032G	Lladro	Open	107.50	220.00
79-02-519	Avoiding the Goose L5033G	Lladro	Open	160.00	350.00
79-02-520	Goose Trying To Eat L5034G	Lladro	Open	135.00	290.00
80-02-521	Act II w/base L5035G	Lladro	Open	700.00	1425.00
79-02-522	Jockey with Lass L5036G	Lladro	Open	950.00	2050.00
80-02-523	Sleighride w/base L5037G	Lladro	Open	585.00	1045.00
80-02-524	Girl with Toy Wagon L5044G	Lladro	Open	115.00	220.00
80-02-525	Belinda with Doll L5045G	Lladro	Open	115.00	205.00
79-02-526	Dancer L5050G	Lladro	Open	85.00	190.00
80-02-527	Clown with Clock L5056	Lladro	Closed	290.00	950.00
80-02-528	Clown with Violin and Top Hat L5057	Lladro	Closed	270.00	750.00
80-02-529	Clown with Concertina L5058	Lladro	Closed	290.00	675.00
80-02-530	Clown with Saxaphone L5059	Lladro	Closed	320.00	575-610.
80-02-531	Girl Clown with Trumpet L5060	Lladro	Closed	290.00	500-575.
80-02-532	Girl Bending/March Wind L5061	Lladro	Closed	370.00	N/A
80-02-533	Dutch Girl with Hands in Back L5062	Lladro	Closed	225.00	350.00
80-02-534	Gretel L5064	Lladro	Closed	255.00	375.00
80-02-535	Ingrid L5065	Lladro	Closed	370.00	400.00
80-02-536	Ilsa L5066	Lladro	Closed	275.00	300.00
81-02-537	Halloween L5067G	Lladro	Closed	450.00	1300.00
80-02-538	Nostalgia L5071G	Lladro	Open	185.00	310.00
80-02-539	Courtship L5072	Lladro	Closed	327.00	525.00
80-02-540	My Hungry Brood L5074G	Lladro	Open	295.00	415.00
80-02-541	Roses for My Mom L5088	Lladro	Closed	645.00	810.00
80-02-542	Scare-Dy Cat/Playful Cat L5091G	Lladro	Open	65.00	95.00
89-02-543	Her Ladyship, numbered L5097G	Lladro	Closed	5900.00	6700.00
82-02-544	Play with Me L5112G	Lladro	Open	40.00	80.00
82-02-545	Feed Me L5113G	Lladro	Open	40.00	80.00
82-02-546	Pet Me L5114G	Lladro	Open	40.00	80.00
82-02-547	August Moon L5122G	Lladro	Open	185.00	310.00
82-02-548	My Precious Bundle L5123G	Lladro	Open	150.00	230.00
82-02-549	Amparo L5125	Lladro	Closed	130.00	200-250.
82-02-550	Sewing A Trousseau L5126G	Lladro	Closed	185.00	400.00
85-02-551	Nippon Lady L5327	Lladro	Open	325.00	470.00
82-02-552	Lost Love L5128	Lladro	Closed	400.00	650-750.
82-02-553	Jester w/base L5129G	Lladro	Open	220.00	405.00
82-02-554	Pensive Clown w/base L5130G	Lladro	Open	250.00	415.00
82-02-555	Cervantes L5132	Lladro	Closed	925.00	1175.00
82-02-556	A New Doll House L5139	Lladro	Closed	185.00	525.00
82-02-557	Balloons for Sale L5141G	Lladro	Open	145.00	250.00
82-02-558	Scooting L5143	Lladro	Closed	575.00	850-1000.
82-02-559	Amy L5145	Lladro	Closed	110.00	1060-1500.
82-02-560	Ellen L5146	Lladro	Closed	110.00	1200.00
82-02-561	Ivy L5147	Lladro	Closed	100.00	600.00
82-02-562	Olivia L5148	Lladro	Closed	100.00	450-500
82-02-563	Ursula L5149	Lladro	Closed	100.00	400-500
82-02-564	Monks at Prayer L5155G	Lladro	Open	130.00	250.00
82-02-565	Bongo Beat L5157G	Lladro	Open	135.00	230.00
82-02-566	A Step In Time L5158G	Lladro	Open	90.00	180.00
82-02-567	Harmony L5159G	Lladro	Open	270.00	495.00
82-02-568	Rhumba L5160G	Lladro	Open	112.50	185.00
82-02-569	Cycling To A Picnic L5161	Lladro	Closed	2000.00	3000.00
82-02-570	A Toast by Sancho L5165	Lladro	Closed	100.00	300.00
82-02-571	Sea Fever L5166M	Lladro	Closed	130.00	480.00
82-02-572	Jesus L5167G	Lladro	Open	130.00	265.00
82-02-573	Moses L5170G	Lladro	Open	175.00	360.00
82-02-574	Madonna with Flowers L5171G	Lladro	Open	172.50	310.00
82-02-575	Fish A'Plenty L5172G	Lladro	Open	190.00	385.00
82-02-576	Pondering L5173G	Lladro	Open	300.00	495.00
82-02-577	Roaring 20's L5174G	Lladro	Open	172.50	295.00
82-02-578	Flapper L5175G	Lladro	Open	185.00	365.00
82-02-579	Rhapsody in Blue L5176	Lladro	Closed	325.00	1250.00
82-02-580	Stubborn Mule L5178G	Lladro	Open	250.00	420.00
82-02-581	Dante L5177	Lladro	Closed	263.00	475.00
83-02-582	Three Pink Roses w/base L5179	Lladro	Closed	70.00	110.00
83-02-583	Dahlia L5180	Lladro	Closed	65.00	95.00
83-02-584	Japanese Camelia w/base L5181	Lladro	Closed	60.00	90.00
83-02-585	White Peony L5182	Lladro	Closed	85.00	125.00
83-02-586	Two Yellow Roses L5183	Lladro	Closed	57.50	85.00
83-02-587	White Carnation L5184	Lladro	Closed	65.00	100.00
83-02-588	Lactiflora Peony L5185	Lladro	Closed	65.00	100.00
83-02-589	Begonia L5186	Lladro	Closed	67.50	100.00
83-02-590	Rhododendrom L5187	Lladro	Closed	67.50	100.00
83-02-591	Miniature Begonia L5188	Lladro	Closed	80.00	120.00
83-02-592	Chrysanthemum L5189	Lladro	Closed	100.00	150.00
83-02-593	California Poppy L5190	Lladro	Closed	97.50	180.00
84-02-594	Lolita L5192G	Lladro	Open	80.00	155.00
84-02-595	Juanita L5193G	Lladro	Open	80.00	155.00
83-02-596	Say "Cheese!" L5195	Lladro	Closed	170.00	450.00
83-02-597	"Maestro, Music Please!" L5196	Lladro	Closed	135.00	250.00
83-02-598	Female Physician L5197	Lladro	Open	120.00	240.00
84-02-599	Boy Graduate L5198G	Lladro	Open	160.00	275.00
84-02-600	Girl Graduate L5199G	Lladro	Open	160.00	260.00
83-02-601	Male Soccer Player L5200	Lladro	Closed	155.00	450-725.
83-02-602	Josefa Feeding Duck L5201G	Lladro	Closed	125.00	215.00
83-02-603	Aracely with Ducks L5202G	Lladro	Closed	125.00	300.00
84-02-604	Little Jester L5203G	Lladro	Open	75.00	140.00
83-02-605	Sharpening the Cutlery L5204	Lladro	Closed	210.00	700.00
83-02-606	Lamplighter L5205G	Lladro	Open	170.00	360.00

Company Number	Name	Series Artist	Edition Limit	Issue Price	Quote
83-02-607	Yachtsman L5206G	Lladro	Open	110.00	210.00
83-02-608	A Tall Yarn L5207G	Lladro	Open	260.00	515.00
83-02-609	Professor L5208	Lladro	Closed	205.00	450-750.
83-02-610	School Marm L5209	Lladro	Closed	205.00	500-850.
84-02-611	Jolie L5210G	Lladro	Open	105.00	195.00
84-02-612	Angela L5211G	Lladro	Open	105.00	195.00
84-02-613	Evita L5212G	Lladro	Open	105.00	195.00
83-02-614	Lawyer L5213G	Lladro	Open	250.00	520.00
83-02-615	Architect L5214	Lladro	Closed	140.00	220.00
83-02-616	Fishing with Gramps w/base L5215G	Lladro	Open	410.00	775.00
83-02-617	On the Lake L5216	Lladro	Closed	660.00	825.00
83-02-618	Spring L5217G/M	Lladro	Open	90.00	170.00
83-02-619	Autumn L5218G/M	Lladro	Open	90.00	170.00
83-02-620	Summer L5219G/M	Lladro	Open	90.00	170.00
83-02-621	Winter L5220G/M	Lladro	Open	90.00	170.00
83-02-622	Sweet Scent L5221G/M	Lladro	Open	80.00	130.00
83-02-623	Pretty Pickings L5222G/M	Lladro	Open	80.00	130.00
83-02-624	Spring is Here L5223G/M	Lladro	Open	80.00	130.00
84-02-625	The Quest L5224G	Lladro	Open	125.00	275.00
84-02-626	Male Candleholder L5226	Lladro	Closed	660.00	660-1000.
84-02-627	Playful Piglets L5228G	Lladro	Open	80.00	135.00
83-02-628	Storytime L5229	Lladro	Closed	245.00	360.00
83-02-629	Graceful Swan L5230G	Lladro	Closed	N/A	80.00
84-02-630	Swan with Wings Spread L5231G	Lladro	Closed	N/A	115.00
83-02-631	Playful Kittens L5232G	Lladro	Open	130.00	255.00
84-02-632	Charlie the Tramp L5233	Lladro	Closed	150.00	500-1050.
84-02-633	Artistic Endeavor L5234	Lladro	Closed	225.00	450-475.
84-02-634	Ballet Trio L5235G	Lladro	Open	785.00	1525.00
84-02-635	Cat and Mouse L5236G	Lladro	Open	55.00	98.00
84-02-636	School Chums L5237G	Lladro	Open	255.00	440.00
84-02-637	Eskimo Boy with Pet L5238G	Lladro	Open	55.00	105.00
84-02-638	Wine Taster L5239G	Lladro	Open	190.00	360.00
84-02-639	Lady from Majorca L5240	Lladro	Closed	120.00	375.00
84-02-640	Best Wishes L5244	Lladro	Closed	185.00	275.00
84-02-641	St. Cristobal L5246	Lladro	Closed	265.00	600.00
84-02-642	Exam Day L5250G	Lladro	Open	115.00	210.00
84-02-643	Torch Bearer L5251	Lladro	Closed	100.00	275.00
84-02-644	Dancing the Polka L5252G	Lladro	Open	205.00	385.00
84-02-645	Cadet L5253	Lladro	Closed	N/A	350-400.
84-02-646	Making Paella L5254G	Lladro	Open	215.00	400.00
84-02-647	Spanish Soldier L5255	Lladro	Closed	N/A	400-650.
84-02-648	Folk Dancing L5256	Lladro	Closed	205.00	300.00
85-02-649	Bust of Lady from Elche L5269	Lladro	Closed	432.00	750.00
85-02-650	Racing Motor Cyclist L5270	Lladro	Closed	360.00	700-850.
85-02-651	Gazelle L5271	Lladro	Closed	205.00	400.00
85-02-652	Biking in the Country L5272	Lladro	Closed	295.00	500-775.
85-02-653	Wedding Day L5274G	Lladro	Open	240.00	415.00
85-02-654	Weary Ballerina L5275G	Lladro	Open	175.00	295.00
85-02-655	Sailor Serenades His Girl L5276	Lladro	Closed	315.00	475.00
85-02-656	Pierrot with Puppy L5277G	Lladro	Open	95.00	160.00
85-02-657	Pierrot with Puppy and Ball L5278G	Lladro	Open	95.00	160.00
85-02-658	Pierrot with Concertina L5279G	Lladro	Open	95.00	160.00
85-02-659	Hiker L5280	Lladro	Closed	195.00	250.00
85-02-660	Nativity Scene "Haute Relief" L5281	Lladro	Closed	210.00	450.00
85-02-661	Over the Threshold L5282G	Lladro	Open	150.00	270.00
85-02-662	Socialite of the Twenties L5283G	Lladro	Open	175.00	340.00
85-02-663	Glorious Spring L5284G	Lladro	Open	355.00	650.00
85-02-664	Summer on the Farm L5285G	Lladro	Open	235.00	440.00
85-02-665	Fall Clean-up L5286G	Lladro	Open	295.00	550.00
85-02-666	Winter Frost L5287G	Lladro	Open	270.00	520.00
85-02-667	Mallard Duck L5288G	Lladro	Open	310.00	520.00
85-02-668	Love in Bloom L5292G	Lladro	Open	225.00	425.00
85-02-669	Mother and Child and Lamb L5299	Lladro	Closed	180.00	425.00
85-02-670	Medieval Courtship L5300	Lladro	Closed	735.00	850.00
85-02-671	Waiting to Tee Off L5301G	Lladro	Open	145.00	285.00
85-02-672	Playing with Ducks at the Pond L5303	Lladro	Closed	425.00	700.00
85-02-673	Children at Play L5304	Lladro	Closed	220.00	450-550.
85-02-674	A Visit with Granny L5305G	Lladro	Open	275.00	515.00
85-02-675	Young Street Musicians L5306	Lladro	Closed	300.00	950.00
85-02-676	Mini Kitten L5307G	Lladro	Open	35.00	70.00
85-02-677	Mini Cat L5308G	Lladro	Open	35.00	70.00
85-02-678	Mini Cocker Spaniel Pup L5309G	Lladro	Open	35.00	70.00
85-02-679	Mini Cocker Spaniel L5310G	Lladro	Open	35.00	70.00
85-02-680	Wistful Centaur Girl L5319	Lladro	Closed	157.00	340.00
85-02-681	Demure Centaur Girl L5320	Lladro	Closed	157.00	300.00
85-02-682	Parisian Lady L5321G	Lladro	Open	192.50	325.00
85-02-683	Viennese Lady L5322G	Lladro	Open	160.00	295.00
85-02-684	Milanese Lady L5323G	Lladro	Open	180.00	340.00
85-02-685	English Lady L5324G	Lladro	Open	225.00	410.00
85-02-686	Ice Cream Vendor L5325G	Lladro	Open	380.00	650.00
85-02-687	The Tailor L5326	Lladro	Closed	335.00	500-800.
85-02-688	Nippon Lady L5327G	Lladro	Open	325.00	545.00
85-02-689	Lady Equestrian L5328	Lladro	Closed	160.00	375.00
85-02-690	Gentleman Equestrian L5329	Lladro	Closed	160.00	325.00
85-02-691	Concert Violinist L5330	Lladro	Closed	220.00	400.00
85-02-692	"La Giaconda" L5337	Lladro	Closed	350.00	450.00
86-02-693	A Stitch in Time L5344G	Lladro	Open	425.00	745.00
86-02-694	A New Hat L5345	Lladro	Closed	200.00	445.00
86-02-695	Nature Girl L5346	Lladro	Closed	450.00	900.00
86-02-697	Bedtime L5347G	Lladro	Open	300.00	545.00
86-02-698	On Guard L5350	Lladro	Closed	50.00	100.00
86-02-699	Woe is Me L5351	Lladro	Closed	45.00	70.00
86-02-700	Hindu Children L5352G	Lladro	Open	250.00	410.00
86-02-701	Eskimo Riders L5353G/M	Lladro	Open	150.00	250.00
86-02-702	A Ride in the Country L5354G	Lladro	Open	225.00	415.00
86-02-703	Consideration L5355	Lladro	Closed	100.00	225.00
86-02-704	Wolf Hound L5356	Lladro	Closed	45.00	55.00
86-02-705	Oration L5357G	Lladro	Open	170.00	275.00
86-02-706	Little Sculptor L5358	Lladro	Closed	160.00	300.00
86-02-707	El Greco L5359	Lladro	Closed	300.00	675.00
86-02-708	Sewing Circle L5360	Lladro	Closed	600.00	1000.00
86-02-709	Try This One L5361G	Lladro	Open	225.00	385.00
86-02-710	Still Life L5363G	Lladro	Open	180.00	365.00
86-02-711	Litter of Fun L5364G	Lladro	Open	275.00	465.00
86-02-712	Sunday in the Park L5365G	Lladro	Open	375.00	625.00
86-02-713	Can Can L5370	Lladro	Closed	700.00	1100-1400.
86-02-714	Family Roots L5371G	Lladro	Open	575.00	895.00
86-02-715	Lolita L5372G	Lladro	Open	120.00	200.00
86-02-716	Carmencita L5373G	Lladro	Open	120.00	200.00
86-02-717	Pepita L5374G	Lladro	Open	120.00	200.00
86-02-718	Teresita L5375G	Lladro	Open	120.00	200.00
86-02-719	This One's Mine L5376G	Lladro	Open	300.00	520.00
86-02-720	A Touch of Class L5377G	Lladro	Open	475.00	795.00
86-02-721	Time for Reflection L5378G	Lladro	Open	425.00	745.00
86-02-722	Children's Games L5379	Lladro	Closed	325.00	675.00
86-02-723	Sweet Harvest L5380	Lladro	Closed	450.00	650-750.
86-02-724	Serenade L5381	Lladro	Closed	450.00	625.00
86-02-725	Lovers Serenade L5382	Lladro	Closed	350.00	600.00
86-02-726	Petite Maiden L5383	Lladro	Closed	110.00	350.00
86-02-727	Petite Pair L5384	Lladro	Closed	225.00	400.00
86-02-728	Scarecrow & the Lady L5385G	Lladro	Open	350.00	625.00
86-02-729	St. Vincent L5387	Lladro	Closed	190.00	350.00
86-02-730	Sidewalk Serenade L5388	Lladro	Closed	750.00	1300.00
86-02-731	Deep in Thought L5389	Lladro	Closed	170.00	250.00
86-02-732	Spanish Dancer L5390	Lladro	Closed	170.00	275.00
86-02-733	A Time to Rest L5391	Lladro	Closed	170.00	225-375.
86-02-734	Balancing Act L5392	Lladro	Closed	35.00	150.00
86-02-735	Curiosity L5393	Lladro	Closed	25.00	40.00
86-02-736	Poor Puppy L5394	Lladro	Closed	25.00	40.00
86-02-737	Valencian Boy L5395G	Lladro	Closed	200.00	325.00
86-02-738	The Puppet Painter L5396G	Lladro	Open	500.00	850.00
86-02-739	The Poet L5397	Lladro	Closed	425.00	550.00
86-02-740	At the Ball L5398G	Lladro	Closed	375.00	700.00
87-02-741	Time To Rest L5399G	Lladro	Open	175.00	295.00
87-02-742	The Wanderer L5400G	Lladro	Open	150.00	245.00
87-02-743	My Best Friend L5401G	Lladro	Open	150.00	240.00
87-02-744	Desert Tour L5402	Lladro	Closed	950.00	1050.00
87-02-745	The Drummer Boy L5403	Lladro	Closed	225.00	320-550.
87-02-746	Cadet Captain L5404	Lladro	Closed	175.00	325.00
87-02-747	The Flag Bearer L5405	Lladro	Closed	200.00	400.00
87-02-748	The Bugler L5406	Lladro	Closed	175.00	300-400.
87-02-749	At Attention L5407	Lladro	Closed	175.00	325.00
87-02-750	Sunday Stroll L5408	Lladro	Closed	250.00	450.00
87-02-751	Courting Time L5409	Lladro	Closed	425.00	550.00
87-02-752	Pilar L5410	Lladro	Closed	200.00	400.00
87-02-753	Teresa L5411	Lladro	Closed	225.00	350-475.
87-02-754	Isabel L5412	Lladro	Closed	225.00	350-500.
87-02-755	Mexican Dancers L5415G	Lladro	Open	800.00	1150.00
87-02-756	In the Garden L5416G	Lladro	Open	200.00	325.00
87-02-757	Artist's Model L5417	Lladro	Closed	425.00	475.00
87-02-758	Short Eared Owl L5418	Lladro	Closed	200.00	225.00
87-02-759	Great Gray Owl L5419	Lladro	Closed	190.00	195-225.
87-02-760	Horned Owl L5420	Lladro	Closed	150.00	180.00
87-02-761	Barn Owl L5421	Lladro	Closed	120.00	145.00
87-02-762	Hawk Owl L5422	Lladro	Closed	120.00	145.00
87-02-763	Intermezzo L5424	Lladro	Closed	325.00	500.00
87-02-764	Studying in the Park L5425G/M	Lladro	Closed	675.00	950.00
87-02-765	One, Two, Three L5426G	Lladro	Open	240.00	365.00
87-02-766	Saint Nicholas L5427G	Lladro	Closed	425.00	700-900.
87-02-767	Feeding the Pigeons L5428	Lladro	Closed	490.00	700.00
87-02-768	Happy Birthday L5429G	Lladro	Open	100.00	155.00
87-02-769	Music Time L5430	Lladro	Closed	500.00	610.00
87-02-770	Midwife L5431	Lladro	Closed	175.00	400-425.
87-02-771	Monkey L5432	Lladro	Closed	60.00	100-150.
87-02-772	Kangaroo L5433	Lladro	Closed	65.00	150.00
87-02-773	Miniature Polar Bear L5434G	Lladro	Open	65.00	100.00
87-02-774	Cougar L5435	Lladro	Closed	65.00	150.00
87-02-775	Lion L5436	Lladro	Closed	50.00	150.00
87-02-776	Rhino L5437	Lladro	Closed	50.00	150.00
87-02-777	Elephant L5438	Lladro	Closed	50.00	100-150.
87-02-778	The Bride L5439G	Lladro	Open	250.00	385.00
87-02-779	Poetry of Love L5442G	Lladro	Open	500.00	825.00
87-02-780	Sleepy Trio L5443G	Lladro	Open	190.00	305.00
87-02-781	Will You Marry Me? L5447G	Lladro	Open	750.00	1250.00
87-02-782	Naptime L5448G/M	Lladro	Open	135.00	225.00
87-02-783	Goodnight L5449	Lladro	Open	225.00	350.00
87-02-784	I Hope She Does L5450G	Lladro	Open	190.00	315.00
88-02-785	Study Buddies L5451G	Lladro	Open	225.00	295.00
88-02-786	Masquerade Ball L5452G	Lladro	Open	220.00	290.00
88-02-787	For You L5453G	Lladro	Open	450.00	595.00
88-02-788	For Me? L5454G	Lladro	Open	290.00	380.00
88-02-789	Bashful Bather L5455G	Lladro	Open	150.00	190.00
88-02-790	New Playmates L5456G	Lladro	Open	160.00	210.00
88-02-791	Bedtime Story L5457G	Lladro	Open	275.00	355.00
88-02-792	A Barrow of Fun L5460G	Lladro	Open	370.00	485.00
88-02-793	Koala Love L5461G	Lladro	Open	115.00	150.00
88-02-794	Practice Makes Perfect L5462G	Lladro	Open	375.00	495.00
88-02-795	Look At Me! L5465G	Lladro	Open	375.00	475.00
88-02-796	Chit-Chat L5466G	Lladro	Open	150.00	190.00
88-02-797	May Flowers L5467G	Lladro	Open	160.00	195.00
88-02-798	Who's The Fairest? L5468G	Lladro	Open	150.00	195.00
88-02-799	Lambkins L5469G	Lladro	Open	150.00	210.00
88-02-800	Tea Time L5470G	Lladro	Open	280.00	360.00
88-02-801	Sad Sax L5471G	Lladro	Open	175.00	205.00
88-02-802	Circus Sam L5472G	Lladro	Open	175.00	205.00
88-02-803	How You've Grown! L5474G	Lladro	Open	180.00	235.00
88-02-804	A Lesson Shared L5475G	Lladro	Open	150.00	180.00
88-02-805	St. Joseph L5476G	Lladro	Open	210.00	270.00
88-02-806	Mary L5477G	Lladro	Open	130.00	165.00
88-02-807	Baby Jesus L5478G	Lladro	Open	55.00	75.00
88-02-808	King Melchior L5479G	Lladro	Open	210.00	265.00
88-02-809	King Gaspar L5480G	Lladro	Open	210.00	265.00
88-02-810	King Balthasar L5481G	Lladro	Open	210.00	265.00
88-02-811	Ox L5482G	Lladro	Open	125.00	165.00
88-02-812	Donkey L5483G	Lladro	Open	125.00	165.00
88-02-813	Lost Lamb L5484G	Lladro	Open	100.00	140.00
88-02-814	Shepherd Boy L5485G	Lladro	Open	140.00	180.00
88-02-815	Debutantes L5486G	Lladro	Open	490.00	695.00
88-02-816	Ingenue L5487G	Lladro	Open	110.00	140.00
88-02-817	Sandcastles L5488G	Lladro	Open	160.00	220.00
88-02-818	Justice L5489G	Lladro	Open	675.00	825.00
88-02-819	Flor Maria L5490G	Lladro	Open	500.00	635.00
88-02-820	Heavenly Strings L5491G	Lladro	Open	140.00	185.00
88-02-821	Heavenly Cellist L5492G	Lladro	Open	240.00	315.00
88-02-822	Angel with Lute L5493G	Lladro	Open	140.00	185.00
88-02-823	Angel with Clarinet L5494G	Lladro	Open	140.00	185.00
88-02-824	Angelic Choir L5495G	Lladro	Open	300.00	395.00
88-02-825	Recital L5496G	Lladro	Open	190.00	265.00
88-02-826	Dress Rehearsal L5497G	Lladro	Open	290.00	385.00
88-02-827	Opening Night L5498G	Lladro	Open	190.00	260.00
88-02-828	Pretty Ballerina L5499G	Lladro	Open	190.00	260.00
88-02-829	Prayerful Moment (blue) L5500G	Lladro	Open	90.00	110.00
88-02-830	Time to Sew (blue) L5501G	Lladro	Open	90.00	110.00
88-02-831	Meditation (blue) L5502G	Lladro	Open	90.00	110.00
88-02-832	Hurry Now L5503G	Lladro	Open	180.00	240.00
89-02-833	Flowers for Sale L5537G	Lladro	Open	1200.00	1550.00

FIGURINES

Company		Series			
Number	Name	Artist	Edition Limit	Issue Price	Quote
89-02-834	Puppy Dog Tails L5539	Lladro	Open	1200.00	1550.00
89-02-835	Melancholy w/base L5542	Lladro	Open	375.00	440.00
89-02-836	"Hello Flowers" L5543	Lladro	Open	385.00	485.00
89-02-837	Reaching the Goal L5546G	Lladro	Open	215.00	275.00
89-02-838	Only the Beginning L5547G	Lladro	Open	215.00	275.00
89-02-839	Pretty Posies L5548	Lladro	Open	425.00	530.00
89-02-840	My New Pet L5549G	Lladro	Open	150.00	185.00
89-02-841	Serene Moment (blue) L5550G	Lladro	Open	115.00	150.00
89-02-842	Call to Prayer (blue) L5551G	Lladro	Open	100.00	135.00
89-02-843	Morning Chores (blue) L5552G	Lladro	Open	115.00	140.00
89-02-844	Wild Goose Chase L5553G	Lladro	Open	175.00	230.00
89-02-845	Pretty and Prim L5554G	Lladro	Open	215.00	270.00
89-02-846	"Let's Make Up" L5555G	Lladro	Open	215.00	265.00
89-02-847	Daddy's Girl L5584G	Lladro	Open	315.00	395.00
89-02-848	Fine Melody w/base L5585G	Lladro	Open	225.00	295.00
89-02-849	Sad Note w/base L5586G	Lladro	Open	185.00	275.00
89-02-850	Wedding Cake L5587G	Lladro	Open	595.00	750.00
89-02-851	Blustery Day L5588G	Lladro	Open	185.00	230.00
89-02-852	Pretty Pose L5589G	Lladro	Open	185.00	230.00
89-02-853	Spring Breeze L5590G	Lladro	Open	185.00	230.00
89-02-854	Garden Treasures L5591G	Lladro	Open	185.00	230.00
89-02-855	Male Siamese Dancer L5592G	Lladro	Open	345.00	420.00
89-02-856	Siamese Dancer L5593G	Lladro	Open	345.00	420.00
89-02-857	Playful Romp L5594G	Lladro	Open	215.00	270.00
89-02-858	Joy in a Basket L5595G	Lladro	Open	215.00	270.00
89-02-859	A Gift of Love L5596G	Lladro	Open	400.00	495.00
89-02-860	Summer Soiree L5597G	Lladro	Open	150.00	180.00
89-02-861	Bridesmaid L5598G	Lladro	Open	150.00	180.00
89-02-862	Coquette L5599G	Lladro	Open	150.00	180.00
89-02-863	The Blues w/base L5600G	Lladro	Open	265.00	340.00
89-02-864	Ole L5601G	Lladro	Open	365.00	450.00
89-02-865	Close To My Heart L5603G	Lladro	Open	125.00	165.00
89-02-866	Spring Token L5604G	Lladro	Open	175.00	230.00
89-02-867	Floral Treasures L5605G	Lladro	Open	195.00	250.00
89-02-868	Quiet Evening L5606G	Lladro	Open	125.00	165.00
89-02-869	Calling A Friend L5607G	Lladro	Open	125.00	165.00
89-02-870	Baby Doll L5608G	Lladro	Open	150.00	180.00
89-02-871	Playful Friends L5609G	Lladro	Open	135.00	170.00
89-02-872	Star Struck w/base L5610G	Lladro	Open	335.00	420.00
89-02-873	Sad Clown w/base L5611G	Lladro	Open	335.00	420.00
89-02-874	Reflecting w/base L5612G	Lladro	Open	335.00	420.00
90-02-875	Cat Nap L5640 G	Lladro	Open	125.00	145.00
90-02-876	The King's Guard w/base L5642 G	Lladro	Open	950.00	1100.00
90-02-877	Cathy L5643G	Lladro	Open	200.00	335.00
90-02-878	Susan L5644 G	Lladro	Open	190.00	215.00
90-02-879	Elizabeth L5645 G	Lladro	Open	190.00	215.00
90-02-880	Cindy L5646 G	Lladro	Open	190.00	215.00
90-02-881	Sara L5647 G	Lladro	Open	200.00	230.00
90-02-882	Courtney L5648 G	Lladro	Open	200.00	230.00
90-02-883	Nothing To Do L5649 G	Lladro	Open	190.00	220.00
90-02-884	Anticipation L5650 G	Lladro	Open	300.00	340.00
90-02-885	Musical Muse L5651 G	Lladro	Open	375.00	440.00
90-02-886	Venetian Carnival L5658 G	Lladro	Open	500.00	575.00
90-02-887	Barnyard Scene L5659 G	Lladro	Open	200.00	235.00
90-02-888	Sunning In Ipanema L5660 G	Lladro	Open	370.00	420.00
90-02-889	Traveling Artist L5661 G	Lladro	Open	250.00	290.00
90-02-890	May Dance L5662 G	Lladro	Open	170.00	190.00
90-02-891	Spring Dance L5663 G	Lladro	Open	170.00	195.00
90-02-892	Giddy Up L5664 G	Lladro	Open	190.00	230.00
90-02-893	Hang On! L5665 G	Lladro	Open	225.00	260.00
90-02-894	Trino At The Beach L5666 G	Lladro	Open	390.00	460.00
90-02-895	Valencian Harvest L5668 G	Lladro	Open	175.00	205.00
90-02-896	Valencian FLowers L5669 G	Lladro	Open	370.00	420.00
90-02-897	Valencian Beauty L5670 G	Lladro	Open	175.00	205.00
90-02-898	Little Dutch Gardener L5671 G	Lladro	Open	400.00	475.00
90-02-899	Hi There! L5672 G	Lladro	Open	450.00	520.00
90-02-900	A Quiet Moment L5673 G	Lladro	Open	450.00	520.00
90-02-901	A Faun And A Friend L5674 G	Lladro	Open	450.00	520.00
90-02-902	Tee Time L5675 G	Lladro	Open	280.00	315.00
90-02-903	Wandering Minstrel L5676 G	Lladro	Open	270.00	310.00
90-02-904	Twilight Years L5677 G	Lladro	Open	370.00	420.00
90-02-905	I Feel Pretty L5678 G	Lladro	Open	190.00	230.00
90-02-906	In No Hurry L5679 G	Lladro	Open	550.00	640.00
90-02-907	Traveling In Style L5680 G	Lladro	Open	425.00	495.00
90-02-908	On The Road L5681 G	Lladro	Closed	320.00	345.00
90-02-909	Breezy Afternoon L5682 G/M	Lladro	Open	180.00	195.00
90-02-910	Beautiful Burro L5683 G	Lladro	Open	280.00	325.00
90-02-911	Barnyard Reflections L5684 G	Lladro	Open	460.00	525.00
90-02-912	Promenade L5685 G	Lladro	Open	275.00	325.00
90-02-913	On The Avenue L5686 G	Lladro	Open	275.00	325.00
90-02-914	Afternoon Stroll L5687 G	Lladro	Open	275.00	325.00
90-02-915	Dog's Best Friend L5688 G	Lladro	Open	250.00	295.00
90-02-916	Can I Help? L5689 G	Lladro	Open	250.00	295.00
90-02-917	Marshland Mates w/base L5691 G	Lladro	Open	950.00	1200.00
90-02-918	Street Harmonies w/base L5692 G	Lladro	Open	3200.00	3750.00
90-02-919	Circus Serenade L5694 G	Lladro	Open	300.00	360.00
90-02-920	Concertina L5695 G	Lladro	Open	300.00	360.00
90-02-921	Mandolin Serenade L5696 G	Lladro	Open	300.00	360.00
90-02-922	Over The Clouds L5697 G	Lladro	Open	275.00	310.00
90-02-923	Don't Look Down L5698 G	Lladro	Open	330.00	375.00
90-02-924	Sitting Pretty L5699 G	Lladro	Open	300.00	340.00
90-02-925	Southern Charm L5700 G	Lladro	Open	675.00	1025.00
90-02-926	Just A Little Kiss L5701 G	Lladro	Open	320.00	375.00
90-02-927	Back To School L5702 G	Lladro	Open	350.00	405.00
90-02-928	Behave! L5703 G	Lladro	Open	230.00	265.00
90-02-929	Swan Song L5704 G	Lladro	Open	350.00	410.00
90-02-930	The Swan And The Princess L5705 G	Lladro	Open	350.00	410.00
90-02-931	We Can't Play L5706 G	Lladro	Open	200.00	235.00
90-02-932	After School L5707G	Lladro	Open	280.00	315.00
90-02-933	My First Class L5708 G	Lladro	Open	280.00	315.00
90-02-934	Between Classes L5709 G	Lladro	Open	280.00	315.00
90-02-935	Fantasy Friend L5710 G	Lladro	Open	420.00	495.00
90-02-936	A Christmas Wish L5711 G	Lladro	Open	350.00	410.00
90-02-937	Sleepy Kitten L5712 G	Lladro	Open	110.00	130.00
90-02-938	The Snow Man L5713 G	Lladro	Open	300.00	350.00
90-02-939	First Ballet L5714 G	Lladro	Open	370.00	420.00
90-02-940	Mommy, it's Cold!L5715G	Lladro	Open	360.00	415.00
90-02-941	Land of The Giants L5716 G	Lladro	Open	275.00	315.00
90-02-942	Rock A Bye Baby L5717 G	Lladro	Open	300.00	350.00
90-02-943	Sharing Secrets L5720 G	Lladro	Open	290.00	335.00
90-02-944	Once Upon A Time L5721 G	Lladro	Open	550.00	615.00
90-02-945	Follow Me L5722 G	Lladro	Open	140.00	160.00
90-02-946	Heavenly Chimes L5723 G	Lladro	Open	100.00	120.00
90-02-947	Angelic Voice L5724 G	Lladro	Open	125.00	145.00
90-02-948	Making A Wish L5725 G	Lladro	Open	125.00	145.00
90-02-949	Sweep Away The Clouds L5726 G	Lladro	Open	125.00	145.00
90-02-950	Angel Care L5727 G	Lladro	Open	190.00	210.00
90-02-951	Heavenly Dreamer L5728 G	Lladro	Open	100.00	120.00
91-02-952	Carousel Charm L5731G	Lladro	Open	1700.00	1850.00
91-02-953	Carousel Canter L5732G	Lladro	Open	1700.00	1850.00
91-02-954	Horticulturist L5733G	Lladro	Open	450.00	495.00
91-02-955	Pilgrim Couple L5734G	Lladro	Open	490.00	525.00
91-02-956	Big Sister L5735G	Lladro	Open	650.00	685.00
91-02-957	Puppet Show L5736G	Lladro	Open	280.00	295.00
91-02-958	Little Prince L5737G	Lladro	Open	295.00	315.00
91-02-959	Best Foot Forward L5738G	Lladro	Open	280.00	305.00
91-02-960	Lap Full Of Love L5739G	Lladro	Open	275.00	295.00
91-02-961	Alice In Wonderland L5740G	Lladro	Open	440.00	485.00
91-02-962	Dancing Class L5741G	Lladro	Open	340.00	365.00
91-02-963	Bridal Portrait L5742G	Lladro	Open	480.00	525.00
91-02-964	Don't Forget Me L5743G	Lladro	Open	150.00	160.00
91-02-965	Bull & Donkey L5744G	Lladro	Open	250.00	275.00
91-02-966	Baby Jesus L5745G	Lladro	Open	170.00	185.00
91-02-967	St. Joseph L5746G	Lladro	Open	350.00	375.00
91-02-968	Mary L5747G	Lladro	Open	275.00	295.00
91-02-969	Shepherd Girl L5748G	Lladro	Open	150.00	165.00
91-02-970	Shepherd Boy L5749G	Lladro	Open	225.00	245.00
91-02-971	Little Lamb L5750G	Lladro	Open	40.00	42.00
91-02-972	Walk With Father L5751G	Lladro	Open	375.00	410.00
91-02-973	Little Virgin L5752G	Lladro	Open	295.00	325.00
91-02-974	Hold Her Still L5753G	Lladro	Open	650.00	695.00
91-02-975	Singapore Dancers L5754G	Lladro	Open	950.00	1025.00
91-02-976	Claudette L5755G	Lladro	Open	265.00	285.00
91-02-977	Ashley L5756G	Lladro	Open	265.00	290.00
91-02-978	Beautiful Tresses L5757G	Lladro	Open	725.00	785.00
91-02-979	Sunday Best L5758G	Lladro	Open	725.00	785.00
91-02-980	Presto! L5759G	Lladro	Open	275.00	295.00
91-02-981	Interrupted Nap L5760G	Lladro	Open	325.00	350.00
91-02-982	Out For A Romp L5761G	Lladro	Open	375.00	410.00
91-02-983	Checking The Time L5762G	Lladro	Open	560.00	595.00
91-02-984	Musical Partners L5763G	Lladro	Open	625.00	675.00
91-02-985	Seeds Of Laughter L5764G	Lladro	Open	525.00	575.00
91-02-986	Hats Off To Fun L5765G	Lladro	Open	475.00	510.00
91-02-987	Charming Duet L5766G	Lladro	Open	575.00	625.00
91-02-988	First Sampler L5767G	Lladro	Open	625.00	680.00
91-02-989	Academy Days L5768G	Lladro	Open	280.00	310.00
91-02-990	Faithful Steed L5769G	Lladro	Open	370.00	395.00
91-02-991	Out For A Spin L5770G	Lladro	Open	390.00	420.00
91-02-992	The Magic Of Laughter L5771G	Lladro	Open	950.00	995.00
91-02-993	Little Dreamers L5772G/M	Lladro	Open	230.00	240.00
91-02-994	Graceful Offering L5773G	Lladro	Open	850.00	895.00
91-02-995	Nature's Gifts L5774G	Lladro	Open	900.00	975.00
91-02-996	Gift Of Beauty L5775G	Lladro	Open	850.00	895.00
91-02-997	Lover's Paradise L5779G	Lladro	Open	2250.00	2450.00
91-02-998	Walking The Fields L5780G	Lladro	Open	725.00	795.00
91-02-999	Not Too Close L5781G	Lladro	Open	365.00	395.00
91-02-1000	My Chores L5782G	Lladro	Open	325.00	355.00
91-02-1001	Special Delivery L5783G	Lladro	Open	525.00	550.00
91-02-1002	A Cradle Of Kittens L5784G	Lladro	Open	360.00	385.00
91-02-1003	Ocean Beauty L5785G	Lladro	Open	625.00	665.00
91-02-1004	Story Hour L5786G	Lladro	Open	550.00	585.00
91-02-1005	Sophisticate L5787G	Lladro	Open	185.00	195.00
91-02-1006	Talk Of The Town L5788G	Lladro	Open	185.00	195.00
91-02-1007	The Flirt L5789G	Lladro	Open	185.00	195.00
91-02-1008	Carefree L5790G	Lladro	Open	300.00	325.00
91-02-1009	Fairy Godmother L5791G	Lladro	Open	375.00	410.00
91-02-1010	Reverent Moment L5792G	Lladro	Open	295.00	320.00
91-02-1011	Precocious Ballerina L5793G	Lladro	Open	575.00	625.00
91-02-1012	Precious Cargo L5794G	Lladro	Open	460.00	495.00
91-02-1013	Floral Getaway L5795G	Lladro	Open	625.00	685.00
91-02-1014	Holy Night L5796G	Lladro	Open	330.00	360.00
91-02-1015	Come Out And Play L5797G	Lladro	Open	275.00	295.00
91-02-1016	Milkmaid L5798G	Lladro	Open	450.00	495.00
91-02-1017	Shall We Dance? L5799G	Lladro	Open	600.00	650.00
91-02-1018	Elegant Promenade L5802G	Lladro	Open	775.00	825.00
91-02-1019	Playing Tag L5804G	Lladro	Open	170.00	190.00
91-02-1020	Tumbling L5805G/M	Lladro	Open	130.00	140.00
91-02-1021	Tickling L5806G/M	Lladro	Open	130.00	145.00
91-02-1022	My Puppies L5807G	Lladro	Open	325.00	360.00
91-02-1023	Musically Inclined L5810G	Lladro	Open	235.00	250.00
91-02-1024	Littlest Clown L5811G	Lladro	Open	225.00	240.00
91-02-1025	Tired Friend L5812G	Lladro	Open	225.00	245.00
91-02-1026	Having A Ball L5813G	Lladro	Open	225.00	240.00
91-02-1027	Curtain Call L5814G/M	Lladro	Open	490.00	520.00
91-02-1028	In Full Relave L5815G/M	Lladro	Open	490.00	520.00
91-02-1029	Prima Ballerina L5816G/M	Lladro	Open	490.00	520.00
91-02-1030	Backstage Preparation L5817G/M	Lladro	Open	490.00	520.00
91-02-1031	On Her Toes L5818G/M	Lladro	Open	490.00	520.00
91-02-1032	Allegory Of Liberty L5819G	Lladro	Open	1950.00	2100.00
91-02-1033	Dance Of Love L5820G	Lladro	Open	575.00	625.00
91-02-1034	Minstrel's Love L5821G	Lladro	Open	525.00	575.00
91-02-1035	Little Unicorn L5826G/M	Lladro	Open	275.00	295.00
91-02-1036	I've Got It L5827G	Lladro	Open	170.00	180.00
91-02-1037	Next At Bat L5828G	Lladro	Open	170.00	180.00
91-02-1038	Jazz Horn L5832G	Lladro	Open	295.00	295.00
91-02-1039	Jazz Sax L5833G	Lladro	Open	295.00	295.00
91-02-1040	Jazz Bass L5834G	Lladro	Open	395.00	405.00
91-02-1041	I Do L5835G	Lladro	Open	165.00	175.00
91-02-1042	Sharing Sweets L5836G	Lladro	Open	220.00	245.00
91-02-1043	Sing With Me L5837G	Lladro	Open	240.00	250.00
91-02-1044	On The Move L5838G	Lladro	Open	340.00	365.00
92-02-1045	A Quiet Afternoon L5843G	Lladro	Open	1050.00	1100.00
92-02-1046	Flirtatious Jester L5844G	Lladro	Open	890.00	925.00
92-02-1047	Dressing The Baby L5845G	Lladro	Open	295.00	295.00
92-02-1048	All Tuckered Out L5846G/M	Lladro	Open	220.00	225.00
92-02-1049	The Loving Family L5848G	Lladro	Open	950.00	985.00
92-02-1050	Inspiring Muse L5850G	Lladro	Open	1200.00	1250.00
92-02-1051	Feathered Fantasy L5851G	Lladro	Open	1200.00	1250.00
92-02-1052	Easter Bonnets L5852G	Lladro	Open	265.00	275.00
92-02-1053	Floral Admiration L5853G	Lladro	Open	690.00	725.00
92-02-1054	Floral Fantasy L5854G	Lladro	Open	690.00	710.00
92-02-1055	Afternoon Jaunt L5855G	Lladro	Open	420.00	440.00
92-02-1056	Circus Concert L5856G	Lladro	Open	570.00	585.00
92-02-1057	Grand Entrance L5857G	Lladro	Open	265.00	275.00
92-02-1058	Waiting to Dance L5858G	Lladro	Open	295.00	310.00
92-02-1059	At The Ball L5859G	Lladro	Open	295.00	295.00

Company Number	Name	Series Artist	Edition Limit	Issue Price	Quote
92-02-1060	Fairy Garland L5860G	Lladro	Open	630.00	650.00
92-02-1061	Fairy Flowers L5861G	Lladro	Open	630.00	655.00
92-02-1062	Fragrant Bouquet L5862G	Lladro	Open	350.00	360.00
92-02-1063	Dressing For The Ballet L5865G	Lladro	Open	395.00	415.00
92-02-1064	Final Touches L5866G	Lladro	Open	395.00	415.00
92-02-1065	Serene Valenciana L5867G	Lladro	Open	365.00	385.00
92-02-1066	Loving Valenciana L5868G	Lladro	Open	365.00	385.00
92-02-1067	Fallas Queen L5869G	Lladro	Open	420.00	440.00
92-02-1068	Olympic Torch w/Fantasy Logo L5870G	Lladro	Open	165.00	145.00
92-02-1069	Olympic Champion w/Fantasy Logo L5871G	Lladro	Open	165.00	145.00
92-02-1070	Olympic Pride w/Fantasy Logo L5872G	Lladro	Open	165.00	495.00
92-02-1071	Modern Mother L5873G	Lladro	Open	325.00	335.00
92-02-1072	Off We Go L5874G	Lladro	Open	365.00	385.00
92-02-1073	Guest Of Honor L5877G	Lladro	Open	195.00	195.00
92-02-1074	Sister's Pride L5878G	Lladro	Open	595.00	615.00
92-02-1075	Shot On Goal L5879G	Lladro	Open	1100.00	1150.00
92-02-1076	Playful Unicorn L5880G	Lladro	Open	295.00	295.00
92-02-1077	Playful Unicorn L5880M	Lladro	Open	295.00	310.00
92-02-1078	Mischievous Mouse L5881G	Lladro	Open	285.00	295.00
92-02-1079	Restful Mouse L5882G	Lladro	Open	285.00	295.00
92-02-1080	Loving Mouse L5883G	Lladro	Open	285.00	295.00
92-02-1081	From This Day Forward L5885G	Lladro	Open	265.00	265.00
92-02-1082	Hippity Hop L5886G	Lladro	Open	95.00	95.00
92-02-1083	Washing Up L5887G	Lladro	Open	95.00	95.00
92-02-1084	That Tickles! L5888G	Lladro	Open	95.00	95.00
92-02-1085	Snack Time L5889G	Lladro	Open	95.00	95.00
92-02-1086	The Aviator L5891G	Lladro	Open	375.00	380.00
92-02-1087	Circus Magic L5892G	Lladro	Open	470.00	495.00
92-02-1088	Friendship In Bloom L5893G	Lladro	Open	650.00	685.00
92-02-1089	Precious Petals L5894G	Lladro	Open	395.00	415.00
92-02-1090	Bouquet of Blossoms L5895G	Lladro	Open	295.00	295.00
92-02-1091	The Loaves & Fishes L5896G	Lladro	Open	695.00	710.00
92-02-1092	Trimming The Tree L5897G	Lladro	Open	900.00	925.00
92-02-1093	Spring Splendor L5898G	Lladro	Open	440.00	450.00
92-02-1094	Just One More L5899G	Lladro	Open	450.00	460.00
92-02-1095	Sleep Tight L5900G	Lladro	Open	450.00	465.00
92-02-1096	Surprise L5901G	Lladro	Open	325.00	335.00
92-02-1097	Easter Bunnies L5902G	Lladro	Open	240.00	250.00
92-02-1098	Down The Aisle L5903G	Lladro	Open	295.00	295.00
92-02-1099	Sleeping Bunny L5904G	Lladro	Open	75.00	75.00
92-02-1100	Attentive Bunny L5905G	Lladro	Open	75.00	75.00
92-02-1101	Preening Bunny L5906G	Lladro	Open	75.00	75.00
92-02-1102	Sitting Bunny L5907G	Lladro	Open	75.00	75.00
92-02-1103	Just A Little More L5908G	Lladro	Open	370.00	380.00
92-02-1104	All Dressed Up L5909G	Lladro	Open	440.00	450.00
92-02-1105	Making A Wish L5910G	Lladro	Open	790.00	825.00
92-02-1106	Swans Take Flight L5912G	Lladro	Open	2850.00	2950.00
92-02-1107	Rose Ballet L5919G	Lladro	Open	210.00	215.00
92-02-1109	Swan Ballet L5920G	Lladro	Open	210.00	215.00
92-02-1110	Take Your Medicine L5921G	Lladro	Open	360.00	370.00
92-02-1111	Jazz Clarinet L5928G	Lladro	Open	295.00	295.00
92-02-1112	Jazz Drums L5929G	Lladro	Open	595.00	610.00
92-02-1113	Jazz Duo L5930G	Lladro	Open	795.00	810.00
93-02-1114	The Ten Commandments w/Base L5933G	Lladro	Open	930.00	930.00
93-02-1115	The Holy Teacher L5934G	Lladro	Open	375.00	375.00
93-02-1116	Nutcracker Suite L5935G	Lladro	Open	620.00	620.00
93-02-1117	Little Skipper L5936G	Lladro	Open	320.00	320.00
93-02-1118	Riding The Waves L5941G	Lladro	Open	405.00	405.00
93-02-1119	World of Fantasy L5943G	Lladro	Open	295.00	295.00
93-02-1120	The Great Adventure L5944G	Lladro	Open	325.00	325.00
93-02-1121	A Mother's Way L5946G	Lladro	Open	1350.00	1350.00
93-02-1122	General Practioner L5947G	Lladro	Open	360.00	360.00
93-02-1123	Physician L5948G	Lladro	Open	360.00	360.00
93-02-1124	Angel Candleholder w/Lyre L5949G	Lladro	Open	295.00	295.00
93-02-1125	Angel Candleholder w/Tambourine L5950G	Lladro	Open	295.00	295.00
93-02-1126	Sounds of Summer L5953G	Lladro	Open	125.00	125.00
93-02-1127	Sounds of Winter L5954G	Lladro	Open	125.00	125.00
93-02-1128	Sounds of Fall L5955G	Lladro	Open	125.00	125.00
93-02-1129	Sounds of Spring L5956G	Lladro	Open	125.00	125.00
93-02-1130	The Glass Slipper L5957G	Lladro	Open	475.00	475.00
93-02-1131	Country Ride w/Base L5958G	Lladro	Open	2850.00	2850.00
93-02-1132	It's Your Turn L5959G	Lladro	Open	365.00	365.00
93-02-1133	On Patrol L5960G	Lladro	Open	395.00	395.00
93-02-1134	The Great Teacher w/Base L5961G	Lladro	Open	850.00	850.00
93-02-1135	The Clipper Ship w/Base L5965M	Lladro	Open	240.00	240.00
93-02-1136	Flowers Forever w/Base L5966G	Lladro	Open	4150.00	4150.00
93-02-1137	Honeymoon Ride w/Base L5968G	Lladro	Open	2750.00	2750.00
93-02-1138	A Special Toy L5971G	Lladro	Open	815.00	815.00
93-02-1139	Before the Dance w/Base L5972G/M	Lladro	Open	3550.00	3550.00
93-02-1140	Family Outing w/Base L5974G	Lladro	Open	4275.00	4275.00
93-02-1141	Up and Away w/Base L5975G	Lladro	Open	2850.00	2850.00
93-02-1142	The Fireman L5976G	Lladro	Open	395.00	395.00
93-02-1143	Revelation w/base (white) L5977G	Lladro	Open	310.00	310.00
93-02-1144	Revelation w/base (black) L5978M	Lladro	Open	310.00	310.00
93-02-1145	Revelation w/base (sand) L5979M	Lladro	Open	310.00	310.00
93-02-1146	The Past w/base (white) L5980G	Lladro	Open	310.00	310.00
93-02-1147	The Past w/base (black) L5981M	Lladro	Open	310.00	310.00
93-02-1148	The Past w/base (sand) L5982M	Lladro	Open	310.00	310.00
93-02-1149	Beauty w/base (white) L5983G	Lladro	Open	310.00	310.00
93-02-1150	Beauty w/base (black) L5984M	Lladro	Open	310.00	310.00
93-02-1151	Beauty w/base (sand) L5985M	Lladro	Open	310.00	310.00
93-02-1152	Sunday Sermon L5986G	Lladro	Open	425.00	425.00
93-02-1153	Talk to Me L5987G	Lladro	Open	145.00	145.00
93-02-1154	Taking Time L5988G	Lladro	Open	145.00	145.00
93-02-1155	A Mother's Touch L5989G	Lladro	Open	470.00	470.00
93-02-1156	Thoughtful Caress L5990G	Lladro	Open	225.00	225.00
93-02-1157	Love Story L5991G	Lladro	Open	2800.00	2800.00
93-02-1158	Unicorn and Friend L5993G/M	Lladro	Open	355.00	355.00
93-02-1159	Meet My Friend L5994G	Lladro	Open	695.00	695.00
93-02-1160	Soft Meow L5995G	Lladro	Open	480.00	480.00
93-02-1161	Bless the Child L5996G	Lladro	Open	465.00	465.00
93-02-1162	One More Try L5997G	Lladro	Open	715.00	715.00
93-02-1163	My Dad L6001G	Lladro	Open	550.00	550.00
93-02-1164	Down You Go L6002G	Lladro	Open	815.00	815.00
93-02-1165	Ready To Learn L6003G	Lladro	Open	650.00	650.00
93-02-1166	Bar Mitzvah Day L6004G	Lladro	Open	395.00	395.00
93-02-1167	Christening Day w/Base L6005G	Lladro	Open	1425.00	1425.00
93-02-1168	Oriental Colonade w/Base L6006G	Lladro	Open	1875.00	1875.00
93-02-1169	The Goddess & the Unicorn w/Base L6007G	Lladro	Open	1675.00	1675.00
93-02-1170	Joyful Event L6008G	Lladro	Open	825.00	825.00
93-02-1171	Monday's Child (Boy) L6011G	Lladro	Open	245.00	245.00
93-02-1172	Monday's Child (Girl) L6012G	Lladro	Open	260.00	260.00
93-02-1173	Tuesday's Child (Boy) L6013G	Lladro	Open	225.00	225.00
93-02-1174	Tuesday's Child (Girl) L6014G	Lladro	Open	245.00	245.00
93-02-1175	Wednesday's Child (Boy) L6015G	Lladro	Open	245.00	245.00
93-02-1176	Wednesday's Child (Girl) L6016G	Lladro	Open	245.00	245.00
93-02-1177	Thursday's Child (Boy) L6017G	Lladro	Open	225.00	225.00
93-02-1178	Thursday's Child (Girl) L6018G	Lladro	Open	245.00	245.00
93-02-1179	Friday's Child (Boy) L6019G	Lladro	Open	225.00	225.00
93-02-1180	Friday's Child (Girl) L6020G	Lladro	Open	225.00	225.00
93-02-1181	Saturday's Child (Boy) L6021G	Lladro	Open	245.00	245.00
93-02-1182	Saturday's Child (Girl) L6022G	Lladro	Open	245.00	245.00
93-02-1183	Sunday's Child (Boy) L6023G	Lladro	Open	225.00	225.00
93-02-1184	Sunday's Child (Girl) L6024G	Lladro	Open	225.00	225.00
93-02-1185	Barnyard See Saw L6025G	Lladro	Open	500.00	500.00
93-02-1186	My Turn L6026G	Lladro	Open	515.00	515.00
93-02-1187	Hanukah Lights L6027G	Lladro	Open	345.00	345.00
93-02-1188	Mazel Tov! L6028G	Lladro	Open	380.00	380.00
93-02-1189	Hebrew Scholar L6029G	Lladro	Open	225.00	225.00
93-02-1190	On The Go L6031G	Lladro	Open	475.00	475.00
93-02-1191	On The Green L6032G	Lladro	Open	645.00	645.00
93-02-1192	Monkey Business L6034G	Lladro	Open	745.00	745.00
93-02-1193	Young Princess L6036G	Lladro	Open	240.00	240.00
85-02-1194	Lladro Plaque L7116	Lladro	Open	17.50	18.00
92-02-1195	Special Torch L7513G	Lladro	Open	165.00	165.00
92-02-1196	Special Champion L7514G	Lladro	Open	165.00	165.00
92-02-1197	Special Pride L7515G	Lladro	Open	165.00	165.00
93-02-1198	Courage L7522G	Lladro	Open	195.00	195.00
89-02-1199	Starting Forward/Lolo L7605G	Lladro	Open	185.00	190.00
92-02-1200	Garden Song L7618G	Lladro	Open	295.00	295.00
91-02-1201	Garden Classic L7617G	Lladro	Closed	295.00	295.00
Lladro		**Limited Edition**			
71-03-001	Hamlet LL 1144	Lladro	Closed	250.00	2500.00
71-03-002	Othello and Desdemona LL 1145	Lladro	Closed	275.00	2500-3300.
71-03-003	Antique Auto LL1146	Lladro	Closed	1000.00	16000.00
73-03-004	Sea Birds LL1174	Lladro	Closed	600.00	2750.00
71-03-005	Floral LL1184	Lladro	Closed	400.00	2200.00
71-03-006	Floral LL1185	Lladro	Closed	475.00	1800.00
71-03-007	Floral LL1186	Lladro	Closed	575.00	2200.00
72-03-008	Eagles LL1189	Lladro	Closed	900.00	3200.00
72-03-009	Sea Birds with Nest LL1194	Lladro	Closed	600.00	2750.00
72-03-010	Turkey Group LL1196	Lladro	Closed	650.00	1800.00
72-03-011	Peace LL1202	Lladro	Closed	550.00	7500.00
72-03-012	Eagle Owl LL1223	Lladro	Closed	450.00	1050.00
72-03-013	Hansom Carriage LL1225	Lladro	Closed	1250.00	10-12000
73-03-014	Hunting Scene LL1238	Lladro	Closed	800.00	3000.00
73-03-015	Turtle Doves LL1240	Lladro	Closed	500.00	2300-2500.
73-03-016	The Forest LL1243	Lladro	Closed	1250.00	3300.00
74-03-017	Soccer Players LL1266	Lladro	Closed	2000.00	7500.00
74-03-018	Man From LaMancha LL1269	Lladro	Closed	700.00	5000.00
74-03-019	Queen Elizabeth II LL 1275	Lladro	Closed	3650.00	4600.00
74-03-020	Judge LL1281	Lladro	Closed	325.00	1400.00
74-03-021	The Hunt LL1308	Lladro	Closed	4750.00	6900.00
74-03-022	Ducks at Pond LL1317	Lladro	Closed	4250.00	6900.00
76-03-023	Impossible Dream LL1318	Lladro	Closed	2400.00	5000.00
76-03-024	Comforting Baby LL1329	Lladro	Closed	700.00	1050.00
76-03-025	Mountain Country Lady LL1330	Lladro	Closed	900.00	1850.00
76-03-026	My Baby LL1331	Lladro	Closed	550.00	2000.00
78-03-027	Flight of Gazelles LL1352	Lladro	Closed	2450.00	3100.00
78-03-028	Car in Trouble LL1375	Lladro	Closed	3000.00	7600.00
78-03-029	Fearful Flight LL1377	Lladro	750	7000.00	14200.00
78-03-030	Henry VIII LL 1384	Lladro	1,200	650.00	995.00
81-03-031	Venus and Cupid LL1392	Lladro	Closed	1100.00	2800.00
82-03-032	First Date LL1393	Lladro	1,500	3800.00	5900.00
82-03-033	Columbus LL 1432	Lladro	Closed	575.00	1100-1500.
83-03-034	Venetian Serenade LL 1433	Lladro	Closed	2600.00	3750.00
85-03-035	Festival in Valencia LL1457	Lladro	3,000	1475.00	2350.00
85-03-036	Camelot LL1458	Lladro	3,000	1000.00	1650.00
85-03-037	Napoleon Planning Battle LL 1459	Lladro	1,500	875.00	1450.00
85-03-038	Youthful Beauty LL1461	Lladro	5,000	800.00	1200.00
85-03-039	Flock of Birds LL1462	Lladro	1,500	1125.00	1750.00
85-03-040	Classic Spring LL1465	Lladro	Closed	650.00	1100-1400.
85-03-041	Classic Fall LL1466	Lladro	Closed	650.00	1000.00
85-03-042	Valencian Couple on Horse LL1472	Lladro	3,000	1175.00	1550.00
85-03-043	Coach XVIII Century LL1485	Lladro	500	14000.00	25500.00
86-03-044	The New World LL 1486	Lladro	4,000	700.00	1350.00
86-03-045	Fantasia LL1487	Lladro	5,000	1500.00	2700.00
86-03-046	Floral Offering LL1490	Lladro	3,000	2500.00	4450.00
86-03-047	Oriental Music LL1491	Lladro	5,000	1350.00	2400.00
86-03-048	Three Sisters LL1492	Lladro	3,000	1850.00	3250.00
86-03-049	At the Stroke of Twelve LL1493	Lladro	1,500	4250.00	7500.00
86-03-050	Hawaiian Festival LL1496	Lladro	4,000	1850.00	3150.00
87-03-051	A Sunday Drive LL1510	Lladro	1,000	2600.00	5250.00
87-03-052	Listen to Don Quixote LL1520	Lladro	750	1800.00	2900.00
87-03-053	A Happy Encounter LL1523	Lladro	1,500	2900.00	4900.00
88-03-054	Garden Party LL1578	Lladro	500	5500.00	7250.00
88-03-055	Return to La Mancha LL1580	Lladro	500	6400.00	8350.00
89-03-056	Southern Tea LL1597	Lladro	1,000	1775.00	2300.00
89-03-057	Kitakami Cruise w/base LL1605	Lladro	500	5800.00	7350.00
89-03-058	Mounted Warriors w/base LL1608	Lladro	500	2850.00	3450.00
89-03-059	Circus Parade w/base LL1609	Lladro	1,000	5200.00	6550.00
89-03-060	"Jesus the Rock" w/baseLL1615	Lladro	1,000	1175.00	1550.00
91-03-061	Valencian Cruise LL1731	Lladro	1,000	2700.00	2950.00
91-03-062	Venice Vows LL1732	Lladro	1,500	3750.00	4100.00
91-03-063	Liberty Eagle LL1738	Lladro	1,500	1000.00	1100.00
91-03-064	Heavenly Swing LL1739	Lladro	1,000	1900.00	2050.00
91-03-065	Columbus, Two Routes LL1740	Lladro	1,000	1500.00	1650.00
91-03-066	Columbus Reflecting LL1741	Lladro	1,000	1850.00	1995.00
91-03-067	Onward! LL1742	Lladro	1,000	2500.00	2700.00
91-03-068	The Princess And The Unicorn LL1755	Lladro	1,500	1750.00	2300.00
91-03-069	Outing In Seville LL1756	Lladro	500	23000.00	24500.00
92-03-070	Hawaiian Ceremony LL1757	Lladro	1,000	9800.00	10250.00
92-03-071	Circus Time LL1758	Lladro	2,500	9200.00	9650.00
92-03-072	Tea In The Garden LL1759	Lladro	2,000	9500.00	9750.00
93-03-073	Paella Valenciano w/Base LL1762	Lladro	500	10000.00	10000.00
93-03-074	Trusting Friends w/Base LL1763	Lladro	350	1200.00	1200.00
93-03-075	He's My Brother w/Base LL1764	Lladro	350	1500.00	1500.00
93-03-076	The Course of Adventure LL1765	Lladro	250	1625.00	1625.00
93-03-077	Ties That Bind LL1766	Lladro	250	1700.00	1700.00
93-03-078	Motherly Love LL1767	Lladro	250	1330.00	1330.00
93-03-079	Travellers' Respite w/Base LL1768	Lladro	250	1825.00	1825.00
93-03-080	Fruitful Harvest LL1769	Lladro	350	1300.00	1300.00
93-03-081	Gypsy Dancers LL1770	Lladro	250	2250.00	2250.00
93-03-082	Country Doctor w/Base LL1771	Lladro	250	1475.00	1475.00
93-03-083	Back To Back LL1772	Lladro	350	1450.00	1450.00

Number	Name	Artist	Edition Limit	Issue Price	Quote
93-03-084	Mischevous Musician LL1773	Lladro	350	975.00	975.00
93-03-085	A Treasured Moment w/Base LL1774	Lladro	350	950.00	950.00
93-03-086	Oriental Garden w/Base LL1775	Lladro	750	22500.00	22500.00
70-03-087	Girl with Guitar LL2016	Lladro	Closed	650.00	1800.00
70-03-088	Madonna with Child LL2018	Lladro	Closed	450.00	1650.00
71-03-089	Oriental Man LL2021	Lladro	Closed	500.00	1650.00
71-03-090	Three Graces LL2028	Lladro	Closed	950.00	3500.00
71-03-091	Eve at Tree LL2029	Lladro	Closed	450.00	3000.00
71-03-092	Oriental Horse LL2030	Lladro	Closed	1100.00	3500-5000.
71-03-093	Lyric Muse LL2031	Lladro	Closed	750.00	2100.00
71-03-094	Madonna and Child LL2043	Lladro	Closed	400.00	1500.00
73-03-095	Peasant Woman LL2049	Lladro	Closed	400.00	1300.00
73-03-096	Passionate Dance LL2051	Lladro	Closed	450.00	2750.00
77-03-097	St. Theresa LL2061	Lladro	Closed	775.00	1600.00
77-03-098	Concerto LL2063	Lladro	Closed	1000.00	1235.00
77-03-099	Flying Partridges LL2064	Lladro	Closed	3500.00	4300.00
87-03-100	Christopher Columbus w/Base LL2176	Lladro	1,000	1000.00	1350.00
90-03-101	Invincible LL2188	Lladro	300	1100.00	1250.00
93-03-102	Flight of Fancy w/Base LL2243	Lladro	300	1400.00	1400.00
93-03-103	The Awakening w/Base LL2244	Lladro	300	1200.00	1200.00
93-03-104	Inspired Voyage w/Base LL2245	Lladro	1,000	4800.00	4800.00
93-03-105	Days of Yore w/Base LL2248	Lladro	1,000	2050.00	2050.00
93-03-106	Holiday Glow w/Base LL2249	Lladro	1,500	750.00	750.00
93-03-107	Autumn Glow w/Base LL2250	Lladro	1,500	750.00	750.00
93-03-108	Humble Grace w/Base LL2255	Lladro	2,000	2150.00	2150.00
83-03-109	Dawn LL3000	Lladro	300	325.00	525.00
83-03-110	Monks LL3001	Lladro	300	1675.00	2550.00
83-03-111	Waiting LL3002	Lladro	Closed	1550.00	1900.00
83-03-112	Indolence LL3003	Lladro	Closed	1465.00	2100.00
83-03-113	Venus in the Bath LL3005	Lladro	Closed	1175.00	1450.00
87-03-114	Classic Beauty w/Base LL3012	Lladro	500	1300.00	1750.00
87-03-115	Youthful Innocence w/Base LL3013	Lladro	500	1300.00	1750.00
87-03-116	The Nymph w/Base LL3014	Lladro	250	1000.00	1450.00
87-03-117	Dignity LL3015	Lladro	150	1400.00	1900.00
88-03-118	Passion w/Base LL3016	Lladro	750	865.00	1100.00
88-03-119	Muse w/Base LL3017	Lladro	300	650.00	875.00
88-03-120	Cellist w/Base LL3018	Lladro	300	650.00	875.00
88-03-121	True Affection w/Base LL3019	Lladro	300	750.00	975.00
89-03-122	Demureness w/Base LL3020	Lladro	300	400.00	550.00
90-03-123	Daydreaming w/Base LL3022	Lladro	500	550.00	775.00
90-03-124	After The Bath w/Base LL3023	Lladro	Closed	350.00	750-1000.
90-03-125	Discoveries w/Base LL3024	Lladro	100	1500.00	1750.00
91-03-126	Resting Nude LL3025	Lladro	200	650.00	725.00
91-03-127	Unadorned Beauty LL3026	Lladro	200	1700.00	1850.00
82-03-128	Elk LL3501	Lladro	Closed	950.00	1200.00
78-03-129	Nude with Dove LL3503	Lladro	Closed	500.00	1400.00
81-03-130	The Rescue LL3504	Lladro	Closed	3500.00	4450.00
78-03-131	St. Michael LL3515	Lladro	1,500	2200.00	4300.00
80-03-132	Turtle Dove Nest LL3519	Lladro	1,200	3600.00	6050.00
80-03-133	Turtle Dove Group LL3520	Lladro	750	6800.00	11500.00
81-03-134	Philippine Folklore LL3522	Lladro	1,500	1450.00	2400.00
81-03-135	Nest of Eagles LL3523	Lladro	300	6900.00	11500.00
81-03-136	Drum Beats/Watusi Queen LL3524	Lladro	1,500	1875.00	3050.00
82-03-137	Togetherness LL3527	Lladro	Closed	750.00	975.00
82-03-138	Wrestling LL3528	Lladro	Closed	950.00	1125.00
82-03-139	Companionship LL3529	Lladro	Closed	1000.00	1700.00
82-03-140	Anxiety LL3530	Lladro	125	1075.00	1875.00
82-03-141	Victory LL3531	Lladro	Closed	1500.00	1800.00
82-03-142	Plentitude LL3532	Lladro	Closed	1000.00	1375.00
82-03-143	The Observer LL3533	Lladro	115	900.00	1650.00
82-03-144	In the Distance LL3534	Lladro	Closed	525.00	1275.00
82-03-145	Slave LL3535	Lladro	Closed	950.00	1150.00
82-03-146	Relaxation LL3536	Lladro	Closed	525.00	1000.00
82-03-147	Dreaming LL3537	Lladro	Closed	950.00	1475.00
82-03-148	Youth LL3538	Lladro	Closed	525.00	1120.00
82-03-149	Dantiness LL3539	Lladro	Closed	1000.00	1400.00
82-03-150	Pose LL3540	Lladro	Closed	1250.00	1450.00
82-03-151	Tranquility LL3541	Lladro	Closed	1000.00	1400.00
82-03-152	Yoga LL3542	Lladro	Closed	650.00	900.00
82-03-153	Demure LL3543	Lladro	Closed	1250.00	1700.00
82-03-154	Reflections LL3544	Lladro	Closed	650.00	1050.00
82-03-155	Adoration LL3545	Lladro	Closed	1050.00	1600.00
82-03-156	African Woman LL3546	Lladro	Closed	1300.00	2000.00
82-03-157	Reclining Nude LL3547	Lladro	Closed	650.00	875.00
82-03-158	Serenity LL3548	Lladro	300	925.00	1550.00
82-03-159	Reposing LL3549	Lladro	Closed	425.00	575.00
82-03-160	Boxer LL3550	Lladro	300	850.00	1450.00
83-03-161	Bather LL3551	Lladro	Closed	975.00	1300.00
82-03-162	Blue God LL3552	Lladro	1,500	900.00	1575.00
82-03-163	Fire Bird LL3553	Lladro	1,500	800.00	1350.00
82-03-164	Desert People w/Base LL3555	Lladro	750	1680.00	3100.00
82-03-165	Road to Mandalay LL3556	Lladro	Closed	1390.00	2500.00
82-03-166	Jesus in Tiberias LL3557	Lladro	1,200	2600.00	4500.00
92-03-167	The Reader LL3560	Lladro	200	2650.00	2750.00
80-03-168	Successful Hunt LL5098	Lladro	1,000	5200.00	5200.00
92-03-169	Tinkerbell LL5186	Lladro	Closed	350.00	2600.00
85-03-170	Napoleon Bonaparte LL 5338	Lladro	5,000	275.00	495.00
85-03-171	Beethoven LL 5339	Lladro	3,000	800.00	1300.00
85-03-172	Thoroughbred Horse LL5340	Lladro	1,000	625.00	1050.00
85-03-173	I Have Found Thee, Dulcinea LL5341	Lladro	Closed	1850.00	2000-3000.
85-03-174	Pack of Hunting Dogs LL5342	Lladro	3,000	925.00	1650.00
85-03-175	Love Boat LL5343	Lladro	3,000	825.00	1350.00
86-03-176	Fox Hunt LL5362	Lladro	Open	5200.00	8750.00
86-03-177	Rey De Copas LL5366	Lladro	2,000	325.00	600.00
86-03-178	Rey De Oros LL5367	Lladro	2,000	325.00	600.00
86-03-179	Rey De Espadas LL5368	Lladro	2,000	325.00	600.00
86-03-180	Rey De Bastos LL5369	Lladro	2,000	325.00	600.00
86-03-181	Pastoral Scene LL5386	Lladro	Open	1100.00	2100.00
87-03-182	Inspiration LL5413	Lladro	500	1200.00	2100.00
87-03-183	Carnival Time LL5423	Lladro	1,000	2400.00	3900.00
89-03-184	"Pious" LL5541	Lladro	Closed	1075.00	1500-2000.
89-03-185	Freedom LL5602	Lladro	Closed	875.00	950.00
90-03-186	A Ride In The Park LL5718	Lladro	1,000	3200.00	3895.00
91-03-187	Youth LL5800	Lladro	500	650.00	725.00
91-03-188	Charm LL5801	Lladro	500	650.00	725.00
91-03-189	New World Medallion LL5808	Lladro	5,000	200.00	215.00
92-03-190	The Voyage of Columbus LL5847	Lladro	7,500	1450.00	1650-2000.
92-03-191	Sorrowful Mother LL5849	Lladro	1,500	1750.00	1850.00
92-03-192	Justice Eagle LL5863	Lladro	1,500	1700.00	1800.00
92-03-193	Maternal Joy LL5864	Lladro	1,500	1600.00	1700.00
92-03-194	Motoring In Style LL5884	Lladro	1,500	3700.00	3850.00
92-03-195	The Way Of The Cross LL5890	Lladro	2,000	975.00	1050.00
92-03-196	Presenting Credentials LL5911	Lladro	1,500	19500.00	20500.00
92-03-197	Young Mozart LL5915	Lladro	2,500	500.00	500.00
93-03-198	Jester's Serenade w/Base LL5932	Lladro	3,000	1995.00	1995.00
93-03-199	The Blessing w/Base LL5942	Lladro	2,000	1345.00	1345.00
93-03-200	Our Lady of Rocio w/Base LL5951	Lladro	2,000	3500.00	3500.00
93-03-201	Where to Sir w/Base LL5952	Lladro	1,500	5250.00	5250.00
93-03-202	Discovery Mug LL5967	Lladro	1,992	90.00	90.00
93-03-203	Graceful LL6033	Lladro	3,000	1475.00	1475.00
93-03-204	The Hand of Justice w/Base LL6035	Lladro	1,000	1250.00	1250.00
Lladro		**Lladro Collectors Society**			
85-04-001	Little Pals S7600	Lladro	Closed	95.00	2500-4000.
86-04-002	Little Traveler S7602	Lladro	Closed	95.00	1000-2000.
87-04-003	Spring Bouquets S7603	Lladro	Closed	125.00	800-1100.
88-04-004	School Days S7604	Lladro	Closed	125.00	500-800.
88-04-005	Flower Song S7607	Lladro	Closed	175.00	450-750
89-04-006	My Buddy S7609	Lladro	Closed	145.00	300-550.
90-04-007	Can I Play? S7610	Lladro	Closed	150.00	400-650.
91-04-008	Summer Stroll S7611	Lladro	Closed	195.00	275-400.
91-04-009	Picture Perfect S7612	Lladro	Closed	350.00	500-750.
92-04-010	All Aboard S7619	Lladro	Closed	165.00	165.00
93-04-011	Best Friend S7620	Lladro	Yr.Iss.	195.00	195.00

Also see Dave Grossman: Series 05 for Lladro Norman Rockwell

Number	Name	Artist	Edition Limit	Issue Price	Quote
Lynell Studios		**Rockwell**			
81-01-001	Snow Queen	N. Rockwell	10,000	85.00	85.00
81-01-002	Cradle of Love	N. Rockwell	10,000	85.00	85.00
81-01-003	Scotty	N. Rockwell	7,500	125.00	125.00
Seymour Mann, Inc.		**Wizard Of Oz - 40th Anniversary**			
79-01-001	Dorothy, Scarecrow, Lion, Tinman	E. Mann	Closed	7.50	45.00
79-01-002	Dorothy, Scarecrow, Lion, Tinman, Musical	E. Mann	Closed	12.50	75.00
Seymour Mann, Inc.		**Christmas In America**			
88-02-001	Doctor's Office Lite Up	E. Mann	Open	27.50	27.50
88-02-002	Set Of 3, Capitol, White House, Mt. Vernon	E. Mann	Closed	75.00	150.00
89-02-003	Santa in Sleigh	E. Mann	Open	25.00	45.00
90-02-004	Cart With People	E. Mann	Open	25.00	35.00
91-02-005	New England Church Lite Up House MER-375	J. White	Open	27.50	27.50
91-02-006	New England General Store Lite Up House MER-377	J. White	Open	27.50	27.50
Seymour Mann, Inc.		**Christmas Village**			
91-03-001	Away, Away	L. Sciola	Open	30.00	30.00
91-03-002	The Fire Station	L. Sciola	Open	60.00	60.00
91-03-003	Curiosity Shop	L. Sciola	Open	45.00	45.00
91-03-004	Scrooge/Marley's Counting House	L. Sciola	Open	45.00	45.00
91-03-005	The Playhouse	L. Sciola	Open	60.00	60.00
91-03-006	Ye Old Gift Shoppe	L. Sciola	Open	50.00	50.00
91-03-007	Emily's Toys	L. Sciola	Open	45.00	45.00
91-03-008	Counsil House	L. Sciola	Open	60.00	60.00
91-03-009	Public Library	L. Sciola	Open	50.00	50.00
91-03-010	On Thin Ice	L. Sciola	Open	30.00	30.00
91-03-011	Story Teller	L. Sciola	Open	20.00	20.00
Seymour Mann, Inc.		**Christmas Collection**			
85-04-001	Trumpeting Angel w/Jesus XMAS-527	J. White	Open	40.00	40.00
85-04-002	Virgin w/Christ Musical XMAS-528	J. White	Open	33.50	33.50
86-04-003	Antique Santa Musical XMAS-364	J. White	Closed	20.00	20.00
86-04-004	Jumbo Santa/Toys XMAS-38	J. White	Open	45.00	45.00
89-04-005	Cat in Teacup Musical XMAS-600	J. White	Open	30.00	30.00
89-04-006	Santa in Sled w/Reindeer CJ-3	Jaimy	Open	25.00	25.00
89-04-007	Santa Musicals CJ-1/4	Jaimy	Open	27.50	27.50
89-04-008	Santa on Horse CJ-33A	Jaimy	Open	33.50	33.50
89-04-009	Santa w/List CJ-23	Jaimy	Open	27.50	27.50
90-04-010	Antique Shope Lite Up House MER-376	J. White	Open	27.50	27.50
90-04-011	Bakery Lite Up House MER-373	J. White	Open	27.50	27.50
90-04-012	Bethlehem Lite Up Set 3 CP-59893	J. White	Open	120.00	120.00
90-04-013	Brick Church Lite Up House MER-360C	J. White	Open	35.00	35.00
90-04-014	Cathedral Lite Up House MER-362	J. White	Open	37.50	37.50
90-04-015	Church Lite Up House MER-310	J. White	Closed	27.50	27.50
90-04-016	Deep Gold Church Lite Up House MER-360D	J. White	Open	35.00	35.00
90-04-017	Double Store Lite Up House MER-311	J. White	Closed	27.50	27.50
90-04-018	Fire Station Lite Up House XMS-1550C	E.Mann	Closed	25.00	25.00
90-04-019	Grist Mill Lite Up House MER-372	J. White	Open	27.50	27.50
90-04-020	Inn Lite Up House MER-316	J. White	Closed	27.50	27.50
90-04-021	Leatherworks Lite Up House MER-371	J. White	Open	27.50	27.50
90-04-022	Library Lite Up House MER-317	J. White	Closed	27.50	27.50
90-04-023	Light House Lite Up House MER-370	J. White	Open	27.50	27.50
90-04-024	Mansion Lite Up House MER-319	J. White	Closed	27.50	27.50
90-04-025	Mr/Mrs Santa Musical CJ-281	Jaimy	Open	37.50	37.50
90-04-026	New England Church Lite Up House MER-375	J. White	Open	27.50	27.50
90-04-027	New England General Store Lite Up House MER-377	J. White	Open	27.50	27.50
90-04-028	Railroad Station Lite Up House MER-374	J. White	Open	27.50	27.50
90-04-029	Roly Poly Santa 3 Asst. CJ-253/4/7	Jaimy	Open	17.50	17.50
90-04-030	Santa on Chimney Musical CJ-212	Jaimy	Open	33.50	33.50
90-04-031	Santa on See Saw TR-14	E. Mann	Open	30.00	30.00
90-04-032	Santa Packing Bag CJ-210	Jaimy	Open	33.50	33.50
90-04-033	Santa w/List CJ-23	Jaimy	Closed	27.50	27.50
90-04-034	School Lite Up House MER-320	J. White	Closed	27.50	27.50
90-04-035	Town Hall Lite Up House MER-315	J. White	Closed	27.50	27.50
91-04-036	Apothecary Lite Up CJ-128	Jaimy	Open	33.50	33.50
91-04-037	Boy and Girl on Bell CJ-132	Jaimy	Open	13.50	13.50
91-04-038	Boy on Horse CJ-457	Jaimy	Open	6.00	6.00
91-04-039	Carolers Under Lamppost CJ-114A	Jaimy	Open	7.50	7.50
91-04-040	Church Lite Up MER-410	J. White	Open	17.50	17.50
91-04-041	Church w/Blue Roof Lite Up House MER-360	J. White	Open	35.00	35.00
91-04-042	Covered Bridge CJ-101	Jaimy	Open	27.50	27.50
91-04-043	Elf w/Doll House CB-14	E. Mann	Open	30.00	30.00
91-04-044	Elf w/Hammer CB-11	E. Mann	Open	30.00	30.00
91-04-045	Elf w/Reindeer CJ-422	Jaimy	Open	9.00	9.00
91-04-046	Elf w/Rocking Horse CB-10	E. Mann	Open	30.00	30.00
91-04-047	Elf w/Teddy Bear CB-12	E. Mann	Open	30.00	30.00
91-04-048	Emily's Toys CJ-127	Jaimy	Open	35.00	35.00
91-04-049	Father and Mother w/Daughter CJ-133	Jaimy	Open	13.50	13.50
91-04-050	Father Christmas CJ-233	Jaimy	Open	33.50	33.50
91-04-051	Father Christmas w/Holly CJ-239	Jaimy	Open	35.00	35.00
91-04-052	Fire Station CJ-129	Jaimy	Open	50.00	50.00
91-04-053	Four Men Talking CJ-138	Jaimy	Closed	27.50	27.50
91-04-054	Gift Shop Lite Up CJ-125	Jaimy	Open	33.50	33.50

Company		Series			
Number	**Name**	**Artist**	**Edition Limit**	**Issue Price**	**Quote**
91-04-055	Girls w/Instruments CJ-131	Jaimy	Open	13.50	13.50
91-04-056	Horse and Coach CJ-207	Jaimy	Open	25.00	25.00
91-04-057	Kids Building Igloo CJ-137	Jaimy	Open	13.50	13.50
91-04-058	Lady w/Dogs CJ-208	Jaimy	Open	13.50	13.50
91-04-059	Man w/Wheelbarrow CJ-134	Jaimy	Open	13.50	13.50
91-04-060	Newsboy Under Lamppost CJ-144B	Jaimy	Closed	15.00	15.00
91-04-061	Old Curiosity Lite Up CJ-201	Jaimy	Open	37.50	37.50
91-04-062	Playhouse Lite Up CJ-122	Jaimy	Open	50.00	50.00
91-04-063	Public Library Lite Up CJ-121	Jaimy	Open	45.00	45.00
91-04-064	Reindeer Barn Lite Up House CJ-421	Jaimy	Open	55.00	55.00
91-04-065	Restaurant Lite Up House MER-354	J. White	Open	27.50	27.50
91-04-066	Santa Cat Roly Poly CJ-252	Jaimy	Open	17.50	17.50
91-04-067	Santa Fixing Sled CJ-237	Jaimy	Open	35.00	35.00
91-04-068	Santa In Barrel Waterball CJ-243	Jaimy	Open	33.50	33.50
91-04-069	Santa In Toy Shop CJ-441	Jaimy	Open	33.50	33.50
91-04-070	Santa On Train CJ-458	Jaimy	Open	6.00	6.00
91-04-071	Santa On White Horse CJ-338	E. Mann	Open	33.50	33.50
91-04-072	Santa Packing Bag CJ-210	Jaimy	Open	33.50	33.50
91-04-073	Santa Packing Bag CJ-236	Jaimy	Open	35.00	35.00
91-04-074	Santa Sleeping Musical CJ-214	Jaimy	Open	30.00	30.00
91-04-075	Santa w/Bag and List CJ-431	Jaimy	Open	33.50	33.50
91-04-076	Santa w/Deer Musical CJ-21R	Jaimy	Open	33.50	33.50
91-04-077	Santa w/Girl Waterball CJ-241	Jaimy	Open	33.50	33.50
91-04-078	Santa w/Lantern Musical CJ-211	Jaimy	Open	33.50	33.50
91-04-079	Santa w/List CJ-23R	Jaimy	Open	27.50	27.50
91-04-080	Snowball Fight CJ-124B	Jaimy	Open	25.00	25.00
91-04-081	Soup Seller Waterball CJ-209	Jaimy	Open	25.00	25.00
91-04-082	Stone Cottage Lite Up CJ-100	Jaimy	Open	37.50	37.50
91-04-083	Stone House Lite Up CJ-102	Jaimy	Open	45.00	45.00
91-04-084	Teddy Bear On Wheels CB-42	E. Mann	Open	25.00	25.00
91-04-085	The Skaters CJ-205	Jaimy	Open	25.00	25.00
91-04-086	The Story Teller CJ-204	Jaimy	Open	20.00	20.00
91-04-087	The Toy Seller CJ-206	Jaimy	Closed	13.50	13.50
91-04-088	Three Ladies w/Food CJ-136	Jaimy	Open	13.50	13.50
91-04-089	Trader Santa Musical CJ-442	Jaimy	Open	30.00	30.00
91-04-090	Train Set MER-378	J. White	Open	25.00	25.00
91-04-091	2 Tone Stone Church MER-360B	J. White	Open	35.00	35.00
91-04-092	Toy Store Lite Up House MER-355	J. White	Open	27.50	27.50
91-04-093	Two Old Men Talking CJ-107	Jaimy	Open	13.50	13.50
91-04-094	Village Mill Lite Up CJ-104	Jaimy	Open	30.00	30.00
91-04-095	Village People CJ-116A	Jaimy	Open	60.00	60.00
91-04-096	Woman w/Cow CJ-135	Jaimy	Open	15.00	15.00
91-04-097	Ye Olde Town Tavern CJ-130	Jaimy	Open	45.00	45.00
Seymour Mann, Inc.		**Dickens Collection**			
89-05-001	Cratchits Lite Up XMS-7000A	J. White	Open	30.00	30.00
89-05-002	Fezziwigs Lite Up XMS-7000C	J. White	Open	30.00	30.00
89-05-003	Gift Shoppe Lite Up XMS-7000D	J. White	Open	30.00	30.00
89-05-004	Scrooge/Marley Lite Up XMS-7000B	J. White	Open	30.00	30.00
90-05-005	Black Swan Inn Lite Up XMS-7000E	J. White	Open	30.00	30.00
90-05-006	Cratchit Family MER-121	J. White	Open	37.50	37.50
90-05-007	Hen Poultry Lite Up XMS-7000H	J. White	Open	30.00	30.00
90-05-008	Tea and Spice Lite Up XMS-7000F	J. White	Open	30.00	30.00
90-05-009	Waite Fish Store Lite Up XMS-7000G	J. White	Open	30.00	30.00
90-05-010	Cratchit/Tiny Tim Musical MER-105	J. White	Open	33.50	33.50
91-05-011	Cratchit/Tiny Tim Musical CJ-117	Jaimy	Open	33.50	33.50
91-05-012	Cratchit's Lite Up House CJ-200	Jaimy	Open	37.50	37.50
91-05-013	Scrooge/Marley Counting House CJ-202	Jaimy	Open	37.50	37.50
91-05-014	Scrooge Musical CJ-118	Jaimy	Open	30.00	30.00
Seymour Mann, Inc.		**Gingerbread Christmas Collection**			
91-06-001	Gingerbread Angel CJ-411	J. Sauerbrey	Open	7.50	7.50
91-06-002	Gingerbread Church Lite Up House CJ-403	J. Sauerbrey	Open	65.00	65.00
91-06-003	Gingerbread House CJ-416	J. Sauerbrey	Open	7.50	7.50
91-06-004	Gingerbread House Lite Up CJ-404	J. Sauerbrey	Open	65.00	65.00
91-06-005	Gingerbread Man CJ-415	J. Sauerbrey	Open	7.50	7.50
91-06-006	Gingerbread Mansion Lite Up CJ-405	J. Sauerbrey	Open	70.00	70.00
91-06-007	Gingerbread Mouse/Boot CJ-409	J. Sauerbrey	Open	7.50	7.50
91-06-008	Gingerbread Mrs. Claus CJ-414	J. Sauerbrey	Open	7.50	7.50
91-06-009	Gingerbread Reindeer CJ-410	J. Sauerbrey	Open	7.50	7.50
91-06-010	Gingerbread Rocking Horse Music CJ-460	J. Sauerbrey	Open	33.50	33.50
91-06-011	Gingerbread Santa CJ-408	J. Sauerbrey	Open	7.50	7.50
91-06-012	Gingerbread Sleigh CJ-406	J. Sauerbrey	Open	7.50	7.50
91-06-013	Gingerbread Snowman CJ-412	J. Sauerbrey	Open	7.50	7.50
91-06-014	Gingerbread Swan Musical CJ-462	J. Sauerbrey	Closed	33.50	33.50
91-06-015	Gingerbread Sweet Shop Lite Up House CJ-417	J. Sauerbrey	Open	60.00	60.00
91-06-016	Gingerbread Teddy Bear Music CJ-461	J. Sauerbrey	Closed	33.50	33.50
91-06-017	Gingerbread Toy Shop Lite Up House CJ-402	J. Sauerbrey	Open	60.00	60.00
91-06-018	Gingerbread Tree CJ-407	J. Sauerbrey	Open	7.50	7.50
91-06-019	Gingerbread Village Lite Up House CJ-400	J. Sauerbrey	Open	60.00	60.00
Seymour Mann, Inc.		**Victorian Christmas Collection**			
90-07-001	Toy/Doll House Lite Up MER-314	J. White	Closed	27.50	27.50
90-07-002	Victorian House Lite Up MER-312	J. White	Open	27.50	27.50
90-07-003	Yarn Shop Lite Up House MER-313	J. White	Open	27.50	27.50
91-07-004	Antique Shop Lite Up House MER-353	J. White	Open	27.50	27.50
91-07-005	Beige Church Lite Up House MER-351	J. White	Open	35.00	35.00
91-07-006	Book Store Lite Up House MER-351	J. White	Open	27.50	27.50
91-07-007	Church Lite Up House MER-350	J. White	Open	37.50	37.50
91-07-008	Country Store Lite Up House MER-356	J. White	Open	27.50	27.50
91-07-009	Inn Lite Up House MER-352	J. White	Open	27.50	27.50
91-07-010	Little Match Girl CJ-419	Jaimy	Open	9.00	9.00
90-07-011	Two Boys w/Snowman CJ-106	Jaimy	Open	12.00	12.00
Seymour Mann, Inc.		**Cat Musical Figurines**			
85-08-001	Cats Ball Shape MH-303A/G	Kenji	Open	25.00	25.00
86-08-002	Cats w/Ribbon MH-481A/C	Kenji	Open	30.00	30.00
87-08-007	Brown Cat in Teacup MH-600VGB16	Kenji	Open	30.00	30.00
87-08-003	Cat in Garbage Can MH-490	Kenji	Open	35.00	35.00
87-08-004	Cat on Tipped Garbage Can MH-498	Kenji	Open	35.00	35.00
87-08-005	Cat in Rose Teacup MH-600VG	Kenji	Open	30.00	30.00
87-08-006	Cat in Teapot Brown MH-600VGB	Kenji	Open	30.00	30.00
87-08-008	Cat in Teacup MH-600VGG	Kenji	Open	30.00	30.00
87-08-009	Valentine Cat in Teacup MH-600VLT	Kenji	Open	33.50	33.50
87-08-010	Musical Bear MH-602	Kenji	Open	27.50	27.50
87-08-011	Kittens w/Balls of Yarn MH-612	Kenji	Open	30.00	30.00
87-08-012	Cat in Bag MH-614	Kenji	Open	30.00	30.00
87-08-013	Cat in Bag MH-617	Kenji	Open	30.00	30.00
87-08-014	Brown Cat in Bag MH-617B/6	Kenji	Open	30.00	30.00
87-08-015	Valentine Cat in Bag Musical MH-600	Kenji	Open	33.50	33.50
87-08-016	Teapot Cat MH-631	Kenji	Open	30.00	30.00
88-08-017	Cat in Hat Box MH-634	Kenji	Open	35.00	35.00

Company		Series			
Number	**Name**	**Artist**	**Edition Limit**	**Issue Price**	**Quote**
88-08-018	Cat in Hat MH-634B	Kenji	Open	35.00	35.00
88-08-019	Brown Cat in Hat MH-634B/6	Kenji	Open	35.00	35.00
89-08-020	Cat w/Coffee Cup Musical MH-706	Kenji	Open	35.00	35.00
89-08-021	Cat in Flower MH-709	Kenji	Open	35.00	35.00
89-08-022	Cat w/Swing Musical MH-710	Kenji	Open	35.00	35.00
89-08-023	Cat in Water Can Musical MH-712	Kenji	Open	35.00	35.00
89-08-024	Cat on Basket MH-713	Kenji	Closed	35.00	35.00
89-08-025	Cat in Basinet MH-714	Kenji	Closed	35.00	35.00
89-08-026	Cat in Basket MH-713B	Kenji	Open	35.00	35.00
89-08-027	Cat in Gift Box Musical MH-732	Kenji	Open	40.00	40.00
89-08-028	Cat in Shoe MH-718	Kenji	Open	30.00	30.00
89-08-029	Cats in Basket XMAS-664	E. Mann	Closed	7.50	7.50
90-08-030	Bride/Groom Cat MH-738	Kenji	Open	37.50	37.50
90-08-031	Cat in Bootie MH-728	Kenji	Open	35.00	35.00
90-08-032	Grey Cat in Bootie MH-728G/6	Kenji	Open	35.00	35.00
90-08-033	Cat Sailor in Rocking Boat MH-734	Kenji	Open	45.00	45.00
90-08-034	Cat Asleep MH-735	Kenji	Open	17.50	17.50
90-08-035	Cat on Gift Box Music MH-740	Kenji	Open	40.00	40.00
90-08-036	Cat on Pillow MH-731	Kenji	Open	17.50	17.50
90-08-037	Cat w/Bow on Pink Pillow MH-741P	Kenji	Open	33.50	33.50
90-08-038	Cat w/Parrot MH-730	Kenji	Open	37.50	37.50
90-08-039	Kitten Trio in Carriage MH-742	Kenji	Open	37.50	37.50
90-08-040	Cat Calico in Easy Chair MH-743VG	Kenji	Open	27.50	27.50
90-08-041	Cats Graduation MH-745	Kenji	Open	27.50	27.50
90-08-042	Cat in Dress MH-751VG	Kenji	Open	37.50	37.50
91-08-043	Brown Cat in Bag	Kenji	Open	30.00	30.00
91-08-044	Brown Cat in Hat	Kenji	Open	35.00	35.00
91-08-045	Brown Cat in Teacup	Kenji	Open	30.00	30.00
91-08-046	Cat in Bag	Kenji	Open	30.00	30.00
91-08-047	Cat in Bag	Kenji	Open	30.00	30.00
91-08-048	Cat in Bootie	Kenji	Open	35.00	35.00
91-08-049	Cat in Garbage Can	Kenji	Open	35.00	35.00
91-08-050	Cat in Hat	Kenji	Open	35.00	35.00
91-08-051	Cat in Hat Box	Kenji	Open	35.00	35.00
91-08-052	Cat in Rose Teacup	Kenji	Open	30.00	30.00
91-08-053	Cat in Teacup	Kenji	Open	30.00	30.00
91-08-054	Cat in Teapot Brown	Kenji	Open	30.00	30.00
91-08-055	Cat Momma MH-758	Kenji	Open	35.00	35.00
91-08-056	Cat on Tipped Garbage Can	Kenji	Open	35.00	35.00
91-08-057	Cats Ball Shape	Kenji	Open	25.00	25.00
91-08-058	Cats w/Ribbon	Kenji	Open	30.00	30.00
91-08-059	Grey Cat in Bootie	Kenji	Open	35.00	35.00
91-08-060	Kittens w/Balls of Yarn	Kenji	Open	30.00	30.00
91-08-061	Musical Bear	Kenji	Open	27.50	27.50
91-08-062	Teapot Cat	Kenji	Open	30.00	30.00
91-08-063	Cat in Basket MH-768	Kenji	Open	35.00	35.00
91-08-064	Cat Watching Butterfly MH-784	Kenji	Open	17.50	17.50
91-08-065	Cat Watching Canary MH-783	Kenji	Open	25.00	25.00
91-08-066	Cat With Bow on Pink Pillow MH-741P	Kenji	Open	33.50	33.50
91-08-067	Family Cat MH-770	Kenji	Open	35.00	35.00
91-08-068	Kitten Picking Tulips MH-756	Kenji	Open	40.00	40.00
91-08-069	Revolving Cat with Butterfly MH-759	Kenji	Open	40.00	40.00
Seymour Mann, Inc.		**Bunny Musical Figurines**			
91-09-001	Bunny In Teacup MH-781	Kenji	Open	25.00	25.00
91-09-002	Bunny In Teapot MH-780	Kenji	Open	25.00	25.00
Marina's Russian Collection		**Nesting Dolls**			
91-01-001	Ruslan & Ludmila	S.&J. Gusev	2	1695.00	1695.00
92-01-002	Heroes from Russian Legends	S.&J. Gusev	2	1495.00	1495.00
92-01-003	Tsar Saltan	S.&J. Gusev	2	1295.00	1295.00
92-01-004	Russian Icons	S. Pudovkina	1	1495.00	1495.00
92-01-005	Golden Ring of Russia	Markevitch	10	995.00	995.00
92-01-006	Scenes from Folklore Life	Solomatin	100	125.00	125.00
92-01-007	Russian Fairy Tales	Sinitchkin	75	145.00	145.00
Marina's Russian Collection		**Laquered Boxes**			
92-02-001	Goyar's Wedding	Tchictov	2	7500.00	7500.00
92-02-002	Girl at the Stove	S. Sidorov	1	1000.00	1000.00
92-02-003	St. Basel Cathedral	Monashov	1	6500.00	6500.00
Maruri USA		**Birds of Prey**			
81-01-001	Screech Owl	W. Gaither	300	960.00	960.00
81-01-002	American Bald Eagle I	W. Gaither	Closed	165.00	1150-1750.
82-01-003	American Bald Eagle II	W. Gaither	Closed	245.00	1000-2750.
83-01-004	American Bald Eagle III	W. Gaither	Closed	445.00	600-1750.
84-01-005	American Bald Eagle IV	W. Gaither	Closed	360.00	500-1250.
86-01-006	American Bald Eagle V	W. Gaither	Closed	325.00	500-1250.
Maruri USA		**North American Waterfowl I**			
81-02-001	Blue Winged Teal	W. Gaither	200	980.00	980.00
81-02-002	Wood Duck, decoy	W. Gaither	950	480.00	480.00
81-02-003	Flying Wood Ducks	W. Gaither	Closed	880.00	880.00
81-02-004	Canvasback Ducks	W. Gaither	300	780.00	780.00
81-02-005	Mallard Drake	W. Gaither	Closed	2380.00	2380.00
Maruri USA		**North American Waterfowl II**			
81-03-001	Mallard Ducks Pair	W. Gaither	1,500	225.00	225.00
82-03-002	Goldeneye Ducks Pair	W. Gaither	Closed	225.00	225.00
82-03-003	Bufflehead Ducks Pair	W. Gaither	1,500	225.00	225.00
82-03-004	Widgeon, male	W. Gaither	Closed	225.00	225.00
82-03-005	Widgeon, female	W. Gaither	Closed	225.00	225.00
82-03-006	Pintail Ducks Pair	W. Gaither	1,500	225.00	225.00
83-03-007	Loon	W. Gaither	Closed	245.00	245.00
Maruri USA		**North American Songbirds**			
82-04-001	Cardinal, male	W. Gaither	Closed	95.00	95.00
82-04-002	Chickadee	W. Gaither	Closed	95.00	95.00
82-04-003	Bluebird	W. Gaither	Closed	95.00	95.00
82-04-004	Mockingbird	W. Gaither	Closed	95.00	95.00
82-04-005	Carolina Wren	W. Gaither	Closed	95.00	95.00
83-04-006	Cardinal, female	W. Gaither	Closed	95.00	95.00
83-04-007	Robin	W. Gaither	Closed	95.00	95.00
Maruri USA		**North American Game Birds**			
81-05-001	Canadian Geese, pair	W. Gaither	Closed	2000.00	2000.00
81-05-002	Eastern Wild Turkey	W. Gaither	Closed	300.00	300.00
82-05-003	Ruffed Grouse	W. Gaither	Closed	1745.00	1745.00
83-05-004	Bobtail Quail, male	W. Gaither	Closed	375.00	375.00
83-05-005	Bobtail Quail, female	W. Gaither	Closed	375.00	375.00
83-05-006	Wild Turkey Hen with Chicks	W. Gaither	Closed	300.00	300.00

Company Number	Name	Series Artist	Edition Limit	Issue Price	Quote
Maruri USA		**Baby Animals**			
81-06-001	African Lion Cubs	W. Gaither	1,500	195.00	195.00
81-06-002	Wolf Cubs	W. Gaither	Closed	195.00	195.00
81-06-003	Black Bear Cubs	W. Gaither	Closed	195.00	195.00
Maruri USA		**Upland Birds**			
81-07-001	Mourning Doves	W. Gaither	Closed	780.00	780.00
Maruri USA		**Americana**			
81-08-001	Grizzley Bear and Indian	W. Gaither	Closed	650.00	650.00
82-08-002	Sioux Brave and Bison	W. Gaither	Closed	985.00	985.00
Maruri USA		**Stump Animals**			
82-09-001	Red Fox	W. Gaither	Closed	175.00	175.00
83-09-002	Raccoon	W. Gaither	Closed	175.00	175.00
83-09-003	Owl	W. Gaither	Closed	175.00	175.00
84-09-004	Gray Squirrel	W. Gaither	1,200	175.00	175.00
84-09-005	Chipmunk	W. Gaither	Closed	175.00	175.00
84-09-006	Bobcat	W. Gaither	Closed	175.00	175.00
Maruri USA		**Shore Birds**			
84-10-001	Pelican	W. Gaither	Closed	260.00	260.00
84-10-002	Sand Piper	W. Gaither	Closed	285.00	285.00
Maruri USA		**North American Game Animals**			
84-11-001	White Tail Deer	W. Gaither	950	285.00	285.00
Maruri USA		**African Safari Animals**			
83-12-001	African Elephant	W. Gaither	Closed	3500.00	3500.00
83-12-002	Southern White Rhino	W. Gaither	150	3200.00	3200.00
83-12-003	Cape Buffalo	W. Gaither	Closed	2200.00	2200.00
83-12-004	Black Maned Lion	W. Gaither	Closed	1450.00	1450.00
83-12-005	Southern Leopard	W. Gaither	300	1450.00	1450.00
83-12-006	Southern Greater Kudu	W. Gaither	Closed	1800.00	1800.00
83-12-007	Southern Impala	W. Gaither	Closed	1200.00	1200.00
81-12-008	Nyala	W. Gaither	300	1450.00	1450.00
83-12-009	Sable	W. Gaither	Closed	1200.00	1200.00
83-12-010	Grant's Zebras, pair	W. Gaither	500	1200.00	1200.00
Maruri USA		**Special Commissions**			
81-13-001	White Bengal Tiger	W. Gaither	240	340.00	340.00
82-13-002	Cheetah	W. Gaither	Closed	995.00	995.00
83-13-003	Orange Bengal Tiger	W. Gaither	240	340.00	340.00
Maruri USA		**Signature Collection**			
85-14-001	American Bald Eagle	W. Gaither	Closed	60.00	60.00
85-14-002	Canada Goose	W. Gaither	Closed	60.00	60.00
85-14-003	Hawk	W. Gaither	Closed	60.00	60.00
85-14-004	Snow Goose	W. Gaither	Closed	60.00	60.00
85-14-005	Pintail Duck	W. Gaither	Closed	60.00	60.00
85-14-006	Swallow	W. Gaither	Closed	60.00	60.00
Maruri USA		**Legendary Flowers of the Orient**			
85-15-001	Iris	Ito	15,000	45.00	55.00
85-15-002	Lotus	Ito	15,000	45.00	45.00
85-15-003	Chinese Peony	Ito	15,000	45.00	55.00
85-15-004	Lily	Ito	15,000	45.00	55.00
85-15-005	Chrysanthemum	Ito	15,000	45.00	55.00
85-15-006	Cherry Blossom	Ito	15,000	45.00	55.00
85-15-007	Orchid	Ito	15,000	45.00	55.00
85-15-008	Wisteria	Ito	15,000	45.00	55.00
Maruri USA		**American Eagle Gallery**			
85-16-001	E-8501	Maruri Studios	Closed	45.00	50.00
85-16-002	E-8502	Maruri Studios	Open	55.00	65.00
85-16-003	E-8503	Maruri Studios	Open	60.00	65.00
85-16-004	E-8504	Maruri Studios	Open	65.00	75.00
85-16-005	E-8505	Maruri Studios	Closed	65.00	70.00
85-16-006	E-8506	Maruri Studios	Open	75.00	90.00
85-16-007	E-8507	Maruri Studios	Open	75.00	90.00
85-16-008	E-8508	Maruri Studios	Closed	75.00	85.00
85-16-009	E-8509	Maruri Studios	Closed	85.00	85.00
85-16-010	E-8510	Maruri Studios	Open	85.00	95.00
85-16-011	E-8511	Maruri Studios	Closed	85.00	95.00
85-16-012	E-8512	Maruri Studios	Open	295.00	325.00
87-16-013	E-8721	Maruri Studios	Open	40.00	50.00
87-16-014	E-8722	Maruri Studios	Open	45.00	55.00
87-16-015	E-8723	Maruri Studios	Closed	55.00	60.00
87-16-016	E-8724	Maruri Studios	Open	175.00	195.00
89-16-017	E-8931	Maruri Studios	Open	55.00	60.00
89-16-018	E-8932	Maruri Studios	Open	75.00	80.00
89-16-019	E-8933	Maruri Studios	Open	95.00	95.00
89-16-020	E-8934	Maruri Studios	Open	135.00	140.00
89-16-021	E-8935	Maruri Studios	Open	175.00	185.00
89-16-022	E-8936	Maruri Studios	Open	185.00	195.00
91-16-023	E-9141 Eagle Landing	Maruri Studios	Open	60.00	60.00
91-16-024	E-9142 Eagle w/ Totem Pole	Maruri Studios	Open	75.00	75.00
91-16-025	E-9143 Pair in Flight	Maruri Studios	Open	95.00	95.00
91-16-026	E-9144 Eagle w/Salmon	Maruri Studios	Open	110.00	110.00
91-16-027	E-9145 Eagle w/Snow	Maruri Studios	Open	135.00	135.00
91-16-028	E-9146 Eagle w/Babies	Maruri Studios	Open	145.00	145.00
Maruri USA		**Wings of Love Doves**			
87-17-001	D-8701 Single Dove	Maruri Studios	Open	45.00	55.00
87-17-002	D-8702 Double Dove	Maruri Studios	Open	55.00	65.00
87-17-003	D-8703 Single Dove	Maruri Studios	Open	65.00	70.00
87-17-004	D-8704 Double Dove	Maruri Studios	Open	75.00	85.00
87-17-005	D-8705 Single Dove	Maruri Studios	Open	95.00	95.00
87-17-006	D-8706 Double Dove	Maruri Studios	Open	175.00	195.00
90-17-007	D-9021 Double Dove	Maruri Studios	Open	50.00	55.00
90-17-008	D-9022 Double Dove	Maruri Studios	Open	75.00	75.00
90-17-009	D-9023 Double Dove	Maruri Studios	Open	115.00	120.00
90-17-010	D-9024 Double Dove	Maruri Studios	Open	150.00	160.00
Maruri USA		**Majestic Owls of the Night**			
87-18-001	Burrowing Owl	D. Littleton	15,000	55.00	55.00
88-18-002	Barred Owl	D. Littleton	15,000	55.00	55.00
88-18-003	Elf Owl	D. Littleton	15,000	55.00	55.00
Maruri USA		**Studio Collection**			
90-19-001	Majestic Eagles-MS100	Maruri Studios	Closed	350.00	500.00
91-19-002	Delicate Motion-MS200	Maruri Studios	3,500	325.00	325.00
92-19-003	Imperial Panda-MS300	Maruri Studios	3,500	350.00	350.00

Company Number	Name	Series Artist	Edition Limit	Issue Price	Quote
93-19-004	Wild Wings-MS400	Maruri Studios	3,500	395.00	395.00
Maruri USA		**Polar Expedition**			
90-20-001	Baby Emperor Penguin-P-9001	Maruri Studios	Open	45.00	50.00
90-20-002	Baby Arctic Fox-P-9002	Maruri Studios	Open	50.00	55.00
90-20-003	Polar Bear Cub Sliding-P-9003	Maruri Studios	Open	50.00	55.00
90-20-004	Polar Bear Cubs Playing-P-9004	Maruri Studios	Open	60.00	65.00
90-20-005	Baby Harp Seals-P-9005	Maruri Studios	Open	65.00	70.00
90-20-006	Mother & Baby Emperor Penguins -P-9006	Maruri Studios	Open	80.00	85.00
90-20-007	Mother & Baby Harp Seals-P-9007	Maruri Studios	Open	90.00	95.00
90-20-008	Mother & Baby Polar Bears-P-9008	Maruri Studios	Open	125.00	130.00
90-20-009	Polar Expedition Sign-PES-001	Maruri Studios	Open	18.00	18.00
92-20-010	Baby Harp Seal-P-9221	Maruri Studios	Open	55.00	55.00
92-20-011	Emperor Penguins-P-9222	Maruri Studios	Open	60.00	60.00
92-20-012	Arctic Fox Cubs Playing-P-9223	Maruri Studios	Open	65.00	65.00
92-20-013	Polar Bear Family-P-9224	Maruri Studios	Open	90.00	90.00
Maruri USA		**Eyes Of The Night**			
90-21-001	Single Screech Owl-O-8801	Maruri Studios	Open	50.00	55.00
90-21-002	Single Snowy Owl-O-8802	Maruri Studios	Open	50.00	55.00
90-21-003	Single Great Horned Owl-O-8803	Maruri Studios	Open	60.00	65.00
90-21-004	Single Tawny Owl-O-8804	Maruri Studios	Open	60.00	65.00
90-21-005	Single Snowy Owl-O-8805	Maruri Studios	Open	80.00	85.00
90-21-006	Single Screech Owl-O-8806	Maruri Studios	Open	90.00	95.00
90-21-007	Double Barn Owl 0-8807	Maruri Studios	Open	125.00	130.00
90-21-008	Single Great Horned Owl-O-8808	Mauurl Studios	Open	145.00	150.00
90-21-009	Double Snowy Owl-O-8809	Maruri Studios	Open	245.00	250.00
Maruri USA		**Songbirds Of Beauty**			
91-22-001	Chickadee With Roses SB-9101	Maruri Studios	Open	85.00	85.00
91-22-002	Goldfinch With Hawthorne SB-9102	Maruri Studios	Open	85.00	85.00
91-22-003	Cardinal With Cherry Blossom SB-9103	Maruri Studios	Open	85.00	85.00
91-22-004	Robin With Lilies SB-9104	Maruri Studios	Open	85.00	85.00
91-22-005	Bluebird With Apple Blossom SB-9105	Maruri Studios	Open	85.00	85.00
91-22-006	Robin & Baby With Azalea SB-9106	Maruri Studios	Open	115.00	115.00
91-22-007	Dbl. Bluebird With Peach Blossom SB-9107	Maruri Studios	Open	145.00	145.00
91-22-008	Dbl. Cardinal With Dogwood SB-9108	Maruri Studios	Open	145.00	145.00
Maruri USA		**Hummingbirds**			
91-23-001	Rufous w/Trumpet Creeper H-8901	Maruri Studios	Open	70.00	75.00
89-23-002	White-eared w/Morning Glory H-8902	Maruri Studios	Open	85.00	85.00
89-23-003	Violet-crowned w/Gentian H-8903	Maruri Studios	Open	90.00	90.00
89-23-004	Calliope w/Azalea H-8904	Maruri Studios	Open	120.00	120.00
91-23-005	Anna's w/Lily H-8905	Maruri Studios	Open	160.00	160.00
91-23-006	Allew's w/Hibiscus H-8906	Maruri Studios	Open	195.00	195.00
91-23-007	Ruby-Throated w/Azalea H-8911	Maruri Studios	Open	75.00	75.00
91-23-008	White-Eared w/Morning Glory H-8912	Maruri Studios	Open	75.00	75.00
91-23-009	Violet-Crowned w/Gentian H-8913	Maruri Studios	Open	75.00	75.00
91-23-010	Ruby-Throated w/Orchid H-8914	Maruri Studios	Open	150.00	150.00
Maruri USA		**Graceful Reflections**			
91-24-001	Single Mute Swan SW-9151	Maruri Studios	Open	85.00	85.00
91-24-002	Mute Swan w/Baby SW-9152	Maruri Studios	Open	95.00	95.00
91-24-003	Pair-Mute Swan SW-9153	Maruri Studios	Open	145.00	145.00
91-24-004	Pair-Mute Swan SW-9154	Maruri Studios	Open	195.00	195.00
Maruri USA		**Precious Panda**			
92-25-001	Snack Time PP-9201	Maruri Studios	Open	60.00	60.00
92-25-002	Lazy Lunch PP-9202	Maruri Studios	Open	60.00	60.00
92-25-003	Tug Of War PP-9203	Maruri Studios	Open	70.00	70.00
92-25-004	Mother's Cuddle-PP-9204	Maruri Studios	Open	120.00	120.00
Maruri USA		**Gentle Giants**			
92-26-001	Baby Elephant Standing GG-9251	Maruri Studios	Open	50.00	50.00
92-26-002	Baby Elephant Sitting GG-9252	Maruri Studios	Open	65.00	65.00
92-26-003	Elephant Pair Playing GG-9253	Maruri Studios	Open	80.00	80.00
92-26-004	Mother & Baby Elephant GG-9254	Maruri Studios	Open	160.00	160.00
92-26-005	Elephant Pair GG-9255	Maruri Studios	Open	220.00	220.00
Maruri USA		**Horses Of The World**			
93-27-001	Clydesdale HW-9351	Maruri Studios	Open	145.00	145.00
93-27-002	Thoroughbred HW-9352	Maruri Studios	Open	145.00	145.00
93-27-003	Quarter Horse HW-9353	Maruri Studios	Open	145.00	145.00
93-27-004	Camargue HW-9354	Maruri Studios	Open	150.00	150.00
93-27-005	Paint Horse HW-9355	Maruri Studios	Open	160.00	160.00
93-27-006	Arabian HW-9356	Maruri Studios	Open	175.00	175.00
June McKenna Collectibles, Inc.		**Limited Edition**			
83-01-001	Father Christmas	J. McKenna	Closed	90.00	2300-6000.
84-01-002	Old Saint Nick	J. McKenna	Closed	100.00	1500-3000.
85-01-003	Woodland	J. McKenna	Closed	140.00	1600-3000.
86-01-004	Victorian	J. McKenna	Closed	150.00	1000-1500.
87-01-005	Christmas Eve	J. McKenna	Closed	170.00	1600.00
87-01-006	Kris Kringle	J. McKenna	Closed	350.00	500-1300.
88-01-007	Bringing Home Christmas	J. McKenna	Closed	170.00	475-1300.
88-01-008	Remembrance of Christmas Past	J. McKenna	4,000	400.00	450.00
89-01-009	Seasons Greetings	J. McKenna	Closed	200.00	225-300.
89-01-010	Santa's Wardrobe	J. McKenna	Closed	750.00	750.00
90-01-011	Wilderness	J. McKenna	Closed	200.00	200.00
90-01-012	Night Before Christmas	J. McKenna	Closed	750.00	750.00
91-01-013	Coming to Town	J. McKenna	4,000	220.00	220.00
91-01-014	Hot Air Balloon	J. McKenna	1,500	800.00	800.00
92-01-015	Christmas Gathering	J. McKenna	4,000	220.00	220.00
93-01-016	The Patriot	J. McKenna	4,000	250.00	250.00
June McKenna Collectibles, Inc.		**Registered Edition**			
86-02-001	Colonial	J. McKenna	Closed	150.00	300-450.
87-02-002	White Christmas	J. McKenna	Closed	170.00	2000-3000.
88-02-003	Jolly Ole St.. Nick	J. McKenna	Closed	170.00	250-350.
89-02-004	Traditional	J. McKenna	Closed	180.00	250-300.
90-02-005	Toy Maker	J. McKenna	Open	200.00	250.00
91-02-006	Checking His List	J. McKenna	Open	230.00	240.00
92-02-007	Forty Winks	J. McKenna	Open	250.00	250.00
93-02-008	Tomorrow's Christmas	J. McKenna	Open	250.00	250.00
June McKenna Collectibles, Inc.		**Special Limited Edition**			
89-03-001	Santa & His Magic Sleigh	J. McKenna	Closed	280.00	280.00
89-03-002	Last Gentle Nudge	J. McKenna	Closed	280.00	N/A
90-03-003	Up On The Rooftop	J. McKenna	Closed	280.00	N/A
90-03-004	Santa's Reindeer	J. McKenna	1,500	400.00	400.00
90-03-005	Christmas Dreams	J. McKenna	Closed	280.00	280.00
91-03-006	Bedtime Stories	J. McKenna	2,000	500.00	500.00
92-03-007	Santa's Arrival	J. McKenna	2,000	300.00	300.00

Company Number	Name	Series Artist	Edition Limit	Issue Price	Quote
93-03-008	Baking Cookies	J. McKenna	2,000	450.00	450.00
June McKenna Collectibles, Inc.		**June McKenna Figurines**			
84-04-001	Tree Topper	J. McKenna	Closed	70.00	225.00
85-04-002	Soldier	J. McKenna	Closed	40.00	150-200.
85-04-003	Father Times - 3D	J. McKenna	Closed	40.00	N/A
86-04-004	Male Angel	J. McKenna	Closed	44.00	1000-2000.
86-04-005	Little St. Nick	J. McKenna	Closed	50.00	75-125.00
87-04-006	Patriotic Santa	J. McKenna	Closed	50.00	100-150.
87-04-007	Name Plaque	J. McKenna	Closed	50.00	N/A
87-04-008	Country Rag Boy	J. McKenna	Closed	40.00	N/A
87-04-009	Country Rag Girl	J. McKenna	Closed	40.00	N/A
88-04-010	Mrs. Santa	J. McKenna	Closed	50.00	100-125.
88-04-011	Mr. Santa - 3D	J. McKenna	Closed	44.00	N/A
89-04-012	16th Century Santa - 3D	J. McKenna	Closed	60.00	N/A
89-04-013	17th Century Santa - 3D	J. McKenna	Closed	70.00	N/A
89-04-014	Jolly Ole Santa - 3D	J. McKenna	Closed	44.00	N/A
90-04-015	Noel - 3D	J. McKenna	Closed	50.00	70.00
92-04-016	Taking A Break	J. McKenna	Open	60.00	70.00
92-04-017	Christmas Santa	J. McKenna	Open	60.00	70.00
92-04-018	Choir of Angels	J. McKenna	Open	60.00	60.00
92-04-019	Let It Snow	J. McKenna	Open	60.00	60.00
93-04-020	A Good Night's Sleep	J. McKenna	Open	70.00	70.00
93-04-021	Santa and Friends	J. McKenna	Open	70.00	70.00
93-04-022	Mr. Snowman	J. McKenna	Open	40.00	40.00
93-04-023	The Snow Family	J. McKenna	Open	40.00	40.00
93-04-024	Santa Name Plaque	J. McKenna	Open	N/A	N/A
93-04-025	Angel Name Plaque	J. McKenna	Open	N/A	N/A
93-04-026	Children Ice Skaters	J. McKenna	Open	N/A	N/A
June McKenna Collectibles, Inc.		**Carolers**			
85-05-001	Man Caroler	J. McKenna	Closed	36.00	75.00
85-05-002	Woman Caroler	J. McKenna	Closed	36.00	75.00
85-05-003	Girl Caroler	J. McKenna	Closed	36.00	75.00
85-05-004	Boy Caroler	J. McKenna	Closed	36.00	75.00
91-05-005	Carolers, Man With Girl	J. McKenna	Open	50.00	50.00
91-05-006	Carolers, Woman With Boy	J. McKenna	Open	50.00	50.00
92-05-007	Carolers, Grandparents	J. McKenna	Open	70.00	70.00
June McKenna Collectibles, Inc.		**Limited Edition Flatback**			
88-06-001	Toys of Joy	J. McKenna	Closed	30.00	N/A
88-06-002	Mystical Santa	J. McKenna	Closed	30.00	N/A
89-06-003	Blue Christmas	J. McKenna	Closed	32.00	N/A
89-06-004	Victorian	J. McKenna	Closed	32.00	N/A
90-06-006	Old Time Santa	J. McKenna	Closed	34.00	34.00
90-06-007	Medieval Santa	J. McKenna	Closed	34.00	34.00
91-06-008	Farewell Santa	J. McKenna	10,000	34.00	40.00
91-06-009	Bag of Stars	J. McKenna	10,000	34.00	40.00
92-06-010	Good Tidings	J. McKenna	10,000	34.00	40.00
92-06-011	Deck The Halls	J. McKenna	10,000	34.00	40.00
93-06-012	Bells of Christmas	J. McKenna	10,000	40.00	40.00
93-06-012	Santa's Love	J. McKenna	10,000	40.00	40.00
June McKenna Collectibles, Inc.		**7" Limited Edition**			
88-07-001	Joyful Christmas	J. McKenna	Closed	90.00	N/A
88-07-002	Christmas Memories	J. McKenna	Closed	90.00	N/A
89-07-003	Old Fashioned Santa	J. McKenna	Closed	100.00	N/A
89-07-004	Santa's Bag of Surprises	J. McKenna	Closed	100.00	N/A
90-07-005	Christmas Delight	J. McKenna	Closed	100.00	100.00
90-07-006	Ethnic Santa	J. McKenna	Closed	100.00	100.00
91-07-007	Christmas Bishop	J. McKenna	7,500	110.00	120.00
92-07-008	Christmas Wizard	J. McKenna	7,500	110.00	120.00
93-07-009	Christmas Cheer	J. McKenna	7,500	120.00	120.00
June McKenna Collectibles, Inc.		**Nativity Set**			
88-08-001	Nativity - 6 Pieces	J. McKenna	Open	130.00	150.00
89-08-002	Three Wise Men	J. McKenna	Open	60.00	90.00
91-08-003	Sheep With Shepherds - 2 Pieces	J. McKenna	Open	60.00	60.00
June McKenna Collectibles, Inc.		**Black Folk Art**			
85-09-001	Mammie With Kids - 3D	J. McKenna	Closed	90.00	N/A
85-09-002	Kids in a Tub - 3D	J. McKenna	Closed	30.00	60.00
85-09-003	Toaster Cover	J. McKenna	Closed	50.00	N/A
85-09-004	Kissing Cousins - sill sitter	J. McKenna	Closed	36.00	85.00
83-09-005	Black Boy With Watermelon	J. McKenna	Closed	12.00	100.00
83-09-006	Black Girl With Watermelon	J. McKenna	Closed	12.00	100.00
84-09-007	Black Man With Pig	J. McKenna	Closed	13.00	40.00
84-09-008	Black Woman With Broom	J. McKenna	Closed	13.00	110.00
84-09-009	Mammie Cloth Doll	J. McKenna	Closed	90.00	N/A
84-09-010	Remus Cloth Doll	J. McKenna	Closed	90.00	N/A
85-09-011	Watermelon Patch Kids	J. McKenna	Closed	24.00	63.00
85-09-012	Mammie With Spoon	J. McKenna	Closed	13.00	N/A
86-09-013	Black Butler	J. McKenna	Closed	13.00	40.00
87-09-014	Aunt Bertha - 3D	J. McKenna	Closed	36.00	72.00
87-09-015	Uncle Jacob- 3D	J. McKenna	Closed	36.00	50-72.00
87-09-016	Lil' Willie -3D	J. McKenna	Closed	36.00	50-72.00
87-09-017	Sweet Prissy -3D	J. McKenna	Closed	36.00	72.00
88-09-018	Renty	J. McKenna	Closed	16.00	40.00
88-09-019	Netty	J. McKenna	Closed	16.00	40.00
89-09-020	Jake	J. McKenna	Closed	16.00	40.00
89-09-021	Delia	J. McKenna	Closed	16.00	40.00
90-09-022	Tasha	J. McKenna	Closed	17.00	40.00
90-09-023	Tyree	J. McKenna	Closed	17.00	40.00
90-09-024	Let's Play Ball -3D	J. McKenna	Open	45.00	N/A
90-09-025	Sunday's Best -3D	J. McKenna	Open	45.00	N/A
92-09-026	Fishing John -3D	J. McKenna	1,000	160.00	N/A
92-09-027	Sweet Sister Sue -3D	J. McKenna	1,000	160.00	N/A
June McKenna Collectibles, Inc.		**Victorian Limited Edition**			
90-10-001	Edward - 3D	J. McKenna	Closed	180.00	450.00
90-10-002	Elizabeth - 3D	J. McKenna	Closed	180.00	450.00
90-10-003	Joseph - 3D	J. McKenna	Closed	50.00	50.00
90-10-004	Victoria - 3D	J. McKenna	Closed	50.00	50.00
Michael's		**Brian Baker's Deja Vu Collection**			
87-01-001	Hotel Couronne (original)White/Brown 1000	B. Baker	Retrd.	49.00	49.00
87-01-002	Parisian Apartment-Golden Brown 1001	B. Baker	Open	53.00	53.00
87-01-003	The Bernese Guesthouse-Golden Brown 1010	B. Baker	Retrd.	49.00	49.00
87-01-004	Bavarian Church-Yellow 1020	B. Baker	Retrd.	38.00	38.00
87-01-005	Bavarian Church-White 1021	B. Baker	Retrd.	38.00	38.00
87-01-006	Japanese House-White/Brown 1100	B. Baker	Retrd.	47.00	47.00
87-01-007	Snow Cabin-Brown/White 1500	B. Baker	Open	51.00	51.00
87-01-008	Colonial House-Blue 1510	B. Baker	Retrd.	49.00	49.00
87-01-009	Colonial House-Wine 1511	B. Baker	Retrd.	40.00	40.00
87-01-010	Colonial Store-Brick 1512	B. Baker	Open	53.00	53.00
87-01-011	Old West General Store-White/Grey 1520	B. Baker	Retrd.	50.00	50.00
87-01-012	Old West General Store-Yellow 1521	B. Baker	Retrd.	50.00	50.00
87-01-013	The Farm House-Beige/Blue 1525	B. Baker	Retrd.	49.00	49.00
87-01-014	The Farm House-Spiced Tan 1526	B. Baker	Retrd.	49.00	49.00
87-01-015	The Cottage House-White 1530	B. Baker	Open	47.00	47.00
87-01-016	The Cottage House-Blue 1531	B. Baker	Retrd.	42.00	42.00
87-01-017	The Lighthouse-White 1535	B. Baker	Retrd.	53.00	53.00
87-01-018	Gothic Victorian-Peach 1536	B. Baker	10/93	51.00	51.00
87-01-019	Queen Ann Victorian-Peach/Green 1540	B. Baker	Open	53.00	53.00
87-01-020	Queen Ann Victorian-Rose 1541	B. Baker	Open	53.00	53.00
87-01-021	Queen Ann Victorian-Rust/Green 1542	B. Baker	Retrd.	49.00	49.00
87-01-022	Italianate Victorian-Brown 1543	B. Baker	Retrd.	51.00	51.00
87-01-023	Italianate Victorian-Rust/Blue 1544	B. Baker	Retrd.	49.00	49.00
87-01-024	Italianate Victorian-Mauve/Blue 1545	B. Baker	Retrd.	49.00	49.00
87-01-025	Turreted Victorian-Beige/Blue 1546	B. Baker	Retrd.	55.00	55.00
87-01-026	Turreted Victorian-Peach 1547	B. Baker	Retrd.	55.00	55.00
87-01-027	Ultimate Victorian-Maroon/Slate 1548	B. Baker	Open	60.00	60.00
87-01-028	Ultimate Victorian-Lt. Blue/Rose 1549	B. Baker	Open	60.00	60.00
87-01-028	Italianate Victorian-Lavendar 1550	B. Baker	Retrd.	45.00	45.00
88-01-029	Roader Gate, Rothenburg-Brown 1022	B. Baker	Retrd.	49.00	49.00
88-01-030	Hampshire House-Brick 1040	B. Baker	Retrd.	49.00	49.00
88-01-031	Andulusian Village-White 1060	B. Baker	Retrd.	53.00	53.00
88-01-032	Fairy Tale Cottage-White/Brown 1200	B. Baker	Retrd.	46.00	46.00
88-01-033	Christmas House-Blue 1225	B. Baker	Retrd.	51.00	51.00
88-01-034	Casa Chiquita-Natural 1400	B. Baker	Retrd.	53.00	53.00
88-01-035	Georgian Colonial House-White/Blue 1514	B. Baker	Retrd.	53.00	53.00
88-01-036	Adam Colonial Cottage-Blue/White 1515	B. Baker	Retrd.	53.00	53.00
88-01-037	French Colonial Cottage-Beige 1516	B. Baker	Retrd.	42.00	42.00
88-01-038	Antebellum Mansion-Peach 1517	B. Baker	Retrd.	49.00	49.00
88-01-039	Antebellum Mansion-White/Green 1518	B. Baker	Retrd.	49.00	49.00
88-01-040	Antebellum Mansion-Blue/White 1519	B. Baker	Retrd.	49.00	49.00
88-01-041	Country Church-White/Blue 1522	B. Baker	Open	49.00	49.00
88-01-042	One Room School House-Red 1524	B. Baker	Open	53.00	53.00
88-01-043	Gothic Victorian-Sea Green 1537	B. Baker	Retrd.	47.00	47.00
88-01-044	Second Empire House-White/Blue 1538	B. Baker	Open	54.00	54.00
88-01-045	Second Empire House-Sea Grn./Desert 1539	B. Baker	Retrd.	50.00	50.00
88-01-046	Stone Victorians Browns 1554	B. Baker	Open	56.00	56.00
89-01-046	Parisian Apartment-Beige/Blue 1002	B. Baker	Open	53.00	53.00
89-01-047	Hotel Couronne-White/Brown 1003	B. Baker	Retrd.	55.00	55.00
89-01-048	Blumen Shop-White/Brown 1023	B. Baker	Open	53.00	53.00
89-01-049	Windmill on the Dike-Beige/Green 1034	B. Baker	Open	60.00	60.00
89-01-050	Hampshire House-Brick 1041	B. Baker	Retrd.	49.00	49.00
89-01-051	Henry VIII Pub-White/Brown 1043	B. Baker	Open	56.00	56.00
89-01-052	Swedish House-Swed.Red 1050	B. Baker	Retrd.	51.00	51.00
89-01-053	Norwegian House-Brown 1051	B. Baker	Retrd.	51.00	51.00
89-01-054	Antebellum Mansion-Blue/Rose 1505	B. Baker	Open	53.00	53.00
89-01-055	Antebellum Mansion-Peach 1506	B. Baker	Retrd.	49.00	49.00
89-01-056	Country Barn-Red 1527	B. Baker	Open	53.00	53.00
89-01-057	Country Barn-Blue 1528	B. Baker	Retrd.	49.00	49.00
89-01-058	Italianate Victorian-Rose/Blue 1551	B. Baker	Retrd.	51.00	51.00
89-01-059	Italianate Victorian-Peach/Teal 1552	B. Baker	Retrd.	51.00	51.00
89-01-060	Ultimate Victorian-Peach/Green 1553	B. Baker	Open	60.00	60.00
89-01-061	Deja Vu Sign-Ivory/Brown 1600	B. Baker	Retrd.	21.00	21.00
90-01-062	Palm Villa-White/Blue 1420	B. Baker	Open	54.00	54.00
90-01-063	Palm Villa-Desert/Green 1421	B. Baker	Open	54.00	54.00
90-01-064	Old Country Cottage-Blue 1502	B. Baker	Retrd.	51.00	51.00
90-01-065	Old Country Cottage-Red 1503	B. Baker	Retrd.	51.00	51.00
90-01-066	Old Country Cottage-Peach 1504	B. Baker	Retrd.	47.00	47.00
90-01-067	Gothic Victorian-Blue/Mauve 1534	B. Baker	Retrd.	47.00	47.00
90-01-068	Classic Victorian-Blue/White 1555	B. Baker	Open	60.00	60.00
90-01-069	Classic Victorian-Rose/Blue 1556	B. Baker	Open	60.00	60.00
90-01-070	Classic Victorian-Peach 1557	B. Baker	Open	60.00	60.00
90-01-071	Victorian Country Estate-Desert/Brown 1560	B. Baker	Open	62.00	62.00
90-01-072	Victorian Country Estate-Rose/Blue 1561	B. Baker	Open	62.00	62.00
90-01-073	Victorian Country Estate-Peach/Blue 1562	B. Baker	Open	62.00	62.00
91-01-074	Wind and Roses-Brick 1470	B. Baker	Open	63.00	63.00
91-01-075	Log Cabin-Brown 1501	B. Baker	Open	55.00	55.00
91-01-076	Colonial Color-Brown 1508	B. Baker	Open	62.00	62.00
91-01-077	Colonial Cottage-White/Blue 1509	B. Baker	Open	59.00	59.00
91-01-078	Victorian Farmhouse-Golden Brown 1565	B. Baker	Open	59.00	59.00
91-01-079	Teddy's Place-Teal/Rose 1570	B. Baker	Open	61.00	61.00
91-01-080	Mayor's Mansion-Blue/Peach 1585	B. Baker	Open	57.00	57.00
92-01-081	Alpine Ski Lodge-Brown/White 1012	B. Baker	Open	62.00	62.00
92-01-082	Firehouse-Brick 1140	B. Baker	Open	60.00	60.00
92-01-083	Flower Store-Tan/Green 1145	B. Baker	Open	67.00	67.00
92-01-084	Country Station-Blue/Rust 1156	B. Baker	Open	64.00	64.00
92-01-085	Tropical Fantasy-Blue/Coral 1410	B. Baker	Open	67.00	67.00
92-01-086	Tropical Fantasy-Rose/Blue 1411	B. Baker	Open	67.00	67.00
92-01-087	Tropical Fantasy-Yellowl/Teal 1412	B. Baker	Open	67.00	67.00
92-01-088	Rose Cottage-Grey 1443	B. Baker	Open	59.00	59.00
92-01-089	Looks Like Nantucket-Grey 1451	B. Baker	Open	62.00	62.00
92-01-090	Victorian Tower House-Blue/Maroon 1558	B. Baker	Open	63.00	63.00
92-01-091	Victorian Tower House-Peach/Blue 1559	B. Baker	Open	63.00	63.00
92-01-092	Victorian Bay View-Rose/Blue 1563	B. Baker	Open	63.00	63.00
92-01-093	Victorian Bay View-Cream/Teal 1564	B. Baker	Open	63.00	63.00
92-01-094	Angel of the Sea-Mauve/White 1586	B. Baker	Open	67.00	67.00
92-01-095	Angel of the Sea-Blue/White 1587	B. Baker	Open	67.00	67.00
92-01-096	Victorian Charm-Cream 1588	B. Baker	Open	61.00	61.00
92-01-097	Victorian Charm-Mauve 1589	B. Baker	Open	61.00	61.00
92-01-098	Deja Vu Sign-Ivory/Brown 1999	B. Baker	Open	21.00	21.00
93-01-099	Dinard Mansion-Beige/Brick 1005	B. Baker	Open	67.00	67.00
93-01-100	Old West Hotel-Cream 1120	B. Baker	Open	62.00	62.00
93-01-101	Corner Grocery-Brick 1141	B. Baker	Open	67.00	67.00
93-01-102	Post Office-Light Green 1146	B. Baker	Open	60.00	60.00
93-01-103	Enchanted Cottage-Natural 1205	B. Baker	Open	63.00	63.00
93-01-104	Homestead Christmas-Red 1224	B. Baker	Open	57.00	57.00
93-01-105	Monday's Wash-White/Blue 1449	B. Baker	Open	62.00	62.00
93-01-106	Monday's Wash-Cream/Blue 1450	B. Baker	Open	62.00	62.00
93-01-107	The Stone House-Stone/Blue 1453	B. Baker	Open	63.00	63.00
93-01-108	Grandpa's Barn-Brown 1498	B. Baker	Open	63.00	63.00
93-01-109	Sunday Afternoon-Brick 1523	B. Baker	Open	62.00	62.00
93-01-110	Smuggler's Cove-Grey/Brown 1529	B. Baker	Open	72.00	72.00
93-01-111	Admiralty Head Lighthouse-White 1532	B. Baker	Open	62.00	62.00
93-01-112	Charlestone Single House-Blue/White 1583	B. Baker	Open	60.00	60.00
93-01-113	Charlestone Single House-Peach/White 1584	B. Baker	Open	60.00	60.00
93-01-114	Mansard Lady-Blue/Rose 1606	B. Baker	Open	64.00	64.00
93-01-115	Mansard Lady-Tan/Green 1607	B. Baker	Open	64.00	64.00
93-01-116	Steiner Street-Peach/Green 1674	B. Baker	Open	63.00	63.00
93-01-117	Steiner Street-Rose/Blue 1675	B. Baker	Open	63.00	63.00

FIGURINES

Company Number	Name	Series Artist	Edition Limit	Issue Price	Quote
Michael's	**Limited Editions From Brian Baker**				
87-02-001	Amsterdam Canal-Brown, S/N 1030	B. Baker	1,000	79.00	79.00
93-02-002	James River Plantation-Brick, Numbrd.1454	B. Baker	500	108.00	108.00
93-02-003	American Classic-Rose, Numbrd.1566	B. Baker	Retrd.	99.00	99.00
Michael's	**Collectors' Corner**				
93-03-001	Brian's House (Redemption House)-Red1496	B. Baker	Yr.Iss.	71.00	71.00
93-03-002	City Cottage (Membership House)-Rose/Grn. 1682	B. Baker	Yr.Iss.	35.00	35.00
Midwest Importers	**Christian Ulbricht Nutcracker Collection**				
86-01-001	Pilgrim Nutcracker, 16 1/2" 03939	C. Ulbricht	Open	145.00	155.00
92-01-002	Father Christmas Nutcracker 70946	C. Ulbricht	Closed	190.00	190.00
93-01-003	Toymaker Nutcracker 95317	C. Ulbricht	2,500	220.00	220.00
93-01-004	Mrs. Claus Nutcracker 95874	C. Ulbricht	5,000	180.00	180.00
93-01-005	Mr. Claus Nutcracker 95881	C. Ulbricht	5,000	180.00	180.00
Midwest Importers	**Christian Ulbricht "A Christmas Carol" Nutcrackers**				
93-02-001	Bob Cratchit and Tiny Tim Nutcracker 95775	C. Ulbricht	6,000	240.00	240.00
93-02-002	Scrooge Nutcracker 95843	C. Ulbricht	6,000	210.00	210.00
Midwest Importers	**Christian Ulbricht "Nutcracker Fantasy" Nutcrackers**				
91-03-001	Herr Drosselmeyer Nutcracker, 16 1/4" 36568	C. Ulbricht	Open	170.00	185.00
91-03-002	Clara Nutcracker, 11 1/2" 36576	C. Ulbricht	Open	125.00	143.00
91-03-003	Prince Nutcracker, 17" 36659	C. Ulbricht	Open	160.00	173.00
91-03-004	Toy Soldier, 14" 36667	C. Ulbricht	Open	160.00	173.00
91-03-005	Mouse King Nutcracker, 13 1/2" 45105	C. Ulbricht	Open	170.00	180.00
Midwest Importers	**Erzgebirge Nutcracker Collection**				
92-04-001	Christopher Columbus Nutcracker 01529	Midwest Importers	Closed	80.00	80.00
84-04-002	Pinocchio Nutcracker 01602	Midwest Importers	Open	60.00	60.00
92-04-003	Victorian Santa Nutcracker 01876	Midwest Importers	Open	130.00	130.00
92-04-004	Pilgrim Nutcracker 01884	Midwest Importers	Open	96.00	97.00
92-04-005	Indian Nutcracker 01959	Midwest Importers	Open	96.00	97.00
92-04-006	Ringmaster Nutcracker 01967	Midwest Importers	Open	135.00	137.00
92-04-007	Cowboy Nutcracker 02981	Midwest Importers	Open	97.00	107.00
92-04-008	Farmer Nutcracker 11099	Midwest Importers	Open	65.00	73.00
92-04-009	Santa with Skis Nutcracker 13053	Midwest Importers	Open	100.00	105.00
91-04-010	Clown Nutcracker 35619	Midwest Importers	Open	115.00	118.00
91-04-011	Nutcracker-Maker Nutcracker 36013	Midwest Importers	Open	62.00	65.00
90-04-012	Elf Nutcracker 41541	Midwest Importers	Open	70.00	73.00
90-04-013	Sea Captain Nutcracker 41575	Midwest Importers	Open	86.00	95.00
90-04-014	Witch Nutcracker 41591	Midwest Importers	Open	75.00	76.00
90-04-015	Windsor Club Nutcracker 41608	Midwest Importers	Open	85.00	86.50
90-04-016	Woodland Santa Nutcracker 41913	Midwest Importers	Open	105.00	109.00
90-04-017	Uncle Sam Nutcracker 42060	Midwest Importers	Open	50.00	61.50
90-04-018	Merlin the Magician Nutcracker 42078	Midwest Importers	Open	67.00	70.00
88-04-019	Santa with Tree & Toys Nutcracker 76663	Midwest Importers	Open	76.00	87.00
88-04-020	Nordic Santa Nutcracker 88725	Midwest Importers	Open	84.00	104.50
89-04-021	Golfer Nutcracker 93253	Midwest Importers	Open	85.00	89.00
89-04-022	Country Santa Nutcracker 93261	Midwest Importers	Open	95.00	120.00
89-04-023	Fisherman Nutcracker 93279	Midwest Importers	Open	90.00	94.00
93-04-024	Fireman with Dog Nutcracker 65921	Midwest Importers	Open	134.00	134.00
93-04-025	Gepetto Santa Nutcracker 94174	Midwest Importers	Open	115.00	115.00
93-04-026	Santa with Animals Nutcracker 94242	Midwest Importers	Open	117.00	117.00
93-04-027	Cat Witch Nutcracker 94266	Midwest Importers	Open	93.00	93.00
93-04-028	White Santa Nutcracker 95331	Midwest Importers	Open	100.00	100.00
Midwest Importers	**Erzgebirge Easter Nutcrackers**				
91-05-001	Bunny with Egg Nutcracker 01454	Midwest Importers	Open	77.00	80.00
84-05-002	March Hare Nutcracker 03129	Midwest Importers	Open	77.00	80.00
92-05-003	Bunny Painter Nutcracker 64808	Midwest Importers	Open	77.00	77.00
Midwest Importers	**Erzgebirge "Nutcracker Fantasy" Nutcrackers**				
91-06-001	Clara Nutcracker, 8" 12542	Midwest Importers	Open	77.00	80.00
88-06-002	Her Drosselmeyer Nutcracker, 14 1/2" 75061	Midwest Importers	Open	75.00	87.00
88-06-003	The Prince Nutcracker, 12 3/4" 75079	Midwest Importers	Open	75.00	79.00
88-06-004	The Toy Soldier Nutcracker, 11" 75087	Midwest Importers	Open	70.00	77.00
88-06-005	The Mouse King Nutcracker, 10" 75095	Midwest Importers	Open	60.00	77.00
93-06-006	The Mouse King Nutcracker 53508	Midwest Importers	5,000	100.00	100.00
Midwest Importers	**Erzgebirge "A Christmas Carol" Nutcrackers**				
93-07-001	Ghost of Christmas Present Nutcracker 55205	Midwest Importers	5,000	116.00	116.00
93-07-002	Scrooge Nutcracker 55229	Midwest Importers	5,000	104.00	104.00
93-07-003	Bob Cratchit Nutcracker 94211	Midwest Importers	5,000	120.00	120.00
Midwest Importers	**Wendt and Kuhn Collection**				
79-08-001	Angel Playing Violin 04036	Wendt/Kuhn	Open	34.00	35.00
83-08-002	Angel Percussion Musicians, set/6 04432	Wendt/Kuhn	Open	110.00	115.00
84-08-003	Angels Bearing Toys, set/6 04515	Wendt/Kuhn	Open	97.00	100.00
83-08-004	Angel String Musicians, set/6 04557	Wendt/Kuhn	Open	105.00	110.00
83-08-005	Angel String & Woodwind Musicians, set/6 04656	Wendt/Kuhn	Open	108.00	112.00
83-08-006	Angel Conductor on Stand 04698	Wendt/Kuhn	Open	21.00	22.00
83-08-007	Angel Brass Musicians, set/6 04705	Wendt/Kuhn	Open	92.00	96.00
79-08-008	Angel Trio, set/3 04713	Wendt/Kuhn	Open	140.00	145.00
76-08-009	Santa with Angel 04739	Wendt/Kuhn	Open	50.00	52.00
83-08-010	Margarita Birthday Angels, set/3 04804	Wendt/Kuhn	Open	44.00	46.00
80-08-011	Angel Pulling Wagon 05539	Wendt/Kuhn	Open	43.00	45.00
81-08-012	Angel w/ Tree & Basket 11908 (wasMI#0468)	Wendt/Kuhn	Open	24.00	25.00
81-08-013	Santa w/Angel in Sleigh 11924(wasMI#0414)	Wendt/Kuhn	Open	52.00	54.00
81-08-014	Angels at Cradle, set/4 11932 (wasMI#0554)	Wendt/Kuhn	Open	73.00	74.00
83-08-015	Girl w/Wagon 11966 (was MI#2935)	Wendt/Kuhn	Open	27.00	28.00
79-08-016	Girl w/Scissors 11974 (was MI#2941)	Wendt/Kuhn	Open	25.00	26.00
79-08-017	Girl w/Porridge Bowl 11982 (was MI#2942)	Wendt/Kuhn	Open	29.00	30.00
91-08-018	Girl with Doll 12005	Wendt/Kuhn	Open	31.50	32.00
91-08-019	Boy on Rocking Horse, 2 asst. 12021	Wendt/Kuhn	Open	35.00	36.00
79-08-020	Girl w/Cradle, set/2 12039 (was MI#2801)	Wendt/Kuhn	Open	37.50	39.00
91-08-021	White Angel with Violin 12055	Wendt/Kuhn	Open	25.50	26.50
78-08-022	Madonna w/Child 12071 (was MI#0428)	Wendt/Kuhn	Open	120.00	125.00
91-08-023	Birdhouse 12097	Wendt/Kuhn	Open	22.50	23.00
91-08-024	Flower Children, set/6 12138	Wendt/Kuhn	Open	130.00	135.00
91-08-025	Display Base for Wendt und Kuhn Figures, 12 1/2 x2" 12146	Wendt/Kuhn	Open	32.00	34.00
79-08-026	Pied Piper and Children, set/7 28432	Wendt/Kuhn	Open	120.00	130.00
79-08-027	Bavarian Moving Van 28549	Wendt/Kuhn	Open	133.50	138.00
79-08-028	Magarita Angels, set/6 29381	Wendt/Kuhn	Open	94.00	98.00
76-08-029	Angel with Sled 29406	Wendt/Kuhn	Open	36.50	38.00
80-08-030	Little People Napkin Rings, 6 asst. 35049	Wendt/Kuhn	Open	21.00	22.00
90-08-031	Angel Duet in Celestial Stars 41583	Wendt/Kuhn	Open	60.00	62.00
87-08-032	Child on Skis, 2 asst. 60830	Wendt/Kuhn	Open	28.00	29.00
87-08-033	Child on Sled 60856	Wendt/Kuhn	Open	25.50	26.50
92-08-034	Wendt und Kuhn Display Sign w/ Sitting Angel 75350	Wendt/Kuhn	Open	20.00	23.00
88-08-035	Lucia Parade Figures, set/3 76671	Wendt/Kuhn	Open	75.00	78.00
88-08-036	Children Carrying Lanterns Procession, set/6 76697	Wendt/Kuhn	Open	117.00	127.00
89-08-037	Angel at Piano 94037	Wendt/Kuhn	Open	31.00	33.00
Midwest Importers	**Wendt and Kuhn Figurines Candleholders**				
76-09-001	Angel Candleholder Pair 04721	Wendt/Kuhn	Open	70.00	73.00
91-09-002	Angel with Friend Candleholder 11916	Wendt/Kuhn	Open	33.30	34.00
91-09-003	Small Angel Candleholder Pair 11958	Wendt/Kuhn	Open	60.00	63.00
80-09-004	Large Angel Candleholder Pair 12013 (wasMI#0463)	Wendt/Kuhn	Open	270.00	277.00
86-09-005	Pair of Angels Candleholder 12047(was MI#0410)	Wendt/Kuhn	Open	30.00	31.50
91-09-006	White Angel Candleholder 12063	Wendt/Kuhn	Open	28.00	29.00
87-09-007	Santa Candleholder 60822	Wendt/Kuhn	Open	53.00	54.00
Midwest Importers	**Wendt and Kuhn Collection Music Boxes**				
91-10-001	Angels & Santa Around Tree 12112	Wendt/Kuhn	Open	300.00	300.00
78-10-002	Rotating Angels 'Round Cradle 19118	Wendt/Kuhn	Open	270.00	270.00
78-10-003	Angel at Pipe Organ 19291	Wendt/Kuhn	Open	176.00	180.00
76-10-004	Girl Rocking Cradle 92156 (was MI#1941)	Wendt/Kuhn	Open	180.00	190.00
Midwest Importers	**Belenes Puig Nativity Collection**				
85-11-001	Nativity, set/6: Holy Family, Angel, Animals 6 3/4" 02056	J.P. Llobera	Open	250.00	250.00
85-11-002	Shepherd, set/2 04581	J.P. Llobera	Open	110.00	110.00
85-11-003	Wise Men, set/3 04599	J.P. Llobera	Open	185.00	185.00
86-11-004	Sheep, set/3 04755	J.P. Llobera	Open	28.00	28.00
89-11-005	Wise Man with Gold on Camel 20751	J.P. Llobera	Open	155.00	155.00
89-11-006	Wise Man with Myrrh on Camel 20769	J.P. Llobera	Open	155.00	155.00
89-11-007	Wise Man with Frankincense on Camel 20777	J.P. Llobera	Open	155.00	155.00
89-11-008	Donkey 20826	J.P. Llobera	Open	26.00	26.00
89-11-009	Ox 20834	J.P. Llobera	Open	26.00	26.00
89-11-010	Mother Mary 20842	J.P. Llobera	Open	62.00	62.00
89-11-011	Baby Jesus 20850	J.P. Llobera	Open	62.00	62.00
89-11-012	Joseph 20868	J.P. Llobera	Open	62.00	62.00
89-11-013	Angel 20876	J.P. Llobera	Open	50.00	50.00
89-11-014	Wise Man with Frankincense 20884	J.P. Llobera	Open	66.00	66.00
89-11-015	Wise Man with Gold 20892	J.P. Llobera	Open	66.00	66.00
89-11-016	Wise Man with Myrrh 20909	J.P. Llobera	Open	66.00	66.00
89-11-017	Shepherd with Staff 20917	J.P. Llobera	Open	56.00	56.00
89-11-018	Shepherd Carrying Lamb 20925	J.P. Llobera	Open	56.00	56.00
90-11-019	Resting Camel 40254	J.P. Llobera	Open	115.00	115.00
87-11-020	Shepherd & Angel Scene, set/7 60848	J.P. Llobera	Open	305.00	305.00
88-11-021	Standing Camel 87925	J.P. Llobera	Open	115.00	115.00
Midwest Importers	**Leo R. Smith III Collection**				
91-12-001	Stars and Stripes Santa 17435	L.R. Smith	5,000	190.00	200.00
91-12-002	Woodsman Santa 33100	L.R. Smith	5,000	230.00	250.00
91-12-003	Pilgrim Riding Turkey 33126	L.R. Smith	5,000	230.00	250.00
91-12-004	Milkmaker 35411	L.R. Smith	5,000	170.00	184.00
91-12-005	'Tis a Witching Time 35445	L.R. Smith	Closed	140.00	145.00
91-12-006	Toymaker 35403	L.R. Smith	5,000	120.00	130.00
91-12-007	Cossack Santa 10926	L.R. Smith	5,000	95.00	103.00
91-12-008	Pilgrim Man 33134	L.R. Smith	5,000	78.00	84.00
91-12-009	Pilgrim Woman 33150	L.R. Smith	5,000	78.00	84.00
91-12-010	Fisherman Santa 33118	L.R. Smith	5,000	270.00	290.00
92-12-011	Dreams of Night Buffalo 79998	L.R. Smith	5,000	250.00	270.00
92-12-012	Santa of Peace 73289	L.R. Smith	5,000	250.00	270.00
92-12-013	Great Plains Santa 80490	L.R. Smith	5,000	270.00	293.00
92-12-014	Ms. Liberty 78669	L.R. Smith	5,000	190.00	210.00
92-12-015	Woodland Brave 78677	L.R. Smith	5,000	87.00	94.00
92-12-016	Leo Smith Name Plaque 78817	Midwest Importers	Open	12.00	12.00
93-12-017	Gnome Santa on Deer 052068	L.R. Smith	5,000	270.00	270.00
93-12-018	Folk Angel 054444	L.R. Smith	5,000	145.00	145.00
93-12-019	Santa Fisherman 089798	L.R. Smith	5,000	250.00	250.00
93-12-020	Dancing Santa 090428	L.R. Smith	5,000	170.00	170.00
93-12-021	Voyageur 090435	L.R. Smith	5,000	170.00	170.00
Midwest Importers	**Heritage Santa Collection**				
90-13-001	Scanda Klaus 05365	Midwest Importers	Open	26.50	27.50
90-13-002	Herr Kristmas 05373	Midwest Importers	Open	26.50	27.50
90-13-003	MacNicholas 05381	Midwest Importers	Open	26.50	27.50
90-13-004	Papa Frost 05399	Midwest Importers	Open	26.50	27.50
91-13-005	Father Christmas 17980	Midwest Importers	Open	26.50	27.50
91-13-006	Santa Niccolo 17972	Midwest Importers	Open	26.50	27.50
92-13-007	Santa Nykolai 67729	Midwest Importers	Open	26.50	26.50
92-13-008	Pere Noel 67711	Midwest Importers	Open	26.50	26.50
93-13-009	Santa España 73681	Midwest Importers	Open	25.00	25.00
93-13-010	Santa O'Nicholas73704	Midwest Importers	Open	25.00	25.00
Midwest Importers	**Heritage Santa Roly-Polys**				
90-14-001	Scanda Klaus Roly-Poly 05282	Midwest Importers	Open	24.00	25.00
90-14-002	Herr Kristmas Roly-Poly 05290	Midwest Importers	Open	24.00	25.00
90-14-003	MacNicholas Roly-Poly 05307	Midwest Importers	Open	24.00	25.00
90-14-004	Papa Frost Roly-Poly 05315	Midwest Importers	Open	24.00	25.00
91-14-005	Father Christmas Roly-Poly 17964	Midwest Importers	Open	24.00	25.00
91-14-006	Santa Niccolo Roly-Poly 17956	Midwest Importers	Open	24.00	25.00
92-14-007	Santa Nykolai Roly-Poly 67696	Midwest Importers	Open	24.00	24.00
92-14-008	Pere Noel Roly-Poly 67688	Midwest Importers	Open	24.00	24.00
93-14-009	Santa España Roly-Poly 73735	Midwest Importers	Open	20.00	20.00
93-14-010	Santa O'Nicholas Roly-Poly 73759	Midwest Importers	Open	20.00	20.00
Midwest Importers	**Heritage Santa Collection Fabric Mache**				
90-15-001	Scanda Klaus Fabric Mache set 05141	Midwest Importers	Closed	160.00	160.00
90-15-002	Herr Kristmas Fabric Mache set 05159	Midwest Importers	Closed	160.00	160.00
90-15-003	MacNicholas Fabric Mache set 05167	Midwest Importers	Open	160.00	170.00
90-15-004	Papa Frost Fabric Mache set 05175	Midwest Importers	Open	160.00	170.00
91-15-005	Father Christmas Fabric Mache set 18003	Midwest Importers	Open	160.00	170.00
91-15-006	Santa Niccolo Fabric Mache set 17998	Midwest Importers	Open	160.00	170.00
92-15-007	Santa Nykolai Fabric Mache set 67670	Midwest Importers	Open	160.00	170.00
92-15-008	Pere Noel Fabric Mache set 67662	Midwest Importers	Open	160.00	170.00
93-15-009	Santa España Fabric Mache set 73575	Midwest Importers	Open	170.00	170.00
93-15-010	Santa O'Nicholas Fabric Mache set 73650	Midwest Importers	Open	170.00	170.00
Midwest Importers	**Heritage Santa Collection Music Boxes**				
90-16-001	Scanda Klaus Music Box 05323	Midwest Importers	Open	53.00	56.00
90-16-002	Herr Kristmas Music Box 05331	Midwest Importers	Closed	53.00	53.00
90-16-003	MacNicholas Music Box 05349	Midwest Importers	Open	53.00	56.00
90-16-004	Papa Frost Music Box 05357	Midwest Importers	Open	53.00	56.00
91-16-005	Father Christmas Music Box 18029	Midwest Importers	Open	53.00	56.00

Company Number	Name	Series Artist	Edition Limit	Issue Price	Quote
91-16-006	Santa Niccolo Music Box 18011	Midwest Importers	Open	53.00	56.00
92-16-007	Santa Nykolai Music Box 67901	Midwest Importers	Open	53.00	56.00
92-16-008	Pere Noel Music Box 67894	Midwest Importers	Open	53.00	56.00
93-16-009	Santa España Music Box 73667	Midwest Importers	Open	56.00	56.00
93-16-010	Santa O'Nicholas Music Box 73674	Midwest Importers	Open	56.00	56.00
Midwest Importers		**Heritage Santa Collection Snowglobes**			
90-17-001	Scanda Klaus Snowglobe 05240	Midwest Importers	Open	40.00	43.00
90-17-002	Herr Kristmas Snowglobe 05258	Midwest Importers	Closed	40.00	41.50
90-17-003	MacNicholas Snowglobe 05266	Midwest Importers	Open	40.00	43.00
90-17-004	Papa Frost Snowglobe 05274	Midwest Importers	Closed	40.00	41.50
91-17-005	Father Christmas Snowglobe 17948	Midwest Importers	Open	40.00	43.00
91-17-006	Santa Niccolo Snowglobe 17930	Midwest Importers	Open	40.00	43.00
92-17-007	Santa Nykolai Snowglobe 67836	Midwest Importers	Open	40.00	43.00
92-17-008	Pere Noel Snowglobe 67787	Midwest Importers	Open	40.00	43.00
93-17-009	Santa España Snowglobe 73711	Midwest Importers	Open	43.00	43.00
93-17-010	Santa O'Nicholas Snowglobe 73728	Midwest Importers	Open	43.00	43.00
Museum Collections, Inc.		**American Family I**			
79-01-001	Baby's First Step	N. Rockwell	22,500	90.00	220.00
80-01-002	Happy Birthday, Dear Mother	N. Rockwell	22,500	90.00	150.00
80-01-003	Sweet Sixteen	N. Rockwell	22,500	90.00	90.00
80-01-004	First Haircut	N. Rockwell	22,500	90.00	195.00
80-01-005	First Prom	N. Rockwell	22,500	90.00	90.00
80-01-006	Wrapping Christmas Presents	N. Rockwell	22,500	90.00	110.00
80-01-007	The Student	N. Rockwell	22,500	110.00	140.00
80-01-008	Birthday Party	N. Rockwell	22,500	110.00	150.00
80-01-009	Little Mother	N. Rockwell	22,500	110.00	110.00
80-01-010	Washing Our Dog	N. Rockwell	22,500	110.00	110.00
81-01-011	Mother's Little Helpers	N. Rockwell	22,500	110.00	110.00
81-01-012	Bride and Groom	N. Rockwell	22,500	110.00	180.00
Museum Collections, Inc.		**Christmas**			
80-02-001	Checking His List	N. Rockwell	Yr.Iss.	65.00	85.00
81-02-002	Ringing in Good Cheer	N. Rockwell	Yr.Iss.	95.00	95.00
82-02-003	Waiting for Santa	N. Rockwell	Yr.Iss.	95.00	95.00
83-02-004	High Hopes	N. Rockwell	Yr.Iss.	95	95.00
84-02-005	Space Age Santa	N. Rockwell	Yr.Iss.	65.00	65.00
Museum Collections, Inc.		**Classic**			
80-03-001	Lighthouse Keeper's Daughter	N. Rockwell	Closed	65.00	65.00
80-03-002	The Cobbler	N. Rockwell	Closed	65.00	85.00
80-03-003	The Toymaker	N. Rockwell	Closed	65.00	85.00
80-03-004	Bedtime	N. Rockwell	Closed	65.00	95.00
80-03-005	Memories	N. Rockwell	Closed	65.00	65.00
80-03-006	For A Good Boy	N. Rockwell	Closed	65.00	75.00
81-03-007	A Dollhouse for Sis	N. Rockwell	Closed	65.00	65.00
81-03-008	Music Master	N. Rockwell	Closed	65.00	65.00
81-03-009	The Music Lesson	N. Rockwell	Closed	65.00	65.00
81-03-010	Puppy Love	N. Rockwell	Closed	65.00	65.00
81-03-011	While The Audience Waits	N. Rockwell	Closed	65.00	65.00
81-03-012	Off to School	N. Rockwell	Closed	65.00	65.00
82-03-013	The Country Doctor	N. Rockwell	Closed	65.00	65.00
82-03-014	Spring Fever	N. Rockwell	Closed	65.00	65.00
82-03-015	Words of Wisdom	N. Rockwell	Closed	65.00	65.00
82-03-016	The Kite Maker	N. Rockwell	Closed	65.00	65.00
82-03-017	Dreams in the Antique Shop	N. Rockwell	Closed	65.00	65.00
83-03-018	Winter Fun	N. Rockwell	Closed	65.00	65.00
83-03-019	A Special Treat	N. Rockwell	Closed	65.00	65.00
83-03-020	High Stepping	N. Rockwell	Closed	65.00	65.00
83-03-021	Bored of Education	N. Rockwell	Closed	65.00	65.00
83-03-022	A Final Touch	N. Rockwell	Closed	65.00	65.00
83-03-023	Braving the Storm	N. Rockwell	Closed	65.00	65.00
84-03-024	Goin' Fishin'	N. Rockwell	Closed	65.00	65.00
84-03-025	The Big Race	N. Rockwell	Closed	65.00	65.00
84-03-026	Saturday's Hero	N. Rockwell	Closed	65.00	65.00
84-03-027	All Wrapped Up	N. Rockwell	Closed	65.00	65.00
Museum Collections, Inc.		**Commemorative**			
81-04-001	Norman Rockwell Display	N. Rockwell	5,000	125.00	150.00
82-04-002	Spirit of America	N. Rockwell	5,000	125.00	125.00
83-04-003	Norman Rockwell, America's Artist	N. Rockwell	5,000	125.00	125.00
84-04-004	Outward Bound	N. Rockwell	5,000	125.00	125.00
85-04-005	Another Masterpiece by Norman Rockwell	N. Rockwell	5,000	125.00	150.00
86-04-006	The Painter and the Pups	N. Rockwell	5,000	125.00	150.00
Napoleon U.S.A.		**Capodimonte Porcelain Flowers**			
89-01-001	Double Mistere Rose, pink-100350	E. Guerra	Open	32.50	32.50
89-01-002	Double Mistere Rose, yellow-100302	E. Guerra	Open	32.50	32.50
89-01-003	Double Mistere Rose, tea-100303	E. Guerra	Open	32.50	32.50
89-01-004	Double Mistere Rose, red-100305	E. Guerra	Open	32.50	32.50
89-01-005	Double Mistere Rose, aurora-100331	E. Guerra	Open	32.50	32.50
89-01-006	Double Mistere Rose, bicolor-100335	E. Guerra	Open	32.50	32.50
89-01-007	Double Mistere Rose, raspberry-100347	E. Guerra	Open	32.50	32.50
89-01-008	Rose & Bud, pink-100450	E. Guerra	Open	29.00	29.00
89-01-009	Rose & Bud, yellow-100402	E. Guerra	Open	29.00	29.00
89-01-010	Rose & Bud, tea-100403	E. Guerra	Open	29.00	29.00
89-01-012	Rose & Bud, red-100405	E. Guerra	Open	30.00	30.00
89-01-013	Rose & Bud, aurora-100431	E. Guerra	Open	29.00	29.00
89-01-014	Rose & Bud, raspberry-100447	E. Guerra	Open	30.00	30.00
89-01-015	Dogwood Single, pink-100901	E. Guerra	Open	15.00	15.00
89-01-016	Dogwood Single, white-100910	E. Guerra	Open	15.00	15.00
89-01-017	Dogwood Single, pink-100911	E. Guerra	Open	15.00	15.00
89-01-018	My Love Single, red-101105	E. Guerra	Open	72.00	72.00
89-01-019	Wild Rose Single, aurora-101331	E. Guerra	Open	75.00	75.00
89-01-020	Dogwood Double, pink-101401	E. Guerra	Open	22.00	22.00
89-01-021	Dogwood Double, white-101410	E. Guerra	Open	22.00	22.00
89-01-022	Dogwood Double, pink-101411	E. Guerra	Open	22.00	22.00
89-01-023	Clarissa Rose, pink-101550	E. Guerra	Open	185.00	185.00
89-01-024	Clarissa Rose, red-101505	E. Guerra	Open	190.00	190.00
89-01-025	Clarissa Rose, aurora-101531	E. Guerra	Open	185.00	185.00
89-01-026	Single Poppy, orange-102007	E. Guerra	Open	22.50	22.50
89-01-027	Single Rose Med., pink-103050	E. Guerra	Open	25.00	25.00
89-01-028	Single Rose Med., tea-103003	E. Guerra	Open	25.00	25.00
89-01-029	Single Rose Med., red-103005	E. Guerra	Open	25.00	25.00
89-01-030	Single Rose Med., aurora-103031	E. Guerra	Open	25.00	25.00
89-01-031	Single Rose Med., bicolor-103035	E. Guerra	Open	25.00	25.00
89-01-032	Single Rose Med., raspberry-103047	E. Guerra	Open	25.00	25.00
89-01-033	Tulip, pink-103101	E. Guerra	Open	65.00	65.00
89-01-034	Queen Rose 2/bud, pink-110150	E. Guerra	Open	47.00	47.00
89-01-035	Queen Rose 2/bud, red-110105	E. Guerra	Open	48.00	48.00
89-01-036	Queen Rose 2/bud, aurora-110131	E. Guerra	Open	47.00	47.00
89-01-037	Queen Rose 2/bud, raspberry-110147	E. Guerra	Open	47.00	47.00

Company Number	Name	Series Artist	Edition Limit	Issue Price	Quote
89-01-038	Poinsettia Sm., red-112806	E. Guerra	Open	30.00	30.00
89-01-039	Poinsettia Med., red-113106	E. Guerra	Open	44.00	44.00
89-01-040	Single Daffodil, yellow-113202	E. Guerra	Open	29.00	29.00
89-01-041	Single Daffodil, yel./wht.-113220	E. Guerra	Open	29.00	29.00
89-01-042	Daffodil Stem, yellow-113502	E. Guerra	Open	62.00	62.00
89-01-043	Triple Daffodil, yellow-113602	E. Guerra	Open	115.00	115.00
89-01-044	Triple Daffodil, yel.wht.-113620	E. Guerra	Open	115.00	115.00
89-01-045	Camellia, pale pink-113911	E. Guerra	Open	75.00	75.00
89-01-046	Magnolia, white-114910	E. Guerra	Open	36.00	36.00
89-01-047	Poinsettia Plant, red-115406	E. Guerra	500	525.00	525.00
89-01-048	Hibiscus Group, purple-121232	E. Guerra	Open	210.00	210.00
89-01-049	Magnolia Large, white-122510	E. Guerra	Open	80.00	80.00
89-01-050	Queen Rose w/2 buds, red-122805	E. Guerra	Open	90.00	90.00
89-01-051	Queen Rose w/2 buds, aurora-122831	E. Guerra	Open	90.00	90.00
89-01-052	Queen Rose w/2 buds, bicolor-122835	E. Guerra	Open	90.00	90.00
89-01-053	Queen Rose w/2 buds, raspberry-122847	E. Guerra	Open	90.00	90.00
89-01-054	Large Rose 2/buds, red-126805	E. Guerra	Open	80.00	80.00
89-01-055	Large Rose 2/buds, aurora-126831	E. Guerra	Open	80.00	80.00
89-01-056	Large Rose 2/buds, bicolor-126835	E. Guerra	Open	80.00	80.00
89-01-057	High Rose Composition, red-126905	E. Guerra	Open	285.00	285.00
89-01-058	High Rose Composition, aurora-126931	E. Guerra	Open	285.00	285.00
89-01-059	High Rose Composition, bicolor-126935	E. Guerra	Open	285.00	285.00
89-01-060	Lying Rose Composition, red-127005	E. Guerra	Open	275.00	275.00
89-01-061	Lying Rose Composition, aurora-127031	E. Guerra	Open	275.00	275.00
89-01-062	Lying Rose Composition, bicolor-127035	E. Guerra	Open	275.00	275.00
89-01-063	Double Crocus, violet-128608	E. Guerra	Open	47.00	47.00
89-01-064	Holly Poinsettia, red-129906	E. Guerra	Open	90.00	90.00
89-01-065	Rose Long Stem, pink-133901	E. Guerra	Open	45.00	45.00
89-01-066	Rose Long Stem, yellow-133902	E. Guerra	Open	45.00	45.00
89-01-067	Rose Long Stem, red-133905	E. Guerra	Open	45.00	45.00
89-01-068	Rose Long Stem, aurora-133931	E. Guerra	Open	45.00	45.00
89-01-069	Rose Long Stem, bicolor-133935	E. Guerra	Open	45.00	45.00
89-01-070	Rose Long Stem, raspberry-133947	E. Guerra	Open	45.00	45.00
89-01-071	Single Iris, violet-134618	E. Guerra	Open	80.00	80.00
89-01-072	Single Iris, white-134620	E. Guerra	Open	80.00	80.00
89-01-073	Iris Stem, violet-134818	E. Guerra	Open	55.00	55.00
89-01-074	Single Hibiscus Large, red-137006	E. Guerra	Open	50.00	50.00
89-01-075	Single Hibiscus, red-137606	E. Guerra	Open	32.00	32.00
89-01-076	Single Hibiscus, purple-137632	E. Guerra	Open	30.00	30.00
89-01-077	Single Hibiscus, white-137611	E. Guerra	Open	30.00	30.00
89-01-078	Double Hibiscus, red-137706	E. Guerra	Open	75.00	75.00
89-01-079	Double Hibiscus, purple-137732	E. Guerra	Open	75.00	75.00
89-01-080	Double Hibiscus, white-137711	E. Guerra	Open	75.00	75.00
89-01-081	Mascotte Rose Branch, red-138205	E. Guerra	Open	75.00	75.00
89-01-082	Azalea, pink-141033	E. Guerra	Open	185.00	185.00
89-01-083	Azalea, yellow-141020	E. Guerra	Open	185.00	185.00
89-01-084	Single Rose Large, pink-141450	E. Guerra	Open	35.00	35.00
89-01-085	Single Rose Large, yellow-141402	E. Guerra	Open	35.00	35.00
89-01-086	Single Rose Large, tea-141403	E. Guerra	Open	35.00	35.00
89-01-087	Single Rose Large, red-141405	E. Guerra	Open	35.00	35.00
89-01-088	Single Rose Large, aurora-141431	E. Guerra	Open	35.00	35.00
89-01-089	Single Rose Large, bicolor-141435	E. Guerra	Open	35.00	35.00
89-01-090	Single Rose Large, raspberry-141447	E. Guerra	Open	35.00	35.00
89-01-091	Small Rose Stem, red-142705	E. Guerra	Open	27.50	27.50
89-01-092	Small Rose Stem, aurora-142731	E. Guerra	Open	27.50	27.50
89-01-093	Trunk Rose, pink-143101	E. Guerra	Open	60.00	60.00
89-01-094	Princess Orchid Group, pink-143511	E. Guerra	Open	200.00	200.00
89-01-095	Double Iris, white-143720	E. Guerra	Open	175.00	175.00
89-01-096	Double Iris, violet--143718	E. Guerra	Open	175.00	175.00
89-01-097	Rose & Bud Candle Holder, pink-150950	E. Guerra	Open	28.00	28.00
89-01-098	Rose & Bud Candle Holder, red-150905	E. Guerra	Open	28.00	28.00
89-01-099	Rose & Bud Candle Holder, aurora-150931	E. Guerra	Open	28.00	28.00
89-01-100	Double Rose Candle Holder, pink-151401	E. Guerra	Open	45.00	45.00
89-01-101	Double Rose Candle Holder, red-151405	E. Guerra	Open	45.00	45.00
89-01-102	Double Rose Candle Holder, aurora-151431	E. Guerra	Open	45.00	45.00
89-01-103	Jenny Rose w/ buds, red-151505	E. Guerra	Open	65.00	65.00
89-01-104	Jenny Rose w/ buds, bicolor-151535	E. Guerra	Open	65.00	65.00
89-01-105	Double Rose Trunk, aurora-151631	E. Guerra	Open	75.00	75.00
89-01-106	Mistere Rose Plant, red-151905	E. Guerra	Open	185.00	185.00
89-01-107	Garden Rose Composition, bicolor-152035	E. Guerra	Open	200.00	200.00
89-01-108	Large Camellia, pink-152811	E. Guerra	Open	55.00	55.00
89-01-109	Three Princess Orchids, yellow-153112	E. Guerra	Open	250.00	250.00
89-01-110	Small Double Azalea, white/yel.-154120	E. Guerra	Open	42.00	42.00
89-01-111	Small Double Azalea, pink-154133	E. Guerra	Open	42.00	42.00
89-01-112	Single Pansy, yellow-157002	E. Guerra	Open	38.00	38.00
89-01-113	Single Pansy, purple-157008	E. Guerra	Open	38.00	38.00
89-01-114	Pansy w/ Cherry Blossom , purple-157108	E. Guerra	Open	60.00	60.00
89-01-115	Double Pansy, purple-157208	E. Guerra	Open	75.00	75.00
89-01-116	Triple Pansy, purple-157308	E. Guerra	Open	95.00	95.00
89-01-117	Rose Plant, spec.pink-158935	E. Guerra	300	1300.00	1300.00
89-01-118	Lily High Branch, pink-159401	E. Guerra	300	1600.00	1600.00
89-01-119	Hibiscus Plant, red-160009	E. Guerra	300	1500.00	1500.00
89-01-120	Double Large Rose, pink-160250	E. Guerra	Open	50.00	50.00
89-01-121	Double Large Rose, yellow-160202	E. Guerra	Open	50.00	50.00
89-01-122	Double Large Rose, tea-160203	E. Guerra	Open	50.00	50.00
89-01-123	Double Large Rose, red-160205	E. Guerra	Open	50.00	50.00
89-01-124	Double Large Rose, aurora-160231	E. Guerra	Open	50.00	50.00
89-01-125	Double Large Rose, bicolor-160235	E. Guerra	Open	50.00	50.00
89-01-126	Double Large Rose, raspberry-160247	E. Guerra	Open	50.00	50.00
89-01-127	Iris Group, violet-160618	E. Guerra	Open	300.00	300.00
89-01-128	Baroness Rose Group, pink-160750	E. Guerra	Open	310.00	310.00
89-01-129	Baroness Rose Group, aurora-160731	E. Guerra	Open	310.00	310.00
89-01-130	Fragrant Rose Composition, red/wht-161205	E. Guerra	Open	350.00	350.00
89-01-131	Queen Rose on Fence, aurora-161431	E. Guerra	Open	260.00	260.00
89-01-132	May Rose, special pink-161535	E. Guerra	500	400.00	400.00
89-01-133	Poinsettia on Branch, red-162106	E. Guerra	Open	68.00	68.00
89-01-134	Trunk Rose & Bud, red-168705	E. Guerra	Open	110.00	110.00
89-01-135	Trunk Rose & Bud, aurora-168731	E. Guerra	Open	110.00	110.00
89-01-136	Small Branch Rose, red-175205	E. Guerra	Open	40.00	40.00
89-01-137	Small Branch Rose, aurora-175231	E. Guerra	Open	40.00	40.00
89-01-138	Small Branch Rose, bicolor-175235	E. Guerra	Open	40.00	40.00
89-01-139	Small Branch Rose, raspberry-175247	E. Guerra	Open	40.00	40.00
89-01-140	Fragrant Rose w/ bud, red-175405	E. Guerra	Open	37.50	37.50
89-01-141	Silver Jubilee Rose, aurora-175731	E. Guerra	Open	35.00	35.00
89-01-142	Rose & bud w/stem, pink-180250	E. Guerra	Open	32.00	32.00
89-01-143	Rose & bud w/stem, tea-180203	E. Guerra	Open	32.00	32.00
89-01-144	Rose & bud w/stem, red-180205	E. Guerra	Open	35.00	35.00
89-01-145	Rose & bud w/stem, aurora-180231	E. Guerra	Open	32.00	32.00
89-01-146	Rose & bud w/stem, bicolor-180235	E. Guerra	Open	32.00	32.00
89-01-147	Rose & bud w/stem, raspberry-180247	E. Guerra	Open	35.00	35.00
89-01-148	Small Branch Orchid, pink-180811	E. Guerra	Open	50.00	50.00
89-01-149	Two Princess Orchid, yellow-181012	E. Guerra	Open	110.00	110.00
89-01-150	Double Orchid, violet-181118	E. Guerra	Open	115.00	115.00

Number	Name	Artist	Edition Limit	Issue Price	Quote
Company		**Series**			
89-01-151	Daffodil Group, yellow-181902	E. Guerra	Open	200.00	200.00
89-01-152	Daffodil Group, yel./wht.-181920	E. Guerra	Open	200.00	200.00
89-01-153	Single Princess Orchid, white-183010	E. Guerra	Open	45.00	45.00
89-01-154	Typhoon Rose Plant, aurora-183131	E. Guerra	Open	190.00	190.00
89-01-155	Cattleya Orchid, violet-183318	E. Guerra	Open	95.00	95.00
89-01-156	Single Cattleya, violet-183518	E. Guerra	Open	55.00	55.00
89-01-157	May Rose Basket, special pink-190135	E. Guerra	500	650.00	650.00
Pemberton & Oakes		**Zolan's Children**			
82-01-001	Erik and the Dandelion	D. Zolan	17,000	48.00	90.00
83-01-002	Sabina in the Grass	D. Zolan	6,800	48.00	130.00
84-01-003	Winter Angel	D. Zolan	8,000	28.00	150.00
85-01-004	Tender Moment	D. Zolan	10,000	29.00	60.00
PenDelfin		**Nursery Rhymes**			
56-01-001	Wee Willie Winkie	J. Heap	Retrd.	Unkn.	N/A
56-01-002	Little Bo Peep	J. Heap	Retrd.	Unkn.	N/A
56-01-003	Miss Muffet	J. Heap	Retrd.	Unkn.	N/A
56-01-004	Mary Mary Quite Contrary	J. Heap	Retrd.	Unkn.	N/A
56-01-005	Tom Tom the Piper's Son	J. Heap	Retrd.	Unkn.	N/A
56-01-006	Little Jack Horner	J. Heap	Retrd.	Unkn.	N/A
53-01-007	Pendle Witch	J. Heap	Retrd.	Unkn.	N/A
53-01-008	Pixie House	J. Heap	Retrd.	Unkn.	N/A
53-01-009	Tipsy Witch	J. Heap	Retrd.	Unkn.	N/A
53-01-010	Cauldron Witch	J. Heap	Retrd.	Unkn.	N/A
54-01-011	Rhinegold Lamp	J. Heap	Retrd.	Unkn.	N/A
55-01-012	Old Adam	J. Heap	Retrd.	Unkn.	N/A
55-01-013	Balloon Woman	J. Heap	Retrd.	Unkn.	N/A
55-01-014	Bell Man	J. Heap	Retrd.	Unkn.	N/A
55-01-015	Elf	J. Heap	Retrd.	Unkn.	N/A
55-01-016	Toper	J. Heap	Retrd.	Unkn.	N/A
55-01-017	Flying Witch	J. Heap	Retrd.	Unkn.	N/A
55-01-018	Phynnodderee (Commissioned-Exclusive)	J. Heap	Retrd.	Unkn.	N/A
55-01-019	Margot	J. Heap	Retrd.	Unkn.	N/A
55-01-020	Old Father	J. Heap	Retrd.	35.00	900.00
56-01-021	Desmond Duck	J. Heap	Retrd.	Unkn.	N/A
56-01-022	Bobbin Woman	J. Heap	Retrd.	Unkn.	N/A
56-01-023	Manx Kitten	J. Heap	Retrd.	Unkn.	N/A
56-01-024	Midge (Replaced by Picnic Midge)	J. Heap	Retrd.	Unkn.	N/A
56-01-025	Original Robert	J. Heap	Retrd.	Unkn.	N/A
56-01-026	Timber Stand	J. Heap	Retrd.	35.00	N/A
57-01-027	Romeo & Juliet	J. Heap	Retrd.	Unkn.	N/A
57-01-028	Old Mother	J. Heap	Retrd.	35.00	N/A
59-01-029	Cha Cha	J. Heap	Retrd.	Unkn.	N/A
58-01-030	Rabbit Book Ends	J. Heap	Retrd.	Unkn.	N/A
60-01-031	Gussie	J. Heap	Retrd.	Unkn.	N/A
60-01-032	Shiner	J. Heap	Retrd.	Unkn.	N/A
60-01-033	Squeezy	J. Heap	Retrd.	Unkn.	N/A
60-01-034	Model Stand	J. Heap	Retrd.	Unkn.	N/A
60-01-035	Lucy Pocket	J. Heap	Retrd.	10.00	N/A
61-01-036	Megan	J. Heap	Retrd.	Unkn.	N/A
61-01-037	Lollipop (Mouse)	J. Heap	Retrd.	Unkn.	N/A
61-01-038	Mother Mouse	J. Heap	Retrd.	Unkn.	N/A
61-01-039	Father Mouse	J. Heap	Retrd.	Unkn.	N/A
62-01-040	Cornish Prayer (Corny)	J. Heap	Retrd.	Unkn.	N/A
63-01-041	Cyril Squirrel	J. Heap	Retrd.	Unkn.	N/A
63-01-042	Aunt Agatha	J. Heap	Retrd.	Unkn.	N/A
65-01-043	Mouse House	J. Heap	Retrd.	Unkn.	N/A
65-01-044	Picnic Stand	J. Heap	Retrd.	20.00	N/A
65-01-045	Muncher	D. Roberts	Retrd.	25.00	N/A
65-01-046	Pixie Bods	J. Heap	Retrd.	Unkn.	N/A
66-01-047	Picnic Basket	J. Heap	Retrd.	Unkn.	N/A
66-01-048	Milk Jug Stand	J. Heap	Retrd.	Unkn.	N/A
66-01-049	Cakestand	J. Heap	Retrd.	Unkn.	200.00
67-01-050	Maud	J. Heap	Retrd.	5.00	300.00
67-01-051	Robert	D. Roberts	Retrd.	7.00	100.00
67-01-052	The Bath Tub	J. Heap	Retrd.	10.00	N/A
67-01-053	Picnic Table	J. Heap	Retrd.	Unkn.	N/A
69-01-054	The Gallery Series: Wakey, Pieface, Poppet, Robert, Dodger	J. Heap	Retrd.	Unkn.	N/A
71-01-055	Totty	J. Heap	Retrd.	20.50	N/A
59-01-056	Uncle Soames	J. Heap	Retrd.	100.00	300.00
67-01-057	Phumf	J. Heap	Retrd.	Unkn.	N/A
57-01-058	Tammy	D. Roberts	Retrd.	10.00	N/A
62-01-059	Pooch	D. Roberts	Retrd.	10.00	N/A
66-01-060	Pieface	D. Roberts	Retrd.	15.00	N/A
64-01-061	Bongo	D. Roberts	Retrd.	15.00	N/A
80-01-062	Crocker	D. Roberts	Retrd.	30.00	N/A
81-01-063	Nipper	D. Roberts	Retrd.	20.00	N/A
84-01-064	Blossom	D. Roberts	Retrd.	20.00	N/A
PenDelfin		**Bed Series**			
XX-02-001	Dodger	J. Heap	Open	24.00	24.00
XX-02-002	Peeps	J. Heap	Open	21.00	21.00
XX-02-003	Poppet	D. Roberts	Open	23.00	23.00
XX-02-004	Snuggles	J. Heap	Open	20.00	20.00
XX-02-005	Twins	J. Heap	Open	25.00	25.00
XX-02-006	Wakey	J. Heap	Open	24.00	24.00
XX-02-007	Victoria	J. Heap	Open	47.50	47.50
XX-02-008	Parsley	D. Roberts	Open	25.00	25.00
XX-02-009	Chirpy	D. Roberts	Retrd.	60.00	60.00
XX-02-010	Snuggles Awake	J. Heap	Open	60.00	60.00
92-02-011	Sunny	D. Roberts	Open	40.00	40.00
PenDelfin		**Band Series**			
XX-03-001	Rocky	J. Heap	Open	32.00	32.00
XX-03-002	Rolly	J. Heap	Open	17.50	17.50
XX-03-003	Thumper	J. Heap	Open	25.00	25.00
XX-03-004	Piano	D. Roberts	Open	25.00	25.00
XX-03-005	Casanova	J. Heap	Open	35.00	35.00
XX-03-006	Clanger	J. Heap	Open	35.00	35.00
XX-03-007	Rosa	J. Heap	Open	40.00	40.00
XX-03-008	Solo	D. Roberts	Open	40.00	40.00
XX-03-009	Jingles	D. Roberts	Retrd.	22.50	22.50
XX-03-010	Bandstand	J. Heap	Open	70.00	70.00
PenDelfin		**Picnic Series**			
XX-04-001	Picnic Midge	J. Heap	Open	25.00	25.00
XX-04-002	Barrow Boy	J. Heap	Open	35.00	35.00
XX-04-003	Oliver	D. Roberts	Open	25.00	25.00
XX-04-004	Apple Barrel	D. Roberts	Retrd.	15.00	15.00
XX-04-005	Scrumpy	J. Heap	Open	35.00	35.00
XX-04-006	Picnic Island	J. Heap	Open	85.00	85.00

Number	Name	Artist	Edition Limit	Issue Price	Quote
Company		**Series**			
PenDelfin		**Toy Shop Series**			
XX-05-001	Jacky	D. Roberts	Open	45.00	45.00
XX-05-002	The Toy Shop	D. Roberts	Open	325.00	325.00
PenDelfin		**Fisherman Series**			
XX-06-001	Whopper	D. Roberts	Open	35.00	35.00
XX-06-002	Jim-Lad	D. Roberts	Retrd.	45.00	45.00
XX-06-003	Little Mo	D. Roberts	Open	35.00	35.00
XX-06-004	The Raft	J. Heap	Open	70.00	70.00
XX-06-005	Shrimp Stand	D. Roberts	Open	70.00	70.00
XX-06-006	The Jetty	J. Heap	Open	180.00	180.00
PenDelfin		**Sport Series**			
XX-07-001	Birdie	J. Heap	Open	47.50	47.50
XX-07-002	Tennyson	D. Roberts	Open	35.00	35.00
XX-07-003	Humphrey Go Kart	J. Heap	Open	70.00	70.00
XX-07-004	Rambler	D. Roberts	Open	65.00	65.00
XX-07-005	Scout	D. Roberts	Open	N/A	N/A
PenDelfin		**School Series**			
XX-08-001	Boswell	J. Heap	Open	37.50	37.50
XX-08-002	Euclid	J. Heap	Open	35.00	35.00
XX-08-003	Digit	D. Roberts	Open	35.00	35.00
XX-08-004	Duffy	J. Heap	Open	50.00	50.00
XX-08-005	Old School House	J. Heap	Open	250.00	250.00
XX-08-006	Angelo	J. Heap	Open	90.00	90.00
XX-08-007	New Boy	D. Roberts	Open	50.00	50.00
XX-08-008	Wordsworth	D. Roberts	Open	60.00	60.00
PenDelfin		**Various**			
XX-09-001	Dandy	D. Roberts	Open	50.00	50.00
XX-09-002	Barney	J. Heap	Open	18.00	18.00
XX-09-003	Honey	D. Roberts	Open	40.00	40.00
XX-09-004	Charlotte	D. Roberts	Retrd.	50.00	50.00
XX-09-005	Butterfingers	D. Roberts	Open	55.00	55.00
XX-09-006	Scoffer	D. Roberts	Open	55.00	55.00
XX-09-007	Mother with baby	J. Heap	Open	150.00	150.00
XX-09-008	Father	J. Heap	Open	150.00	150.00
PenDelfin		**Village Series**			
XX-10-001	Fruit Shop	J. Heap	Open	125.00	125.00
XX-10-002	Castle Tavern	D. Roberts	Open	120.00	120.00
XX-10-003	Caravan	D. Roberts	Open	350.00	350.00
XX-10-004	Large House	J. Heap	Open	275.00	275.00
XX-10-005	Cobble Cottage	D. Roberts	Open	80.00	80.00
XX-10-006	Curiosity Shop	J. Heap	Open	350.00	350.00
XX-10-007	Balcony Scene	D. Roberts	Open	175.00	175.00
XX-10-008	Grand Stand	J. Heap	Open	150.00	150.00
PenDelfin		**PenDelfin Family Circle Collectors' Club**			
92-11-001	Herald	J. Heap	Yr. Iss.	30.00	30.00
Polland Studios		**Collectible Bronzes**			
67-01-001	Bull Session	D. Polland	11	200.00	1200.00
69-01-002	Blowin' Cold	D. Polland	30	375.00	1250.00
69-01-003	The Breed	D. Polland	30	350.00	975.00
68-01-004	Buffalo Hunt	D. Polland	30	450.00	1250.00
69-01-005	Comanchero	D. Polland	30	350.00	750.00
69-01-006	Dancing Indian with Lance	D. Polland	50	250.00	775.00
69-01-007	Dancing Indian with Tomahawk	D. Polland	50	250.00	775.00
69-01-008	Dancing Medicine Man	D. Polland	50	250.00	775.00
69-01-009	Drawn Sabers	D. Polland	50	2000.00	5650.00
69-01-010	Lookouts	D. Polland	30	375.00	1300.00
69-01-011	Top Money	D. Polland	30	275.00	800.00
69-01-012	Trail Hazzard	D. Polland	30	700.00	1750.00
69-01-013	War Cry	D. Polland	30	350.00	975.00
69-01-014	When Enemies Meet	D. Polland	30	700.00	2350.00
70-01-015	Coffee Time	D. Polland	50	1200.00	2900.00
70-01-016	The Lost Dispatch	D. Polland	50	1200.00	2950.00
70-01-017	Wanted	D. Polland	50	500.00	1150.00
70-01-018	Dusted	D. Polland	50	400.00	1175.00
71-01-019	Ambush at Rock Canyon	D. Polland	5	20000.00	45000.00
71-01-020	Oh Sugar!	D. Polland	40	700.00	1525.00
71-01-021	Shakin' Out a Loop	D. Polland	40	500.00	1075.00
72-01-022	Buffalo Robe	D. Polland	50	1000.00	2350.00
73-01-023	Bunch Quitter	D. Polland	60	750.00	1975.00
73-01-024	Challenge	D. Polland	60	750.00	1800.00
73-01-025	War Party	D. Polland	60	1500.00	5500.00
73-01-026	Tracking	D. Polland	60	500.00	1150.00
75-01-027	Cheyenne	D. Polland	6	1300.00	1800.00
75-01-028	Counting Coup	D. Polland	6	1450.00	1950.00
75-01-029	Crow Scout	D. Polland	6	1300.00	1800.00
75-01-030	Buffalo Hunt	D. Polland	6	2200.00	3500.00
76-01-031	Rescue	D. Polland	6	2400.00	3000.00
76-01-032	Painting the Town	D. Polland	6	3000.00	4200.00
76-01-033	Monday Morning Wash	D. Polland	6	2800.00	2800.00
76-01-034	Mandan Hunter	D. Polland	12	775.00	775.00
80-01-035	Buffalo Prayer	D. Polland	25	375.00	675.00
Polland Studios		**Collector Society**			
87-02-001	I Come In Peace	D. Polland	Closed	35.00	400-550.
87-02-002	Silent Trail	D. Polland	Closed	300.00	1200.00
87-02-003	I Come In Peace, Silent Trail-Matched Numbered Set	D. Polland	Closed	335.00	1500-1895.
88-02-004	The Hunter	D. Polland	Closed	35.00	400-500.
88-02-005	Disputed Trail	D. Polland	Closed	300.00	700-960.
88-02-006	The Hunter, Disputed Trail-Matched Numbered Set	D. Polland	Closed	335.00	1100-1450.
89-02-007	Crazy Horse	D. Polland	Closed	35.00	300-550.
89-02-008	Apache Birdman	D. Polland	Closed	300.00	700-960.
89-02-009	Crazy Horse, Apache Birdman-Matched Numbered Set	D. Polland	Closed	335.00	1300-1700.
90-02-010	Chief Pontiac	D. Polland	Closed	35.00	200-430.
90-02-011	Buffalo Pony	D. Polland	Closed	300.00	600-900.
90-02-012	Chief Pontiac, Buffalo Pony-Matched Numbered Set	D. Polland	Closed	335.00	900-1350.
91-02-013	War Dancer	D. Polland	Closed	35.00	200-400.
91-02-014	The Signal	D. Polland	Closed	350.00	500-650.
91-02-015	War Drummer & The Signal-Matched Numbered Set	D. Polland	Closed	385.00	900-1150.
92-02-016	Cabinet Sign	D. Polland	Closed	35.00	65.00
92-02-017	Warrior's Farewell	D. Polland	Closed	350.00	400.00

Company Number	Name	Series Artist	Edition Limit	Issue Price	Quote
92-02-018	Cabinet Sign & Warrior's Farewell-Matched Numbered Set	D. Polland	Closed	385.00	465.00
Polland Studios		**Pewter/Porcelain Collection**			
84-03-001	Federal Stallion	D. Polland	1,500	145.00	185.00
85-03-003	Running Free	D. Polland	1,500	250.00	300.00
86-03-003	Hunting Cougar	D. Polland	1,500	145.00	180.00
91-03-004	Mermaid	D. Polland	2,000	250.00	250.00
91-03-005	Mermaid (Tinted)	D. Polland	2,500	275.00	275.00
91-03-006	Turtle Hounds (Tinted)	D. Polland	2,500	150.00	150.00
91-03-007	Double Play	D. Polland	2,500	150.00	150.00
91-03-008	Double Play (Tinted)	D. Polland	2,500	165.00	165.00
91-03-009	4th And Goal	D. Polland	2,500	150.00	150.00
91-03-010	4th And Goal (Tinted)	D. Polland	2,500	165.00	165.00
91-03-011	Ballerina	D. Polland	1,500	100.00	100.00
91-03-012	Ballerina (Tinted)	D. Polland	1,500	115.00	115.00
91-03-013	Ballerina (Porcelain)	D. Polland	1,500	125.00	125.00
91-03-014	Stalking Cougar (Porcelain)	D. Polland	2,500	85.00	85.00
91-03-015	Indian Pony Grey (Porcelain)	D. Polland	2,500	115.00	115.00
91-03-016	Indian Pony Bay (Porcelain)	D. Polland	2,500	115.00	115.00
91-03-017	Indian Pony Buckskin (Porcelain)	D. Polland	2,500	115.00	115.00
Possible Dreams®		**Clothtique® The Saturday Evening Post Norman Rockwell Collection**			
90-01-001	Dear Santa-3050	N. Rockwell	Closed	160.00	180.00
90-01-002	Santa with Globe-3051	N. Rockwell	Closed	154.00	175.00
90-01-003	Hobo-3052	N. Rockwell	Open	159.00	159.00
90-01-004	Love Letters-3053	N. Rockwell	Open	172.00	172.00
91-01-005	Gone Fishing-3054	N. Rockwell	Open	250.00	250.00
91-01-006	Doctor and Doll-3055	N. Rockwell	Open	196.00	196.00
91-01-007	Springtime-3056	N. Rockwell	Open	130.00	130.00
91-01-008	The Gift-3057	N. Rockwell	Open	160.00	160.00
91-01-009	Gramps at the Reins-3058	N. Rockwell	Open	290.00	290.00
91-01-010	Man with Geese-3059	N. Rockwell	Open	120.00	120.00
91-01-011	Plotting His Course-3060	N. Rockwell	Open	160.00	160.00
92-01-012	Triple Self Portrait-3061	N. Rockwell	Open	230.00	230.00
92-01-013	Marriage License-3062	N. Rockwell	Open	195.00	195.00
92-01-014	Santa's Helpers-3063	N. Rockwell	Open	170.00	170.00
92-01-015	Balancing the Budget-3064	N. Rockwell	Open	120.00	120.00
Possible Dreams®		**Clothtique® The Saturday Evening Post J.C. Leyendecker Collection**			
90-02-001	Santa and Baby-3600	J. Leyendecker	Closed	100.00	110.00
91-02-002	Hugging Santa-3599	J. Leyendecker	Open	129.00	129.00
92-02-003	Santa on Ladder-3598	J. Leyendecker	Open	135.00	135.00
Possible Dreams®		**Clothtique® The American Artist Collection**			
91-03-001	Magic of Christmas-15001	L. Bywaters	Open	132.00	132.00
91-03-002	A Peaceful Eve-15002	L. Bywaters	Open	99.50	99.50
91-03-003	Alpine Christmas-15003	J. Brett	Open	129.00	129.00
91-03-004	Traditions-15004	T. Blackshear	Open	50.00	50.00
91-03-005	A Friendly Visit-15005	T. Browning	Open	99.50	99.50
91-03-006	Santa's Cuisine-15006	T. Browning	Open	137.50	137.50
91-03-007	Father Christmas-15007	J. Vaillancourt	Open	59.50	59.50
92-03-008	An Angel's Kiss-15008	J. Griffith	Open	85.00	85.00
92-03-009	Peace on Earth-15009	M. Alvin	Open	87.50	87.50
92-03-010	Lighting the Way-15012	L. Bywaters	Open	85.00	85.00
92-03-011	Out of the Forrest-15013	J. Vaillancourt	Open	60.00	60.00
92-03-012	Heralding the Way-15014	J. Griffith	Open	72.00	72.00
92-03-013	Music Makers-15010	T. Browning	Open	135.00	135.00
93-03-015	Strumming the Lute-15015	M. Alvin	Open	79.00	79.00
93-03-016	Nature's Love-15016	M. Alvin	Open	75.00	75.00
93-03-017	Father Earth-15017	M. Monteiro	Open	77.00	77.00
93-03-018	Easy Putt-15018	T. Browning	Open	110.00	110.00
93-03-019	The Workshop-15019	T. Browning	Open	140.00	140.00
93-03-020	The Tree Planter-15020	J. Griffith	Open	79.50	79.50
93-03-021	A Beacon of Light-15022	J. Vaillancourt	Open	60.00	60.00
93-03-022	Just Scooting Along-15023	J. Vaillancourt	Open	79.50	79.50
93-03-023	A Brighter Day-15024	J. St. Denis	Open	67.50	67.50
93-03-024	Ice Capers-15025	T. Browning	Open	99.50	99.50
Possible Dreams®		**Clothtique® Limited Edition Santas**			
88-04-001	Patriotic Santa-3000	Unknown	Closed	240.00	240.00
88-04-002	Father Christmas-3001	Unknown	Closed	240.00	240.00
88-04-003	Kris Kringle-3002	Unknown	Closed	240.00	240.00
89-04-004	Traditional Santa 40's-3003	Unknown	10,000	240.00	240.00
Possible Dreams®		**Clothtique® Pepsi® Santa Collection**			
90-05-001	Traditional Pepsi Santa 1940's-3601	Unknown	Open	68.00	70.00
91-05-002	Pepsi Santa 1952-3602	N. Rockwell	Open	75.00	77.50
92-05-003	Santa and Friend-3603	Unknown	Open	84.00	84.00
Possible Dreams®		**Clothtique® Santas Collection**			
87-06-001	Traditional Santa-713028	Unknown	Closed	34.50	34.50
87-06-002	Ukko-713031	Unknown	Closed	38.00	38.00
87-06-003	Colonial Santa-713032	Unknown	Closed	38.00	38.00
87-06-004	Christmas Man-713027	Unknown	Closed	34.50	34.50
87-06-005	Santa with Pack-713026	Unknown	Closed	34.50	34.50
87-06-006	Traditional Deluxe Santa-713030	Unknown	Closed	38.00	38.00
88-06-007	Frontier Santa-713034	Unknown	Closed	40.00	42.00
88-06-008	St. Nicholas-713035	Unknown	Closed	40.00	42.00
88-06-009	Weinachtsmann-713037	Unknown	Closed	40.00	43.00
88-06-010	Carpenter Santa-713033	Unknown	Closed	38.00	44.00
88-06-011	Russian St. Nicholas-713036	Unknown	Closed	40.00	43.00
89-06-012	Traditional Santa-713038	Unknown	Closed	42.00	43.00
89-06-013	Pelze Nichol-713039	Unknown	Closed	40.00	47.00
89-06-014	Mrs. Claus w/doll-713041	Unknown	Closed	42.00	43.00
89-06-015	Baby's First Christmas-713042	Unknown	Closed	42.00	46.00
89-06-016	Exhausted Santa-713043	Unknown	Closed	60.00	65.00
89-06-017	Santa with Embroidered Coat-713040	Unknown	Closed	43.00	47.00
90-06-018	Santa At Workbench-713044	Unknown	Closed	72.00	75.50
90-06-019	Santa "Please Stop Here"-713045	Unknown	Closed	63.00	66.00
90-06-020	Harlem Santa-713046	Unknown	Open	46.00	52.50
90-06-021	Santa Skiing-713047	Unknown	Closed	62.00	65.00
90-06-022	Blue Robed Santa-713048	Unknown	Closed	46.00	50.00
91-06-023	The True Spirit of Christmas-713075	Unknown	Closed	97.00	97.00
91-06-024	Santa in Bed-713076	Unknown	Open	76.00	79.50
91-06-025	Siberian Santa-713077	Unknown	Closed	49.00	51.50
91-06-026	Mrs. Claus in Coat -713078	Unknown	Open	47.00	49.50
91-06-027	Decorating the Tree-713079	Unknown	Closed	60.00	60.00
91-06-028	Father Christmas-713087	Unknown	Open	43.00	45.20
91-06-029	Kris Kringle-713088	Unknown	Closed	43.00	45.20
91-06-030	Santa Shelf Sitter-713089	Unknown	Open	55.50	58.00
92-06-031	1940's Traditional Santa-713049	Unknown	Open	44.00	44.00
92-06-032	Santa on Sled-713050	Unknown	Open	75.00	75.00

Company Number	Name	Series Artist	Edition Limit	Issue Price	Quote
92-06-033	Nicholas-713052	Unknown	Open	57.50	57.50
92-06-034	Fireman Santa-713053	Unknown	Open	60.00	60.00
92-06-035	African American Santa-713056	Unknown	Open	65.00	65.00
92-06-036	Engineer Santa-713057	Unknown	Open	130.00	130.00
92-06-037	Santa on Reindeer-713058	Unknown	Open	75.00	79.00
92-06-038	Santa in Rocking Chair-713090	M. Monteiro	Open	85.00	85.00
92-06-039	Santa on Sleigh-713091	Unknown	Open	79.00	79.00
92-06-040	Santa on Motorbike-713054	Unknown	Open	115.00	115.00
93-06-041	European Santa-713095	Unknown	Open	53.00	53.00
93-06-042	May Your Wishes Come True-713095	Unknown	Open	59.00	59.00
93-06-043	Victorian Santa-713097	Unknown	Open	55.50	55.50
93-06-044	His Favorite Color-713098	Unknown	Open	48.00	48.00
93-06-045	Santa w/Groceries-713099	Unknown	Open	47.50	47.50
93-06-046	Afro Santa & Doll-713102	Unknown	Open	40.00	40.00
93-06-047	The Modern Shopper-713103	Unknown	Open	40.00	40.00
93-06-048	Nigel as Santa-713104	Unknown	Open	53.50	53.50
93-06-049	A Long Trip-713105	Unknown	Open	95.00	95.00
93-06-050	Fireman & Child-713106	Unknown	Open	55.00	55.00
Possible Dreams®		**The Citizens of Londonshire**			
92-07-001	Beth-713417	Unknown	Open	35.00	35.00
92-07-002	Albert-713426	Unknown	Open	65.00	65.00
89-07-003	Lady Ashley-713405	Unknown	Open	65.00	65.00
89-07-004	Lord Winston of Riverside-713403	Unknown	Open	65.00	65.00
89-07-005	Sir Robert-713401	Unknown	Open	65.00	65.00
89-07-006	Rodney-713404	Unknown	Open	65.00	65.00
90-07-007	Dr. Isaac-713409	Unknown	Open	65.00	65.00
90-07-008	Admiral Waldo-713407	Unknown	Open	65.00	65.00
91-07-009	Sir Red-713415	Unknown	Open	72.00	72.00
91-07-010	Bernie-713414	Unknown	Open	68.00	68.00
92-07-011	Tiffany Sorbet-713416	Unknown	Open	65.00	65.00
90-07-012	Margaret of Foxcroft-713408	Unknown	Open	65.00	65.00
90-07-013	Officer Kevin-713406	Unknown	Open	65.00	65.00
89-07-014	Lord Nicholas-713402	Unknown	Open	72.00	72.00
92-07-015	Countess of Hamlett-713419	Unknown	Open	65.00	65.00
89-07-016	Earl of Hamlett-713400	Unknown	Open	65.00	65.00
92-07-017	Rebecca-713424	Unknown	Open	35.00	35.00
90-07-018	Dianne-713413	Unknown	Open	33.00	33.00
90-07-019	Phillip-713412	Unknown	Open	33.00	33.00
90-07-020	Walter-713410	Unknown	Open	33.00	33.00
90-07-021	Wendy-713411	Unknown	Open	33.00	33.00
92-07-022	Jean Claude-713421	Unknown	Open	35.00	35.00
92-07-023	Nicole-713420	Unknown	Open	35.00	35.00
92-07-024	David-713423	Unknown	Open	37.50	37.50
92-07-025	Debbie-713422	Unknown	Open	37.50	37.50
92-07-026	Christopher-713418	Unknown	Open	35.00	35.00
92-07-027	Richard-713425	Unknown	Open	35.00	35.00
93-07-028	Nigel As Santa-713104	Unknown	Open	53.50	53.50
Possible Dreams®		**Santa Claus Network Collectors Club**			
92-08-001	The Gift Giver	Unknown	Yr. Iss.	Gift	40.00
93-08-002	Woodland Santa	Unknown	Yr. Iss.	Gift	59.00
Precious Art/Panton		**World of Krystonia**			
87-01-001	Small Graffyn/Grunch-1012	Panton	Retrd.	45.00	175-250.
87-01-002	Small N'Borg-1091	Panton	Retrd.	50.00	250-325.
87-01-003	Large Rueggan-1701	Panton	Retrd.	55.00	160-450.
87-01-004	Owhey-1071	Panton	Retrd.	32.00	90-125.00
87-01-005	Medium Stoope-1101	Panton	Retrd.	52.00	200-275.
87-01-006	Small Shepf-1152	Panton	Retrd.	40.00	85-125.00
87-01-007	Large Wodema-1301	Panton	Retrd.	50.00	125-300.
88-01-008	Large N'Grall-2201	Panton	Retrd.	108.00	250-400.
87-01-009	Large Krak N'Borg-3001	Panton	Retrd.	240.00	500-800.
87-01-010	Large Moplos-1021	Panton	Retrd.	90.00	175-300.
87-01-011	Large Myzer-1201	Panton	Retrd.	50.00	150-250.
87-01-012	Large Turfen-1601	Panton	Retrd.	50.00	150-250.
87-01-013	Large Haapf-1901	Panton	Retrd.	38.00	85-125.00
88-01-014	Small Tulan Captain-2502	Panton	Retrd.	44.00	80-125.00
87-01-015	Small Groc-1042B	Panton	Retrd.	24.00	4600.00
87-01-016	Large Graffyn on Grumblypeg Grunch-1011	Panton	Retrd.	52.00	90-125.00
87-01-017	Grumblypeg Grunch-1081	Panton	Retrd.	52.00	95-120.00
88-01-018	Tarnhold - Med.-3202	Panton	Retrd.	120.00	140-185.
89-01-019	Caught At Last!-1107	Panton	Retrd.	150.00	175-240.
89-01-020	Stoope (waterglobe) -9003	Panton	Retrd.	40.00	N/A
89-01-021	Graffyn on Grunch (waterglobe) -9006	Panton	Retrd.	42.00	N/A
Precious Art/Panton		**Krystonia Collector's Club**			
89-02-001	Pultzr	Panton	Retrd.	55.00	250-500.
89-02-002	Key	Panton	Retrd.	Gift	100.00
91-02-003	Dragons Play	Panton	Retrd.	65.00	150-200.
91-02-004	Kephrens Chest	Panton	Retrd.	Gift	65-100.00
92-02-005	Vaaston	Panton	Yr. Iss.	65.00	65.00
92-02-006	Lantern	Panton	Yr. Iss.	Gift	N/A
Princeton Gallery		**Unicorn Collection**			
90-01-001	Love's Delight	Unknown	Open	75.00	75.00
90-01-002	Love's Sweetness	Unknown	Open	75.00	75.00
91-01-003	Love's Devotion	Unknown	Open	119.00	119.00
91-01-004	Love's Purity	Unknown	Open	95.00	95.00
91-01-005	Love's Majesty	Unknown	Open	95.00	95.00
91-01-006	Christmas Unicorn	Unknown	Yr.Iss.	85.00	85.00
92-01-007	Love's Fancy	Unknown	Open	95.00	95.00
93-01-008	Love's Courtship	Unknown	Open	95.00	95.00
Princeton Gallery		**Playful Pups**			
90-02-001	Dalmation-Where's The Fire	Unknown	Open	19.50	19.50
90-02-002	Beagle	Unknown	Open	19.50	19.50
91-02-003	St. Bernard	Unknown	Open	19.50	19.50
91-02-004	Labrador Retriever	Unknown	Open	19.50	19.50
91-02-005	Wrinkles (Shar Pei)	Unknown	Open	19.50	19.50
Princeton Gallery		**Garden Capers**			
90-03-001	Any Mail?	Unknown	Open	29.50	29.50
91-03-002	Blue Jays	Unknown	Open	29.50	29.50
91-03-003	Robin	Unknown	Open	29.50	29.50
92-03-004	Goldfinch, Home Sweet Home	Unknown	Open	29.50	29.50
92-03-005	Bluebird, Spring Planting	Unknown	Open	29.50	29.50
Princeton Gallery		**Baby bird Trios**			
91-04-001	Woodland Symphony (Bluebirds)	Unknown	Open	45.00	45.00
91-04-002	Cardinals	Unknown	Open	45.00	45.00

Company / Number	Series / Name	Artist	Edition Limit	Issue Price	Quote
Princeton Gallery	**Pegasus**				
92-05-001	Wings of Magic	Unknown	Open	95.00	95.00
Princeton Gallery	**Enchanted Nursery**				
92-06-001	Caprice	Unknown	Open	57.00	57.00
93-06-002	Pegasus	Unknown	Open	57.00	57.00
Princeton Gallery	**Lady And The Unicorn**				
92-07-001	Love's Innocence	Unknown	Open	119.00	119.00
Reco International	**Granget Crystal Sculpture**				
73-01-001	Long Earred Owl, Asio Otus	G. Granget	350	2250.00	2250.00
XX-01-002	Ruffed Grouse	G. Granget	350	1000.00	1000.00
Reco International	**Porcelains in Miniature by John McClelland**				
XX-02-001	John	J. McClelland	10,000	34.50	34.50
XX-02-002	Alice	J. McClelland	10,000	34.50	34.50
XX-02-003	Chimney Sweep	J. McClelland	10,000	34.50	34.50
XX-02-004	Dressing Up	J. McClelland	10,000	34.50	34.50
XX-02-005	Autumn Dreams	J. McClelland	Open	29.50	29.50
XX-02-006	Tuck-Me-In	J. McClelland	Open	29.50	29.50
XX-02-007	Country Lass	J. McClelland	Open	29.50	29.50
XX-02-008	Sudsie Suzie	J. McClelland	Open	29.50	29.50
XX-02-009	Smooth Smailing	J. McClelland	Open	29.50	29.50
XX-02-010	The Clown	J. McClelland	Open	29.50	29.50
XX-02-011	The Baker	J. McClelland	Open	29.50	29.50
XX-02-012	Quiet Moments	J. McClelland	Open	29.50	29.50
XX-02-013	The Farmer	J. McClelland	Open	29.50	29.50
XX-02-014	The Nurse	J. McClelland	Open	29.50	29.50
XX-02-015	The Policeman	J. McClelland	Open	29.50	29.50
XX-02-016	The Fireman	J. McClelland	Open	29.50	29.50
XX-02-017	Winter Fun	J. McClelland	Open	29.50	29.50
XX-02-018	Cowgirl	J. McClelland	Open	29.50	29.50
XX-02-019	Cowboy	J. McClelland	Open	29.50	29.50
XX-02-020	Doc	J. McClelland	Open	29.50	29.50
XX-02-021	Lawyer	J. McClelland	Open	29.50	29.50
XX-02-022	Farmer's Wife	J. McClelland	Open	29.50	29.50
XX-02-023	First Outing	J. McClelland	Open	29.50	29.50
XX-02-024	Club Pro	J. McClelland	Open	29.50	29.50
XX-02-025	Batter Up	J. McClelland	Open	29.50	29.50
XX-02-026	Love 40	J. McClelland	Open	29.50	29.50
XX-02-027	The Painter	J. McClelland	Open	29.50	29.50
XX-02-028	Special Delivery	J. McClelland	Open	29.50	29.50
XX-02-029	Center Ice	J. McClelland	Open	29.50	29.50
XX-02-030	First Solo	J. McClelland	Open	29.50	29.50
XX-02-031	Highland Fling	J. McClelland	7,500	34.50	34.50
XX-02-032	Cheerleader	J. McClelland	Open	29.50	29.50
Reco International	**The Reco Clown Collection**				
85-03-001	Whoopie	J. McClelland	Open	12.00	13.00
85-03-002	The Professor	J. McClelland	Open	12.00	13.00
85-03-003	Top Hat	J. McClelland	Open	12.00	13.00
85-03-004	Winkie	J. McClelland	Open	12.00	13.00
85-03-005	Scamp	J. McClelland	Open	12.00	13.00
85-03-006	Curly	J. McClelland	Open	12.00	13.00
85-03-007	Bow Jangles	J. McClelland	Open	12.00	13.00
85-03-008	Sparkles	J. McClelland	Open	12.00	13.00
85-03-009	Ruffles	J. McClelland	Open	12.00	13.00
85-03-010	Arabesque	J. McClelland	Open	12.00	13.00
85-03-011	Hobo	J. McClelland	Open	12.00	13.00
85-03-012	Sad Eyes	J. McClelland	Open	12.00	13.00
87-03-013	Love	J. McClelland	Open	12.00	13.00
87-03-014	Mr. Big	J. McClelland	Open	12.00	13.00
87-03-015	Twinkle	J. McClelland	Open	12.00	13.00
87-03-016	Disco Dan	J. McClelland	Open	12.00	13.00
87-03-017	Smiley	J. McClelland	Open	12.00	13.00
87-03-018	The Joker	J. McClelland	Open	12.00	13.00
87-03-019	Jolly Joe	J. McClelland	Open	12.00	13.00
87-03-020	Zany Jack	J. McClelland	Open	12.00	13.00
87-03-021	Domino	J. McClelland	Open	12.00	13.00
87-03-022	Happy George	J. McClelland	Open	12.00	13.00
87-03-023	Tramp	J. McClelland	Open	12.00	13.00
87-03-024	Wistful	J. McClelland	Open	12.00	13.00
Reco International	**The Reco Angel Collection**				
86-04-001	Innocence	J. McClelland	Open	12.00	12.00
86-04-002	Harmony	J. McClelland	Open	12.00	12.00
86-04-003	Love	J. McClelland	Open	12.00	12.00
86-04-004	Gloria	J. McClelland	Open	12.00	12.00
86-04-005	Praise	J. McClelland	Open	20.00	20.00
86-04-006	Devotion	J. McClelland	Open	15.00	15.00
86-04-007	Faith	J. McClelland	Open	24.00	24.00
86-04-008	Joy	J. McClelland	Open	15.00	15.00
86-04-009	Adoration	J. McClelland	Open	24.00	24.00
86-04-010	Peace	J. McClelland	Open	24.00	24.00
86-04-011	Serenity	J. McClelland	Open	24.00	24.00
86-04-012	Hope	J. McClelland	Open	24.00	24.00
88-04-013	Reverence	J. McClelland	Open	12.00	12.00
88-04-014	Minstral	J. McClelland	Open	12.00	12.00
Reco International	**Sophisticated Ladies Figurines**				
87-05-001	Felicia	A. Fazio	9,500	29.50	32.50
87-05-002	Samantha	A. Fazio	9,500	29.50	32.50
87-05-003	Phoebe	A. Fazio	9,500	29.50	32.50
87-05-004	Cleo	A. Fazio	9,500	29.50	32.50
87-05-005	Cerissa	A. Fazio	9,500	29.50	32.50
87-05-006	Natasha	A. Fazio	9,500	29.50	32.50
87-05-007	Bianka	A. Fazio	9,500	29.50	32.50
87-05-008	Chelsea	A. Fazio	9,500	29.50	32.50
Reco International	**Clown Figurines by John McClelland**				
87-06-001	Mr. Tip	J. McClelland	9,500	35.00	35.00
87-06-002	Mr. Cure-All	J. McClelland	9,500	35.00	35.00
87-06-003	Mr. One-Note	J. McClelland	9,500	35.00	35.00
87-06-004	Mr. Lovable	J. McClelland	9,500	35.00	35.00
88-06-005	Mr. Magic	J. McClelland	9,500	35.00	35.00
88-06-006	Mr. Cool	J. McClelland	9,500	35.00	35.00
88-06-007	Mr. Heart-Throb	J. McClelland	9,500	35.00	35.00
Reco International	**The Reco Angel Collection Miniatures**				
87-07-001	Innocence	J. McClelland	Open	7.50	7.50
87-07-002	Harmony	J. McClelland	Open	7.50	7.50
87-07-003	Love	J. McClelland	Open	7.50	7.50
87-07-004	Gloria	J. McClelland	Open	7.50	7.50
87-07-005	Devotion	J. McClelland	Open	7.50	7.50
87-07-006	Joy	J. McClelland	Open	7.50	7.50
87-07-007	Adoration	J. McClelland	Open	10.00	10.00
87-07-008	Peace	J. McClelland	Open	10.00	10.00
87-07-009	Serenity	J. McClelland	Open	10.00	10.00
87-07-010	Hope	J. McClelland	Open	10.00	10.00
87-07-011	Praise	J. McClelland	Open	10.00	10.00
87-07-012	Faith	J. McClelland	Open	10.00	10.00
Reco International	**Faces of Love**				
88-08-001	Cuddles	J. McClelland	Open	29.50	32.50
88-08-002	Sunshine	J. McClelland	Open	29.50	32.50
Reco International	**Reco Creche Collection**				
87-09-001	Holy Family (3 Pieces)	J. McClelland	Open	49.00	49.00
87-09-002	Lamb	J. McClelland	Open	9.50	9.50
87-09-003	Shepherd-Kneeling	J. McClelland	Open	22.50	22.50
87-09-004	Shepherd-Standing	J. McClelland	Open	22.50	22.50
88-09-005	King/Frankincense	J. McClelland	Open	22.50	22.50
88-09-006	King/Myrrh	J. McClelland	Open	22.50	22.50
88-09-007	King/Gold	J. McClelland	Open	22.50	22.50
88-09-008	Donkey	J. McClelland	Open	16.50	16.50
88-09-009	Cow	J. McClelland	Open	15.00	15.00
Reco International	**The Reco Collection Clown Busts**				
88-10-001	Hobo	J. McClelland	5,000	40.00	40.00
88-10-002	Love	J. McClelland	5,000	40.00	40.00
88-10-003	Sparkles	J. McClelland	5,000	40.00	40.00
88-10-004	Bow Jangles	J. McClelland	5,000	40.00	40.00
88-10-005	Domino	J. McClelland	5,000	40.00	40.00
Reco International	**Wedding Gifts**				
91-11-001	Cake Topper Bride & Groom	J. McClelland	Open	35.00	35.00
91-11-002	Bride & Groom- Musical	J. McClelland	Open	90.00	90.00
91-11-003	Bride-Blond-Musical	J. McClelland	Open	80.00	80.00
91-11-004	Bride-Brunette-Musical	J. McClelland	Open	80.00	80.00
91-11-005	Bride & Groom	J. McClelland	Open	85.00	85.00
91-11-006	Bride-Blond	J. McClelland	Open	60.00	60.00
91-11-007	Bride-Brunette	J. McClelland	Open	60.00	60.00
Rhodes Studio	**Rockwell's Main Street**				
90-01-001	Rockwell's Studio	Rockwell-Inspired	150-day	28.00	75-150.00
90-01-002	The Antique Shop	Rockwell-Inspired	150-day	28.00	28.00
90-01-003	The Town Offices	Rockwell-Inspired	150-day	32.00	32.00
90-01-004	The Country Store	Rockwell-Inspired	150-day	32.00	32.00
91-01-005	The Library	Rockwell-Inspired	150-day	36.00	36.00
91-01-006	The Bank	Rockwell-Inspired	150-day	36.00	36.00
91-01-007	Red Lion Inn	Rockwell-Inspired	150-day	39.00	39.00
Rhodes Studio	**Rockwell's Hometown**				
91-02-001	Rockwell's Residence	Rhodes	Closed	34.95	34.95
91-02-002	Greystone Church	Rhodes	12/92	34.95	34.95
91-02-003	Bell Tower	Rockwell-Inspired	3/93	36.95	36.95
91-02-004	Firehouse	Rockwell-Inspired	3/93	36.95	36.95
91-02-005	Church On The Green	Rockwell-Inspired	9/93	39.95	39.95
92-02-006	Town Hall	Rockwell-Inspired	12/93	39.95	39.95
92-02-007	Citizen's Hall	Rockwell-Inspired	3/94	42.95	42.95
92-02-008	The Berkshire Playhouse	Rockwell-Inspired	6/94	42.95	42.95
92-02-009	Mission House	Rockwell-Inspired	9/94	42.95	42.95
92-02-010	Old Corner House	Rockwell-Inspired	12/94	42.95	42.95
Rhodes Studio	**Rockwell's Heirloom Santa Collection**				
90-03-001	Santa's Workshop	Rockwell-Inspired	150-day	49.95	49.95
91-03-002	Christmas Dream	Rockwell-Inspired	150-day	49.95	49.95
92-03-003	Making His List	Rockwell-Inspired	12/93	49.95	49.95
Rhodes Studio	**Rockwell's Age of Wonder**				
91-04-001	Splish Splash	Rockwell-Inspired	Closed	34.95	34.95
91-04-002	Hush-A-Bye	Rockwell-Inspired	12/92	34.95	34.95
91-04-003	Stand by Me	Rockwell-Inspired	3/93	36.95	36.95
91-04-004	School Days	Rockwell-Inspired	6/93	36.95	36.95
91-04-005	Summertime	Rockwell-Inspired	9/93	39.95	39.95
92-04-006	The Birthday Party	Rockwell-Inspired	12/93	39.95	39.95
Rhodes Studios	**Rockwell's Beautiful Dreamers**				
91-05-001	Sitting Pretty	Rockwell-Inspired	12/92	37.95	37.95
91-05-002	Dear Diary	Rockwell-Inspired	6/93	37.95	37.95
91-05-003	Secret Sonnets	Rockwell-Inspired	9/93	39.95	39.95
91-05-004	Springtime Serenade	Rockwell-Inspired	12/93	39.95	39.95
92-05-005	Debutante's Dance	Rockwell-Inspired	3/94	42.95	42.95
92-05-006	Walk in the Park	Rockwell-Inspired	6/94	42.95	42.95
Rhodes Studio	**Rockwell's Gems of Wisdom**				
91-06-001	Love Cures All	Rockwell-Inspired	12/92	39.95	39.95
91-06-002	Practice Makes Perfect	Rockwell-Inspired	9/93	39.95	39.95
91-06-003	A Stitch In Time	Rockwell-Inspired	12/93	42.95	42.95
Also see Norman Rockwell Gallery					
River Shore	**Loveable-Baby Animals**				
78-01-001	Akiku-Seal	R. Brown	15,000	37.50	150.00
78-01-002	Alfred-Raccoon	R. Brown	15,000	42.50	45.00
79-01-003	Scooter-Chipmunk	R. Brown	15,000	45.00	55.00
79-01-004	Matilda-Koala	R. Brown	15,000	45.00	45.00
River Shore	**Wildlife Baby Animals**				
78-02-001	Fanny-Fawn	R. Brown	15,000	45.00	90.00
79-02-002	Roosevelt-Bear	R. Brown	15,000	50.00	65.00
79-02-003	Roscoe-Red Fox	R. Brown	15,000	50.00	50.00
80-02-004	Priscilla-Skunk	R. Brown	15,000	50.00	50.00
River Shore	**Rockwell Single Issues**				
81-03-001	Looking Out To Sea	N. Rockwell	9,500	85.00	225.00
82-03-002	Grandpa's Guardian	N. Rockwell	9,500	125.00	125.00
River Shore	**Babies of Endangered Species**				
84-04-001	Sidney (Cougar)	R. Brown	15,000	45.00	45.00
84-04-002	Baxter (Bear)	R. Brown	15,000	45.00	45.00
84-04-003	Caroline (Antelope)	R. Brown	15,000	45.00	45.00
84-04-004	Webster (Timberwolf)	R. Brown	15,000	45.00	45.00
84-04-005	Violet (Otter)	R. Brown	15,000	45.00	45.00
84-04-006	Chester (Prairie Dog)	R. Brown	15,000	45.00	45.00

Number	Name	Artist	Edition Limit	Issue Price	Quote
84-04-007	Trevor (Fox)	R. Brown	15,000	45.00	45.00
84-04-008	Daisy (Wood Bison)	R. Brown	15,000	45.00	45.00
River Shore		**Wilderness Babies**			
85-05-001	Penelope (Deer)	R. Brown	15,000	45.00	45.00
85-05-002	Carmen (Burro)	R. Brown	15,000	45.00	45.00
85-05-003	Rocky (Bobcat)	R. Brown	15,000	45.00	45.00
85-05-004	Abercrombie (Polar Bear)	R. Brown	15,000	45.00	45.00
85-05-005	Elrod (Fox)	R. Brown	15,000	45.00	45.00
85-05-006	Reggie (Raccoon)	R. Brown	15,000	45.00	45.00
85-05-007	Arianne (Rabbit)	R. Brown	15,000	45.00	45.00
85-05-008	Annabel (Mountain Goat)	R. Brown	15,000	45.00	45.00
River Shore		**Lovable Teddies Musical Figurine Collection**			
87-06-001	Gilbert	M. Hague	Open	29.50	29.50
87-06-002	William	M. Hague	Open	29.50	29.50
87-06-003	Austin	M. Hague	Open	29.50	29.50
87-06-004	April	M. Hague	Open	29.50	29.50
88-06-005	Henry	M. Hague	Open	29.50	29.50
88-06-006	Harvey	M. Hague	Open	29.50	29.50
88-06-007	Adam	M. Hague	Open	29.50	29.50
88-06-008	Katie	M. Hague	Open	29.50	29.50
Norman Rockwell Gallery		**Rockwell's Family Album**			
91-01-001	Baby's First Steps	Rockwell-Inspired	6/93	39.95	39.95
91-01-002	Little Shaver	Rockwell-Inspired	12/93	39.95	39.95
92-01-003	Happy Birthday Dear Mother	Rockwell-Inspired	3/94	22.95	22.95
Norman Rockwell Gallery		**Young At Heart**			
92-02-001	Batter up	Rockwell-Inspired	N/A	34.95	34.95
92-02-002	Figure Eight	Rockwell-Inspired	N/A	34.95	34.95
Norman Rockwell Gallery		**Rockwell's Sugar And Spice**			
92-03-001	The Winner	Rockwell-Inspired	N/A	39.95	39.95
92-03-002	Dressing Up	Rockwell-Inspired	N/A	39.95	39.95
92-03-003	The Valedictorian	Rockwell-Inspired	N/A	39.95	39.95
92-03-004	The Little Gourmet	Rockwell-Inspired	N/A	42.95	42.95
Norman Rockwell Gallery		**Rockwell's Joys Of Motherhood**			
92-04-001	Mother's Little Angels	Rockwell-Inspired	N/A	34.95	34.95
92-04-002	Sweet Dreams	Rockwell-Inspired	N/A	34.95	34.95
Norman Rockwell Gallery		**Rockwell's Living Treasures**			
91-05-001	Grandpa's Gift Of Love	Rockwell-Inspired	N/A	39.95	39.95
92-05-002	Grandpa's Expert Advise	Rockwell-Inspired	N/A	39.95	39.95
92-05-003	Grandpa's First Mate	Rockwell-Inspired	N/A	39.95	39.95
Norman Rockwell Gallery		**Rockwell's Puppy Love**			
91-06-001	Buttercup	Rockwell-Inspired	6/93	44.95	44.95
91-06-002	Swingin'	Rockwell-Inspired	9/93	44.95	44.95
91-06-003	Schoolin'	Rockwell-Inspired	12/93	44.95	44.95
91-06-004	Sleddin'	Rockwell-Inspired	3/93	44.95	44.95
Norman Rockwell Gallery		**Rockwell's Best Friends**			
91-07-001	Bark If They Bite	Rockwell-Inspired	6/93	39.95	39.95
92-07-002	Two-Part Harmony	Rockwell-Inspired	9/93	39.95	39.95
92-07-003	Day Dreamers	Rockwell-Inspired	12/94	42.95	42.95
92-07-004	Gone Fishin'	Rockwell-Inspired	3/95	42.95	42.95
92-07-005	The Wishing Well	Rockwell-Inspired	6/95	44.95	44.95
93-07-006	Puppy Proud	Rockwell-Inspired	9/95	44.95	44.95
Norman Rockwell Gallery		**Reflections of Rockwell**			
91-08-001	When I Grow Up	Rockwell-Inspired	12/93	39.95	39.95
92-08-002	A Young Girl's Dream	Rockwell-Inspired	3/94	39.95	39.95
92-08-003	The Finishing Touch	Rockwell-Inspired	6/94	39.95	39.95
Norman Rockwell Gallery		**Rockwell's Winter Wonderland Snowglobes**			
91-09-001	Skater's Waltz	Rockwell-Inspired	12/93	29.95	29.95
92-09-002	All Wrapped Up	Rockwell-Inspired	6/94	29.95	29.95
92-09-003	Young At Heart	Rockwell-Inspired	9/94	32.95	32.95
92-09-004	Downhill Dash	Rockwell-Inspired	12/94	32.95	32.95
92-09-005	Scotty Gets HisTree	Rockwell-Inspired	3/95	34.95	34.95
Norman Rockwell Gallery		**Rockwell's Classic Santa Snowglobes**			
92-10-001	Santa's Workshop	Rockwell-Inspired	N/A	29.95	29.95
92-10-002	Around the World	Rockwell-Inspired	N/A	29.95	29.95
Norman Rockwell Gallery		**Rockwell's Boys Will Be Boys**			
92-11-001	No Swimming	Rockwell-Inspired	N/A	29.95	29.95
92-11-002	Mischief Makers	Rockwell-Inspired	N/A	29.95	29.95
93-11-003	Space Rangers	Rockwell-Inspired	N/A	32.95	32.95
Norman Rockwell Gallery		**Rockwell's Main Street Snow Globes**			
92-12-001	The Studio	Rockwell-Inspired	N/A	29.95	29.95
92-12-002	The Antique Shop	Rockwell-Inspired	N/A	29.95	29.95
93-12-003	Town Offices	Rockwell-Inspired	N/A	29.95	29.95
Also See Rhodes Studio					
Rohn		**Around the World**			
71-01-001	Coolie	E. Rohn	100	700.00	1200.00
72-01-002	Gypsy	E. Rohn	125	1450.00	1850.00
73-01-003	Matador	E. Rohn	90	2400.00	3100.00
73-01-004	Sherif	E. Rohn	100	1500.00	2250.00
74-01-005	Aussie-Hunter	E. Rohn	90	1000.00	1300.00
Rohn		**Clowns-Big Top Series**			
79-02-001	White Face	E. Rohn	100	1000.00	3500.00
80-02-002	Tramp	E. Rohn	100	1200.00	2500.00
81-02-003	Auguste	E. Rohn	100	1400.00	1700.00
83-02-004	Sweetheart	E. Rohn	200	925.00	1500.00
Rohn		**Famous People**			
75-03-001	Harry S. Truman	E. Rohn	75	2400.00	4000.00
79-03-002	Norman Rockwell	E. Rohn	200	1950.00	2300.00
81-03-003	Ronald Reagan	E. Rohn	200	3000.00	3000.00
85-03-004	Sherlock Holmes	E. Rohn	2,210	155.00	190.00
86-03-005	Dr. John Watson	E. Rohn	2,210	155.00	155.00
Rohn		**Remember When**			
71-04-001	Riverboat Captain	E. Rohn	100	1000.00	2400.00
71-04-002	American GI	E. Rohn	100	600.00	1750.00
73-04-003	Apprentice	E. Rohn	175	500.00	850.00

Number	Name	Artist	Edition Limit	Issue Price	Quote
74-04-004	Recruit (set w/FN-5)	E. Rohn	250	250.00	500.00
74-04-005	Missy	E. Rohn	250	250.00	500.00
77-04-006	Flapper	E. Rohn	500	325.00	500.00
77-04-007	Sou' Wester	E. Rohn	450	300.00	500.00
77-04-008	Casey	E. Rohn	300	275.00	500.00
77-04-009	Wally	E. Rohn	250	250.00	500.00
73-04-010	Jazz Man	E. Rohn	150	750.00	3500.00
80-04-011	Showman (W.C. Fields)	E. Rohn	300	220.00	500.00
81-04-012	Clown Prince	E. Rohn	25	2000.00	2400.00
Rohn		**Religious & Biblical**			
77-05-001	Zaide	E. Rohn	70	1950.00	5000.00
78-05-002	Sabbath	E. Rohn	70	1825.00	5000.00
85-05-003	The Mentor	E. Rohn	15	9500.00	9500.00
Rohn		**Small World Series**			
74-06-001	Big Brother	E. Rohn	250	90.00	90.00
74-06-002	Burglers	E. Rohn	250	120.00	120.00
74-06-003	Quackers	E. Rohn	250	75.00	75.00
74-06-004	Knee Deep	E. Rohn	500	60.00	60.00
75-06-005	Field Mushrooms	E. Rohn	250	90.00	90.00
75-06-006	Oyster Mushroom	E. Rohn	250	140.00	140.00
XX-06-007	Johnnie's	E. Rohn	1,500	90.00	90.00
Rohn		**Western**			
71-07-001	Trail-Hand	E. Rohn	100	1200.00	1600.00
71-07-002	Crow Indian	E. Rohn	100	800.00	1500.00
71-07-003	Apache Indian	E. Rohn	125	800.00	2000.00
71-07-004	Chosen One (Indian Maid)	E. Rohn	125	850.00	2000.00
Rohn		**Clowns-Hey Rube**			
79-08-001	Whiteface	E. Rohn	300	190.00	350.00
79-08-002	Tramp	E. Rohn	300	190.00	350.00
79-08-003	Auguste	E. Rohn	300	190.00	350.00
Rohn		**Famous People-Bisque**			
79-09-001	Norman Rockwell	E. Rohn	Yr.Iss.	100.00	200.00
79-09-002	Lincoln	E. Rohn	500	100.00	500.00
81-09-003	Reagan	E. Rohn	2,500	140.00	200.00
83-09-004	J. F. Kennedy	E. Rohn	500	140.00	400.00
Rohn		**Wild West**			
82-10-001	Rodeo Clown	E. Rohn	100	2600.00	3500.00
Roman, Inc.		**Fontanini, The Collectible Creche**			
73-01-001	10cm., (15 piece Set)	E. Simonetti	Closed	63.60	88.50
73-01-002	12cm., (15 piece Set)	E. Simonetti	Closed	76.50	102.00
79-01-003	16cm., (15 piece Set)	E. Simonetti	Closed	178.50	285.00
82-01-004	17cm., (15 piece Set)	E. Simonetti	Closed	189.00	305.00
73-01-005	19cm., (15 piece Set)	E. Simonetti	Closed	175.50	280.00
80-01-006	30cm., (15 piece Set)	E. Simonetti	Closed	670.00	758.50
Roman, Inc.		**A Child's World 1st Edition**			
80-02-001	Nighttime Thoughts	F. Hook	Closed	25.00	65.00
80-02-002	Kiss Me Good Night	F. Hook	15,000	29.00	40.00
80-02-003	Sounds of the Sea	F. Hook	15,000	45.00	140.00
80-02-004	Beach Buddies, signed	F. Hook	15,000	29.00	600.00
80-02-005	My Big Brother	F. Hook	Closed	39.00	200.00
80-02-006	Helping Hands	F. Hook	Closed	45.00	75.00
80-02-007	Beach Buddies, unsigned	F. Hook	15,000	29.00	450.00
Roman, Inc.		**A Child's World 2nd Edition**			
81-03-001	Making Friends	F. Hook	15,000	42.00	46.00
81-03-002	Cat Nap	F. Hook	15,000	42.00	100.00
81-03-003	The Sea and Me	F. Hook	15,000	39.00	43.00
81-03-004	Sunday School	F. Hook	15,000	39.00	70.00
81-03-005	I'll Be Good	F. Hook	15,000	36.00	70.00
81-03-006	All Dressed Up	F. Hook	15,000	36.00	70.00
Roman, Inc.		**A Child's World 3rd Edition**			
81-04-001	Pathway to Dreams	F. Hook	15,000	47.00	50.00
81-04-002	Road to Adventure	F. Hook	15,000	47.00	50.00
81-04-003	Sisters	F. Hook	15,000	64.00	69.00
81-04-004	Bear Hug	F. Hook	15,000	42.00	45.00
81-04-005	Spring Breeze	F. Hook	15,000	37.50	40.00
81-04-006	Youth	F. Hook	15,000	37.50	40.00
Roman, Inc.		**A Child's World 4th Edition**			
82-05-001	All Bundled Up	F. Hook	15,000	37.50	40.00
82-05-002	Bedtime	F. Hook	15,000	35.00	38.00
82-05-003	Birdie	F. Hook	15,000	37.50	40.00
82-05-004	My Dolly!	F. Hook	15,000	39.00	40.00
82-05-005	Ring Bearer	F. Hook	15,000	39.00	40.00
82-05-006	Flower Girl	F. Hook	15,000	42.00	45.00
Roman, Inc.		**A Child's World 5th Edition**			
83-06-001	Ring Around the Rosie	F. Hook	15,000	99.00	105.00
83-06-002	Handful of Happiness	F. Hook	15,000	36.00	40.00
83-06-003	He Loves Me...	F. Hook	15,000	49.00	55.00
83-06-004	Finish Line	F. Hook	15,000	39.00	42.00
83-06-005	Brothers	F. Hook	15,000	64.00	70.00
83-06-006	Puppy's Pal	F. Hook	15,000	39.00	42.00
Roman, Inc.		**A Child's World 6th Edition**			
84-07-001	Good Doggie	F. Hook	15,000	47.00	50.00
84-07-002	Sand Castles	F. Hook	15,000	37.50	40.00
84-07-003	Nature's Wonders	F. Hook	15,000	29.00	31.00
84-07-004	Let's Play Catch	F. Hook	15,000	33.00	35.00
84-07-005	Can I Help?	F. Hook	15,000	37.50	40.00
84-07-006	Future Artist	F. Hook	15,000	42.00	45.00
Roman, Inc.		**A Child's World 7th Edition**			
85-08-001	Art Class	F. Hook	15,000	99.00	105.00
85-08-002	Please Hear Me	F. Hook	15,000	29.00	30.00
85-08-003	Don't Tell Anyone	F. Hook	15,000	49.00	50.00
85-08-004	Mother's Helper	F. Hook	15,000	45.00	50.00
85-08-005	Yummm!	F. Hook	15,000	36.00	39.00
85-08-006	Look at Me!	F. Hook	15,000	42.00	45.00
Roman, Inc.		**A Child's World 8th Edition**			
85-09-001	Private Ocean	F. Hook	15,000	29.00	31.00
85-09-002	Just Stopped By	F. Hook	15,000	36.00	40.00
85-09-003	Dress Rehearsal	F. Hook	15,000	33.00	35.00

Company		Series			
Number	**Name**	**Artist**	**Edition Limit**	**Issue Price**	**Quote**
85-09-004	Chance of Showers	F. Hook	15,000	33.00	35.00
85-09-005	Engine	F. Hook	15,000	36.00	40.00
85-09-006	Puzzling	F. Hook	15,000	36.00	40.00
Roman, Inc.		**A Child's World 9th Edition**			
87-10-001	Li'l Brother	F. Hook	15,000	60.00	65.00
87-10-002	Hopscotch	F. Hook	15,000	67.50	70.00
Roman, Inc.		**Rohn's Clowns**			
84-11-001	White Face	E. Rohn	7,500	95.00	95.00
84-11-002	Auguste	E. Rohn	7,500	95.00	95.00
84-11-003	Hobo	E. Rohn	7,500	95.00	95.00
Roman, Inc.		**The Masterpiece Collection**			
79-12-001	Adoration	F. Lippe	5,000	73.00	73.00
80-12-002	Madonna with Grapes	P. Mignard	5,000	85.00	85.00
81-12-003	The Holy Family	G. delle Notti	5,000	98.00	98.00
82-12-004	Madonna of the Streets	R. Ferruzzi	5,000	65.00	65.00
Roman, Inc.		**Ceramica Excelsis**			
77-13-001	Madonna and Child with Angels	Unknown	5,000	60.00	60.00
77-13-002	What Happened to Your Hand?	Unknown	5,000	60.00	60.00
77-13-003	Madonna with Child	Unknown	5,000	65.00	65.00
77-13-004	St. Francis	Unknown	5,000	60.00	60.00
77-13-005	Christ Knocking at the Door	Unknown	5,000	60.00	60.00
78-13-006	Infant of Prague	Unknown	5,000	37.50	60.00
78-13-007	Christ in the Garden of Gethsemane	Unknown	5,000	40.00	60.00
78-13-008	Flight into Egypt	Unknown	5,000	59.00	90.00
78-13-009	Christ Entering Jerusalem	Unknown	5,000	96.00	96.00
78-13-010	Holy Family at Work	Unknown	5,000	96.00	96.00
78-13-011	Assumption Madonna	Unknown	5,000	56.00	56.00
78-13-012	Guardian Angel with Girl	Unknown	5,000	69.00	69.00
78-13-013	Guardian Angel with Boy	Unknown	5,000	69.00	69.00
79-13-014	Moses	Unknown	5,000	77.00	77.00
79-13-015	Noah	Unknown	5,000	77.00	77.00
79-13-016	Jesus Speaks in Parables	Unknown	5,000	90.00	90.00
80-13-017	Way to Emmaus	Unknown	5,000	155.00	155.00
80-13-018	Daniel in the Lion's Den	Unknown	5,000	80.00	80.00
80-13-019	David	Unknown	5,000	77.00	77.00
81-13-020	Innocence	Unknown	5,000	95.00	95.00
81-13-021	Journey to Bethlehem	Unknown	5,000	89.00	89.00
81-13-022	Way of the Cross	Unknown	5,000	59.00	59.00
81-13-023	Sermon on the Mount	Unknown	5,000	56.00	56.00
83-13-024	Good Shepherd	Unknown	5,000	49.00	49.00
83-13-025	Holy Family	Unknown	5,000	72.00	72.00
83-13-026	St. Francis	Unknown	5,000	59.50	59.50
83-13-027	St. Anne	Unknown	5,000	49.00	49.00
83-13-028	Jesus with Children	Unknown	5,000	74.00	74.00
83-13-029	Kneeling Santa	Unknown	5,000	95.00	95.00
Roman, Inc.		**Hook**			
82-14-001	Sailor Mates	F. Hook	2,000	290.00	315.00
82-14-002	Sun Shy	F. Hook	2,000	290.00	315.00
Roman, Inc.		**Frances Hook's Four Seasons**			
84-15-001	Winter	F. Hook	12,500	95.00	100.00
85-15-002	Spring	F. Hook	12,500	95.00	100.00
85-15-003	Summer	F. Hook	12,500	95.00	100.00
85-15-004	Fall	F. Hook	12,500	95.00	100.00
Roman, Inc.		**Jam Session**			
85-16-001	Trombone Player	E. Rohn	7,500	145.00	145.00
85-16-002	Bass Player	E. Rohn	7,500	145.00	145.00
85-16-003	Banjo Player	E. Rohn	7,500	145.00	145.00
85-16-004	Coronet Player	E. Rohn	7,500	145.00	145.00
85-16-005	Clarinet Player	E. Rohn	7,500	145.00	145.00
85-16-006	Drummer	E. Rohn	7,500	145.00	145.00
Roman, Inc.		**Spencer**			
85-17-001	Moon Goddess	I. Spencer	5,000	195.00	195.00
85-17-002	Flower Princess	I. Spencer	5,000	195.00	195.00
Roman, Inc.		**Hook**			
86-18-001	Carpenter Bust	F. Hook	Yr.Iss.	95.00	95.00
86-18-002	Carpenter Bust-Heirloom Edition	F. Hook	Yr.Iss.	95.00	95.00
87-18-003	Madonna and Child	F. Hook	15,000	39.50	39.50
87-18-004	Little Children, Come to Me	F. Hook	15,000	45.00	45.00
Roman, Inc.		**Catnippers**			
85-19-001	The Paw that Refreshes	I. Spencer	15,000	45.00	45.00
85-19-002	A Christmas Mourning	I. Spencer	15,000	45.00	49.50
85-19-003	A Tail of Two Kitties	I. Spencer	15,000	45.00	45.00
85-19-004	Sandy Claws	I. Spencer	15,000	45.00	45.00
85-19-005	Can't We Be Friends	I. Spencer	15,000	45.00	45.00
85-19-006	A Baffling Yarn	I. Spencer	15,000	45.00	45.00
85-19-007	Flying Tiger-Retired	I. Spencer	15,000	45.00	45.00
85-19-008	Flora and Felina	I. Spencer	15,000	45.00	49.50
Roman, Inc.		**Heartbeats**			
86-20-001	Miracle	I. Spencer	5,000	145.00	145.00
87-20-002	Storytime	I. Spencer	5,000	145.00	145.00
Roman, Inc.		**Classic Brides of the Century**			
89-21-001	1900-Flora	E. Williams	5,000	175.00	175.00
89-21-002	1910-Elizabeth Grace	E. Williams	5,000	175.00	175.00
89-21-003	1920-Mary Claire	E. Williams	5,000	175.00	175.00
89-21-004	1930-Kathleen	E. Williams	5,000	175.00	175.00
89-21-005	1940-Margaret	E. Williams	5,000	175.00	175.00
89-21-006	1950-Barbara Ann	E. Williams	5,000	175.00	175.00
89-21-007	1960-Dianne	E. Williams	5,000	175.00	175.00
89-21-008	1970-Heather	E. Williams	5,000	175.00	175.00
89-21-009	1980-Jennifer	E. Williams	5,000	175.00	175.00
92-21-010	1990-Stephanie Helen	E. Williams	5,000	175.00	175.00
Roman Inc.		**Dolfi Original-5" Wood**			
89-22-001	My First Kitten	L. Martin	5,000	230.00	230.00
89-22-002	Flower Child	L. Martin	5,000	230.00	230.00
89-22-003	Pampered Puppies	L. Martin	5,000	230.00	230.00
89-22-004	Wrapped In Love	L. Martin	5,000	230.00	230.00
89-22-005	Garden Secrets	L. Martin	5,000	230.00	230.00
89-22-006	Puppy Express	L. Martin	5,000	230.00	230.00
89-22-007	Sleepyhead	L. Martin	5,000	230.00	230.00
89-22-008	Mother Hen	L. Martin	5,000	230.00	230.00
89-22-009	Holiday Herald	L. Martin	5,000	230.00	230.00
89-22-010	Birdland Cafe	L. Martin	5,000	230.00	230.00
89-22-011	My First Cake	L. Martin	5,000	230.00	230.00
89-22-012	Mud Puddles	L. Martin	5,000	230.00	230.00
89-22-013	Study Break	L. Martin	5,000	250.00	250.00
89-22-014	Dress Rehearsal	L. Martin	5,000	375.00	375.00
89-22-015	Friends & Flowers	L. Martin	5,000	300.00	300.00
89-22-016	Merry Little Light	L. Martin	5,000	250.00	250.00
89-22-017	Mary & Joey	L. Martin	5,000	375.00	375.00
89-22-018	Little Santa	L. Martin	5,000	250.00	250.00
89-22-019	Sing a Song of Joy	L. Martin	5,000	300.00	300.00
89-22-020	Barefoot In Spring	L. Martin	5,000	300.00	300.00
89-22-021	My Favorite Things	L. Martin	5,000	300.00	300.00
89-22-022	Have I Been That Good	L. Martin	5,000	375.00	375.00
89-22-023	A Shoulder to Lean On	L. Martin	5,000	300.00	300.00
89-22-024	Big Chief Sitting Dog	L. Martin	5,000	250.00	250.00
Roman, Inc.		**Dolfi Original-7" Stoneart**			
89-23-001	My First Kitten	L. Martin	Open	110.00	110.00
89-23-002	Flower Child	L. Martin	Open	110.00	110.00
89-23-003	Pampered Puppies	L. Martin	Open	110.00	110.00
89-23-004	Wrapped In Love	L. Martin	Open	110.00	110.00
89-23-005	Garden Secrets	L. Martin	Open	110.00	110.00
89-23-006	Puppy Express	L. Martin	Open	110.00	110.00
89-23-007	Sleepyhead	L. Martin	Open	110.00	110.00
89-23-008	Mother Hen	L. Martin	Open	110.00	110.00
89-23-009	Holiday Herald	L. Martin	Open	110.00	110.00
89-23-010	Birdland Cafe	L. Martin	Open	110.00	110.00
89-23-011	My First Cake	L. Martin	Open	110.00	110.00
89-23-012	Mud Puddles	L. Martin	Open	110.00	110.00
89-23-013	Study Break	L. Martin	Open	120.00	120.00
89-23-014	Dress Rehearsal	L. Martin	Open	185.00	185.00
89-23-015	Friends & Flowers	L. Martin	Open	150.00	150.00
89-23-016	Merry Little Light	L. Martin	Open	120.00	120.00
89-23-017	Mary & Joey	L. Martin	Open	185.00	185.00
89-23-018	Little Santa	L. Martin	Open	120.00	120.00
89-23-019	Sing a Song of Joy	L. Martin	Open	150.00	150.00
89-23-020	Barefoot In Spring	L. Martin	Open	150.00	150.00
89-23-021	My Favorite Things	L. Martin	Open	150.00	150.00
89-23-022	Have I Been That Good	L. Martin	Open	185.00	185.00
89-23-023	A Shoulder to Lean On	L. Martin	Open	150.00	150.00
89-23-024	Big Chief Sitting Dog	L. Martin	Open	120.00	120.00
Roman, Inc.		**Dolfi Original-10" Stoneart**			
89-24-001	My First Kitten	L. Martin	Open	300.00	300.00
89-24-002	Flower Child	L. Martin	Open	300.00	300.00
89-24-003	Pampered Puppies	L. Martin	Open	300.00	300.00
89-24-004	Wrapped in Love	L. Martin	Open	300.00	300.00
89-24-005	Garden Secrets	L. Martin	Open	300.00	300.00
89-24-006	Puppy Express	L. Martin	Open	300.00	300.00
89-24-007	Sleepyhead	L. Martin	Open	300.00	300.00
89-24-008	Mother Hen	L. Martin	Open	300.00	300.00
89-24-009	Holiday Herald	L. Martin	Open	300.00	300.00
89-24-010	Birdland Cafe	L. Martin	Open	300.00	300.00
89-24-011	My First Cake	L. Martin	Open	300.00	300.00
89-24-012	Mud Puddles	L. Martin	Open	300.00	300.00
89-24-013	Study Break	L. Martin	Open	325.00	325.00
89-24-014	Dress Rehearsal	L. Martin	Open	495.00	495.00
89-24-015	Friends & Flowers	L. Martin	Open	400.00	400.00
89-24-016	Merry Little Light	L. Martin	Open	325.00	325.00
89-24-017	Mary & Joey	L. Martin	Open	495.00	495.00
89-24-018	Little Santa	L. Martin	Open	325.00	325.00
89-24-019	Sing a Song of Joy	L. Martin	Open	400.00	400.00
89-24-020	Barefoot In Spring	L. Martin	Open	400.00	400.00
89-24-021	My Favorite Things	L. Martin	Open	400.00	400.00
89-24-022	Have I Been That Good	L. Martin	Open	495.00	495.00
89-24-023	A Shoulder to Lean On	L. Martin	Open	400.00	400.00
89-24-024	Big Chief Sitting Dog	L. Martin	Open	325.00	325.00
Roman, Inc.		**Dolfi Original-10" Wood**			
89-26-001	My First Kitten	L. Martin	2,000	750.00	750.00
89-26-002	Flower Child	L. Martin	2,000	750.00	750.00
89-26-003	Pampered Puppies	L. Martin	2,000	750.00	750.00
89-26-004	Wrapped in Love	L. Martin	2,000	750.00	750.00
89-26-005	Garden Secrets	L. Martin	2,000	750.00	750.00
89-26-006	Puppy Express	L. Martin	2,000	750.00	750.00
89-26-007	Sleepyhead	L. Martin	2,000	750.00	750.00
89-26-008	Mother Hen	L. Martin	2,000	750.00	750.00
89-26-009	Holiday Herald	L. Martin	2,000	750.00	750.00
89-26-010	Birdland Cafe	L. Martin	2,000	750.00	750.00
89-26-011	My First Cake	L. Martin	2,000	750.00	750.00
89-26-012	Mud Puddles	L. Martin	2,000	750.00	750.00
89-26-013	Study Break	L. Martin	2,000	825.00	825.00
89-26-014	Dress Rehearsal	L. Martin	2,000	1250.00	1250.00
89-26-015	Friends & Flowers	L. Martin	2,000	1000.00	1000.00
89-26-016	Merry Little Light	L. Martin	2,000	825.00	825.00
89-26-017	Mary & Joey	L. Martin	2,000	1250.00	1250.00
89-26-018	Little Santa	L. Martin	2,000	825.00	825.00
89-26-019	Sing a Song of Joy	L. Martin	2,000	1000.00	1000.00
89-26-020	Barefoot In Spring	L. Martin	2,000	1000.00	1000.00
89-26-021	My Favorite Things	L. Martin	2,000	1000.00	1000.00
89-26-022	Have I Been That Good	L. Martin	2,000	1250.00	1250.00
89-26-023	A Shoulder to Lean On	L. Martin	2,000	1000.00	1000.00
89-26-024	Big Chief Sitting Dog	L. Martin	2,000	825.00	825.00
Roman, Inc.		**The Museum Collection by Angela Tripi**			
90-27-001	The Mentor	A. Tripi	1,000	290.00	290.27
91-27-002	The Fiddler	A. Tripi	1,000	175.00	175.27
91-27-003	Christopher Columbus	A. Tripi	1,000	250.00	250.00
91-27-004	St. Francis of Assisi	A. Tripi	1,000	175.00	175.00
91-27-005	The Caddie	A. Tripi	1,000	135.00	135.00
91-27-006	A Gentleman's Game	A. Tripi	1,000	175.00	175.00
91-27-007	Tee Time at St. Andrew's	A. Tripi	1,000	175.00	175.00
92-27-008	Prince of the Plains	A. Tripi	1,000	175.00	175.00
92-27-009	The Fur Trapper	A. Tripi	1,000	175.00	175.00
92-27-010	Justice for All	A. Tripi	1,000	95.00	95.00
92-27-011	Flying Ace	A. Tripi	1,000	95.00	95.00
92-27-012	Our Family Doctor	A. Tripi	1,000	95.00	95.00
92-27-013	To Serve and Protect	A. Tripi	1,000	95.00	95.00
92-27-014	Ladies' Day	A. Tripi	1,000	175.00	175.00
92-27-015	Ladies' Tee	A. Tripi	1,000	250.00	250.00
92-27-016	The Tap In	A. Tripi	1,000	175.00	175.00
92-27-017	Fore!	A. Tripi	1,000	175.00	175.00

FIGURINES

Company Number	Name	Series Artist	Edition Limit	Issue Price	Quote
92-27-018	Checking It Twice	A. Tripi	2,500	95.00	95.00
92-27-019	The Tannenbaum Santa	A. Tripi	2,500	95.00	95.00
92-27-020	This Way, Santa	A. Tripi	2,500	95.00	95.00
92-27-021	The Gift Giver	A. Tripi	2,500	95.00	95.00
92-27-022	8-pc. Nativity Set	A. Tripi	2,500	425.00	425.00
Roman, Inc.		**Fontanini Heirloom Nativity**			
74-28-001	5" Mary (5")	E. Simonetti	Closed	2.50	9.50
74-28-002	Jesus (5")	E. Simonetti	Closed	2.50	9.50
74-28-003	Joseph (5")	E. Simonetti	Closed	2.50	9.50
91-28-004	New (5") Joseph	E. Simonetti	Open	11.50	11.50
91-28-005	New (5") Mary	E. Simonetti	Open	11.50	11.50
91-28-006	New (5") Jesus	E. Simonetti	Open	11.50	11.50
Roman, Inc.		**Fontanini Presepio Collection**			
90-29-001	Gideon	E. Simonetti.	Yr.Iss.	15.00	15.00
92-29-002	Ariel	E. Simonetti	Yr.Iss.	29.50	29.50
93-29-003	Jeshua & Adin	E. Simonetti	Yr.Iss.	29.50	29.50
Roman, Inc.		**Fontanini Collectors' Club Member Only**			
91-30-001	The Pilgrimage	E. Simonetti	Yr.Iss.	24.95	24.95
92-30-002	She Rescued Me	E. Simonetti	Yr.Iss.	23.50	23.50
92-30-003	He Comforts Me	E. Simonetti	Yr.Iss.	12.50	12.50
93-30-004	Christmas Symphony	E. Simonetti	Yr.Iss.	13.50	13.50
Roman, Inc.		**The Richard Judson Zolan Collection**			
92-31-001	Summer at the Seashore	R.J. Zolan	1,200	125.00	125.00
Roman, Inc.		**Tender Expressions**			
92-32-001	You Are Always in the Thoughts That Fill My Day	B. Sargent	Open	27.50	27.50
92-32-002	I Even Love the Rain When You Share My Umbrella	B. Sargent	Open	27.50	27.50
92-32-003	I Tell Everyone How Special You Are	B. Sargent	Open	27.50	27.50
92-32-004	The Greatest Love Shines From A Mother's Face	B. Sargent	Open	27.50	27.50
92-32-005	I Count My Blessings...And There You Are!	B. Sargent	Open	27.50	27.50
92-32-006	Thoughts Of You Are In My Heart	B. Sargent	Open	27.50	27.50
Royal Doulton		**Royal Doulton Figurines**			
XX-01-001	Indian Brave	P. Davies	500	2500.00	5700.00
XX-01-002	The Palio	P. Davies	500	2500.00	6500.00
XX-01-003	Beethoven	R. Garbe	25	N/A	6500.00
Royal Doulton		**Royalty**			
XX-02-001	Queen Elizabeth II	P. Davies	750	200.00	1950-2050.
XX-02-002	Queen Mother	P. Davies	1,500	650.00	1200.00
XX-02-003	Duchess Of York	E. Griffiths	1,500	495.00	650.00
XX-02-004	Duke Of Edinburgh	P. Davies	750	395.00	395.00
XX-02-005	Prince Of Wales HN2883	E. Griffiths	1,500	395.00	450-850.
XX-02-006	Prince Of Wales HN2884	E. Griffiths	1,500	750.00	750.00
XX-02-007	Princess Of Wales HN2887	E. Griffiths	1,500	750.00	1250.00
XX-02-008	Lady Diana Spencer	E. Griffiths	1,500	395.00	650-750.
Royal Doulton		**Lady Musicians**			
XX-03-001	Cello	P. Davies	750	250.00	1000.00
XX-03-002	Chitarrone	P. Davies	750	250.00	600-1200.
XX-03-003	Cymbals	P. Davies	750	325.00	550-950.
XX-03-004	Dulcimer	P. Davies	750	375.00	600-1500.
XX-03-005	Flute	P. Davies	750	250.00	950-1100.
XX-03-006	French Horn	P. Davies	750	400.00	600-950.
XX-03-007	Harp	P. Davies	750	275.00	1500-1800.
XX-03-008	Hurdy Gurdy	P. Davies	750	375.00	600-1300.
XX-03-009	Lute	P. Davies	750	250.00	950.00
XX-03-010	Viola d'Amore	P. Davies	750	400.00	550-1000.
XX-03-011	Violin	P. Davies	750	250.00	900-950.
XX-03-012	Virginals	P. Davies	750	250.00	1200-1500.
Royal Doulton		**Dancers Of The World**			
XX-04-001	Dancers, Balinese	P. Davies	750	950.00	950.00
XX-04-002	Dancers, Breton	P. Davies	750	850.00	850-900.
XX-04-003	Dancers, Chinese	P. Davies	750	750.00	750-900.
XX-04-004	Dancers, Indian Temple	P. Davies	750	400.00	1000.00
XX-04-005	Dancers, Kurdish	P. Davies	750	550.00	550.00
XX-04-006	Dancers, Mexican	P. Davies	750	550.00	550-900.
XX-04-007	Dancers, No. American Indian	P. Davies	750	950.00	950.00
XX-04-008	Dancers, Philippine	P. Davies	750	450.00	750-900.
XX-04-009	Dancers, Polish	P. Davies	750	750.00	850-1500.
XX-04-010	Dancers, Scottish	P. Davies	750	450.00	850-1200.
XX-04-011	Dancers, Flamenco	P. Davies	750	400.00	1200-1500.
XX-04-012	Dancers, West Indian	P. Davies	750	850.00	850.00
Royal Doulton		**Soldiers of The Revolution**			
XX-05-001	Soldiers, New York	E. Griffiths	350	750.00	750.00
XX-05-002	Soldiers, New Hampshire	E. Griffiths	350	750.00	750.00
XX-05-003	Soldiers, New Jersey	E. Griffiths	350	750.00	2000.00
XX-05-004	Soldiers, Connecticut	E. Griffiths	350	750.00	750.00
XX-05-005	Soldiers, Delaware	E. Griffiths	350	750.00	750.00
XX-05-006	Soldiers, Georgia	E. Griffiths	350	750.00	850.00
XX-05-007	Soldiers, Massachusetts	E. Griffiths	350	750.00	750.00
XX-05-008	Soldiers, Pennsylvania	E. Griffiths	350	750.00	750.00
XX-05-009	Soldiers, Rhode Island	E. Griffiths	350	750.00	750.00
XX-05-010	Soldiers, South Carolina	E. Griffiths	350	750.00	850.00
XX-05-011	Soldiers, North Carolina	E. Griffiths	350	750.00	750.00
XX-05-012	Soldiers, Maryland	E. Griffiths	350	750.00	750.00
XX-05-013	Soldiers, Virginia	E. Griffiths	350	1500.00	2500.00
XX-05-014	Soldiers, Washington	Ispanky	750	N/A	2000.00
Royal Doulton		**Femmes Fatales**			
XX-06-001	Cleopatra	P. Davies	750	750.00	1350.00
XX-06-002	Helen of Troy	P. Davies	750	1250.00	1250-1400.
XX-06-003	Queen of Sheba	P. Davies	750	1250.00	1250-1400.
XX-06-004	Tz'u-Hsi	P. Davies	750	1250.00	1250.00
XX-06-005	Eve	P. Davies	750	1250.00	1250.00
XX-06-006	Lucrezia Borgia	P. Davies	750	1250.00	1250.00
Royal Doulton		**Myths & Maidens**			
XX-07-001	Lady & Unicorn	R. Jefferson	S/O	2500.00	2500-3500.
XX-07-002	Leda & Swan	R. Jefferson	300	2950.00	2950-3200.
XX-07-003	Juno & Peacock	R. Jefferson	300	2950.00	2950-3200.
XX-07-004	Europa & Bull	R. Jefferson	300	2950.00	2950-3200.
XX-07-005	Diana The Huntress	R. Jefferson	300	2950.00	2950-3200.

Company Number	Name	Series Artist	Edition Limit	Issue Price	Quote
Royal Doulton		**Gentle Arts**			
XX-08-001	Spinning	P. Davies	750	1250.00	1250-1400.
XX-08-002	Tapestry Weaving	P. Parsons	750	1250.00	1250.00
XX-08-003	Writing	P. Parsons	750	1350.00	1350.00
XX-08-004	Painting	P. Parsons	750	1350.00	1350.00
XX-08-005	Adornment	N/A	750	1350.00	1350.00
XX-08-006	Flower Arranging	N/A	750	1350.00	1350.00
Royal Doulton		**Ships Figureheads**			
XX-09-001	Ajax	S. Keenan	950	N/A	550-700.
XX-09-002	Benmore	S. Keenan	950	N/A	550-700.
XX-09-003	Chieftain	S. Keenan	950	N/A	750.00
XX-09-004	Hibernia	S. Keenan	950	N/A	950.00
XX-09-005	Lalla Rookh	S. Keenan	950	N/A	750.00
XX-09-006	Mary, Queen of Scots	S. Keenan	950	N/A	1200.00
XX-09-007	Lord Nelson	S. Keenan	950	N/A	850.00
XX-09-008	Pocahontas	S. Keenan	950	N/A	950.00
Royal Doulton		**Les Saisons**			
XX-10-001	Automne	R. Jefferson	300	850.00	950.00
XX-10-002	Printemps	R. Jefferson	300	850.00	850.00
XX-10-003	L'Hiver	R. Jefferson	300	850.00	850.00
XX-10-004	L'Ete	R. Jefferson	300	850.00	895.00
Royal Doulton		**Queens of Realm**			
XX-11-001	Queen Elizabeth I	P. Parsons	S/O	495.00	495-1200.
XX-11-002	Queen Victoria	P Parsons	S/O	495.00	850-1000
XX-11-003	Queen Anne	N/A	5,000	525.00	550.00
XX-11-004	Mary, Queen of Scots	N/A	S/O	550.00	750-950.
Royal Doulton		**Gainsborough Ladies**			
XX-12-001	Mary, Countess Howe	P. Gee	5,000	650.00	650-700.
91-12-002	Lady Sheffield	P. Gee	5,000	650.00	650-700.
91-12-003	Hon Frances Duncombe	P. Gee	5,000	650.00	650-700.
91-12-004	Countess of Sefton	P. Gee	5,000	650.00	650-700.
Royal Doulton		**Reynolds Collection**			
91-13-001	Lady Worsley HN3318	P. Gee	5,000	550.00	600.00
92-13-002	Countess Harrington HN3317	P. Gee	5,000	550.00	600.00
92-13-003	Mrs. Hugh Bonfoy HN3319	P. Gee	5,000	550.00	600.00
93-13-004	Countess Spencer HN3320	P. Gee	5,000	595.00	595.00
Royal Doulton		**Age of Innocence**			
91-14-001	Feeding Time	N. Pedley	9,500	245.00	275.00
91-14-002	Making Friends	N. Pedley	9,500	270.00	295.00
91-14-003	Puppy Love	N. Pedley	9,500	270.00	295.00
92-14-004	First Outing	N. Pedley	9,500	275.00	295.00
Royal Doulton		**Character Jugs**			
91-15-001	Henry VIII	W. Harper	1,991	395.00	850.00
91-15-002	Santa Claus Miniature	N/A	5,000	50.00	75-85.00
92-15-003	King Charles I	W. Harper	2,500	450.00	450.00
93-15-004	William Shakespeare	W. Harper	2,500	625.00	625.00
93-15-005	Abraham Lincoln	S. Taylor	2,500	190.00	190.00
Royal Doulton		**Character Jug of the Year**			
91-16-001	Fortune Teller	N/A	Closed	130.00	150.00
92-16-002	Winston Churchill	N/A	Closed	195.00	195.00
93-16-003	Vice-Admiral Lord Nelson	S. Taylor	Yr.Iss.	225.00	225.00
Royal Doulton		**Star Crossed Lovers Character Jugs**			
86-17-001	Napoleon & Josephine	M. Abberley	9,500	195.00	195.00
XX-17-002	Anthony & Cleopatra	M. Abberley	S/O	195.00	195.00
89-17-003	King Arthur & Guinevere	S. Taylor	9,500	195.00	195.00
88-17-004	Samson & Delilah	S. Taylor	9,500	195.00	195.00
Royal Doulton		**Antagonists Character Jugs**			
86-18-001	George III & George Washington	M. Abberley	9,500	195.00	195.00
Royal Doulton		**Prestige Figures**			
91-19-001	Columbine	N/A	N/A	1250.00	1350.00
91-19-002	Fighter Elephant	N/A	N/A	2500.00	2500.00
91-19-003	Fox	N/A	N/A	1550.00	1550.00
91-19-004	Harlequin	N/A	N/A	1250.00	1350.00
91-19-005	Jack Point	N/A	N/A	2900.00	3000.00
91-19-006	King Charles	N/A	N/A	2500.00	2500.00
91-19-007	Leopard on Rock	N/A	N/A	3000.00	3000.00
91-19-008	Lion on Rock	N/A	N/A	3000.00	3000.00
91-19-009	Matador and Bull	N/A	N/A	21500.00	23000.00
91-19-010	The Moor	N/A	N/A	2500.00	2700.00
91-19-011	Princess Badoura	N/A	N/A	28000.00	30000.00
91-19-012	St George and Dragon	N/A	N/A	13600.00	14500.00
91-19-013	Tiger	N/A	N/A	1950.00	1950.00
91-19-014	Tiger on Rock	N/A	N/A	3000.00	3000.00
92-19-015	Christopher Columbus	A. Maslankowski	1,492	1950.00	1950.00
92-19-016	Napoleon at Waterloo	A. Maslankowski	1,500	1900.00	1900.00
Royal Doulton		**Figure of the Year**			
91-20-001	Amy	P. Gee	Closed	195.00	250.00
92-20-002	Mary	P. Gee	Closed	225.00	250.00
93-20-003	Patricia	V. Annand	Yr.Iss.	250.00	250.00
Royal Doulton		**British Sporting Heritage**			
93-21-001	Henley	V. Annand	5,000	475.00	475.00
Royal Doulton		**Limited Editions**			
93-22-001	Lt. General Ulysses S. Grant	R. Tabbenor	5,000	1175.00	1175.00
93-22-002	General Robert E. Lee	R. Tabbenor	5,000	1175.00	1175.00
93-22-003	Duke of Wellington	A. Maslankowski	1,500	1750.00	1750.00
93-22-004	Winston S. Churchill	A. Maslankowski	5,000	595.00	595.00
Royal Doulton		**Royal Doulton Collectors' Club**			
80-23-001	John Doulton Jug (8 O'Clock)	N/A	Yr.Iss.	70.00	125.00
81-23-002	Sleepy Darling Figure	N/A	Yr.Iss.	100.00	195.00
82-23-003	Dog of Fo	N/A	Yr.Iss.	50.00	150.00
82-23-004	Prized Possessions Figure	N/A	Yr.Iss.	125.00	475.00
83-23-005	Loving Cup	N/A	Yr.Iss.	75.00	275.00
83-23-006	Springtime	N/A	Yr.Iss.	125.00	350.00
84-23-007	Sir Henry Doulton Jug	N/A	Yr.Iss.	50.00	125.00
84-23-008	Pride & Joy Figure	N/A	Yr.Iss.	125.00	225.00
85-23-009	Top of the Hill Plate	N/A	Yr.Iss.	34.95	75.00
85-23-010	Wintertime Figure	N/A	Yr.Iss.	125.00	195.00
86-23-011	Albert Sagger Toby Jug	N/A	Yr.Iss.	34.95	70.00

Company / Number	Name	Series / Artist	Edition Limit	Issue Price	Quote
86-23-012	Auctioneer Figure	N/A	Yr.Iss.	150.00	195.00
87-23-013	Collector Bunnykins	N/A	Yr.Iss.	40.00	295.00
87-23-014	Summertime Figurine	N/A	Yr.Iss.	140.00	150.00
88-23-015	Top of the Hill Miniature Figurine	N/A	Yr.Iss.	95.00	125.00
88-23-016	Beefeater Tiny Jug	N/A	Yr.Iss.	25.00	125.00
88-23-017	Old Salt Tea Pot	N/A	Yr.Iss.	135.00	250.00
89-23-018	Geisha Flambe Figure	N/A	Yr.Iss.	195.00	195.00
89-23-019	Flower Sellers Children Plate	N/A	Yr.Iss.	65.00	65.00
90-23-020	Autumntime Figure	N/A	Yr.Iss.	190.00	190.00
90-23-021	Jester Mini Figure	N/A	Yr.Iss.	115.00	115.00
90-23-022	Old King Cole Tiny Jug	N/A	Yr.Iss.	35.00	100.00
91-23-023	Bunny's Bedtime Figure	N/A	Yr.Iss.	195.00	250.00
91-23-024	Charles Dickens Jug	N/A	Yr.Iss.	100.00	100.00
91-23-025	L'Ambiteuse Figure (Tissot Lady)	N/A	Yr.Iss.	295.00	295.00
91-23-026	Christopher Columbus Jug	N/A	Yr.Iss.	95.00	95.00
92-23-027	Discovery Figure	N/A	Yr.Iss.	160.00	160.00
92-23-028	King Edward Jug	N/A	Yr.Iss.	250.00	250.00
92-23-029	Master Potter Bunnykins	N/A	Yr.Iss.	50.00	50.00
92-23-030	Eliza Farren Prestige Figure	N/A	Yr.Iss.	335.00	335.00
93-23-031	Barbara Figure	N/A	Yr.Iss.	285.00	285.00
Royal Worcester		**Dorothy Doughty Porcelains**			
35-01-001	American Redstarts and Hemlock	D. Doughty	66	Unkn.	5500.00
41-01-002	Apple Blossoms	D. Doughty	250	400.00	1400-3750.
63-01-003	Audubon Warblers	D. Doughty	500	1350.00	2100-4200.
38-01-004	Baltimore Orioles	D. Doughty	250	350.00	Unkn.
56-01-005	Bewick's Wrens & Yellow Jasmine	D. Doughty	500	600.00	2100-3800.
36-01-006	Bluebirds	D. Doughty	350	500.00	8500-9000.
64-01-007	Blue Tits & Pussy Willow	D. Doughty	500	250.00	3000.00
40-01-008	Bobwhite Quail	D. Doughty	22	275.00	11000.
59-01-009	Cactus Wrens	D. Doughty	500	1250.00	1700-4500.
60-01-010	Canyon Wrens	D. Doughty	500	750.00	2000-4000.
37-01-011	Cardinals	D. Doughty	500	500.00	20000-9250.
68-01-012	Carolina Paroquet, Color	D. Doughty	350	1200.00	1900-2200.
68-01-013	Carolina Paroquet, White	D. Doughty	75	600.00	Unkn.
65-01-014	Cerulean Warblers & Red Maple	D. Doughty	500	1350.00	1400-3000.
38-01-015	Chickadees & Larch	D. Doughty	300	350.00	8500-8900.
65-01-016	Chuffchaff	D. Doughty	500	1500.00	1300-2900.
42-01-017	Crabapple Blossom Sprays And A Butterfly	D. Doughty	250	Unkn.	800.00
40-01-018	Crabapples	D. Doughty	250	400.00	3700-4250.
67-01-019	Downy Woodpecker & Pecan, Color	D. Doughty	400	1500.00	1000-2400.
67-01-020	Downy Woodpecker & Pecan, White	D. Doughty	75	1000.00	1900.00
59-01-021	Elf Owl	D. Doughty	500	875.00	Unkn.
55-01-022	Gnatcatchers	D. Doughty	500	600.00	2700-4900.
72-01-023	Goldcrests, Pair	D. Doughty	500	4200.00	Unkn.
36-01-024	Goldfinches & Thistle	D. Doughty	250	350.00	2000-7000.
68-01-025	Gray Wagtail	D. Doughty	500	600.00	Unkn.
61-01-026	Hooded Warblers	D. Doughty	500	950.00	4300.00
50-01-027	Hummingbirds And Fuchsia	D. Doughty	500	Unkn.	2800.00
42-01-028	Indigo Bunting And Plum Twig	D. Doughty	5,000	Unkn.	Unkn.
42-01-029	Indigo Buntings, Blackberry Sprays	D. Doughty	500	375.00	1700-3500.
65-01-030	Kingfisher Cock & Autumn Beech	D. Doughty	500	1250.00	1900-2300.
52-01-031	Kinglets & Noble Pine	D. Doughty	500	450.00	1300-4800.
66-01-032	Lark Sparrow	D. Doughty	500	750.00	Unkn.
62-01-033	Lazuli Bunting & Chokecherries, Color	D. Doughty	500	1350.00	3000-4500.
62-01-034	Lazuli Bunting & Chokecherries, White	D. Doughty	100	1350.00	2600-3000.
64-01-035	Lesser Whitethroats	D. Doughty	500	350.00	1200-4000.
50-01-036	Magnolia Warbler	D. Doughty	150	1100.00	1900-3600.
77-01-037	Meadow Pipit	D. Doughty	500	1800.00	1800.00
50-01-038	Mexican Feijoa	D. Doughty	250	600.00	2600-4900.
40-01-039	Mockingbirds	D. Doughty	500	450.00	7200-7750.
42-01-040	Mockingbirds and Peach Blossom	D. Doughty	500	Unkn.	Unkn.
64-01-041	Moorhen Chick	D. Doughty	500	1000.00	Unkn.
64-01-042	Mountain Bluebirds	D. Doughty	500	950.00	1700-2300.
55-01-043	Myrtle Warblers	D. Doughty	500	550.00	1300-4000.
71-01-044	Nightingale & Honeysuckle	D. Doughty	500	2500.00	2500-2750.
47-01-045	Orange Blossoms & Butterfly	D. Doughty	250	500.00	4200-4500.
57-01-046	Ovenbirds	D. Doughty	250	650.00	4500.00
57-01-047	Parula Warblers	D. Doughty	500	600.00	1700-3600.
58-01-048	Phoebes On Flame Vine	D. Doughty	500	750.00	2200-5500.
52-01-049	Red-Eyed Vireos	D. Doughty	500	450.00	2000.00
68-01-050	Redstarts & Gorse	D. Doughty	500	1900.00	2300.00
64-01-051	Robin	D. Doughty	500	750.00	Unkn.
56-01-052	Scarlet Tanagers	D. Doughty	500	675.00	3000-4200.
62-01-053	Scissor-Tailed Flycatcher, Color	D. Doughty	250	950.00	Unkn.
62-01-054	Scissor-Tailed Flycatcher, White	D. Doughty	75	950.00	1300-1600.
63-01-055	Vermillion Flycatchers	D. Doughty	500	250.00	1100-3400.
64-01-056	Wrens & Burnet Rose	D. Doughty	500	650.00	1000.00
52-01-057	Yellow-Headed Blackbirds	D. Doughty	350	650.00	2000-2400.
58-01-058	Yellowthroats on Water Hyacinth	D. Doughty	350	750.00	1700-4000.
Royal Worcester		**Ronald Van Ruyckevelt Porcelains**			
XX-02-001	Alice	R. Van Ruyckevelt	500	1875.00	1875.00
70-02-002	American Pintail, Pair	R. Van Ruyckevelt	500	Unkn.	3000.00
69-02-003	Argenteuil A-108	R. Van Ruyckevelt	338	Unkn.	Unkn.
68-02-004	Blue Angel Fish	R. Van Ruyckevelt	500	375.00	900.00
67-02-005	Bluefin Tuna	R. Van Ruyckevelt	500	500.00	Unkn.
65-02-006	Blue Marlin	R. Van Ruyckevelt	500	500.00	1000.00
69-02-007	Bobwhite Quail, Pair	R. Van Ruyckevelt	500	Unkn.	2000.00
67-02-008	Butterfly Fish	R. Van Ruyckevelt	500	375.00	1600.00
69-02-009	Castelneau Pink	R. Van Ruyckevelt	429	Unkn.	825-875.
69-02-010	Castelneau Yellow	R. Van Ruyckevelt	163	Unkn.	825-875.
XX-02-011	Cecilia	R. Van Ruyckevelt	500	1875.00	1875.00
68-02-012	Dolphin	R. Van Ruyckevelt	500	500.00	900.00
71-02-013	Elaine	R. Van Ruyckevelt	750	600.00	600-650.
62-02-014	Flying Fish	R. Van Ruyckevelt	300	400.00	450.00
71-02-015	Green-Winged Teal	R. Van Ruyckevelt	500	1450.00	1450.00
62-02-016	Hibiscus	R. Van Ruyckevelt	500	300.00	350.00
56-02-017	Hogfish & Sergeant Major	R. Van Ruyckevelt	500	375.00	650.00
68-02-018	Honfleur A-105	R. Van Ruyckevelt	290	Unkn.	600.00
68-02-019	Honfleur A-106	R. Van Ruyckevelt	290	Unkn.	600.00
71-02-020	Languedoc	R. Van Ruyckevelt	216	Unkn.	1150.00
68-02-021	Mallards	R. Van Ruyckevelt	500	Unkn.	2000.00
68-02-022	Mennecy A-101	R. Van Ruyckevelt	338	Unkn.	675-725.
68-02-023	Mennecy A-102	R. Van Ruyckevelt	334	Unkn.	675-725.
61-02-024	Passionflower	R. Van Ruyckevelt	500	300.00	400.00
76-02-025	Picnic	R. Van Ruyckevelt	250	2850.00	2850.00
76-02-026	Queen Elizabeth I	R. Van Ruyckevelt	250	3850.00	3850.00
77-02-027	Queen Elizabeth II	R. Van Ruyckevelt	250	Unkn.	Unkn.
76-02-028	Queen Mary I	R. Van Ruyckevelt	250	4850.00	4850.00
68-02-029	Rainbow Parrot Fish	R. Van Ruyckevelt	500	1500.00	1500.00
58-02-030	Red Hind	R. Van Ruyckevelt	500	375.00	900.00
68-02-031	Ring-Necked Pheasants	R. Van Ruyckevelt	500	Unkn.	3200-3400.
64-02-032	Rock Beauty	R. Van Ruyckevelt	500	425.00	850.00
62-02-033	Sailfish	R. Van Ruyckevelt	500	400.00	550.00
69-02-034	Saint Denis A-109	R. Van Ruyckevelt	500	Unkn.	925-950.
61-02-035	Squirrelfish	R. Van Ruyckevelt	500	400.00	9000.00
66-02-036	Swordfish	R. Van Ruyckevelt	500	575.00	650.00
64-02-037	Tarpon	R. Van Ruyckevelt	500	500.00	975.00
72-02-038	White Doves	R. Van Ruyckevelt	25	3600.00	27850.00
Royal Worcester		**Ruth Van Ruyckevelt Porcelains**			
60-03-001	Beatrice	R. Van Ruyckevelt	500	125.00	Unkn.
69-03-002	Bridget	R. Van Ruyckevelt	500	300.00	600-700.
60-03-003	Caroline	R. Van Ruyckevelt	500	125.00	Unkn.
68-03-004	Charlotte and Jane	R. Van Ruyckevelt	500	1000.00	1500-1650.
67-03-005	Elizabeth	R. Van Ruyckevelt	750	300.00	750-800.
69-03-006	Emily	R. Van Ruyckevelt	500	300.00	600.00
78-03-007	Esther	R. Van Ruyckevelt	500	Unkn.	Unkn.
71-03-008	Felicity	R. Van Ruyckevelt	750	600.00	600.00
59-03-009	Lisette	R. Van Ruyckevelt	500	100.00	Unkn.
62-03-010	Louisa	R. Van Ruyckevelt	500	400.00	975.00
68-03-011	Madeline	R. Van Ruyckevelt	500	300.00	750-800.
68-03-012	Marion	R. Van Ruyckevelt	500	275.00	575-625.
64-03-013	Melanie	R. Van Ruyckevelt	500	150.00	Unkn.
59-03-014	Penelope	R. Van Ruyckevelt	500	100.00	Unkn.
64-03-015	Rosalind	R. Van Ruyckevelt	500	150.00	Unkn.
63-03-016	Sister of London Hospital	R. Van Ruyckevelt	500	Unkn.	475-500.
63-03-017	Sister of St. Thomas Hospital	R. Van Ruyckevelt	500	Unkn.	475-500.
70-03-018	Sister of the Red Cross	R. Van Ruyckevelt	750	Unkn.	525-500.
66-03-019	Sister of University College Hospital	R. Van Ruyckevelt	500	Unkn.	475-500.
64-03-020	Tea Party	R. Van Ruyckevelt	250	400.00	7000.00
Royal Worcester		**Bicentennial L.E. Commemoratives**			
73-04-001	Potter	P.W. Baston	500	Unkn.	300-400.
73-04-002	Cabinetmaker	P.W. Baston	500	Unkn.	300-400.
73-04-003	Blacksmith	P.W. Baston	500	Unkn.	500.00
75-04-004	Clockmaker	P.W. Baston	Unkn.	Unkn.	500.00
Sarah's Attic, Inc.		**Angels In The Attic**			
89-01-001	St. Gabbe	Sarah's Attic	Closed	30.00	33.00
89-01-002	St. Anne	Sarah's Attic	Closed	29.00	32.00
89-01-003	Angel Wendall	Sarah's Attic	Closed	10.00	14.00
89-01-004	Angel Winnie	Sarah's Attic	Closed	10.00	14.00
89-01-005	Angel Wendy	Sarah's Attic	Closed	10.00	14.00
89-01-006	Angel Wilbur	Sarah's Attic	Closed	9.50	21.50
89-01-007	Angel Bonnie	Sarah's Attic	Closed	17.00	20.00
89-01-008	Angel Clyde	Sarah's Attic	Closed	17.00	20.00
89-01-009	Angel Floppy	Sarah's Attic	Closed	10.00	20.00
89-01-010	Angel Eddie	Sarah's Attic	Closed	10.00	10.00
89-01-011	Angel Jessica	Sarah's Attic	Closed	14.00	14.00
89-01-012	Angel Jeffrey	Sarah's Attic	Closed	14.00	14.00
89-01-013	Angel Amelia	Sarah's Attic	Closed	10.00	14.00
89-01-014	Angel Alex	Sarah's Attic	Closed	10.00	14.00
89-01-015	Angel Abbee	Sarah's Attic	Closed	9.50	13.00
89-01-016	Angel Ashbee	Sarah's Attic	Closed	9.50	13.00
89-01-017	Angel Rayburn	Sarah's Attic	Closed	12.00	19.00
89-01-018	Angel Reggie	Sarah's Attic	Closed	12.00	15.00
89-01-019	Angel Reba	Sarah's Attic	Closed	12.00	12.00
89-01-020	Angel Ruthie	Sarah's Attic	Closed	12.00	12.00
89-01-021	Angel Daisy	Sarah's Attic	Closed	14.00	14.00
89-01-022	Angel Patsy	Sarah's Attic	Closed	13.00	13.00
89-01-023	Angel Ashlee	Sarah's Attic	Closed	14.00	14.00
89-01-024	Angel Shooter	Sarah's Attic	Closed	12.50	18.00
89-01-025	Angel Grams	Sarah's Attic	Closed	17.00	35.00
89-01-026	Angel Gramps	Sarah's Attic	Closed	17.00	95.00
89-01-027	Angel Dusty	Sarah's Attic	Closed	12.00	95.00
89-01-028	Angel Emmy Lou	Sarah's Attic	Closed	12.00	12.00
89-01-029	Saint Willie Bill	Sarah's Attic	Closed	30.00	40.00
89-01-030	Angel Bevie	Sarah's Attic	Closed	10.00	10.00
89-01-031	St. George	Sarah's Attic	Closed	60.00	65.00
90-01-032	Angel Rabbit in Basket	Sarah's Attic	Closed	25.00	25.00
90-01-033	Angel Bear in Basket	Sarah's Attic	Closed	23.00	23.00
90-01-034	Angel Billi	Sarah's Attic	Closed	18.00	22.00
90-01-035	Angel Cindi	Sarah's Attic	Closed	18.00	22.00
90-01-036	Angel Lena	Sarah's Attic	Closed	36.00	40.00
90-01-037	Angel Trudy	Sarah's Attic	Closed	36.00	36.00
90-01-038	Angel Trapper	Sarah's Attic	Closed	17.00	20.00
90-01-039	Angel Louise	Sarah's Attic	Closed	17.00	20.00
90-01-040	Angel Flossy	Sarah's Attic	Closed	15.00	15.00
90-01-041	Angel Buster	Sarah's Attic	Closed	15.00	15.00
91-01-042	Angel Donald with Dog	Sarah's Attic	Closed	50.00	50.00
91-01-043	Angel Bert Golfing	Sarah's Attic	Closed	60.00	60.00
91-01-044	Contentment	Sarah's Attic	Closed	100.00	100.00
91-01-045	Love	Sarah's Attic	Closed	80.00	80.00
92-01-046	Angelle Guardian Angel	Sarah's Attic	2,000	170.00	170.00
92-01-047	Kiah Guardian Angel	Sarah's Attic	2,000	170.00	170.00
92-01-048	Heavenly Caring	Sarah's Attic	2,500	70.00	70.00
92-01-049	Heavenly Sharing	Sarah's Attic	2,500	70.00	70.00
92-01-050	Heavenly Giving	Sarah's Attic	2,500	70.00	70.00
92-01-051	Heavenly Loving	Sarah's Attic	2,500	70.00	70.00
92-01-052	Harmony Angel	Sarah's Attic	3,500	26.00	26.00
92-01-053	Joy Angel	Sarah's Attic	3,500	26.00	26.00
92-01-054	Noble Angel	Sarah's Attic	3,500	24.00	24.00
92-01-055	Sincerity Angel	Sarah's Attic	3,500	24.00	24.00
92-01-056	White Baby Peace	Sarah's Attic	3,500	14.00	14.00
92-01-057	Black Baby Peace	Sarah's Attic	3,500	14.00	14.00
92-01-058	Tree w/ White Angel	Sarah's Attic	Open	22.00	22.00
92-01-059	Tree w/ Black Angel	Sarah's Attic	Open	22.00	22.00
92-01-060	Heavenly Heart Base	Sarah's Attic	Open	40.00	40.00
93-01-061	Heavenly Uniting	Sarah's Attic	2,500	45.00	45.00
93-01-062	Heavenly Protecting	Sarah's Attic	2,500	40.00	40.00
Sarah's Attic, Inc.		**Americana Collection**			
88-02-001	Amer. Bear	Sarah's Attic	Closed	17.50	17.50
88-02-002	Betsy Ross	Sarah's Attic	Closed	34.00	40.00
88-02-003	Americana Bear	Sarah's Attic	Closed	70.00	70.00
88-02-004	Americana Bunny	Sarah's Attic	Closed	70.00	70.00
88-02-005	Betsy Bear W/Flag	Sarah's Attic	Closed	22.50	27.50
88-02-006	Colonial Bear W/Hat	Sarah's Attic	Closed	22.50	25.00
88-02-007	Turkey	Sarah's Attic	Closed	10.00	12.00
88-02-008	Indian Brave	Sarah's Attic	Closed	10.00	10.00
88-02-009	Indian Girl	Sarah's Attic	Closed	10.00	10.00
88-02-010	Pilgrim Boy	Sarah's Attic	Closed	12.50	12.50
88-02-011	Pilgrim Girl	Sarah's Attic	Closed	12.50	12.50
88-02-012	Americana Clown	Sarah's Attic	Closed	80.00	80.00

Company Number	Name	Series Artist	Edition Limit	Issue Price	Quote
90-02-013	Iron Hawk	Sarah's Attic	Closed	70.00	140.00
90-02-014	Bright Sky	Sarah's Attic	Closed	70.00	140.00
90-02-015	Little Dove	Sarah's Attic	Closed	40.00	80.00
90-02-016	Spotted Eagle	Sarah's Attic	Closed	30.00	60.00
Sarah's Attic, Inc.		**Beary Adorables Collection**			
87-03-001	Alex Bear	Sarah's Attic	Closed	11.50	11.50
87-03-002	Amelia Bear	Sarah's Attic	Closed	11.50	11.50
87-03-003	Abbee Bear	Sarah's Attic	Closed	10.00	10.00
87-03-004	Ashbee Bear	Sarah's Attic	Closed	10.00	10.00
87-03-005	Collectible Bear	Sarah's Attic	Closed	16.00	16.00
88-03-006	Ghost Bear	Sarah's Attic	Closed	12.00	12.00
88-03-007	Lefty Bear	Sarah's Attic	Closed	80.00	80.00
89-03-008	Sid Bear	Sarah's Attic	Closed	18.00	25.00
89-03-009	Sophie Bear	Sarah's Attic	Closed	18.00	25.00
89-03-010	Daisy Bear	Sarah's Attic	Closed	48.00	55.00
89-03-011	Griswald Bear	Sarah's Attic	Closed	48.00	55.00
89-03-012	Missy Bear	Sarah's Attic	Closed	26.00	30.00
89-03-013	Mikey Bear	Sarah's Attic	Closed	26.00	26.00
89-03-014	Angel Bear	Sarah's Attic	Closed	24.50	24.50
89-03-015	Sugar Bear	Sarah's Attic	Closed	12.00	12.00
89-03-016	Mini Teddy Bear	Sarah's Attic	Closed	5.00	5.00
89-03-017	Sammy Bear	Sarah's Attic	Closed	12.00	15.00
89-03-018	Spice Bear	Sarah's Attic	Closed	12.00	15.00
90-03-019	Bailey 50's Bear	Sarah's Attic	Closed	25.00	30.00
90-03-020	Beulah 50's Bear	Sarah's Attic	Closed	25.00	30.00
90-03-021	Birkey 50's Bear	Sarah's Attic	Closed	20.00	25.00
90-03-022	Belinda 50's Bear	Sarah's Attic	Closed	20.00	25.00
88-03-023	Bear in Basket	Sarah's Attic	Closed	48.00	48.00
87-03-024	Bear On Trunk	Sarah's Attic	Closed	20.00	20.00
88-03-025	Einstein Bear	Sarah's Attic	Closed	8.50	8.50
88-03-026	Benni Bear	Sarah's Attic	Closed	7.00	7.00
88-03-027	Jester Clown Bear	Sarah's Attic	Closed	12.50	12.50
88-03-028	Honey Picnic Bear	Sarah's Attic	Closed	16.50	20.00
88-03-029	Rufus Picnic Bear	Sarah's Attic	Closed	15.00	20.00
88-03-030	Marti Picnic Bear	Sarah's Attic	Closed	12.50	20.00
88-03-031	Arti Picnic Bear	Sarah's Attic	Closed	7.00	15.00
90-03-032	Miss Love Brown Bear	Sarah's Attic	Closed	42.00	42.00
90-03-033	Dudley Brown Bear	Sarah's Attic	Closed	32.00	32.00
90-03-034	Margie Brown Bear	Sarah's Attic	Closed	32.00	32.00
90-03-035	Joey Brown Bear	Sarah's Attic	Closed	32.00	32.00
90-03-036	Franny Brown Bear	Sarah's Attic	Closed	32.00	32.00
90-03-037	Oliver Black Bear	Sarah's Attic	Closed	32.00	32.00
92-03-038	Mandy Mother Bear	Sarah's Attic	3,500	20.00	20.00
92-03-039	Andy Father Bear	Sarah's Attic	3,500	20.00	20.00
92-03-040	Brandy Baby Bear	Sarah's Attic	3,500	14.00	14.00
93-03-041	You're Beary Huggable	Sarah's Attic	Open	18.00	18.00
93-03-042	I Miss You Beary Much	Sarah's Attic	Open	18.00	18.00
93-03-043	You're Beary Special Bear	Sarah's Attic	Open	18.00	18.00
93-03-044	I'm Beary Sorry	Sarah's Attic	Open	18.00	18.00
Sarah's Attic, Inc.		**Black Heritage Collection**			
89-04-001	Quilting Ladies	Sarah's Attic	Closed	80.00	200-295.
89-04-002	Pappy Jake	Sarah's Attic	Closed	33.00	100-135.
90-04-003	Susie Mae	Sarah's Attic	Open	20.00	22.00
90-04-004	Caleb	Sarah's Attic	Open	21.00	23.00
90-04-005	Hattie	Sarah's Attic	4,000	35.00	100-135.
90-04-006	Whoopie & Wooster	Sarah's Attic	Closed	50.00	250-350.00
90-04-007	Carpet Bag	Sarah's Attic	Closed	10.00	25.00
90-04-008	Portia	Sarah's Attic	Closed	26.00	45-65.00
90-04-009	Harpster W/Banjo	Sarah's Attic	Closed	60.00	250-350.
90-04-010	Libby W/Bibs	Sarah's Attic	Closed	36.00	70-135.00
90-04-011	Lucas W/Bibs	Sarah's Attic	Closed	36.00	75-135.00
90-04-012	Praise the Lord I (Preacher I)	Sarah's Attic	Closed	50.00	75-135.00
90-04-013	Pearl-Tap Dancer	Sarah's Attic	Closed	40.00	75.00
90-04-014	Percy-Tap Dancer	Sarah's Attic	5,000	40.00	75.00
90-04-015	Brotherly Love	Sarah's Attic	Closed	80.00	80.00
87-04-016	Gramps	Sarah's Attic	Closed	16.00	16.00
87-04-017	Grams	Sarah's Attic	Closed	16.00	16.00
90-04-018	Nighttime Pearl	Sarah's Attic	10,000	50.00	50.00
90-04-019	Nighttime Percy	Sarah's Attic	10,000	50.00	50.00
90-04-020	Sadie & Osie Mae	Sarah's Attic	8,000	70.00	70.00
90-04-021	Corporal Pervis	Sarah's Attic	8,000	60.00	60.00
90-04-022	Victorian Portia	Sarah's Attic	Closed	35.00	35.00
90-04-023	Victorian Webster	Sarah's Attic	Closed	35.00	35.00
90-04-024	Caleb W/Vegetables	Sarah's Attic	Closed	50.00	50.00
90-04-025	Praise the Lord II	Sarah's Attic	5,000	100.00	100.00
90-04-026	Harpster W/Harmonica	Sarah's Attic	8,000	60.00	60.00
90-04-027	Whoopie & Wooster II	Sarah's Attic	8,000	70.00	70.00
90-04-028	Libby W/Puppy	Sarah's Attic	10,000	50.00	50.00
90-04-029	Lucas W/Dog	Sarah's Attic	10,000	50.00	50.00
90-04-030	Black Baby Tansy	Sarah's Attic	10,000	40.00	40.00
90-04-031	Uncle Reuben	Sarah's Attic	8,000	70.00	70.00
91-04-032	Pappy Jake & Susie Mae	Sarah's Attic	6,000	60.00	60.00
91-04-033	Hattie Quilting	Sarah's Attic	6,000	60.00	60.00
91-04-034	Portia Quilting	Sarah's Attic	6,000	40.00	40.00
91-04-035	Caleb With Football	Sarah's Attic	6,000	40.00	40.00
91-04-036	Black Teacher Miss Lettie	Sarah's Attic	6,000	50.00	50.00
91-04-037	Buffalo Soldier	Sarah's Attic	5,000	80.00	80.00
91-04-038	Clarence - Porter	Sarah's Attic	5,000	80.00	80.00
91-04-039	Cricket - Black Girl Graduate	Sarah's Attic	6,000	46.00	46.00
91-04-040	Chips - Black Boy Graduate	Sarah's Attic	6,000	46.00	46.00
91-04-041	Music Masters	Sarah's Attic	Closed	300.00	310-375.
91-04-042	"Gen. of Love" Cookstove	Sarah's Attic	Unkn.	100.00	100.00
91-04-043	Granny Wynne & Olivia	Sarah's Attic	5,000	85.00	85.00
91-04-044	Esther with Butter Churn	Sarah's Attic	5,000	70.00	70.00
91-04-045	Braided Rug	Sarah's Attic	Unkn.	35.00	35.00
91-04-046	Pie	Sarah's Attic	Unkn.	7.00	7.00
91-04-047	Kettles	Sarah's Attic	Unkn.	13.00	13.00
92-04-048	Rhythm & Blues	Sarah's Attic	5,000	80.00	80.00
92-04-049	Music Masters II	Sarah's Attic	1,000	250.00	250.00
92-04-050	Sojourner Truth	Sarah's Attic	3,000	80.00	80.00
92-04-051	Booker T. Washington	Sarah's Attic	3,000	80.00	80.00
92-04-052	Ida B. Wells & Frederick Douglass	Sarah's Attic	3,000	160.00	160.00
92-04-053	Jomo	Sarah's Attic	4,000	27.00	27.00
92-04-054	Kaminda	Sarah's Attic	4,000	50.00	50.00
92-04-055	Shamba	Sarah's Attic	4,000	50.00	50.00
92-04-056	Boys Night Out	Sarah's Attic	2,000	350.00	350.00
92-04-057	Harpster w/Banjo	Sarah's Attic	Closed	250.00	250.00
92-04-058	Whoopie	Sarah's Attic	Closed	200.00	200.00
92-04-059	Wooster	Sarah's Attic	Closed	160.00	160.00
92-04-060	Harriet Tubman	Sarah's Attic	3,000	60.00	60.00
92-04-061	Nurturing with Love	Sarah's Attic	2,000	60.00	60.00
93-04-062	Miles Boy Angel Gospel Singer	Sarah's Attic	2,500	27.00	27.00
93-04-063	Praise the Lord III	Sarah's Attic	2,500	44.00	44.00
93-04-064	Bessie Gospel Singer	Sarah's Attic	2,500	40.00	40.00
93-04-065	Jesse Gospel Singer	Sarah's Attic	2,500	40.00	40.00
93-04-066	Vanessa Gospel Singer	Sarah's Attic	2,500	40.00	40.00
93-04-067	Claudia Gospel Singer	Sarah's Attic	2,500	27.00	27.00
93-04-068	Brewster Boy	Sarah's Attic	2,500	27.00	27.00
93-04-069	Moriah Girl Angel	Sarah's Attic	2,500	27.00	27.00
93-04-070	Nat Love Cowboy	Sarah's Attic	2,500	45.00	45.00
Sarah's Attic, Inc.		**Cuddly Critters Collection**			
87-05-001	Sparky	Sarah's Attic	Closed	9.00	10.00
88-05-002	Kitty Cat W/Bonnet	Sarah's Attic	Closed	12.00	12.00
89-05-003	Madam Donna	Sarah's Attic	Closed	35.50	45.00
89-05-004	Messieur Pierre	Sarah's Attic	Closed	35.50	45.00
88-05-005	Cow W/Bell	Sarah's Attic	Closed	35.00	35.00
88-05-006	Papa Mouse	Sarah's Attic	Closed	17.50	22.00
89-05-007	Whiskers Boy Cat	Sarah's Attic	Closed	10.00	10.00
89-05-008	Puddin Girl Cat	Sarah's Attic	Closed	10.00	10.00
89-05-009	Otis Papa Cat	Sarah's Attic	Closed	13.00	13.00
89-05-010	Wiggly Pig	Sarah's Attic	Closed	17.00	25.00
90-05-011	Pa Squirrel Sherman	Sarah's Attic	Closed	19.00	19.00
90-05-012	Ma Squirrel Sasha	Sarah's Attic	Closed	19.00	19.00
90-05-013	Boy Squirrel Sonny	Sarah's Attic	Closed	18.00	18.00
90-05-014	Girl Squirrel Sis	Sarah's Attic	Closed	18.00	18.00
90-05-015	Horace & Sissy Dogs	Sarah's Attic	Closed	50.00	50.00
90-05-016	Rebecca Mom Dog	Sarah's Attic	Closed	40.00	40.00
90-05-017	Penny Girl Dog	Sarah's Attic	Closed	35.00	35.00
90-05-018	Scooter Boy Dog	Sarah's Attic	Closed	30.00	30.00
90-05-019	Jasper Dad Cat	Sarah's Attic	Closed	36.00	36.00
90-05-020	Winnie Mom Cat	Sarah's Attic	Closed	36.00	36.00
90-05-021	Scuffy Boy Cat	Sarah's Attic	Closed	26.00	26.00
90-05-022	Lulu Girl Cat	Sarah's Attic	Closed	26.00	26.00
88-05-023	Lila Mrs. Mouse	Sarah's Attic	Closed	17.50	26.00
88-05-024	Lucky Boy Mouse	Sarah's Attic	Closed	13.00	16.00
88-05-025	Lucky Girl Mouse	Sarah's Attic	Closed	12.00	16.00
88-05-026	Rocking Horse	Sarah's Attic	Closed	56.00	56.00
88-05-027	Lazy-cat On Back	Sarah's Attic	Closed	13.00	13.00
88-05-028	Buster Boy Cat	Sarah's Attic	Closed	14.00	14.00
88-05-029	Flossy Girl Cat	Sarah's Attic	Closed	9.50	15.00
88-05-030	Trapper Papa Cat	Sarah's Attic	Closed	20.00	25.00
88-05-031	Louise Mama Cat	Sarah's Attic	Closed	20.00	25.00
88-05-032	Sleeping Cat	Sarah's Attic	Closed	6.00	6.00
88-05-033	Carousel Horse	Sarah's Attic	Closed	31.00	31.00
88-05-034	Myrtle The Pig	Sarah's Attic	Closed	38.00	45.00
91-05-035	Jiggs - Sleeping Cat	Sarah's Attic	Unkn.	10.00	10.00
Sarah's Attic, Inc.		**Classroom Memories**			
88-06-001	Miss Pritchett	Sarah's Attic	Open	28.00	35.00
91-06-002	Achieving Our Goals	Sarah's Attic	10,000	80.00	80.00
91-06-003	Classroom Memories	Sarah's Attic	6,000	80.00	80.00
Sarah's Attic, Inc.		**Cotton Tale Collection**			
87-07-001	Winnie Mom Rabbit	Sarah's Attic	Closed	17.00	17.00
88-07-002	Girl Rabbit Res. Candle	Sarah's Attic	Closed	14.00	14.00
88-07-003	Boy Rabbit Res. Candle	Sarah's Attic	Closed	14.00	14.00
88-07-004	Lizzy Hare	Sarah's Attic	Closed	10.00	10.00
88-07-005	Izzy Hare	Sarah's Attic	Closed	10.00	10.00
88-07-006	Maddy Hare	Sarah's Attic	Closed	11.00	11.00
88-07-007	Amos Hare	Sarah's Attic	Closed	11.00	11.00
89-07-008	Crumb Rabbit	Sarah's Attic	Closed	29.00	35-40.00
89-07-009	Cookie Rabbit	Sarah's Attic	Closed	29.00	35-40.00
89-07-010	Papa Rabbit	Sarah's Attic	Closed	50.00	60-65.00
89-07-011	Nana Rabbit	Sarah's Attic	Closed	50.00	60-65.00
89-07-012	Thelma Rabbit	Sarah's Attic	Closed	33.00	40.00
89-07-013	Thomas Rabbit	Sarah's Attic	Closed	33.00	40.00
89-07-014	Tessy Rabbit	Sarah's Attic	Closed	15.00	20.00
89-07-015	Toby Rabbit	Sarah's Attic	Closed	17.00	20.00
89-07-016	Sleeping Baby Bunny	Sarah's Attic	Closed	15.50	25.00
90-07-017	Zeb W/Carrots	Sarah's Attic	Closed	18.00	18.00
90-07-018	Zelda W/Carrots	Sarah's Attic	Closed	18.00	18.00
90-07-019	Zeke W/Carrots	Sarah's Attic	Closed	17.00	17.00
90-07-020	Zoe W/Carrots	Sarah's Attic	Closed	17.00	17.00
90-07-021	Olly Rabbit W/Vest	Sarah's Attic	Closed	65.00	75.00
90-07-022	Molly Rabbit W/Vest	Sarah's Attic	Closed	65.00	75.00
90-07-023	Henry Rabbit W/Pipe	Sarah's Attic	Open	30.00	32.00
90-07-024	Hannah Rabbit Ouilting	Sarah's Attic	Open	30.00	32.00
90-07-025	Herbie Rabbit W/Book	Sarah's Attic	Open	20.00	22.00
90-07-026	Hether Rabbit W/Doll	Sarah's Attic	Open	20.00	22.00
90-07-027	X-Mas Toby	Sarah's Attic	Closed	20.00	20.00
90-07-028	Zeb Sailor Dad	Sarah's Attic	Closed	26.00	28.00
90-07-029	Zelda Sailor Mom	Sarah's Attic	Closed	26.00	28.00
90-07-030	Zeke Sailor Boy	Sarah's Attic	Closed	24.00	26.00
90-07-031	Zoe Sailor Girl	Sarah's Attic	Closed	24.00	26.00
88-07-032	Rabbit In Basket	Sarah's Attic	Closed	48.00	55.00
87-07-033	Wendall Pa Rabbit	Sarah's Attic	Closed	17.00	25.00
87-07-034	Wendy Girl Rabbit	Sarah's Attic	Closed	15.00	25.00
87-07-035	Wilbur Boy Rabbit	Sarah's Attic	Closed	13.00	25.00
87-07-036	Bonnie	Sarah's Attic	Closed	38.00	38.00
87-07-037	Clyde	Sarah's Attic	Closed	38.00	38.00
87-07-038	Floppy	Sarah's Attic	Closed	21.00	21.00
88-07-039	Mini Papa Rabbit	Sarah's Attic	Closed	8.50	12.00
88-07-040	Mini Boy Rabbit	Sarah's Attic	Closed	7.50	12.00
88-07-041	Mini Girl Rabbit	Sarah's Attic	Closed	7.50	12.00
88-07-042	Mini Mama Rabbit	Sarah's Attic	Closed	8.50	12.00
88-07-043	Cind Rabbit	Sarah's Attic	Closed	27.00	35.00
88-07-044	Billi Rabbit	Sarah's Attic	Closed	27.00	35.00
90-07-045	Papa Farm Rabbit	Sarah's Attic	6/93	80.00	80.00
90-07-046	Nana Farm Rabbit	Sarah's Attic	6/93	100.00	100.00
90-07-047	Chuckles Farm Rabbit	Sarah's Attic	6/93	53.00	53.00
90-07-048	Cookie Farm Rabbit	Sarah's Attic	6/93	47.00	47.00
90-07-049	Crumb Farm Rabbit	Sarah's Attic	6/93	53.00	53.00
90-07-050	Sleepy Farm Rabbit	Sarah's Attic	6/93	35.00	35.00
90-07-051	Victorian Thomas	Sarah's Attic	6/93	60.00	60.00
90-07-052	Victorian Thelma	Sarah's Attic	6/93	60.00	60.00
90-07-053	Victorian Toby	Sarah's Attic	6/93	40.00	40.00
90-07-054	Victorian Tessy	Sarah's Attic	6/93	20.00	20.00
90-07-055	Victorian Tabitha	Sarah's Attic	6/93	30.00	30.00
90-07-056	Victorian Tucker	Sarah's Attic	6/93	37.00	37.00
92-07-057	Christmas Tabitha w/Basket	Sarah's Attic	2,500	24.00	24.00
92-07-058	Cowboy Toby w/Hobby Horse	Sarah's Attic	2,500	32.00	32.00
92-07-059	Higgins Dad Rabbit	Sarah's Attic	2,500	40.00	40.00
92-07-060	Annabelle Mom Rabbit	Sarah's Attic	2,500	40.00	40.00

FIGURINES

Company Number	Name	Series Artist	Edition Limit	Issue Price	Quote
92-07-061	Pockets Boy Rabbit	Sarah's Attic	2,500	30.00	30.00
92-07-062	Petals Girl Rabbit	Sarah's Attic	2,500	30.00	30.00
92-07-063	Dustin Baking Boy Rabbit	Sarah's Attic	2,500	32.00	32.00
92-07-064	Flower Baking Girl Rabbit	Sarah's Attic	2,500	32.00	32.00
93-07-065	Hannah With Muff	Sarah's Attic	12/93	30.00	30.00
93-07-066	Henry With Wreath	Sarah's Attic	12/93	30.00	30.00
93-07-067	Heather In Sled	Sarah's Attic	12/93	30.00	30.00
93-07-068	Herbie Sitting	Sarah's Attic	12/93	25.00	25.00
93-07-069	Christmas Toby w/Book	Sarah's Attic	2,500	20.00	20.00
93-07-070	Tabitha Cowgirl Rabbit	Sarah's Attic	2,500	30.00	30.00
Sarah's Attic, Inc.		**Daisy Collection**			
89-08-001	Sally Booba	Sarah's Attic	Open	30.00	40.00
90-08-002	Jack Boy Ball & Glove	Sarah's Attic	Open	30.00	40.00
90-08-003	Sparky	Sarah's Attic	6/93	53.00	55.00
90-08-004	Spike	Sarah's Attic	Open	44.00	46.00
90-08-005	Bomber	Sarah's Attic	Open	50.00	52.00
90-08-006	Jewel	Sarah's Attic	Open	60.00	62.00
90-08-007	Stretch	Sarah's Attic	Open	50.00	52.00
Sarah's Atttic, Inc.		**Ginger Babies Collection**			
89-09-001	Ginger	Sarah's Attic	Closed	17.00	17.00
89-09-002	Molasses	Sarah's Attic	Closed	17.00	17.00
90-09-003	Ginger Girl Cinnamon	Sarah's Attic	Closed	15.50	20.00
90-09-004	Ginger Boy Nutmeg	Sarah's Attic	Closed	15.50	20.00
92-09-005	Home Sweet Home	Sarah's Attic	12/93	100.00	100.00
92-09-006	Cookie Base	Sarah's Attic	12/93	50.00	50.00
92-09-007	Ginger Bench w/Cat	Sarah's Attic	12/93	10.00	10.00
92-09-008	Gingerbread Fence	Sarah's Attic	12/93	13.00	1300
92-09-009	Vanilla Gingerbread Girl	Sarah's Attic	12/93	18.00	18.00
92-09-010	Almond Gingerbread Boy	Sarah's Attic	12/93	18.00	18.00
92-09-011	Cinnamon & Nutmeg w/Wagon	Sarah's Attic	12/93	36.00	36.00
92-09-012	Ginger Tree	Sarah's Attic	12/93	20.00	20.00
Sarah's Attic, Inc.		**Happy Collection**			
87-10-001	Sitting Happy	Sarah's Attic	Closed	26.00	26.00
87-10-002	Happy W/Balloons	Sarah's Attic	Closed	22.00	22.00
90-10-003	Encore Clown W/Dog	Sarah's Attic	Closed	100.00	100.00
87-10-004	Lge. Happy Clown	Sarah's Attic	Closed	22.00	22.00
88-10-005	Lady Clown	Sarah's Attic	Closed	20.00	20.00
Sarah's Attic, Inc.		**Heavenly Wings Collection**			
89-11-001	Angelica Angel	Sarah's Attic	Closed	21.00	25.00
89-11-002	Regina	Sarah's Attic	Closed	24.00	30.00
89-11-003	Heavenly Guardian	Sarah's Attic	Closed	40.00	40.00
90-11-004	Boy Angel Inst. Adair	Sarah's Attic	Closed	29.00	29.00
90-11-005	Enos W/ Blue Gown	Sarah's Attic	Closed	33.00	75-135.00
90-11-006	Adora W/Pink Gown	Sarah's Attic	Closed	35.00	75-135.00
90-11-007	Adora W/Bunny	Sarah's Attic	10,000	50.00	50.00
90-11-008	Enos W/Frog	Sarah's Attic	10,000	50.00	50.00
Sarah's Attic, Inc.		**Little Charmers Collection**			
89-12-001	Jennifer & Dog	Sarah's Attic	Closed	57.00	57.00
87-12-002	Daisy	Sarah's Attic	Closed	36.00	36.00
88-12-003	Girl W/Teacup	Sarah's Attic	Closed	37.00	37.00
88-12-004	Girl W/Dog	Sarah's Attic	Closed	43.00	43.00
89-12-005	Moose Boy Sitting	Sarah's Attic	Open	18.00	20.00
88-12-006	Jessica	Sarah's Attic	Closed	44.00	44.00
87-12-007	Bevie	Sarah's Attic	Closed	18.00	18.00
87-12-008	Dusty	Sarah's Attic	Closed	19.00	19.00
87-12-009	Twinkle W/Pole	Sarah's Attic	Closed	19.00	19.00
87-12-010	Willie Bill	Sarah's Attic	Closed	20.00	20.00
87-12-011	Shooter	Sarah's Attic	Closed	19.00	19.00
87-12-012	Emmy Lou	Sarah's Attic	Closed	14.00	14.00
87-12-013	Cupcake W/Rope	Sarah's Attic	Closed	19.00	19.00
87-12-014	Cheerleader	Sarah's Attic	Closed	16.00	16.00
87-12-015	Eddie	Sarah's Attic	Closed	18.00	18.00
87-12-016	Ashlee	Sarah's Attic	Closed	60.00	60.00
87-12-017	Corky-Boy Sailor Suit	Sarah's Attic	Closed	14.50	14.50
87-12-018	Clementine-Girl Sailor Suit	Sarah's Attic	Closed	14.50	14.50
87-12-019	Butch-Boy Book Sitting	Sarah's Attic	Closed	16.00	16.00
87-12-020	Blondie-Girl Doll Sitting	Sarah's Attic	Closed	16.00	16.00
87-12-021	Amber-Sm. Girl Standing	Sarah's Attic	Closed	15.00	15.00
87-12-022	Archie-Sm.Boy Standing	Sarah's Attic	Closed	15.00	15.00
87-12-023	Bare Bottom Baby	Sarah's Attic	Closed	9.50	9.50
87-12-024	Baseball Player	Sarah's Attic	Closed	24.00	24.00
87-12-025	Football Player	Sarah's Attic	Closed	24.00	24.00
87-12-026	Woman Golfer	Sarah's Attic	Closed	24.00	24.00
87-12-027	Man Golfer	Sarah's Attic	Closed	24.00	24.00
87-12-028	Beau-Cupie Boy	Sarah's Attic	Closed	20.00	20.00
87-12-029	Buttons-Cupie Giri	Sarah's Attic	Closed	20.00	20.00
88-12-030	Boy W/Clown Doll	Sarah's Attic	Closed	40.00	40.00
88-12-031	Bowler	Sarah's Attic	Closed	24.00	24.00
88-12-032	Basketball Player	Sarah's Attic	Closed	24.00	24.00
90-12-033	White Baby Tansy	Sarah's Attic	10,000	40.00	40.00
93-12-034	Lottie White Girl Graduate	Sarah's Attic	2,000	35.00	35.00
93-12-035	Logan White Boy Graduate	Sarah's Attic	2,000	35.00	35.00
Sarah's Attic, Inc.		**Memory Lane Collection**			
89-13-001	Fire Station	Sarah's Attic	Closed	20.00	20.00
89-13-002	Post Office	Sarah's Attic	Closed	25.00	25.00
89-13-003	Mini Depot	Sarah's Attic	Closed	7.00	7.00
89-13-004	Mini Bank	Sarah's Att!c	Closed	6.00	6.00
89-13-005	Briton Church	Sarah's Attic	Closed	25.00	25.00
87-13-006	House W/Dormers	Sarah's Attic	Closed	15.00	15.00
87-13-007	Barn	Sarah's Attic	Closed	16.50	16.50
87-13-008	Mill	Sarah's Attic	Closed	16.50	16.50
87-13-009	Cottage	Sarah's Attic	Closed	13.00	13.00
87-13-010	Barber Shop	Sarah's Attic	Closed	13.00	13.00
87-13-011	Grandma's House	Sarah's Attic	Closed	13.00	13.00
87-13-012	Church	Sarah's Attic	Closed	19.00	19.00
87-13-013	School	Sarah's Attic	Closed	14.00	14.00
87-13-014	General Store	Sarah's Attic	Closed	13.00	13.00
87-13-015	Drug Store	Sarah's Attic	Closed	13.00	13.00
88-13-016	Mini Barber Shop	Sarah's Attic	Closed	6.50	6.50
88-13-017	Mini Drug Store	Sarah's Attic	Closed	6.00	6.00
88-13-018	Mini General Store	Sarah's Attic	Closed	6.00	6.00
88-13-019	Mini Salt Box	Sarah's Attic	Closed	6.00	6.00
88-13-020	Mini Church	Sarah's Attic	Closed	6.50	6.50
88-13-021	Mini School	Sarah's Attic	Closed	6.50	6.50
88-13-022	Mini Barn	Sarah's Attic	Closed	6.00	6.00
88-13-023	Mini Grandma's House	Sarah's Attic	Closed	7.00	7.00
88-13-024	Mini Mill	Sarah's Attic	Closed	6.50	6.50
88-13-025	Bank	Sarah's Attic	Closed	13.00	13.00
88-13-026	Train Depot	Sarah's Attic	Closed	13.50	13.50
Sarah's Attic, Inc.		**Rose Collection**			
89-14-001	Sweet Rose	Sarah's Attic	Closed	50.00	50.00
90-14-002	Victorian Boy Cody	Sarah's Attic	Closed	46.00	46.00
90-14-003	Tyler Vict. Boy	Sarah's Attic	Closed	40.00	40.00
90-14-004	Tiffany Vict. Girl	Sarah's Attic	Closed	40.00	40.00
92-14-005	Misty	Sarah's Attic	4,000	60.00	60.00
Sarah's Attic, Inc.		**Snowflake Collection**			
89-15-001	Flurry	Sarah's Attic	Open	10.00	12.00
89-15-002	Boo Mini Snowman	Sarah's Attic	Open	6.00	6.00
89-15-003	Winter Frolic	Sarah's Attic	Closed	60.00	70.00
90-15-004	Amer. Snow Old Glory	Sarah's Attic	Closed	24.00	26.00
92-15-005	Crystal Mother Snowman	Sarah's Attic	3,500	20.00	20.00
92-15-006	Topper Father Snowman	Sarah's Attic	3,500	20.00	20.00
92-15-007	Sparkles Baby Snowman	Sarah's Attic	3,500	14.00	14.00
Sarah's Attic, Inc.		**Sarah's Gang Collection**			
89-16-001	Small Country Willie	Sarah's Attic	Closed	13.00	26.00
89-16-002	Small Country Tillie	Sarah's Attic	Closed	13.00	26.00
87-16-003	Sitting Whimpy	Sarah's Attic	Closed	14.00	20.00
87-16-004	Sitting Katie	Sarah's Attic	Closed	14.00	20.00
87-16-005	Willie Candle Holder	Sarah's Attic	Closed	15.00	20.00
87-16-006	Tillie Candle Holder	Sarah's Attic	Closed	15.00	20.00
87-16-007	Original Tillie	Sarah's Attic	Closed	14.00	20.00
87-16-008	Original Willie	Sarah's Attic	Closed	14.00	20.00
87-16-009	Original Whimpy	Sarah's Attic	Closed	14.00	20.00
87-16-010	Original Katie	Sarah's Attic	Closed	14.00	20.00
87-16-011	Originl Twinkie	Sarah's Attic	Closed	14.00	20.00
87-16-012	Original Cupcake	Sarah's Attic	Closed	14.00	20.00
89-16-013	Americana Willie	Sarah's Attic	Open	17.00	21.00
89-16-014	Americana Tillie	Sarah's Attic	Open	17.00	21.00
89-16-015	Americana Katie	Sarah's Attic	Open	19.00	21.00
89-16-016	Americana Whimpy	Sarah's Attic	Open	19.00	21.00
89-16-017	Americana Cupcake	Sarah's Attic	Open	19.00	21.00
89-16-018	Americana Twinkie	Sarah's Attic	Open	19.00	21.00
90-16-019	Americana Rachel	Sarah's Attic	Open	30.00	30.00
89-16-020	Baby Rachel	Sarah's Attic	Open	17.00	20.00
89-16-021	Small Sailor Katie	Sarah's Attic	Closed	14.00	20.00
89-16-022	Small Sailor Whimpy	Sarah's Attic	Closed	14.00	20.00
89-16-023	Small School Cupcake	Sarah's Attic	Closed	11.00	20.00
89-16-024	Small School Twinkie	Sarah's Attic	Closed	11.00	20.00
89-16-025	Beachtime Katie & Whimpy	Sarah's Attic	Closed	53.00	60.00
90-16-026	Beachtime Cupcake	Sarah's Attic	Closed	30.00	35.00
90-16-027	Beachtime Twinkie	Sarah's Attic	Closed	30.00	35.00
90-16-028	Beachtime Willie	Sarah's Attic	Closed	30.00	35.00
90-16-029	Beachtime Tillie	Sarah's Attic	Closed	30.00	35.00
90-16-030	Beachtime Baby Rachel	Sarah's Attic	Closed	30.00	35.00
90-16-031	Witch Katie	Sarah's Attic	Closed	40.00	40.00
90-16-032	Scarecrow Whimpy	Sarah's Attic	Closed	40.00	40.00
90-16-033	Devil Cupcake	Sarah's Attic	Closed	36.00	40.00
90-16-034	Devil Twinkie	Sarah's Attic	Closed	36.00	40.00
90-16-035	Clown Tillie	Sarah's Attic	Closed	40.00	40.00
90-16-036	Clown Willie	Sarah's Attic	Closed	40.00	40.00
90-16-037	Pumpkin Rachel	Sarah's Attic	Closed	36.00	40.00
88-16-038	Cupcake	Sarah's Attic	Open	18.00	20.00
88-16-039	Twinkie	Sarah's Attic	Open	18.00	20.00
88-16-040	Katie	Sarah's Attic	Open	18.00	20.00
88-16-041	Whimpy	Sarah's Attic	Open	18.00	20.00
88-16-042	Willie	Sarah's Attic	Open	18.00	20.00
88-16-043	Tillie	Sarah's Attic	Open	18.00	20.00
87-16-044	Cupcake On Heart	Sarah's Attic	Closed	12.00	20.00
87-16-045	Katie On Heart	Sarah's Attic	Closed	12.00	20.00
87-16-046	Whimpy On Heart	Sarah's Attic	Closed	12.00	20.00
87-16-047	Twinkie On Heart	Sarah's Attic	Closed	12.00	20.00
87-16-048	Tillie On Heart	Sarah's Attic	Closed	12.00	20.00
87-16-049	Willie On Heart	Sarah's Attic	Closed	12.00	20.00
91-16-050	Whimpy - White Groom	Sarah's Attic	12/94	47.00	47.00
91-16-051	Katie - White Bride	Sarah's Attic	12/94	47.00	47.00
91-16-052	Rachel - White Flower Girl	Sarah's Attic	12/94	40.00	40.00
91-16-053	Tyler - White Ring Bearer	Sarah's Attic	12/94	40.00	40.00
91-16-054	Cracker - Cocker Spanial	Sarah's Attic	12/94	9.00	9.00
91-16-055	Twinkie - White Minister	Sarah's Attic	12/94	50.00	50.00
91-16-056	Tillie - Black Bride	Sarah's Attic	12/94	47.00	47.00
91-16-057	Willie - Black Groom	Sarah's Attic	12/94	47.00	47.00
91-16-058	Peaches - Black Flower Girl	Sarah's Attic	12/94	40.00	40.00
91-16-059	Pug - Black Ring Bearer	Sarah's Attic	12/94	40.00	40.00
91-16-060	Percy - Black Minister	Sarah's Attic	12/94	50.00	50.00
91-16-061	Thanksgiving Katie	Sarah's Attic	10,000	32.00	32.00
91-16-062	Thanksgiving Whimpy	Sarah's Attic	10,000	32.00	32.00
91-16-063	Thanksgiving Tillie	Sarah's Attic	10,000	32.00	32.00
91-16-064	Thanksgiving Willie	Sarah's Attic	10,000	32.00	32.00
91-16-065	Thanksgiving Rachel	Sarah's Attic	10,000	32.00	32.00
91-16-066	Nurse Cupcake	Sarah's Attic	6,000	46.00	46.00
91-16-067	Doctor Twinkie	Sarah's Attic	6,000	50.00	50.00
91-16-068	Teacher Tillie	Sarah's Attic	6,000	50.00	50.00
91-16-069	Executive Whimpy	Sarah's Attic	6,000	46.00	46.00
92-16-070	Winter Tillie on Log	Sarah's Attic	2,500	35.00	35.00
92-16-071	Winter Willie w/ Skates	Sarah's Attic	2,500	35.00	35.00
92-16-072	Winter Katie	Sarah's Attic	2,500	35.00	35.00
92-16-073	Winter Whimpy	Sarah's Attic	2,500	35.00	35.00
93-16-074	Katie & Rachel in Chair	Sarah's Attic	12/94	60.00	60.00
93-16-075	Twinkie w/ Football	Sarah's Attic	12/94	28.00	28.00
93-16-076	Cupcake on Bench	Sarah's Attic	12/94	28.00	28.00
93-16-077	Whimpy w/ Train	Sarah's Attic	12/94	28.00	28.00
93-16-078	Willie w/ Pillow	Sarah's Attic	12/94	28.00	28.00
93-16-079	Tillie	Sarah's Attic	12/94	28.00	28.00
Sarah's Attic, Inc.		**Santas Of The Month**			
88-17-001	January White Santa	Sarah's Attic	Closed	50.00	125-150.
88-17-002	January Black Santa	Sarah's Attic	Closed	50.00	250-375.
88-17-003	February White Santa	Sarah's Attic	Closed	50.00	125-150.
88-17-004	February Black Santa	Sarah's Attic	Closed	50.00	250-375.
88-17-005	March White Santa	Sarah's Attic	Closed	50.00	125-150.
88-17-006	March Black Santa	Sarah's Attic	Closed	50.00	250-375.
88-17-007	April White Santa	Sarah's Attic	Closed	50.00	125-150.
88-17-008	April Black Santa	Sarah's Attic	Closed	50.00	250-375.
88-17-009	May White Santa	Sarah's Attic	Closed	50.00	125-150.
88-17-010	May Black Santa	Sarah's Attic	Closed	50.00	250-375.
88-17-011	June White Santa	Sarah's Attic	Closed	50.00	125-150.
88-17-012	June Black Santa	Sarah's Attic	Closed	50.00	250-375.

Number	Name	Artist	Edition Limit	Issue Price	Quote
88-17-013	July White Santa	Sarah's Attic	Closed	50.00	125-150.
88-17-014	July Black Santa	Sarah's Attic	Closed	50.00	250-375.
88-17-015	August White Santa	Sarah's Attic	Closed	50.00	125-150.
88-17-016	August Black Santa	Sarah's Attic	Closed	50.00	250-375.
88-17-017	September White Santa	Sarah's Attic	Closed	50.00	125-150.
88-17-018	September Black Santa	Sarah's Attic	Closed	50.00	250-375.
88-17-019	October White Santa	Sarah's Attic	Closed	50.00	125-150.
88-17-020	October Black Santa	Sarah's Attic	Closed	50.00	250-375.
88-17-021	November White Santa	Sarah's Attic	Closed	50.00	125-150.
88-17-022	November Black Santa	Sarah's Attic	Closed	50.00	250-375.
88-17-023	December White Santa	Sarah's Attic	Closed	50.00	125-150.
88-17-024	December Black Santa	Sarah's Attic	Closed	50.00	250-350.
88-17-025	Mini January White Santa	Sarah's Attic	Closed	14.00	20.00
88-17-026	Mini January Black Santa	Sarah's Attic	Closed	14.00	50.00
88-17-027	Mini February White Santa	Sarah's Attic	Closed	14.00	20.00
88-17-028	Mini February Black Santa	Sarah's Attic	Closed	14.00	50.00
88-17-029	Mini March White Santa	Sarah's Attic	Closed	14.00	20.00
88-17-030	Mini March Black Santa	Sarah's Attic	Closed	14.00	50.00
88-17-031	Mini April White Santa	Sarah's Attic	Closed	14.00	20.00
88-17-032	Mini April Black Santa	Sarah's Attic	Closed	14.00	50.00
88-17-033	Mini May White Santa	Sarah's Attic	Closed	14.00	20.00
88-17-034	Mini May Black Santa	Sarah's Attic	Closed	14.00	50.00
88-17-035	Mini June White Santa	Sarah's Attic	Closed	14.00	20.00
88-17-036	Mini June Black Santa	Sarah's Attic	Closed	14.00	50.00
88-17-037	Mini July White Santa	Sarah's Attic	Closed	14.00	20.00
88-17-038	Mini July Black Santa	Sarah's Attic	Closed	14.00	50.00
88-17-039	Mini August White Santa	Sarah's Attic	Closed	14.00	20.00
88-17-040	Mini August Black Santa	Sarah's Attic	Closed	14.00	50.00
88-17-041	Mini September White Santa	Sarah's Attic	Closed	14.00	20.00
88-17-042	Mini September Black Santa	Sarah's Attic	Closed	14.00	50.00
88-17-043	Mini October White Santa	Sarah's Attic	Closed	14.00	20.00
88-17-044	Mini October Black Santa	Sarah's Attic	Closed	14.00	50.00
88-17-045	Mini November White Santa	Sarah's Attic	Closed	14.00	20.00
88-17-046	Mini November Black Santa	Sarah's Attic	Closed	14.00	50.00
88-17-047	Mini December White Santa	Sarah's Attic	Closed	14.00	20.00
88-17-048	Mini December Black Santa	Sarah's Attic	Closed	14.00	50.00
90-17-049	Jan. Santa Winter Fun	Sarah's Attic	Closed	80.00	80.00
90-17-050	Feb. Santa Cupids Help	Sarah's Attic	Closed	120.00	120.00
90-17-051	Mar. Santa Irish Delight	Sarah's Attic	Closed	120.00	120.00
90-17-052	Apr. Santa Spring/Joy	Sarah's Attic	Closed	150.00	150.00
90-17-053	May Santa Par For Course	Sarah's Attic	Closed	100.00	100.00
90-17-054	June Santa Graduation	Sarah's Attic	Closed	70.00	70.00
90-17-055	July Santa God Bless	Sarah's Attic	Closed	100.00	100.00
90-17-056	Aug. Santa Summers Trn.	Sarah's Attic	Closed	110.00	110.00
90-17-057	Sep. Santa Touchdown	Sarah's Attic	Closed	90.00	90.00
90-17-058	Oct. Santa Seasons Plenty	Sarah's Attic	Closed	120.00	120.00
90-17-059	Nov. Santa Give Thanks	Sarah's Attic	Closed	100.00	100.00
90-17-060	Dec. Santa Peace	Sarah's Attic	Closed	120.00	120.00
90-17-061	Mrs. January	Sarah's Attic	Closed	80.00	80.00
90-17-062	Mrs. February	Sarah's Attic	Closed	110.00	110.00
90-17-063	Mrs. March	Sarah's Attic	Closed	80.00	80.00
90-17-064	Mrs. April	Sarah's Attic	Closed	110.00	110.00
90-17-065	Mrs. May	Sarah's Attic	Closed	80.00	80.00
90-17-066	Mrs. June	Sarah's Attic	Closed	70.00	70.00
90-17-067	Mrs. July	Sarah's Attic	Closed	100.00	100.00
90-17-068	Mrs. August	Sarah's Attic	Closed	90.00	90.00
90-17-069	Mrs. September	Sarah's Attic	Closed	90.00	90.00
90-17-070	Mrs. October	Sarah's Attic	Closed	90.00	90.00
90-17-071	Mrs. November	Sarah's Attic	Closed	90.00	90.00
90-17-072	Mrs. December	Sarah's Attic	Closed	110.00	110.00
90-17-073	Jan. Fruits of Love	Sarah's Attic	12/94	90.00	90.00
90-17-074	Feb. From The Heart	Sarah's Attic	12/94	90.00	90.00
90-17-075	Mar. Irish Love	Sarah's Attic	12/94	100.00	100.00
90-17-076	Apr. Spring Time	Sarah's Attic	12/94	90.00	90.00
90-17-077	May Caddy Chatter	Sarah's Attic	12/94	100.00	100.00
90-17-078	June Homerun	Sarah's Attic	12/94	90.00	90.00
90-17-079	July Celebrate Amer.	Sarah's Attic	12/94	90.00	90.00
90-17-080	Aug. Fun In The Sun	Sarah's Attic	12/94	90.00	90.00
90-17-081	Sept. Lessons In Love	Sarah's Attic	12/94	90.00	90.00
90-17-082	Oct. Masquerade	Sarah's Attic	12/94	120.00	120.00
90-17-083	Nov. Harvest Of Love	Sarah's Attic	12/94	120.00	120.00
90-17-084	Dec. A Gift Of Peace	Sarah's Attic	12/94	90.00	90.00
90-17-085	Masquerade Tillie	Sarah's Attic	12/94	45.00	45.00
92-17-086	Oct. White Halloween Santa	Sarah's Attic	12/94	35.00	35.00
92-17-087	Oct. Black Halloween Santa	Sarah's Attic	12/94	35.00	35.00
92-17-088	Nov. White Harvest Santa	Sarah's Attic	12/94	35.00	35.00
92-17-089	Nov. Black Harvest Santa	Sarah's Attic	12/94	35.00	35.00
92-17-090	Dec. White Father X-Mas Santa	Sarah's Attic	12/94	35.00	35.00
92-17-091	Dec. Black Father X-Mas Santa	Sarah's Attic	12/94	35.00	35.00
93-17-092	April White Easter Santa	Sarah's Attic	12/94	35.00	35.00
93-17-093	April Black Easter Santa	Sarah's Attic	12/94	35.00	35.00
93-17-094	May White Springtime Santa	Sarah's Attic	12/94	35.00	35.00
93-17-095	May Black Springtime Santa	Sarah's Attic	12/94	35.00	35.00
93-17-096	June White Summertime Santa	Sarah's Attic	12/94	35.00	35.00
93-17-097	June White Summertime Santa	Sarah's Attic	12/94	35.00	35.00

Sarah's Attic, Inc. — **Sarah's Neighborhood Friends**

Number	Name	Artist	Edition Limit	Issue Price	Quote
90-18-001	Bubba W/Lantern	Sarah's Attic	Closed	35.00	35.00
90-18-002	Pansy W/Sled	Sarah's Attic	Closed	30.00	30.00
90-18-003	Bud W/Book	Sarah's Attic	Closed	35.00	35.00
90-18-004	Weasel W/Cap	Sarah's Attic	Closed	35.00	35.00
90-18-005	Annie W/Violin	Sarah's Attic	Closed	35.00	35.00
90-18-006	Hewett W/Drum	Sarah's Attic	Closed	35.00	35.00
90-18-007	Waldo Dog	Sarah's Attic	Closed	10.00	10.00
90-18-008	Hewett W/Apples	Sarah's Attic	Closed	40.00	40.00
90-18-009	Bud W/Newspaper	Sarah's Attic	Closed	40.00	40.00
90-18-010	Waldo W/Flowers	Sarah's Attic	Closed	14.00	14.00
90-18-011	Annie W/Flower Basket	Sarah's Attic	Closed	56.00	56.00
90-18-012	Pansy W/Buggy	Sarah's Attic	Closed	50.00	50.00
90-18-013	Bubba W/Lemonade	Sarah's Attic	Closed	54.00	54.00
90-18-014	Weasel W/Paper	Sarah's Attic	Closed	40.00	40.00
91-18-015	Dolly - White Baby Jesus	Sarah's Attic	12/94	20.00	20.00
91-18-016	Annie - White Mary	Sarah's Attic	12/94	30.00	30.00
91-18-017	Bud - White Joseph	Sarah's Attic	12/94	34.00	34.00
91-18-019	Kitten in Basket	Sarah's Attic	12/94	15.00	15.00
91-18-020	Bubba - Black King	Sarah's Attic	12/94	40.00	40.00
91-18-021	Weasel - White King W/Kitten	Sarah's Attic	12/94	40.00	40.00
91-18-022	Hewitt - White King W/Drum	Sarah's Attic	12/94	40.00	40.00
91-18-023	Pansy - Black Angel	Sarah's Attic	12/94	30.00	30.00
91-18-024	Waldo - Dog W/Shoe	Sarah's Attic	12/94	15.00	15.00
91-18-025	Babes - Black Baby Jesue	Sarah's Attic	12/94	20.00	20.00
91-18-026	Noah - Black Joseph	Sarah's Attic	12/94	36.00	36.00
91-18-027	Shelby - Black Mary	Sarah's Attic	12/94	30.00	30.00
91-18-028	Crate of Love - White	Sarah's Attic	12/94	40.00	40.00
91-18-029	Crate of Love - Black	Sarah's Attic	12/94	40.00	40.00
91-18-030	Nurse Pansy	Sarah's Attic	6,000	46.00	46.00
91-18-031	Dr. Bubba	Sarah's Attic	6,000	60.00	60.00
91-18-032	Teacher Annie	Sarah's Attic	6,000	55.00	55.00
91-18-033	Executive Noah	Sarah's Attic	6,000	46.00	46.00
92-18-034	Stitches Donkey	Sarah's Attic	12/94	26.00	26.00
92-18-035	Rags Cow	Sarah's Attic	12/94	30.00	30.00
92-18-036	Patches Sheep	Sarah's Attic	12/94	20.00	20.00
92-18-037	Angel Hope	Sarah's Attic	12/94	40.00	40.00

Sarah's Attic, Inc. — **Tattered n' Torn Collection**

Number	Name	Artist	Edition Limit	Issue Price	Quote
90-19-001	Boy Rag Doll Opie	Sarah's Attic	Closed	50.00	50.00
90-19-002	Girl Rag Doll Polly	Sarah's Attic	Closed	50.00	50.00
90-19-003	Muffin Black Rag Doll	Sarah's Attic	Closed	30.00	30.00
90-19-004	Puffin Black Rag Doll	Sarah's Attic	Closed	30.00	30.00
90-19-005	White Prissy & Peanut	Sarah's Attic	Closed	120.00	120.00
90-19-006	White Muffin & Puffin	Sarah's Attic	Closed	55.00	55.00
90-19-007	Black Prissy & Peanut	Sarah's Attic	Closed	120.00	120.00
90-19-008	Black Muffin & Puffin	Sarah's Attic	Closed	55.00	55.00

Sarah's Attic, Inc. — **Spirit of Christmas Collection**

Number	Name	Artist	Edition Limit	Issue Price	Quote
87-20-001	Naughty Or Nice Santa At D	Sarah's Attic	Closed	100.00	100.00
87-20-002	Father Snow	Sarah's Attic	Closed	46.00	46.00
87-20-003	Jingle Bells	Sarah's Attic	Closed	28.00	28.00
87-20-004	Long Journey	Sarah's Attic	Closed	28.00	35.00
88-20-005	Joseph-Natural	Sarah's Attic	Closed	11.00	11.00
88-20-006	Mary-Natural	Sarah's Attic	Closed	11.00	11.00
88-20-007	Jesus-Natural	Sarah's Attic	Closed	7.00	7.00
88-20-008	Mini Mary-Natural	Sarah's Attic	Closed	5.00	5.00
88-20-009	Mini Joseph-Natural	Sarah's Attic	Closed	5.00	5.00
88-20-010	Mini Jesus-Natural	Sarah's Attic	Closed	3.50	3.50
88-20-011	Cow/Ox	Sarah's Attic	Closed	16.50	16.50
88-20-012	Sheep	Sarah's Attic	Closed	8.00	8.00
88-20-013	Spirit of Christmas	Sarah's Attic	4,000	80.00	80.00
89-20-014	Silent Night	Sarah's Attic	Closed	33.00	40.00
89-20-015	Woodland Santa	Sarah's Attic	Closed	100.00	125.00
89-20-016	Jolly 2	Sarah's Attic	6,000	15.00	17.00
89-20-017	Yule Tidings 2	Sarah's Attic	Closed	23.00	30.00
89-20-018	St. Nick 2	Sarah's Attic	Closed	43.00	43.00
88-20-019	Blessed Christmas	Sarah's Attic	7,500	100.00	100.00
89-20-020	Father Snow 2	Sarah's Attic	Closed	32.00	36.00
87-20-021	Santa W/Pockets	Sarah's Attic	Closed	34.00	34.00
87-20-022	Santa's Workshop	Sarah's Attic	Closed	54.00	54.00
87-20-023	Colonel Santa	Sarah's Attic	Closed	40.00	40.00
88-20-024	Mini Mary	Sarah's Attic	Closed	8.00	8.00
88-20-025	Mini Joseph	Sarah's Attic	Closed	8.00	8.00
88-20-026	Mini Jesus	Sarah's Attic	Closed	8.00	8.00
88-20-027	Elf Grabbing Hat	Sarah's Attic	Closed	10.00	10.00
88-20-028	Santa W/Elf	Sarah's Attic	Closed	90.00	90.00
88-20-029	Lge. Santa Res. Candle	Sarah's Attic	Closed	14.50	14.50
88-20-030	Lge. Mrs. Claus Res. Candle	Sarah's Attic	Closed	14.50	14.50
88-20-031	Sm. Angel Res. Candle	Sarah's Attic	Closed	9.50	9.50
88-20-032	Sm. Santa Res. Candle	Sarah's Attic	Closed	10.50	10.50
88-20-033	Sm. Mrs. Claus Res. Candle	Sarah's Attic	Closed	10.50	10.50
88-20-034	Mini Santa Res. Candle	Sarah's Attic	Closed	8.00	8.00
89-20-035	Christmas Joy	Sarah's Attic	Closed	32.00	32.00
89-20-036	Jingle Bells 2	Sarah's Attic	Closed	25.50	25.50
89-20-037	Colonel Santa 2	Sarah's Attic	Closed	35.00	35.00
89-20-038	Papa Santa Sitting	Sarah's Attic	Closed	30.00	40.00
69-20-039	Mama Santa Sitting	Sarah's Attic	Closed	30.00	40.00
89-20-040	Papa Santa Stocking	Sarah's Attic	Closed	50.00	60.00
89-20-041	Mama Santa Stocking	Sarah's Attic	Closed	50.00	60.00
89-20-042	Long Journey 2	Sarah's Attic	Closed	35.00	40.00
89-20-043	Stinky Elf Sitting	Sarah's Attic	Closed	16.00	20.00
89-20-044	Winky Elf Letter	Sarah's Attic	Closed	16.00	20.00
89-20-045	Blinkey Elf Ball	Sarah's Attic	Closed	16.00	20.00
89-20-046	Mini Colonel Santa	Sarah's Attic	Closed	14.00	20.00
89-20-047	Mini St. Nick	Sarah's Attic	Closed	14.00	14.00
89-20-048	Mini Jingle Bells	Sarah's Attic	Closed	16.00	16.00
89-20-049	Mini Father Snow	Sarah's Attic	Closed	16.00	16.00
88-20-050	Mini Long Journey	Sarah's Attic	Closed	11.00	11.00
89-20-051	Mini Jolly	Sarah's Attic	Closed	10.00	10.00
89-20-052	Mini Naughty Or Nice	Sarah's Attic	Closed	20.00	20.00
90-20-053	X-Mas Wonder Santa	Sarah's Attic	Closed	50.00	50.00
90-20-054	Santa Claus Express	Sarah's Attic	4,000	150.00	150.00
90-20-055	Christmas Music	Sarah's Attic	Closed	60.00	60.00
90-20-056	Love The Children	Sarah's Attic	5,000	75.00	75.00
90-20-057	Christmas Wishes	Sarah's Attic	5,000	50.00	50.00
90-20-058	Bells of X-Mas	Sarah's Attic	Closed	35.00	35.00
88-20-059	Santa Kneeling	Sarah's Attic	Closed	22.00	22.00
88-20-060	Santa In Chimney	Sarah's Attic	Closed	110.00	110.00
88-20-061	Christmas Clown	Sarah's Attic	Closed	88.00	88.00
87-20-062	Santa Sitting	Sarah's Attic	Closed	20.50	20.50
87-20-063	Mini Santa W/Cane	Sarah's Attic	Closed	11.00	11.00
87-20-064	Large Santa W/Cane	Sarah's Attic	Closed	33.00	33.00
87-20-065	Sm. Santa W/Tree	Sarah's Attic	Closed	17.00	17.00
87-20-066	Mrs. Claus	Sarah's Attic	Closed	28.00	28.00
87-20-067	Kris Kringle	Sarah's Attic	Closed	120.00	120.00
88-20-068	Sitting Elf	Sarah's Attic	Closed	7.00	7.00
88-20-069	Elf W/Gift	Sarah's Attic	Closed	8.50	8.50
88-20-070	Sm.Sitting Santa	Sarah's Attic	Closed	11.00	11.00
88-20-071	Sm. Mrs. Claus	Sarah's Attic	Closed	8.50	8.50
91-20-072	Treasures of Love Santa	Sarah's Attic	3,000	140.00	140.00
91-20-073	Sharing Love Santa	Sarah's Attic	3,000	120.00	120.00
92-20-074	Peace on Earth Santa Doll	Sarah's Attic	Closed	320.00	320.00
92-20-075	Small Blessed Christmas Flat Back	Sarah's Attic	5,000	40.00	40.00
92-20-076	Small Emily & Gideon Flat Back	Sarah's Attic	5,000	40.00	40.00
92-20-077	Small Enos & Adora Flat Back	Sarah's Attic	5,000	35.00	35.00
92-20-078	Small Love the Children Flat Back	Sarah's Attic	5,000	35.00	35.00
92-20-079	Small Toby w/Train Flat Back	Sarah's Attic	5,000	35.00	35.00
92-20-080	Small Christmas Love Flat Back	Sarah's Attic	5,000	30.00	30.00
93-20-081	Let There Be Love White Santa	Sarah's Attic	2,000	70.00	70.00
93-20-082	Let There Be Peace Black Santa	Sarah's Attic	2,000	70.00	70.00

Sarah's Attic — **United Hearts Collection**

Number	Name	Artist	Edition Limit	Issue Price	Quote
91-21-001	Tillie With Skates	Sarah's Attic	Closed	32.00	32.00
91-21-002	Willie on Sled	Sarah's Attic	Closed	32.00	32.00
91-21-003	Chilly Snowman	Sarah's Attic	Closed	33.00	33.00
91-21-004	Valentine Prissy with Dog	Sarah's Attic	Closed	36.00	36.00
91-21-005	Valentine Peanut w/Candy	Sarah's Attic	Closed	32.00	32.00
91-21-006	Shelby w/Shamrock	Sarah's Attic	Closed	36.00	36.00
91-21-007	Noah w/Pot of Gold	Sarah's Attic	Closed	36.00	36.00

Company		Series			
Number	**Name**	**Artist**	**Edition Limit**	**Issue Price**	**Quote**
91-21-008	Hawitt w/Leprechaun	Sarah's Attic	Closed	56.00	56.00
91-21-009	Tabitha Rabbit w/Bunny	Sarah's Attic	Closed	32.00	32.00
91-21-010	Toby & Tessie w/Wheelbarrow	Sarah's Attic	Closed	44.00	44.00
91-21-011	Wooly Lamb	Sarah's Attic	Closed	16.00	16.00
91-21-012	Emily w/Buggy	Sarah's Attic	Closed	53.00	53.00
91-21-013	Gideon with Bear & Rose	Sarah's Attic	Closed	40.00	40.00
91-21-014	Sally Booba Graduation	Sarah's Attic	Closed	45.00	45.00
91-21-015	Jack Boy Graduation	Sarah's Attic	Closed	40.00	40.00
91-21-016	Sparky Dog Graduation	Sarah's Attic	Closed	16.00	16.00
91-21-017	Bibi - Miss Liberty Bear	Sarah's Attic	Closed	30.00	30.00
91-21-018	Liberty Papa Barney & Biff	Sarah's Attic	Closed	64.00	64.00
91-21-019	Beach Pansy with Kitten	Sarah's Attic	Closed	34.00	34.00
91-21-020	Beach Annie & Waldo	Sarah's Attic	Closed	40.00	40.00
91-21-021	Beach Bubba w/Innertube	Sarah's Attic	Closed	34.00	34.00
91-21-022	School Cookie Rabbit w/Kit	Sarah's Attic	Closed	28.00	28.00
91-21-023	School Crumb Rabbit-Dunce	Sarah's Attic	Closed	32.00	32.00
91-21-024	School Chuckles Rabbit	Sarah's Attic	Closed	26.00	26.00
91-21-025	School Desk with Book	Sarah's Attic	Closed	15.00	15.00
91-21-026	Barney the Great Bear	Sarah's Attic	Closed	40.00	40.00
91-21-027	Clown Bibi & Biff Bears	Sarah's Attic	Closed	35.00	55.00
91-21-028	Thanksgiving Cupcake	Sarah's Attic	Closed	36.00	36.00
91-21-029	Thanksgiving Twinkie	Sarah's Attic	Closed	32.00	32.00
91-21-030	Thanksgiving Cornstalk	Sarah's Attic	Closed	30.00	30.00
91-21-031	Christmas Adora	Sarah's Attic	Closed	36.00	36.00
91-21-032	Christmas Enos	Sarah's Attic	Closed	36.00	36.00
91-21-033	Christmas Tree with Hearts	Sarah's Attic	Closed	40.00	40.00
92-21-034	Hether Rabbit w/Doll	Sarah's Attic	12/93	26.00	26.00
92-21-035	Herbie Rabbit sitting	Sarah's Attic	12/93	26.00	26.00
92-21-036	Mr. Carrotman	Sarah's Attic	12/93	30.00	30.00
92-21-037	Fluffy Bear on blanket	Sarah's Attic	12/93	35.00	35.00
92-21-038	Puffy Bear w/Roses	Sarah's Attic	12/93	35.00	35.00
92-21-039	Young Kim w/Kite	Sarah's Attic	12/93	40.00	40.00
92-21-040	Kyu Lee w/Sailboat	Sarah's Attic	12/93	40.00	40.00
92-21-041	Jewel w/Umbrella	Sarah's Attic	12/93	60.00	60.00
92-21-042	Stretch w/Rabbit	Sarah's Attic	12/93	50.00	50.00
92-21-043	Angel Adora w/Doll	Sarah's Attic	12/93	50.00	50.00
92-21-044	Angel Enos w/Bear	Sarah's Attic	12/93	50.00	50.00
92-21-045	May Pole	Sarah's Attic	12/93	35.00	35.00
92-21-046	Toby w/Bat	Sarah's Attic	12/93	34.00	34.00
92-21-047	Tabitha w/Ball	Sarah's Attic	12/93	34.00	34.00
92-21-048	Tessie on Blanket w/Ball	Sarah's Attic	12/93	34.00	34.00
92-21-049	Cookie w/Torch	Sarah's Attic	12/93	34.00	34.00
92-21-050	Crumb w/Flag	Sarah's Attic	12/93	34.00	34.00
92-21-051	Zena w/Shells	Sarah's Attic	12/93	46.00	46.00
92-21-052	Ethan w/Sandcastle	Sarah's Attic	12/93	46.00	46.00
92-21-053	Katie w Planner	Sarah's Attic	12/93	35.00	35.00
92-21-054	Willie w/Pail	Sarah's Attic	12/93	35.00	35.00
92-21-055	Teacher's Desk	Sarah's Attic	12/93	36.00	36.00
92-21-056	Pug w/Pumpkin	Sarah's Attic	12/93	47.00	47.00
92-21-057	Peaches w/Cat	Sarah's Attic	12/93	30.00	30.00
92-21-058	Cupcake w/Pumkins	Sarah's Attic	12/93	35.00	35.00
92-21-059	Twinkie w/Basket	Sarah's Attic	12/93	35.00	35.00
92-21-060	Hay Bal	Sarah's Attic	12/93	23.00	23.00
92-21-061	Mrs. Claus w/Ribbon	Sarah's Attic	12/93	45.00	45.00
92-21-062	Santa w/Train	Sarah's Attic	12/93	45.00	45.00
92-21-063	Tree of Love	Sarah's Attic	12/93	40.00	40.00
Sarah's Attic		**Children of Love**			
91-22-001	Charity Sewing Flags	Sarah's Attic	10,000	46.00	46.00
91-22-002	Benjamin with Drums	Sarah's Attic	10,000	46.00	46.00
91-22-003	Susie Painting Train	Sarah's Attic	10,000	46.00	46.00
91-22-004	Skip Building House	Sarah's Attic	10,000	50.00	50.00
91-22-005	Blossom w/Wash Tub	Sarah's Attic	5,000	50.00	50.00
91-22-006	Madge w/Watering Can	Sarah's Attic	2,500	50.00	50.00
91-22-007	Marty with Shovel	Sarah's Attic	2,500	50.00	50.00
91-22-008	Prayer Time Muffy	Sarah's Attic	5,000	46.00	46.00
91-22-009	Prayer Time Calvin	Sarah's Attic	5,000	46.00	46.00
91-22-010	Guardian Angel Priscilla	Sarah's Attic	5,000	46.00	46.00
91-22-011	Prayer Time Bed	Sarah's Attic	N/A	40.00	40.00
91-22-012	Angel Pup	Sarah's Attic	N/A	14.00	14.00
Sarah's Attic		**Cherished Memories**			
91-23-001	Black Baby Boy (Birth-1 yr.)	Sarah's Attic	N/A	50.00	50.00
91-23-002	Black Baby Girl (1-2 yrs.)	Sarah's Attic	N/A	50.00	50.00
91-23-003	Black Baby Boy (1-2 yrs.)	Sarah's Attic	N/A	50.00	50.00
91-23-004	Black Baby Girl (Birth- yr.)	Sarah's Attic	N/A	50.00	50.00
91-23-005	White Baby Boy (Birth-1 yr.)	Sarah's Attic	N/A	60.00	60.00
91-23-006	White Baby Girl (Birth-1 yr.)	Sarah's Attic	N/A	60.00	60.00
91-23-007	White Baby Girl (1-2 yrs.)	Sarah's Attic	N/A	60.00	60.00
91-23-008	White Baby Boy (1-2 yrs.)	Sarah's Attic	N/A	60.00	60.00
92-23-009	White Girl (2-3 yrs.)	Sarah's Attic	N/A	30.00	30.00
92-23-010	White Boy (2-3 yrs.)	Sarah's Attic	N/A	30.00	30.00
92-23-011	Black Girl (2-3 yrs.)	Sarah's Attic	N/A	25.00	25.00
92-23-012	Black Boy (2-3 yrs.)	Sarah's Attic	N/A	25.00	25.00
92-23-009	White Girl (3-4 yrs.)	Sarah's Attic	Open	50.00	50.00
92-23-010	White Boy (3-4 yrs.)	Sarah's Attic	Open	50.00	50.00
93-23-011	Black Girl (3-4 yrs.) w/ Tricycle	Sarah's Attic	Open	40.00	40.00
93-23-012	Black Boy (3-4 yrs.) w/ Wagon	Sarah's Attic	Open	40.00	40.00
Sarah's Attic		**Matt & Maggie Series**			
86-24-001	Matt Candle Holder	Sarah's Attic	Closed	12.00	12.00
86-24-002	Maggie Candle Holder	Sarah's Attic	Closed	12.00	12.00
86-24-003	Maggie	Sarah's Attic	Closed	14.00	14.00
86-24-004	Matt	Sarah's Attic	Closed	14.00	14.00
87-24-005	Standing Matt	Sarah's Attic	Closed	11.00	11.00
87-24-006	Standing Maggie	Sarah's Attic	Closed	11.00	11.00
87-24-007	Matt on Heart	Sarah's Attic	Closed	9.00	9.00
87-24-008	Maggie on Heart	Sarah's Attic	Closed	9.00	9.00
87-24-009	Matt & Maggie w/ Bear	Sarah's Attic	Closed	100.00	100.00
88-24-010	Large Matt	Sarah's Attic	Closed	48.00	48.00
88-24-011	Large Maggie	Sarah's Attic	Closed	48.00	48.00
88-24-012	Small Sitting Matt	Sarah's Attic	Closed	11.50	11.50
88-24-013	Small Sitting Maggie	Sarah's Attic	Closed	11.50	11.50
89-24-014	Mini Matt	Sarah's Attic	Closed	6.00	6.00
89-24-015	Mini Maggie	Sarah's Attic	Closed	6.00	6.00
89-24-016	Matt Bench Sitter	Sarah's Attic	Closed	32.00	32.00
89-24-017	Maggie Bench Sitter	Sarah's Attic	Closed	32.00	32.00
Sarah's Attic		**Dreams of Tomorrow**			
92-25-001	Executive Katie	Sarah's Attic	6,000	23.00	23.00
92-25-002	Executive Shelby	Sarah's Attic	6,000	23.00	23.00
92-25-003	Fireman Wilie	Sarah's Attic	6,000	23.00	23.00
92-25-004	Fireman Bud	Sarah's Attic	6,000	25.00	25.00

Company		Series			
Number	**Name**	**Artist**	**Edition Limit**	**Issue Price**	**Quote**
92-25-005	Ballerina Pansy	Sarah's Attic	3,000	26.00	26.00
92-25-006	Ballerina Cupcake	Sarah's Attic	3,000	26.00	26.00
92-25-007	Policeman Bubba	Sarah's Attic	3,000	26.00	26.00
92-25-008	Policeman Twinkie	Sarah's Attic	3,000	26.00	26.00
93-25-009	Tillie Basketball Player	Sarah's Attic	Open	32.00	32.00
93-25-010	Willie Baseball Player	Sarah's Attic	Open	32.00	32.00
93-25-011	Champ Baseball Player	Sarah's Attic	Open	32.00	32.00
93-25-012	JoJo Basketball Player	Sarah's Attic	Open	32.00	32.00
93-25-013	Waitress Pansy	Sarah's Attic	2,000	40.00	40.00
93-25-014	Waitress Dana	Sarah's Attic	2,000	34.00	34.00
93-25-015	Pharmacist Noah	Sarah's Attic	2,000	34.00	34.00
93-25-016	Pharmacist Jack Boy	Sarah's Attic	2,000	34.00	34.00
Sarah's Attic		**Tender Moments**			
93-26-001	Love of My Life- Black Couple	Sarah's Attic	1,000	70.00	70.00
93-26-002	True Love-White Couple	Sarah's Attic	1,000	70.00	70.00
93-26-003	New Beginnings- Pregnant White Lady	Sarah's Attic	1,000	55.00	55.00
93-26-004	Joy of Motherhood- Pregnant Black Lady	Sarah's Attic	1,000	55.00	55.00
93-26-005	Grams w/ Rolling Pin	Sarah's Attic	12/93	50.00	50.00
93-26-006	Rosie on Crate	Sarah's Attic	12/93	50.00	50.00
93-26-007	Ellie w/ Cookbook	Sarah's Attic	12/93	28.00	28.00
93-26-008	Evan w/ Bowl	Sarah's Attic	12/93	28.00	28.00
Sarah's Attic		**Spirit of America**			
92-27-001	Gray Wolf Father Indian	Sarah's Attic	2,000	46.00	46.00
92-27-002	Morning Flower Mother Indian	Sarah's Attic	2,000	46.00	46.00
92-27-003	Red Feather Boy Indian	Sarah's Attic	2,000	30.00	30.00
92-27-004	Moon Dance Girl Indian	Sarah's Attic	2,000	30.00	30.00
Sarah's Attic		**Sarah's Attic Accessories**			
92-28-001	Respect Gift	Sarah's Attic	Open	7.00	7.00
92-28-002	Dignity Gift	Sarah's Attic	Open	7.00	7.00
92-28-003	Large Flatbed Wagon	Sarah's Attic	Open	100.00	100.00
92-28-004	Large Park Bench	Sarah's Attic	Open	50.00	50.00
92-28-005	Snow Base	Sarah's Attic	Open	40.00	40.00
92-28-006	Evergreen Tree	Sarah's Attic	Open	10.00	10.00
92-28-007	Barrel of Love	Sarah's Attic	Open	10.00	10.00
92-28-008	Cart of Love	Sarah's Attic	Open	13.00	13.00
92-28-009	Banjo's Dog Bowl	Sarah's Attic	Open	10.00	10.00
93-28-010	Base with Steps	Sarah's Attic	Open	35.00	35.00
93-28-011	ABC 123 Blocks	Sarah's Attic	12/94	4.00	4.00
93-28-012	Toy Horse	Sarah's Attic	12/94	6.00	6.00
93-28-013	Staircase	Sarah's Attic	12/94	28.00	28.00
93-28-014	Seasonal Trunk	Sarah's Attic	12/94	10.00	10.00
93-28-015	Bunny Love Rabbit	Sarah's Attic	12/94	18.00	18.00
93-28-016	Happy Easter Sign	Sarah's Attic	12/94	6.00	6.00
93-28-017	USA Banner w/ Drum	Sarah's Attic	12/94	15.00	15.00
93-28-018	Happy 4th of July Sign	Sarah's Attic	12/94	6.00	6.00
93-28-019	Trick or Treat Pumpkin	Sarah's Attic	12/94	15.00	15.00
93-28-020	Happy Halloween Sign	Sarah's Attic	12/94	6.00	6.00
93-28-021	Harvest Doll w/ Pumpkin	Sarah's Attic	12/94	18.00	18.00
93-28-022	Happy Thanksgiving Sign	Sarah's Attic	12/94	6.00	6.00
93-28-023	Mery Christmas Wreath	Sarah's Attic	12/94	6.00	6.00
93-28-024	Teddy Tree	Sarah's Attic	12/94	35.00	35.00
93-28-025	Large Floor Base w/ Rug	Sarah's Attic	12/94	34.00	34.00
93-28-026	Lamp	Sarah's Attic	12/94	6.00	6.00
93-28-027	Book	Sarah's Attic	12/94	5.00	5.00
93-28-028	Cookie Jar w/ Pan	Sarah's Attic	12/94	6.00	6.00
93-28-029	Squeaks Dog	Sarah's Attic	12/94	7.00	7.00
Sarah's Attic		**Forever Friends Collector's Club**			
91-29-001	Ruby	Sarah's Attic	Closed	36.00	36.00
91-29-002	Diamond	Sarah's Attic	Closed	42.00	42.00
91-29-003	Ruby, Diamond, pair	Sarah's Attic	Closed	78.00	325.00
91-29-004	Forever Frolicking Friends	Sarah's Attic	Closed	Gift	50.00
92-29-005	Love Starts With Children	Sarah's Attic	Closed	Gift	70.00
92-29-006	Sharing Dreams	Sarah's Attic	Closed	75.00	75.00
92-29-007	Lifetime Friends	Sarah's Attic	Closed	75.00	75.00
Schmid/B.F.A.		**Don Polland Figurines I**			
83-01-001	Young Bull	D. Polland	2,750	125.00	250.00
83-01-002	Escape	D. Polland	2,500	175.00	650.00
83-01-003	Fighting Bulls	D. Polland	2,500	200.00	600.00
83-01-004	Hot Pursuit	D. Polland	2,500	225.00	550.00
83-01-005	The Hunter	D. Polland	2,500	225.00	500.00
83-01-006	Downed	D. Polland	2,500	250.00	600.00
83-01-007	Challenge	D. Polland	2,000	275.00	600.00
83-01-008	A Second Chance	D. Polland	2,000	350.00	650.00
83-01-009	Dangerous Moment	D. Polland	2,000	250.00	350.00
83-01-010	The Great Hunt	D. Polland	350	3750.00	3750.00
86-01-011	Running Wolf-War Chief	D. Polland	2,500	170.00	295.00
86-01-012	Eagle Dancer	D. Polland	2,500	170.00	295.00
86-01-013	Plains Warrior	D. Polland	1,250	350.00	550.00
86-01-014	Second Chance	D. Polland	2,000	125.00	650.00
86-01-015	Shooting the Rapids	D. Polland	2,500	195.00	495.00
86-01-016	Down From The High Country	D. Polland	2,250	225.00	295.00
86-01-017	War Trophy	D. Polland	2,250	225.00	500.00
Schmid/B.F.A.		**RFD America**			
79-02-001	Country Road 25030	L. Davis	Closed	100.00	700-750.
79-02-002	Ignorance is Bliss 25031	L. Davis	Closed	165.00	1250-1300.
79-02-003	Blossom 25032	L. Davis	Closed	180.00	1500-1600.
79-02-004	Fowl Play 25033	L. Davis	Closed	100.00	275-325.
79-02-005	Slim Pickins 25034	L. Davis	Closed	165.00	825-850.
79-02-006	Broken Dreams 25035	L. Davis	Closed	165.00	1000-1300.
80-02-007	Good, Clean Fun 25020	L. Davis	Closed	40.00	125-160.
80-02-008	Strawberry Patch 25021	L. Davis	Closed	25.00	95.00
80-02-009	Forbidden Fruit 25022	L. Davis	Closed	25.00	175-250.
80-02-010	Milking Time 25023	L. Davis	Closed	20.00	200-240.
80-02-011	Sunday Afternoon 25024	L. Davis	Closed	22.50	225-250.
80-02-012	New Day 25025	L. Davis	Closed	20.00	165.00
80-02-013	Wilbur 25029	L. Davis	Closed	100.00	600-750.
80-02-014	Itching Post 25037	L. Davis	Closed	30.00	100-115.
80-02-015	Creek Bank Bandit 25038	L. Davis	Closed	37.50	400.00
81-02-016	Split Decision 25210	L. Davis	Closed	45.00	175-325.
81-02-017	Double Trouble 25211	L. Davis	Closed	35.00	475.00
81-02-018	Under the Weather 25212	L. Davis	Closed	25.00	85.00
81-02-019	Country Boy 25213	L. Davis	Closed	37.50	250-375.
81-02-020	Hightailing It 25214	L. Davis	Closed	50.00	375-500.
81-02-021	Studio Mouse 25215	L. Davis	Closed	60.00	275-325.
81-02-022	Dry as a Bone 25216	L. Davis	Closed	45.00	275-325
81-02-023	Rooted Out 25217	L. Davis	Closed	45.00	100-115.
81-02-024	Up To No Good 25218	L. Davis	Closed	200.00	850-950.

Company Number	Name	Series Artist	Edition Limit	Issue Price	Quote
81-02-025	Punkin' Seeds 25219	L. Davis	Closed	225.00	1200-1750.
81-02-026	Scallawags 25221	L. Davis	Closed	65.00	125-200.
82-02-027	Baby Bobs 25222	L. Davis	Closed	47.50	200-250.
82-02-028	Stray Dog 25223	L. Davis	Closed	35.00	75.00
82-02-029	Two's Company 25224	L. Davis	Closed	43.50	200-250.
82-02-030	Moving Day 25225	L. Davis	Closed	43.50	225-300.
82-02-031	Brand New Day 25226	L. Davis	Closed	23.50	150-175.
82-02-032	Baby Blossom 25227	L. Davis	Closed	40.00	175-300.
82-02-033	When Mama Gets Mad 25228	L. Davis	Closed	37.50	300-375.
82-02-034	A Shoe to Fill 25229	L. Davis	Closed	37.50	150-175.
82-02-035	Idle Hours 25230	L. Davis	Closed	37.50	225-300.
82-02-036	Thinking Big 25231	L. Davis	Closed	35.00	100.00
82-02-037	Country Crook 25280	L. Davis	Closed	37.50	300-400.
82-02-038	Waiting for His Master 25281	L. Davis	Closed	50.00	225-300.
82-02-039	Moon Raider 25325	L. Davis	Closed	190.00	325-400.
82-02-040	Blossom and Calf 25326	L. Davis	Closed	250.00	700-1000.
82-02-041	Treed 25327	L. Davis	Closed	155.00	250-300.
83-02-042	Woman's Work 25232	L. Davis	Closed	35.00	90-95.00
83-02-043	Counting the Days 25233	L. Davis	Closed	40.00	60.00
83-02-044	Licking Good 25234	L. Davis	Closed	35.00	200-250.
83-02-045	Mama's Prize Leghorn 25235	L. Davis	Closed	55.00	100-135.
83-02-046	Fair Weather Friend 25236	L. Davis	Closed	25.00	75.00
83-02-047	False Alarm 25237	L. Davis	Closed	65.00	150-185.
83-02-048	Makin' Tracks 25238	L. Davis	Closed	70.00	125-185.
83-02-049	Hi Girls, The Name's Big Jack 25328	L. Davis	Closed	200.00	325.00
83-02-050	City Slicker 25329	L. Davis	Closed	150.00	300-375.
83-02-051	Happy Hunting Ground 25330	L. Davis	Closed	160.00	240.00
83-02-052	Stirring Up Trouble 25331	L. Davis	Closed	160.00	250.00
83-02-053	His Eyes Are Bigger Than His Stomach 25332	L. Davis	Closed	235.00	325-350.
84-02-054	Courtin' 25220	L. Davis	Closed	45.00	125-135.
84-02-055	Anybody Home 25239	L. Davis	Closed	35.00	100-130.
84-02-056	Headed Home 25240	L. Davis	Closed	25.00	50.00
84-02-057	One for the Road 25241	L. Davis	Open	37.50	60-70.00
84-02-058	Huh? 25242	L. Davis	Closed	40.00	95.00
84-02-059	Gonna Pay for His Sins 25243	L. Davis	Open	27.50	90.00
84-02-060	His Master's Dog 25244	L. Davis	Closed	45.00	120-175.
84-02-061	Pasture Pals 25245	L. Davis	Closed	52.00	75.00
84-02-062	Country Kitty 25246	L. Davis	Closed	52.00	115-125.
84-02-063	Catnapping Too? 25247	L. Davis	Closed	70.00	100-125.
84-02-064	Gossips 25248	L. Davis	Closed	110.00	250.00
84-02-066	Prairie Chorus 25333	L. Davis	Closed	135.00	1000-1500.
84-02-067	Mad As A Wet Hen 25334	L. Davis	Closed	185.00	700-800.
85-02-068	Country Crooner 25256	L. Davis	Open	25.00	65.00
85-02-069	Barn Cats 25257	L. Davis	Open	39.50	80.00
85-02-070	Don't Play with Your Food 25258	L. Davis	Open	28.50	80.00
85-02-071	Out-of-Step 25259	L. Davis	Open	45.00	90.00
85-02-072	Renoir 25261	L. Davis	Closed	45.00	80.00
85-02-073	Too Good to Waste on Kids 25262	L. Davis	Open	70.00	130.00
85-02-074	Ozark Belle 25264	L. Davis	Closed	35.00	80.00
85-02-075	Will You Still Respect Me in the Morning 25265	L. Davis	Open	35.00	70.00
85-02-076	Country Cousins 25266	L. Davis	Open	42.50	80.00
85-02-077	Love at First Sight 25267	L. Davis	Open	70.00	105.00
85-02-078	Feelin' His Oats 25275	L. Davis	1,500	150.00	275-300.
85-02-079	Furs Gonna Fly 25335	L. Davis	1,500	145.00	175-225.
85-02-080	Hog Heaven 25336	L. Davis	1,500	165.00	260-450.
86-02-081	Comfy? 25273	L. Davis	Open	40.00	80.00
86-02-082	Mama? 25277	L. Davis	Closed	15.00	40.00
86-02-083	Bit Off More Than He Could Chew 25279	L. Davis	Open	15.00	60.00
87-02-084	Mail Order Bride 25263	L. Davis	Closed	150.00	185-325.
87-02-085	Glutton for Punishment 25268	L. Davis	Closed	95.00	150.00
87-02-086	Easy Pickins 25269	L. Davis	Closed	45.00	85.00
87-02-087	Bottoms Up 25270	L. Davis	Open	80.00	105.00
87-02-088	The Orphans 25271	L. Davis	Open	50.00	85.00
87-02-089	When the Cat's Away 25276	L. Davis	Open	40.00	60.00
87-02-090	Two in the Bush 25337	L. Davis	Closed	150.00	245-350.
87-02-091	Chicken Thief 25338	L. Davis	Closed	200.00	300-380.
88-02-092	Sawin' Logs 25260	L. Davis	Open	85.00	105.00
88-02-093	Fleas 25272	L. Davis	Open	20.00	24.00
88-02-094	Making a Bee Line 25274	L. Davis	Closed	75.00	125.00
88-02-095	Missouri Spring 25278	L. Davis	Open	115.00	130.00
88-02-096	Perfect Ten 25282	L. Davis	Closed	95.00	105-177.
88-02-097	Goldie and Her Peeps 25283	L. Davis	Open	25.00	36.50
88-02-098	In a Pickle 25284	L. Davis	Open	40.00	50.00
88-02-099	Wishful Thinking 25285	L. Davis	Open	55.00	70.00
88-02-100	Brothers 25286	L. Davis	Closed	55.00	85.00
88-02-101	Happy Hour 25287	L. Davis	Open	57.50	65-80.00
88-02-102	When Three Foot's a Mile 25315	L. Davis	Closed	230.00	300-450.
88-02-103	No Private Time 25316	L. Davis	Closed	200.00	250-325.
88-02-104	Wintering Lamb 25317	L. Davis	Closed	200.00	270.00
89-02-105	New Friend 25288	L. Davis	Open	45.00	60.00
89-02-106	Family Outing 25289	L. Davis	Open	45.00	60.00
89-02-107	Left Overs 25290	L. Davis	Open	90.00	100.00
89-02-108	Coon Capers 25291	L. Davis	Open	67.50	90.00
89-02-109	Mother Hen 25292	L. Davis	Open	37.50	50.00
89-02-110	Meeting of Sheldon 25293	L. Davis	Open	120.00	150.00
89-02-111	Boy's Night Out 25339	L. Davis	1,500	190.00	225.00
89-02-112	A Tribute to Hooker 25340	L. Davis	Closed	180.00	250-300.
89-02-113	Woodscolt 25342	L. Davis	Closed	300.00	350-500.
90-02-114	Corn Crib Mouse 25295	L. Davis	Open	35.00	45.00
90-02-115	Seein' Red 25296	L. Davis	Open	35.00	47.00
90-02-116	Little Black Lamb (Baba) 25297	L. Davis	Open	30.00	37.50
90-02-117	Hanky Panky 25298	L. Davis	Open	65.00	100.00
90-02-118	Finder's Keepers 25299	L. Davis	Open	39.50	45.00
90-02-119	Foreplay 25300	L. Davis	Open	59.50	80.00
90-02-120	The Last Straw 25301	L. Davis	Open	125.00	147-162.50
90-02-121	Long Days, Cold Nights 25344	L. Davis	2,500	175.00	190.00
90-02-122	Piggin' Out 25345	L. Davis	Closed	190.00	300-400.
90-02-123	Tricks Of The Trade 25346	L. Davis	Closed	300.00	300-375.
91-02-124	First Offense 25304	L. Davis	Open	70.00	70.00
91-02-125	Gun Shy 25305	L. Davis	Open	70.00	70.00
91-02-126	Heading For The Persimmon Grove 25306	L. Davis	Open	80.00	80.00
91-02-127	Kissin' Cousins 25307	L. Davis	Open	80.00	80.00
91-02-128	Washed Ashore 25308	L. Davis	Open	70.00	70.00
91-02-129	Long, Hot Summer 25343	L. Davis	1,950	250.00	250.00
91-02-130	Cock Of The Walk 25347	L. Davis	2,500	300.00	300.00
91-02-131	Sooieee 25360	L. Davis	1,500	350.00	350.00
92-02-132	Ozark's Vittles 25318	L. Davis	Open	60.00	60.00
92-02-133	Don't Play With Fire 25319	L. Davis	Open	120.00	120.00
92-02-134	Safe Haven 25320	L. Davis	Open	95.00	95.00
92-02-135	Free Lunch 25321	L. Davis	Open	85.00	85.00
92-02-136	Headed South 25327	L. Davis	Open	45.00	45.00

Company Number	Name	Series Artist	Edition Limit	Issue Price	Quote
92-02-137	My Favorite Chores 25362	L. Davis	1,500	750.00	750.00
92-02-138	OH Sheeeit . . . 25363	L. Davis	Open	120.00	120.00
92-02-139	She Lay Low 25364	L. Davis	Open	120.00	120.00
92-02-140	Snake Doctor 25365	L. Davis	Open	70.00	70.00
92-02-141	The Grass is Always Greener 25367	L. Davis	Open	195.00	195.00
92-02-142	School Yard Dogs 25369	L. Davis	Open	100.00	100.00
92-02-143	The Honeymoon's Over 25370	L. Davis	1,950	300.00	300.00
93-02-144	Sweet Tooth 25373	L. Davis	Open	60.00	60.00
93-02-145	Dry Hole 25374	L. Davis	Open	30.00	30.00
93-02-146	No Hunting 25375	L. Davis	1,000	95.00	95.00
93-02-147	Peep Show 25376	L. Davis	Open	35.00	35.00
93-02-148	If You Can't Beat Em Join Em 25379	L. Davis	1,750	250.00	250.00
93-02-149	King of The Mountain 25380	L. Davis	750	500.00	500.00
93-02-150	Sheep Sheerin Time 25388	L. Davis	1,200	500.00	500.00
93-02-151	Happy Birthday My Sweet 25560	L. Davis	Open	35.00	35.00
93-02-152	Be My Valentine 25561	L. Davis	Open	35.00	35.00
93-02-153	Don't Open Till Christmas 25562	L. Davis	Open	35.00	35.00
93-02-154	I'm Thankful For You 25563	L. Davis	Open	35.00	35.00
93-02-155	You're a Basket Full of Fun 25564	L. Davis	Open	35.00	35.00
93-02-156	Oh Where is He Now 95041	L. Davis	Open	250.00	250.00
93-02-157	The Freeloaders 95042	L. Davis	Open	230.00	230.00
Schmid/B.F.A.		**Farm Set**			
85-03-001	Privy 25348	L. Davis	Closed	12.50	40.00
85-03-002	Windmill 25349	L. Davs	Closed	25.00	50.00
85-03-003	Remus' Cabin 25350	L. Davis	Closed	42.50	45-65.00
85-03-004	Main House 25351	L. Davis	Closed	42.50	125-150.
85-03-005	Barn 25352	L. Davis	Closed	47.50	350.00
85-03-006	Goat Yard and Studio 25353	L. Davis	Closed	32.50	45-75.00
85-03-007	Corn Crib and Sheep Pen 25354	L. Davis	Closed	25.00	50-85.00
85-03-008	Hog House 25355	L. Davis	Closed	27.50	60-85.00
85-03-009	Hen House 25356	L. Davis	Closed	32.50	60-85.00
85-03-010	Smoke House 25357	L. Davis	Closed	12.50	35-65.00
85-03-011	Chicken House 25358	L. Davis	Closed	19.00	65.00
85-03-012	Garden and Wood Shed 25359	L. Davis	Closed	25.00	65.00
Schmid/B.F.A.		**Davis Cat Tales Figurines**			
82-04-001	Right Church, Wrong Pew 25204	L. Davis	Closed	70.00	350-400.
82-04-002	Company's Coming 25205	L. Davis	Closed	60.00	250-275.
82-04-003	On the Move 25206	L. Davis	Closed	70.00	650-675.
82-04-004	Flew the Coop 25207	L. Davis	Closed	60.00	275-325.
Schmid/B.F.A.		**Davis Special Edition Figurines**			
83-05-001	The Critics 23600	L. Davis	Closed	400.00	1350-1650.
85-05-002	Home from Market 23601	L. Davis	Closed	400.00	1500.00
89-05-003	From A Friend To A Friend 23602	L. Davis	1,200	750.00	1500-1600.
90-05-004	What Rat Race? 23603	L. Davis	1,200	800.00	950.00
92-05-005	Last Laff 23604	L. Davis	1,200	900.00	900.00
Schmid/B.F.A.		**Davis Country Christmas Figurines**			
83-06-001	Hooker at Mailbox with Presents 23550	L. Davis	Closed	80.00	750.00
84-06-002	Country Christmas 23551	L. Davis	Closed	80.00	450.00
85-06-003	Christmas at Fox Fire Farm 23552	L. Davis	Closed	80.00	200 250.
86-06-004	Christmas at Red Oak 23553	L. Davis	Closed	80.00	225.00
87-06-005	Blossom's Gift 23554	L. Davis	Closed	150.00	350-500.
88-06-006	Cutting the Family Christmas Tree 23555	L. Davis	Closed	80.00	300-350.
89-06-007	Peter and the Wren 23556	L. Davis	Closed	165.00	300-450.
90-06-008	Wintering Deer 23557	L. Davis	Closed	165.00	250.00
91-06-009	Christmas At Red Oak II 23558	L. Davis	Closed	250.00	250.00
92-06-010	Born on a Starry Night 23559	L. Davis	2,500	225.00	225.00
93-06-011	Waiting For Mr. Lowell 23606	L. Davis	2,500	250.00	250.00
Schmid/B.F.A.		**Little Critters**			
89-07-001	Gittin' a Nibble 25294	L. Davis	Open	50.00	57.00
90-07-002	Outing With Grandpa 25502	L. Davis	2,500	200.00	250.00
90-07-003	Home Squeezins 25504	L. Davis	Open	90.00	90.00
90-07-004	Punkin' Pig 25505	L. Davis	2,500	250.00	350.00
90-07-005	Private Time 25506	L. Davis	Open	18.00	40.00
91-07-006	Great American Chicken Race 25500	L. Davis	2,500	225.00	275.00
91-07-007	Punkin' Wine 25501	L. Davis	Open	100.00	150.00
91-07-008	Milk Mouse 25503	L. Davis	2,500	175.00	228.00
91-07-009	When Coffee Never Tasted So Good 25507	L. Davis	1,250	800.00	800.00
91-07-010	Toad Strangler 25509	L. Davis	Open	57.00	57.00
91-07-011	Hittin' The Sack 25510	L. Davis	Open	70.00	70.00
91-07-012	Itiskit, Itasket 25511	L. Davis	Open	45.00	45.00
91-07-013	Christopher Critter 25514	L. Davis	1,992	150.00	150.00
92-07-014	Double Yolker 25516	L. Davis	Yr.Iss.	70.00	70.00
92-07-015	Miss Private Time 25517	L. Davis	Yr.Iss.	35.00	35.00
92-07-016	A Wolf in Sheep's Clothing 25518	L. Davis	Yr.Iss.	110.00	110.00
92-07-017	Charivari 25707	L. Davis	950	250.00	250.00
Schmid/B.F.A.		**Lowell Davis Farm Club**			
85-08-001	The Bride 221001 / 20993	L. Davis	Closed	45.00	400-475.
87-08-002	The Party's Over 221002 / 20994	L. Davis	Closed	50.00	100-190.
88-08-003	Chow Time 221003 / 20995	L. Davis	Closed	55.00	125-150.
89-08-004	Can't Wait 221004 / 20996	L. Davis	Closed	75.00	125.00
90-08-005	Pit Stop 221005 / 20997	L. Davis	Closed	75.00	125.00
91-08-006	Arrival Of Stanley 221006 / 20998	L. Davis	Yr.Iss.	100.00	100.00
91-08-007	Don't Pick The Flowers 221007 / 21007	L. Davis	Yr.Iss.	100.00	100.00
92-08-008	Hog Wild	L. Davis	Yr.Iss.	100.00	100.00
92-08-009	Check's in the Mail	L. Davis	Yr.Iss.	100.00	100.00
93-08-010	The Survivor	L. Davis	Yr.Iss.	70.00	70.00
93-08-011	Summer Days	L. Davis	Yr.Iss.	100.00	100.00
Schmid/B.F.A.		**Lowell Davis Farm Club Renewal Figurine**			
85-09-001	Thirsty? 892050 / 92050	L. Davis	Yr.Iss.	Gift	N/A
87-09-002	Cackle Berries 892051 / 92051	L. Davis	Yr.Iss.	Gift	N/A
88-09-003	Ice Cream Churn 892052 / 92052	L. Davis	Yr.Iss.	Gift	39.00
90-09-004	Not A Sharing Soul 892053 / 92053	L. Davis	Yr.Iss.	Gift	40.00
91-09-005	New Arrival 892054 / 92054	L. Davis	Yr.Iss.	Gift	20.00
92-09-006	Garden Toad	L. Davis	Yr.Iss.	Gift	N/A
93-09-007	Luke 12:6	L. Davis	Yr.Iss.	Gift	N/A
Schmid/B.F.A.		**Country Pride**			
81-10-001	Surprise in the Cellar 25200	L. Davis	Closed	100.00	900-1200.
81-10-002	Plum Tuckered Out 25201	L. Davis	Closed	100.00	600-950.
81-10-003	Bustin' with Pride 25202	L. Davis	Closed	100.00	225-250.
81-10-004	Duke's Mixture 25203	L. Davis	Closed	100.00	375-450.
Schmid/B.F.A.		**Uncle Remus**			
81-11-001	Brer Fox 25250	L. Davis	Closed	70.00	900-950.
81-11-002	Brer Bear 25251	L. Davis	Closed	80.00	900-1200.
81-11-003	Brer Rabbit 25252	L. Davis	Closed	85.00	1500-2000.

Number	Name	Artist	Edition Limit	Issue Price	Quote
81-11-004	Brer Wolf 25253	L. Davis	Closed	85.00	425-475.
81-11-005	Brer Weasel 25254	L. Davis	Closed	80.00	475-700.
81-11-006	Brer Coyote 25255	L. Davis	Closed	80.00	425-475.
Schmid/B.F.A.		**Promotional Figurine**			
91-12-001	Leavin' The Rat Race 225512	L. Davis	N/A	125.00	175-200.
92-12-002	Hen Scratch Prom 225968	L. Davis	N/A	95.00	95.00
Schmid/B.F.A.		**Route 66**			
91-13-001	Just Check The Air 25600	L. Davis	350	700.00	900-1400.
91-13-002	Nel's Diner 25601	L. Davis	350	700.00	900-1400.
91-13-003	Little Bit Of Shade 25602	L. Davis	Open	100.00	100.00
91-13-004	Just Check The Air 25603	L. Davis	2,500	550.00	550.00
91-13-005	Nel's Diner 25604	L. Davis	2,500	550.00	550.00
92-13-006	Relief 25605	L. Davis	Open	80.00	80.00
92-13-007	Welcome Mat (w/ wooden base)25606	L. Davis	1,500	400.00	400.00
92-13-008	Fresh Squeezed? 25608	L. Davis	2,500	450.00	450.00
92-13-009	Fresh Squeezed? (w/ wooden base) 25609	L. Davis	350	600.00	600.00
92-13-010	Quiet Day at Maple Grove 25618	L. Davis	Open	130.00	130.00
92-13-011	Going To Grandma's 25619	L. Davis	Open	80.00	80.00
92-13-012	What Are Pals For? 25620	L. Davis	Open	100.00	100.00
93-13-013	Home For Christmas 25621	L. Davis	Open	80.00	80.00
93-13-014	Kickin' Himself 25622	L. Davis	Open	80.00	80.00
Schmid/B.F.A.		**Friends of Mine**			
89-14-001	Sun Worshippers 23620	L. Davis	5,000	120.00	134.00
89-14-002	Sun Worshippers Mini Figurine 23621	L. Davis	Open	32.50	32.50
90-14-003	Sunday Afternoon Treat 23625	L. Davis	5,000	120.00	130-170.
90-14-004	Sunday Afternoon Treat Mini Figurine 23626	L. Davis	Open	32.50	37.50
91-14-005	Warm Milk 23629	L. Davis	5,000	120.00	200.00
91-14-006	Warm Milk Mini Figurine 23630	L. Davis	Open	32.50	37.50
92-14-007	Cat and Jenny Wren 23633	L. Davis	5,000	170.00	170.00
92-14-008	Cat and Jenny Wren Mini Figurine 23634	L. Davis	Open	35.00	35.00
Schmid/B.F.A.		**Pen Pals**			
93-15-001	The Old Home Place Mini Figurine 25801	L. Davis	Open	30.00	30.00
93-15-002	The Old Home Place 25802	L. Davis	1,200	200.00	200.00
Schmid/B.F.A.		**Dealer Counter Signs**			
80-16-001	RFD America 888902	L. Davis	Closed	40.00	175-275.
81-16-002	Uncle Remus 888904	L. Davis	Closed	30.00	300.00
85-16-003	Fox Fire Farm 888907	L. Davis	Closed	30.00	150-275.
90-16-004	Mr. Lowell's Farm 25302	L. Davis	Open	50.00	55-70.00
92-16-005	Little Critters 25515	L. Davis	Open	50.00	50.00
Schmid/B.F.A.		**Kitty Cucumber Musical Figurine**			
92-17-001	Dance 'Round the Maypole 30215	M. Lillemoe	5,000	55.00	55.00
92-17-002	Butterfly 30221	M. Lillemoe	5,000	50.00	50.00

Sebastian Studios: See also Lance Corporation

Number	Name	Artist	Edition Limit	Issue Price	Quote
Sebastian Studios		**Large Ceramastone Figures**			
39-01-001	Paul Revere Plaque	P.W. Baston	Closed	Unkn.	400-500.
40-01-002	Jesus	P.W. Baston	Closed	Unkn.	300-400.
40-01-003	Mary	P.W. Baston	Closed	Unkn.	600-1000.
40-01-004	Caroler	P.W. Baston	Closed	Unkn.	300-400.
40-01-005	Candle Holder	P.W. Baston	Closed	Unkn.	300-400.
40-01-006	Lamb	P.W. Baston	Closed	Unkn.	300-400.
40-01-007	Basket	P.W. Baston	Closed	Unkn.	300-400.
40-01-008	Horn of Plenty	P.W. Baston	Closed	Unkn.	300-400.
40-01-009	Breton Man	P.W. Baston	Closed	Unkn.	600-1000.
40-01-010	Breton Woman	P.W. Baston	Closed	Unkn.	600-1000.
47-01-011	Large Victorian Couple	P.W. Baston	Closed	Unkn.	600-1000.
48-01-012	Woody at Three	P.W. Baston	Closed	Unkn.	600-1000.
56-01-013	Jell-O Cow Milk Pitcher	P.W. Baston	Closed	Unkn.	175-225.
58-01-014	Swift Instrument Girl	P.W. Baston	Closed	Unkn.	500-750.
59-01-015	Wasp Plaque	P.W. Baston	Closed	Unkn.	500-750.
63-01-016	Henry VIII	P.W. Baston	Closed	Unkn.	600-1000.
63-01-017	Anne Boleyn	P.W. Baston	Closed	Unkn.	600-1000.
63-01-018	Tom Sawyer	P.W. Baston	Closed	Unkn.	600-1000.
63-01-019	Mending Time	P.W. Baston	Closed	Unkn.	600-1000.
63-01-020	David Copperfield	P.W. Baston	Closed	Unkn.	600-1000.
63-01-021	Dora	P.W. Baston	Closed	Unkn.	600-1000.
63-01-022	George Washington Toby Jug	P.W. Baston	Closed	Unkn.	600-1000.
63-01-023	Abraham Lincoln Toby Jug	P.W. Baston	Closed	Unkn.	600-1000.
63-01-024	John F. Kennedy Toby Jug	P.W. Baston	Closed	Unkn.	600-1000.
64-01-025	Colonial Boy	P.W. Baston	Closed	Unkn.	600-1000.
64-01-026	Colonial Man	P.W. Baston	Closed	Unkn.	600-1000.
64-01-027	Colonial Woman	P.W. Baston	Closed	Unkn.	600-1000.
64-01-028	Colonial Girl	P.W. Baston	Closed	Unkn.	600-1000.
64-01-029	IBM Mother	P.W. Baston	Closed	Unkn.	600-1000.
64-01-030	IBM Father	P.W. Baston	Closed	Unkn.	600-1000.
64-01-031	IBM Son	P.W. Baston	Closed	Unkn.	600-1000.
64-01-032	IBM Woman	P.W. Baston	Closed	Unkn.	600-1000.
64-01-033	IBM Photographer	P.W. Baston	Closed	Unkn.	600-1000.
65-01-034	N.E. Home For Little Wanderers	P.W. Baston	Closed	Unkn.	600-1000.
65-01-035	Stanley Music Box	P.W. Baston	Closed	Unkn.	300-500.
65-01-036	The Dentist	P.W. Baston	Closed	Unkn.	600-1000.
66-01-037	Guitarist	P.W. Baston	Closed	Unkn.	600-1000.
67-01-038	Infant of Prague	P.W. Baston	Closed	Unkn.	600-1000.
73-01-039	Potter	P.W. Baston	Closed	Unkn.	300-400.
73-01-040	Cabinetmaker	P.W. Baston	Closed	Unkn.	300-400.
73-01-041	Blacksmith	P.W. Baston	Closed	Unkn.	300-400.
73-01-042	Clockmaker	P.W. Baston	Closed	Unkn.	600-1000.
75-01-043	Minuteman	P.W. Baston	Closed	Unkn.	600-1000.
78-01-044	Mt. Rushmore	P.W. Baston	Closed	Unkn.	400-500.
XX-01-045	Santa Fe...All The Way	P.W. Baston	Closed	Unkn.	600-1000.
XX-01-046	St. Francis (Plaque)	P.W. Baston	Closed	Unkn.	600-1000.
Sebastian Studios		**Sebastian Miniatures**			
38-02-001	Shaker Man	P.W. Baston	Closed	Unkn.	75-100.00
38-02-002	Shaker Lady	P.W. Baston	Closed	Unkn.	75-100.00
39-02-003	George Washington	P.W. Baston	Closed	Unkn.	35-75.00
39-02-004	Martha Washington	P.W. Baston	Closed	Unkn.	35-75.00
39-02-005	John Alden	P.W. Baston	Closed	Unkn.	35-50.00
39-02-006	Priscilla	P.W. Baston	Closed	Unkn.	35-50.00
39-02-007	Williamsburg Governor	P.W. Baston	Closed	Unkn.	75-100.00
39-02-008	Williamsburg Lady	P.W. Baston	Closed	Unkn.	75-100.00
39-02-009	Benjamin Franklin	P.W. Baston	Closed	Unkn.	75-100.00
39-02-010	Deborah Franklin	P.W. Baston	Closed	Unkn.	75-100.00
39-02-011	Gabriel	P.W. Baston	Closed	Unkn.	100-125.
39-02-012	Evangeline	P.W. Baston	Closed	Unkn.	100-125.
39-02-013	Coronado	P.W. Baston	Closed	Unkn.	75-100.00
39-02-014	Coronado's Senora	P.W. Baston	Closed	Unkn.	75-100.00
39-02-015	Sam Houston	P.W. Baston	Closed	Unkn.	75-100.00
39-02-016	Margaret Houston	P.W. Baston	Closed	Unkn.	75-100.00
39-02-017	Indian Warrior	P.W. Baston	Closed	Unkn.	100-125.
39-02-018	Indian Maiden	P.W. Baston	Closed	Unkn.	100-125.
40-02-019	Jean LaFitte	P.W. Baston	Closed	Unkn.	75-100.00
40-02-020	Catherine LaFitte	P.W. Baston	Closed	Unkn.	75-100.00
40-02-021	Dan'l Boone	P.W. Baston	Closed	Unkn.	75-100.00
40-02-022	Mrs. Dan'l Boone	P.W. Baston	Closed	Unkn.	75-100.00
40-02-023	Peter Stvyvesant	P.W. Baston	Closed	Unkn.	75-100.00
40-02-024	Ann Stvyvesant	P.W. Baston	Closed	Unkn.	75-100.00
40-02-025	John Harvard	P.W. Baston	Closed	Unkn.	125-150.
40-02-026	Mrs. Harvard	P.W. Baston	Closed	Unkn.	125-150.
40-02-027	John Smith	P.W. Baston	Closed	Unkn.	75-150.00
40-02-028	Pocohontas	P.W. Baston	Closed	Unkn.	75-150.00
40-02-029	William Penn	P.W. Baston	Closed	Unkn.	100-150.
40-02-030	Hannah Penn	P.W. Baston	Closed	Unkn.	100-150.
40-02-031	Buffalo Bill	P.W. Baston	Closed	Unkn.	75-100.00
40-02-032	Annie Oakley	P.W. Baston	Closed	Unkn.	75-100.00
40-02-033	James Monroe	P.W. Baston	Closed	Unkn.	150-175.
40-02-034	Elizabeth Monroe	P.W. Baston	Closed	Unkn.	150-175.
41-02-035	Rooster	P.W. Baston	Closed	Unkn.	600-1000.
41-02-036	Ducklings	P.W. Baston	Closed	Unkn.	600-1000.
41-02-037	Peacock	P.W Baston	Closed	Unkn.	600-1000.
41-02-038	Doves	P.W. Baston	Closed	Unkn.	600-1000.
41-02-039	Pheasant	P.W. Baston	Closed	Unkn.	600-1000.
41-02-040	Swan	P.W. Baston	Closed	Unkn.	600-1000.
41-02-041	Secrets	P.W. Baston	Closed	Unkn.	600-1000.
41-02-042	Kitten (Sleeping)	P.W. Baston	Closed	Unkn.	600-1000.
41-02-043	Kitten (Sitting)	P.W. Baston	Closed	Unkn.	600-1000.
42-02-044	Majorette	P.W. Baston	Closed	Unkn.	325.-375.
42-02-045	Cymbals	P.W. Baston	Closed	Unkn.	325-375.
42-02-046	Horn	P.W. Baston	Closed	Unkn.	325-375.
42-02-047	Tuba	P.W. Baston	Closed	Unkn.	325-375.
42-02-048	Drum	P.W. Baston	Closed	Unkn.	325-375.
42-02-049	Accordion	P.W. Baston	Closed	Unkn.	325-375.
46-02-050	Puritan Spinner	P.W. Baston	Closed	Unkn.	600-1000.
46-02-051	Satchel-Eye Dyer	P.W. Baston	Closed	Unkn.	125-150.
47-02-052	Down East	P.W. Baston	Closed	Unkn.	125-150.
47-02-053	First Cookbook Author	P.W. Baston	Closed	Unkn.	125-150.
47-02-054	Fisher Pair PS	P.W. Baston	Closed	Unkn.	600-1000.
47-02-055	Mr. Beacon Hill	P.W. Baston	Closed	Unkn.	75-125.00
47-02-056	Mrs. Beacon Hill	P.W. Baston	Closed	Unkn.	75-125.00
47-02-057	Dahl's Fisherman	P.W. Baston	Closed	Unkn.	150-175.
47-02-058	Dilemma	P.W. Baston	Closed	Unkn.	275-300.
47-02-059	Princess Elizabeth	P.W. Baston	Closed	Unkn.	200-300.
47-02-060	Prince Philip	P.W. Baston	Closed	Unkn.	200-300.
47-02-061	Howard Johnson Pieman	P.W. Baston	Closed	Unkn.	300-450.
47-02-062	Tollhouse Town Crier	P.W. Baston	Closed	Unkn.	125-175.
48-02-063	Slalom	P.W. Baston	Closed	Unkn.	175-200.
48-02-064	Sitzmark	P.W. Baston	Closed	Unkn.	175-200.
48-02-065	Mr. Rittenhouse Square	P.W. Baston	Closed	Unkn.	150-175.
48-02-066	Mrs. Rittenhouse Square	P.W. Baston	Closed	Unkn.	150-175.
48-02-067	Swedish Boy	P.W. Baston	Closed	Unkn.	300-500.
48-02-068	Swedish Girl	P.W. Baston	Closed	Unkn.	300-500.
48-02-069	Democratic Victory	P.W. Baston	Closed	Unkn.	350-500.
48-02-070	Republican Victory	P.W. Baston	Closed	Unkn.	600-1000.
48-02-071	Nathaniel Hawthorne	P.W. Baston	Closed	Unkn.	175-200.
48-02-072	Jordan Marsh Observer	P.W. Baston	Closed	Unkn.	150-175.
48-02-073	Mr. Sheraton	P.W. Baston	Closed	Unkn.	350-400.
48-02-074	A Harvey Girl	P.W. Baston	Closed	Unkn.	250-300.
48-02-075	Mary Lyon	P.W. Baston	Closed	Unkn.	250-300.
49-02-076	Uncle Mistletoe	P.W. Baston	Closed	Unkn.	250-300.
49-02-077	Eustace Tilly	P.W. Baston	Closed	Unkn.	750-1500.
49-02-078	Menotomy Indian	P.W. Baston	Closed	Unkn.	175-250.
49-02-079	Boy Scout Plaque	P.W. Baston	Closed	Unkn.	300-350.
49-02-080	Patrick Henry	P.W. Baston	Closed	Unkn.	100-125.
49-02-081	Sarah Henry	P.W. Baston	Closed	Unkn.	100-125.
49-02-082	Paul Bunyan	P.W. Baston	Closed	Unkn.	250.00
49-02-083	Emmett Kelly	P.W. Baston	Closed	Unkn.	250-300.
49-02-084	Giant Royal Bengal Tiger	P.W. Baston	Closed	Unkn.	1000-1500.
49-02-085	The Thinker	P.W. Baston	Closed	Unkn.	175-250.
49-02-086	The Mark Twain Home in Hannibal, MO	P.W. Baston	Closed	Unkn.	600-1000.
49-02-087	Dutchman's Pipe	P.W. Baston	Closed	Unkn.	175-225.
49-02-088	Gathering Tulips	P.W. Baston	Closed	Unkn.	225-250.
50-02-089	Phoebe, House of 7 Gables	P.W. Baston	Closed	Unkn.	150-175.
50-02-090	Mr. Obocell	P.W. Baston	Closed	Unkn.	75-125.00
50-02-091	National Diaper Service	P.W. Baston	Closed	Unkn.	250-300.
51-02-092	Judge Pyncheon	P.W. Baston	Closed	Unkn.	175-225.
51-02-093	Seb. Dealer Plaque (Marblehead)	P.W. Baston	Closed	Unkn.	300-350.
51-02-094	Great Stone Face	P.W. Baston	Closed	Unkn.	600-1000.
51-02-095	Christopher Columbus	P.W. Baston	Closed	Unkn.	250-300.
51-02-096	Sir Frances Drake	P.W. Baston	Closed	Unkn.	250-300.
51-02-097	Jesse Buffman (WEEI)	P.W. Baston	Closed	Unkn.	200-350.
51-02-098	Carl Moore (WEEI)	P.W. Baston	Closed	Unkn.	200-300.
51-02-099	Caroline Cabot (WEEI)	P.W. Baston	Closed	Unkn.	200-350.
51-02-100	Mother Parker (WEEI)	P.W. Baston	Closed	Unkn.	200-350.
51-02-101	Charles Ashley (WEEI)	P.W. Baston	Closed	Unkn.	200-350.
51-02-102	E. B. Rideout (WEEI)	P.W. Baston	Closed	Unkn.	200-350.
51-02-103	Priscilla Fortesue (WEEI)	P.W. Baston	Closed	Unkn.	200-350.
51-02-104	Chiquita Banana	P.W. Baston	Closed	Unkn.	350-400.
51-02-105	Mlt Seal	P.W. Baston	Closed	Unkn.	350-425.
51-02-106	The Observer & Dame New England.	P.W. Baston	Closed	Unkn.	325-375.
51-02-107	Jordon Marsh Observer Rides the A.W. Horse	P.W. Baston	Closed	Unkn.	300-325.
51-02-108	The Iron Master's House	P.W. Baston	Closed	Unkn.	350-500.
51-02-109	Chief Pontiac	P.W. Baston	Closed	Unkn.	400-700.
52-02-110	The Favored Scholar	P.W. Baston	Closed	Unkn.	200-300.
52-02-111	Neighboring Pews	P.W. Baston	Closed	Unkn.	200-300.
52-02-112	Weighing the Baby	P.W. Baston	Closed	Unkn.	200-300.
52-02-113	The First House, Plimoth Plantation	P.W. Baston	Closed	Unkn.	150-195.
52-02-114	Scottish Girl (Jell-O)	P.W. Baston	Closed	Unkn.	350-375.
52-02-115	Lost in the Kitchen (Jell-O)	P.W. Baston	Closed	Unkn.	350-375.
52-02-116	The Fat Man (Jell-O)	P.W. Baston	Closed	Unkn.	525-600.
52-02-117	Baby (Jell-O)	P.W. Baston	Closed	Unkn.	525-600.
52-02-118	Stork (Jell-O)	P.W. Baston	Closed	Unkn.	425-525.
52-02-119	Tabasco Sauce	P.W. Baston	Closed	Unkn.	400-500.
52-02-120	Aerial Tramway	P.W. Baston	Closed	Unkn.	300-600.
52-02-121	Marblehead High School Plaque	P.W. Baston	Closed	Unkn.	200-300.
52-02-122	St. Joan d'Arc	P.W. Baston	Closed	Unkn.	300-350.
52-02-123	St. Sebastian	P.W. Baston	Closed	Unkn.	300-350.
52-02-124	Our Lady of Good Voyage	P.W. Baston	Closed	Unkn.	200-250.
52-02-125	Old Powder House	P.W. Baston	Closed	Unkn.	250-300.
53-02-126	Holgrave the Daguerrotypist	P.W. Baston	Closed	Unkn.	200-250.

Company Number	Name	Series Artist	Edition Limit	Issue Price	Quote
53-02-127	St. Teresa of Lisieux	P.W. Baston	Closed	Unkn.	225-275.
53-02-128	Darned Well He Can	P.W. Baston	Closed	Unkn.	300-350.
53-02-129	R.H. Stearns Chestnut Hill Mall	P.W. Baston	Closed	Unkn.	225-275.
53-02-130	Boy Jesus in the Temple	P.W. Baston	Closed	Unkn.	350-400.
53-02-131	Blessed Julie Billart	P.W. Baston	Closed	Unkn.	400-500.
53-02-132	"Old Put" Enjoys a Licking	P.W. Baston	Closed	Unkn.	300-350.
53-02-133	Lion (Jell-O)	P.W. Baston	Closed	Unkn.	350-375.
53-02-134	The Schoolboy of 1850	P.W. Baston	Closed	Unkn.	350-400.
54-02-135	Whale (Jell-O)	P.W. Baston	Closed	Unkn.	350-375.
54-02-136	Rabbit (Jell-O)	P.W. Baston	Closed	Unkn.	350-375.
54-02-137	Moose (Jell-O)	P.W. Baston	Closed	Unkn.	350-375.
54-02-138	Scuba Diver	P.W. Baston	Closed	Unkn.	400-450.
54-02-139	Stimalose (Woman)	P.W. Baston	Closed	Unkn.	175-200.
54-02-140	Stimalose (Men)	P.W. Baston	Closed	Unkn.	600-1000.
54-02-141	Bluebird Girl	P.W. Baston	Closed	Unkn.	400-450.
54-02-142	Campfire Girl	P.W. Baston	Closed	Unkn.	400-450.
54-02-143	Horizon Girl	P.W. Baston	Closed	Unkn.	400-450.
54-02-144	Kernel-Fresh Ashtray	P.W. Baston	Closed	Unkn.	400-450.
54-02-145	William Penn	P.W. Baston	Closed	Unkn.	175-225.
54-02-146	St. Pius X	P.W. Baston	Closed	Unkn.	400-475.
54-02-147	Resolute Ins. Co. Clipper PS	P.W. Baston	Closed	Unkn.	300-325.
54-02-148	Dachshund (Audiovox)	P.W. Baston	Closed	Unkn.	300-350.
54-02-149	Our Lady of Laleche	P.W. Baston	Closed	Unkn.	300-350.
54-02-150	Swan Boat Brooch-Empty Seats	P.W. Baston	Closed	Unkn.	600-1000.
54-02-151	Swan Boat Brooch-Full Seats	P.W. Baston	Closed	Unkn.	600-1000.
55-02-152	Davy Crockett	P.W. Baston	Closed	Unkn.	225-275.
55-02-153	Giraffe (Jell-O)	P.W. Baston	Closed	Unkn.	350-375.
55-02-154	Old Woman in the Shoe (Jell-O)	P.W. Baston	Closed	Unkn.	500-600.
55-02-155	Santa (Jell-O)	P.W. Baston	Closed	Unkn.	500-600.
55-02-156	Captain Doliber	P.W. Baston	Closed	Unkn.	300-350.
55-02-157	Second Bank-State St. Trust PS	P.W. Baston	Closed	Unkn.	300-325.
55-02-158	Horse Head PS	P.W. Baston	Closed	Unkn.	350-375.
56-02-159	Robin Hood & Little John	P.W. Baston	Closed	Unkn.	400-500.
56-02-160	Robin Hood & Friar Tuck	P.W. Baston	Closed	Unkn.	400-500.
56-02-161	77th Bengal Lancer (Jell-O)	P.W. Baston	Closed	Unkn.	600-1000.
56-02-162	Three Little Kittens (Jell-O)	P.W. Baston	Closed	Unkn.	375-400.
56-02-163	Texcel Tape Boy	P.W. Baston	Closed	Unkn.	350-425.
56-02-164	Permacel Tower of Tape Ashtray	P.W. Baston	Closed	Unkn.	600-1000.
56-02-165	Arthritic Hands (J & J)	P.W. Baston	Closed	Unkn.	600-1000.
56-02-166	Rarical Blacksmith	P.W. Baston	Closed	Unkn.	300-500.
56-02-167	Praying Hands	P.W. Baston	Closed	Unkn.	250-300.
56-02-168	Eastern Paper Plaque	P.W. Baston	Closed	Unkn.	350-400.
56-02-169	Girl on Diving Board	P.W. Baston	Closed	Unkn.	400-450.
56-02-170	Elsie the Cow Billboard	P.W. Baston	Closed	Unkn.	600-1000.
56-02-171	Mrs. Obocell	P.W. Baston	Closed	Unkn.	400-450.
56-02-172	Alike, But Oh So Different	P.W. Baston	Closed	Unkn.	300-350.
56-02-173	NYU Grad School of Bus. Admin. Bldg.	P.W. Baston	Closed	Unkn.	300-350.
56-02-174	The Green Giant	P.W. Baston	Closed	Unkn.	400-500.
56-02-175	Michigan Millers PS	P.W. Baston	Closed	Unkn.	200-275.
57-02-176	Mayflower PS	P.W. Baston	Closed	Unkn.	300-325.
57-02-177	Jamestown Church	P.W. Baston	Closed	Unkn.	400-450.
57-02-178	Olde James Fort	P.W. Baston	Closed	Unkn.	250-300.
57-02-179	Jamestown Ships	P.W. Baston	Closed	Unkn.	350-475.
57-02-180	IBM 305 Ramac	P.W. Baston	Closed	Unkn.	400-450.
57-02-181	Colonial Fund Doorway PS	P.W. Baston	Closed	Unkn.	600-1000.
57-02-182	Speedy Alka Seltzer	P.W. Baston	Closed	Unkn.	600-1000.
57-02-183	Nabisco Spoonmen	P.W. Baston	Closed	Unkn.	600-1000.
57-02-184	Nabisco Buffalo Bee	P.W. Baston	Closed	Unkn.	600-1000.
57-02-185	Borden's Centennial (Elsie the Cow)	P.W. Baston	Closed	Unkn.	600-1000.
57-02-186	Along the Albany Road PS	P.W. Baston	Closed	Unkn.	600-1000.
58-02-187	Romeo & Juliet	P.W. Baston	Closed	Unkn.	400-500.
58-02-188	Mt. Vernon	P.W. Baston	Closed	Unkn.	400-500.
58-02-189	Hannah Duston PS	P.W. Baston	Closed	Unkn.	250-325.
58-02-190	Salem Savings Bank	P.W. Baston	Closed	Unkn.	250-300.
58-02-191	CBS Miss Columbia PS	P.W. Baston	Closed	Unkn.	600-1000.
58-02-192	Connecticut Bank & Trust	P.W. Baston	Closed	Unkn.	225-275.
58-02-193	Jackie Gleason	P.W. Baston	Closed	Unkn.	600-1000.
58-02-194	Harvard Trust Colonial Man	P.W. Baston	Closed	Unkn.	275-325.
58-02-195	Jordan Marsh Observer	P.W. Baston	Closed	Unkn.	175-275.
58-02-196	Cliquot Club Eskimo PS	P.W. Baston	Closed	Unkn.	1000-2300.
58-02-197	Commodore Stephen Decatur	P.W. Baston	Closed	Unkn.	125-175.
59-02-198	Siesta Coffee PS	P.W. Baston	Closed	Unkn.	600-1000.
59-02-199	Harvard Trust Co. Town Crier	P.W. Baston	Closed	Unkn.	350-400.
59-02-200	Mrs. S.O.S.	P.W. Baston	Closed	Unkn.	300-350.
59-02-201	H.P. Hood Co. Cigar Store Indian	P.W. Baston	Closed	Unkn.	600-1000.
59-02-202	Alexander Smith Weaver	P.W. Baston	Closed	Unkn.	350-425.
59-02-203	Fleischman's Margarine PS	P.W. Baston	Closed	Unkn.	225-325.
59-02-204	Alcoa Wrap PS	P.W. Baston	Closed	Unkn.	350-400.
59-02-205	Fiorello LaGuardia	P.W. Baston	Closed	Unkn.	125-175.
59-02-206	Henry Hudson	P.W. Baston	Closed	Unkn.	125-175.
59-02-207	Giovanni Verrazzano	P.W. Baston	Closed	Unkn.	125-175.
60-02-208	Peter Stvyvesant	P.W. Baston	Closed	Unkn.	125-175.
60-02-209	Masonic Bible	P.W. Baston	Closed	Unkn.	300-400.
60-02-210	Son of the Desert	P.W. Baston	Closed	Unkn.	200-275.
60-02-211	Metropolitan Life Tower PS	P.W. Baston	Closed	Unkn.	350-400.
60-02-212	Supp-Hose Lady	P.W. Baston	Closed	Unkn.	300-350.
60-02-213	Marine Memorial	P.W. Baston	Closed	Unkn.	300-400.
60-02-214	The Infantryman	P.W. Baston	Closed	Unkn.	600-1000.
61-02-215	Tony Piet	P.W. Baston	Closed	Unkn.	600-1000.
61-02-216	Bunky Knudsen	P.W. Baston	Closed	Unkn.	600-1000.
61-02-217	Merchant's Warren Sea Capt.	P.W. Baston	Closed	Unkn.	200-250.
61-02-218	Pope John 23rd	P.W. Baston	Closed	Unkn.	400-450.
61-02-219	St. Jude Thaddeus	P.W. Baston	Closed	Unkn.	400-500.
62-02-220	Seaman's Bank for Savings	P.W. Baston	Closed	Unkn.	300-350.
62-02-221	Yankee Clipper Sulfide	P.W. Baston	Closed	Unkn.	600-1000.
62-02-222	Big Brother Bob Emery	P.W. Baston	Closed	Unkn.	600-1000.
62-02-223	Blue Belle Highlander	P.W. Baston	Closed	Unkn.	200-250.
63-02-224	John F. Kennedy Toby Jug	P.W. Baston	Closed	Unkn.	600-1000.
63-02-225	Jackie Kennedy Toby Jug	P.W. Baston	Closed	Unkn.	600-1000.
63-02-226	Naumkeag Indian	P.W. Baston	Closed	Unkn.	225-275.
63-02-227	Dia-Mel Fat Man	P.W. Baston	Closed	Unkn.	375-400.
65-02-228	Pope Paul VI	P.W. Baston	Closed	Unkn.	400-500.
65 02 229	Henry Wadsworth Longfellow	P.W. Baston	Closed	Unkn.	275-325.
65-02-230	State Street Bank Globe	P.W. Baston	Closed	Unkn.	250-300.
65-02-231	Panti-Legs Girl PS	P.W. Baston	Closed	Unkn.	250-300.
66-02-232	Paul Revere Plaque (W.T. Grant)	P.W. Baston	Closed	Unkn.	300-350.
66-02-233	Massachusetts SPCA	P.W. Baston	Closed	Unkn.	250-350.
66-02-234	Little George	P.W. Baston	Closed	Unkn.	350-450.
66-02-235	Gardeners (Thermometer)	P.W. Baston	Closed	Unkn.	300-400.
66-02-236	Gardener Man	P.W. Baston	Closed	Unkn.	250-300.
66-02-237	Gardener Women	P.W. Baston	Closed	Unkn.	250-300.
66-02-238	Town Lyne Indian	P.W. Baston	Closed	Unkn.	600-1000.
67-02-239	Doc Berry of Berwick (yellow shirt)	P.W. Baston	Closed	Unkn.	300-350.
67-02-240	Ortho-Novum	P.W. Baston	Closed	Unkn.	600-1000.
68-02-241	Captain John Parker	P.W. Baston	Closed	Unkn.	300-350.
68-02-242	Watermill Candy Plaque	P.W. Baston	Closed	Unkn.	600-1000.
70-02-243	Uncle Sam in Orbit	P.W. Baston	Closed	Unkn.	350-400.
71-02-244	Town Meeting Plaque	P.W. Baston	Closed	Unkn.	350-400.
71-02-245	Boston Gas Tank	P.W. Baston	Closed	Unkn.	300-500.
72-02-246	George & Hatchet	P.W. Baston	Closed	Unkn.	400-450.
72-02-247	Martha & the Cherry Pie	P.W. Baston	Closed	Unkn.	350-400.
XX-02-248	The King	P.W. Baston	Closed	Unkn.	600-1000.
XX-02-249	Bob Hope	P.W. Baston	Closed	Unkn.	600-1000.
XX-02-250	Coronation Crown	P.W. Baston	Closed	Unkn.	600-1000.
XX-02-251	Babe Ruth	P.W. Baston	Closed	Unkn.	600-1000.
XX-02-252	Sylvania Electric-Bulb Display	P.W. Baston	Closed	Unkn.	600-1000.
XX-02-252	Ortho Gynecic	P.W. Baston	Closed	Unkn.	600-1000.
XX-02-254	Eagle Plaque	P.W. Baston	Closed	Unkn.	1000-1500.
Shelia's, Inc.		**Painted Ladies I**			
90-01-001	San Francisco Stick House-yellow	S.Thompson	Retrd.	10.00	35.00
90-01-002	San Francisco Stick House-blue	S.Thompson	Retrd.	10.00	35.00
90-01-003	San Francisco Italianate-yellow	S.Thompson	Retrd.	10.00	35.00
90-01-004	Colorado Queen Anne	S.Thompson	Retrd.	10.00	35.00
90-01-005	Atlanta Queen Anne	S.Thompson	Retrd.	10.00	35.00
90-01-006	Savannah Gingerbread	S.Thompson	Retrd.	10.00	35.00
90-01-007	Cape May Gothic Revival	S.Thompson	Retrd.	10.00	35.00
90-01-008	Malden Mass. Victorian Inn	S.Thompson	Retrd.	10.00	35.00
90-01-009	Illinois Queen Anne	S.Thompson	Retrd.	10.00	35-50.00
90-01-010	Cincinnati Gothic	S.Thompson	Retrd.	10.00	20-35.00
Shelia's, Inc.		**Painted Ladies II**			
90-02-001	The Gingerbread Mansion	S.Thompson	Open	15.00	15.00
90-02-002	Pitkin House	S.Thompson	Open	15.00	15.00
90-02-003	The Young-Larson House	S.Thompson	Open	15.00	15.00
90-02-004	Queen Anne Rowhouse	S.Thompson	Open	15.00	15.00
90-02-005	Pink Gothic	S.Thompson	Open	15.00	15.00
90-02-006	The Victorian Blue Rose	S.Thompson	Open	15.00	15.00
90-02-007	Morningstar Inn	S.Thompson	Open	15.00	15.00
90-02-008	Cape May Victorian Pink House	S.Thompson	Open	15.00	15.00
Shelia's, Inc.		**Dicken's Village '91**			
91-03-001	Scrooge & Marley's Shop	S.Thompson	7/93	15.00	15.00
91-03-002	Butcher Shop	S.Thompson	7/93	15.00	15.00
91-03-003	Toy Shoppe	S.Thompson	7/93	15.00	15.00
91-03-004	Scrooge's Home	S.Thompson	7/93	15.00	15.00
91-03-005	Victorian Apartment Building	S.Thompson	7/93	15.00	15.00
91-03-006	Gazebo & Carolers	S.Thompson	7/93	12.00	12.00
91-03-007	Victorian Skaters	S.Thompson	7/93	12.00	12.00
91-03-008	Evergreen Tree	S.Thompson	7/93	11.00	11.00
Shelia's, Inc.		**Dicken's Village '92**			
92-04-001	Victorian Church	S.Thompson	7/93	15.00	15.00
Shelia's, Inc.		**Charleston**			
88-05-001	Rainbow Row-rust	S.Thompson	7/93	9.00	9.00
88-05-002	Rainbow Row-tan	S.Thompson	7/93	9.00	9.00
88-05-003	Rainbow Row-cream	S.Thompson	7/93	9.00	9.00
88-05-004	Rainbow Row-green	S.Thompson	7/93	9.00	9.00
88-05-005	Rainbow Row-lavender	S.Thompson	7/93	9.00	9.00
88-05-006	Rainbow Row-pink	S.Thompson	7/93	9.00	9.00
88-05-007	Rainbow Row-blue	S.Thompson	7/93	9.00	9.00
88-05-008	Rainbow Row-yellow	S.Thompson	7/93	9.00	9.00
88-05-009	Rainbow Row-lt. yellow	S.Thompson	7/93	9.00	9.00
89-05-010	Middleton Plantation	S.Thompson	Retrd.	9.00	50.00
89-05-011	Powder Magazine	S.Thompson	Retrd.	9.00	50.00
90-05-012	Beth Elohim Temple	S.Thompson	7/93	15.00	15.00
90-05-013	Manigault House	S.Thompson	Open	15.00	15.00
90-05-014	Heyward-Washington House	S.Thompson	Open	15.00	15.00
90-05-015	Magnolia Plantation House	S.Thompson	Open	16.00	16.00
90-05-016	Edmonston-Alston	S.Thompson	Open	15.00	15.00
90-05-017	St. Philip's Church	S.Thompson	Open	15.00	15.00
90-05-018	#2 Meeting Street	S.Thompson	Open	15.00	15.00
90-05-019	City Market	S.Thompson	Open	15.00	15.00
90-05-020	Dock Street Theater	S.Thompson	Open	15.00	15.00
90-05-021	Pink House	S.Thompson	Open	12.00	12.00
90-05-022	90 Church St.	S.Thompson	Open	12.00	12.00
90-05-023	St. Michael's Church	S.Thompson	Open	15.00	15.00
90-05-024	Exchange Building	S.Thompson	Open	15.00	15.00
Shelia's, Inc.		**Charleston Gold Seal**			
88-06-001	Rainbow Row-rust (gold seal)	S.Thompson	Retrd.	9.00	N/A
88-06-002	Rainbow Row-tan (gold seal)	S.Thompson	Retrd.	9.00	N/A
88-06-003	Rainbow Row-cream (gold seal)	S.Thompson	Retrd.	9.00	N/A
88-06-004	Rainbow Row-green (gold seal)	S.Thompson	Retrd.	9.00	N/A
88-06-005	Rainbow Row-lavender (gold seal)	S.Thompson	Retrd.	9.00	N/A
88-06-006	Rainbow Row-pink (gold seal)	S.Thompson	Retrd.	9.00	N/A
88-06-007	Rainbow Row-blue (gold seal)	S.Thompson	Retrd.	9.00	N/A
88-06-008	Rainbow Row-yellow (gold seal)	S.Thompson	Retrd.	9.00	N/A
88-06-009	Rainbow Row-lt. yellow (gold seal)	S.Thompson	Retrd.	9.00	N/A
88-06-010	Pink House (gold seal)	S.Thompson	Retrd.	9.00	N/A
88-06-011	90 Church St. (gold seal)	S.Thompson	Retrd.	9.00	N/A
89-06-012	Middleton Plantation (gold seal)	S.Thompson	Retrd.	9.00	N/A
89-06-013	Powder Magazine (gold seal)	S.Thompson	Retrd.	9.00	N/A
89-06-014	St. Michael's Church (gold seal)	S.Thompson	Retrd.	9.00	N/A
89-06-015	Exchange Building (gold seal)	S.Thompson	Retrd.	9.00	N/A
Shelia's, Inc.		**Texas**			
90-07-001	The Alamo	S.Thompson	Retrd.	15.00	15.00
90-07-001	Mission Concepcion	S.Thompson	Retrd.	15.00	15.00
90-07-001	Mission San Francisco	S.Thompson	Retrd.	15.00	15.00
90-07-001	Mission San Jose'	S.Thompson	Retrd.	15.00	15.00
Shelia's, Inc.		**New England**			
90-08-001	Old North Church	S.Thompson	Retrd.	15.00	19.00
90-08-002	Martha's Vineyard Cottage-blue/mauve	S.Thompson	Retrd.	15.00	19.00
90-08-003	Martha's Vineyard Cottage-blue/orange	S.Thompson	Retrd.	15.00	19.00
90-08-004	President Bush Home	S.Thompson	Retrd.	15.00	19.00
90-08-005	Longfellow's Home	S.Thompson	Retrd.	15.00	19.00
90-08-006	Motif #1 Boathouse	S.Thompson	Retrd.	15.00	19.00
90-08-007	Paul Revere's Home	S.Thompson	Retrd.	15.00	19.00
90-08-008	Faneuil Hall	S.Thompson	Retrd.	15.00	19.00
90-08-009	Stage Harbor Lighthouse	S.Thompson	Retrd.	15.00	19.00
90-08-010	Wedding Cake House	S.Thompson	Retrd.	15.00	19.00

Company Number	Name	Series Artist	Edition Limit	Issue Price	Quote
Shelia's, Inc.		**Williamsburg**			
90-09-001	Governor's Palace	S.Thompson	Open	15.00	15.00
90-09-002	Printer-Bookbinder	S.Thompson	7/93	12.00	12.00
90-09-003	Milliner	S.Thompson	Open	12.00	12.00
90-09-004	Silversmith	S.Thompson	Open	12.00	12.00
90-09-005	Nicolson Store	S.Thompson	Open	12.00	12.00
90-09-006	Apothecary	S.Thompson	Open	12.00	12.00
90-09-007	King's Arm Tavern	S.Thompson	Open	15.00	15.00
90-09-008	Courthouse	S.Thompson	Open	15.00	15.00
90-09-009	Homesite	S.Thompson	Open	15.00	15.00
Shelia's, Inc.		**Philadelphia**			
90-10-001	Carpenter's Hall	S.Thompson	Open	15.00	15.00
90-10-002	Market St. Post Office	S.Thompson	Open	15.00	15.00
90-10-003	Betsy Ross House	S.Thompson	Open	15.00	15.00
90-10-004	Independence Hall	S.Thompson	Open	15.00	15.00
90-10-005	Elphreth's Alley	S.Thompson	Open	15.00	15.00
90-10-006	Old Tavern	S.Thompson	Open	15.00	15.00
90-10-007	Graff House	S.Thompson	Retrd.	15.00	15.00
90-10-008	Old City Hall	S.Thompson	Open	15.00	15.00
Shelia's, Inc.		**Washington D.C.**			
90-11-001	National Archives	S.Thompson	7/93	16.00	16.00
90-11-002	Library of Congress	S.Thompson	7/93	16.00	16.00
90-11-003	White House	S.Thompson	7/93	16.00	16.00
90-11-004	Washington Monument	S.Thompson	7/93	16.00	16.00
90-11-005	Cherry Trees	S.Thompson	7/93	12.00	12.00
Shelia's, Inc.		**North Carolina**			
90-12-001	Josephus Hall House	S.Thompson	7/93	15.00	15.00
90-12-002	Presbyterian Bell Tower	S.Thompson	7/93	15.00	15.00
90-12-003	Cape Hateras Lighthouse	S.Thompson	Open	15.00	15.00
90-12-004	The Tryon Palace	S.Thompson	7/93	15.00	15.00
Shelia's, Inc.		**South Carolina**			
90-13-001	The Hermitage	S.Thompson	Open	15.00	15.00
90-13-002	The Governor's Mansion	S.Thompson	Open	15.00	15.00
90-13-003	The Lace House	S.Thompson	Open	15.00	15.00
90-13-004	The State House	S.Thompson	Open	15.00	15.00
90-13-005	All Saints' Church	S.Thompson	7/93	15.00	15.00
Shelia's, Inc.		**St. Augustine**			
90-14-001	The "Oldest House"	S.Thompson	7/93	15.00	15.00
90-14-002	Old City Gates	S.Thompson	7/93	15.00	15.00
90-14-003	Anastasia Lighthouse	S.Thompson	Open	15.00	15.00
90-14-004	Anastasia Lighthousekeeper's house	S.Thompson	7/93	15.00	15.00
90-14-005	Mission Nombre deDios	S.Thompson	7/93	15.00	15.00
Shelia's, Inc.		**Savannah**			
90-15-001	Olde Pink House	S.Thompson	Open	15.00	15.00
90-15-002	Andrew Low Mansion	S.Thompson	Open	15.00	15.00
90-15-003	Davenport House	S.Thompson	Open	15.00	15.00
90-15-004	Juliette Low House	S.Thompson	Open	15.00	15.00
90-15-005	Herb House	S.Thompson	Open	15.00	15.00
90-15-006	Mikve Israel Temple	S.Thompson	Open	15.00	15.00
90-15-007	Tybee Lighthouse	S.Thompson	Open	15.00	15.00
90-15-008	Gingerbread House	S.Thompson	Retrd.	15.00	35.00
92-15-009	Catherdral of St. John	S.Thompson	Open	16.00	16.00
Shelia's, Inc.		**East Coast Lighthouse**			
90-16-001	Tybee Lighthouse	S.Thompson	Open	15.00	15.00
90-16-002	Stage Harbor Lighthouse	S.Thompson	Retrd.	15.00	19.00
91-16-003	Cape Hatteras Lighthouse	S.Thompson	Open	15.00	15.00
91-16-004	Anastasia Lighthouse	S.Thompson	Open	15.00	15.00
Shelia's, Inc.		**Collectible Accessories**			
90-17-001	Wrought Iron Gate With Magnolias	S.Thompson	Open	11.00	11.00
90-17-002	Gazebo With Victorian Lady	S.Thompson	Open	11.00	11.00
90-17-003	Oak Bower	S.Thompson	Open	11.00	11.00
90-17-004	Fence 5"	S.Thompson	Open	9.00	9.00
90-17-005	Fence 8"	S.Thompson	Open	10.00	10.00
90-17-006	Lake With Swan	S.Thompson	Open	11.00	11.00
90-17-007	Tree With Bush	S.Thompson	Open	10.00	10.00
Silver Deer, Ltd.		**Crystal Collectibles**			
84-01-001	Pinocchio, 120mm -02059	G. Truex	Closed	195.00	195-320.00
87-01-002	Bloomer-02102	G. Truex	5,000	140.00	170.00
90-01-003	Joe Cool Cruisin'- 02018	G. Truex	Closed	165.00	165.00
90-01-004	Snoopy's Suppertime- 01973	G. Truex	Closed	160.00	160.00
90-01-005	King Of Beasts- 02017	G. Truex	1,500	170.00	194.00
90-01-006	Romance- 02002	S. Dailey	2,500	250.00	290.00
91-01-007	Dreamland Teddy- 02643	S. Dailey	2,500	97.50	105.00
91-01-008	Tea For Two- 02639	S. Dailey	1,500	150.00	157.50
91-01-009	Flying Ace- 02649	S. Dailey	Open	140.00	150.00
92-01-010	Proud Spirit- 02823	S. Dailey	500	550.00	580.00
92-01-011	Make A Wish!- 02818	S. Dailey	1,500	210.00	220.00
92-01-012	Joe Cool 'Vette- 02807	S. Dailey	1,500	165.00	175.00
92-01-013	Schoolhouse Mouse- 02805	S. Dailey	Open	45.00	47.50
92-01-014	Teetering Twosome- 02808	S. Dailey	Open	75.00	80.00
92-01-015	Checkmate- 02812	S. Dailey	Open	130.00	137.50
92-01-016	Literary Ace- 02810	S. Dailey	Open	90.00	95.00
93-01-017	Morning Star Muse- 03550	G. Truex	40	3,000.00	3,000.00
93-01-018	Lady of the Fountains- 03559	G. Truex	Open	420.00	420.00
93-01-019	Pool of Flowers- 03560	G. Truex	Open	230.00	230.00
93-01-020	Star Catcher Bunny- 03747	G. Truex	Open	75.00	75.00
93-01-021	Hoppy Trails Bunny- 03748	G. Truex	Open	85.00	85.00
93-01-022	Come Follow Me Bunny- 03749	G. Truex	Open	85.00	85.00
93-01-023	Pinwheel Bunny- 03750	G. Truex	Open	75.00	75.00
93-01-024	Little Big Rig- 03785	G. Truex	Open	70.00	70.00
93-01-025	Teapot Twosome- 03793	G. Truex	Open	110.00	110.00
93-01-026	Toe Tappin' Snoopy- 03794	G. Truex	Open	120.00	120.00
93-01-027	The Outfield Comic- 03796	G. Truex	Open	40.00	40.00
93-01-028	The Outfield Comic w/Snoopy- 03797	G. Truex	Open	130.00	130.00
93-01-029	The Psychiatrist is in Comic- 03798	G. Truex	Open	40.00	40.00
93-01-030	The Psychiatrist is in Comic w/Snoopy - 03799	G. Truex	Open	130.00	130.00
93-01-031	Literary Ace Comic- 03800	G. Truex	Open	40.00	40.00
93-01-032	Literary Ace Comic w/Snoopy- 03801	G. Truex	Open	130.00	130.00
93-01-033	Wedding Day- 03802	G. Truex	Open	157.50	157.50
93-01-034	Snail's Pace- 03803	G. Truex	2,500	170.00	170.00
93-01-035	Joe Cool T-Bird- 03804	G. Truex	1,500	175.00	175.00
93-01-036	Card Game- 03805	G. Truex	1,500	300.00	300.00
93-01-037	Fairyland Frolic- 03806	G. Truex	1,200	350.00	350.00

Company Number	Name	Series Artist	Edition Limit	Issue Price	Quote
93-01-038	Balancing Act- 03807	G. Truex	1,200	300.00	300.00
93-01-039	The Malt Shop- 03808	G. Truex	1,200	400.00	400.00
93-01-040	Pinocchio, AB- 03809	G. Truex	400	500.00	500.00
93-01-041	U.S.S. Enterprise- 03812	G. Truex	1,200	375.00	375.00
Silver Deer, Ltd.		**Crystal Zoo Collectors' Club**			
91-02-001	Le Printemps	S. Dailey	Closed	Gift	N/A
91-02-002	Victoriana (Redemption)	S. Dailey	Closed	195.00	195.00
92-02-003	Garden Party	S. Dailey	Closed	Gift	N/A
92-02-004	Garden Guest (Redemption)	S. Dailey	8/93	175.00	175.00
93-02-005	Busy Bee	G. Truex	12/93	Gift	N/A
93-02-006	Debonair Bear	G. Truex	12/93	125.00	125.00
Silver Deer, Ltd.		**Ark Collectors' Club**			
91-03-001	Christmas Puppy	T. Rubel	Closed	Gift	N/A
91-03-002	Snowy Egret (Redemption)	T. Rubel	Closed	75.00	75.00
92-03-003	Snowball	T. Rubel	Closed	Gift	N/A
Sports Impressions/Enesco		**Baseball Superstar Figurines**			
87-01-001	Wade Boggs	S. Impressions	Closed	90-125.	150-225.
88-01-002	Jose Canseco	S. Impressions	Closed	90-125.	125-200.
89-01-003	Will Clark	S. Impressions	Closed	90-125.	125-250.
88-01-004	Andre Dawson	S. Impressions	2,500	90-125.	125-200.
88-01-005	Bob Feller	S. Impressions	2,500	90-125.	125-200.
89-01-006	Kirk Gibson	S. Impressions	Closed	90-125.	125-200.
87-01-007	Keith Hernandez	S. Impressions	2,500	90-125.	125-200.
88-01-008	Reg Jackson (Yankees)	S. Impressions	Closed	90-125.	125-200.
89-01-009	Reg Jackson (Angels)	S. Impressions	Closed	90-125.	125-250.
88-01-010	Al Kaline	S. Impressions	2,500	90-125.	125.00
87-01-011	Mickey Mantle	S. Impressions	Closed	90-125.	175-375.
87-01-012	Don Mattingly	S. Impressions	Closed	90-125.	225-650.
88-01-013	Paul Molitor	S. Impressions	2,500	90-125.	125.00
89-01-014	Duke Snider	S. Impressions	2,500	90-125.	125.00
89-01-015	Alan Trammell	S. Impressions	2,500	90-125.	125.00
89-01-016	Frank Viola	S. Impressions	2,500	90-125.	125.00
87-01-017	Ted Williams	S. Impressions	Closed	90-125.	200-375.
Sports Impressions/Enesco		**Collectors' Club Members Only**			
90-02-001	The Mick-Mickey Mantle 5000-1	S. Impressions	Yr.Iss.	75.00	95.00
91-02-002	Rickey Henderson-Born to Run 5001-11	S. Impressions	Yr.Iss.	49.95	49.95
91-02-003	Nolan Ryan-300 Wins 5002-01	S. Impressions	Yr.Iss.	195.00	195.00
91-02-004	Willie, Mickey & Duke plate 5003-04	S. Impressions	Yr.Iss.	39.95	39.95
92-02-005	Babe Ruth 5006-11	S. Impressions	Yr.Iss.	40.00	40.00
92-02-006	Walter Payton 5015-01	S. Impressions	Yr.Iss.	50.00	50.00
Sports Impressions/Enesco		**Collectors' Club Symbol of Membership**			
91-03-001	Mick/7 plate 5001-02	S. Impressions	Yr.Iss.	Gift	N/A
92-03-002	USA Basketball team plate 5008-30	S. Impressions	Yr.Iss.	Gift	N/A
93-03-003	Nolan Ryan porcelain card	S. Impressions	Yr.Iss.	Gift	N/A
Summerhill Crystal		**Summerhill Crystal**			
92-01-001	Venus	Summerhill	500	96.00	96.00
92-01-002	Sacre Coeur	Summerhill	5,000	190.00	190.00
92-01-003	L'arc du Triomphe	Summerhill	5,000	220.00	220.00
92-01-004	Bicycle	Summerhill	500	64.00	64.00
92-01-005	Princess Coach	Summerhill	1,500	700.00	700.00
92-01-006	Large Dragon	Summerhill	1,500	320.00	320.00
92-01-007	Mickey Mouse, Lg.	Summerhill	Open	295.00	295.00
92-01-008	Mickey Mouse, Med.	Summerhill	Open	165.00	165.00
92-01-009	Minnie Mouse, Lg.	Summerhill	Open	295.00	295.00
92-01-010	Minnie Mouse, Med.	Summerhill	Open	165.00	165.00
92-01-011	Epcot Center, Lg.	Summerhill	Open	245.00	245.00
92-01-012	Epcot Center, Med.	Summerhill	Open	110.00	110.00
92-01-013	Epcot Center, Sm.	Summerhill	Open	75.00	75.00
Summerhill Crystal		**Warner Brothers Collection**			
92-02-001	Tasmanian Devil.	Summerhill	2,750	220.00	220.00
92-02-002	Speedy Gonzales	Summerhill	2,750	164.00	164.00
92-02-003	Tweety Bird	Summerhill	Open	120.00	120.00
Summerhill Crystal		**Collector Society**			
92-03-001	Robbie Rabbit	Summerhill	Yr.Iss.	125.00	125.00
Swarovski America		**Our Woodland Friends**			
79-01-001	Mini Owl	M. Schreck	Open	16.00	29.50
79-01-002	Small Owl	M. Schreck	Open	59.00	85.00
79-01-003	Large Owl	M. Schreck	Open	90.00	120.00
83-01-004	Giant Owl	M. Schreck	Open	1200.00	2000.00
85-01-005	Mini Bear	M. Schreck	Open	16.00	55.00
82-01-006	Small Bear	M. Schreck	Open	44.00	75.00
81-01-007	Large Bear	M. Schreck	Open	75.00	95.00
87-01-008	Fox	A. Stocker	Open	50.00	75.00
88-01-009	Mini Sitting Fox	A. Stocker	Open	35.00	42.50
88-01-010	Mini Running Fox	A. Stocker	Open	35.00	42.50
85-01-011	Squirrel	M. Schreck	Open	35.00	55.00
89-01-012	Mushrooms	A. Stocker	Open	35.00	42.50
Swarovski America		**African Wildlife**			
89-02-001	Small Elephant	A. Stocker	Open	50.00	65.00
88-02-002	Large Elephant	A. Stocker	Open	70.00	95.00
89-02-003	Small Hippopotamus	A. Stocker	Open	70.00	75.00
90-02-004	Small Rhinoceros	A. Stocker	Open	70.00	75.00
Swarovski America		**Kingdom Of Ice And Snow**			
86-03-001	Mini Baby Seal	A. Stocker	Open	30.00	42.50
85-03-002	Large Seal	M. Schreck	Open	44.00	85.00
84-03-003	Mini Penguin	M. Schreck	Open	16.00	37.50
84-03-004	Large Penguin	M. Schreck	Open	44.00	95.00
86-03-005	Large Polar Bear	A. Stocker	Open	140.00	195.00
89-03-006	Walrus	M. Stamey	Open	120.00	135.00
Swarovski America		**In A Summer Meadow**			
87-04-001	Small Hedgehog	M. Schreck	Open	50.00	55.00
85-04-002	Medium Hedgehog	M. Schreck	Open	70.00	85.00
85-04-003	Large Hedgehog	M. Schreck	Open	120.00	135.00
88-04-004	Mini Lying Rabbit	A. Stocker	Open	35.00.	42.50
88-04-005	Mini Sitting Rabbit	A. Stocker	Open	35.00	42.50
88-04-006	Mother Rabbit	A. Stocker	Open	60.00	75.00
76-04-007	Medium Mouse	M. Schreck	Open	48.00	85.00
86-04-008	Mini Butterfly	Team	Open	16.00	42.50
82-04-009	Butterfly	Team	Open	44.00	85.00
86-04-010	Snail	M. Stamey	Open	35.00	55.00
91-04-011	Field Mouse	A. Stocker	Open	47.50	49.50

Company / Number	Name	Series / Artist	Edition Limit	Issue Price	Quote
92-04-012	Sparrow	Schneiderbauer	Open	29.50	29.50
Swarovski America		**Beauties of the Lake**			
89-05-001	Small Swan	M. Schreck	Open	35.00	49.50
77-05-002	Medium Swan	M. Schreck	Open	44.00	75.00
77-05-003	Large Swan	M. Schreck	Open	55.00	95.00
86-05-004	Mini Standing Duck	A. Stocker	Open	22.00	37.50
86-05-005	Mini Swimming Duck	M. Schreck	Open	16.00	37.50
83-05-006	Mini Drake	M. Schreck	Open	20.00	42.50
86-05-007	Mallard	M. Schreck	Open	80.00	135.00
89-05-008	Giant Mallard	M. Stamey	Open	2000.00	4500.00
Swarovski America		**Silver Crystal City**			
90-06-001	Silver Crystal City-Cathedral	G. Stamey	Open	95.00	120.00
90-06-002	Silver Crystal City-Houses I& II(Set of 2)	G. Stamey	Open	75.00	75.00
90-06-003	Silver Crystal City-Houses III & IV(Set of 2)	G. Stamey	Open	75.00	75.00
90-06-004	Silver Crystal City-Poplars (Set of 3)	G. Stamey	Open	40.00	49.50
91-06-005	City Tower	G. Stamey	Open	37.50	42.50
91-06-006	City Gates	G. Stamey	Open	95.00	95.00
Swarovski America		**Nativity Scene**			
91-07-001	Holy Family With Arch	Team	Open	250.00	250.00
92-07-002	Wise Men (Set of 3)	Team	Open	175.00	175.00
92-07-003	Shepherd	Team	Open	65.00	65.00
92-07-004	Angel	Team	Open	65.00	65.00
Swarovski America		**When We Were Young**			
88-08-001	Locomotive	G. Stamey	Open	150.00	150.00
88-08-002	Tender	G. Stamey	Open	55.00	55.00
88-08-003	Wagon	G. Stamey	Open	85.00	85.00
90-08-004	Petrol Wagon	G. Stamey	Open	75.00	85.00
89-08-005	Old Timer Automobile	G. Stamey	Open	130.00	150.00
90-08-006	Airplane	A. Stocker	Open	135.00	150.00
91-08-007	Santa Maria	G. Stamey	Open	375.00	375.00
Swarovski America		**Exquisite Accents**			
80-09-001	Birdbath	M. Schreck	Open	150.00	195.00
87-09-002	Birds' Nest	Team	Open	90.00	120.00
87-09-003	Small Dinner Bell	M. Schreck	Open	60.00	65.00
87-09-004	Medium Dinner Bell	M. Schreck	Open	80.00	95.00
Swarovski America		**Sparkling Fruit**			
86-10-001	Small Pineapple/Gold	M. Schreck	Open	55.00	85.00
81-10-002	Large Pineapple/Gold	M. Schreck	Open	150.00	250.00
81-10-003	Giant Pineapple/Gold	M. Schreck	Open	1750.00	3250.00
85-10-004	Small Grapes	Team	Open	200.00	250.00
85-10-005	Medium Grapes	Team	Open	300.00	375.00
91-10-006	Apple	M. Stamey	Open	175.00	175.00
91-10-007	Pear	M. Stamey	Open	175.00	175.00
Swarovski America		**A Pet's Corner**			
90-11-001	Beagle Puppy	A. Stocker	Open	40.00	49.50
90-11-002	Scotch Terrier	A. Stocker	Open	60.00	75.00
87-11-003	Mini Dachshund	A. Stocker	Open	20.00	49.50
91-11-004	Sitting Cat	M. Stamey	Open	75.00	75.00
91-11-005	Kitten	M. Stamey	Open	47.50	49.50
92-11-006	Poodle	A. Stocker	Open	125.00	135.00
Swarovski America		**South Sea**			
91-12-001	South Sea Shell	M. Stamey	Open	110.00	120.00
88-12-002	Open Shell With Pearl	M. Stamey	Open	120.00	150.00
87-12-003	Mini Blowfish	Team	Open	22.00	29.50
86-12-004	Small Blowfish	Team	Open	35.00	55.00
91-12-005	Butterfly Fish	M. Stamey	Open	150.00	165.00
Swarovski America		**Endangered Species**			
91-13-001	Kiwi	M. Stamey	Open	37.50	37.50
89-13-002	Mini Koala	A. Stocker	Open	35.00	42.50
87-13-003	Koala	A. Stocker	Open	50.00	65.00
77-13-004	Small Turtle	M. Schreck	Open	35.00	49.50
77-13-005	Large Turtle	M. Schreck	Open	48.00	75.00
81-13-006	Giant Turtle	M. Schreck	Open	2500.00	4500.00
92-13-007	Mother Beaver	A. Stocker	Open	110.00	120.00
92-13-008	Sitting Baby Beaver	A. Stocker	Open	47.50	49.50
92-13-009	Lying Baby Beaver	A. Stocker	Open	47.50	49.50
Swarovski America		**Barnyard Friends**			
82-14-001	Mini Pig	M. Schreck	Open	16.00	29.50
84-14-002	Medium Pig	M. Schreck	Open	35.00	55.00
88-14-003	Mini Chicks (Set of 3)	G. Stamey	Open	35.00	37.50
87-14-004	Mini Rooster	G. Stamey	Open	35.00	55.00
87-14-005	Mini Hen	G. Stamey	Open	35.00	42.50
Swarovski America		**The Game of Kings**			
84-15-001	Chess Set	M. Schreck	Open	950.00	1375.00
Swarovski America		**Among Flowers And Foliage**			
92-16-001	Hummingbird	Schneiderbauer	Open	195.00	195.00
92-16-002	Bumblebee	Schneiderbauer	Open	85.00	85.00
Swarovski America		**Our Candleholders**			
85-17-001	Small Water Lily 7600NR124	M. Schreck	Open	100.00	165.00
83-17-002	Medium Water Lily 7600NR123	M. Schreck	Open	150.00	250.00
85-17-003	Large Water Lily 7600NR125	M. Schreck	Open	200.00	375.00
89-17-004	Medium Star 7600NR143001	Team	Open	200.00	250.00
87-17-005	Large Star 7600NR143	Team	Open	250.00	375.00
Swarovski America		**Decorative Items For The Desk (Paperweights)**			
87-18-001	Small Chaton 7433NR50	M. Schreck	Open	50.00	65.00
87-18-002	Large Chaton 7433NR80	M. Schreck	Open	190.00	250.00
90-18-003	Giant Chaton 7433NR180000	M. Schreck	Open	3900.00	4500.00
87-18-004	Small Pyramid CC/VM7450NR40	M. Schreck	Open	100.00	120.00
87-18-005	Large Pyramid CC/VM7450NR50	M. Schreck	Open	90.00	195.00
Swarovski America		**Crystal Melodies**			
92-19-001	Lute	M. Zendron	Open	125.00	135.00
92-19-002	Harp	M. Zendron	Open	175.00	195.00
Swarovski America		**Collectors Society Editions**			
87-20-001	Togetherness-The Lovebirds	Schreck/Stocker	Retrd.	150.00	2500-4000.
88-20-002	Sharing-The Woodpeckers	A. Stocker	Retrd.	165.00	1100-1400.
89-20-003	Amour-The Turtledoves	A. Stocker	Retrd.	195.00	600-900.
90-20-004	Lead Me-The Dolphins	M. Stamey	Retrd.	225.00	700-1500.

Company / Number	Name	Series / Artist	Edition Limit	Issue Price	Quote
91-20-005	Save Me-The Seals	M. Stamey	Retrd.	225.00	450-700.
92-20-006	Care For Me - The Whales	M. Stamey	Retrd.	265.00	350-495.
92-20-007	5th Anniversary Edition-The Birthday Cake	G. Stamey	Retrd.	85.00	125.00
93-20-008	Inspiration Africa-The Elephant	M. Zendron	12/93	325.00	325.00
Swarovski America		**Retired**			
84-21-001	Dachshund 7641NR75	M. Schreck	Retrd.	48.00	100-125.
82-21-002	Mini Cat 7659NR31	M. Schreck	Retrd.	16.00	45-65.00
77-21-003	Large Cat 7634NR70	M. Schreck	Retrd.	44.00	90-140.00
84-21-004	Large Blowfish 7644NR41	Team	Retrd.	40.00	100-132.
88-21-005	Whale 7628NR80	M. Stamey	Retrd.	70.00	110-200.
86-21-006	Small Falcon Head 7645NR45	M. Schreck	Retrd.	60.00	100-125.
84-21-007	Large Falcon Head 7645NR100	M. Schreck	Retrd.	600.00	1200.00
XX-21-008	Small Mouse 7631NR30	M. Schreck	Retrd.	35.00	50-80.00
79-21-009	Mini Sparrow7650NR20	M. Schreck	Retrd.	16.00	35.00
84-21-010	Frog 7642NR48	M. Schreck	Retrd.	30.00	55-82.00
XX-21-011	Mini Chicken 7651NR20	Team	Retrd.	16.00	45-90.00
XX-21-012	Mini Rabbit 7652NR20	Team	Retrd.	16.00	50-95.00
XX-21-013	Mini Duck 7653NR45	Team	Retrd.	16.00	36-45.00
XX-21-014	Mini Mouse 7655NR23	Team	Retrd.	16.00	45-75.00
XX-21-015	Mini Swan 7658NR27	M. Schreck	Retrd.	16.00	65-115.00
84-21-016	Mini Bear 7670NR32	M. Schreck	Retrd.	16.00	65-100.00
XX-21-017	Mini Butterfly 7671NR30	Team	Retrd.	16.00	50-100.00
XX-21-018	Mini Dachshund 7672NR42	A. Stocker	Retrd.	20.00	50-100.00
XX-21-019	Small Hedgehog 7630NR30	M. Schreck	Retrd.	38.00	250-300.
XX-21-020	Medium Hedgehog 7630NR40	M. Schreck	Retrd.	44.00	150-250.
XX-21-021	Large Hedgehog 7630NR50	M. Schreck	Retrd.	65.00	150-300.
XX-21-022	King Size Hedgehog 7630NR60	M. Schreck	Retrd.	98.00	300-450.
XX-21-023	Large Mouse 7631NR50	M. Schreck	Retrd.	69.00	175-250.
XX-21-024	King Size Mouse 7631NR60	M. Schreck	Retrd.	95.00	300-350.
XX-21-025	King Size Turtle 7632NR75	M. Schreck	Retrd.	58.00	200.00
XX-21-026	Medium Cat 7634NR52	Team	Retrd.	38.00	130-200.
XX-21-027	Dog 7635NR70	Team	Retrd.	44.00	85-90.00
XX-21-028	King Size Bear7637NR92	M. Schreck	Retrd.	95.00	550-935.
XX-21-029	Giant Size Bear 7637NR112	M. Schreck	Retrd.	125.00	650-1100.
XX-21-030	Large Pig 7638NR65	M. Schreck	Retrd.	50.00	150-275.
XX-21-031	Elephant 7640NR55	Team	Retrd.	90.00	180-250.
XX-21-032	Large Sparrow 7650NR32	Team	Retrd.	38.00	70-120.00
XX-21-033	Large Rabbit 7652NR45	Team	Retrd.	38.00	125-175.
XX-21-034	Medium Duck 7653NR55	Team	Retrd.	38.00	60-100.00
XX-21-035	Large Duck 7653NR75	Team	Retrd.	44.00	125-250.
87-21-036	Partridge 7625NR50	A. Stocker	Retrd.	85.00	200-250.
88-21-037	Hippopotamus 7626NR65	A. Stocker	Retrd.	70.00	95-200.00
88-21-038	Rhinoceros 7622NR70	A. Stocker	Retrd.	70.00	125-200.
90-21-039	Kingfisher 7621NR000001	M. Stamey	Retrd.	75.00	125-150.
89-21-040	Toucan 7621NR000002	M. Stamey	Retrd.	70.00	125-150.
89-21-041	Owl 7621NR000003	M. Stamey	Retrd.	70.00	125-150.
89-21-042	Parrot 7621NR000004	M. Stamey	Retrd.	70.00	125.00
XX-21-043	Sm. Apple Photo Stand(Gold) 7504NR030G	Team	Retrd.	40.00	200.00
XX-21-044	Sm. Apple Photo Stand 7504NR030R	Team	Retrd.	40.00	175-250.
XX-21-045	Lg. Apple Photo Stand(Gold) 7504NR050G	Team	Retrd.	80.00	265-300.
XX-21-046	Lg. Apple Photo Stand 7504NR050R	Team	Retrd.	80.00	200-250.
XX-21-047	Kg Sz Apple Photo Stand(Gold) 7504NR060G	Team	Retrd.	120.00	425-500.
XX-21-048	Large Grapes 7550NR30015	Team	Retrd.	250.00	600-700.
85-21-049	Butterfly (Gold) 7551NR100	Team	Retrd.	200.00	500-1000.
85-21-050	Butterfly (Rhodium) 7551NR200	Team	Retrd.	200.00	500-1000.
85-21-051	Hummingbird (Gold) 7552NR100	Team	Retrd.	200.00	550-1000.
85-21-052	Hummingbird (Rhodium) 7552NR200	Team	Retrd.	200.00	950-1750.
85-21-053	Bee (Gold) 7553NR100	Team	Retrd.	200.00	550-900.
85-21-054	Bee (Rhodium) 7553NR200	Team	Retrd.	200.00	1100-1500.
87-21-055	Sm. Pineapple/Rhodium 7507NR060002	M. Schreck	Retrd.	55.00	150-200.
82-21-056	Lg. Pineapple/Rhodium 7507NR105002	M. Schreck	Retrd.	150.00	330-500.
85-21-057	Giant Pineapple/Rhodium 7507NR26002	M. Schreck	Retrd.	1750.00	3000.00
81-21-058	Large Dinner Bell 7467NR071000	M. Schreck	Retrd.	80.00	150-175.
XX-21-059	Rd. Pprwgt-Green 7404NR40	Team	Retrd.	20.00	75-150.00
XX-21-060	Rd. Pprwgt-Sahara 7404NR40	Team	Retrd.	20.00	75-150.00
XX-21-061	Rd. Pprwgt-Berm Blue 7404NR40	Team	Retrd.	20.00	75-150.00
XX-21-062	Rd. Pprwgt-Green 7404NR30	Team	Retrd.	15.00	50-150.00
XX-21-063	Rd. Pprwgt-Sahara 7404NR30	Team	Retrd.	15.00	50-150.00
XX-21-064	Rd. Pprwgt-Berm. Blue 7404NR30	Team	Retrd.	15.00	50-150.00
XX-21-065	Rd. Pprwgt-Green 7404NR50	Team	Retrd.	40.00	75-150.00
XX-21-066	Rd. Pprwgt-Sahara 7404NR50	Team	Retrd.	40.00	75-150.00
XX-21-067	Rd. Pprwgt-Berm. Blue 7404NR50	Team	Retrd.	40.00	75-150.00
XX-21-068	Carousel Pprwgt-Vitrl Med 7451NR60087	Team	Retrd.	80.00	750-1000.
XX-21-069	Carousel Pprwgt-Crystal Cal 7451NR60095	Team	Retrd.	80.00	750-1000.
XX-21-070	Atomic Pprwgt-Vitrl Med 7454NR60087	Team	Retrd.	80.00	1000-1500.
XX-21-071	Atomic Pprwgt-Crystal Cal 7454NR60095	Team	Retrd.	80.00	960-1200.
XX-21-072	Barrel Pprwgt 7453NR60087 Vitrl Med	Team	Retrd.	80.00	300-500.
XX-21-073	Barrel Pprwgt 7453NR60095 Crystal Cal	Team	Retrd.	80.00	280-420.
XX-21-074	Rd. Pprwgt-Crystal Cal 7404NR30095	Team	Retrd.	15.00	75.00
XX-21-075	Rd. Pprwgt-Vitrl Med 7404NR30087	Team	Retrd.	15.00	75.00
XX-21-076	Rd. Pprwgt-Crystal Cal 7404NR40095	Team	Retrd.	20.00	75-95.00
XX-21-077	Rd. Pprwgt-Vitrl Med 7404NR40087	Team	Retrd.	20.00	75-95.00
XX-21-078	Rd. Pprwgt-Crystal Cal 7404NR50095	Team	Retrd.	40.00	100-200.
XX-21-079	Rd. Pprwgt-Vitrl Med 7404NR50087	Team	Retrd.	40.00	100-200.
XX-21-080	Rd. Pprwgt-Crystal Cal 7404NR60095	Team	Retrd.	50.00	150-250.
XX-21-081	Rd. Pprwgt-Vitrl Med 7404NR60087	Team	Retrd.	50.00	150-250.
XX-21-082	Geometric Pprwgt 7432NR57002n	Team	Retrd.	75.00	125-300.
XX-21-083	One Ton Pprwgt 7495NR65	Team	Retrd.	75.00	100-200.
XX-21-084	Octron Pprwgt 7456NR41	Team	Retrd.	75.00	150-275.
XX-21-085	Octron Pprwgt 7456NR1087	Team	Retrd.	90.00	125-200.
XX-21-086	Candleholder 7600NR101	Team	Retrd.	23.00	350-600.
XX-21-087	Candleholder 7600NR102	Team	Retrd.	35.00	125-150.
XX-21-088	Candleholder 7600NR103	Team	Retrd.	40.00	125-175.
XX-21-089	Candleholder European Style 7600NR103	Team	Retrd.	N/A	750.00
XX-21-090	Candleholder 7600NR104	Team	Retrd.	95.00	300.00
XX-21-091	Candleholder 7600NR106	Team	Retrd.	85.00	225-350.
XX-21-092	Candleholder 7600NR107	Team	Retrd.	100.00	300-500.
XX-21-093	Candleholder European Style 7600NR108	Team	Retrd.	N/A	850.00
XX-21-094	Candleholder 7600NR109	Team	Retrd.	37.00	125-175.
XX-21-095	Candleholder 7600NR110	Team	Retrd.	40.00	125-150.
XX-21-096	Candleholder 7600NR111	Team	Retrd.	100.00	300-400.
XX-21-097	Candleholder 7600NR112	Team	Retrd.	75.00	300-400.
XX-21-098	Candleholder 7600NR114	Team	Retrd.	37.00	150-200.
XX-21-099	Candleholder 7600NR115	Team	Retrd.	185.00	300-400.
XX-21-100	Candleholder 7600NR116	Team	Retrd.	350.00	1000-1500.
XX-21-101	Candleholder 7600NR119	Team	Retrd.	N/A	500.00
XX-21-102	Sm.Candleholder w/ Flowers 7600NR120	Team	Retrd.	60.00	200-250.
XX-21-103	Baroque Candleholder 7600NR121	Team	Retrd.	150.00	250-450.
XX-21-104	Candleholder 7600NR122	Team	Retrd.	85.00	200-240.
XX-21-105	Sm.Candleholder w/ Leaves 7600NR126	Team	Retrd.	100.00	250-300.
XX-21-106	Candleholder 7600NR127	Team	Retrd.	65.00	125-200.
XX-21-107	Candleholder 7600NR128	Team	Retrd.	100.00	200-250.

Number	Name	Artist	Edition Limit	Issue Price	Quote
Company		**Series**			
XX-21-108	Candleholder 7600NR129	Team	Retrd.	120.00	250-300.
XX-21-109	Candleholder 7600NR130	Team	Retrd.	275.00	1000-1500.
XX-21-110	Candleholder 7600NR131(Set of 6)	Team	Retrd.	43.00	960.00
XX-21-111	Small Global Candleholder (4) 7600NR132	Team	Retrd.	60.00	150-250.
XX-21-112	Med. Global Candleholder (2) 7600NR133	Team	Retrd.	40.00	100.00
XX-21-113	Large Global Candleholder 7600NR134	Team	Retrd.	40.00	60-90.00
XX-21-114	Kingsize Global Candleholder 7600NR135	Team	Retrd.	50.00	150-200.
XX-21-115	Pineapple Candleholder 7600NR136	Team	Retrd.	150.00	400-500.
XX-21-116	Large Candleholderw/Flowers 7600NR137	Team	Retrd.	150.00	190-225.
XX-21-117	Candleholder 7600NR138	Team	Retrd.	160.00	300-350.
XX-21-118	Candleholder 7600NR139	Team	Retrd.	140.00	300-500.
XX-21-119	Candleholder 7600NR140	Team	Retrd.	120.00	300-400.
XX-21-120	Candleholder European Style 7600NR141	Team	Retrd.	N/A	750.00
XX-21-121	Candleholder European Style 7600NR142	Team	Retrd.	N/A	500.00
90-21-122	Sm. Neo-Classic Candlehldr7600NR144070	A. Stocker	Retrd.	170.00	175.00
90-21-123	Med. Neo-ClassicCandlehldr7600NR144080	A. Stocker	Retrd.	190.00	250.00
90-21-124	Large Neo-Classic Candlehldr7600NR144090	A. Stocker	Retrd.	220.00	225.00
XX-21-125	Beetle Bottle Opener (Rodium) 7505NR76	Team	Retrd.	80.00	1300-2500.
XX-21-126	Beetle Bottle Opener (Gold) 7505NR76	Team	Retrd.	80.00	2500.00
XX-21-127	Table Magnifyer 7510NR01	Team	Retrd.	80.00	1200-2000.
XX-21-128	Treasure Box (Round/Butterfly) 7464NR50/10	Team	Retrd.	80.00	175-250.
XX-21-129	Treasure Box (Heart/Flower)7465NR52	Team	Retrd.	80.00	175-250.
XX-21-130	Treasure Box (Oval/Butterfly)7466NR063100	Team	Retrd.	80.00	175-250.
XX-21-131	Salt and Pepper Shakers 7508NR068034	Team	Retrd.	80.00	175-250.
XX-21-132	Picture Frame/Oval 7505NR75G	Team	Retrd.	90.00	200-275.
XX-21-133	Picture Frame/Square 7506NR60G	Team	Retrd.	100.00	200-300.
XX-21-134	Treasure Box (Round/Flower) 7464NR50	Team	Retrd.	80.00	150-250.
XX-21-135	Treasure Box (Heart/Butterfly)7465NR52/100	Team	Retrd.	80.00	200-250.
XX-21-136	Treasure Box (Oval/Flower) 7466NR063000	Team	Retrd.	80.00	150-250.
XX-21-137	Vase 7511NR70	Team	Retrd.	50.00	75-125.00
XX-21-138	Schnapps Glasses, Set of 6-7468NR039000	Team	Retrd.	150.00	350-375.
XX-21-139	Ashtray 7461NR100	Team	Retrd.	45.00	200-300.
XX-21-140	Lighter 7462NR062	Team	Retrd.	160.00	200-400.
XX-21-141	Cigarette Holder 7463NR062	Team	Retrd.	85.00	150.00
XX-21-142	Small Cardholders, Set of 4 -7403NR20095	Team	Retrd.	25.00	125-200.
XX-21-143	Large Cardholders, Set of 4 -7403NR30095	Team	Retrd.	45.00	250-400.
82-21-144	Cone Vitrail Medium 7452NR60087	M. Schreck	Retrd.	80.00	200-250.
82-21-145	Cone Crystal Cal 7452NR60095	M. Schreck	Retrd.	80.00	200-250.
81-21-146	Egg 7458NR63069	M. Schreck	Retrd.	60.00	110-175.
81-21-147	Chess Set/Wooden Board	Team	Retrd.	950.00	2500-3000.
Swarovski America		**Commemorative Single Issue**			
90-22-001	Elephant*(Introduced by Swarovski America as a commemorative item test during Design Celebration/January '90 in Walt Disney World)	Team	Closed	125.00	1200-1500.
United Design Corp.		**Legend of Santa Claus**			
86-01-001	Santa At Rest CF-001	L. Miller	Retrd.	70.00	400-600.
86-01-002	Kris Kringle CF-002	L. Miller	Retrd.	60.00	125-140.
86-01-003	Santa With Pups CF-003	S. Bradford	Retrd.	65.00	350-550.
86-01-004	Rooftop Santa CF-004	S. Bradford	Retrd.	65.00	100-175.
86-01-005	Elf Pair CF-005	L. Miller	Retrd.	60.00	125-150.
87-01-006	Mrs. Santa CF-006	S. Bradford	Retrd.	60.00	175-200.
87-01-007	On Santa's Knee-CF007	S. Bradford	15,000	65.00	79.00
87-01-008	Dreaming Of Santa CF-008	S. Bradford	Retrd.	65.00	225-375.
87-01-009	Checking His List CF-009	L. Miller	15,000	75.00	85.00
87-01-010	Loading Santa's Sleigh CF-010	L. Miller	Retrd.	100.00	100.00
87-01-011	Santa On Horseback CF-011	S. Bradford	Retrd.	75.00	200-350.
88-01-012	St. Nicholas CF-015	L. Miller	Retrd.	75.00	135-150.
88-01-013	Load 'Em Up CF-016	S. Bradford	Retrd.	79.00	300-350.
88-01-014	Assembly Required CF-017	L. Miller	7,500	79.00	95.00
88-01-015	Father Christmas CF-018	S. Bradford	7,500	75.00	85.00
89-01-016	A Purrr-Fect Christmas CF-019	S. Bradford	7,500	95.00	95.00
89-01-017	Christmas Harmony CF-020	S. Bradford	Retrd.	85.00	150.00
89-01-018	Hitching Up CF-021	L. Miller	Retrd.	90.00	90.00
90-01-019	Puppy Love CF-024	L. Miller	7,500	100.00	100.00
90-01-020	Forest Friends CF-025	L. Miller	Retrd.	90.00	90.00
90-01-021	Waiting For Santa CF-026	S. Bradford	7,500	100.00	100.00
90-01-022	Safe Arrival CF-027	Memoli/Jonas	7,500	150.00	150.00
90-01-023	Victorian Santa CF-028	S. Bradford	Retrd.	125.00	175-200.
91-01-024	For Santa CF-029	L. Miller	7,500	99.00	99.00
91-01-025	Santa At Work CF-030	L. Miller	7,500	99.00	99.00
91-01-026	Reindeer Walk CF-031	K. Memoli	7,500	150.00	150.00
91-01-027	Blessed Flight CF-032	K. Memoli	Retrd.	159.00	159.00
91-01-028	Victorian Santa w/ Teddy CF-033	S. Bradford	7,500	150.00	150.00
92-01-029	Arctic Santa CF-035	S. Bradford	7,500	90.00	90.00
92-01-030	Letters to Santa CF-036	L. Miller	7,500	125.00	125.00
92-01-031	Santa and Comet CF-037	L. Miller	7,500	110.00	110.00
92-01-032	The Christmas Tree CF-038	L. Miller	7,500	90.00	90.00
92-01-031	Santa and Mrs. Claus CF-039	K. Memoli	7,500	150.00	150.00
92-01-032	Earth Home Santa CF-040	S. Bradford	7,500	135.00	135.00
92-01-033	Loads of Happiness CF-041	K. Memoli	7,500	100.00	100.00
92-01-034	Santa and Mrs. Claus, Victorian CF-042	K. Memoli	7,500	135.00	135.00
93-01-035	The Night Before Christmas CF-043	L. Miller	7,500	75.00	75.00
93-01-036	Santa's Friend CF-044	L. Miller	7,500	85.00	85.00
93-01-037	Jolly St. Nick CF-045	K. Memoli	7,500	100.00	100.00
93-01-038	Dear Santa CF-046	K. Memoli	7,500	159.00	159.00
93-01-039	Northwoods Santa CF-047	S. Bradford	7,500	85.00	85.00
93-01-040	Victorian Lion & Lamb Santa CF-048	S. Bradford	7,500	64.00	64.00
93-01-041	Jolly St. Nick, Victorian CF 050	K. Memoli	7,500	100.00	100.00
United Design Corp.		**Legend Of The Little People**			
89-02-001	Woodland Cache LL-001	L. Miller	Retrd.	35.00	45.00
89-02-002	Adventure Bound LL-002	L. Miller	Retrd.	35.00	45.00
89-02-003	A Friendly Toast LL-003	L. Miller	Retrd.	35.00	45.00
89-02-004	Treasure Hunt LL-004	L. Miller	7,500	45.00	45.00
89-02-005	Magical Discovery LL-005	L. Miller	Retrd.	45.00	45.00
89-02-006	Spring Water Scrub LL-006	L. Miller	7,500	35.00	45.00
89-02-007	Caddy's Helper LL-007	L. Miller	Retrd.	35.00	45.00
90-02-008	Husking Acorns LL-008	L. Miller	7,500	60.00	60.00
90-02-009	Traveling Fast LL-009	L. Miller	7,500	45.00	45.00
90-02-010	Hedgehog In Harness LL-010	L. Miller	7,500	45.00	45.00
90-02-011	Woodland Scout LL-011	L. Miller	7,500	40.00	45.00
90-02-012	Fishin' Hole LL-012	L. Miller	7,500	35.00	45.00
90-02-013	A Proclamation LL-013	L. Miller	7,500	45.00	50.00
90-02-014	Gathering Acorns LL-014	L. Miller	7,500	100.00	100.00
90-02-015	A Look Through The Spyglass LL-015	L. Miller	7,500	40.00	45.00
90-02-016	Writing The Legend LL-016	L. Miller	7,500	65.00	65.00
90-02-017	Ministral Magic LL-017	L. Miller	7,500	45.00	45.00
90-02-018	A Little Jig LL-018	L. Miller	7,500	45.00	45.00
91-02-019	Viking LL-019	L. Miller	7,500	45.00	45.00
91-02-020	The Easter Bunny's Cart LL-020	L. Miller	7,500	45.00	45.00
91-02-021	Got It LL-021	L. Miller	7,500	45.00	45.00
91-02-022	It's About Time LL-022	L. Miller	7,500	55.00	55.00
91-02-023	Fire it Up LL-023	L. Miller	7,500	50.00	50.00
United Design Corp.		**Music Makers**			
89-03-001	Coming To Town MM-001	L. Miller	Open	69.00	69.00
89-03-002	Merry Little Christmas MM-002	L. Miller	Open	69.00	69.00
89-03-003	Merry Making MM-003	L. Miller	Retrd.	69.00	80-100.00
89-03-004	Santa's Sleigh MM-004	L. Miller	Open	69.00	69.00
89-03-005	Evening Carolers MM-005	D. Kennicutt	Open	69.00	69.00
89-03-006	Winter Fun MM-006	D. Kennicutt	Open	69.00	69.00
89-03-007	Snowshoe Sled Ride MM-007	D. Kennicutt	Open	69.00	69.00
89-03-008	Christmas Tree MM-008	D. Kennicutt	Open	69.00	69.00
89-03-009	Teddy Drummers MM-009	D. Kennicutt	Open	69.00	69.00
89-03-010	Teddies And Frosty MM-010	D. Kennicutt	Open	69.00	69.00
89-03-011	Herald Angel MM-011	S. Bradford	Retrd.	79.00	79.00
89-03-012	Teddy Bear Band MM-012	S. Bradford	12,000	99.00	99.00
91-03-013	Dashing Through The Snow MM-013	D. Kennicutt	Open	59.00	59.00
91-03-014	Two Faeries MM-014	D. Kennicutt	Open	59.00	59.00
91-03-015	A Christmas Gift MM-015	D. Kennicutt	Open	59.00	59.00
91-03-016	Crystal Angel MM-017	D. Kennicutt	Open	59.00	59.00
91-03-017	Teddy Soldiers MM-018	D. Kennicutt	Open	69.00	69.00
United Design Corp.		**Easter Bunny Family**			
88-04-001	Bunnies, Basket Of SEC-001	D. Kennicutt	Retrd.	13.00	17.50
88-04-002	Bunny Boy W/Duck SEC-002	D. Kennicutt	Retrd.	13.00	17.50
88-04-003	Bunny, Easter SEC-003	D. Kennicutt	Retrd.	15.00	17.50
88-04-004	Bunny Girl W/Hen SEC-004	D. Kennicutt	Retrd.	13.00	17.50
88-04-005	Rabbit, Grandma SEC-005	D. Kennicutt	Retrd.	15.00	20.00
88-04-006	Rabbit, Grandpa SEC-006	D. Kennicutt	Retrd.	15.00	20.00
88-04-007	Rabbit, Momma w/Bonnet SEC-007	D. Kennicutt	Retrd.	15.00	20.00
89-04-008	Auntie Bunny SEC-008	D. Kennicutt	Retrd.	20.00	23.00
89-04-009	Little Sis W/Lolly SEC-009	D. Kennicutt	Retrd.	14.50	17.50
89-04-010	Bunny W/Prize Egg SEC-010	D. Kennicutt	Retrd.	19.50	20.00
89-04-011	Sis & Bubba Sharing SEC-011	D. Kennicutt	Open	22.50	23.00
89-04-012	Easter Egg Hunt SEC-012	D. Kennicutt	Open	16.50	20.00
89-04-013	Rock-A-Bye Bunny SEC-013	D. Kennicutt	Open	20.00	23.00
89-04-014	Ducky W/Bonnet, Pink SEC-014	D. Kennicutt	Retrd.	10.00	12.00
89-04-015	Ducky W/Bonnet,Blue SEC-015	D. Kennicutt	Retrd.	10.00	12.00
90-04-016	Bubba w/Wagon SEC-016	D. Kennicutt	Retrd.	16.50	17.50
90-04-017	Easter Bunny w/Crystal SEC 017	D. Kennicutt	Open	23.00	23.00
90-04-018	Hen w/Chick SEC-018	D. Kennicutt	Retrd.	23.00	23.00
90-04-019	Momma Making Basket SEC-019	D. Kennicutt	Retrd.	23.00	23.00
90-04-020	Mother Goose SEC-020	D. Kennicutt	Retrd.	16.50	20.00
91-04-021	Bubba In Wheelbarrow SEC-021	D. Kennicutt	Retrd.	20.00	20.00
91-04-022	Lop-Ear W/Crystal SEC-022	D. Kennicutt	Open	23.00	23.00
91-04-023	Nest of Bunny Eggs SEC-023	D. Kennicutt	Open	17.50	17.50
91-04-024	Victorian Momma SEC-024	D. Kennicutt	Retrd.	20.00	20.00
91-04-025	Bunny Boy W/Basket SEC-025	D. Kennicutt	Retrd.	20.00	20.00
91-04-026	Victorian Auntie Bunny SEC-026	D. Kennicutt	Retrd.	20.00	20.00
91-04-027	Baby in Buggy, Boy SEC-027	D. Kennicutt	Open	20.00	20.00
91-04-028	Fancy Find SEC-028	D. Kennicutt	Open	20.00	20.00
91-04-029	Baby in Buggy, Girl SEC-029	D. Kennicutt	Open	20.00	20.00
92-04-030	Easter Bunny w/Back Pack SEC-030	D. Kennicutt	Open	20.00	20.00
92-04-031	Grandma w/ Bible SEC-031	D. Kennicutt	Open	20.00	20.00
92-04-032	Grandpa w/Carrots SEC-032	D. Kennicutt	Open	20.00	20.00
92-04-033	Auntie Bunny w/Cake SEC-033	D. Kennicutt	Open	20.00	20.00
92-04-034	Boy Bunny w/Large Egg SEC-034	D. Kennicutt	Open	20.00	20.00
92-04-035	Girl Bunny w/Large Egg SEC-035	D. Kennicutt	Open	20.00	20.00
93-04-036	Egg Roll SEC-036	D. Kennicutt	Open	23.00	23.00
93-04-037	Grandma & Quilt SEC-037	D. Kennicutt	Open	23.00	23.00
93-04-038	Rocking Horse SEC-038	D. Kennicutt	Open	20.00	20.00
93-04-039	Girl Bunny w/Basket SEC-039	D. Kennicutt	Open	20.00	20.00
93-04-040	Christening Day SEC-040	D. Kennicutt	Open	20.00	20.00
93-04-041	Easter Bunny, Chocolate Egg SEC-041	D. Kennicutt	Open	23.00	23.00
93-04-042	Lop Ear Dying Eggs SEC-042	D. Kennicutt	Open	23.00	23.00
93-04-043	Mom Storytime SEC-043	D. Kennicutt	Open	20.00	20.00
United Design Corp.		**Backyard Birds**			
88-05-001	Bluebird, Small BB-001	S. Bradford	Open	10.00	10.00
88-05-002	Cardinal, Small BB-002	S. Bradford	Open	10.00	10.00
88-05-003	Chickadee, Small BB-003	S. Bradford	Open	10.00	10.00
88-05-004	Hummingbird Flying, Small BB-004	S. Bradford	Open	10.00	10.00
88-05-005	Hummingbird Female, Small BB-005	S. Bradford	Retrd.	10.00	10.00
88-05-006	Robin Baby, Small BB-006	S. Bradford	Open	10.00	10.00
88-05-007	Sparrow, Small BB-007	S. Bradford	Open	10.00	10.00
88-05-008	Robin Babies BB-008	S. Bradford	Open	15.00	18.00
88-05-009	Bluebird BB-009	S. Bradford	Open	15.00	20.00
88-05-010	Chickadee BB-010	S. Bradford	Open	15.00	17.00
88-05-011	Cardinal, Female BB-011	S. Bradford	Open	15.00	17.00
88-05-012	Humingbird BB-012	S. Bradford	Open	15.00	17.00
88-05-013	Cardinal, Male BB-013	S. Bradford	Open	15.00	17.00
88-05-014	Red-winged Blackbird BB-014	S. Bradford	Retrd.	15.00	16.50
88-05-015	Robin BB-015	S. Bradford	Open	15.00	20.00
88-05-016	Sparrow BB-016	S. Bradford	Open	15.00	17.00
88-05-017	Bluebird Hanging BB-017	S. Bradford	Retrd.	11.00	16.50
88-05-018	Cardinal Hanging BB-018	S. Bradford	Retrd.	11.00	11.00
88-05-019	Chickadee Hanging BB-019	S. Bradford	Retrd.	11.00	11.00
88-05-020	Robin Hanging BB-020	S. Bradford	Retrd.	11.00	11.00
88-05-021	Sparrow Hanging BB-021	S. Bradford	Retrd.	11.00	11.00
88-05-022	Hummingbird Sm., Hanging BB-022	S. Bradford	Retrd.	11.00	11.00
88-05-023	Humingbird, Lg., Hanging BB-023	S. Bradford	Retrd.	15.00	15.00
89-05-024	Baltimore Oriole BB-024	S. Bradford	Open	19.50	22.00
89-05-025	Hoot Owl BB-025	S. Bradford	Open	15.00	20.00
89-05-026	Blue Jay BB-026	S. Bradford	Open	19.50	22.00
89-05-027	Blue Jay, Baby BB-027	S. Bradford	Open	15.00	15.00
89-05-028	Goldfinch BB-028	S. Bradford	Open	16.50	20.00
89-05-029	Saw-Whet Owl BB-029	S. Bradford	Open	15.00	18.00
89-05-030	Woodpecker BB-030	S. Bradford	Open	16.50	20.00
90-05-031	Bluebird (Upright) BB-031	S. Bradford	Open	20.00	20.00
90-05-032	Cedar Waxwing BB-032	S. Bradford	Open	20.00	20.00
90-05-033	Cedar Waxwing Babies BB-033	S. Bradford	Open	22.00	22.00
90-05-034	Indigo Bunting BB-036	S. Bradford	Open	20.00	20.00
90-05-035	Indigo Bunting, Female BB-039	S. Bradford	Open	20.00	20.00
90-05-036	Nuthatch, White-throated BB-037	S. Bradford	Open	20.00	20.00
90-05-037	Painted Bunting BB-040	S. Bradford	Open	20.00	20.00
90-05-038	Painted Bunting, Female BB-041	S. Bradford	Open	20.00	20.00
90-05-039	Purple Finch BB-038	S. Bradford	Open	20.00	20.00
90-05-040	Rose Breasted Grosbeak BB-042	S. Bradford	Open	20.00	20.00
90-05-041	Evening Grosbeak BB-034	S. Bradford	Open	22.00	22.00

FIGURINES

Company / Number	Name	Series / Artist	Edition Limit	Issue Price	Quote
United Design Corp.		**PenniBears™**			
89-06-001	Bouquet Girl PB-001	P.J. Jonas	Retrd.	20.00	45-50.00
89-06-002	Honey Bear PB-002	P.J. Jonas	Retrd.	20.00	45-50.00
89-06-003	Bouquet Boy PB-003	P.J. Jonas	Retrd.	20.00	45-50.00
89-06-004	Beautiful Bride PB-004	P.J. Jonas	12/92	20.00	45-50.00
89-06-005	Butterfly Bear PB-005	P.J. Jonas	Retrd.	20.00	45-50.00
89-06-006	Cookie Bandit PB-006	P.J. Jonas	12/92	20.00	22.00
89-06-007	Baby Hugs PB-007	P.J. Jonas	12/92	20.00	22.00
89-06-008	Doctor Bear PB-008	P.J. Jonas	12/92	20.00	22.00
89-06-009	Lazy Days PB-009	P.J. Jonas	12/92	20.00	22.00
89-06-010	Petite Mademoiselle PB-010	P.J. Jonas	12/92	20.00	22.00
90-06-011	Giddiap Teddy PB-011	P.J. Jonas	Retrd.	20.00	45-50.00
90-06-012	Buttons & Bows PB-012	P.J. Jonas	Retrd.	20.00	45-50.00
90-06-013	Country Spring PB-013	P.J. Jonas	Retrd.	20.00	45-50.00
90-06-014	Garden Path PB-014	P.J. Jonas	Retrd.	20.00	45-50.00
89-06-015	Handsome Groom PB-015	P.J. Jonas	12/92	20.00	22.00
89-06-016	Nap Time PB-016	P.J. Jonas	12/92	20.00	22.00
89-06-017	Nurse Bear PB-017	P.J. Jonas	12/92	20.00	22.00
89-06-018	Birthday Bear PB-018	P.J. Jonas	12/92	20.00	24.00
89-06-019	Attic Fun PB-019	P.J. Jonas	12/92	20.00	22.00
89-06-020	Puppy Bath PB-020	P.J. Jonas	12/92	20.00	22.00
89-06-021	Puppy Love PB-021	P.J. Jonas	12/92	20.00	22.00
89-06-022	Tubby Teddy PB-022	P.J. Jonas	12/92	20.00	22.00
89-06-023	Bathtime Buddies PB-023	P.J. Jonas	12/92	20.00	22.00
89-06-024	Southern Belle PB-024	P.J. Jonas	Retrd.	20.00	45-50.00
90-06-025	Boooo Bear PB-025	P.J. Jonas	4/93	20.00	22.00
90-06-026	Sneaky Snowball PB-026	P.J. Jonas	4/93	20.00	22.00
90-06-027	Count Bearacula PB-027	P.J. Jonas	4/93	22.00	24.00
90-06-028	Dress Up Fun PB-028	P.J. Jonas	4/93	22.00	24.00
90-06-029	Scarecrow Teddy PB-029	P.J. Jonas	4/93	24.00	24.00
90-06-030	Country Quilter PB-030	P.J. Jonas	4/93	22.00	26.00
90-06-031	Santa Bear-ing Gifts PB-031	P.J. Jonas	4/93	24.00	26.00
90-06-032	Stocking Surprise PB-032	P.J. Jonas	4/93	22.00	26.00
91-06-033	Bearly Awake PB-033	P.J. Jonas	12/93	22.00	22.00
91-06-034	Lil' Mer-teddy PB-034	P.J. Jonas	12/93	24.00	24.00
91-06-035	Bump-bear-Crop PB-035	P.J. Jonas	12/93	26.00	26.00
91-06-036	Country Lullabye PB-036	P.J. Jonas	12/93	24.00	24.00
91-06-037	Bear Footin' it PB-037	P.J. Jonas	12/93	24.00	24.00
91-06-038	Windy Day PB-038	P.J. Jonas	12/93	24.00	24.00
91-06-039	Summer Sailing PB-039	P.J. Jonas	12/93	26.00	26.00
91-06-040	Goodnight Sweet Princess PB-040	P.J. Jonas	12/93	26.00	26.00
91-06-041	Goodnight Little Prince PB-041	P.J. Jonas	12/93	26.00	26.00
91-06-042	Bunny Buddies PB-042	P.J. Jonas	12/93	22.00	22.00
91-06-043	Baking Goodies PB-043	P.J. Jonas	12/93	26.00	26.00
91-06-044	Sweetheart Bears PB-044	P.J. Jonas	12/93	28.00	28.00
91-06-045	Bountiful Harvest PB-045	P.J. Jonas	4/94	24.00	24.00
91-06-046	Christmas Reinbear PB-046	P.J. Jonas	4/94	28.00	28.00
91-06-047	Pilgrim Provider PB-047	P.J. Jonas	4/94	32.00	32.00
91-06-048	Sweet Lil 'Sis PB-048	P.J. Jonas	4/94	22.00	22.00
91-06-049	Curtain Call PB-049	P.J. Jonas	4/94	24.00	24.00
91-06-050	Boo Hoo Bear PB-050	P.J. Jonas	4/94	22.00	22.00
91-06-051	Happy Hobo PB-051	P.J. Jonas	4/94	26.00	26.00
91-06-052	A Wild Ride PB-052	P.J. Jonas	4/94	26.00	26.00
92-06-053	Spanish Rose PB-053	P.J. Jonas	12/94	24.00	24.00
92-06-054	Tally Ho! PB-054	P.J. Jonas	12/94	22.00	22.00
92-06-055	Smokey's Nephew PB-055	P.J. Jonas	12/94	22.00	22.00
92-06-056	Cinderella PB-056	P.J. Jonas	12/94	22.00	22.00
92-06-057	Puddle Jumper PB-057	P.J. Jonas	12/94	24.00	24.00
92-06-058	After Every Meal PB-058	P.J. Jonas	12/94	22.00	22.00
92-06-059	Pot O' Gold PB-059	P.J. Jonas	12/94	22.00	22.00
92-06-050	"I Made It" Girl PB-060	P.J. Jonas	12/94	22.00	22.00
92-06-061	"I Made It" Boy PB-061	P.J. Jonas	12/94	22.00	22.00
92-06-062	Dust Bunny Roundup PB-062	P.J. Jonas	12/94	22.00	22.00
92-06-063	Sandbox Fun PB-063	P.J. Jonas	12/94	22.00	22.00
92-06-064	First Prom PB-064	P.J. Jonas	12/94	22.00	22.00
92-06-065	Clowning Around PB-065	P.J. Jonas	12/94	22.00	22.00
92-06-066	Batter Up PB-066	P.J. Jonas	12/94	22.00	22.00
92-06-067	Will You Be Mine? PB-067	P.J. Jonas	12/94	22.00	22.00
92-06-068	On Your Toes PB-068	P.J. Jonas	12/94	24.00	24.00
92-06-069	Apple For Teacher PB-069	P.J. Jonas	12/94	24.00	24.00
92-06-070	Downhill Thrills PB-070	P.J. Jonas	12/94	24.00	24.00
92-06-071	Lil' Devil PB-071	P.J. Jonas	12/94	24.00	24.00
92-06-072	Touchdown PB-072	P.J. Jonas	12/94	22.00	22.00
92-06-073	Bear-Capade PB-073	P.J. Jonas	12/94	22.00	22.00
92-06-074	Lil' Sis Makes Up PB-074	P.J. Jonas	12/94	22.00	22.00
92-06-075	Christmas Cookies PB-075	P.J. Jonas	12/94	22.00	22.00
92-06-076	Decorating The Wreath PB-076	P.J. Jonas	12/94	22.00	22.00
93-06-077	A Happy Camper PB-077	P.J. Jonas	12/95	28.00	28.00
93-06-078	My Forever Love PB-078	P.J. Jonas	12/95	28.00	28.00
93-06-079	Rest Stop PB-079	P.J. Jonas	12/95	24.00	24.00
93-06-080	May Joy Be Yours PB-080	P.J. Jonas	12/95	24.00	24.00
93-06-081	Santa's Helper PB-081	P.J. Jonas	12/95	28.00	28.00
93-06-082	Gotta Try Again PB-082	P.J. Jonas	12/95	24.00	24.00
93-06-083	Little Bear Peep PB-083	P.J. Jonas	12/95	24.00	24.00
93-06-084	Happy Birthday PB-084	P.J. Jonas	12/95	26.00	26.00
93-06-085	Getting 'Round On My Own PB-085	P.J. Jonas	12/95	26.00	26.00
93-06-086	Summer Belle PB-086	P.J. Jonas	12/95	24.00	24.00
93-06-087	Making It Better PB-087	P.J. Jonas	12/95	24.00	24.00
93-06-088	Big Chief Little Bear PB-088	P.J. Jonas	12/95	28.00	28.00
United Design Corp.	**PenniBears™ Collector's Club Members Only Editions**				
91-07-001	First Collection PB-C90	P.J. Jonas	Retrd.	26.00	100.00
92-07-002	Collecting Makes Cents PB-C91	P.J. Jonas	Retrd.	26.00	75.00
93-07-003	Today's Pleasures, Tomorrow's Treasures	P.J. Jonas	Yr.Iss.	26.00	50.00
United Design Corp.		**Party Animals™**			
84-08-001	Democratic Donkey ('84)	D. Kennicutt	Retrd.	14.50	16.00
84-08-002	GOP Elephant ('84)	L. Miller	Retrd.	14.50	16.00
86-08-003	Democratic Donkey ('86)	L. Miller	Retrd.	14.50	14.50
86-08-004	GOP Elephant ('86)	L. Miller	Retrd.	14.50	14.50
88-08-005	Democratic Donkey ('88)	L. Miller	Retrd.	14.50	16.00
88-08-006	GOP Elephant ('88)	L. Miller	Retrd.	14.50	16.00
90-08-007	Democratic Donkey ('90)	D. Kennicutt	Open	16.00	16.00
90-08-008	GOP Elephant ('90)	D. Kennicutt	Retrd.	16.00	16.00
92-08-009	Democratic Donkey ('92)	K. Memoli	Open	20.00	20.00
92-08-010	GOP Elephant ('92)	K. Memol	Open	20.00	20.00
United Design Corp.		**Angels Collection**			
91-09-001	Christmas Angel AA-003	S. Bradford	10,000	125.00	125.00
91-09-002	Trumpeter Angel AA-004	S. Bradford	10,000	99.00	99.00
91-09-003	Classical Angel AA-005	S. Bradford	10,000	79.00	79.00
91-09-004	Messenger of Peace AA-006	S. Bradford	10,000	75.00	75.00
91-09-005	Winter Rose Angel AA-007	S. Bradford	10,000	65.00	65.00
91-09-006	Heavenly Shepherdess AA-008	S. Bradford	10,000	99.00	99.00
91-09-007	The Gift AA-009	S. Bradford	Retrd.	135.00	300-350.
91-09-008	Victorian Cupid Angel AA-010	P.J. Jonas	Open	15.00	15.00
91-09-009	Rosetti Angel AA-011	P.J. Jonas	Open	20.00	20.00
91-09-010	Angel Waif AA-012	P.J. Jonas	Open	15.00	15.00
91-09-011	Peace Descending Angel AA-013	P.J. Jonas	Open	20.00	20.00
92-09-012	Joy To The World AA-016	D. Newburn	10,000	90.00	90.00
92-09-013	Peaceful Encounter AA-017	D. Newburn	10,000	100.00	100.00
92-09-014	The Gift '92 AA-018	S. Bradford	3,500	140.00	140.00
92-09-015	Winter Angel AA-019	D. Newburn	10,000	75.00	75.00
92-09-016	Angel, Lion & Lamb AA-020	K. Memoli	10,000	135.00	135.00
92-09-017	Angel, Lamb & Critters AA-021	S. Bradford	10,000	90.00	90.00
92-09-018	Crystal Angel AA-022	P.J. Jonas	Open	20.00	20.00
92-09-019	Rose Of Sharon AA-023	P.J. Jonas	Open	20.00	20.00
92-09-020	Victorian Angel AA-024	P.J. Jonas	Open	20.00	20.00
92-09-021	Star Glory AA-025	P.J. Jonas	Open	20.00	20.00
93-09-022	Madonna AA-031	K. Memoli	Open	65.00	65.00
93-09-023	Angel of Flight AA-032	K. Memoli	Open	79.00	79.00
93-09-024	Angel w/ Lillies-033	D. Newburn	Open	55.00	55.00
93-09-025	Angel w/ Birds AA-034	D. Newburn	Open	55.00	55.00
93-09-026	Angel w/ Leaves AA-035	D. Newburn	Open	55.00	55.00
93-09-027	The Gift '93 AA-037	S. Bradford	Open	100.00	100.00
93-09-028	Angel w/ Lillies, Dark AA-039	D. Newburn	Open	55.00	55.00
93-09-029	Angel w/ Leaves, Dark AA-041	D. Newburn	Open	55.00	55.00
United Design Corp.		**Lil' Dolls**			
91-10-001	Georgie Bear LD-001	P.J. Jonas	10,000	35.00	35.00
91-10-002	Jenny Bear LD-002	P.J. Jonas	10,000	35.00	35.00
91-10-003	Amy LD-003	D. Newburn	10,000	35.00	35.00
91-10-004	Sam LD-004	D. Newburn	10,000	35.00	35.00
91-10-005	Becky Bunny LD-005	D. Newburn	10,000	35.00	35.00
91-10-006	Nutcracker LD-006	P.J. Jonas	10,000	35.00	35.00
91-10-007	Marching In Time LD-007	D. Newburn	10,000	35.00	35.00
91-10-008	Betty Button's Surprise LD-008	Newburn/Jonas	10,000	35.00	35.00
91-10-009	Archibald Bear LD-009	P.J. Jonas	10,000	35.00	35.00
91-10-010	Angela Bear LD-010	P.J. Jonas	10,000	35.00	35.00
91-10-011	Sara LD-011	D. Newburn	10,000	35.00	35.00
91-10-012	Tom LD-012	D. Newburn	10,000	35.00	35.00
91-10-013	Addie LD-013	D. Newburn	10,000	35.00	35.00
91-10-014	Krista LD-014	D. Newburn	10,000	35.00	35.00
91-10-015	Tess LD-015	D. Newburn	10,000	35.00	35.00
92-10-016	Purr-Cila LD-016	D. Newburn	10,000	35.00	35.00
92-10-017	Clara & The Nutcracker LD-017	D. Newburn	10,000	35.00	35.00
92-10-018	Buster Button LD-018	D. Newburn	10,000	35.00	35.00
United Design Corp.		**Storytime Rhymes & Tales**			
91-11-001	Mother Goose-001	H. Henriksen	3,500	64.00	64.00
91-11-002	Mistress Mary-002	H. Henriksen	3,500	64.00	64.00
91-11-003	Simple Simon-003	H. Henriksen	3,500	90.00	90.00
91-11-004	Owl & Pussy Cat-004	H. Henriksen	3,500	100.00	100.00
91-11-005	Three Little Pigs-005	H. Henriksen	3,500	100.00	100.00
91-11-006	Little Miss Muffet-006	H. Henriksen	3,500	64.00	64.00
91-11-007	Little Jack Horner-007	H. Henriksen	3,500	50.00	50.00
91-11-008	Humpty Dumpty-008	H. Henriksen	3,500	64.00	64.00
VickiLane		**Sweet Thumpins**			
90-01-001	Venture into Sweet Thumpins	V. Anderson	2,500	60.00	73.00
91-01-002	Tea Time	V. Anderson	2,500	79.00	82.00
91-01-003	Making Memories	V. Anderson	2,500	70.00	73.00
92-01-004	Cookie Peddler	V. Anderson	1,500	90.00	90.00
VickiLane		**Mice Memories**			
90-02-001	Happiness Together	V. Anderson	2,500	65.00	73.00
Wee Forest Folk		**Bunnies**			
72-01-001	Double Bunnies B-1	A. Petersen	Closed	9.00	N/A
72-01-002	Housekeeping Bunny B-2	A. Petersen	Closed	11.00	N/A
73-01-003	Sir Rabbit B-3	W. Petersen	Closed	11.50	N/A
73-01-004	The Professor B-4	A. Petersen	Closed	12.00	N/A
73-01-005	Sunday Bunny B-5	A. Petersen	Closed	9.50	N/A
73-01-006	Broom Bunny B-6	A. Petersen	Closed	9.50	N/A
73-01-007	Muff Bunny B-7	A. Petersen	Closed	9.00	N/A
73-01-008	Market Bunny B-8	A. Petersen	Closed	9.00	N/A
77-01-009	Batter Bunny B-9	A. Petersen	Closed	17.00	275-400.
77-01-010	Tennis Bunny BS-10	A. Petersen	Closed	10.50	250-300.
78-01-011	Wedding Bunnies B-11	W. Petersen	Closed	33.50	300-600.
80-01-012	Professor Rabbit B-12	W. Petersen	Closed	16.00	400-450.
92-01-014	Windy Day B-13	D. Petersen	Open	37.00	37.00
85-01-013	Tiny Easter Bunny B-14	D. Petersen	Closed	25.00	75.00
Wee Forest Folk		**Bears**			
77-02-001	Blueberry Bears BR-1	A. Petersen	Closed	31.50	500-700.
77-02-002	Girl Blueberry Bear BR-2	A. Petersen	Closed	15.00	200-400.
77-02-003	Boy Blueberry Bear BR-3	A. Petersen	Closed	17.00	200-400.
78-02-004	Big Lady Bear BR-4	A. Petersen	Closed	16.00	N/A
78-02-005	Traveling Bear BR-5	A. Petersen	Closed	21.50	250-375.
Wee Forest Folk		**Tiny Teddies**			
83-03-001	Tiny Teddy TT-1	D. Petersen	Closed	16.00	100-200.
84-03-002	Little Teddy T-1	D. Petersen	Closed	26.00	100-150.
84-03-003	Sailor Teddy T-2	D. Petersen	Suspd.	26.00	85-125.00
84-03-004	Boo Bear T-3	D. Petersen	Suspd.	26.00	N/A
84-03-005	Drummer Bear T-4	D. Petersen	Suspd.	28.00	75.00
84-03-006	Santa Bear T-5	D. Petersen	Suspd.	33.00	150.00
85-03-007	Ride 'em Teddy! T-6	D. Petersen	Suspd.	38.00	110-135.
85-03-008	Seaside Teddy T-7	D. Petersen	Suspd.	32.00	90.00
86-03-009	Huggy Bear T-8	D. Petersen	Suspd.	26.00	N/A
87-03-010	Wedding Bears T-9	D. Petersen	Suspd.	54.00	145.00
87-03-011	Christmas Teddy T-10	D. Petersen	Suspd.	26.00	85.00
88-03-012	Hansel & Gretel Bears@Witch's House T-11	D. Petersen	Suspd.	175.00	245.00
89-03-013	Momma Bear T-12	D. Petersen	Suspd.	27.00	36.00
Wee Forest Folk		**Fairy Tale Series**			
80-04-001	Red Riding Hood & Wolf FT-1	A. Petersen	Closed	34.00	850-1300.
80-04-002	Red Riding Hood FT-2	A. Petersen	Closed	14.00	250-400.
Wee Forest Folk		**Wind in the Willows**			
82-05-001	Mole WW-1	A. Petersen	Closed	18.00	200-300.
82-05-002	Badger WW-2	A. Petersen	Closed	18.00	200-300.
82-05-003	Toad WW-3	W. Petersen	Closed	18.00	200-300.
82-05-004	Ratty WW-4	A. Petersen	Closed	18.00	200-300.

Company Number	Name	Series Artist	Edition Limit	Issue Price	Quote
Wee Forest Folk		**Frogs**			
74-06-001	Prince Charming F-1	W. Petersen	Closed	7.50	N/A
74-06-002	Frog on Rock F-2	A. Petersen	Closed	6.00	N/A
77-06-003	Frog Friends F-3	W. Petersen	Closed	17.50	N/A
77-06-004	Spring Peepers F-4	A. Petersen	Closed	9.00	N/A
77-06-005	Grampa Frog F-5	W. Petersen	Closed	17.50	N/A
78-06-006	Singing Frog F-6	A. Petersen	Closed	12.00	N/A
Wee Forest Folk		**Owls**			
74-07-001	Mr. and Mrs. Owl O-1	A. Petersen	Closed	19.00	300-375.
74-07-002	Mrs. Owl O-2	A. Petersen	Closed	8.50	100-200.
74-07-003	Mr. Owl O-3	A. Petersen	Closed	10.50	100-200.
75-07-004	Colonial Owls O-4	A. Petersen	Closed	11.50	N/A
79-07-005	"Grad" Owl O-5	W. Petersen	Closed	12.50	N/A
80-07-006	Graduate Owl O-6	W. Petersen	Closed	12.00	N/A
Wee Forest Folk		**Raccoons**			
77-08-001	Mother Raccoon RC-1	A. Petersen	Closed	11.50	300-450.
77-08-002	Hiker Raccoon RC-2	A. Petersen	Closed	12.00	325-475.
78-08-003	Bird Watcher Raccoon RC-3	A. Petersen	Closed	22.50	350-425.
78-08-004	Raccoon Skater RCS-1	A. Petersen	Closed	12.00	200-400.
78-08-005	Raccoon Skier RCS-2	A. Petersen	Closed	14.00	300-450.
Wee Forest Folk		**Foxes**			
77-09-001	Fancy Fox FX-1	A. Petersen	Closed	10.00	325-450.
77-09-002	Dandy Fox FX-2	A. Petersen	Closed	12.50	N/A
78-09-003	Barrister Fox FX-3	A. Petersen	Closed	21.00	450.00
Wee Forest Folk		**Piggies**			
78-10-001	Miss Piggy School Marm P-1	A. Petersen	Closed	12.00	225-300.
78-10-002	Piggy Baker P-2	A. Petersen	Closed	14.50	225-400.
78-10-003	Jolly Tar Piggy P-3	A. Petersen	Closed	10.00	175-225.
78-10-004	Picnic Piggies P-4	A. Petersen	Closed	24.00	200-300.
78-10-005	Girl Piglet/Picnic Piggy P-5	A. Petersen	Closed	12.00	100-125.
78-10-006	Boy Piglet/ Picnic Piggy P-6	A. Petersen	Closed	12.00	100-125.
78-10-007	Piggy Jogger PS-1	A. Petersen	Closed	13.50	125-200.
80-10-008	Piggy Ballerina P-7	A. Petersen	Closed	15.50	175-250.
80-10-009	Piggy Policeman P-8	A. Petersen	Closed	17.50	200-325.
80-10-010	Pig O' My Heart P-9	A. Petersen	Closed	13.50	175-250.
80-10-011	Nurse Piggy P-10	A. Petersen	Closed	15.50	200-250.
81-10-012	Holly Hog P-11	A. Petersen	Closed	25.00	300-400.
Wee Forest Folk		**Animals**			
73-11-001	Miss Ducky D-1	A. Petersen	Closed	8.00	N/A
74-11-002	Miss Hippo H-1	A. Petersen	Closed	8.00	N/A
74-11-003	Baby Hippo H-2	A. Petersen	Closed	7.00	N/A
74-11-004	Miss and Baby Hippo H-3	A. Petersen	Closed	15.00	N/A
75-11-005	Seedy Rat R-1	A. Petersen	Closed	11.50	200-350.
75-11-006	"Doc" Rat R-2.	W. Petersen	Closed	12.00	200-350.
77-11-007	Nutsy Squirrel SQ-1	W. Petersen	Closed	6.00	N/A
78-11-008	Beaver Wood Cutter BV-1	W. Petersen	Closed	23.00	225-450.
78-11-009	Mole Scout MO-1	A. Petersen	Closed	9.00	225-375.
79-11-010	Turtle Jogger TS-1	A. Petersen	Closed	9.00	N/A
Wee Forest Folk		**Mouse Sports**			
75-12-001	Bobsled Three MS-1	A. Petersen	Closed	12.00	N/A
75-12-002	Skater Mouse MS-2	A. Petersen	Closed	14.00	300-500.
76-12-003	Mouse Skier MS-3	A. Petersen	Closed	12.50	250-400.
76-12-004	Tennis Star MS-4	A. Petersen	Closed	7.50	100-275.
76-12-005	Tennis Star MS-5	A. Petersen	Closed	10.50	100-275.
77-12-006	Skating Star Mouse MS-6	A. Petersen	Closed	9.00	250-400.
77-12-007	Golfer Mouse MS-7	A. Petersen	Closed	15.50	350-700.
80-12-008	Skater Mouse MS-8	A. Petersen	Closed	18.00	375-600.
80-12-009	Skier Mouse MS-9	A. Petersen	Open	13.00	35.00
81-12-010	Golfer Mouse MS-10	A. Petersen	Closed	17.00	200-350.
82-12-011	Two in a Canoe MS-11	W. Petersen	Open	29.00	56.00
84-12-012	Land Ho! MS-12	A. Petersen	Closed	46.00	200-300.
84-12-013	Tennis Anyone? MS-13	A. Petersen	Closed	18.00	100-130.
85-12-014	Fishin' Chip MS-14	W. Petersen	Closed	46.00	125-150.
89-12-015	Joe Di'Mousio MS-15	A. Petersen	Open	39.00	43.00
Wee Forest Folk		**Forest Scene**			
88-13-001	Woodland Serenade FS-1	W. Petersen	Open	125.00	130.00
89-13-002	Hearts and Flowers FS-2	W. Petersen	Open	110.00	112.00
90-13-003	Mousie Comes A-Calling FS-3	W. Petersen	Open	128.00	130.00
91-13-004	Mountain Stream FS-4	W. Petersen	Open	128.00	130.00
92-13-005	Love Letter FS-5	W. Petersen	Open	98.00	98.00
Wee Forest Folk		**Mice**			
72-14-001	Miss Mouse M-1	A. Petersen	Closed	8.00	300-350.
72-14-002	Market Mouse M-1a	A. Petersen	Closed	8.00	57.00
72-14-003	Miss Mousey M-2	A. Petersen	Closed	7.50	N/A
72-14-004	Miss Mousey Straw Hat M-2a	A. Petersen	Closed	8.00	225-325.
72-14-005	Miss Mousey Bow Hat M-2b	A. Petersen	Closed	8.00	N/A
73-14-006	Miss Nursey M-3	A. Petersen	Closed	7.50	200-400.
74-14-007	Good Knight Mouse M-4	W. Petersen	Closed	7.50	N/A
74-14-008	Farmer Mouse M-5	A. Petersen	Closed	7.00	N/A
74-14-009	Wood Sprite M-6a	A. Petersen	Closed	7.50	300-550.
74-14-010	Wood Sprite M-6b	A. Petersen	Closed	7.50	300-550.
74-14-011	Wood Sprite M-6c	A. Petersen	Closed	7.50	300-550.
75-14-012	Two Mice with Candle M-7	A. Petersen	Closed	8.00	300-400.
75-14-013	Two Tiny Mice M-8	A. Petersen	Closed	7.50	300-500.
75-14-014	Bride Mouse M-9	A. Petersen	Closed	7.50	375-500.
76-14-015	Fan Mouse M-10	A. Petersen	Closed	10.50	N/A
76-14-016	Tea Mouse M-11	A. Petersen	Closed	10.50	N/A
76-14-017	May Belle M-12	A. Petersen	Closed	8.00	225-425.
76-14-018	June Belle M-13	A. Petersen	Closed	7.50	225-425.
76-14-019	Nightie Mouse M-14	A. Petersen	Closed	9.50	300-500.
76-14-020	Mrs. Mousey M-15	A. Petersen	Closed	8.00	N/A
76-14-021	Mrs. Mousey with Hat M-15a	A. Petersen	Closed	8.50	N/A
76-14-022	Mouse with Muff M-16	A. Petersen	Closed	9.00	N/A
76-14-023	Shawl Mouse M-17	A. Petersen	Closed	9.00	N/A
76-14-024	Mama Mouse with Baby M-18	A. Petersen	Closed	12.00	325-450.
77-14-025	King "Tut" Mouse TM-1	A. Petersen	Closed	9.50	450-600.
77-14-026	Queen "Tut" Mouse TM-2	A. Petersen	Closed	9.50	450-600.
77-14-027	Baby Sitter M-19	A. Petersen	Closed	9.50	225-325.
78-14-028	Bridge Club Mouse M-20	A. Petersen	Closed	12.00	N/A
78-14-029	Bridge Club Mouse Partner M-21	A. Petersen	Closed	12.00	N/A
78-14-030	Secretary, Miss Spell/Miss Pell M-22	A. Petersen	Closed	9.50	375-400.
78-14-031	Picnic Mice M-23	W. Petersen	Closed	14.50	325-400.
78-14-032	Wedding Mice M-24	W. Petersen	Closed	15.00	375-550.
78-14-033	Cowboy Mouse M-25	A. Petersen	Closed	12.00	300-500.
78-14-034	Chief Nip-a-Way Mouse M-26	A. Petersen	Closed	14.00	300-400.
78-14-035	Pirate Mouse M-27	A. Petersen	Closed	13.00	300-700.
78-14-036	Town Crier Mouse M-28	A. Petersen	Closed	10.50	N/A
79-14-037	Mouse Duet M-29	A. Petersen	Closed	25.00	550-700.
79-14-038	Mouse Pianist M-30	A. Petersen	Closed	17.00	300-500.
79-14-039	Mouse Violinist M-31	A. Petersen	Closed	9.00	200-350.
79-14-040	Chris-Miss M-32	A. Petersen	Closed	9.00	200-350.
79-14-041	Chris-Mouse M-33	A. Petersen	Closed	9.00	250-350.
79-14-042	Mousey Baby, heart book M-34	A. Petersen	Closed	9.50	250-375.
79-14-043	Rock-a-bye Baby Mouse M-35	A. Petersen	Closed	17.00	300-450.
79-14-044	Raggedy and Mouse M-36	A. Petersen	Closed	12.00	250-350.
79-14-045	Gardener Mouse M-37	A. Petersen	Closed	12.00	375-400.
79-14-046	Mouse Ballerina M-38	A. Petersen	Closed	12.50	N/A
79-14-047	Mouse Artiste M-39	A. Petersen	Closed	12.50	300-525.
80-14-048	Miss Bobbin M-40	A. Petersen	Open	22.00	54.00
80-14-049	Fishermouse M-41	A. Petersen	Closed	16.00	450-650.
80-14-050	Commo-Dormouse M-42	W. Petersen	Closed	14.00	500-700.
80-14-051	Santa Mouse M-43	A. Petersen	Closed	12.50	200-250.
80-14-052	Witch Mouse M-44	A. Petersen	Closed	12.00	125-200.
80-14-053	Miss Teach M-45	A. Petersen	Closed	18.00	350-450.
80-14-054	Miss Polly Mouse M-46	A. Petersen	Closed	23.00	300-450.
80-14-055	Pirate Mouse M-47	W. Petersen	Closed	16.00	800-900.
80-14-056	Photographer Mouse M-48	W. Petersen	Closed	23.00	400-700.
80-14-057	Carpenter Mouse M-49	A. Petersen	Closed	15.00	375-450.
80-14-058	Mrs. Tidy and Helper M-50	A. Petersen	Closed	24.00	450-650.
80-14-059	Mrs. Tidy M-51	A. Petersen	Closed	19.50	350-450.
81-14-060	Mother's Helper M-52	A. Petersen	Closed	11.00	200-300.
81-14-061	Flower Girl M-53	A. Petersen	Closed	15.00	275-350.
81-14-062	Nurse Mousey M-54	A. Petersen	Closed	14.00	200-400.
81-14-063	Doc Mouse & Patient M-55	W. Petersen	Closed	14.00	500.00
81-14-064	School Marm Mouse M-56	A. Petersen	Closed	19.50	450-550.
81-14-065	Barrister Mouse M-57	A. Petersen	Closed	16.00	400-495.
81-14-066	Graduate Mouse M-58	A. Petersen	Closed	15.00	75-125.00
81-14-067	Pearl Knit Mouse M-59	A. Petersen	Closed	20.00	200-250.
81-14-068	Mom and Squeaky Clean M-60	A. Petersen	Open	27.00	51.00
81-14-069	Little Devil M-61	A. Petersen	Open	12.50	26.00
81-14-070	Blue Devil M-61	A. Petersen	Closed	12.50	N/A
81-14-071	Little Ghost M-62	A. Petersen	Open	8.50	19.00
81-14-072	The Carolers M-63	A. Petersen	Closed	29.00	300-450.
81-14-073	Lone Caroler M-64	A. Petersen	Closed	15.50	375-500.
81-14-074	Mousey Express M-65	A. Petersen	Open	22.00	48.00
82-14-075	Baby Sitter M-66	A. Petersen	Open	23.50	41.00
82-14-076	Wedding Mice M-67	W. Petersen	Open	29.50	54.00
82-14-077	Office Mousey M-68	A. Petersen	Closed	23.00	300-400.
82-14-078	Beddy-bye Mousey M-69	A. Petersen	Open	29.00	48.00
82-14-079	Me and Raggedy Ann M-70	A. Petersen	Open	18.50	32.00
82-14-080	Arty Mouse M-71	A. Petersen	Closed	19.00	50-100.
82-14-081	Say "Cheese" M-72	W. Petersen	Closed	15.50	250-450.
82-14-082	Miss Teach & Pupil M-73	A. Petersen	Closed	29.50	350-575.
82-14-083	Tea for Two M-74	A. Petersen	Closed	26.00	300-400.
82-14-084	Mousey's Teddy M-75	A. Petersen	Closed	29.00	300-375.
82-14-085	Beach Mousey M-76	A. Petersen	Open	19.00	32.00
82-14-086	Little Fire Chief M-77	W. Petersen	Closed	29.00	350-475.
82-14-087	Moon Mouse M-78	A. Petersen	Closed	15.50	375-450.
82-14-088	Sweethearts M-79	A. Petersen	Closed	26.00	375-500.
82-14-089	Girl Sweetheart M-80	A. Petersen	Open	13.50	21.00
82-14-090	Boy Sweetheart M-81	A. Petersen	Closed	13.50	300-350.
82-14-091	Easter Bunny Mouse M-82	A. Petersen	Open	18.00	31.00
82-14-092	Happy Birthday! M-83	A. Petersen	Open	17.50	30.00
82-14-093	Snowmouse & Friend M-84	A. Petersen	Closed	23.50	300-450.
82-14-094	Little Sledders M-85	A. Petersen	Closed	33.50	175-275.
82-14-095	Lamplight Carolers M-86	A. Petersen	Closed	46.00	225-350.
82-14-096	Holly Mouse M-87	A. Petersen	Open	13.50	26.00
82-14-097	Littlest Angel M-88	A. Petersen	Closed	15.00	100.00
82-14-098	Poorest Angel M-89	A. Petersen	Closed	15.00	85-100.00
83-14-099	Merry Chris-Miss M-90	A. Petersen	Closed	17.50	150-250.
83-14-100	Merry Chris-Mouse M-91	A. Petersen	Closed	16.00	150-250.
83-14-101	Christmas Morning M-92	A. Petersen	Closed	35.00	175-350.
83-14-102	First Christmas M-93	A. Petersen	Closed	16.00	200-350.
83-14-103	Cupid Mouse M-94	W. Petersen	Open	22.00	36.00
83-14-104	Mousey Nurse M-95	A. Petersen	Open	15.00	25.00
83-14-105	Get Well Soon! M-96	A. Petersen	Closed	15.00	225-350.
83-14-106	Mouse Call M-97	W. Petersen	Closed	24.00	250-400.
83-14-107	Clown Mouse M-98	A. Petersen	Closed	22.00	250-350.
83-14-108	Birthday Girl M-99	A. Petersen	Open	18.50	29.00
83-14-109	Mousey's Cone M-100	A. Petersen	Open	22.00	33.00
83-14-110	Mousey's Tricycle M-101	A. Petersen	Open	24.00	42.00
83-14-111	Mousey's Dollhouse M-102	A. Petersen	Closed	30.00	275-475.
83-14-112	Rocking Tot M-103	A. Petersen	Closed	19.50	50-100.00
83-14-113	Harvest Mouse M-104	W. Petersen	Closed	23.00	250-350.
83-14-114	Wash Day M-105	A. Petersen	Closed	23.00	300-400
83-14-115	Pack Mouse M-106	W. Petersen	Closed	19.00	280-375.
83-14-116	Chief Geronimouse M-107a	A. Petersen	Open	21.00	37.00
83-14-117	Running Doe/Little Deer M-107b	A. Petersen	Open	35.00	39.00
83-14-118	Rope 'em Mousey M-108	A. Petersen	Closed	19.00	200-350.
84-14-119	Campfire Mouse M-109	W. Petersen	Closed	26.00	300-395.
84-14-120	Traveling Mouse M-110	A. Petersen	Closed	28.00	225-275.
84-14-121	Spring Gardener M-111	A. Petersen	Open	26.00	38.00
84-14-122	First Day of School M-112	A. Petersen	Closed	27.00	350-550.
84-14-123	Tidy Mouse M-113	A. Petersen	Closed	38.00	300-400.
84-14-124	Pen Pal Mousey M-114	A. Petersen	Closed	26.00	350-400.
84-14-125	Mom & Ginger Baker M-115	W. Petersen	Open	38.00	58.00
84-14-126	Santa's Trainee M-116	W. Petersen	Closed	36.50	375-475.
84-14-127	Chris-Mouse Pageant M-117	A. Petersen	Open	38.00	52.00
84-14-128	Peter's Pumpkin M-118	A. Petersen	Closed	19.00	64-66.00
84-14-129	Prudence Pie Maker M-119	A. Petersen	Closed	18.50	58-66.00
84-14-130	Witchy Boo! M-120	A. Petersen	Open	21.00	33.00
85-14-131	Pageant Wiseman M-121	A. Petersen	Closed	58.00	125-200.
85-14-132	Wise Man with Turban M-121a	A. Petersen	Open	28.00	32.00
85-14-133	Wise Man in Robe M-121b	A. Petersen	Open	26.00	31.00
85-14-134	Wise Man Kneeling M-121c	A. Petersen	Open	29.00	34.00
85-14-135	Pageant Shepherds M-122	A. Petersen	Closed	35.00	100-200.
85-14-136	Shepherd Kneeling M-122a	A. Petersen	Open	20.00	26.00
85-14-137	Shepherd Standing M-122b	A. Petersen	Open	20.00	26.00
85-14-138	Under the Chris-Mouse Tree M-123	A. Petersen	Open	48.00	71.00
85-14-139	Chris-Mouse Tree M-124	A. Petersen	Open	28.00	42.00
85-14-140	Quilting Bee M-125	W. Petersen	Open	30.00	39.00
85-14-141	Attic Treasure M-126	A. Petersen	Open	42.00	54.00
85-14-142	Family Portrait M-127	A. Petersen	Closed	54.00	200-275.
85-14-143	Strolling with Baby M-128	A. Petersen	Open	42.00	54.00
85-14-144	Piggy-Back Mousey M-129	W. Petersen	Closed	28.00	250-395.
85-14-145	Mouse Talk M-130	A. Petersen	Open	44.00	58.00
85-14-146	Come Play! M-131	A. Petersen	Closed	18.00	50-100.00
85-14-147	Sunday Drivers M-132	W. Petersen	Open	58.00	108.00

Number	Name	Artist	Edition Limit	Issue Price	Quote
85-14-148	Field Mouse M-133	W. Petersen	Open	46.00	79.00
86-14-149	First Date M-134	W. Petersen	Open	60.00	64.00
86-14-150	Waltzing Matilda M-135	W. Petersen	Open	48.00	51.00
86-14-151	Sweet Dreams M-136	A. Petersen	Closed	58.00	100-150.
86-14-152	First Haircut M-137	W. Petersen	Closed	58.00	110-135.
86-14-153	Fun Float M-138	W. Petersen	Open	34.00	36.00
86-14-154	Mouse on Campus M-139	W. Petersen	Closed	25.00	100.00
86-14-155	Just Checking M-140	A. Petersen	Open	34.00	38.00
86-14-156	Come & Get It! M-141	A. Petersen	Closed	34.00	100-165.
86-14-157	Christ-Mouse Stocking M-142	A. Petersen	Open	34.00	38.00
86-14-158	Down the Chimney M-143	A. Petersen	Closed	48.00	200-295.
87-14-159	Pageant Stable M-144	A. Petersen	Open	56.00	65.00
87-14-160	Pageant Angel M-145	A. Petersen	Open	19.00	23.00
87-14-161	Miss Noel M-146	A. Petersen	Open	32.00	37.00
87-14-162	Choir Mouse M-147	W. Petersen	Closed	23.00	65.00
87-14-163	Tooth Fairy M-148	A. Petersen	Open	32.00	36.00
87-14-164	Don't Cry! M-149	A. Petersen	Closed	33.00	50-70.00
87-14-165	Market Mouse M-150	W. Petersen	Open	49.00	57.00
87-14-166	The Red Wagon M-151	W. Petersen	Closed	59.00	125-175.
87-14-167	Scooter Mouse M-152	W. Petersen	Open	38.00	38.00
87-14-168	Trumpeter M-153a	W. Petersen	Closed	29.00	50-90.00
87-14-169	Drummer M-153b	W. Petersen	Closed	29.00	50-90.00
87-14-170	Tuba Player M-153c	W. Petersen	Closed	29.00	50-90.00
87-14-171	Bat Mouse M-154	A. Petersen	Open	25.00	29.00
87-14-172	Littlest Witch and Skeleton M-155	A. Petersen	Open	49.00	56.00
87-14-173	Littlest Witch M-156	A. Petersen	Open	24.00	28.00
87-14-174	Skeleton Mousey M-157	A. Petersen	Open	27.00	31.00
88-14-175	Aloha! M-158	A. Petersen	Open	32.00	36.00
88-14-176	Forty Winks M-159	W. Petersen	Open	36.00	41.00
88-14-177	Mousey's Easter Basket M-160	A. Petersen	Open	32.00	36.00
89-14-178	Commencement Day M-161	W. Petersen	Open	28.00	31.00
89-14-179	Prima Ballerina M-162	A. Petersen	Open	35.00	38.00
89-14-180	Elf Tales M-163	A. Petersen	Open	48.00	49.00
89-14-181	Father Chris-Mouse M-164	A. Petersen	Open	34.00	36.00
89-14-182	Haunted Mouse House M-165	D. Petersen	Open	125.00	165.00
90-14-183	Chris-Mouse Slipper M-166	A. Petersen	Open	35.00	37.00
90-14-184	Colleen O'Green M-167	A. Petersen	Open	40.00	42.00
90-14-185	Stars & Stripes M-168	A. Petersen	Open	34.00	36.00
90-14-186	Hans & Greta M-169	A. Petersen	Closed	64.00	100-125.
90-14-187	Polly's Parasol M-170	A. Petersen	Open	39.00	42.00
90-14-188	Zelda M-171	A. Petersen	Open	37.00	41.00
91-14-189	Red Riding Hood at Grandmother's House M-172	D. Petersen	Open	295.00	295.00
91-14-190	Silent Night M-173	A. Petersen	Open	64.00	68.00
91-14-191	The Nutcracker M-174	A. Petersen	Open	49.00	52.00
91-14-192	Mousie's Egg Factory M-175	A. Petersen	Open	73.00	78.00
91-14-193	Grammy-Phone M-176	A. Petersen	Open	75.00	79.00
91-14-194	Tea For Three M-177	D. Petersen	Open	135.00	145.00
91-14-195	Night Prayer M-178	A. Petersen	Open	52.00	56.00
91-14-196	Sea Sounds M-179	A. Petersen	Open	34.00	36.00
91-14-197	April Showers M-180	A. Petersen	Open	27.00	29.00
91-14-198	Little Squirt M-181	W. Petersen	Open	49.00	51.00
92-14-199	Miss Daisy M-182	A. Petersen	Open	42.00	42.00
92-14-200	Peekaboo! M-183	A. Petersen	Open	52.00	52.00
92-14-201	Mrs. Mousey's Studio M-184	W. Petersen	Open	150.00	150.00
92-14-202	The Old Black Stove M-185	A. Petersen	Open	130.00	130.00
92-14-203	High on the Hog M-186	A. Petersen	Open	52.00	52.00
92-14-204	Adam's Apples M-187	A. Petersen	Open	148.00	148.00
92-14-205	Snow Buddies M-188	D. Petersen	Open	58.00	58.00
Wee Forest Folk		**Christmas Carol Series**			
87-15-001	Scrooge CC-1	A. Petersen	Open	23.00	29.00
87-15-002	Bob Cratchit and Tiny Tim CC-2	A. Petersen	Open	36.00	43.00
87-15-003	Marley's Ghost CC-3	A. Petersen	Open	24.00	30.00
87-15-004	Ghost of Christmas Past CC-4	A. Petersen	Open	24.00	30.00
87-15-005	Ghost of Christmas Present CC-5	A. Petersen	Open	54.00	60.00
87-15-006	Ghost of Christmas Yet to Come CC-6	A. Petersen	Open	24.00	29.00
88-15-007	The Fezziwigs CC-7	A. Petersen	Open	65.00	79.00
Wee Forest Folk		**Cinderella Series**			
88-16-001	Cinderella's Slipper C-1	A. Petersen	Closed	62.00	150-200.
89-16-002	Cinderella's Slipper C-1a	A. Petersen	Open	32.00	36.00
88-16-003	The Ugly Stepsisters C-2	A. Petersen	Open	62.00	68.00
88-16-004	The Mean Stepmother C-3	A. Petersen	Open	32.00	38.00
88-16-005	The Flower Girls C-4	A. Petersen	Open	42.00	51.00
88-16-006	Cinderella's Wedding C-5	A. Petersen	Open	62.00	72.00
88-16-007	Flower Girl C-6	A. Petersen	Open	22.00	27.00
89-16-008	The Fairy Godmother C-7	A. Petersen	Open	69.00	81.00
Wee Forest Folk		**Robin Hood Series**			
90-17-001	Robin Hood RH-1	A. Petersen	Open	37.00	39.00
90-17-002	Maid Marion RH-2	A. Petersen	Open	32.00	34.00
90-17-003	Friar Tuck RH-3	A. Petersen	Open	32.00	34.00
Wee Forest Folk		**Limited Edition**			
81-18-001	Beauty and the Beast BB-1	W. Petersen	Closed	89.00	N/A
84-18-002	Postmouster LTD-1	W. Petersen	Closed	46.00	500-750.
85-18-002	Helping Hand LTD-2	A. Petersen	Closed	62.00	500-650.
87-18-003	Statue in the Park LTD-3	W. Petersen	Closed	93.00	400-750.
88-18-004	Uncle Sammy LTD-4	A. Petersen	Closed	85.00	150-295.
Wee Forest Folk		**Minutemice**			
74-19-001	Mouse on Drum with Fife MM-1	A. Petersen	Closed	9.00	N/A
74-19-002	Mouse on Drum with Fife Wood Base MM-1a	A. Petersen	Closed	9.00	N/A
74-19-003	Mouse on Drum with Black Hat MM-2	A. Petersen	Closed	9.00	N/A
74-19-004	Mouse Carrying Large Drum MM-3	A. Petersen	Closed	8.00	N/A
74-19-005	Concordian On Drum with Glasses MM-4	A. Petersen	Closed	9.00	N/A
74-19-006	Concordian Wood Base w/Tan Coat MM-4a	A. Petersen	Closed	7.50	N/A
74-19-007	Concordian Wood Base w/Hat MM-4b	A. Petersen	Closed	8.00	N/A
74-19-008	Little Fifer on Drum with Fife MM-5	A. Petersen	Closed	8.00	N/A
74-19-009	Little Fifer on Wood Base MM-5a	A. Petersen	Closed	8.00	N/A
74-19-010	Little Fifer on Drum MM-5b	A. Petersen	Closed	8.00	N/A
79-19-011	Minute Mouse and Red Coat MM-9	W. Petersen	Open	28.00	28.00
79-19-012	Concord Minute Mouse MM-10	W. Petersen	Open	14.00	14.00
79-19-013	Red Coat Mouse MM-11	W. Petersen	Open	14.00	14.00
Wee Forest Folk		**Single Issues**			
72-20-001	Party Mouse in Sailor Suit	A. Petersen	Closed	N/A	N/A
72-20-002	Party Mouse with Bow Tie	A. Petersen	Closed	N/A	N/A
72-20-003	Party Mouse in Plain Dress	A. Petersen	Closed	N/A	N/A
72-20-004	Party Mouse in Polka-Dot Dress	A. Petersen	Closed	N/A	N/A
79-20-005	Ezra Ripley	A. Petersen	Open	40.00	40.00
79-20-006	Sarah Ripley	A. Petersen	Open	48.00	48.00
80-20-007	Cave Mouse	W. Petersen	Closed	N/A	500-600.
80-20-008	Cave Mouse with Baby	W. Petersen	Closed	26.00	N/A
83-20-009	Wee Forest Folk Display Piece	A. Petersen	Open	70.00	70.00

GRAPHICS

Number	Name	Artist	Edition Limit	Issue Price	Quote
American Legacy		**Etem**			
XX-01-001	Indiana Summer	S. Etem	Closed	150.00	150.00
XX-01-002	Little Bandit	S. Etem	Closed	150.00	150.00
XX-01-003	The Fountain	S. Etem	Closed	150.00	150.00
Anna-Perenna Porcelain		**Krumeich Hector's Window**			
XX-01-001	Genuine Stone Litho	T. Krumeich	325	175.00	225.00
XX-01-002	13-Color Litho, framed	T. Krumeich	995	95.00	95.00
Artaffects		**Perillo**			
77-01-001	Madre, S/N	G. Perillo	500	125.00	250-950.
78-01-002	Madonna of the Plains, S/N	G. Perillo	500	125.00	200-600.
78-01-003	Snow Pals, S/N	G. Perillo	500	125.00	150-550.
79-01-004	Sioux Scout and Buffalo Hunt, matched set	G. Perillo	500	150.00	250-850.
80-01-005	Babysitter, S/N	G. Perillo	3,000	45.00	125-350.
80-01-006	Puppies, S/N	G. Perillo	3,000	45.00	200-450.
81-01-007	Peaceable Kingdom, S/N	G. Perillo	950	100.00	375-800.
82-01-008	Tinker, S/N	G. Perillo	3,000	45.00	100-350.
82-01-009	Tender Love, S/N	G. Perillo	950	75.00	125-450.
82-01-010	Lonesome Cowboy, S/N	G. Perillo	950	75.00	100-450.
82-01-011	Chief Pontiac, S/N	G. Perillo	950	75.00	100.00
82-01-012	Hoofbeats, S/N	G. Perillo	950	100.00	150.00
82-01-013	Indian Style, S/N	G. Perillo	950	75.00	100.00
82-01-014	Maria, S/N	G. Perillo	550	150.00	350.00
82-01-015	Papoose, S/N	G. Perillo	950	125.00	125.00
83-01-016	The Moment Poster, S/N	G. Perillo	495	20.00	60.00
84-01-017	Out of the Forest, S/N	G. Perillo	Unkn.	Unkn.	450.00
84-01-018	Navajo Love, S/N	G. Perillo	300	125.00	700.00
85-01-019	Chief Crazy Horse, S/N	G. Perillo	950	125.00	450.00
85-01-020	Chief Sitting Bull, S/N	G. Perillo	500	125.00	350.00
85-01-021	Marigold, S/N	G. Perillo	500	125.00	150-450.
85-01-022	Whirlaway, S/N	G. Perillo	950	125.00	150.00
85-01-023	Secretariat, S/N	G. Perillo	950	125.00	150.00
86-01-024	The Rescue, S/N	G. Perillo	325	150.00	200-550.
86-01-025	War Pony, S/N	G. Perillo	325	150.00	250.00
86-01-026	Learning His Ways, S/N	G. Perillo	325	150.00	250.00
86-01-027	The Pout, S/N	G. Perillo	325	150.00	200-450.
88-01-028	Magnificent Seven, S/N	G. Perillo	950	125.00	125.00
88-01-029	By the Stream, S/N	G. Perillo	950	100.00	150.00
90-01-030	The Pack, S/N	G. Perillo	950	150.00	250.00
Artaffects		**Grand Gallery Collection (Framed)**			
88-02-001	Tender Love	G. Perillo	2,500	75.00	90.00
88-02-002	Brave & Free	G. Perillo	2,500	75.00	175.00
88-02-003	Noble Heritage	G. Perillo	2,500	75.00	90.00
88-02-004	Chief Crazy Horse	G. Perillo	2,500	75.00	90.00
88-02-005	The Cheyenne Nation	G. Perillo	2,500	75.00	90.00
88-02-006	Late Mail	G. Perillo	2,500	75.00	90.00
88-02-007	The Peaceable Kingdom	G. Perillo	2,500	75.00	100.00
88-02-008	Chief Red Cloud	G. Perillo	2,500	75.00	90.00
88-02-009	The Last Frontier	G. Perillo	2,500	75.00	95.00
88-02-010	Native American	G. Perillo	2,500	75.00	90.00
88-02-011	Blackfoot Hunter	G. Perillo	2,500	75.00	90.00
88-02-012	Lily of the Mohawks	G. Perillo	2,500	75.00	90.00
88-02-013	Amy	MaGo	2,500	75.00	90.00
88-02-014	Mischief	MaGo	2,500	75.00	90.00
88-02-015	Tomorrows	MaGo	2,500	75.00	90.00
88-02-016	Lauren	MaGo	2,500	75.00	90.00
88-02-017	Visiting the Doctor	R. Sauber	2,500	75.00	90.00
88-02-018	Home Sweet Home	R. Sauber	2,500	75.00	90.00
88-02-019	God Bless America	R. Sauber	2,500	75.00	90.00
88-02-020	The Wedding	R. Sauber	2,500	75.00	90.00
88-02-021	Motherhood	R. Sauber	2,500	75.00	90.00
88-02-022	Venice	L. Marchetti	2,500	75.00	90.00
88-02-023	Paris	L. Marchetti	2,500	75.00	90.00
Artaffects		**Captured On Canvas**			
91-03-001	Brave and Free	G. Perillo	Open	195.00	195.00
Artaffects		**Members Only Limited Edition Redemption Offerings**			
84-04-001	Out of the Forest (Litho)	G. Perillo	Yr.Iss.	50.00	50.00
Artaffects		**Limited Edition Free Gifts to Members**			
83-05-001	Perillo/Cougar (Poster)	G. Perillo	Yr.Iss.	Gift	N/A
85-05-002	Litte Plum Blossom (Poster)	G. Perillo	Yr.Iss.	Gift	N/A
Artaffects		**Sauber**			
82-06-001	Butterfly	R. Sauber	3,000	45.00	100.00
Artaffects		**Mago**			
88-07-001	Serenity	Mago	950	95.00	200.00
88-07-002	Beth	Mago	950	95.00	200.00
88-07-003	Jessica	Mago	550	225.00	325.00
88-07-004	Sebastian	Mago	Pair	Pair	Pair
Artaffects		**Deneen**			
88-08-001	Twentieth Century Limited	J. Deneen	950	75.00	75.00
88-08-002	Santa Fe	J. Deneen	950	75.00	75.00
88-08-003	Empire Builder	J. Deneen	950	75.00	75.00
Art World of Bourgeault		**Royal Literary Series**			
89-01-001	John Bunyan Cottage	R. Bourgeault	Unkn.	75.00	175.00
89-01-002	Thomas Hardy Cottage	R. Bourgeault	Unkn.	75.00	175.00
89-01-003	John Milton Cottage	R. Bourgeault	Unkn.	75.00	175.00
89-01-004	Anne Hathaway Cottage	R. Bourgeault	Unkn.	75.00	175.00
Art World of Bourgeault		**The English Countryside Handtouched**			
89-02-001	The Country Squire	R. Bourgeault	550	75.00	475.00
Marty Bell		**Limited Edition Lithographs**			
87-01-001	Alderton Village	M. Bell	S/O	264.00	500-899.
88-01-002	Allington Castle, Kent	M. Bell	S/O	540.00	540.00
90-01-003	Arbor Cottage	M. Bell	S/O	130.00	150-250.
91-01-004	Bay Tree Cottage, Rye	M. Bell	S/O	230.00	230-520.
82-01-005	Bibury Cottage	M. Bell	S/O	290.00	800-1000.
82-01-006	Big Daddy's Shoe	M. Bell	S/O	64.00	150-300.
88-01-007	Bishop's Roses, The	M. Bell	S/O	220.00	300-500.
89-01-008	Blush of Spring	M. Bell	S/O	96.00	120-160.

Company Number	Name	Series Artist	Edition Limit	Issue Price	Quote
88-01-009	Bodiam Twilight	M. Bell	S/O	128.00	200-900.
87-01-010	Broughton Village	M. Bell	S/O	128.00	400-500.
90-01-011	Bryants Puddle Thatch	M. Bell	S/O	130.00	150-295.
86-01-012	Burford Village Store	M. Bell	S/O	120.00	500-1500.
82-01-013	Castle Combe Cottage	M. Bell	S/O	264.00	400-1000.
91-01-014	Christmas in Rochester	M. Bell	S/O	148.00	275-350.
87-01-015	Chaplains Garden, The	M. Bell	S/O	264.00	1000-2000.
87-01-016	Chippenham Farm	M. Bell	S/O	120.00	300-900.
88-01-017	Clove Cottage	M. Bell	S/O	128.00	225-600.
88-01-018	Clover Lane Cottage	M. Bell	S/O	272.00	595-1400.
86-01-019	Cotswold Parish Church	M. Bell	S/O	98.00	500-1500.
88-01-020	Cotswold Twilight	M. Bell	S/O	128.00	200-495.
82-01-021	Crossroads Cottage	M. Bell	S/O	38.00	200.00
85-01-022	Devon Roses	M. Bell	S/O	78.00	195-500.
91-01-023	Dorset Roses	M. Bell	S/O	96.00	195.00
87-01-024	Dove Cottage Garden	M. Bell	S/O	272.00	304-495.
87-01-025	Driftstone Manor	M. Bell	S/O	440.00	2500.00
87-01-026	Ducksbridge Cottage	M. Bell	S/O	430.00	2000.00
87-01-027	Eashing Cottage	M. Bell	S/O	128.00	200-400.
92-01-028	East Sussex Roses (Archival)	M. Bell	S/O	184.00	184.00
85-01-029	Fiddleford Cottage	M. Bell	S/O	78.00	500-1950.
89-01-030	Fireside Christmas	M. Bell	S/O	136.00	200-500.
88-01-031	Friday Street Lane	M. Bell	S/O	320.00	450.00
89-01-032	The Game Keeper's Cottage	M. Bell	S/O	560.00	900-1800.
88-01-033	Ginger Cottage	M. Bell	S/O	320.00	550-800.
90-01-034	Goater's Cottage	M. Bell	S/O	368.00	400-560.
90-01-035	Gomshall Flower Shop	M. Bell	S/O	396.00	1200-2000.
87-01-036	Halfway Cottage	M. Bell	S/O	272.00	300-600.
86-01-037	Housewives Choice	M. Bell	S/O	98.00	400-1000.
88-01-038	Icomb Village Garden	M. Bell	S/O	620.00	800-1500.
88-01-039	Jasmine Thatch	M. Bell	S/O	272.00	400-600.
89-01-040	Larkspur Cottage	M. Bell	S/O	220.00	300-450.
85-01-041	Little Boxford	M. Bell	S/O	78.00	300-900.
91-01-042	Little Timbers	M. Bell	S/O	130.00	130.00
87-01-043	Little Tulip Thatch	M. Bell	S/O	120.00	400-700.
90-01-044	Little Well Thatch	M. Bell	S/O	130.00	150-250.
90-01-045	Longparrish Cottage	M. Bell	S/O	130.00	300-550.
90-01-046	Longstock Lane	M. Bell	S/O	130.00	150-250.
86-01-047	Lorna Doone Cottage	M. Bell	S/O	380.00	8000-9000.
90-01-048	Lower Brockhampton Manor	M. Bell	S/O	730.00	850-1800.
88-01-049	Lullabye Cottage	M. Bell	S/O	220.00	300-400.
87-01-050	May Cottage	M. Bell	S/O	128.00	200-699.
88-01-051	Meadow School	M. Bell	S/O	220.00	350.00
85-01-052	Meadowlark Cottage	M. Bell	S/O	78.00	450-699.
87-01-053	The Millpond, Stockbridge	M. Bell	S/O	120.00	1000-1699.
87-01-054	Morning Glory Cottage	M. Bell	S/O	120.00	450-599.
88-01-055	Morning's Glow	M. Bell	S/O	280.00	320-650.
88-01-056	Murrle Cottage	M. Bell	S/O	320.00	450-650.
83-01-057	Nestlewood	M. Bell	S/O	325.00	1700-4950.
89-01-058	Old Beams Cottage	M. Bell	S/O	368.00	550-700.
88-01-059	Old Bridge, Grasmere	M. Bell	S/O	640.00	640.00
90-01-060	Old Hertfordshire Thatch	M. Bell	S/O	396.00	700-1500.
84-01-061	Penshurst Tea Rooms (Archival)	M. Bell	S/O	335.00	795-1800.
84-01-062	Penshurst Tea Rooms (Canvas)	M. Bell	S/O	335.00	1500-3600.
89-01-063	Periwinkle Tea Rooms, The	M. Bell	S/O	694.00	694.00
89-01-064	Pride of Spring	M. Bell	S/O	96.00	200-400.
90-01-065	Ready For Christmas	M. Bell	S/O	148.00	200-800.
88-01-066	Rodway Cottage	M. Bell	S/O	620.00	700-1500.
90-01-067	Sanctuary	M. Bell	S/O	220.00	350.00
82-01-068	Sandhills Cottage	M. Bell	S/O	38.00	38.00
88-01-069	Sandy Lane Thatch	M. Bell	S/O	396.00	500.00
82-01-070	School Lane Cottage	M. Bell	S/O	38.00	38.00
88-01-071	Shere Village Antiques	M. Bell	S/O	272.00	304-699.
82-01-072	Spring in the Santas Ynez	M. Bell	S/O	428.00	428.00
91-01-073	Springtime at Scotney	M. Bell	S/O	730.00	400-1000.
90-01-074	Summer's Garden	M. Bell	S/O	78.00	400-800.
85-01-075	Summers Glow	M. Bell	S/O	98.00	600-1000.
87-01-076	Sunrise Thatch	M. Bell	S/O	128.00	200-300.
85-01-077	Surrey Garden House	M. Bell	S/O	98.00	850-1499.
85-01-078	Sweet Pine Cottage	M. Bell	S/O	78.00	350-1499.
88-01-079	Sweet Twilight	M. Bell	S/O	220.00	350-600.
91-01-080	Tea Time	M. Bell	S/O	130.00	130-350.
82-01-081	Thatchcolm Cottage	M. Bell	S/O	38.00	38.00
91-01-082	Upper Chute	M. Bell	S/O	496.00	1100-1500.
87-01-083	The Vicar's Gate	M. Bell	S/O	110.00	600-1500.
87-01-084	Wakehurst Place	M. Bell	S/O	520.00	2000-2500.
87-01-085	Well Cottage, Sandy Lane	M. Bell	S/O	440.00	650-1500.
91-01-086	Wepham Cottage	M. Bell	S/O	396.00	1100.00
84-01-087	West Kington Dell	M. Bell	S/O	240.00	480-999.
92-01-088	West Sussex Roses (Archival)	M. Bell	S/O	184.00	184.00
87-01-089	White Lilac Thatch	M. Bell	S/O	272.00	400-700.
85-01-090	Windsong Cottage	M. Bell	S/O	78.00	350-799.
85-01-091	Windward Cottage, Rye	M. Bell	S/O	228.00	550-635.
86-01-092	York Garden Shop	M. Bell	S/O	110.00	250-999.
Marty Bell		**Members Only Collectors Club**			
91-02-001	Little Thatch Twilight	M. Bell	Closed	288.00	320-380.
91-02-002	Charter Rose, The	M. Bell	Closed	Gift	N/A
92-02-003	Candle At Eventide	M. Bell	Yr.Iss.	Gift	N/A
92-02-004	Blossom Lane	M. Bell	Yr.Iss.	288.00	288.00
Circle Fine Art		**Rockwell**			
XX-01-001	American Family Folio	N. Rockwell	200	Unkn.	17500.00
XX-01-002	The Artist at Work	N. Rockwell	130	Unkn.	3500.00
XX-01-003	At the Barber	N. Rockwell	200	Unkn.	4900.00
XX-01-004	Autumn	N. Rockwell	200	Unkn.	3500.00
XX-01-005	Autumn/Japon	N. Rockwell	25	Unkn.	3600.00
XX-01-006	Aviary	N. Rockwell	200	Unkn.	4200.00
XX-01-007	Barbershop Quartet	N. Rockwell	200	Unkn.	4200.00
XX-01-008	Baseball	N. Rockwell	200	Unkn.	3600.00
XX-01-009	Ben Franklin's Philadelphia	N. Rockwell	200	Unkn.	3600.00
XX-01-010	Ben's Belles	N. Rockwell	200	Unkn.	3500.00
XX-01-011	The Big Day	N. Rockwell	200	Unkn.	3400.00
XX-01-012	The Big Top	N. Rockwell	148	Unkn.	2800.00
XX-01-013	Blacksmith Shop	N. Rockwell	200	Unkn.	6300.00
XX-01-014	Bookseller	N. Rockwell	200	Unkn.	2700.00
XX-01-015	Bookseller/Japon	N. Rockwell	25	Unkn.	2750.00
XX-01-016	The Bridge	N. Rockwell	200	Unkn.	3100.00
XX-01-017	Cat	N. Rockwell	200	Unkn.	3400.00
XX-01-018	Cat/Collotype	N. Rockwell	200	Unkn.	4000.00
XX-01-019	Cheering	N. Rockwell	200	Unkn.	3600.00
XX-01-020	Children at Window	N. Rockwell	200	Unkn.	3600.00
XX-01-021	Church	N. Rockwell	200	Unkn.	3400.00
XX-01-022	Church/Collotype	N. Rockwell	200	Unkn.	4000.00
XX-01-023	Circus	N. Rockwell	200	Unkn.	2650.00
XX-01-024	County Agricultural Agent	N. Rockwell	200	Unkn.	3900.00
XX-01-025	The Critic	N. Rockwell	200	Unkn.	4650.00
XX-01-026	Day in the Life of a Boy	N. Rockwell	200	Unkn.	6200.00
XX-01-027	Day in the Life of a Boy/Japon	N. Rockwell	25	Unkn.	6500.00
XX-01-028	Debut	N. Rockwell	200	Unkn.	3600.00
XX-01-029	Discovery	N. Rockwell	200	Unkn.	5900.00
XX-01-030	Doctor and Boy	N. Rockwell	200	Unkn.	9400.00
XX-01-031	Doctor and Doll-Signed	N. Rockwell	200	Unkn.	11900.00
XX-01-032	Dressing Up/Pencil	N. Rockwell	200	Unkn.	3700.00
XX-01-033	Dressing Up/Ink	N. Rockwell	60	Unkn.	4400.00
XX-01-034	The Drunkard	N. Rockwell	200	Unkn.	3600.00
XX-01-035	The Expected and Unexpected	N. Rockwell	200	Unkn.	3700.00
XX-01-036	Family Tree	N. Rockwell	200	Unkn.	5900.00
XX-01-037	Fido's House	N. Rockwell	200	Unkn.	3600.00
XX-01-038	Football Mascot	N. Rockwell	200	Unkn.	3700.00
XX-01-039	Four Seasons Folio	N. Rockwell	200	Unkn.	13500.00
XX-01-040	Four Seasons Folio/Japon	N. Rockwell	25	Unkn.	14000.00
XX-01-041	Freedom from Fear-Signed	N. Rockwell	200	Unkn.	6400.00
XX-01-042	Freedom from Want-Signed	N. Rockwell	200	Unkn.	6400.00
XX-01-043	Freedom of Speech-Signed	N. Rockwell	200	Unkn.	6400.00
XX-01-044	Freedom of Religion-Signed	N. Rockwell	200	Unkn.	6400.00
XX-01-045	Gaiety Dance Team	N. Rockwell	200	Unkn.	4300.00
XX-01-046	Girl at Mirror-Signed	N. Rockwell	200	Unkn.	8400.00
XX-01-047	The Golden Age	N. Rockwell	200	Unkn.	3500.00
XX-01-048	Golden Rule-Signed	N. Rockwell	200	Unkn.	4400.00
XX-01-049	Golf	N. Rockwell	200	Unkn.	3600.00
XX-01-050	Gossips	N. Rockwell	200	Unkn.	5000.00
XX-01-051	Gossips/Japon	N. Rockwell	25	Unkn.	5100.00
XX-01-052	Grotto	N. Rockwell	200	Unkn.	3400.00
XX-01-053	Grotto/Collotype	N. Rockwell	200	Unkn.	4000.00
XX-01-054	High Dive	N. Rockwell	200	Unkn.	3400.00
XX-01-055	The Homecoming	N. Rockwell	200	Unkn.	3700.00
XX-01-056	The House	N. Rockwell	200	Unkn.	3700.00
XX-01-057	Huck Finn Folio	N. Rockwell	200	Unkn.	35000.00
XX-01-058	Ichabod Crane	N. Rockwell	200	Unkn.	6700.00
XX-01-059	The Inventor	N. Rockwell	200	Unkn.	4100.00
XX-01-060	Jerry	N. Rockwell	200	Unkn.	4700.00
XX-01-061	Jim Got Down on His Knees	N. Rockwell	200	Unkn.	4500.00
XX-01-062	Lincoln	N. Rockwell	200	Unkn.	11400.00
XX-01-063	Lobsterman	N. Rockwell	200	Unkn.	5500.00
XX-01-064	Lobsterman/Japon	N. Rockwell	25	Unkn.	5750.00
XX-01-065	Marriage License	N. Rockwell	200	Unkn.	6900.00
XX-01-066	Medicine	N. Rockwell	200	Unkn.	3400.00
XX-01-067	Medicine/Color Litho	N. Rockwell	200	Unkn.	4000.00
XX-01-068	Miss Mary Jane	N. Rockwell	200	Unkn.	4500.00
XX-01-069	Moving Day	N. Rockwell	200	Unkn.	3900.00
XX-01-070	My Hand Shook	N. Rockwell	200	Unkn.	4500.00
XX-01-071	Music Hath Charms	N. Rockwell	200	Unkn.	4200.00
XX-01-072	Out the Window	N. Rockwell	200	Unkn.	3400.00
XX-01-073	Out the Window/ Collotype	N. Rockwell	200	Unkn.	4000.00
XX-01-074	Outward Bound-Signed	N. Rockwell	200	Unkn.	7900.00
XX-01-075	Poor Richard's Almanac	N. Rockwell	200	Unkn.	24000.00
XX-01-076	Prescription	N. Rockwell	200	Unkn.	4900.00
XX-01-077	Prescription/Japon	N. Rockwell	25	Unkn.	5000.00
XX-01-078	The Problem We All Live With	N. Rockwell	200	Unkn.	4500.00
XX-01-079	Puppies	N. Rockwell	200	Unkn.	3700.00
XX-01-080	Raliegh the Dog	N. Rockwell	200	Unkn.	3900.00
XX-01-081	Rocket Ship	N. Rockwell	200	Unkn.	3650.00
XX-01-082	The Royal Crown	N. Rockwell	200	Unkn.	3500.00
XX-01-083	Runaway	N. Rockwell	200	Unkn.	3800.00
XX-01-084	Runaway/Japon	N. Rockwell	200	Unkn.	5700.00
XX-01-085	Safe and Sound	N. Rockwell	200	Unkn.	3800.00
XX-01-086	Saturday People	N. Rockwell	200	Unkn.	3300.00
XX-01-087	Save Me	N. Rockwell	200	Unkn.	3600.00
XX-01-088	Saying Grace-Signed	N. Rockwell	200	Unkn.	7400.00
XX-01-089	School Days Folio	N. Rockwell	200	Unkn.	14000.00
XX-01-090	Schoolhouse	N. Rockwell	200	Unkn.	4500.00
XX-01-091	Schoolhouse/Japon	N. Rockwell	25	Unkn.	4650.00
XX-01-092	See America First	N. Rockwell	200	Unkn.	5650.00
XX-01-093	See America First/Japon	N. Rockwell	25	Unkn.	6100.00
XX-01-094	Settling In	N. Rockwell	200	Unkn.	3600.00
XX-01-095	Shuffelton's Barbershop	N. Rockwell	200	Unkn.	7400.00
XX-01-096	Smoking	N. Rockwell	200	Unkn.	3400.00
XX-01-097	Smoking/Collotype	N. Rockwell	200	Unkn.	4000.00
XX-01-098	Spanking	N. Rockwell	200	Unkn.	3400.00
XX-01-099	Spanking/ Collotype	N. Rockwell	200	Unkn.	4000.00
XX-01-100	Spelling Bee	N. Rockwell	200	Unkn.	6500.00
XX-01-101	Spring	N. Rockwell	200	Unkn.	3500.00
XX-01-102	Spring/Japon	N. Rockwell	25	Unkn.	3600.00
XX-01-103	Spring Flowers	N. Rockwell	200	Unkn.	5200.00
XX-01-104	Study for the Doctor's Office	N. Rockwell	200	Unkn.	6000.00
XX-01-105	Studying	N. Rockwell	200	Unkn.	3600.00
XX-01-106	Summer	N. Rockwell	200	Unkn.	3500.00
XX-01-107	Summer/Japon	N. Rockwell	25	Unkn.	3600.00
XX-01-108	Summer Stock	N. Rockwell	200	Unkn.	4900.00
XX-01-109	Summer Stock/Japon	N. Rockwell	25	Unkn.	5000.00
XX-01-110	The Teacher	N. Rockwell	200	Unkn.	3400.00
XX-01-111	The Teacher/Japon	N. Rockwell	25	Unkn.	3500.00
XX-01-112	Teacher's Pet	N. Rockwell	200	Unkn.	3600.00
XX-01-113	The Texan	N. Rockwell	200	Unkn.	3700.00
XX-01-114	Then For Three Minutes	N. Rockwell	200	Unkn.	4500.00
XX-01-115	Then Miss Watson	N. Rockwell	200	Unkn.	4500.00
XX-01-116	There Warn't No Harm	N. Rockwell	200	Unkn.	4500.00
XX-01-117	Three Farmers	N. Rockwell	200	Unkn.	3600.00
XX-01-118	Ticketseller	N. Rockwell	200	Unkn.	4200.00
XX-01-119	Ticketseller/Japon	N. Rockwell	25	Unkn.	4400.00
XX-01-120	Tom Sawyer Color Suite	N. Rockwell	200	Unkn.	30000.00
XX-01-121	Tom Sawyer Folio	N. Rockwell	200	Unkn.	26500.00
XX-01-122	Top of the World	N. Rockwell	200	Unkn.	4200.00
XX-01-123	Trumpeter	N. Rockwell	200	Unkn.	3900.00
XX-01-124	Trumpeter/Japon	N. Rockwell	25	Unkn.	4100.00
XX-01-125	Two O'Clock Feeding	N. Rockwell	200	Unkn.	3600.00
XX-01-126	The Village Smithy	N. Rockwell	200	Unkn.	3500.00
XX-01-127	Welcome	N. Rockwell	200	Unkn.	3500.00
XX-01-128	Wet Paint	N. Rockwell	200	Unkn.	3800.00
XX-01-129	When I Lit My Candle	N. Rockwell	200	Unkn.	4500.00
XX-01-130	White Washing	N. Rockwell	200	Unkn.	3400.00
XX-01-131	Whitewashing the Fence/Collotype	N. Rockwell	200	Unkn.	4000.00
XX-01-132	Window Washer	N. Rockwell	200	Unkn.	4800.00
XX-01-133	Winter	N. Rockwell	200	Unkn.	3500.00
XX-01-134	Winter/Japon	N. Rockwell	25	Unkn.	3600.00

Company / Number	Name	Series / Artist	Edition Limit	Issue Price	Quote
XX-01-135	Ye Old Print Shoppe	N. Rockwell	200	Unkn.	3500.00
XX-01-136	Your Eyes is Lookin'	N. Rockwell	200	Unkn.	4500.00
Cross Gallery, Inc.		**Limited Edition Prints**			
83-01-001	Isbaaloo Eetshiileehcheek(Sorting Her Beads)	P.A. Cross	S/0	150.00	1750.00
83-01-002	Ayla-Sah-Xuh-Xah (Pretty Colours, Many Designs)	P.A. Cross	S/0	150.00	450.00
84-01-003	Blue Beaded Hair Ties	P.A. Cross	S/0	85.00	330.00
84-01-004	Profile of Caroline	P.A. Cross	S/0	85.00	185.00
84-01-005	Whistling Water Clan Girl: Crow Indian	P.A. Cross	S/0	85.00	85.00
84-01-006	Thick Lodge Clan Boy: Crow Indian	P.A. Cross	475	85.00	85.00
85-01-007	The Water Vision	P.A. Cross	S/0	150.00	325.00
86-01-008	The Winter Shawl	P.A. Cross	S/0	150.00	1600.00
86-01-009	The Red Capote	P.A. Cross	S/0	150.00	850.00
86-01-010	Grand Entry	P.A. Cross	S/0	85.00	85.00
84-01-011	Winter Morning	P.A. Cross	S/0	185.00	1450.00
84-01-012	Dii-tah-shteh Ee-wihza-ahook (A Coat of much Value)	P.A. Cross	S/0	90.00	740.00
87-01-013	Caroline	P.A. Cross	S/0	45.00	145.00
87-01-014	Tina	P.A. Cross	S/0	45.00	110.00
87-01-015	The Red Necklace	P.A. Cross	S/0	90.00	210.00
87-01-016	The Elkskin Robe	P.A. Cross	S/0	190.00	640.00
88-01-017	Ma-a-luppis-she-La-dus (She is above everything, nothing can touch her)	P.A. Cross	S/0	190.00	525.00
88-01-018	Dance Apache	P.A. Cross	S/0	190.00	360.00
89-01-019	The Dreamer	P.A. Cross	S/0	190.00	600.00
89-01-020	Chey-ayjeh: Prey	P.A. Cross	S/0	190.00	600.00
89-01-021	Teesa Waits To Dance	P.A. Cross	S/0	135.00	180.00
89-01-022	B' Achua Dlubh-bia Bii Noskiiyahi The Gift, Part II	P.A. Cross	S/0	225.00	650.00
89-01-023	Biaachee-itah Bah-achbeh	P.A. Cross	S/0	225.00	525.00
90-01-024	Baape Ochia (Night Wind, Turquoise)	P.A. Cross	S/0	185.00	185.00
90-01-025	Ishia-Kahda #1 (Quiet One)	P.A. Cross	S/0	185.00	185.00
90-01-026	Eshte	P.A. Cross	S/0	185.00	185.00
91-01-027	The Blue Shawl	P.A. Cross	S/0	185.00	185.00
91-01-028	Ashpahdua Hagay Ashae-Gyoke (My Home & Heart Is Crow)	P.A. Cross	S/0	225.00	225-350.
Cross Gallery, Inc		**Star Quilt Series**			
85-02-001	Winter Warmth	P.A. Cross	S/0	150.00	900-1215.
86-02-002	Reflections	P.A. Cross	S/0	185.00	865.00
88-02-003	The Quilt Makers	P.A. Cross	S/0	190.00	1200.00
Cross Gallery, Inc.		**Wolf Series**			
85-03-001	Dii-tah-shteh Bii-wik; Chedah-bah liidah	P.A. Cross	S/0	185.00	3275.00
87-03-002	The Morning Star Gives Long Otter His Hoop Medicine Power	P.A. Cross	S/0	190.00	1800-2500.
89-03-003	Biagoht Eecuebeh Hehsheesh-Checah: (Red Ridinghood and Her Wolves)	P.A. Cross	S/0	225.00	1500-2500.
90-03-004	Agnjnaug Amaguut;Inupiag (Women With Her Wolves)	P.A. Cross	1,050	325.00	325-750.
Cross Gallery, Inc.		**Half Breed Series**			
89-04-001	Ach-hua Dlubh: (Body Two), Half Breed	P.A. Cross	S/0	190.00	1450.00
89-04-002	Ach-hua Dlubh: (Body Two), Half Breed II	P.A. Cross	S/0	225.00	1100.00
90-04-003	Ach-hua Dlubh: (Body Two), Half Breed III	P.A. Cross	S/0	225.00	850.00
Cross Gallery, Inc.		**Limited Edition Original Graphics**			
87-05-001	Caroline, Stone Lithograph	P.A. Cross	S/0	300.00	600.00
88-05-002	Maidenhood Hopi, Stone Lithograph	P.A. Cross	S/0	950.00	1150.00
89-05-003	The Red Capote, Serigraph	P.A. Cross	S/0	750.00	1150.00
89-05-004	Rosapina, Etching	P.A. Cross	74	1200.00	1200.00
90-05-005	Nighteyes, I, Serigraph	P.A. Cross	S/0	225.00	425.00
Cross Gallery, Inc.		**Miniature Line**			
91-06-001	BJ	P.A. Cross	447	80.00	80.00
91-06-002	Watercolour Study #2 For Half Breed	P.A. Cross	447	80.00	80.00
91-06-003	The Floral Shawl	P.A. Cross	447	80.00	80.00
91-06-004	Kendra	P.A. Cross	447	80.00	80.00
Cross Gallery, Inc.		**The Painted Ladies' Suite**			
92-07-001	The Painted Ladies	P.A. Cross	S/0	225.00	225.00
92-07-002	Avisola	P.A. Cross	475	185.00	185.00
92-07-003	Itza-chu (Apache; The Eagle)	P.A. Cross	475	185.00	185.00
92-07-004	Kel'hoya (Hopi; Little Sparrow Hawk)	P.A. Cross	475	185.00	185.00
92-07-005	Dah-say (Crow; Heart)	P.A. Cross	475	185.00	185.00
92-07-006	Tze-go-juni (Chiricahua Apache)	P.A. Cross	447	80.00	80.00
92-07-007	Sus(h)gah-daydus(h) (Crow; Quick)	P.A. Cross	447	80.00	80.00
92-07-008	Acoria (Crow; Seat of Honor)	P.A. Cross	475	185.00	185.00
Cross Gallery, Inc.		**The Gift**			
93-08-001	The Gift, Part III	P.A. Cross	475	225.00	225.00
Gartlan USA		**Lithograph**			
86-01-001	George Brett-"The Swing"	J. Martin	2,000	85.00	150.00
87-01-002	Roger Staubach	C. Soileau	1,979	85.00	125.00
89-01-003	Kareem Abdul Jabbar-The Record Setter	M. Taylor	1,989	85.00	175-225.
90-01-004	Darryl Strawberry	M. Taylor	500	295.00	295.00
91-01-005	Darryl Strawberry, signed Artist Proof	M. Taylor	50	395.00	395.00
91-01-006	Joe Montana	M. Taylor	500	495.00	495.00
91-01-007	Negro League 1st World Series (print)	Unknown	1,924	109.00	109.00
Gartlan USA		**Gallery Series I**			
92-02-001	Wayne Gretzky (16x20) Tri-Cut	M. Taylor	500	195.00	195.00
92-02-002	Ken Griffey Jr. (16x20) Tri-Cut	M. Taylor	500	195.00	195.00
92-02-003	Joe Montana (16x20) Tri-Cut	M. Taylor	500	195.00	195.00
92-02-004	Brett Hull (16x20) Tri-Cut	M. Taylor	500	195.00	195.00
Gartlan USA		**Gallery Series 2**			
92-03-001	Yogi Berra (12x20 w/8 1/2" plate)	M. Taylor	950	89.00	89.00
92-03-002	Rod Carew (12x20 w/8 1/2" plate)	M. Taylor	950	89.00	89.00
92-03-003	Carlton Fisk (12x20 w/8 1/2" plate)	M. Taylor	950	89.00	89.00
92-03-004	Whitey Ford (12x20 w/8 1/2" plate)	M. Taylor	950	89.00	89.00
92-03-005	Wayne Gretzky (12x20 w/8 1/2" plate)	M. Taylor	950	89.00	89.00
92-03-006	Ken Griffey Jr. (12x20 w/8 1/2" plate)	M. Taylor	950	89.00	89.00
92-03-007	Gordy Howe (12x20 w/8 1/2" plate)	M. Taylor	950	89.00	89.00
92-03-008	Joe Montana (12x20 w/8 1/2" plate)	M. Taylor	950	89.00	89.00
92-03-009	Tom Seaver (12x20 w/8 1/2" plate)	M. Taylor	950	89.00	89.00
92-03-010	John Wooden (12x20 w/8 1/2" plate)	M. Taylor	950	89.00	89.00
92-03-011	Carl Yastrzemski (12x20 w/8 1/2" plate)	M. Taylor	950	89.00	89.00
92-03-012	Brett & Bobby Hull (12x20 w/8 1/2" plate)	M. Taylor	950	89.00	89.00
Gartlan USA		**Gallery Series 3**			
92-04-001	Wayne Gretzky (12x16 w/photo)	M. Taylor	Open	79.00	79.00
92-04-002	Ken Griffey, Jr. (12x16 w/photo)	M. Taylor	Open	79.00	79.00
92-04-003	Joe Montana (12x16 w/photo)	M. Taylor	Open	79.00	79.00
92-04-004	Brett Hull (12x16 w/photo)	M. Taylor	Open	79.00	79.00
Gartlan USA		**Gallery Series 4**			
92-05-001	Wayne Gretzky (8x10 w/mini fig.)	M. Taylor	950	89.00	89.00
92-05-002	Carlton Fisk (8x10 w/mini fig.)	M. Taylor	950	89.00	89.00
92-05-003	Ken Griffey, Jr. (8x10 w/mini fig.)	M. Taylor	950	89.00	89.00
92-05-004	Brett Hull (8x10 w/mini fig.)	M. Taylor	950	89.00	89.00
92-05-005	Gordie Howe (8x10 w/mini fig.)	M. Taylor	950	89.00	89.00
92-05-006	Joe Montana (8x10 w/mini fig.)	M. Taylor	950	89.00	89.00
92-05-007	Tom Seaver (8x10 w/mini fig.)	M. Taylor	950	89.00	89.00
92-05-008	Carl Yastrzemski (8x10 w/mini fig.)	M. Taylor	950	89.00	89.00
92-05-009	George Brett (8x10 w/mini fig. & signed rounder)	Martin	300	125.00	125.00
Gartlan USA		**Gallery Series 5**			
92-06-001	Carlton Fisk (8x10)	M. Taylor	950	69.00	69.00
92-06-002	Wayne Gretzky (8x10)	M. Taylor	950	69.00	69.00
92-06-003	Ken Griffey, Jr. (8x10)	M. Taylor	950	69.00	69.00
92-06-004	Brett Hull (8x10)	M. Taylor	950	69.00	69.00
92-06-005	Gordie Howe (8x10)	M. Taylor	950	69.00	69.00
92-06-006	Joe Montana (8x10)	M. Taylor	950	69.00	69.00
92-06-007	Tom Seaver (8x10)	M. Taylor	950	69.00	69.00
92-06-008	Carl Yastrzemski (8x10)	M. Taylor	950	69.00	69.00
92-06-009	George Brett (8x10)	Martin	3,000	59.00	59.00
Graphics Buying Service		**Stone**			
79-01-001	Mare and Foal	F. Stone	500	90.00	500.00
79-01-002	Affirmed, Steve Cauthen Up	F. Stone	750	100.00	600.00
79-01-003	The Rivals-Affirmed & Alydar	F. Stone	500	90.00	500.00
79-01-004	Patience	F. Stone	1,000	90.00	1200.00
79-01-005	One, Two, Three	F. Stone	500	100.00	1000.00
79-01-006	The Moment After	F. Stone	500	90.00	350.00
80-01-007	Genuine Risk	F. Stone	500	100.00	700.00
80-01-008	The Belmont-Bold Forbes	F. Stone	500	100.00	375.00
80-01-009	The Kentucky Derby	F. Stone	750	100.00	650.00
80-01-010	The Pasture Pest	F. Stone	500	100.00	875.00
80-01-011	Exceller-Bill Shoemaker	F. Stone	500	90.00	800.00
80-01-012	Spectacular Bid	F. Stone	500	65.00	350-400.
80-01-013	Kidnapped Mare-Franfreluche	F. Stone	750	115.00	575.00
81-01-014	The Shoe-8,000 Wins	F. Stone	395	200.00	7000.00
81-01-015	The Arabians	F. Stone	750	115.00	525.00
81-01-016	The Thoroughbreds	F. Stone	750	115.00	425.00
81-01-017	Contentment	F. Stone	750	115.00	525.00
81-01-018	John Henry-Bill Shoemaker Up	F. Stone	595	160.00	1500.00
82-01-019	Off and Running	F. Stone	750	125.00	250-350.
82-01-020	The Water Trough	F. Stone	750	125.00	575.00
82-01-021	The Power Horses	F. Stone	750	125.00	250.00
82-01-022	Man O'War "Final Thunder"	F. Stone	750	175.00	2500-3100.
83-01-023	The Duel	F. Stone	750	150.00	400.00
83-01-024	The Andalusian	F. Stone	750	150.00	350.00
83-01-025	Tranquility	F. Stone	750	150.00	525.00
83-01-026	Secretariat	F. Stone	950	175.00	995-1200.
83-01-027	Ruffian-For Only a Moment	F. Stone	750	175.00	1100.00
84-01-028	Turning For Home	F. Stone	750	150.00	425.00
84-01-029	Northern Dancer	F. Stone	950	175.00	625.00
85-01-030	John Henry-McCarron Up	F. Stone	750	175.00	500-750.
85-01-031	Eternal Legacy	F. Stone	950	175.00	950.00
85-01-032	Fred Stone Paints the Sport of Kings	F. Stone	750	265.00	750.00
85-01-033	Kelso	F. Stone	950	175.00	750.00
86-01-034	Ruffian & Foolish Pleasure	F. Stone	950	175.00	375.00
86-01-035	Nijinski II	F. Stone	950	175.00	275.00
86-01-036	Forever Friends	F. Stone	950	175.00	725.00
87-01-037	Lady's Secret	F. Stone	950	175.00	425.00
87-01-038	The First Day	F. Stone	950	175.00	225.00
87-01-039	The Rivalry-Alysheba and Bet Twice	F. Stone	950	195.00	550.00
88-01-040	Alysheba	F. Stone	950	195.00	650.00
88-01-041	Cam-Fella	F. Stone	950	175.00	350.00
89-01-042	Shoe Bald Eagle	F. Stone	950	195.00	675.00
89-01-043	Phar Lap	F. Stone	950	195.00	275.00
89-01-044	Battle For The Triple Crown	F. Stone	950	225.00	650.00
90-01-045	Final Tribute- Secretariat	F. Stone	1,150	265.00	1300.00
90-01-046	Old Warriors Shoemaker-John Henry	F. Stone	1,950	265.00	595.00
91-01-047	Black Stallion	F. Stone	1,500	225.00	250.00
91-01-048	Forego	F. Stone	1,150	225.00	250.00
91-01-049	Go For Wand-A Candle in the Wind	F. Stone	1,150	225.00	225.00
92-01-050	Dance Smartly	F. Stone	950	225.00	325.00
Greenwich Workshop		**Doolittle**			
80-01-001	Bugged Bear	B. Doolittle	1,000	85.00	3000-3800.
83-01-002	Christmas Day, Give or Take a Week	B. Doolittle	4,581	80.00	1950-2500.
82-01-003	Eagle's Flight	B. Doolittle	1,500	185.00	3000-5000.
83-01-004	Escape by a Hare	B. Doolittle	1,500	80.00	950-1100.
84-01-005	Forest Has Eyes, The	B. Doolittle	8,544	175.00	3800-5200.
80-01-006	Good Omen, The	B. Doolittle	1,000	85.00	3500-5000.
87-01-007	Guardian Spirits	B. Doolittle	13,238	295.00	1200-1700.
84-01-008	Let My Spirit Soar	B. Doolittle	1,500	195.00	3600-5000.
79-01-009	Pintos	B. Doolittle	1,000	65.00	10-12000.00
83-01-010	Runs With Thunder	B. Doolittle	1,500	150.00	1800-2400.
83-01-011	Rushing War Eagle	B. Doolittle	1,500	150.00	1500-2000.
81-01-012	Spirit of the Grizzly	B. Doolittle	1,500	150.00	3700-4600.
86-01-013	Two Bears of the Blackfeet	B. Doolittle	2,650	225.00	1100-1850.
85-01-014	Two Indian Horses	B. Doolittle	12,253	225.00	3000-4700.
81-01-015	Unknown Presence	B. Doolittle	1,500	150.00	3000-4000.
86-01-016	Where Silence Speaks, Doolittle The Art of Bev Doolittle	B. Doolittle	3,500	650.00	3500-4200.
80-01-017	Whoo !?	B. Doolittle	1,000	75.00	1600-1800.
85-01-018	Wolves of the Crow	B. Doolittle	2,650	225.00	1900-2900.
81-01-019	Woodland Encounter	B. Doolittle	1,500	145.00	9000-11000.
87-01-020	Calling the Buffalo	B. Doolittle	8,500	245.00	1100-1700.
87-01-021	Season of the Eagle	B. Doolittle	36,548	245.00	675-1000.
88-01-022	Doubled Back	B. Doolittle	15,000	245.00	1350-1900.
89-01-023	Sacred Ground	B. Doolittle	69,996	265.00	500-1000.
90-01-024	Hide and Seek Suite	B. Doolittle	25,000	1200.00	900-1200.
91-01-025	The Sentinel	B. Doolittle	35,000	275.00	800-1200.
91-01-026	Sacred Circle (PC)	B. Doolittle	40,192	325.00	480-750.
Greenwich Workshop		**McCarthy**			
80-02-001	A Time Of Decision	F. McCarthy	1,150	125.00	250.00
77-02-002	An Old Time Mountain Man	F. McCarthy	1,000	65.00	275.00

Company Number	Name	Series Artist	Edition Limit	Issue Price	Quote
84-02-003	After the Dust Storm	F. McCarthy	1,000	145.00	165.00
82-02-004	Alert	F. McCarthy	1,000	135.00	160.00
84-02-005	Along the West Fork	F. McCarthy	1,000	175.00	225-285.
78-02-006	Ambush, The	F. McCarthy	1,000	125.00	300-345.
82-02-007	Apache Scout	F. McCarthy	1,000	165.00	175-190.
88-02-008	Apache Trackers (C)	F. McCarthy	1,000	95.00	135-150.
82-02-009	Attack on the Wagon Train	F. McCarthy	1,400	150.00	220-395.
77-02-010	The Beaver Men	F. McCarthy	1,000	75.00	500-710.
80-02-011	Before the Charge	F. McCarthy	1,000	115.00	200-400.
78-02-012	Before the Norther	F. McCarthy	1,000	90.00	400-525.
90-02-013	Below The Breaking Dawn	F. McCarthy	1,250	225.00	185-225.
89-02-014	Big Medicine	F. McCarthy	1,000	225.00	375-425.
83-02-015	Blackfoot Raiders	F. McCarthy	1,000	90.00	250.00
86-02-016	The Buffalo Runners	F. McCarthy	1,000	195.00	195-250.
83-02-017	Burning the Way Station	F. McCarthy	1,000	175.00	375-500.
89-02-018	Canyon Lands	F. McCarthy	1,250	225.00	235.00
82-02-019	Challenge, The	F. McCarthy	1,000	175.00	425.00
85-02-020	Charging the Challenger	F. McCarthy	1,000	150.00	200-300.
86-02-021	Children of the Raven	F. McCarthy	1,000	185.00	185-600.
87-02-022	Chiricahua Raiders	F. McCarthy	1,000	165.00	165-275.
77-02-023	Comanche Moon	F. McCarthy	1,000	75.00	250.00
86-02-024	Comanche War Trail	F. McCarthy	1,000	165.00	165-225.
89-02-025	The Coming Of The Iron Horse	F. McCarthy	1,500	225.00	225-375.
89-02-026	The Coming Of The Iron Horse (Print/Pewter Train Special Publ. Ed.)	F. McCarthy	100	1500.00	1650-2150.
81-02-027	The Coup	F. McCarthy	1,000	125.00	375-450.
81-02-028	Crossing the Divide/The Old West	F. McCarthy	1,500	850.00	900-1250.
84-02-029	The Decoys	F. McCarthy	450	325.00	500.00
77-02-030	Distant Thunder	F. McCarthy	1,500	75.00	650-900.
89-02-031	Down From The Mountains	F. McCarthy	1,500	245.00	245-290.
86-02-032	The Drive (C)	F. McCarthy	1,000	95.00	95-175.
77-02-033	Dust Stained Posse	F. McCarthy	1,000	75.00	675-915.
85-02-034	The Fireboat	F. McCarthy	1,000	175.00	200.00
87-02-035	Following the Herds	F. McCarthy	1,000	195.00	250-300.
80-02-036	Forbidden Land	F. McCarthy	1,000	125.00	225.00
78-02-037	The Fording	F. McCarthy	1,000	75.00	300-360.
87-02-038	From the Rim	F. McCarthy	1,000	225.00	225-310.
81-02-039	Headed North	F. McCarthy	1,000	150.00	225-275.
90-02-040	Hoka Hey: Sioux War Cry	F. McCarthy	1,250	225.00	225.00
88-02-041	The Hostile Land	F. McCarthy	1,000	225.00	235.00
76-02-042	The Hostiles	F. McCarthy	1,000	75.00	600.00
74-02-043	The Hunt	F. McCarthy	1,000	75.00	620-930.
88-02-044	In Pursuit of the White Buffalo	F. McCarthy	1,500	225.00	420-450.
83-02-045	In The Land Of The Sparrow Hawk People	F. McCarthy	1,000	165.00	180.00
87-02-046	In The Land Of The Winter Hawk	F. McCarthy	1,000	225.00	350-525.
78-02-047	In The Pass	F. McCarthy	1,500	90.00	200.00
85-02-048	The Last Crossing	F. McCarthy	550	350.00	450-500.
88-02-049	The Last Stand: Little Big Horn	F. McCarthy	2,250	225.00	225-250.
74-02-050	Lone Sentinel	F. McCarthy	1,000	55.00	1465-1800.
79-02-051	The Loner	F. McCarthy	1,000	75.00	400-600.
74-02-052	Long Column	F. McCarthy	1,000	75.00	750-1250.
85-02-053	The Long Knives	F. McCarthy	1,000	175.00	250-275.
89-02-054	Los Diablos	F. McCarthy	1,250	225.00	225-275.
83-02-055	Moonlit Trail	F. McCarthy	1,000	90.00	210.00
78-02-056	Night Crossing	F. McCarthy	1,000	75.00	200-250.
74-02-057	The Night They Needed a Good Ribbon Man	F. McCarthy	1,000	65.00	350-475.
79-02-058	On the Warpath	F. McCarthy	1,000	75.00	195-250.
83-02-059	Out Of The Mist They Came	F. McCarthy	1,000	165.00	225-325.
90-02-060	Out Of The Windswept Ramparts	F. McCarthy	1,250	225.00	225.00
76-02-061	Packing In	F. McCarthy	1,000	65.00	375-500.
91-02-062	Pony Express	F. McCarthy	1,000	225.00	225.00
79-02-063	The Prayer	F. McCarthy	1,500	90.00	550-600.
91-02-064	The Pursuit	F. McCarthy	650	550.00	550.00
81-02-065	Race with the Hostiles	F. McCarthy	1,000	135.00	170-225.
86-02-066	Red Bull's War Party	F. McCarthy	1,000	165.00	165-225.
79-02-067	Retreat to Higher Ground	F. McCarthy	2,000	90.00	350-500.
75-02-068	Returning Raiders	F. McCarthy	1,000	75.00	450.00
80-02-069	Roar of the Norther	F. McCarthy	1,000	90.00	250-450.
77-02-070	Robe Signal	F. McCarthy	850	60.00	420-500.
88-02-071	Saber Charge	F. McCarthy	2,250	225.00	250.00
84-02-072	The Savage Taunt	F. McCarthy	1,000	225.00	250-375.
85-02-073	Scouting The Long Knives	F. McCarthy	1,400	195.00	250-300.
78-02-074	Single File	F. McCarthy	1,000	75.00	300-490.
76-02-075	Sioux Warriors	F. McCarthy	650	55.00	375-450.
75-02-076	Smoke Was Their Ally	F. McCarthy	1,000	75.00	425-455.
80-02-077	Snow Moon	F. McCarthy	1,000	115.00	250-300.
86-02-078	Spooked	F. McCarthy	1,400	195.00	200.00
81-02-079	Surrounded	F. McCarthy	1,000	150.00	195-275.
75-02-080	The Survivor	F. McCarthy	1,000	65.00	350.00
85-02-081	The Traders	F. McCarthy	1,000	195.00	275-195.
80-02-082	The Trooper	F. McCarthy	1,000	90.00	295.00
78-02-083	To Battle	F. McCarthy	1,000	75.00	370.00
88-02-084	Turning The Leaders	F. McCarthy	1,500	225.00	240.00
83-02-085	Under Attack	F. McCarthy	5,676	125.00	295-350.
81-02-086	Under Hostile Fire	F. McCarthy	1,000	150.00	210-250.
75-02-087	Waiting for the Escort	F. McCarthy	1,000	75.00	225-250.
76-02-088	The Warrior	F. McCarthy	650	50.00	450-600.
82-02-089	The Warriors	F. McCarthy	1,000	150.00	200.00
84-02-090	Watching the Wagons	F. McCarthy	1,400	175.00	440.00
87-02-091	When Omens Turn Bad	F. McCarthy	1,000	165.00	490-525.
86-02-092	Where Tracks Will Be Lost	F. McCarthy	550	350.00	350-375.
84-02-093	Whirling He Raced to Meet the Challenge	F. McCarthy	1,000	175.00	275-340.
91-02-094	The Wild Ones	F. McCarthy	1,000	225.00	225.00
90-02-095	Winter Trail	F. McCarthy	1,500	235.00	235-300.
Greenwich Workshop		**Wysocki**			
88-03-001	The Americana Bowl	C. Wysocki	3,500	295.00	295.00
83-03-002	Amish Neighbors	C. Wysocki	1,000	150.00	475-600.
89-03-003	Another Year At Sea	C. Wysocki	2,500	175.00	250-410.
83-03-004	Applebutter Makers	C. Wysocki	1,000	135.00	375-675.
87-03-005	Bach's Magnificat in D Minor	C. Wysocki	2,250	150.00	350-400.
91-03-006	Beauty And The Beast	C. Wysocki	2,000	125.00	125.00
90-03-007	Belly Warmers	C. Wysocki	2,500	150.00	150-225.
84-03-008	Bird House (C)	C. Wysocki	1,000	85.00	175-250.
85-03-009	Birds of a Feather	C. Wysocki	1,250	145.00	300-400.
89-03-010	Bostonians And Beans (PC)	C. Wysocki	6,711	225.00	350-400.
79-03-011	Butternut Farms	C. Wysocki	1,000	75.00	1150-1300.
80-03-012	Caleb's Buggy Barn	C. Wysocki	1,000	80.00	275-325.
84-03-013	Cape Cod Cold Fish Party	C. Wysocki	1,000	150.00	175-250.
81-03-014	Carver Coggins	C. Wysocki	1,000	145.00	800-1200.
89-03-015	Christmas Greeting	C. Wysocki	11,000	125.00	125-250.
82-03-016	Christmas Print, 1982	C. Wysocki	2,000	80.00	600-850.
85-03-017	Clammers at Hodge's Horn	C. Wysocki	1,000	150.00	900-1200.

Company Number	Name	Series Artist	Edition Limit	Issue Price	Quote
83-03-018	Commemorative Print, 1983	C. Wysocki	2,000	55.00	55-100.00
84-03-019	Cotton Country	C. Wysocki	1,000	150.00	200-250.
83-03-020	Country Race	C. Wysocki	1,000	150.00	190-325.
86-03-021	Daddy's Coming Home	C. Wysocki	1,250	150.00	1100-1500.
87-03-022	Dahalia Dinalhaven Makes a Dory Deal	C. Wysocki	2,250	150.00	230-375.
86-03-023	Dancing Pheasant Farms	C. Wysocki	1,750	165.00	325-450.
85-03-024	Devilstone Harbor/An American Celebration (B & P)	C. Wysocki	3,500	195.00	350-600.
89-03-025	Dreamers	C. Wysocki	3,000	175.00	175-275.
80-03-026	Derby Square	C. Wysocki	1,000	90.00	825-975.
86-03-027	Devilbelly Bay	C. Wysocki	1,000	145.00	275-375.
79-03-028	Farhaven by the Sea	C. Wysocki	1,000	75.00	750-950.
88-03-029	Feathered Critics	C. Wysocki	2,500	150.00	150-195.
79-03-030	Fox Run	C. Wysocki	1,000	75.00	1400-1900.
84-03-031	The Foxy Fox Outfoxes the Fox Hunters	C. Wysocki	1,500	150.00	500-650.
89-03-032	Fun Lovin' Silly Folks	C. Wysocki	3,000	185.00	185-300.
86-03-033	Hickory Haven Canal	C. Wysocki	1,500	165.00	725-850.
88-03-034	Home Is My Sailor	C. Wysocki	2,500	150.00	150-250.
90-03-035	Jingle Bell Teddy and Friends	C. Wysocki	5,000	125.00	125.00
80-03-036	Jolly Hill Farms	C. Wysocki	1,000	75.00	700-900.
86-03-037	Lady Liberty's Independence Day Enterprising Immigrants	C. Wysocki	1,500	140.00	200-300.
89-03-038	The Memory Maker	C. Wysocki	2,500	165.00	165.00
85-03-039	Merrymakers Serenade	C. Wysocki	1,250	135.00	135.00
86-03-040	Mr. Swallobark	C. Wysocki	2,000	145.00	450-575.
82-03-041	The Nantucket	C. Wysocki	1,000	145.00	145-400.
81-03-042	Olde America	C. Wysocki	1,500	125.00	475-750.
81-03-043	Page's Bake Shoppe	C. Wysocki	1,000	115.00	450-575.
81-03-044	Prairie Wind Flowers	C. Wysocki	1,000	125.00	900-1500.
90-03-045	Robin Hood	C. Wysocki	2,000	165.00	165.00
91-03-046	Rockland Breakwater Light	C. Wysocki	2,500	165.00	165.00
85-03-047	Salty Witch Bay	C. Wysocki	475	350.00	1500-2000.
91-03-048	Sea Captain's Wife Abiding	C. Wysocki	1,500	150.00	150-400.
79-03-049	Shall We?	C. Wysocki	1,000	75.00	425-475.
82-03-050	Sleepy Town West	C. Wysocki	1,500	150.00	400-575.
84-03-051	Storin' Up	C. Wysocki	450	325.00	750-1125.
82-03-052	Sunset Hills, Texas Wildcatters	C. Wysocki	1,000	125.00	125-170.
84-03-053	Sweetheart Chessmate	C. Wysocki	1,000	95.00	275-375.
83-03-054	Tea by the Sea	C. Wysocki	1,000	145.00	1200-1950.
87-03-055	'Twas the Twilight Before Christmas	C. Wysocki	7,500	95.00	150.00
84-03-056	Warm Christmas Love, A	C. Wysocki	3,951	80.00	300-450.
90-03-057	Wednesday Night Checkers	C. Wysocki	2,500	175.00	175.00
90-03-058	Where The Bouys Are	C. Wysocki	2,750	175.00	175.00
91-03-059	Whistle Stop Christmas	C. Wysocki	5,000	125.00	125-190.
84-03-060	Yankee Wink Hollow	C. Wysocki	1,000	95.00	900-1125.
87-03-061	Yearning For My Captain	C. Wysocki	2,000	150.00	300-400.
87-03-062	You've Been So Long at Sea, Horatio	C. Wysocki	2,500	150.00	150-350.
Greenwich Workshop		**Lyman**			
90-04-001	Among The Wild Brambles	Lyman	1,750	185.00	180-275.
87-04-002	An Elegant Couple	Lyman	1,000	125.00	150-235.
85-04-003	Autumn Gathering	Lyman	850	115.00	250.00
85-04-004	Bear & Blossoms (C)	Lyman	850	75.00	75-220.00
87-04-005	Canadian Autumn	Lyman	1,500	165.00	175.00
89-04-006	Color In The Snow	Lyman	1,500	165.00	165-250.
86-04-007	Colors of Twilight	Lyman	850	N/A	N/A
91-04-008	Dance of Cloud and Cliff	Lyman	1,500	225.00	325-450.
83-04-009	Early Winter In The Mountains	Lyman	850	95.00	150-500.
91-04-010	Embers at Dawn	Lyman	3,500	225.00	650-1200.
83-04-011	End Of The Ridge	Lyman	850	95.00	200-275.
90-04-012	Evening Light	Lyman	2,500	225.00	525-900.
84-04-013	Free Flight (C)	Lyman	850	70.00	70-120.00
87-04-014	High Creek Crossing	Lyman	1,000	165.00	775-1000.
89-04-015	High Light	Lyman	1,250	165.00	200-350.
86-04-016	High Trail At Sunset	Lyman	1,000	125.00	545-695.
88-04-017	The Intruder	Lyman	1,500	150.00	150.00
89-04-018	Last Light of Winter	Lyman	1,500	175.00	500-600.
87-04-019	Moon Shadows	Lyman	1,500	135.00	135-185.
86-04-020	Morning Solitude	Lyman	850	115.00	150-250.
90-04-021	A Mountain Campfire	Lyman	1,500	195.00	1300-3000.
87-04-022	New Territories	Lyman	1,000	135.00	210-235.
84-04-023	Noisy Neighbors	Lyman	650	95.00	600-900.
84-04-024	Noisy Neighbors (R)	Lyman	25	215.00	520-1800.
83-04-025	The Pass	Lyman	850	95.00	400-575.
89-04-026	Quiet Rain	Lyman	1,500	165.00	260-475.
88-04-027	The Raptor's Watch	Lyman	1,500	150.00	275-325.
88-04-028	Return Of The Falcon	Lyman	1,500	150.00	150.00
88-04-029	Return Of The Falcon (P)	Lyman	Open	20.00	20.00
91-04-030	Secret Watch	Lyman	2,250	150.00	150.00
90-04-031	Silent Snows	Lyman	1,750	210.00	225.00
88-04-032	Snow Hunter	Lyman	1,500	135.00	135.00
86-04-033	Snowy Throne (C)	Lyman	850	85.00	85-295.
87-04-034	Twilight Snow (C)	Lyman	950	85.00	85-225.
88-04-035	Uzumati: Great Bear of Yosemite	Lyman	1,750	150.00	150.00
88-04-036	Uzumati: Great Bear of Yosemite (P)	Lyman	Open	20.00	20.00
Guildhall, Inc.		**De Haan**			
79-01-001	Foggy Mornin' Wait	C. De Haan	650	75.00	2525.00
80-01-002	Texas Panhandle	C. De Haan	650	75.00	1525.00
81-01-003	MacTavish	C. De Haan	650	75.00	1425.00
81-01-004	Forgin' The Keechi	C. De Haan	650	85.00	725.00
81-01-005	Surprise Encounter	C. De Haan	750	85.00	475.00
82-01-006	O' That Strawberry Roan	C. De Haan	750	85.00	125.00
83-01-007	Ridin' Ol' Paint	C. De Haan	750	85.00	625.00
83-01-008	Crossin' Horse Creek	C. De Haan	750	100.00	625.00
83-01-009	Keep A Movin' Dan	C. De Haan	750	85.00	125.00
84-01-010	Jake	C. De Haan	650	100.00	600.00
84-01-011	Spooked	C. De Haan	650	95.00	1825.00
85-01-012	Up the Chisholm	C. De Haan	750	85.00	125.00
85-01-013	Keechi Country	C. De Haan	750	100.00	375.00
85-01-014	Oklahoma Paints	C. De Haan	750	100.00	425.00
85-01-015	Horsemen of the West (Suite of 3)	C. De Haan	650	145.00	975.00
86-01-016	The Mustangers	C. De Haan	750	100.00	400.00
86-01-017	The Searchers	C. De Haan	650	100.00	375.00
86-01-018	Moondancers	C. De Haan	750	100.00	165.00
86-01-019	The Loner (with matching buckle)	C. De Haan	750	145.00	425.00
87-01-020	Snow Birds	C. De Haan	750	100.00	350.00
87-01-021	Murphy's Law	C. De Haan	750	100.00	225.00
87-01-022	Crow Ceremonial Dress	C. De Haan	750	100.00	175.00
87-01-023	Supremacy	C. De Haan	750	100.00	175.00
88-01-024	Mornin' Gather	C. DeHaan	750	100.00	350.00
88-01-025	Stage To Deadwood	C. DeHaan	750	100.00	275.00
88-01-026	Water Breakin'	C. DeHaan	750	125.00	600.00

Company / Number	Name	Series / Artist	Edition Limit	Issue Price	Quote
89-01-027	Kentucky Blue	C. DeHaan	750	125.00	575.00
89-01-028	Village Markers	C. DeHaan	750	125.00	525.00
89-01-029	The Quarter Horse	C. DeHaan	800	125.00	325.00
89-01-030	Crows	C. DeHaan	800	135.00	525.00
90-01-031	War Cry	C. DeHaan	925	135.00	275.00
90-01-032	Crow Autumn	C. DeHaan	925	135.00	250.00
90-01-033	Escape	C. DeHaan	925	135.00	200.00
90-01-034	High Plains Drifters	C. DeHaan	925	140.00	200.00
90-01-035	The Pipe Carrier	C. DeHaan	925	140.00	175.00
Guildhall, Inc.		**Baize**			
88-02-001	Best of Friends	W. Baize	575	85.00	85.00
88-02-002	Winter Arrival	W. Baize	575	85.00	85.00
Guildhall, Inc.		**Moline**			
88-03-001	Companions	B. Moline	575	85.00	85.00
88-03-002	Portraying His Heritage	B. Moline	575	85.00	85.00
Hadley Companies		**Blaylock**			
87-01-001	Evening Hayride	T. Blaylock	950	85.00	85.00
87-01-002	Anasazi Nest Builder I	T. Blaylock	950	150.00	325.00
87-01-003	Anasazi Nest Builder II	T. Blaylock	950	150.00	150.00
87-01-004	Morning Snack	T. Blaylock	950	100.00	100.00
87-01-005	Just in Time for Breakfast	T. Blaylock	400	75.00	100.00
87-01-006	Rocky Mountain Courtship	T. Blaylock	950	150.00	150.00
87-01-007	Easy Landing	T. Blaylock	Open	60.00	60.00
87-01-008	Honkers on an Updraft	T. Blaylock	950	150.00	200.00
88-01-009	Anasazi Nest Builder III	T. Blaylock	950	225.00	225.00
88-01-010	Two's Company	T. Blaylock	Open	60.00	60.00
88-01-011	Teton Trumpeters	T. Blaylock	950	150.00	150.00
88-01-012	Daybreak on Cinnamon Creek	T. Blaylock	950	100.00	150.00
89-01-013	Climbing Eagle Pass	T. Blaylock	950	100.00	100.00
89-01-014	Sawtooth Point	T. Blaylock	950	80.00	80.00
89-01-015	Homestead on Blackberry Lane	T. Blaylock	950	40.00	40.00
89-01-016	Country Bouquet	T. Blaylock	950	40.00	40.00
90-01-017	Bighorn Hideaway	T. Blaylock	950	150.00	150.00
90-01-018	Sunrise Cascade	T. Blaylock	950	150.00	150.00
90-01-019	Arrival of the 9:59	T. Blaylock	950	100.00	200.00
91-01-020	Bring Up a Grandchild	T. Blaylock	950	150.00	150.00
91-01-021	Black Canyon Express	T. Blaylock	950	100.00	100.00
92-01-022	When Gold Ran the Rails	T. Blaylock	950	150.00	150.00
92-01-023	Black River Reunion	T. Blaylock	950	150.00	150.00
Hadley Companies		**Bush**			
92-02-001	Cliff Divers	D. Bush	750	100.00	100.00
92-02-002	Twilight Encounter	D. Bush	999	125.00	125.00
92-02-003	Shallow Crossing	D. Bush	999	125.00	125.00
92-02-004	Puddle Jumpers	D. Bush	Open	30.00	30.00
93-02-005	The Hiding Place	D. Bush	750	100.00	100.00
Hadley Companies		**Capser**			
92-03-001	Comes the Dawn	M. Capser	600	100.00	100.00
92-03-002	Silence Unbroken	M. Capser	600	100.00	100.00
92-03-003	The Watch	M. Capser	600	100.00	100.00
92-03-004	Reflections	M. Capser	600	100.00	100.00
93-03-005	Skyline Serenade	M. Capser	600	100.00	100.00
Hadley Companies		**Daniel**			
92-04-001	Puppy Love	K. Daniel	850	75.00	75.00
92-04-002	Nightwatch	K. Daniel	999	150.00	150.00
92-04-003	Forever Friends	K. Daniel	850	185.00	185.00
92-04-004	Lone Drifter	K. Daniel	999	150.00	150.00
93-04-005	Mystic Point	K. Daniel	999	150.00	150.00
Hadley Companies		**Franca**			
88-05-001	Sitting Bull	O. Franca	950	70.00	250.00
88-05-002	The Apache	O. Franca	950	70.00	175.00
88-05-003	Slow Bull	O. Franca	950	70.00	250.00
88-05-004	Cacique	O. Franca	950	70.00	175.00
88-05-005	The Red Shawl	O. Franca	600	80.00	300.00
88-05-006	Feathered Hair Ties	O. Franca	600	80.00	300.00
89-05-007	Young Warrior	O. Franca	999	80.00	425.00
89-05-008	Navajo Fantasy	O. Franca	999	80.00	150.00
89-05-009	Winter	O. Franca	999	80.00	300.00
89-05-010	Pink Navajo	O. Franca	999	80.00	250.00
90-05-011	Cecy	O. Franca	1,500	125.00	175.00
90-05-012	Santa Fe	O. Franca	1,500	125.00	125.00
90-05-013	Blue Navajo	O. Franca	1,500	125.00	125.00
90-05-014	Destiny	O. Franca	999	100.00	100.00
90-05-015	Blue Tranquility	O. Franca	999	100.00	100.00
90-05-016	Wind Song	O. Franca	999	100.00	425.00
90-05-017	Navajo Summer	O. Franca	999	100.00	240.00
90-05-018	Feathered Hair Ties II	O. Franca	999	100.00	300.00
90-05-019	Turqoise Necklace	O. Franca	999	100.00	450.00
91-05-020	Early Morning	O. Franca	3,600	125.00	125.00
91-05-021	Red Wolf	O. Franca	1,500	125.00	175.00
91-05-022	Olympia	O. Franca	1,500	125.00	250.00
91-05-023	The Lovers	O. Franca	2,400	125.00	650.00
91-05-024	The Model	O. Franca	1,500	125.00	400.00
92-05-025	Navajo Reflection	O. Franca	4,000	80.00	225.00
92-05-026	Wind Song II	O. Franca	4,000	80.00	150.00
92-05-027	Navajo Daydream	O. Franca	3,600	175.00	175.00
92-05-028	Navajo Meditating	O. Franca	4,000	80.00	125.00
Hadley Companies		**Hanks**			
90-06-001	Contemplation	S. Hanks	999	100.00	150.00
90-06-002	Quiet Rapport	S. Hanks	999	150.00	300.00
90-06-003	Emotional Appeal	S. Hanks	999	150.00	200.00
91-06-004	Duet	S. Hanks	999	150.00	250.00
91-06-005	A World For Our Children	S. Hanks	999	125.00	475.00
91-06-006	Sunday Afternoon	S. Hanks	Open	40.00	40.00
92-06-007	Stepping Stones	S. Hanks	999	150.00	250.00
92-06-008	An Innocent View	S. Hanks	999	150.00	350.00
92-06-009	Sometimes It's the Little Things	S. Hanks	999	125.00	225.00
92-06-010	Things Worth Keeping	S. Hanks	999	125.00	450.00
92-06-011	Conferring With the Sea	S. Hanks	999	125.00	250.00
93-06-012	Gathering Thoughts	S. Hanks	1,500	150.00	150.00
93-06-013	The Thinkers	S. Hanks	1,500	150.00	150.00
93-06-014	The New Arrival	S. Hanks	1,500	150.00	150.00
Hadley Companies		**Hulings**			
88-07-001	Ile de la Cite - Paris	C. Hulings	580	150.00	225.00
88-07-002	Onteniente	C. Hulings	580	150.00	425.00
88-07-003	Three Cats on a Grapevine	C. Hulings	580	65.00	225.00
89-07-004	Chechaquene - Morrocco Market Square	C. Hulings	999	150.00	150.00
89-07-005	Portuguese Vegetable Woman	C. Hulings	999	85.00	85.00
90-07-006	The Lonely Man	C. Hulings	999	150.00	150.00
90-07-007	Spanish Shawl	C. Hulings	999	125.00	125.00
90-07-008	Ancient French Farmhouse	C. Hulings	999	150.00	150.00
91-07-009	Place des Ternes	C. Hulings	580	195.00	195.00
92-07-010	Cuernavaca Flower Market	C. Hulings	580	225.00	225.00
92-07-011	Sunday Afternoon	C. Hulings	580	195.00	195.00
93-07-012	Spring Flowers	C. Hulings	580	225.00	225.00
Hadley Companies		**Moon**			
87-08-001	Father of the Loins	B. Moon	250	90.00	90.00
87-08-002	Boldy	B. Moon	250	100.00	100.00
87-08-003	Catnap	B. Moon	300	60.00	60.00
87-08-004	Born Free	B. Moon	500	80.00	80.00
88-08-005	Bonnie & Clyde	B. Moon	Open	30.00	30.00
88-08-006	The Cats of Anderson House Hotel	B. Moon	Open	30.00	30.00
88-08-007	The James-Younger Gangs Last Raid	B. Moon	Open	30.00	30.00
89-08-008	The Hunt Club	B. Moon	Open	30.00	30.00
89-08-009	The Odd Couple	B. Moon	Open	30.00	30.00
89-08-010	HMS Bounty Approached Pitcarian Island	B. Moon	725	300.00	300.00
91-08-011	Hotdoggers	B. Moon	Open	30.00	30.00
91-08-012	Doolittle Raiders	B. Moon	980	200.00	300.00
91-08-013	Gone Fishin'	B. Moon	Open	30.00	30.00
92-08-014	Tidalwave Over Ploesti	B. Moon	1,800	200.00	200.00
92-08-015	The Spirit of Christmas	B. Moon	Open	30.00	30.00
92-08-016	The Card Players	B. Moon	Open	30.00	30.00
Hadley Companies		**Redlin**			
77-09-001	Apple River Mallards	T. Redlin	Open	10.00	150.00
77-09-002	Over the Blowdown	T. Redlin	Open	20.00	70.00
77-09-003	Winter Snows	T. Redlin	Open	20.00	100.00
78-09-004	Back from the Fields	T. Redlin	720	40.00	325.00
78-09-005	Backwater Mallards	T. Redlin	720	40.00	650.00
78-09-006	Old Loggers Trail	T. Redlin	720	40.00	550.00
78-09-007	Over the Rushes	T. Redlin	720	40.00	400.00
78-09-008	Quiet Afternoon	T. Redlin	720	40.00	400.00
78-09-009	Startled	T. Redlin	720	30.00	400.00
79-09-010	Ageing Shoreline	T. Redlin	960	40.00	250.00
79-09-011	Colorful Trio	T. Redlin	960	40.00	400.00
79-09-012	Fighting a Headwind	T. Redlin	960	30.00	250.00
79-09-013	Morning Chores	T. Redlin	960	40.00	1100.00
79-09-014	The Loner	T. Redlin	960	40.00	200.00
79-09-015	Whitecaps	T. Redlin	960	40.00	375.00
80-09-016	Autumn Run	T. Redlin	960	60.00	450.00
80-09-017	Breaking Away	T. Redlin	960	60.00	300.00
80-09-018	Clearing the Rail	T. Redlin	960	60.00	350.00
80-09-019	Country Road	T. Redlin	960	60.00	375.00
80-09-020	Drifting	T. Redlin	960	60.00	300.00
80-09-021	The Homestead	T. Redlin	960	60.00	375.00
80-09-022	Intruders	T. Redlin	960	60.00	200.00
80-09-023	Night Watch	T. Redlin	2,400	60.00	700.00
80-09-024	Rusty Refuge	T. Redlin	960	60.00	475.00
80-09-025	Secluded Pond	T. Redlin	960	60.00	250.00
80-09-026	Silent Sunset	T. Redlin	960	60.00	850.00
80-09-027	Spring Thaw	T. Redlin	960	60.00	350.00
80-09-028	Squall Line	T. Redlin	960	60.00	300.00
81-09-029	1981 Mn Duck Stamp Print	T. Redlin	7,800	125.00	200.00
81-09-030	All Clear	T. Redlin	960	150.00	350.00
81-09-031	April Snow	T. Redlin	960	100.00	450.00
81-09-032	Broken Covey	T. Redlin	960	100.00	325.00
81-09-033	High Country	T. Redlin	960	100.00	450.00
81-09-034	Hightailing	T. Redlin	960	75.00	200.00
81-09-035	The Landmark	T. Redlin	960	100.00	400.00
81-09-036	Morning Retreat (AP)	T. Redlin	240	400.00	2700.00
81-09-037	Passing Through	T. Redlin	960	100.00	225.00
81-09-038	Rusty Refuge II	T. Redlin	960	100.00	375.00
81-09-039	Sharing the Bounty	T. Redlin	960	100.00	550.00
81-09-040	Soft Shadows	T. Redlin	960	100.00	225.00
81-09-041	Spring Run-Off	T. Redlin	1,700	125.00	350.00
82-09-042	1982 Mn Trout Stamp Print	T. Redlin	960	125.00	600.00
82-09-043	Evening Retreat (AP)	T. Redlin	300	400.00	2500.00
82-09-044	October Evening	T. Redlin	960	100.00	450.00
82-09-045	Reflections	T. Redlin	960	100.00	400.00
82-09-046	Seed Hunters	T. Redlin	960	100.00	450.00
82-09-047	Spring Mapling	T. Redlin	960	100.00	450.00
82-09-048	The Birch Line	T. Redlin	960	100.00	500.00
82-09-049	The Landing	T. Redlin	Open	30.00	80.00
82-09-050	Whitewater	T. Redlin	960	100.00	400.00
82-09-051	Winter Haven	T. Redlin	500	85.00	800.00
83-09-052	1983 ND Duck Stamp Print	T. Redlin	3,438	135.00	135.00
83-09-053	Autumn Shoreline	T. Redlin	Open	50.00	200.00
83-09-054	Backwoods Cabin	T. Redlin	960	150.00	675.00
83-09-055	Evening Glow	T. Redlin	960	150.00	1400.00
83-09-056	Evening Surprise	T. Redlin	960	150.00	900.00
83-09-057	Hidden Point	T. Redlin	960	150.00	350.00
83-09-058	On the Alert	T. Redlin	960	125.00	400.00
83-09-059	Peaceful Evening	T. Redlin	960	100.00	350.00
83-09-060	Prairie Springs	T. Redlin	960	150.00	325.00
83-09-061	Rushing Rapids	T. Redlin	960	125.00	400.00
84-09-062	1984 Quail Conservation	T. Redlin	1,500	135.00	135.00
84-09-063	Bluebill Point (AP)	T. Redlin	240	300.00	400.00
84-09-064	Changing Seasons-Summer	T. Redlin	960	150.00	800.00
84-09-065	Closed for the Season	T. Redlin	960	150.00	300.00
84-09-066	Leaving the Sanctuary	T. Redlin	960	150.00	475.00
84-09-067	Morning Glow	T. Redlin	960	150.00	1200.00
84-09-068	Night Harvest	T. Redlin	960	150.00	575.00
84-09-069	Nightflight (AP)	T. Redlin	360	600.00	2800.00
84-09-070	Prairie Skyline	T. Redlin	960	150.00	550.00
84-09-071	Rural Route	T. Redlin	960	150.00	350.00
84-09-072	Rusty Refuge III	T. Redlin	960	150.00	400.00
84-09-073	Silent Wings Suite (set of 4)	T. Redlin	960	200.00	450.00
84-09-074	Sundown	T. Redlin	960	300.00	575.00
84-09-075	Sunny Afternoon	T. Redlin	960	150.00	375.00
84-09-076	Winter Windbreak	T. Redlin	960	150.00	450.00
85-09-077	1985 MN Duck Stamp	T. Redlin	4,385	135.00	135.00
85-09-078	Afternoon Glow	T. Redlin	960	150.00	1000.00
85-09-079	Breaking Cover	T. Redlin	960	150.00	325.00
85-09-080	Brousing	T. Redlin	960	150.00	350.00
85-09-081	Clear View	T. Redlin	1,500	300.00	450.00
85-09-082	Delayed Departure	T. Redlin	1,500	150.00	450.00
85-09-083	Evening Company	T. Redlin	960	150.00	450.00

Company Number	Name	Series Artist	Edition Limit	Issue Price	Quote
85-09-084	Night Light	T. Redlin	1,500	300.00	600.00
85-09-085	Riverside Pond	T. Redlin	960	150.00	525.00
85-09-086	Rusty Refuge IV	T. Redlin	960	150.00	500.00
85-09-087	The Sharing Season	T. Redlin	Open	60.00	150.00
85-09-088	Whistle Stop	T. Redlin	960	150.00	550.00
85-09-089	Back to the Sanctuary	T. Redlin	960	150.00	450.00
86-09-090	Changing Seasons-Autumn	T. Redlin	960	150.00	400.00
86-09-091	Changing Seasons-Winter	T. Redlin	960	200.00	400.00
86-09-092	Coming Home	T. Redlin	2,400	100.00	1200.00
86-09-093	Hazy Afternoon	T. Redlin	2,560	200.00	650.00
86-09-094	Night Mapling	T. Redlin	960	200.00	550.00
86-09-095	Prairie Monuments	T. Redlin	960	200.00	400.00
86-09-096	Sharing Season II	T. Redlin	Open	60.00	150.00
86-09-097	Silent Flight	T. Redlin	960	150.00	250.00
86-09-098	Stormy Weather	T. Redlin	1,500	200.00	550.00
86-09-099	Sunlit Trail	T. Redlin	960	150.00	325.00
86-09-100	Twilight Glow	T. Redlin	960	200.00	700.00
87-09-101	Autumn Afternoon	T. Redlin	4,800	100.00	750.00
87-09-102	Changing Seasons-Spring	T. Redlin	960	200.00	450.00
87-09-103	Deer Crossing	T. Redlin	2,400	200.00	450.00
87-09-104	Evening Chores (print & book)	T. Redlin	2,400	400.00	500.00
87-09-105	Evening Harvest	T. Redlin	960	200.00	475.00
87-09-106	Golden Retreat (AP)	T. Redlin	500	800.00	1600.00
87-09-107	Prepared for the Season	T. Redlin	Open	70.00	100.00
87-01-108	Sharing the Solitude	T. Redlin	2,400	125.00	700.00
87-09-109	That Special Time	T. Redlin	2,400	125.00	650.00
87-09-110	Together for the Season	T. Redlin	Open	70.00	150.00
88-09-111	Boulder Ridge	T. Redlin	4,800	150.00	200.00
88-09-112	Catching the Scent	T. Redlin	2,400	200.00	250.00
88-09-113	Country Neighbors	T. Redlin	4,800	150.00	350.00
88-09-114	Homeward Bound	T. Redlin	Open	70.00	125.00
88-09-115	Lights of Home	T. Redlin	9,500	125.00	750.00
88-09-116	Moonlight Retreat (AP)	T. Redlin	530	1000.00	1000.00
88-09-117	Prairie Morning	T. Redlin	4,800	150.00	250.00
88-09-118	Quiet of the Evening	T. Redlin	4,800	150.00	850.00
88-09-119	The Master's Domain	T. Redlin	2,400	225.00	700.00
88-09-120	Wednesday Afternoon	T. Redlin	6,800	175.00	400.00
88-09-121	House Call	T. Redlin	6,800	175.00	450.00
89-09-122	Office Hours	T. Redlin	6,800	175.00	450.00
89-09-123	Morning Rounds	T. Redlin	6,800	175.00	350.00
89-09-124	Indian Summer	T. Redlin	4,800	200.00	300.00
89-09-125	Aroma of Fall	T. Redlin	6,800	200.00	1250.00
89-09-126	Homeward Bound	T. Redlin	Open	80.00	100.00
89-09-127	Special Memories (AP Only)	T. Redlin	570	1000.00	1000.00
90-09-128	Family Traditions	T. Redlin	Open	80.00	100.00
90-09-129	Pure Contentment	T. Redlin	9,500	150.00	350.00
90-09-130	Master of the Valley	T. Redlin	6,800	200.00	200.00
90-09-131	Evening Solitude	T. Redlin	9,500	200.00	500-650.
90-09-132	Best Friends (AP Only)	T. Redlin	570	1000.00	1000.00
90-09-133	Heading Home	T. Redlin	Open	80.00	100.00
90-09-134	Welcome to Paradise	T. Redlin	14,500	150.00	300.00
90-09-135	Evening With Friends	T. Redlin	19,500	225.00	575-975.
91-09-136	Morning Solitude	T. Redlin	12,107	250.00	475.00
91-09-137	Flying Free	T. Redlin	14,500	200.00	200.00
91-09-138	Hunter's Haven (AP Only)	T. Redlin	N/A	175.00	175.00
91-09-140	Pleasures of Winter	T. Redlin	24,500	150.00	200.00
91-09-141	Comforts of Home	T. Redlin	22,900	175.00	350.00
92-09-142	Summertime	T. Redlin	24,900	225.00	225.00
92-09-143	Oh Beautiful for Spacious Skies	T. Redlin	29,500	250.00	250.00
92-09-144	Winter Wonderland	T. Redlin	29,500	150.00	150.00
92-09-145	The Conservationists	T. Redlin	29,500	175.00	175.00
93-09-146	For Amber Waves of Grain	T. Redlin	29,500	250.00	250.00
Hadley Companies		**Van Zyle**			
92-10-001	On the Upper Kenai	J. Van Zyle	999	125.00	125.00
92-10-002	Eminent Domain	J. Van Zyle	999	150.00	150.00
92-10-003	Iditarod Memories - Stone Litho	J. Van Zyle	100	485.00	485.00
92-10-004	Alpenglow Evening - Stone Litho	J. Van Zyle	100	350.00	350.00
92-10-005	Trail into the Mystic/Bashful	J. Van Zyle	580	125.00	125.00
Hallmark Galleries		**Innocent Wonders**			
92-01-001	Pinkie Poo	T. Blackshear	9,500	75.00	75.00
Hallmark Galleries		**Majestic Wilderness**			
92-02-001	White-tailed Deer	M. Newman	9,500	75.00	75.00
92-02-002	Timber Wolves	M. Newman	9,500	75.00	75.00
John Hine		**Rambles**			
89-01-001	Two for Joy	A. Wyatt	Closed	59.90	59.90
89-01-002	Riverbank	A. Wyatt	Closed	59.90	59.90
89-01-003	Waters Edge	A. Wyatt	Closed	59.90	59.90
89-01-004	Summer Harvest	A. Wyatt	Closed	59.90	59.90
89-01-005	Garden Gate	A. Wyatt	Closed	59.90	59.90
89-01-006	Hedgerow	A. Wyatt	Closed	59.90	59.90
89-01-007	Frog	A. Wyatt	Closed	33.00	33.00
89-01-008	Wren	A. Wyatt	Closed	33.00	33.00
89-01-009	Kingfisher	A. Wyatt	Closed	33.00	33.00
89-01-010	Blue Tit	A. Wyatt	Closed	33.00	33.00
89-01-011	Lobster Pot	A. Wyatt	Closed	50.00	50.00
89-01-012	Puffin Rock	A. Wyatt	Closed	50.00	50.00
89-01-013	Otter's Holt	A. Wyatt	Closed	50.00	50.00
89-01-014	Bluebell Cottage	A. Wyatt	Closed	50.00	50.00
89-01-015	Shirelarm	A. Wyatt	Closed	42.00	42.00
89-01-016	St. Mary's Church	A. Wyatt	Closed	42.00	42.00
89-01-017	The Swan	A. Wyatt	Closed	42.00	42.00
89-01-018	Castle Street	A. Wyatt	Closed	42.00	42.00
Lightpost Group Inc./ Lightpost Publishing		**Canvas Editions-Framed**			
89-01-001	Carmel, Ocean Avenue	T. Kinkade	Closed	645.00	1800-4000.
89-01-002	San Francisco, Union Square	T. Kinkade	Closed	595.00	1500-3000.
89-01-003	Entrance to the Manor House	T. Kinkade	Closed	495.00	900-1000.
89-01-004	Evening at Merritt's Cottage	T. Kinkade	Closed	495.00	850-2000.
90-01-005	Hidden Cottage	T. Kinkade	Closed	495.00	1000-2000.
90-01-006	Chandler's Cottage	T. Kinkade	Closed	495.00	1000-2000.
90-01-007	Christmas Cottage 1990	T. Kinkade	Closed	295.00	600-1500.
90-01-008	Christmas Eve	T. Kinkade	Closed	395.00	500-1800.
90-01-009	Morning Light A/P	T. Kinkade	Closed	695.00	900-950.
90-01-010	Rose Arbor	T. Kinkade	Closed	495.00	750-900.
90-01-011	Spring At Stonegate	T. Kinkade	550	295.00	295.00
91-01-012	Home For The Holidays	T. Kinkade	Closed	595.00	1250-1395.
91-01-013	Afternoon Light, Dogwoods	T. Kinkade	980	495.00	495.00
91-01-014	The Autumn Gate	T. Kinkade	Closed	595.00	595-1000
91-01-015	Boston	T. Kinkade	550	495.00	495.00
91-01-016	Carmel, Tuck Box Tea Room	T. Kinkade	980	595.00	595.00
91-01-017	Cedar Nook Cottage	T. Kinkade	1,960	185.00	185.00
91-01-018	Flags Over The Capitol	T. Kinkade	980	595.00	595.00
91-01-019	Home For The Evening	T. Kinkade	Closed	195.00	195.00
91-01-020	The Lit Path	T. Kinkade	1,960	195.00	195.00
91-01-021	McKenna's Cottage	T. Kinkade	980	495.00	495.00
90-01-022	Olde Porterfield Tea Room	T. Kinkade	Closed	495.00	595-2000
91-01-023	Open Gate, Sussex	T. Kinkade	980	195.00	195.00
91-01-024	Pye Corner Cottage	T. Kinkade	1,960	195.00	195.00
91-01-025	Victorian Evening	T. Kinkade	980	495.00	495.00
91-01-026	Woodman's Thatch	T. Kinkade	1,960	195.00	195.00
92-01-027	Broadwater Bridge	T. Kinkade	Closed	495.00	495-795.
92-01-028	Swanbrooke Cottage	T. Kinkade	Closed	595.00	595-795.
92-01-029	Sweetheart Cottage	T. Kinkade	980	495.00	495.00
92-01-030	Blossom Hill Church	T. Kinkade	980	595.00	595.00
92-01-031	Cottage-By-The-Sea	T. Kinkade	980	595.00	595.00
92-01-032	Home is Where the Heart Is	T. Kinkade	Closed	595.00	595-895.
92-01-033	Miller's Cottage	T. Kinkade	980	495.00	495.00
92-01-034	Sunday at Apple Hill	T. Kinkade	Closed	495.00	495.00
92-01-035	Victorian Garden	T. Kinkade	980	795.00	795.00
92-01-036	San Francisco, Nob Hill	T. Kinkade	Closed	645.00	645-1500.
92-01-037	Julianne's Cottage	T. Kinkade	Closed	395.00	395-695.
92-01-038	Weathervane Hutch	T. Kinkade	1,960	295.00	295.00
92-01-039	Yosemite	T. Kinkade	980	595.00	595.00
92-01-040	Country Memories	T. Kinkade	Closed	395.00	395-695.
92-01-041	The Garden Party	T. Kinkade	980	495.00	495.00
92-01-042	Victorian Christmas	T. Kinkade	Closed	595.00	595-895.
92-01-043	Moonlit Sleigh Ride	T. Kinkade	980	285.00	285.00
92-01-044	Olde Porterfield Gift Shoppe	T. Kinkade	980	495.00	495.00
92-01-045	Amber Afternoon	T. Kinkade	980	495.00	495.00
92-01-046	Silent Night	T. Kinkade	Closed	395.00	495.00
92-01-047	Evening Carolers	T. Kinkade	980	295.00	295.00
92-01-048	Christmas At the Ahwahnee	T. Kinkade	980	495.00	495.00
93-01-049	Sweetheart Cottage	T. Kinkade	980	495.00	495.00
93-01-050	Beside Still Waters	T. Kinkade	1280	495.00	495.00
Lightpost Group Inc./ Lightpost Publishing		**Archival Paper-Framed**			
85-02-001	Birth of a City	T. Kinkade	Closed	150.00	195-250.
89-02-002	Carmel, Ocean Avenue	T. Kinkade	Closed	225.00	650-1000.
90-02-003	Chandler's Cottage	T. Kinkade	Closed	125.00	350.00
90-02-004	Christmas Cottage 1990	T. Kinkade	Closed	95.00	150.00
84-02-005	Dawson	T. Kinkade	Closed	150.00	150.00
89-02-006	Entrance to the Manor House	T. Kinkade	Closed	125.00	500-675.
89-02-007	Evening at Merritt's Cottage	T. Kinkade	Closed	125.00	675.00
85-02-008	Evening Service	T. Kinkade	Closed	90.00	90-200.00
90-02-009	Hidden Cottage	T. Kinkade	Closed	125.00	650.00
85-02-010	Moonlight on the Waterfront	T. Kinkade	Closed	150.00	150-200.
86-02-011	New York, 6th Avenue	T. Kinkade	Closed	150.00	450.00
84-02-012	Placerville, 1916	T. Kinkade	Closed	90.00	1500-2200.
88-02-013	Room with a View	T. Kinkade	Closed	150.00	650.00
86-02-014	San Francisco, 1909	T. Kinkade	Closed	150.00	900-1450.
89-02-015	San Francisco, Union Square	T. Kinkade	Closed	225.00	650-900.
90-02-016	Rose Arbor	T. Kinkade	Closed	125.00	300.00
90-02-017	Spring At Stonegate	T. Kinkade	550	95.00	95.00
91-02-018	Afternoon Light, Dogwoods	T. Kinkade	980	185.00	185.00
91-02-019	The Autumn Gate	T. Kinkade	980	225.00	225.00
91-02-020	Boston	T. Kinkade	550	175.00	175.00
91-02-021	Carmel, Tuck Box Tea Room	T. Kinkade	980	275.00	275.00
91-02-022	Christmas Eve	T. Kinkade	980	125.00	125.00
91-02-023	Flags Over The Capitol	T. Kinkade	1,991	195.00	195.00
91-02-024	Home For The Evening	T. Kinkade	980	100.00	100.00
91-02-025	Home For The Holidays	T. Kinkade	980	225.00	225.00
91-02-026	McKenna's Cottage	T. Kinkade	980	150.00	150.00
91-02-027	Olde Porterfield Tea Room	T. Kinkade	980	150.00	150.00
91-02-028	Open Gate, Sussex	T. Kinkade	980	100.00	100.00
91-02-029	Victorian Evening	T. Kinkade	980	150.00	150.00
92-02-030	Blossom Hill Church	T. Kinkade	980	225.00	225.00
92-02-031	Broadwater Bridge	T. Kinkade	980	225.00	225.00
92-02-032	Swanbrooke Cottage	T. Kinkade	980	250.00	225.00
92-02-033	Sweetheart Cottage	T. Kinkade	980	150.00	150.00
92-02-034	Cottage-By-The-Sea	T. Kinkade	980	250.00	250.00
92-02-035	Home is Where the Heart Is	T. Kinkade	980	225.00	225.00
92-02-036	Miller's Cottage	T. Kinkade	980	175.00	175.00
92-02-037	Sunday At Apple Hill	T. Kinkade	980	175.00	175.00
92-02-038	Victorian Garden	T. Kinkade	980	275.00	275.00
92-02-039	San Francisco, Nob Hill	T. Kinkade	980	275.00	275.00
92-02-040	Julianne's Cottage	T. Kinkade	980	185.00	185.00
92-02-041	Yosemite	T. Kinkade	980	225.00	225.00
92-02-042	Country Memories	T. Kinkade	980	185.00	185.00
92-02-043	The Garden Party	T. Kinkade	980	175.00	175.00
92-02-044	Victorian Christmas	T. Kinkade	980	225.00	225.00
92-02-045	Olde Porterfield Gift Shoppe	T. Kinkade	980	175.00	175.00
92-02-046	Amber Afternoon	T. Kinkade	980	175.00	175.00
92-02-047	Silent Night	T. Kinkade	980	185.00	185.00
92-02-048	Christmas At the Ahwahnee	T. Kinkade	980	175.00	175.00
92-02-049	Paris, City of Lights	T. Kinkade	980	225.00	225.00
93-02-050	Sweetheart Cottage	T. Kinkade	980	387.00	387.00
93-02-051	Beside Still Waters	T. Kinkade	1280	422.00	422.00
Lightpost Group Inc./ Lightpost Publishing		**Archival Paper/Canvas-Combined Edition-Framed**			
90-03-001	Blue Cottage(Paper)	T. Kinkade	750	125.00	125.00
90-03-002	Blue Cottage(Canvas)	T. Kinkade	Combined	495.00	495.00
90-03-003	Moonlit Village(Paper)	T. Kinkade	Closed	225.00	300.00
90-03-004	Moonlit Village(Canvas)	T. Kinkade	Closed	595.00	1145-1500.
90-03-005	New York, 1932(Paper)	T. Kinkade	Closed	225.00	225.00
90-03-006	New York, 1932(Canvas)	T. Kinkade	Closed	595.00	595-1200.
90-03-007	Skating in the Park(Paper)	T. Kinkade	750	275.00	275.00
90-03-008	Skating in the Park(Canvas)	T. Kinkade	Combined	645.00	645.00
Lightpost Group Inc./ National Heritage Gallery		**Gone With The Wind™ Collection-Framed**			
93-04-001	Scarlett & Her Beaux	N. Heritage	12,500	160.00	160.00
93-04-002	Not A Marrying Man	N. Heritage	12,500	160.00	160.00
93-04-003	You Need Kissing	N. Heritage	12,500	190.00	190.00
93-04-004	You Do Waltz Divinely	N. Heritage	12,500	190.00	190.00
Lightpost Group Inc./ National Heritage Gallery		**U.S. Presidents Collection-Framed**			
93-05-001	George Washington	N. Heritage	7,500	225.00	225.00
93-05-002	Abraham Lincoln	N. Heritage	7,500	225.00	225.00
93-05-003	John F. Kennedy	N. Heritage	7,500	225.00	225.00
93-05-004	Mark Twain	N. Heritage	7,500	225.00	225.00
Mill Pond Press		**Bateman**			
86-01-001	A Resting Place-Cape Buffalo	R. Bateman	950	265.00	265.00

Company Number	Name	Series Artist	Edition Limit	Issue Price	Quote
82-01-002	Above the River -Trumpeter Swans	R. Bateman	950	200.00	850-925.
84-01-003	Across the Sky-Snow Geese	R. Bateman	950	220.00	650-750.
80-01-004	African Amber-Lioness Pair	R. Bateman	950	175.00	525-900.
79-01-005	Afternoon Glow-Snowy Owl	R. Bateman	950	125.00	550-625.
90-01-006	Air, The Forest and The Watch	R. Bateman	42,558	325.00	325-400.
84-01-007	Along the Ridge-Grizzly Bears	R. Bateman	950	200.00	700-950.
84-01-008	American Goldfinch-Winter Dress	R. Bateman	950	75.00	200-300.
79-01-009	Among the Leaves-Cottontail Rabbit	R. Bateman	950	75.00	1200.00
80-01-010	Antarctic Elements	R. Bateman	950	125.00	150.00
91-01-011	Arctic Cliff-White Wolves	R. Bateman	13,000	325.00	450-800.
82-01-012	Arctic Evening-White Wolf	R. Bateman	950	185.00	950-1200.
80-01-013	Arctic Family-Polar Bears	R. Bateman	950	150.00	1100-2000.
82-01-014	Arctic Portrait-White Gyrfalcon	R. Bateman	950	175.00	250.00
85-01-015	Arctic Tern Pair	R. Bateman	950	175.00	200.00
81-01-016	Artist and His Dog	R. Bateman	950	150.00	550.00
80-01-017	Asleep on the Hemlock-Screech Owl	R. Bateman	950	125.00	1150.00
91-01-018	At the Cliff-Bobcat	R. Bateman	12,500	325.00	325.00
87-01-019	At the Nest-Secretary Birds	R. Bateman	950	290.00	290.00
82-01-020	At the Roadside-Red-Tailed Hawk	R. Bateman	950	185.00	550.00
80-01-021	Autumn Overture-Moose	R. Bateman	950	245.00	1450.00
80-01-022	Awesome Land-American Elk	R. Bateman	950	245.00	1450.00
89-01-023	Backlight-Mute Swan	R. Bateman	950	275.00	600.00
83-01-024	Bald Eagle Portrait	R. Bateman	950	185.00	300.00
82-01-025	Baobab Tree and Impala	R. Bateman	950	245.00	350.00
80-01-026	Barn Owl in the Churchyard	R. Bateman	950	125.00	775.00
89-01-027	Barn Swallow and Horse Collar	R. Bateman	950	225.00	225.00
82-01-028	Barn Swallows in August	R. Bateman	950	245.00	425.00
85-01-029	Beaver Pond Reflections	R. Bateman	950	185.00	225.00
84-01-030	Big Country, Pronghorn Antelope	R. Bateman	950	185.00	200.00
86-01-031	Black Eagle	R. Bateman	950	200.00	200.00
86-01-032	Black-Tailed Deer in the Olympics	R. Bateman	950	245.00	300.00
86-01-033	Blacksmith Plover	R. Bateman	950	185.00	185.00
91-01-034	Bluebird and Blossoms	R. Bateman	4,500	235.00	235.00
91-01-035	Bluebird and Blossoms-Prestige Ed.	R. Bateman	450	625.00	625.00
80-01-036	Bluffing Bull-African Elephant	R. Bateman	950	135.00	1125.00
81-01-037	Bright Day-Atlantic Puffins	R. Bateman	950	175.00	875.00
89-01-038	Broad-Tailed Hummingbird Pair	R. Bateman	950	225.00	225.00
80-01-039	Brown Pelican and Pilings	R. Bateman	950	165.00	950.00
79-01-040	Bull Moose	R. Bateman	950	125.00	1275.00
78-01-041	By the Tracks-Killdeer	R. Bateman	950	75.00	1200.00
83-01-042	Call of the Wild-Bald Eagle	R. Bateman	950	200.00	250.00
81-01-043	Canada Geese-Nesting	R. Bateman	950	295.00	2950.00
85-01-044	Canada Geese Family(stone lithograph)	R. Bateman	260	350.00	1000.00
85-01-045	Canada Geese Over the Escarpment	R. Bateman	950	135.00	175.00
86-01-046	Canada Geese With Young	R. Bateman	950	195.00	325.00
88-01-047	Cardinal and Wild Apples	R. Bateman	950	235.00	235.00
89-01-048	Catching The Light-Barn Owl	R. Bateman	2,000	295.00	295.00
88-01-049	Cattails, Fireweed and Yellowthroat	R. Bateman	950	235.00	275.00
89-01-050	Centennial Farm	R. Bateman	950	295.00	450.00
80-01-051	Chapel Doors	R. Bateman	950	135.00	375.00
86-01-052	Charging Rhino	R. Bateman	950	325.00	500.00
88-01-053	Cherrywood with Juncos	R. Bateman	950	245.00	245-345.
82-01-054	Cheetah Profile	R. Bateman	950	245.00	500.00
78-01-055	Cheetah With Cubs	R. Bateman	950	95.00	450.00
90-01-056	Chinstrap Penguin	R. Bateman	810	150.00	150.00
92-01-057	Clan of the Raven	R. Bateman	950	235.00	235.00
81-01-058	Clear Night-Wolves	R. Bateman	950	245.00	6500-8100.
88-01-059	Colonial Garden	R. Bateman	950	245.00	245.00
87-01-060	Continuing Generations-Spotted Owls	R. Bateman	950	525.00	1150.00
91-01-061	Cottage Lane-Red Fox	R. Bateman	950	285.00	285.00
84-01-062	Cougar Portrait	R. Bateman	950	95.00	200.00
79-01-063	Country Lane-Pheasants	R. Bateman	950	85.00	300.00
81-01-064	Courting Pair-Whistling Swans	R. Bateman	950	245.00	550.00
81-01-065	Courtship Display-Wild Turkey	R. Bateman	950	175.00	175.00
80-01-066	Coyote in Winter Sage	R. Bateman	950	245.00	3600.00
92-01-067	Cries of Courtship-Red Crowned Cranes	R. Bateman	950	350.00	350.00
80-01-068	Curious Glance-Red Fox	R. Bateman	950	135.00	1200.00
86-01-069	Dark Gyrfalcon	R. Bateman	950	225.00	325.00
82-01-070	Dipper By the Waterfall	R. Bateman	950	165.00	200.00
89-01-071	Dispute Over Prey	R. Bateman	950	325.00	325.00
89-01-072	Distant Danger-Raccoon	R. Bateman	1,600	225.00	225.00
84-01-073	Down for a Drink-Morning Dove	R. Bateman	950	135.00	200.00
78-01-074	Downy Woodpecker on Goldenrod Gall	R. Bateman	950	50.00	1425.00
88-01-075	Dozing Lynx	R. Bateman	950	335.00	1750.00
86-01-076	Driftwood Perch-Striped Swallows	R. Bateman	950	195.00	250.00
83-01-077	Early Snowfall-Ruffed Grouse	R. Bateman	950	195.00	225.00
83-01-078	Early Spring-Bluebird	R. Bateman	950	185.00	450.00
81-01-079	Edge of the Ice-Ermine	R. Bateman	950	175.00	475.00
82-01-080	Edge of the Woods-Whitetail Deer, w/Book	R. Bateman	950	745.00	1400.00
91-01-081	Elephant Cow and Calf	R. Bateman	950	300.00	300.00
86-01-082	Elephant Herd and Sandgrouse	R. Bateman	950	235.00	235.00
91-01-083	Encounter in the Bush-African Lions	R. Bateman	950	295.00	325.00
87-01-084	End of Season-Grizzly	R. Bateman	950	325.00	500.00
91-01-085	Endangered Spaces-Grizzly	R. Bateman	4,008	325.00	325.00
85-01-086	Entering the Water-Common Gulls	R. Bateman	950	195.00	200.00
86-01-087	European Robin and Hydrangeas	R. Bateman	950	130.00	225.00
89-01-088	Evening Call-Common Loon	R. Bateman	950	235.00	525.00
80-01-089	Evening Grosbeak	R. Bateman	950	125.00	1175.00
83-01-090	Evening Idyll-Mute Swans	R. Bateman	950	245.00	525.00
81-01-091	Evening Light-White Gyrfalcon	R. Bateman	950	245.00	1100.00
79-01-092	Evening Snowfall-American Elk	R. Bateman	950	150.00	1900.00
87-01-093	Everglades	R. Bateman	950	360.00	360.00
80-01-094	Fallen Willow-Snowy Owl	R. Bateman	950	200.00	950.00
87-01-095	Farm Lane and Blue Jays	R. Bateman	950	225.00	450.00
86-01-096	Fence Post and Burdock	R. Bateman	950	130.00	130.00
91-01-097	Fluid Power-Orca	R. Bateman	290	2500.00	2500.00
80-01-098	Flying High-Golden Eagle	R. Bateman	950	150.00	975.00
82-01-099	Fox at the Granary	R. Bateman	950	165.00	225.00
82-01-100	Frosty Morning-Blue Jay	R. Bateman	950	185.00	1000.00
82-01-101	Gallinule Family	R. Bateman	950	135.00	135.00
81-01-102	Galloping Herd-Giraffes	R. Bateman	950	175.00	1200.00
85-01-103	Gambel's Quail Pair	R. Bateman	950	95.00	350.00
82-01-104	Gentoo Penguins and Whale Bones	R. Bateman	950	205.00	300.00
83-01-105	Ghost of the North-Great Gray Owl	R. Bateman	950	200.00	2675.00
82-01-106	Golden Crowned Kinglet and Rhododendron	R. Bateman	950	150.00	2575.00
79-01-107	Golden Eagle	R. Bateman	950	150.00	250.00
85-01-108	Golden Eagle Portrait	R. Bateman	950	115.00	175.00
89-01-109	Goldfinch In the Meadow	R. Bateman	1,600	150.00	200.00
83-01-110	Goshawk and Ruffed Grouse	R. Bateman	950	185.00	400-700.
88-01-111	Grassy Bank-Great Blue Heron	R. Bateman	950	285.00	285.00
81-01-112	Gray Squirrel	R. Bateman	950	180.00	1250.00
79-01-113	Great Blue Heron	R. Bateman	950	125.00	1300.00
87-01-114	Great Blue Heron in Flight	R. Bateman	950	295.00	550.00
88-01-115	Great Crested Grebe	R. Bateman	950	135.00	135.00
87-01-116	Great Egret Preening	R. Bateman	950	315.00	500.00
83-01-117	Great Horned Owl in the White Pine	R. Bateman	950	225.00	575.00
87-01-118	Greater Kudu Bull	R. Bateman	950	145.00	145.00
91-01-119	Gulls on Pilings	R. Bateman	1,950	265.00	265.00
88-01-120	Hardwood Forest-White-Tailed Buck	R. Bateman	950	345.00	2100.00
88-01-121	Harlequin Duck-Bull Kelp-Executive Ed.	R. Bateman	950	550.00	550.00
88-01-122	Harlequin Duck-Bull Kelp-Gold Plated	R. Bateman	950	300.00	300.00
80-01-123	Heron on the Rocks	R. Bateman	950	75.00	300.00
81-01-124	High Camp at Dusk	R. Bateman	950	245.00	300.00
79-01-125	High Country-Stone Sheep	R. Bateman	950	125.00	325.00
87-01-126	High Kingdom-Snow Leopard	R. Bateman	950	325.00	700-850.
90-01-127	Homage to Ahmed	R. Bateman	290	3300.00	3300.00
84-01-128	Hooded Mergansers in Winter	R. Bateman	950	210.00	650-700.
84-01-129	House Finch and Yucca	R. Bateman	950	95.00	175.00
86-01-130	House Sparrow	R. Bateman	950	125.00	150.00
87-01-131	House Sparrows and Bittersweet	R. Bateman	950	220.00	400.00
86-01-132	Hummingbird Pair Diptych	R. Bateman	950	330.00	475.00
87-01-133	Hurricane Lake-Wood Ducks	R. Bateman	950	135.00	200.00
81-01-134	In for the Evening	R. Bateman	950	150.00	1500.00
84-01-135	In the Brier Patch-Cottontail	R. Bateman	950	165.00	350.00
86-01-136	In the Grass-Lioness	R. Bateman	950	245.00	245.00
85-01-137	In the Highlands-Golden Eagle	R. Bateman	950	235.00	425.00
85-01-138	In the Mountains-Osprey	R. Bateman	950	95.00	125.00
92-01-139	Intrusion-Mountain Gorilla	R. Bateman	2,250	325.00	325.00
90-01-140	Ireland House	R. Bateman	950	265.00	318.00
85-01-141	Irish Cottage and Wagtail	R. Bateman	950	175.00	175.00
90-01-142	Keeper of the Land	R. Bateman	290	3300.00	3300.00
79-01-143	King of the Realm	R. Bateman	950	125.00	675.00
87-01-144	King Penguins	R. Bateman	950	130.00	135.00
81-01-145	Kingfisher and Aspen	R. Bateman	950	225.00	600.00
80-01-146	Kingfisher in Winter	R. Bateman	950	175.00	825.00
80-01-147	Kittiwake Greeting	R. Bateman	950	75.00	550.00
81-01-148	Last Look-Bighorn Sheep	R. Bateman	950	195.00	225.00
87-01-149	Late Winter-Black Squirrel	R. Bateman	950	165.00	165.00
81-01-150	Laughing Gull and Horseshoe Crab	R. Bateman	950	125.00	125.00
82-01-151	Leopard Ambush	R. Bateman	950	245.00	600.00
88-01-152	Leopard and Thomson Gazelle Kill	R. Bateman	950	275.00	275.00
85-01-153	Leopard at Seronera	R. Bateman	950	175.00	280.00
80-01-154	Leopard in a Sausage Tree	R. Bateman	950	150.00	1250.00
84-01-155	Lily Pads and Loon	R. Bateman	950	200.00	1875.00
87-01-156	Lion and Wildebeest	R. Bateman	950	265.00	265.00
80-01-157	Lion at Tsavo	R. Bateman	950	150.00	275.00
78-01-158	Lion Cubs	R. Bateman	950	125.00	800.00
87-01-159	Lioness at Serengeti	R. Bateman	950	325.00	325.00
85-01-160	Lions in the Grass	R. Bateman	950	265.00	1250.00
81-01-161	Little Blue Heron	R. Bateman	950	95.00	275.00
82-01-162	Lively Pair-Chickadees	R. Bateman	950	160.00	450.00
83-01-163	Loon Family	R. Bateman	950	200.00	750.00
90-01-164	Lunging Heron	R. Bateman	1,250	225.00	225.00
78-01-165	Majesty on the Wing-Bald Eagle	R. Bateman	950	150.00	4000.00
88-01-166	Mallard Family at Sunset	R. Bateman	950	235.00	235.00
86-01-167	Mallard Family-Misty Marsh	R. Bateman	950	130.00	175.00
86-01-168	Mallard Pair-Early Winter	R. Bateman	41,740	135.00	200.00
86-01-169	Mallard Pair-Early Winter Gold Plated	R. Bateman	7,691	250.00	375.00
85-01-170	Mallard Pair-Early Winter 24K Gold	R. Bateman	950	1650.00	2000.00
89-01-171	Mangrove Morning-Roseate Spoonbills	R. Bateman	2,000	325.00	325.00
91-01-172	Mangrove Shadow-Common Egret	R. Bateman	1,250	285.00	285.00
86-01-173	Marginal Meadow	R. Bateman	950	220.00	350.00
79-01-174	Master of the Herd-African Buffalo	R. Bateman	950	150.00	2250.00
84-01-175	May Maple-Scarlet Tanager	R. Bateman	950	175.00	825.00
82-01-176	Meadow's Edge-Mallard	R. Bateman	950	175.00	900.00
82-01-177	Merganser Family in Hiding	R. Bateman	950	200.00	525.00
89-01-178	Midnight-Black Wolf	R. Bateman	25,352	325.00	1650-2200.
80-01-179	Mischief on the Prowl-Raccoon	R. Bateman	950	85.00	350.00
80-01-180	Misty Coast-Gulls	R. Bateman	950	135.00	600.00
84-01-181	Misty Lake-Osprey	R. Bateman	950	95.00	300.00
81-01-182	Misty Morning-Loons	R. Bateman	950	150.00	3000.00
86-01-183	Moose at Water's Edge	R. Bateman	950	130.00	225.00
90-01-184	Morning Cove-Common Loon	R. Bateman	950	165.00	165.00
85-01-185	Morning Dew-Roe Deer	R. Bateman	950	175.00	175.00
83-01-186	Morning on the Flats-Bison	R. Bateman	950	200.00	300.00
84-01-187	Morning on the River-Trumpeter Swans	R. Bateman	950	185.00	300.00
90-01-188	Mossy Branches-Spotted Owl	R. Bateman	4,500	300.00	525.00
90-01-189	Mowed Meadow	R. Bateman	950	190.00	190.00
86-01-190	Mule Deer in Aspen	R. Bateman	950	175.00	175.00
83-01-191	Mule Deer in Winter	R. Bateman	950	200.00	350.00
88-01-192	Muskoka Lake-Common Loons	R. Bateman	950	265.00	450.00
89-01-193	Near Glenburnie	R. Bateman	950	265.00	265.00
83-01-194	New Season-American Robin	R. Bateman	950	200.00	450.00
86-01-195	Northern Reflections-Loon Family	R. Bateman	8,631	255.00	2100.00
85-01-196	Old Whaling Base and Fur Seals	R. Bateman	950	195.00	550.00
87-01-197	Old Willow and Mallards	R. Bateman	950	325.00	390.00
80-01-198	On the Alert-Chipmunk	R. Bateman	950	60.00	500.00
85-01-199	On the Garden Wall	R. Bateman	950	115.00	300.00
85-01-200	Orca Procession	R. Bateman	950	245.00	2525.00
81-01-201	Osprey Family	R. Bateman	950	245.00	325.00
83-01-202	Osprey in the Rain	R. Bateman	950	110.00	650.00
87-01-203	Otter Study	R. Bateman	950	235.00	375.00
81-01-204	Pair of Skimmers	R. Bateman	950	150.00	150.00
88-01-205	Panda's At Play (stone lithograph)	R. Bateman	160	400.00	2500.00
84-01-206	Peregrine and Ruddy Turnstones	R. Bateman	950	200.00	350.00
85-01-207	Peregrine Falcon and White-Throated Swifts	R. Bateman	950	245.00	550.00
87-01-208	Peregrine Falcon on the Cliff-Stone Litho	R. Bateman	525	350.00	625.00
83-01-209	Pheasant in Cornfield	R. Bateman	950	200.00	375.00
88-01-210	Pheasants at Dusk	R. Bateman	950	325.00	525.00
82-01-211	Pileated Woodpecker on Beech Tree	R. Bateman	950	175.00	525.00
90-01-212	Pintails in Spring	R. Bateman	9,651	135.00	135.00
82-01-213	Pioneer Memories-Magpie Pair	R. Bateman	950	175.00	250.00
87-01-214	Plowed Field-Snowy Owl	R. Bateman	950	145.00	400.00
90-01-215	Polar Bear	R. Bateman	290	3300.00	3300.00
82-01-216	Polar Bear Profile	R. Bateman	950	210.00	2350.00
82-01-217	Polar Bears at Bafin Island	R. Bateman	950	245.00	875.00
90-01-218	Power Play-Rhinoceros	R. Bateman	950	320.00	320.00
80-01-219	Prairie Evening-Short-Eared Owl	R. Bateman	950	150.00	200.00
88-01-220	Preening Pair-Canada Geese	R. Bateman	950	235.00	300.00
87-01-221	Pride of Autumn-Canada Goose	R. Bateman	950	135.00	245.00
86-01-222	Proud Swimmer-Snow Goose	R. Bateman	950	185.00	185.00
89-01-223	Pumpkin Time	R. Bateman	950	195.00	195.00
82-01-224	Queen Anne's Lace and AmericanGoldfinch	R. Bateman	950	150.00	1000.00
84-01-225	Ready for Flight-Peregrine Falcon	R. Bateman	950	185.00	500.00
82-01-226	Ready for the Hunt-Snowy Owl	R. Bateman	950	245.00	550.00
88-01-227	Red Crossbills	R. Bateman	950	125.00	125.00

GRAPHICS

Company Number	Name	Series Artist	Edition Limit	Issue Price	Quote
84-01-228	Red Fox on the Prowl	R. Bateman	950	245.00	1500.00
82-01-229	Red Squirrel	R. Bateman	950	175.00	700.00
86-01-230	Red Wolf	R. Bateman	950	250.00	525.00
81-01-231	Red-Tailed Hawk by the Cliff	R. Bateman	950	245.00	550.00
81-01-232	Red-Winged Blackbird and Rail Fence	R. Bateman	950	195.00	225.00
84-01-233	Reeds	R. Bateman	950	185.00	575.00
86-01-234	Resting Place-Cape Buffalo	R. Bateman	950	265.00	265.00
87-01-235	Rhino at Ngoro Ngoro	R. Bateman	950	325.00	325.00
86-01-236	Robins at the Nest	R. Bateman	950	185.00	225.00
87-01-237	Rocky Point-October	R. Bateman	950	195.00	275.00
80-01-238	Rocky Wilderness-Cougar	R. Bateman	950	175.00	1425.00
90-01-239	Rolling Waves-Lesser Scaup	R. Bateman	3,330	125.00	125.00
81-01-240	Rough-Legged Hawk in the Elm	R. Bateman	950	175.00	250.00
81-01-241	Royal Family-Mute Swans	R. Bateman	950	245.00	1100.00
83-01-242	Ruby Throat and Columbine	R. Bateman	950	150.00	2200.00
87-01-243	Ruddy Turnstones	R. Bateman	950	175.00	175.00
81-01-244	Sarah E. with Gulls	R. Bateman	950	245.00	2625.00
91-01-245	Sea Otter Study	R. Bateman	950	150.00	150.00
81-01-246	Sheer Drop-Mountain Goats	R. Bateman	950	245.00	2800.00
88-01-247	Shelter	R. Bateman	950	325.00	1000.00
92-01-248	Siberian Tiger	R. Bateman	4,500	325.00	325.00
84-01-249	Smallwood	R. Bateman	950	200.00	500.00
90-01-250	Snow Leopard	R. Bateman	290	2500.00	3500.00
85-01-251	Snowy Hemlock-Barred Owl	R. Bateman	950	245.00	400.00
87-01-252	Snowy Owl and Milkweed	R. Bateman	950	235.00	950.00
83-01-253	Snowy Owl on Driftwood	R. Bateman	950	245.00	1450.00
83-01-254	Spirits of the Forest	R. Bateman	950	170.00	1750.00
86-01-255	Split Rails-Snow Buntings	R. Bateman	950	220.00	220.00
80-01-256	Spring Cardinal	R. Bateman	950	125.00	600.00
82-01-257	Spring Marsh-Pintail Pair	R. Bateman	950	200.00	275.00
80-01-258	Spring Thaw-Killdeer	R. Bateman	950	85.00	150.00
82-01-259	Still Morning-Herring Gulls	R. Bateman	950	200.00	250.00
87-01-260	Stone Sheep Ram	R. Bateman	950	175.00	175.00
85-01-261	Stream Bank June	R. Bateman	950	160.00	175.00
84-01-262	Stretching-Canada Goose	R. Bateman	950	225.00	3600-3900.
85-01-263	Strutting-Ring-Necked Pheasant	R. Bateman	950	225.00	325.00
85-01-264	Sudden Blizzard-Red-Tailed Hawk	R. Bateman	950	245.00	600.00
84-01-265	Summer Morning-Loon	R. Bateman	950	185.00	1250.00
90-01-266	Summer Morning Pasture	R. Bateman	950	175.00	175.00
86-01-267	Summertime-Polar Bears	R. Bateman	950	225.00	475.00
79-01-268	Surf and Sanderlings	R. Bateman	950	65.00	450.00
81-01-269	Swift Fox	R. Bateman	950	175.00	350.00
86-01-270	Swift Fox Study	R. Bateman	950	115.00	150.00
87-01-271	Sylvan Stream-Mute Swans	R. Bateman	950	125.00	125.00
84-01-272	Tadpole Time	R. Bateman	950	135.00	475.00
88-01-273	Tawny Owl In Beech	R. Bateman	950	325.00	600.00
92-01-274	Tembo (African Elephant)	R. Bateman	1,550	350.00	350.00
88-01-275	The Challenge-Bull Moose	R. Bateman	10,671	325.00	325.00
91-01-276	The Scolding-Chickadees & Screech Owl	R. Bateman	12,500	235.00	235.00
84-01-277	Tiger at Dawn	R. Bateman	950	225.00	2500.00
83-01-278	Tiger Portrait	R. Bateman	950	130.00	400.00
88-01-279	Tree Swallow over Pond	R. Bateman	950	290.00	290.00
91-01-280	Trumpeter Swan Family	R. Bateman	290	2500.00	2500.00
85-01-281	Trumpeter Swans and Aspen	R. Bateman	950	245.00	550.00
79-01-282	Up in the Pine-Great Horned Owl	R. Bateman	950	150.00	550.00
80-01-283	Vantage Point	R. Bateman	950	245.00	1200.00
81-01-284	Watchful Repose-Black Bear	R. Bateman	950	245.00	700.00
89-01-285	Vulture And Wildebeest	R. Bateman	550	295.00	295.00
85-01-286	Weathered Branch-Bald Eagle	R. Bateman	950	115.00	300.00
91-01-287	Whistling Swan-Lake Erie	R. Bateman	1,950	325.00	325.00
85-01-288	White-Breasted Nuthatch on a Beech Tree	R. Bateman	950	175.00	300.00
80-01-289	White Encounter-Polar Bear	R. Bateman	950	245.00	4200-4800.
80-01-290	White-Footed Mouse in Wintergreen	R. Bateman	950	60.00	650.00
82-01-291	White-Footed Mouse on Aspen	R. Bateman	950	90.00	180.00
92-01-292	White-Tailed Deer Through the Birches	R. Bateman	10,000	335.00	335.00
84-01-293	White-Throated Sparrow and Pussy Willow	R. Bateman	950	150.00	580.00
90-01-294	White on White-Snowshoe Hare	R. Bateman	950	195.00	590.00
82-01-295	White World-Dall Sheep	R. Bateman	950	200.00	450.00
91-01-296	Wide Horizon-Tundra Swans	R. Bateman	2,862	325.00	135-325.
91-01-297	Wide Horizon-Tundra Swans Companion	R. Bateman	2,862	325.00	325.00
86-01-298	Wildbeest	R. Bateman	950	185.00	185.00
82-01-299	Willet on the Shore	R. Bateman	950	125.00	225.00
79-01-300	Wily and Wary-Red Fox	R. Bateman	950	125.00	1500.00
84-01-301	Window into Ontario	R. Bateman	950	265.00	1500.00
83-01-302	Winter Barn	R. Bateman	950	170.00	400.00
79-01-303	Winter Cardinal	R. Bateman	950	75.00	3550.00
85-01-304	Winter Companion	R. Bateman	950	175.00	500.00
80-01-305	Winter Elm-American Kestrel	R. Bateman	950	135.00	600.00
86-01-306	Winter in the Mountains-Raven	R. Bateman	950	200.00	200.00
83-01-307	Winter-Lady Cardinal	R. Bateman	950	200.00	1500.00
81-01-308	Winter Mist-Great Horned Owl	R. Bateman	950	245.00	900.00
79-01-309	Winter-Snowshoe Hare	R. Bateman	950	95.00	1200.00
80-01-310	Winter Song-Chickadees	R. Bateman	950	95.00	900.00
84-01-311	Winter Sunset-Moose	R. Bateman	950	245.00	2700.00
81-01-312	Winter Wren	R. Bateman	950	135.00	250.00
87-01-313	Wise One, The	R. Bateman	950	325.00	800.00
79-01-314	Wolf Pack in Moonlight	R. Bateman	950	95.00	3000.00
83-01-315	Wolves on the Trail	R. Bateman	950	225.00	700.00
85-01-316	Wood Bison Portrait	R. Bateman	950	165.00	200.00
83-01-317	Woodland Drummer-Ruffed Grouse	R. Bateman	950	185.00	250.00
81-01-318	Wrangler's Campsite-Gray Jay	R. Bateman	950	195.00	550.00
79-01-319	Yellow-Rumped Warbler	R. Bateman	950	50.00	575.00
78-01-320	Young Barn Swallow	R. Bateman	950	75.00	700.00
83-01-321	Young Elf Owl-Old Saguaro	R. Bateman	950	95.00	250.00
91-01-322	Young Giraffe	R. Bateman	290	850.00	850.00
89-01-323	Young Kittiwake	R. Bateman	950	195.00	195.00
88-01-324	Young Sandhill-Cranes	R. Bateman	950	325.00	325.00
89-01-325	Young Snowy Owl	R. Bateman	950	195.00	195.00
Mill Pond Press		**Reece**			
48-02-001	Federal Duck Stamp-Buffleheads	M. Reece	200	15.00	1200.00
51-02-002	Federal Duck Stamp-Gadwalls	M. Reece	250	15.00	1200.00
59-02-003	Federal Duck Stamp-Retriever	M. Reece	400	15.00	3750.00
69-02-004	Federal Duck Stamp-White-Winged Scoters	M. Reece	750	50.00	940.00
71-02-005	Federal Duck Stamp-Cinnamon Teal	M. Reece	950	75.00	2850.00
91-02-006	Offshore Lunch-Common Loons	M. Reece	550	195.00	195.00
91-02-007	The Chase-Wolf Pack	M. Reece	550	150.00	150.00
91-02-008	Upland Series IV-Ruffed Goose	M. Reece	950	125.00	125.00
Mill Pond Press		**Calle**			
84-03-001	A Brace for the Spit	P. Calle	950	110.00	275.00
83-03-002	A Winter Surprise	P. Calle	950	195.00	800.00
81-03-003	Almost Home	P. Calle	950	150.00	150.00

Company Number	Name	Series Artist	Edition Limit	Issue Price	Quote
91-03-004	Almost There	P. Calle	950	165.00	165.00
89-03-005	And A Good Book For Company	P. Calle	950	135.00	190.00
81-03-006	And Still Miles to Go	P. Calle	950	245.00	300.00
81-03-007	Andrew At The Falls	P. Calle	950	150.00	175.00
89-03-008	The Beaver Men	P. Calle	950	125.00	125.00
80-03-009	Caring for the Herd	P. Calle	950	110.00	110.00
84-03-010	Chance Encounter	P. Calle	950	225.00	300.00
81-03-011	Chief High Pipe (Color)	P. Calle	950	265.00	275.00
80-03-012	Chief High Pipe (Pencil)	P. Calle	950	75.00	165.00
80-03-013	Chief Joseph-Man of Peace	P. Calle	950	135.00	150.00
90-03-014	Children of Walpi	P. Calle	350	160.00	160.00
90-03-015	The Doll Maker	P. Calle	950	95.00	95.00
82-03-016	Emerging from the Woods	P. Calle	950	110.00	110-160.
81-03-017	End of a Long Day	P. Calle	950	150.00	150-190.
84-03-018	Fate of the Late Migrant	P. Calle	950	110.00	300.00
83-03-019	Free Spirits	P. Calle	950	195.00	325.00
83-03-020	Free Trapper Study	P. Calle	550	75.00	125-300.
81-03-021	Fresh Tracks	P. Calle	950	150.00	165.00
81-03-022	Friend of Foe	P. Calle	950	125.00	125.00
81-03-023	Friends	P. Calle	950	150.00	150.00
89-03-024	The Fur Trapper	P. Calle	550	75.00	175.00
82-03-025	Generations in the Valley	P. Calle	950	245.00	245.00
85-03-026	Grandmother, The	P. Calle	950	150.00	150.00
92-03-027	Hunter of Geese	P. Calle	950	125.00	125.00
83-03-028	In Search of Beaver	P. Calle	950	225.00	600.00
91-03-029	In the Beginning . . . Friends	P. Calle	1,250	250.00	250.00
87-03-030	In the Land of the Giants	P. Calle	950	245.00	780.00
90-03-031	Interrupted Journey	P. Calle	1,750	265.00	265.00
90-03-032	Interrupted Journey-Prestige Ed.	P. Calle	290	465.00	465.00
87-03-033	Into the Great Alone	P. Calle	950	245.00	600.00
81-03-034	Just Over the Ridge	P. Calle	950	245.00	325.00
80-03-035	Landmark Tree	P. Calle	950	125.00	225.00
91-03-036	Man of the Fur Trade	P. Calle	550	110.00	110.00
84-03-037	Mountain Man	P. Calle	950	95.00	250-550.
89-03-038	Navajo Madonna	P. Calle	650	95.00	95.00
81-03-039	One With The Land	P. Calle	950	245.00	325.00
81-03-040	Pause at the Lower Falls	P. Calle	950	110.00	125.00
80-03-041	Prayer to the Great Mystery	P. Calle	950	245.00	400.00
82-03-042	Return to Camp	P. Calle	950	245.00	400.00
80-03-043	Sioux Chief	P. Calle	950	85.00	85-140.00
90-03-044	Son of Sitting Bull	P. Calle	950	95.00	95.00
86-03-045	Snow Hunter	P. Calle	950	150.00	250-410.
80-03-046	Something for the Pot	P. Calle	950	175.00	1000.00
85-03-047	Storyteller of the Mountains	P. Calle	950	225.00	575.00
83-03-048	Strays From the Flyway	P. Calle	950	195.00	250-340.
81-03-049	Teton Friends	P. Calle	950	150.00	200.00
91-03-050	The Silenced Honkers	P. Calle	1,250	250.00	250.00
91-03-051	They Call Me Matthew	P. Calle	950	125.00	125.00
92-03-052	Through the Tall Grass	P. Calle	950	175.00	175.00
82-03-053	Two from the Flock	P. Calle	950	245.00	400.00
80-03-054	View from the Heights	P. Calle	950	245.00	350.00
80-03-055	When Snow Came Early	P. Calle	950	85.00	250-340.
84-03-056	When Trails Cross	P. Calle	950	245.00	750.00
91-03-057	When Trails Grow Cold	P. Calle	2,500	265.00	265.00
91-03-058	When Trails Grow Cold-Prestige Ed.	P. Calle	290	465.00	465-600.
81-03-059	Winter Hunter (Color)	P. Calle	950	245.00	725.00
80-03-060	Winter Hunter (Pencil)	P. Calle	950	65.00	450.00
Mill Pond Press		**Peterson**			
76-04-001	Adelie Penguins	R. Peterson	950	35.00	35.00
74-04-002	Bald Eagle	R. Peterson	950	150.00	440.00
73-04-003	Baltimore Oriole S/N	R. Peterson	450	150.00	300.00
76-04-004	Barn Owl	R. Peterson	950	225.00	300.00
74-04-005	Barn Swallow S/N	R. Peterson	750	150.00	250 350.
76-04-006	Blue Jays	R. Peterson	950	150.00	350.00
77-04-007	BlueBird	R. Peterson	950	75.00	225.00
74-04-008	Bobolink S/N	R. Peterson	750	150.00	275.00
75-04-009	Bobwhites	R. Peterson	950	150.00	285.00
73-04-010	Cardinal S/N	R. Peterson	450	150.00	525.00
73-04-011	Flicker	R. Peterson	450	150.00	225.00
76-04-012	Golden Eagle	R. Peterson	950	200.00	210.00
74-04-013	Great Horned Owl	R. Peterson	950	150.00	450.00
79-04-014	Gyrfalcon	R. Peterson	950	225.00	360.00
78-04-015	Mockingbird	R. Peterson	950	125.00	250-300.
77-04-016	Peregrine Falcon	R. Peterson	950	175.00	300.00
78-04-017	Ring-Necked Pheasant	R. Peterson	950	200.00	250-300.
78-04-018	Robin	R. Peterson	950	125.00	410.00
78-04-019	Rose-Breasted Grosbeak	R. Peterson	950	125.00	125.00
75-04-020	Ruffed Grouse	R. Peterson	950	150.00	350.00
77-04-021	Scarlet Tanager	R. Peterson	950	125.00	200.00
75-04-022	Sea Otters	R. Peterson	950	25.00	100.00
76-04-023	Snowy Owl	R. Peterson	950	175.00	475.00
77-04-024	Sooty Terns S/N	R. Peterson	450	50.00	85.00
77-04-025	Willets S/N	R. Peterson	450	50.00	75.00
73-04-026	Wood Thrush	R. Peterson	450	150.00	295.00
Mill Pond Press		**Machetanz**			
79-05-001	Beginnings	F. Machetanz	950	175.00	425.00
88-05-002	Change of Direction	F. Machetanz	950	320.00	320-670.
89-05-003	The Chief Dances	F. Machetanz	950	235.00	235.00
79-05-004	Decision on the Ice Field	F. Machetanz	950	150.00	450.00
84-05-005	End of a Long Day	F. Machetanz	950	200.00	200-370.
85-05-006	End of the Hunt	F. Machetanz	950	245.00	255.00
78-05-007	Face to Face	F. Machetanz	950	150.00	1500.00
92-05-008	First Day in Harness	F. Machetanz	950	225.00	225.00
90-05-009	Glory of the Trail	F. Machetanz	950	225.00	275.00
81-05-010	Golden Years	F. Machetanz	950	245.00	590.00
90-05-011	The Grass is Always Greener	F. Machetanz	950	200.00	200.00
92-05-012	Harpooner's Moment	F. Machetanz	950	225.00	225.00
84-05-013	The Heritage of Alaska	F. Machetanz	950	400.00	800.00
78-05-014	Hunter's Dawn	F. Machetanz	950	125.00	500.00
78-05-015	Into the Home Stretch	F. Machetanz	950	175.00	700.00
91-05-016	Kayak Man	F. Machetanz	950	215.00	215-275.
80-05-017	King of the Mountain	F. Machetanz	950	200.00	200.00
86-05-018	Kyrok-Eskimo Seamstress	F. Machetanz	950	225.00	225.00
85-05-019	Land of the Midnight Sun	F. Machetanz	950	245.00	245-270.
85-05-020	Language of the Snow	F. Machetanz	950	195.00	195-240.
86-05-021	Leaving the Nest	F. Machetanz	950	245.00	245.00
86-05-022	Lone Musher	F. Machetanz	950	245.00	145-275.
84-05-023	Many Miles Together	F. Machetanz	950	245.00	245-285.
81-05-024	Midday Moonlight	F. Machetanz	950	265.00	425.00
84-05-025	Midnight Watch	F. Machetanz	950	250.00	250-300.
82-05-026	Mighty Hunter	F. Machetanz	950	265.00	400.00

Company Number	Name	Series Artist	Edition Limit	Issue Price	Quote
82-05-027	Moonlit Stakeout	F. Machetanz	950	265.00	525.00
82-05-028	Moose Tracks	F. Machetanz	950	265.00	300.00
86-05-029	Mt. Blackburn-Sovereign of the Wrangells	F. Machetanz	950	245.00	245.00
83-05-030	Nanook	F. Machetanz	950	295.00	295.00
80-05-031	Nelchina Trail	F. Machetanz	950	245.00	450.00
79-05-032	Pick of the Litter	F. Machetanz	950	165.00	1050.00
90-05-033	Quality Time	F. Machetanz	950	200.00	200-240.
79-05-034	Reaching the Campsite	F. Machetanz	950	200.00	400.00
85-05-035	Reaching the Pass	F. Machetanz	950	265.00	465.00
84-05-036	Smoke Dreams	F. Machetanz	950	250.00	400-450.
80-05-037	Sourdough	F. Machetanz	950	245.00	1125.00
87-05-038	Spring Fever	F. Machetanz	950	225.00	225.00
84-05-039	Story of the Beads	F. Machetanz	950	245.00	245.00
91-05-040	The Search for Gold	F. Machetanz	950	225.00	225.00
82-05-041	The Tender Arctic	F. Machetanz	950	295.00	750.00
83-05-042	They Opened the North Country	F. Machetanz	950	245.00	245.00
91-05-043	Tundra Flower	F. Machetanz	950	235.00	235-350.
81-05-044	What Every Hunter Fears	F. Machetanz	950	245.00	375.00
80-05-045	When Three's a Crowd	F. Machetanz	950	225.00	825.00
81-05-046	Where Men and Dogs Seem Small	F. Machetanz	950	245.00	400.00
81-05-047	Winter Harvest	F. Machetanz	950	265.00	325.00
Mill Pond Press		**Parker**			
86-06-001	Above the Breakers-Osprey	R. Parker	950	150.00	175.00
86-06-002	At End of Day-Wolves	R. Parker	950	235.00	325.00
86-06-003	Autumn Foraging-Moose	R. Parker	950	175.00	425.00
86-06-004	Autumn Leaves-Red Fox	R. Parker	950	95.00	100.00
89-06-005	Autumn Maples-Wolves	R. Parker	950	195.00	195.00
86-06-006	Autumn Meadow-Elk	R. Parker	950	195.00	200.00
90-06-007	Breaking the Silence-Wolves	R. Parker	1,250	195.00	300.00
86-06-008	Cardinal In Blue Spruce	R. Parker	950	125.00	150.00
86-06-009	Cardinal in Brambles	R. Parker	950	125.00	150.00
84-06-010	Chickadees In Autumn	R. Parker	950	75.00	75.00
86-06-011	Creekside-Cougar	R. Parker	950	225.00	350.00
91-06-012	Deep Snow-Whitetail	R. Parker	950	175.00	175.00
89-06-013	Deep Water-Orcas	R. Parker	1,250	195.00	195.00
89-06-014	Early Snowfall-Elk	R. Parker	950	185.00	185.00
87-06-015	Evening Glow-Wolf Pack	R. Parker	950	245.00	275.00
84-06-016	Face of the North	R. Parker	950	95.00	250.00
89-06-017	Flying Redtail	R. Parker	290	295.00	295.00
86-06-018	Following Mama-Mute Swans	R. Parker	950	165.00	475.00
91-06-019	Forest Trek-Gray Wolf	R. Parker	950	185.00	185.00
87-06-020	Freeze Up-Canada Geese	R. Parker	950	85.00	100.00
91-06-021	Gila Woodpecker	R. Parker	950	135.00	135.00
84-06-022	Gray Wolf Portrait	R. Parker	950	115.00	175.00
90-06-023	Icy Morning-Red Fox	R. Parker	950	150.00	150.00
90-06-024	Inside Passage-Orcas	R. Parker	1,500	195.00	195.00
86-06-025	Just Resting-Sea Otter	R. Parker	950	85.00	250.00
90-06-026	Lioness and Cubs	R. Parker	150	295.00	295.00
83-06-027	Mallard Family	R. Parker	950	95.00	95.00
85-06-028	Misty Dawn-Loon	R. Parker	950	120.00	525.00
91-06-029	Moonlit Tracks-Wolves	R. Parker	1,500	200.00	225-400.
90-06-030	Moose in the Brush	R. Parker	950	195.00	195.00
86-06-031	Morning on the Lagoon-Mute Swan	R. Parker	950	95.00	100.00
91-06-032	Mother and Son-Orcas	R. Parker	950	185.00	185.00
86-06-033	Northern Morning-Arctic Fox	R. Parker	950	125.00	175.00
87-06-034	On the Run-Wolf Pack	R. Parker	950	245.00	300.00
82-06-035	Racoon Pair	R. Parker	950	95.00	400.00
87-06-036	Rail Fence-Bluebirds	R. Parker	950	105.00	125.00
85-06-037	Reflections-Mallard	R. Parker	950	85.00	175.00
86-06-038	Rimrock-Cougar	R. Parker	950	200.00	900.00
83-06-039	Riverside Pause-River Otter	R. Parker	950	95.00	150.00
88-06-040	Silent Passage-Orcas	R. Parker	950	175.00	175.00
84-06-041	Silent Steps-Lynx	R. Parker	950	145.00	325.00
82-06-042	Snow on the Pine-Chickadees	R. Parker	950	95.00	100.00
85-06-043	Spring Arrivals-Canada Geese	R. Parker	950	120.00	200.00
82-06-044	Spring Mist-Gray Wolf	R. Parker	950	155.00	375.00
85-06-045	Waiting Out the Storm	R. Parker	950	105.00	400.00
82-06-046	Weathered Wood-Bluebirds	R. Parker	950	75.00	175.00
84-06-047	When Paths Cross	R. Parker	950	185.00	400.00
86-06-048	Whitetail and Wolves	R. Parker	950	180.00	300.00
85-06-049	Wings Over Winter-Bald Eagle	R. Parker	950	135.00	350.00
87-06-050	Winter Creek and Whitetails	R. Parker	950	185.00	185.00
86-06-051	Winter Creek-Coyote	R. Parker	950	130.00	275.00
87-06-052	Winter Encounter-Wolf	R. Parker	950	235.00	350.00
84-06-053	Winter Jay	R. Parker	950	95.00	150.00
90-06-054	Winter Lookout-Cougar	R. Parker	950	175.00	175.00
87-06-055	Winter Sage-Coyote	R. Parker	950	225.00	350.00
87-06-056	Winter Storm-Coyotes	R. Parker	950	245.00	325.00
83-06-057	Yellow Dawn-American Elk	R. Parker	950	130.00	200.00
Mill Pond Press		**Seerey-Lester**			
86-07-001	Above the Treeline-Cougar	J. Seerey-Lester	950	130.00	175.00
87-07-002	Alpenglow-Artic Wolf	J. Seerey-Lester	950	200.00	275.00
84-07-003	Among the Cattails-Canada Geese	J. Seerey-Lester	950	130.00	425.00
84-07-004	Artic Procession-Willow Ptarmigan	J. Seerey-Lester	950	220.00	600.00
90-07-005	Artic Wolf Pups	J. Seerey-Lester	290	500.00	500.00
87-07-006	Autumn Mist-Barred Owl	J. Seerey-Lester	950	160.00	225.00
92-07-007	Banyan Ambush- Black Panther	J. Seerey-Lester	950	235.00	235.00
84-07-008	Basking-Brown Pelicans	J. Seerey-Lester	950	115.00	125.00
90-07-009	Bittersweet Winter-Cardinal	J. Seerey-Lester	1,250	150.00	275.00
92-07-010	Black Magic-Panther	J. Seerey-Lester	750	195.00	195.00
87-07-011	Canyon Creek-Cougar	J. Seerey-Lester	950	195.00	450.00
85-07-012	Children of the Forest-Red Fox Kits	J. Seerey-Lester	950	110.00	150.00
85-07-013	Children of the Tundra-Artic Wolf Pup	J. Seerey-Lester	950	110.00	225.00
84-07-014	Close Encounter-Bobcat	J. Seerey-Lester	950	130.00	190.00
83-07-015	Cool Retreat-Lynx	J. Seerey-Lester	950	85.00	100.00
89-07-016	Cougar Run	J. Seerey-Lester	950	185.00	450.00
90-07-017	Dawn Majesty	J. Seerey-Lester	1,250	185.00	185.00
91-07-018	Denali Family-Grizzly Bear	J. Seerey-Lester	950	195.00	195.00
88-07-019	Edge of the Forest-Timber Wolves	J. Seerey-Lester	950	500.00	700.00
89-07-020	Evening Duet-Snowy Egrets	J. Seerey-Lester	1,250	185.00	185.00
91-07-021	Evening Encounter-Grizzly & Wolf	J. Seerey-Lester	1,250	185.00	185.00
91-07-022	Face to Face	J. Seerey-Lester	1,250	200.00	200.00
85-07-023	Fallen Birch-Chipmunk	J. Seerey-Lester	950	60.00	250.00
85-07-024	First Light-Gray Jays	J. Seerey-Lester	950	130.00	200.00
83-07-025	First Snow-Grizzly Bears	J. Seerey-Lester	950	95.00	250.00
85-07-026	Gathering-Gray Wolves, The	J. Seerey-Lester	950	165.00	350.00
89-07-027	Gorilla	J. Seerey-Lester	290	400.00	600.00
90-07-028	Grizzly Litho	J. Seerey-Lester	290	400.00	400.00
89-07-029	Heavy Going-Grizzly	J. Seerey-Lester	950	175.00	175.00
86-07-030	Hidden Admirer-Moose	J. Seerey-Lester	950	165.00	275.00
89-07-031	High and Mighty-Gorilla	J. Seerey-Lester	950	185.00	225.00

Company Number	Name	Series Artist	Edition Limit	Issue Price	Quote
86-07-032	High Country Champion-Grizzly	J. Seerey-Lester	950	175.00	275.00
84-07-033	High Ground-Wolves	J. Seerey-Lester	950	130.00	325.00
84-07-034	Icy Outcrop-White Gyrfalcon	J. Seerey-Lester	950	115.00	200.00
90-07-035	In Their Presence	J. Seerey-Lester	1,250	200.00	200.00
85-07-036	Island Sanctuary-Mallards	J. Seerey-Lester	950	95.00	175.00
83-07-037	Lone Fisherman-Great Blue Heron	J. Seerey-Lester	950	85.00	300.00
84-07-038	Lying Low-Cougar	J. Seerey-Lester	950	85.00	450.00
91-07-039	Monsoon-White Tiger	J. Seerey-Lester	950	195.00	195.00
91-07-040	Moonlight Chase-Cougar	J. Seerey-Lester	1,250	195.00	195-220.
88-07-041	Morning Display-Common Loons	J. Seerey-Lester	950	135.00	300.00
84-07-042	Morning Mist-Snowy Owl	J. Seerey-Lester	950	95.00	95-180.00
90-07-043	Mountain Cradle	J. Seerey-Lester	1,250	200.00	200.00
90-07-044	Night Run-Artic Wolves	J. Seerey-Lester	1,250	200.00	250.00
87-07-045	Out of the Blizzard-Timber Wolves	J. Seerey-Lester	950	215.00	350.00
92-07-046	Out of the Darkness	J. Seerey-Lester	290	200.00	200.00
91-07-047	Out on a Limb-Young Barred Owl	J. Seerey-Lester	950	185.00	185.00
91-07-048	Panda Trilogy	J. Seerey-Lester	950	375.00	375.00
90-07-049	The Plunge-Northern Sea Lions	J. Seerey-Lester	1,250	200.00	200.00
86-07-050	Racing the Storm-Artic Wolves	J. Seerey-Lester	950	200.00	350.00
92-07-051	Regal Majesty	J. Seerey-Lester	290	200.00	200.00
90-07-052	Seasonal Greeting-Cardinal	J. Seerey-Lester	1,250	150.00	150.00
91-07-053	Sisters-Artic Wolves	J. Seerey-Lester	1,250	185.00	185.00
89-07-054	Sneak Peak	J. Seerey-Lester	950	185.00	185.00
89-07-055	Softly, Softly-White Tiger	J. Seerey-Lester	950	220.00	490.00
91-07-056	Something Stirred (Bengal Tiger)	J. Seerey-Lester	950	195.00	195.00
84-07-057	Spirit of the North-White Wolf	J. Seerey-Lester	950	130.00	185.00
90-07-058	Spout	J. Seerey-Lester	290	500.00	500.00
86-07-059	Spring Mist Chickadees	J. Seerey-Lester	950	105.00	150.00
89-07-060	Spring Flurry-Adelie Penguins	J. Seerey-Lester	950	185.00	185.00
91-07-061	Suitors-Wood Ducks	J. Seerey-Lester	3,313	135.00	135.00
90-07-062	Summer Rain-Common Loons	J. Seerey-Lester	4,500	200.00	200.00
90-07-063	Summer Rain-Common Loons(Prestige)	J. Seerey-Lester	450	425.00	425.00
92-07-064	The Chase-Snow Leopard	J. Seerey-Lester	950	200.00	200.00
83-07-065	The Refuge-Raccoon	J. Seerey-Lester	950	85.00	300.00
90-07-066	Their First Season	J. Seerey-Lester	1,250	200.00	200.00
90-07-067	Togetherness	J. Seerey-Lester	1,250	125.00	185.00
85-07-068	Under the Pines-Bobcat	J. Seerey-Lester	950	95.00	275.00
89-07-069	Water Sport-Bobcat	J. Seerey-Lester	950	185.00	185.00
90-07-070	Whitetail Spring	J. Seerey-Lester	1,250	185.00	185.00
83-07-071	Winter Lookout-Cougar	J. Seerey-Lester	950	85.00	500.00
86-07-072	Winter Perch-Cardinal	J. Seerey-Lester	950	85.00	175.00
85-07-073	Winter Rendezvous-Coyotes	J. Seerey-Lester	950	140.00	225.00
Mill Pond Press		**Brenders**			
88-08-001	A Hunter's Dream	C. Brenders	950	165.00	750-875.
90-08-002	A Threatened Symbol	C. Brenders	1,950	145.00	300.00
88-08-003	Apple Harvest	C. Brenders	950	115.00	295.00
87-08-004	Autumn Lady	C. Brenders	950	150.00	375.00
89-08-005	A Young Generation	C. Brenders	1,250	165.00	375-425.
86-08-006	Black-Capped Chickadees	C. Brenders	950	40.00	400.00
90-08-007	Blond Beauty	C. Brenders	1,950	185.00	185.00
86-08-008	Bluebirds	C. Brenders	950	40.00	200-350.
91-08-009	Calm Before the Challenge-Moose	C. Brenders	1,950	225.00	225.00
87-08-010	Close to Mom	C. Brenders	950	150.00	900-1450.
86-08-011	Colorful Playground-Cottontails	C. Brenders	950	75.00	475.00
92-08-012	Den Mother-Pencil Sketch	C. Brenders	2,500	135.00	135.00
92-08-013	Den Mother-Wolf Family	C. Brenders	25,000	250.00	250.00
86-08-014	Disturbed Daydreams	C. Brenders	950	95.00	425.00
87-08-015	Double Trouble-Raccoons	C. Brenders	950	120.00	500-750.
88-08-016	Forest Sentinel-Bobcat	C. Brenders	950	135.00	500.00
90-08-017	Full House-Fox Family	C. Brenders	20,106	235.00	235.00
90-08-018	Ghostly Quiet-Spanish Lynx	C. Brenders	1,950	200.00	200.00
86-08-019	Golden Season-Gray Squirrel	C. Brenders	950	85.00	525.00
86-08-020	Harvest Time-Chipmunk	C. Brenders	950	65.00	150-250.
88-08-021	Hidden In the Pines-Immature Great Hor	C. Brenders	950	175.00	1500.00
88-08-022	High Adventure-Black Bear Cubs	C. Brenders	950	105.00	375.00
87-08-023	Ivory-Billed Woodpecker	C. Brenders	950	95.00	500.00
88-08-024	Long Distance Hunters	C. Brenders	950	175.00	1400-2250.
89-08-025	Lord of the Marshes	C. Brenders	1,250	135.00	175.00
86-08-026	Meadowlark	C. Brenders	950	40.00	150.00
89-08-027	Merlins at the Nest	C. Brenders	1,250	165.00	300-375.
85-08-028	Mighty Intruder	C. Brenders	950	95.00	275.00
87-08-029	Migration Fever-Barn Swallows	C. Brenders	950	150.00	295-350.
90-08-030	Mountain Baby-Bighorn Sheep	C. Brenders	1,950	165.00	165.00
87-08-031	Mysterious Visitor-Barn Owl	C. Brenders	950	150.00	295-375.
91-08-032	The Nesting Season-House Sparrow	C. Brenders	1,950	195.00	250.00
89-08-033	Northern Cousins-Black Squirrels	C. Brenders	950	150.00	250.00
84-08-034	On the Alert-Red Fox	C. Brenders	950	95.00	475.00
90-08-035	On the Old Farm Door	C. Brenders	1,500	225.00	450.00
91-08-036	One to One-Gray Wolf	C. Brenders	10,000	245.00	450-500.
92-08-037	Pathfinder-Red Fox	C. Brenders	5,000	245.00	245.00
84-08-038	Playful Pair-Chipmunks	C. Brenders	950	60.00	400.00
92-08-039	Red Fox Study	C. Brenders	1,250	125.00	125.00
86-08-040	Robins	C. Brenders	950	40.00	125.00
92-08-041	Rocky Kingdom-Bighorn Sheep	C. Brenders	1,750	255.00	255.00
91-08-042	Shadows in the Grass-Young Cougars	C. Brenders	1,950	235.00	235.00
90-08-043	Shoreline Quartet-White Ibis	C. Brenders	1,950	265.00	265.00
84-08-044	Silent Hunter-Great Horned Owl	C. Brenders	950	95.00	450.00
84-08-045	Silent Passage	C. Brenders	950	150.00	495.00
90-08-046	Small Talk	C. Brenders	1,500	125.00	150-250.
90-08-047	Spring Fawn	C. Brenders	1,500	125.00	300.00
90-08-048	Squirrel's Dish	C. Brenders	1,950	110.00	110.00
89-08-049	Steller's Jay	C. Brenders	1,250	135.00	175.00
91-08-050	Study for One to One	C. Brenders	1,950	120.00	200.00
88-08-051	Talk on the Old Fence	C. Brenders	950	165.00	495-725.
86-08-052	The Acrobat's Meal-Red Squirrel	C. Brenders	950	65.00	275.00
89-08-053	The Apple Lover	C. Brenders	1,500	125.00	275.00
91-08-054	The Balance of Nature	C. Brenders	1,950	225.00	225.00
89-08-055	The Companions	C. Brenders	18,036	200.00	850-1250.
89-08-056	The Predator's Walk	C. Brenders	1,250	150.00	375.00
89-08-057	The Survivors-Canada Geese	C. Brenders	1,500	225.00	850-950.
84-08-058	Waterside Encounter	C. Brenders	950	95.00	1000.00
87-08-059	White Elegance-Trumpeter Swans	C. Brenders	950	115.00	390.00
92-08-060	Wolf Scout #1	C. Brenders	2,500	105.00	105.00
92-08-061	Wolf Scout #2	C. Brenders	2,500	105.00	105.00
91-08-062	Wolf Study	C. Brenders	950	125.00	125.00
87-08-063	Yellow-Bellied Marmot	C. Brenders	950	95.00	425.00
Mill Pond Press		**Daly**			
91-09-001	A New Beginning	J. Daly	5,000	125.00	125.00
90-09-002	The Big Moment	J. Daly	1,500	125.00	125.00
91-09-003	Cat's Cradle Prestige Edition	J. Daly	950	450.00	450.00
90-09-004	Confrontation	J. Daly	1,500	85.00	85.00

Number	Name	Artist	Edition Limit	Issue Price	Quote
90-09-005	Contentment	J. Daly	1,500	95.00	275.00
92-09-006	Dominoes	J. Daly	1,500	155.00	155.00
86-09-007	Flying High	J. Daly	950	50.00	350.00
92-09-008	Her Secret Place	J. Daly	1,500	135.00	135.00
91-09-009	Home Team: Zero	J. Daly	1,500	150.00	150.00
91-09-010	Homemade	J. Daly	1,500	125.00	125.00
90-09-011	Honor and Allegiance	J. Daly	1,500	110.00	110.00
90-09-012	The Ice Man	J. Daly	1,500	125.00	125.00
89-09-013	In the Doghouse	J. Daly	1,500	75.00	250.00
90-09-014	It's That Time Again	J. Daly	1,500	120.00	120.00
92-09-015	Left Out	J. Daly	1,500	110.00	110.00
89-09-016	Let's Play Ball	J. Daly	1,500	75.00	150.00
90-09-017	Make Believe	J. Daly	1,500	75.00	125.00
91-09-018	Pillars of a Nation-Charter Edition	J. Daly	20,000	175.00	175.00
92-09-019	Playmates	J. Daly	1,500	155.00	155.00
90-09-020	Radio Daze	J. Daly	1,500	150.00	150.00
83-09-021	Saturday Night	J. Daly	950	85.00	1125.00
90-09-022	The Scholar	J. Daly	1,500	110.00	110.00
82-09-023	Spring Fever	J. Daly	950	85.00	750.00
89-09-024	The Thief	J. Daly	1,500	95.00	175.00
92-09-025	The Flying Horse	J. Daly	950	325.00	325.00
91-09-026	Time-Out	J. Daly	1,500	125.00	125.00

New Masters Publishing — **Bannister**

Number	Name	Artist	Edition Limit	Issue Price	Quote
78-01-001	Bandstand	P. Bannister	250	75.00	450.00
80-01-002	Dust of Autumn	P. Bannister	200	200.00	1225.00
80-01-003	Faded Glory	P. Bannister	200	200.00	1225.00
80-01-004	Gift of Happiness	P. Bannister	200	200.00	2000.00
80-01-005	Girl on the Beach	P. Bannister	200	200.00	1200.00
80-01-006	The Silver Bell	P. Bannister	200	200.00	2000.00
81-01-007	April	P. Bannister	S/O	200.00	1100.00
81-01-008	Crystal	P. Bannister	300	260.00	300.00
81-01-009	Easter	P. Bannister	S/O	260.00	950.00
81-01-010	Juliet	P. Bannister	S/O	260.00	5000.00
81-01-011	My Special Place	P. Bannister	S/O	260.00	1850.00
81-01-012	Porcelain Rose	P. Bannister	S/O	260.00	2000.00
81-01-013	Rehearsal	P. Bannister	S/O	260.00	1850.00
81-01-014	Sea Haven	P. Bannister	S/O	260.00	1100.00
81-01-015	Titania	P. Bannister	S/O	260.00	900.00
82-01-016	Amaryllis	P. Bannister	S/O	285.00	1900.00
82-01-017	Cinderella	P. Bannister	500	285.00	285.00
82-01-018	Emily	P. Bannister	S/O	285.00	800.00
82-01-019	Ivy	P. Bannister	S/O	285.00	700.00
82-01-020	Jasmine	P. Bannister	S/O	285.00	650.00
82-01-021	Lily	P. Bannister	500	235.00	235.00
82-01-022	Mail Order Brides	P. Bannister	S/O	325.00	2300.00
82-01-023	Memories	P. Bannister	S/O	235.00	500.00
82-01-024	Nuance	P. Bannister	S/O	235.00	470.00
82-01-025	Parasols	P. Bannister	500	235.00	235.00
82-01-026	The Present	P. Bannister	S/O	260.00	800.00
83-01-027	The Duchess	P. Bannister	S/O	250.00	1800.00
84-01-028	The Fan Window	P. Bannister	S/O	195.00	450.00
84-01-029	Window Seat	P. Bannister	S/O	150.00	600.00
83-01-030	Ophelia	P. Bannister	S/O	150.00	675.00
84-01-031	Scarlet Ribbons	P. Bannister	S/O	150.00	325.00
83-01-032	Mementos	P. Bannister	S/O	150.00	1400.00
84-01-033	April Light	P. Bannister	S/O	150.00	600.00
84-01-034	Make Believe	P. Bannister	S/O	150.00	600.00
88-01-035	Summer Choices	P. Bannister	300	250.00	800.00
88 01 036	Guinevere	P. Bannister	485	265.00	1000.00
88-01-037	Love Seat	P. Bannister	S/O	230.00	500.00
88-01-038	Apples and Oranges	P. Bannister	S/O	265.00	600.00
89-01-039	Daydreams	P. Bannister	S/O	265.00	530.00
86-01-040	Pride & Joy	P. Bannister	S/O	150.00	300.00
86-01-041	Soiree	P. Bannister	950	150.00	225.00
87-01-042	Autumn Fields	P. Bannister	950	150.00	225.00
87-01-043	September Harvest	P. Bannister	S/O	150.00	300.00
87-01-044	Quiet Corner	P. Bannister	S/O	115.00	300.00
87-01-045	First Prize	P. Bannister	950	115.00	175.00
88-01-046	Floribunda	P. Bannister	S/O	265.00	550.00
89-01-047	March Winds	P. Bannister	S/O	265.00	530.00
89-01-048	Peace	P. Bannister	S/O	265.00	1100.00
89-01-049	The Quilt	P. Bannister	S/O	265.00	900.00
89-01-050	Low Tide	P. Bannister	S/O	265.00	550.00
89-01-051	Chapter One	P. Bannister	S/O	265.00	1300.00
90-01-052	Lavender Hill	P. Bannister	S/O	265.00	625.00
90-01-053	Rendezvous	P. Bannister	S/O	265.00	650.00
90-01-054	Sisters	P. Bannister	S/O	265.00	950.00
90-01-055	Seascapes	P. Bannister	S/O	265.00	550.00
90-01-056	Songbird	P. Bannister	S/O	265.00	550.00
90-01-057	Good Friends	P. Bannister	S/O	265.00	750.00
91-01-058	String of Pearls	P. Bannister	S/O	265.00	850.00
91-01-059	Wildflowers	P. Bannister	S/O	295.00	590.00
91-01-060	Crossroads	P. Bannister	S/O	295.00	590.00
91-01-060	Teatime	P. Bannister	S/O	295.00	600.00
91-01-061	Celebration	P. Bannister	S/O	350.00	700.00
91-01-062	Pudding & Pies	P. Bannister	S/O	265.00	265.00

Past Impressions — **Maley**

Number	Name	Artist	Edition Limit	Issue Price	Quote
84-01-001	Secluded Garden	A. Maley	Closed	150.00	970.00
84-01-002	Glorious Summer	A. Maley	Closed	150.00	725.00
85-01-003	Secret Thoughts	A. Maley	Closed	150.00	850.00
85-01-004	Passing Elegance	A. Maley	Closed	150.00	750.00
86-01-005	Winter Romance	A. Maley	Closed	150.00	750.00
86-01-006	Tell Me	A. Maley	Closed	150.00	850.00
88-01-007	Opening Night	A. Maley	Closed	250.00	2000.00
67-01-008	Love Letter	A. Maley	Closed	200.00	450-550.
87-01-009	The Promise	A. Maley	450	200.00	315.00
88-01-010	Day Dreams	A. Maley	500	200.00	350-450.
88-01-011	The Boardwalk	A. Maley	500	250.00	340.00
88-01-012	Tranquil Moment	A. Maley	Closed	250.00	315.00
88-01-013	Joys of Childhood	A. Maley	500	250.00	250.00
88-01-014	Victorian Trio	A. Maley	500	250.00	340.00
89-01-015	English Rose	A. Maley	750	250.00	285.00
89-01-016	Winter Impressions	A. Maley	750	250.00	315.00
89-01-017	In Harmony	A. Maley	750	250.00	250.00
90-01-018	Festive Occasion	A. Maley	750	250.00	250.00
90-01-019	Summer Pastime	A. Maley	750	250.00	250.00
90-01-020	Cafe Royale	A. Maley	750	275.00	275.00
90-01-021	Romantic Engagement	A. Maley	750	275.00	275.00
90-01-022	Gracious Era	A. Maley	750	275.00	275.00
90-01-023	Evening Performance	A. Maley	750	150.00	150.00
91-01-024	Between Friends	A. Maley	750	275.00	275.00
91-01-025	Summer Carousel	A. Maley	750	200.00	200.00
91-01-026	Sunday Afternoon	A. Maley	750	275.00	275.00
91-01-027	Winter Carousel	A. Maley	750	200.00	200.00
92-01-028	Evening Performance	A. Maley	750	150.00	150.00
92-01-029	Intimate Moment	A. Maley	750	250.00	250.00
92-01-030	A Walk in the Park	A. Maley	500	260.00	260.00
92-01-031	An Elegant Affair	A. Maley	500	260.00	260.00
92-01-032	Circle of Love	A. Maley	500	250.00	250.00

Past Impressions, Inc. — **Women of Elegance**

Number	Name	Artist	Edition Limit	Issue Price	Quote
89-02-001	Victoria	A. Maley	750	125.00	125.00
89-02-002	Catherine	A. Maley	750	125.00	125.00
89-02-003	Beth	A. Maley	750	125.00	125.00
89-02-004	Alexandra	A. Maley	750	125.00	125.00

Pemberton & Oaks — **Zolan's Children-Lithographs**

Number	Name	Artist	Edition Limit	Issue Price	Quote
82-01-001	By Myself	D. Zolan	880	98.00	250-289.
82-01-002	Erik and the Dandelion	D. Zolan	880	98.00	400-460.
84-01-003	Sabina in the Grass	D. Zolan	880	98.00	640-710.
86-01-004	Tender Moment	D. Zolan	880	98.00	295-375.
87-01-005	Touching the Sky	D. Zolan	880	98.00	290-350.
88-01-006	Tiny Treasures	D. Zolan	450	150.00	235-275.
88-01-007	Winter Angel	D. Zolan	980	98.00	275-350.
88-01-009	Small Wonder	D. Zolan	880	98.00	312.00
88-01-010	Day Dreamer	D. Zolan	1,000	35.00	150.00
88-01-011	Waiting to Play	D. Zolan	1,000	35.00	130-195.
89-01-012	Christmas Prayer	D. Zolan	880	98.00	175-245.
89-01-013	Almost Home	D. Zolan	880	98.00	275-309.
89-01-014	Brotherly Love	D. Zolan	880	98.00	360.00
89-01-015	Daddy's Home	D. Zolan	880	98.00	305.00
89-01-016	Grandma's Mirror	D. Zolan	880	98.00	170.00
89-01-017	Mother's Angels	D. Zolan	880	98.00	310.00
89-01-018	Rodeo Girl	D. Zolan	880	98.00	170.00
89-01-019	Snowy Adventure	D. Zolan	880	98.00	295.00
89-01-020	Summer's Child	D. Zolan	880	98.00	98.00
90-01-021	Colors of Spring	D. Zolan	880	98.00	185-325.
90-01-022	Crystal's Creek	D. Zolan	880	98.00	195-325.
90-01-023	First Kiss	D. Zolan	880	98.00	260.00
90-01-024	Laurie and the Creche	D. Zolan	880	98.00	98.00
91-01-025	Autumn Leaves	D. Zolan	880	98.00	175.00
91-01-026	Flowers for Mother	D. Zolan	880	98.00	98.00
91-01-027	Summer Suds	D. Zolan	880	98.00	98.00
92-01-028	Enchanted Forest	D. Zolan	880	98.00	98.00
92-01-029	New Shoes	D. Zolan	880	98.00	98.00

Pemberton & Oaks — **Zolan's Children-Miniature Lithographs**

Number	Name	Artist	Edition Limit	Issue Price	Quote
91-02-001	Morning Discovery	D. Zolan	Yr.Iss.	35.00	35.00

Pemberton & Oaks — **Grandparents Day-Miniature Lithographs**

Number	Name	Artist	Edition Limit	Issue Price	Quote
92-03-001	Letter to Grandma	D. Zolan	Yr.Iss.	35.00	35.00

Pemberton & Oaks — **Single Issues-Miniature Lithographs**

Number	Name	Artist	Edition Limit	Issue Price	Quote
91-04-001	Tender Moment	D. Zolan	Yr.Iss.	35.00	35.00
92-04-002	Brotherly Love	D. Zolan	Yr.Iss.	18.00	18.00

Pemberton & Oaks — **Miniature Replicas of Oils**

Number	Name	Artist	Edition Limit	Issue Price	Quote
90-05-001	Brotherly Love	D. Zolan	Yr.Iss.	24.40	24.40
90-05-002	Daddy's Home	D. Zolan	Yr.Iss.	24.40	24.40
91-05-003	Crystal's Creek	D. Zolan	Yr.Iss.	24.40	24.40
92-05-004	It's Grandma & Grandpa	D. Zolan	Yr.Iss.	24.40	24.40
92-05-005	Mother's Angels	D. Zolan	Yr.Iss.	24.40	24.40
92-05-006	Touching the Sky	D. Zolan	Yr.Iss.	24.40	24.40

Pemberton & Oaks — **Canvas Replicas**

Number	Name	Artist	Edition Limit	Issue Price	Quote
92-06-001	Quiet Time	D. Zolan	Yr.Iss.	18.80	18.80

Reco International — **Limited Edition Print**

Number	Name	Artist	Edition Limit	Issue Price	Quote
84-01-001	Jessica	S. Kuck	500	60.00	400.00
85-01-002	Heather	S. Kuck	500	75.00	150.00
86-01-003	Ashley	S. Kuck	500	85.00	150.00

Reco International — **McClelland**

Number	Name	Artist	Edition Limit	Issue Price	Quote
XX-02-001	Olivia	J. McClelland	300	175.00	175.00
XX-02-002	Sweet Dreams	J. McClelland	300	145.00	145.00
XX-02-003	Just for You	J. McClelland	300	155.00	155.00
XX-02-004	Reverie	J. McClelland	300	110.00	110.00
XX-02-005	I Love Tammy	J. McClelland	500	75.00	100.00

Reco International — **Fine Art Canvas Reproduction**

Number	Name	Artist	Edition Limit	Issue Price	Quote
90-03-001	Beach Play	J. McClelland	350	80.00	80.00
91-03-002	Flower Swing	J. McClelland	350	100.00	100.00
91-03-003	Summer Conversation	J. McClelland	350	80.00	80.00

Norman Rockwell Galleries — **Rockwell Graphics**

Number	Name	Artist	Edition Limit	Issue Price	Quote
91-01-001	Rockwell's Santa's Workshop (Canvas Reproduction)	Rockwell-Inspired	N/A	34.95	34.95
91-01-002	Rockwell's Main Street (Canvas Reproduction)	Rockwell-Inspired	N/A	69.95	69.95
92-01-003	Rockwell's Springtime in Stockbridge (Canvas Reproduction)	Rockwell-Inspired	N/A	79.95	79.95

Norman Rockwell Galleries — **Rockwell's Masterpiece Collection**

Number	Name	Artist	Edition Limit	Issue Price	Quote
92-02-001	Spring Flowers (Canvas Reproduction)	Rockwell-Inspired	N/A	59.95	59.95

Roman, Inc. — **Hook**

Number	Name	Artist	Edition Limit	Issue Price	Quote
81-01-001	The Carpenter	F. Hook	Yr.Iss	100.00	1000.00
81-01-002	The Carpenter (remarque)	F. Hook	Yr.Iss	100.00	3000.00
82-01-003	Frolicking	F. Hook	1,200	60.00	350.00
82-01-004	Gathering	F. Hook	1,200	60.00	350.00
82-01-005	Poulets	F. Hook	1,200	60.00	350.00
82-01-006	Bouquet	F. Hook	1,200	70.00	350.00
82-01-007	Surprise	F. Hook	1,200	50.00	350.00
82-01-008	Posing	F. Hook	1,200	70.00	350.00
82-01-009	Little Children, Come to Me	F. Hook	1,950	50.00	500.00
82-01-010	Little Children, Come to Me, remarque	F. Hook	50	100.00	500.00

Roman, Inc. — **Portraits of Love**

Number	Name	Artist	Edition Limit	Issue Price	Quote
88-02-001	Sharing	F. Hook	2,500	25.00	25.00
88-02-002	Expectation	F. Hook	2,500	25.00	25.00
88-02-003	Remember When...	F. Hook	2,500	25.00	25.00
88-02-004	My Kitty	F. Hook	2,500	25.00	25.00
88-02-005	In Mother's Arms	F. Hook	2,500	25.00	25.00
88-02-006	Sunkissed Afternoon	F. Hook	2,500	25.00	25.00

Company Number	Name	Series Artist	Edition Limit	Issue Price	Quote
Roman, Inc.		**Abble Williams**			
88-03-001	Mary, Mother of the Carpenter	A. Williams	Closed	100.00	100.00
Roman, Inc.		**The Discovery of America Miniature Art Print**			
91-04-001	The Discovery of America	I. Spencer	Open	2.00	2.00
Schmid		**Lowell Davis Lithographs**			
81-01-001	Surprise in the Cellar, remarque	L. Davis	101	100.00	400.00
81-01-002	Surprise in the Cellar, regular edition	L. Davis	899	75.00	375.00
81-01-003	Plum Tuckered Out, remarque	L. Davis	101	100.00	350.00
81-01-004	Plum Tuckered Out, regular edition	L. Davis	899	75.00	300.00
81-01-005	Duke's Mixture, remarque	L. Davis	101	150.00	350.00
81-01-006	Duke's Mixture, regular edition	L. Davis	899	75.00	125.00
82-01-007	Bustin' with Pride, remarque	L. Davis	101	150.00	250.00
82-01-008	Bustin' with Pride, regular edition	L. Davis	899	75.00	125.00
82-01-009	Birth of a Blossom, remarque	L. Davis	50	200.00	450.00
82-01-010	Birth of a Blossom, regular edition	L. Davis	400	125.00	300.00
82-01-011	Suppertime, remarque	L. Davis	50	200.00	450.00
82-01-012	Suppertime, regular edition	L. Davis	400	125.00	300.00
82-01-013	Foxfire Farm, remarque	L. Davis	100	200.00	250.00
82-01-014	Foxfire Farm, regular edition	L. Davis	800	125.00	125.00
85-01-015	Self Portrait	L. Davis	450	75.00	192.00
87-01-016	Blossom's Gift	L. Davis	450	75.00	75.00
89-01-017	Sun Worshippers	L. Davis	750	100.00	100.00
90-01-018	Sunday Afternoon Treat	L. Davis	750	100.00	100.00
91-01-019	Warm Milk	L. Davis	750	100.00	179.00
92-01-020	Cat and Jenny Wren	L. Davis	750	100.00	100.00
93-01-021	The Old Home Place	L. Davis	750	130.00	130.00
Schmid		**Berta Hummel Lithographs**			
80-02-001	Moonlight Return	B. Hummel	900	150.00	850.00
80-02-002	1984 American Visit	B. Hummel	5	550.00	1000.00
81-02-003	A Time to Remember	B. Hummel	720	150.00	300.00
81-02-004	1984 American Visit	B. Hummel	5	550.00	1100.00
81-02-005	Remarqued	B. Hummel	180	250.00	1250.00
81-02-006	1984 American Visit	B. Hummel	2	1100.00	1700.00
82-02-007	Poppies	B. Hummel	450	150.00	650.00
82-02-008	1984 American Visit	B. Hummel	3	250.00	850.00
83-02-009	Angelic Messenger, 75th Anniversary	B. Hummel	195	375.00	700.00
83-02-010	Angelic Messenger, Christmas Message	B. Hummel	400	275.00	450.00
83-02-011	1984 American Visit	B. Hummel	10	275.00	600.00
83-02-012	Regular	B. Hummel	100	175.00	350.00
83-02-013	1984 American Visit	B. Hummel	10	175.00	400.00
85-02-014	Birthday Bouquet, Edition 1	B. Hummel	195	450.00	550.00
85-02-015	Birthday Bouquet, Edition 2	B. Hummel	225	375.00	375.00
85-02-016	Birthday Bouquet, Edition 3	B. Hummel	100	195.00	395.00
Schmid		**Ferrandiz Lithographs**			
80-03-001	Most Precious Gift, remarque	J. Ferrandiz	50	225.00	2800.00
80-03-002	Most Precious Gift, regular edition	J. Ferrandiz	425	125.00	1200.00
80-03-003	My Star, remarque	J. Ferrandiz	75	175.00	1800.00
80-03-004	My Star, regular edition	J. Ferrandiz	675	100.00	650.00
81-03-005	Heart of Seven Colors, remarque	J. Ferrandiz	75	175.00	1300.00
81-03-006	Heart of Seven Colors, regular edition	J. Ferrandiz	600	100.00	395.00
82-03-007	Oh Small Child, remarque	J. Ferrandiz	50	225.00	1450.00
82-03-008	Oh Small Child, regular edition	J. Ferrandiz	450	125.00	495.00
82-03-009	Spreading the Word, remarque	J. Ferrandiz	75	225.00	1075.00
82-03-010	Spreading the Word, regular edition	J. Ferrandiz	675	125.00	190-250.
82-03-011	On the Threshold of Life, remarque	J. Ferrandiz	50	275.00	1350.00
82-03-012	On the Threshold of Life, regular edition	J. Ferrandiz	425	150.00	450.00
82-03-013	Riding Through the Rain, remarque	J. Ferrandiz	100	300.00	950.00
82-03-014	Riding Through the Rain, regular edition	J. Ferrandiz	900	165.00	350.00
82-03-015	Mirror of the Soul, regular edition	J. Ferrandiz	225	150.00	425.00
82-03-016	Mirror of the Soul, remarque	J. Ferrandiz	35	250.00	2400.00
82-03-017	He Seems to Sleep, regular edition	J. Ferrandiz	450	150.00	700.00
82-03-018	He Seems to Sleep, remarque	J. Ferrandiz	25	300.00	3200.00
83-03-019	Friendship, remarque	J. Ferrandiz	15	1200.00	2300.00
83-03-020	Friendship, regular edition	J. Ferrandiz	460	165.00	450.00
84-03-021	Star in the Teapot; regular edition	J. Ferrandiz	410	165.00	165.00
84-03-022	Star in the Teapot; remarque	J. Ferrandiz	15	1200.00	2100.00
Terry Arts International		**Graphics**			
92-01-001	Blonde À La Rose-1915 31 Colors, framed	P.A.Renoir/P.Renoir	950	595.00	595.00
92-01-002	Blonde À La Rose-1915 31 Colors, unframed	P.A.Renoir/P.Renoir	950	395.00	395.00
92-01-003	Blonde À La Rose-1915 31 Colors, framed-AP	P.A.Renoir/P.Renoir	50	595.00	595.00
92-01-004	Blonde À La Rose-1915 31 Colors, unframed-AP	P.A.Renoir/P.Renoir	50	395.00	395.00
92-01-005	Alphonsine Fournaise-1879 24 Colors, framed	P.A.Renoir/P.Renoir	950	595.00	595.00
92-01-006	Alphonsine Fournaise-1879 24 Colors, unframed	P.A.Renoir/P.Renoir	950	395.00	395.00
92-01-007	Alphonsine Fournaise-1879 24 Colors, framed-AP	P.A.Renoir/P.Renoir	50	595.00	595.00
92-01-008	Alphonsine Fournaise-1879 24 Colors, unframed-AP	P.A.Renoir/P.Renoir	50	395.00	395.00
93-01-009	La Balançoire (The Swing)-1876 34 Colors, framed	P.A.Renoir/P.Renoir	950	750.00	750.00
93-01-010	La Balançoire (The Swing)-1876 34 Colors, unframed	P.A.Renoir/P.Renoir	950	550.00	550.00
93-01-011	La Balançoire (The Swing)-1876 34 Colors, framed-AP	P.A.Renoir/P.Renoir	50	750.00	750.00
93-01-012	La Balançoire (The Swing)-1876 34 Colors, unframed-AP	P.A.Renoir/P.Renoir	50	550.00	550.00
93-01-013	Les Marronniers Roses-1881 28 Colors, framed	P.A.Renoir/P.Renoir	950	625.00	625.00
93-01-014	Les Marronniers Roses-1881 28 Colors, unframed	P.A.Renoir/P.Renoir	950	425.00	425.00
93-01-015	Les Marronniers Roses-1881 28 Colors, framed-AP	P.A.Renoir/P.Renoir	50	625.00	625.00
93-01-016	Les Marronniers Roses-1881 28 Colors, unframed-AP	P.A.Renoir/P.Renoir	50	425.00	425.00
93-01-017	Jeunes Filles Au Piano-1892 34 Colors, framed	P.A.Renoir/P.Renoir	950	635.00	635.00
93-01-018	Jeunes Filles Au Piano-1892 34 Colors, unframed	P.A.Renoir/P.Renoir	950	465.00	465.00
93-01-019	Jeunes Filles Au Piano-1892 34 Colors, framed-AP	P.A.Renoir/P.Renoir	50	635.00	635.00
93-01-020	Jeunes Filles Au Piano-1892 34 Colors, unframed-AP	P.A.Renoir/P.Renoir	50	465.00	465.00
93-01-021	Bouquet De Tulipes-1905 24 Colors, framed	P.A.Renoir/P.Renoir	950	595.00	595.00
93-01-022	Bouquet De Tulipes-1905 24 Colors, unframed	P.A.Renoir/P.Renoir	950	395.00	395.00
93-01-023	Bouquet De Tulipes-1905 24 Colors, framed-AP	P.A.Renoir/P.Renoir	50	595.00	595.00
93-01-024	Bouquet De Tulipes-1905 24 Colors, unframed-AP	P.A.Renoir/P.Renoir	50	395.00	395.00
V.F. Fine Arts		**Kuck**			
86-01-001	Tender Moments, proof	S. Kuck	50	80.00	295.00
86-01-002	Tender Moments, S/N	S. Kuck	500	70.00	250.00
86-01-003	Summer Reflections, proof	S. Kuck	90	70.00	300.00
86-01-004	Summer Reflections, S/N	S. Kuck	900	60.00	250.00
86-01-005	Silhouette, proof	S. Kuck	25	90.00	250.00
86-01-006	Silhouette, S/N	S. Kuck	250	80.00	220.00
87-01-007	Le Papillion, remarque	S. Kuck	7	150.00	250.00
87-01-008	Le Papillion, proof	S. Kuck	35	110.00	175.00
87-01-009	Le Papillion, S/N	S. Kuck	350	90.00	150.00
87-01-010	The Reading Lesson, proof	S. Kuck	90	70.00	190-250.
87-01-011	The Reading Lesson, S/N	S. Kuck	900	60.00	200.00
87-01-012	The Daisy, proof	S. Kuck	90	40.00	100.00
87-01-013	The Daisy, S/N	S. Kuck	900	30.00	75.00
87-01-014	The Loveseat, proof	S. Kuck	90	40.00	50-75.00
87-01-015	The Loveseat, S/N	S. Kuck	900	30.00	50.00
87-01-016	A Quiet Time, proof	S. Kuck	90	50.00	75.00
87-01-017	A Quiet Time, S/N	S. Kuck	900	40.00	50.00
87-01-018	The Flower Girl, proof	S. Kuck	90	50.00	75.00
87-01-019	The Flower Girl, S/N	S. Kuck	900	40.00	50-60.00
87-01-020	Mother's Love, proof	S. Kuck	12	225.00	1800.00
87-01-021	Mother's Love, S/N	S. Kuck	150	195.00	1200.00
88-01-022	My Dearest, S/N	S. Kuck	350	160.00	775.00
88-01-023	My Dearest, proof	S. Kuck	50	200.00	900.00
88-01-024	My Dearest, remarque	S. Kuck	25	325.00	1100.00
88-01-025	The Kitten, S/N	S. Kuck	350	120.00	1200.00
88-01-026	The Kitten, proof	S. Kuck	50	150.00	1300.00
88-01-027	The Kitten, remarque	S. Kuck	25	250.00	950-1450.
88-01-028	Wild Flowers, S/N	S. Kuck	350	160.00	250.00
88-01-029	Wild Flowers, proof	S. Kuck	50	175.00	300.00
88-01-030	Wild Flowers, remarque	S. Kuck	25	250.00	350.00
88-01-031	Little Ballerina, S/N	S. Kuck	150	110.00	300.00
88-01-032	Little Ballerina, proof	S. Kuck	25	150.00	350.00
88-01-033	Little Ballerina, remarque	S. Kuck	25	225.00	450.00
88-01-034	First Recital, S/N	S. Kuck	150	200.00	900.00
88-01-035	First Recital, proof	S. Kuck	25	250.00	1000.00
88-01-036	First Recital, remarque	S. Kuck	25	400.00	1200.00
89-01-037	Sisters, S/N	S. Kuck	900	95.00	190.00
89-01-038	Sisters, proof	S. Kuck	90	150.00	395.00
89-01-039	Sisters, remarque	S. Kuck	50	200.00	375.00
89-01-040	Rose Garden, S/N	S. Kuck	500	95.00	400.00
89-01-041	Rose Garden, proof	S. Kuck	50	150.00	450.00
89-01-042	Rose Garden, remarque	S. Kuck	50	200.00	600.00
89-01-043	Sonatina, S/N	S. Kuck	900	150.00	350.00
89-01-044	Sonatina, proof	S. Kuck	90	225.00	450.00
89-01-045	Sonatina, remarque	S. Kuck	50	300.00	600.00
89-01-046	Puppy, S/N	S. Kuck	500	120.00	600.00
89-01-047	Puppy, proof	S. Kuck	50	180.00	650.00
89-01-048	Puppy, remarque	S. Kuck	50	240.00	750-950.
89-01-049	Innocence, S/N	S. Kuck	900	150.00	200.00
89-01-050	Innocence, proof	S. Kuck	90	225.00	250.00
89-01-051	Innocence, remarque	S. Kuck	50	300.00	350.00
89-01-052	Bundle of Joy, S/N	S. Kuck	1,000	125.00	250.00
89-01-053	Day Dreaming, S/N	S. Kuck	900	150.00	200.00
89-01-054	Day Dreaming, proof	S. Kuck	90	225.00	225.00
89-01-055	Day Dreaming, remarque	S. Kuck	50	300.00	300.00
90-01-056	Lilly Pond, S/N	S. Kuck	750	150.00	150.00
90-01-057	Lilly Pond, proof	S. Kuck	75	200.00	200.00
90-01-058	Lilly Pond, color remarque	S. Kuck	125	500.00	500.00
90-01-059	First Snow, S/N	S. Kuck	500	95.00	225.00
90-01-060	First Snow, proof	S. Kuck	50	150.00	275.00
90-01-061	First Snow, remarque	S. Kuck	25	200.00	325.00
90-01-062	Le Beau, S/N	S. Kuck	1,500	80.00	160.00
90-01-063	Le Beau, proof	S. Kuck	150	120.00	200.00
90-01-064	Le Beau, remarque	S. Kuck	25	160.00	250.00
90-01-065	Chopsticks, S/N	S. Kuck	1,500	80.00	80.00
90-01-066	Chopsticks, proof	S. Kuck	150	120.00	120.00
90-01-067	Chopsticks, remarque	S. Kuck	25	160.00	160.00
91-01-068	Memories, S/N	S. Kuck	5,000	195.00	195.00
91-01-069	God's Gift, proof	S. Kuck	150	150.00	150.00
91-01-070	God's Gift, S/N	S. Kuck	1,500	95.00	95.00
92-01-071	Joyous Day S/N	S. Kuck	1,200	125.00	125.00
92-01-072	Joyous Day, proof	S. Kuck	120	175.00	175.00
92-01-073	Joyous Day Canvas Transfer	S. Kuck	250	250.00	250.00
92-01-074	Yesterday, S/N	S. Kuck	950	95.00	95.00
92-01-075	Yesterday, proof	S. Kuck	95	150.00	150.00
92-01-076	Yesterday, Canvas Framed	S. Kuck	550	195.00	195.00
92-01-077	Duet, S/N	S. Kuck	950	125.00	125.00
92-01-078	Duet, proof	S. Kuck	95	175.00	175.00
92-01-079	Duet,Canvas Framed	S. Kuck	500	255.00	255.00
World Art Editions		**Masseria**			
80-01-001	Eduardo	F. Masseria	300	275.00	2700.00
80-01-002	Rosanna	F. Masseria	300	275.00	3200.00
80-01-003	Nina	F. Masseria	300	325.00	1950.00
80-01-004	First Kiss	F. Masseria	300	375.00	2200.00
81-01-005	Selene	F. Masseria	300	325.00	2200.00
81-01-006	First Flower	F. Masseria	300	325.00	2200.00
81-01-007	Elisa with Flower	F. Masseria	300	325.00	2200.00
81-01-008	Solange	F. Masseria	300	325.00	2200.00
81-01-009	Susan Sewing	F. Masseria	300	375.00	2500.00
81-01-010	Jessica	F. Masseria	300	375.00	2300.00
81-01-011	Eleanor	F. Masseria	300	375.00	1900.00
81-01-012	Julie	F. Masseria	300	375.00	950.00
82-01-013	Robin	F. Masseria	300	425.00	975.00
82-01-014	Jodie	F. Masseria	300	425.00	950.00
82-01-015	Jill	F. Masseria	300	425.00	750.00
82-01-016	Jamie	F. Masseria	300	425.00	750.00
82-01-017	Yasmin	F. Masseria	300	425.00	720.00
82-01-018	Yvette	F. Masseria	300	425.00	620.00
82-01-019	Judith	F. Masseria	300	425.00	750.00
82-01-020	Amy	F. Masseria	300	425.00	720.00
83-01-021	Tara	F. Masseria	300	450.00	1100.00
83-01-022	Antonio	F. Masseria	300	450.00	1100.00
84-01-023	Memoirs	F. Masseria	300	450.00	700.00
84-01-024	Christopher	F. Masseria	300	450.00	700.00
84-01-025	Bettina	F. Masseria	250	550.00	700.00
84-01-026	Vincente	F. Masseria	360	550.00	1000.00

Company		Series			
Number	Name	Artist	Edition Limit	Issue Price	Quote
85-01-027	Christina	F. Masseria	300	500.00	700.00
85-01-028	Jorgito	F. Masseria	300	500.00	700.00
84-01-029	Regina	F. Masseria	950	395.00	495.00
84-01-030	Peter	F. Masseria	950	395.00	495.00
85-01-031	Marquerita	F. Masseria	950	495.00	495.00
85-01-032	To Catch a Butterfly	F. Masseria	950	495.00	495.00
PLATES					
American Artists		**The Horses of Fred Stone**			
82-01-001	Patience	F. Stone	9,500	55.00	145.00
82-01-002	Arabian Mare and Foal	F. Stone	9,500	55.00	125.00
82-01-003	Safe and Sound	F. Stone	9,500	55.00	80-120.00
83-01-004	Contentment	F. Stone	9,500	55.00	70-120.00
American Artists		**The Stallion Series**			
83-02-001	Black Stallion	F. Stone	12,500	49.50	100.00
83-02-002	Andalusian	F. Stone	12,500	49.50	80.00
American Artists		**Sport of Kings Series**			
84-03-001	Man O'War	F. Stone	9,500	65.00	150-200.
84-03-002	Secretariat	F. Stone	9,500	65.00	295.00
85-03-003	John Henry	F. Stone	9,500	65.00	100.00
86-03-004	Seattle Slew	F. Stone	9,500	65.00	65.00
American Artists		**Mare and Foal Series**			
86-04-001	Water Trough	F. Stone	12,500	49.50	125.00
86-04-002	Tranquility	F. Stone	12,500	49.50	65.00
86-04-003	Pasture Pest	F. Stone	12,500	49.50	100.00
87-04-004	The Arabians	F. Stone	12,500	49.50	49.50
American Artists		**Famous Fillies**			
87-05-001	Lady's Secret	F. Stone	9,500	65.00	85.00
88-05-002	Ruffian	F. Stone	9,500	65.00	85.00
88-05-003	Genuine Risk	F. Stone	9,500	65.00	85.00
92-05-004	Go For The Wand	F. Stone	9,500	65.00	85.00
American Artists		**Fred Stone Classic Series**			
86-06-001	The Shoe-8,000 Wins	F. Stone	9,500	75.00	95.00
86-06-002	The Eternal Legacy	F. Stone	9,500	75.00	95.00
88-06-003	Forever Friends	F. Stone	9,500	75.00	85.00
89-06-004	Alysheba	F. Stone	9,500	75.00	85.00
American Artists		**Family Treasures**			
81-07-001	Cora's Recital	R. Zolan	18,500	39.50	39.50
82-07-002	Cora's Tea Party	R. Zolan	18,500	39.50	39.50
83-07-003	Cora's Garden Party	R. Zolan	18,500	39.50	39.50
American Rose Society		**All-American Rose**			
75-01-001	Oregold	Unknown	9,800	39.00	142.00
75-01-002	Arizona	Unknown	9,800	39.00	142.00
75-01-003	Rose Parade	Unknown	9,800	39.00	137.00
76-01-004	Yankee Doodle	Unknown	9,800	39.00	135.50
76-01-005	America	Unknown	9,800	39.00	135.50
76-01-006	Cathedral	Unknown	9,800	39.00	135.50
76-01-007	Seashell	Unknown	9,800	39.00	135.50
77-01-008	Double Delight	Unknown	9,800	39.00	115.00
77-01-009	Prominent	Unknown	9,800	39.00	115.00
77-01-010	First Edition	Unknown	9,800	39.00	115.00
78-01-011	Color Magic	Unknown	9,800	39.00	107.00
78-01-012	Charisma	Unknown	9,800	39.00	58-89.00
79-01-013	Paradise	Unknown	9,800	39.00	39-58.00
79-01-014	Sundowner	Unknown	9,800	39.00	67-75.00
79-01-015	Friendship	Unknown	9,800	39.00	74-79.00
80-01-016	Love	Unknown	9,800	49.00	80.00
80-01-017	Honor	Unknown	9,800	49.00	55-77.00
80-01-018	Cherish	Unknown	9,800	49.00	80.00
81-01-019	Bing Crosby	Unknown	9,800	49.00	49.00
81-01-020	White Lightnin'	Unknown	9,800	49.00	69.00
81-01-021	Marina	Unknown	9,800	49.00	61-69.00
82-01-022	Shreveport	Unknown	9,800	49.00	50-54.00
82-01-023	French Lace	Unknown	9,800	49.00	54.00
82-01-024	Brandy	Unknown	9,800	49.00	69.00
82-01-025	Mon Cheri	Unknown	9,800	49.00	49.00
83-01-026	Sun Flare	Unknown	9,800	49.00	69.00
83-01-027	Sweet Surrender	Unknown	9,800	49.00	55.00
84-01-028	Impatient	Unknown	9,800	49.00	55.00
84-01-029	Olympiad	Unknown	9,800	49.00	55.00
84-01-030	Intrigue	Unknown	9,800	49.00	58.00
85-01-031	Showbiz	Unknown	9,800	49.50	49.50
85-01-032	Peace	Unknown	9,800	49.50	49.50
85-01-033	Queen Elizabeth	Unknown	9,800	49.50	49.50
Anheuser-Busch, Inc.		**Holiday Plate Series**			
89-01-001	Winters Day N2295	B. Kemper	Retrd.	30.00	50-150.00
90-01-002	An American Tradition N2767	S. Sampson	Retrd.	30.00	30-35.00
91-01-003	The Season's Best N3034	S. Sampson	25-day	30.00	30.00
92-01-004	A Perfect Christmas N3440	S. Sampson	25-day	27.50	27.50
93-01-005	Special Delivery N4002	N. Koerber	25-day	N/A	N/A
Anheuser-Busch, Inc.		**Man's Best Friend Series**			
90-02-001	Buddies N2615	M. Urdahl	Retrd.	30.00	30-45.00
90-02-002	Six Pack N3005	M. Urdahl	Retrd.	30.00	30.00
92-02-003	Something's Brewing N3147	M. Urdahl	25-day	30.00	30.00
93-02-004	Outstanding in Their Field N4003	M. Urdahl	25-day	30.00	30.00
Anheuser-Busch, Inc.		**1992 Olympic Team Series**			
91-03-001	1992 Olympic Team Winter Plate N3180	A-Busch, Inc.	25-day	35.00	35.00
92-03-002	1992 Olympic Team Summer Plate N3122	A-Busch, Inc.	25-day	35.00	35.00
Anheuser-Busch, Inc.		**Civil War Series**			
92-04-001	General Grant N3478	D. Langeneckert	25-day	45.00	45.00
93-04-002	General Robert E. Lee N3590	D. Langeneckert	25-day	45.00	45.00
93-04-003	President Abraham Lincoln N3591	D. Langeneckert	25-day	45.00	45.00
Anheuser-Busch, Inc.		**Archives Plate Series**			
92-05-001	1893 Columbian Exposition N3477	D. Langeneckert	25-day	27.50	27.50
92-05-002	Ganymede	D. Langeneckert	25-day	N/A	N/A
Anna-Perenna Porcelain		**Uncle Tad's Cats**			
79-01-001	Oliver's Birthday	T. Krumeich	5,000	75.00	220.00
80-01-002	Peaches & Cream	T. Krumeich	5,000	75.00	80.00
81-01-003	Princess Aurora	T. Krumeich	5,000	80.00	85.00

Company		Series			
Number	Name	Artist	Edition Limit	Issue Price	Quote
81-01-004	Walter's Window	T. Krumeich	5,000	80.00	95.00
Anna-Perenna Porcelain		**Annual Christmas Plate**			
84-02-001	Noel, Noel	P. Buckley Moss	5,000	67.50	325.00
85-02-002	Helping Hands	P. Buckley Moss	5,000	67.50	225.00
86-02-003	Night Before Christmas	P. Buckley Moss	5,000	67.50	150.00
87-02-004	Christmas Sleigh	P. Buckley Moss	5,000	75.00	95.00
88-02-005	Christmas Joy	P. Buckley Moss	7,500	75.00	75.00
89-02-006	Christmas Carol	P. Buckley Moss	7,500	80.00	95.00
90-02-007	Christmas Eve	P. Buckley Moss	7,500	80.00	80.00
91-02-008	The Snowman	P. Buckley Moss	7,500	80.00	80.00
92-02-009	Christmas Warmth	P. Buckley Moss	7,500	85.00	85.00
Anna-Perenna Porcelain		**American Silhouettes-Childrens Series**			
81-03-001	Fiddlers Two	P. Buckley Moss	5,000	75.00	95.00
83-03-002	Mary With The Lambs	P. Buckley Moss	5,000	75.00	85.00
84-03-003	Ring-Around-the-Rosie	P. Buckley Moss	5,000	75.00	200.00
84-03-004	Waiting For Tom	P. Buckley Moss	5,000	75.00	175.00
Anna-Perenna Porcelain		**The Celebration Series**			
86-04-001	Wedding Joy	P. Buckley Moss	5,000	100.00	200-350.
87-04-002	The Christening	P. Buckley Moss	5,000	100.00	175.00
88-04-003	The Anniversary	P. Buckley Moss	5,000	100.00	120-190.
89-04-004	Family Reunion	P. Buckley Moss	5,000	100.00	150.00
Anna-Perenna Porcelain		**American Silhouettes Family Series**			
81-05-001	Family Outing	P. Buckley Moss	5,000	75.00	95.00
82-05-002	John and Mary	P. Buckley Moss	5,000	75.00	95.00
82-05-003	Homemakers Quilting	P. Buckley Moss	5,000	75.00	85-195.00
84-05-004	Leisure Time	P. Buckley Moss	5,000	75.00	85.00
Anna-Perenna Porcelain		**American Silhouettes Valley Series**			
81-06-001	Frosty Frolic	P. Buckley Moss	5,000	75.00	85-95.00
82-06-002	Hay Ride	P. Buckley Moss	5,000	75.00	85.00
83-06-003	Sunday Ride	P. Buckley Moss	5,000	75.00	85-100.00
84-06-004	Market Day	P. Buckley Moss	5,000	75.00	120.00
ANRI		**Ferrandiz Christmas**			
72-01-001	Christ In The Manger	J. Ferrandiz	Closed	35.00	230.00
73-01-002	Christmas	J. Ferrandiz	Unkn.	40.00	225.00
74-01-003	Holy Night	J. Ferrandiz	Unkn.	50.00	100.00
75-01-004	Flight into Egypt	J. Ferrandiz	Unkn.	60.00	95.00
76-01-005	Tree of Life	J. Ferrandiz	Unkn.	60.00	85.00
76-01-006	Girl with Flowers	J. Ferrandiz	Closed	65.00	185.00
78-01-007	Leading the Way	J. Ferrandiz	Closed	77.50	180.00
79-01-008	The Drummer	J. Ferrandiz	Closed	120.00	175.00
80-01-009	Rejoice	J. Ferrandiz	Closed	150.00	160.00
81-01-010	Spreading the Word	J. Ferrandiz	Closed	150.00	150.00
82-01-011	The Shepherd Family	J. Ferrandiz	Closed	150.00	150.00
83-01-012	Peace Attend Thee	J. Ferrandiz	Closed	150.00	150.00
ANRI		**Ferrandiz Mother's Day Series**			
72-02-001	Mother Sewing	J. Ferrandiz	Closed	35.00	200.00
73-02-002	Alpine Mother & Child	J. Ferrandiz	Closed	40.00	150.00
74-02-003	Mother Holding Child	J. Ferrandiz	Closed	50.00	150.00
75-02-004	Dove Girl	J. Ferrandiz	Closed	60.00	150.00
76-02-005	Mother Knitting	J. Ferrandiz	Closed	60.00	200.00
77-02-006	Alpine Stroll	J. Ferrandiz	Closed	65.00	125.00
78-02-007	The Beginning	J. Ferrandiz	Closed	75.00	150.00
79-02-008	All Hearts	J. Ferrandiz	Closed	120.00	170.00
80-02-009	Spring Arrivals	J. Ferrandiz	Closed	150.00	165.00
81-02-010	Harmony	J. Ferrandiz	Closed	150.00	150.00
82-02-011	With Love	J. Ferrandiz	Closed	150.00	150.00
ANRI		**Ferrandiz Wooden Wedding Plates**			
72-03-001	Boy and Girl Embracing	J. Ferrandiz	Unkn.	40.00	150.00
73-03-002	Wedding Scene	J. Ferrandiz	Unkn.	40.00	150.00
74-03-003	Wedding	J. Ferrandiz	Unkn.	48.00	150.00
75-03-004	Wedding	J. Ferrandiz	Unkn.	60.00	150.00
76-03-005	Wedding	J. Ferrandiz	Unkn.	60.00	90-150.00
ANRI		**Christmas**			
71-04-001	St. Jakob in Groden	J. Malfertheiner	10,000	37.50	65.00
72-04-002	Pipers at Alberobello	J. Malfertheiner	10,000	45.00	75.00
73-04-003	Alpine Horn	J. Malfertheiner	10,000	45.00	390.00
74-04-004	Young Man and Girl	J. Malfertheiner	10,000	50.00	95.00
75-04-005	Christmas in Ireland	J. Malfertheiner	10,000	60.00	60.00
76-04-006	Alpine Christmas	J. Malfertheiner	6,000	65.00	190.00
77-04-007	Legend of Heligenblut	J. Malfertheiner	6,000	65.00	91.00
78-04-008	Klockler Singers	J. Malfertheiner	6,000	80.00	80.00
79-04-009	Moss Gatherers	Unknown	6,000	135.00	177.00
80-04-010	Wintry Churchgoing	Unknown	6,000	165.00	165.00
81-04-011	Santa Claus in Tyrol	Unknown	6,000	165.00	200.00
82-04-012	The Star Singers	Unknown	6,000	165.00	165.00
83-04-013	Unto Us a Child is Born	Unknown	6,000	165.00	310.00
84-04-014	Yuletide in the Valley	Unknown	6,000	165.00	170.00
85-04-015	Good Morning, Good Cheer	J. Malfertheiner	6,000	165.00	165.00
86-04-016	A Groden Christmas	J. Malfertheiner	6,000	165.00	200.00
87-04-017	Down From the Alps	J. Malfertheiner	6,000	195.00	250.00
88-04-018	Christkindl Markt	J. Malfertheiner	6,000	220.00	230.00
88-04-019	Flight Into Egypt	J. Malfertheiner	6,000	275.00	275.00
90-04-020	Holy Night	J. Malfertheiner	6,000	300.00	300.00
ANRI		**ANRI Mother's Day**			
72-05-001	Alpine Mother & Children	Unknown.	5,000	35.00	50.00
73-05-002	Alpine Mother & Children	Unknown	5,000	40.00	50.00
74-05-003	Alpine Mother & Children	Unknown	5,000	50.00	55.00
75-05-004	Alpine Stroll	Unknown	5,000	60.00	65.00
76-05-005	Knitting	Unknown	5,000	60.00	65.00
ANRI		**ANRI Father's Day**			
72-06-001	Alpine Father & Children	Unknown	5,000	35.00	100.00
73-06-002	Alpine Father & Children	Unknown	5,000	40.00	95.00
74-06-003	Cliff Gazing	Unknown	5,000	50.00	100.00
76-06-004	Sailing	Unknown	5,000	60.00	90.00
ANRI		**Disney Four Star Collection**			
89-07-001	Mickey Mini Plate	Disney Studios	5,000	40.00	45.00
90-07-002	Minnie Mini Plate	Disney Studios	5,000	40.00	45.00
91-07-003	Donald Mini Plate	Disney Studios	5,000	50.00	50.00
Arabia Annual		**Kalevala**			
76-01-001	Vainamoinen's Sowing	R. Uosikkinen	Unkn.	30.00	230.00

Company / Number	Name	Series / Artist	Edition Limit	Issue Price	Quote
77-01-002	Aino's Fate	R. Uosikkinen	Unkn.	30.00	30.00
78-01-003	Lemminkainen's Chase	R. Uosikkinen	2,500	39.00	39.00
79-01-004	Kullervo's Revenge	R. Uosikkinen	Annual	39.50	39.50
80-01-005	Vainomoinen's Rescue	R. Uosikkinen	Annual	45.00	52.00
81-01-006	Vainomoinen's Magic	R. Uosikkinen	Annual	49.50	49.50
82-01-007	Joukahainen Shoots the Horse	R. Uosikkinen	Annual	55.50	56.00
83-01-008	Lemminkainen's Escape	R. Uosikkinen	Annual	60.00	76.00
84-01-009	Lemminkainen's Magic Feathers	R. Uosikkinen	Annual	49.50	87.00
85-01-010	Lemminkainen's Grief	R. Uosikkinen	Annual	60.00	76.00
86-01-011	Osmatar Creating Ale	R. Uosikkinen	Annual	60.00	85.00
87-01-012	Valnamoinen Tricks Ilmarinen	R. Uosikkinen	Annual	65.00	90.00
88-01-013	Hears Vainamolnen Weep	R. Uosikkinen	Annual	69.00	115.00
89-01-014	Four Maidens	R. Uosikkinen	Annual	75.00	87.00
90-01-015	Annikka	R. Uosikkinen	Annual	85.00	105.00
91-01-013	Lemminkain's Mother Says Don't/ War	R. Uosikkinen	Annual	85.00	89.00
Armstrong's		**Infinite Love**			
87-01-001	A Pair of Dreams	S. Etem	14-day	24.50	24.50
87-01-002	The Eyes Say "I Love You"	S. Etem	14-day	24.50	24.50
87-01-003	Once Upon a Smile	S. Etem	14-day	24.50	24.50
87-01-004	Kiss a Little Giggle	S. Etem	14-day	24.50	24.50
88-01-005	Love Goes Forth in Little Feet	S. Etem	14-day	24.50	24.50
88-01-006	Bundle of Joy	S. Etem	14-day	24.50	24.50
88-01-007	Grins For Grandma	S. Etem	14-day	24.50	24.50
89-01-008	A Moment to Cherish	S. Etem	14-day	24.50	24.50
Armstrong's		**Statue of Liberty**			
86-02-001	Dedication	A. D'Estrehan	10,000	39.50	49.50
86-02-002	The Immigrants	A. D'Estrehan	10,000	39.50	49.50
86-02-003	Independence	A. D'Estrehan	10,000	39.50	49.50
86-02-004	Re-Dedication	A. D'Estrehan	10,000	39.50	49.50
Armstrong's		**Commemorative Issues**			
83-03-001	70 Years Young (10 1/2")	R. Skelton	15,000	85.00	125.00
84-03-002	Freddie the Torchbearer (8 1/2")	R. Skelton	15,000	62.50	85.00
Armstrong's		**The Signature Collection**			
86-04-001	Anyone for Tennis?	R. Skelton	9,000	62.50	62.50
86-04-002	Anyone for Tennis? (signed)	R. Skelton	1,000	125.00	650.00
87-04-003	Ironing the Waves	R. Skelton	9,000	62.50	75.00
87-04-004	Ironing the Waves (signed)	R. Skelton	1,000	125.00	175.00
88-04-005	The Cliffhanger	R. Skelton	9,000	62.50	65.00
88-04-006	The Cliffhanger (signed)	R. Skelton	1,000	150.00	150.00
Armstrong's		**Happy Art Series**			
81-05-001	Woody's Triple Self-Portriat, Signed	W. Lantz	1,000	100.00	100.00
81-05-002	Woody's Triple Self-Portrait	W. Lantz	9,000	39.50	39.50
83-05-003	Gothic Woody, Signed	W. Lantz	1,000	100.00	100.00
83-05-004	Gothic Woody	W. Lantz	9,000	39.50	39.50
84-05-005	Blue Boy Woody, Signed	W. Lantz	1,000	100.00	100.00
84-05-006	Blue Boy Woody	W. Lantz	9,000	39.50	39.50
Armstrong's		**The Constitution Series**			
87-06-001	U.S. Constitution vs. Guerriere	A. D'Estrehan	10,000	39.50	39.50
87-06-002	U.S. Constitution vs. Tripoli	A. D'Estrehan	10,000	39.50	50.00
87-06-003	U.S. Constitution vs. Java	A. D'Estrehan	10,000	39.50	39.50
87-06-004	The Great Chase	A. D'Estrehan	10,000	39.50	39.50
Armstrong's		**The Mischief Makers**			
86-07-001	Puddles	S. Etem	10,000	39.95	39.95
86-07-002	Buckles	S. Etem	10,000	39.95	39.95
87-07-003	Trix	S. Etem	10,000	39.95	39.95
88-07-004	Naps	S. Etem	10,000	39.95	45.00
Armstrong's		**Faces of the World**			
88-08-001	Erin (Ireland)	L. De Winne	14-day	24.50	24.50
88-08-002	Clara (Belgium)	L. De Winne	14-day	24.50	24.50
88-08-003	Luisa (Spain)	L. De Winne	14-day	24.50	24.50
88-08-004	Tamiko (Japan)	L. De Winne	14-day	24.50	24.50
88-08-005	Colette (France)	L. De Winne	14-day	24.50	24.50
88-08-006	Heather (England)	L. De Winne	14-day	24.50	24.50
88-08-007	Greta (Austria)	L. De Winne	14-day	24.50	24.50
88-08-008	Maria (Italy)	L. De Winne	14-day	24.50	24.50
Armstrong's/Crown Parlan		**Freddie The Freeloader**			
79-01-001	Freddie in the Bathtub	R. Skelton	10,000	60.00	200-240.
80-01-002	Freddie's Shack	R. Skelton	10,000	60.00	95-125.00
81-01-003	Freddie on the Green	R. Skelton	10,000	60.00	69.00
82-01-004	Love that Freddie	R. Skelton	10,000	60.00	70.00
Armstrong's/Crown Parlan		**Freddie's Adventures**			
82-02-001	Captain Freddie	R. Skelton	15,000	60.00	65-95.00
82-02-002	Bronco Freddie	R. Skelton	15,000	60.00	65-75.00
83-02-003	Sir Freddie	R. Skelton	15,000	62.50	65-79.00
84-02-004	Gertrude and Heathcliffe	R. Skelton	15,000	62.50	70.00
Artaffects		**Portraits of American Brides**			
86-01-001	Caroline	R. Sauber	10-day	29.50	75-85.00
86-01-002	Jacqueline	R. Sauber	10-day	29.50	30-45.00
87-01-003	Elizabeth	R. Sauber	10-day	29.50	37-45.00
87-01-004	Emily	R. Sauber	10-day	29.50	45.00
87-01-005	Meredith	R. Sauber	10-day	29.50	45-55.00
87-01-006	Laura	R. Sauber	10-day	29.50	45.00
87-01-007	Sarah	R. Sauber	10-day	29.50	46.00
87-01-008	Rebecca	R. Sauber	10-day	29.50	64.00
Artaffects		**How Do I Love Thee?**			
82-02-001	Alaina	R. Sauber	19,500	39.95	60.00
82-02-002	Taylor	R. Sauber	19,500	39.95	60.00
83-02-003	Rendezvouse	R. Sauber	19,500	39.95	60.00
83-02-004	Embrace	R. Sauber	19,500	39.95	60.00
Artaffects		**Childhood Delights**			
83-03-001	Amanda	R. Sauber	7,500	45.00	75.00
Artaffects		**Songs of Stephen Foster**			
84-04-001	Oh! Susannah	R. Sauber	3,500	60.00	80.00
84-04-002	Jeanie with the Light Brown Hair	R. Sauber	3,500	60.00	80.00
84-04-003	Beautiful Dreamer	R. Sauber	3,500	60.00	80.00
Artaffects		**Times of Our Lives Collection**			
84-05-001	Happy Birthday-(10 1/4")	R. Sauber	Open	37.50	39.50
88-05-002	Happy Birthday-(6 1/2")	R. Sauber	Open	19.50	22.50
85-05-003	Home Sweet Home-(10 1/4")	R. Sauber	Open	37.50	39.50
88-05-004	Home Sweet Home-(6 1/2")	R. Sauber	Open	19.50	22.50
82-05-005	The Wedding-(10 1/4")	R. Sauber	Open	37.50	39.50
88-05-006	The Wedding-(6 1/2")	R. Sauber	Open	19.50	22.50
86-05-007	The Anniversary-(10 1/4")	R. Sauber	Open	37.50	39.50
88-05-008	The Anniversary-(6 1/2")	R. Sauber	Open	19.50	22.50
86-05-009	Sweethearts-(10 1/4")	R. Sauber	Open	37.50	49.00
88-05-010	Sweethearts-(6 1/2")	R. Sauber	Open	19.50	22.50
86-05-011	The Christening-(10 1/4")	R. Sauber	Open	37.50	39.50
88-05-012	The Christening-(6 1/2")	R. Sauber	Open	19.50	22.50
85-05-013	All Adore Him-(10 1/4")	R. Sauber	Open	37.50	39.50
88-05-014	All Adore Him-(6 1/2")	R. Sauber	Open	19.50	22.50
87-05-015	Motherhood-(10 1/4")	R. Sauber	Open	37.50	39.50
88-05-016	Motherhood-(6 1/2")	R. Sauber	Open	19.50	22.50
87-05-017	Fatherhood-(10 1/4")	R. Sauber	Open	37.50	39.50
88-05-018	Fatherhood-(6 1/2")	R. Sauber	Open	19.50	22.50
87-05-019	Sweet Sixteen-(10 1/4")	R. Sauber	Open	37.50	39.50
89-05-020	God Bless America-(10 1/4")	R. Sauber	14-day	39.50	39.50
89-05-021	God Bless America-(6 1/4")	R. Sauber	14-day	21.50	22.50
89-05-022	Visiting the Doctor-(10 1/4")	R. Sauber	14-day	39.50	39.50
90-05-023	Mother's Joy-(6 1/2")	R. Sauber	Open	22.50	22.50
90-05-024	Mother's Joy-(10 1/4")	R. Sauber	Open	39.50	39.50
Artaffects		**Timeless Love**			
89-06-001	The Proposal	R. Sauber	14-day	35.00	38.00
89-06-002	Sweet Embrace	R. Sauber	14-day	35.00	35.00
90-06-003	Afternoon Light	R. Sauber	14-day	35.00	35.00
90-06-004	Quiet Moments	R. Sauber	14-day	35.00	35.00
Artaffects		**Winter Mindscape**			
89-07-001	Peaceful Village	R. Sauber	14-day	29.50	65.00
89-07-002	Snowbound	R. Sauber	14-day	29.50	40.00
90-07-003	Papa's Surprise	R. Sauber	14-day	29.50	40.00
90-07-004	Well Traveled Road	R. Sauber	14-day	29.50	40.00
90-07-005	First Freeze	R. Sauber	14-day	29.50	40.00
90-07-006	Country Morning	R. Sauber	14-day	29.50	40.00
90-07-007	Sleigh Ride	R. Sauber	14-day	29.50	40.00
90-07-008	January Thaw	R. Sauber	14-day	29.50	40.00
Artaffects		**Baby's Firsts**			
89-08-001	Visiting the Doctor (6 1/2")	R. Sauber	14-day	21.50	22.50
89-08-002	Baby's First Step (6 1/2")	R. Sauber	14-day	21.50	22.50
89-08-003	First Birthday (6 1/2")	R. Sauber	14-day	21.50	22.50
89-08-004	Christmas Morn (6 1/2")	R. Sauber	14-day	21.50	22.50
89-08-005	Picture Perfect (6 1/2")	R. Sauber	14-day	21.50	22.50
Artaffects		**Masterpieces of Rockwell**			
80-09-001	After the Prom	N. Rockwell	17,500	42.50	150.00
80-09-002	The Challenger	N. Rockwell	17,500	50.00	75.00
82-09-003	Girl at the Mirror	N. Rockwell	17,500	50.00	100.00
82-09-004	Missing Tooth	N. Rockwell	17,500	50.00	75.00
Artaffects		**Rockwell Americana**			
81-10-001	Shuffleton's Barbershop	N. Rockwell	17,500	75.00	150.00
82-10-002	Breaking Home Ties	N. Rockwell	17,500	75.00	125.00
83-10-003	Walking to Church	N. Rockwell	17,500	75.00	125.00
Artaffects		**Rockwell Trilogy**			
81-11-001	Stockbridge in Winter 1	N. Rockwell	Open	35.00	50-65.00
82-11-002	Stockbridge in Winter 2	N. Rockwell	Open	35.00	50-65.00
82-11-003	Stockbridge in Winter 3	N. Rockwell	Open	35.00	50-75.00
Artaffects		**Simpler Times Series**			
84-12-001	Lazy Daze	N. Rockwell	7,500	35.00	75.00
84-12-002	One for the Road	N. Rockwell	7,500	35.00	75.00
Artaffects		**On the Road Series**			
84-13-001	Pride of Stockbridge	N. Rockwell	Open	35.00	75.00
84-13-002	City Pride	N. Rockwell	Open	35.00	75.00
84-13-003	Country Pride	N. Rockwell	Open	35.00	75.00
Artaffects		**Special Occasions**			
82-14-001	Bubbles	F. Tipton Hunter	Open	29.95	50.00
82-14-002	Butterflies	F. Tipton Hunter	Open	29.95	50.00
Artaffects		**Masterpieces of Impressionism**			
80-15-001	Woman with Parasol	Monet/Cassat	17,500	35.00	75.00
81-15-002	Young Mother Sewing	Monet/Cassat	17,500	35.00	60.00
82-15-003	Sara in Green Bonnet	Monet/Cassat	17,500	35.00	60.00
83-15-004	Margot in Blue	Monet/Cassat	17,500	35.00	50.00
Artaffects		**Magical Moment**			
81-16-001	Happy Dreams	B. P. Gutmann	Open	29.95	100.00
81-16-002	Harmony	B. P. Gutmann	Open	29.95	90.00
82-16-003	His Majesty	B. P. Gutmann	Open	29.95	60.00
83-16-003	The Lullaby	B. P. Gutmann	Open	29.95	50.00
82-16-004	Waiting for Daddy	B. P. Gutmann	Open	29.95	50.00
82-16-005	Thank You God	B. P .Gutmann	Open	29.95	50.00
Artaffects		**Mother's Love**			
84-17-001	Daddy's Here	B. P. Gutmann	Open	29.95	60.00
Artaffects		**Bessie's Best**			
84-18-001	Oh! Oh! A Bunny	B. P. Gutmann	Open	29.95	65.00
84-18-002	The New Love	B. P. Gutmann	Open	29.95	65.00
84-18-003	My Baby	B. P. Gutmann	Open	29.95	65.00
84-18-004	Looking for Trouble	B. P. Gutmann	Open	29.95	65.00
84-18-005	Taps	B. P. Gutmann	Open	29.95	65.00
Artaffects		**Masterpieces of the West**			
80-19-001	Texas Night Herder	Johnson	17,500	35.00	75.00
80-19-002	Indian Trapper	Remington	17,500	35.00	100.00
82-19-003	Cowboy Style	Leigh	17,500	35.00	75.00
82-19-004	Indian Style	Perillo	17,500	35.00	150.00
Artaffects		**Playful Pets**			
82-20-001	Curiosity	J. H. Dolph	7,500	45.00	75.00
82-20-002	Master's Hat	J. H. Dolph	7,500	45.00	75.00
Artaffects		**The Tribute Series**			
82-21-001	I Want You	J. M. Flagg	Open	29.95	50.00
82-21-002	Gee, I Wish	H. C. Christy	Open	29.95	50.00
83-21-003	Soldier's Farewell	N. Rockwell	Open	29.95	50.00

Company Number	Name / Series	Artist	Edition Limit	Issue Price	Quote
Artaffects	**The Carnival Series**				
82-22-001	Knock em' Down	T. Newsom	19,500	35.00	50.00
82-22-002	Carousel	T. Newsom	19,500	35.00	50.00
Artaffects	**The Adventures of Peter Pan**				
90-23-001	Flying Over London	T. Newsom	14-day	29.50	40.00
90-23-002	Look At Me	T. Newsom	14-day	29.50	40.00
90-23-003	The Encounter	T. Newsom	14-day	29.50	40.00
90-23-004	Never land	T. Newsom	14-day	29.50	40.00
Artaffects	**Nursery Pair**				
83-24-001	In Slumberland	C. Becker	Open	25.00	60.00
83-24-002	The Awakening	C. Becker	Open	25.00	60.00
Artaffects	**Becker Babies**				
83-25-001	Snow Puff	C. Becker	Open	29.95	60.00
84-25-002	Smiling Through	C. Becker	Open	29.95	60.00
84-25-003	Pals	C. Becker	Open	29.95	60.00
Artaffects	**Melodies of Childhood**				
83-26-001	Twinkle, Twinkle Little Star	H. Garrido	19,500	35.00	50.00
83-26-002	Row, Row, Row Your Boat	H. Garrido	19,500	35.00	50.00
83-26-003	Mary had a Little Lamb	H. Garrido	19,500	35.00	50.00
Artaffects	**Unicorn Magic**				
83-27-001	Morning Encounter	J. Terreson	7,500	50.00	60.00
83-27-002	Afternoon Offering	J. Terreson	7,500	50.00	60.00
Artaffects	**Baker Street**				
83-28-001	Sherlock Holmes	M. Hooks	9,800	55.00	55-95.00
83-28-002	Watson	M. Hooks	9,800	55.00	55-75.00
Artaffects	**Angler's Dream**				
83-29-001	Brook Trout	J. Eggert	9,800	55.00	75.00
83-29-002	Striped Bass	J. Eggert	9,800	55.00	75.00
83-29-003	Largemouth Bass	J. Eggert	9,800	55.00	75.00
83-29-004	Chinook Salmon	J. Eggert	9,800	55.00	75.00
Artaffects	**Portrait Series**				
86-30-001	Chantilly	J. Eggert	14-day	24.50	40.00
86-30-002	Dynasty	J. Eggert	14-day	24.50	40.00
86-30-003	Velvet	J. Eggert	14-day	24.50	40.00
86-30-004	Jambalaya	J. Eggert	14-day	24.50	40.00
Artaffects	**The Great Trains**				
85-31-001	Santa Fe	J. Deneen	7,500	35.00	100.00
85-31-002	Twentieth Century Ltd.	J. Deneen	7,500	35.00	100.00
86-31-003	Empire Builder	J. Deneen	7,500	35.00	100.00
Artaffects	**Classic American Trains**				
88-32-001	Homeward Bound	J. Deneen	14-day	35.00	53.00
88-32-002	A Race Against Time	J. Deneen	14-day	35.00	35.00
88-32-003	Midday Stop	J. Deneen	14-day	35.00	35.00
88-32-004	The Silver Bullet	J. Deneen	14-day	35.00	54.00
88-32-005	Traveling in Style	J. Deneen	14-day	35.00	50.00
88-32-006	Round the Bend	J. Deneen	14-day	35.00	35.00
88-32-007	Taking the High Road	J. Deneen	14-day	35.00	45.00
88-32-008	Competition	J. Deneen	14-day	35.00	40.00
Artaffects	**Classic American Cars**				
89-33-001	Duesenberg	J. Deneen	14-day	35.00	40.00
89-33-002	Cadillac	J. Deneen	14-day	35.00	35.00
89-33-003	Cord	J. Deneen	14-day	35.00	35.00
89-33-004	Ruxton	J. Deneen	14-day	35.00	35.00
90-33-005	Lincoln	J. Deneen	14-day	35.00	35.00
90-33-006	Packard	J. Deneen	14-day	35.00	35.00
90-33-007	Hudson	J. Deneen	14-day	35.00	35.00
90-33-008	Pierce-Arrow	J. Deneen	14-day	35.00	35.00
Artaffects	**Great American Trains**				
92-34-001	The Alton Limited	J. Deneen	75-day	27.00	27.00
92-34-002	The Capitol Limited	J. Deneen	75-day	27.00	27.00
92-34-003	The Merchants Limited	J. Deneen	75-day	27.00	27.00
92-34-004	The Broadway Limited	J. Deneen	75-day	27.00	27.00
92-34-005	The Southwestern Limited	J. Deneen	75-day	27.00	27.00
92-34-006	The Blackhawk Limited	J. Deneen	75-day	27.00	27.00
92-34-007	The Sunshine Special Limited	J. Deneen	75-day	27.00	27.00
92-34-008	The Panama Special Limited	J. Deneen	75-day	27.00	27.00
Artaffects	**Sailing Through History**				
86-35-001	Flying Cloud	K. Soldwedel	14-day	29.50	60.00
86-35-002	Santa Maria	K. Soldwedel	14-day	29.50	60.00
86-35-003	Mayflower	K. Soldwedel	14-day	29.50	60.00
Artaffects	**American Maritime Heritage**				
87-36-001	U.S.S. Constitution	K. Soldwedel	14 Day	35.00	35.00
Artaffects	**Christian Collection**				
87-37-001	Bring to Me the Children	A. Tobey	Unkn.	35.00	35.00
87-37-002	Wedding Feast at Cana	A. Tobey	Unkn.	35.00	35.00
87-37-003	The Healer	A. Tobey	Unkn.	35.00	35.00
Artaffects	**Reflections of Youth**				
88-38-001	Julia	Mago	14-day	29.50	45-55.00
88-38-002	Jessica	Mago	14-day	29.50	35.00
88-38-003	Sebastian	Mago	14-day	29.50	35.00
88-38-004	Michelle	Mago	14-day	29.50	55.00
88-38-005	Andrew	Mago	14-day	29.50	35.00
88-38-006	Beth	Mago	14-day	29.50	39.00
88-38-007	Amy	Mago	14-day	29.50	39.00
88-38-008	Lauren	Mago	14-day	29.50	39.00
Artaffects	**MaGo's Motherhood**				
90-39-001	Serenity	MaGo	14-day	50.00	50.00
Artaffects	**Studies of Early Childhood**				
90-40-001	Christopher & Kate	MaGo	150-day	34.90	36-59.00
90-40-002	Peek-A-Boo	MaGo	150-day	34.90	40-49.00
90-40-003	Anybody Home?	MaGo	150-day	34.90	35-49.00
90-40-004	Three-Part Harmony	MaGo	150-day	34.90	50-59.00
Artaffects	**Heavenly Angels**				
92-41-001	Hush-A-Bye	MaGo	75-day	27.00	27.00
92-41-002	Heavenly Helper	MaGo	75-day	27.00	27.00
92-41-003	Heavenly Light	MaGo	75-day	27.00	27.00
92-41-004	The Angel's Kiss	MaGo	75-day	27.00	27.00
92-41-005	Caught In The Act	MaGo	75-day	27.00	27.00
92-41-006	My Angel	MaGo	75-day	27.00	27.00
92-41-007	Angel Cake	MaGo	75-day	27.00	27.00
92-41-008	Sleepy Sentinel	MaGo	75-day	27.00	27.00
Artaffects	**Good Sports**				
89-42-001	Purrfect Game (6 1/2")	S. Miller-Maxwell	14-day	22.50	25.00
89-42-002	Alley Cats (6 1/2")	S. Miller-Maxwell	14-day	22.50	25.00
89-42-003	Tee Time (6 1/2")	S. Miller-Maxwell	14-day	22.50	25.00
89-42-004	Two/Love (6 1/2")	S. Miller-Maxwell	14-day	22.50	25.00
89-42-005	What's the Catch (6 1/2")	S. Miller-Maxwell	14-day	22.50	25.00
89-42-006	Quaterback Sneak (6 1/2")	S. Miller-Maxwell	14-day	22.50	25.00
Artaffects	**Romantic Cities of Europe**				
89-43-001	Venice	L. Marchetti	14-day	35.00	65.00
89-43-002	Paris	L. Marchetti	14-day	35.00	50.00
90-43-003	London	L. Marchetti	14-day	35.00	50.00
90-43-004	Moscow	L. Marchetti	14-day	35.00	35.00
Artaffects	**The Life of Jesus**				
92-44-001	The Last Supper	L. Marchetti	25-day	27.00	27.00
92-44-002	The Sermon on the Mount	L. Marchetti	25-day	27.00	27.00
92-44-003	The Agony in the Garden	L. Marchetti	25-day	27.00	27.00
92-44-004	The Entry Into Jerusalem	L. Marchetti	25-day	27.00	27.00
92-44-005	The Blessing of the Children	L. Marchetti	25-day	27.00	27.00
92-44-006	The Resurrection	L. Marchetti	25-day	27.00	27.00
92-44-007	The Healing of the Sick	L. Marchetti	25-day	27.00	27.00
92-44-008	The Descent from the Cross	L. Marchetti	25-day	27.00	27.00
Artaffects	**Backstage**				
90-45-001	The Runaway	B. Leighton-Jones	14-day	29.50	29.50
90-45-002	The Letter	B. Leighton-Jones	14-day	29.50	29.50
90-45-003	Bubbling Over	B. Leighton-Jones	14-day	29.50	29.50
Artaffects	**Chieftains I**				
79-46-001	Chief Sitting Bull	G. Perillo	7,500	65.00	399.00
79-46-002	Chief Joseph	G. Perillo	7,500	65.00	124-199.
80-46-003	Chief Red Cloud	G. Perillo	7,500	65.00	148-175.
80-46-004	Chief Geronimo	G. Perillo	7,500	65.00	100-199.
81-46-005	Chief Crazy Horse	G. Perillo	7,500	65.00	185-250.
Artaffects	**The Plainsmen**				
78-47-001	Buffalo Hunt (Bronze)	G. Perillo	2,500	350.00	500.00
79-47-002	The Proud One (Bronze)	G. Perillo	2,500	350.00	800.00
Artaffects	**The Professionals**				
79-48-001	The Big Leaguer	G. Perillo	15,000	29.95	33-55.00
80-48-002	Ballerina's Dilemma	G. Perillo	15,000	32.50	33-55.00
81-48-003	Quarterback	G. Perillo	15,000	32.50	40-55.00
81-48-004	Rodeo Joe	G. Perillo	15,000	35.00	40.00
82-48-005	Major Leaguer	G. Perillo	15,000	35.00	40-55.00
83-48-006	The Hockey Player	G. Perillo	15,000	35.00	40-55.00
Artaffects	**Pride of America's Indians**				
86-49-001	Brave and Free	G. Perillo	10-day	24.50	80-125.00
86-49-002	Dark-Eyed Friends	G. Perillo	10-day	24.50	40-85.00
86-49-003	Noble Companions	G. Perillo	10-day	24.50	30-65.00
87-49-004	Kindred Spirits	G. Perillo	10-day	24.50	45-75.00
87-49-005	Loyal Alliance	G. Perillo	10-day	24.50	80-100.00
87-49-006	Small and Wise	G. Perillo	10-day	24.50	35-50.00
87-49-007	Winter Scouts	G. Perillo	10-day	24.50	35-58.00
87-49-008	Peaceful Comrades	G. Perillo	10-day	24.50	40-75.00
Artaffects	**Legends of the West**				
82-50-001	Daniel Boone	G. Perillo	10,000	65.00	80.00
83-50-002	Davy Crockett	G. Perillo	10,000	65.00	80.00
83-50-003	Kit Carson	G. Perillo	10,000	65.00	80.00
83-50-004	Buffalo Bill	G. Perillo	10,000	65.00	80.00
Artaffects	**Chieftains II**				
83-51-001	Chief Pontiac	G. Perillo	7,500	70.00	85.00
83-51-002	Chief Victorio	G. Perillo	7,500	70.00	85.00
84-51-003	Chief Tecumseh	G. Perillo	7,500	70.00	85.00
84-51-004	Chief Cochise	G. Perillo	7,500	70.00	85.00
84-51-005	Chief Black Kettle	G. Perillo	7,500	70.00	110.00
Artaffects	**Child's Life**				
83-52-001	Siesta	G. Perillo	10,000	45.00	50.00
84-52-002	Sweet Dreams	G. Perillo	10,000	45.00	50.00
Artaffects	**Indian Nations**				
83-53-001	Blackfoot	G. Perillo	7,500	140.00	350-500.
83-53-002	Cheyenne	G. Perillo	7,500	Set	Set
83-53-003	Apache	G. Perillo	7,500	Set	Set
83-53-004	Sioux	G. Perillo	7,500	Set	Set
Artaffects	**The Storybook Collection**				
80-54-001	Little Red Ridinghood	G. Perillo	18-day	29.95	30-52.00
81-54-002	Cinderella	G. Perillo	18-day	29.95	30-60.00
81-54-003	Hansel & Gretel	G. Perillo	18-day	29.95	30-52.00
82-54-004	Goldilocks & 3 Bears	G. Perillo	18-day	29.95	30-60.00
Artaffects	**Perillo Santas**				
80-55-001	Santa's Joy	G. Perillo	Open	29.95	50.00
81-55-002	Santa's Bundle	G. Perillo	Open	29.95	48.00
Artaffects	**The Princesses**				
82-56-001	Lily of the Mohawks	G. Perillo	7,500	50.00	85.00
82-56-002	Pocahontas	G. Perillo	7,500	50.00	50-65.00
82-56-003	Minnehaha	G. Perillo	7,500	50.00	65.00
82-56-004	Sacajawea	G. Perillo	7,500	50.00	85.00
Artaffects	**Nature's Harmony**				
82-57-001	The Peaceable Kingdom	G. Perillo	12,500	100.00	200-250.
82-57-002	Zebra	G. Perillo	12,500	50.00	60.00
82-57-003	Bengal Tiger	G. Perillo	12,500	50.00	60.00
83-57-004	Black Panther	G. Perillo	12,500	50.00	70.00
83-57-005	Elephant	G. Perillo	12,500	50.00	80.00

PLATES

Company Number	Name	Series Artist	Edition Limit	Issue Price	Quote
Artaffects		**Arctic Friends**			
82-58-001	Siberian Love	G. Perillo	7,500	100.00	175.00
82-58-002	Snow Pals	G. Perillo	7,500	Set	Set
Artaffects		**Motherhood Series**			
83-59-001	Madre	G. Perillo	10,000	50.00	75.00
84-59-002	Madonna of the Plains	G. Perillo	3,500	50.00	75-100.00
85-59-003	Abuela	G. Perillo	3,500	50.00	75.00
86-59-004	Nap Time	G. Perillo	3,500	50.00	75.00
Artaffects		**The War Ponies**			
83-60-001	Sioux War Pony	G. Perillo	7,500	60.00	95-125.00
83-60-002	Nez Perce War Pony	G. Perillo	7,500	60.00	149-195.
83-60-003	Apache War Pony	G. Perillo	7,500	60.00	95-125.00
Artaffects		**The Tribal Ponies**			
84-61-001	Arapaho Tribal Pony	G. Perillo	3,500	65.00	150.00
84-61-002	Comanche Tribal Pony	G. Perillo	3,500	65.00	150.00
84-61-003	Crow Tribal Pony	G. Perillo	3,500	65.00	200.00
Artaffects		**The Thoroughbreds**			
84-62-001	Whirlaway	G. Perillo	9,500	50.00	250.00
84-62-002	Secretariat	G. Perillo	9,500	50.00	350.00
84-62-003	Man o' War	G. Perillo	9,500	50.00	150.00
84-62-004	Seabiscuit	G. Perillo	9,500	50.00	150.00
Artaffects		**Special Issue**			
81-63-001	Apache Boy	G. Perillo	5,000	95.00	175.00
83-63-002	Papoose	G. Perillo	3,000	100.00	125.00
83-63-003	Indian Style	G. Perillo	17,500	50.00	50.00
84-63-004	The Lovers	G. Perillo	Open	50.00	100.00
84-63-005	Navajo Girl	G. Perillo	3,500	95.00	350.00
86-63-006	Navajo Boy	G. Perillo	3,500	95.00	250.00
87-63-007	We The People	H.C. Christy	Open	35.00	35.00
Artaffects		**The Arabians**			
86-64-001	Silver Streak	G. Perillo	3,500	95.00	150.00
Artaffects		**The Colts**			
85-65-001	Appaloosa	G. Perillo	5,000	40.00	100.00
85-65-002	Pinto	G. Perillo	5,000	40.00	110.00
85-65-003	Arabian	G. Perillo	5,000	40.00	100.00
85-65-004	Thoroughbred	G. Perillo	5,000	40.00	100.00
Artaffects		**Tender Moments**			
85-66-001	Sunset	G. Perillo	2,000	150.00	250.00
85-66-002	Winter Romance	G. Perillo	2,000	Set	Set
Artaffects		**Young Emotions**			
86-67-001	Tears	G. Perillo	5,000	75.00	250.00
86-67-002	Smiles	G. Perillo	5,000	Set	Set
Artaffects		**The Maidens**			
85-68-001	Shimmering Waters	G. Perillo	5,000	60.00	150.00
85-68-002	Snow Blanket	G. Perillo	5,000	60.00	150.00
85-68-003	Song Bird	G. Perillo	5,000	60.00	150.00
Artaffects		**The Young Chieftains**			
85-69-001	Young Sitting Bull	G. Perillo	5,000	50.00	75-150.00
85-69-002	Young Joseph	G. Perillo	5,000	50.00	100.00
86-69-003	Young Red Cloud	G. Perillo	5,000	50.00	100.00
86-69-004	Young Geronimo	G. Perillo	5,000	50.00	100.00
86-69-005	Young Crazy Horse	G. Perillo	5,000	50.00	100.00
Artaffects		**Perillo Christmas**			
87-70-001	Shining Star	G. Perillo	Yr.Iss	29.50	125-300.
88-70-002	Silent Light	G. Perillo	Yr.Iss	35.00	50-200.00
89-70-003	Snow Flake	G. Perillo	Yr.Iss	35.00	50.00
90-70-004	Bundle Up	G. Perillo	Yr.Iss	39.50	75.00
91-70-005	Christmas Journey	G. Perillo	Yr.Iss	39.50	50.00
Artaffects		**America's Indian Heritage**			
87-71-001	Cheyenne Nation	G. Perillo	10-day	24.50	45-85.00
88-71-002	Arapaho Nation	G. Perillo	10-day	24.50	45.00
88-71-003	Kiowa Nation	G. Perillo	10-day	24.50	45.00
88-71-004	Sioux Nation	G. Perillo	10-day	24.50	30-55.00
88-71-005	Chippewa Nation	G. Perillo	10-day	24.50	50.00
88-71-006	Crow Nation	G. Perillo	10-day	24.50	60.00
88-71-007	Nez Perce Nation	G. Perillo	10-day	24.50	50.00
88-71-008	Blackfoot Nation	G. Perillo	10-day	24.50	95.00
Artaffects		**Mother's Love**			
88-72-001	Feelings	G. Perillo	Yr.Iss	35.00	90.00
89-72-002	Moonlight	G. Perillo	Yr.Iss	35.00	65.00
90-72-003	Pride & Joy	G. Perillo	Yr.Iss	39.50	50.00
91-72-004	Little Shadow	G. Perillo	Yr.Iss	39.50	45.00
Artaffects		**North American Wildlife**			
89-73-001	Mustang	G. Perillo	14-day	29.50	45.00
89-73-002	White-Tailed Deer	G. Perillo	14-day	29.50	35.00
89-73-003	Mountain Lion	G. Perillo	14-day	29.50	45.00
90-73-004	American Bald Eagle	G. Perillo	14-day	29.50	29.50
90-73-005	Timber Wolf	G. Perillo	14-day	29.50	35.00
90-73-006	Polar Bear	G. Perillo	14-day	29.50	39.00
90-73-007	Buffalo	G. Perillo	14-day	29.50	39.00
90-73-008	Bighorn Sheep	G. Perillo	14-day	29.50	39.00
Artaffects		**Portraits By Perillo-Mini Plates**			
89-74-001	Smiling Eyes-(4 1/4")	G. Perillo	9,500	19.50	19.50
89-74-002	Bright Sky-(4 1/4")	G. Perillo	9,500	19.50	19.50
89-74-003	Running Bear-(4 1/4")	G. Perillo	9,500	19.50	19.50
89-74-004	Little Feather-(4 1/4")	G. Perillo	9,500	19.50	19.50
90-74-005	Proud Eagle-(4 1/4")	G. Perillo	9,500	19.50	19.50
90-74-006	Blue Bird-(4 1/4")	G. Perillo	9,500	19.50	19.50
90-74-007	Wildflower-(4 1/4")	G. Perillo	9,500	19.50	19.50
90-74-008	Spring Breeze-(4 1/4")	G. Perillo	9,500	19.50	19.50
Artaffects		**March of Dimes: Our Children, Our Future**			
89-75-001	A Time to Be Born	G. Perillo	150-day	29.00	35-49.00
Artaffects		**Indian Bridal**			
90-76-001	Yellow Bird (6 1/2")	G. Perillo	14-day	25.00	25.00
90-76-002	Autumn Blossom (6 1/2")	G. Perillo	14-day	25.00	25.00
90-76-003	Misty Waters (6 1/2")	G. Perillo	14-day	25.00	25.00
90-76-004	Sunny Skies (6 1/2")	G. Perillo	14-day	25.00	25.00
Artaffects		**Proud Young Spirits**			
90-77-001	Protector of the Plains	G. Perillo	14-day	29.50	40-65.00
90-77-002	Watchful Eyes	G. Perillo	14-day	29.50	40-50.00
90-77-003	Freedom's Watch	G. Perillo	14-day	29.50	35-45.00
90-77-004	Woodland Scouts	G. Perillo	14-day	29.50	35-45.00
90-77-005	Fast Friends	G. Perillo	14-day	29.50	35-45.00
90-77-006	Birds of a Feather	G. Perillo	14-day	29.50	35-45.00
90-77-007	Prairie Pals	G. Perillo	14-day	29.50	35-45.00
90-77-008	Loyal Guardian	G. Perillo	14-day	29.50	35-45.00
Artaffects		**Perillo's Four Seasons**			
91-78-001	Summer (6 1/2")	G. Perillo	14-day	25.00	25.00
91-78-002	Autumn (6 1/2")	G. Perillo	14-day	25.00	25.00
91-78-003	Winter (6 1/2")	G. Perillo	14-day	25.00	25.00
91-78-004	Spring (6 1/2")	G. Perillo	14-day	25.00	25.00
Artaffects		**Council of Nations**			
92-79-001	Strength of the Sioux	G. Perillo	14-day	29.50	45.00
92-79-002	Pride of the Cheyenne	G. Perillo	14-day	29.50	29.50
92-79-003	Dignity of the Nez Perce	G. Perillo	14-day	29.50	29.50
92-79-004	Courage of the Arapaho	G. Perillo	14-day	29.50	29.50
92-79-005	Power of the Blackfoot	G. Perillo	14-day	29.50	29.50
92-79-006	Nobility of the Algonquin	G. Perillo	14-day	29.50	29.50
92-79-007	Wisdom of the Cherokee	G. Perillo	14-day	29.50	29.50
92-79-008	Boldness of the Seneca	G. Perillo	14-day	29.50	29.50
Artaffects		**War Ponies of the Plains**			
92-80-001	Nightshadow	G. Perillo	75-day	27.00	27.00
92-80-002	Windcatcher	G. Perillo	75-day	27.00	27.00
92-80-003	Prairie Prancer	G. Perillo	75-day	27.00	27.00
92-80-004	Thunderfoot	G. Perillo	75-day	27.00	27.00
92-80-005	Proud Companion	G. Perillo	75-day	27.00	27.00
92-80-006	Sun Dancer	G. Perillo	75-day	27.00	27.00
92-80-007	Free Spirit	G. Perillo	75-day	27.00	27.00
92-80-008	Gentle Warrior	G. Perillo	75-day	27.00	27.00
Artaffects		**Living In Harmony**			
91-81-001	Peaceable Kingdom	G. Perillo	75-day	29.50	29.50
Artaffects		**Studies in Black and White-Collector's Club Only(Miniatures)**			
92-82-001	Dignity	G. Perillo	Yr. Iss.	75/Set	75/Set
92-82-002	Determination	G. Perillo	Yr. Iss.	Set	Set
92-82-003	Diligence	G. Perillo	Yr. Iss.	Set	Set
92-82-004	Devotion	G. Perillo	Yr. Iss.	Set	Set
Artaffects		**Club Member Limited Edition Redemption Offerings**			
92-83-001	The Pencil	G. Perillo	Yr. Iss.	35.00	35.00
92-83-002	Studies in Black and White (Set of 4)	G. Perillo	Yr. Iss.	75/Set	75/Set
93-83-003	Watcher of the Wilderness	G. Perillo	Yr. Iss.	60.00	60.00
Artists of the World		**Holiday**			
76-01-001	Festival of Lights	T. DeGrazia	9,500	45.00	98-195.00
77-01-002	Bell of Hope	T. DeGrazia	9,500	45.00	53.00
78-01-003	Little Madonna	T. DeGrazia	9,500	45.00	58-95.00
79-01-004	The Nativity	T. DeGrazia	9,500	50.00	85-150.00
80-01-005	Little Pima Drummer	T. DeGrazia	9,500	50.00	60.00
81-01-006	A Little Prayer	T. DeGrazia	9,500	55.00	65.00
82-01-007	Blue Boy	T. DeGrazia	10,000	60.00	65-95.00
83-01-008	Heavenly Blessings	T. DeGrazia	10,000	65.00	65.00
84-01-009	Navajo Madonna	T. DeGrazia	10,000	65.00	125.00
85-01-010	Saguaro Dance	T. DeGrazia	10,000	65.00	100.00
Artists of the World		**Holiday**			
76-02-001	Festival of Lights, signed	T. DeGrazia	500	100.00	350.00
77-02-002	Bell of Hope, signed	T. DeGrazia	500	100.00	200.00
78-02-003	Little Madonna, signed	T. DeGrazia	500	100.00	350.00
79-02-004	The Nativity, signed	T. DeGrazia	500	100.00	200.00
80-02-005	Little Pima Drummer, signed	T. DeGrazia	500	100.00	200.00
81-02-006	A Little Prayer, signed	T. DeGrazia	500	100.00	200.00
82-02-007	Blue Boy, signed	T. DeGrazia	96	100.00	200.00
Artists of the World		**Holiday Mini-Plates**			
80-03-001	Festival of Lights	T. DeGrazia	5,000	15.00	250.00
81-03-002	Bell of Hope	T. DeGrazia	5,000	15.00	95.00
82-03-003	Little Madonna	T. DeGrazia	5,000	15.00	95.00
82-03-004	The Nativity	T. DeGrazia	5,000	15.00	95.00
83-03-005	Little Pima Drummer	T. DeGrazia	5,000	15.00	25.00
83-03-006	Little Prayer	T. DeGrazia	5,000	20.00	25.00
84-03-007	Blue Boy	T. DeGrazia	5,000	20.00	25.00
84-03-008	Heavenly Blessings	T. DeGrazia	5,000	20.00	25.00
85-03-009	Navajo Madonna	T. DeGrazia	5,000	20.00	25.00
85-03-010	Saguaro Dance	T. DeGrazia	5,000	20.00	25.00
Artists of the World		**Children**			
76-04-001	Los Ninos	T. DeGrazia	5,000	35.00	900-1000.
77-04-002	White Dove	T. DeGrazia	5,000	40.00	60-100.00
78-04-003	Flower Girl	T. DeGrazia	9,500	45.00	90.00
79-04-004	Flower Boy	T. DeGrazia	9,500	45.00	69.00
80-04-005	Little Cocopah	T. DeGrazia	9,500	50.00	70.00
81-04-006	Beautiful Burden	T. DeGrazia	9,500	50.00	55.00
82-04-007	Merry Little Indian	T. DeGrazia	9,500	55.00	85.00
83-04-008	Wondering	T. DeGrazia	10,000	60.00	60.00
84-04-009	Pink Papoose	T. DeGrazia	10,000	65.00	65.00
85-04-010	Sunflower Boy	T. DeGrazia	10,000	65.00	65-125.00
Artists of the World		**Children (Signed)**			
78-05-001	Los Ninos, signed	T. DeGrazia	500	100.00	3000.00
78-05-002	White Dove, signed	T. DeGrazia	500	100.00	450.00
78-05-003	Flower Girl, signed	T. DeGrazia	500	100.00	450.00
79-05-004	Flower Boy, signed	T. DeGrazia	500	100.00	450.00
80-05-005	Little Cocopah Girl, signed	T. DeGrazia	500	100.00	320.00
81-05-006	Beautiful Burden, signed	T. DeGrazia	500	100.00	320.00
81-05-007	Merry Little Indian, signed	T. DeGrazia	500	100.00	450.00
Artists of the World		**Children Mini-Plates**			
80-06-001	Los Ninos	T. DeGrazia	5,000	15.00	300.00
81-06-002	White Dove	T. DeGrazia	5,000	15.00	35.00
82-06-003	Flower Girl	T. DeGrazia	5,000	15.00	35.00
82-06-004	Flower Boy	T. DeGrazia	5,000	15.00	35.00
83-06-005	Little Cocopah Indian Girl	T. DeGrazia	5,000	15.00	25.00

Number	Name	Artist	Edition Limit	Issue Price	Quote
83-06-006	Beautiful Burden	T. DeGrazia	5,000	20.00	53.00
84-06-007	Merry Little Indian	T. DeGrazia	5,000	20.00	25.00
84-06-008	Wondering	T. DeGrazia	5,000	20.00	25.00
85-06-009	Pink Papoose	T. DeGrazia	5,000	20.00	25.00
85-06-010	Sunflower Boy	T. DeGrazia	5,000	20.00	25.00
Artists of the World		**Children at Play**			
85-07-001	My First Horse	T. DeGrazia	15,000	65.00	75.00
86-07-002	Girl With Sewing Machine	T. DeGrazia	15,000	65.00	75.00
87-07-003	Love Me	T. DeGrazia	15,000	65.00	75.00
88-07-004	Merrily, Merrily, Merrily	T. DeGrazia	15,000	65.00	75.00
89-07-005	My First Arrow	T. DeGrazia	15,000	65.00	75.00
90-07-006	Away With My Kite	T. DeGrazia	15,000	65.00	75.00
Artists of the World		**Western**			
86-08-001	Morning Ride	T. DeGrazia	5,000	65.00	85.00
87-08-002	Bronco	T. DeGrazia	5,000	65.00	85.00
88-08-003	Apache Scout	T. DeGrazia	5,000	65.00	85.00
89-08-004	Alone	T. DeGrazia	5,000	65.00	85.00
Artists of the World		**Children of the Sun**			
87-09-001	Spring Blossoms	T. DeGrazia	150-day	34.50	34.50
87-09-002	My Little Pink Bird	T. DeGrazia	150-day	34.50	34.50
87-09-003	Bright Flowers of the Desert	T. DeGrazia	150-day	37.90	37.90
88-09-004	Gifts from the Sun	T. DeGrazia	150-day	37.90	37.90
88-09-005	Growing Glory	T. DeGrazia	150-day	37.90	37.90
88-09-006	The Gentle White Dove	T. DeGrazia	150-day	37.90	37.90
88-09-007	Sunflower Maiden	T. DeGrazia	150-day	39.90	39.90
89-09-008	Sun Showers	T. DeGrazia	150-day	39.90	45.00
Artists of the World		**Fiesta of the Children**			
90-10-001	Welcome to the Fiesta	T. DeGrazia	150-day	34.50	34.50-49.00
90-10-002	Castanets in Bloom	T. DeGrazia	150-day	34.50	34.50
91-10-003	Fiesta Flowers	T. DeGrazia	150-day	34.50	34.50
91-10-004	Fiesta Angels	T. DeGrazia	150-day	34.50	34.50
Artists of the World		**Children of Aberdeen**			
79-11-001	Girl with Little Brother	K. Fung Ng	Undis.	50.00	50.00
80-11-002	Sampan Girl	K. Fung Ng	Undis.	50.00	55.00
81-11-003	Girl with Little Sister	K. Fung Ng	Undis.	55.00	60.00
82-11-004	Girl with Seashells	K. Fung Ng	Undis.	60.00	60.00
83-11-005	Girl with Seabirds	K. Fung Ng	Undis.	60.00	60.00
84-11-006	Brother and Sister	K. Fung Ng	Undis.	60.00	60.00
Art World of Bourgeault		**The English Countryside Series**			
80-01-001	The Country Squire	R. Bourgeault	1,500	70.00	395.00
81-01-002	The Willows	R. Bourgeault	1,500	85.00	395.00
82-01-003	Rose Cottage	R. Bourgeault	1,500	90.00	395.00
83-01-004	Thatched Beauty	R. Bourgeault	1,500	95.00	395.00
Art World of Bourgeault		**The English Countryside-Single Issues**			
84-02-001	The Anne Hathaway Cottage	R. Bourgeault	500	150.00	750.00
85-02-002	Lilac Cottage	R, Bourgeault	500	125.00	395.00
87-02-003	Suffolk Pink	R. Bourgeault	50	220.00	625.00
88-02-004	Stuart House	R. Bourgeault	50	325.00	625.00
89-02-005	Lark Rise	R. Bourgeault	50	450.00	625.00
Art World of Bourgeault		**The Royal Literary Series**			
85-03-001	The John Bunyan Cottage	R. Bourgeault	4,500	60.00	95.00
87-03-002	The Thomas Hardy Cottage	R. Bourgeault	4,500	65.00	95.00
88-03-003	The John Milton Cottage	R. Bourgeault	4,500	65.00	95.00
89-03-004	The Anne Hathaway Cottage	R. Bourgeault	4,500	65.00	95.00
Art World of Bourgeault		**Where Is England Series**			
90-04-001	Forget-Me-Not	R. Bourgeault	50	525.00	705.00
91-04-002	The Fleece Inn	R. Bourgeault	50	525.00	705.00
92-04-003	Millbrook House	R. Bourgeault	50	525.00	525.00
93-04-004	Cotswold Beauty	R. Bourgeault	50	525.00	525.00
Art World of Bourgeault		**Where Is Scotland Series**			
91-05-001	Eilean Donan Castle	R. Bourgeault	50	525.00	705.00
Art World of Bourgeault		**The Royal Gainsborough Series**			
90-06-001	The Lisa-Caroline	R. Bourgeault	N/A	75.00	85.00
91-06-002	A Gainsborough Lady	R. Bourgeault	N/A	N/A	N/A
Bareuther		**Christmas**			
67-01-001	Stiftskirche	H. Mueller	10,000	12.00	85.00
68-01-002	Kapplkirche	H. Mueller	10,000	12.00	25.00
69-01-003	Christkindlesmarkt	H. Mueller	10,000	12.00	18.00
70-01-004	Chapel in Oberndorf	H. Mueller	10,000	12.50	22.00
71-01-005	Toys for Sale From Drawing By	L. Richter	10,000	12.75	27.00
72-01-006	Christmas in Munich	H. Mueller	10,000	14.50	25.00
73-01-007	Sleigh Ride	H. Mueller	10,000	15.00	35.00
74-01-008	Black Forest Church	H. Mueller	10,000	19.00	19.00
75-01-009	Snowman	H. Mueller	10,000	21.50	30.00
76-01-010	Chapel in the Hills	H. Mueller	10,000	23.50	26.00
77-01-011	Story Time	H. Mueller	10,000	24.50	40.00
78-01-012	Mittenwald	H. Mueller	10,000	27.50	31.00
79-01-013	Winter Day	H. Mueller	10,000	35.00	35.00
80-01-014	Mittenberg	H. Mueller	10,000	37.50	39.00
81-01-015	Walk in the Forest	H. Mueller	10,000	39.50	39.50
82-01-016	Bad Wimpfen	H. Mueller	10,000	39.50	43.00
83-01-017	The Night before Christmas	H. Mueller	10,000	39.50	39.50
84-01-018	Zeil on the River Main	H. Mueller	10,000	42.50	45.00
85-01-019	Winter Wonderland	H. Mueller	10,000	42.50	57.00
86-01-020	Christmas in Forchheim	H. Mueller	10,000	42.50	70.00
87-01-021	Decorating the Tree	H. Mueller	10,000	42.50	85.00
88-01-022	St. Coloman Church	H. Mueller	10,000	52.50	65.00
89-01-023	Sleigh Ride	H. Mueller	10,000	52.50	80-90.00
90-01-024	The Old Forge in Rothenburg	H. Mueller	10,000	52.50	52.50
91-01-025	Christmas Joy	H. Mueller	10,000	56.50	56.50
92-01-026	Market Place in Heppenheim	H. Mueller	10,000	59.50	59.50
93-01-027	Winter Fun	H. Mueller	5,000	59.50	59.50
Belleek		**Christmas**			
70-01-001	Castle Caldwell	Unknown	7,500	25.00	70-85.00
71-01-002	Celtic Cross	Unknown	7,500	25.00	60.00
72-01-003	Flight of the Earls	Unknown	7,500	30.00	35.00
73-01-004	Tribute To Yeats	Unknown	7,500	38.50	40.00
74-01-005	Devenish Island	Unknown	7,500	45.00	190.00
75-01-006	The Celtic Cross	Unknown	7,500	48.00	80.00
76-01-007	Dove of Peace	Unknown	7,500	55.00	55.00
77-01-008	Wren	Unknown	7,500	55.00	55.00
Belleek		**Holiday Scenes in Ireland**			
91-02-001	Traveling Home	Unknown	7,500	75.00	75.00
92-02-001	Bearing Gifts	Unknown	7,500	75.00	75.00
Berlin Design		**Christmas**			
70-01-001	Christmas in Bernkastel	Unknown	4,000	14.50	125.00
71-01-002	Christmas in Rothenburg	Unknown	20,000	14.50	45.00
72-01-003	Christmas in Michelstadt	Unknown	20,000	15.00	55.00
73-01-004	Christmas in Wendlestein	Unknown	20,000	20.00	55.00
74-01-005	Christmas in Bremen	Unknown	20,000	25.00	53.00
75-01-006	Christmas in Dortland	Unknown	20,000	30.00	35.00
76-01-007	Christmas in Augsburg	Unknown	20,000	32.00	75.00
77-01-008	Christmas in Hamburg	Unknown	20,000	32.00	32.00
78-01-009	Christmas in Berlin	Unknown	20,000	36.00	85.00
79-01-010	Christmas in Greetsiel	Unknown	20,000	47.50	60.00
80-01-011	Christmas in Mittenberg	Unknown	20,000	50.00	55.00
81-01-012	Christmas Eve In Hahnenklee	Unknown	20,000	55.00	55.00
82-01-013	Christmas Eve In Wasserberg	Unknown	20,000	55.00	50.00
83-01-014	Christmas in Oberndorf	Unknown	20,000	55.00	65.00
84-01-015	Christmas in Ramsau	Unknown	20,000	55.00	55.00
85-01-016	Christmas in Bad Wimpfen	Unknown	20,000	55.00	59.00
86-01-017	Christmas Eve in Gelnhaus	Unknown	20,000	65.00	65.00
87-01-018	Christmas Eve in Goslar	Unknown	20,000	65.00	65.00
88-01-019	Christmas Eve in Ruhpolding	Unknown	20,000	65.00	90.00
89-01-020	Christmas Eve in Friedechsdadt	Unknown	20,000	80.00	80.00
90-01-021	Christmas Eve in Partenkirchen	Unknown	20,000	80.00	80.00
91-01-022	Christmas Eve in Allendorf	Unknown	20,000	80.00	80.00
Berlin Design		**Historical**			
75-02-001	Washington Crossing the Delaware	Unknown	Annual	30.00	40.00
76-02-002	Tom Thumb	Unknown	Annual	32.00	35.00
77-02-003	Zeppelin	Unknown	Annual	32.00	35.00
78-02-004	Benz Motor Car Munich	Unknown	10,000	36.00	36.00
79-02-005	Johannes Gutenberg	Unknown	10,000	47.50	48.00
Berlin Design		**Holiday Week of the Family Kappelmann**			
84-03-001	Monday	Unknown	Undis.	33.00	33.00
84-03-002	Tuesday	Unknown	Undis.	33.00	37.00
85-03-003	Wednesday	Unknown	Undis.	33.00	37.00
85-03-004	Thursday	Unknown	Undis.	35.00	38.00
85-03-005	Friday	Unknown	Undis.	35.00	40.00
86-03-006	Saturday	Unknown	Undis.	35.00	40.00
86-03-007	Sunday	Unknown	Undis.	35.00	40.00
Bing & Grondahl		**Christmas**			
95-01-001	Behind The Frozen Window	F.A. Hallin	Annual	.50	4500-5900.
96-01-002	New Moon	F.A. Hallin	Annual	.50	1200-2299.
97-01-003	Sparrows	F.A. Hallin	Annual	.75	1125-1499.
98-01-004	Roses and Star	F. Garde	Annual	.75	825-900.
99-01-005	Crows	F. Garde	Annual	.75	910-1759.
00-01-006	Church Bells	F. Garde	Annual	.75	850-1309.
01-01-007	Three Wise Men	S. Sabra	Annual	1.00	500.00
02-01-008	Gothic Church Interior	D. Jensen	Annual	1.00	300-429.
03-01-009	Expectant Children	M. Hyldahl	Annual	1.00	300-429.
04-01-010	Fredericksberg Hill	C. Olsen	Annual	1.00	125-175.
05-01-011	Christmas Night	D. Jensen	Annual	1.00	175-186.
06-01-012	Sleighing to Church	D. Jensen	Annual	1.00	98-110.00
07-01-013	Little Match Girl	E. Plockross	Annual	1.00	135.00
08-01-014	St. Petri Church	P. Jorgensen	Annual	1.00	95-105.
09-01-015	Yule Tree	Aarestrup	Annual	1.50	99-110.00
10-01-016	The Old Organist	C. Ersgaard	Annual	1.50	79-100.00
11-01-017	Angels and Shepherds	H. Moltke	Annual	1.50	96.00
12-01-018	Going to Church	E. Hansen	Annual	1.50	100.00
13-01-019	Bringing Home the Tree	T. Larsen	Annual	1.50	94.00
14-01-020	Amalienborg Castle	T. Larsen	Annual	1.50	85-150.00
15-01-021	Dog Outside Window	D. Jensen	Annual	1.50	155-160.
16-01-022	Sparrows at Christmas	P. Jorgensen	Annual	1.50	87.00
17-01-023	Christmas Boat	A. Friis	Annual	1.50	70-93.00
18-01-024	Fishing Boat	A. Friis	Annual	1.50	87.00
19-01-025	Outside Lighted Window	A. Friis	Annual	2.00	85-126.00
20-01-026	Hare in the Snow	A. Friis	Annual	2.00	95-120.00
21-01-027	Pigeons	A. Friis	Annual	2.00	90.00
22-01-028	Star of Bethlehem	A. Friis	Annual	2.00	75-126.00
23-01-029	The Ermitage	A. Friis	Annual	2.00	79-93.00
24-01-030	Lighthouse	A. Friis	Annual	2.50	82-87.00
25-01-031	Child's Christmas	A. Friis	Annual	2.50	90-126.00
26-01-032	Churchgoers	A. Friis	Annual	2.50	82-93.00
27-01-033	Skating Couple	A. Friis	Annual	2.50	87-110.00
28-01-034	Eskimos	A. Friis	Annual	2.50	69-126.00
29-01-035	Fox Outside Farm	A. Friis	Annual	2.50	85-125.00
30-01-036	Christmas Train	A. Friis	Annual	2.50	97.00
31-01-037	Town Hall Square	H. Flugenring	Annual	2.50	87.00
32-01-038	Life Boat	H. Flugenring	Annual	2.50	82-95.00
33-01-039	Korsor-Nyborg Ferry	H. Flugenring	Annual	3.00	80-101.00
34-01-040	Church Bell in Tower	H. Flugenring	Annual	3.00	75.00
35-01-041	Lillebelt Bridge	O. Larson	Annual	3.00	75-109.00
36-01-042	Royal Guard	O. Larson	Annual	3.00	82.00
37-01-043	Arrival of Christmas Guests	O. Larson	Annual	3.00	90-97.00
38-01-044	Lighting the Candles	I. Tjerne	Annual	3.00	145-162.
39-01-045	Old Lock-Eye, The Sandman	I. Tjerne	Annual	3.00	187-238.
40-01-046	Christmas Letters	O. Larson	Annual	4.00	187-200.
41-01-047	Horses Enjoying Meal	O. Larson	Annual	4.00	255.00
42-01-048	Danish Farm	O. Larson	Annual	4.00	212-225.
43-01-049	Ribe Cathedral	O. Larson	Annual	5.00	180.00
44-01-050	Sorgenfri Castle	O. Larson	Annual	5.00	107-140.
45-01-051	The Old Water Mill	O. Larson	Annual	5.00	160.00
46-01-052	Commemoration Cross	M. Hyldahl	Annual	5.00	85-148.00
47-01-053	Dybbol Mill	M. Hyldahl	Annual	5.00	130-238.
48-01-054	Watchman	M. Hyldahl	Annual	5.50	214.00
49-01-055	Landsoldaten	M. Hyldahl	Annual	5.50	100-250.
50-01-056	Kronborg Castle	M. Hyldahl	Annual	5.50	141.00
51-01-057	Jens Bang	M. Hyldahl	Annual	6.00	100.00
52-01-058	Thorsvaldsen Museum	B. Pramvig	Annual	6.00	121.00
53-01-059	Snowman	B. Pramvig	Annual	7.50	89-95.00
54-01-060	Royal Boat	K. Bonfils	Annual	7.00	100-106.
55-01-061	Kaulundorg Church	K. Bonfils	Annual	8.00	105-127.
56-01-062	Christmas in Copenhagen	K. Bonfils	Annual	8.50	150-164.
57-01-063	Christmas Candles	K. Bonfils	Annual	9.00	144-150.
58-01-064	Santa Claus	K. Bonfils	Annual	9.50	119.00
59-01-065	Christmas Eve	K. Bonfils	Annual	10.00	135-140.
60-01-066	Village Church	K. Bonfils	Annual	10.00	149-169.

Company / Number	Name	Series / Artist	Edition Limit	Issue Price	Quote
61-01-067	Winter Harmony	K. Bonfils	Annual	10.50	75-107.00
62-01-068	Winter Night	K. Bonfils	Annual	11.00	52-100.00
63-01-069	The Christmas Elf	H. Thelander	Annual	11.00	89-105.00
64-01-070	The Fir Tree and Hare	H. Thelander	Annual	11.50	36-47.00
65-01-071	Bringing Home the Tree	H. Thelander	Annual	12.00	45-49.00
66-01-072	Home for Christmas	H. Thelander	Annual	12.00	28-47.00
67-01-073	Sharing the Joy	H. Thelander	Annual	13.00	25-39.00
68-01-074	Christmas in Church	H. Thelander	Annual	14.00	20-39.00
69-01-075	Arrival of Guests	H. Thelander	Annual	14.00	20-30.00
70-01-076	Pheasants in Snow	H. Thelander	Annual	14.50	15-25.00
71-01-077	Christmas at Home	H. Thelander	Annual	15.00	25.00
72-01-078	Christmas in Greenland	H. Thelander	Annual	16.50	20-25.00
73-01-079	Country Christmas	H. Thelander	Annual	19.50	19.50-25.00
74-01-080	Christmas in the Village	H. Thelander	Annual	22.00	25.00
75-01-081	Old Water Mill	H. Thelander	Annual	27.50	27.50
76-01-082	Christmas Welcome	H. Thelander	Annual	27.50	27.50
77-01-083	Copenhagen Christmas	H. Thelander	Annual	29.50	29.50
78-01-084	Christmas Tale	H. Thelander	Annual	32.00	35.00
79-01-085	White Christmas	H. Thelander	Annual	36.50	50.00
80-01-086	Christmas in Woods	H. Thelander	Annual	42.50	42.50
81-01-087	Christmas Peace	H. Thelander	Annual	49.50	49.50
82-01-088	Christmas Tree	H. Thelander	Annual	54.50	54.50
83-01-089	Christmas in Old Town	H. Thelander	Annual	54.50	54.50
84-01-090	The Christmas Letter	E. Jensen	Annual	54.50	54.50
85-01-091	Christmas Eve at the Farmhouse	E. Jensen	Annual	54.50	54.50
86-01-092	Silent Night, Holy Night	E. Jensen	Annual	54.50	54.50
87-01-093	The Snowman's Christmas Eve	E. Jensen	Annual	59.50	55-70.00
88-01-094	In the Kings Garden	E. Jensen	Annual	64.50	65.00
89-01-095	Christmas Anchorage	E. Jensen	Annual	59.50	60-80.00
90-01-096	Changing of the Guards	E. Jensen	Annual	64.50	60-80.00
91-01-097	Copenhagen Stock Exchange	E. Jensen	Annual	69.50	70-85.00
92-01-098	Christmas At the Rectory	J. Steensen	Annual	69.50	69.50
93-01-099	Father Christmas in Copenhagen	J. Nielson	Annual	69.50	69.50
Bing & Grondahl		**Jubilee-5 Year Cycle**			
15-02-001	Frozen Window	F.A. Hallin	Annual	Unkn.	155.00
20-02-002	Church Bells	F. Garde	Annual	Unkn.	65.00
25-02-003	Dog Outside Window	D. Jensen	Annual	Unkn.	130.00
30-02-004	The Old Organist	C. Ersgaard	Annual	Unkn.	169.00
35-02-005	Little Match Girl	E. Plockross	Annual	Unkn.	720.00
40-02-006	Three Wise Men	S. Sabra	Annual	Unkn.	1839.00
45-02-007	Amalienborg Castle	T. Larsen	Annual	Unkn.	199.00
50-02-008	Eskimos	A. Friis	Annual	Unkn.	199.00
55-02-009	Dybbol Mill	M. Hyldahl	Annual	Unkn.	210.00
60-02-010	Kronborg Castle	M. Hyldahl	Annual	25.00	129.00
65-02-011	Chruchgoers	A. Friis	Annual	25.00	69.00
70-02-012	Amalienborg Castle	T. Larsen	Annual	30.00	30.00
75-02-013	Horses Enjoying Meal	O. Larson	Annual	40.00	50.00
80-02-014	Yule Tree	Aarestrup	Annual	60.00	60.00
85-02-015	Lifeboat at Work	H. Flugenring	Annual	65.00	93.00
90-02-016	The Royal Yacht Dannebrog	J. Bonfils	Annual	95.00	95.00
Bing & Grondahl		**Mother's Day**			
69-03-001	Dogs and Puppies	H. Thelander	Annual	9.75	350-400.
70-03-002	Bird and Chicks	H. Thelander	Annual	10.00	14-25.00
71-03-003	Cat and Kitten	H. Thelander	Annual	11.00	15.00
72-03-004	Mare and Foal	H. Thelander	Annual	12.00	15.00
73-03-005	Duck and Ducklings	H. Thelander	Annual	13.00	15.00
74-03-006	Bear and Cubs	H. Thelander	Annual	16.50	16.50
75-03-007	Doe and Fawns	H. Thelander	Annual	19.50	19.50
76-03-008	Swan Family	H. Thelander	Annual	22.50	22.50
77-03-009	Squirrel and Young	H. Thelander	Annual	23.50	25.00
78-03-010	Heron	H. Thelander	Annual	24.50	25.00
79-03-011	Fox and Cubs	H. Thelander	Annual	27.50	27.50
80-03-012	Woodpecker and Young	H. Thelander	Annual	29.50	39.00
81-03-013	Hare and Young	H. Thelander	Annual	36.50	36.50
82-03-014	Lioness and Cubs	H. Thelander	Annual	39.50	39.50
83-03-015	Raccoon and Young	H. Thelander	Annual	39.50	39.50
84-03-016	Stork and Nestlings	H. Thelander	Annual	39.50	39.50
85-03-017	Bear and Cubs	H. Thelander	Annual	39.50	40.00
86-03-018	Elephant with Calf	H. Thelander	Annual	39.50	43.00
87-03-019	Sheep with Lambs	H. Thelander	Annual	42.50	69.00
88-03-020	Crested Ployer & Young	H. Thelander	Annual	47.50	55.00
88-03-021	Lapwing Mother with Chicks	H. Thelander	Annual	49.50	55.00
89-03-022	Cow With Calf	H. Thelander	Annual	49.50	50.00
90-03-023	Hen with Chicks	L. Jensen	Annual	52.50	65.00
91-03-024	The Nanny Goat and her Two Frisky Kids	L. Jensen	Annual	54.50	70.00
92-03-025	Panda With Cubs	L. Jensen	Annual	59.50	59.50
93-03-026	St. Bernard Dog and Puppies	A. Therkelsen	Annual	59.50	59.50
Bing & Grondahl		**Children's Day Plate Series**			
85-04-001	The Magical Tea Party	C. Roller	Annual	24.50	25.00
86-04-002	A Joyful Flight	C. Roller	Annual	26.50	28.00
86-04-003	The Little Gardeners	C. Roller	Annual	29.50	40.00
88-04-004	Wash Day	C. Roller	Annual	34.50	34.50
89-04-005	Bedtime	C. Roller	Annual	37.00	50.00
90-04-006	My Favorite Dress	S. Vestergaard	Annual	37.00	40.00
91-04-007	Fun on the Beach	S. Vestergaard	Annual	45.00	45.00
92-04-008	A Summer Day in the Meadow	S. Vestergaard	Annual	45.00	45.00
93-04-009	The Carousel	S. Vestergaard	Annual	45.00	45.00
Bing & Grondahl		**Statue of Liberty**			
85-05-001	Statue of Liberty	Unknown	10,000	60.00	100.00
Bing & Grondahl		**Christmas In America**			
86-06-001	Christmas Eve in Williamsburg	J. Woodson	Annual	29.50	69-150.00
87-06-002	Christmas Eve at the White House	J. Woodson	Annual	34.50	45-80.00
88-06-003	Christmas Eve at Rockefeller Center	J. Woodson	Annual	34.50	45-75.00
89-06-004	Christmas In New England	J. Woodson	Annual	37.00	60-65.00
90-06-005	Christmas Eve at the Capitol	J. Woodson	Annual	39.50	40-55.00
91-06-006	Christmas Eve at Independence Hall	J. Woodson	Annual	45.00	45-85.00
92-06-007	Christmas in San Francisco	J. Woodson	Annual	47.50	47.50
93-06-008	Coming Home For Christmas	J. Woodson	Annual	47.50	47.50
Bing & Grondahl		**Santa Claus Collection**			
89-07-001	Santa's Workshop	H. Hansen	Annual	59.50	60-65.00
90-07-002	Santa's Sleigh	H. Hansen	Annual	59.50	60-85.00
91-07-003	Santa's Journey	H. Hansen	Annual	69.50	60-85.00
92-07-004	Santa's Arrival	H. Hansen	Annual	74.50	74.50
93-07-005	Santa's Gifts	H. Hansen	Annual	74.50	74.50
Bing & Grondahl		**Young Adventurer Plate**			
90-08-001	The Little Viking	S. Vestergaard	Annual	52.50	65.00
Bing & Grondahl		**Christmas in America Anniversary Plate**			
91-09-001	Christmas Eve in Williamsburg	J. Woodson	Annual	69.50	69.50
Bing & Grondahl		**Centennial Collection**			
91-10-001	Crows Enjoying Christmas	D. Jensen	Annual	59.50	59.50
92-10-002	Copenhagen Christmas	H. Vlugenring	Annual	59.50	59.50
93-10-003	Christmas Elf	H. Thelander	Annual	59.50	59.50
94-10-004	Christmas in Church	H. Thelander	Annual	59.50	59.50
95-10-005	Behind The Frozen Window	A. Hallin	Annual	59.50	59.50
Boehm Studios		**Egyptian Commemorative**			
78-01-001	Tutankhamun	Boehm	5,000	125.00	170.00
78-01-002	Tutankhamun, handpainted	Boehm	225	975.00	975.00
Boehm Studios		**Panda**			
82-16-001	Panda, Harmony	Boehm	5,000	65.00	65.00
82-16-002	Panda, Peace	Boehm	5,000	65.00	65.00
Curator Collection: See Artaffects					
C.U.I./Carolina Collection/Dram Tree		**Native American Series**			
91-01-001	Hunt for the Buffalo Edition I	P. Kethley	4,950	39.50	39.50
92-01-002	Story Teller	P. Kethley	4,950	40.00	40.00
C.U.I./Carolina Collection/Dram Tree		**Christmas Series**			
91-02-001	Checkin' it Twice Edition I	CUI	4,950	39.50	39.50
C.U.I./Carolina Collection/Dram Tree		**Environmental Series**			
91-03-001	Rainforest Magic Edition I	C. L. Bragg	4,950	39.50	39.50
92-03-002	First Breath	M. Hoffman	4,950	40.00	40.00
C.U.I./Carolina Collection/Dram Tree		**Girl In The Moon**			
91-04-001	Miller Girl in the Moon Edition I	CUI	9,950	39.50	39.50
C.U.I./Carolina Collection/Dram Tree		**DU Great American Sporting Dogs**			
92-05-001	Black Lab Edition I	J. Killen	20,000	40.00	40.00
93-05-002	Golden Retriever Edition II	J. Killen	28-day	40.00	40.00
93-05-003	Springer Spaniel Edition III	J. Killen	28-day	40.00	40.00
93-05-004	Yellow Labrador Edition IV	J. Killen	28-day	40.00	40.00
93-05-005	English Setter Edition V	J. Killen	28-day	40.00	40.00
93-05-006	Brittany Spaniel Edition VI	J. Killen	28-day	40.00	40.00
C.U.I./Carolina Collection/Dram Tree		**Classic Car Series**			
92-06-001	1957 Chevy	G. Geivette	28-day	40.00	40.00
C.U.I./Carolina Collection/Dram Tree		**Corvette Series**			
92-07-001	1953 Corvette	G. Geivette	28-day	40.00	40.00
D'Arceau Limoges		**Lafayette**			
73-01-001	The Secret Contract	A. Restieau	Unkn.	14.82	20.00
73-01-002	North Island Landing	A. Restieau	Unkn.	19.82	22.00
74-01-003	City Tavern Meeting	A. Restieau	Unkn.	19.82	22.00
74-01-004	Battle of Brandywine	A. Restieau	Unkn.	19.82	22.00
75-01-005	Messages to Franklin	A. Restieau	Unkn.	19.82	23.00
75-01-006	Siege at Yorktown	A. Restieau	Unkn.	19.82	20.00
D'Arceau Limoges		**Christmas**			
75-02-001	La Fruite en Egypte	A. Restieau	Unkn.	24.32	30.00
76-02-002	Dans la Creche	A. Restieau	Unkn.	24.32	29.00
77-02-003	Refus d' Hebergement	A. Restieau	Unkn.	24.32	29.00
78-02-004	La Purification	A. Restieau	Yr.Iss.	26.81	29.00
79-02-005	L' Adoration des Rois	A. Restieau	Yr.Iss.	26.81	31.00
80-02-006	Joyeuse Nouvelle	A. Restieau	Yr.Iss.	28.74	32.00
81-02-007	Guides par L' Etoile	A. Restieau	Yr.Iss.	28.74	30.00
82-02-008	L' Annuciation	A. Restieau	Yr.Iss.	30.74	35.00
Delphi		**Elvis Presley: Looking At A Legend**			
88-01-001	Elvis at/Gates of Graceland	B. Emmett	150-day	24.75	125-150.
89-01-002	Jailhouse Rock	B. Emmett	150-day	24.75	75-99.00
89-01-003	The Memphis Flash	B. Emmett	150-day	27.75	45-85.00
89-01-004	Homecoming	B. Emmett	150-day	27.75	45-95.00
90-01-005	Elvis and Gladys	B. Emmett	150-day	27.75	52-95.00
90-01-006	A Studio Session	B. Emmett	150-day	27.75	40-75.00
90-01-007	Elvis in Hollywood	B. Emmett	150-day	29.75	50-55.00
90-01-008	Elvis on His Harley	B. Emmett	150-day	29.75	48-68.00
90-01-009	Stage Door Autographs	B. Emmett	150-day	29.75	29.75
91-01-010	Christmas at Graceland	B. Emmett	150-day	32.75	32.75
91-01-011	Entering Sun Studio	B. Emmett	150-day	32.75	32.75
91-01-012	Going for the Black Belt	B. Emmett	150-day	32.75	32.75
91-01-013	His Hand in Mine	B. Emmett	150-day	32.75	32.75
91-01-014	Letters From Fans	B. Emmett	150-day	32.75	32.75
91-01-015	Closing the Deal	B. Emmett	150-day	34.75	34.75
92-01-016	Elvis Returns to the Stage	B. Emmett	150-day	34.75	34.75
Delphi		**Elvis Presley: In Performance**			
90-02-001	'68 Comeback Special	B. Emmett	150-day	24.75	24.75
91-02-002	King of Las Vegas	B. Emmett	150-day	24.75	47.00
91-02-003	Aloha From Hawaii	B. Emmett	150-day	27.75	125.00
91-02-004	Back in Tupelo, 1956	B. Emmett	150-day	27.75	27.75
91-02-005	If I Can Dream	B. Emmett	150-day	27.75	27.75
91-02-006	Benefit for the USS Arizona	B. Emmett	150-day	29.75	29.75
91-02-007	Madison Square Garden, 1972	B. Emmett	150-day	29.75	29.75
91-02-008	Tampa, 1955	B. Emmett	150-day	29.75	29.75
91-02-009	Concert in Baton Rouge, 1974	B. Emmett	150-day	29.75	29.75
92-02-010	On Stage in Wichita, 1974	B. Emmett	150-day	31.75	31.75
92-02-011	In the Spotlight: Hawaii, '72	B. Emmett	150-day	31.75	31.75
Delphi		**Portraits of the King**			
91-03-001	Love Me Tender	D. Zwierz	150-day	27.75	27.75
91-03-002	Are You Lonesome Tonight?	D. Zwierz	150-day	27.75	27.75
91-03-003	I'm Yours	D. Zwierz	150-day	30.75	30.75
91-03-004	Treat Me Nice	D. Zwierz	150-day	30.75	30.75
92-03-005	The Wonder of You	D. Zwierz	150-day	30.75	30.75
92-03-006	You're a Heartbreaker	D. Zwierz	150-day	32.75	32.75
92-03-007	Just Because	D. Zwierz	150-day	32.75	32.75
Delphi		**The Elvis Presley Hit Parade**			
92-04-001	Heartbreak Hotel	N. Giorgio	150-day	29.75	29.75
92-04-002	Blue Suede Shoes	N. Giorgio	150-day	29.75	29.75
92-04-003	Hound Dog	N. Giorgio	150-day	32.75	32.75
Delphi		**Elvis on the Big Screen**			
92-05-001	Loving You	B. Emmett	150-day	29.75	29.75

PLATES

Company Number	Name	Series Artist	Edition Limit	Issue Price	Quote
92-05-002	G.I. Blues	B. Emmett	150-day	29.75	29.75
Delphi		**Dream Machines**			
88-06-001	'56 T-Bird	P. Palma	150-day	24.75	30-55.00
88-06-002	'57 'Vette	P. Palma	150-day	24.75	39.00
89-06-003	'58 Biarritz	P. Palma	150-day	27.75	27.75
89-06-004	'56 Continental	P. Palma	150-day	27.75	27.75
89-06-005	'57 Bel Air	P. Palma	150-day	27.75	55.00
89-06-006	'57 Chrysler 300C	P. Palma	150-day	27.75	38.00
Delphi		**Indiana Jones**			
89-07-001	Indiana Jones	V. Gadino	150-day	24.75	29-35.00
89-07-002	Indiana Jones and His Dad	V. Gadino	150-day	24.75	54.00
90-07-003	Indiana Jones/Dr. Schneider	V. Gadino	150-day	27.75	39.00
90-07-004	A Family Discussion	V. Gadino	150-day	27.75	45-49.00
90-07-005	Young Indiana Jones	V. Gadino	150-day	27.75	55-69.00
91-07-006	Indiana Jones/The Holy Grail	V. Gadino	150-day	27.75	63-68.00
Delphi		**The Marilyn Monroe Collection**			
89-08-001	Marilyn Monroe/7 Year Itch	C. Notarile	150-day	24.75	65-85.00
90-08-002	Diamonds/Girls Best Friend	C. Notarile	150-day	24.75	65-75.00
91-08-003	Marilyn Monroe/River of No Return	C. Notarile	150-day	27.75	65-80.00
92-08-004	How to Marry a Millionaire	C. Notarile	150-day	27.75	65-85.00
92-08-005	There's No Business/Show Business	C. Notarile	150-day	27.75	60-85.00
92-08-006	Marilyn Monroe in Niagra	C. Notarile	150-day	29.75	65.00
Delphi		**The Beatles Collection**			
91-09-001	The Beatles, Live In Concert	N. Giorgio	150-day	24.75	24.75
91-09-002	Hello America	N. Giorgio	150-day	24.75	24.75
91-09-003	A Hard Day's Night	N. Giorgio	150-day	27.75	27.75
Delphi		**Legends of Baseball**			
92-10-001	Babe Ruth: The Called Shot	B. Benger	150-day	24.95	24.95
Department 56		**Dickens' Village**			
87-01-001	Dickens' Village Porcelain Plates, 5917-0 Set of 4	Department 56	Closed	140.00	140.00
Department 56		**A Christmas Carol**			
91-02-001	The Cratchit's Christmas Pudding, 5706-1	R. Innocenti	18,000	60.00	75-125.00
92-02-002	Marley's Ghost Appears To Scrooge, 5721-5	R. Innocenti	18,000	60.00	60.00
93-02-003	The Spirit of Christmas Present, 5722-3	R. Innocenti	18,000	60.00	60.00
Duncan Royale		**History of Santa Claus I**			
85-01-001	Medieval	S. Morton	Retrd.	40.00	75.00
85-01-002	Kris Kringle	S. Morton	Retrd.	40.00	65.00
85-01-003	Pioneer	S. Morton	10,000	40.00	40.00
86-01-004	Russian	S. Morton	Retrd.	40.00	40.00
86-01-005	Soda Pop	S. Morton	Retrd.	40.00	65.00
86-01-006	Civil War	S. Morton	10,000	40.00	40.00
86-01-007	Nast	S. Morton	Retrd.	40.00	75.00
87-01-008	St. Nicholas	S. Morton	Retrd.	40.00	75.00
87-01-009	Dedt Moroz	S. Morton	10,000	40.00	40.00
87-01-010	Black Peter	S. Morton	10,000	40.00	40.00
87-01-011	Victorian	S. Morton	Retrd.	40.00	40.00
87-01-012	Wassail	S. Morton	Retrd.	40.00	40.00
XX-01-013	Collection of 12 Plates	S. Morton	Retrd.	480.00	480.00
Enesco Corporation		**Precious Moments Inspired Thoughts**			
85-01-001	Love One Another-E-5215	S. Butcher	15,000	40.00	65.00
82-01-002	Make a Joyful Noise-E-7174	S. Butcher	15,000	40.00	40.00
83-01-003	I Believe In Miracles-E-9257	S. Butcher	15,000	40.00	40.00
84-01-004	Love is Kind-E-2847	S. Butcher	15,000	40.00	45.00
Enesco Corporation		**Precious Moments Mother's Love**			
81-02-001	Mother Sew Dear-E-5217	S. Butcher	15,000	40.00	70.00
82-02-002	The Purr-fect Grandma-E-7173	S. Butcher	15,000	40.00	40.00
83-02-003	The Hand that Rocks the Future-E-9256	S. Butcher	15,000	40.00	40.00
84-02-004	Loving Thy Neighbor-E-2848	S. Butcher	15,000	40.00	40.00
Enesco Corporation		**Precious Moments Christmas Collection**			
81-03-001	Come Let Us Adore Him-E-5646	S. Butcher	15,000	40.00	60-65.00
82-03-002	Let Heaven and Nature Sing-E-2347	S. Butcher	15,000	40.00	45.00
83-03-003	Wee Three Kings-E-0538	S. Butcher	15,000	40.00	50.00
84-03-004	Unto Us a Child Is Born-E-5395	S. Butcher	15,000	40.00	40-45.00
Enesco Corporation		**Precious Moments Joy of Christmas**			
82-04-001	I'll Play My Drum For Him-E-2357	S. Butcher	Yr.Iss.	40.00	90.00
83-04-002	Christmastime is for Sharing-E-0505	S. Butcher	Yr.Iss.	40.00	90.00
84-04-003	The Wonder of Christmas-E-5396	S. Butcher	Yr.Iss.	40.00	70.00
85-04-004	Tell Me the Story of Jesus-15237	S. Butcher	Yr.Iss.	40.00	90-105.00
Enesco Corporation		**Precious Moments The Four Seasons**			
85-05-001	The Voice of Spring-12106	S. Butcher	Yr.Iss.	40.00	80-90.00
85-05-002	Summer's Joy-12114	S. Butcher	Yr.Iss.	40.00	75-80.00
86-05-003	Autumn's Praise-12122	S. Butcher	Yr.Iss.	40.00	55-100.00
86-05-004	Winter's Song-12130	S. Butcher	Yr.Iss.	40.00	60-65.00
Enesco Corporation		**Precious Moments Open Editions**			
82-06-001	Our First Christmas Together-E-2378	S. Butcher	Suspd.	30.00	45-55.00
81-06-002	The Lord Bless You and Keep You-E-5216	S. Butcher	Suspd.	30.00	40-45.00
82-06-003	Rejoicing with You-E-7172	S. Butcher	Suspd.	30.00	40.00
83-06-004	Jesus Loves Me-E-9275	S. Butcher	Suspd.	30.00	45.00
83-06-005	Jesus Loves Me-E-9276	S. Butcher	Suspd.	30.00	45.00
Enesco Corporation		**Precious Moments Christmas Love**			
86-07-001	I'm Sending You a White Christmas-101834	S. Butcher	Yr.Iss.	45.00	75.00
87-07-002	My Peace I Give Unto Thee-102954	S. Butcher	Yr.Iss.	45.00	95.00
88-07-003	Merry Christmas Deer-520284	S. Butcher	Yr.Iss.	50.00	80.00
89-07-004	May Your Christmas Be A Happy Home-523003	S. Butcher	Yr.Iss.	50.00	75.00
Enesco Corporation		**Precious Moments Christmas Blessings**			
90-08-001	Wishing You A Yummy Christmas-523801	S. Butcher	Yr.Iss.	50.00	70.00
91-08-002	Blessings From Me To Thee-523860	S. Butcher	Yr.Iss.	50.00	60.00
92-08-003	But The Greatest of These Is Love-527742	S. Butcher	Yr.Iss.	50.00	50.00
Ernst Enterprises		**Women of the West**			
79-01-001	Expectations	D. Putnam	10,000	39.50	39.50
81-01-002	Silver Dollar Sal	D. Putnam	10,000	39.50	45.00
82-01-003	School Marm	D. Putnam	10,000	39.50	39.50
83-01-004	Dolly	D. Putnam	10,000	39.50	39.50

Company Number	Name	Series Artist	Edition Limit	Issue Price	Quote
Ernst Enterprises		**A Beautiful World**			
81-02-001	Tahitian Dreamer	S. Morton	27,500	27.50	30.00
82-02-002	Flirtation	S. Morton	27,500	27.50	27.50
84-02-003	Elke of Oslo	S. Morton	27,500	27.50	27.50
Ernst Enterprises		**Seems Like Yesterday**			
81-03-001	Stop & Smell the Roses	R. Money	10-day	24.50	24.50
82-03-002	Home by Lunch	R. Money	10-day	24.50	24.50
82-03-003	Lisa's Creek	R. Money	10-day	24.50	24.50
83-03-004	It's Got My Name on It	R. Money	10-day	24.50	24.50
83-03-005	My Magic Hat	R. Money	10-day	24.50	24.50
84-03-006	Little Prince	R. Money	10-day	24.50	24.50
Ernst Enterprises		**Turn of The Century**			
81-04-001	Riverboat Honeymoon	R. Money	10-day	35.00	35.00
82-04-002	Children's Carousel	R. Money	10-day	35.00	37.50
84-04-003	Flower Market	R. Money	10-day	35.00	35.00
85-04-004	Balloon Race	R. Money	10-day	35.00	35.00
Ernst Enterprises		**Hollywood Greats**			
81-05-001	John Wayne	S. Morton	27,500	29.95	50-165.00
81-05-002	Gary Cooper	S. Morton	27,500	29.95	32.50
82-05-003	Clark Gable	S. Morton	27,500	29.95	65-85.00
84-05-004	Alan Ladd	S. Morton	27,500	29.95	95.00
Ernst Enterprises		**Commemoratives**			
81-06-001	John Lennon	S. Morton	30-day	39.50	155.00
82-06-002	Elvis Presley	S. Morton	30-day	39.50	150.00
82-06-003	Marilyn Monroe	S. Morton	30-day	39.50	75.00
83-06-004	Judy Garland	S. Morton	30-day	39.50	75.00
84-06-005	John Wayne	S. Morton	2,500	39.50	75.00
Ernst Enterprises		**Classy Cars**			
82-07-001	The 26T	S. Kuhnly	20-day	24.50	32.00
82-07-002	The 31A	S. Kuhnly	20-day	24.50	30.00
83-07-003	The Pickup	S. Kuhnly	20-day	24.50	27.50
84-07-004	Panel Van	S. Kuhnly	20-day	24.50	35.00
Ernst Enterprises		**Star Trek**			
84-08-001	Mr. Spock	S. Morton	90-day	29.50	150.00
85-08-002	Dr. McCoy	S. Morton	90-day	29.50	95.00
85-08-003	Sulu	S. Morton	90-day	29.50	75.00
85-08-004	Scotty	S. Morton	90-day	29.50	85.00
85-08-005	Uhura	S. Morton	90-day	29.50	75.00
85-08-006	Chekov	S. Morton	90-day	29.50	75.00
85-08-007	Captain Kirk	S. Morton	90-day	29.50	150.00
85-08-008	Beam Us Down Scotty	S. Morton	90-day	29.50	125.00
85-08-009	The Enterprise	S. Morton	90-day	39.50	85-150.00
Ernst Enterprises		**Elvira**			
86-09-001	Night Rose	S. Morton	90-day	29.50	29.50
Fairmont		**Spencer Special**			
78-01-001	Hug Me	I. Spencer	10,000	55.00	150.00
78-01-002	Sleep Little Baby	I. Spencer	10,000	65.00	125.00
Fairmont		**Famous Clowns**			
76-02-001	Freddie the Freeloader	R. Skelton	10,000	55.00	400-550.
77-02-002	W. C. Fields	R. Skelton	10,000	55.00	99.00
78-02-003	Happy	R. Skelton	10,000	55.00	110.00
79-02-004	The Pledge	R. Skelton	10,000	55.00	99.00
Fenton Art Glass		**American Craftsman Carnival**			
70-01-001	Glassmaker	Unknown	600	10.00	140.00
70-01-002	Glassmaker	Unknown	200	10.00	220.00
70-01-003	Glassmaker	Unknown	Annual	10.00	68.00
71-01-004	Printer	Unknown	Annual	10.00	80.00
72-01-005	Blacksmith	Unknown	Annual	10.00	150.00
73-01-006	Shoemaker	Unknown	Annual	12.50	70.00
74-01-007	Cooper	Unknown	Annual	12.50	55.00
75-01-008	Silversmith Revere	Unknown	Annual	12.50	60.00
76-01-009	Gunsmith	Unknown	Annual	15.00	45.00
77-01-010	Potter	Unknown	Annual	15.00	35.00
78-01-011	Wheelwright	Unknown	Annual	15.00	25.00
79-01-012	Cabinetmaker	Unknown	Annual	15.00	23.00
80-01-013	Tanner	Unknown	Annual	16.50	20.00
81-01-014	Housewright	Unknown	Annual	17.50	18.00
Fitz and Floyd, Inc.		**Fitz and Floyd Annual Christmas Plate**			
92-01-001	Nutcracker Sweets "The Magic of the Nutcracker"	R. Havins	Closed	65.00	65.00
93-01-002	Charles Dickens' "A Christmas Carol"	T. Kerr	5,000	70.00	70.00
Fitz and Floyd, Inc.		**Wonderland**			
93-02-001	A Mad Tea Party	R. Havins	5,000	70.00	70.00
Fitz and Floyd, Inc.		**The Twelve Days of Christmas**			
93-03-001	A Partridge in a Pear Tree	T. Kerr	5,000	70.00	70.00
Fitz and Floyd, Inc.		**The Myth of Santa Claus**			
93-04-001	Russian Santa	R. Havins	5,000	70.00	70.00
Flambro Imports		**Emmett Kelly, Jr. Plates**			
83-01-001	Why Me? Plate I	C. Kelly	10,000	40.00	348-400.
84-01-002	Balloons For Sale Plate II	C. Kelly	10,000	40.00	300.00
85-01-003	Big Business Plate III	C. Kelly	10,000	40.00	228-300.
86-01-004	And God Bless America IV	C. Kelly	10,000	40.00	300.
88-01-005	Tis the Season	D. Rust	10,000	40.00	40-75.00
89-01-006	Looking Back- 65th Birthday	D. Rust	6,500	50.00	150-200.
91-01-007	Winter	D. Rust	10,000	60.00	60.00
92-01-008	Spring	D. Rust	10,000	60.00	60.00
92-01-009	Summer	D. Rust	10,000	60.00	60.00
92-01-010	Autumn	D. Rust	10,000	60.00	60.00
Flambro Imports		**Raggedy Ann & Andy**			
88-02-001	70 Years Young	C. Beylon	10,000	35.00	55-59.00
Fleetwood Collection		**Christmas**			
80-01-001	The Magi	F. Wenger	5,000	45.00	75.00
81-01-002	The Holy Child	F. Wenger	7,500	49.50	58.00
82-01-003	The Shepherds	F. Wenger	5,000	50.00	50.00
85-01-004	Coming Home for Christmas	F. Jacques	5,000	50.00	50.00

Company		Series			
Number	**Name**	**Artist**	**Edition Limit**	**Issue Price**	**Quote**
Fleetwood Collection		**Mother's Day**			
80-02-001	Cottontails	D. Balke	5,000	45.00	75.00
81-02-002	Raccoons	D. Balke	5,000	45.00	58.00
82-02-003	Whitetail Deer	D. Balke	5,000	50.00	50.00
83-02-004	Canada Geese	D. Balke	5,000	50.00	50.00
Fleetwood Collection		**Royal Wedding**			
81-03-001	Prince Charles/Lady Diana	J. Mathews	9,500	49.50	75.00
86-03-002	Prince Andrew/Sarah Ferguson	J. Mathews	10,000	50.00	50.00
Fleetwood Collection		**Statue of Liberty**			
86-04-001	Statue of Liberty Plate	J. Mathews	10,000	50.00	50.00
Fountainhead		**The Wings of Freedom**			
85-01-001	Courtship Flight	M. Fernandez	2,500	250.00	2400.00
86-01-002	Wings of Freedom	M. Fernandez	2,500	250.00	1100.00
Fountainhead		**As Free As The Wind**			
89-02-001	As Free As The Wind	M. Fernandez	Unkn.	295.00	300-600.
Fukagawa		**Warabe No Haiku Series**			
77-01-001	Beneath The Plum Branch	Suetomi	Undis.	38.00	45.00
78-01-002	Child of Straw	Suetomi	Undis.	42.00	47.50
79-01-003	Dragon Dance	Suetomi	Undis.	42.00	45.00
80-01-004	Mask Dancing	Suetomi	Undis.	42.00	90.00
Gartlan USA, Inc.		**Pete Rose Platinum Edition**			
85-01-001	Pete Rose "The Best of Baseball"(3 1/4")	T. Sizemore	Open	12.95	19.00
85-01-002	Pete Rose "The Best of Baseball"(10 1/4")	T. Sizemore	4,192	100.00	300-600.
Gartlan USA, Inc.		**The Round Tripper**			
86-02-001	Reggie Jackson (3 1/4" diameter)	J. Martin	Open	12.95	19.00
Gartlan USA, Inc.		**George Brett Gold Crown Collection**			
86-03-001	George Brett "Baseball's All Star"(3 1/4")	J. Martin	Open	12.95	19.00
86-03-002	George Brett "Baseball's All Star"(10 1/4") signed	J. Martin	2,000	100.00	200-400.
Gartlan USA, Inc.		**Roger Staubach Sterling Collection**			
87-04-001	Roger Staubach (3 1/4" diameter)	C. Soileau	Open	12.95	19.00
87-04-002	Roger Staubach (10 1/4" diameter), signed	C. Soileau	1,979	100.00	100-150.
Gartlan USA, Inc.		**Magic Johnson Gold Rim Collection**			
87-05-001	Magic Johnson-"The Magic Show"(10 1/4") signed	R. Winslow	1,987	100.00	300-600.
87-05-002	Magic Johnson-"The Magic Show"(3 1/4")	R. Winslow	Closed	14.50	25-35.00
Gartlan USA, Inc.		**Mike Schmidt "500th" Home Run Edition**			
87-06-001	Mike Schmidt-"Power at the Plate"(10 1/4") signed	C. Paluso	1,987	100.00	280-450.
87-06-002	Mike Schmidt-"Power at the Plate"(3 1/4")	C. Paluso	Open	14.50	19.00
87-06-003	Mike Schmidt, Artist Proof	C. Paluso	56	150.00	150.00
Gartlan USA, Inc.		**Pete Rose Diamond Collection**			
88-07-001	Pete Rose-"The Reigning Legend" (10 1/4"), signed	Forbes	950	195.00	225-250.
88-07-002	Pete Rose-"The Reigning Legend" (10 1/4"), signed, Artist Proof	Forbes	50	300.00	450.00
88-07-003	Pete Rose-"The Reigning Legend"(3 1/4")	Forbes	Open	14.50	19.00
Gartlan USA, Inc		**Kareem Abdul-Jabbar Sky-Hook Collection**			
89-08-001	Kareem Abdul-Jabbar- "Path of Glory" (10 1/4"), signed	M. Taylor	1,989	100.00	200-300.
89-08-002	Collector plate (3 1/4")	M. Taylor	Closed	16.00	18.00
Gartlan USA, Inc.		**Johnny Bench**			
89-09-001	Collector Plate (10 1/4"), signed	M. Taylor	1,989	100.00	150-250.
89-09-002	Collector Plate (3 1/4"),	M. Taylor	Open	16.00	19.00
Gartlan USA, Inc.		**Coaching Classics-John Wooden**			
89-10-001	Collector Plate (10 1/4"), signed	M. Taylor	1,975	100.00	100.00
89-10-002	Collector Plate (8 1/2")	M. Taylor	10,000	45.00	45.00
89-10-003	Collector Plate (3 1/4")	M. Taylor	Open	16.00	19.00
Gartlan USA, Inc.		**Wayne Gretzky**			
89-11-001	Collector Plate (10 1/4") signed by Gretzky and Howe	M. Taylor	1,851	225.00	225-450.
89-11-002	Collector Plate (10 1/4") Artist Proof, signed by Gretzky and Howe	M. Taylor	300	300.00	425-500.
89-11-003	Collector Plate (8 1/2")	M. Taylor	10,000	45.00	45-75.00
89-11-004	Collector Plate (3 1/4")	M. Taylor	Open	16.00	19.00
Gartlan USA, Inc.		**Yogi Berra**			
89-12-001	Collector Plate (10 1/4"), signed	M. Taylor	2,150	125.00	125-150.
89-12-002	Collector Plate (10 1/4"), signed, Artist Proof	M. Taylor	250	175.00	175.00
89-12-003	Collector Plate (3 1/4")	M. Taylor	Open	16.00	19.00
89-12-004	Collector Plate (8 1/2")	M. Taylor	10,000	45.00	45.00
Gartlan USA, Inc.		**Whitey Ford**			
90-13-001	Signed Plate (10 1/4")	M. Taylor	2,360	125.00	125-150.
90-13-002	Signed Plate (10 1/4"), Artist Proof	M. Taylor	250	175.00	175.00
90-13-003	Plate (8 1/2")	M. Taylor	10,000	45.00	45.00
90-13-004	Plate (3 1/4")	M. Taylor	Open	16.00	19.00
Gartlan USA, Inc.		**Darryl Strawberry**			
90-14-001	Signed Plate (10 1/4")	M. Taylor	2,500	125.00	125.00
90-14-002	Plate (8 1/2")	M. Taylor	10,000	45.00	45.00
90-14-003	Plate (3 1/4")	M. Taylor	Open	16.00	19.00
Gartlan USA, Inc.		**Luis Aparicio**			
90-15-001	Signed Plate (10 1/4")	M. Taylor	1,984	125.00	125.00
90-15-002	Signed Plate (10 1/4"), Artist Proof	M. Taylor	250	150.00	150.00
90-15-003	Plate (8 1/2")	M. Taylor	10,000	45.00	45.00
90-15-004	Plate (3 1/4")	M. Taylor	Open	16.00	19.00
Gartlan USA, Inc.		**Rod Carew**			
91-16-001	Hitting For The Hall(10 1/4"), signed	M. Taylor	950	150.00	150.00
91-16-002	Hitting For The Hall(8 1/2")	M. Taylor	10,000	45.00	45.00
91-16-003	Hitting For The Hall(3 1/4")	M. Taylor	Open	16.00	19.00
Gartlan USA, Inc.		**Brett & Bobby Hull**			
91-17-001	Hockey's Golden Boys(10 1/4"), signed	M. Taylor	950	250.00	250-400.
92-17-002	Plate, Artist Proof	M. Taylor	300	350.00	350.00
91-17-003	Hockey's Golden Boys(8 1/2")	M. Taylor	10,000	45.00	45.00
91-17-004	Hockey's Golden Boys(3 1/4")	M. Taylor	Open	16.00	19.00
Gartlan USA, Inc.		**Joe Montana**			
91-18-001	Signed Plate (10 1/4")	M. Taylor	2,250	125.00	125.00
91-18-002	Signed Plate (10 1/4"), Artist Proof	M. Taylor	250	195.00	195.00
91-18-003	Plate (8 1/2")	M. Taylor	10,000	45.00	45.00
91-18-004	Plate (3 1/4")	M. Taylor	Open	16.00	19.00
Gartlan USA, Inc.		**Al Barlick**			
91-19-001	Plate (3 1/4")	M. Taylor	Open	16.00	19.00
Gartlan USA, Inc.		**Carlton Fisk**			
92-20-001	Signed Plate (10 1/4")	M. Taylor	950	150.00	150.00
92-20-002	Signed Plate (10 1/4"), Artist Proof	M. Taylor	300	175.00	225.00
92-20-003	Plate (8 1/2")	M. Taylor	10,000	45.00	45.00
92-20-004	Plate (3 1/4")	M. Taylor	Open	19.00	19.00
Gartlan USA, Inc.		**Ken Griffey Jr.**			
92-21-001	Signed Plate (10 1/4")	M. Taylor	1,989	125.00	125.00
92-21-002	Signed Plate (10 1/2"), Artist Proof	M. Taylor	300	195.00	195.00
92-21-003	Plate (8 1/2")	M. Taylor	10,000	45.00	45.00
92-21-004	Plate (3 1/4")	M. Taylor	Open	19.00	19.00
Gartlan USA, Inc.		**Phil Esposito**			
92-22-001	Signed Plate (10 1/4")	M. Taylor	1,984	150.00	150.00
92-22-002	Signed Plate (10 1/2"), Artist Proof	M. Taylor	300	195.00	195.00
92-22-003	Plate (8 1/2")	M. Taylor	10,000	49.00	49.00
92-22-004	Plate (3 1/4")	M. Taylor	Open	19.00	19.00
Gartlan USA, Inc.		**Carl Yastrzemski**			
92-23-001	Signed Plate (10 1/4")	M. Taylor	1,989	150.00	150.00
92-23-002	Signed Plate (10 1/2"), Artist Proof	M. Taylor	300	195.00	195.00
92-23-003	Plate (8 1/2")	M. Taylor	10,000	49.00	49.00
92-23-004	Plate (3 1/4")	M. Taylor	Open	19.00	19.00
Gartlan USA, Inc.		**Tom Seaver**			
92-24-001	Signed Plate (10 1/4")	M. Taylor	1,992	150.00	150-195.
92-24-002	Signed Plate (10 1/4"), Artist Proof	M. Taylor	250	195.00	195.00
92-24-003	Signed Plate (8 1/2")	M. Taylor	10,000	45.00	45.00
92-24-004	Signed Plate (3 1/4)	M. Taylor	Open	19.00	19.00
Gartlan USA, Inc.		**Gordie Howe**			
92-25-001	Signed Plate (10 1/4")	M. Taylor	2,358	150.00	150.00
92-25-002	Signed Plate (10 1/4"), Artist Proof	M. Taylor	250	195.00	195.00
92-25-003	Signed Plate (8 1/2")	M. Taylor	10,000	45.00	45.00
92-25-004	Signed Plate (3 1/4")	M. Taylor	Open	19.00	19.00
W. S. George		**Gone With the Wind: Golden Anniversary**			
88-01-001	Scarlett and Her Suitors	H. Rogers	150-day	24.50	75-149.00
88-01-002	The Burning of Atlanta	H. Rogers	150-day	24.50	85-125.00
88-01-003	Scarlett and Ashley After the War	H. Rogers	150-day	27.50	90-110.00
88-01-004	The Proposal	H. Rogers	150-day	27.50	125.00
89-01-005	Home to Tara	H. Rogers	150-day	27.50	55-89.00
89-01-006	Strolling in Atlanta	H. Rogers	150-day	27.50	45-89.00
89-01-007	A Question of Honor	H. Rogers	150-day	29.50	68-89.00
89-01-008	Scarlett's Resolve	H. Rogers	150-day	29.50	90-125.00
89-01-009	Frankly My Dear	H. Rogers	150-day	29.50	50-65.00
89-01-010	Melane and Ashley	H. Rogers	150-day	32.50	32.50
90-01-011	A Toast to Bonnie Blue	H. Rogers	150-day	32.50	32.50
90-01-012	Scarlett and Rhett's Honeymoon	H. Rogers	150-day	32.50	32.50
W. S. George		**Scenes of Christmas Past**			
87-02-001	Holiday Skaters	L. Garrison	150-day	27.50	50-75.00
88-02-002	Christmas Eve	L. Garrison	150-day	27.50	45-50.00
89-02-003	The Homecoming	L. Garrison	150-day	30.50	35-60.00
90-02-004	The Toy Store	L. Garrison	150-day	30.50	30-45.00
91-02-005	The Carollers	L. Garrison	150-day	30.50	45-50.00
92-02-006	Family Traditions	L. Garrison	150-day	32.50	32.50
W. S. George		**On Gossamer Wings**			
88-03-001	Monarch Butterflies	L. Liu	150-day	24.50	38-50.00
88-03-002	Western Tiger Swallowtails	L. Liu	150-day	24.50	30-47.00
88-03-003	Red-Spotted Purple	L. Liu	150-day	27.50	35-49.00
88-03-004	Malachites	L. Liu	150-day	27.50	40.00
88-03-005	White Peacocks	L. Liu	150-day	27.50	36.00
89-03-006	Eastern Tailed Blues	L. Liu	150-day	27.50	49.00
89-03-007	Zebra Swallowtails	L. Liu	150-day	29.50	37.50
89-03-008	Red Admirals	L. Liu	150-day	29.50	35.00
W. S. George		**Flowers of Your Garden**			
88-04-001	Roses	V. Morley	150-day	24.50	42-69.00
88-04-002	Lilacs	V. Morley	150-day	24.50	70-95.00
88-04-003	Daisies	V. Morley	150-day	27.50	40-55.00
88-04-004	Peonies	V. Morley	150-day	27.50	30-60.00
88-04-005	Chrysanthemums	V. Morley	150-day	27.50	30-45.00
89-04-006	Daffodils	V. Morley	150-day	27.50	30-55.00
89-04-007	Tulips	V. Morley	150-day	29.50	30-55.00
89-04-008	Irises	V. Morley	150-day	29.50	35-65.00
W. S. George		**Beloved Hymns of Childhood**			
88-05-001	The Lord's My Shepherd	C. Barker	150-day	29.50	57.00
88-05-002	Away In a Manger	C. Barker	150-day	29.50	31.00
89-05-003	Now Thank We All Our God	C. Barker	150-day	32.50	32.50
89-05-004	Love Divine	C. Barker	150-day	32.50	32.50
89-05-005	I Love to Hear the Story	C. Barker	150-day	32.50	32.50
89-05-006	All Glory, Laud and Honour	C. Barker	150-day	32.50	32.50
90-05-007	All People on Earth Do Dwell	C. Barker	150-day	34.50	34.50
90-05-008	Loving Shepherd of Thy Sheep	C. Barker	150-day	34.50	34.50
W. S. George		**Classic Waterfowl: The Ducks Unlimited**			
88-06-001	Mallards at Sunrise	L. Kaatz	150-day	36.50	70.00
88-06-002	Geese in the Autumn Fields	L. Kaatz	150-day	36.50	40-45.00
89-06-003	Green Wings/Morning Marsh	L. Kaatz	150-day	39.50	45-50.00
89-06-004	Canvasbacks, Breaking Away	L. Kaatz	150-day	39.50	39-50.00
89-06-005	Pintails in Indian Summer	L. Kaatz	150-day	39.50	39.50
90-06-006	Wood Ducks Taking Flight	L. Kaatz	150-day	39.50	60.00
90-06-007	Snow Geese Against November Skies	L. Kaatz	150-day	41.50	45.00
90-06-008	Bluebills Comin In	L. Kaatz	150-day	41.50	41.50
W. S. George		**The Elegant Birds**			
88-07-001	The Swan	J. Faulkner	150-day	32.50	35-39.00
88-07-002	Great Blue Heron	J. Faulkner	150-day	32.50	35.50

Company / Number	Name / Series	Artist	Edition Limit	Issue Price	Quote
89-07-003	Snowy Egret	J. Faulkner	150-day	32.50	40-45.00
89-07-004	The Anhinga	J. Faulkner	150-day	35.50	35-40.00
89-07-005	The Flamingo	J. Faulkner	150-day	35.50	35-40.00
90-07-006	Sandhill and Whooping Crane	J. Faulkner	150-day	35.50	35-40.00
W. S. George	**Last of Their Kind: The Endangered Species**				
88-08-001	The Panda	W. Nelson	150-day	27.50	50-75.00
89-08-002	The Snow Leopard	W. Nelson	150-day	27.50	35-55.00
89-08-003	The Red Wolf	W. Nelson	150-day	30.50	35-40.00
89-08-004	The Asian Elephant	W. Nelson	150-day	30.50	30-45.00
90-08-005	The Slender-Horned Gazelle	W. Nelson	150-day	30.50	35.00
90-08-006	The Bridled Wallaby	W. Nelson	150-day	30.50	30.50
90-08-007	The Black-Footed Ferret	W. Nelson	150-day	33.50	33.50
90-08-008	The Siberian Tiger	W. Nelson	150-day	33.50	33.50
91-08-009	The Vicuna	W. Nelson	150-day	33.50	33.50
91-08-010	Przewalski's Horse	W. Nelson	150-day	33.50	33.50
W. S. George	**America the Beautiful**				
88-09-001	Yosemite Falls	H. Johnson	150-day	34.50	45-49.00
89-09-002	The Grand Canyon	H. Johnson	150-day	34.50	38.00
89-09-003	Yellowstone River	H. Johnson	150-day	37.50	39.00
89-09-004	The Great Smokey Mountains	H. Johnson	150-day	37.50	45.00
90-09-005	The Everglades	H. Johnson	150-day	37.50	45.00
90-09-006	Acadia	H. Johnson	150-day	37.50	45.00
90-09-007	The Grand Tetons	H. Johnson	150-day	39.50	65.00
90-09-008	Crater Lake	H. Johnson	150-day	39.50	49.00
W. S. George	**Bonds of Love**				
89-10-001	Precious Embrace	B. Burke	150-day	29.50	45-60.00
90-10-002	Cherished Moment	B. Burke	150-day	29.50	37-59.00
91-10-003	Tender Caress	B. Burke	150-day	32.50	40-69.00
92-10-004	Loving Touch	B. Burke	150-day	32.50	39-45.00
W. S. George	**The Golden Age of the Clipper Ships**				
89-11-001	The Twilight Under Full Sail	C. Vickery	150-day	29.50	31-39.00
89-11-002	The Blue Jacket at Sunset	C. Vickery	150-day	29.50	35.00
89-11-003	Young America, Homeward	C. Vickery	150-day	32.50	38.00
90-11-004	Flying Cloud	C. Vickery	150-day	32.50	50.00
90-11-005	Davy Crocket at Daybreak	C. Vickery	150-day	32.50	45.00
90-11-006	Golden Eagle Conquers Wind	C. Vickery	150-day	32.50	40.00
90-11-007	The Lightning in Lifting Fog	C. Vickery	150-day	34.50	34.50
90-11-008	Sea Witch, Mistress/Oceans	C. Vickery	150-day	34.50	34.50
W. S. George	**Romantic Gardens**				
89-12-001	The Woodland Garden	C. Smith	150-day	29.50	29.50
89-12-002	The Plantation Garden	C. Smith	150-day	29.50	29.50
90-12-003	The Cottage Garden	C. Smith	150-day	32.50	55.00
90-12-004	The Colonial Garden	C. Smith	150-day	32.50	32.50
W. S. George	**Country Nostalgia**				
89-13-001	The Spring Buggy	M. Harvey	150-day	29.50	36.00
89-13-002	The Apple Cider Press	M. Harvey	150-day	29.50	45.00
89-13-003	The Vintage Seed Planter	M. Harvey	150-day	29.50	45.00
89-13-004	The Old Hand Pump	M. Harvey	150-day	32.50	40-45.00
90-13-005	The Wooden Butter Churn	M. Harvey	150-day	32.50	45-49.00
90-13-006	The Dairy Cans	M. Harvey	150-day	32.50	32.50
90-13-007	The Forgotten Plow	M. Harvey	150-day	34.50	44-48.00
90-13-008	The Antique Spinning Wheel	M. Harvey	150-day	34.50	36.00
W. S. George	**Hollywood's Glamour Girls**				
89-14-001	Jean Harlow-Dinner at Eight	E. Dzenis	150-day	24.50	50.00
90-14-002	Lana Turner-Postman Ring Twice	E. Dzenis	150-day	29.50	40-49.00
90-14-003	Carol Lombard-The Gay Bride	E. Dzenis	150-day	29.50	40.00
90-14-004	Greta Garbo-In Grand Hotel	E. Dzenis	150-day	29.50	60-69.00
W. S. George	**Purebred Horses of the Americas**				
89-15-001	The Appalosa	D. Schwartz	150-day	34.50	34.50
89-15-002	The Tenessee Walker	D. Schwartz	150-day	34.50	34.50
90-15-003	The Quarterhorse	D. Schwartz	150-day	37.50	45.00
90-15-004	The Saddlebred	D. Schwartz	150-day	37.50	55.00
90-15-005	The Mustang	D. Schwartz	150-day	37.50	60.00
90-15-006	The Morgan	D. Schwartz	150-day	37.50	76.00
W. S. George	**Nature's Poetry**				
89-16-001	Morning Serenade	L. Liu	150-day	24.50	45.00
89-16-002	Song of Promise	L. Liu	150-day	24.50	35-40.00
90-16-003	Tender Lullaby	L. Liu	150-day	27.50	45-57.00
90-16-004	Nature's Harmony	L. Liu	150-day	27.50	40-42.00
90-16-005	Gentle Refrain	L. Liu	150-day	27.50	30-54.00
90-16-006	Morning Chorus	L. Liu	150-day	27.50	45.00
90-16-007	Melody at Daybreak	L. Liu	150-day	29.50	30.00
91-16-008	Delicate Accord	L. Liu	150-day	29.50	30.00
91-16-009	Lyrical Beginnings	L. Liu	150-day	29.50	30.00
91-16-010	Song of Spring	L. Liu	150-day	32.50	32.50
91-16-011	Mother's Melody	L. Liu	150-day	32.50	32.50
91-16-012	Cherub Chorale	L. Liu	150-day	32.50	32.50
W. S. George	**Art Deco**				
89-17-001	A Flapper With Greyhounds	M. McDonald	150-day	39.50	50-57.00
90-17-002	Tango Dancers	M. McDonald	150-day	39.50	50-65.00
90-17-003	Arriving in Style	M. McDonald	150-day	39.50	69-79.00
90-17-004	On the Town	M. McDonald	150-day	39.50	59-90.00
W. S. George	**Our Woodland Friends**				
89-18-001	Fascination	C. Brenders	150-day	29.50	47-50.00
90-18-002	Beneath the Pines	C. Brenders	150-day	29.50	35-45.00
90-18-003	High Adventure	C. Brenders	150-day	32.50	35.00
90-18-004	Shy Explorers	C. Brenders	150-day	32.50	40.00
91-18-005	Golden Season:Gray Squirrel	C. Brenders	150-day	32.50	35.00
91-18-006	Full House Fox Family	C. Brenders	150-day	32.50	45.00
91-18-007	A Jump Into Life: Spring Fawn	C. Brenders	150-day	34.50	34.50
91-18-008	Forest Sentinel:Bobcat	C. Brenders	150-day	34.50	34.50
W. S. George	**The Federal Duck Stamp Plate Collection**				
90-19-001	The Lesser Scaup	N. Anderson	150-day	27.50	45-50.00
90-19-002	Mallard	N. Anderson	150-day	27.50	55.00
90-19-003	The Ruddy Ducks	N. Anderson	150-day	30.50	45.00
90-19-004	Canvasbacks	N. Anderson	150-day	30.50	55.00
91-19-005	Pintails	N. Anderson	150-day	30.50	30.50
91-19-006	Wigeons	N. Anderson	150-day	30.50	30.50
91-19-007	Cinnamon Teal	N. Anderson	150-day	32.50	32.50
91-19-008	Fulvous Wistling Duck	N. Anderson	150-day	32.50	32.50
91-19-009	The Redheads	N. Anderson	150-day	32.50	32.50
91-19-010	Snow Goose	N. Anderson	150-day	32.50	32.50
W. S. George	**Dr. Zhivago**				
90-20-001	Zhivago and Lara	G. Bush	150-day	39.50	45.00
91-20-002	Love Poems For Lara	G. Bush	150-day	39.50	49.00
91-20-003	Zhivago Says Farewell	G. Bush	150-day	39.50	39.50
91-20-004	Lara's Love	G. Bush	150-day	39.50	39.50
W. S. George	**Blessed Are The Children**				
90-21-001	Let the/Children Come To Me	W. Rane	150-day	29.50	30-40.00
90-21-002	I Am the Good Shepherd	W. Rane	150-day	29.50	29.50
91-21-003	Whoever Welcomes/Child	W. Rane	150-day	32.50	33-51.00
91-21-004	Hosanna in the Highest	W. Rane	150-day	32.50	32.50
91-21-005	Jesus Had Compassion on Them	W. Rane	150-day	32.50	32.50
91-21-006	Blessed are the Peacemakers	W. Rane	150-day	34.50	34.50
91-21-007	I am the Vine, You are the Branches	W. Rane	150-day	34.50	34.50
91-21-008	Seek and You Will Find	W. Rane	150-day	34.50	34.50
W. S. George	**The Vanishing Gentle Giants**				
91-22-001	Jumping For Joy	A. Casay	150-day	32.50	75.00
91-22-002	Song of the Humpback	A. Casay	150-day	32.50	32.50
91-22-003	Monarch of the Deep	A. Casay	150-day	35.50	35.50
91-22-004	Travelers of the Sea	A. Casay	150-day	35.50	35.50
91-22-005	White Whale of the North	A. Casay	150-day	35.50	35.50
91-22-006	Unicorn of the Sea	A. Casay	150-day	35.50	35.50
W. S. George	**Spirit of Christmas**				
90-23-001	Silent Night	J. Sias	150-day	29.50	36-55.00
91-23-002	Jingle Bells	J. Sias	150-day	29.50	30-39.50
91-23-003	Deck The Halls	J. Sias	150-day	32.50	75.00
91-23-004	I'll Be Home For Christmas	J. Sias	150-day	32.50	60.00
91-23-005	Winter Wonderland	J. Sias	150-day	32.50	32.50
91-23-006	O Christmas Tree	J. Sias	150-day	32.50	32.50
W. S. George	**Flowers From Grandma's Garden**				
90-24-001	Country Cuttings	G. Kurz	150-day	24.50	45-59.00
90-24-002	The Morning Bouquet	G. Kurz	150-day	24.50	45-49.00
91-24-003	Homespun Beauty	G. Kurz	150-day	27.50	27.50
91-24-004	Harvest in the Meadow	G. Kurz	150-day	27.50	27.50
91-24-005	Gardener's Delight	G. Kurz	150-day	27.50	27.50
91-24-006	Nature's Bounty	G. Kurz	150-day	27.50	27.50
91-24-007	A Country Welcome	G. Kurz	150-day	29.50	29.50
91-24-008	The Springtime Arrangement	G. Kurz	150-day	29.50	29.50
W. S. George	**The Secret World Of The Panda**				
90-25-001	A Mother's Care	J. Bridgett	150-day	27.50	35-49.00
91-25-002	A Frolic in the Snow	J. Bridgett	150-day	27.50	27.50
91-25-003	Lazy Afternoon	J. Bridgett	150-day	30.50	30.50
91-25-004	A Day of Exploring	J. Bridgett	150-day	30.50	30.50
91-25-005	A Gentle Hug	J. Bridgett	150-day	32.50	32.50
91-25-006	A Bamboo Feast	J. Bridgett	150-day	32.50	32.50
W. S. George	**Wonders Of The Sea**				
91-26-001	Stand By Me	R.Harm	150-day	34.50	35-49.00
91-26-002	Heart to Heart	R.Harm	150-day	34.50	34.50
91-26-003	Warm Embrace	R.Harm	150-day	34.50	34.50
91-26-004	A Family Affair	R.Harm	150-day	34.50	34.50
W. S. George	**Critic's Choice: Gone With The Wind**				
91-27-001	Marry Me, Scarlett	P. Jennis	150-day	27.50	27.50
91-27-002	Waiting for Rhett	P. Jennis	150-day	27.50	27.50
91-27-003	A Declaration of Love	P. Jennis	150-day	30.50	30.50
91-27-004	The Paris Hat	P. Jennis	150-day	30.50	30.50
91-27-005	Scarlett Asks a Favor	P. Jennis	150-day	30.50	30.50
92-27-006	Scarlett Gets Her Way	P. Jennis	150-day	32.50	32.50
92-27-007	The Smitten Suitor	P. Jennis	150-day	32.50	32.50
92-27-008	Scarlett's Shopping Spree	P. Jennis	150-day	32.50	32.50
92-27-009	The Buggy Ride	P. Jennis	150-day	32.50	32.50
W. S. George	**Gone With The Wind: The Passions of Scarlett O'Hara**				
92-28-001	Fiery Embrace	P. Jennis	150-day	29.50	29.50
92-28-002	Pride and Passion	P. Jennis	150-day	29.50	29.50
92-28-003	Dreams of Ashley	P. Jennis	150-day	32.50	32.50
92-28-004	The Fond Farewell	P. Jennis	150-day	32.50	32.50
W. S. George	**Victorian Cat**				
90-29-001	Mischief With The Hatbox	H. Bonner	150-day	24.50	60.00
91-29-002	String Quartet	H. Bonner	150-day	24.50	24.50
91-29-003	Daydreams	H. Bonner	150-day	27.50	27.50
91-29-004	Frisky Felines	H. Bonner	150-day	27.50	27.50
91-29-005	Kittens at Play	H. Bonner	150-day	27.50	27.50
91-29-006	Playing in the Parlor	H. Bonner	150-day	29.50	29.50
91-29-007	Perfectly Poised	H. Bonner	150-day	29.50	29.50
92-29-008	Midday Repose	H. Bonner	150-day	29.50	29.50
W. S. George	**Victorian Cat Capers**				
92-30-001	Who's the Fairest of Them All?	F. Paton	150-day	24.50	24.50
92-30-002	Puss in Boots	Unknown	150-day	24.50	24.50
92-30-003	My Bowl is Empty	W. Hepple	150-day	27.50	27.50
W. S. George	**Glorious Songbirds**				
91-31-001	Cardinals on a Snowy Branch	R. Cobane	150-day	29.50	45.00
91-31-002	Indigo Buntings and/Blossoms	R. Cobane	150-day	29.50	29-35.00
91-31-003	Chickadees Among The Lilacs	R. Cobane	150-day	32.50	35.00
91-31-004	Goldfinches in/Thistle	R. Cobane	150-day	32.50	32.50
91-31-005	Cedar Waxwing/Winter Berries	R. Cobane	150-day	32.50	32.50
91-31-006	Bluebirds in a Blueberry Bush	R. Cobane	150-day	34.50	34.50
91-31-007	Baltimore Orioles/Autumn Leaves	R. Cobane	150-day	34.50	34.50
91-31-008	Robins with Dogwood in Bloom	R. Cobane	150-day	34.50	34.50
W. S. George	**Nature's Lovables**				
90-32-001	The Koala	C. Frace	150-day	27.50	50.00
91-32-002	New Arrival	C. Frace	150-day	27.50	27.50
91-32-003	Chinese Treasure	C. Frace	150-day	27.50	27.50
91-32-004	Baby Harp Seal	C. Frace	150-day	30.50	30.50
91-32-005	Bobcat: Nature's Dawn	C. Frace	150-day	30.50	30.50
91-32-006	Clouded Leopard	C. Frace	150-day	32.50	32.50
91-32-007	Zebra Foal	C. Frace	150-day	32.50	32.50
91-32-008	Bandit	C. Frace	150-day	32.50	32.50
W. S. George	**Soaring Majesty**				
91-33-001	Freedom	C. Frace	150-day	29.50	55.00
91-33-002	The Northern Goshhawk	C. Frace	150-day	29.50	45.00

Number	Name	Artist	Edition Limit	Issue Price	Quote
91-33-003	Peregrine Falcon	C. Frace	150-day	32.50	32.50
91-33-004	Red-Tailed Hawk	C. Frace	150-day	32.50	32.50
91-33-005	The Osprey	C. Frace	150-day	32.50	32.50
91-33-006	The Gyrfalcon	C. Frace	150-day	34.50	34.50
91-33-007	The Golden Eagle	C. Frace	150-day	34.50	34.50
92-33-008	Red-Shouldered Hawk	C. Frace	150-day	34.50	34.50
W. S. George		**The World's Most Magnificent Cats**			
91-34-001	Fleeting Encounter	C. Frace	150-day	24.50	40-60.00
91-34-002	Cougar	C. Frace	150-day	24.50	24.50
91-34-003	Royal Bengal	C. Frace	150-day	27.50	27.50
91-34-004	Powerful Presence	C. Frace	150-day	27.50	27.50
91-34-005	Jaguar	C. Frace	150-day	27.50	27.50
91-34-006	The Clouded Leopard	C. Frace	150-day	29.50	29.50
91-34-007	The African Leopard	C. Frace	150-day	29.50	29.50
91-34-008	Mighty Warrior	C. Frace	150-day	29.50	29.50
92-34-009	The Cheetah	C. Frace	150-day	31.50	31.50
92-34-010	Siberian Tiger	C. Frace	150-day	31.50	31.50
W. S. George		**A Loving Look: Duck Families**			
90-35-001	Family Outing	B. Langton	150-day	34.50	37.00
91-35-002	Sleepy Start	B. Langton	150-day	34.50	34.50
91-35-003	Quiet Moment	B. Langton	150-day	37.50	37.50
91-35-004	Safe and Sound	B. Langton	150-day	37.50	37.50
91-35-005	Spring Arrivals	B. Langton	150-day	37.50	37.50
91-35-006	The Family Tree	B. Langton	150-day	37.50	37.50
W. S. George		**Nature's Legacy**			
90-36-001	Blue Snow at Half Dome	J. Sias	150-day	24.50	40.00
91-36-002	Misty Morning/Mt. McKinley	J. Sias	150-day	24.50	24.50
91-36-003	Mount Ranier	J. Sias	150-day	27.50	27.50
91-36-004	Havasu Canyon	J. Sias	150-day	27.50	27.50
91-36-005	Autumn Splendor in the Smoky Mts.	J. Sias	150-day	27.50	27.50
91-36-006	Winter Peace in Yellowstone Park	J. Sias	150-day	29.50	29.50
91-36-007	Golden Majesty/Rocky Mountains	J. Sias	150-day	29.50	29.50
91-36-008	Radiant Sunset Over the Everglades	J. Sias	150-day	29.50	29.50
W. S. George		**Symphony of Shimmering Beauties**			
91-37-001	Iris Quartet	L. Liu	150-day	29.50	39.00
91-37-002	Tulip Ensemble	L. Liu	150-day	29.50	29.50
91-37-003	Poppy Pastorale	L. Liu	150-day	32.50	32.50
91-37-004	Lily Concerto	L. Liu	150-day	32.50	32.50
91-37-005	Peony Prelude	L. Liu	150-day	32.50	32.50
91-37-006	Rose Fantasy	L. Liu	150-day	34.50	34.50
91-37-007	Hibiscus Medley	L. Liu	150-day	34.50	34.50
92-37-008	Dahlia Melody	L. Liu	150-day	34.50	34.50
92-37-009	Hollyhock March	L. Liu	150-day	34.50	34.50
W. S. George		**Portraits of Christ**			
91-38-001	Father, Forgive Them	J. Salamanca	150-day	29.50	29.50
91-38-002	Thy Wil Be Done	J. Salamanca	150-day	29.50	29.50
91-38-003	This is My Beloved Son	J. Salamanca	150-day	32.50	32.50
91-38-004	Lo, I Am With You	J. Salamanca	150-day	32.50	32.50
91-38-005	Become as Little Children	J. Salamanca	150-day	32.50	32.50
91-38-006	Peace I Leave With You	J. Salamanca	150-day	34.50	34.50
92-38-007	For God So Loved the World	J. Salamanca	150-day	34.50	34.50
92-38-008	I Am the Way, the Truth and the Life	J. Salamanca	150-day	34.50	34.50
W. S. George		**Portraits of Exquisite Birds**			
90-39-001	Backyard Treasure/Chickadee	C. Brenders	150-day	29.50	29.50-50.00
90-39-002	The Beautiful Bluebird	C. Brenders	150-day	29.50	35-61.00
91-39-003	Summer Gold: The Robin	C. Brenders	150-day	32.50	35.00
91-39-004	The Meadowlark's Song	C. Brenders	150-day	32.50	32.50
91-39-005	Ivory-Billed Woodpecker	C. Brenders	150-day	32.50	32.50
91-39-006	Red-Winged Blackbird	C. Brenders	150-day	32.50	32.50
W. S. George		**Alaska: The Last Frontier**			
91-40-001	Icy Majesty	H. Lambson	150-day	34.50	34.50
91-40-002	Autumn Grandeur	H. Lambson	150-day	34.50	34.50
92-40-003	Mountain Monarch	H. Lambson	150-day	37.50	37.50
92-40-004	Down the Trail	H. Lambson	150-day	37.50	37.50
92-40-005	Moonlight Lookout	H. Lambson	150-day	37.50	37.50
W. S. George		**On Wings of Snow**			
91-41-001	The Swans	L. Liu	150-day	34.50	34.50
91-41-002	The Doves	L. Liu	150-day	34.50	34.50
91-41-003	The Peacocks	L. Liu	150-day	37.50	37.50
91-41-004	The Egrets	L. Liu	150-day	37.50	37.50
91-41-005	The Cockatoos	L. Liu	150-day	37.50	37.50
92-41-006	The Herons	L. Liu	150-day	37.50	37.50
W. S. George		**Nature's Playmates**			
91-42-001	Partners	C. Frace	150-day	29.50	29.50
91-42-002	Secret Heights	C. Frace	150-day	29.50	29.50
91-42-003	Recess	C. Frace	150-day	32.50	32.50
91-42-004	Double Trouble	C. Frace	150-day	32.50	32.50
91-42-005	Pals	C. Frace	150-day	32.50	32.50
92-42-006	Curious Trio	C. Frace	150-day	34.50	34.50
92-42-007	Playmates	C. Frace	150-day	34.50	34.50
92-42-008	Surprise	C. Frace	150-day	34.50	34.50
W. S. George		**Field Birds of North America**			
91-43-001	Winter Colors: Ring-Necked Pheasant	D. Bush	150-day	39.50	39.50
91-43-002	In Display: Ruffed Goose	D. Bush	150-day	39.50	39.50
91-43-003	Morning Light: Bobwhite Quail	D. Bush	150-day	42.50	42.50
91-43-004	Misty Clearing: Wild Turkey	D. Bush	150-day	42.50	42.50
92-43-005	Autumn Moment: American Woodcock	D. Bush	150-day	42.50	42.50
92-43-006	Season's End: Willow Ptarmigan	D. Bush	150-day	42.50	42.50
W. S. George		**Country Bouquets**			
91-44-001	Morning Sunshine	G. Kurz	150-day	29.50	40.00
91-44-002	Summer Perfume	G. Kurz	150-day	29.50	29.50
91-44-003	Warm Welcome	G. Kurz	150-day	32.50	32.50
91-44-004	Garden's Bounty	G. Kurz	150-day	32.50	32.50
W. S. George		**Gentle Beginnings**			
91-45-001	Tender Loving Care	W. Nelson	150-day	34.50	34.50
91-45-002	A Touch of Love	W. Nelson	150-day	34.50	34.50
91-45-003	Under Watchful Eyes	W. Nelson	150-day	37.50	37.50
91-45-004	Lap of Love	W. Nelson	150-day	37.50	37.50
W. S. George		**Garden of the Lord**			
92-46-001	Love One Another	C. Gillies	150-day	29.50	29.50
92-46-002	Perfect Peace	C. Gillies	150-day	29.50	29.50
92-46-003	Trust in the Lord	C. Gillies	150-day	32.50	32.50
W. S. George		**The Majestic Horse**			
92-47-001	Classic Beauty: Thoroughbred	P. Wildermuth	150-day	34.50	34.50
92-47-002	American Gold: The Quarterhorse	P. Wildermuth	150-day	34.50	34.50
92-47-003	Regal Spirit: The Arabian	P. Wildermuth	150-day	34.50	34.50
W. S. George		**Columbus Discovers America: The 500th Anniversary**			
92-48-001	Under Full Sail	J. Penalva	150-day	29.50	29.50
92-48-002	Ashore at Dawn	J. Penalva	150-day	29.50	29.50
92-48-003	Columbus Raises the Flag	J. Penalva	150-day	32.50	32.50
92-48-004	Bringing Together Two Cultures	J. Penalva	150-day	32.50	32.50
W. S. George		**Lena Liu's Basket Bouquets**			
92-49-001	Roses	L. Liu	150-day	29.50	29.50
92-49-002	Pansies	L. Liu	150-day	29.50	29.50
W. S. George		**Tomorrow's Promise**			
92-50-001	Curiosity: Asian Elephants	W. Nelson	150-day	29.50	29.50
W. S. George		**Sonnets in Flowers**			
92-51-001	Sonnet of Beauty	G. Kurz	150-day	29.50	29.50
W. S. George		**On the Wing**			
92-52-001	Winged Splendor	T. Humphrey	150-day	29.50	29.50
92-52-002	Rising Mallard	T. Humphrey	150-day	29.50	29.50
92-52-003	Glorious Ascent	T. Humphrey	150-day	32.50	32.50
W. S. George		**The Sound of Music: Silver Anniversary**			
91-53-001	The Hills are Alive	V. Gadino	150-day	29.50	29.50
92-53-002	Let's Start at the Very Beginning	V. Gadino	150-day	29.50	29.50
92-53-003	Something Good	V. Gadino	150-day	32.50	32.50
92-53-004	Maria's Wedding Day	V. Gadino	150-day	32.50	32.50
W. S. George		**Grand Safari: Images of Africa**			
92-54-001	A Moment's Rest	C. Frace	150-day	34.50	34.50
W. S. George		**A Treasury of Songbirds**			
92-55-001	Springtime Splendor	R. Stine	150-day	29.50	29.50
92-55-002	Morning's Glory	R. Stine	150-day	29.50	29.50
92-55-003	Golden Daybreak	R. Stine	150-day	32.50	32.50
W. S. George		**Heart of the Wild**			
91-56-001	A Gentle Touch	G. Beecham	150-day	29.50	29.50
92-56-002	Mother's Pride	G. Beecham	150-day	29.50	29.50
W. S. George		**Spirits of the Sky**			
92-57-001	Twilight Glow	C. Fisher	150-day	29.50	29.50
92-57-002	First Light	C. Fisher	150-day	29.50	29.50
W. S. George		**Poetic Cottages**			
92-58-001	Garden Paths of Oxfordshire	C. Valente	150-day	29.50	29.50
92-58-002	Twilight at Woodgreen Pond	C. Valente	150-day	29.50	29.50
92-58-003	Stonewall Brook Blossoms	C. Valente	150-day	32.50	32.50
W. S. George		**Memories of a Victorian Childhood**			
92-59-001	You'd Better Not Pout	Unknown	150-day	29.50	29.50
92-59-002	Sweet Slumber	Unknown	150-day	29.50	29.50
W. S. George		**Petal Pals**			
92-60-001	Garden Discovery	L. Chang	150-day	24.50	24.50
92-60-002	Flowering Fascination	L. Chang	150-day	24.50	24.50
Ghent Collection		**April Fool Annual**			
78-01-001	April Fool	N. Rockwell	10,000	35.00	60.00
79-01-002	April Fool	N. Rockwell	10,000	35.00	35.00
80-01-003	April Fool	N. Rockwell	10,000	37.50	45.00
Ghent Collection		**American Bicentennial Wildlife**			
76-02-001	American Bald Eagle	H. Moeller	2,500	95.00	95.00
76-02-002	American Whitetail Deer	E. Bierly	2,500	95.00	95.00
76-02-003	American Bison	C. Frace	2,500	95.00	95.00
76-02-004	American Wild Turkey	A. Gilbert	2,500	95.00	95.00
Goebel/Schmid		**M.I. Hummel Collectibles-Annual Plates**			
71-01-001	Heavenly Angel 264	M.I. Hummel	Closed	25.00	500-675.
72-01-002	Hear Ye, Hear Ye 265	M.I. Hummel	Closed	30.00	40-100.00
73-01-003	Glober Trotter 266	M.I. Hummel	Closed	32.50	100-300.
74-01-004	Goose Girl 267	M.I. Hummel	Closed	40.00	52-125.00
75-01-005	Ride into Christmas 268	M.I. Hummel	Closed	50.00	100-225.
76-01-006	Apple Tree Girl 269	M.I. Hummel	Closed	50.00	100-125.
77-01-007	Apple Tree Boy 270	M.I. Hummel	Closed	52.50	54-150.00
78-01-008	Happy Pastime 271	M.I. Hummel	Closed	65.00	100-150.
79-01-009	Singing Lesson 272	M.I. Hummel	Closed	90.00	100-125.
80-01-010	School Girl 273	M.I. Hummel	Closed	100.00	80-100.00
81-01-011	Umbrella Boy 274	M.I. Hummel	Closed	100.00	125.00
82-01-012	Umbrella Girl 275	M.I. Hummel	Closed	100.00	135-200.
83-01-013	The Postman 276	M.I. Hummel	Closed	108.00	150-250.
84-01-014	Little Helper 277	M.I. Hummel	Closed	108.00	125.00
85-01-015	Check Girl 278	M.I. Hummel	Closed	110.00	110-175.
86-01-016	Playmates 279	M.I. Hummel	Closed	125.00	150-175.
87-01-017	Feeding Time 283	M.I. Hummel	Closed	135.00	290-350.
88-01-018	Little Goat Herder 284	M.I. Hummel	Closed	145.00	145-175.
89-01-019	Farm Boy 285	M.I. Hummel	Closed	160.00	175.00
90-01-020	Shepherd's Boy 286	M.I. Hummel	Closed	170.00	196.00
91-01-021	Just Resting 287	M.I. Hummel	Closed	196.00	196.00
92-01-022	Wayside Harmony 288	M.I. Hummel	Closed	210.00	210.00
93-01-023	Doll Bath 289	M.I. Hummel	Yr.Iss.	210.00	210.00
Goebel/Schmid		**M.I. Hummel Collectibles Anniversary Plates**			
75-02-001	Stormy Weather 280	M.I. Hummel	Closed	100.00	100-200.
80-02-002	Spring Dance 281	M.I. Hummel	Closed	225.00	225.00
85-02-003	Auf Wiedersehen 282	M.I. Hummel	Closed	225.00	250-280.
Goebel/Schmid		**M.I. Hummel-Little Music Makers**			
84-03-001	Little Fiddler 744	M.I. Hummel	Closed	30.00	70-125.00
85-03-002	Serenade 741	M.I. Hummel	Closed	30.00	70-125.00
86-03-003	Soloist 743	M.I. Hummel	Closed	35.00	70-125.00
87-03-004	Band Leader 742	M.I. Hummel	Closed	40.00	70-125.00
Goebel/Schmid		**M.I. Hummel Club Exclusive-Celebration**			
86-04-001	Valentine Gift (Hum 738)	M.I. Hummel	Closed	90.00	100-150.

PLATES

Company		Series			
Number	Name	Artist	Edition Limit	Issue Price	Quote
87-04-002	Valentine Joy (Hum 737)	M.I. Hummel	Closed	98.00	130-150.
88-04-003	Daisies Don't Tell (Hum 736)	M.I. Hummel	Closed	115.00	130-150.
89-04-004	It's Cold (Hum 735)	M.I. Hummel	Closed	120.00	130-150.
Goebel/Schmid		**M.I. Hummel-The Little Homemakers**			
88-05-001	Little Sweeper (Hum 745)	M.I. Hummel	Closed	45.00	70-90.00
89-05-002	Wash Day (Hum 746)	M.I. Hummel	Closed	50.00	70-90.00
90-05-003	A Stitch in Time (Hum 747)	M.I. Hummel	Closed	50.00	70-90.00
91-05-004	Chicken Licken (Hum 748)	M.I. Hummel	Closed	70.00	70-99.00
Goebel/Schmid		**M.I. Hummel-Friends Forever**			
92-06-001	Meditation 292	M.I. Hummel	Open	180.00	180.00
93-06-002	For Father 293	M.I. Hummel	Open	195.00	195.00
Gorham		**Christmas**			
74-01-001	Tiny Tim	N. Rockwell	Annual	12.50	35.00
75-01-002	Good Deeds	N. Rockwell	Annual	17.50	35.00
76-01-003	Christmas Trio	N. Rockwell	Annual	19.50	20.00
77-01-004	Yuletide Reckoning	N. Rockwell	Annual	19.50	30.00
78-01-005	Planning Christmas Visit	N. Rockwell	Annual	24.50	24.50
79-01-006	Santa's Helpers	N. Rockwell	Annual	24.50	24.50
80-01-007	Letter to Santa	N. Rockwell	Annual	27.50	32.00
81-01-008	Santa Plans His Visit	N. Rockwell	Annual	29.50	50.00
82-01-009	Jolly Coachman	N. Rockwell	Annual	29.50	30.00
83-01-010	Christmas Dancers	N. Rockwell	Annual	29.50	35.00
84-01-011	Christmas Medley	N. Rockwell	17,500	29.95	29.95
85-01-012	Home For The Holidays	N. Rockwell	17,500	29.95	30.00
86-01-013	Merry Christmas Grandma	N. Rockwell	17,500	29.95	65.00
87-01-014	The Homecoming	N. Rockwell	17,500	35.00	52.00
88-01-015	Discovery	N. Rockwell	17,500	37.50	37.50
Gorham		**A Boy and His Dog Four Seasons Plates**			
71-02-001	Boy Meets His Dog	N. Rockwell	Annual	50.00	200-400.
71-02-002	Adventures Between Adventures	N. Rockwell	Annual	Set	Set
71-02-003	The Mysterious Malady	N. Rockwell	Annual	Set	Set
71-02-004	Pride of Parenthood	N. Rockwell	Annual	Set	Set
Gorham		**Young Love Four Seasons Plates**			
72-03-001	Downhill Daring	N. Rockwell	Annual	60.00	140.00
72-03-002	Beguiling Buttercup	N. Rockwell	Annual	Set	Set
72-03-003	Flying High	N. Rockwell	Annual	Set	Set
72-03-004	A Scholarly Pace	N. Rockwell	Annual	Set	Set
Gorham		**Four Ages of Love**			
73-04-001	Gaily Sharing Vintage Time	N. Rockwell	Annual	60.00	229.00
73-04-002	Flowers in Tender Bloom	N. Rockwell	Annual	Set	Set
73-04-003	Sweet Song So Young	N. Rockwell	Annual	Set	Set
73-04-004	Fondly We Do Remember	N. Rockwell	Annual	Set	Set
Gorham		**Grandpa and Me Four Seasons Plates**			
74-05-001	Gay Blades	N. Rockwell	Annual	60.00	85-100.00
74-05-002	Day Dreamers	N. Rockwell	Annual	Set	Set
74-05-003	Goin' Fishing	N. Rockwell	Annual	Set	Set
74-05-004	Pensive Pals	N. Rockwell	Annual	Set	Set
Gorham		**Me and My Pals Four Seasons Plates**			
75-06-001	A Lickin' Good Bath	N. Rockwell	Annual	70.00	150.00
75-06-002	Young Man's Fancy	N. Rockwell	Annual	Set	Set
75-06-003	Fisherman's Paradise	N. Rockwell	Annual	Set	Set
75-06-004	Disastrous Daring	N. Rockwell	Annual	Set	Set
Gorham		**Grand Pals Four Seasons Plates**			
76-07-001	Snow Sculpturing	N. Rockwell	Annual	70.00	160.00
76-07-002	Soaring Spirits	N. Rockwell	Annual	Set	Set
76-07-003	Fish Finders	N. Rockwell	Annual	Set	Set
76-07-004	Ghostly Gourds	N. Rockwell	Annual	Set	Set
Gorham		**Going on Sixteen Four Seasons Plates**			
77-08-001	Chilling Chore	N. Rockwell	Annual	75.00	110.00
77-08-002	Sweet Serenade	N. Rockwell	Annual	Set	Set
77-08-003	Shear Agony	N. Rockwell	Annual	Set	Set
77-08-004	Pilgrimage	N. Rockwell	Annual	Set	Set
Gorham		**Tender Years Four Seasons Plates**			
78-09-001	New Year Look	N. Rockwell	Annual	100.00	100.00
78-09-002	Spring Tonic	N. Rockwell	Annual	Set	Set
78-09-003	Cool Aid	N. Rockwell	Annual	Set	Set
78-09-004	Chilly Reception	N. Rockwell	Annual	Set	Set
Gorham		**A Helping Hand Four Seasons Plates**			
79-10-001	Year End Court	N. Rockwell	Annual	100.00	100.00
79-10-002	Closed for Business	N. Rockwell	Annual	Set	Set
79-10-003	Swatter's Rights	N. Rockwell	Annual	Set	Set
79-10-004	Coal Season's Coming	N. Rockwell	Annual	Set	Set
Gorham		**Dad's Boys Four Seasons Plates**			
80-11-001	Ski Skills	N. Rockwell	Annual	135.00	135.00
80-11-002	In His Spirits	N. Rockwell	Annual	Set	Set
80-11-003	Trout Dinner	N. Rockwell	Annual	Set	Set
80-11-004	Careful Aim	N. Rockwell	Annual	Set	Set
Gorham		**Old Timers Four Seasons Plates**			
81-12-001	Canine Solo	N. Rockwell	Annual	100.00	100.00
81-12-002	Sweet Surprise	N. Rockwell	Annual	Set	Set
81-12-003	Lazy Days	N. Rockwell	Annual	Set	Set
81-12-004	Fancy Footwork	N. Rockwell	Annual	Set	Set
Gorham		**Life with Father Four Seasons Plates**			
82-13-001	Big Decision	N. Rockwell	Annual	100.00	200-300.
82-13-002	Blasting Out	N. Rockwell	Annual	Set	Set
82-13-003	Cheering the Champs	N. Rockwell	Annual	Set	Set
82-13-004	A Tough One	N. Rockwell	Annual	Set	Set
Gorham		**Old Buddies Four Seasons Plates**			
83-14-001	Shared Success	N. Rockwell	Annual	115.00	115.00
83-14-002	Endless Debate	N. Rockwell	Annual	Set	Set
83-14-003	Hasty Retreat	N. Rockwell	Annual	Set	Set
83-14-004	Final Speech	N. Rockwell	Annual	Set	Set
Gorham		**Bas Relief**			
81-15-001	Sweet Song So Young	N. Rockwell	Undis.	100.00	100.00
81-15-002	Beguiling Buttercup	N. Rockwell	Undis.	62.50	70.00
82-15-003	Flowers in Tender Bloom	N. Rockwell	Undis.	100.00	100.00
82-15-004	Flying High	N. Rockwell	Undis.	62.50	65.00
Gorham		**Single Release**			
74-16-001	Weighing In	N. Rockwell	Annual	12.50	80-99.00
Gorham		**Single Release**			
74-17-001	The Golden Rule	N. Rockwell	Annual	12.50	30.00
Gorham		**Single Release**			
75-18-001	Ben Franklin	N. Rockwell	Annual	19.50	35.00
Gorham		**Boy Scout Plates**			
75-19-001	Our Heritage	N. Rockwell	18,500	19.50	40.00
76-19-002	A Scout is Loyal	N. Rockwell	18,500	19.50	55.00
77-19-003	The Scoutmaster	N. Rockwell	18,500	19.50	60.00
77-19-004	A Good Sign	N. Rockwell	18,500	19.50	50.00
78-19-005	Pointing the Way	N. Rockwell	18,500	19.50	50.00
78-19-006	Campfire Story	N. Rockwell	18,500	19.50	25.00
80-19-007	Beyond the Easel	N. Rockwell	18,500	45.00	45.00
Gorham		**Single Release**			
76-20-001	The Marriage License	N. Rockwell	Numbrd	37.50	52.00
Gorham		**Presidential**			
76-21-001	John F. Kennedy	N. Rockwell	9,800	30.00	65.00
76-21-002	Dwight D. Eisenhower	N. Rockwell	9,800	30.00	35.00
Gorham		**Single Release**			
78-22-001	Triple Self Portrait Memorial Plate	N. Rockwell	Annual	37.50	75.00
Gorham		**Four Seasons Landscapes**			
80-23-001	Summer Respite	N. Rockwell	Annual	45.00	67.50
81-23-002	Autumn Reflection	N. Rockwell	Annual	45.00	65.00
82-23-003	Winter Delight	N. Rockwell	Annual	50.00	62.50
83-23-004	Spring Recess	N. Rockwell	Annual	60.00	60.00
Gorham		**Single Release**			
80-24-001	The Annual Visit	N. Rockwell	Annual	32.50	35.00
Gorham		**Single Release**			
81-25-001	Day in Life of Boy	N. Rockwell	Annual	50.00	80.00
81-25-002	Day in Life of Girl	N. Rockwell	Annual	50.00	80-108.00
Gorham		**Gallery of Masters**			
71-26-001	Man with a Gilt Helmet	Rembrandt	10,000	50.00	50.00
72-26-002	Self Portrait with Saskia	Rembrandt	10,000	50.00	50.00
73-26-003	The Honorable Mrs. Graham	Gainsborough	7,500	50.00	50.00
Gorham		**Barrymore**			
71-27-001	Quiet Waters	Barrymore	15,000	25.00	25.00
72-27-002	San Pedro Harbor	Barrymore	15,000	25.00	25.00
Gorham		**Barrymore**			
72-28-001	Nantucket, Sterling	Barrymore	1,000	100.00	100.00
72-28-002	Little Boatyard, Sterling	Barrymore	1,000	100.00	145.00
Gorham		**Pewter Bicentennial**			
71-29-001	Burning of the Gaspee	R. Pailthorpe	5,000	35.00	35.00
72-29-002	Boston Tea Party	R. Pailthorpe	5,000	35.00	35.00
Gorham		**Vermeil Bicentennial**			
72-30-001	1776 Plate	Gorham	250	750.00	800.00
Gorham		**Silver Bicentennial**			
72-31-001	1776 Plate	Gorham	500	500.00	500.00
72-31-002	Burning of the Gaspee	R. Pailthorpe	750	500.00	500.00
73-31-003	Boston Tea Party	R. Pailthorpe	750	550.00	575.00
Gorham		**China Bicentennial**			
72-32-001	1776 Plate	Gorham	18,500	17.50	35.00
76-32-002	1776 Bicentennial	Gorham	8,000	17.50	35.00
Gorham		**Remington Western**			
73-33-001	A New Year on the Cimarron	F. Remington	Annual	25.00	35-50.00
73-33-002	Aiding a Comrade	F. Remington	Annual	25.00	30-125.00
73-33-003	The Flight	F. Remington	Annual	25.00	30-95.00
73-33-004	The Fight for the Water Hole	F. Remington	Annual	25.00	30-125.00
75-33-005	Old Ramond	F. Remington	Annual	20.00	35-60.00
75-33-006	A Breed	F. Remington	Annual	20.00	35-65.00
76-33-007	Cavalry Officer	F. Remington	5,000	37.50	60-75.00
76-33-008	A Trapper	F. Remington	5,000	37.50	60-75.00
Gorham		**Moppet Plates-Christmas**			
73-34-001	M. Plate Christmas	Unknown	Annual	10.00	35.00
74-34-002	M. Plate Christmas	Unknown	Annual	12.00	12.00
75-34-003	M. Plate Christmas	Unknown	Annual	13.00	13.00
76-34-004	M. Plate Christmas	Unknown	Annual	13.00	15.00
77-34-005	M. Plate Christmas	Unknown	Annual	13.00	14.00
78-34-006	M. Plate Christmas	Unknown	Annual	10.00	10.00
79-34-007	M. Plate Christmas	Unknown	Annual	12.00	12.00
80-34-008	M. Plate Christmas	Unknown	Annual	12.00	12.00
81-34-009	M. Plate Christmas	Unknown	Annual	12.00	12.00
82-34-010	M. Plate Christmas	Unknown	Annual	12.00	12.00
83-34-011	M. Plate Christmas	Unknown	Annual	12.00	12.00
Gorham		**Moppet Plates-Mother's Day**			
73-35-001	M. Plate Mother's Day	Unknown	Annual	10.00	30.00
74-35-002	M. Plate Mother's Day	Unknown	Annual	12.00	20.00
75-35-003	M. Plate Mother's Day	Unknown	Annual	13.00	15.00
76-35-004	M. Plate Mother's Day	Unknown	Annual	13.00	15.00
77-35-005	M. Plate Mother's Day	Unknown	Annual	13.00	15.00
78-35-006	M. Plate Mother's Day	Unknown	Annual	10.00	10.00
Gorham		**Moppet Plates-Anniversary**			
76-36-001	M. Plate Anniversary	Unknown	20,000	13.00	13.00
Gorham		**Julian Ritter, Fall In Love**			
77-37-001	Enchantment	J. Ritter	5,000	100.00	100.00
77-37-002	Frolic	J. Ritter	5,000	Set	Set
77-37-003	Gutsy Gal	J. Ritter	5,000	Set	Set
77-37-004	Lonely Chill	J. Ritter	5,000	Set	Set

PLATES

Company Number	Name	Series Artist	Edition Limit	Issue Price	Quote
Gorham		**Julian Ritter**			
77-38-001	Christmas Visit	J. Ritter	9,800	24.50	29.00
Gorham		**Julian Ritter, To Love a Clown**			
78-39-001	Awaited Reunion	J. Ritter	5,000	120.00	120.00
78-39-002	Twosome Time	J. Ritter	5,000	120.00	120.00
78-39-003	Showtime Beckons	J. Ritter	5,000	120.00	120.00
78-39-004	Together in Memories	J. Ritter	5,000	120.00	120.00
Gorham		**Julian Ritter**			
78-40-001	Valentine, Fluttering Heart	J. Ritter	7,500	45.00	45.00
Gorham		**Christmas/Children's Television Workshop**			
81-41-001	Sesame Street Christmas	Unknown	Annual	17.50	17.50
82-41-002	Sesame Street Christmas	Unknown	Annual	17.50	17.50
83-41-003	Sesame Street Christmas	Unknown	Annual	19.50	19.50
Gorham		**Pastoral Symphony**			
82-42-001	When I Was a Child	B. Felder	7,500	42.50	50.00
82-42-002	Gather the Children	B. Felder	7,500	42.50	50.00
84-42-003	Sugar and Spice	B. Felder	7,500	42.50	50.00
XX-42-004	He Loves Me	B. Felder	7,500	42.50	50.00
Gorham		**Encounters, Survival and Celebrations**			
82-43-001	A Fine Welcome	J. Clymer	7,500	50.00	75.00
83-43-002	Winter Trail	J. Clymer	7,500	50.00	125.00
83-43-003	Alouette	J. Clymer	7,500	62.50	62.50
83-43-004	The Trader	J. Clymer	7,500	62.50	62.50
83-43-005	Winter Camp	J. Clymer	7,500	62.50	75.00
83-43-006	The Trapper Takes a Wife	J. Clymer	7,500	62.50	62.50
Gorham		**Charles Russell**			
80-44-001	In Without Knocking	C. Russell	9,800	38.00	75.00
81-44-002	Bronc to Breakfast	C. Russell	9,800	38.00	75-115.00
82-44-003	When Ignorance is Bliss	C. Russell	9,800	45.00	75-115.00
83-44-004	Cowboy Life	C. Russell	9,800	45.00	100.00
Gorham		**Gorham Museum Doll Plates**			
84-45-001	Lydia	Gorham	5,000	29.00	125.00
84-45-002	Belton Bebe	Gorham	5,000	29.00	55.00
84-45-003	Christmas Lady	Gorham	7,500	32.50	32.50
85-45-004	Lucille	Gorham	5,000	29.00	35.00
85-45-005	Jumeau	Gorham	5,000	29.00	29.00
Gorham		**Time Machine Teddies Plates**			
86-46-001	Miss Emily, Bearing Up	B. Port	5,000	32.50	32.50
87-46-002	Big Bear, The Toy Collector	B. Port	5,000	32.50	32.50
88-46-003	Hunny Munny	B. Port	5,000	37.50	37.50
Gorham		**Leyendecker Annual Christmas Plates**			
88-47-001	Christmas Hug	J. C. Leyendecker	10,000	37.50	37.50
Gorham		**Single Release**			
76-48-001	The Black Regiment 1778	F. Quagon	7,500	25.00	58.00
Gorham		**American Artist**			
76-49-001	Apache Mother & Child	R. Donnelly	9,800	25.00	56.00
Dave Grossman Creations		**Emmett Kelly Plates**			
86-01-001	Christmas Carol	B. Leighton-Jones	Yr.Iss.	20.00	20.00
87-01-002	Christmas Wreath	B. Leighton-Jones	Yr.Iss.	20.00	20.00
88-01-003	Christmas Dinner	B. Leighton-Jones	Yr.Iss.	20.00	49.00
89-01-004	Christmas Feast	B. Leighton-Jones	Yr.Iss.	20.00	39.00
90-01-005	Just What I Needed	B. Leighton-Jones	Yr.Iss.	24.00	39.00
91-01-006	Emmett The Snowman	B. Leighton-Jones	Yr.Iss.	25.00	35.00
92-01-007	Christmas Tunes	B. Leighton-Jones	Yr.Iss.	25.00	25.00
Dave Grossman Creations		**Saturday Evening Post Collection**			
91-02-001	Downhill Daring BRP-91	Rockwell-Inspired	Yr.Iss.	25.00	25.00
91-02-002	Missed BRP-101	Rockwell-Inspired	Yr Iss.	25.00	25.00
92-02-003	Choosin Up BRP-102	Rockwell-Inspired	Y. Iss.	25.00	25.00
Dave Grossman Creations		**Native American Series**			
91-03-001	Lone Wolf	E. Roberts	10,000	45.00	45.00
92-03-002	Tortoise Lady	E. Roberts	10,000	45.00	45.00
Dave Grossman Designs		**Norman Rockwell Collection**			
79-01-001	Leapfrog NRP-79	Rockwell-Inspired	Retrd.	50.00	50.00
80-01-002	Lovers NRP-80	Rockwell-Inspired	Retrd.	60.00	60.00
81-01-003	Dreams of Long Ago NRP-81	Rockwell-Inspired	Retrd.	60.00	60.00
82-01-004	Doctor and Doll NRP-82	Rockwell-Inspired	Retrd.	65.00	95.00
83-01-005	Circus NRP-83	Rockwell-Inspired	Retrd.	65.00	65.00
84-01-006	Visit With Rockwell NRP-84	Rockwell-Inspired	Retrd.	65.00	65.00
80-01-007	Christmas Trio RXP-80	Rockwell-Inspired	Retrd.	75.00	75.00
81-01-008	Santa's Good Boys RXP-81	Rockwell-Inspired	Retrd.	75.00	75.00
82-01-009	Faces of Christmas RXP-82	Rockwell-Inspired	Retrd.	75.00	75.00
83-01-010	Christmas Chores RXP-83	Rockwell-Inspired	Retrd.	75.00	75.00
84-01-011	Tiny Tim RXP-84	Rockwell-Inspired	Retrd.	75.00	75.00
80-01-012	Back To School RMP-80	Rockwell-Inspired	Retrd.	24.00	24.00
81-01-013	No Swimming RMP-81	Rockwell-Inspired	Retrd.	25.00	25.00
82-01-014	Love Letter RMP-82	Rockwell-Inspired	Retrd.	27.00	30.00
83-01-015	Doctor and Doll RMP-83	Rockwell-Inspired	Retrd.	27.00	27.00
84-01-016	Big Moment RMP-84	Rockwell-Inspired	Retrd.	27.00	27.00
79-01-017	Butterboy RP-01	Rockwell-Inspired	Retrd.	40.00	40.00
82-01-018	American Mother RGP-42	Rockwell-Inspired	Retrd.	45.00	45.00
83-01-019	Dreamboat RGP-83	Rockwell-Inspired	Retrd.	24.00	30.00
78-01-020	Young Doctor RDP-26	Rockwell-Inspired	Retrd.	50.00	65.00
Dave Grossman Designs		**Norman Rockwell Collection-Tom Sawyer Plates**			
75-02-001	Whitewashing the Fence TSP-01	Rockwell-Inspired	Retrd.	26.00	35.00
76-02-002	First Smoke TSP-02	Rockwell-Inspired	Retrd.	26.00	35.00
77-02-003	Take Your Medicine TSP-03	Rockwell-Inspired	Retrd.	26.00	40.00
78-02-004	Lost in Cave TSP-04	Rockwell-Inspired	Retrd.	26.00	40.00
Dave Grossman Designs		**Norman Rockwell Collection-Huck Finn Plates**			
79-03-001	Secret HFP-01	Rockwell-Inspired	Retrd.	40.00	40.00
80-03-002	ListeningHFP-02	Rockwell-Inspired	Retrd.	40.00	40.00
80-03-003	No Kings HFP-03	Rockwell-Inspired	Retrd.	40.00	40.00
81-03-004	Snake Escapes HFP-04	Rockwell-Inspired	Retrd.	40.00	40.00
Dave Grossman Designs		**Norman Rockwell Collection-Boy Scout Plates**			
81-04-001	Can't Wait BSP-01	Rockwell-Inspired	Retrd.	30.00	45.00
82-04-002	Guiding Hand BSP-02	Rockwell-Inspired	Retrd.	30.00	35.00

Company Number	Name	Series Artist	Edition Limit	Issue Price	Quote
83-04-003	Tomorrow's Leader BSP-03	Rockwell-Inspired	Retrd.	30.00	45.00
Grande Copenhagen		**Christmas**			
75-01-001	Alone Together	Unknown	Undis.	24.50	24.50
76-01-002	Christmas Wreath	Unknown	Undis.	24.50	24.50
77-01-003	Fishwives at Gammelstrand	Unknown	Undis.	26.50	26.50
78-01-004	Hans Christian Anderson	Unknown	Undis.	32.50	32.50
79-01-005	Pheasants	Unknown	Undis.	34.50	56.00
80-01-006	Snow Queen in the Tivoli	Unknown	Undis.	39.50	39.50
81-01-007	Little Match Girl in Nyhavn	Unknown	Undis.	42.50	43.00
82-01-008	Shepherdess/Chimney Sweep	Unknown	Undis.	45.00	49.00
83-01-009	Little Mermaid Near Kronborg	Unknown	Undis.	45.00	104.00
84-01-010	Sandman at Amalienborg	Unknown	Undis.	45.00	50.00
Hadley Companies		**Glow Series**			
85-01-001	Evening Glow	T. Redlin	5,000	55.00	350-450.
85-01-002	Morning Glow	T. Redlin	5,000	55.00	125-250.
85-01-003	Twilight Glow	T. Redlin	5,000	55.00	95-125.00
87-01-004	Morning Retreat	T. Redlin	9,500	65.00	65-125.00
87-01-005	Evening Retreat	T. Redlin	9,500	65.00	65-75.00
88-01-006	Golden Retreat	T. Redlin	9,500	65.00	95.00
89-01-007	Moonlight Retreat	T. Redlin	9,500	65.00	65.00
87-01-008	Coming Home	T. Redlin	9,500	85.00	85.00
88-01-009	Lights of Home	T. Redlin	9,500	85.00	85.00
89-01-010	Homeward Bound	T. Redlin	9,500	85.00	85.00
88-01-011	Afternoon Glow	T. Redlin	5,000	55.00	55.00
Hallmark Galleries		**Enchanted Garden**			
92-01-001	Swan Lake (tile)	E. Richardson	9,500	35.00	35.00
92-01-002	Fairy Bunny Tale: The Beginning (tile)	E. Richardson	14,500	25.00	25.00
92-01-003	Fairy Bunny Tale: Beginning II (tile)	E. Richardson	14,500	35.00	35.00
92-01-004	Neighborhood Dreamer	E. Richardson	9,500	45.00	45.00
Hallmark Galleries		**Days to Remember-The Art of Norman Rockwell**			
92-02-001	Sweet Song So Young (pewter medallion)	D. Unruh	9,500	45.00	45.00
92-02-002	Sleeping Children (pewter medallion)	D. Unruh	9,500	45.00	45.00
92-02-003	A Boy Meets His Dog (pewter medallion)	D. Unruh	9,500	45.00	45.00
92-02-004	Fisherman's Paradise (pewter medallion)	D. Unruh	9,500	45.00	45.00
Hallmark Galleries		**Innocent Wonders**			
92-03-001	Dinky Toot	T. Blackshear	9,500	35.00	35.00
92-03-002	Pinky Poo	T. Blackshear	9,500	35.00	35.00
Hallmark Galleries		**Tobin Fraley Carousels**			
92-04-001	Philadelphia Toboggan Co/1920 (pewter medallion)	T. Fraley	9,500	45.00	45.00
Hallmark Galleries		**Majestic Wilderness**			
92-05-001	Vixen & Kits	M. Newman	9,500	35.00	35.00
92-05-002	Timber Wolves (porcelain)	M. Newman	9,500	35.00	35.00
Hamilton/Boehm		**Award Winning Roses**			
79-01-001	Peace Rose	Boehm	15,000	45.00	62.50
79-01-002	White Masterpiece Rose	Boehm	15,000	45.00	45-62.50
79-01-003	Tropicana Rose	Boehm	15,000	45.00	45-62.50
79-01-004	Elegance Rose	Boehm	15,000	45.00	45-62.50
79-01-005	Queen Elizabeth Rose	Boehm	15,000	45.00	62.50
79-01-006	Royal Highness Rose	Boehm	15,000	45.00	45-62.50
79-01-007	Angel Face Rose	Boehm	15,000	45.00	45-62.50
79-01-008	Mr. Lincoln Rose	Boehm	15,000	45.00	45-62.50
Hamilton/Boehm		**Owl Collection**			
80-02-001	Boreal Owl	Boehm	15,000	45.00	75.00
80-02-002	Snowy Owl	Boehm	15,000	45.00	62.50
80-02-003	Barn Owl	Boehm	15,000	45.00	62.50
80-02-004	Saw Whet Owl	Boehm	15,000	45.00	62.50
80-02-005	Great Horned Owl	Boehm	15,000	45.00	62.50
80-02-006	Screech Owl	Boehm	15,000	45.00	62.50
80-02-007	Short Eared Owl	Boehm	15,000	45.00	62.50
80-02-008	Barred Owl	Boehm	15,000	45.00	62.50
Hamilton/Boehm		**Hummingbird Collection**			
80-03-001	Calliope	Boehm	15,000	62.50	80.00
80-03-002	Broadbilled	Boehm	15,000	62.50	62.50
80-03-003	Rufous Flame Bearer	Boehm	15,000	62.50	80.00
80-03-004	Broadtail	Boehm	15,000	62.50	62.50
80-03-005	Streamertail	Boehm	15,000	62.50	80.00
80-03-006	Blue Throated	Boehm	15,000	62.50	80.00
80-03-007	Crimson Topaz	Boehm	15,000	62.50	62.50
80-03-008	Brazilian Ruby	Boehm	15,000	62.50	80.00
Hamilton/Boehm		**Water Birds**			
81-04-001	Canada Geese	Boehm	15,000	62.50	75.00
81-04-002	Wood Ducks	Boehm	15,000	62.50	62.50
81-04-003	Hooded Merganser	Boehm	15,000	62.50	87.00
81-04-004	Ross's Geese	Boehm	15,000	62.50	62.50
81-04-005	Common Mallard	Boehm	15,000	62.50	62.50
81-04-006	Canvas Back	Boehm	15,000	62.50	62.50
81-04-007	Green Winged Teal	Boehm	15,000	62.50	62.50
81-04-008	American Pintail	Boehm	15,000	62.50	62.50
Hamilton/Boehm		**Gamebirds of North America**			
84-05-001	Ring-Necked Pheasant	Boehm	15,000	62.50	62.50
84-05-002	Bob White Quail	Boehm	15,000	62.50	62.50
84-05-003	American Woodcock	Boehm	15,000	62.50	62.50
84-05-004	California Quail	Boehm	15,000	62.50	62.50
84-05-005	Ruffed Grouse	Boehm	15,000	62.50	62.50
84-05-006	Wild Turkey	Boehm	15,000	62.50	62.50
84-05-007	Willow Partridge	Boehm	15,000	62.50	62.50
84-05-008	Prairie Grouse	Boehm	15,000	62.50	62.50
Hamilton Collection		**Precious Portraits**			
87-01-001	Sunbeam	B. P. Gutmann	14-day	24.50	30-45.00
87-01-002	Mischief	B. P. Gutmann	14-day	24.50	30-45.00
87-01-003	Peach Blossom	B. P. Gutmann	14-day	24.50	36-45.00
87-01-004	Goldilocks	B. P. Gutmann	14-day	24.50	30-45.00
87-01-005	Fairy Gold	B. P. Gutmann	14-day	24.50	36-45.00
87-01-006	Bunny	B. P. Gutmann	14-day	24.50	30-45.00
Hamilton Collection		**Bundles of Joy**			
88-02-001	Awakening	B. P. Gutmann	14-day	24.50	75-125.00
88-02-002	Happy Dreams	B. P. Gutmann	14-day	24.50	60-95.00
88-02-003	Tasting	B. P. Gutmann	14-day	24.50	55.00

Company		Series			
Number	**Name**	**Artist**	**Edition Limit**	**Issue Price**	**Quote**
88-02-004	Sweet Innocence	B. P. Gutmann	14-day	24.50	30.00
88-02-005	Tommy	B. P. Gutmann	14-day	24.50	30-55.00
88-02-006	A Little Bit of Heaven	B. P. Gutmann	14-day	24.50	75.00
88-02-007	Billy	B. P. Gutmann	14-day	24.50	30-50.00
88-02-008	Sun Kissed	B. P. Gutmann	14-day	24.50	30-35.00
Hamilton Collection		**The Nutcracker Ballet**			
78-03-001	Clara	S. Fisher	28-day	19.50	36.00
79-03-002	Godfather	S. Fisher	28-day	19.50	19.50
79-03-003	Sugar Plum Fairy	S. Fisher	28-day	19.50	45.00
79-03-004	Snow Queen and King	S. Fisher	28-day	19.50	40.00
80-03-005	Waltz of the Flowers	S. Fisher	28-day	19.50	19.50
80-03-006	Clara and the Prince	S. Fisher	28-day	19.50	45.00
Hamilton Collection		**Precious Moments Plates**			
79-04-001	Friend in the Sky	T. Utz	28-day	21.50	50.00
80-04-002	Sand in her Shoe	T. Utz	28-day	21.50	27.00
80-04-003	Snow Bunny	T. Utz	28-day	21.50	25.00
80-04-004	Seashells	T. Utz	28-day	21.50	37.50
81-04-005	Dawn	T. Utz	28-day	21.50	27.00
82-04-006	My Kitty	T. Utz	28-day	21.50	36.00
Hamilton Collection		**The Greatest Show on Earth**			
81-05-001	Clowns	F. Moody	10-day	30.00	45.00
81-05-002	Elephants	F. Moody	10-day	30.00	30.00
81-05-003	Aerialists	F. Moody	10-day	30.00	30.00
81-05-004	Great Parade	F. Moody	10-day	30.00	30.00
81-05-005	Midway	F. Moody	10-day	30.00	30.00
81-05-006	Equestrians	F. Moody	10-day	30.00	30.00
82-05-007	Lion Tamer	F. Moody	10-day	30.00	30.00
82-05-008	Grande Finale	F. Moody	10-day	30.00	30.00
Hamilton Collection		**Rockwell Home of the Brave**			
81-06-001	Reminiscing	N. Rockwell	18,000	35.00	75.00
81-06-002	Hero's Welcome	N. Rockwell	18,000	35.00	50.00
81-06-003	Back to his Old Job	N. Rockwell	18,000	35.00	40.00
81-06-004	War Hero	N. Rockwell	18,000	35.00	35.00
82-06-005	Willie Gillis in Church	N. Rockwell	18,000	35.00	35.00
82-06-006	War Bond	N. Rockwell	18,000	35.00	35.00
82-06-007	Uncle Sam Takes Wings	N. Rockwell	18,000	35.00	48.00
82-06-008	Taking Mother over the Top	N. Rockwell	18,000	35.00	35.00
Hamilton Collection		**Japanese Floral Calendar**			
81-07-001	New Year's Day	Shuho/Kage	10-day	32.50	32.50
82-07-002	Early Spring	Shuho/Kage	10-day	32.50	32.50
82-07-003	Spring	Shuho/Kage	10-day	32.50	32.50
82-07-004	Girl's Doll Day Festival	Shuho/Kage	10-day	32.50	32.50
82-07-005	Buddha's Birthday	Shuho/Kage	10-day	32.50	32.50
82-07-006	Early Summer	Shuho/Kage	10-day	32.50	32.50
82-07-007	Boy's Doll Day Festival	Shuho/Kage	10-day	32.50	32.50
82-07-008	Summer	Shuho/Kage	10-day	32.50	32.50
82-07-009	Autumn	Shuho/Kage	10-day	32.50	32.50
83-07-010	Festival of the Full Moon	Shuho/Kage	10-day	32.50	32.50
83-07-011	Late Autumn	Shuho/Kage	10-day	32.50	32.50
83-07-012	Winter	Shuho/Kage	10-day	32.50	32.50
Hamilton Collection		**Portraits of Childhood**			
81-08-001	Butterfly Magic	T. Utz	28-day	24.95	24.95
82-08-002	Sweet Dreams	T. Utz	28-day	24.95	24.95
83-08-003	Turtle Talk	T. Utz	28-day	24.95	36.00
84-08-004	Friends Forever	T. Utz	28-day	24.95	24.95
Hamilton Collection		**Carefree Days**			
82-09-001	Autumn Wanderer	T. Utz	10-day	24.50	24.50
82-09-002	Best Friends	T. Utz	10-day	24.50	30.00
82-09-003	Feeding Time	T. Utz	10-day	24.50	24.50
82-09-004	Bathtime Visitor	T. Utz	10-day	24.50	30.00
82-09-005	First Catch	T. Utz	10-day	24.50	30.00
82-09-006	Monkey Business	T. Utz	10-day	24.50	30.00
82-09-007	Touchdown	T. Utz	10-day	24.50	24.50
82-09-008	Nature Hunt	T. Utz	10-day	24.50	24.50
Hamilton Colletion		**Utz Mother's Day**			
83-10-001	A Gift of Love	T. Utz	N/A	27.50	37.50
83-10-002	Mother's Helping Hand	T. Utz	N/A	27.50	27.50
83-10-003	Mother's Angel	T. Utz	N/A	27.50	27.50
Hamilton Collection		**Single Issues**			
83-11-001	Princess Grace	T. Utz	21-day	39.50	60.00
93-11-002	The Official Honeymooner's Commemorative Plate	D. Bobnick	28-day	37.50	37.50
Hamilton Collection		**Summer Days of Childhood**			
83-12-001	Mountain Friends	T. Utz	10-day	29.50	29.50
83-12-002	Garden Magic	T. Utz	10-day	29.50	29.50
83-12-003	Little Beachcomber	T. Utz	10-day	29.50	29.50
83-12-004	Blowing Bubbles	T. Utz	10-day	29.50	29.50
83-12-005	The Birthday Party	T. Utz	10-day	29.50	29.50
83-12-006	Playing Doctor	T. Utz	10-day	29.50	29.50
83-12-007	A Stolen Kiss	T. Utz	10-day	29.50	29.50
83-12-008	Kitty's Bathtime	T. Utz	10-day	29.50	29.50
83-12-009	Cooling Off	T. Utz	10-day	29.50	29.50
83-12-010	First Customer	T. Utz	10-day	29.50	29.50
83-12-011	A Jumping Contest	T. Utz	10-day	29.50	29.50
83-12-012	Balloon Carnival	T. Utz	10-day	29.50	29.50
Hamilton Collection		**Passage to China**			
83-13-001	Empress of China	R. Massey	15,000	55.00	55.00
83-13-002	Alliance	R. Massey	15,000	55.00	55.00
85-13-003	Grand Turk	R. Massey	15,000	55.00	55.00
85-13-004	Sea Witch	R. Massey	15,000	55.00	55.00
85-13-005	Flying Cloud	R. Massey	15,000	55.00	55.00
85-13-006	Romance of the Seas	R. Massey	15,000	55.00	55.00
85-13-007	Sea Serpent	R. Massey	15,000	55.00	55.00
85-13-008	Challenge	R. Massey	15,000	55.00	55.00
Hamilton Collection		**Springtime of Life**			
85-14-001	Teddy's Bathtime	T. Utz	14-day	29.50	29.50
85-14-002	Just Like Mommy	T. Utz	14-day	29.50	29.50
85-14-003	Among the Daffodils	T. Utz	14-day	29.50	29.50
85-14-004	My Favorite Dolls	T. Utz	14-day	29.50	29.50
85-14-005	Aunt Tillie's Hats	T. Utz	14-day	29.50	29.50
85-14-006	Little Emily	T. Utz	14-day	29.50	29.50

Company		Series			
Number	**Name**	**Artist**	**Edition Limit**	**Issue Price**	**Quote**
85-14-007	Granny's Boots	T. Utz	14-day	29.50	29.50
85-14-008	My Masterpiece	T. Utz	14-day	29.50	29.50
Hamilton Collection		**A Child's Best Friend**			
85-15-001	In Disgrace	B. P. Gutmann	14-day	24.50	90-185.00
85-15-002	The Reward	B. P. Gutmann	14-day	24.50	50-125.00
85-15-003	Who's Sleepy	B. P. Gutmann	14-day	24.50	45-90.00
85-15-004	Good Morning	B. P. Gutmann	14-day	24.50	45-75.00
85-15-005	Sympathy	B. P. Gutmann	14-day	24.50	54.00
85-15-006	On the Up and Up	B. P. Gutmann	14-day	24.50	75.00
85-15-007	Mine	B. P. Gutmann	14-day	24.50	90.00
85-15-008	Going to Town	B. P. Gutmann	14-day	24.50	60-69.00
Hamilton Collection		**A Country Summer**			
85-16-001	Butterfly Beauty	N. Noel	10-day	29.50	36.00
85-16-002	The Golden Puppy	N. Noel	10-day	29.50	29.50
86-16-003	The Rocking Chair	N. Noel	10-day	29.50	36.00
86-16-004	My Bunny	N. Noel	10-day	29.50	33.00
88-16-005	The Piglet	N. Noel	10-day	29.50	29.50
88-16-006	Teammates	N. Noel	10-day	29.50	29.50
Hamilton Collection		**The Little Rascals**			
85-17-001	Three for the Show	Unknown	10-day	24.50	30-45.00
85-17-002	My Gal	Unknown	10-day	24.50	24.50
85-17-003	Skeleton Crew	Unknown	10-day	24.50	24.50
85-17-004	Roughin' It	Unknown	10-day	24.50	24.50
85-17-005	Spanky's Pranks	Unknown	10-day	24.50	24.50
85-17-006	Butch's Challenge	Unknown	10-day	24.50	24.50
85-17-007	Darla's Debut	Unknown	10-day	24.50	24.50
85-17-008	Pete's Pal	Unknown	10-day	24.50	24.50
Hamilton Collection		**The Japanese Blossoms of Autumn**			
85-18-001	Bellflower	Koseki/Ebihara	10-day	45.00	45.00
85-18-002	Arrowroot	Koseki/Ebihara	10-day	45.00	45.00
85-18-003	Wild Carnation	Koseki/Ebihara	10-day	45.00	45.00
85-18-004	Maiden Flower	Koseki/Ebihara	10-day	45.00	45.00
85-18-005	Pampas Grass	Koseki/Ebihara	10-day	45.00	45.00
85-18-006	Bush Clover	Koseki/Ebihara	10-day	45.00	45.00
85-18-007	Purple Trousers	Koseki/Ebihara	10-day	45.00	45.00
Hamilton Collection		**The Star Wars Plate Collection**			
87-19-001	Hans Solo	T. Blackshear	14-day	29.50	36-60.00
87-19-002	R2-D2 and Wicket	T. Blackshear	14-day	29.50	45-55.00
87-19-003	Luke Skywalker and Darth Vader	T. Blackshear	14-day	29.50	60-75.00
87-19-004	Princess Leia	T. Blackshear	14-day	29.50	60-85.00
87-19-005	The Imperial Walkers	T. Blackshear	14-day	29.50	60-85.00
87-19-006	Luke and Yoda	T. Blackshear	14-day	29.50	60-69.00
88-19-007	Space Battle	T. Blackshear	14-day	29.50	185-295.
88-19-008	Crew in Cockpit	T. Blackshear	14-day	29.50	60-85.00
Hamilton Collection		**America's Greatest Sailing Ships**			
88-20-001	USS Constitution	T. Freeman	14-day	29.50	36.00
88-20-002	Great Republic	T. Freeman	14-day	29.50	36.00
88-20-003	America	T. Freeman	14-day	29.50	45.00
88-20-004	Charles W. Morgan	T. Freeman	14-day	29.50	36.00
88-20-005	Eagle	T. Freeman	14-day	29.50	48.00
88-20-006	Bonhomme Richard	T. Freeman	14-day	29.50	36.00
88-20-007	Gertrude L. Thebaud	T. Freeman	14-day	29.50	45.00
88-20-008	Enterprise	T. Freeman	14-day	29.50	36.00
Hamilton Collection		**Noble Owls of America**			
86-21-001	Morning Mist	J. Seerey-Lester	15,000	55.00	55.00
87-21-002	Prairie Sundown	J. Seerey-Lester	15,000	55.00	55.00
87-21-003	Winter Vigil	J. Seerey-Lester	15,000	55.00	55.00
87-21-004	Autumn Mist	J. Seerey-Lester	15,000	55.00	75.00
87-21-005	Dawn in the Willows	J. Seerey-Lester	15,000	55.00	55.00
87-21-006	Snowy Watch	J. Seerey-Lester	15,000	55.00	90.00
88-21-007	Hiding Place	J. Seerey-Lester	15,000	55.00	55.00
88-21-008	Waiting for Dusk	J. Seerey-Lester	15,000	55.00	55.00
Hamilton Collection		**Treasured Days**			
87-22-001	Ashley	H. Bond	14-day	29.50	60.00
87-22-002	Christopher	H. Bond	14-day	24.50	45.00
87-22-003	Sara	H. Bond	14-day	24.50	30.00
87-22-004	Jeremy	H. Bond	14-day	24.50	48.00
87-22-005	Amanda	H. Bond	14-day	24.50	48.00
88-22-006	Nicholas	H. Bond	14-day	24.50	48.00
88-22-007	Lindsay	H. Bond	14-day	24.50	48.00
88-22-008	Justin	H. Bond	14-day	24.50	48.00
Hamilton Collection		**Butterfly Garden**			
87-23-001	Spicebush Swallowtail	P. Sweany	14-day	29.50	45.00
87-23-002	Common Blue	P. Sweany	14-day	29.50	37.50
87-23-003	Orange Sulphur	P. Sweany	14-day	29.50	30.00
87-23-004	Monarch	P. Sweany	14-day	29.50	37.50
87-23-005	Tiger Swallowtail	P. Sweany	14-day	29.50	30.00
87-23-006	Crimson Patched Longwing	P. Sweany	14-day	29.50	37.50
88-23-007	Morning Cloak	P. Sweany	14-day	29.50	29.50
88-23-008	Red Admiral	P. Sweany	14-day	29.50	37.50
Hamilton Collection		**The Golden Classics**			
87-24-001	Sleeping Beauty	C. Lawson	10-day	37.50	37.50
87-24-002	Rumpelstiltskin	C. Lawson	10-day	37.50	37.50
87-24-003	Jack and the Beanstalk	C. Lawson	10-day	37.50	37.50
87-24-004	Snow White and Rose Red	C. Lawson	10-day	37.50	37.50
87-24-005	Hansel and Gretel	C. Lawson	10-day	37.50	37.50
88-24-006	Cinderella	C. Lawson	10-day	37.50	37.50
88-24-007	The Golden Goose	C. Lawson	10-day	37.50	37.50
88-24-008	The Snow Queen	C. Lawson	10-day	37.50	37.50
Hamilton Collection		**Children of the American Frontier**			
86-25-001	In Trouble Again	D. Crook	10-day	24.50	35.00
86-25-002	Tubs and Suds	D. Crook	10-day	24.50	27.00
86-25-003	A Lady Needs a Little Privacy	D. Crook	10-day	24.50	24.50
86-25-004	The Desperadoes	D. Crook	10-day	24.50	27.00
86-25-005	Riders Wanted	D. Crook	10-day	24.50	30.00
87-25-006	A Cowboy's Downfall	D. Crook	10-day	24.50	24.50
87-25-007	Runaway Blues	D. Crook	10-day	24.50	24.50
87-25-008	A Special Patient	D. Crook	10-day	24.50	24.50
Hamilton Collection		**The Official Honeymooners Plate Collection**			
87-26-001	The Honeymooners	D. Kilmer	14-day	24.50	60-150.00
87-26-002	The Hucklebuck	D. Kilmer	14-day	24.50	85-150.00

Number	Name	Artist	Edition Limit	Issue Price	Quote
87-26-003	Baby, You're the Greatest	D. Kilmer	14-day	24.50	75-175.00
88-26-004	The Golfer	D. Kilmer	14-day	24.50	90-175.00
88-26-005	The TV Chefs	D. Kilmer	14-day	24.50	120-175.
88-26-006	Bang! Zoom!	D. Kilmer	14-day	24.50	67-175.00
88-26-007	The Only Way to Travel	D. Kilmer	14-day	24.50	120-175.
88-26-008	The Honeymoon Express	D. Kilmer	14-day	24.50	150-220.
Hamilton Collection		**North American Waterbirds**			
88-27-001	Wood Ducks	R. Lawrence	14-day	37.50	55.00
88-27-002	Hooded Mergansers	R. Lawrence	14-day	37.50	54.00
88-27-003	Pintails	R. Lawrence	14-day	37.50	45.00
88-27-004	Canada Geese	R. Lawrence	14-day	37.50	45.00
89-27-005	American Widgeons	R. Lawrence	14-day	37.50	54.00
89-27-006	Canvasbacks	R. Lawrence	14-day	37.50	55.00
89-27-007	Mallard Pair	R. Lawrence	14-day	37.50	60.00
89-27-008	Snow Geese	R. Lawrence	14-day	37.50	45.00
Hamilton Collection		**Nature's Quiet Moments**			
88-28-001	A Curious Pair	R. Parker	14-day	37.50	37.50
88-28-002	Northern Morning	R. Parker	14-day	37.50	37.50
88-28-003	Just Resting	R. Parker	14-day	37.50	37.50
89-28-004	Waiting Out the Storm	R. Parker	14-day	37.50	37.50
89-28-005	Creekside	R. Parker	14-day	37.50	37.50
89-28-006	Autumn Foraging	R. Parker	14-day	37.50	37.50
89-28-007	Old Man of the Mountain	R. Parker	14-day	37.50	37.50
89-28-008	Mountain Blooms	R. Parker	14-day	37.50	37.50
Hamilton Collection		**Wizard of Oz Commemorative**			
88-29-001	We're Off to See the Wizard	T. Blackshear	14-day	24.50	250.00
88-29-002	Dorothy Meets the Scarecrow	T. Blackshear	14-day	24.50	90-125.00
89-29-003	The Tin Man Speaks	T. Blackshear	14-day	24.50	105-150
89-29-004	A Glimpse of the Munchkins	T. Blackshear	14-day	24.50	90-100.00
89-29-005	The Witch Casts A Spell	T. Blackshear	14-day	24.50	112-125.
89-29-006	If I Were King Of The Forest	T. Blackshear	14-day	24.50	150.00
89-29-007	The Great and Powerful Oz	T. Blackshear	14-day	24.50	150-175.
89-29-008	There's No Place Like Home	T. Blackshear	14-day	24.50	120-175.
Hamilton Collection		**Petals and Purrs**			
88-30-001	Blushing Beauties	B. Harrison	14-day	24.50	45.00
88-30-002	Spring Fever	B. Harrison	14-day	24.50	37.50
88-30-003	Morning Glories	B. Harrison	14-day	24.50	36.00
88-30-004	Forget-Me-Not	B. Harrison	14-day	24.50	36.00
89-30-005	Golden Fancy	B. Harrison	14-day	24.50	30.00
89-30-006	Pink Lillies	B. Harrison	14-day	24.50	30.00
89-30-007	Summer Sunshine	B. Harrison	14-day	24.50	24.50
89-30-008	Siamese Summer	B. Harrison	14-day	24.50	24.50
Hamilton Collection		**The Jeweled Hummingbirds Plate Collection**			
89-31-001	Ruby-throated Hummingbirds	J. Landenberger	14-day	37.50	37.50
89-31-002	Great Sapphire Wing Hummingbirds	J. Landenberger	14-day	37.50	37.50
89-31-003	Ruby-Topaz Hummingbirds	J. Landenberger	14-day	37.50	37.50
89-31-004	Andean Emerald Hummingbirds	J. Landenberger	14-day	37.50	37.50
89-31-005	Garnet-throated Hummingbirds	J. Landenberger	14-day	37.50	37.50
89-31-006	Blue-Headed Sapphire Hummingbirds	J. Landenberger	14-day	37.50	37.50
89-31-007	Pearl Coronet Hummingbirds	J. Landenberger	14-day	37.50	37.50
89-31-008	Amethyst-throated Sunangels	J. Landenberger	14-day	37.50	37.50
Hamilton Collection		**Stained Glass Gardens**			
89-32-001	Peacock and Wisteria	Unknown	15,000	55.00	55.00
89-32-002	Garden Sunset	Unknown	15,000	55.00	55.00
89-32-003	The Cockatoo's Garden	Unknown	15,000	55.00	55.00
89-32-004	Waterfall and Iris	Unknown	15,000	55.00	55.00
90-32-005	Roses and Magnolias	Unknown	15,000	55.00	55.00
90-32-006	A Hollyhock Sunrise	Unknown	15,000	55.00	55.00
90-32-007	Peaceful Waters	Unknown	15,000	55.00	55.00
90-32-008	Springtime in the Valley	Unknown	15,000	55.00	55.00
Hamilton Collection		**The I Love Lucy Plate Collection**			
89-33-001	California, Here We Come	J. Kritz	14-day	29.50	50-55.00
89-33-002	It's Just Like Candy	J. Kritz	14-day	29.50	60-125.00
90-33-003	The Big Squeeze	J. Kritz	14-day	29.50	55-135.00
90-33-004	Eating the Evidence	J. Kritz	14-day	29.50	75-149.00
90-33-005	Two of a Kind	J. Kritz	14-day	29.50	50-85.00
91-33-006	Queen of the Gypsies	J. Kritz	14-day	29.50	60-125.00
92-33-007	Night at the Copa	J. Kritz	14-day	29.50	45-90.00
92-33-008	A Rising Problem	J. Kritz	14-day	29.50	36-50.00
Hamilton Collection		**Great Fighter Planes Of World War II**			
92-34-001	Old Crow	R. Waddey	14-day	29.50	29.50
92-34-002	Big Hog	R. Waddey	14-day	29.50	29.50
92-34-003	P-47 Thunderbolt	R. Waddey	14-day	29.50	29.50
92-34-004	P-40 Flying Tiger	R. Waddey	14-day	29.50	29.50
92-34-005	F4F Wildcat	R. Waddey	14-day	29.50	29.50
92-34-006	P-38F Lightning	R. Waddey	14-day	29.50	29.50
93-34-007	F6F Hellcat	R. Waddey	14-day	29.50	29.50
93-34-008	P-39M Airacobra	R. Waddey	14-day	29.50	29.50
Hamilton Collection		**Birds of the Temple Gardens**			
89-35-001	Doves of Fidelity	J. Cheng	14-day	29.50	29.50
89-35-002	Cranes of Eternal Life	J. Cheng	14-day	29.50	29.50
89-35-003	Honorable Swallows	J. Cheng	14-day	29.50	29.50
89-35-004	Oriental White Eyes of Beauty	J. Cheng	14-day	29.50	29.50
89-35-005	Pheasants of Good Fortune	J. Cheng	14-day	29.50	29.50
89-35-006	Imperial Goldcrest	J. Cheng	14-day	29.50	29.50
89-35-007	Goldfinches of Virtue	J. Cheng	14-day	29.50	29.50
89-35-008	Magpies: Birds of Good Omen	J. Cheng	14-day	29.50	29.50
Hamilton Collection		**Winter Wildlife**			
89-36-001	Close Encounters	J. Seerey-Lester	15,000	55.00	55.00
89-36-002	Among the Cattails	J. Seerey-Lester	15,000	55.00	55.00
89-36-003	The Refuge	J. Seerey-Lester	15,000	55.00	55.00
89-36-004	Out of the Blizzard	J. Seerey-Lester	15,000	55.00	55.00
89-36-005	First Snow	J. Seerey-Lester	15,000	55.00	55.00
89-36-006	Lying In Wait	J. Seerey-Lester	15,000	55.00	55.00
89-36-007	Winter Hiding	J. Seerey-Lester	15,000	55.00	55.00
89-36-008	Early Snow	J. Seerey-Lester	15,000	55.00	55.00
Hamilton Collection		**Big Cats of the World**			
89-37-001	African Shade	D. Manning	14-day	29.50	29.50
89-37-002	View from Above	D. Manning	14-day	29.50	29.50
90-37-003	On The Prowl	D. Manning	14-day	29.50	29.50
90-37-004	Deep In The Jungle	D. Manning	14-day	29.50	29.50
90-37-005	Spirit Of The Mountain	D. Manning	14-day	29.50	29.50

Number	Name	Artist	Edition Limit	Issue Price	Quote
90-37-006	Spotted Sentinel	D. Manning	14-day	29.50	29.50
90-37-007	Above the Treetops	D. Manning	14-day	29.50	29.50
90-37-008	Mountain Dweller	D. Manning	14-day	29.50	29.50
92-37-009	Jungle Habitat	D. Manning	14-day	29.50	29.50
92-37-010	Solitary Sentry	D. Manning	14-day	29.50	29.50
Hamilton Collection		**Mixed Company**			
90-38-001	Two Against One	P. Cooper	14-day	29.50	36.00
90-38-002	A Sticky Situation	P. Cooper	14-day	29.50	36.00
90-38-003	What's Up	P. Cooper	14-day	29.50	29.50
90-38-004	All Wrapped Up	P. Cooper	14-day	29.50	36.00
90-38-005	Picture Perfect	P. Cooper	14-day	29.50	29.50
91-38-006	A Moment to Unwind	P. Cooper	14-day	29.50	33.00
91-38-007	Ole	P. Cooper	14-day	29.50	33.00
91-38-008	Picnic Prowlers	P. Cooper	14-day	29.50	29.50
Hamilton Collection		**Portraits From Oz**			
89-39-001	Dorothy	T. Blackshear	14-day	29.50	120-199.
89-39-002	Scarecrow	T. Blackshear	14-day	29.50	70-96.00
89-39-003	Tin Man	T. Blackshear	14-day	29.50	60-99.00
90-39-004	Cowardly Lion	T. Blackshear	14-day	29.50	55-99.00
90-39-005	Glinda	T. Blackshear	14-day	29.50	66-89.00
90-39-006	Wizard	T. Blackshear	14-day	29.50	75.00
90-39-007	Wicked Witch	T. Blackshear	14-day	29.50	90.00
90-39-008	Toto	T. Blackshear	14-day	29.50	145-150.
Hamilton Collection		**Delights of Childhood**			
89-40-001	Crayon Creations	J. Lamb	14-day	29.50	29.50
89-40-002	Little Mother	J. Lamb	14-day	29.50	29.50
90-40-003	Bathing Beauty	J. Lamb	14-day	29.50	29.50
90-40-004	Is That You, Granny?	J. Lamb	14-day	29.50	29.50
90-40-005	Nature's Little Helper	J. Lamb	14-day	29.50	29.50
90-40-006	So Sorry	J. Lamb	14-day	29.50	33.00
90-40-007	Shower Time	J. Lamb	14-day	29.50	33.00
90-40-008	Storytime Friends	J. Lamb	14-day	29.50	29.50
Hamilton Collection		**Classic Sporting Dogs**			
89-41-001	Golden Retrievers	B. Christie	14-day	24.50	54.00
89-41-002	Labrador Retrievers	B. Christie	14-day	24.50	60.00
89-41-003	Beagles	B. Christie	14-day	24.50	36.00
89-41-004	Pointers	B. Christie	14-day	24.50	30.00
89-41-005	Springer Spaniels	B. Christie	14-day	24.50	39.00
90-41-006	German Short-Haired Pointers	B. Christie	14-day	24.50	54.00
90-41-007	Irish Setters	B. Christie	14-day	24.50	36.00
90-41-008	Brittany Spaniels	B. Christie	14-day	24.50	48.00
Hamilton Collection		**Majesty of Flight**			
89-42-001	The Eagle Soars	T. Hirata	14-day	37.50	48.00
89-42-002	Realm of the Red-Tail	T. Hirata	14-day	37.50	39.00
89-42-003	Coastal Journey	T. Hirata	14-day	37.50	45.00
89-42-004	Sentry of the North	T. Hirata	14-day	37.50	48.00
89-42-005	Commanding the Marsh	T. Hirata	14-day	37.50	45.00
90-42-006	The Vantage Point	T. Hirata	14 day	29.50	45.00
90-42-007	Silent Watch	T. Hirata	14-day	29.50	48.00
90-42-008	Fierce and Free	T. Hirata	14-day	29.50	45.00
Hamilton Collection		**The Proud Nation**			
89-43-001	Navajo Little One	R. Swanson	14-day	24.50	45.00
89-43-002	In a Big Land	R. Swanson	14-day	24.50	31.00
89-43-003	Out with Mama's Flock	R. Swanson	14-day	24.50	33.00
89-43-004	Newest Little Sheepherder	R. Swanson	14-day	24.50	35.00
89-43-005	Dressed Up for the Powwow	R. Swanson	14-day	24.50	35.00
89-43-006	Just a Few Days Old	R. Swanson	14-day	24.50	30-49.00
89-43-007	Autumn Treat	R. Swanson	14-day	24.50	45.00
89-43-008	Up in the Red Rocks	R. Swanson	14-day	24.50	30.00
Hamilton Collection		**Thornton Utz 10th Anniversary Commemorative Plate Collection**			
89-44-001	Dawn	T. Utz	14-day	29.50	29.50
89-44-002	Just Like Mommy	T. Utz	14-day	29.50	29.50
89-44-003	Playing Doctor	T. Utz	14-day	29.50	29.50
89-44-004	My Kitty	T. Utz	14-day	29.50	29.50
89-44-005	Turtle Talk	T. Utz	14-day	29.50	29.50
89-44-006	Best Friends	T. Utz	14-day	29.50	29.50
89-44-007	Among the Daffodils	T. Utz	14-day	29.50	39.00
89-44-008	Friends in the Sky	T. Utz	14-day	29.50	29.50
89-44-009	Teddy's Bathtime	T. Utz	14-day	29.50	29.50
89-44-010	Little Emily	T. Utz	14-day	29.50	29.50
Hamilton Collection		**Country Kitties**			
89-45-001	Mischief Makers	G. Gerardi	14-day	24.50	45.00
89-45-002	Table Manners	G. Gerardi	14-day	24.50	36.00
89-45-003	Attic Attack	G. Gerardi	14-day	24.50	45.00
89-45-004	Rock and Rollers	G. Gerardi	14-day	24.50	27-35.00
89-45-005	Just For the Fern of It	G. Gerardi	14-day	24.50	27.00
89-45-006	All Washed Up	G. Gerardi	14-day	24.50	39.00
89-45-007	Stroller Derby	G. Gerardi	14-day	24.50	39.00
89-45-008	Captive Audience	G. Gerardi	14-day	24.50	39.00
Hamilton Collection		**Winged Reflections**			
89-46-001	Following Mama	R. Parker	14-day	37.50	37.50
89-46-002	Above the Breakers	R. Parker	14-day	37.50	37.50
89-46-003	Among the Reeds	R. Parker	14-day	37.50	37.50
89-46-004	Freeze Up	R. Parker	14-day	37.50	37.50
89-46-005	Wings Above the Water	R. Parker	14-day	37.50	37.50
90-46-006	Summer Loon	R. Parker	14-day	29.50	29.50
90-46-007	Early Spring	R. Parker	14-day	29.50	29.50
90-46-008	At The Water's Edge	R. Parker	14-day	29.50	29.50
Hamilton Collection		**Elvis Remembered**			
89-47-001	Loving You	S. Morton	90-day	37.50	75-99.00
89-47-002	Early Years	S. Morton	90-day	37.50	65-99.00
89-47-003	Tenderly	S. Morton	90-day	37.50	80-99.00
89-47-004	The King	S. Morton	90-day	37.50	70-125.00
89-47-005	Forever Yours	S. Morton	90-day	37.50	85.00
89-47-006	Rockin in the Moonlight	S. Morton	90-day	37.50	60-99.00
89-47-007	Moody Blues	S. Morton	90-day	37.50	75-99.00
89-47-008	Elvis Presley	S. Morton	90-day	37.50	75-125.00
Hamilton Collection		**Fifty Years of Oz**			
89-48-001	Fifty Years of Oz	T. Blackshear	14-day	37.50	135-199.
Hamilton Collection		**Small Wonders of the Wild**			
89-49-001	Hideaway	C. Frace	14-day	29.50	29.50

Number	Name	Artist	Edition Limit	Issue Price	Quote
Company		**Series**			
90-49-002	Young Explorers	C. Frace	14-day	29.50	29.50
90-49-003	Three of a Kind	C. Frace	14-day	29.50	75.00
90-49-004	Quiet Morning	C. Frace	14-day	29.50	29.50
90-49-005	Eyes of Wonder	C. Frace	14-day	29.50	29.50
90-49-006	Ready for Adventure	C. Frace	14-day	29.50	29.50
90-49-007	Uno	C. Frace	14-day	29.50	29.50
90-49-008	Exploring a New World	C. Frace	14-day	29.50	29.50
Hamilton Collection		**Dear to My Heart**			
90-50-001	Cathy	J. Hagara	14-day	29.50	29.50
90-50-002	Addie	J. Hagara	14-day	29.50	29.50
90-50-003	Jimmy	J. Hagara	14-day	29.50	29.50
90-50-004	Dacy	J. Hagara	14-day	29.50	29.50
90-50-005	Paul	J. Hagara	14-day	29.50	29.50
91-50-006	Shelly	J. Hagara	14-day	29.50	29.50
91-50-007	Jenny	J. Hagara	14-day	29.50	29.50
91-50-008	Joy	J. Hagara	14-day	29.50	29.50
Hamilton Collection		**North American Gamebirds**			
90-51-001	Ring-necked Pheasant	J. Killen	14-day	37.50	37.50
90-51-002	Bobwhite Quail	J. Killen	14-day	37.50	45.00
90-51-003	Ruffed Grouse	J. Killen	14-day	37.50	37.50
90-51-004	Gambel Quail	J. Killen	14-day	37.50	42.00
90-51-005	Mourning Dove	J. Killen	14-day	37.50	45.00
90-51-006	Woodcock	J. Killen	14-day	37.50	45.00
91-51-007	Chukar Partridge	J. Killen	14-day	37.50	45.00
91-51-008	Wild Turkey	J. Killen	14-day	37.50	45.00
Hamilton Collection		**The Saturday Evening Post Plate Collection**			
89-52-001	The Wonders of Radio	N. Rockwell	14-day	35.00	35.00
89-52-002	Easter Morning	N. Rockwell	14-day	35.00	50-60.00
89-52-003	The Facts of Life	N. Rockwell	14-day	35.00	35.00
90-52-004	The Window Washer	N. Rockwell	14-day	35.00	45.00
90-52-005	First Flight	N. Rockwell	14-day	35.00	54.00
90-52-006	Traveling Companion	N. Rockwell	14-day	35.00	35.00
90-52-007	Jury Room	N. Rockwell	14-day	35.00	35.00
90-52-008	Furlough	N. Rockwell	14-day	35.00	35.00
Hamilton Collection		**Favorite American Songbirds**			
89-53-001	Blue Jays of Spring	D. O'Driscoll	14-day	29.50	35.00
89-53-002	Red Cardinals of Winter	D. O'Driscoll	14-day	29.50	29.50
89-53-003	Robins & Apple Blossoms	D. O'Driscoll	14-day	29.50	35.00
89-53-004	Goldfinches of Summer	D. O'Driscoll	14-day	29.50	36.00
90-53-005	Autumn Chickadees	D. O'Driscoll	14-day	29.50	29.50
90-53-006	Bluebirds and Morning Glories	D. O'Driscoll	14-day	29.50	35.00
90-53-007	Tufted Titmouse and Holly	D. O'Driscoll	14-day	29.50	29.50
91-53-008	Carolina Wrens of Spring	D. O'Driscoll	14-day	29.50	29.50
Hamilton Collection		**Coral Paradise**			
89-54-001	The Living Oasis	H. Bond	14-day	29.50	29.50
90-54-002	Riches of the Coral Sea	H. Bond	14-day	29.50	29.50
90-54-003	Tropical Pageantry	H. Bond	14-day	29.50	36.00
90-54-004	Caribbean Spectacle	H. Bond	14-day	29.50	33.00
90-54-005	Undersea Village	H. Bond	14-day	29.50	36.00
90-54-006	Shimmering Reef Dwellers	H. Bond	14-day	29.50	36.00
90-54-007	Mysteries of the Galapagos	H. Bond	14-day	29.50	33.00
90-54-008	Forest Beneath the Sea	H. Bond	14-day	29.50	29.50
Hamilton Collection		**Noble American Indian Women**			
89-55-001	Sacajawea	D. Wright	14-day	29.50	45.00
90-55-002	Pocahontas	D. Wright	14-day	29.50	45.00
90-55-003	Minnehaha	D. Wright	14-day	29.50	36.00
90-55-004	Pine Leaf	D. Wright	14-day	29.50	45.00
90-55-005	Lily of the Mohawk	D. Wright	14-day	29.50	36.00
90-55-006	White Rose	D. Wright	14-day	29.50	45.00
91-55-007	Lozen	D. Wright	14-day	29.50	33.00
91-55-008	Falling Star	D. Wright	14-day	29.50	45.00
Hamilton Collection		**Little Ladies**			
89-56-001	Playing Bridesmaid	M.H. Bogart	14-day	29.50	60-100.00
90-56-002	The Seamstress	M.H. Bogart	14-day	29.50	60-99.00
90-56-003	Little Captive	M.H. Bogart	14-day	29.50	45-60.00
90-56-004	Playing Mama	M.H. Bogart	14-day	29.50	54-99.00
90-56-005	Susanna	M.H. Bogart	14-day	29.50	60-80.00
90-56-006	Kitty's Bath	M.H. Bogart	14-day	29.50	54-99.00
90-56-007	A Day in the Country	M.H. Bogart	14-day	29.50	60-99.00
91-56-008	Sarah	M.H. Bogart	14-day	29.50	45-80.00
Hamilton Collection		**A Country Season of Horses**			
90-57-001	First Day of Spring	J.M. Vass	14-day	29.50	36.00
90-57-002	Summer Splendor	J.M. Vass	14-day	29.50	33.00
90-57-003	A Winter's Walk	J.M. Vass	14-day	29.50	33.00
90-57-004	Autumn Grandeur	J.M. Vass	14-day	29.50	29.50
90-57-005	Cliffside Beauty	J.M. Vass	14-day	29.50	29.50
90-57-006	Frosty Morning	J.M. Vass	14-day	29.50	29.50
90-57-007	Crisp Country Morning	J.M. Vass	14-day	29.50	29.50
90-57-008	River Retreat	J.M. Vass	14-day	29.50	29.50
Hamilton Collection		**Good Sports**			
90-58-001	Wide Retriever	J. Lamb	14-day	29.50	36.00
90-58-002	Double Play	J. Lamb	14-day	29.50	36.00
90-58-003	Hole in One	J. Lamb	14-day	29.50	39.00
90-58-004	The Bass Masters	J. Lamb	14-day	29.50	29.50
90-58-005	Spotted on the Sideline	J. Lamb	14-day	29.50	33.00
90-58-006	Slap Shot	J. Lamb	14-day	29.50	33.00
91-58-007	Net Play	J. Lamb	14-day	29.50	36.00
91-58-008	Bassetball	J. Lamb	14-day	29.50	29.50
92-58-009	Boxer Rebellion	J. Lamb	14-day	29.50	29.50
92-58-010	Great Try	J. Lamb	14-day	29.50	29.50
Hamilton Collection		**Curious Kittens**			
90-59-001	Rainy Day Friends	B. Harrison	14-day	29.50	29.50-35.00
90-59-002	Keeping in Step	B. Harrison	14-day	29.50	36.00
91-59-003	Delightful Discovery	B. Harrison	14-day	29.50	36.00
91-59-004	Chance Meeting	B. Harrison	14-day	29.50	36.00
91-59-005	All Wound Up	B. Harrison	14-day	29.50	29.50
91-59-006	Making Tracks	B. Harrison	14-day	29.50	29.50
91-59-007	Playing Cat and Mouse	B. Harrison	14-day	29.50	36.00
91-59-008	A Paw's in the Action	B. Harrison	14-day	29.50	29.50
92-59-009	Little Scholar	B. Harrison	14-day	29.50	29.50
92-59-010	Cat Burglar	B. Harrison	14-day	29.50	29.50

Number	Name	Artist	Edition Limit	Issue Price	Quote
Company		**Series**			
Hamilton Collection		**The American Civil War**			
90-60-001	General Robert E. Lee	D. Prechtel	14-day	37.50	48.00
90-60-002	Generals Grant and Lee At Appomattox	D. Prechtel	14-day	37.50	48.00
90-60-003	General Thomas "Stonewall" Jackson	D. Prechtel	14-day	37.50	54.00
90-60-004	Abraham Lincoln	D. Prechtel	14-day	37.50	60.00
91-60-005	General J.E.B. Stuart	D. Prechtel	14-day	37.50	45.00
91-60-006	General Philip Sheridan	D. Prechtel	14-day	37.50	45.00
91-60-007	A Letter from Home	D. Prechtel	14-day	37.50	60.00
91-60-008	Going Home	D. Prechtel	14-day	37.50	45.00
92-60-009	Assembling The Troop	D. Prechtel	14-day	37.50	37.50
92-60-010	Standing Watch	D. Prechtel	14-day	37.50	37.50
Hamilton Collection		**Growing Up Together**			
90-61-001	My Very Best Friends	P. Brooks	14-day	29.50	36.00
90-61-002	Tea for Two	P. Brooks	14-day	29.50	29.50
90-61-003	Tender Loving Care	P. Brooks	14-day	29.50	29.50
90-61-004	Picnic Pals	P. Brooks	14-day	29.50	29.50
91-61-005	Newfound Friends	P. Brooks	14-day	29.50	29.50
91-61-006	Kitten Caboodle	P. Brooks	14-day	29.50	29.50
91-61-007	Fishing Buddies	P. Brooks	14-day	29.50	29.50
91-61-008	Bedtime Blessings	P. Brooks	14-day	29.50	29.50
Hamilton Collection		**Classic TV Westerns**			
90-62-001	The Lone Ranger and Tonto	K. Milnazik	14-day	29.50	45-55.00
90-62-002	Bonanza ™	K. Milnazik	14-day	29.50	49-60.00
90-62-003	Roy Rogers and Dale Evans	K. Milnazik	14-day	29.50	60.00
91-62-004	Rawhide	K. Milnazik	14-day	29.50	36-60.00
91-62-005	Wild Wild West	K. Milnazik	14-day	29.50	60.00
91-62-006	Have Gun, Will Travel	K. Milnazik	14-day	29.50	36-59.00
91-62-007	The Virginian	K. Milnazik	14-day	29.50	29.50-49.00
91-62-008	Hopalong Cassidy	K. Milnazik	14-day	29.50	60-80.00
Hamilton Collection		**Timeless Expressions of the Orient**			
90-63-001	Fidelity	M. Tsang	15,000	75.00	95.00
91-63-002	Femininity	M. Tsang	15,000	75.00	75.00
91-63-003	Longevity	M. Tsang	15,000	75.00	75.00
91-63-004	Beauty	M. Tsang	15,000	55.00	55.00
92-63-005	Courage	M. Tsang	15,000	55.00	55.00
Hamilton Collection		**Star Wars 10th Anniversary Commemorative**			
90-64-001	Star Wars 10th Anniversary Commemorative Plates	T. Blackshear	14-day	39.50	90-149.00
Hamilton Collection		**Romantic Castles of Europe**			
90-65-001	Ludwig's Castle	D. Sweet	19,500	55.00	55.00
91-65-002	Palace of the Moors	D. Sweet	19,500	55.00	55.00
91-65-003	Swiss Isle Fortress	D. Sweet	19,500	55.00	55.00
91-65-004	The Legendary Castle of Leeds	D. Sweet	19,500	55.00	55.00
91-65-005	Davinci's Chambord	D. Sweet	19,500	55.00	55.00
91-65-006	Eilean Donan	D. Sweet	19,500	55.00	55.00
92-65-007	Eltz Castle	D. Sweet	19,500	55.00	55.00
92-65-008	Kylemore Abbey	D. Sweet	19,500	55.00	55.00
Hamilton Collection		**The American Rose Garden**			
88-66-001	American Spirit	P.J. Sweany	14-day	29.50	29.50
88-66-002	Peace Rose	P.J. Sweany	14-day	29.50	29.50
89-66-003	White Knight	P.J. Sweany	14-day	29.50	36.00
89-66-004	American Heritage	P.J. Sweany	14-day	29.50	36.00
89-66-005	Eclipse	P.J. Sweany	14-day	29.50	33.00
89-66-006	Blue Moon	P.J. Sweany	14-day	29.50	36.00
89-66-007	Coral Cluster	P.J. Sweany	14-day	29.50	33.00
89-66-008	President Herbert Hoover	P.J. Sweany	14-day	29.50	29.50
Hamilton Collection		**English Country Cottages**			
90-67-001	Periwinkle Tea Room	M. Bell	14-day	29.50	36.00
91-67-002	Gamekeeper's Cottage	M. Bell	14-day	29.50	60.00
91-67-003	Ginger Cottage	M. Bell	14-day	29.50	60.00
91-67-004	Larkspur Cottage	M. Bell	14-day	29.50	36.00
91-67-005	The Chaplain's Garden	M. Bell	14-day	29.50	33.00
91-67-006	Lorna Doone Cottage	M. Bell	14-day	29.50	29.50
91-67-007	Murrle Cottage	M. Bell	14-day	29.50	29.50
91-67-008	Lullabye Cottage	M. Bell	14-day	29.50	29.50
Hamilton Collection		**The Angler's Prize**			
91-68-001	Trophy Bass	M. Susinno	14-day	29.50	36.00
91-68-002	Blue Ribbon Trout	M. Susinno	14-day	29.50	33.00
91-68-003	Sun Dancers	M. Susinno	14-day	29.50	29.50
91-68-004	Freshwater Barracuda	M. Susinno	14-day	29.50	36.00
91-68-005	Bronzeback Fighter	M. Susinno	14-day	29.50	36.00
91-68-006	Autumn Beauty	M. Susinno	14-day	29.50	36.00
92-68-007	Old Mooneyes	M. Susinno	14-day	29.50	36.00
92-68-008	Silver King	M. Susinno	14-day	29.50	33.00
Hamilton Collection		**Woodland Encounters**			
91-69-001	Want to Play?	G. Giordano	14-day	29.50	29.50
91-69-002	Peek-a-boo!	G. Giordano	14-day	29.50	29.50
91-69-003	Lunchtime Visitor	G. Giordano	14-day	29.50	29.50
91-69-004	Anyone for a Swim?	G. Giordano	14-day	29.50	29.50
91-69-005	Nature Scouts	G. Giordano	14-day	29.50	29.50
91-69-006	Meadow Meeting	G. Giordano	14-day	29.50	29.50
91-69-007	Hi Neighbor	G. Giordano	14-day	29.50	29.50
92-69-008	Field Day	G. Giordano	14-day	29.50	29.50
Hamilton Collection		**Childhood Reflections**			
91-70-001	Harmony	B.P. Gutmann	14-day	29.50	36.00
91-70-002	Kitty's Breakfast	B.P. Gutmann	14-day	29.50	29.50
91-70-003	Friendly Enemies	B.P. Gutmann	14-day	29.50	29.50
91-70-004	Smile, Smile, Smile	B.P. Gutmann	14-day	29.50	29.50
91-70-005	Lullaby	B.P. Gutmann	14-day	29.50	29.50
91-70-006	Oh! Oh! A Bunny	B.P. Gutmann	14-day	29.50	29.50
91-70-007	Little Mother	B.P. Gutmann	14-day	29.50	29.50
91-70-008	Thank You, God	B.P. Gutmann	14-day	29.50	29.50
Hamilton Collection		**Great Mammals of the Sea**			
91-71-001	Orca Trio	Wyland	14-day	35.00	45-50.00
91-71-002	Hawaii Dolphins	Wyland	14-day	35.00	37.50
91-71-003	Orca Journey	Wyland	14-day	35.00	42.00
91-71-004	Dolphin Paradise	Wyland	14-day	35.00	45.00
91-71-005	Children of the Sea	Wyland	14-day	35.00	35.00
91-71-006	Kissing Dolphins	Wyland	14-day	35.00	39.00
91-71-007	Islands	Wyland	14-day	35.00	45.00
91-71-008	Orcas	Wyland	14-day	35.00	45.00

Company Number	Name	Series Artist	Edition Limit	Issue Price	Quote
Hamilton Collection		**The West of Frank McCarthy**			
91-72-001	Attacking the Iron Horse	F. McCarthy	14-day	37.50	50-60.00
91-72-002	Attempt on the Stage	F. McCarthy	14-day	37.50	45-50.00
91-72-003	The Prayer	F. McCarthy	14-day	37.50	50-54.00
91-72-004	On the Old North Trail	F. McCarthy	14-day	37.50	50.00
91-72-005	The Hostile Threat	F. McCarthy	14-day	37.50	45-50.00
91-72-006	Bringing Out the Furs	F. McCarthy	14-day	37.50	45-50.00
91-72-007	Kiowa Raider	F. McCarthy	14-day	37.50	45-50.00
91-72-008	Headed North	F. McCarthy	14-day	37.50	37.50-50.00
Hamilton Collection		**The Quilted Countryside: A Signature Collection by Mel Steele**			
91-73-001	The Old Country Store	M. Steele	14-day	29.50	36.00
91-73-002	Winter's End	M. Steele	14-day	29.50	29.50
91-73-003	The Quilter's Cabin	M. Steele	14-day	29.50	33.00
91-73-004	Spring Cleaning	M. Steele	14-day	29.50	29.50
91-73-005	Summer Harvest	M. Steele	14-day	29.50	29.50
91-73-006	The Country Merchant	M. Steele	14-day	29.50	29.50
92-73-007	Wash Day	M. Steele	14-day	29.50	29.50
92-73-008	The Antiques Store	M. Steele	14-day	29.50	29.50
Hamilton Collection		**Sporting Generation**			
91-74-001	Like Father, Like Son	J. Lamb	14-day	29.50	29.50
91-74-002	Golden Moments	J. Lamb	14-day	29.50	29.50
91-74-003	The Lookout	J. Lamb	14-day	29.50	29.50
92-74-004	Picking Up The Scent	J. Lamb	14-day	29.50	29.50
92-74-005	First Time Out	J. Lamb	14-day	29.50	29.50
92-74-006	Who's Tracking Who	J. Lamb	14-day	29.50	29.50
92-74-007	Springing Into Action	J. Lamb	14-day	29.50	29.50
92-74-008	Point of Interest	J. Lamb	14-day	29.50	29.50
Hamilton Collection		**Seasons of the Bald Eagle**			
91-75-001	Autumn in the Mountains	J. Pitcher	14-day	37.50	37.50
91-75-002	Winter in the Valley	J. Pitcher	14-day	37.50	37.50
91-75-003	Spring on the River	J. Pitcher	14-day	37.50	37.50
91-75-004	Summer on the Seacoast	J. Pitcher	14-day	37.50	37.50
Hamilton Collection		**The STAR TREK 25th Anniversary Commemorative Collection**			
91-76-001	SPOCK	T. Blackshear	14-day	35.00	75-99.00
91-76-002	Kirk	T. Blackshear	14-day	35.00	35-75.00
92-76-003	McCoy	T. Blackshear	14-day	35.00	35.00
92-76-004	Uhura	T. Blackshear	14-day	35.00	35.00
92-76-005	Scotty	T. Blackshear	14-day	35.00	35.00
93-76-006	Sulu	T. Blackshear	14-day	35.00	35.00
Hamilton Collection		**The Spock® Commemorative Wall Plaque**			
93-77-001	Spock® Commemorative Wall Plaque	N/A	2,500	195.00	195.00
Hamilton Collection		**STAR TREK 25th Anniversary Commemorative Plate**			
91-78-001	STAR TREK 25th Anniversary Commemorative Plate	T. Blackshear	14-day	37.50	75.00
Hamilton Collection		**Vanishing Rural America**			
91-79-001	Quiet Reflections	J. Harrison	14-day	29.50	45.00
91-79-002	Autumn's Passage	J. Harrison	14-day	29.50	45.00
91-79-003	Storefront Memories	J. Harrison	14-day	29.50	45.00
91-79-004	Country Path	J. Harrison	14-day	29.50	36.00
91-79-005	When the Circus Came To Town	J. Harrison	14-day	29.50	36.00
91-79-006	Covered in Fall	J. Harrison	14-day	29.50	45.00
91-79-007	America's Heartland	J. Harrison	14-day	29.50	33.00
91-79-008	Rural Delivery	J. Harrison	14-day	29.50	33.00
Hamilton Collection		**North American Ducks**			
91-80-001	Autumn Flight	R. Lawrence	14-day	29.50	29.50
91-80-002	The Resting Place	R. Lawrence	14-day	29.50	29.50
91-80-003	Twin Flight	R. Lawrence	14-day	29.50	29.50
92-80-004	Misty Morning	R. Lawrence	14-day	29.50	29.50
92-80-005	Springtime Thaw	R. Lawrence	14-day	29.50	29.50
92-80-006	Summer Retreat	R. Lawrence	14-day	29.50	29.50
92-80-007	Overcast	R. Lawrence	14-day	29.50	29.50
92-80-008	Perfect Pintails	R. Lawrence	14-day	29.50	29.50
Hamilton Collection		**Proud Indian Families**			
91-81-001	The Storyteller	K. Freeman	14-day	29.50	35-40.00
91-81-002	The Power of the Basket	K. Freeman	14-day	29.50	35-40.00
91-81-003	The Naming Ceremony	K. Freeman	14-day	29.50	35-40.00
92-81-004	Playing With Tradition	K. Freeman	14-day	29.50	35-40.00
92-81-005	Preparing the Berry Harvest	K. Freeman	14-day	29.50	35-40.00
92-81-006	Ceremonial Dress	K. Freeman	14-day	29.50	35-40.00
92-81-007	Sounds of the Forest	K. Freeman	14-day	29.50	35-40.00
92-81-008	The Marriage Ceremony	K. Freeman	14-day	29.50	35-40.00
Hamilton Collection		**Little Shopkeepers**			
90-82-001	Sew Tired	G. Gerardi	14-day	29.50	29.50
91-82-002	Break Time	G. Gerardi	14-day	29.50	29.50
91-82-003	Purrfect Fit	G. Gerardi	14-day	29.50	29.50
91-82-004	Toying Around	G. Gerardi	14-day	29.50	36.00
91-82-005	Chain Reaction	G. Gerardi	14-day	29.50	45.00
91-82-006	Inferior Decorators	G. Gerardi	14-day	29.50	36.00
91-82-007	Tulip Tag	G. Gerardi	14-day	29.50	36.00
91-82-008	Candy Capers	G. Gerardi	14-day	29.50	36.00
Hamilton Collection		**Our Cherished Seas**			
92-83-001	Whale Song	S. Barlowe	48-day	37.50	37.50
92-83-002	Lions of the Sea	S. Barlowe	48-day	37.50	37.50
92-83-003	Flight of the Dolphins	S. Barlowe	48-day	37.50	37.50
92-83-004	Palace of the Seals	S. Barlowe	48-day	37.50	37.50
Hamilton Collection		**Republic Pictures Film Library Collection**			
92-84-001	Show With Laredo	S. Morton	28-day	37.50	37.50
92-84-002	The Ride Home	S. Morton	28-day	37.50	37.50
92-84-003	Attack at Tarawa	S. Morton	28-day	37.50	37.50
92-84-004	Thoughts of Angelique	S. Morton	28-day	37.50	37.50
92-84-005	War of the Wildcats	S. Morton	28-day	37.50	37.50
92-84-006	The Fightning Seabees	S. Morton	28-day	37.50	37.50
92-84-007	The Quiet Man	S. Morton	28-day	37.50	37.50
93-84-008	Angel & The Badman	S. Morton	28-day	37.50	37.50
93-84-009	Sands of Iwo Jima	S. Morton	28-day	37.50	37.50
Hamilton Collection		**Unbridled Spirit**			
92-85-001	Surf Dancer	C. DeHaan	28-day	29.50	29.50
92-85-002	Winter Renegade	C. DeHaan	28-day	29.50	29.50
92-85-003	Desert Shadows	C. DeHaan	28-day	29.50	29.50

Company Number	Name	Series Artist	Edition Limit	Issue Price	Quote
Hamilton Collection		**Victorian Playtime**			
91-86-001	A Busy Day	M. H. Bogart	14-day	29.50	29.50
92-86-002	Little Masterpiece	M. H. Bogart	14-day	29.50	29.50
92-86-003	Playing Bride	M. H. Bogart	14-day	29.50	29.50
92-86-004	Waiting for a Nibble	M. H. Bogart	14-day	29.50	29.50
92-86-005	Tea and Gossip	M. H. Bogart	14-day	29.50	29.50
92-86-006	Cleaning House	M. H. Bogart	14-day	29.50	29.50
92-86-007	A Little Persuasion	M. H. Bogart	14-day	29.50	29.50
92-86-008	Peek-a-Boo	M. H. Bogart	14-day	29.50	29.50
Hamilton Collection		**Winter Rails**			
92-87-001	Winter Crossing	T. Xaras	28-day	29.50	29.50
93-87-002	Coal Country	T. Xaras	28-day	29.50	29.50
93-87-003	Daylight Run	T. Xaras	28-day	29.50	29.50
Hamilton Collection		**Farmyard Friends**			
92-88-001	Mistaken Identity	J. Lamb	28-day	29.50	29.50
92-88-002	Little Cowhands	J. Lamb	28-day	29.50	29.50
93-88-003	Shreading the Evidence	J. Lamb	28-day	29.50	29.50
93-88-004	Partners in Crime	J. Lamb	28-day	29.50	29.50
Hamilton Collection		**Man's Best Friend**			
92-89-001	Special Delivery	L. Picken	28-day	29.50	29.50
92-89-002	Making Waves	L. Picken	28-day	29.50	29.50
92-89-003	Good Catch	L. Picken	28-day	29.50	29.50
93-89-004	Time For a Walk	L. Picken	28-day	29.50	29.50
93-89-005	Faithful Friend	L. Picken	28-day	29.50	29.50
93-89-006	Let's Play Ball	L. Picken	28-day	29.50	29.50
Hamilton Collection		**Nature's Nightime Realm**			
92-90-001	Bobcat	G. Murray	28-day	29.50	29.50
92-90-002	Cougar	G. Murray	28-day	29.50	29.50
93-90-003	Jaguar	G. Murray	28-day	29.50	29.50
93-90-004	White Tiger	G. Murray	28-day	29.50	29.50
Hamilton Collection		**Precious Moments Bible Story**			
91-91-001	Come Let Us Adore Him	S. Butcher	28-day	29.50	29.50
92-91-002	They Followed The Star	S. Butcher	28-day	29.50	29.50
92-91-003	The Flight Into Egypt	S. Butcher	28-day	29.50	29.50
92-91-004	The Carpenter Shop	S. Butcher	28-day	29.50	29.50
92-91-005	Jesus In The Temple	S. Butcher	28-day	29.50	29.50
92-91-006	The Crucifixion	S. Butcher	28-day	29.50	29.50
93-91-007	He Is Not Here	S. Butcher	28-day	29.50	29.50
Hamilton Collection		**The Wonder Of Christmas**			
91-92-001	Santa's Secret	J. McClelland	28-day	29.50	29.50
92-92-002	My Favorite Ornament	J. McClelland	28-day	29.50	29.50
92-92-003	Waiting For Santa	J. McClelland	28-day	29.50	29.50
Hamilton Collection		**Romantic Victorian Keepsake**			
92-93-001	Dearest Kiss	J. Grossman	28-day	35.00	35.00
93-93-002	First Love	J. Grossman	28-day	35.00	35.00
93-93-003	As Fair as a Rose	J. Grossman	28-day	35.00	35.00
Hamilton Collection		**The World Of Zolan**			
92-94-001	First Kiss	D. Zolan	28-day	29.50	29.50
92-94-002	Morning Discovery	D. Zolan	28-day	29.50	29.50
93-94-003	Little Fisherman	D. Zolan	28-day	29.50	29.50
93-94-004	Letter to Grandma	D. Zolan	28-day	29.50	29.50
93-94-005	Twilight Prayer	D. Zolan	28-day	29.50	29.50
93-94-006	Flowers for Mother	D. Zolan	28-day	29.50	29.50
Hamilton Collection		**Mystic Warriors**			
92-95-001	Deliverance	C. Ren	28-day	29.50	29.50
92-95-002	Mystic Warrior	C. Ren	28-day	29.50	29.50
92-95-003	Sun Seeker	C. Ren	28-day	29.50	29.50
92-95-004	Top Gun	C. Ren	28-day	29.50	29.50
92-95-005	Man Who Walks Alone	C. Ren	28-day	29.50	29.50
92-95-006	Windrider	C. Ren	28-day	29.50	29.50
92-95-007	Spirit of the Plains	C. Ren	28-day	29.50	29.50
93-95-008	Blue Thunder	C. Ren	28-day	29.50	29.50
93-95-009	Sun Glow	C. Ren	28-day	29.50	29.50
93-95-010	Peace Maker	C. Ren	28-day	29.50	29.50
Hamilton Collection		**Andy Griffith**			
92-96-001	Sheriff Andy Taylor	R. Tannenbaum	28-day	29.50	29.50
92-96-002	A Startling Conclusion	R. Tannenbaum	28-day	29.50	29.50
Hamilton Collection		**Madonna And Child**			
92-97-001	Madonna Della Seida	R. Sanzio	28-day	37.50	37.50
92-97-002	Virgin of the Rocks	L. DaVinci	28-day	37.50	37.50
Hamilton Collection		**Council Of Nations**			
91-98-001	Strength of the Sioux	G. Perillo	28-day	29.50	29.50
92-98-002	Pride of the Cheyenne	G. Perillo	28-day	29.50	29.50
92-98-003	Dignity of the Nez Parce	G. Perillo	28-day	29.50	29.50
92-98-004	Courage of the Arapaho	G. Perillo	28-day	29.50	29.50
92-98-005	Power of the Blackfoot	G. Perillo	28-day	29.50	29.50
92-98-006	Nobility of the Algonqui	G. Perillo	28-day	29.50	29.50
92-98-007	Wisdom of the Cherokee	G. Perillo	28-day	29.50	29.50
92-98-008	Boldness of the Seneca	G. Perillo	28-day	29.50	29.50
Hamilton Collection		**Beauty Of Winter**			
92-99-001	Silent Night	N/A	28-day	19.50	19.50
93-99-002	Moonlight Sleighride	N/A	28-day	19.50	19.50
Hamilton Collection		**Bialosky®& Friends**			
92-100-001	Family Addition	P./A.Bialosky	28-day	29.50	29.50
93-100-002	Sweetheart	P./A.Bialosky	28-day	29.50	29.50
93-100-003	Let's Go Fishing	P./A.Bialosky	28-day	29.50	29.50
93-100-004	U.S. Mail	P./A.Bialosky	28-day	29.50	29.50
Hamilton Collection		**Country Garden Cottages**			
92-101-001	Riverbank Cottage	E. Dertner	28-day	29.50	29.50
92-101-002	Sunday Outing	E. Dertner	28-day	29.50	29.50
92-101-003	Shepherd's Cottage	E. Dertner	28-day	19.50	19.50
93-101-004	Daydream Cottage	E. Dertner	28-day	19.50	19.50
93-101-005	Garden Glorious	E. Dertner	28-day	29.50	29.50
93-101-006	This Side of Heaven	E. Dertner	28-day	29.50	29.50
Hamilton Collection		**Quiet Moments Of Childhood**			
91-102-001	Elizabeth's Afternoon Tea	D. Green	14-day	29.50	33.00
91-102-002	Christina's Secret Garden	D. Green	14-day	29.50	29.50

Company		Series			
Number	Name	Artist	Edition Limit	Issue Price	Quote
91-102-003	Eric & Erin's Storytime	D. Green	14-day	29.50	29.50
92-102-004	Jessica's Tea Party	D. Green	14-day	29.50	29.50
92-102-005	Megan & Monique's Bakery	D. Green	14-day	29.50	29.50
92-102-006	Children's Day By The Sea	D. Green	14-day	29.50	29.50
92-102-007	Jordan's Playful Pups	D. Green	14-day	29.50	29.50
92-102-008	Daniel's Morning Playtime	D. Green	14-day	29.50	29.50
Hamilton Collection		**Star Trek: The Next Generation**			
93-103-001	Captain Jean-Luc Picard	T. Blackshear	28-day	35.00	35.00
93-103-002	Commander William Riker	T. Blackshear	28-day	35.00	35.00
Hamilton Collection		**Portraits of the Bald Eagle**			
93-104-001	Ruler of the Sky	J. Pitcher	28-day	37.50	37.50
93-104-002	In Bold Defiance	J. Pitcher	28-day	37.50	37.50
Hamilton Collection		**A Lisi Martin Christmas**			
92-105-001	Santa's Littlest Reindeer	L. Martin	28-day	29.50	29.50
93-105-002	Not A Creature Was Stirring	L. Martin	28-day	29.50	29.50
Hamilton Collection		**Glory of Christ**			
92-106-001	The Ascension	C. Micarelli	48-day	29.50	29.50
Hamilton Collection		**Star Wars Trilogy**			
93-107-001	Star Wars	M. Weistling	28-day	37.50	37.50
Hamilton Collection		**Normas Rockwell's Saturday Evening Post Baseball Plate Collection**			
92-108-001	100th Year of Baseball	N. Rockwell	Open	19.50	19.50
93-108-002	The Rookie	N. Rockwell	Open	19.50	19.50
93-108-003	The Dugout	N. Rockwell	Open	19.50	19.50
93-108-004	Bottom of the Sixth	N. Rockwell	Open	19.50	19.50
Hamilton Collection		**Cameo Kittens**			
93-109-001	Ginger Snap	Q. Lemonds	28-day	29.50	29.50
Hamilton Collection		**Princesses of the Plains**			
93-110-001	Prairie Flower	D. Wright	28-day	29.50	29.50
93-110-002	Snow Princess	D. Wright	28-day	29.50	29.50
Hamilton Collection		**Victorian Christmas Memories**			
92-111-001	A Visit from St. Nicholas	J. Grossman	28-day	29.50	29.50
93-111-002	Christmas Delivery	J. Grossman	28-day	29.50	29.50
Haviland		**Twelve Days of Christmas**			
70-01-001	Partridge	R. Hetreau	30,000	25.00	54.00
71-01-002	Two Turtle Doves	R. Hetreau	30,000	25.00	25.00
72-01-003	Three French Hens	R. Hetreau	30,000	27.50	27.50
73-01-004	Four Calling Birds	R. Hetreau	30,000	28.50	30.00
74-01-005	Five Golden Rings	R. Hetreau	30,000	30.00	30.00
75-01-006	Six Geese a'laying	R. Hetreau	30,000	32.50	32.50
76-01-007	Seven Swans	R. Hetreau	30,000	38.00	38.00
77-01-008	Eight Maids	R. Hetreau	30,000	40.00	40.00
78-01-009	Nine Ladies Dancing	R. Hetreau	30,000	45.00	67.00
79-01-010	Ten Lord's a'leaping	R. Hetreau	30,000	50.00	50.00
80-01-011	Eleven Pipers Piping	R. Hetreau	30,000	55.00	65.00
81-01-012	Twelve Drummers	R. Hetreau	30,000	60.00	60.00
Haviland & Parlon		**Tapestry I**			
71-01-001	Unicorn in Captivity	Unknown	10,000	35.00	63.00
72-01-002	Start of the Hunt	Unknown	10,000	35.00	50.00
73-01-003	Chase of the Unicorn	Unknown	10,000	35.00	76.00
74-01-004	End of the Hunt	Unknown	10,000	37.50	69.00
75-01-005	Unicorn Surrounded	Unknown	10,000	40.00	70.00
76-01-006	Brought to the Castle	Unknown	10,000	42.50	65.00
Haviland & Parlon		**The Lady and the Unicorn**			
77-02-001	To My Only Desire	Unknown	20,000	45.00	45.00
78-02-002	Sight	Unknown	20,000	45.00	45.00
79-02-003	Sound	Unknown	20,000	47.50	47.50
80-02-004	Touch	Unknown	15,000	52.50	100.00
81-02-005	Scent	Unknown	10,000	59.00	59.00
82-02-006	Taste	Unknown	10,000	59.00	59.00
Haviland & Parlon		**Christmas Madonnas**			
72-03-001	By Raphael	Raphael	5,000	35.00	42.00
73-03-002	By Feruzzi	Feruzzi	5,000	40.00	78.00
74-03-003	By Raphael	Raphael	5,000	42.50	42.50
75-03-004	By Murillo	Murillo	7,500	42.50	42.50
76-03-005	By Botticelli	Botticelli	7,500	45.00	45.00
77-03-006	By Bellini	Bellini	7,500	48.00	48.00
78-03-007	By Lippi	Lippi	7,500	48.00	53.00
79-03-008	Madonna of The Eucharist	Botticelli	7,500	49.50	112.00
Edna Hibel Studios		**Arte Ovale**			
80-01-001	Takara, Gold	E. Hibel	300	1000.00	2500.00
80-01-002	Takara, Blanco	E. Hibel	700	450.00	1100.00
80-01-003	Takara, Cobalt Blue	E. Hibel	1,000	595.00	2000.00
84-01-004	Taro-kun, Gold	E. Hibel	300	1000.00	2500.00
84-01-005	Taro-kun, Blanco	E. Hibel	700	450.00	750.00
84-01-006	Taro-kun, Cobalt Blue	E. Hibel	1,000	595.00	975.00
Edna Hibel Studios		**The World I Love**			
81-02-001	Leah's Family	E. Hibel	17,500	85.00	85.00
82-02-002	Kaylin	E. Hibel	17,500	85.00	85.00
83-02-003	Edna's Music	E. Hibel	17,500	85.00	85.00
83-02-004	O, Hana	E. Hibel	17,500	85.00	85.00
Edna Hibel Studios		**March of Dimes: Our Children, Our Future**			
90-03-001	A Time To Embrace	E. Hibel	150-days	29.00	29.00
John Hine N.A. Ltd.		**David Winter Plate Collection**			
91-01-001	A Christmas Carol	M. Fisher	10,000	30.00	30.00
91-01-002	Cotswold Village Plate	M. Fisher	10,000	30.00	30.00
92-01-003	Chichester Cross Plate	M. Fisher	10,000	30.00	30.00
92-01-004	Little Mill Plate	M. Fisher	10,000	30.00	30.00
92-01-005	Old Curiosity Shop	M. Fisher	10,000	30.00	30.00
92-01-006	Scrooge's Counting House	M. Fisher	10,000	30.00	30.00
93-01-007	Dove Cottage	M. Fisher	10,000	30.00	30.00
93-01-008	Little Forge	M. Fisher	10,000	30.00	30.00
Hutschenreuther		**Gunther Granget**			
72-01-001	American Sparrows	G. Granget	5,000	50.00	150.00
72-01-002	European Sparrows	G. Granget	5,000	30.00	65.00
73-01-003	American Kildeer	G. Granget	2,250	75.00	90.00

Company		Series			
Number	Name	Artist	Edition Limit	Issue Price	Quote
73-01-004	American Squirrel	G. Granget	2,500	75.00	75.00
73-01-005	European Squirrel	G. Granget	2,500	35.00	50.00
74-01-006	American Partridge	G. Granget	2,500	75.00	90.00
75-01-007	American Rabbits	G. Granget	2,500	90.00	90.00
76-01-008	Freedom in Flight	G. Granget	5,000	100.00	100.00
76-01-009	Wrens	G. Granget	2,500	100.00	110.00
76-01-010	Freedom in Flight, Gold	G. Granget	200	200.00	200.00
77-01-011	Bears	G. Granget	2,500	100.00	100.00
78-01-012	Foxes' Spring Journey	G. Granget	1,000	125.00	200.00
Hutschenreuther		**The Glory of Christmas**			
82-02-001	The Nativity	W./C. Hallett	25,000	80.00	125.00
83-02-002	The Annunciation	W./C. Hallett	25,000	80.00	115.00
84-02-003	The Shepherds	W./C. Hallett	25,000	80.00	100.00
85-02-004	The Wiseman	W./C. Hallett	25,000	80.00	100.00
Imperial Ching-te Chen		**Beauties of the Red Mansion**			
86-01-001	Pao-chai	Z. HuiMin	115-day	27.92	35.00
86-01-002	Yuan-chun	Z. HuiMin	115-day	27.92	30.00
87-01-003	Hsi-feng	Z. HuiMin	115-day	30.92	40.00
87-01-004	Hsi-chun	Z. HuiMin	115-day	30.92	35.00
88-01-005	Miao-yu	Z. HuiMin	115-day	30.92	35.00
88-01-006	Ying-chun	Z. HuiMin	115-day	30.92	40.00
88-01-007	Tai-yu	Z. HuiMin	115-day	32.92	40.00
88-01-008	Li-wan	Z. HuiMin	115-day	32.92	35.00
88-01-009	Ko-Ching	Z. HuiMin	115-day	32.92	35.00
88-01-010	Hsiang-yun	Z. HuiMin	115-day	34.92	40.00
89-01-011	Tan-Chun	Z. HuiMin	115-day	34.92	49.00
89-01-012	Chiao-chieh	Z. HuiMin	115-day	34.92	34.92
Imperial Ching-te Chen		**Scenes from the Summer Palace**			
88-02-001	The Marble Boat	Z. Song Mao	175-day	29.92	35.00
88-02-002	Jade Belt Bridge	Z. Song Mao	175-day	29.92	30.00
89-02-003	Hall that Dispels the Clouds	Z. Song Mao	175-day	32.92	32.92
89-02-004	The Long Promenade	Z. Song Mao	175-day	32.92	32.92
89-02-005	Garden/Harmonious Pleasure	Z. Song Mao	175-day	32.92	32.92
89-02-006	The Great Stage	Z. Song Mao	175-day	32.92	32.92
89-02-007	Seventeen Arch Bridge	Z. Song Mao	175-day	34.92	34.92
89-02-008	Boaters on Kumming Lake	Z. Song Mao	175-day	34.92	34.92
Imperial Ching-te Chen		**Blessings From a Chinese Garden**			
88-03-001	The Gift of Purity	Z. Song Mao	175 day	39.92	35.00
89-03-002	The Gift of Grace	Z. Song Mao	175-day	39.92	43.00
89-03-003	The Gift of Beauty	Z. Song Mao	175-day	42.92	49.00
89-03-004	The Gift of Happiness	Z. Song Mao	175-day	42.92	44.00
90-03-005	The Gift of Truth	Z. Song Mao	175-day	42.92	42.92
90-03-006	The Gift of Joy	Z. Song Mao	175-day	42.92	42.92
Imperial Ching-te Chen		**Legends of West Lake**			
89-04-001	Lady White	J. Xue-Bing	175-day	29.92	44.00
90-04-002	Lady Silkworm	J. Xue-Bing	175-day	29.92	41.00
90-04-003	Laurel Peak	J. Xue-Bing	175-day	29.92	33.00
90-04-004	Rising Sun Terrace	J. Xue-Bing	175-day	32.92	32.92
90-04-005	The Apricot Fairy	J. Xue-Bing	175-day	32.92	40.00
90-04-006	Bright Pearl	J. Xue-Bing	175-day	32.92	32.92
90-04-007	Thread of Sky	J. Xue-Bing	175-day	34.92	34.92
91-04-008	Phoenix Mountain	J. Xue-Bing	175-day	34.92	34.92
91-04-009	Ancestors of Tea	J. Xue-Bing	175-day	34.92	34.92
91-04-010	Three Pools Mirroring/Moon	J. Xue-Bing	175-day	36.92	36.92
91-04-011	Fly-In Peak	J. Xue-Bing	175-day	36.92	36.92
91-04-012	The Case of the Folding Fans	J. Xue-Bing	175-day	36.92	36.92
Imperial Ching-te Chen		**Flower Goddesses of China**			
91-05-001	The Lotus Goddess	Z. HuiMin	175-day	34.92	34.92
91-05-002	The Chrysanthemum Goddess	Z. HuiMin	175-day	34.92	38.00
91-05-003	The Plum Blossom Goddess	Z. HuiMin	175-day	37.92	37.92
91-05-004	The Peony Goddess	Z. HuiMin	175-day	37.92	37.92
91-05-005	The Narcissus Goddess	Z. HuiMin	175-day	37.92	37.92
91-05-006	The Camellia Goddess	Z. HuiMin	175-day	37.92	37.92
Imperial Ching-te Chen		**The Forbidden City**			
90-06-001	Pavilion of 10,000 Springs	S. Fu	150-day	39.92	39.92
90-06-002	Flying Kites/Spring Day	S. Fu	150-day	39.92	39.92
90-06-003	Pavilion/Floating Jade Green	S. Fu	150-day	42.92	42.92
91-06-004	The Lantern Festival	S. Fu	150-day	42.92	42.92
91-06-005	Nine Dragon Screen	S. Fu	150-day	42.92	42.92
91-06-006	The Hall of the Cultivating Mind	S. Fu	150-day	42.92	42.92
91-06-007	Dressing the Empress	S. Fu	150-day	45.92	45.92
91-06-008	Pavilion of Floating Cups	S. Fu	150-day	45.92	45.92
Imperial Ching-te Chen		**Maidens of the Folding Sky**			
92-07-001	Lady Lu	J. Xue-Bing	175-day	29.92	29.92
92-07-002	Mistress Yang	J. Xue-Bing	175-day	29.92	29.92
92-07-003	Bride Yen Chun	J. Xue-Bing	175-day	32.92	32.92
International Silver		**Bicentennial**			
72-01-001	Signing Declaration	M. Deoliveira	7,500	40.00	310.00
73-01-002	Paul Revere	M. Deoliveira	7,500	40.00	160.00
74-01-003	Concord Bridge	M. Deoliveira	7,500	40.00	115.00
75-01-004	Crossing Delaware	M. Deoliveira	7,500	50.00	80.00
76-01-005	Valley Forge	M. Deoliveira	7,500	50.00	65.00
77-01-006	Surrender at Yorktown	M. Deoliveira	7,500	50.00	60.00
Kaiser		**Oberammergau Passion Play**			
70-01-001	Oberammergau	T. Schoener	Closed	25.00	30.00
70-01-002	Oberammergau	K. Bauer	Closed	40.00	40.00
91-01-003	Oberammergau, sepia	Unknown	700	38.00	38.00
91-01-004	Oberammergau, cobalt	Unknown	400	64.00	64.00
Kaiser		**Christmas Plates**			
70-02-001	Waiting for Santa Claus	T. Schoener	Closed	12.50	25.00
71-02-002	Silent Night	K. Bauer	Closed	13.50	23.00
72-02-003	Welcome Home	K. Bauer	Closed	16.50	43.00
73-02-004	Holy Night	T. Schoener	Closed	18.00	44.00
74-02-005	Christmas Carolers	K. Bauer	Closed	25.00	30.00
75-02-006	Bringing Home the Tree	J. Northcott	Closed	25.00	30.00
76-02-007	Christ/Saviour Born	C. Maratti	Closed	25.00	35.00
77-02-008	The Three Kings	T. Schoener	Closed	25.00	25.00
78-02-009	Shepherds in The Field	T. Schoener	Closed	30.00	30.00
79-02-010	Christmas Eve	H. Blum	Closed	32.00	45.00
80-02-011	Joys of Winter	H. Blum	Closed	40.00	43.00
81-02-012	Adoration by Three Kings	K. Bauer	Closed	40.00	41.00
82-02-013	Bringing Home the Tree	K. Bauer	Closed	40.00	45.00

PLATES

Company / Number	Name	Series / Artist	Edition Limit	Issue Price	Quote
Kaiser		**Memories of Christmas**			
83-03-001	The Wonder of Christmas	G. Neubacher	Closed	42.50	42.50
84-03-002	A Christmas Dream	G. Neubacher	Closed	39.50	42.50
85-03-003	Christmas Eve	G. Neubacher	Closed	39.50	39.50
86-03-004	A Vist with Santa	G. Neubacher	Closed	39.50	39.50
Kaiser		**Mother's Day**			
71-04-001	Mare and Foal	T. Schoener	Closed	13.00	25.00
72-04-002	Flowers for Mother	T. Schoener	Closed	16.50	20.00
73-04-003	Cats	T. Schoener	Closed	17.00	40.00
74-04-004	Fox	T. Schoener	Closed	20.00	40.00
75-04-005	German Shepherd	T. Schoener	Closed	25.00	100.00
76-04-006	Swan and Cygnets	T. Schoener	Closed	25.00	27.50
77-04-007	Mother Rabbit and Young	T. Schoener	Closed	25.00	30.00
78-04-008	Hen and Chicks	T. Schoener	Closed	30.00	50.00
79-04-009	A Mother's Devotion	N. Peterner	Closed	32.00	40.00
80-04-010	Raccoon Family	J. Northcott	Closed	40.00	45.00
81-04-011	Safe Near Mother	H. Blum	Closed	40.00	40.00
82-04-012	Pheasant Family	K. Bauer	Closed	40.00	44.00
83-04-013	Tender Care	K. Bauer	Closed	40.00	65.00
Kaiser		**Anniversary**			
72-05-001	Love Birds	T. Schoener	Closed	16.50	30.00
73-05-002	In the Park	T. Schoener	Closed	16.50	24.50
74-05-003	Canoeing	T. Schoener	Closed	20.00	30.00
75-05-004	Tender Moment	K. Bauer	Closed	25.00	27.50
76-05-005	Serenade	T. Schoener	Closed	25.00	25.00
77-05-006	Simple Gift	T. Schoener	Closed	25.00	25.00
78-05-007	Viking Toast	T. Schoener	Closed	30.00	30.00
79-05-008	Romantic Interlude	H. Blum	Closed	32.00	32.00
80-05-009	Love at Play	H. Blum	Closed	40.00	40.00
81-05-010	Rendezvous	H. Blum	Closed	40.00	40.00
82-05-011	Betrothal	K. Bauer	Closed	40.00	40.00
83-05-012	Sunday Afternoon	T. Schoener	Closed	40.00	40.00
Kaiser		**King Tut**			
78-06-001	King Tut	Unknown	Closed	65.00	100.00
Kaiser		**Feathered Friends**			
78-07-001	Blue Jays	G. Loates	Closed	70.00	100.00
79-07-002	Cardinals	G. Loates	Closed	80.00	90.00
80-07-003	Waxwings	G. Loates	Closed	80.00	85.00
81-07-004	Goldfinch	G. Loates	Closed	80.00	85.00
Kaiser		**Egyptian**			
80-08-001	Nefertiti	Unknown	10,000	275.00	458.00
80-08-002	Tutankhamen	Unknown	10,000	275.00	458.00
Kaiser		**Four Seasons**			
81-09-001	Spring	I. Cenkovcan	Unkn.	50.00	64.00
81-09-002	Summer	I. Cenkovcan	Unkn.	50.00	64.00
81-09-003	Autumn	I. Cenkovcan	Unkn.	50.00	64.00
81-09-004	Winter	I. Cenkovcan	Unkn.	50.00	64.00
Kaiser		**On The Farm**			
81-10-001	The Duck	A. Lohmann	Unkn.	50.00	108.00
82-10-002	The Rooster	A. Lohmann	Unkn.	50.00	108.00
83-10-003	The Pond	A. Lohmann	Unkn.	50.00	108.00
83-10-004	The Horses	A. Lohmann	Unkn.	50.00	108.00
XX-10-005	White Horse	A. Lohmann	Unkn.	50.00	108.00
XX-10-006	Ducks on the Pond	A. Lohmann	Unkn.	50.00	108.00
XX-10-007	Girl with Goats	A. Lohmann	Unkn.	50.00	108.00
XX-10-008	Girl Feeding Animals	A. Lohmann	Unkn.	50.00	108.00
Kaiser		**Water Fowl**			
85-11-001	Mallard Ducks	E. Bierly	19,500	55.00	89.00
85-11-002	Canvas Back Ducks	E. Bierly	19,500	55.00	89.00
85-11-003	Wood Ducks	E. Bierly	19,500	55.00	89.00
85-11-004	Pintail Ducks	E. Bierly	19,500	55.00	89.00
Kaiser		**Wildflowers**			
86-12-001	Trillium	G. Neubacher	Closed	39.50	65.00
87-12-002	Spring Beauty	G. Neubacher	9,500	45.00	64.00
87-12-003	Wild Asters	G. Neubacher	9,500	49.50	59.00
87-12-004	Wild Roses	G. Neubacher	9,500	49.50	59.00
Kaiser		**Famous Lullabies**			
85-13-001	Sleep Baby Sleep	G. Neubacher	Unkn.	39.50	40.00
86-13-002	Rockabye Baby	G. Neubacher	Unkn.	39.50	41.00
86-13-003	A Mockingbird	G. Neubacher	Unkn.	39.50	46.00
86-13-004	Au Clair De Lune	G. Neubacher	Unkn.	39.50	44.00
87-13-005	Welsh Lullabye	G. Neubacher	Unkn.	39.50	57.00
88-13-006	Brahms' Lullabye	G. Neubacher	Unkn.	39.50	45.00
Kaiser		**Bicentennial Plate**			
76-14-001	Signing Declaration	J. Trumball	Closed	75.00	150.00
Edwin M. Knowles		**Wizard of Oz**			
77-01-001	Over the Rainbow	J. Auckland	100-day	19.00	50.00
78-01-002	If I Only Had a Brain	J. Auckland	100-day	19.00	44.00
78-01-003	If I Only Had a Heart	J. Auckland	100-day	19.00	30.00
78-01-004	If I Were King of the Forest	J. Auckland	100-day	19.00	35.00
79-01-005	Wicked Witch of the West	J. Auckland	100-day	19.00	30-49.00
79-01-006	Follow the Yellow Brick Road	J. Auckland	100-day	19.00	30-49.00
79-01-007	Wonderful Wizard of Oz	J. Auckland	100-day	19.00	44.00
80-01-008	The Grand Finale	J. Auckland	100-day	24.00	35-59.00
Edwin M. Knowles		**Gone with the Wind**			
78-02-001	Scarlett	R. Kursar	100-day	21.50	220-280.
79-02-002	Ashley	R. Kursar	100-day	21.50	125-195.
80-02-003	Melanie	R. Kursar	100-day	21.50	80.00
81-02-004	Rhett	R. Kursar	100-day	23.50	60-79.00
82-02-005	Mammy Lacing Scarlett	R. Kursar	100-day	23.50	75-90.00
83-02-006	Melanie Gives Birth	R. Kursar	100-day	23.50	90.00
84-02-007	Scarlet's Green Dress	R. Kursar	100-day	25.50	70.00
85-02-008	Rhett and Bonnie	R. Kursar	100-day	25.50	76.00
85-02-009	Scarlett and Rhett: The Finale	R. Kursar	100-day	29.50	80-85.00
Edwin M. Knowles		**Csatari Grandparent**			
80-03-001	Bedtime Story	J. Csatari	100-day	18.00	18.00
81-03-002	The Skating Lesson	J. Csatari	100-day	20.00	23.00
82-03-003	The Cookie Tasting	J. Csatari	100-day	20.00	20.00
83-03-004	The Swinger	J. Csatari	100-day	20.00	20.00

Company / Number	Name	Series / Artist	Edition Limit	Issue Price	Quote
84-03-005	The Skating Queen	J. Csatari	100-day	22.00	25.00
85-03-006	The Patriot's Parade	J. Csatari	100-day	22.00	22.00
86-03-007	The Home Run	J. Csatari	100-day	22.00	29.00
87-03-008	The Sneak Preview	J. Csatari	100-day	22.00	26.00
Edwin M. Knowles		**Americana Holidays**			
78-04-001	Fourth of July	D. Spaulding	Yr.Iss.	26.00	26.00
79-04-002	Thanksgiving	D. Spaulding	Yr.Iss.	26.00	26.00
80-04-003	Easter	D. Spaulding	Yr.Iss.	26.00	26.00
81-04-004	Valentine's Day	D. Spaulding	Yr.Iss.	26.00	26.00
82-04-005	Father's Day	D. Spaulding	Yr.Iss.	26.00	26.00
83-04-006	Christmas	D. Spaulding	Yr.Iss.	26.00	26.00
84-04-007	Mother's Day	D. Spaulding	Yr.Iss.	26.00	27.00
Edwin M. Knowles		**Annie**			
83-05-001	Annie and Sandy	W. Chambers	100-day	19.00	22-50.00
83-05-002	Daddy Warbucks	W. Chambers	100-day	19.00	21-39.00
83-05-003	Annie and Grace	W. Chambers	100-day	19.00	22.00
84-05-004	Annie and the Orphans	W. Chambers	100-day	21.00	24-49.00
85-05-005	Tomorrow	W. Chambers	100-day	21.00	22.00
86-05-006	Annie and Miss Hannigan	W. Chambers	100-day	21.00	29.50
86-05-007	Annie, Lily and Rooster	W. Chambers	100-day	24.00	24.00
86-05-008	Grand Finale	W. Chambers	100-day	24.00	24.00
Edwin M. Knowles		**The Four Ancient Elements**			
84-06-001	Earth	G. Lambert	75-day	27.50	35.00
84-06-002	Water	G. Lambert	75-day	27.50	35.00
85-06-003	Air	G. Lambert	75-day	29.50	35.00
85-06-004	Fire	G. Lambert	75-day	29.50	40.00
Edwin M. Knowles		**Biblical Mothers**			
83-07-001	Bethsheba and Solomon	E. Licea	Yr.Iss.	39.50	39.50
84-07-002	Judgment of Solomon	E. Licea	Yr.Iss.	39.50	39.50
84-07-003	Pharaoh's Daughter and Moses	E. Licea	Yr.Iss.	39.50	39.50
85-07-004	Mary and Jesus	E. Licea	Yr.Iss.	39.50	41-52.00
85-07-005	Sarah and Isaac	E. Licea	Yr.Iss.	44.50	51.00
86-07-006	Rebekah, Jacob and Esau	E. Licea	Yr.Iss.	44.50	45.00
Edwin M. Knowles		**Hibel Mother's Day**			
84-08-001	Abby and Lisa	E. Hibel	Yr.Iss.	29.50	45-50.00
85-08-002	Erica and Jamie	E. Hibel	Yr.Iss.	29.50	30-49.00
86-08-003	Emily and Jennifer	E. Hibel	Yr.Iss.	29.50	55.00
87-08-004	Catherine and Heather	E. Hibel	Yr.Iss.	34.50	45.00
88-08-005	Sarah and Tess	E. Hibel	Yr.Iss.	34.90	34.90
89-08-006	Jessica and Kate	E. Hibel	Yr.Iss.	34.90	35-45.00
90-08-007	Elizabeth, Jordan & Janie	E. Hibel	Yr.Iss.	36.90	42.00
91-08-008	Michele and Anna	E. Hibel	Yr.Iss.	36.90	40-45.00
Edwin M. Knowles		**Friends I Remember**			
83-09-001	Fish Story	J. Down	97-day	17.50	17.50
84-09-002	Office Hours	J. Down	97-day	17.50	17.50
85-09-003	A Coat of Paint	J. Down	97-day	17.50	25.00
85-09-004	Here Comes the Bride	J. Down	97-day	19.50	19.50
85-09-005	Fringe Benefits	J. Down	97-day	19.50	19.50
86-09-006	High Society	J. Down	97-day	19.50	19.50
86-09-007	Flower Arrangement	J. Down	97-day	21.50	22-29.00
86-09-008	Taste Test	J. Down	97-day	21.50	21.50
Edwin M. Knowles		**Father's Love**			
84-10-001	Open Wide	B. Bradley	100-day	19.50	20-25.00
84-10-002	Batter Up	B. Bradley	100-day	19.50	20-29.00
85-10-003	Little Shaver	B. Bradley	100-day	19.50	20.00
85-10-004	Swing Time	B. Bradley	100-day	22.50	22.50
Edwin M. Knowles		**The King and I**			
84-11-001	A Puzzlement	W. Chambers	150-day	19.50	19.50
85-11-002	Shall We Dance?	W. Chambers	150-day	19.50	42.00
85-11-003	Getting to Know You	W. Chambers	150-day	19.50	29.00
85-11-004	We Kiss in a Shadow	W. Chambers	150-day	19.50	39.00
Edwin M. Knowles		**Ency. Brit. Birds of Your Garden**			
85-12-001	Cardinal	K. Daniel	100-day	19.50	40.00
85-12-002	Blue Jay	K. Daniel	100-day	19.50	40.00
85-12-003	Oriole	K. Daniel	100-day	22.50	40.00
86-12-004	Chickadees	K. Daniel	100-day	22.50	40.00
86-12-005	Bluebird	K. Daniel	100-day	22.50	35.00
86-12-006	Robin	K. Daniel	100-day	22.50	24.00
86-12-007	Hummingbird	K. Daniel	100-day	24.50	28.00
87-12-008	Goldfinch	K. Daniel	100-day	24.50	40.00
87-12-009	Downy Woodpecker	K. Daniel	100-day	24.50	25-29.00
87-12-010	Cedar Waxwing	K. Daniel	100-day	24.90	29.00
Edwin M. Knowles		**Frances Hook Legacy**			
85-13-001	Fascination	F. Hook	100-day	19.50	29.00
85-13-002	Daydreaming	F. Hook	100-day	19.50	29.00
86-13-003	Discovery	F. Hook	100-day	22.50	29.00
86-13-004	Disappointment	F. Hook	100-day	22.50	29.00
86-13-005	Wonderment	F. Hook	100-day	22.50	25.00
87-13-006	Expectation	F. Hook	100-day	22.50	35.00
Edwin M. Knowles		**Hibel Christmas**			
85-14-001	The Angel's Message	E. Hibel	Yr.Iss.	45.00	44-59.00
86-14-002	The Gifts of the Magi	E. Hibel	Yr.Iss.	45.00	50-69.00
87-14-003	The Flight Into Egypt	E. Hibel	Yr.Iss.	49.00	50-69.00
88-14-004	Adoration of the Shepherd	E. Hibel	Yr.Iss.	49.00	50.00
89-14-005	Peaceful Kingdom	E. Hibel	Yr.Iss.	49.00	49-55.00
90-14-006	Nativity	E. Hibel	Yr.Iss.	49.00	70.00
Edwin M. Knowles		**Upland Birds of North America**			
86-15-001	The Pheasant	W. Anderson	150-day	24.50	25.00
86-15-002	The Grouse	W. Anderson	150-day	24.50	25.00
87-15-003	The Quail	W. Anderson	150-day	27.50	28.00
87-15-004	The Wild Turkey	W. Anderson	150-day	27.50	28.00
87-15-005	The Gray Partridge	W. Anderson	150-day	27.50	28.00
87-15-006	The Woodcock	W. Anderson	150-day	27.90	28.00
Edwin M. Knowles		**Oklahoma!**			
85-16-001	Oh, What a Beautiful Mornin'	M. Kunstler	150-day	19.50	19.50
86-16-002	Surrey with the Fringe on Top'	M. Kunstler	150-day	19.50	19.50
86-16-003	I Cain't Say No	M. Kunstler	150-day	19.50	19.50
86-16-004	Oklahoma	M. Kunstler	150-day	19.50	19.50

PLATES

Company / Number	Name	Series / Artist	Edition Limit	Issue Price	Quote
Edwin M. Knowles		**Sound of Music**			
86-17-001	Sound of Music	T. Crnkovich	150-day	19.50	22-29.00
86-17-002	Do-Re-Mi	T. Crnkovich	150-day	19.50	25.00
86-17-003	My Favorite Things	T. Crnkovich	150-day	22.50	25-29.00
86-17-004	Laendler Waltz	T. Crnkovich	150-day	22.50	35.00
87-17-005	Edelweiss	T. Crnkovich	150-day	22.50	35.00
87-17-006	I Have Confidence	T. Crnkovich	150-day	22.50	29-42.00
87-17-007	Maria	T. Crnkovich	150-day	24.90	39-50.00
87-17-008	Climb Ev'ry Mountain	T. Crnkovich	150-day	24.90	45-50.00
Edwin M. Knowles		**American Innocents**			
86-18-001	Abigail in the Rose Garden	Marsten/Mandrajji	100-day	19.50	19.50
86-18-002	Ann by the Terrace	Marsten/Mandrajji	100-day	19.50	19.50
86-18-003	Ellen and John in the Parlor	Marsten/Mandrajji	100-day	19.50	19.50
86-18-004	William on the Rocking Horse	Marsten/Mandrajji	100-day	19.50	48.00
Edwin M. Knowles		**J. W. Smith Childhood Holidays**			
86-19-001	Easter	J. W. Smith	97-day	19.50	21.00
86-19-002	Thanksgiving	J. W. Smith	97-day	19.50	21.00
86-19-003	Christmas	J. W. Smith	97-day	19.50	24.00
86-19-004	Valentine's Day	J. W. Smith	97-day	22.50	25.00
87-19-005	Mother's Day	J. W. Smith	97-day	22.50	25.00
87-19-006	Fourth of July	J. W. Smith	97-day	22.50	30.00
Edwin M. Knowles		**Living with Nature-Jerner's Ducks**			
86-20-001	The Pintail	B. Jerner	150-day	19.50	60.00
86-20-002	The Mallard	B. Jerner	150-day	19.50	50.00
87-20-003	The Wood Duck	B. Jerner	150-day	22.50	40.00
87-20-004	The Green-Winged Teal	B. Jerner	150-day	22.50	55.00
87-20-005	The Northern Shoveler	B. Jerner	150-day	22.90	34.00
87-20-006	The American Widgeon	B. Jerner	150-day	22.90	35.00
87-20-007	The Gadwall	B. Jerner	150-day	24.90	35.00
88-20-008	The Blue-Winged Teal	B. Jerner	150-day	24.90	38.00
Edwin M. Knowles		**Lincoln Man of America**			
86-21-001	The Gettysburg Address	M. Kunstler	150-day	24.50	25.00
87-21-002	The Inauguration	M. Kunstler	150-day	24.50	26.00
87-21-003	The Lincoln-Douglas Debates	M. Kunstler	150-day	27.50	27.50
87-21-004	Beginnings in New Salem	M. Kunstler	150-day	27.90	30.00
88-21-005	The Family Man	M. Kunstler	150-day	27.90	27.90
88-21-006	Emancipation Proclamation	M. Kunstler	150-day	27.90	45.00
Edwin M. Knowles		**Portraits of Motherhood**			
87-22-001	Mother's Here	W. Chambers	150-day	29.50	35.00
88-22-002	First Touch	W. Chambers	150-day	29.50	32.00
Edwin M. Knowles		**A Swan is Born**			
87-23-001	Hopes and Dreams	L. Roberts	150-day	24.50	30.00
87-23-002	At the Barre	L. Roberts	150-day	24.50	34.00
87-23-003	In Position	L. Roberts	150-day	24.50	40-65.00
88-23-004	Just For Size	L. Roberts	150-day	24.50	45.00
Edwin M. Knowles		**South Pacific**			
87-24-001	Some Enchanted Evening	E. Gignilliat	150-day	24.50	24.50
87-24-002	Happy Talk	E. Gignilliat	150-day	24.50	34.00
87-24-003	Dites Moi	E. Gignilliat	150-day	24.90	40.00
88-24-004	Honey Bun	E. Gignilliat	150-day	24.90	24.90
Edwin M. Knowles		**Tom Sawyer**			
87-25-001	Whitewashing the Fence	W. Chambers	150-day	27.50	27.50
87-25-002	Tom and Becky	W. Chambers	150-day	27.90	27.90
87-25-003	Tom Sawyer the Pirate	W. Chambers	150-day	27.90	27.90
88-25-004	First Pipes	W. Chambers	150-day	27.90	27.90
Edwin M. Knowles		**Friends of the Forest**			
87-26-001	The Rabbit	K. Daniel	150-day	24.50	42.00
87-26-002	The Raccoon	K. Daniel	150-day	24.50	60.00
87-26-003	The Squirrel	K. Daniel	150-day	27.90	28-30.00
88-26-004	The Chipmunk	K. Daniel	150-day	27.90	28-30.00
88-26-005	The Fox	K. Daniel	150-day	27.90	43.00
88-26-006	The Otter	K. Daniel	150-day	27.90	29.00
Edwin M. Knowles		**Amy Brackenbury's Cat Tales**			
87-27-001	A Chance Meeting: White American Shorthairs	A. Brackenbury	150-day	21.50	40.00
87-27-002	Gone Fishing: Maine Coons	A. Brackenbury	150-day	21.50	55.00
88-27-003	Strawberries and Cream: Cream Persians	A. Brackenbury	150-day	24.90	75.00
88-27-004	Flower Bed: British Shorthairs	A. Brackenbury	150-day	24.90	30.00
88-27-005	Kittens and Mittens: Silver Tabbies	A. Brackenbury	150-day	24.90	30.00
88-27-006	All Wrapped Up: Himalayans	A. Brackenbury	150-day	24.90	55.00
Edwin M. Knowles		**The Story of Christmas by Eve Licea**			
87-28-001	The Annunciation	E. Licea	Yr.Iss.	44.90	46.00
88-28-002	The Nativity	E. Licea	Yr.Iss.	44.90	45.00
89-28-003	Adoration Of The Shepherds	E. Licea	Yr.Iss.	49.90	53.00
90-28-004	Journey Of The Magi	E. Licea	Yr.Iss.	49.90	59.00
91-28-005	Gifts Of The Magi	E. Licea	Yr.Iss.	49.90	65.00
92-28-006	Rest on the Flight into Egypt	E. Licea	Yr.Iss.	49.90	49.90
Edwin M. Knowles		**Carousel**			
87-29-001	If I Loved You	D. Brown	150-day	24.90	24.90
88-29-002	Mr. Snow	D. Brown	150-day	24.90	24.90
88-29-003	The Carousel Waltz	D. Brown	150-day	24.90	55.00
88-29-004	You'll Never Walk Alone	D. Brown	150-day	24.90	47.00
Edwin M. Knowles		**Field Puppies**			
87-30-001	Dog Tired-The Springer Spaniel	L. Kaatz	150-day	24.90	65-70.00
87-30-002	Caught in the Act-The Golden Retriever	L. Kaatz	150-day	24.90	60.00
88-30-003	Missing/Point/Irish Setter	L. Kaatz	150-day	27.90	40.00
88-30-004	A Perfect Set-Labrador	L. Kaatz	150-day	27.90	52.00
88-30-005	Fritz's Folly-German Shorthaired Pointer	L. Kaatz	150-day	27.90	42-44.00
88-30-006	Shirt Tales: Cocker Spaniel	L. Kaatz	150-day	27.90	35.00
89-30-007	Fine Feathered Friends-English Setter	L. Kaatz	150-day	29.90	46.00
89-30-008	Command Performance/ Wiemaraner	L. Kaatz	150-day	29.90	34.00
Edwin M. Knowles		**The American Journey**			
87-31-001	Westward Ho	M. Kunstler	150-day	29.90	29.90
88-31-002	Kitchen With a View	M. Kunstler	150-day	29.90	32.00
88-31-003	Crossing the River	M. Kunstler	150-day	29.90	39.00
88-31-004	Christmas at the New Cabin	M. Kunstler	150-day	29.90	45.00
Edwin M. Knowles		**Precious Little Ones**			
88-32-001	Little Red Robins	M. T. Fangel	150-day	29.90	29.90
88-32-002	Little Fledglings	M. T. Fangel	150-day	29.90	29.90
88-32-003	Saturday Night Bath	M. T. Fangel	150-day	29.90	34.00
88-32-004	Peek-A-Boo	M. T. Fangel	150-day	29.90	47.00
Edwin M. Knowles		**Aesop's Fables**			
88-33-001	The Goose That Laid the Golden Egg	M. Hampshire	150-day	27.90	27.90
88-33-002	The Hare and the Tortoise	M. Hampshire	150-day	27.90	30.00
88-33-003	The Fox and the Grapes	M. Hampshire	150-day	30.90	35.00
89-33-004	The Lion And The Mouse	M. Hampshire	150-day	30.90	33.00
89-33-005	The Milk Maid And Her Pail	M. Hampshire	150-day	30.90	57.00
89-33-006	The Jay And The Peacock	M. Hampshire	150-day	30.90	38.00
Edwin M. Knowles		**Not So Long Ago**			
88-34-001	Story Time	J. W. Smith	150-day	24.90	24.90
88-34-002	Wash Day for Dolly	J. W. Smith	150-day	24.90	24.90
88-34-003	Suppertime for Kitty	J. W. Smith	150-day	24.90	48.00
88-34-004	Mother's Little Helper	J. W. Smith	150-day	24.90	35.00
Edwin M. Knowles		**Jerner's Less Travelled Road**			
88-35-001	The Weathered Barn	B. Jerner	150-day	29.90	29.90
88-35-002	The Murmuring Stream	B. Jerner	150-day	29.90	29.90
88-35-003	The Covered Bridge	B. Jerner	150-day	32.90	36.00
89-35-004	Winter's Peace	B. Jerner	150-day	32.90	36.00
89-35-005	The Flowering Meadow	B. Jerner	150-day	32.90	33.00
89-35-006	The Hidden Waterfall	B. Jerner	150-day	32.90	33.00
Edwin M. Knowles		**Once Upon a Time**			
88-36-001	Little Red Riding Hood	K. Pritchett	150-day	24.90	24.90
88-36-002	Rapunzel	K. Pritchett	150-day	24.90	24.90
88-36-003	Three Little Pigs	K. Pritchett	150-day	27.90	36.00
89-36-004	The Princess and the Pea	K. Pritchett	150-day	27.90	27.90
89-36-005	Goldilocks and the Three Bears	K. Pritchett	150-day	27.90	43.00
89-36-006	Beauty and the Beast	K. Pritchett	150-day	27.90	60.00
Edwin M. Knowles		**Majestic Birds of North America**			
88-37-001	The Bald Eagle	D. Smith	150-day	29.90	45.00
88-37-002	Peregrine Falcon	D. Smith	150-day	29.90	29.90
88-37-003	The Great Horned Owl	D. Smith	150-day	32.90	32.90
89-37-004	The Red-Tailed Hawk	D. Smith	150-day	32.90	32.90
89-37-005	The White Gyrfalcon	D. Smith	150-day	32.90	32.90
89-37-006	The American Kestral	D. Smith	150-day	32.90	32.90
90-37-007	The Osprey	D. Smith	150-day	34.90	34.90
90-37-008	The Golden Eagle	D. Smith	150-day	34.90	34.90
Edwin M. Knowles		**Cinderella**			
88-38-001	Bibbidi, Bobbidi, Boo	Disney Studios	150-day	29.90	90-100.00
88-38-002	A Dream Is A Wish Your Heart Makes	Disney Studios	150-day	29.90	90-100.00
89-38-003	Oh Sing Sweet Nightingale	Disney Studios	150-day	32.90	60-100.00
89-38-004	A Dress For Cinderelly	Disney Studios	150-day	32.90	90-110.00
89-38-005	So This Is Love	Disney Studios	150-day	32.90	60-70.00
90-38-006	At The Stroke Of Midnight	Disney Studios	150-day	32.90	54-60.00
90-38-007	If The Shoe Fits	Disney Studios	150-day	34.90	60-90.00
90-38-008	Happily Ever After	Disney Studios	150-day	34.90	60-80.00
Edwin M. Knowles		**Mary Poppins**			
89-40-001	Mary Poppins	M. Hampshire	150-day	29.90	40-55.00
89-40-002	A Spoonful of Sugar	M. Hampshire	150-day	29.90	40.00
90-40-003	A Jolly Holiday With Mary	M. Hampshire	150-day	32.90	45.00
90-40-004	We Love To Laugh	M. Hampshire	150-day	32.90	55-65.00
91-40-005	Chim Chim Cher-ee	M. Hampshire	150-day	32.90	40-65.00
91-40-006	Tuppence a Bag	M. Hampshire	150-day	32.90	55-65.00
Edwin M. Knowles		**Home Sweet Home**			
89-41-001	The Victorian	R. McGinnis	150-day	39.90	39.90
89-41-002	The Greek Revival	R. McGinnis	150-day	39.90	39.90
89-41-003	The Georgian	R. McGinnis	150-day	39.90	39.90
90-41-004	The Mission	R. McGinnis	150-day	39.90	39.90
Edwin M. Knowles		**My Fair Lady**			
89-42-001	Opening Day at Ascot	W. Chambers	150-day	24.90	30-39.00
89-42-002	I Could Have Danced All Night	W. Chambers	150-day	24.90	35.00
89-42-003	The Rain in Spain	W. Chambers	150-day	27.90	27.90
89-42-004	Show Me	W. Chambers	150-day	27.90	30-35.00
90-42-005	Get Me To/Church On Time	W. Chambers	150-day	27.90	35-55.00
90-42-006	I've Grown Accustomed/Face	W. Chambers	150-day	27.90	35-55.00
Edwin M. Knowles		**Sundblom Santas**			
89-43-001	Santa By The Fire	H. Sundblom	Closed	27.90	44.00
90-43-002	Christmas Vigil	H. Sundblom	Closed	27.90	36-50.00
91-43-003	To All A Good Night	H. Sundblom	Closed	32.90	45.00
92-43-004	Santa's on His Way	H. Sundblom	Closed	32.90	32.90
Edwin M. Knowles		**Great Cats Of The Americas**			
89-44-001	The Jaguar	L. Cable	150-day	29.90	65-100.00
89-44-002	The Cougar	L. Cable	150-day	29.90	44.00
89-44-003	The Lynx	L. Cable	150-day	32.90	44.00
90-44-004	The Ocelot	L. Cable	150-day	32.90	50.00
90-44-005	The Bobcat	L. Cable	150-day	32.90	44.00
90-44-006	The Jaguarundi	L. Cable	150-day	32.90	52.00
90-44-007	The Margay	L. Cable	150-day	34.90	44.00
91-44-008	The Pampas Cat	L. Cable	150-day	34.90	50.00
Edwin M. Knowles		**Heirlooms And Lace**			
89-45-001	Anna	C. Layton	150-day	34.90	60-90.00
89-45-022	Victoria	C. Layton	150-day	34.90	60-90.00
90-45-003	Tess	C. Layton	150-day	37.90	80-90.00
90-45-004	Olivia	C. Layton	150-day	37.90	135-139.
91-45-005	Bridget	C. Layton	150-day	37.90	110-131.
91-45-006	Rebecca	C. Layton	150-day	37.90	95-125.00
Edwin M. Knowles		**Stately Owls**			
89-46-001	The Snowy Owl	J. Beaudoin	150-day	29.90	47.00
89-46-002	The Great Horned Owl	J. Beaudoin	150-day	29.90	40.00
90-46-003	The Barn Owl	J. Beaudoin	150-day	32.90	40.00
90-46-004	The Screech Owl	J. Beaudoin	150-day	32.90	42.00
90-46-005	The Short-Eared Owl	J. Beaudoin	150-day	32.90	32.90
90-46-006	The Barred Owl	J. Beaudoin	150-day	32.90	32.90
90-46-007	The Great Grey Owl	J. Beaudoin	150-day	34.90	34.90
91-46-008	The Saw-Whet Owl	J. Beaudoin	150-day	34.90	34.90
Edwin M. Knowles		**Singin' In The Rain**			
90-47-001	Singin' In The Rain	M. Skolsky	150-day	32.90	35-40.00
90-47-002	Good Morning	M. Skolsky	150-day	32.90	45.00

Company		Series			
Number	Name	Artist	Edition Limit	Issue Price	Quote
91-47-003	Broadway Melody	M. Skolsky	150-day	32.90	45-55.00
91-47-004	We're Happy Again	M. Skolsky	150-day	32.90	40-65.00
Edwin M. Knowles		**Pinocchio**			
89-48-001	Gepetto Creates Pinocchio	Disney Studios	150-day	29.90	57.00
90-48-002	Pinocchio And The Blue Fairy	Disney Studios	150-day	29.90	55-65.00
90-48-003	It's an Actor's Life For Me	Disney Studios	150-day	32.90	50.00
90-48-004	I've Got No Strings On Me	Disney Studios	150-day	32.90	50-65.00
91-48-005	Pleasure Island	Disney Studios	150-day	32.90	50-60.00
91-48-006	A Real Boy	Disney Studios	150-day	32.90	65-70.00
Edwin M. Knowles		**Nature's Child**			
90-49-001	Sharing	M. Jobe	150-day	29.90	44.00
90-49-002	The Lost Lamb	M. Jobe	150-day	29.90	35.00
90-49-003	Seems Like Yesterday	M. Jobe	150-day	32.90	40.00
90-49-004	Faithful Friends	M. Jobe	150-day	32.90	43.00
90-49-005	Trusted Companion	M. Jobe	150-day	32.90	55.00
91-49-006	Hand in Hand	M. Jobe	150-day	32.90	32.90
Edwin M. Knowles		**Fantasia: (The Sorcerer's Apprentice) Golden Anniversary**			
90-50-001	The Apprentice's Dream	Disney Studios	150-day	29.90	29.90
90-50-002	Mischievous Apprentice	Disney Studios	150-day	29.90	29.90
91-50-003	Dreams of Power	Disney Studios	150-day	32.90	32.90
91-50-004	Mickey's Magical Whirlpool	Disney Studios	150-day	32.90	32.90
91-50-005	Wizardry Gone Wild	Disney Studios	150-day	32.90	32.90
91-50-006	Mickey Makes Magic	Disney Studios	150-day	34.90	34.90
91-50-007	The Penitent Apprentice	Disney Studios	150-day	34.90	34.90
92-50-008	An Apprentice Again	Disney Studios	150-day	34.90	34.90
Edwin M. Knowles		**Casablanca**			
90-51-001	Here's Looking At You, Kid	J. Griffin	150-day	34.90	62.00
90-51-002	We'll Always Have Paris	J. Griffin	150-day	34.90	34.90
91-51-003	We Loved Each Other Once	J. Griffin	150-day	37.90	37.90
91-51-004	Rick's Cafe Americain	J. Griffin	150-day	37.90	37.90
91-51-005	A Franc For Your Thoughts	J. Griffin	150-day	37.90	37.90
91-51-006	Play it Sam	J. Griffin	150-day	37.90	37.90
Edwin M. Knowles		**Field Trips**			
90-52-001	Gone Fishing	L. Kaatz	150-day	24.90	24.90
91-52-002	Ducking Duty	L. Kaatz	150-day	24.90	24.90
91-52-003	Boxed In	L. Kaatz	150-day	27.90	27.90
91-52-004	Pups 'N Boots	L. Kaatz	150-day	27.90	27.90
91-52-005	Puppy Tales	L. Kaatz	150-day	27.90	27.90
91-52-006	Pail Pals	L. Kaatz	150-day	29.90	29.90
91-52-007	Chesapeake Bay Retrievers	L. Kaatz	150-day	29.90	29.90
91-52-008	Hat Trick	L. Kaatz	150-day	29.90	29.90
Edwin M. Knowles		**The Old Mill Stream**			
90-53-001	New London Grist Mill	C. Tennant	150-day	39.90	39.90
91-53-002	Wayside Inn Grist Mill	C. Tennant	150-day	39.90	39.90
91-53-003	Old Red Mill	C. Tennant	150-day	39.90	39.90
91-53-004	Glade Creek Grist Mill	C. Tennant	150-day	39.90	39.90
Edwin M. Knowles		**Birds of the Seasons**			
90-54-001	Cardinals In Winter	S. Timm	150-day	24.90	24.90-60.00
90-54-002	Bluebirds In Spring	S. Timm	150-day	24.90	24.90-68.00
91-54-003	Nuthatches In Fall	S. Timm	150-day	27.90	27.90
91-54-004	Baltimore Orioles In Summer	S. Timm	150-day	27.90	43.00
91-54-005	Blue Jays In Early Fall	S. Timm	150-day	27.90	27.90
91-54-006	Robins In Early Spring	S. Timm	150-day	27.90	27.90
91-54-007	Cedar Waxwings in Fall	S. Timm	150-day	29.90	29.90
91-54-008	Chickadees in Winter	S. Timm	150-day	29.90	29.90
Edwin M. Knowles		**Cozy Country Corners**			
90-55-001	Lazy Morning	H. H. Ingmire	150-day	24.90	45-48.00
90-55-002	Warm Retreat	H. H. Ingmire	150-day	24.90	45-50.00
91-55-003	A Sunny Spot	H. H. Ingmire	150-day	27.90	27.90
91-55-004	Attic Afternoon	H. H. Ingmire	150-day	27.90	27.90
91-55-005	Mirror Mischief	H. H. Ingmire	150-day	27.90	27.90
91-55-006	Hide and Seek	H. H. Ingmire	150-day	29.90	29.90
91-55-007	Apple Antics	H. H. Ingmire	150-day	29.90	29.90
91-55-008	Table Trouble	H. H. Ingmire	150-day	29.90	29.90
Edwin M. Knowles		**Jewels of the Flowers**			
91-56-001	Sapphire Wings	T.C. Chiu	150-day	29.90	29.90
91-56-002	Topaz Beauties	T.C. Chiu	150-day	29.90	29.90
91-56-003	Amethyst Flight	T.C. Chiu	150-day	32.90	32.90
91-56-004	Ruby Elegance	T.C. Chiu	150-day	32.90	32.90
91-56-005	Emerald Pair	T.C. Chiu	150-day	32.90	32.90
91-56-006	Opal Splendor	T.C. Chiu	150-day	34.90	34.90
92-56-007	Pearl Luster	T.C. Chiu	150-day	34.90	34.90
92-56-008	Aquamarine Glimmer	T.C. Chiu	150-day	34.90	34.90
Edwin M. Knowles		**Pussyfooting Around**			
91-57-001	Fish Tales	C. Wilson	150-day	24.90	34.00
91-57-002	Teatime Tabbies	C. Wilson	150-day	24.90	24.90
91-57-003	Yarn Spinners	C. Wilson	150-day	24.90	24.90
91-57-004	Two Maestros	C. Wilson	150-day	24.90	24.90
Edwin M. Knowles		**Baby Owls of North America**			
91-58-001	Peek-A-Whoo:Screech Owls	J. Thornbrugh	150-day	27.90	27.90
91-58-002	Forty Winks: Saw-Whet Owls	J. Thornbrugh	150-day	29.90	29.90
91-58-003	The Tree House: Northern Pygmy Owls	J. Thornbrugh	150-day	30.90	30.90
91-58-004	Three of a Kind: Great Horned Owls	J. Thornbrugh	150-day	30.90	30.90
91-58-005	Out on a Limb: Great Gray Owls	J. Thornbrugh	150-day	30.90	30.90
91-58-006	Beginning to Explore: Boreal Owls	J. Thornbrugh	150-day	32.90	32.90
92-58-007	Three's Company: Long Eared Owls	J. Thornbrugh	150-day	32.90	32.90
92-58-008	Whoo's There: Barred Owl	J. Thornbrugh	150-day	32.90	32.90
Edwin M. Knowles		**Season For Song**			
91-59-001	Winter Concert	M. Jobe	150-day	34.90	60.00
91-59-002	Snowy Symphony	M. Jobe	150-day	34.90	45.00
91-59-003	Frosty Chorus	M. Jobe	150-day	34.90	34.90
91-59-004	Silver Serenade	M. Jobe	150-day	34.90	34.90
Edwin M. Knowles		**Garden Cottages of England**			
91-60-001	Chandler's Cottage	T. Kinkade	150-day	27.90	30.00
91-60-002	Cedar Nook Cottage	T. Kinkade	150-day	27.90	27.90
91-60-003	Candlelit Cottage	T. Kinkade	150-day	30.90	30.90
91-60-004	Open Gate Cottage	T. Kinkade	150-day	30.90	30.90
91-60-005	McKenna's Cottage	T. Kinkade	150-day	30.90	30.90
91-60-006	Woodsman's Thatch Cottage	T. Kinkade	150-day	32.90	32.90
92-60-007	Merritt's Cottage	T. Kinkade	150-day	32.90	32.90
92-60-008	Stonegate Cottage	T. Kinkade	150-day	32.90	32.90
Edwin M. Knowles		**Sleeping Beauty**			
91-61-001	Once Upon A Dream	Disney Studios	150-day	39.90	39.90
91-61-002	Awakened by a Kiss	Disney Studios	150-day	39.90	39.90
91-61-003	Happy Birthday Briar Rose	Disney Studios	150-day	42.90	42.90
Edwin M. Knowles		**Snow White and the Seven Dwarfs**			
91-62-001	The Dance of Snow White/Seven Dwarfs	Disney Studios	150-day	29.90	29.90
91-62-002	With a Smile and a Song	Disney Studios	150-day	29.90	29.90
91-62-003	A Special Treat	Disney Studios	150-day	32.90	32.90
92-62-004	A Kiss for Dopey	Disney Studios	150-day	32.90	32.90
92-62-005	The Poison Apple	Disney Studios	150-day	32.90	32.90
Edwin M. Knowles		**Classic Fairy Tales**			
91-63-001	Goldilocks and the Three Bears	S. Gustafson	150-day	29.90	29.90
91-63-002	Little Red Riding Hood	S. Gustafson	150-day	29.90	29.90
91-63-003	The Three Little Pigs	S. Gustafson	150-day	32.90	32.90
91-63-004	The Frog Prince	S. Gustafson	150-day	32.90	32.90
92-63-005	Jack and the Beanstalk	S. Gustafson	150-day	32.90	32.90
92-63-006	Hansel and Gretel	S. Gustafson	150-day	34.90	34.90
92-63-007	Puss in Boots	S. Gustafson	150-day	34.90	34.90
Edwin M. Knowles		**Wizard of Oz: A National Treasure**			
91-64-001	Yellow Brick Road	R. Laslo	150-day	29.90	29.90
92-64-002	I Haven't Got a Brain	R. Laslo	150-day	29.90	29.90
92-64-003	I'm a Little Rusty Yet	R. Laslo	150-day	32.90	32.90
92-64-004	I Even Scare Myself	R. Laslo	150-day	32.90	32.90
92-64-005	We're Off To See the Wizard	R. Laslo	150-day	32.90	32.90
92-64-006	I'll Never Get Home	R. Laslo	150-day	34.90	34.90
Edwin M. Knowles		**First Impressions**			
91-65-001	Taking a Gander	J. Giordano	150-day	29.90	40-50.00
91-65-002	Two's Company	J. Giordano	150-day	29.90	29.90
91-65-003	Fine Feathered Friends	J. Giordano	150-day	32.90	32.90
91-65-004	What's Up?	J. Giordano	150-day	32.90	32.90
91-65-005	All Ears	J. Giordano	150-day	32.90	32.90
92-65-006	Between Friends	J. Giordano	150-day	32.90	32.90
Edwin M. Knowles		**Santa's Christmas**			
91-66-001	Santa's Love	T. Browning	150-day	29.90	50-55.00
91-66-002	Santa's Cheer	T. Browning	150-day	29.90	35.00
91-66-003	Santa's Promise	T. Browning	150-day	32.90	50.00
91-66-004	Santa's Gift	T. Browning	150-day	32.90	32.90
92-66-005	Santa's Surprise	T. Browning	150-day	32.90	32.90
92-66-006	Santa's Magic	T. Browning	150-day	32.90	32.90
Edwin M. Knowles		**Home for the Holidays**			
91-67-001	Sleigh Ride Home	T. Kinkade	150-day	29.90	29.90
91-67-002	Home to Grandma's	T. Kinkade	150-day	29.90	29.90
91-67-003	Home Before Christmas	T. Kinkade	150-day	32.90	32.90
91-67-004	The Warmth of Home	T. Kinkade	150-day	32.90	32.90
92-67-005	Homespun Holiday	T. Kinkade	150 day	32.90	32.90
92-67-006	Hometime Yuletide	T. Kinkade	150-day	34.90	34.90
Edwin M. Knowles		**Call of the Wilderness**			
91-68-001	First Outing	K. Daniel	150-day	29.90	29.90
91-68-002	Howling Lesson	K. Daniel	150-day	29.90	29.90
91-68-003	Silent Watch	K. Daniel	150-day	32.90	32.90
91-68-004	Winter Travelers	K. Daniel	150-day	32.90	32.90
92-68-005	Ahead of the Pack	K. Daniel	150-day	32.90	32.90
92-68-006	Northern Spirits	K. Daniel	150-day	34.90	34.90
92-68-007	Twilight Friends	K. Daniel	150-day	34.90	34.90
Edwin M. Knowles		**Old-Fashioned Favorites**			
91-69-001	Apple Crisp	M. Weber	150-day	29.90	50-60.00
91-69-002	Blueberry Muffins	M. Weber	150-day	29.90	29.90
91-69-003	Peach Cobbler	M. Weber	150-day	29.90	29.90
91-69-004	Chocolate Chip Oatmeal Cookies	M. Weber	150-day	29.90	29.90
Edwin M. Knowles		**Songs of the American Spirit**			
91-70-001	The Star Spangled Banner	H. Bond	150-day	29.90	29.90
91-70-002	Battle Hymn of the Republic	H. Bond	150-day	29.90	29.90
91-70-003	America the Beautiful	H. Bond	150-day	29.90	29.94
91-70-004	My Country 'Tis of Thee	H. Bond	150-day	29.90	29.90
Edwin M. Knowles		**Backyard Harmony**			
91-71-001	The Singing Lesson	J. Thornbrugh	150-day	27.90	27.90
91-71-002	Welcoming a New Day	J. Thornbrugh	150-day	27.90	27.90
91-71-003	Announcing Spring	J. Thornbrugh	150-day	30.90	30.90
92-71-004	The Morning Harvest	J. Thornbrugh	150-day	30.90	30.90
92-71-005	Spring Time Pride	J. Thornbrugh	150-day	30.90	30.90
92-71-006	Treetop Serenade	J. Thornbrugh	150-day	32.90	32.90
Edwin M. Knowles		**Bambi**			
92-72-001	Bashful Bambi	Disney Studios	150-day	34.90	34.90
92-72-002	Bambi's New Friends	Disney Studios	150-day	34.90	34.90
92-72-003	Hello Little Prince	Disney Studios	150-day	37.90	37.90
92-72-004	Bambi's Morning Greetings	Disney Studios	150-day	37.90	37.90
Edwin M. Knowles		**Purrfect Point of View**			
92-73-001	Unexpected Visitors	J. Giordano	150-day	29.90	29.90
92-73-002	Wistful Morning	J. Giordano	150-day	29.90	29.90
92-73-003	Afternoon Catnap	J. Giordano	150-day	29.90	29.90
Edwin M. Knowles		**China's Natural Treasures**			
92-74-001	The Siberian Tiger	T.C. Chiu	150-day	29.90	29.90
92-74-002	The Snow Leopard	T.C. Chiu	150-day	29.90	29.90
92-74-003	The Giant Panda	T.C. Chiu	150-day	32.90	32.90
92-74-004	The Tibetan Brown Bear	T.C. Chiu	150-day	32.90	32.90
92-74-005	The Asian Elephant	T.C. Chiu	150-day	32.90	32.90
92-74-006	The Golden Monkey	T.C. Chiu	150-day	34.90	34.90
Edwin M. Knowles		**Under Mother's Wing**			
92-75-001	Arctic Spring: Snowy Owls	J. Beaudoin	150-day	29.90	29.90
92-75-002	Forest's Edge: Great Gray Owls	J. Beaudoin	150-day	29.90	29.90
92-75-003	Treetop Trio: Long-Eared Owls	J. Beaudoin	150-day	32.90	32.90
92-75-004	Woodland Watch: Spotted Owls	J. Beaudoin	150-day	32.90	32.90
Edwin M. Knowles		**Classic Mother Goose**			
92-76-001	Little Miss Muffet	S. Gustafson	150-day	29.90	29.90
92-76-002	Mary had a Little Lamb	S. Gustafson	150-day	29.90	29.90
92-76-003	Mary, Mary, Quite Contrary	S. Gustafson	150-day	29.90	29.90

Company / Number	Name / Series	Artist	Edition Limit	Issue Price	Quote
Edwin M. Knowles	**Keepsake Rhymes**				
92-77-001	Humpty Dumpty	S. Gustafson	150-day	29.90	29.90
Edwin M. Knowles	**Thomas Kinkade's Thomashire**				
92-78-001	Olde Porterfield Tea Room	T. Kinkade	150-day	29.90	29.90
92-78-002	Olde Thomashire Mill	T. Kinkade	150-day	29.90	29.90
92-78-003	Swanbrook Cottage	T. Kinkade	150-day	32.90	32.90
Edwin M. Knowles	**Small Blessings**				
92-79-001	Now I Lay Me Down to Sleep	C. Layton	150-day	29.90	29.90
92-79-002	Bless Us O Lord For These, Thy Gifts	C. Layton	150-day	29.90	29.90
Edwin M. Knowles	**Seasons of Splendor**				
92-80-001	Autumn's Grandeur	K. Randle	150-day	29.90	29.90
92-80-002	School Days	K. Randle	150-day	29.90	29.90
92-80-003	Woodland Mill Stream	K. Randle	150-day	32.90	32.90
Edwin M. Knowles	**Lady and the Tramp**				
92-81-001	First Date	Disney Studios	150-day	34.90	34.90
92-81-002	Puppy Love	Disney Studios	150-day	34.90	34.90
Edwin M. Knowles	**Sweetness and Grace**				
92-82-001	God Bless Teddy	J. Welty	150-day	34.90	34.90
92-82-002	Sunshine and Smiles	J. Welty	150-day	34.90	34.90
Edwin M. Knowles	**Thomas Kinkade's Yuletide Memories**				
92-83-001	The Magic of Christmas	T. Kinkade	150-day	29.90	29.90
Edwin M. Knowles	**It's a Dog's Life**				
92-84-001	We've Been Spotted	L. Kaatz	150-day	29.90	29.90
Edwin M. Knowles	**Mickey's Christmas Carol**				
92-85-001	Bah Humbug	Disney Studios	150-day	29.90	29.90
Edwin M. Knowles	**The Disney Treasured Moments Collection**				
92-86-001	Cinderella	Disney Studios	150-day	29.90	29.90
Edwin M. Knowles	**Christmas in the City**				
92-87-001	A Christmas Snowfall	A. Leimanis	150-day	34.90	34.90
Edwin M. Knowles	**Romantic Age of Steam**				
92-88-001	The Empire Builder	R.B. Pierce	150-day	29.90	29.90
Konigszelt Bayern	**Hedi Keller Christmas**				
79-01-001	The Adoration	H. Keller	Unkn.	29.50	29.50
80-01-002	Flight into Egypt	H. Keller	Unkn.	29.50	29.50
81-01-003	Return into Galilee	H. Keller	Unkn.	29.50	29.50
82-01-004	Following the Star	H. Keller	Unkn.	29.50	29.50
83-01-005	Rest on the Flight	H. Keller	Unkn.	29.50	29.50
84-01-006	The Nativity	H. Keller	Unkn.	29.50	29.50
85-01-007	Gift of the Magi	H. Keller	Unkn.	34.50	34.50
86-01-008	Annunciation	H. Keller	Unkn.	34.50	34.50
KPM-Royal Berlin	**Christmas**				
69-01-001	Christmas Star	Unknown	5,000	28.00	380.00
70-01-002	Three Kings	Unknown	5,000	28.00	300.00
71-01-003	Christmas Tree	Unknown	5,000	28.00	290.00
72-01-004	Christmas Angel	Unknown	5,000	31.00	300.00
73-01-005	Christ Child on Sled	Unknown	5,000	33.00	280.00
74-01-006	Angel and Horn	Unknown	5,000	35.00	180.00
75-01-007	Shepherds	Unknown	5,000	40.00	165.00
76-01-008	Star of Bethlehem	Unknown	5,000	43.00	140.00
77-01-009	Mary at Crib	Unknown	5,000	46.00	100.00
78-01-010	Three Wise Men	Unknown	5,000	49.00	54.00
79-01-011	The Manger	Unknown	5,000	55.00	55.00
80-01-012	Shepherds in Fields	Unknown	5,000	55.00	55.00
Lalique	**Annual**				
65-01-001	Deux Oiseaux (Two Birds)	M. Lalique	2,000	25.00	1200.00
66-01-002	Rose de Songerie (Dream Rose)	M. Lalique	5,000	25.00	160.00
67-01-003	Ballet de Poisson (Fish Ballet)	M. Lalique	5,000	25.00	120.00
68-01-004	Gazelle Fantaisie (Gazelle Fantasy)	M. Lalique	5,000	25.00	115.00
69-01-005	Papillon (Butterfly)	M. Lalique	5,000	30.00	80.00
70-01-006	Paon (Peacock)	M. Lalique	5,000	30.00	70.00
71-01-007	Hibou (Owl)	M. Lalique	5,000	35.00	70.00
72-01-008	Coquillage (Shell)	M. Lalique	5,000	40.00	65.00
73-01-009	Petit Geai (Jayling)	M. Lalique	5,000	42.50	125.00
74-01-010	Sous d'Argent (Silver Pennies)	M. Lalique	5,000	47.50	115.00
75-01-011	Duo de Poisson (Fish Duet)	M. Lalique	5,000	50.00	135.00
76-01-012	Aigle (Eagle)	M. Lalique	5,000	60.00	100.00
Lance Corporation	**Sebastian Plates**				
78-01-001	Motif No. 1	P.W. Baston	Closed	75.00	50-75.00
79-01-002	Grand Canyon	P.W. Baston	Closed	75.00	50-75.00
80-01-003	Lone Cypress	P.W. Baston	Closed	75.00	150-175.
80-01-004	In The Candy Store	P.W. Baston	Closed	39.50	39.50
81-01-005	The Doctor	P.W. Baston	Closed	39.50	39.50
83-01-006	Little Mother	P.W. Baston	Closed	39.50	39.50
84-01-007	Switching The Freight	P.W. Baston	Closed	42.50	80-100.00
Lance Corporation	**The American Expansion (Hudson Pewter)**				
75-02-001	Spirit of '76 (6" Plate)	P.W. Baston	Closed	Unkn.	100-120.
75-02-002	American Independence	P.W. Baston	Closed	Unkn.	100-125.
75-02-003	American Expansion	P.W. Baston	Closed	Unkn.	50-75.00
75-02-004	The American War Between the States	P.W. Baston	Closed	Unkn.	150-200.
Lance Corporation	**A Child's Christmas (Hudson Pewter)**				
78-03-001	Bedtime Story	A. Petitto	10,000	35.00	60.00
79-03-002	Littlest Angels	A. Petitto	10,000	35.00	60.00
80-03-003	Heaven's Christmas Tree	A. Petitto	10,000	42.50	60.00
81-03-004	Filling The Sky	A. Petitto	10,000	47.50	60.00
Lance Corporation	**Twas The Night Before Christmas (Hudson Pewter)**				
82-04-001	Not A Creature Was Stirring	A. Hollis	10,000	47.50	60.00
83-04-002	Visions Of Sugar Plums	A. Hollis	10,000	47.50	60.00
84-04-003	His Eyes How They Twinkled	A. Hollis	10,000	47.50	60.00
85-04-004	Happy Christmas To All	A. Hollis	10,000	47.50	60.00
86-04-005	Bringing Home The Tree	J. Wanat	10,000	47.50	60.00
Lance Corporation	**Walt Disney (Hudson Pewter)**				
86-05-001	God Bless Us, Every One	D. Everhart	10,000	47.50	60.00
87-05-002	The Caroling Angels	A. Petitto	10,000	47.50	60.00
87-05-003	Jolly Old Saint Nick	D. Everhart	10,000	55.00	60.00
88-05-004	He's Checking It Twice	D. Everhart	10,000	50.00	60.00
Lance Corporaton	**The Songs of Christmas (Hudson Pewter)**				
88-06-001	Silent Night	A. McGrory	2,500	55.00	60.00
89-06-002	Hark! The Herald Angels Sing	A. McGrory	2,500	60.00	60.00
90-06-003	The First Noel	A. McGrory	2,500	60.00	60.00
91-06-004	We Three Kings	A. McGrory	2,500	60.00	60.00
Lenox China	**Boehm Birds**				
70-01-001	Wood Thrush	E. Boehm	Yr.Iss.	35.00	140.00
71-01-002	Goldfinch	E. Boehm	Yr.Iss.	35.00	65.00
72-01-003	Mountain Bluebird	E. Boehm	Yr.Iss.	37.50	39.00
73-01-004	Meadowlark	E. Boehm	Yr.Iss.	50.00	50.00
74-01-005	Rufous Hummingbird	E. Boehm	Yr.Iss.	45.00	45-50.00
75-01-006	American Redstart	E. Boehm	Yr.Iss.	50.00	50.00
76-01-007	Cardinals	E. Boehm	Yr.Iss.	53.00	55.00
77-01-008	Robins	E. Boehm	Yr.Iss.	55.00	55.00
78-01-009	Mockingbirds	E. Boehm	Yr.Iss.	58.00	75.00
79-01-010	Golden-Crowned Kinglets	E. Boehm	Yr.Iss.	65.00	75-95.00
80-01-011	Black-Throated Blue Warblers	E. Boehm	Yr.Iss.	80.00	85.00
81-01-012	Eastern Phoebes	E. Boehm	Yr.Iss.	92.50	92.50
Lenox China	**Boehm Woodland Wildlife**				
73-02-001	Racoons	E. Boehm	Yr.Iss.	50.00	50.00
74-02-002	Red Foxes	E. Boehm	Yr.Iss.	52.50	52.50
75-02-003	Cottontail Rabbits	E. Boehm	Yr.Iss.	58.50	58.50
76-02-004	Eastern Chipmunks	E. Boehm	Yr.Iss.	62.50	62.50
77-02-005	Beaver	E. Boehm	Yr.Iss.	67.50	67.50
78-02-006	Whitetail Deer	E. Boehm	Yr.Iss.	70.00	70.00
79-02-007	Squirrels	E. Boehm	Yr.Iss.	76.00	76.00
80-02-008	Bobcats	E. Boehm	Yr.Iss.	82.50	82.50
81-02-009	Martens	E. Boehm	Yr.Iss.	100.00	150.00
82-02-010	River Otters	E. Boehm	Yr.Iss.	100.00	180.00
Lenox China	**Colonial Christmas Wreath**				
81-03-001	Colonial Virginia	Unknown	Yr.Iss.	65.00	76.00
82-03-002	Massachusetts	Unknown	Yr.Iss.	70.00	93.00
83-03-003	Maryland	Unknown	Yr.Iss.	70.00	79.00
84-03-004	Rhode Island	Unknown	Yr.Iss.	70.00	82.00
85-03-005	Connecticut	Unknown	Yr.Iss.	70.00	75.00
86-03-006	New Hampshire	Unknown	Yr.Iss.	70.00	75.00
87-03-007	Pennsylvania	Unknown	Yr.Iss.	70.00	75.00
88-03-008	Delaware	Unknown	Yr.Iss.	70.00	70.00
89-03-009	New York	Unknown	Yr.Iss.	75.00	82.00
90-03-010	New Jersey	Unknown	Yr.Iss.	75.00	78.00
91-03-011	South Carolina	Unknown	Yr.Iss.	75.00	75.00
92-03-012	North Carolina	Unknown	Yr.Iss.	75.00	75.00
Lenox Collections	**American Wildlife**				
82-01-001	Red Foxes	N. Adams	9,500	65.00	65.00
82-01-002	Ocelots	N. Adams	9,500	65.00	65.00
82-01-003	Sea Lions	N. Adams	9,500	65.00	65.00
82-01-004	Raccoons	N. Adams	9,500	65.00	65.00
82-01-005	Dall Sheep	N. Adams	9,500	65.00	65.00
82-01-006	Black Bears	N. Adams	9,500	65.00	65.00
82-01-007	Mountain Lions	N. Adams	9,500	65.00	65.00
82-01-008	Polar Bears	N. Adams	9,500	65.00	65.00
82-01-009	Otters	N. Adams	9,500	65.00	65.00
82-01-010	White Tailed Deer	N. Adams	9,500	65.00	65.00
82-01-011	Buffalo	N. Adams	9,500	65.00	65.00
82-01-012	Jack Rabbits	N. Adams	9,500	65.00	65.00
Lenox Collections	**Garden Bird Plate Collection**				
88-02-001	Chickadee	Unknown	Open	48.00	48.00
88-02-002	Bluejay	Unknown	Open	48.00	48.00
89-02-003	Hummingbird	Unknown	Open	48.00	48.00
91-02-004	Dove	Unknown	Open	48.00	48.00
91-02-005	Cardinal	Unknown	Open	48.00	48.00
92-02-006	Goldfinch	Unknown	Open	48.00	48.00
Lenox Collections	**Christmas Trees Around the World**				
91-03-001	Germany	Unknown	Yr.Iss.	75.00	75.00
92-03-002	France	Unknown	Yr.Iss.	75.00	75.00
Lenox Collections	**Annual Holiday**				
91-04-001	Sleigh	Unknown	Yr.Iss.	75.00	75.00
Lenox Collections	**Nature's Collage**				
92-05-001	Cedar Waxwing, Among The Berries	C. McClung	Open	34.50	34.50
92-05-002	Gold Finches, Golden Splendor	C. McClung	Open	34.50	34.50
Lihs Linder	**Christmas**				
72-01-001	Little Drummer Boy	J. Neubauer	6,000	25.00	35.00
73-01-002	Carolers	J. Neubauer	6,000	25.00	25.00
74-01-003	Peace	J. Neubauer	6,000	25.00	25.00
75-01-004	Christmas Cheer	J. Neubauer	6,000	30.00	34.00
76-01-005	Joy of Christmas	J. Neubauer	6,000	30.00	30.00
77-01-006	Holly Jolly Christmas	J. Neubauer	6,000	30.00	30.00
78-01-007	Holy Night	J. Neubauer	6,000	40.00	40.00
Lightpost Publishing	**Thomas Kinkade Signature Collection**				
91-01-001	Chandler's Cottage	T. Kinkade	2,500	49.95	49.95
91-01-002	Cedar Nook	T. Kinkade	2,500	49.95	49.95
91-01-003	Sleigh Ride Home	T. Kinkade	2,500	49.95	49.95
91-01-004	Home To Grandma's	T. Kinkade	2,500	49.95	49.95
Lilliput Lane, Ltd.	**American Landmarks Collection**				
90-01-001	Country Church	R. Day	5,000	35.00	35.00
90-01-002	Riverside Chapel	R. Day	5,000	35.00	35.00
Lladro	**Lladro Plate Collection**				
93-01-001	The Great Voyage L5964G	Lladro	Open	50.00	50.00
93-01-002	Looking Out L5998G	Lladro	Open	38.00	38.00
93-01-003	Swinging L5999G	Lladro	Open	38.00	38.00
93-01-004	Duck Plate L6000G	Lladro	Open	38.00	38.00
March of Dimes	**Our Children, Our Future**				
89-01-001	A Time for Peace	D. Zolan	150-day	29.00	45-50.00
89-01-002	A Time To Love	S. Kuck	150-day	29.00	45-69.00
89-01-003	A Time To Plant	J. McClelland	150-day	29.00	35.00
89-01-004	A Time To Be Born	G. Perillo	150-day	29.00	35.00
90-01-005	A Time To Embrace	E. Hibel	150-day	29.00	35.00
90-01-006	A Time To Laugh	A. Williams	150-day	29.00	39-49.00

PLATES

Company		Series			
Number	Name	Artist	Edition Limit	Issue Price	Quote
Maruri USA		**Eagle Plate Series**			
84-01-001	Free Flight	W. Gaither	Closed	150.00	150-198.
Mingolla/Home Plates		**Christmas**			
73-01-001	Copper, Enamel	Mingolla	1,000	95.00	165.00
74-01-002	Copper, Enamel	Mingolla	1,000	110.00	145.00
75-01-003	Copper, Enamel	Mingolla	1,000	125.00	145.00
76-01-004	Copper, Enamel	Mingolla	1,000	125.00	125.00
77-01-005	Winter Wonderland (Copper Enamel)	Mingolla	2,000	200.00	200.00
Mingolla/Home Plates		**Christmas**			
74-02-001	Porcelain	Mingolla	5,000	35.00	65.00
75-02-002	Porcelain	Mingolla	5,000	35.00	45.00
76-02-003	Porcelain	Mingolla	5,000	35.00	30.00
Museum Collections, Inc.		**American Family I**			
79-01-001	Baby's First Step	N. Rockwell	9,900	28.50	48.00
79-01-002	Happy Birthday Dear Mother	N. Rockwell	9,900	28.50	45.00
79-01-003	Sweet Sixteen	N. Rockwell	9,900	28.50	35.00
79-01-004	First Haircut	N. Rockwell	9,900	28.50	60.00
79-01-005	First Prom	N. Rockwell	9,900	28.50	35.00
79-01-006	Wrapping Christmas Presents	N. Rockwell	9,900	28.50	35.00
79-01-007	The Student	N. Rockwell	9,900	28.50	35.00
79-01-008	Birthday Party	N. Rockwell	9,900	28.50	35.00
79-01-009	Little Mother	N. Rockwell	9,900	28.50	35.00
79-01-010	Washing Our Dog	N. Rockwell	9,900	28.50	35.00
79-01-011	Mother's Little Helpers	N. Rockwell	9,900	28.50	35.00
79-01-012	Bride and Groom	N. Rockwell	9,900	28.50	35.00
Museum Collections, Inc.		**Christmas**			
79-02-001	Day After Christmas	N. Rockwell	Yr.Iss	75.00	75.00
80-02-002	Checking His List	N. Rockwell	Yr.Iss	75.00	75.00
81-02-003	Ringing in Good Cheer	N. Rockwell	Yr.Iss	75.00	75.00
82-02-004	Waiting for Santa	N. Rockwell	Yr.Iss	75.00	75.00
83-02-005	High Hopes	N. Rockwell	Yr.Iss	75.00	75.00
84-02-006	Space Age Santa	N. Rockwell	Yr.Iss	55.00	55.00
Museum Collections, Inc.		**American Family II**			
80-03-001	New Arrival	N. Rockwell	22,500	35.00	55.00
80-03-002	Sweet Dreams	N. Rockwell	22,500	35.00	37.50
80-03-003	Little Shaver	N. Rockwell	22,500	35.00	40.00
80-03-004	We Missed You Daddy	N. Rockwell	22,500	35.00	37.50
80-03-005	Home Run Slugger	N. Rockwell	22,500	35.00	37.50
80-03-006	Giving Thanks	N. Rockwell	22,500	35.00	37.50
80-03-007	Space Pioneers	N. Rockwell	22,500	35.00	37.50
80-03-008	Little Salesman	N. Rockwell	22,500	35.00	37.50
80-03-009	Almost Grown up	N. Rockwell	22,500	35.00	37.50
80-03-010	Courageous Hero	N. Rockwell	22,500	35.00	37.50
81-03-011	At the Circus	N. Rockwell	22,500	35.00	37.50
81-03-012	Good Food, Good Friends	N. Rockwell	22,500	35.00	37.50
Pemberton & Oakes		**Zolan's Children**			
78-01-001	Erik and Dandelion	D. Zolan	22-day	19.00	225-270.
79-01-002	Sabina in the Grass	D. Zolan	22-day	22.00	220-250.
80-01-003	By Myself	D. Zolan	22-day	24.00	55-65.00
81-01-004	For You	D. Zolan	22-day	24.00	50-100.00
Pemberton & Oakes		**Wonder of Childhood**			
82-02-001	Touching the Sky	D. Zolan	22-day	19.00	35-65.00
83-02-002	Spring Innocence	D. Zolan	22-day	19.00	43-75.00
84-02-003	Winter Angel	D. Zolan	22-day	22.00	60-100.00
85-02-004	Small Wonder	D. Zolan	22-day	22.00	40-70.00
86-02-005	Grandma's Garden	D. Zolan	22-day	22.00	50-70.00
87-02-006	Day Dreamer	D. Zolan	22-day	22.00	40-65.00
Pemberton & Oakes		**Children and Pets**			
84-03-001	Tender Moment	D. Zolan	28-day	19.00	52-90.00
84-03-002	Golden Moment	D. Zolan	28-day	19.00	45-60.00
85-03-003	Making Friends	D. Zolan	28-day	19.00	40-75.00
85-03-004	Tender Beginning	D. Zolan	28-day	19.00	40-65.00
86-03-005	Backyard Discovery	D. Zolan	28-day	19.00	40-70.00
86-03-006	Waiting to Play	D. Zolan	28-day	19.00	45-65.00
Pemberton & Oakes		**Children at Christmas**			
81-04-001	A Gift for Laurie	D. Zolan	15,000	48.00	80-100.00
82-04-002	Christmas Prayer	D. Zolan	15,000	48.00	100-150.00
83-04-003	Erik's Delight	D. Zolan	15,000	48.00	70-95.00
84-04-004	Christmas Secret	D. Zolan	15,000	48.00	75-110.00
85-04-005	Christmas Kitten	D. Zolan	15,000	48.00	85-125.00
86-04-006	Laurie and the Creche	D. Zolan	15,000	48.00	80-100.00
Pemberton & Oakes		**Special Moments of Childhood Collection**			
88-05-001	Brotherly Love	D. Zolan	19-day	19.00	60-75.00
88-05-002	Sunny Surprise	D. Zolan	19-day	19.00	40-65.00
89-05-003	Summer's Child	D. Zolan	19-day	22.00	40-50.00
90-05-004	Meadow Magic	D. Zolan	19-day	22.00	35.00
90-05-005	Cone For Two	D. Zolan	19-day	24.60	28-42.00
90-05-006	Rodeo Girl	D. Zolan	19-day	24.60	30-50.00
Pemberton & Oakes		**Childhood Friendship Collection**			
86-06-001	Beach Break	D. Zolan	17-day	19.00	55-65.00
87-06-002	Little Engineers	D. Zolan	17-day	19.00	75-125.00
88-06-003	Tiny Treasures	D. Zolan	17-day	19.00	50-95.00
88-06-004	Sharing Secrets	D. Zolan	17-day	19.00	45-60.00
88-06-005	Dozens of Daisies	D. Zolan	17-day	19.00	40-65.00
90-06-006	Country Walk	D. Zolan	17-day	19.00	40-55.00
Pemberton & Oakes		**Tenth Anniversary**			
88-07-001	Ribbons and Roses	D. Zolan	19-day	24.40	50-75.00
Pemberton & Oakes		**Father's Day**			
86-08-001	Daddy's Home	D. Zolan	19-day	19.00	65-90.00
Pemberton & Oakes		**Mother's Day**			
88-09-001	Mother's Angels	D. Zolan	19-day	19.00	65-75.00
Pemberton & Oakes		**Grandparent's Day**			
90-10-001	It's Grandma & Grandpa	D. Zolan	19-day	24.40	36.00
Pemberton & Oakes		**Adventures of Childhood Collection**			
89-11-001	Almost Home	D. Zolan	44-day	19.60	60-85.00
89-11-002	Crystal's Creek	D. Zolan	44-day	19.60	50-75.00
89-11-003	Summer Suds	D. Zolan	44-day	22.00	30-60.00
90-11-004	Snowy Adventure	D. Zolan	44-day	22.00	40-75.00
91-11-005	Forests & Fairy Tales	D. Zolan	44-day	24.40	35.00
Pemberton & Oakes		**Thanksgiving**			
81-12-001	I'm Thankful Too	D. Zolan	19-day	19.00	70-100.00
Pemberton & Oakes		**Nutcracker II**			
81-13-001	Grand Finale	S. Fisher	Undis.	24.40	36.00
82-13-002	Arabian Dancers	S. Fisher	Undis.	24.40	67.50
83-13-003	Dew Drop Fairy	S. Fisher	Undis.	24.40	40-70.00
84-13-004	Clara's Delight	S. Fisher	Undis.	24.40	42.00
85-13-005	Bedtime for Nutcracker	S. Fisher	Undis.	24.40	45.00
86-13-006	The Crowning of Clara	S. Fisher	Undis.	24.40	36.00
87-13-007	Dance of the Snowflakes	D. Zolan	Undis.	24.40	50-100.00
88-13-008	The Royal Welcome	R. Anderson	Undis.	24.40	24.40
89-13-009	The Spanish Dancer	M. Vickers	Undis.	24.40	24.40
Pemberton & Oakes		**March of Dimes: Our Children, Our Future**			
89-14-001	A Time for Peace	D. Zolan	150-day	29.00	45-50.00
Pemberton & Oakes		**Christmas**			
91-15-001	Candlelight Magic	D. Zolan	Open	24.80	24.80
Pemberton & Oakes		**Companion to Brotherly Love**			
89-16-001	Sisterly Love	D. Zolan	19-day	22.00	42.00
Pemberton & Oakes		**Single Issue Day to Day Spode**			
91-17-001	Daisy Days	D. Zolan	15,000	48.00	48.00
Pemberton & Oakes		**The Best of Zolan in Miniature**			
85-18-001	Sabina	D. Zolan	22-day	12.50	112-145.
86-18-002	Erik and Dandelion	D. Zolan	22-day	12.50	96-102.00
86-18-003	Tender Moment	D. Zolan	22-day	12.50	65.00
86-18-004	Touching the Sky	D. Zolan	22-day	12.50	55-65.00
87-18-005	A Gift for Laurie	D. Zolan	22-day	12.50	50-75.00
87-18-006	Small Wonder	D. Zolan	22-day	12.50	40-75.00
Pemberton & Oakes		**Childhood Discoveries (Miniature)**			
90-19-001	Colors of Spring	D. Zolan	19-day	14.40	40-45.00
90-19-002	Autumn Leaves	D. Zolan	19-day	14.40	35-45.00
91-19-003	Enchanted Forest	D. Zolan	19-day	16.60	30-45.00
91-19-004	Just Ducky	D. Zolan	19-day	16.60	30-45.00
91-19-005	Rainy Day Pals	D. Zolan	19-day	16.60	35.00
92-19-006	Double Trouble	D. Zolan	19-day	16.60	30-45.00
Pemberton & Oakes		**Valentine's Day (Miniature)**			
90-20-001	First Kiss	D. Zolan	19-day	14.40	60-65.00
93-20-002	Peppermint Kiss	D. Zolan	19-day	16.60	16.60
Pemberton & Oakes		**Easter (Miniature)**			
91-21-001	Easter Morning	D. Zolan	19-day	16.60	30-60.00
Pemberton & Oakes		**Mother's Day (Miniature)**			
90-22-001	Flowers for Mother	D. Zolan	19-day	14.40	50-65.00
92-22-002	Twilight Prayer	D. Zolan	19-day	16.60	25-40.00
Pemberton & Oakes		**Moments To Remember (Miniature)**			
92-23-001	Just We Two	D. Zolan	19-day	16.60	16.60
92-23-002	Almost Home	D. Zolan	19-day	16.60	16.60
93-23-003	Tiny Treasures	D. Zolan	19-day	16.60	16.60
Pemberton & Oakes		**Single Issues (Miniature)**			
86-24-001	Backyard Discovery	D. Zolan	22-day	12.50	55.00
86-24-002	Daddy's Home	D. Zolan	19-day	12.50	810.00
89-24-003	Sunny Surprise	D. Zolan	19-day	12.50	62.00
89-24-004	My Pumpkin	D. Zolan	19-day	14.40	40-70.00
91-24-005	Backyard Buddies	D. Zolan	19-day	16.60	35.00
91-24-006	The Thinker	D. Zolan	19-day	16.60	30-45.00
Pemberton & Oakes		**Plaques**			
91-25-001	New Shoes	D. Zolan	Yr. Iss.	18.80	25-27.00
92-25-002	Grandma's Garden	D. Zolan	Yr. Iss.	18.80	25-27.00
92-25-003	Small Wonder	D. Zolan	Yr. Iss.	18.80	25-27.00
Pemberton & Oakes		**Plaques-Single Issues**			
91-26-001	Flowers for Mother	D. Zolan	Yr. Iss.	16.80	25-30.00
Pemberton & Oakes		**Heirloom Ovals**			
92-27-001	My Kitty	D. Zolan	Yr. Iss.	18.80	18.80
Pemberton & Oakes		**Membership (Miniature)**			
87-28-001	For You	D. Zolan	19-day	12.50	100.00
88-28-002	Making Friends	D. Zolan	19-day	12.50	72.00
89-28-003	Grandma's Garden	D. Zolan	19-day	12.50	71.00
90-28-004	A Christmas Prayer	D. Zolan	19-day	14.40	95.00
90-28-005	By Myself	D. Zolan	19-day	14.40	14.40
91-28-006	Golden Moment	D. Zolan	19-day	15.00	15.00
92-28-007	Brotherly Love	D. Zolan	19-day	15.00	65.00
PenDelfin		**Plate Series**			
XX-01-001	Mother With Baby	J. Heap	Retrd.	40.00	200.00
XX-01-002	Father	J. Heap	7,500	40.00	40.00
XX-01-003	Whopper	D. Roberts	7,500	50.00	50.00
XX-01-004	Gingerbread Day	J. Heap	7,500	55.00	55.00
XX-01-005	Caravan	D. Roberts	7,500	60.00	60.00
XX-01-006	Old Schoolhouse	J. Heap	7,500	60.00	60.00
Pickard		**Lockhart Wildlife**			
70-01-001	Woodcock/Ruffed Grouse, pair	J. Lockhart	2,000	150.00	210.00
71-01-002	Teal/Mallard, pair	J. Lockhart	2,000	150.00	160.00
72-01-003	Mockingbird/Cardinal, pair	J. Lockhart	2,000	162.50	140.00
73-01-004	Turkey/Pheasant, pair	J. Lockhart	2,000	162.50	225.00
74-01-005	American Bald Eagle	J. Lockhart	2,000	150.00	675.00
75-01-006	White Tailed Deer	J. Lockhart	2,500	100.00	100.00
76-01-007	American Buffalo	J. Lockhart	2,500	165.00	165.00
77-01-008	Great Horn Owl	J. Lockhart	2,500	100.00	115.00
78-01-009	American Panther	J. Lockhart	2,000	175.00	175.00
79-01-010	Red Foxes	J. Lockhart	2,500	120.00	120.00
80-01-011	Trumpeter Swan	J. Lockhart	2,000	200.00	200.00
Pickard		**Annual Christmas**			
76-02-001	Alba Madonna	Raphael	7,500	60.00	100.00
77-02-002	The Nativity	L. Lotto	7,500	65.00	65.00

Company / Number	Name	Series / Artist	Edition Limit	Issue Price	Quote
78-02-003	Rest on Flight into Egypt	G. David	10,000	65.00	65.00
79-02-004	Adoration of the Magi	Botticelli	10,000	70.00	70.00
80-02-005	Madonna and Child	Sodoma	10,000	80.00	80.00
81-02-006	Madonna and Child with Angels	Memling	10,000	90.00	90.00
Pickard		**Mother's Love**			
80-03-001	Miracle	I. Spencer	7,500	95.00	95.00
81-03-002	Story Time	I. Spencer	7,500	110.00	110.00
82-03-003	First Edition	I. Spencer	7,500	115.00	115.00
83-03-004	Precious Moment	I. Spencer	7,500	120.00	145.00
Pickard		**Children of Mexico**			
81-04-001	Maria	J. Sanchez	5,000	85.00	85.00
81-04-002	Miguel	J. Sanchez	5,000	85.00	85.00
82-04-003	Regina	J. Sanchez	5,000	90.00	90.00
83-04-004	Raphael	J. Sanchez	5,000	90.00	90.00
Pickard		**Symphony of Roses**			
82-05-001	Wild Irish Rose	I. Spencer	10,000	85.00	95.00
83-05-002	Yellow Rose of Texas	I. Spencer	10,000	90.00	100-110.
84-05-003	Honeysuckle Rose	I. Spencer	10,000	95.00	135.00
85-05-004	Rose of Washington Square	I. Spencer	10,000	100.00	175.00
Porsgrund		**Christmas**			
68-01-001	Church Scene	G. Bratile	Annual	12.00	125.00
69-01-002	Three Kings	G. Bratile	Annual	12.00	12.00
70-01-003	Road to Bethlehem	G. Bratile	Annual	12.00	12.00
71-01-004	A Child is Born	G. Bratile	Annual	12.00	12.00
72-01-005	Hark the Herald Angels	G. Bratile	Annual	12.00	12.00
73-01-006	Promise of the Savior	G. Bratile	Annual	12.00	12.00
74-01-007	The Shepherds	G. Bratile	Annual	15.00	36.00
75-01-008	Road to Temple	G. Bratile	Annual	19.50	19.50
76-01-009	Jesus and the Elders	G. Bratile	Annual	22.00	43.00
77-01-010	Draught of the Fish	G. Bratile	Annual	24.00	28.00
Princeton Gallery		**Circus Friends Collection**			
89-01-001	Don't Be Shy	R. Sanderson	Unkn.	29.50	29.50
90-01-002	Make Me A Clown	R. Sanderson	Unkn.	29.50	29.50
90-01-003	Looks Like Rain	R. Sanderson	Unkn.	29.50	29.50
90-01-004	Cheer Up Mr. Clown	R. Sanderson	Unkn.	29.50	29.50
Princeton Gallery		**Cubs Of The Big Cats**			
90-02-001	Cougar Cub	Q. Lemond	Unkn.	29.50	29.50
91-02-002	Lion Cub	Q. Lemond	90-day	29.50	29.50
91-02-003	Snow Leopard	Q. Lemond	90-day	29.50	29.50
91-02-004	Cheetah	Q. Lemond	90-day	29.50	29.50
91-02-005	Tiger	Q. Lemond	90-day	29.50	29.50
92-02-006	Lynx Cub	Q. Lemond	90-day	29.50	29.50
92-02-007	White Tiger Cub	Q. Lemond	90-day	29.50	29.50
Princeton Gallery		**Arctic Wolves**			
91-03-001	Song of the Wilderness	J. Van Zyle	90-day	29.50	29.50
92-03-002	In The Eye of the Moon	J. Van Zyle	90-day	29.50	29.50
Princeton Gallery		**Enchanted World of the Unicorn**			
91-04-001	Rainbow Valley	R. Sanderson	90-day	29.50	29.50
92-04-002	Golden Shore	R. Sanderson	90-day	29.50	29.50
Princeton Gallery		**Darling Dalmatians**			
91-05-001	Dalmatian	L. Picken	90-day	29.50	29.50
92-05-002	Firehouse Frolic	L. Picken	90-day	29.50	29.50
Reco International		**Bohemian Annuals**			
74-01-001	1974	Unknown	500	130.00	155.00
75-01-002	1975	Unknown	500	140.00	160.00
76-01-003	1976	Unknown	500	150.00	160.00
Reco International		**Americanna**			
72-02-001	Gaspee Incident	S. Devlin	1,500	200.00	325.00
Reco International		**Dresden Christmas**			
71-03-001	Shepherd Scene	Unknown	3,500	15.00	50.00
72-03-002	Niklas Church	Unknown	6,000	15.00	25.00
73-03-003	Schwanstein Church	Unknown	6,000	18.00	35.00
74-03-004	Village Scene	Unknown	5,000	20.00	30.00
75-03-005	Rothenburg Scene	Unknown	5,000	24.00	30.00
76-03-006	Village Church	Unknown	5,000	26.00	35.00
77-03-007	Old Mill (Issue Closed)	Unknown	5,000	28.00	30.00
Reco International		**Dresden Mother's Day**			
72-04-001	Doe and Fawn	Unknown	8,000	15.00	20.00
73-04-002	Mare and Colt	Unknown	6,000	16.00	25.00
74-04-003	Tiger and Cub	Unknown	5,000	20.00	23.00
75-04-004	Dachshunds	Unknown	5,000	24.00	28.00
76-04-005	Owl and Offspring	Unknown	5,000	26.00	30.00
77-04-006	Chamois (Issue Closed)	Unknown	5,000	28.00	30.00
Reco International		**Furstenberg Christmas**			
71-05-001	Rabbits	Unknown	7,500	15.00	30.00
72-05-002	Snowy Village	Unknown	6,000	15.00	20.00
73-05-003	Christmas Eve	Unknown	4,000	18.00	35.00
74-05-004	Sparrows	Unknown	4,000	20.00	30.00
75-05-005	Deer Family	Unknown	4,000	22.00	30.00
76-05-006	Winter Birds	Unknown	4,000	25.00	25.00
Reco International		**Furstenberg Deluxe Christmas**			
71-06-001	Wise Men	E. Grossberg	1,500	45.00	45.00
72-06-002	Holy Family	E. Grossberg	2,000	45.00	45.00
73-06-003	Christmas Eve	E. Grossberg	2,000	60.00	65.00
Reco International		**Furstenberg Easter**			
71-07-001	Sheep	Unknown	3,500	15.00	150.00
72-07-002	Chicks	Unknown	6,500	15.00	60.00
73-07-003	Bunnies	Unknown	4,000	16.00	80.00
74-07-004	Pussywillow	Unknown	4,000	20.00	32.50
75-07-005	Easter Window	Unknown	4,000	22.00	30.00
76-07-006	Flower Collecting	Unknown	4,000	25.00	25.00
Reco International		**Furstenberg Mother's Day**			
72-08-001	Hummingbirds, Fe	Unknown	6,000	15.00	45.00
73-08-002	Hedgehogs	Unknown	5,000	16.00	40.00
74-08-003	Doe and Fawn	Unknown	4,000	20.00	30.00
75-08-004	Swans	Unknown	4,000	22.00	23.00
76-08-005	Koala Bears	Unknown	4,000	25.00	30.00
Reco International		**Furstenberg Olympic**			
72-09-001	Munich	J. Poluszynski	5,000	20.00	75.00
76-09-002	Montreal	J. Poluszynski	5,000	37.50	37.50
Reco International		**Grafburg Christmas**			
75-10-001	Black-Capped Chickadee	Unknown	5,000	20.00	60.00
76-10-002	Squirrels	Unknown	5,000	22.00	22.00
Reco International		**King's Christmas**			
73-11-001	Adoration	Merli	1,500	100.00	265.00
74-11-002	Madonna	Merli	1,500	150.00	250.00
75-11-003	Heavenly Choir	Merli	1,500	160.00	235.00
76-11-004	Siblings	Merli	1,500	200.00	225.00
Reco International		**King's Flowers**			
73-12-001	Carnation	A. Falchi	1,000	85.00	130.00
74-12-002	Red Rose	A. Falchi	1,000	100.00	145.00
75-12-003	Yellow Dahlia	A. Falchi	1,000	110.00	162.00
76-12-004	Bluebells	A. Falchi	1,000	130.00	165.00
77-12-005	Anemones	A. Falchi	1,000	130.00	175.00
Reco International		**King's Mother's Day**			
73-13-001	Dancing Girl	Merli	1,500	100.00	225.00
74-13-002	Dancing Boy	Merli	1,500	115.00	250.00
75-13-003	Motherly Love	Merli	1,500	140.00	225.00
76-13-004	Maiden	Merli	1,500	180.00	200.00
Reco International		**Four Seasons**			
73-14-001	Spring	J. Poluszynski	2,500	50.00	75.00
73-14-002	Summer	J. Poluszynski	2,500	50.00	75.00
73-14-003	Fall	J. Poluszynski	2,500	50.00	75.00
73-14-004	Winter	J. Poluszynski	2,500	50.00	75.00
Reco International		**Marmot Father's Day**			
70-15-001	Stag	Unknown	3,500	12.00	100.00
71-15-002	Horse	Unknown	3,500	12.50	40.00
Reco International		**Marmot Christmas**			
70-16-001	Polar Bear, Fe	Unknown	5,000	13.00	60.00
71-16-002	Buffalo Bill	Unknown	6,000	16.00	55.00
72-16-003	Boy and Grandfather	Unknown	5,000	20.00	50.00
71-16-004	American Buffalo	Unknown	6,000	14.50	35.00
73-16-005	Snowman	Unknown	3,000	22.00	45.00
74-16-006	Dancing	Unknown	2,000	24.00	30.00
75-16-007	Quail	Unknown	2,000	30.00	40.00
76-16-008	Windmill	Unknown	2,000	40.00	40.00
Reco International		**Marmot Mother's Day**			
72-17-001	Seal	Unknown	6,000	16.00	60.00
73-17-002	Bear with Cub	Unknown	3,000	20.00	140.00
74-17-003	Penguins	Unknown	2,000	24.00	50.00
75-17-004	Raccoons	Unknown	2,000	30.00	45.00
76-17-005	Ducks	Unknown	2,000	40.00	40.00
Reco International		**Moser Christmas**			
70-18-001	Hradcany Castle	Unknown	400	75.00	170.00
71-18-002	Karlstein Castle	Unknown	1,365	75.00	80.00
72-18-003	Old Town Hall	Unknown	1,000	85.00	85.00
73-18-004	Karlovy Vary Castle	Unknown	500	90.00	100.00
Reco International		**Moser Mother's Day**			
71-19-001	Peacocks	Unknown	350	75.00	100.00
72-19-002	Butterflies	Unknown	750	85.00	90.00
73-19-003	Squirrels	Unknown	500	90.00	95.00
Reco International		**Royale**			
69-20-001	Apollo Moon Landing	Unknown	2,000	30.00	80.00
Reco International		**Royale Christmas**			
69-21-001	Christmas Fair	Unknown	6,000	12.00	125.00
70-21-002	Vigil Mass	Unknown	10,000	13.00	110.00
71-21-003	Christmas Night	Unknown	8,000	16.00	50.00
72-21-004	Elks	Unknown	8,000	16.00	45.00
73-21-005	Christmas Down	Unknown	6,000	20.00	37.50
74-21-006	Village Christmas	Unknown	5,000	22.00	60.00
75-21-007	Feeding Time	Unknown	5,000	26.00	35.00
76-21-008	Seaport Christmas	Unknown	5,000	27.50	30.00
77-21-009	Sledding	Unknown	5,000	30.00	30.00
Reco International		**Royal Mother's Day**			
70-22-001	Swan and Young	Unknown	6,000	12.00	80.00
71-22-002	Doe and Fawn	Unknown	9,000	13.00	55.00
72-22-003	Rabbits	Unknown	9,000	16.00	40.00
73-22-004	Owl Family	Unknown	6,000	18.00	40.00
74-22-005	Duck and Young	Unknown	5,000	22.00	40.00
75-22-006	Lynx and Cubs	Unknown	5,000	26.00	40.00
76-22-007	Woodcock and Young	Unknown	5,000	27.50	32.50
77-22-008	Koala Bear	Unknown	5,000	30.00	30.00
Reco International		**Royale Father's Day**			
70-23-001	Frigate Constitution	Unknown	5,000	13.00	80.00
71-23-002	Man Fishing	Unknown	5,000	13.00	35.00
72-23-003	Mountaineer	Unknown	5,000	16.00	55.00
73-23-004	Camping	Unknown	4,000	18.00	45.00
74-23-005	Eagle	Unknown	2,500	22.00	35.00
75-23-006	Regatta	Unknown	2,500	26.00	35.00
76-23-007	Hunting	Unknown	2,500	27.50	32.50
77-23-008	Fishing	Unknown	2,500	30.00	30.00
Reco International		**Royale Game Plates**			
72-24-001	Setters	J. Poluszynski	500	180.00	200.00
73-24-002	Fox	J. Poluszynski	500	200.00	250.00
74-24-003	Osprey	W. Schiener	250	250.00	250.00
75-24-004	California Quail	W. Schiener	250	265.00	265.00
Reco International		**Royale Germania Christmas Annual**			
70-25-001	Orchid	Unknown	600	200.00	650.00
71-25-002	Cyclamen	Unknown	1,000	200.00	325.000
72-25-003	Silver Thistle	Unknown	1,000	250.00	290.00
73-25-004	Tulips	Unknown	600	275.00	310.00
74-25-005	Sunflowers	Unknown	500	300.00	320.00

Company		Series			
Number	**Name**	**Artist**	**Edition Limit**	**Issue Price**	**Quote**
75-25-006	Snowdrops	Unknown	350	450.00	500.00
Reco International		**Royale Germania Crystal Mother's Day**			
71-26-001	Roses	Unknown	250	135.00	650.00
72-26-002	Elephant and Youngster	Unknown	750	180.00	250.00
73-26-003	Koala Bear and Cub	Unknown	600	200.00	225.00
74-26-004	Squirrels	Unknown	500	240.00	250.00
75-26-005	Swan and Young	Unknown	350	350.00	360.00
Reco International		**Western**			
74-27-001	Mountain Man	E. Berke	1,000	165.00	165.00
Reco International		**The World of Children**			
77-28-001	Rainy Day Fun	J. McClelland	10,000	50.00	50.00
78-28-002	When I Grow Up	J. McClelland	15,000	50.00	50.00
79-28-003	You're Invited	J. McClelland	15,000	50.00	51.00
80-28-004	Kittens for Sale	J. McClelland	15,000	50.00	75.00
Reco International		**Mother Goose**			
79-29-001	Mary, Mary	J. McClelland	Yr.Iss.	22.50	100-120.
80-29-002	Little Boy Blue	J. McClelland	Yr.Iss.	22.50	35-50.00
81-29-003	Little Miss Muffet	J. McClelland	Yr.Iss.	24.50	35-55.00
82-29-004	Little Jack Horner	J. McClelland	Yr.Iss.	24.50	30-45.00
83-29-005	Little Bo Peep	J. McClelland	Yr.Iss.	24.50	24.50
84-29-006	Diddle, Diddle Dumpling	J. McClelland	Yr.Iss.	24.50	24.50
85-29-007	Mary Had a Little Lamb	J. McClelland	Yr.Iss.	27.50	30-39.00
86-29-008	Jack and Jill	J. McClelland	Yr.Iss.	27.50	35-45.00
Reco International		**The McClelland Children's Circus Collection**			
82-30-001	Tommy the Clown	J. McClelland	100-day	29.50	49.00
82-30-002	Katie, the Tightrope Walker	J. McClelland	100-day	29.50	49.00
83-30-003	Johnny the Strongman	J. McClelland	100-day	29.50	39.00
84-30-004	Maggie the Animal Trainer	J. McClelland	100-day	29.50	30.00
Reco International		**Becky's Day**			
85-31-001	Awakening	J. McClelland	90-day	24.50	29.00
85-31-002	Getting Dressed	J. McClelland	90-day	24.50	29.00
86-31-003	Breakfast	J. McClelland	90-day	27.50	35.00
86-31-004	Learning is Fun	J. McClelland	90-day	27.50	27.50
86-31-005	Muffin Making	J. McClelland	90-day	27.50	27.50
86-31-006	Tub Time	J. McClelland	90-day	27.50	35.00
86-31-007	Evening Prayer	J. McClelland	90-day	27.50	27.50
Reco International		**Treasured Songs of Childhood**			
87-32-001	Twinkle, Twinkle, Little Star	J. McClelland	150-day	29.50	30-45.00
88-32-002	A Tisket, A Tasket	J. McClelland	150-day	29.50	39.00
88-32-003	Baa, Baa, Black Sheep	J. McClelland	150-day	32.90	35-45.00
89-32-004	Round The Mulberry Bush	J. McClelland	150-day	32.90	35-45.00
89-32-005	Rain, Rain Go Away	J. McClelland	150-day	32.90	35-45.00
89-32-006	I'm A Little Teapot	J. McClelland	150-day	32.90	38-45.00
89-32-007	Pat-A-Cake	J. McClelland	150-day	34.90	39.00
90-32-008	Hush Little Baby	J. McClelland	150-day	34.90	39.00
Reco International		**The Wonder of Christmas**			
91-33-001	Santa's Secret	J. McClelland	48-day	29.50	29.50
92-33-002	My Favorite Ornament	J. McClelland	48-day	29.50	29.50
92-33-003	Waiting For Santa	J. McClelland	48-day	29.50	29.50
93-33-004	Candlelight Christmas	J. McClelland	48-day	29.50	29.50
Reco International		**The Premier Collection**			
91-34-001	Love	J. McClelland	7,500	75.00	75.00
Reco International		**Golf Collection**			
92-35-001	Par Excellence	J. McClelland	180-day	35.00	35.00
Reco International		**The Children's Garden**			
93-36-001	Garden Friends	J. McClelland	120-day	29.50	29.50
93-36-002	Tea for Three	J. McClelland	120-day	29.50	29.50
93-36-003	TBA	J. McClelland	120-day	29.50	29.50
Reco International		**March of Dimes: Our Children, Our Future**			
89-37-001	A Time to Love (2nd in Series)	S. Kuck	150-day	29.00	45-69.00
89-37-002	A Time to Plant (3rd in Series)	J. McClelland	150-day	29.00	35.00
Reco International		**Games Children Play**			
79-38-001	Me First	S. Kuck	10,000	45.00	50.00
80-38-002	Forever Bubbles	S. Kuck	10,000	45.00	48.00
81-38-003	Skating Pals	S. Kuck	10,000	45.00	47.50
82-38-004	Join Me	S. Kuck	10,000	45.00	45.00
Reco International		**The Grandparent Collector's Plates**			
81-39-001	Grandma's Cookie Jar	S. Kuck	Yr.Iss.	37.50	37.50
81-39-002	Grandpa and the Dollhouse	S. Kuck	Yr.Iss.	37.50	37.50
Reco International		**Little Professionals**			
82-40-001	All is Well	S. Kuck	10,000	39.50	43-65.00
83-40-002	Tender Loving Care	S. Kuck	10,000	39.50	50-75.00
84-40-003	Lost and Found	S. Kuck	10,000	39.50	45.00
85-40-004	Reading, Writing and...	S. Kuck	10,000	39.50	45.00
Reco International		**Days Gone By**			
83-41-001	Sunday Best	S. Kuck	14-day	29.50	60-75.00
83-41-002	Amy's Magic Horse	S. Kuck	14-day	29.50	45-55.00
84-41-003	Little Anglers	S. Kuck	14-day	29.50	35-45.00
84-41-004	Afternoon Recital	S. Kuck	14-day	29.50	65-70.00
84-41-005	Little Tutor	S. Kuck	14-day	29.50	45.00
85-41-006	Easter at Grandma's	S. Kuck	14-day	29.50	45.00
85-41-007	Morning Song	S. Kuck	14-day	29.50	40-50.00
85-41-008	The Surrey Ride	S. Kuck	14-day	29.50	45.00
Reco International		**A Childhood Almanac**			
85-42-001	Fireside Dreams-January	S. Kuck	14-day	29.50	45-49.00
85-42-002	Be Mine-February	S. Kuck	14-day	29.50	45.00
86-42-003	Winds of March-March	S. Kuck	14-day	29.50	45-49.00
85-42-004	Easter Morning-April	S. Kuck	14-day	29.50	55.00
85-42-005	For Mom-May	S. Kuck	14-day	29.50	45.00
85-42-006	Just Dreaming-June	S. Kuck	14-day	29.50	55.00
85-42-007	Star Spangled Sky-July	S. Kuck	14-day	29.50	45.00
85-42-008	Summer Secrets-August	S. Kuck	14-day	29.50	49-55.00
85-42-009	School Days-September	S. Kuck	14-day	29.50	50-60.00
86-42-010	Indian Summer-October	S. Kuck	14-day	29.50	45.00
86-42-011	Giving Thanks-November	S. Kuck	14-day	29.50	45-49.00
85-42-012	Christmas Magic-December	S. Kuck	14-day	35.00	45-55.00

Company		Series			
Number	**Name**	**Artist**	**Edition Limit**	**Issue Price**	**Quote**
Reco International		**Mother's Day Collection**			
85-43-001	Once Upon a Time	S. Kuck	Yr.Iss.	29.50	55-75.00
86-43-002	Times Remembered	S. Kuck	Yr.Iss.	29.50	50-75.00
87-43-003	A Cherished Time	S. Kuck	Yr.Iss.	29.50	55.00
88-43-004	A Time Together	S. Kuck	Yr.Iss.	29.50	59.00
Reco International		**A Children's Christmas Pageant**			
86-44-001	Silent Night	S. Kuck	Yr.Iss.	32.50	35-55.00
87-44-002	Hark the Herald Angels Sing	S. Kuck	Yr.Iss.	32.50	35.00
88-44-003	While Shepherds Watched...	S. Kuck	Yr.Iss.	32.50	32.50
89-44-004	We Three Kings	S. Kuck	Yr.Iss.	32.50	32.50
Reco International		**Barefoot Children**			
87-45-001	Night-Time Story	S. Kuck	14-day	29.50	40.00
87-45-002	Golden Afternoon	S. Kuck	14-day	29.50	40.00
88-45-003	Little Sweethearts	S. Kuck	14-day	29.50	40.00
88-45-004	Carousel Magic	S. Kuck	14-day	29.50	49.00
88-45-005	Under the Apple Tree	S. Kuck	14-day	29.50	40.00
88-45-006	The Rehearsal	S. Kuck	14-day	29.50	45-55.00
88-45-007	Pretty as a Picture	S. Kuck	14-day	29.50	45.00
88-45-008	Grandma's Trunk	S. Kuck	14-day	29.50	45.00
Reco International		**Special Occasions by Reco**			
88-46-001	The Wedding	S. Kuck	Open	35.00	35.00
89-46-002	Wedding Day (6 1/2")	S. Kuck	Open	25.00	25.00
90-46-003	The Special Day	S. Kuck	Open	25.00	25.00
Reco International		**Victorian Mother's Day**			
89-47-001	Mother's Sunshine	S. Kuck	Yr.Iss.	35.00	45-85.00
90-47-002	Reflection Of Love	S. Kuck	Yr.Iss.	35.00	50-80.00
91-47-003	A Precious Time	S. Kuck	Yr.Iss.	35.00	45-75.00
92-47-004	Loving Touch	S. Kuck	Yr.Iss.	35.00	45-49.00
Reco International Corp.		**Plate Of The Month Collection**			
90-48-001	January	S. Kuck	28-day	25.00	25.00
90-48-002	February	S. Kuck	28-day	25.00	25.00
90-48-003	March	S. Kuck	28-day	25.00	25.00
90-48-004	April	S. Kuck	28-day	25.00	25.00
90-48-005	May	S. Kuck	28-day	25.00	25.00
90-48-006	June	S. Kuck	28-day	25.00	25.00
90-48-007	July	S. Kuck	28-day	25.00	25.00
90-48-008	August	S. Kuck	28-day	25.00	25.00
90-48-009	September	S. Kuck	28-day	25.00	25.00
90-48-010	October	S. Kuck	28-day	25.00	25.00
90-48-011	November	S. Kuck	28-day	25.00	25.00
90-48-012	December	S. Kuck	28-day	25.00	25.00
Reco International Corp.		**Premier Collection**			
91-49-001	Puppy	S. Kuck	7,500	95.00	150.00
91-49-002	Kitten	S. Kuck	7,500	95.00	200-250.
92-49-003	La Belle	S. Kuck	7,500	95.00	95.00
92-49-004	Le Beau	S. Kuck	7,500	95.00	95.00
Reco International Corp.		**Hearts And Flowers**			
91-50-001	Patience	S. Kuck	120-day	29.50	45.00
91-50-002	Tea Party	S. Kuck	120-day	29.50	29.50
92-50-003	Cat's In The Cradle	S. Kuck	120-day	32.50	32.50
92-50-004	Carousel of Dreams	S. Kuck	120-day	32.50	32.50
92-50-005	Storybook Memories	S. Kuck	120-day	32.50	32.50
93-50-006	Delightful Bundle	S. Kuck	120-day	34.50	34.50
93-50-007	Easter Morning Visitor	S. Kuck	120-day	34.50	34.50
93-50-008	Me and My Pony	S. Kuck	120-day	34.50	34.50
Reco International Corp.		**Gift of Love Mother's Day Collection**			
93-51-001	Morning Glory	S. Kuck	10,000	65.00	65.00
Reco International Corp.		**Tidings Of Joy**			
92-52-001	Peace on Earth	S. Kuck	N/A	35.00	35.00
Reco International		**The Sophisticated Ladies Collection**			
85-53-001	Felicia	A. Fazio	21-day	29.50	32.50
85-53-002	Samantha	A. Fazio	21-day	29.50	32.50
85-53-003	Phoebe	A. Fazio	21-day	29.50	32.50
85-53-004	Cleo	A. Fazio	21-day	29.50	32.50
86-53-005	Cerissa	A. Fazio	21-day	29.50	32.50
86-53-006	Natasha	A. Fazio	21-day	29.50	32.50
86-53-007	Bianka	A. Fazio	21-day	29.50	32.50
86-53-008	Chelsea	A. Fazio	21-day	29.50	32.50
Reco International		**Gardens of Beauty**			
88-54-001	English Country Garden	D. Barlowe	14-day	29.50	29.50
88-54-002	Dutch Country Garden	D. Barlowe	14-day	29.50	29.50
88-54-003	New England Garden	D. Barlowe	14-day	29.50	29.50
88-54-004	Japanese Garden	D. Barlowe	14-day	29.50	29.50
89-54-005	Italian Garden	D. Barlowe	14-day	29.50	29.50
89-54-006	Hawaiian Garden	D. Barlowe	14-day	29.50	29.50
89-54-007	German Country Garden	D. Barlowe	14-day	29.50	29.50
89-54-008	Mexican Garden	D. Barlowe	14-day	29.50	29.50
Reco International		**Gardens of America**			
92-55-001	Colonial Splendor	D. Barlowe	48-day	29.50	29.50
Reco International		**Vanishing Animal Kingdoms**			
86-56-001	Rama the Tiger	S. Barlowe	21,500	35.00	35.00
86-56-002	Olepi the Buffalo	S. Barlowe	21,500	35.00	35.00
87-56-003	Coolibah the Koala	S. Barlowe	21,500	35.00	42.00
87-56-004	Ortwin the Deer	S. Barlowe	21,500	35.00	39.00
87-56-005	Yen-Poh the Panda	S. Barlowe	21,500	35.00	40.00
88-56-006	Mamakuu the Elephant	S. Barlowe	21,500	35.00	59.00
Reco International Corp.		**Town And Country Dogs**			
90-57-001	Fox Hunt	S. Barlowe	36-day	35.00	35.00
91-57-002	The Retrieval	S. Barlowe	36-day	35.00	35.00
91-57-003	Golden Fields (Golden Retriever)	S. Barlowe	36-day	35.00	35.00
93-57-004	Faithful Companions (Cocker Spaniel)	S. Barlowe	36-day	35.00	35.00
Reco International		**Our Cherished Seas**			
91-58-001	Whale Song	S. Barlowe	48-day	37.50	37.50
91-58-002	Lions of the Sea	S. Barlowe	48-day	37.50	37.50
91-58-003	Flight of the Dolphins	S. Barlowe	48-day	37.50	37.50
92-58-004	Palace of the Seals	S. Barlowe	48-day	37.50	37.50
92-58-005	Orca Ballet	S. Barlowe	48-day	37.50	37.50
93-58-006	Emperors of the Ice	S. Barlowe	48-day	37.50	37.50

Company / Number	Series / Name	Artist	Edition Limit	Issue Price	Quote
93-58-007	Turtle Treasure	S. Barlowe	48-day	37.50	37.50
93-58-008	Splendor of the Sea	S. Barlowe	48-day	37.50	37.50
Reco International	**Great Stories from the Bible**				
87-59-001	Moses in the Bulrushes	G. Katz	14-day	29.50	35.00
87-59-002	King Saul & David	G. Katz	14-day	29.50	35.00
87-59-003	Moses and the Ten Commandments	G. Katz	14-day	29.50	38.00
87-59-004	Joseph's Coat of Many Colors	G. Katz	14-day	29.50	35.00
88-59-005	Rebekah at the Well	G. Katz	14-day	29.50	35.00
88-59-006	Daniel Reads the Writing on the Wall	G. Katz	14-day	29.50	35.00
88-59-007	The Story of Ruth	G. Katz	14-day	29.50	35.00
88-59-008	King Solomon	G. Katz	14-day	29.50	35.00
Reco International	**The Nutcracker Ballet**				
89-60-001	Christmas Eve Party	C. Micarelli	14-day	35.00	35.00
90-60-002	Clara And Her Prince	C. Micarelli	14-day	35.00	37.00
90-60-003	The Dream Begins	C. Micarelli	14-day	35.00	35.00
91-60-004	Dance of the Snow Fairies	C. Micarelli	14-day	35.00	35.00
92-60-005	The Land of Sweets	C. Micarelli	14-day	35.00	35.00
92-60-006	The Sugar Plum Fairy	C. Micarelli	14-day	35.00	35.00
Reco International	**Special Occasions-Wedding**				
91-61-001	From This Day Forward (9 1/2")	C. Micarelli	Open	35.00	35.00
91-61-002	From This Day Forward (6 1/2")	C. Micarelli	Open	25.00	25.00
91-61-003	To Have And To Hold (9 1/2")	C. Micarelli	Open	35.00	35.00
91-61-004	To Have And To Hold (6 1/2")	C. Micarelli	Open	25.00	25.00
Reco International	**The Glory Of Christ**				
92-62-001	The Ascension	C. Micarelli	48-day	29.50	29.50
93-62-002	Jesus Teaching	C. Micarelli	48-day	29.50	29.50
93-62-003	The Last Supper	C. Micarelli	48-day	29.50	29.50
Reco International	**J. Bergsma Mother's Day Series**				
90-63-001	The Beauty Of Life	J. Bergsma	14-day	35.00	35.00
92-63-002	Life's Blessing	J. Bergsma	14-day	35.00	35.00
93-63-003	My Greatest Treasures	J. Bergsma	14-day	35.00	35.00
Reco International	**Guardians Of The Kingdom**				
90-64-001	Rainbow To Ride On	J. Bergsma	17,500	35.00	37.00
90-64-002	Special Friends Are Few	J. Bergsma	17,500	35.00	35.00
90-64-003	Guardians Of The Innocent Children	J. Bergsma	17,500	35.00	38.00
90-64-004	The Miracle Of Love	J. Bergsma	17,500	35.00	37.00
91-64-005	The Magic Of Love	J. Bergsma	17,500	35.00	35.00
91-64-006	Only With The Heart	J. Bergsma	17,500	35.00	35.00
91-64-007	To Fly Without Wings	J. Bergsma	17,500	35.00	35.00
91-64-008	In Faith I Am Free	J. Bergsma	17,500	35.00	35.00
Reco International	**Castles & Dreams**				
92-65-001	The Birth of a Dream	J. Bergsma	48-day	29.50	29.50
92-65-002	Dreams Come True	J. Bergsma	48-day	29.50	29.50
93-65-003	TBA	J. Bergsma	48-day	29.50	29.50
93-65-004	TBA	J. Bergsma	48-day	29.50	29.50
Reco International	**The Christmas Series**				
90-66-001	Down The Glistening Lane	J. Bergsma	14-day	35.00	39.00
91-66-002	A Child Is Born	J. Bergsma	14-day	35.00	35.00
92-66-003	Christmas Day	J. Bergsma	14-day	35.00	35.00
93-66-004	TBA	J. Bergsma	14-day	35.00	35.00
Reco International	**God's Own Country**				
90-67-001	Daybreak	I. Drechsler	14-day	30.00	30.00
90-67-002	Coming Home	I. Drechsler	14-day	30.00	30.00
90-67-003	Peaceful Gathering	I. Drechsler	14-day	30.00	30.00
90-67-004	Quiet Waters	I. Drechsler	14-day	30.00	30.00
Reco International	**The Flower Fairies Year Collection**				
90-68-001	The Red Clover Fairy	C.M. Barker	14-day	29.50	29.50
90-68-002	The Wild Cherry Blossom Fairy	C.M. Barker	14-day	29.50	29.50
90-68-003	The Pine Tree Fairy	C.M. Barker	14-day	29.50	29.50
90-68-004	The Rose Hip Fairy	C.M. Barker	14-day	29.50	29.50
Reco International	**Oscar & Bertie's Edwardian Holiday**				
91-69-001	Snapshot	P.D. Jackson	48-day	29.50	29.50
92-69-002	Early Rise	P.D. Jackson	48-day	29.50	29.50
92-69-003	All Aboard	P.D. Jackson	48-day	29.50	29.50
92-69-004	Learning To Swim	P.D. Jackson	48-day	29.50	29.50
Reco International	**In The Eye of The Storm**				
91-70-001	First Strike	W. Lowe	120-day	29.50	29.50
92-70-002	Night Force	W. Lowe	120-day	29.50	29.50
92-70-003	Tracks Across The Sand	W. Lowe	120-day	29.50	29.50
92-70-004	The Storm Has Landed	W. Lowe	120-day	29.50	29.50
Reco International	**Celebration Of Love**				
92-71-001	Happy Anniversary (9 1/4")	J. Hall	Open	35.00	35.00
92-71-002	10th (9 1/4")	J. Hall	Open	35.00	35.00
92-71-003	25th (9 1/4")	J. Hall	Open	35.00	35.00
92-71-004	50th (9 1/4")	J. Hall	Open	35.00	35.00
92-71-005	Happy Anniversary (6 1/2")	J. Hall	Open	25.00	35.00
92-71-006	10th (6 1/2")	J. Hall	Open	25.00	35.00
92-71-007	25th (6 1/2")	J. Hall	Open	25.00	35.00
92-71-008	50th (6 1/2")	J. Hall	Open	25.00	35.00
Reco International	**The Heart Of The Family**				
92-72-001	Sharing Secrets	J. York	48-day	29.50	29.50
93-72-002	Spinning Dreams	J. York	48-day	29.50	29.50
Reece	**Waterfowl**				
73-01-001	Mallards & Wood Ducks (Pair)	Unknown	900	250.00	375.00
74-01-002	Canvasback & Canadian Geese (Pair)	Unknown	900	250.00	375.00
75-01-003	Pintails & Teal (Pair)	Unknown	900	250.00	425.00
Reed and Barton	**Audubon**				
70-01-001	Pine Siskin	Unknown	5,000	60.00	175.00
71-01-002	Red-Shouldered Hawk	Unknown	5,000	60.00	75.00
72-01-003	Stilt Sandpiper	Unknown	5,000	60.00	70.00
73-01-004	Red Cardinal	Unknown	5,000	60.00	65.00
74-01-005	Boreal Chickadee	Unknown	5,000	65.00	65.00
75-01-006	Yellow-Breasted Chat	Unknown	5,000	65.00	65.00
76-01-007	Bay-Breasted Warbler	Unknown	5,000	65.00	65.00
77-01-008	Purple Finch	Unknown	5,000	65.00	65.00

Company / Number	Series / Name	Artist	Edition Limit	Issue Price	Quote
River Shore	**Famous Americans**				
76-01-001	Brown's Lincoln	Rockwell-Brown	9,500	40.00	40.00
77-01-002	Rockwell's Triple Self-Portrait	Rockwell-Brown	9,500	45.00	45.00
78-01-003	Peace Corps	Rockwell-Brown	9,500	45.00	45.00
79-01-004	Spirit of Lindbergh	Rockwell-Brown	9,500	50.00	50.00
River Shore	**Norman Rockwell Single Issue**				
79-02-001	Spring Flowers	N. Rockwell	17,000	75.00	145.00
80-02-002	Looking Out to Sea	N. Rockwell	17,000	75.00	130.00
82-02-003	Grandpa's Guardian	N. Rockwell	17,000	80.00	80.00
82-02-004	Grandpa's Treasures	N. Rockwell	17,000	80.00	80.00
River Shore	**Baby Animals**				
79-03-001	Akiku	R. Brown	20,000	50.00	80.00
80-03-002	Roosevelt	R. Brown	20,000	50.00	90.00
81-03-003	Clover	R. Brown	20,000	50.00	65.00
82-03-004	Zuela	R. Brown	20,000	50.00	65.00
River Shore	**Rockwell Four Freedoms**				
81-04-001	Freedom of Speech	N. Rockwell	17,000	65.00	80-99.00
82-04-002	Freedom of Worship	N. Rockwell	17,000	65.00	80.00
82-04-003	Freedom from Fear	N. Rockwell	17,000	65.00	65-200.00
82-04-004	Freedom from Want	N. Rockwell	17,000	65.00	65-400.00
River Shore	**Puppy Playtime**				
87-05-001	Double Take	J. Lamb	14-day	24.50	32-35.00
88-05-002	Catch of the Day	J. Lamb	14-day	24.50	24.50
88-05-003	Cabin Fever	J. Lamb	14-day	24.50	24.50
88-05-004	Weekend Gardener	J. Lamb	14-day	24.50	24.50
88-05-005	Getting Acquainted	J. Lamb	14-day	24.50	24.50
88-05-006	Hanging Out	J. Lamb	14-day	24.50	24.50
88-05-007	A New Leash On Life	J. Lamb	14-day	24.50	29.50
87-05-008	Fun and Games	J. Lamb	14-day	24.50	29.50
River Shore	**Lovable Teddies**				
85-06-001	Bedtime Blues	M. Hague	10-day	21.50	21.50
85-06-002	Bearly Frightful	M. Hague	10-day	21.50	21.50
85-06-003	Caught in the Act	M. Hague	10-day	21.50	21.50
85-06-004	Fireside Friends	M. Hague	10-day	21.50	21.50
85-06-005	Harvest Time	M. Hague	10-day	21.50	21.50
85-06-006	Missed a Button	M. Hague	10-day	21.50	21.50
85-06-007	Tender Loving Bear	M. Hague	10-day	21.50	21.50
85-06-008	Sunday Stroll	M. Hague	10-day	21.50	21.50
River Shore	**Little House on the Prairie**				
85-07-001	Founder's Day Picnic	E. Christopherson	10-day	29.50	50.00
85-07-002	Women's Harvest	E. Christopherson	10-day	29.50	45.00
85-07-003	Medicine Show	E. Christopherson	10-day	29.50	45.00
85-07-004	Caroline's Eggs	E. Christopherson	10-day	29.50	45.00
85-07-005	Mary's Gift	E. Christopherson	10-day	29.50	45.00
85-07-006	A Bell for Walnut Grove	E. Christopherson	10-day	29.50	45.00
85-07-007	Ingall's Family	E. Christopherson	10-day	29.50	45.00
85-07-008	The Sweetheart Tree	E. Christopherson	10-day	29.50	45.00
River Shore	**We the Children**				
87-08-001	The Freedom of Speech	D. Crook	14-day	24.50	24.50
88-08-002	Right to Vote	D. Crook	14-day	24.50	24.50
88-08-003	Unreasonable Search and Seizure	D. Crook	14-day	24.50	24.50
88-08-004	Right to Bear Arms	D. Crook	14-day	24.50	24.50
88-08-005	Trial by Jury	D. Crook	14-day	24.50	24.50
88-08-006	Self Incrimination	D. Crook	14-day	24.50	24.50
88-08-007	Cruel and Unusual Punishment	D. Crook	14-day	24.50	24.50
88-08-008	Quartering of Soldiers	D. Crook	14-day	24.50	24.50
Norman Rockwell Gallery	**Rockwell's Christmas Legacy**				
92-01-001	Santa's Workshop	Rockwell-Inspired	4/94	49.90	49.90
Rockwell Society	**Christmas**				
74-01-001	Scotty Gets His Tree	N. Rockwell	Yr.Iss.	24.50	90.00
75-01-002	Angel with Black Eye	N. Rockwell	Yr.Iss.	24.50	40-45.00
76-01-003	Golden Christmas	N. Rockwell	Yr.Iss.	24.50	32.00
77-01-004	Toy Shop Window	N. Rockwell	Yr.Iss.	24.50	35.00
78-01-005	Christmas Dream	N. Rockwell	Yr.Iss.	24.50	35-45.00
79-01-006	Somebody's Up There	N. Rockwell	Yr.Iss.	24.50	35.00
80-01-007	Scotty Plays Santa	N. Rockwell	Yr.Iss.	24.50	24.50
81-01-008	Wrapped Up in Christmas	N. Rockwell	Yr.Iss.	25.50	26.50
82-01-009	Christmas Courtship	N. Rockwell	Yr.Iss.	25.50	25.50
83-01-010	Santa in the Subway	N. Rockwell	Yr.Iss.	25.50	25.50
84-01-011	Santa in the Workshop	N. Rockwell	Yr.Iss.	27.50	27.50
85-01-012	Grandpa Plays Santa	N. Rockwell	Yr.Iss.	27.90	35.00
86-01-013	Dear Santy Claus	N. Rockwell	Yr.Iss.	27.90	27.90
87-01-014	Santa's Golden Gift	N. Rockwell	Yr.Iss.	27.90	27.90
88-01-015	Santa Claus	N. Rockwell	Yr.Iss.	29.90	29.90
89-01-016	Jolly Old St. Nick	N. Rockwell	Yr.Iss.	29.90	29.90
90-01-017	A Christmas Prayer	N. Rockwell	Yr.Iss.	29.90	34-49.00
91-01-018	Santa's Helpers	N. Rockwell	Yr.Iss.	32.90	49.00
92-01-019	The Christmas Surprise	N. Rockwell	Yr.Iss.	32.90	32.90
Rockwell Society	**Mother's Day**				
76-02-001	A Mother's Love	N. Rockwell	Yr.Iss.	24.50	55.00
77-02-002	Faith	N. Rockwell	Yr.Iss.	24.50	35.00
78-02-003	Bedtime	N. Rockwell	Yr.Iss.	24.50	45-55.00
79-02-004	Reflections	N. Rockwell	Yr.Iss.	24.50	24.50
80-02-005	A Mother's Pride	N. Rockwell	Yr.Iss.	24.50	24.50
81-02-006	After the Party	N. Rockwell	Yr.Iss.	24.50	24.50
82-02-007	TheCooking Lesson	N. Rockwell	Yr.Iss.	24.50	26.00
83-02-008	Add Two Cups and Love	N. Rockwell	Yr.Iss.	25.50	30-49.00
84-02-009	Grandma's Courting Dress	N. Rockwell	Yr.Iss.	25.50	30-42.00
85-02-010	Mending Time	N. Rockwell	Yr.Iss.	27.50	28.00
86-02-011	Pantry Raid	N. Rockwell	Yr.Iss.	27.90	40-45.00
87-02-012	Grandma's Surprise	N. Rockwell	Yr.Iss.	29.90	40.00
88-02-013	My Mother	N. Rockwell	Yr.Iss.	29.90	29.90
89-02-014	Sunday Dinner	N. Rockwell	Yr.Iss.	29.90	36-45.00
90-02-015	Evening Prayers	N. Rockwell	Yr.Iss.	29.90	35.00
91-02-016	Building Our Future	N. Rockwell	Yr.Iss.	32.90	38.00
91-02-017	Gentle Reassurance	N. Rockwell	Yr.Iss.	32.90	32.90
Rockwell Society	**Heritage**				
77-03-001	Toy Maker	N. Rockwell	Yr.Iss.	14.50	100-125
78-03-002	Cobbler	N. Rockwell	Yr.Iss.	19.50	70-75.00
79-03-003	Lighthouse Keeper's Daughter	N. Rockwell	Yr.Iss.	19.50	28-35.00
80-03-004	Ship Builder	N. Rockwell	Yr.Iss.	19.50	25-39.00
81-03-005	Music maker	N. Rockwell	Yr.Iss.	19.50	19.50

Number	Name	Artist	Edition Limit	Issue Price	Quote
82-03-006	Tycoon	N. Rockwell	Yr.Iss.	19.50	19.50
83-03-007	Painter	N. Rockwell	Yr.Iss.	19.50	19.50
84-03-008	Storyteller	N. Rockwell	Yr.Iss.	19.50	19.50
85-03-009	Gourmet	N. Rockwell	Yr.Iss.	19.50	19.50
86-03-010	Professor	N. Rockwell	Yr.Iss.	22.90	22.90
87-03-011	Shadow Artist	N. Rockwell	Yr.Iss.	22.90	35.00
88-03-012	The Veteran	N. Rockwell	Yr.Iss.	22.90	30.00
88-03-013	The Banjo Player	N. Rockwell	Yr.Iss.	22.90	29.00
90-03-014	The Old Scout	N. Rockwell	Yr.Iss.	24.90	36.00
91-03-015	The Young Scholar	N. Rockwell	Yr.Iss.	24.90	43-49.00
91-03-016	The Family Doctor	N. Rockwell	Yr.Iss.	27.90	35-49.00
Rockwell Society		**Rockwell's Rediscovered Women**			
84-04-001	Dreaming in the Attic	N. Rockwell	100-day	19.50	30-39.00
84-04-002	Waiting on the Shore	N. Rockwell	100-day	22.50	23.00
84-04-003	Pondering on the Porch	N. Rockwell	100-day	22.50	23-32.00
84-04-004	Making Believe at the Mirror	N. Rockwell	100-day	22.50	30.00
84-04-005	Waiting at the Dance	N. Rockwell	100-day	22.50	23.00
84-04-006	Gossiping in the Alcove	N. Rockwell	100-day	22.50	23.00
84-04-007	Standing in the Doorway	N. Rockwell	100-day	22.50	23-30.00
84-04-008	Flirting in the Parlor	N. Rockwell	100-day	22.50	30.00
84-04-009	Working in the Kitchen	N. Rockwell	100-day	22.50	30.00
84-04-010	Meeting on the Path	N. Rockwell	100-day	22.50	23.00
84-04-011	Confiding in the Den	N. Rockwell	100-day	22.50	25-27.00
84-04-012	Reminiscing in the Quiet	N. Rockwell	100-day	22.50	22.50
XX-04-013	Complete Collection	N. Rockwell	100-day	267.00	370.00
Rockwell Society		**Rockwell on Tour**			
83-05-001	Walking Through Merrie Englande	N. Rockwell	150-day	16.00	29.00
83-05-002	Promenade a Paris	N. Rockwell	150-day	16.00	29.00
83-05-003	When in Rome	N. Rockwell	150-day	16.00	29.00
84-05-004	Die Walk am Rhein	N. Rockwell	150-day	16.00	35.00
Rockwell Society		**Rockwell's Light Compaign**			
83-06-001	This is the Room that Light Made	N. Rockwell	150-day	19.50	35-39.00
84-06-002	Grandpa's Treasure Chest	N. Rockwell	150-day	19.50	35.00
84-06-003	Father's Help	N. Rockwell	150-day	19.50	19.50
84-06-004	Evening's Ease	N. Rockwell	150-day	19.50	19.50
84-06-005	Close Harmony	N. Rockwell	150-day	21.50	21.50
84-06-006	The Birthday Wish	N. Rockwell	150-day	21.50	23.00
Rockwell Society		**Rockwell's American Dream**			
85-07-001	A Young Girl's Dream	N. Rockwell	150-day	19.90	20-35.00
85-07-002	A Couple's Commitment	N. Rockwell	150-day	19.90	20-30.00
85-07-003	A Family's Full Measure	N. Rockwell	150-day	22.90	22.90
86-07-004	A Mother's Welcome	N. Rockwell	150-day	22.90	35.00
86-07-005	A Young Man's Dream	N. Rockwell	150-day	22.90	34.00
86-07-006	The Musician's Magic	N. Rockwell	150-day	22.90	22.90
87-07-007	An Orphan's Hope	N. Rockwell	150-day	24.90	24.90
87-07-008	Love's Reward	N. Rockwell	150-day	24.90	50.00
Rockwell Society		**Colonials-The Rarest Rockwells**			
85-08-001	Unexpected Proposal	N. Rockwell	150-day	27.90	27.90
86-08-002	Words of Comfort	N. Rockwell	150-day	27.90	27.90
86-08-003	Light for the Winter	N. Rockwell	150-day	30.90	30.90
87-08-004	Portrait for a Bridegroom	N. Rockwell	150-day	30.90	30.90
87-08-005	The Journey Home	N. Rockwell	150-day	30.90	30.90
87-08-006	Clinching the Deal	N. Rockwell	150-day	30.90	30.90
88-08-007	Sign of the Times	N. Rockwell	150-day	32.90	32.90
88-08-008	Ye Glutton	N. Rockwell	150-day	32.90	32.90
Rockwell Society		**A Mind of Her Own**			
86-09-001	Sitting Pretty	N. Rockwell	150-day	24.90	25-35.00
87-09-002	Serious Business	N. Rockwell	150-day	24.90	30-38.00
87-09-003	Breaking the Rules	N. Rockwell	150-day	24.90	43-47.00
87-09-004	Good Intentions	N. Rockwell	150-day	27.90	27.90
88-09-005	Second Thoughts	N. Rockwell	150-day	27.90	27.90
88-09-006	World's Away	N. Rockwell	150-day	27.90	30.00
88-09-007	Kiss and Tell	N. Rockwell	150-day	29.90	29.90
88-09-008	On My Honor	N. Rockwell	150-day	29.90	35.00
Rockwell Society		**Rockwell's Golden Moments**			
87-10-001	Grandpa's Gift	N. Rockwell	150-day	19.90	35-39.00
87-10-002	Grandma's Love	N. Rockwell	150-day	19.90	35-39.00
88-10-003	End of day	N. Rockwell	150-day	22.90	35.00
88-10-004	Best Friends	N. Rockwell	150-day	22.90	35.00
89-10-005	Love Letters	N. Rockwell	150-day	22.90	35.00
89-10-006	Newfound Worlds	N. Rockwell	150-day	22.90	32-35.00
89-10-007	Keeping Company	N. Rockwell	150-day	24.90	24.90
89-10-008	Evening's Repose	N. Rockwell	150-day	24.90	24.90
Rockwell Society		**Rockwell's The Ones We Love**			
88-11-001	Tender Loving Care	N. Rockwell	150-day	19.90	40-49.00
89-11-002	A Time to Keep	N. Rockwell	150-day	19.90	19.90
89-11-003	The Inventor And The Judge	N. Rockwell	150-day	22.90	22.90
89-11-004	Ready For The World	N. Rockwell	150-day	22.90	22.90
89-11-005	Growing Strong	N. Rockwell	150-day	22.90	30.00
90-11-006	The Story Hour	N. Rockwell	150-day	22.90	22.90
90-11-007	The Country Doctor	N. Rockwell	150-day	24.90	35-51.00
90-11-008	Our Love of Country	N. Rockwell	150-day	24.90	35.00
90-11-009	The Homecoming	N. Rockwell	150-day	24.90	35.00
91-11-010	A Helping Hand	N. Rockwell	150-day	24.90	24.90
Rockwell Society		**Coming Of Age**			
90-12-001	Back To School	N. Rockwell	150-day	29.90	39.00
90-12-002	Home From Camp	N. Rockwell	150-day	29.90	30-35.00
90-12-003	Her First Formal	N. Rockwell	150-day	32.90'	49.00
90-12-004	The Muscleman	N. Rockwell	150-day	32.90	37.00
90-12-005	A New Look	N. Rockwell	150-day	32.90	44.00
91-12-006	A Balcony Seat	N. Rockwell	150-day	32.90	35.00
91-12-007	Men About Town	N. Rockwell	150-day	34.90	60.00
91-12-008	Paths of Glory	N. Rockwell	150-day	34.90	34.90
91-12-009	Doorway to the Past	N. Rockwell	150-day	34.90	34.90
91-12-010	School's Out!	N. Rockwell	150-day	34.90	34.90
Rockwell Society		**Innocence and Experience**			
91-13-001	The Sea Captain	N. Rockwell	150-day	29.90	39-45.00
91-13-002	The Radio Operator	N. Rockwell	150-day	29.90	39-45.00
91-13-003	The Magician	N. Rockwell	150-day	32.90	32.90
92-13-004	The American Heroes	N. Rockwell	150-day	32.90	32.90
Rockwell Society		**Rockwell's Treasured Memories**			
91-14-001	Quiet Reflections	N. Rockwell	150-day	29.90	31.00

Number	Name	Artist	Edition Limit	Issue Price	Quote
91-14-002	Romantic Reverie	N. Rockwell	150-day	29.90	29.90
91-14-003	Tender Romance	N. Rockwell	150-day	32.90	32.90
91-14-004	Evening Passage	N. Rockwell	150-day	32.90	32.90
91-14-005	Heavenly Dreams	N. Rockwell	150-day	32.90	32.90
91-14-006	Sentimental Shores	N. Rockwell	150-day	32.90	32.90
Roman, Inc.		**The Masterpiece Collection**			
79-01-001	Adoration	F. Lippe	5,000	65.00	65.00
80-01-002	Madonna with Grapes	P. Mignard	5,000	87.50	87.50
81-01-003	The Holy Family	G. Delle Notti	5,000	95.00	95.00
82-01-004	Madonna of the Streets	R. Ferruzzi	5,000	85.00	85.00
Roman, Inc.		**A Child's World**			
80-02-001	Little Children, Come to Me	F. Hook	15,000	45.00	49.00
Roman, Inc.		**A Child's Play**			
82-03-001	Breezy Day	F. Hook	30-day	29.95	39.00
82-03-002	Kite Flying	F. Hook	30-day	29.95	39.00
84-03-003	Bathtub Sailor	F. Hook	30-day	29.95	35.00
84-03-004	The First Snow	F. Hook	30-day	29.95	35.00
Roman, Inc.		**Frances Hook Collection-Set I**			
82-04-001	I Wish, I Wish	F. Hook	15,000	24.95	35-39.00
82-04-002	Baby Blossoms	F. Hook	15,000	24.95	35-39.00
82-04-003	Daisy Dreamer	F. Hook	15,000	24.95	35-39.00
82-04-004	Trees So Tall	F. Hook	15,000	24.95	35-39.00
Roman, Inc.		**Frances Hook Collection-Set II**			
83-05-001	Caught It Myself	F. Hook	15,000	24.95	25.00
83-05-002	Winter Wrappings	F. Hook	15,000	24.95	25.00
83-05-003	So Cuddly	F. Hook	15,000	24.95	25.00
83-05-004	Can I Keep Him?	F. Hook	15,000	24.95	25.00
Roman, Inc.		**Pretty Girls of the Ice Capades**			
83-06-001	Ice Princess	G. Petty	30-day	24.50	24.50
Roman, Inc.		**The Ice Capades Clown**			
83-07-001	Presenting Freddie Trenkler	G. Petty	30-day	24.50	24.50
Roman, Inc.		**Roman Memorial**			
84-08-001	The Carpenter	F. Hook	Yr.Iss.	100.00	135.00
Roman, Inc.		**Roman Cats**			
84-09-001	Grizabella	Unknown	30-day	29.50	29.50
84-09-002	Mr. Mistoffelees	Unknown	30-day	29.50	29.50
84-09-003	Rum Rum Tugger	Unknown	30-day	29.50	29.50
Roman, Inc.		**The Magic of Childhood**			
85-10-001	Special Friends	A. Williams	10-day	24.50	35.00
85-10-002	Feeding Time	A. Williams	10-day	24.50	35.00
85-10-003	Best Buddies	A. Williams	10-day	24.50	35.00
85-10-004	Getting Acquainted	A. Williams	10-day	24.50	35.00
86-10-005	Last One In	A. Williams	10-day	24.50	35.00
86-10-006	A Handful Of Love	A. Williams	10-day	24.50	35.00
86-10-007	Look Alikes	A. Williams	10-day	24.50	35.00
86-10-008	No Fair Peeking	A. Williams	10-day	24.50	35.00
Roman, Inc.		**Frances Hook Legacy**			
85-11-001	Fascination	F. Hook	100-day	19.50	35-39.00
85-11-002	Daydreaming	F. Hook	100-day	19.50	35-39.00
85-11-003	Discovery	F. Hook	100-day	22.50	35-39.00
85-11-004	Disappointment	F. Hook	100-day	22.50	35-39.00
85-11-005	Wonderment	F. Hook	100-day	22.50	35-39.00
85-11-006	Expectation	F. Hook	100-day	22.50	35-39.00
Roman, Inc.		**The Lord's Prayer**			
86-12-001	Our Father	A. Williams	10-day	24.50	24.50
86-12-002	Thy Kingdom Come	A. Williams	10-day	24.50	24.50
86-12-003	Give Us This Day	A. Williams	10-day	24.50	24.50
86-12-004	Forgive Our Trespasses	A. Williams	10-day	24.50	34.00
86-12-005	As We Forgive	A. Williams	10-day	24.50	24.50
86-12-006	Lead Us Not	A. Williams	10-day	24.50	24.50
86-12-007	Deliver Us From Evil	A. Williams	10-day	24.50	24.50
86-12-008	Thine Is The Kingdom	A. Williams	10-day	24.50	24.50
Roman, Inc.		**The Sweetest Songs**			
86-13-001	A Baby's Prayer	I. Spencer	30-day	39.50	45.00
86-13-002	This Little Piggie	I. Spencer	30-day	39.50	39.50
88-13-003	Long, Long Ago	I. Spencer	30-day	39.50	39.50
89-13-004	Rockabye	I. Spencer	30-day	39.50	39.50
Roman, Inc.		**Fontanini Annual Christmas Plate**			
86-14-001	A King Is Born	E. Simonetti	Yr.Iss.	60.00	60.00
87-14-002	O Come, Let Us Adore Him	E. Simonetti	Yr.Iss.	60.00	65.00
88-14-003	Adoration of the Magi	E. Simonetti	Yr.Iss.	70.00	75.00
89-14-004	Flight Into Egypt	E. Simonetti	Yr.Iss.	75.00	85.00
Roman, Inc.		**The Love's Prayer**			
88-15-001	Love Is Patient and Kind	A. Williams	14-day	29.50	29.50
88-15-002	Love Is Never Jealous or Boastful	A. Williams	14-day	29.50	29.50
88-15-003	Love Is Never Arrogant or Rude	A. Williams	14-day	29.50	29.50
88-15-004	Love Does Not Insist on Its Own Way	A. Williams	14-day	29.50	29.50
88-15-005	Love Is Never Irritable or Resentful	A. Williams	14-day	29.50	29.50
88-15-006	Love Rejoices In the Right	A. Williams	14-day	29.50	29.50
88-15-007	Love Believes All Things	A. Williams	14-day	29.50	29.50
88-15-008	Love Never Ends	A. Williams	14-day	29.50	29.50
Roman, Inc.		**March of Dimes: Our Children, Our Future**			
90-16-001	A Time To Laugh	A. Williams	150-day	29.00	39-49.00
Roman, Inc.		**Abbie Williams Collection**			
91-17-001	Legacy of Love	A. Williams	Open	29.50	29.50
91-17-002	Bless This Child	A. Williams	Open	29.50	29.50
Roman, Inc.		**Catnippers**			
86-18-001	Christmas Mourning	I. Spencer	9,500	34.50	34.50
92-18-002	Happy Holidaze	I. Spencer	9,500	34.50	34.50
Roman, Inc.		**God Bless You, Little One**			
91-19-001	Baby's First Birthday (Girl)	A. Williams	Open	29.50	29.50
91-19-002	Baby's First Birthday (Boy)	A. Williams	Open	29.50	29.50
91-19-003	Baby's First Smile	A. Williams	Open	19.50	19.50
91-19-004	Baby's First Word	A. Williams	Open	19.50	19.50

Number	Name	Artist	Edition Limit	Issue Price	Quote
91-19-005	Baby's First Step	A. Williams	Open	19.50	19.50
91-19-006	Baby's First Tooth	A. Williams	Open	19.50	19.50
Roman, Inc.		**Millenium Series**			
92-20-001	Silent Night	Morcaldo/Lucchesi	2,000	49.50	49.50
93-20-002	The Annunciation	Morcaldo/Lucchesi	5,000	49.50	49.50
Roman, Inc.		**Tender Expressions**			
92-21-001	Thoughts of You Are In My Heart	B. Sargent	100-day	29.50	29.50
Roman, Inc.		**The Richard Judson Zolan Collection**			
92-22-001	The Butterfly Net	R.J. Zolan	100-day	29.50	29.50
Rorstrand		**Christmas**			
68-01-001	Bringing Home the Tree	G. Nylund	Annual	12.00	500.00
69-01-002	Fisherman Sailing Home	G. Nylund	Annual	13.50	18-30.00
70-01-003	Nils with His Geese	G. Nylund	Annual	13.50	13.50-15.00
71-01-004	Nils in Lapland	G. Nylund	Annual	15.00	15.00
72-01-005	Dalecarlian Fiddler	G. Nylund	Annual	15.00	20-22.00
73-01-006	Farm in Smaland	G. Nylund	Annual	16.00	60.00
74-01-007	Vadslena	G. Nylund	Annual	19.00	43.00
75-01-008	Nils in Vastmanland	G. Nylund	Annual	20.00	35.00
76-01-009	Nils in Uapland	G. Nylund	Annual	20.00	43-49.00
77-01-010	Nils in Varmland	G. Nylund	Annual	29.50	29.50
78-01-011	Nils in Fjallbacka	G. Nylund	Annual	32.50	49.00
79-01-012	Nils in Vaestergoetland	G. Nylund	Annual	38.50	38.50
80-01-013	Nils in Halland	G. Nylund	Annual	55.00	60.00
81-01-014	Nils in Gotland	G. Nylund	Annual	55.00	45.00
82-01-015	Nils at Skansen	G. Nylund	Annual	47.50	40.00
83-01-016	Nils in Oland	G. Nylund	Annual	42.50	55.00
84-01-017	Angerman land	G. Nylund	Annual	42.50	35.00
85-01-018	Nils in Jamtland	G. Nylund	Annual	42.50	70.00
86-01-019	Nils in Karlskr	G. Nylund	Annual	42.50	50.00
87-01-020	Christmas	G. Nylund	Annual	47.50	150.00
88-01-021	Christmas	G. Nylund	Annual	55.00	60.00
89-01-022	Nils Visits Gothenborg	G. Nylund	Annual	60.00	61.00
Rosenthal		**Christmas**			
10-01-001	Winter Peace	Unknown	Annual	Unkn.	550.00
11-01-002	Three Wise Men	Unknown	Annual	Unkn.	325.00
12-01-003	Stardust	Unknown	Annual	Unkn.	255.00
13-01-004	Christmas Lights	Unknown	Annual	Unkn.	235.00
14-01-005	Christmas Song	Unknown	Annual	Unkn.	350.00
15-01-006	Walking to Church	Unknown	Annual	Unkn.	180.00
16-01-007	Christmas During War	Unknown	Annual	Unkn.	240.00
17-01-008	Angel of Peace	Unknown	Annual	Unkn.	200.00
18-01-009	Peace on Earth	Unknown	Annual	Unkn.	200.00
19-01-010	St. Christopher with Christ Child	Unknown	Annual	Unkn.	225.00
20-01-011	Manger in Bethlehem	Unknown	Annual	Unkn.	325.00
21-01-012	Christmas in Mountains	Unknown	Annual	Unkn.	200.00
22-01-013	Advent Branch	Unknown	Annual	Unkn.	200.00
23-01-014	Children in Winter Woods	Unknown	Annual	Unkn.	200.00
24-01-015	Deer in the Woods	Unknown	Annual	Unkn.	200.00
25-01-016	Three Wise Men	Unknown	Annual	Unkn.	200.00
26-01-017	Christmas in Mountains	Unknown	Annual	Unkn.	195.00
27-01-018	Station on the Way	Unknown	Annual	Unkn.	200.00
28-01-019	Chalet Christmas	Unknown	Annual	Unkn.	185.00
29-01-020	Christmas in Alps	Unknown	Annual	Unkn.	225.00
30-01-021	Group of Deer Under Pines	Unknown	Annual	Unkn.	225.00
31-01-022	Path of the Magi	Unknown	Annual	Unkn.	225.00
32-01-023	Christ Child	Unknown	Annual	Unkn.	185.00
33-01-024	Thru the Night to Light	Unknown	Annual	Unkn.	190.00
34-01-025	Christmas Peace	Unknown	Annual	Unkn.	190.00
35-01-026	Christmas by the Sea	Unknown	Annual	Unkn.	190.00
36-01-027	Nurnberg Angel	Unknown	Annual	Unkn.	195.00
37-01-028	Berchtesgaden	Unknown	Annual	Unkn.	195.00
38-01-029	Christmas in the Alps	Unknown	Annual	Unkn.	195.00
39-01-030	Schneekoppe Mountain	Unknown	Annual	Unkn.	195.00
40-01-031	Marien Chruch in Danzig	Unknown	Annual	Unkn.	250.00
41-01-032	Strassburg Cathedral	Unknown	Annual	Unkn.	250.00
42-01-033	Marianburg Castle	Unknown	Annual	Unkn.	300.00
43-01-034	Winter Idyll	Unknown	Annual	Unkn.	300.00
44-01-035	Wood Scape	Unknown	Annual	Unkn.	300.00
45-01-036	Christmas Peace	Unknown	Annual	Unkn.	400.00
46-01-037	Christmas in an Alpine Valley	Unknown	Annual	Unkn.	240.00
47-01-038	Dillingen Madonna	Unknown	Annual	Unkn.	985.00
48-01-039	Message to the Shepherds	Unknown	Annual	Unkn.	875.00
49-01-040	The Holy Family	Unknown	Annual	Unkn.	185.00
50-01-041	Christmas in the Forest	Unknown	Annual	Unkn.	185.00
51-01-042	Star of Bethlehem	Unknown	Annual	Unkn.	450.00
52-01-043	Christmas in the Alps	Unknown	Annual	Unkn.	195.00
53-01-044	The Holy Light	Unknown	Annual	Unkn.	195.00
54-01-045	Christmas Eve	Unknown	Annual	Unkn.	195.00
55-01-046	Christmas in a Village	Unknown	Annual	Unkn.	195.00
56-01-047	Christmas in the Alps	Unknown	Annual	Unkn.	195.00
57-01-048	Christmas by the Sea	Unknown	Annual	Unkn.	195.00
58-01-049	Christmas Eve	Unknown	Annual	Unkn.	195.00
59-01-050	Midnight Mass	Unknown	Annual	Unkn.	195.00
60-01-051	Christmas in a Small Village	Unknown	Annual	Unkn.	195.00
61-01-052	Solitary Christmas	Unknown	Annual	Unkn.	225.00
62-01-053	Christmas Eve	Unknown	Annual	Unkn.	195.00
63-01-054	Silent Night	Unknown	Annual	Unkn.	195.00
64-01-055	Christmas Market in Nurnberg	Unknown	Annual	Unkn.	225.00
65-01-056	Christmas Munich	Unknown	Annual	Unkn.	185.00
66-01-057	Christmas in Ulm	Unknown	Annual	Unkn.	275.00
67-01-058	Christmas in Reginburg	Unknown	Annual	Unkn.	185.00
68-01-059	Christmas in Bremen	Unknown	Annual	Unkn.	195.00
69-01-060	Christmas in Rothenburg	Unknown	Annual	Unkn.	220.00
70-01-061	Christmas in Cologne	Unknown	Annual	Unkn.	175.00
71-01-062	Christmas in Garmisch	Unknown	Annual	42.00	100.00
72-01-063	Christmas in Franconia	Unknown	Annual	50.00	95.00
73-01-064	Lubeck-Holstein	Unknown	Annual	77.00	105.00
74-01-065	Christmas in Wurzburg	Unknown	Annual	85.00	100.00
Rosenthal		**Wiinblad Christmas**			
71-02-001	Maria & Child	B. Wiinblad	Undis.	100.00	700.00
72-02-002	Caspar	B. Wiinblad	Undis.	100.00	290.00
73-02-003	Melchior	B. Wiinblad	Undis.	125.00	335.00
74-02-004	Balthazar	B. Wiinblad	Undis.	125.00	300.00
75-02-005	The Annunciation	B. Wiinblad	Undis.	195.00	195.00
76-02-006	Angel with Trumpet	B. Wiinblad	Undis.	195.00	195.00
77-02-007	Adoration of Shepherds	B. Wiinblad	Undis.	225.00	225.00
78-02-008	Angel with Harp	B. Wiinblad	Undis.	275.00	295.00

Number	Name	Artist	Edition Limit	Issue Price	Quote
79-02-009	Exodus from Egypt	B. Wiinblad	Undis.	310.00	310.00
80-02-010	Angel with Glockenspiel	B. Wiinblad	Undis.	360.00	360.00
81-02-011	Christ Child Visits Temple	B. Wiinblad	Undis.	375.00	375.00
82-02-012	Christening of Christ	B. Wiinblad	Undis.	375.00	375.00
Rosenthal		**Nobility of Children**			
76-03-001	La Contessa Isabella	E. Hibel	12,750	120.00	120.00
77-03-002	La Marquis Maurice-Pierre	E. Hibel	12,750	120.00	120.00
78-03-003	Baronesse Johanna	E. Hibel	12,750	130.00	140.00
79-03-004	Chief Red Feather	E. Hibel	12,750	140.00	180.00
Rosenthal		**Oriental Gold**			
76-04-001	Yasuko	E. Hibel	2,000	275.00	650.00
77-04-002	Mr. Obata	E. Hibel	2,000	275.00	500.00
78-04-003	Sakura	E. Hibel	2,000	295.00	400.00
79-04-004	Michio	E. Hibel	2,000	325.00	375.00
Royal Bayreuth		**Christmas**			
72-01-001	Carriage in the Village	Unknown	4,000	15.00	80.00
73-01-002	Scow Scene	Unknown	4,000	16.50	20.00
74-01-003	The Old Mill	Unknown	4,000	24.00	24.00
75-01-004	Forest Chalet "Serenity"	Unknown	4,000	27.50	27.50
76-01-005	Christmas in the Country	Unknown	5,000	40.00	40.00
77-01-006	Peace on Earth	Unknown	5,000	40.00	40.00
78-01-007	Peaceful Interlude	Unknown	5,000	45.00	45.00
79-01-008	Homeward Bound	Unknown	5,000	50.00	50.00
Royal Copenhagen		**Christmas**			
08-01-001	Madonna and Child	C. Thomsen	Annual	1.00	2500-4000.
09-01-002	Danish Landscape	S. Ussing	Annual	1.00	180.00
10-01-003	The Magi	C. Thomsen	Annual	1.00	143.00
11-01-004	Danish Landscape	O. Jensen	Annual	1.00	180.00
12-01-005	Christmas Tree	C. Thomsen	Annual	1.00	180.00
13-01-006	Frederik Church Spire	A. Boesen	Annual	1.50	149.00
14-01-007	Holy Spirit Church	A. Boesen	Annual	1.50	189.00
15-01-008	Danish Landscape	A. Krog	Annual	1.50	194.00
16-01-009	Shepherd at Christmas	R. Bocher	Annual	1.50	112.00
17-01-010	Our Savior Church	O. Jensen	Annual	2.00	99.00
18-01-011	Sheep and Shepherds	O. Jensen	Annual	2.00	102.00
19-01-012	In the Park	O. Jensen	Annual	2.00	102.00
20-01-013	Mary and Child Jesus	G. Rode	Annual	2.00	102.00
21-01-014	Aabenraa Marketplace	O. Jensen	Annual	2.00	93.00
22-01-015	Three Singing Angels	E. Selschau	Annual	2.00	85.00
23-01-016	Danish Landscape	O. Jensen	Annual	2.00	85.00
24-01-017	Sailing Ship	B. Olsen	Annual	2.00	124.00
25-01-018	Christianshavn	O. Jensen	Annual	2.00	102.00
26-01-019	Christianshavn Canal	R. Bocher	Annual	2.00	113.00
27-01-020	Ship's Boy at Tiller	B. Olsen	Annual	2.00	138-169.
28-01-021	Vicar's Family	G. Rode	Annual	2.00	99.00
29-01-022	Grundtvig Church	O. Jensen	Annual	2.00	99.00
30-01-023	Fishing Boats	B. Olsen	Annual	2.50	127.00
31-01-024	Mother and Child	G. Rode	Annual	2.50	127.00
32-01-025	Frederiksberg Gardens	O. Jensen	Annual	2.50	119.00
33-01-026	Ferry and the Great Belt	B. Olsen	Annual	2.50	173.00
34-01-027	The Hermitage Castle	O. Jensen	Annual	2.50	173.00
35-01-028	Kronborg Castle	B. Olsen	Annual	2.50	260.00
36-01-029	Roskilde Cathedral	R. Bocher	Annual	2.50	205.00
37-01-030	Main Street Copenhagen	N. Thorsson	Annual	2.50	100-230.
38-01-031	Round Church in Osterlars	H. Nielsen	Annual	3.00	355.00
39-01-032	Greenland Pack-Ice	S. Nielsen	Annual	3.00	459.00
40-01-033	The Good Shepherd	K. Lange	Annual	3.00	473.00
41-01-034	Danish Village Church	T. Kjolner	Annual	3.00	473.00
42-01-035	Bell Tower	N. Thorsson	Annual	4.00	455.00
43-01-036	Flight into Egypt	N. Thorsson	Annual	4.00	620.00
44-01-037	Danish Village Scene	V. Olson	Annual	4.00	330.00
45-01-038	A Peaceful Motif	R. Bocher	Annual	4.00	495.00
46-01-039	Zealand Village Church	N. Thorsson	Annual	4.00	219.00
47-01-040	The Good Shepherd	K. Lange	Annual	4.50	285.00
48-01-041	Nodebo Church	T. Kjolner	Annual	4.50	245.00
49-01-042	Our Lady's Cathedral	H. Hansen	Annual	5.00	280.00
50-01-043	Boeslunde Church	V. Olson	Annual	5.00	220.00
51-01-044	Christmas Angel	R. Bocher	Annual	5.00	430.00
52-01-045	Christmas in the Forest	K. Lange	Annual	5.00	155.00
53-01-046	Frederiksberg Castle	T. Kjolner	Annual	6.00	155.00
54-01-047	Amalienborg Palace	K. Lange	Annual	6.00	155.00
55-01-048	Fano Girl	K. Lange	Annual	7.00	230.00
56-01-049	Rosenborg Castle	K. Lange	Annual	7.00	217.00
57-01-050	The Good Shepherd	H. Hansen	Annual	8.00	121-177.
58-01-051	Sunshine over Greenland	H. Hansen	Annual	9.00	83-125.00
59-01-052	Christmas Night	H. Hansen	Annual	9.00	130-140.
60-01-053	The Stag	H. Hansen	Annual	10.00	138-169.
61-01-054	Training Ship	K. Lange	Annual	10.00	110-189.
62-01-055	The Little Mermaid	Unknown	Annual	11.00	140-250.
63-01-056	Hojsager Mill	K. Lange	Annual	11.00	51-97.00
64-01-057	Fetching the Tree	K. Lange	Annual	11.00	49-69.00
65-01-058	Little Skaters	K. Lange	Annual	12.00	45-74.00
66-01-059	Blackbird	K. Lange	Annual	12.00	27-35.00
67-01-060	The Royal Oak	K. Lange	Annual	13.00	24-38.00
68-01-061	The Last Umiak	K. Lange	Annual	13.00	15-38.00
69-01-062	The Old Farmyard	K. Lange	Annual	14.00	21-38.00
70-01-063	Christmas Rose and Cat	K. Lange	Annual	14.00	29-40.00
71-01-064	Hare In Winter	K. Lange	Annual	15.00	15-25.00
72-01-065	In the Desert	K. Lange	Annual	16.00	27-45.00
73-01-066	Train Homeward Bound	K. Lange	Annual	22.00	23.00
74-01-067	Winter Twilight	K. Lange	Annual	22.00	23.00
75-01-068	Queen's Palace	K. Lange	Annual	27.50	27.50
76-01-069	Danish Watermill	S. Vestergaard	Annual	27.50	28.00
77-01-070	Immervad Bridge	K. Lange	Annual	32.00	32.00
78-01-071	Greenland Scenery	K. Lange	Annual	35.00	80.00
79-01-072	Choosing Christmas Tree	K. Lange	Annual	42.50	78.00
80-01-073	Bringing Home the Tree	K. Lange	Annual	49.50	49.50
81-01-074	Admiring Christmas Tree	K. Lange	Annual	52.50	52.50
82-01-075	Waiting for Christmas	K. Lange	Annual	54.50	60.00
83-01-076	Merry Christmas	K. Lange	Annual	54.50	54.50
84-01-077	Jingle Bells	K. Lange	Annual	54.50	54.50
85-01-078	Snowman	K. Lange	Annual	54.50	54.50-66.00
86-01-079	Christmas Vacation	K. Lange	Annual	54.50	58.00
87-01-080	Winter Birds	S. Vestergaard	Annual	59.50	59.50
88-01-081	Christmas Eve in Copenhagen	S. Vestergaard	Annual	59.50	59.50
89-01-082	The Old Skating Pond	S. Vestergaard	Annual	59.50	69.00
90-01-083	Christmas at Tivoli	S. Vestergaard	Annual	64.50	76.00
91-01-084	The Festival of Santa Lucia	S. Vestergaard	Annual	69.50	69.50
92-01-085	The Queen's Carriage	S. Vestergaard	Annual	69.50	69.50

Company		Series			
Number	**Name**	**Artist**	**Edition Limit**	**Issue Price**	**Quote**
93-01-086	Christmas Guests	S. Vestergaard	Annual	69.50	69.50
Royal Copenhagen		**Nature's Children**			
93-02-001	The Robins	J. Nielsen	Annual	39.50	39.50
Royal Cornwall		**Creation**			
77-01-001	In the Beginning	Y. Koutsis	10,000	37.50	90.00
77-01-002	In His Image	Y. Koutsis	10,000	45.00	55.00
78-01-003	Adam's Rib	Y. Koutsis	10,000	45.00	52.50
78-01-004	Banished from Eden	Y. Koutsis	10,000	45.00	47.50
78-01-005	Noah and the Ark	Y. Koutsis	10,000	45.00	45.00
80-01-006	Tower of Babel	Y. Koutsis	10,000	45.00	75.00
80-01-007	Sodom and Gomorrah	Y. Koutsis	10,000	45.00	45.00
80-01-008	Jacob's Wedding	Y. Koutsis	10,000	45.00	45.00
80-01-009	Rebekah at the Well	Y. Koutsis	10,000	45.00	75.00
80-01-010	Jacob's Ladder	Y. Koutsis	10,000	45.00	75.00
80-01-011	Joseph's Coat of Many Colors	Y. Koutsis	10,000	45.00	75.00
80-01-012	Joseph Interprets Pharaoh's Dream	Y. Koutsis	10,000	45.00	75.00
Royal Cornwall		**Creation Calhoun Charter Release**			
77-01-001	In The Beginning	Y. Koutsis	19,500	29.50	152.00
77-01-002	In His Image	Y. Koutsis	19,500	29.50	120.00
77-01-003	Adam's Rib	Y. Koutsis	19,500	29.50	100.00
77-01-004	Banished from Eden	Y. Koutsis	19,500	29.50	90.00
77-01-005	Noah and the Ark	Y. Koutsis	19,500	29.50	90.00
78-01-006	Tower of Babel	Y. Koutsis	19,500	29.50	80.00
78-01-007	Sodom and Gomorrah	Y. Koutsis	19,500	29.50	80.00
78-01-008	Jacob's Wedding	Y. Koutsis	19,500	29.50	80.00
78-01-009	Rebekah at the Well	Y. Koutsis	19,500	29.50	80.00
78-01-010	Jacob's Ladder	Y. Koutsis	19,500	29.50	80.00
78-01-011	Joseph's Coat of Many Colors	Y. Koutsis	19,500	29.50	80.00
78-01-012	Joseph Interprets Pharaoh's Dream	Y. Koutsis	19,500	29.50	80.00
Royal Devon		**Rockwell Christmas**			
75-01-001	Downhill Daring	N. Rockwell	Yr.Iss.	24.50	30.00
76-01-002	The Christmas Gift	N. Rockwell	Yr.Iss.	24.50	35.00
77-01-003	The Big Moment	N. Rockwell	Yr.Iss.	27.50	50.00
78-01-004	Puppets for Christmas	N. Rockwell	Yr.Iss.	27.50	27.50
79-01-005	One Present Too Many	N. Rockwell	Yr.Iss.	31.50	31.50
80-01-006	Gramps Meets Gramps	N. Rockwell	Yr.Iss.	33.00	33.00
Royal Devon		**Rockwell Mother's Day**			
75-02-001	Doctor and Doll	N. Rockwell	Yr.Iss.	23.50	50.00
76-02-002	Puppy Love	N. Rockwell	Yr.Iss.	24.50	104.00
77-02-003	The Family	N. Rockwell	Yr.Iss.	24.50	85.00
78-02-004	Mother's Day Off	N. Rockwell	Yr.Iss.	27.00	35.00
79-02-005	Mother's Evening Out	N. Rockwell	Yr.Iss.	30.00	32.00
80-02-006	Mother's Treat	N. Rockwell	Yr.Iss.	32.50	35.00
Royal Doulton		**Family Christmas Plates**			
91-01-001	Dad Plays Santa	N/A	Yr.Iss.	60.00	60.00
Royal Worcester		**Birth Of A Nation**			
72-01-001	Boston Tea Party	P.W. Baston	10,000	45.00	275-325.
73-01-002	Paul Revere	P.W. Baston	10,000	45.00	250-300.
74-01-003	Concord Bridge	P.W. Baston	10,000	50.00	150.00
75-01-004	Signing Declaration	P.W. Baston	10,000	65.00	150.00
76-01-005	Crossing Delaware	P.W. Baston	10,000	65.00	150.00
77-01-006	Washington's Inauguration	P.W. Baston	1,250	65.00	250-300.
Royal Worcester		**Currier and Ives Plates**			
74-02-001	Road in Winter	P.W. Baston	5,570	59.50	100-125.
75-02-002	Old Grist Mill	P.W. Baston	3,200	59.50	100-125.
76-02-003	Winter Pastime	P.W. Baston	1,500	59.50	125-150.
77-02-004	Home to Thanksgiving	P.W. Baston	546	59.50	200-250.
Royal Worcester		**Water Birds of North America**			
85-03-001	Mallards	J. Cooke	15,000	55.00	55.00
85-03-002	Canvas Backs	J. Cooke	15,000	55.00	55.00
85-03-003	Wood Ducks	J. Cooke	15,000	55.00	55.00
85-03-004	Snow Geese	J. Cooke	15,000	55.00	55.00
85-03-005	American Pintails	J. Cooke	15,000	55.00	55.00
85-03-006	Green Winged Teals	J. Cooke	15,000	55.00	55.00
85-03-007	Hooded Mergansers	J. Cooke	15,000	55.00	55.00
85-03-008	Canada Geese	J. Cooke	15,000	55.00	55.00
Royal Worcester		**Kitten Encounters**			
87-04-001	Fishful Thinking	P. Cooper	14-day	29.50	54.00
87-04-002	Puppy Pal	P. Cooper	14-day	29.50	36.00
87-04-003	Just Ducky	P. Cooper	14-day	29.50	36.00
87-04-004	Bunny Chase	P. Cooper	14-day	29.50	30.00
87-04-005	Flutter By	P. Cooper	14-day	29.50	30.00
87-04-006	Bedtime Buddies	P. Cooper	14-day	29.50	30.00
88-04-007	Cat and Mouse	P. Cooper	14-day	29.50	33.00
88-04-008	Stablemates	P. Cooper	14-day	29.50	48.00
Royal Worcester		**Kitten Classics**			
85-05-001	Cat Nap	P. Cooper	14-day	29.50	36.00
85-05-002	Purrfect Treasure	P. Cooper	14-day	29.50	29.50
85-05-003	Wild Flower	P. Cooper	14-day	29.50	29.50
85-05-004	Birdwatcher	P. Cooper	14-day	29.50	29.50
85-05-005	Tiger's Fancy	P. Cooper	14-day	29.50	33.00
85-05-006	Country Kitty	P. Cooper	14-day	29.50	33.00
85-05-007	Little Rascal	P. Cooper	14-day	29.50	29.50
86-05-008	First Prize	P. Cooper	14-day	29.50	29.50
Sarah's Attic		**Classroom Memories**			
91-01-001	Classroom Memories	Sarah's Attic	6,000	80.00	80.00
Schmid		**Davis Red Oak Sampler**			
86-01-001	General Store	L. Davis	5,000	45.00	100-135.
87-01-002	Country Wedding	L. Davis	5,000	45.00	90.00
89-01-003	Country School	L. Davis	5,000	45.00	60.00
90-01-004	Blacksmith Shop	L. Davis	5,000	52.50	60.00
Schmid		**Davis Country Pride Plates**			
81-02-001	Surprise in the Cellar	L. Davis	7,500	35.00	175-200.
81-02-002	Plum Tuckered Out	L. Davis	7,500	35.00	150-185.
81-02-003	Duke's Mixture	L. Davis	7,500	35.00	100-175.
82-02-004	Bustin' with Pride	L. Davis	7,500	35.00	100-125.
Schmid		**Davis Cat Tales Plates.**			
82-03-001	Right Church, Wrong Pew	L. Davis	12,500	37.50	100-175.

Company		Series			
Number	**Name**	**Artist**	**Edition Limit**	**Issue Price**	**Quote**
82-03-002	Company's Coming	L. Davis	12,500	37.50	100-150.
82-03-003	On the Move	L. Davis	12,500	37.50	100-125.
82-03-004	Flew the Coop	L. Davis	12,500	37.50	100-125.
Schmid		**Davis Special Edition Plates**			
83-04-001	The Critics	L. Davis	12,500	45.00	65-100.00
84-04-002	Good Ole Days Privy Set 2	L. Davis	5,000	60.00	135-175.
86-04-003	Home From Market	L. Davis	7,500	55.00	115-125.
Schmid		**Davis Christmas Plates**			
83-05-001	Hooker at Mailbox With Present	L. Davis	7,500	45.00	85-100.00
84-05-002	Country Christmas	L. Davis	7,500	45.00	100.00
85-05-003	Christmas at Foxfire Farm	L. Davis	7,500	45.00	75-120.00
86-05-004	Christmas at Red Oak	L. Davis	7,500	45.00	75-95.00
87-05-005	Blossom's Gift	L. Davis	7,500	47.50	75.00
88-05-006	Cutting the Family Christmas Tree	L. Davis	7,500	47.50	75.00
89-05-007	Peter and the Wren	L. Davis	7,500	47.50	75.00
90-05-008	Wintering Deer	L. Davis	7,500	47.50	47.50
91-05-009	Christmas at Red Oak II	L. Davis	7,500	55.00	55.00
92-05-010	Born On A Starry Night	L. Davis	7,500	55.00	55.00
93-05-011	Waiting For Mr. Lowell	L. Davis	5,000	55.00	55.00
Schmid		**Friends of Mine**			
89-06-001	Sun Worshippers	L. Davis	7,500	53.00	53.00
90-06-002	Sunday Afternoon Treat	L. Davis	7,500	53.00	53.00
91-06-003	Warm Milk	L. Davis	7,500	55.00	55.00
92-06-004	Cat and Jenny Wren	L. Davis	7,500	55.00	55.00
Schmid		**Pen Pals**			
93-07-001	The Old Home Place	L. Davis	5,000	50.00	50.00
Schmid		**Disney Annual**			
83-08-001	Sneak Preview	Disney Studios	20,000	22.50	22.50
84-08-002	Command Performance	Disney Studios	20,000	22.50	22.50
85-08-003	Snow Biz	Disney Studios	20,000	22.50	22.50
86-08-004	Tree For Two	Disney Studios	20,000	22.50	22.50
87-08-005	Merry Mouse Medley	Disney Studios	20,000	25.00	25.00
88-08-006	Warm Winter Ride	Disney Studios	20,000	25.00	25.00
89-08-007	Merry Mickey Claus	Disney Studios	20,000	32.50	60.00
90-08-008	Holly Jolly Christmas	Disney Studios	20,000	32.50	32.50
91-08-009	Mickey and Minnie's Rockin' Christmas	Disney Studios	20,000	37.00	37.00
Schmid		**Disney Christmas**			
73-09-001	Sleigh Ride	Disney Studio	Annual	10.00	300-350.
74-09-002	Decorating The Tree	Disney Studio	Annual	10.00	80.00
75-09-003	Caroling	Disney Studio	Annual	12.50	18.00
76-09-004	Building A Snowman	Disney Studio	Annual	13.00	17.00
77-09-005	Down The Chimney	Disney Studio	Annual	13.00	15.00
78-09-006	Night Before Christmas	Disney Studio	Annual	15.00	35.00
79-09-007	Santa's Suprise	Disney Studio	15,000	17.50	29.00
80-09-008	Sleigh Ride	Disney Studio	15,000	17.50	40.00
81-09-009	Happy Holidays	Disney Studio	15,000	17.50	22.00
82-09-010	Winter Games	Disney Studio	15,000	18.50	29.00
Schmid		**Disney Mother's Day**			
74-10-001	Flowers For Mother	Disney Studio	Annual	10.00	45.00
75-10-002	Snow White & Dwarfs	Disney Studio	Annual	12.50	50.00
76-10-003	Minnie Mouse	Disney Studio	Annual	13.00	25.00
77-10-004	Pluto's Pals	Disney Studio	Annual	13.00	18.00
78-10-005	Flowers For Bambi	Disney Studio	Annual	15.00	40.00
79-10-006	Happy Feet	Disney Studio	10,000	17.50	20.00
80-10-007	Minnie's Surprise	Disney Studio	10,000	17.50	30.00
81-10-008	Playmates	Disney Studio	10,000	17.50	35.00
82-10-009	A Dream Come True	Disney Studio	10,000	18.50	40.00
Schmid		**Disney Special Edition Plates**			
78-11-001	Mickey Mouse At Fifty	Disney Studios	15,000	25.00	65-100.00
80-11-002	Happy Birthday Pinocchio	Disney Studios	7,500	17.50	25-60.00
81-11-003	Alice in Wonderland	Disney Studios	7,500	17.50	17.50
82-11-004	Happy Birthday Pluto	Disney Studios	7,500	17.50	39.00
82-11-005	Goofy's Golden Jubilee	Disney Studios	7,500	18.50	29.00
87-11-006	Snow White Golden Anniversary	Disney Studios	5,000	47.50	47.50
88-11-007	Mickey Mouse & Minnie Mouse 60th	Disney Studios	10,000	50.00	95-125.00
89-11-008	Sleeping Beauty 30th Anniversary	Disney Studios	5,000	80.00	95.00
90-11-009	Fantasia-Sorcerer's Apprentice	Disney Studios	5,000	59.00	59-99.00
90-11-010	Pinocchio's Friend	Disney Studios	Annual	25.00	25.00
90-11-011	Fantasia Relief Plate	Disney Studios	20,000	25.00	39.00
Schmid		**Ferrandiz Music Makers Porcelain Plates**			
81-12-001	The Flutist	J. Ferrandiz	10,000	25.00	29.00
81-12-002	The Entertainer	J. Ferrandiz	10,000	25.00	29.00
82-12-003	Magical Medley	J. Ferrandiz	10,000	25.00	29.00
82-12-004	Sweet Serenade	J. Ferrandiz	10,000	25.00	32.00
Schmid		**Ferrandiz Beautiful Bounty Porcelain Plates**			
82-13-001	Summer's Golden Harvest	J. Ferrandiz	10,000	40.00	40.00
82-13-002	Autumn's Blessing	J. Ferrandiz	10,000	40.00	40.00
82-13-003	A Mid-Winter's Dream	J. Ferrandiz	10,000	40.00	42.50
82-13-004	Spring Blossoms	J. Ferrandiz	10,000	40.00	40.00
Schmid		**Ferrandiz Wooden Birthday Plates**			
72-14-001	Boy	J. Ferrandiz	Unkn.	15.00	150.00
72-14-002	Girl	J. Ferrandiz	Unkn.	15.00	160.00
73-14-003	Boy	J. Ferrandiz	Unkn.	20.00	200.00
73-14-004	Girl	J. Ferrandiz	Unkn.	20.00	150.00
74-14-005	Boy	J. Ferrandiz	Unkn.	22.00	160.00
74-14-006	Girl	J. Ferrandiz	Unkn.	22.00	160.00
Schmid		**Juan Ferrandiz Porcelain Christmas Plates**			
72-15-001	Christ in the Manger	J. Ferrandiz	Unkn.	30.00	179.00
73-15-002	Christmas	J. Ferrandiz	Unkn.	30.00	229.00
Schmid		**Christmas**			
71-16-001	Angel	B. Hummel	Annual	15.00	19-39.00
72-16-002	Angel With Flute	B. Hummel	Annual	15.00	15.00
73-16-003	The Nativity	B. Hummel	Annual	15.00	73.00
74-16-004	The Guardian Angel	B. Hummel	Annual	18.50	18.50
75-16-005	Christmas Child	B. Hummel	Annual	25.00	25.00
76-16-006	Sacred Journey	B. Hummel	Annual	27.50	32.00
77-16-007	Herald Angel	B. Hummel	Annual	27.50	32.00
78-16-008	Heavenly Trio	B. Hummel	Annual	32.50	32.50
79-16-009	Starlight Angel	B. Hummel	Annual	38.00	38.00
80-16-010	Parade Into Toyland	B. Hummel	Annual	45.00	45.00

Company Number	Name	Series Artist	Edition Limit	Issue Price	Quote
81-16-011	A Time To Remember	B. Hummel	Annual	45.00	45.00
82-16-012	Angelic Procession	B. Hummel	Annual	45.00	49.00
83-16-013	Angelic Messenger	B. Hummel	Annual	45.00	45.00
84-16-014	A Gift from Heaven	B. Hummel	Annual	45.00	48.00
85-16-015	Heavenly Light	B. Hummel	Annual	45.00	46.50
86-16-016	Tell The Heavens	B. Hummel	Annual	45.00	56.00
87-16-017	Angelic Gifts	B. Hummel	Annual	47.50	47.50
88-16-018	Cheerful Cherubs	B. Hummel	Annual	53.00	66.00
89-16-019	Angelic Musician	B. Hummel	Annual	53.00	53.00
90-16-020	Angel's Light	B. Hummel	Annual	53.00	57.00
91-16-021	Message From Above	B. Hummel	Annual	60.00	60.00
92-16-022	Sweet Blessings	B. Hummel	Annual	65.00	65.00
Schmid		**Mother's Day**			
72-17-001	Playing Hooky	B. Hummel	Annual	15.00	15.00
73-17-002	Little Fisherman	B. Hummel	Annual	15.00	33.00
74-17-003	Bumblebee	B. Hummel	Annual	18.50	20.00
75-17-004	Message of Love	B. Hummel	Annual	25.00	29.00
76-17-005	Devotion For Mother	B. Hummel	Annual	27.50	30.00
77-17-006	Moonlight Return	B. Hummel	Annual	27.50	29.00
78-17-007	Afternoon Stroll	B. Hummel	Annual	32.50	32.50
79-17-008	Cherub's Gift	B. Hummel	Annual	38.00	38.00
80-17-009	Mother's Little Helpers	B. Hummel	Annual	45.00	52.00
81-17-010	Playtime	B. Hummel	Annual	45.00	52.00
82-17-011	The Flower Basket	B. Hummel	Annual	45.00	47.50
83-17-012	Spring Bouquet	B. Hummel	Annual	45.00	54.00
84-17-013	A Joy to Share	B. Hummel	Annual	45.00	45.00
85-17-014	A Mother's Journey	B. Hummel	Annual	45.00	45.00
86-17-015	Home From School	B. Hummel	Annual	45.00	55.00
88-17-016	Young Reader	B. Hummel	Annual	52.50	81.00
89-17-017	Pretty as a Picture	B. Hummel	Annual	53.00	75.00
90-17-018	Mother's Little Athlete	B. Hummel	Annual	53.00	53.00
91-17-019	Soft & Gentle	B. Hummel	Annual	55.00	55.00
Schmid		**The Littlest Night**			
93-18-001	The Littlest Night	B. Hummel	Annual	25.00	25.00
Schmid		**Paddington Bear/Musician's Dream Plates**			
83-19-001	The Beat Goes On	Unknown	10,000	17.50	22.50
83-19-002	Knowing the Score	Unknown	10,000	17.50	20.00
83-19-003	Perfect Harmony	Unknown	10,000	17.50	17.50
83-19-004	Tickling The Ivory	Unknown	10,000	17.50	17.50
Schmid		**A Year With Paddington Bear Plates**			
79-20-001	Pyramid of Presents	Unknown	25,000	12.50	27.50
80-20-002	Springtime	Unknown	25,000	12.50	25.00
81-20-003	Sandcastles	Unknown	25,000	12.50	22.50
82-20-004	School Days	Unknown	25,000	12.50	12.50
Schmid		**Peanuts Mother's Day Plates**			
72-21-001	Linus	C. Schulz	Unkn.	10.00	10.00
73-21-002	Mom?	C. Schulz	Unkn.	10.00	10.00
74-21-003	Snoopy/Woodstock/Parade	C. Schulz	Unkn.	10.00	10.00
75-21-004	A Kiss for Lucy	C. Schulz	Unkn.	12.50	10.00
76-21-005	Linus and Snoopy	C. Schulz	Unkn.	13.00	35.00
77-21-006	Dear Mom	C. Schulz	Unkn.	13.00	30.00
78-21-007	Thoughts That Count	C. Schulz	Unkn.	15.00	25.00
79-21-008	A Special Letter	C. Schulz	Unkn.	17.50	22.50
80-21-009	A Tribute to Mom	C. Schulz	Unkn.	17.50	22.50
81-21-010	Mission for Mom	C. Schulz	Unkn.	17.50	20.00
82-21-011	Which Way to Mother	C. Schulz	Unkn.	18.50	18.50
Schmid		**Peanuts Valentine's Day Plates**			
77-22-001	Home Is Where the Heart is	C. Schulz	Unkn.	13.00	32.50
78-22-002	Heavenly Bliss	C. Schulz	Unkn.	13.00	30.00
79-22-003	Love Match	C. Schulz	Unkn.	17.50	27.50
80-22-004	From Snoopy, With Love	C. Schulz	Unkn.	17.50	25.00
81-22-005	Hearts-A-Flutter	C. Schulz	Unkn.	17.50	20.00
82-22-006	Love Patch	C. Schulz	Unkn.	17.50	17.50
Schmid		**Peanuts World's Greatest Athlete**			
82-23-001	Go Deep	C. Schulz	10,000	17.50	25.00
82-23-002	The Puck Stops Here	C. Schulz	10,000	17.50	22.50
82-23-003	The Way You Play The Game	C. Schulz	10,000	17.50	20.00
82-23-004	The Crowd Went Wild	C. Schulz	10,000	17.50	17.50
Schmid		**Peanuts Special Edition Plate**			
76-24-001	Bi-Centennial	C. Schulz	Unkn.	13.00	30.00
Schmid		**Peanuts Christmas**			
72-25-001	Snoopy Guides the Sleigh	C. Schulz	Annual	10.00	32.00
73-25-002	Christmas Eve at Doghouse	C. Schulz	Annual	10.00	90.00
74-25-003	Christmas At Fireplace	C. Schulz	Annual	10.00	45.00
75-25-004	Woodstock and Santa Claus	C. Schulz	Annual	12.50	14.00
76-25-005	Woodstock's Christmas	C. Schulz	Annual	13.00	24-25.00
77-25-006	Deck The Doghouse	C. Schulz	Annual	13.00	26.00
78-25-007	Filling the Stocking	C. Schulz	Annual	15.00	50.00
79-25-008	Christmas at Hand	C. Schulz	15,000	17.50	31.00
80-25-009	Waiting for Santa	C. Schulz	15,000	17.50	30.00
81-25-010	A Christmas Wish	C. Schulz	15,000	17.50	17.50
82-25-011	Perfect Performance	C. Schulz	15,000	18.50	55.00
Schmid		**Raggedy Ann Annual Plates**			
80-26-001	The Sunshine Wagon	Unknown	10,000	17.50	80-100.00
81-26-002	The Raggedy Shuffle	Unknown	10,000	17.50	27.50-75.00
82-26-003	Flying High	Unknown	10,000	18.50	18.50
83-26-004	Winning Streak	Unknown	10,000	22.50	22.50
84-26-005	Rocking Rodeo	Unknown	10,000	22.50	22.50
Schmid		**Raggedy Ann Bicentennial Plate**			
76-27-001	Bicentennial Plate	Unknown	Unkn.	13.00	30-60.00
Schmid		**Raggedy Ann Christmas Plates**			
75-28-001	Gifts of Love	Unknown	Unkn.	12.50	45.00
76-28-002	Merry Blades	Unknown	Unkn.	13.00	37.50
77-28-003	Christmas Morning	Unknown	Unkn.	13.00	22.50
78-28-004	Checking the List	Unknown	Unkn.	15.00	20.00
79-28-005	Little Helper	Unknown	Unkn.	17.50	19.50
Schmid		**Raggedy Ann Valentine's Day Plates**			
78-29-001	As Time Goes By	Unknown	Unkn.	13.00	25.00
79-29-002	Daisies Do Tell	Unknown	Unkn.	17.50	20.00

Company Number	Name	Series Artist	Edition Limit	Issue Price	Quote
Schmid		**Kitty Cucumber Annual**			
89-30-001	Ring Around the Rosie	M. Lillemoe	20,000	25.00	45.00
90-30-002	Swan Lake	M. Lillemoe	20,000	25.00	45.00
91-30-003	Tea Party	M. Lillemoe	2,500	25.00	45.00
92-30-004	Dance 'Round the Maypole	M. Lillemoe	2,500	25.00	45.00
Spode		**Christmas**			
70-01-001	Partridge	G. West	Undis.	35.00	35.00
71-01-002	Angel's Singing	G. West	Undis.	35.00	35.00
72-01-003	Three Ships A'Sailing	G. West	Undis.	35.00	35.00
73-01-004	We Three Kings of Orient	G. West	Undis.	35.00	35.00
74-01-005	Deck the Halls	G. West	Undis.	35.00	35.00
75-01-006	Christbaum	G. West	Undis.	45.00	45.00
76-01-007	Good King Wenceslas	G. West	Undis.	45.00	45.00
77-01-008	Holly & Ivy	G. West	Undis.	45.00	45.00
78-01-009	While Shepherds Watched	G. West	Undis.	45.00	45.00
79-01-010	Away in a Manger	G. West	Undis.	50.00	50.00
80-01-011	Bringing in the Boar's Head	P. Wood	Undis.	60.00	60.00
81-01-012	Make We Merry	P. Wood	Undis.	65.00	65.00
Spode		**American Song Birds**			
72-02-001	Set of Twelve	R. Harm	Undis.	350.00	765.00
Sports Impressions/Enesco		**Gold Edition Plates**			
86-01-001	Mickey Mantle At Night	R. Simon	Closed	125.00	225-350.
87-01-002	Darryl Strawberry #1	R. Simon	Closed	125.00	125-195.
87-01-003	Ted Williams	R. Simon	Closed	125.00	225-250.
88-01-004	Brooks Robinson	R. Simon	Closed	125.00	225.00
88-01-005	Larry Bird	R. Simon	Closed	125.00	275.00
88-01-006	Magic Johnson	R. Simon	Closed	125.00	350.00
Vague Shadows: See Artaffects					
V-Palekh Art Studios		**Russian Legends**			
88-01-001	Ruslan and Ludmilla	G. Lubimov	195-day	29.87	40.00
88-01-002	The Princess/Seven Bogatyrs	A. Kovalev	195-day	29.87	38.00
88-01-003	The Golden Cockerel	V. Vleshko	195-day	32.87	32.87
88-01-004	Lukomorya	R. Belousov	195-day	32.87	32.87
89-01-005	Fisherman and the Magic Fish	N. Lopatin	195-day	32.87	32.87
89-01-006	Tsar Saltan	G. Zhiryakova	195-day	32.87	32.87
89-01-007	The Priest and His Servant	O. An	195-day	34.87	34.87
90-01-008	Stone Flower	V. Bolshakova	195-day	34.87	34.87
90-01-009	Sadko	E. Populor	195-day	34.87	34.87
90-01-010	The Twelve Months	N. Lopatin	195-day	36.87	36.87
90-01-011	Silver Hoof	S. Adeyanor	195-day	36.87	36.87
90-01-012	Morozko	N. Lopatin	195-day	36.87	36.87
Veneto Flair		**Bellini**			
71-01-001	Madonna	V. Tiziano	500	45.00	400.00
Veneto Flair		**Christmas**			
71-02-001	Three Kings	V. Tiziano	1,500	55.00	160.00
72-02-002	Shepherds	V. Tiziano	2,000	55.00	90.00
73-02-003	Christ Child	V. Tiziano	2,000	55.00	55.00
74-02-004	Angel	V. Tiziano	Pair	55.00	55.00
Veneto Flair		**Wildlife**			
71-03-001	Deer	V. Tiziano	500	37.50	450.00
72-03-002	Elephant	V. Tiziano	1,000	37.50	275.00
73-03-003	Puma	V. Tiziano	2,000	37.50	65.00
74-03-004	Tiger	V. Tiziano	2,000	40.00	50.00
Veneto Flair		**Birds**			
72-04-001	Owl	Unknown	2,000	37.50	100.00
72-04-002	Falcon	Unknown	2,000	37.50	37.50
73-04-003	Mallard	Unknown	2,000	45.00	45.00
Veneto Flair		**Easter**			
73-05-001	Rabbits	Unknown	2,000	50.00	90.00
74-05-002	Chicks	Unknown	2,000	50.00	55.00
75-05-003	Lamb	Unknown	2,000	50.00	55.00
76-05-004	Composite	Unknown	2,000	55.00	55.00
Viletta		**Disneyland**			
76-01-001	Signing The Declaration	Unknown	3,000	15.00	100.00
76-01-002	Crossing The Delaware	Unknown	3,000	15.00	100.00
76-01-003	Betsy Ross	Unknown	3,000	15.00	100.00
76-01-004	Spirit of '76	Unknown	3,000	15.00	100.00
79-01-005	Mickey's 50th Anniversary	Unknown	5,000	37.00	50.00
Villeroy & Boch		**Russian Fairytales Snow Maiden**			
80-01-001	The Snow Maiden	B. Zvorykin	27,500	70.00	130.00
81-01-002	Snegurochka at the Court of Tsar Berendei	B. Zvorykin	27,500	70.00	70.00
81-01-003	Snegurochka and Lei, the Shepherd Boy	B. Zvorykin	27,500	70.00	73.00
Villeroy & Boch		**Russian Fairytales The Red Knight**			
81-02-001	The Red Knight	B. Zvorykin	27,500	70.00	70-135.00
81-02-002	Vassilissa and Her Stepsisters	B. Zvorykin	27,500	70.00	77.00
81-02-003	Vassilissa is Presented to the Tsar	B. Zvorykin	27,500	70.00	75.00
Villeroy & Boch		**Russian Fairytales The Firebird**			
81-03-001	In Search of the Firebird	B. Zvorykin	27,500	70.00	90-112.00
81-03-002	Ivan and Tsarevna on the Grey Wolf	B. Zvorykin	27,500	70.00	78.00
81-03-003	The Wedding of Tsarevna Elena the Fair	B. Zvorykin	27,500	70.00	100-118.
Villeroy & Boch		**Russian Fairytales Maria Morevna**			
82-04-001	Maria Morevna and Tsarevich Ivan	B. Zvorykin	27,500	70.00	70.00
82-04-002	Koshchey Carries Off Maria Morevna	B. Zvorykin	27,500	70.00	81.00
82-04-003	Tsarevich Ivan and the Beautiful Castle	B. Zvorykin	27,500	70.00	95-115.00
Villeroy & Boch		**Flower Fairy**			
79-05-001	Lavender	C. Barker	21-day	35.00	125.00
80-05-002	Sweet Pea	C. Barker	21-day	35.00	125.00
80-05-003	Candytuft	C. Barker	21-day	35.00	89.00
81-05-004	Heliotrope	C. Barker	21-day	35.00	75.00
81-05-005	Blackthorn	C. Barker	21-day	35.00	75.00
81-05-006	Appleblossom	C. Barker	21-day	35.00	95.00
Waterford Wedgwood USA		**Wedgwood Christmas**			
69-01-001	Windsor Castle	T. Harper	Annual	25.00	100.00
70-01-002	Trafalgar Square	T. Harper	Annual	30.00	30.00
71-01-003	Picadilly Circus	T. Harper	Annual	30.00	40.00
72-01-004	St. Paul's Cathedral	T. Harper	Annual	35.00	40.00

Company		Series			
Number	**Name**	**Artist**	**Edition Limit**	**Issue Price**	**Quote**
73-01-005	Tower of London	T. Harper	Annual	40.00	90.00
74-01-006	Houses of Parliament	T. Harper	Annual	40.00	40.00
75-01-007	Tower Bridge	T. Harper	Annual	45.00	45.00
76-01-008	Hampton Court	T. Harper	Annual	50.00	50.00
77-01-009	Westminister Abbey	T. Harper	Annual	55.00	60.00
78-01-010	Horse Guards	T. Harper	Annual	60.00	60.00
79-01-011	Buckingham Palace	Unknown	Annual	65.00	65.00
80-01-012	St. James Palace	Unknown	Annual	70.00	70.00
81-01-013	Marble Arch	Unknown	Annual	75.00	75.00
82-01-014	Lambeth Palace	Unknown	Annual	80.00	90.00
83-01-015	All Souls, Langham Palace	Unknown	Annual	80.00	80.00
84-01-016	Constitution Hill	Unknown	Annual	80.00	80.00
85-01-017	The Tate Gallery	Unknown	Annual	80.00	80.00
86-01-018	The Albert Memorial	Unknown	Annual	80.00	150.00
87-01-019	Guildhall	Unknown	Annual	80.00	85.00
88-01-020	The Observatory/Greenwich	Unknown	Annual	80.00	90.00
89-01-021	Winchester Cathedral	Unknown	Annual	88.00	88.00
Waterford Wedgwood USA		**Mother's Day**			
71-02-001	Sportive Love	Unknown	Unkn.	20.00	20.00
72-02-002	The Sewing Lesson	Unknown	Unkn.	20.00	20.00
73-02-003	The Baptism of Achilles	Unknown	Unkn.	20.00	25.00
74-02-004	Domestic Employment	Unknown	Unkn.	30.00	33.00
75-02-005	Mother and Child	Unknown	Unkn.	35.00	37.00
76-02-006	The Spinner	Unknown	Unkn.	35.00	35.00
77-02-007	Leisure Time	Unknown	Unkn.	35.00	35.00
78-02-008	Swan and Cygnets	Unknown	Unkn.	40.00	40.00
79-02-009	Deer and Fawn	Unknown	Unkn.	45.00	45.00
80-02-010	Birds	Unknown	Unkn.	47.50	47.50
81-02-012	Mare and Foal	Unknown	Unkn.	50.00	60.00
82-02-013	Cherubs with Swing	Unknown	Unkn.	55.00	60.00
83-02-014	Cupid and Butterfly	Unknown	Unkn.	55.00	55.00
84-02-015	Musical Cupids	Unknown	Unkn.	55.00	59.00
85-02-016	Cupids and Doves	Unknown	Annual	55.00	80.00
86-02-017	Cupids Fishing	Unknown	Annual	55.00	55.00
87-02-018	Spring Flowers	Unknown	Annual	55.00	80.00
88-02-019	Tiger Lily	Unknown	Annual	55.00	59.00
89-02-020	Irises	Unknown	Annual	65.00	65.00
91-02-021	Peonies	Unknown	Annual	65.00	65.00
Waterford Wedgwood USA		**Bicentennial**			
72-03-001	Boston Tea Party	Unknown	Annual	40.00	40.00
73-03-002	Paul Revere's Ride	Unknown	Annual	40.00	115.00
74-03-003	Battle of Concord	Unknown	Annual	40.00	55.00
75-03-004	Across the Delaware	Unknown	Annual	40.00	105.00
75-03-005	Victory at Yorktown	Unknown	Annual	45.00	53.00
76-03-006	Declaration Signed	Unknown	Annual	45.00	45.00

STEINS

Company		Series			
Anheuser-Busch, Inc.		**Specialty Steins**			
75-01-001	Bud Man CS1	A-Busch,Inc.	Retrd.	N/A	300-400.
75-01-002	A&Eagle CS2	A-Busch,Inc.	Retrd.	N/A	175-250.
75-01-003	A&Eagle Lidded CSL2	A-Busch,Inc.	Retrd.	N/A	275-375.
75-01-004	Katakombe CS3	A-Busch,Inc.	Retrd.	N/A	250-275.
75-01-005	Katakombe Lidded CSL3	A-Busch,Inc.	Retrd.	N/A	250-350.
75-01-006	German Olympia CS4	A-Busch,Inc.	Retrd.	N/A	100-175.
75-01-007	Senior Grande Lidded CSL4	A-Busch,Inc.	Retrd.	N/A	450-600.
75-01-008	German Pilique CS5	A-Busch,Inc.	Retrd.	N/A	275-350.
75-01-009	German Pilique Lidded CSL5	A-Busch,Inc.	Retrd.	N/A	450-550.
75-01-010	Senior Grande CS6	A-Busch,Inc.	Retrd.	N/A	450-600.
75-01-011	German Olympia Lidded CSL6	A-Busch,Inc.	Retrd.	N/A	250-300.
75-01-012	Miniature Bavarian CS7	A-Busch,Inc.	Retrd.	N/A	200-300.
76-01-013	Budweiser Centennial Lidded CSL7	A-Busch,Inc.	Retrd.	N/A	450-500.
76-01-014	U.S. Bicentennial Lidded CSL8	A-Busch,Inc.	Retrd.	N/A	450-550.
76-01-015	Natural Light CS9	A-Busch,Inc.	Retrd.	N/A	100-250.
76-01-016	Clydesdales Hofbrau Lidded CSL9	A-Busch,Inc.	Retrd.	N/A	275-300.
76-01-017	Blue Delft (4 assorted) CS11	A-Busch,Inc.	Retrd.	N/A	N/A
76-01-018	Clydesdales CS12	A-Busch,Inc.	Retrd.	N/A	375-410.
76-01-019	Budweiser Centennial CS13	A-Busch,Inc.	Retrd.	N/A	400-500.
76-01-020	U.S. Bicentennial CS14	A-Busch,Inc.	Retrd.	N/A	400-500.
76-01-021	Clydesdales Grants Farm CS15	A-Busch,Inc.	Retrd.	N/A	225-325.
76-01-022	German Cities (6 assorted) CS16	A-Busch,Inc.	Retrd.	N/A	1500-1800.
76-01-023	Americana CS17	A-Busch,Inc.	Retrd.	N/A	350-450.
76-01-024	Budweiser Label CS18	A-Busch,Inc.	Retrd.	N/A	350-625.
80-01-025	Budweiser Ladies (4 assorted) CS20	A-Busch,Inc.	Retrd.	N/A	2000-2500.
77-01-026	Budweiser Girl CS21	A-Busch,Inc.	Retrd.	N/A	N/A
76-01-027	Budweiser Centennial CS22	A-Busch,Inc.	Retrd.	N/A	350-450.
77-01-028	A&Eagle CS24	A-Busch,Inc.	Retrd.	N/A	350.00
76-01-029	A&Eagle Barrel CS26	A-Busch,Inc.	Retrd.	N/A	95-150.
76-01-030	Michelob CS27	A-Busch,Inc.	Retrd.	N/A	150-175.
76-01-031	A&Eagle Lidded CS28	A-Busch,Inc.	Retrd.	N/A	275-375.
76-01-032	Clydesdales Lidded CS29	A-Busch,Inc.	Retrd.	N/A	275-350.
76-01-033	Coracao Decanter Set (7 piece) CS31	A-Busch,Inc.	Retrd.	N/A	400-500.
76-01-034	Geraman Wine Set (7 piece) CS32	A-Busch,Inc.	Retrd.	N/A	400-500.
76-01-035	Clydesdales Decanter CS33	A-Busch,Inc.	Retrd.	N/A	1000-1200.
76-01-036	Holanda Brown Decanter Set (7 piece) CS34	A-Busch,Inc.	Retrd.	N/A	275.00
76-01-037	Holanda Blue Decanter Set (7 piece) CS35	A-Busch,Inc.	Retrd.	N/A	N/A
76-01-038	Canteen Decanter Set (7 piece) CS36	A-Busch,Inc.	Retrd.	N/A	N/A
76-01-039	St. Louis Decanter CS37	A-Busch,Inc.	Retrd.	N/A	N/A
76-01-040	St. Louis Decanter Set (7 piece) CS38	A-Busch,Inc.	Retrd.	N/A	1000-1200.
80-01-041	Wurzburger Hofbrau CS39	A-Busch,Inc.	Retrd.	N/A	350-450.
80-01-042	Budweiser Chicago Skyline CS40	A-Busch,Inc.	Retrd.	N/A	135-175.
78-01-043	Busch Gardens CS41	A-Busch,Inc.	Retrd.	N/A	350-450.
80-01-044	Oktoberfest-- "The Old Country" CS42	A-Busch,Inc.	Retrd.	N/A	350-450.
80-01-045	Natural Light Label CS43	A-Busch,Inc.	Retrd.	N/A	100-200.
80-01-046	Busch Label CS44	A-Busch,Inc.	Retrd.	N/A	125-200.
80-01-047	Michelob Label CS45	A-Busch,Inc.	Retrd.	N/A	100-125.
80-01-048	Budweiser Label CS46	A-Busch,Inc.	Retrd.	N/A	75-150.00
81-01-049	Budweiser Chicagoland CS51	A-Busch,Inc.	Retrd.	N/A	50-75.00
81-01-050	Budweiser Texas CS52	A-Busch,Inc.	Retrd.	N/A	60-65.00
81-01-051	Budweiser California CS56	A-Busch,Inc.	Retrd.	N/A	40-85.00
83-01-052	Budweiser San Francisco CS59	A-Busch,Inc.	Retrd.	N/A	175-200.
84-01-053	Budweiser Olympic Games CS60	A-Busch,Inc.	Retrd.	N/A	20-50.00
83-01-054	Bud Light Baron CS61	A-Busch,Inc.	Retrd.	N/A	25-50.00
87-01-055	Santa Claus CS79	A-Busch,Inc.	Retrd.	N/A	60-85.00
87-01-056	King Cobra CS80	A-Busch,Inc.	Retrd.	N/A	150.00
87-01-057	Winter Olympic Games, Lidded CS81	A-Busch,Inc.	Retrd.	49.95	65-90.00
88-01-058	Budweiser Winter Olympic Games CS85	A-Busch,Inc.	Retrd.	24.95	27.00
88-01-059	Summer Olympic Games, Lidded CS91	A-Busch,Inc.	Retrd.	54.95	65.00
88-01-060	Budweiser Summer Olympic Games CS92	A-Busch,Inc.	Retrd.	54.95	54.95
88-01-061	Budweiser/ Field&Stream Set (4 piece) CS95	A-Busch,Inc.	Retrd.	69.95	175-225.
89-01-062	Bud Man CS100	A-Busch,Inc.	Open	29.95	29.95
90-01-063	Baseball Cardinal Stein CS125	A-Busch,Inc.	Retrd.	30.00	30.00
91-01-064	Bevo Fox Stein CS160	A-Busch,Inc.	Retrd.	250.00	250.00
92-01-065	U.S. Olympic Team CS168	A-Busch,Inc.	Open	16.00	19.00
92-01-066	1992 Rodeo CS184	A-Busch,Inc.	Open	18.00	25.00
93-01-067	Bill Elliott CS196	H. Droog	25,000	150.00	150.00
93-01-068	Bill Elliott CS196SE	H. Droog	1,500	N/A	N/A
93-01-069	Bud Man Character Stein CS213	A-Busch,Inc.	Open	N/A	N/A
Anheuser-Busch, Inc.		**Clydesdales Holiday Series**			
80-02-001	1st Holiday CS19	A-Busch,Inc.	Retrd.	9.95	100-200.
81-02-002	2nd Holiday CS50	A-Busch,Inc.	Retrd.	9.95	225-275.
82-02-003	3rd Holiday CS57 50th Anniversary	A-Busch,Inc.	Retrd.	9.95	80-140.00
83-02-004	4th Holiday CS58	A-Busch,Inc.	Retrd.	9.95	25-40.00
84-02-005	5th Holiday CS62	A-Busch,Inc.	Retrd.	9.95	15-30.00
85-02-006	6th Holiday CS63	A-Busch,Inc.	Retrd.	9.95	20-30.00
86-02-007	7th Holiday CS66	A-Busch,Inc.	Retrd.	9.95	15-30.00
87-02-008	8th Holiday CS70	A-Busch,Inc.	Retrd.	9.95	13-20.00
88-02-009	9th Holiday CS88	A-Busch,Inc.	Retrd.	9.95	13-20.00
89-02-010	10th Holiday CS89	A-Busch,Inc.	Retrd.	12.95	13-20.00
Anheuser-Busch, Inc.		**Clydesdales Series**			
87-03-001	Eight Horse Hitch CS74	A-Busch,Inc.	Retrd.	9.95	18-22.00
88-03-002	Mare & Foal CS90	A-Busch,Inc.	Retrd.	11.50	22-28.00
89-03-003	Parade Dress CS99	A-Busch,Inc.	Retrd.	11.50	28-30.00
91-03-004	Training Hitch CS131	A-Busch,Inc.	Retrd.	13.00	16-20.00
92-03-005	Clydesdales on Parade CS161	A-Busch,Inc.	Open	16.00	16.00
Anheuser-Busch, Inc.		**Horseshoe Series**			
86-04-001	Horseshoe CS68	A-Busch,Inc.	Retrd.	14.95	45-50.00
87-04-002	Horsehead CS76	A-Busch,Inc.	Retrd.	16.00	20-25.00
86-04-003	Horseshoe CS77	A-Busch,Inc.	Retrd.	16.00	20-25.00
87-04-004	Horsehead CS78	A-Busch,Inc.	Retrd.	14.95	45-50.00
88-04-005	Harness CS94	A-Busch,Inc.	Retrd.	16.00	45-75.00
Anheuser-Busch, Inc.		**Limited Edition Series**			
85-05-001	Ltd. Ed. I Brewing & Fermenting CS64	A-Busch,Inc.	Retrd.	29.95	175-200.
86-05-002	Ltd. Ed. II Aging & Cooperage CS65	A-Busch,Inc.	Retrd.	29.95	45-75.00
87-05-003	Ltd. Ed. III Transportation CS71	A-Busch,Inc.	Retrd.	29.95	35-50.00
88-05-004	Ltd. Ed. IV Taverns & Public Houses CS75	A-Busch,Inc.	Retrd.	29.95	30-35.00
89-05-005	Ltd. Ed.V Festival Scene CS98	A-Busch,Inc.	Retrd.	34.95	34.95
Anheuser-Busch, Inc.		**Historical Landmark Series**			
86-06-001	Brew House CS67 (First)	A-Busch,Inc.	Retrd.	19.95	22-35.00
87-06-002	Stables CS73 (Second)	A-Busch,Inc.	Retrd.	19.95	22-35.00
88-06-003	Grant Cabin CS83 (Third)	A-Busch,Inc.	Retrd.	19.95	22-35.00
88-06-004	Old School House CS84 (Fourth)	A-Busch,Inc.	Retrd.	19.95	22-35.00
Anheuser-Busch, Inc.		**Classic Series**			
88-07-001	1st Edition CS93	A-Busch,Inc.	Retrd.	34.95	150-200.
89-07-002	2nd Edition CS104	A-Busch,Inc.	Retrd.	54.95	100-149.
90-07-003	3rd Edition CS113	A-Busch,Inc.	Retrd.	75.00	75-110.00
91-07-004	4th Edition CS130	A-Busch,Inc.	Retrd.	75.00	75.00
Anheuser-Busch, Inc.		**Endangered Species Series**			
89-08-001	Bald Eagle CS106(First)	A-Busch,Inc.	Retrd.	24.95	125-175.
90-08-002	Asian Tiger CS126 (Second)	A-Busch,Inc.	Retrd.	27.50	29-39.00
91-08-003	African Elephant CS135 (Third)	A-Busch,Inc.	100,000	29.00	29.00
92-08-004	Giant Panda CS173(Fourth)	B. Kemper	100,000	29.00	29.00
92-08-005	Grizzly CS204(Fifth)	B. Kemper	100,000	N/A	N/A
Anheuser-Busch, Inc.		**Porcelain Heritage Series**			
90-09-001	Berninghaus CS105	Berninghaus	Retrd.	75.00	75.00
91-09-002	After The Hunt CS155	A-Busch,Inc.	25,000	100.00	100.00
92-09-003	Cherub CS182	D. Langeneckert	25,000	100.00	100.00
Anheuser-Busch, Inc.		**Discover America Series**			
90-10-001	Nina CS107	A-Busch,Inc.	100,000	40.00	40.00
91-10-002	Pinta CS129	A-Busch,Inc.	100,000	40.00	40.00
92-10-003	Santa Maria CS138	A-Busch,Inc.	100,000	40.00	40.00
Anheuser-Busch, Inc.		**Wholesaler Holiday Series**			
90-11-001	An American Tradition CS112-Signature Edition, 1990	S. Sampson	Retrd.	13.50	16-80.00
91-11-002	The Season's Best CS133, 1991	S. Sampson	Open	14.50	16-50.00
92-11-003	The Perfect Christmas CS167	S. Sampson	Open	14.50	14.50
93-11-004	Special Delivery CS192	N. Koerber	Open	15.00	15.00
Anheuser-Busch, Inc.		**Sports History Series**			
90-12-001	Baseball, America's Favorite Pastime CS124	A-Busch,Inc.	Retrd.	20.00	22-25.00
90-12-002	Football, Gridiron Legacy CS128	A-Busch,Inc.	Retrd.	20.00	22.00
91-12-003	Auto Racing, Chasing The Checkered Flag CS132	A-Busch,Inc.	100,000	22.00	22.00
91-12-004	Basketball, Heroes of the Hardwood CS134	A-Busch,Inc.	100,000	22.00	22.00
92-12-005	Golf, Par For The Course CS165	A-Busch,Inc.	100,000	22.00	22.00
93-12-006	Hockey, Center Ice CS209	A-Busch,Inc.	100,000	N/A	N/A
Anheuser-Busch, Inc.		**Bud Label Series**			
89-13-001	Budweiser Label CS101	A-Busch,Inc.	Open	N/A	13-16.00
90-13-002	Antique Label II CS127	A-Busch,Inc.	Open	14.00	14-16.00
90-13-003	Bottled Beer III CS136	A-Busch,Inc.	Open	15.00	15.00
Anheuser-Busch, Inc.		**St. Patrick's Day Series**			
91-14-001	1991 St. Patrick's Day CS109	A-Busch,Inc.	Retrd.	15.00	20-60.00
92-14-002	1992 St. Patrick's Day CS166	A-Busch,Inc.	100,000	15.00	15.00
93-14-003	1993 St. Patrick's Day CS193	A-Busch,Inc.	50,000	15.30	15.30
Anheuser-Busch, Inc.		**Sports Legend Series**			
91-15-001	Babe Ruth CS142	A-Busch,Inc.	50,000	85.00	85.00
92-15-002	Jim Thorpe CS171	M. Caito	50,000	85.00	85.00
93-15-003	Joe Lewis CS206	M. Caito	50,000	N/A	N/A
Anheuser-Busch, Inc.		**Logo Series Steins**			
91-16-001	Budweiser CS143	A-Busch,Inc.	Open	16.00	16.00
91-16-002	Bud Light CS144	A-Busch,Inc.	Open	16.00	16.00
91-16-003	Michelob CS145	A-Busch,Inc.	Open	16.00	16.00
91-16-004	Michelob Dry CS146	A-Busch,Inc.	Open	16.00	16.00
91-16-005	Busch CS147	A-Busch,Inc.	Open	16.00	16.00
91-16-006	A&Eagle CS148	A-Busch,Inc.	Open	16.00	16.00
91-16-007	Bud Dry Draft CS156	A-Busch,Inc.	Open	16.00	16.00
Anheuser-Busch, Inc.		**1992 Olympic Team Series**			
91-17-001	1992 Winter Olympic Stein CS162	A-Busch,Inc.	25,000	85.00	85.00

Company Number	Name	Series Artist	Edition Limit	Issue Price	Quote
92-17-002	1992 Summer Olympic Stein CS163	A-Busch,Inc.	25,000	85.00	85.00
Anheuser-Busch, Inc.		**Birds of Prey Series**			
91-18-001	American Bald Eagle CS164	P. Ford	25,000	125.00	125.00
92-18-002	Peregrine Falcon CS183	P. Ford	25,000	125.00	183.00
93-18-003	Osprey CS212	P. Ford	25,000	N/A	N/A
Anheuser-Busch, Inc.		**Archives Series**			
92-19-001	1893 Columbian Exposition CS169	A-Busch,Inc.	150,000	35.00	35.00
92-19-002	Ganymede CS190	D. Langeneckert	75,000	N/A	N/A
Anheuser-Busch, Inc.		**Civil War Series**			
92-20-001	General Grant CS181	D. Langeneckert	25,000	150.00	150.00
93-20-002	General Robert E. Lee CS188	D. Langeneckert	25,000	150.00	150.00
93-20-003	President Abraham Lincoln CS189	D. Langeneckert	25,000	150.00	150.00
Anheuser-Busch, Inc.		**Sea World Series**			
92-21-001	Killer Whale CS186	A-Busch, Inc.	25,000	100.00	100.00
92-21-002	Dolphin CS187	A-Busch, Inc.	22,500	90.00	90.00
Anheuser-Busch, Inc.		**Hunter's Companion Series**			
93-22-001	Labrador Retriever CS195	L. Freeman	50,000	32.50	32.50
Anheuser-Busch, Inc.		**A & Eagle Historical Trademark Series**			
93-23-001	The 1872 Edition CS193	D. Langeneckert	50,000	22.00	22.00
Anheuser-Busch, Inc./Gerz Meisterwerke Collection		**First Hunt Series**			
92-24-001	Golden Retriever GM-2	P. Ford	10,000	150.00	150.00
Anheuser-Busch, Inc./Gerz Meisterwerke Collection		**Saturday Evening Post Series**			
93-25-001	Santa's Mailbag GM-1	Gerz	Retrd.	195.00	195.00
Anheuser-Busch, Inc.		**Octoberfest Series**			
92-26-001	1992 Octoberfest CS185	A-Busch,Inc.	35,000	16.00	16.00
93-26-002	1993 Octoberfest CS202	A-Busch,Inc.	35,000	N/A	N/A
Anheuser-Busch, Inc.		**Budweiser Racing Series**			
92-27-001	Budweiser Racing-Elliot/Johnson N3553	T. Watts	Retrd.	18.00	18.00
93-27-002	Budweiser RacingTeam CS194	H. Droog	Open	19.00	19.00
Anheuser-Busch, Inc.		**Marine Conservation Series**			
93-28-001	Manatee CS215	A-Busch,Inc.	N/A	N/A	N/A
Anheuser-Busch, Inc.		**Anheuser-Busch Founder Series**			
93-29-001	Adophus Busch CS216	A-Busch,Inc.	N/A	N/A	N/A
Artaffects		**Perillo Steins**			
89-01-001	Buffalo Hunt	G. Perillo	5,000	125.00	125.00
91-01-002	Hoofbeats	G. Perillo	5,000	125.00	125.00
CUI/Carolina Collection/Dram Tree		**Ducks Unlimited**			
87-01-001	Wood Duck Edition I	K. Bloom	Retrd.	80.00	125-150.
88-01-002	Mallard Edition II	M. Bradford	25,000	80.00	80.00
89-01-003	Canvasbacks Edition III	L. Barnicle	25,000	80.00	80.00
90-01-004	Pintails Edition IV	R. Plasschaert	20,000	80.00	80.00
91-01-005	Canada Geese Edition V	J. Meger	20,000	80.00	80.00
CUI/Carolina Collection/Dram Tree		**Federal Duck Stamp**			
90-02-001	Lesser Scaup Edition I	N. Anderson	6,950	80.00	80.00
91-02-002	Black Bellied Whistling Duck Edition II	J. Hautman	6,950	80.00	80.00
92-02-003	King Eiders Edition III	N. Howe	6,950	80.00	80.00
CUI/Carolina Collection/Dram Tree		**National Wild Turkey Federation**			
90-03-001	The Apprentice Edition I	M.T. Noe	9,950	125.00	125.00
91 03 002	Sultan's Sunrise Edition II	A. Agnew	6,950	100.00	100.00
92-03-003	Double Gobble Edition III	J.S. Eberhardt	6,950	100.00	100.00
CUI/Carolina Collection		**North American Hunting Club**			
90-04-001	Deer Crossing Edition I	R. McGovern	6,950	85.00	85.00
92-04-002	Yukon Grizzly Edition II	L. Anderson	6,950	90.00	90.00
CUI/Carolina Collection/Dram Tree		**Nat'l. Foundation to Protect America's Eagles**			
91-05-001	Great American Patriots Edition I	R.J. McDonald	6,950	80.00	80.00
CUI/Carolina Collection/Dram Tree		**American Angler Series Limited Edition**			
90-06-001	Large Mouth Bass	J.R. Hook	Retrd.	25.00	25.00
CUI/Carolina Collection/Dram Tree		**Big Horn Sheep**			
90-07-001	Wind Blown Ridge	J. Antolik	3,950	70.00	70.00
CUI/Carolina Collection/Dram Tree		**Pheasants Forever**			
91-08-001	Jumping Ringnecks Edition I	J. Killen	6,950	100.00	100.00
92-08-002	Foggy Morning Magic Edition II	P. Crowe	6,950	100.00	100.00
CUI/Carolina Collection/Dram Tree		**Trout Unlimited**			
91-09-001	Rainbow Edition I	M. Stidham	6,950	90.00	90.00
92-09-002	Downstream & Across Edition II	E. Hardle	6,950	90.00	90.00
CUI/Carolina Collection/Dram Tree		**Quail Unlimited**			
91-10-001	Hedgerow Bobs Edition I	D. Chapple	6,950	90.00	90.00
92-10-002	California Trio Edition II	J. Garcia	6.950	90.00	90.00
CUI/Carolina Collection/Dram Tree		**Whitetails Unlimited**			
91-11-001	Whitetails in Retreat Edition I	J. Paluh	6,950	90.00	90.00
92-11-002	Indian Summer Flight Edition II	B. Miller	6,950	90.00	90.00
CUI/Carolina Collection/Dram Tree		**Jack Russell Terrier**			
91-12-001	Jack Russell Terrier Edition I	B.B. Atwater	6,950	90.00	90.00
CUI/Carolina Collection/Dram Tree		**Statue of Liberty**			
91-13-001	Lady Liberty	CUI	Open	50.00	50.00
86-13-002	Statue of Liberty	CUI	Retrd.	42.50	42.50
CUI/Carolina Collection/Dram Tree		**Civil War**			
91-14-001	Firing on Fort Sumter Edition I	CUI	4,950	125.00	125.00
92-14-002	Stonewall Jackson Edition II	CUI	4,950	125.00	125.00
92-14-003	J.E.B. Stuart Edition III	CUI	4,950	128.00	128.00
93-14-004	Robert E. Lee Edition IV	CUI	4,950	128.00	128.00
CUI/Carolina Collection/Dram Tree		**Native American Series**			
91-15-001	Hunt for the Buffalo Edition I	P. Kethley	4,950	100.00	100.00
92-15-002	Story Teller	P. Kethley	4,950	50.00	50.00

Company Number	Name	Series Artist	Edition Limit	Issue Price	Quote
CUI/Carolina Collection/Dram Tree		**Christmas Series**			
91-16-001	Checkin' It Twice Edition I	CUI	4,950	125.00	125.00
92-16-002	With A Finger Aside His Nose	CUI	4,950	125.00	128.00
93-16-003	Mrs. Claus	CUI	4,950	128.00	128.00
CUI/Carolina Collection/Dram Tree		**Environmental Series**			
91-17-001	Rain Forest Magic Edition I	C.L. Bragg	4,950	90.00	90.00
92-17-002	First Breath Edition II	M. Hoffman	4,950	90.00	90.00
CUI/Carolina Collection/Dram Tree		**Miller Girl in the Moon**			
90-18-001	Miller Girl in the Moon	CUI	Open	50.00	50.00
CUI/Carolina Collection/Dram Tree		**Great American Achievements**			
86-19-001	First Successful Flight Edition I	CUI	Retrd.	10.95	75-95.00
87-19-002	The Model T Edition II	CUI	Retrd.	12.95	30 50.00
88-19-003	First Transcontinental Railway Edition III	CUI	Retrd.	15.95	28-40.00
89-19-004	The First River Steamer Edition IV	CUI	Retrd.	25.00	25.00
90-19-005	Man's First Walk on the Moon Edition V	CUI	Retrd.	25.00	25.00
CUI/Carolina Collection/Dram Tree		**Birth of a Nation**			
91-20-001	Paul Revere's Ride Edition I	CUI	Open	25.00	25.00
91-20-002	Paul Revere's Ride Lidded Edition I	CUI	10,000	70.00	70.00
92-20-003	Signing Of The Declaration Of Independence-Edition II	CUI	Open	25.00	25.00
92-20-004	Signing Of The Declaration Of Independence-Special Pewter Lidden Edition II	CUI	10,000	70.00	70.00
CUI/Carolina Collection/Dram Tree		**Miller Plank Road**			
91-21-001	Miller Plank Road Edition I	CUI	9,850	90.00	90.00
CUI/Carolina Collection/Dram Tree		**Miller Historical Collection**			
90-22-001	Frederic Miller Edition I	CUI	Retrd.	136.00	136.00
91-22-002	Miller's Delivery Wagon Edition II	CUI	Retrd.	130.00	130.00
92-22-003	Coopersmith Edition III	CUI	9,950	130.00	130.00
CUI/Carolina Collection/Dram Tree		**Miller Holiday Series**			
91-23-001	Milwaukee Waterfront Edition I	CUI	9,950	50.00	50.00
92-23-002	Christmas on Old World Third St. Edition II	CUI	9,950	50.00	50.00
92-23-003	Miller Inn Edition III	CUI	9,950	50.00	50.00
CUI/Carolina Collection/Dram Tree		**Coors Historical Collection**			
88-24-001	Rocky Mountain Brewry Edition I	CUI	Retrd.	15.95	15.95
89-24-002	Old Time Delivery Wagon Edition II	CUI	Retrd.	16.95	16.95
90-24-003	Waterfall Edition III	CUI	Retrd.	25.00	25.00
CUI/Carolina Collection/Dram Tree		**Rocky Mountain Legends**			
91-25-001	Skier Edition I	CUI	Open	25.00	25.00
91-25-002	Skier Lidded Edition I	CUI	10,000	70.00	70.00
92-25-003	White Water Rafting Edition II	CUI	Open	25.00	25.00
92-25-004	White Water Rafting Special Lidded Edition II	CUI	10,000	70.00	70.00
CUI/Carolina Collection/Dram Tree		**Coors Rodeo Collection**			
91-26-001	Jack Hammer Edition I	M.H. Scott	20,000	90.00	90.00
92-26-002	Born To Buck Edition II	M.H. Scott	20,000	90.00	90.00
93-26-003	Bulldogger Edition III	M.H. Scott	20,000	90.00	90.00
93-26-004	Ride on the Wild Side Edition IV	M.H. Scott	20,000	90.00	90.00
93-26-005	Teamwork Edition V	M.H. Scott	20,000	90.00	90.00
93-26-006	Turning Tight Edition VI	M.H. Scott	20,000	90.00	90.00
CUI/Carolina Collection/Dram Tree		**Winterfest**			
89-27-001	Outdoor Skating Edition I	T. Stortz	9,950	50.00	50.00
90-27-002	Christmas Square Edition II	T. Stortz	9,950	50.00	50.00
91-27-003	Horsedrawn Sleighs Edition III	T. Stortz	9,950	50.00	50.00
92-27-004	Skating Party Edition IV	T. Stortz	9,950	50.00	50.00
CUI/Carolina Collection/Dram Tree		**Coors Legacy Series**			
91-28-001	Coors Rams Head Edition I	CUI	6,950	130.00	130.00
92-28-002	Bock Beer Edition II	CUI	6,950	120.00	120.00
CUI/Carolina Collection/Dram Tree		**Miller Racing Team**			
91-29-001	Penske/Wallace	CUI	6,950	50.00	50.00
92-29-002	Bobby Rahal	CUI	6,950	53.00	53.00
CUI/Carolina Collection/Dram Tree		**Ruffed Grouse Society**			
90-30-001	Northwoods Grouse Edition I	G. Moss	3,950	50.00	50.00
91-30-002	Edition II	Z. Jones	3,950	50.00	50.00
CUI/Carolina Collection/Dram Tree		**Phillip Morris**			
91-31-001	London's Bond St. Edition I	D. Hilburn	9,950	50.00	50.00
CUI/Carolina Collection/Dram Tree		**The Fleet Reserve**			
91-32-001	The Arizona Edition I	T. Freeman	6,950	60.00	60.00
92-32-002	Old Salts Edition II	Unknown	6,950	63.50	63.50
CUI/Carolina Collection/Dram Tree		**Experimental Aircraft Association**			
91-33-001	Into the Teeth of a Tiger Edition I	W.S. Phillips	4,950	80.00	80.00
92-33-002	Tokyo Raiders Ready For Launch Edition II	J. Dietz	4,950	80.00	80.00
CUI/Carolina Collection/Dram Tree		**National Football League**			
91-34-001	First NFL Championship Game Edition I -Pewter Edition	CUI	4,950	80.00	80.00
CUI/Carolina Collection/Dram Tree		**N.F.L. National Football League**			
91-35-001	Historically Speaking Pewter Edition I	CUI	4,950	80.00	80.00
CUI/Carolina Collection/Dram Tree		**N.B.A. National Basketball Association**			
91-36-001	100 Years of Basketball-Pewter Edition I	CUI	4,950	80.00	80.00
CUI/Carolina Collection/Dram Tree		**Stroh Heritage Collection**			
84-37-001	Horsedrawn Wagon - Heritage I	CUI	Retrd.	11.95	15-25.00
85-37-002	Kirn Inn Germany - Heritage II	CUI	Retrd.	12.95	15-22.00
86-37-003	Lion Brewing Company - Heritage III	CUI	Retrd.	13.95	25-35.00
87-37-004	Bohemian Beer - Heritage IV	CUI	Retrd.	14.95	19-21.00
88-37-005	Delivery Vehicles - Heritage V	CUI	Open	25.00	25.00
89-37-006	Fire Brewed - Heritage V I	CUI	Retrd.	16.95	19.00
CUI/Carolina Collection/Dram Tree		**Stroh Bavaria Collection**			
90-38-001	Dancers Edition I - Bavaria I	CUI	Open	45.00	45.00
90-38-002	Dancers Pewter Figure Edition I - Bavaria I	CUI	10,000	70.00	70.00
91-38-003	Barrel Pusher Edition II - Bavaria II	CUI	Open	45.00	45.00
91-38-004	Barrel Pusher Pewter Edition II - Bavaria II	CUI	10,000	70.00	70.00
92-38-005	The Aging Cellar-Edition III	CUI	Open	45.00	45.00

Company / Number	Name	Series / Artist	Edition Limit	Issue Price	Quote
92-38-006	The Aging Cellar-Pewter Edition III	CUI	10,000	70.00	70.00
93-38-007	Bavaria-Pewter Edition IV	CUI	10,000	70.00	70.00
93-38-008	Bavaria IV	CUI	Open	45.00	45.00
CUI/Carolina Collection/Dram Tree		**Beck's**			
90-39-001	Beck's Purity Law Edition I	CUI	3,950	115.00	115.00
CUI/Carolina Collection/Dra Tree		**Northern Solitude**			
90-40-001	Moosehead Northern Solitude	N. Anderson	3,950	72.00	72.00
CUI/Carolina Collection/Dram Tree		**Team of the Decade - NFL**			
90-41-001	NFL 49ers	CUI	9,950	60.00	60.00
CUI/Carolina Collection/Dram Tree		**SuperBowl XXV - NFL**			
91-42-001	NFL	CUI	4,950	60.00	60.00
CUI/Carolina Collection/Dram Tree		**SuperBowl Champions - NFL**			
91-43-001	NY Giants - NFL	CUI	4,950	60.00	60.00
92-43-002	Washington Redskins - NFL	CUI	4,950	60.00	60.00
CUI/Carolina Collection/Dram Tree		**World Series Champions - MLB**			
90-44-001	Cincinnati Reds - MLB	CUI	4,950	60.00	60.00
91-44-002	Minnesota Twins - MLB	CUI	4,950	60.00	60.00
92-44-003	Toronto Blue Jays-MLB	CUI	4,950	60.00	60.00
CUI/Carolina Collection/Dram Tree		**Stanley Cup Champions - NHL**			
91-45-001	Pittsburgh Penguins - NHL	CUI	4,950	60.00	60.00
92-45-002	Pittsburgh Penguins - NHL	CUI	4,950	60.00	60.00
CUI/Carolina Collection/Dram Tree		**World Champions - NBA**			
91-46-001	Chicago Bulls - NBA	CUI	4,950	60.00	60.00
92-46-002	Chicago Bulls - NBA	CUI	4,950	60.00	60.00
CUI/Carolina Collection/Dram Tree		**Anniversary Series**			
91-47-001	Chicago Bulls 25th Anniversary	CUI	4,950	60.00	60.00
92-47-002	Philadelphia Eagles 60th Anniversary	CUI	4,950	60.00	60.00
92-47-003	Cincinnati Bengals	CUI	4,950	60.00	60.00
CUI/Carolina Collection/Dram Tree		**Ducks Unlimited Classic Decoy Series**			
92-48-001	1930's Bert Graves Mallard Decoys Edition I	D. Boncela	20,000	100.00	100.00
CUI/Carolina Collection/Dram Tree		**North American Fishing Club**			
92-49-001	Jumpin' Hog	V. Beck	6,950	90.00	90.00
CUI/Carolina Collection/Dram Tree		**Lighthouse Collectors Series**			
92-50-001	Boston Light Edition I	CUI	4,950	100.00	100.00
92-50-001	Cape Hatteras Lighthouse Edition II	CUI	4,950	100.00	100.00
CUI/Carolina Collection/Dram Tree		**American Conference Champion - NFL**			
91-51-001	Buffalo Bills - 91 ACC	CUI	4,950	60.00	60.00
CUI/Carolina Collection/Dram Tree		**National League Champion - MLB**			
91-52-001	Atlanta Braves - 91 NLC	CUI	4,950	60.00	60.00
CUI/Carolina Collection/Dram Tree		**Ducks Unlimited Waterfowl of North America**			
92-53-001	Spring Reflections	P. Crowe	4,950	100.00	100.00
93-53-002	Into the Wind	T. Burleson	45-day	60.00	60.00
CUI/Carolina Collection/Dram Tree		**Classic Car Series**			
92-54-001	1957 Chevy	G. Geivette	6,950	100.00	100.00
CUI/Carolina Collection/Dram Tree		**The Corvette Series**			
92-55-001	1953 Corvette	G. Geivette	6,950	100.00	100.00
CUI/Carolina Collection/Dram Tree		**Moosehead**			
92-56-001	Moosehead 125th Anniversary	CUI	9,950	100.00	100.00
CUI/Carolina Collection/Dram Tree		**Quarterback Legends**			
92-57-001	Hall of Fame - John Unitas Edition I	CUI	4,950	175.00	175.00
92-57-002	Hall of Fame - Y.A. Tittle Edition II	CUI	4,950	175.00	175.00
92-57-003	Hall of Fame - Bart Starr	CUI	4,950	175.00	175.00
CUI/Carolina Collection/Dram Tree		**Cooperstown Collection**			
92-58-001	St. Louis Cardinals 100th Anniversary	CUI	Open	70.00	70.00
CUI/Carolina Collection/Dram Tree		**Cooperstown Team Collection**			
92-59-001	Brooklyn Dodgers	CUI	Open	60.00	60.00
92-59-002	Boston Braves	CUI	Open	60.00	60.00
92-59-003	Washington Senators	CUI	Open	60.00	60.00
CUI/Carolina Collection/Dram Tree		**The History of Billiards**			
93-60-001	King Louis XIV at Billiards-1694	Trouvian	2,450	39.50	39.50
93-60-002	Ich Mache Nur Collee-1745	Unknown	2,450	39.50	39.50
93-60-003	Indifference-1823	D.T. Egerton	2,450	39.50	39.50
93-60-004	First Major Stake Match-1859	Unknown	2,450	39.50	39.50
93-60-005	Grand union Hotel, Saratoga NY-1875	Unknown	2,450	39.50	39.50
93-60-006	Untitled Print-1905	M. Neuman	2,450	39.50	39.50
CUI/Carolina Collection/Dram Tree		**Coors Racing**			
92-61-001	Keystone/Wally Dallenbach, Jr.	CUI	9,950	53.00	53.00
CUI/Carolina Collection/Dram Tree		**Elvis Presley**			
92-62-001	Postal Stamp-"Still the King"	Unknown	45-day	60.00	60.00
CUI/Carolina Collection/Dram Tree		**Texaco Heritage Collection**			
92-63-001	Return From a Holiday	Unknown	9,950	90.00	90.00
Hamilton Collection		**Warriors Of The Plains Tankards**			
92-01-001	Thundering Hooves	G. Stewart	Open	125.00	125.00
Norman Rockwell Gallery		**Rockwell**			
92-01-001	Jolly Santa	Rockwell-Inspired	N/A	49.95	49.95
Norman Rockwell Gallery		**Rockwell Mugs**			
92-02-001	Saturday Evening Post(Set of 4)	Rockwell-Inspired	N/A	29.95	29.95
92-02-002	Santa Mugs(Set of 4)	Rockwell-Inspired	N/A	29.95	29.95
92-02-003	Main Street Mug Collection(Set of 2)	Rockwell-Inspired	N/A	17.00	17.00